THE WAR
ILLUSTRATED

FRANKLIN D. ROOSEVELT, PRESIDENT OF THE U.S.A.

THE WAR
Illustrated

Complete Record of the Conflict
by Land and Sea and in the Air

Edited by
SIR JOHN HAMMERTON

Volume Four

The FOURTH VOLUME OF THE WAR ILLUSTRATED contains the weekly issues from No. 71 to No. 100. None of the preceding volumes of the series is so crowded with events of vital importance to the shaping of the War. It is difficult to imagine that, until we are within sight of the end, the drama of World War will move at a swifter tempo than during the first seven months of 1941, with which the following pages are concerned.

Our literary and pictorial contents comprise, indeed, a picture-record of what will prove to be one of the most historic periods of the world-wide conflict. The startling success of General Wavell's campaign against the Italians in North Africa, resulting in the destruction of so much of Mussolini's Army ; the vitally important battle of Cape Matapan, which crippled the Italian Navy ; the heroic stand of Greece against Fascist aggression ; the sensational turn of affairs in Yugoslavia ; the treachery of Bulgaria, Rumania and Hungary, leading to the Nazi domination of the Balkans ; the short-lived revolution in Irak ; the war in Syria, where the degenerate Vichy government forced the former allies of France to turn their arms against hostile French forces under the command of General Dentz, and fortunately in so doing gave a new direction to Germany's Eastward thrust, little to the liking of Hitler ; the tremendous increase in Britain's air power, with its promise of the coming day when the command of the sky will pass into the hands of Britain's incomparable Air Force ; the sensational break between Germany and Russia, vastly extending the area of the War ; America's no less sensational steps to make secure her means of cooperation with Great Britain— these are but a few of the many new chapters in the history of the world that have been written in the seven months covered by this volume.

We need not emphasize the extraordinary difficulties under which the production of THE WAR ILLUSTRATED has been maintained while Britain has been one of the central targets of Nazi attack, but our pages bear little evidence of the trying conditions in which they have been compiled, printed, and circulated widely throughout the British Empire and all friendly lands. No effort will be spared to maintain the series, and every ingenuity will be exercised to the carrying through of its original aim : the completion of a vivid picture-record of the Second World War, whose historic interest must in a future day eclipse all that has gone before.

Published 2000
Cover Design © 2000
TRIDENT PRESS INTERNATIONAL
ISBN 1-58279-103-1 Single Edition
Printed in Croatia

AIR CHIEF MARSHAL SIR PHILIP JOUBERT DE LA FERTE, K.C.B., C.M.G., D.S.O.

Sir Philip Joubert was Air Officer Commanding R.A.F., India, when war broke out. In October 1939 he was recalled for service at home and was appointed adviser on combined operations, later becoming Assistant Chief of the Air Staff. On June 14, 1941, he succeeded Sir Frederick Bowhill as Air Officer C.-in-C. Coastal Command.

LT.-GEN. SIR HENRY MAITLAND WILSON, K.C.B., G.B.E., D.S.O.

After commanding 2nd Division at Aldershot, 1937-1939, General Wilson became General Officer Commanding-in-Chief in Egypt.   As General Wavell's right-hand man he played a large part in the British advance in the Western Desert to Benghazi and later led the Allied forces in Greece and Syria.

LT.-GEN. SIR ALAN GORDON CUNNINGHAM, K.C.B., D.S.O., M.C.

Commander of the 5th Anti-Aircraft Division, T.A., in 1938, General Cunningham was sent, shortly after the outbreak of war, to command the Imperial troops in East Africa. It was his brilliant leadership which directed the swift campaign in Abyssinia to its successful conclusion.

General Index to Volume Four

*T*HIS *Index is designed to give ready reference to the whole of the literary and pictorial contents of* THE WAR ILLUSTRATED. *Individual subjects and persons of importance are indexed under their own headings, while references are included to general subjects such as Greece, War in ; France ; Italy, etc. Page Numbers in italics indicate illustrations.*

9

List of Maps and Plans

Errata and Addenda

The WAR ILLUSTRATED

Vol. 4   A Permanent Picture Record of the Second Great War   No. 71

LONDON'S GUILDHALL, most famous building of its kind in the world, was destroyed during the fierce fire raid made by Nazi airmen on the City in the course of the evening of December 29, 1940. Home of the City Corporation and scene of innumerable historic and civic ceremonies and political gatherings, the Guildhall was partly destroyed by the Great Fire of 1666, but the Nazis were more successful in the work of destruction. Gog and Magog, the famous wooden figures of the legendary giants, perished with other Guildhall treasures, but most of the statues—the photograph above, taken on the morning after the raid, shows clearly that of the Duke of Wellington—were left to survey the ruins of the Great Hall.

Photo, " The Star," Exclusive to THE WAR ILLUSTRATED

In Bardia the Italians Were Surrounded

Swept out of Egypt by the Army of the Nile, Graziani's army of invasion sought a refuge
in the fortfied harbour of Bardia. There, as we tell below, they were soon closely
beleaguered, and it was held to be merely a question of time before they would be
compelled to hoist the white flag of surrender.

LITTLE more than a few huts and warehouses, with a jetty which gives it
the right to call itself a port, and an
airfield on the top of the desert hills beyond,
Bardia was soon crammed to suffocation as
the defeated Italians streamed in from the
positions they had been forced to abandon
in Egypt. Many of them would have liked to
have continued their retreat, so severely
mauled had they been during the preceding
days of battle, but General Berti, who was in
command of Bardia, had apparently received
orders from Mussolini to dig himself in and
to hold out as long as possible. So the fugitives were collected and sorted out, and,
stiffened by fresh troops brought up from
the west, were sent to their stations in the
perimeter of forts. These were distributed
roughly in a semi-circle some miles beyond
Bardia itself—little outposts built of rock
and concrete, defended by artillery and linked
by entrenchments.

Meanwhile, Wavell's troops—British and
Indians, Australians and New Zealanders and
Free French—drew ever closer until every line
of retreat had been cut off. Just before the
British cut the coast road to the west which
linked Bardia to Tobruk and beyond, Berti
managed to evacuate most of his air arm and
its equipment, and henceforth the Italian
advanced air-striking base was at El Adem,
70 miles distant along the coast. Then the
ring was closed finally and completely, for the
ships of the British Mediterranean Fleet kept
close watch off shore.

So the siege of Bardia began, and day by
day, even hour by hour, the strength of the
encircling army grew apace. Way back across
the desert for more than 150 miles poured
the tide of reinforcements; tanks and
armoured cars, lorries packed with men, and
supplies, moved in a never-ending stream,
their progress marked by vast, billowing
clouds of sand. Once again the excellence
of British staff work was clearly demonstrated

as the great convoys of men and materials
moved on with clockwork regularity and precision. The coast road from Alexandria to
Sollum was packed with vehicles and columns
of marching troops, and the rock walls of
" Hellfire " Pass, which had been so stubbornly defended by the Italians only a few
hours before, echoed and re-echoed with the
roar of the mechanized army.

General Berti's position in the beleaguered
port was not enviable, for the 20,000 men
whom he was reported to have under his
command were now compelled to rely entirely
upon the supplies which had been accumulated before the ring was closed. But the
British, too, had their difficulties. First, there
was the urgent need to overhaul and repair
the numbers of tanks, armoured cars and
motor lorries which for days and weeks had
been driven hard across the rough and stony
surface of the desert. Then there was the
necessity to replenish the stores of petrol
which had been eaten into during the top-
speed rush; and there was the same necessity,
of course, in the matter of provisions and

The Australian soldier, top, is protected
against sandstorms by an improvised respirator
and mica goggles. Above is the commander of
the unit that bore the brunt of the attack on
Sidi Barrani with his staff amid the ruins.

ammunition for the troops. So swift had
been the advance that the communications
had been sorely tried, and several days were
required to complete the chain afresh. Then,
for Maitland Wilson as for Graziani before
him, the question of water supplies was one
of ever-present urgency; just before the
Italians left Sollum they blew up the two big
wells on which they had relied during their
occupancy of the place, but on the other hand
their retreat was so precipitate that they
abandoned a number of their motor water-
tanks, without stopping to open the cocks.
We may surmise that these supply problems,
whether of water or of provisions, were solved
in large measure by the use of sea transport.

Some time must probably still elapse before details of the guns, ammunition and stores captured
by the Army of the Nile in its first rush to victory are known. It has, however, provided useful
work for the Italian prisoners, who are here loading up material into their own lorries—also
among the booty—ready to be taken to the British base.   *Photos, British Official: Crown Copyright*

Wavell's Men Were Worthy of Their General

British soldiers in Libya with their motor cycles have stopped to read the message sent to General Wavell by Mr. Anthony Eden, then Secretary of State for War, in the second week in December. Offering the congratulations of all ranks of the Army on the great victory in the Western Desert, Mr. Eden added, "Your brilliant stroke has delighted us and filled us all with pride."

Like the Italian Navy, Egypt's contains several small vessels designed and used for the conveyance of water, and as likely as not these vessels were now brought into service.

For both besiegers and besieged the weather was now decidedly unpleasant. Towards the end of December and in the opening weeks of January the weather on the Libyan coast is usually regarded as being at its worst. Strong gales sweep in from the south, giving rise to sand storms which make aerial reconnaissance next to impossible and, indeed, make it difficult for aeroplanes either to take off or to land, so often is the ground obliterated by the heavy, dust-laden clouds. Blowing as they do from the heart of the sun-baked Sahara, these simoons are as fiercely hot in the summer as they are bitterly cold in the winter ; and now it was winter, and the men who had marched miles in the blazing sun shivered at night about their camp fires.

Christmas brought no lull in the desert war. On December 23 Cairo announced that " Our artillery has continued to harass the enemy inside the defences of Bardia, while our preparations outside are progressing," and on December 28 a similar statement was supplemented by the words, " Operations by our mobile detachments to clear the country to the westwards are proceeding." Then it went on to announce that the number of prisoners counted to date since the beginning of the operations in the Western Desert now numbered 38,114, of whom 24,845 were Italian officers and other ranks.

Just after Christmas British G.H.Q. in Cairo stated that Bardia's garrison, harassed by our artillery fire, continued passively to await events. What else, indeed, could they do, cut off as they were from their comrades to the west ? These comrades themselves were threatened, for the first news from the Western Desert in 1941 was to the effect that British armoured car patrols had penetrated over 70 miles into Libya, reaching a point only a few miles south of Tobruk. There were skirmishes with Italian columns, but these, it was reported, fled in surprise when they found themselves being challenged by the British advance guard.

THE ARMY OF THE NILE far out in the desert has had to find everything for itself, for in these dreary wastes there are no buildings that can be used as headquarters or billets. Here the problem of finding accommodation for headquarters has been solved by digging deep, and these stairs give access to a dugout fairly safe—and, what is more, comfortably cool.

Photos, British Official: Crown Copyright

How the Indians Triumphed in the Desert War

In General Wavell's smashing victory over the Italians in the Western Desert, a great part was played by men of the Indian Army ; in particular Indian troops distinguished themselves in the operations against Sidi Barrani's system of forts. Here we give details of the fighting as disclosed in communiqués issued from New Delhi.

AMONG the first troops to go " over the top " in the Army of the Nile's great onslaught on the Italian positions in the Western Desert, it was officially announced in Delhi on December 13, were a number of Indian soldiers. Moslems and Sikhs, Rajputs, Jats, Garhwalis, Madrassi— all were mentioned for the gallant part they had played, and were playing, in the battle.

Fuller details of the Indians' exploits were given in a communiqué issued by the Indian High Command on December 26.

" Between December 6 and 7," it said, " an Indian division left their concentration area near Mersa Matruh and concentrated, apparently unobserved, after a 25-30 miles march. On the following day the division moved some 50 miles farther to the west into an area about 15 miles south-east of Nibeiwa Camp, where the Italian armoured forces under General Maletti were located. These included elements of a Blackshirt division. Here our troops were joined by armoured units.

"The Italian positions had been reconnoitred during the hours of darkness, and it was found that the defences were definitely weaker on the south-west than elsewhere. It was accordingly decided to attack the camp from the south-west, and at the same time make a move with some artillery and infantry to create the impression of an attack from the south-east. During the night on December 8-9 our troops moved to their assembly positions of attack, their movements being covered by aircraft which flew over the camp and dropped bombs. Artillery was drawn up into position within 700 yards of the enemy forces. The attack began at 7 o'clock on the morning of the 9th, and was preceded by short but heavy concentration of artillery fire on the enemy defences. Simultaneously our tanks attacked and reached the defences about 7 a.m. They were followed closely by British and Indian infantry which had been brought up in motor transport to within 800 yards of the enemy positions.

" The tank attack was covered by a smoke screen, and broke through the enemy lines. Many enemy tanks were caught while warming up their engines. They were fired on while still in a row, and were soon on fire. The Italians were evidently heavily shaken by the tank attack following so closely on the artillery bombardment and by the almost simultaneous arrival of British and Indian infantry who swept through the camp. There was, however, considerable resistance, especially in the south-east corner of the camp, where hand-to-hand fighting took place. By a quarter to nine the whole of this defensive camp was ours. Some 2,000 prisoners were taken immediately ; 30 enemy tanks were destroyed and 20-30 guns of various calibre captured in addition to many rounds of ammunition.

" The Indian division then moved north to Himaref, which formed part of another Italian defensive position. An attack was launched along the normal line of entry into the camp. Our tanks entered, followed by two infantry battalions, one British and one Indian, who swept to the right and left respectively. A further infantry battalion formed a defensive flank to the east to guard against any possible counter-attack. Our attack was completely successful, and 3,000 prisoners and many guns were taken.

" Simultaneously other troops of the division attacked the Italian position of Somaref. This was executed by a detachment of tanks and an Indian battalion. These tanks ran into an enemy counter-attack. One company of Indian troops got out of lorries and, bringing their automatic weapons into action, killed about 400 of the enemy, while another company captured about 700 more. Altogether 1,000 prisoners were taken in this action. The main position at Somaref was occupied early next morning.

" The attack was continued on December 10 against further minor positions between Somaref and Sidi Barrani more Italian prisoners being captured. In the afternoon an attack started by artillery and tanks was launched to secure the Sidi Barrani road to the east of that place. This attack reached its objectives quickly, opposition being only slight. The next morning our operations were continued to draw the enemy in Sidi Barrani, and were carried out in cooperation with other of our forces operating to the east. In this fight the remnants of a Blackshirt division of the Libyan Division were caught and surrendered. Some 3,000 to 4,000 more prisoners were taken. Then the Indian units proceeded to mop up the area."

Indian Troops held an honoured place in the Army of the Nile which advanced so triumphantly across the Western Desert. These men of an Indian division are part of a tank-hunting squad ; between them are two anti-tank guns. The men are armed with rifles and hand grenades. The bottles in front of the soldiers are " Molotov cocktails "—most effective weapons for dealing with tanks.

Unhappy the Caproni They Happen to Spot

IN THE WESTERN DESERT these men on the look-out for enemy aircraft have as their only protection a small sand-bagged emplacement, which leaves them very much exposed to machine-gun fire from dive-bombers. The spotter-telescope crew consists of three men: one scans the sky with binoculars to give warning of the approach of hostile aircraft, another operates the "spotter," while the third is at the field telephone that keeps contact with the anti-aircraft guns.

Photo, British Official : Crown Copyright

Our Navy's Contribution to Italy's Defeat

General Wavell's smashing victory over Graziani in the Western Desert was due in large
measure to the complete coordination and perfect timing of the Imperial forces on land,
sea, and in the air. In other pages we have described the fighting on land ; now we go on
to tell something of the Navy's part in the triumph.

WHILE the Imperial Army of the Nile was moving across the desert by the light of the stars, ships of our Mediterranean Fleet were taking up their positions within range of the African shore, ready at zero hour to send great shells whistling through the air on Graziani's forts and encampments.

The naval operations were timed in perfect coordination with the military. During the night of December 8 the Italian base camps at Maktila and Sidi Barrani itself were bombarded by heavy and light units, and these bombardments—highly successful they proved to be—were carried out in cooperation with 'planes of the Fleet Air Arm and the Royal Air Force. Aircraft reported that all salvoes fell in the target area. The next night saw a repetition of the bombardment from the sea. By December 10 the enemy were in full retreat westwards along the coastal road, and they were speeded on their march by our naval units, who shelled the Italian columns seen on the roads in the neighbourhood of Sollum. Sollum was again a target during the im-

portant period between 1 a.m. on December 11 and 1 a.m. on December 12, when the Italian command was doing its utmost to withdraw its troops from the imminent threat of encirclement by General O'Connor's armoured units. During the 24 hours both heavy and light units of the Mediterranean Fleet were firing practically continuously,

strong westerly winds that were then blowing. December 13 was comparatively quiet ; no naval bombardments were carried out, since the exceedingly rapid advance of the Imperial troops had led to some degree of uncertainty as to the military situation. But on the following night the Navy's big guns were in action again, blazing away at Bardia, and

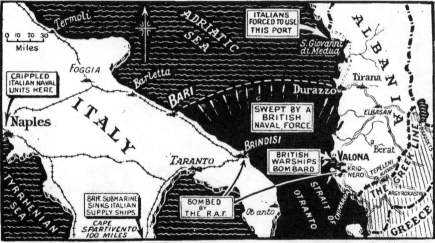

NAVAL AND R.A.F. OPERATIONS in Italy, the Adriatic, and Albania are shown in this map, together with the extent of the sweep of Vice-Admiral Pridham-Wippel's ships on December 18, 1940. The bombardment of Valona by battleships under the command of Admiral Sir Andrew Cunningham, C.-in-C. of the Mediterranean Fleet, took place on the same day as the sweep.
Courtesy of " The Daily Telegraph "

and the range was frequently closed so that pom-poms could be used when the enemy personnel abandoned their armoured vehicles. The Italian shore batteries fired in reply but no hits were sustained by any of the ships.

During December 12 low visibility curtailed naval bombardment, but many of the ships were engaged in conveying supplies to our forward troops—now many miles beyond their advanced bases—and in evacuating the thousands of prisoners whose numbers were growing hour by hour. This called for a high degree of seamanship, owing to the

during the same night Swordfish aircraft of the Fleet Air Arm carried out a heavy attack on the enemy harbour of Tripoli, dropping four tons of bombs, scoring direct hits on supply ships lying alongside the jetties, and giving rise to numerous fires and explosions among the warehouses and supply dumps. Once again enemy opposition was ineffective. An attack by E-boats on the bombarding ship off Bardia was driven off, and on December 14 the Italian submarine "Naiade," which attempted to interfere with our operations, was promptly sunk.

Daring Raid on Bardia

Bardia was again the target during the following days, when at frequent intervals both heavy and light forces of the Mediterranean Fleet pumped shells into the blazing harbour. The Italian shore batteries and torpedo-carrying aircraft did their best to drive off the attackers, but no hits were sustained by any of our ships and the bombardment went on. In the early hours of December 17 a British light unit carried out a very close range attack on the port of Bardia —now lit by huge fires—penetrating into the inner harbour under heavy machine-gun fire and sinking three supply ships.

Not content with battering the Italian positions in Libya, the Mediterranean Fleet suddenly swept northwards, and one of the most striking demonstrations of sea power so far enacted in the present struggle ensued when it slipped through the Straits of Otranto to the Adriatic Sea, with a view to harassing the Italian sea communications with Albania. "On the night of December 18," reported Admiral Cunningham, "a cruising and destroyer force, under the command of Vice-

WAR IN THE ADRIATIC—this in effect was the result of the daring incursion described in this page. Vice-Admiral Pridham-Wippel, who commanded the squadron of cruisers and destroyers, was operating in familiar waters as he served in the Adriatic during the last war ; the photograph, top, shows him as a Captain. In the lower photograph is one of the streets of Valona, the port which was shelled by the British battleships.
Photos, G.P.U. and Percy G. Luck

They Blasted the Italians at Valona and Bardia

Battleships of the British Fleet in the Eastern Mediterranean took a great part in preparing the way for the advance of Sir Archibald Wavell's army against the Italian positions by bombarding the coast. These units of the Fleet steaming out towards the coast of Libya to attack the enemy positions were photographed from one of the line of ships. Their principal objectives were Bardia and Capuzzo, just west of Sollum, at which the army's attack was directed.

Bristling with guns, a British battleship is here seen at practice. She is firing only her secondary armament of 6-in. guns, of which there are from eight to twelve on most battleships. They are used only at short range. In addition to the 6-in. guns, between six and ten guns of from 15 to 16 ins. are carried. Beside the superstructure can be seen some of the machine-guns, useful in dealing with aerial attack, that form part of the armament of all warships.

Photos, British Official : Crown Copyright

Cunningham Gives the Lie to Mussolini

DESTROYERS took part in the sweep of the Adriatic and in the subsequent bombardment of Valona on December 18, 1940, for they are the watch-dogs of all the big ships at sea, their duty being to ward off enemy submarines or, if it is a Fleet action, to act as "mosquito" ships, dashing in to attack the enemy with torpedoes at close quarters.   *Photo, British Official : Crown Copyright*

Admiral H. D. Pridham-Wippell, swept the Adriatic as far north as Bari and Durazzo, when they encountered no enemy shipping." During the same night a force of battleships under the command of the Commander-in-Chief himself passed through the Straits of Otranto and carried out a heavy bombardment of Valona, the vital supply port of the Italian forces in southern Albania.

Nearly a hundred tons of high-explosive shells were fired, and it may be presumed that not only Valona but Saseno, the Italian island at the entrance to the bay, received due attention. Throughout these operations no enemy opposition of any kind was encountered.

In yet another quarter Italy felt the heavy hand of British sea power. Since the Fleet Air Arm's smashing attack on Taranto Italian convoys to North Africa had avoided the direct route southwards across the Mediterranean, and were developing instead a much longer route, by way of the Straits of Messina and then round the north and west of Sicily. But now even this route, within sight of the Italian shores though it was for most of the way, was no longer safe. An official Admiralty communiqué issued on December 20 stated that H.M. Submarine "Truant" (Lt.-Comdr. H. A. V. Haggard, R.N.) had been operating with great success against the Italian sea communications off the south of Italy. During the night of December 13-14 H.M.S. "Truant" attacked an escorted convoy of heavily-laden supply ships off Cape Spartivento (the very tip of the Italian boot, near the southern entrance to the Straits of Messina). One of the enemy supply ships was sunk, and a second possibly sunk. During the next night H.M.S. "Truant" torpedoed and sank a large Italian tanker, deeply laden and steering south, off the Calabrian coast of southern Italy.

In the light of these operations, Mussolini must have been hard put to it to decide what portion of the Mediterranean or of the Adriatic might still be described as "ours."

H.M.S. "ORION," a cruiser of 7,215 tons completed in 1932, was Vice-Admiral Pridham-Wippell's flagship in his sweep of the Adriatic on December 18. No Italian ships were encountered, but the Fleet ran into a field of waterspouts and the weather was decidedly unpleasant—a strong nor'-wester blowing, with bad visibility and a high sea. Despite the hoped-for possibility of an enemy appearance, the ship's cooks went on with preparing the Xmas menu. *Photo, Sport & General*

Catapulted into Action from a Ship at Sea

Fairey 'Sea Fox' Light Reconnaisance Plane operating mostly from Cruisers

Electric Crane Port & Starboard

Hangars for Four Planes

Wings folded

Plane being prepared for Launching

Supermarine 'Walrus' Reconnaisance Plane being launched from Catapult

Launching Trolley

LAUNCHING MECHANISM BELOW DECKS

Piston

Cable

Crew Operators

Electric Cranes can hoist Planes aboard whilst Ship is in Motion

'Walrus' can cover 600 Miles before returning to 'Warspite'

DETAIL OF FOREPART OF 'WALRUS' AMPHIBIAN

Lewis Gunner　Camera

Wheels retract into Wings

Even before the last war, launching aircraft by catapult was the subject of experiments, but it is only of late years that the technique has reached its present high state of development. Today, every capital ship and nearly every cruiser carries one or more aircraft for scouting and other purposes.

Time and again the value of these ship-carried 'planes has been proved. Thus in the action off Montevideo on December 13, 1939—the Battle of the River Plate—the small Fairey Sea Fox, which has a speed of 125 m.p.h. and can stay in the air for four hours at a time, was catapulted from the deck of H.M.S. "Ajax" and contributed in large measure to the deadly aim of the British gun-layers. Again, when H.M.S. "Warspite" entered Narvik Fjord on April 13, and smashed the Nazi destroyers one of our aircraft flew back along the course she had come and sank a U-boat which was following in the great ship's wake.

HOW A 'PLANE LEAVES ITS FLOATING AERODROME

Specially drawn for

THE WAR ILLUSTRATED

by Haworth

Here in this diagrammatic drawing we have an impression of the Supermarine Walrus being launched from the decks of H.M.S. "Warspite," the battleship which was Admiral Cunningham's flagship in his incursion, successful as it was daring, into the Adriatic just before Christmas, 1940.

The aircraft are housed in hangars on the deck, immediately below which is the launching mechanism. The 'plane is placed on the launching trolley, whence it is catapulted into the air. Its flight completed—a Walrus can cover some 600 miles before re-fuelling—the 'plane is hoisted aboard whilst the ship is still in motion by electric cranes. Detail of the forepart of the Walrus Amphibian is shown at the foot of the diagram, and in the circle appears a Fairey Sea Fox.

The Supermarine Walrus is strongly built, and can ride out heavy weather; it has a speed of 130 m.p.h. and a range of some 600 miles. The wheels when not required are retractable.

Slow but Sure Was the Greeks' Progress

There was nothing hurried, not a suggestion of rashness, about the Greek campaign against the Italians in the mountains of Albania. Rather it was a question of slow but sustained pressure, so that step by step the enemy were driven back and forced to cede one town, abandon one line of defence, after the other.

CHRISTMAS DAY, 1940, will long be remembered by the people of Corfu, for it was on that day that the little town was twice raided—first by British airmen and then by Italian. "British airmen," stated the Athens newspaper "Estia," "showed their truly civilized nature by dropping Christmas gifts from their aeroplanes for the children of Corfu. Hardly had the British

mand strove its utmost to hold the town. Italian infantry and artillery were strongly entrenched on two peaks to the west and south-west, and for days their airmen bombed and machine-gunned the only road along the coast. Yet the Greeks pressed on across the mountains, repeating the flanking tactics which had proved so successful in earlier engagements. Overcoming terrific obstacles

—the precipitous country, the bitter weather (the ground was several feet deep in snow) and determined enemy resistance—they looked down at length on the little town, and once again the Italians were forced to retreat. Some managed to escape along the road to the north, but a complete battalion of Blackshirts, the 153rd, consisting of 30 officers and 800 men, were compelled to surrender, together with the whole of their material. Questioned after the battle, some of the prisoners explained the disaster by the British

Valona Harbour has been heavily attacked by the R.A.F., and this photograph, taken from a bomber, shows remarkable accuracy of aim in hitting one of the narrow piers that enclose the port.

gone, however, than the Italian assassins flew over to sow death and destruction among children who had barely had time to enjoy the British gifts."

Later it was reported that the gifts included leather jerkins, which must have been exceedingly welcome to those people of the island who had lost their homes through Italian bombing and were now spending the bitter winter nights in caves in the hills. The British airmen flew so low that the crew of one machine said that they were able to see an old woman standing before her cottage, signalling vigorously that one of the parcels should be dropped at her doorstep ! As for Italians, their gifts were bombs, and they left behind them 15 killed and some 30 wounded.

On the mainland the Greek advance went on unchecked. It was announced in Athens on December 23 that the Greek forces had captured the town of Chimara (Himara), on the Adriatic coast, some 30 miles south of Valona. For ten days the Italian High Com-

+++++++++++++++++++++++++++++

THE POETS & THE WAR

XLII

GREECE, 1940

By I.F.B.

Greece, undismayed, in ages gone
Saved the world's soul at Marathon.
A darkness greater than before
Seeks to eclipse the world once more :
So Greece, in fearless, swift disdain,
Strikes for the soul of man again.

—*Daily Telegraph*

+++++++++++++++++++++++++++++

naval bombardment of Valona on December 18, news of which had been spread by drivers of army motor vehicles coming from the port. They felt that they were cut off.

Just after Christmas the Greek High Command stated that "limited local operations were continuing successfully." These operations were, for the most part, in the triangle formed by Argyrokastro, Tepelini, and the recently-captured Chimara. Such was the weather and the nature of the ground that they were necessarily limited, but they were none the less highly successful : a number of guns were taken and the toll of prisoners grew apace as the ground from which the Italians had been driven was mopped up.

With Valona bombed and bombarded as to be practically useless, the little port of Chimara might have been valuable to the Italians, though, as can be seen, it does not offer much accommodation for shipping. On December 23, 1940, however, it was announced in Athens that it had been captured by the victorious Greek Army.   *Photos, British Official : Crown Copyright ; and P. G. Luck*

Chimara's Fall Opened the Road to Valona

Then the Greeks pushed on, never giving the Italians time to re-form and consolidate a fresh position. A two-pronged attack was developed towards Valona, from Chimara on the one side and Tepelini on the other. Progress was most marked along the coast, where the Greeks secured the mountains whose cliffs rose into the clouds 4,000 to 6,000 feet above the snow-bound road beside the Adriatic along which the Italians were struggling.

By the end of the year the war had lasted a little more than two months. On October 27, the day before the Italians started their invasion, the Italian General Rossi issued an Order of the Day. "In a few hours," he said, "you will be called upon to cross the border into Greece. . . . You will be

Greek morale is as high as that of any army can possibly be. Reinforcements for the troops that are gradually driving the Italians out of Albania are seen above on their way to the front. Every man wears the smile of victory.

Mussolini probably regarded the Adriatic as even more "our own sea" than the Mediterranean. But proof that he no longer rules it is given by the photograph below of Italian troop-carrier aeroplanes, the only means of transport, disembarking troops in Albania.

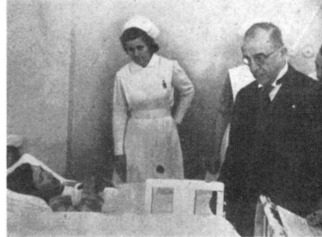

The Greek Prime Minister, General Metaxas, is visiting wounded Greek soldiers in hospital just before Christmas to offer them his good wishes for a speedy recovery.
Photos, G.P.U. and Keystone

worthy of your predecessors in the Great War, and the campaigns in Spain and Africa. The enemy cannot resist your impetuous onslaught. Your glorious flags and banners, kissed by victory, will soon wave over the places captured in your headlong and irresistible advance." Three weeks later, the "irresistible advance" carried the Italians to the Kalamas River, well across the frontier inside Greece. Yet on November 18 General Geloso found it necessary to issue an order that "no detachment must retreat from any position without superior orders. Positions must be maintained at all costs. . . ."

But a few weeks more, and the Italians were now no longer in Greece, but in full retreat through Albania. The orders just quoted were captured at the headquarters of the 32nd Infantry of the Siena Division when they were driven out of the positions which they held behind a peak south of Chimara. By the end of the year more than a quarter of Albania had been conquered by the Greeks and they were still advancing.

Greek Thanksgiving for the Rout of the Invader

The Greek Navy is small, and its largest ship is the "Averoff," on board of which the Patriarch of the Greek Orthodox Church is here seen conducting a thanksgiving service for the successes of the Allies. The "Averoff," a cruiser of 9,450 tons built in 1910, is the only large ship in the Greek Navy, but destroyers built within the last ten years have shown their mettle against Italy's shy warships.

Photo, Keystone

The Second Great Fire of London

In the pages of history and the diarists Pepys and Evelyn we are told of London's Great Fire of 1666 ; now from our personal experience we know of another Great Fire, rivalling the first in its destructiveness though caused not by human carelessness but by inhuman savagery.   Below we tell the story of this Second Great Fire of London.

THOUSANDS of incendiary bombs were showered on the City of London on the night of Sunday, December 29, 1940, by Goering's airmen in a savage and wanton attempt to burn down this historic area—the " square mile " packed with irreplaceable architectural treasures, enshrining undying memories of national and civic worthies who raised the City to its present greatness.

This same square mile is probably the world's most dangerous spot from the fire-fighting point of view, and even in peacetime an outbreak here sends men and equipment racing to its aid from all the surrounding fire stations. On Sunday night, of course, the London Fire Brigade was reinforced by that magnificent body of civilian firemen, the A.F.S., and help reached the Metropolitan area from the outlying districts within a radius of some score miles or so. Alongside their comrades of the L.F.B., they toiled all night with hardly a break, until by daylight all the many conflagrations had been got under control and a greater danger had been averted.

Workers making their way to desk or shop or bench on Monday morning found the streets criss-crossed with fire-hoses, into which hundreds of the new motor-pumps were sending water to damp down the piles of still smoking debris. Here and there a roof or some interior woodwork was still blazing, but never after the first few strenuous hours was there much risk of further spread – London's fire-fighters had seen to that before they were relieved at daybreak by others who had stood by ready at their local stations throughout the night.

There were some who would never return to answer the roll, and others lay in hospital beds where their wounds were being cared for. Four firemen were buried beneath a wall which collapsed in City Road ; though flames leapt half-way across the road, their comrades dug with bare hands in the endeavour to save them, but only the bodies were recovered. From every area tales of heroism came in.

Despite everything that men could do, the City suffered grievous loss, and the night of December 29-30 will be remembered with horror. The ancient Guildhall was a blackened shell ; eight of Wren's churches had been destroyed ; a large part of Paternoster Row, the traditional home of booksellers and publishers for centuries, was a smoking ruin. St. Paul's Cathedral had been ringed around by fires that raged in commercial buildings in its Churchyard, but was itself practically unharmed by the conflagrations. Its Chapter House was gutted.

The churches destroyed or gutted included some of the City's finest : St. Lawrence Jewry in Gresham St., the church of the City Corporation ; St. Mary the Virgin, Aldermanbury ; St. Andrew-by-the-Wardrobe ; St. Stephen's, Coleman St. ; St. Vedast, Foster Lane ; Christ Church, Newgate St., in whose galleries the boys of Christ's Hospital used to sit ; St. Anne and St. Agnes, Gresham St. ; and St. Bride's Fleet St. In Gough Square, Dr. Johnson's house was damaged by fire ; so, too, was the Central Criminal Court in the Old Bailey, but prompt action saved it from destruction.

The wreckage of the famous Guildhall was a piteous sight, with the Banqueting Hall a mass of smoking rubble. Fortunately the Guildhall Library, with the Museum and the Art Gallery, were saved. The escape of St. Paul's was due largely to the alert and efficient work of the Cathedral staff of watchers and firemen, who extinguished fire-bombs as they fell on the roof. But to anyone who visited the scene next day and saw how buildings on each side had been burned out it seemed little short of a miracle that somewhere or other the blaze had not spread to the great Church in their midst, at some places only a short span away. Here indeed was evidence of the untiring, skilful and well-directed efforts of London's firemen in the biggest task that had ever come to their lot.

The raid, which began early in the evening, ceased before midnight, and there has been some speculation as to why the Nazis did not carry it further, and follow up the fire-bombs with myriads of high-explosive missiles. The explanation seems to be that the enemy bombers were recalled on account of bad weather conditions prevailing on the Continent. Another theory is that this massed attack on the Capital was intended to be a prelude to an attempted invasion which, for some unexplained reason, was called off.

If ever evidence was needed as to how the Nazis misjudge the British temperament it was furnished indubitably by this stupid attack on London's square mile. When the Premier and Mrs. Churchill paid a two-hour visit to the ravaged streets on the next afternoon they were greeted with intense enthusiasm by A.R.P. workers and the public. And there were also cries of " When are we going to give it back to them ? "

MR. AND MRS. CHURCHILL made a lengthy tour of the City of London on December 30, 1940. For two hours they viewed the wanton damage to famous City streets and buildings—the grim results of the Nazis' fierce fire-raid on the previous evening. In particular the Premier noted the ruins of St. Bride's Church, in Fleet Street, and all that was left of the Guildhall, where he had spoken on so many historic occasions. Firemen and demolition squads gave Mr. Churchill a very enthusiastic welcome.

Photo, Topical Press

Sunday Evening in December: 'A Most Horrid

" As far as we could see up the hill of the City," wrote Samuel Pepys in his Diary on September 2, 1666, " a most horrid, malicious, bloody flame . . ."
So a diarist of this present age might have described the scene on the night of Sunday, December 29, 1940, when the City of London was set aflame by
the Nazi fire-raisers. Some 150 'planes were estimated to have taken part in the attack, and before midnight at least 10,000 fire bombs had been
dropped. The Guildhall was left a gaunt and blackened skeleton (see page 1) ; nine churches, eight of them built by Sir Christopher Wren—including

alicious, Bloody Flame Up the Hill of the City'

what many people regard as his masterpiece, St. Bride's in Fleet Street—were burnt out or seriously damaged, and amongst the other buildings affected were the Old Bailey, Trinity House, Dr. Johnson's House, the Guildhall School of Music, and the offices of the " Daily Telegraph," as well as a large number of business premises. But for the magnificent efforts of the London Fire Brigade the devastation would have been even greater. Above is the scene of flaming fury when at its height : against the firelit sky are picked out in sharp relief the steeple of St. Bride's and the dome of St. Paul's.

Battle in the Air: 'Shots' With a Camera-Gun

These unique photographs have been enlarged from recent film records taken with camera-guns which are fitted in the wings of Hurricanes and Spitfires; they are loaded with 16 mm. film and "shoot" when and as long as the guns are fired, thus making an automatic record of the firing and its effect. (1) Five Heinkel 111's are being attacked. The aircraft at the bottom right of the formation is receiving a burst of fire as shown by the streaks of light from the tracer bullets. Its port engine is on fire. (2) A Heinkel 111 caught in a burst of fire. (3) Part of a large formation of Heinkel 111's. (4) A Heinkel 111 in flight. (5) A Dornier being heavily attacked. The dark object on the left is one of the crew baling out.
Photos, British Official: Crown Copyright.

Mighty Blows at the Italians by the R.A.F.

Many pages would be required to do full justice to the part played by the Royal Air Force in the defeat of the Italians in the Western Desert and in support of the Greeks fighting so valiantly against the common foe in the mountains of Albania. Below we give just a suggestion of their mighty operations.

LATER information which becomes available about the British offensive in the Western Desert shows how largely the success of this fine exploit depended upon the splendid work of the Royal Air Force. In the twelve days that followed the attack on Castel Benito (on the night of December 7-8) the Italians lost 144 aircraft for certain, and probably more : eighty-eight of these were destroyed in the air, and fifty-six were captured or destroyed on the ground. Our own losses amounted to thirteen aircraft (five pilots saved) ; during the five days December 15-19 there were no British losses.

Whatever may be said about the poor morale of the Italian army, its airmen have showed no lack of courage in the Libyan operations, and some of our own airmen expressed the view that the Italian pilots had put up a better fight than those of the Luftwaffe encountered over Britain. In fact, the air arm seemed to be the only fighting force on which Marshal Graziani could count for offensive action during the encirclement of Sidi Barrani, the retreat along the coast, and the defence of Bardia—now being hemmed in by our army. The weakness of the Regia Aeronautica appeared to have lain rather in its aircraft than in its pilots.

A recapitulation of the leading events of the twelve days from December 7-19 is impressive :

December 7-8.—Aerodrome at Castel Benito bombed by the R.A.F. and five hangars put out of action.

December 8-9.—Attack on Benina ; when our pilots reported the aerodrome to be carpeted with flame.

December 9.—R.A.F. attack coastal aerodromes, bombing every one from Derna to Sidi Barrani. Our pilots also " thoroughly harassed " Italian troops and transports.

December 10.—El Adem bombed and the aerodrome " gutted."

December 11.—R.A.F. attacked Blackshirt troops retreating towards Sollum, the enemy columns were bombed and machine-gunned and thrown into confusion.

December 18-19.—Our bombers attack the camp at Derna and set it on fire.

Apart from these operations the R.A.F. (aided by the R.A.A.F.) was continually employed in cooperation with our Army and Navy. The Italian air force was compelled to draw back ever farther and to abandon its bases upon which so much labour had been lavished in readiness for the advance on Egypt. On December 22, for example, the Italian air striking base had been shifted to El Adem, some 70 miles back.

Attack on Castel Benito

Continuing with the battering of enemy aerodromes, the R.A.F. struck again at Castel Benito on Friday night (December 20-21). The attack was made in two waves : the first scored four direct hits on three hangars ; eleven enemy aircraft were destroyed by flames or by bombing, and others damaged. The second wave of our bombers obtained seven direct hits on or near hangars, three bombs falling on buildings left unattacked by the first wave ; eight enemy aircraft were destroyed. Our aircraft, after bombing the hangars and other buildings with most marked results, dive-attacked and machine-gunned the aerodrome.

On the same night (December 20-21) other of our bombers went westward to raid Benghazi and Berka. Next evening another attack was made on Berka, and Benina also was bombed. Away to the east the harbour and other objectives at Tobruk were attacked. So, under relentless and increasing pressure, the Italians were obliged to withdraw their air bases ever farther into the interior of Libya.

Over Albania our fighters and bombers relentlessly harassed the Italian ground forces, driving off enemy fighter 'planes which sought to protect the hard-pressed columns now trying to find a defensive line that could be held. (Up till December 21 the R.A.F. had lost only nine aircraft in Greece since Italy began her invasion.) By intensive bombing attacks on the Italian mainland ports the R.A.F. stopped the flow of reinforcements and supplies to Albania. Fleet Air Arm machines bombed important islands of the Dodecanese group.

While light and heavy units of our Mediterranean Fleet attacked Valona on the night of Dec. 18, pouring in 100 tons of H.E. shells, the R.A.F. attacked Valona and Krionero from the air. Oil tanks and railways at Brindisi were bombed on December 19. On Saturday (Dec. 21), in a battle over Argyrokastro, nine British fighters attacked fifty Italian 'planes and shot down eight of them. The enemy force consisted of bombers escorted by fighters. Two of our own aircraft were lost in this Homeric battle. R.A.F. heavy bombers flew from Britain on Saturday night to bomb an oil refinery at Porto Marghera, near Venice.

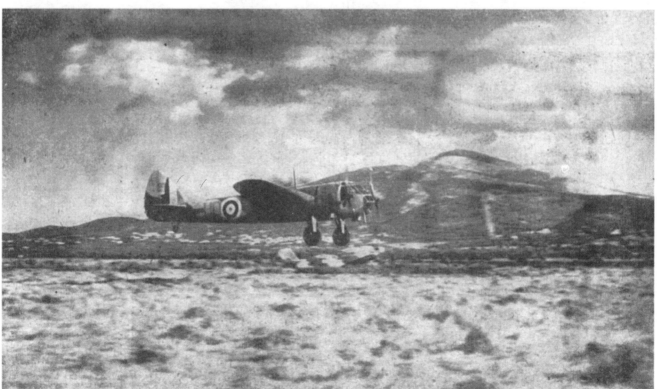

BRISTOL BLENHEIM bombers are among the aircraft used by the R.A.F. (G.) in support of the Greek Army in Albania. Here one of them, its undercarriage lowered in readiness for landing, is returning to its base after a successful raid on the Italian forces. Bristol Blenheims have also done magnificent work in raids on Germany and the invasion ports, and in a modified form the same type has been employed as long-range fighters.

Photo, British Official : Crown Copyright

Sheffield Could Take It As Well As London

"The City of Steel" was bombed by the Nazis on December 12, 1940, and again two days later. Some material damage was done, but the Pioneer Corps, right, were brought on the scene and were soon at work clearing away debris and salving everything that was still of value.

Like London, Sheffield took Nazi frightfulness with a smile, the women no less than the men. Below, a bombed-out family in front of a small house in Sheffield wear a "winning" smile that Hitler and his Nazis would not like to see.

"Carry On" was the slogan of the people of Sheffield, and typical of it is the young woman above sweeping glass from the window of a shop that is "open" in two senses of the word. The glass has gone, but customers will be served as usual.

The Ministry of Information did its best to help the people of Sheffield with one of its loudspeaker vans that toured the bombed areas giving advice to the homeless and those who sought shelter. Wherever it stopped people gathered round it, and not a question was unanswered.

Photos, Central Press and Keystone

'Worthy of the Men Who Fly for Britain'

BOMBERS that will rain destruction on the strongholds of the Axis Powers, under construction (left). In this huge workshop the electrical installation, one of the most important and delicate parts of these huge machines, is being completed. In his broadcast on December 17, 1940 Lord Beaverbrook addressed these words to those engaged in the production of aircraft : " We have the inspiring knowledge that the aircraft we make will be directed by firm and strong hands. It is our task to assure the pilots that the supply is adequate to the necessities and worthy of the men who fly for Britain over land and sea."

Great responsibilities and great risks are the lot of the test pilots who take the bombers on their first flights. Below is one of them chatting with some of the girl workers at the factory after a flight.

Girl workers (circle) applying dope to a completed wing, the last stage in its construction.

MECHANICAL PERFECTION is essential in these monster machines. Men and machines continue to ensure it. Above is a rolling machine fed at one end with raw material and producing a "tophat-shaped" duralumin bar at the other end. These bars form part of the wonderful interior of a bomber (right) 64 feet in length.

Photos, Fox and Topical

In at the Kill with a 'Terrier of the Sea'

Lying in wait for the convoys that bring food and munitions to Britain are the U-boats
of the enemy. And ready for them, too, are the trawlers of the Royal Navy. Sometimes—
all too often – the U-boat gets his victim; but often, too, the "sea-terrier" gets his "rat."

IT is getting on towards sunset, and the inbound convoy is ploughing steadily along over the last stage of its Atlantic voyage. Already a landfall has been made. The sudden boom of a gun from one of the ships ; then a spurt of water where the shell has fallen more than a mile away. A periscope has been sighted. Now watch the escorting anti-submarine trawler go into action.

Round she swings towards the point where that shell fell. The engine-room telegraph rings for full speed and the alarm bell clangs in the mess deck. Little need for the alarm bell because that sound of a gun has brought the men below racing on deck. By the time that the alarm bell is ringing, a broad Scots voice is already reporting up the voice-pipe from the depth charge racks at the stern that all is ready to give that lurking U-boat hell.

position on his head. The minutes tick by. At last comes the report the whole ship has been waiting for—that the U-boat has been located. A bearing is given. An order is called to the man at the wheel just below the top bridge. Again the fighting trawler swings round, slowed for the moment by the thrust of the rudder hard over. Now she is picking up again, moving to full speed.

The commanding officer bends over another of the copper voice-pipes which sprout around the bridge. He whistles down to the engine-room. "Give her another shovelful and let's have all she's got," is his cheerful order. "Tell the Chief to hold on to his hat and watch his dynamos."

Now the U-boat has been identified and it has been discovered that it is trying to sneak

laugh. Now the trawler is closing in fast upon the U-boat. Already there is some thin oil on the surface of the sea. It seems that the U-boat is badly hit. Again the depth charges go hurtling over the side ; again the explosions and the shuddering of the little ship. This time the swirl of the waters brings black pieces of debris boiling to the surface. This looks like the kill. Cheers from aft suggest that revenge is sweet.

The trawler turns again to investigate. There is a strong smell from the oil which is rising to the surface of the sea, and a small stream of bubbles tells of the death-throes of the U-boat. "The Chief" comes on deck from the engine-room. "Any bodies yet ?" he asks grimly. He also has a score to settle. He lost his brother in a minesweeper only a week ago. The engine-room reports that no damage has been done by the shock of the depth charges, except that the clock below there has stopped.

It seems that finish can be written to that U-boat, but no chances can be taken. Again the trawler takes up position for a third attack. Once more she runs in. Once more the depth charges go over. Once more comes the great shudder as they explode. Then the coxswain drops over the side a buoy carrying a red flag and a lamp to mark the spot.

"Sparks" has long since passed the running commentary of the attack over the air to the base, and back comes the wireless message ordering the trawler to stand by during the night and see that no sign of life comes from the submarine. With the daylight comes a destroyer to check evidence and make sure that it is safe to write off that U-boat. Then another message, this time from the C.-in-C. "Well done." Now the trawler can make for port again. The sea-terrier has finished off another rat.

THIS ITALIAN SUBMARINE was attacked with depth charges by a British destroyer in the Mediterranean and forced to surface. The conning-tower was shot away and the ammunition in her fore part exploded. The crew were taken aboard the destroyer. The submarine was subsequently sunk by gunfire.
Photo, Associated Press

And that Scot aft has a personal interest in giving the Germans plenty of hell. Last winter he was not in the Navy. He was a fisherman. He was in a defenceless little fishing fleet in the North Sea which was shelled out of existence by a U-boat, and he spent an hour-and-a-half fighting for life in the icy waters after the Germans had machine-gunned the boats in which he and his mates were trying to escape. That's just one big reason why he joined the Navy. Now he is on the personal warpath.

Every member of the crew is keyed up to top pitch. On the main gun platform above the break of the fo'c'sle they are standing by in the faint and vain hope of some target practice on a real U-boat instead of a barrel. But this is a job for depth charges. High up on the bridge you can feel the rising thrill of the hunt. All is ready. Cigarettes are lit. The young Reserve officer who commands the ship discusses with his two junior officers the probable tactics of the hunted U-boat commander as he tries to escape. A seaman, seated on a high stool before which stands a compass, listens carefully on the earphones as he swings the detector carefully round in search of the German submarine. "Number One"—the First Lieutenant, who will shout the order to release the charges—stands near with another set of earphones in

away ; it must have tried to circle to safety when it heard the trawler pick up speed again. But the trawler, too, alters course, and is fast closing in. Five hundred yards, three hundred yards, one hundred yards. Stand by. Now ! Over the side go the depth charges and the trawler races on. Half-a-minute later the water spouts astern tell that the depth charges have exploded. The little trawler gives a great shudder at the force of the explosions.

Way below the surface the crew of the U-boat hold their breath in agony as their craft heaves and strains to breaking point at the shattering blast. The submarine heels far over and the lights go out. Way below the sea they are fighting desperately but vainly to escape from the trap. And at the after rail of the trawler the gleeful Scots fisherman is ready again. The trawler turns to run in for the second attack. Now the submarine lies still, either stricken or foxing.

On the platform forward the gunner and his crew look a little glum at being out of the immediate fun. Some of them also have scores to pay off for the strafing which the Germans gave them in the Norwegian fiords months ago. They look up in response to a hail from the bridge. "That last lot was for Namsos," shouts the commanding officer with a grin, and the gun's crew cheer up and

These members of a U-boat crew are being helped aboard a British ship. They look up hopefully at their rescuers as they are hauled to safety from their indiarubber raft.
Photo, Keystone

Above Deck and Below in the Fighting Navy

The Stoker P.O. in the boiler-room of a modern oil-fired warship has his eyes constantly on dials and gauges and his hands on controls.

Practically all the ships of the Royal Navy from battleships to destroyers, except the very newest battleships, carry torpedo tubes. The torpedo-room in which the 21-in. "tin fish" are kept is seen in the photograph above. A torpedo is just being placed in the tube, while another is being lowered into position ready to follow it.

LIFE on the ocean wave : the photographs in this page give some idea of life in a battleship today when, except during their watch below, most of the men are engaged in handling complicated machinery both for fighting and propulsion. The stokers, for instance, are no longer the "black squad" who once shovelled coal into the furnaces, but experts in handling the elaborate gear required for oil fuelling. Torpedoes require expert mechanical knowledge for their handling, while gun control and navigation demand that the gunnery and navigation officers should have an intimate knowledge of the scientific instruments used.

The control of a battleship is a very complicated matter compared with what it was thirty or forty years ago—as the photograph above, taken on the compass platform of a battleship at sea, shows. The navigating officer, centre, is giving instructions ; on his left is the officer of the watch, while one of innumerable "gadgets" is the magnetic compass, right.

Jack's watch below in wartime is even more welcome than in peacetime, and in winter weather the lower deck is the best place for it. Reading and table games help pass the time away, and it is warm enough for such scanty clothing as the man in the hammock wears.

Photos, British Official: Crown Copyright ; and "Daily Mirror"

OUR SEARCHLIGHT ON THE WAR

Lord Halifax Goes to Washington

VISCOUNT HALIFAX, Secretary of State for Foreign Affairs, succeeds Lord Lothian as Ambassador to the U.S.A. Mr. Churchill's choice is approved on both sides of the Atlantic, for the new Ambassador's courage, high integrity of character, and complete grasp of the aims and direction of Britain's foreign policy, have long been recognized and well qualify him to be the successor of a man regarded at the time of his tragically sudden death as almost irreplaceable. The "New York Times," commenting on the appointment, remarked : "Lord Halifax may be counted upon to serve his country in a critical hour not as a diplomat but as a peculiarly sincere and eloquent

Viscount Halifax, left, is one of the few statesmen who have been both Viceroy of India and Foreign Secretary. Mr. Anthony Eden, centre, who succeeds him at the Foreign Office, was, when first he was Foreign Secretary in 1935, only 38 years of age. Captain David Margesson, right, the new Secretary of State for War, was a Whip—Conservative or National Government—since 1924.
Photo, Press Portrait Bureau and Planet News

exponent of the thesis that peace on earth is contingent on men's good will. . . . The most uncompromising fighter is the man of peace who is forced to take up the sword." Lord Halifax is succeeded at the Foreign Office by Mr. Anthony Eden, who is already well acquainted with this Ministry. In 1926 he became Parliamentary Private Secretary to Sir Austen Chamberlain, who was at that time Foreign Minister, and later served there while Lord Privy Seal and Minister without Portfolio. In 1935 Mr. Eden succeeded Sir Samuel Hoare as Foreign Secretary, but resigned in February 1938 owing to his disagreement with Mr. Chamberlain's Italian policy. The post of War Minister, relinquished by Mr. Eden, will be filled by Capt. David Margesson, who has been Government Chief Whip since 1931.

Defenceless Island Shelled by Raider

NAURU, a British South Pacific island well known for its rich phosphate deposits, was heavily shelled on December 27 by a German raider which approached the island disguised under a Japanese name and bearing Japanese colours. Just before opening fire she hoisted the Nazi flag. The raider appeared soon after daybreak and signalled in Morse : "Don't use wireless or I will shoot the mast down. I am going to shoot at stores and the phosphate jetties." The helpless inhabitants had perforce to obey the instruction and save their radio station. Great damage was done by shells to plant, stores, and fuel tanks. Nauru, which now has a population of 3,000, mostly natives, was annexed by Germany in 1888. At the outbreak of the Great War it was occupied and garrisoned by Australian soldiers, and since the Peace Conference has been jointly administered, under the terms of a League of

Nations mandate, by the United Kingdom, Australia, and New Zealand. The erection of fortifications and the establishment of naval, or military bases is strictly forbidden, facts which are, of course, well known to the enemy. It has been officially stated that the production of phosphates will be impossible for some months to come.

Air Successes in Africa

ONE fighter squadron of the R.A.F., now serving in the Western Desert, has destroyed 51 Italian aircraft since war began, and has recorded in addition twelve unconfirmed victories. The Empire is well represented in this particular squadron, for in it are pilots from India, South Africa, Rhodesia, and British Columbia, as well as from Britain. An all-Australian fighter squadron is also piling up a remarkable total of successes in Libya. On December 28 it was announced that the immediate award of the Distinguished Flying Cross had been made to four Squadron Leaders serving in the Middle East Command.

Nazis Say : Enough Food For All

THERE are two schools of opinion about the need for sending food to German-occupied countries. Mr. Hoover and others in U.S.A. have been pleading for food ships from America to be allowed through the blockade, and this point of view receives support from accounts by neutral observers of food queues and shortage of necessities in Europe. Britain's contention that there is no reason for the American food ships receives corroboration from an unexpected quarter : a report issued by the Berlin Institute for Business Research. This claims that Germany is able to feed adequately every individual on the Continent. A list is attached to the report showing that German stocks and production equal 90 per cent. of requirements, South-Eastern Europe 110 per cent., and other countries as follows : Denmark, 108 per cent. ; Italy, 95 per cent ; France, 83 per cent. ; Holland, 67 per cent. ; and Belgium, 51 per cent.. Figures for Poland and Norway are omitted.

German Reprisals in Norway

EVEN less kindly than some of the other occupied countries has Norway taken to Nazi control, and the Quisling regime is being opposed, actively or passively, all over the country. The recent sit-down strike of buyers transacting business on the Oslo Stock Exchange was a clear indication that Nor-

wegian financiers are of the same opinion as the general public. This action was stigmatized in Quisling's newspaper, "Fritt Folk," as a form of high treason. The German authorities are becoming more and more vindictive in their manner of dealing with opposition, supposed or active. Several teachers and 50 pupils of a high school at Oslo were recently arrested on the charge of tolerating or inciting the maltreatment of pupils whose fathers belong to the National Assembly or to the Hirden organization, the counterpart of the German S.S. troops. Others were attacked and their pockets searched for photographs of King Haakon. On December 16 the 18,000 inhabitants of the town of Aalesund were forbidden to stay out of doors after dark for four nights a week. This punishment was enforced because, in spite of warnings, crowds had assembled outside the German barracks, when two Norwegians were shot dead by troops who charged. More severe reprisals will be made on whole towns unless demonstrations against the supporters of Quisling cease. Norwegian prisons are now so full that special gaols have been opened for political prisoners.

Round-Up of Englishwomen in Paris

MORE than three thousand British women living in Paris have been recently arrested and interned by order of the German authorities. For the most part they are elderly women, some being over eighty, and a large proportion have been nannies or governesses in French households. In most districts each woman was visited by a French policeman who gave her two hours in which to pack her belongings and to report at the police station ; but in one area the unhappy women were detained under arrest when they went to make their compulsory daily report, and were not allowed to return home for necessaries. Later they were removed by special trains to distant internment camps, one of which is at Val Dajol, near Plombieres, in the Vosges. This action has caused much indignation among the prominent French aristocratic and industrial families who employed and became attached to these Englishwomen, and the American Red Cross has been busy endeavouring at their request to secure the release of individuals. The question of arranging for the repatriation of German women interned in this country in exchange for British women detained by Germany is receiving Government attention.

Spain Tricked by the Axis

A SECRET document which was discovered, with other papers, in an Italian submarine disabled by the Royal Navy, proves once more that the good will so often professed by the Axis partners towards Spain has no basis in fact. The text of this remarkable order, which is signed by Admiral Falangola, officer in command of submarines, is as follows :

Inform the units under your command that the ships flying the Spanish flag belonging to the Ybarra and Pinillos shipping companies leaving or coming from Casablanca and sailing towards Lisbon must be attacked without warning. The steamers of the Ybarra company have a black funnel with the letters A.V. interlaced in white. The house flag is blue and bears the same monogram in white. The Pinillos company has not any particular markings ; it appears to own the ships Sil, Ario, Celta, of 2,500, 800, and 1,200 tons respectively.

The reason for sinking without warning the merchant ships of these two inoffensive Spanish lines is not given, but it has been surmised that it was in order to spread abroad the tale that they had been sunk by Britain, and in this way to rouse anti-English feeling in Spain.

I Saw Shells Pumped into Valona

The British battleships which shelled Valona by moonlight on the
night of December 18, 1940 took the sleeping Italians completely by
surprise, as is shown in this eye-witness story by an Associated Press
correspondent who was aboard one of the attacking battleships. An
account of the naval operation is given in page 6.

Millicent Pennington, Section Officer in the
A.F.S., whose story of how she gained the
M.B.E. is told in this page.
Photo, " Daily Express "

WHEN Valona, Mussolini's chief supply
base in Albania, was shelled by
British naval units I watched the
bombardment through narrow slits in the
after control tower of a British battleship.
The ship's commander had posted bulletins
before the attack saying : " Objective—to
discomfort the Italians."

Mussolini's shore batteries remained silent
during the bombardment, leaving no doubt
that the enemy had been so taken by surprise
that he was unable to fire his guns in the
direction of the flashes, even though he could
not immediately determine the warships'
exact positions.

Scores of shells hurtled through the air
from the warships, each carrying more than
2,000 lb. of destruction. For 12 minutes
shells were pumped into Valona, the sound of
the guns reverberating miles along the
Albanian coast.

Shells exploded with tremendous force in
the naval yards, amid ships, warehouses and
military establishments. A reddish glow,
which soon lit the peaks of the 2,000-ft.
mountains surrounding Valona, showed that
great fires had been started.

The warships then moved slowly southward, and the Italian batteries fired star
shells, vainly trying to light up the attacking
forces, but not a single enemy bomber

attempted to attack us as we retired. As the
light of fires crept over the mountains, a
youthful midshipman in the top control tower
sang " One Night of Love."

This was the first time that the Battle
Fleet had ventured so far north in the
Adriatic. It fought its way through heavy
seas, strong winds and blinding rain for two
days before turning into the Straits of
Otranto.

There a break in the weather came, and
at Valona the warships went close enough
inshore to see the lone light of the harbour
before firing their terrific broadsides.

'It Was Funny When We Ducked'

Among awards for heroism granted in December to members of
the London A.F.S. and Women's A.F.S. was that of the medal
of the civil division of the Order of the British Empire to Section
Officer Millicent Pennington. Section Officer Pennington's own story of
her exploit was published in the W.A.F.S. magazine and is given below.

THE official announcement of awards to
Millicent Pennington and Winifred
Eustace, Women's A.F.S., states that
" during several serious fires on oil depots,
wharves, and factories, they attended with
the canteen van for 12 hours each night, and
carried out their work under heavy bombardment with outstanding coolness." In a

vivid description of this incident, Section
Officer Pennington said :

On the night we took the long trip to
—— we went " in convoy," preceded by
dispatch rider and control car and followed
by the canteen van from H.Q.

We sat—" hovered " expresses it better—
on the front seat and proceeded through a
darkness which was sometimes brilliantly lit
by gun flashes and searchlights, which was
decidedly helpful when we had to wriggle
our way round bomb craters.

Bombs were dropping around us all the
time, and often we had the further light of
fires.

It was more than an hour's drive, and when
we got to our destination we had to be ready
as soon as possible. The urns had been lit
en route, so in fifteen minutes we were serving.
We were so close to the fires we could feel
the heat quite intensely.

The men were strange to see. They were
hot and wet, and their faces were as black as
niggers' from dirt, oil, and perspiration.
Only their teeth and eyes gleamed.

When the Bombs Came Over

Still more extraordinary was the moment—
many moments—when the bombs came over.
The sub-officer controlling the queue every
now and then would yell, " Duck ! "

Then everyone bent down, and as I ducked,
too, all I could see would be rows and rows
of steel helmets . . . like a sort of
armadillo.

The effect was really quite funny.

One man told me his one thought when
ducking was how to steady his cup of tea—
much more important to save it than to duck
quickly !

We served hundreds of men, and as the
hours went on we also gave them " iron
rations," that is, stewed meat, Irish stew, etc.
Altogether we were out more than thirteen
hours.—" *Daily Express.*"

FIFTEEN-INCH GUNS of British battleships were among those that poured their rain of shells
into Valona on December 18, 1940. Here a battleship of the Mediterranean Fleet is firing one of
the salvos that took heart out of the Italians, and whose thunder put heart into the Greeks.
Photo, British Official : Crown Copyright

||||||||||||||||||||||||||||||||||||||||||||||||||||||||||||| **I WAS THERE!** |||||||||||||||||||||||||||||||||||||||||||||||||||||||||||||

We Heard Captain Reid's Last Farewell

As the British steamer " Western Prince " sank after being torpedoed in the Atlantic, her commander, Captain Reid, stood alone on the bridge waving farewell to the passengers and crew. The following eye-witness stories of this sea tragedy pay tribute to the captain's heroism and self-sacrifice.

Stepping safely ashore at a British port is Mrs. Dent, whose dramatic description of the escape of herself and her baby from the torpedoed " Western Prince " is given in this page.   *Photos, Associated Press*

AMONG the survivors from the torpedoed " Western Prince " was Mr. C. D. Howe, Canadian Minister of Munitions, who, describing the sinking of the ship, said :

We stayed up until after midnight to see Friday the 13th safely out, and I was in bed asleep when the ship was torpedoed at ten minutes to six on Saturday morning. We wakened to the sound of the explosion and the ringing of bells. Twenty minutes later we were in the lifeboats and we saw the ship sink. We went back over the wreckage after the " Western Prince " went down, but there was no sign of any survivor.

Among those who were lost was the captain's steward, a man named Franks. He had gone back to the sinking ship to get the crew's Spitfire fund money. I understand the crew had collected about £100 from their tips and wages. Franks obtained the keys and went back to salvage it. He went down with the ship with the money in his hand.

We heard Captain Reid give three hoots on the siren in token of farewell.

After the first torpedo hit the ship the submarine surfaced and we saw the Nazis taking pictures of the sinking by flashlight. When the ship disappeared our

The 10,926-ton liner "Western Prince," torpedoed on December 13, 1940, on her way to England (left). Above: Capt. John Reid, who went down with his ship, after sounding the siren in farewell.

lifeboats cruised over the floating debris. Suddenly the submarine, partially submerged, passed within 50 feet of us.

We had been some time in the boat when the rescue ship, a British freighter, came along. It was a difficult job to pick us up in the heavy seas that were running, but the captain did a grand job.

It took us over four days to reach port. The captain of the freighter had accommodation for only 32 on his ship, but he undertook the task of feeding an extra 140 with great promptness.

It was due to the magnificent seamanship shown by Captain Reid in getting the lifeboats away in dangerous seas and to the skill shown by the captain of our rescue ship that the casualty list was so light. The crews of both ships behaved marvellously and the passengers were grand. There was not a single trace of panic.

Mr. Cunningham, of São Paulo, Brazil, said that Captain Reid stood gallantly on the bridge sounding his siren in farewell. He went on :

We could easily have found a place for him on the boat, but he

thought there were enough in it and refused to come. After the ship went down we rowed over the spot, but all we saw was wreckage.

We encountered mountainous seas, and it was little short of miraculous how we survived. At the outset the seas were lifting the lifeboats as high as the promenade deck of the ship. Five lifeboats got away safely but the sixth overturned.

Describing how this lifeboat capsized after being swept against the side of the ship, one of the men aboard said :

The seas were too much for us, and we crashed against the hull. The motor-boat capsized. There were 25 of us in the boat, including four passengers. I was picked up after struggling in the water for some time, but some of the others were lost.

Babies ' as Good as Gold '

Three babies— three-months-old Alexandra Bankoff, eleven-months-old Frances Dent, and Roderick Henderson— were among the rescued. With a number of women passengers they were hoisted in baskets from the lifeboats to the rescue ship by a crane. A woman passenger said that " all the babies were as good as gold."

Telling the story of her rescue, Mrs. Dent said : Luckily I had thought of the possibility of being torpedoed, and only the night before I packed a small kitbag with warm clothes for baby.

I never dressed so quickly in my life, but baby was still in her pyjamas when I carried her to the boat station. As soon as we got clear of the ship I pulled on baby's warm clothes, and after that I never heard a murmur from her. I tried to keep her as warm as possible by snuggling her close to me.

The trouble was food, but we solved the problem by giving her tinned curried rice and tinned salmon. She seemed to thrive on it, and I don't think I shall worry about her diet after this ! —" *Daily Telegraph* " and " *Daily Mail*."

Sidelights on France Under the Nazis

The Nazis in France have ranged A.A. guns along the sands on the Channel coast to form part of their defences against the R.A.F. The German caption of the photo, right, explains the fact that such light guns are used only to keep the gun crews in practice, though of late the R.A.F. has given them what might be thought quite sufficient opportunities to shoot in earnest!

Vital roads and railways by which supplies might reach the Nazi invasion ports constitute highly legitimate objectives of the R.A.F. The German motor scouts, right centre, are looking out for any bombs that may have fallen in open country.

The commanding officer of a German submarine that has just returned from a raid on British shipping, salutes as his ship enters one of the Atlantic ports now used as U-boat bases.

OCCUPIED FRANCE has now its "Jeune Front," with its offices in Paris (left). Above, Marshal Pétain greeting children who have been expelled from Alsace by the Nazis.

Photos, Wide World, Keystone, E.N.A., and Associated Press

Cartoon Commentary on the War

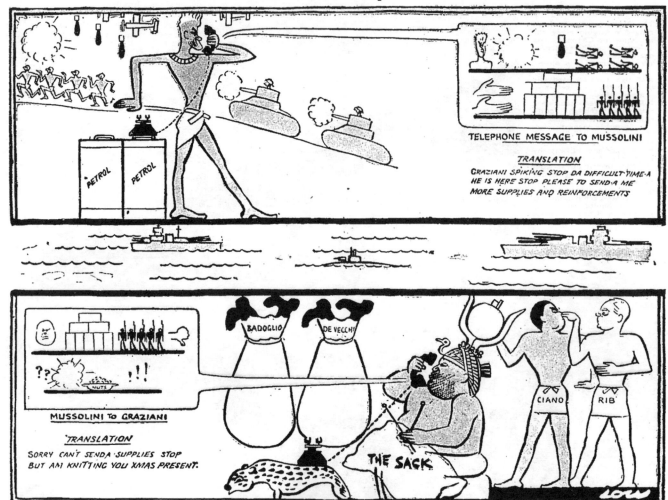

AN EGYPTIAN FREEZE

Cartoon by Low, courtesy of the "Evening Standard"

"MOTHOLINI" AROUND THE CANDLE

From the "Melbourne Argus"

"A DIRTY STAIN!—BUT IT WILL WEAR OFF!"

Cartoon by ZEC, courtesy of the "Daily Mirror"

Take Cover, Aussies! Raiders Approaching!

ANTI-DIVE BOMBER TACTICS now form part of the training of all the British and Dominion Armies. In these two photographs, Australian troops in training at Bonegilla camp are going through this part of their course. Top, troops are warned that enemy aircraft are approaching. Below, the men disperse on either side of the road and lie prone until danger has passed.

Photos, Associated Press

OUR DIARY OF THE WAR

SUNDAY, DEC. 22, 1940　　　*477th day*

On the Sea⁓Admiralty announced that H.M. submarine " Swordfish " was overdue and must be considered lost.

In the Air⁓At dawn Coastal Command aircraft attacked dockyard at Wilhelmshaven and enemy bases at Brest and Lorient.

R.A.F. bombed targets in Rhineland, including Mannheim and Ludwigshaven. Inland docks at Cologne were hit and oil stocks at Frankfort-on-Main were fired. Attacks also made on Channel ports and aerodromes.

War against Italy⁓British troops in Bardia area being steadily reinforced. Italian garrison putting up strong resistance. R.A.F. made successful night raid on Benina.

Home Front⁓No daylight activity except for few bombs dropped in west of Scotland. During night raids were again made on Merseyside and on Manchester, which had its first long and severe attack. Much damage done and many casualties. Enemy bombers were also reported from many other parts of the country.

Greek War⁓Severe battles reported from all sectors in Albania in spite of heavy snow. Chimara reported to be under heavy fire from Greek artillery. Eighteen Italian aeroplanes brought down.

Fierce air battle over Argyrokastro, when 9 R.A.F. machines attacked force exceeding 50, brought down 8 and damaged 3 others. Two British 'planes lost. R.A.F. raided oil wells at Kucove, Central Albania.

General⁓Lord Halifax appointed Ambassador to U.S.A., Mr. Anthony Eden to be Foreign Minister and Capt. David Margesson to be War Minister.

MONDAY, DEC. 23　　　*478th day*

In the Air⁓R.A.F. attacked Boulogne, Dunkirk, and Ostend, and industrial targets in the Rhineland, including Ludwigshaven.

War against Italy⁓British artillery constantly harassed Italians inside Bardia defences. Prisoners evacuated from Sidi Barrani battle stated to number 35,949, including 1,704 officers.

R.A.F. made heavy night attacks on Castel Benito and Tripoli.

Home Front⁓No daylight activity. During night enemy aircraft were active over widely separated districts, including London. Bombs dropped were mostly incendiaries.

Three enemy bombers shot down.

Greek War⁓Athens announced fall of Chimara and capture of 153rd battalion of Blackshirts. Battle continuing near Klisura.

General⁓Mr. Churchill broadcast to the Italian people.

TUESDAY, DEC. 24　　　*479th day*

On the Sea⁓C.-in-C. Mediterranean reported that on Dec. 21 naval aircraft attacked with torpedoes a convoy of three merchant ships and sank two.

War against Italy⁓Situation quiet around Bardia. No attempt made to relieve or support beleaguered garrison. R.A.F. bombed aerodromes at Tmimi and Gazala.

C.-in-C. Mediterranean announced that naval aircraft successfully attacked harbour of Tripoli on night of Dec. 20-21.

Home Front⁓No bombs dropped over Britain, but two trains in East England were machine-gunned from the air.

Greek War⁓Greeks continued successful advance. R.A.F. attacked Valona aerodrome.

WEDNESDAY, DEC. 25　　　*480th day*

On the Sea⁓Enemy warship attacked British convoy in North Atlantic. One ship hit and slightly damaged. Escorting force pursued raider and engaged it at long range. H.M.S. " Berwick " sustained slight damage. During pursuit German steamer " Baden " was intercepted and set herself on fire.

War against Italy⁓British reinforcements continued to mass round Bardia. Enemy air attacks were ineffective.

R.A.F. made numerous reconnaissance and patrol flights, one being over Naples, where an Italian bomber was shot down.

Home Front⁓No raids made over Britain. Enemy aircraft shot down in Orkneys.

Greek War⁓Greeks launched vigorous attack north of Pogradets in direction of Lin. Greek pressure very strong in valley of R. Devoli. Italians organizing defences on heights protecting port of Valona.

Italian aircraft bombed town of Corfu.

THE DRAGON-SLAYER
" So much for that one, and now to face the next "
From the cartoon by E. H. Shepard, by permission of the Proprietors of " Punch "

THURSDAY, DEC. 26　　　*481st day*

On the Sea⁓Admiralty announced that H.M. destroyer " Acheron " had been sunk.

In the Air⁓Coastal Command aircraft bombed several aerodromes in Brittany and shipping at Le Treport. During night Bordeaux aerodrome was attacked.

War against Italy⁓G.H.Q. Cairo reported no change in the situation in Libya. During night R.A.F. successfully raided Tobruk.

On Sudan frontier British patrols carried out successful raid east of Kassala. Growing revolt reported in Southern Abyssinia.

Home Front⁓Enemy aircraft dropped bombs on Isle of Sheppey. No night raids.

Greek War⁓Athens reported successful local operations which enabled enemy positions to be occupied. Italian retreat continued north and east from Chimara.

R.A.F. raided Krionero. Shipping and military targets at Valona were bombed.

FRIDAY, DEC. 27　　　*482nd day*

On the Sea⁓Pacific island of Nauru (British) heavily shelled by enemy raider disguised under Japanese name and colours. Severe damage done to buildings and plant.

In the Air⁓R.A.F. raided enemy ports from Norway to Normandy. Shipping and harbour works in Haugesund area hit.

Coastal Command aircraft bombed submarine base at Lorient and aerodromes in Brittany. Merignac aerodrome, near Bordeaux, again attacked. Docks at Cherbourg and ship yards at St. Nazaire bombed.

War against Italy⁓G.H.Q. Cairo reported that situation remained unchanged.

Home Front⁓Enemy aircraft dropped bombs during morning on town in S.E. England. Night raids were resumed and many bombs fell in London during 4-hour onslaught, causing casualties and damage.

Dover shelled before dawn by long-range guns from Channel coast.

SATURDAY, DEC. 28　　　*483rd day*

In the Air⁓R.A.F. attacked oil targets at Rotterdam and Antwerp. Lorient was again raided.

Wave after wave of bombers plastered German invasion ports and long-range gun positions.

War against Italy⁓Cairo reported that concentration of British forces round Bardia was proceeding. Mobile detachments were clearing country to westwards.

Patrols again active on frontier of Sudan and Kenya.

Home Front⁓Lone raider dropped bombs over Southampton in daylight. At night intensive raid made on town in S.W. England and hundreds of people rendered homeless.

Greek War⁓Greeks pushing slowly but steadily ahead. Italians raided Greek naval base of Preveza and claimed to have hit a ship.

SUNDAY, DEC. 29　　　*484th day*

On the Sea⁓Greek submarine "Papanikolis" reported to have torpedoed three Italian troopships in the Adriatic.

In the Air⁓During night two waves of R.A.F. heavy bombers raided Naples.

Despite very bad weather aerodromes and Channel invasion ports were attacked, as well as targets in Frankfort area, Germany.

War against Italy⁓Cairo reported that in Bardia area British artillery had again been active with some slight response from the garrison. Enemy abandoned fort of Sidi Aziz, south-west of Bardia.

Enemy landing-grounds at Tmimi, Derna and Gazala were bombed.

South-west of Kassala and east of Gallabat British patrols, supported by artillery, harassed the enemy.

Home Front⁓Slight enemy activity over Britain by daylight. At night waves of aircraft made determined attempt on London, showering incendiary bombs over both City and outskirts. Many buildings destroyed by fire, including the Guildhall, nine City churches, Trinity House, several halls of City Companies, a museum, two hospitals, several schools and innumerable commercial buildings and houses.

Greek War⁓Athens stated that enemy had been driven from fortified positions north and north-west of Chimara. Greeks won important positions on R. Drinos. R.A.F. raided Valona twice.

General⁓Mr. Roosevelt in a broadcast warned the Americas of danger from the Axis.

'SO THIS IS ONE OF THE TANKS THE ITALIANS LEFT BEHIND THEM!'

After months of routine training and a weary period of waiting, units of the Australian Imperial Force have gone into action against the Italians in Libya with all the enthusiasm shown by the Anzacs of the previous generation. In the great pursuit across the sandy wastes of the Western Desert vast quantities of guns, tanks, stores and equipment were captured from the defeated Italian army, and above a couple of Australian soldiers are making a thorough examination of one of the many abandoned Italian tanks.

Photo, Australian Official: Crown Copyright

Bardia Was Another Glorious Victory

After Sidi Barrani and Sollum, the fall of Bardia. It was a bitter cup for Mussolini, and all the more bitter because this stronghold of Italian power in North Africa was stormed by the soldiers of one of the most democratic of those democracies at which the Duce has so often gibed.

BLASTED from the air, bombarded from the sea, and shelled from the land, Bardia surrendered on the afternoon of January 4.

The town had been completely surrounded by the Imperial Army of the Nile since December 20, and every day that passed the iron ring about it grew tighter as Wavell brought up more troops and guns, tanks and 'planes. The first wave of the assault was delivered by the R.A.F. on the night of Wednesday, January 1, when they bombarded the place throughout the night. The Italians expected—as they were intended to expect—that the attack would follow at dawn, and when dawn came but no attack, they breathed again. The next night there was another terrific bombardment, described by those who witnessed it as the heaviest yet seen in the Middle East. For hours the British bombers roared above the town, dropping tons of bombs at every flight, while artillery from their emplacements out in the desert kept up a continuous fire. The garrison were

MAJ.-GEN. IVEN G. MACKAY, who commanded the Australian forces in their attack on Bardia. Soon after the outbreak of war he was appointed to command the 6th Div. 2nd A.I.F.   *Photo, Sport & General*

tanks anywhere,'' they said later—came the Australians, with bayonets fixed, shouting their war cries and absolutely thirsting for battle.

Once through the gap the Australians and the tanks swiftly cleaned up the strong points and machine-gun nests opposing them and then wheeled sharply to the right. Here they had before them a long stretch of high ground unbroken by ravines and offering a good terrain for tank manoeuvres.

With guns blazing they swept on southwards so that they took Bardia's southwesterly and southern defences from the rear. All the gun emplacements were facing directly away from them, and the pill-boxes and machine-gun nests were similarly built only for firing outwards against an enemy making a frontal attack. Now, to the Italians' consternation, the Australians were attacking not from the front but from the rear, and position after position was turned with scarcely a fight. Bardia's defences, to whose making had gone four years' labour by men who are generally regarded as amongst the world's finest military engineers, crumbled like a pack of cards as the British tanks crushed beneath them what the artillery barrage had left of the concrete pill-boxes, the thick ring of trenches, and the dragon's teeth of barbed wire and mines.

The Italians, haggard and dazed by the gun fire, poured out from the defence works with their hands raised in surrender; within a few hours 5,000 prisoners had been taken and were staggering away across the battlefield to the places of concentration. Meanwhile, there was no stopping the Australians. Led by Major-General Mackay—himself a veteran of Gallipoli—they fought as their fathers fought before them on Gallipoli's stricken beaches and mountain slopes, on the muddy and bloody hillsides of the Somme.

We may follow the battle's progress in a series of communiqués. The first, issued on the night of January 3, merely stated that '' Just before dawn this morning Australian forces supported by tanks penetrated a sector

BARDIA, captured by the British on Jan. 5, 1941, is shown on this sketch map with its fortified ring of defence works, 15 miles in extent. The outer defences of the port were pierced by the Australians on Jan. 3, and detachments of the same troops, supported by tanks, delivered their final attack two days later.   *By courtesy of the " Daily Telegraph"*

not unduly perturbed; as the attack had not followed the bombardment of Wednesday night, they argued that neither would it follow the bombardment of Thursday. There, however, they were mistaken, for at dawn on Friday, January 3, the British land forces moved to the assault, while from the air and sea 'planes and ships joined in delivering a terrific onslaught.

Particularly powerful was the bombardment of Graziani's fortress by the Royal Navy. Battleships supported by a screen of destroyers defied the fire of the shore batteries and hurled 300 tons of shells into Bardia in the course of one 90 minutes' bombardment, and another terrific bombardment was launched at 5.30 a.m. on Friday—zero hour—when the ships at sea saw star shells burst in the sky above the Australians' position—the signal that the Aussies were there and were keeping their appointment to the minute. For hours the ships, great and small, pounded

away at the Italian defences, and the whole coastline was covered in clouds of smoke and dust.

The troops chosen for the attack were the Australians. First to go over were the sappers, who cut the wire in front of the Italian first line. Then they wormed their way forward under heavy enemy fire and succeeded at several points in bridging the wide ditch which surrounded the defence perimeter; they also located and touched off a whole string of land mines and blew up tank traps or filled them with earth.

These daring operations opened the door for the advance of the Australian infantry and the British tanks—a famous regiment of Hussars. At zero hour — 5.30 a.m.— the tanks raced forward through the gaps made in the western side of the perimeter, and fought their way straight forward to the east along a deep ravine named Wadi el Gerfan. Close behind them—'' We'd go with your

GENERAL BERGANZOLI, who commanded the Italian forces at Bardia, was taken prisoner, together with another Corps Commander and four senior generals.   *Photo, E.N.A.*

Italy's Tanks Were No Match for Our 'Cavalry'

BRITISH MECHANIZED FORCES played a great part in the battles of the Western Desert and proved themselves vastly superior to those of the enemy, whose tanks—as the upper photograph, taken after the capture of Nibeiwa, shows—were left abandoned though often intact all over the vast battlefield. The striking photograph above shows Australian troops in Bren gun carriers moving forward in formation in desert manoeuvres. Like ships of the desert they ride over the undulating sand dunes, following close upon the clearly defined tracks of other armoured units.

Photos, Australian Official : Crown Copyright

Navy, Army and Air Force Triumphed Together

Perfect coordination of the three arms, the Navy, the Army, and the R.A.F. brought about the sweeping victories of Britain in Egypt and Libya. Above are some of the victors.

The town of Bardia fell at dusk on Saturday, when an Australian officer hauled down the Italian flag from Government House and raised instead the Union Jack. The final attack was a matter of a few minutes. The Australians, still full of fight after two days of fierce battle, made the assault, supported by British tanks.

As they lay amongst the rocks waiting the final word to charge, they were in the highest spirits. " Boy, what do you think of us now ? " they asked, and " What time do the " pubs " shut in Bardia tonight ? We mean to get there this evening." And get there they did—though whether they found any " pubs " open may be doubted—for by now the Italians had had more than enough, and with the exception of some of the artillery who continued to fire until the Australians attacked them with the bayonet, resistance was weak. There was one case of a batch of 2,000 who took refuge in a cave and

of the defences of Bardia. Operations are continuing." On Saturday, Cairo gave out that by " Friday evening our troops had penetrated the centre defences of Bardia to a depth of two miles on a frontage of nine miles. The attack was carried out with great dash by Australians, whose casualties have been comparatively light." And a little later came the news that over 8,000 prisoners had already been taken. Then on Sunday evening there came a communiqué which read : " Before nightfall on Saturday Italian troops occupying the whole of the northern sector of the defences of Bardia were forced to surrender. Our patrols have penetrated into Bardia itself, and enemy resistance is now confined to a restricted area in the south-east zone of the perimeter defences. More than 15,000 prisoners have now been captured, and operations to mop up remaining centres of resistance are continuing satisfactorily."

Maj.-Gen. Beresford-Peirse, D.S.O., seen above with two of his officers, commanded the Indian Division which took part in the attack on Sidi Barrani. Prior to the war he was in India.

surrendered at the order of an Australian officer, backed by eight men, to " Come on out ! "

With the fall of Bardia resistance was practically at an end ; only in the ravines south of the town were Italian guns still firing. But throughout the night the Australians mopped up relentlessly, and on Sunday morning the last pockets of Italian resistance were subdued. Then late at night that same day a special communiqué was issued in Cairo. " All resistance at Bardia ceased at 13.30 hours today. The town, with total forces defending it and all stores and equipment, is now in our hands. General Berganzoli, commanding the Italian forces at Bardia, another corps commander, and four senior generals are prisoners of war. It is not yet possible to make a full count, but prisoners so far captured exceed 25,000. Among other booty captured or destroyed are 45 light and five medium tanks."

Report had it that Graziani had urged Bardia's evacuation, but had been overruled by Mussolini. If so, then on the Duce's head lay the blood of those who died in Bardia's defence.

BRITISH SOLDIERS show an almost quixotic generosity to prisoners. To the Italian soldiers who were captured during General Wavell's sweep towards Bardia a cigarette was their great need, and the outstretched hands of the prisoners as a soldier distributes his stock bear witness to the straits to which Graziani's men were reduced.   *Photos, Australian & British Official : Crown Copyright*

Graziani's Men were not Sorry to be Prisoners

IN THE WESTERN DESERT the Italians captured by the British during the rapid advance which marked the close of 1940 were so resigned to their fate that, although only one sentry could be spared for each 500 prisoners, none tried to escape. By December 24, 1940 the prisoners evacuated following the capture of Sidi Barrani totalled 35,900, and the capture of Bardia led to an equally large haul. These prisoners, awaiting transportation, are assisting in the unloading of a store ship.

Photo, British Official : Crown Copyright

A New City Will Start like a Phoenix

St. Paul's was ringed by flames after the " arson raid " on the night of Sunday, December 29, 1940, and this scene, photographed from the roof of the Cathedral when the fires were at their height, shows that it was only by a miracle that the City's proudest building escaped unscathed.

Above is the scene in Addle Street, connecting Wood Street and Aldermanbury, photographed the day after London's great fire. Left, is the lovely steeple of St. Bride's, Fleet Street, which was still burning when daylight came. " Some of our losses are irreparable," said the Lord Mayor, Sir George Wilkinson, but " a new City will start like a Phoenix from the ashes of the desolated streets."

Photos, " Daily Mirror " and Wide World

From the Ashes of the Desolated Streets

Fore Street, in the heart of the devastated area of the City of London, is seen above as it was until the fearful night of December 29, 1940, while top right is the street next day.

The Halls of the Great City Companies also suffered severely; those of the Girdlers' Coopers', Saddlers' and Haberdashers' Companies were practically destroyed. Left, the ruins of the last-named.

ST. LAWRENCE JEWRY was one of the Wren churches that were reduced to ruins. These photographs, above and right, show it as it was on December 29, 1940, and on the following day. It was the sparks from this burning building that set fire to the Guildhall.
Photos, Fox, Associated Press, Topical, W. F. Taylor and Central Press

It Was Manchester's Turn for the 'Blitz'

Beneath the ruins of this building, destroyed during one of the mass attacks by Nazi bombers on Manchester during December, 1940, some 200 people remained unharmed in a deep underground shelter.

Manchester Cathedral did not escape damage, the Military Chapel, formerly the Derby Chapel, of this 14th-century building being wrecked by a bomb during one of the December raids.

A.F.S. MEN of Manchester showed an endurance which vied with that of their comrades in London. Above, after working all through the night, they are still on duty. Left, Manchester Royal Exchange, one of the finest buildings of its kind in the Kingdom, as the Nazis left it.   *Photos, G.P.U. and Planet News*

Solving the Identity of the Nazi Raiders

Baffled by the defences of the British fortress, Hitler is relying more and more on his surface-raiders to sink our Mercantile Marine and so starve us into surrender. This article by Haworth, whose diagrams are so well-known a feature of these pages, deals with some of the ships which are believed to be among those which are preying on Britain's commerce.

IT seems certain that at least one of Germany's remaining warships is at work in the Atlantic in a determined attempt to destroy our commerce. Of her

Scuttled by her crew after she had been set on fire, the 4,137-ton German freighter "Phrygia" was one of four that attempted to escape from Tampico, Mexico, in the early autumn. The others scurried back to port.

action seems to show that she brought into play a considerable weight of metal.

It is often overlooked that Germany has several old battleships of the Schleswig-Holstein class, which carry four 11-inch guns, although the "Schleswig-Holstein" (which will be remembered for her shelling of the Polish Westerplatte garrison at Gdynia) is thought to have been sunk in the Baltic. These vessels are normally used as training ships, but it is possible that one of them is operating as a raider. Then there are the battle-cruisers "Gneisenau" and the much damaged 26,000-ton "Scharnhorst," but it is hardly likely that such valuable vessels as these would be used as commerce raiders. There are left the fast modern cruisers of the Hipper class, vessels of 10,000 tons mounting eight 8-inch guns. Whether one or more of these vessels are at work in the Atlantic remains to be seen, but there is ample evidence that there is in addition at least one armed merchantman taking toll of our shipping in the same way.

Since the sinking of the "Jervis Bay" several British merchantmen have been attacked in the Atlantic; according to the Mackay radio messages the "Ridley" was attacked and set on fire on the same date, the "Port Hobart" was shelled off the West Indies on November 23, and the "Trehata" was attacked on the same date 500 miles

German raider flying Greek colours and firing four 6-inch guns sank the "Haxby" near Bermuda, killing 16 of her crew and taking the skipper, Captain Cornelius Arundell, on board, where he stayed a prisoner for four months. This same raider, using the name and colours of the "Narvik" (which Lloyd's Register classes as a Swedish ship of 4,234 tons), sank the Yugoslav "Santa Margareta" on July 7, 400 miles east of the Virgin Isles, West Indies. She followed this up with the sinkings of the "Davisian" and "King John" in approximately the same position.

It seems reasonable to suppose that the raider, turning south when the West Indies became too hot for her, met the British merchant cruiser "Alcantara" near Trinidad on July 29. Escaping from this encounter, the Nazi vessel turned north again, was refuelled by the German oil-tanker "Winnetou," and captured her next victim, the Norwegian "Tropic Sea," in the North Atlantic during the month of August. A German prize crew and the English prisoners were put aboard, but the "Tropic Sea's" journey to Germany was interrupted on September 3, when H.M. submarine "Truant" challenged her, rescued the prisoners and later surfaced near the English shores. The "Tropic Sea" was scuttled by the German prize crew and sank.

Meanwhile, the raider hunted fresh prey, and possibly attacked and sank the freighter "Anglo-Saxon" in the North Atlantic, from which two survivors, George Tapscott and Wilbert Widdicombe, landed at Eleuthera Isle, 40 miles from Nassau, after a 70 days' voyage in a small boat.

Captain Arundell of the "Haxby" speaks of the raider as an armed liner (with one funnel and two masts) of the Hamburg-Amerika Line, about 10,000 tons, mounting six 6-inch guns and carrying a crew of about 300. The raider had a telescopic funnel, and could change her superstructure. Brazilian

H.M.S. DIOMEDE, a 4,850-ton light cruiser, was waiting for the German freighters when they made another attempt to slip out to sea on November 29, 1940. One of them, the 5,033-ton "Idarwald," after being captured in the Caribbean, attempted to follow the example of the "Phrygia," but men from the "Diomede" extinguished the fires and took the ship back to port.

three pocket-battleships there remain the "Admiral von Scheer" and the "Lützow" (formerly "Deutschland"), which can last be placed on April 23, 1940, when she was beached 50 miles west of Trondheim. Possibly she escaped from Norway before the British Navy mined the Arctic between Norway and Iceland in May, and she may have been in hiding at some West African harbour after the French collapse on June 17.

The evidence of the crews of the "Rangitiki" and "Cornish City," members of the convoy escorted by the "Jervis Bay," that the German vessel fired from a range of 15,000 yards, indicates that the raider might have been equipped with anything from a 6-inch gun upwards, but the brevity of the

west of Ireland. Since the last two attacks were made on the same date, there must be at least two raiders in the Atlantic, one of them being, perhaps, the armed merchantman which had been preying on British and neutral shipping throughout the summer. The log of this raider, so far as can be ascertained from available evidence, is as follows:

On April 24, 1940, a

The "Idarwald" is here seen in port at Tampico between her two attempts to escape the British blockading warships. It is believed that the captains of the Nazi ships were suffering badly from nerves when they put to sea the first time and that they fled, not from the British, but from two American destroyers on neutrality patrol.

Photos, Stephen Cribb, Wide World and Associated Press

From Arctic to Pacific the Chase Goes On

COUNT FELIX VON LUCKNER, believed to be in command of the German raider operating in the Pacific. He won fame in the last war in the same field of activity.

and Dutch colours had been used, besides the Greek and Swedish already mentioned. A huge supply of mines was on board, and the vessel was equipped for a three years' voyage. There are several German liners of the Hamburg-Amerika service, as well as those of the Norddeutscher Lloyd and the German African lines, any of which may have been armed at Hamburg early in the war.

The "Eisenach" (4,177 tons) is known to have been fitted out with 6-inch guns at Corinto, Nicaragua, on September 25, 1939. Another vessel which might be considered is the "Triderun" (2,464 tons), an armed merchantman reported at the Celebes Isles, Dutch East Indies, on May 6, 1940, before the invasion of Holland. It would appear more probable, however, that this ship is operating in the Pacific. There is also the "Scharnhorst," Norddeutscher Lloyd express liner of 18,184 tons, which refuelled at Kobe, Japan, on September 13, 1940, and left for an unknown destination.

The "Orinoco" (9,660 tons), one of the Hamburg-Amerika liners, which was an auxiliary cruiser in the last war, left Cuba in March of last year. The next date by which she can definitely be placed is in mid-November, when she limped into Tampico, Mexico, with engine and boiler trouble due to sabotage aboard. It is noteworthy that this occurred after the "Phrygia" scuttled herself on November 15 off Panuco River, Mexico, on sighting four American patrolling destroyers. The "Phrygia," formerly a supply ship to the "Graf Spee," had left Tampico with full cargo to supply a German Atlantic raider.

Scuttling of the 'Idarwald'

The latest supply ship to be scuttled by her crew is the "Idarwald," which left Tampico in November with full cargo, bound ostensibly for Vigo, Spain, but actually steaming due north to meet a German raider. The crew opened the sea-cocks and set fire to their ship on sighting the British cruiser "Diomede"; the British boarding-party, although unable to save the ship, hauled down the Swastika and hoisted the White Ensign.

Then there was the "Rhein," also a supply ship, which left Tampico at the same time as the "Idarwald" and was intercepted and sunk by a Dutch man-of-war, "Van Kinsbergen," on December 11.

The "Windhoek," formerly a supply ship to the "Graf Spee," is known to be still at Santos, Brazil, unable to leave port as harbour dues are unpaid. The "Hermonthis" and three other German ships are reported to have been bottled up at Callao, Peru, since August 1939. The Peruvian Senate recently refused departure papers, on the ground that the hostile intent of such supply ships might provoke an incident with the British Navy within the American neutrality zone. A notable capture was the Norddeutscher Lloyd S.S. "Weser" (9,179 tons), intercepted on September 25, 1940, off Manzanillo, Mexico, by the Canadian merchant cruiser "Prince Robert." The cargo of hides, mercury, oil, food and stores, was captured intact. But several German vessels which may be acting as supply ships are still at large, among them the "Dresden," supply ship to the "Graf Spee"; "Helgoland," which left Barranquilla with full cargo and carrying twenty German civilian air pilots about October 25; "Havelland," last placed at Punta Arenas in October; and the Hamburg-Amerika liner "Rio Grande," which left a Brazilian port with full cargo on November 1.

Raiders in the Pacific

The Pacific Ocean also has been the scene of sinkings of our merchantmen, both by surface raiders and by mines. The "Niagara" was mined in the Tasman Sea on June 19. A cargo boat struck a mine off the Australian coast on November 8, but her crew was saved; and on the same date the American S.S. "City of Rayville" was blown up by a German mine (on the evidence of the Cape Otway lighthouse-keeper) 120 miles S.W.

of Melbourne. Enemy mines were also discovered on May 17 off Cape Agulhas, S. Africa.

On August 17 the "Turakina" was attacked by an armed raider in the Tasman Sea, and this event was followed by the German claim of the sinking of the "British Commander" 300 miles south of Madagascar. Some 500 survivors from seven ships—sunk by several raiders in the Pacific since August 1940 — were landed in the Bismarck Archipelago, on December 21, and a few days later were taken to an Australian port.

The ships in question were six British— the "Komata" (3,900 tons), "Ranitane" (16,712 tons), "Holmwood," "Triona" (4,413 tons), "Triaster" (6,032 tons), and "Triadic" (6,378 tons), and one Norwegian vessel, the "Vinni" (5,181 tons). Survivors from three other sunk ships— the "Turakina," mentioned above (British, 9,161 tons), "Notou" (French, 2,489 tons), and "Ringwood" (Norwegian, 7,203 tons), were believed to be still aboard the raider.

Although the survivors were unable to give for certain the name of the ship which had marooned them, it was suspected that she was the "Glengarry," a British ship of 9,460 tons of the Glen Line which was seized in Copenhagen when the Germans invaded Denmark. She was reported to have had a Japanese flag painted on her sides, and to be commanded by Count Felix von Luckner, whose exploits as the captain of a German raider in the Great War won him the name of "Sea Devil."

Two attacks were made on ships in the Indian Ocean during November—the "Maimoa" and the "Port Brisbane." The passengers and crew (including one woman) from these vessels were taken prisoner aboard the raider, with the exception of the survivors from one of the "Port Brisbane's" three lifeboats, who escaped to tell the tale.

THE "CARNARVON CASTLE," formerly a Union Castle liner, is one of several similar ships that have put up gallant fights against Nazi raiders that slipped out into the Atlantic and Pacific. After an encounter with a raider in the Atlantic on Dec. 5, 1940 she put into port, and above is her bridge spattered with shrapnel (see page 695, Vol. 3). *Photos, Planet News and Keystone*

Across the Mountains Winds the Victors' Trail

GREEK SOLDIERS, well clad to resist the inclement weather, which nevertheless failed to halt their advance, are seen marching forward in open country after the capture of Koritza from the Italians. As this picture from a Paramount newsreel shows, the Greeks, owing to the difficult nature of the terrain, advanced mainly on foot, supplies and ammunition being carried on sure-footed pack mules well used to the mountainous country. Such country provides a strategic obstacle which should favour the Italians, but in practice it favoured the skilled and hardy Greek troops.

Photo, E. P. Genock, British Paramount News

A Winter's Tale of War in the Balkans

While the Italians were surrendering in their tens of thousands in Libya, their comrades in Albania were slowly but surely being forced back by the Greeks on to Valona. From the one field of battle as from the other there was no cheering news for Mussolini. Below we tell of the Greek successes that accompanied the turn of the year.

WHILE the Greek soldiers were battling their way along the snow-bound roads and mountain tracks of Albania, driving the Italians steadily before them, their comrades of the Royal Hellenic Navy were also playing a manful part in the war of liberation. Greece is sorely deficient in big ships, but the spirit of the men who triumphed at Salamis nearly 2,500 years ago is still present in her little ships—the submarines in particular. Thus, just before Christmas there came the story of the Greek submarine "Papanicolis."

Ordered to patrol the Straits of Otranto, the "Papanicolis"—a submarine of 576 tons—entered the Adriatic and, arrived in the Gulf of Valona without molestation. There she remained submerged for many hours until at midday on Christmas Eve, Lieut.-Commander Milton Iatrides saw through his periscope an Italian convoy steaming towards Valona from Brindisi. It consisted of six transports—one a liner of 15,000 tons—moving in a double line, shepherded by six destroyers, two at the head, two in the middle, and two bringing up the rear.

Careful not to make a sound for fear of detection by the destroyers' hydrophones, the "Papanicolis" remained just below the surface until the ships of the convoy were passing on either side of her. Then her commander took aim and launched four torpedoes. With the first he hit a transport at a distance of 800 yards; the second hit another ship at 1,000 yards, and a third one at 1,200 yards. As for the fourth, it probably hit one of the destroyers.

Then the submarine dived to 170 feet, but as she went down her crew heard three explosions, proof positive that three of the torpedoes had scored direct hits. The Italian destroyers came rushing up and attacked the submarine with depth charges, rocking

the "Papanicolis" with their explosions. Italian 'planes, too, bombed her time and again. But the little ship was unhurt and made never a sound. Swept northwards by a strong current, she surfaced five hours later off the coast of Dalmatia. Again she submerged, this time for between 30 and 40 hours, and throughout Christmas Day she was hunted by Italian aircraft. Finally, however, she reached one of the Ionian Islands and on December 27 regained her base. Lieut.-Commander Iatrides was promoted to Commander and decorated for his bravery, and all his officers and crew were awarded the War Cross.

Exploits of the "Katsonis"

Another of the Greek submarines, the "Katsonis," distinguished itself a few days later. The Greek Ministry of Marine announced on January 5 that the "Katsonis," when patrolling ten miles south of Menders Point on the Albanian coast, sighted an Italian munitions-carrying tanker making towards San Giovanni di Medua. The Italian ship mounted two guns of greater calibre than those of the "Katsonis," but the submarine released both torpedoes. The tanker avoided them by swinging on to a zig-zag course, whereupon the "Katsonis" surfaced, approached to 500 yards and, although out-gunned, scored a direct hit on the tanker, which took fire and blew up.

Yet a third Greek ship whose exploits should be remembered is the destroyer "Aetos," which sank an Italian submarine.

On land the fierce struggle for Valona, Klisura and Tepelini continued. It was not a battle so much as a competition in endurance. So bitter, indeed, was the winter weather that for days at a time there was little to break the silence in the mountains save the occasional crack of a rifle and the

roar of an avalanche. The Italians were strongly entrenched between Tepelini and Klisura; in Tepelini itself was the 17th Battalion of the 3rd Julia Alpini Division, and to the west were some twelve batteries of Italian artillery. Then between Klisura and Berat was a regiment of Blackshirts. All three villages— they are hardly more—were strongly defended with barbed wire and machine-gun posts made of rough timber and rocks. But for the Italians as for the Greeks the war had now entered a very unpleasant phase. Not only were there no dry and warm dug-outs, but many of the soldiers on both sides were without shelter. They were lacking, too, in winter clothing; hot food was generally unobtainable, and the men often went hungry. The mules suffered even more greatly from the cold and exposure, and it was reported that they were dying like flies, simply collapsing at the sides of the tracks and lying there until they were frozen stiff.

But the Italians bore the strain far worse than the Greeks since for the most part they had been accustomed to the warm climate of the Mediterranean lowlands. Italians taken prisoner were terribly exhausted by cold, hunger and weariness, and some of the artillerymen said that they had been strapped to their guns by their officers to prevent them deserting. "It is not true to assert," wrote the Special Correspondent of the Athens newspaper "Ethnos," "that the Italian soldier cannot fight. They are keen fighters, but probably this war does not inspire them. Italian soldiers who have been made prisoner, after having first taken food and gained assurance that they will be treated as well as possible, begin to laugh and joke. They give the impression that the nightmare of war is over for them, and they look very pleased."

MACHINE-GUNS have proved a very valuable weapon to the Greeks, for in the mountainous regions of Albania through which artillery could not easily pass, they can be transported on mules or pack-horses. Such weapons as these, skilfully handled by the Greeks, were not at all to the liking of the Italians. The machine-guns in use amongst the Greek troops are the Hotchkiss (used in the Great War by the French and to some extent by the British armies), the St. Etienne, and Schwarzlose—an Austrian production. Greek mountain artillery—made by Schneider and Krupp for the most part—has also proved its worth.

Photo, G.P.U.

Into Koritza with the Victorious Greeks

On November 22, 1940, the Greeks completed the occupation of Koritza, and a few days afterwards King George of Greece visited his victorious troops. Left he is seen during his inspection accompanied by two officers of the High Command.

Photo, G.P.U.

Koritza was an Italian stronghold, and when the Italians evacuated it they left a great quantity of guns, ammunition, and other stores behind them. Below, Greek soldiers examining bombs for aircraft which were among the booty. The captured stores were a most welcome addition to the Greek resources.

Photo, Paramount Newsreel

In 1925, while Albania was still a Republic, Italy obtained well-nigh complete control of its finances; the National Bank of Albania was established in Rome with practically all its capital subscribed from Italian sources. Only branches were set up in Albania; the Greek soldiers above are standing outside that in Koritza.

Photo, Paramount Newsreel

When the Greeks entered Koritza with the long train of mules which formed a great part of their transport, they passed the Greek and Albanian flags flying side by side, right. In this display of bunting the Albanians may well have read a promise of future independence.

Photo, G.P.U.

Not as Conquerors but as Captives the

Pho

MARCH
Sid
trail of
a fractio
during th
through
marked t
Barrani w
little mor
the ope
offensive.
were tak
Graziani'
the town
no fewer
had bee
tured gu
300 and
with equ
worth mi
the whir
revenges
graph of
mechaniz
the obe
Italians
capture

lians Resume Their March Into Egypt

uins of
long
is but
aptured
dvance
which
Sidi
Dec. 11,
rs after
British
isoners
fall of
ore in
ec. 30
isoners
cap-
o over
strewn
aterial
How
ngs its
photo-
ain's
assing
the
their
i on

Britain Has 'Flown' to the Aid of Greece

The R.A.F. is playing a big part in attack and patrol in the Eastern Mediterranean. A Sunderland flying boat of the R.A.F., top, is flying above the still waters of the Mediterranean dotted with the Isles of Greece. Above, an R.A.F. bomber starting off from a Greek aerodrome.

BLENHEIM BOMBERS, as well as Sunderland flying boats, are among the aircraft that the R.A.F. are using in support of the Greeks against the Italians. Above, against a sunset sky, one of these machines is returning from a raid. In the foreground is a camouflaged tent at the aerodrome. In the circle, a sergeant of the R.A.F. offers his bald head to be " touched for luck " by two of his comrades just off on a flight. One of the chief objectives of the R.A.F. has been the Albanian port of Valona, which up to December 29, 1940, had been bombed 22 times.

Photos, British Official : Crown Copyright

Fire Over Germany: The Year's Lurid End

Only a short while after the Nazi fire-raising raid on the City of London, the R.A.F. delivered yet another smashing attack on the great German city and port of Bremen. This attack was one of many, as we tell in our review of some of the principal aspects of the air war given below.

THE big drop in day bombing attacks is clearly reflected in the table printed in this page : German losses during December were 48 aircraft, as compared with 201 in the previous month plus 20 Italian 'planes ; British losses were 8 in December, compared with 53 in November. During the 16 months from the beginning of the war Germany lost in raids over Britain at least 3,045 aircraft, whereas our own losses in defending these islands were 847 'planes, 427 of our pilots being saved. In all theatres of war combined the total German loss for 1940 was computed to be in the neighbourhood of 4,500 aircraft, and the Italian loss was put at 550. It has also been estimated that the cost of the year's aerial operations in man-power to Germany was 11,000, and that incurred by Italy about 1,200.

Manchester was heavily raided on the night of Dec. 22, many casualties being caused. Three enemy 'planes were shot down in all by our night patrols. During the attack on Merseyside the night before our A.A. guns had shot down two bombers. London and the Midlands, with the N.W. and S. of Britain, were raided during the night of Monday, Dec. 23, but there was little activity by day. Christmas Day and Boxing Day passed peacefully ; a stray enemy machine dropped bombs in the Isle of Sheppey on the afternoon of the 25th, and next day a German bomber was shot down in the Orkneys. Apart from this Britain was untroubled by the Luftwaffe, and for three nights there was no Alert.

On Friday, Dec. 27, a town in the South-east was bombed in daylight, with few casualties. At night London underwent a heavy attack for some four hours. Next evening it was the turn of a town in the south-west which experienced one of its worst raids. Earlier in the day Southampton had been attacked, when a lone raider suddenly appeared and dropped bombs. The City of London was singled out on Sunday night for that strange raid which began with a mass-attack by fire-bombs and then stopped short ; it has already been described in page 13. By day there had been only isolated incidents, at coastal and N.W. towns. After this there came a lull—one of those strange pauses which are difficult to explain, since it is of the essence of strategy to keep on hammering at an enemy. Bombs were dropped in Kent and East Anglia during daylight on Monday, Dec. 30, but

ENEMY AND BRITISH AIRCRAFT LOSSES			
	German	Italian	British
May	1,990	—	258
June	276	—	177
July	245	—	115
Aug.	1,110	—	310
Sept.	1,114	—	311
Oct.	241	—	119
Nov.	201	20	53
Dec. 1-31	48	—	8
Totals, May to Dec. 31	5,225	20	1,351

Daily Results

Dec.	Ger. Losses	Br. Losses	Br. Pilots Saved	Dec.	Ger. Losses	Br. Losses	Br. Pilots Saved
1 ...	8	5	5	15 ...	—	—	—
2 ...	2	—	—	16 ...	—	—	—
3 ...	—	—	—	17 ...	1	—	—
4 ...	1	—	—	18 ...	1	—	—
5 ...	14	2	1	19 ...	1	—	—
6 ...	—	—	—	20 ...	—	—	—
7 ...	2	—	—	21 ...	5	1	1
8 ...	1	—	—	22 ...	3	—	—
9 ...	1	—	—	24 ...	—	—	—
10 ...	1	—	—	25 ...	1	—	—
11 ...	2	—	—	26-31 ...	—	—	—
12 ...	4	—	—				
13 ...	—	—	—	Totals	48	8	7
14 ...	—	—	—				

From the beginning of the war up to **Dec. 31, 1940, 3,045 enemy aircraft** destroyed during raids on Britain. R.A.F. losses **847**, but **427** pilots saved.

In the **Western Desert operations**, since Italy entered the war, she has lost the following aircraft in combat or destroyed on the ground. British losses are given for the same period :

	Italy Combat	Italy Ground	Britain Combat		Italy Combat	Italy Ground	Britain Combat
June	13	6	3	Oct. ...	8	2	4
July ...	22	4	1	Nov.	14	3	2
Aug.	27	8	4	Dec. ...	104	83	12
Sept.	10	5	3	Totals	198	111	29

there were no night raids. The last night of the year passed without an Alert, and during daylight there were only isolated attacks on Kent and Essex coastal towns.

During 1940 London's Alerts numbered more than 400, and lasted for roughly 1,180 hours. The first daylight attack on the Capital came early in September ; in the big raid of Sept. 8 the Nazis lost 99 aircraft, 78 being shot down by our fighters. On the next day, when again between three and four hundred Nazi 'planes attacked London, our Spitfires and Hurricanes accounted for 47. Then the Metropolitan area—and the country generally—began to feel secure under the protection of its incomparable Air Force and ground defences. Work and traffic no longer ceased for the Alert, and only when danger became imminent did the workers resort to shelters. The enemy had failed to stop our productive effort. During the year the A.A. guns of Britain destroyed 444 enemy aircraft. The figures for enemy aircraft destroyed by Allied naval units from the beginning of the war up to Dec. 1, 1940 are 192 ; in addition there were 91 whose destruction was unconfirmed, and another hundred which were " damaged."

In spite of the intense provocation, no reprisal raids on German cities were carried out : and the R.A.F. bombers continued their operations according to the strategical pattern worked out by the High Command. On Tuesday, Dec. 31, during reconnaissance flights in daylight over Western Germany, one of our Blenheims swooped down on a bridge near Emmerich, and at below 500 feet he loosed off a stick of bombs ; some of them hit the bridge fair and square. Another pilot bombed a factory at Cologne, while yet others attacked objectives at Rotterdam and Ymuiden.

On Jan. 1 a very large force of our bombers raided Bremen for 3½ hours. In this great industrial centre —second only to Hamburg in importance—the main objectives were the shipbuilding yards and docks, where submarines are built ; the Deutsche Vacuum Oil Refinery ; rice and starch mills and many other industrial targets ; the Focke-Wulf air-frame works ; and railways and other communications. Twenty thousand incendiaries, more than twice the number dropped by the Germans on the City of London during the great fire-raising attack, fell on Bremen, besides loads of high explosives. Repeat visits were paid to the great city on the next two nights.

In London the Royal Engineers on Jan. 4, 1941, began their task of blowing up bomb-shattered buildings that threatened to collapse. Here is a photograph taken while they were on the job in Newgate Street. Before the roar of the explosion has subsided the building comes down in a cloud of dust and smoke.
Photo, Sport & General

Let Us Now Praise Those Who Fought the Fire

Shocking as was the damage done to London by the Nazi fire-raisers on the night of December 29-30, 1940, it would have been far greater but for the tremendous efforts, the self-sacrificing toil, of the men and women of London's Fire Service. This article is in the nature of a tribute to that fine body of civilian warriors.

ONLY a glimpse or two through the smoke is yet visible of the wonderful saga of the Second Great Fire of London: of the half-dozen night porters and spotters who strove in vain to save St. Bride's; of the St. Paul's Churchyard caretakers who threw fire-bombs from the roofs of the world's most inflammable buildings, the soft goods warehouses; of the Auxiliaries—former clerks and cooks, commercial travellers and "counter-jumpers"—who held the struggling hoses for a night and a day almost without relief in face of poisonous smoke and searing flame; of the "regulars" of the London Fire Brigade, who darted in the fire-floats from one side of the Thames to the other in an astonishing attempt to cope with a colossal outburst of flame in Southwark as well as the inferno of the City.

Fire-fighting in peacetime is a dangerous job enough and claims its casualties. But the peacetime fireman does not have to extinguish, to rescue, and to brave fumes with tons of high-explosives descending upon himself and the burning buildings around him, as in the "Dunkirk of Dockland," for instance, at the beginning of the "blitz." Nor does he have to work at his terrible task for such long periods without relief, since in peacetime the fire services are never called out to their full capacity. But in war fires are beacons to bombers as well as threats to property, and when half a city is engulfed the reliefs are not forthcoming—they are at work themselves. Small wonder that on the morning of Monday, December 30, one saw firemen not only dirty but dazed; they had worked to, and beyond, exhaustion

point, until they were literally "fit to drop." So worn with fatigue were some parties that one might see three exhausted men struggling to control a snaking hose which one fresh man would normally be capable of handling. An occasional drop of tea—and the bravery of the tea providers of the Y.M.C.A. and other mobile canteens, who served thousands of cups that one night, must not be forgotten—was the sole refreshment some of our civilian heroes received for twelve or fifteen hours. But they saved the day; they won the battle and the acclaim of the world. Next day hundreds of them, part-time volunteers, went back to their offices, sat on their stools, picked up their pens, and went on where they left off at Saturday noon. "Have a nice week-end?" "Pretty fair. Rather warm, though."

At the corner of Ave Maria Lane and Paternoster Row there was a nest of book publishers. Their premises made one of the biggest of the two hundred separate fires which were at one time visible from St. Paul's roof. They were old buildings, of stucco and brick for the most part, containing many wooden partitions, and they "went up like a petrol dump." Burning books and paper make a thick smoke, and through it came hurtling down from the top storeys great half-ton lumps of masonry, each enough to kill a half-dozen men. But the work went on.

A hundred yards away, on the roof of St. Paul's Cathedral, the volunteer fire-watchers laboured to save the sacred edifice—and with success. They were not firemen, but architects, surveyors, solicitors and other

A.F.S. girls, one of whom is seen in the top photograph, brought much-needed food to their firemen comrades who night and day fought the City fires without thought of rest

Photos, Planet News and L.N.A

They Served Like Heroes in London's Front Line

Thousands of cups of tea and slices of cake were supplied to London's heroic firemen by the Y.M.C.A. canteens. One of them was in the very building in St. Paul's Churchyard where the Y.M.C.A. was founded in 1844.

professional men, some of whom, seeing the glow of the burning City from their Hampstead homes, drove their cars through the furnace to do their duty to the Cathedral. They wielded their rakes and stirrup pumps, and kept Wren's building inviolate while hell raged round the holy place.

At the bottom of Ludgate Hill another scene : one solitary, immobile figure, silhouetted black against the crimson glow—a fireman mounted on a water-tower, directing a silver jet upon yet another top-storey blaze. Just one of the bravest men in London. Others were at work round the Guildhall in the close-packed streets and alleys of " Fire Danger Zone No. 1."

There were between ten and twenty thousand firemen in the front line that night ; in supreme control was Mr. F. W. Jackson, Deputy Chief Officer and London Regional Fire Officer, while one of his officers, Mr. C. M. Kerr, established a central control and arranged for water to be relayed from the Thames. The men were not all Londoners ; brigades were sent to help with the Second Great Fire from many towns in the surrounding area, and four hundred sub-stations were put into a state of emergency, ready to answer all calls for more men and more pumps. They drove through the night at breakneck pace to the rescue and fought for London until the battle was won and their strength all but spent. Then, reeling with fatigue, dizzy with the flames and smoke, grimed and unshaven, they packed up their

equipment and went back to their home stations in the quiet counties.

Some did not go back. Four firemen were killed when the wall of a burning building in the City Road collapsed upon and killed them. Their comrades tore at the masonry with their bare hands, but they were dead when found. Many were seriously injured by falling stone, others badly burned by streams of fire from ignited gas mains. Some 60 men were entrapped by the flames in the Fore Street area, and only escaped by dropping over the parapet on to the Underground railway line. But the casualties were small for a major battle.

If civilians were amazed at the heroism of the firemen, the firemen were no less astonished by the calmness and courage of civilians. Passers-by and late homegoers, shelterers who had emerged for a cigarette, and all the shifting population of a blacked-out city on a Sunday night joined in the battle without a thought for themselves, while the raiders zoomed overhead and the streets were showered with cascades of glass splinters and torrents of fire and water. Of these heroes no one will ever know the names.

Lest Londoners should imagine that theirs is the only city where dwell such heroes, let us not forget that the same experiences, the same heroism, and the same glorious victory have been endured, demonstrated and won by the firemen and people of Coventry, Manchester, Bristol, Southampton, Sheffield, and half a dozen other great provincial cities. Truly " you can't lick the people " when they are fighting for their own homes.

When dawn came on December 30, 1940, London's firemen and many others who had come in from outer areas to fight the flames were still pouring water on the ruins, some only smouldering, some still burning. Pasted to the wall on the right of these three firemen are the remains of a poster headed, " How to fight a fire." The rest is washed away. It no longer matters, for the firemen know all there is to know.   *Photos, Planet News and L.N.A.*

Echoes of War in Far-off South Africa

'I Take Off My Hat to England!'

GEN. SMUTS, in a speech at Wynburg, Orange Free State, on Dec. 11, 1940, expressed his confidence in the ultimate victory of Britain. He said:

The end of 1940 finds me more hopeful than I was at the end of 1939. Greece is trampling on Italy. That part of Italy's fleet which is not under water has vanished.

Hitler has used the greatest air fleet at his disposal, but military damage is negligible.

Britain is immeasurably stronger than before the war, and is no longer on the defensive. When I speak of England I take off my hat.

We must choose our friends for the future. I choose the country under which we suffered 40 or 50 years ago, but who, when we were at their mercy, treated us as a Christian people.

(1) The "Commands on Wheels," the mobile column which is touring S. Africa to show the mechanized army to the country, is here seen passing along the sea front of East London, Cape Province. (2) General Smuts, who combines the roles of Minister of Defence and Officer Commanding the Union Forces with that of Prime Minister of the Union, is in conference with Lieut.-General Sir Pierre Van Ryneveld, Chief of the General Staff. (3) Young evacuees at Westbrooke, the Governor-General's residence at Cape Town, send cables home on their arrival. (4) On the Kenya frontier South African troops are fighting against the Italians. Infantry are here seen returning to camp after a 17-hour route march.   *Photos, South African Official and G.P.U.*

The Mediterranean Fleet is in Good Heart & Fettle

Shortly before Christmas Lieut.-Commander A. M. Kimmins, R.N., well known as a playwright, visited Gibraltar, Malta and Alexandria under official auspices. Here is his report, broadcast as " War Commentary " on December 26, of what he saw and heard.

My first port of call was Gibraltar—the famous rock fortress which guards the narrow entrance to the western end of the Mediterranean. As we approached I began to wonder what it must feel like to be stationed on a tiny and very isolated promontory—which is what Gib is.

I know the saying " as safe as the Rock of Gibraltar " has become a sort of trademark of security throughout the world. It was coined, though, in the days of cutlasses and cannon balls—not under modern conditions of long-range armour-piercing shells, aircraft bombing, and all the rest of it.

Frankly, I expected to find everyone digging deeper and deeper holes inside the Rock as a refuge from these new methods of onslaught. But did I ? Most certainly not. Admittedly, squads of men, white from head to foot from the dust and muck shooting out from their pneumatic drills, were working

day and night building new galleries. But these galleries were not to take cover in ; they were to feed the new gun positions, the new observation posts, and so on. In fact, although preparing for siege—an essentially defensive operation—offensive tactics were being employed. There was no question of locking doors, cutting down the rations, and seeing how long they would be able to last out. It was much more a question of locking the doors, then rolling up the sleeves and seeing how many of the enemy they would be able to wipe out before being relieved.

Down below in the harbour under the very shadow of the Rock lay the units of our Western Mediterranean Fleet, fresh from their successes against the Italians. Wherever I went I found nothing but unbounded optimism and terrific enthusiasm. Hardly surprising really, because these ships and aircraft had already had a crack at the

enemy, and their one ambition now is to have more and more. In the Admiral's cabin in the flagship I had a long talk with Admiral Sir James Somerville.

" It is noteworthy, but curious," he told me, " that when we meet the enemy fleet at sea in the Mediterranean it declines battle. Why is this ? Well, in my opinion, it is because our enemies know in their hearts full well that theirs is not a just cause. That they have been wrongly led. I feel sure of this." And then he went on : " The facts are simple, and since they are simple they appeal to us sailors. We know what we are fighting for ; the enemy does not. And that knowledge, coupled with the knowledge that our people at home are resisting so magnificently, justifies us in the belief that 1941 will be a red letter year in our history."

Those were Admiral Somerville's words. Perhaps at this very moment he and his ships

Gibraltar has two harbours—the commercial, seen in the foreground, and the naval harbour, beyond it. On the right is the coast of Spain, and on the horizon can be seen the coast of Africa.   *Photo, Charles E. Brown*

GIBRALTAR'S BIG THREE responsible for its defence during the first critical months of the war are here seen in consultation. They are, left to right, Vice-Admiral Sir Dudley North, Naval C.-in-C.; Lieut.-General Sir Clive Liddell, Governor and C.-in-C., and Major-General MacFarlane, Military Commander. In December, 1940, Sir Dudley North was succeeded by Vice-Admiral Sir Frederick Edward-Collins.   *Photo, Topical*

are slipping out of harbour in the light of the half moon. On their starboard side are the gay, bright lights of Algeciras in neutral Spain —a reminder of the days of peace we are fighting for. Astern of them, as they turn out of the narrow harbour entrance, is the vast towering silhouette of the Rock. The ships are steaming out hoping for the chance to attack. From inside the Rock there comes at intervals the sound of muffled explosions. Another gallery has been blasted. Another gun is being put into position so that, should their turn come, they'll be able to hit out, mighty hard too.

From Gibraltar I flew on east to Malta, our island stronghold in the middle of the Mediterranean. As we passed over the blue waters I saw many British warships patrolling and searching for the enemy. But I never saw an Italian.

Now Malta, like Gib, is so small that on the average political map of the world— where the British Empire is shown in red— neither of them presents a sufficient area to

From East to West 'Thumbs Up!' All the Way

EAST OF GIBRALTAR the Italian Fleet dare not show its flag, though day after day British battle-ships such as these have swept the Mediterranean asking nothing better than to decide with guns whose sea it really is. The result would well justify the British C.-in-C. in hoisting a broom at his masthead, like the famous Dutch Admiral Tromp, 300 years ago, to show that he was master of the seas.
Photo, Central Press

MAJ.-GEN. DOBBIE, Acting Governor of Malta, is one of the best-known personalities in the Royal Engineers and, like that other Engineer, "Chinese" Gordon, believes that a soldier is all the better for being a good Christian.
Photo, Russell

allow for even the smallest red splodge; they have to be content with red lines under their names. And, like Gib, Malta lies nearly a thousand miles from its nearest British neighbour. What's more, Malta with Sicily to the north, Libya to the south and various Italian islands dotted around, is surrounded by the enemy on all sides.

Not a particularly healthy place one would imagine, but in Malta, to my surprise, I found everything going on much the same as before. Everyone, Navy, Army, Air Force and civilians, was of course, working overtime, but—for their moments of relaxation—the cinemas, bars and so on were open as before. When the British warships return the inhabitants crowd the Barracca—the high ground overlooking the Grand Harbour—and cheer like mad. When they see an Italian aircraft shot down, they yell themselves hoarse.

Before this trip I had not been in Malta for some years, and so, in all innocence, I approached a cheerful-looking Karozzi driver (Karozzis are the local cabs) and asked him to take me to the main street, the Strada Reale. In a flash his expression changed and he stared down at me with stinking contempt.

I repeated my request, but he only eyed me with greater suspicion and asked me who I was and where I came from

By now somewhat peeved, I replied haughtily that I should have thought that my uniform was sufficient evidence that I was a naval officer and, if he must know, I had arrived that afternoon. At this news he wilted completely, bowed me into his cab and then said with terrific pride: "In Malta we no longer have Italian names for our streets. The Strada Reale is now The Kingsway."

When we reached our destination I asked him what he thought about the Italian air raids. He didn't accept the question for himself, but turned proudly and patted his best friend, his horse. "Charlie," he said, "not like the sirens, but Charlie not give a damn for the Italian bombs!"

In Malta, you see, the whole civil population are just as much part of the defence organization of the islands as they are here at home. His Excellency the Governor and the Vice-Admiral Commanding the Dockyard—Admiral Ford—were both lost in admiration for the way the Maltese had faced up to the air raids and all the rest of it. The last thing Admiral Ford said to me was: " You can tell all at home that as far as Malta is concerned it's 'Thumbs up.' "

From Malta I flew on to Alexandria, the naval base in Egypt from which the main portion of the Mediterranean Fleet has been operating. On the way I looked down upon British warships heading for Greece; others were steaming at full speed to bombard the Libyan coastline. Again I never saw one single Italian. Just as in the Western Mediterranean, the control of the seas was completely ours.

At Gib and Malta I think the thing that had impressed me more than anything else was the spirit of the individuals. Now as we glided down into the harbour of Alexandria I felt a new sensation: a feeling of bursting pride in the strength and might of the British and Allied Navies lying there below. Powerful ships of all classes were grouped in formidable array. The traffic problem at the harbour entrance was acute. Ships were steaming out to play their part alongside the land forces in bombarding the retreating Italians and their coastal positions:

others were returning for more and yet more ammunition. Even from the air one could tell that those at anchor in the harbour were by no means idle. The numbers of small craft, ammunition lighters, oilers and so on hurrying from warship to warship told clearly enough that the men-o'-war were not in harbour for a rest or shelter. They were here for one reason only, to replenish with stores and ammunition and get back to sea on the job.

Later, when talking to the individuals, the sailors who had chased and harried the Italian Fleet on so many occasions, the Fleet Air Arm pilots who had carried out that amazing raid on Taranto—in fact all those who had played their part in gaining control of the Mediterranean, I found one very noticeable thing. Except from a purely technical point of view they had little to say of what had happened in the past. Their whole conversation hinged on two factors. Where and how often could they strike in the future? And what news could I give them of their folks at home?

'A. B. C.' the C.-in-C.

While in Alexandria I had a talk with the Commander-in-Chief, Admiral Sir Andrew B. Cunningham. His is a name which has been on everyone's lips and yet in the street he wouldn't be recognized. He is a Scot and is known affectionately by those who serve under him as "A.B.C." He is short, rugged, and with rather close-cut greying hair above blue eyes which pierce right through you. For many months he has shouldered tremendous responsibilities, and yet there is not one sign of fatigue. Like most Scots, once he gets an idea into his head nothing will deter him from seeing it through. At present his one idea is to sink every enemy ship in the Mediterranean. Given the chance, he will.

This is what the Commander-in-Chief asked me to say: " Perhaps the best news I can give those at home is the fact that the fleet in the Mediterranean is in good heart and fettle for the reason that experience has shown that we can rely unquestionably on the vital support of the factories and munition works of the Home Front."

**Eye Witness Stories of Episodes
and Adventures in the
Second Great War**

I Saw the City Burning at Midnight

The German attempt to fire London on December 29, 1940, made the
night memorable even to the city which had already been so heavily
raided. A "Daily Mail" reporter, who was on the spot while the
fires were at their height, wrote this graphic impression of the scene.

MIDNIGHT was not far away when, on
December 29, 1940, I walked up
Ludgate Hill, buildings blazing to
my left, buildings blazing to my right. A
mighty glare lit the sky above, tinting the
high clouds with a tinge of pink.

Even at this hour a great crowd of
Londoners were out to watch the attempted
destruction of their beloved city. They
walked slowly—men, smartly dressed girls,
Cockney matrons, here and there a child.
And they walked almost in silence.

In the glare of many fires their faces
showed white and bitter. They said little.
They were awed and deeply angry. Every
now and then you would hear someone
mutter to himself, " They'll pay for this."

We picked our course across tangled lines
of hose, moved quietly out of the way of
firemen, glanced warily behind to dodge
the motors and appliances that heralded
their approach with the jangling of bells.

St. Paul's loomed ahead, its ancient walls
strangely lovely in the glow of a hundred
fires. The grey stones shone scarlet ; every
now and then a pall of smoke from a building

opposite would momentarily douse a blaze
of flame, and black shadows would chase
each other across the dome..

Here was a sight at which to marvel.
Fire blazed all around, flames dangerously
close. The cathedral itself, its cross above the
dome calm and aloof above a sea of fire, stood
out, an island of God, safe and untouched.

On, and deeper into the City. Fires, always fires ; to the left, to the right, before
and behind.

Every now and then a shower of burning
rubble would whirl down from a rooftop,
caught by the wind, dance along the road and
clothe one for a second in a sea of sparks.

Everywhere great armies of firemen, professional and amateur, worked grimly on,
too absorbed in their own fierce business to
worry about the danger to fools like myself,
drawn to this scene of destruction by an
instinct too deep to be denied.

Now I reach a wide cross-roads. One
great block of buildings is alight. Scores of
firemen grapple with it.

The wind is rising. The flames leap and
roar at its touch. Suddenly from one side

of the burning block a great tongue of flame
leaps out. It is caught by the wind. It
swells in size, leaps sheer across a wide road
horizontal, like some gigantic blow-lamp.

The end of the flames lick the facing
building. The second building catches. . .

As I watch, fascinated, I become conscious
of a roaring close at hand. I glance through
the door of a darkened building beside me.

The Shower of Fire Grows Heavier

What I see there makes me catch my breath.
Inside is a wide, square hall. To the left there
are lifts. Ahead is a fine, wide stairway. All is
lighted by great showers of sparks falling
through from somewhere above. I had not
known that the building was afire. The
sparks now are coming down thick and fast.

A heavy pile carpet on the hall floor begins
to smoulder. The shower of fire grows
crazier and heavier. The carpet flames.
The fire spreads to the staircase. It is like
some scene from a Hollywood magnate's
dream. Soon the whole staircase is ablaze.

Firemen rush to their new task. Ten
minutes later there is a mighty roar. Flames
burst from the roof and through the upper
windows.

I turn back sickened. I make my way
through the same silent crowds, hear the
same muttered remark, " They'll pay for
this."

Pray God they will.

LONDON'S GREAT FIRE on the night of December 29, 1940, lit up the square mile of the City almost as brightly as daylight, and seen from any
point of the compass it presented such an awe-inspiring spectacle of flames, sparks and smoke as has never been seen since the great fire of 1666.
The scene above could be multiplied many times over, but it bears witness to the fact that amidst all the devastation many famous buildings still
stood and were even unscorched.
Photo, Planet News

'Don't You British Women Ever Cry?'

On her way from Australia to England the "Rangitane" was attacked by a German raider in the Pacific, and sunk. After weeks of imprisonment in a German supply ship, the "Tokyo Maru," survivors were marooned on the little South Sea island of Emirau (see page 38). Below we print some of the stories they had to tell.

"IT was early in the morning of November 26, 1940," said Miss Mundie, who was returning to England after acting as an escort to a number of British children evacuated to Australia, "when the raider shelled the 'Rangitane.'

"After the first shells I was trapped in a cabin; the passage-way was filled with flames. Then there was an explosion below and heavy gas-like fumes enveloped me. My clothes began to sizzle, and soon I was naked. I tried to get out of the cabin, but the flames were too fierce. The ship was so quiet that I thought she had been deserted and I was given up as lost. You see, two other women and a man on either side of my cabin were killed.

"Then I heard someone call for help. I called out but there was no response. Another woman called for help, and I again called out. Then a man appeared beside the flames. He spoke reassuringly and led me

sighted," he said, "a radio signal was sent out advising 'raiders sighted.' Without warning the raider fired a shot which went through the steering-gear; other shells followed rapidly. Mr. Crawford, the ship's surgeon, worked under fire giving first aid to the injured. Stewards gathered the dead and injured in blankets—there was no time to get them on to stretchers—and carried them to the lifeboats. Two ship's stewardesses

were killed and a third wounded. Others helped the women and children to bandage wounds and remained level-headed and cheerful. Two brothers named Stickfuss, both engine-room workers, were seen helping each other, though they were mortally wounded. Neither murmured. They died together."

Of the 46 women aboard the "Rangitane," six were killed by the raider's shells, and of the rest many were wounded, some seriously. Then for days they were half-starved and kept short of drinking-water. Yet nothing could break their spirit. "Don't you British women ever cry?" the raider's captain, said to be Count Felix von Luckner, is stated to have asked them.

Our Flight Was a Regular Nightmare

Pilots of the Bomber Command returning to their bases on the night of December 10, 1940 brought reports of icing, electrical storms, dense cloud and snow over the North Sea and Germany. The experience of one crew, narrated below, serves to show what our aircraft are often up against.

A HEAVY bomber of the R.A.F. had been detailed to attack a target in Germany. As soon as they reached the Dutch

Six searchlights caught the machine and fastened on to us. I could hear the shells bursting underneath and to the side. Every now and then we kept going into those horrible spirals. The wireless operator was thrown across the aircraft and broke his ankle, but he got back to his wireless and kept working it. I had already told the crew to get their parachutes on, but with the front gunner injured it would have been impossible for us to have left the aircraft. We couldn't have got him out. I had a feeling at the back of my mind, too, that the starboard engine would pick up again once we got out of cloud.

The whole thing was a nightmare. I don't know how the guns missed us. With only one engine I couldn't take any evasive action. We ran slap through a balloon barrage. We were still on one engine then and I just flew on. I was sweating hot. We had dropped to about a thousand feet when the starboard engine picked up at last and so we got home.

THE "RANGITANE," some of the survivors from which tell of their experiences in this page, was a liner of 16,712 tons belonging to the New Zealand Shipping Company. When she was attacked she had about 100 passengers on board. Survivors from six ships flying the Union Jack, and one Norwegian, were "marooned" on the South Sea island of Emirau.   *Photo, Central Press*

away. I do not know his name, but he saved my life."

'Jimmie Never Made a Murmur'

Mrs. Langan, another of the passengers said:

"When the raider began firing I screamed, 'Jimmie, come to me!' The cabin became full of fumes and we could not breathe. We heard the bursting of shells above us. I half carried Jimmie and his brother Brian to the lifeboat. As I did so I realized that people were being killed and injured all around me. It was not until I reached the boat that I realized Jimmie had been hit. He never made a murmur. The Germans may have been polite afterwards, but as a mother I say nothing can forgive them for injuring a child like this."

Then the Quartermaster, Mr. L. Valerie, who was at the wheel when the raider opened fire, added his contribution to what he well described as "one of the ghastliest incidents of the war":

"As soon as the sinister vessel was

coast they ran into heavy cloud. Describing their experiences the sergeant-pilot said:

We tried to climb through it, but couldn't. We went up to 14,000 feet without getting clear. Then it started to snow, and very soon the outside of the front turret was thickly covered. The front gunner couldn't see a thing so he came out. There was snow all over the top part of his clothing. Things got worse. The airspeed indicators froze up. I asked the second pilot what he thought, and he agreed that it seemed pretty useless trying to get through.

We were about 80 miles inland and, turning, we set course for base. Ten minutes later the starboard engine started missing, then the engine failed altogether, probably because of ice in the carburettor. I decided to get rid of the bombs to lighten the aircraft. By this time we had got down to about 11,000 feet. I couldn't keep height at all, and we kept going into steep spirals, losing a thousand feet at a time with the aircraft temporarily out of control. At one time we were actually heading east again.

At a bomber station "somewhere in England" final adjustments are being made to a 250 lb. bomb carried under the wing. In the background a bomber, fully laden with bombs, is taking off.   *Photo, Mrs. T. Muir*

Now in the City the Noise of Crashing Walls

After the fierce Nazi fire-raid of December 29, 1940 on the City of London, demolition squads got rapidly to work and many buildings that had been rendered unsafe in the fire-devastated areas were blown away by charges of gun-cotton or pulled down. Wreckage was cleared away from world-famous streets and order restored to business thoroughfares. Masonry from a building in the process of being destroyed is here seen crashing down into the street. The building is being demolished with the aid of a mobile caterpillar crane.   *Photo, T. G. Kirby, Staff Photographer, "News-Chronicle"*

OUR SEARCHLIGHT ON THE WAR

Plot to Assassinate Ibn Saud

FROM Mecca comes the news of the frustration of a conspiracy to kill King Ibn Saud of Arabia. The ring-leader was Sherif Abdul Hamid Ibn Ohn, a member of the famous Hussein family and so a relative of the Emir Abdullah of Trans-jordania and of the Royal family of Iran. He claims descent from the Prophet Mahomet and so gained Arab clemency, his sentence to death being commuted to life imprisonment. Two of the other conspirators, who were his servants, were executed and others imprisoned. It appears that in the summer of 1939 he was in Berlin interviewing high Nazi officials. He then returned to Egypt, where he has property, but three months ago went to Arabia on the pretext that he wished to take part in a pilgrimage to Mecca. Arrangements were then made to assassinate the King during the excitement that prevails at Mecca when the city is crowded with pilgrims. Ibn Saud, who was proclaimed King of the Hejaz in 1926, signed a treaty with Britain by which, the following year, the independence of his country was recognized. He unified the Hejaz and Nejd territories under the name of Saudi Arabia in 1932. This is the second attempt to assassinate the King. The first was in March, 1935, again at Mecca, as he and his son were making the devout circuit of the sacred Kaaba.

British Honours for Polish Airmen

THE first British awards to be given to Polish airmen were made in December, 1940, when four pilots of the Polish Squadron of the R.A.F. were decorated with the Distinguished Flying Cross by the Air Officer C.-in-C., Fighter Command, Air Marshal W. Sholto Douglas, at an aerodrome in the north of England. A fifth D.F.C. was awarded to a pilot who had been killed in action. After decorating the men the Air Marshal said: "The R.A.F. is proud to have its Polish comrades, whose deeds are known throughout the Air Force. I hope your Squadron will do equally well in the months to come. I look forward to the victory of our cause and to a free and independent Poland." The Polish Squadron played an important part in the defence of London in September, and between them these five pilots destroyed 44 German aircraft and severely damaged others. The officer commanding the Polish fighters is Squadron-Leader R. G. Kellett, D.S.O., D.F.C., who was leader of the R.A.F. long-distance flight to Australia in 1938. To him Poland has given her highest award for valour, the "Virtuti Militari."

FOUR POLISH AIRMEN were decorated with the D.F.C. by Air Marshal Sholto Douglas in December, 1940. Addressing the officers after decorating them he said, "The R.A.F. is proud to have its Polish comrades whose deeds are known throughout the whole Air Force."
Photo, British Official: Crown Copyright

Medal for Brave Merchant Seamen

LLOYD'S have decided to add to their medals and, with the approval of the Admiralty and the Ministry of Shipping, intend to strike one to be awarded to officers and men of the Merchant Navy and fishing fleet in recognition of exceptional gallantry at sea in time of war. It will be known as "Lloyd's War Medal for Bravery at Sea." The design is as follows:

LLOYD'S WAR MEDAL, recently instituted to reward bravery at sea. Like Lloyd's Meritorious Medal it will be a coveted distinction amongst merchant seamen.

Obverse. A heroic figure symbolizing courage and endurance is seated looking out over the sea, on which is seen in the distance a vessel of the mercantile marine. In his right hand the figure holds a wreath. The inscription is: "Awarded by Lloyd's."

Reverse. A trident, symbolizing sea power, is surrounded by an endless wreath of oak leaves and acorns. On a ribbon across the centre of the design is the single word "Bravery."

The ribbon is blue and silver, similar in design to that of the ribbon for Lloyd's Meritorious Medal, but with the colours reversed. The new medal is the work of Mr. Allan G. Wyon, F.R.B.S., member of a family responsible for designing all Lloyd's medals.

Japanese Anti-British Activities

IN the Japanese port of Kobe there have been anchored since the beginning of the war a number of ships ready to make for the open sea when the word is given. Among them is the liner "Scharnhorst," a 21-knot turbo-electric vessel belonging to the Norddeutscher Lloyd. A correspondent of the "Daily Telegraph" reports that this ship is being fully re-conditioned below decks and that guns and other armaments have been seen. If it is true that she is being fitted out as an armed ship the Japanese Government renders itself liable under international law for any damage she may do. German prize crews have made use of both Chinese and Japanese ports for the purpose of provisioning and arming. Quite recently a captured Norwegian tanker, converted by the Nazis into a prison ship, entered Kobe harbour, discharged her prisoners, took aboard provisions and water, and steamed away without interference. In the early days of the war British ships patrolled outside Japanese ports to prevent this sort of thing from happening, but the Navy can no longer spare enough vessels for this purpose.

British Submarine in German Navy

ACCORDING to the Nazis, H.M. submarine "Seal," reported by the British Admiralty on May 12, 1940, to be overdue and considered lost, is now being used under the German flag and in the service of their Government. Foreign reports at the time of her disappearance suggested that some of the crew might be prisoners of war, but the Germans state that the entire crew were made prisoner when the submarine was taken in tow after being mined off the Swedish coast. The "Seal" was the last of the six mine-laying submarines of the Porpoise class and was completed at Chatham in 1938. Her commander, Lieut.-Commander R. P. Lonsdale, was mentioned in despatches in May for "daring endurance and resource in the conduct of hazardous and successful operations."

German Bombs on Eire

EIRE, the only neutral country associated with the British Commonwealth of Nations, was first bombed by Nazi aircraft on August 27, 1940. Germany admitted liability for this raid and it was thought that the pilot had lost his bearings. On October 21 bombs fell in open country in Co. Wicklow, injuring nobody. On December 21 bombs were dropped near Dublin, and there were two casualties. On December 29 aircraft flying over Co. Donegal and the Lough Swilly coastal forts were fired on by A.A. guns. More decisive raids were made during the nights of January 1 and 2, 1941. On the 1st the raiders flew along a 100-mile line on the eastern side of the country, apparently using the sea as a directional guide, and bombs fell in four counties. On the night of the 2nd further bombs fell in another county, Wexford, and in addition magnetic mines intended for sowing at sea were dropped near Enniskerry, in Co. Wicklow. Experts who examined the bombs were in no doubt as to the nationality of the aircraft, and at least one incendiary picked up near the Curragh, where there is not only a military camp but one for interned airmen, was definitely identified as German. The mines, which had come down by parachute, were destroyed by army engineers on January 3. It is difficult to explain the bombing of Eire as other than deliberate, for German aircraft crews are fully supplied with navigating instruments. If for some reason the bombs were being jettisoned it would be better policy to do this over the sea than to violate the neutrality of a non-belligerent country.

Pre-War Family Budget

AN inquiry carried out by the Ministry of Labour into the cost of living before the outbreak of war among manual workers and non-manual workers earning less than £250 a year provides some interesting side-lights on the family budget of fifteen months ago. It was found that the average home in the 9,000 under survey spent £4 6s. 3d. a week, of which only £1 14s. 1d. went in food. The biggest single item of this was milk, which cost 3s. 0¾d. Bread cost 2s. 8¾d., meat 2s. 8d., eggs 1s. 10½d., and tea 1s. 7¾d. Fuel and light together were 7s. 6½d. in the winter and 5s. 2½d. in summer. Other items were as follows:

	s.	*d.*
Cigarettes and Tobacco	2	6½
Travelling	2	3
Entertainment (Cinema 10¾d. of this) ..	1	4½
Clothing (woman)	2	7½
Clothing (man)	2	3¾
Clothing (children, and boot repairs) ..	4	4¾

If a new cost of living index figure is adopted in view of wartime prices and the new Purchase Tax, millions of workers, whose wage rates are based on the present index, will be affected and the repercussions in industry will be considerable.

They Have Won Honour in Freedom's Cause

Sergt. E. Powell, R.A.F. wireless operator and air gunner, **D.F.M.**, for 36 successful flights over enemy territory.

Flight Sergt. G. C. Unwin, D.F.M., for destroying 13 enemy aircraft and assisting in the destruction of others.

Cpl. J. M. G. Robins, W.A.A.F., M.M., for assisting wounded and rendering first aid in a bombed shelter.

Pilot Officer H. M. Stephen, D.S.O., for destroying more than 20 enemy aircraft. First D.S.O. on the Home Front.

Sergt.-Gunner W. H. Sturdy, D.F.M., for actions over enemy territory before the evacuation from France.

Chief Engineer A. H. Singleton, D.S.M., for devotion to duty during the evacuation of Narvik and Namsos.

Skipper W. H. Pollock, of Hull, **D.S.C.**, for conspicuous service against the enemy off the French coast.

Lieut.-Cdr. S. H. Norris, R.N., D.S.O., for courage and resource in successful actions against Italian submarines.

Lieut. L. J. Tillie, R.N., a bar to his **D.S.C.**, for courage and resource in successful action against Italian submarines.

Capt. E. Small, of South Shields, **M.B.E.** (Civil Div.), for bravery displayed during a bombing attack in the Channel.

Skipper G. Mitchell, of Brighton, a **Shield of Honour**, for displaying courage and devotion to duty at Dunkirk.

Staff Officer R. T. Harris, of Croydon A.R.P. Engineers' Service, **G.C.**, for conspicuous bravery in carrying out dangerous duties.

Wolf Cub R. Newman, aged 10, Boy Scouts' Silver Cross, for saving the life of his baby brother during an air raid.

Cpl. K. F. Clements, aged 18, Boy's Brigade Cross for Heroism, for rescuing his mother and grandmother from their blazing house.

Deputy Chief Inspector T. Breaks (Fire Brigade Div., Home Office), **O.B.E.**, for outstanding work during fire caused by enemy action.

Act. Capt. W. J. S. Fletcher, M.C., for gallantry in bombed London area. Winner of the first M.C. awarded in the Battle of London.

Capt. D. W. Cunnington of Calgary, Alberta, **G.M.**, for displaying conspicuous bravery in carrying out dangerous duties.

Lieut. J. M. S. Patton, G.C., who, with Capt. Cunnington, dragged an unexploded bomb from an important building.

Capt. R. T. H. Lonsdale, Leicestershires, **M.C.**, for displaying conspicuous bravery and devotion to duty on active service.

Lieut.-Col. (temp. Col.) **F. S. Morgan, Royal Corps of Signals, C.B.E.** (Military Div.), for courage and outstanding devotion to duty.

Aux. Fireman H. B. Neale, G.M., for helping to save two oil tanks from destruction during air raid.

Mr. C. E. Burridge, G.M., for helping to save a large gasholder from destruction. Gas was issuing under pressure.

Miss B. Quin, of Coventry, **G.M.**, for smothering 5 bombs and digging out 7 people from a shelter.

Mr. F. R. Cox, G.M., for assisting Mr. Burridge to save a gasholder. Enemy aircraft were bombing close by.

Station Inspector Gahan, O.B.E. (Civil Div.), for courage in air raids and outstanding organizing ability.

OUR DIARY OF THE WAR

MONDAY, DEC. 30, 1940   *485th day*

In the Air—R.A.F. fighters on patrol shot down two Italian seaplanes over Adriatic.

War against Italy—British still shelling Bardia. On night of 29-30 R.A.F. heavy bombers raided landing-grounds at Gazala and Tobruk.

During night of 30-31 R.A.F. bombed Taranto, Naples, and Palermo harbour.

Offensive reconnaissance carried out over large area of Somaliland by S. African Air Force. Enemy bomber destroyed at Bardera.

Home Front—During day single enemy aircraft dropped bombs in East Anglia and Kent. Diving bomber machine-gunned streets of one town. No night air activity.

Greek War—Athens announced successful local operations on different parts of front. More than 1,000 prisoners taken and much material. Greeks now about 16 miles S.E. of Berat. Italian ski detachment broken up.

TUESDAY, DEC. 31   *486th day*

On the Sea—British warship reported to have sunk four Italian supply ships in Adriatic.

Five hundred survivors from ships sunk by Pacific raiders landed at Australian port.

In the Air—Bombers of R.A.F. carried out series of daylight raids on Cologne, oil supplies at Rotterdam and docks at Ymuiden. Important Rhine bridge near Emmerich, N.W. of Ruhr, also hit. Haamstede aerodrome and A.A. ship at Flushing bombed.

War against Italy—Siege of Bardia continued. British patrols now operating more than 70 miles inside Libya. R.A.F. attacked enemy troops and motor transport in and to west of Bardia.

R.A.F. raided Gubba, Assab and Danghila, Italian East Africa.

Guerilla warfare being carried out against Italians by bands of Abyssinian rebels.

Home Front—Few isolated raids by single aircraft in Kent and Essex. Passenger train in Kent attacked. No night raids.

Greek War—Greeks occupied more fortified enemy positions north of Chimara. Farther east, Italian withdrawal continued either side of Aoos river. During night fierce battle was fought in Klisura sector. Valona bombed by R.A.F. for 23rd time.

WEDNESDAY, JAN. 1, 1941   *487th day*

In the Air—Twenty thousand incendiaries and load of high explosive bombs dropped on Bremen during R.A.F. night raid lasting 3½ hours. Ports of Flushing, Ostend and Brest were also attacked.

War against Italy—Italian garrison of Bardia showed no sign of activity. R.A.F. bombed it during night and also raided aerodromes at Tmimi, Gazala and Derna.

During night R.A.F. carried out heavy raid on shipping in Tripoli harbour, sinking motor vessel of 10,000 tons.

Aircraft of a Rhodesian squadron bombed enemy positions at Keru, east of Kassala.

Home Front—Incendiary bombs fell at several points in Eastern England during night. Enemy 'planes were also reported over Liverpool, near a northern Midlands own and over London.

Greek War—Italians constructing new fortified positions across central Albania to provide line of withdrawal should Valona, Tepelini and Klisura fall. Fighting continued in deep snow in mountains around Skumbi valley, near Lake Ochrida.

General—Bombs fell on Eire during night, in various parts of eastern counties.

THURSDAY, JAN. 2   *488th day*

In the Air—R.A.F. again attacked Bremen, bombs being dropped on naval base, shipyards and railway station. Other aircraft attacked targets at Emden and Amsterdam.

War against Italy—Bardia subjected to very heavy air attack, both by day and night. Tobruk and Gazala were also bombed.

Hitler sent air squadrons to Italy to form integral part of Italian Air Force.

Home Front—Slight enemy day activity in some coastal districts. Violent night raid made on Cardiff, with thousands of incendiaries followed by high explosive bombs.

Greek War—In Southern Albania Greeks crossed R. Bence and advanced three miles, taking 500 prisoners. They also occupied village of Dobrenje, 18 miles S.E. of Berat. R.A.F. made successful raid on Elbasan.

FRIDAY, JAN. 3   *489th day*

On the Sea—Admiralty announced that H.M. submarine " Thunderbolt " (formerly " Thetis ") had sunk an Italian submarine which was on its way to occupied territory.

In the Air—R.A.F. heavily attacked Bremen for third night in succession.

War against Italy—Just after dawn Australian forces, supported by tanks, penetrated sector of Bardia defences. Navy hurled at least 300 tons of shells into the fortress. By evening British troops had penetrated centre defences to depth of 2 miles on frontage of 9 miles.

Home Front—Slight enemy activity in some coastal districts. At night Bristol was heavily raided, fire bombs being dropped more than high explosives.

German bomber destroyed by A.A. fire.

Greek War—Italian counter-attacks against mountain positions in Klisura district repulsed by Greeks with heavy enemy losses. British and Greek aircraft bombed Italian positions along whole of northern front.

General—Vichy Cabinet reorganized. Admiral Darlan made Minister of Interior ; General Huntziger, Defence Minister ; M. Flandin took over direction of economic affairs as well as foreign relations.

Eire had third raid in 24 hours, bombs being dropped over Dublin. Mr. de Valera sent strong protest to Germany.

SATURDAY, JAN. 4   *490th day*

In the Air—Coastal Command aircraft attacked Brest, scoring three direct hits on enemy destroyer. Two German merchant vessels bombed off S.W. coast of Norway.

Bad weather hampered night operations, but Brest and Hamburg were again attacked.

War against Italy—Italian troops occupying northern sector of defences of Bardia were forced to surrender. British patrols penetrated into Bardia itself and enemy resistance was confined to south-east zone of perimeter defences.

R.A.F. bombers continued incessant attack on enemy aerodromes in Eastern Libya.

Home Front—During day bombs fell on two S.E. coast towns. During night enemy made long series of attacks, mainly directed against a West of England town.

Two enemy aircraft shot down into sea off South coast.

Greek War—Struggle for key towns of Klisura and Tepelini proceeding, but both armies hampered by bitter winter weather. Highly successful R.A.F. raid on Elbasan.

SUNDAY, JAN. 5   *491st day*

On the Sea—Admiralty announced that H.M. trawler " Kennymore " and H.M. drifter " Harvest Gleaner " had been sunk.

In the Air—Coastal Command aircraft attacked shipping in docks at Brest and an enemy aerodrome.

War against Italy—All resistance at Bardia ceased and garrison surrendered. Prisoners so far captured exceeded 25,000.

Home Front—Few bombs fell during day in East Anglia. At night baskets of incendiaries were dropped over London, and some high explosives.

Greek War—Limited local actions in Albania. Greeks took over 200 more prisoners and much material.

MONDAY, JAN. 6   *492nd day*

In the Air—Coastal Command aircraft attacked three enemy merchant vessels off Norway and badly damaged one. Enemy tanker off Dutch coast received direct hit.

War against Italy—More than 30,000 prisoners captured at Bardia, and quantities of tanks, guns, equipment and stores.

British advanced elements now approaching Tobruk area, on which R.A.F. bombers made intensive attacks. Fighter aircraft destroyed 11 enemy machines and badly damaged many others.

During night of 6-7 R.A.F. heavy bombers again raided Tripoli.

Raid carried out on Massawa.

Home Front—During day bombs fell in London area, on Kent and in Eastern Counties. No enemy activity at night.

Greek War—R.A.F. again raided Valona. Greeks captured still more Italian prisoners.

OUR WAR GAZETTEER

Bardia. Libyan port, strongly fortified and a vital Italian base ; 12 miles from Egyptian-Libyan frontier ; on coastal road to Tobruk, 65 miles west. Captured by British on January 5, 1941.

Benghazi. Important seaport of Libya, pop. 64,000 (19,000 Italians). There is a first-class motor road between Benghazi and Tripoli. Benina aerodrome, one of the principal Italian air bases in Libya, has been repeatedly bombed by the R.A.F. Cap. of Cyrenaica.

Berat. On r. Osum, 30 miles northeast of Valona ; pop. 10,000 ; near site of ancient Elyma ; formerly exported olives and oil ; the seat of a Greek archbishop. Captured by the Italians from the Austrians in 1918.

Chimara. (Himara). Albanian port on the Adriatic, 28 miles south of Valona. Captured by Greeks on December 23, 1940. It lies on the coastal road from Valona to Santi Quaranta.

Durazzo. (Durrës). Principal Albanian port on the Adriatic ; pop. 9,000 ; the ancient Dyrrhachium ; used during present Italo-Greek conflict as place of disembarkation of Italian troops.

Elbasan. Albanian town, on r. Skumbi 65 miles west of Monastir ; pop. 13,000 ; one of the most important towns in the country ; occupied by Austrians in 1916, it was recovered by the Allies in 1918.

Sidi Barrani. Sixty miles east from Bardia, on Egyptian coast. It was General Graziani's forward base in the Italian plan of campaign for the invasion of Egypt. Captured by the British on December 12, 1940.

Sollum. On Egyptian-Libyan frontier, captured by British from the Italians on December 16, 1940. **Fort Capuzzo** on Libyan side of frontier was likewise taken by British forces on December 16.

Tirana. Capital of Albania, 20 miles east of Durazzo ; pop. 30,000 ; overlooking Rushka valley ; former seat of Albanian Government.

Tobruk. Important Italian naval base on Libyan coast ; Italian troops retreated to Tobruk as British Army of the Nile encircled Bardia.

Valona. (Vlone). Port on the Strait of Otranto ; pop. 9,000 ; the independence of Albania was proclaimed at Valona in 1912 ; heavily attacked by R.A.F.

PAST GRAZIANI'S SHATTERED STRONGHOLD LIES THE CONQUERORS' ROAD

Fort Capuzzo, whose wrecked buildings these British Bren-gun carriers are passing, was an Italian stronghold south of Bardia. It was captured by British troops on the same day that they occupied Sollum, Dec. 16, 1940. With the capture of the fort the Army of the Nile found itself over the Libyan frontier inside the enemy's own territory. Thence the victorious army of General Wavell proceeded to Bardia, which early in the New Year was stormed by the Australians and British mechanized cavalry.

Photo, British Official : Crown Copyright

On to Tobruk Swept the Army of the Nile

Continuing his masterly strategy in the Western Desert, General Wavell followed up his capture of Bardia by the investment of Tobruk, the next centre of Italian power along the coast. Meanwhile, the full extent of the Bardia victory became apparent as the prisoners and the spoil were counted.

EVEN before Bardia fell the mechanized patrols of Wavell's army were reported to be south of Tobruk, Graziani's naval base and military stronghold some 80 miles along the coast to the west. A few days more, and the place was closely invested. No reinforcements could reach it from the west, nor could any of the troops leave it who had formed its garrison or had struggled into it before the British onrush.

FREE FRENCH units operating with the British forces in the Western Desert contributed to the fall of Bardia. At the same time a detachment of French marines cut the road from Bardia to Tobruk. These two Frenchmen are seen with an Italian A.A. gun.

Once again the desert rose in dust as the Imperial Army of the Nile thundered across it. Guns rattled into position, heavy tanks lumbered up to support their lighter brethren, thousands of troops marched along the sandy tracks or were borne swiftly on motor lorries. (What an improvement on the way their fathers had " foot-slogged " through the Flanders mud !)

Tobruk was strongly defended—stronger even than Bardia had been—but it was not anticipated that it would stand a prolonged siege. Its garrison was believed to be fewer in numbers than that which had endeavoured to hold Bardia, and it was entrusted with the defence of a far larger area ; the outer perimeter of the defences, indeed, was some 25 miles in length, although in front of the town itself was a much shorter line of trenches, plentifully supplied with anti-tank obstacles and machine-gun posts. There

was good reason to believe that the equipment of the defenders was decidedly inadequate, as so much had been lost in the disasters of the preceding weeks. Then while the defenders were dispirited by those disasters, the attackers were cheered by the consciousness of victories already won and filled with hope of even greater victories to come.

Steadily the Italian outposts were driven in, while their defences were plastered day after day by the British bombers. Tobruk's aerodrome at El Adem, 18 miles to the south in the heart of the desert, was so heavily bombed that on January 6 it was abandoned by the Italians. Well might it be described as the graveyard of the Regia Aeronautica in Libya, for when the British troops entered they found the burnt out remains of 25 Italian bombers and 43 fighters which had been put out of action on the ground by the R.A.F. The Italians had removed much of their material and several aeroplane engines, but such was their haste they made no attempt to destroy the hangars or plant.

Meanwhile, the battlefield at Bardia was being carefully cleared. For miles the desert was strewn with abandoned guns, tanks, and lorries. So great was the spoil that it was days before it could be properly enumerated. Then it was announced in Cairo that the

The Italians were bombed out of their air bases in Eastern Libya during the British stranglehold on Tobruk. On this map the lines of attack are shown by arrows (land) and 'planes. *Courtesy of the " Daily Telegraph "*

British had captured or destroyed in the Bardia action 368 medium and field guns, 26 heavy anti-aircraft guns, 68 light guns, 13 medium tanks and 117 light tanks, and 708 transport vehicles of one kind or another. " The high degree of unserviceability in the equipment and, more especially, in the mechanical transport, resulted largely from our bombardment of Bardia, but it also shows complete lack of maintenance during and after the Italian rout from Sidi Barrani."

The Italian casualties in the Bardia battle were stated to amount to 2,041 officers and 42,837 men killed or captured. More than 40,000 of these were prisoners—10,000 more than had been announced at first, for it was found that the Italian army in Bardia included a number of departmental and administrative units. The total British and Australian casualties incurred in the capture of Bardia were less than 600.

TOBRUK, Italian naval base in Libya, about 60 miles west of Bardia, was subjected to increasing air bombardment by the R.A.F. after the fall of Bardia on January 5. Tobruk became the next vital objective for the British in their advance into Libya. Part of its extensive harbour is here shown.
Photos, Dorien Leigh and British Official ; Crown Copyright

At Bardia They Counted the Captives and the Spoil

THE CAPTURE OF BARDIA, had the place been garrisoned by other than dispirited troops, might have been no easy matter, since for three years the Italians had been strengthening what was already a natural fortress. Top, our artillery bombard Bardia. Note the greatcoats, suggesting how chilly the desert can be in the early hours. Below, British in the line at Bardia.

Another communiqué issued by G.H.Q., Cairo, struck a rather amusing note. " It transpires that on the night before Bardia fell the Blackshirt corps commander and his two Blackshirt divisional generals deserted their troops, leaving the Regular commander to fight on. One of the Blackshirt commanders has since been picked up with the bulk of his staff, north of Bardia. General Berganzoli " Electric Beard " as he was nicknamed by his troops in Spain because of the black profusion of his facial appendage and the others are still missing. It is possible that they may have decamped by motor-boat, specially reserved for the purpose." The search is still continuing, concluded the communiqué dryly ; and two days later one of the missing three was captured while plodding across the desert in the direction of Tobruk.

Italian losses since the Western Desert offensive began on December 9 now totalled nearly 80,000 killed, wounded and prisoners, while the war material captured included 41 medium and 162 light tanks, 589 guns with more than 3,000 rounds of ammunition, more than 600 machine-guns, 700 light guns, and 11,000,000 rounds of small arms and machine-gun ammunition, and at least 1,700 lorries. Not a word of these crippling losses

was permitted to be told to the Italian people by Mussolini, who on his own declaration writes the Italian communiqués so that he may be sure that they tell the truth. On January 11 the Italian General Staff announced that the Italian losses in the North African campaign during December, i.e. the

Battle for Sidi Barrani, amounted to 77 killed, 307 wounded, and 343 missing !

News of the fate of their comrades in Bardia was conveyed to the Tobruk garrison by leaflets dropped by the R.A.F. Gifts of another kind were showered by our bombers on the Italian aerodromes along the Libyan shore. Soon it was reported by our patrolling aircraft that the aerodromes at Derna, Martuba, El Tmimi, and El Gazala were all empty of enemy aircraft, except for a considerable number that were lying on the ground unserviceable. The seaplane base at Bomba also appeared to have been abandoned by the enemy. Our fighter squadrons were active, too, destroying many enemy 'planes, either in combat or on the ground.

From Rome there came suggestions that the Italians were concentrating their forces still to the west, possibly in the neighbourhood of Benghazi, now Marshal Graziani's headquarters since he had been chased out of Cirene by the R.A.F. (They gave him no peace, however, at Benghazi.) And to Benghazi came a horde of panic-stricken settlers, who had abandoned the olive groves which they had so laboriously established in the more fertile tracts of Cyrenaica.

GUN POSITIONS had been erected all round the perimeter of the Bardia defences, but most of them were rapidly put out of action and captured, as was this one. Some 200 field guns of this kind were captured during the Bardia battle.
Photos, British Official : Crown Copyright

Bardia Was a Resounding Victory for the R.A.F.

In the operations in Libya the Regia Aeronautica was singularly ineffective, so great and decisive was the mastery of the air scored by Sir Arthur Longmore's airmen. Reasons for the predominance of the R.A.F. are not difficult to find ; indeed, more than sufficient were given by the Italians themselves when they were interrogated on the morrow of the fall of Bardia.

WHEN two Italian generals and a number of senior officers, included amongst the first batch of Bardia prisoners, were flown to the Middle East Headquarters of the Imperial Army of the Nile, they explained the defeat of the Italian arms as

That extreme cold is not one of the adverse conditions with which pilots of the R.A.F. in the Libyan desert have to contend, as do those operating from Britain, is obvious from the scanty clothing that these two men, sprinting to their machines, are wearing.

being very largely due to the bombing of the R.A.F. One commented, " No force in the world could have stood up to it. They came as regularly as the hour chimes of the Bardia clock." Another middle - aged Italian officer said, " Your airmen and your ships never gave us any rest. Bombs and shells seemed to be exploding among our defences night and day. No wonder it wore down the morale of our troops. Your heavy bombers are terrifying."

So much for the Italian evidence ; now let us hear what a young flying officer of the R.A.F. who flew over the battlefield in a reconnaissance aircraft had to say. " On Sunday I was detailed to fly over the Bardia defences," he said. " Only one complete Italian battery was firing, but other isolated guns were still pumping shells into a wadi (dried-up bed of a river) to the north where our infantry had established a base. At about half-past nine I saw six of our tanks snaking their way towards the battery, pouring out yellow flashes of fire without interruption. Their fire must have been very accurate, because when I was within 200 yards of the enemy the opposing fire ceased and I saw the Italian gunners running forward waving their hats and jackets. I was circling round at about 150 feet and got

a wonderful view of our infantry, who were following the tanks and mopping-up the Italians as they came running from their entrenchments. I dived on a detachment of our troops and dropped a message directing them to some isolated groups of Italians who were obviously anxious to surrender. I saw one column of prisoners about 1,000 yards long slowly winding its way from Bardia towards Capuzzo, apparently unescorted."

When they landed, the R.A.F. pilots mixed with the prisoners and listened with interest to the tales they had to tell. Some of the Italians, it transpired, had not eaten for three days, and the water shortage had been very acute. Many

Big bombs for the remaining Italian strongholds in Libya are here laid out on the desert for a final examination by the armourers before they are loaded on to the bomb-racks.

were barefooted as their boots were completely worn out ; men otherwise quite fit had to be given lifts on British transport vehicles because their feet were lacerated and bleeding. Some of the more temperamental officers were weeping.

On a plateau near Fort Capuzzo a solitary A.P.M. with a handful of good-natured Tommies

marshalled thousands of prisoners and kept them in some kind of order. Down the hill which leads to the port of Sollum a column of seventeen hundred Italians was headed by one British military policeman. " Who are you—the Pied Piper of Bardia ? " shouted a Tommy to the Red Cap. Some of the prisoners left the column and climbed over the rocks, taking a short cut to the port. No one minded. In any case they all reached the bottom in time to catch the ship. Before going aboard the ship which took them to safe custody, many of the Italians rushed into the sea to bathe their tired feet. Others retrieved oranges which were floating in the sea, and until restrained ate them ravenously.

Next we may give the story of an R.A.F. sergeant who, when piloting a Hurricane over Bardia, dived into a formation of five Italian S 79s which were bombing a British naval unit. " At 300 yards," he said, " I fired my first burst. Within half a minute one of the Savoias had caught fire and was plunging into the sea. I turned to attack another and saw two of the crew bale out as my fire was again successful. The third in my bag got it in the starboard motor, and the aircraft went into a long glide which finished in the Mediterranean. I silenced the return fire of the fourth Savoia, and pieces of metal flew off to starboard. There was little chance of her ever making her base. It was a pity my ammunition ran out, as the fifth was a sitter."

But, in fact, there was little air fighting over the Western Desert, for our Hurricanes and Gladiators were demonstrably superior to the Italian 'planes. Every aerodrome in Libya was bombed, some of them many times, while tons of bombs were dropped on shipping and the harbour of Tripoli, capital of Libya, 600 miles west of Tobruk. Wellingtons and Blenheims, Hurricanes and Gladiators, together with American Glenn Martins — between them they smashed Graziani's air arm to bits.

BOMBERS, too, undergo a thorough overhaul before every flight. Here an aircraftman is pumping up the huge balloon tires of a Bristol Bombay bomber before it takes off.   *Photos, British Official : Crown Copyright*

British Bombers Swoop from Desert Skies

BLENHEIMS IN LIBYA have proved a thorn in the side of Marshal Graziani's forces on account of their relentless bombardment of Italian aerodromes, camps, motor transport, troop concentrations and lines of communication. This formation of Blenheim bombers, aircraft which are among the fastest medium bombers in the world, is seen far out over the Western Desert on its way to attack Italian military objectives. A large share of the credit for the fall of Bardia must go to the R.A.F.

From these Ports Hitler Plans to Invade Us

For many months past the Fuehrer, with practically the whole of the Continent beneath his heel, has threatened Britain with invasion. So far it has not materialized, but here we give some account of the ports from which the great Nazi Armada may be expected to come—if it comes at all.

LIKE Napoleon before him, Hitler controls the whole of the European coasts that face the west. From the Pyrenees to the Arctic Circle and beyond stretches his dominion, some 1,500 miles of ocean-washed coast, rich in harbours where fleets may anchor, armadas congregate, and U-boats and raiders lurk. We may well imagine that as he looks at the map spread out before him on his desk in the Chancellery, the Fuehrer must tell himself and the yes-men peeping over his shoulder that with so vast a sweep of territory under his control nothing can save England now. "From here I will strike— and here—and here," and down comes Adolf's finger on this port and on that.

Most northerly of the "invasion ports" are those on the coast of Norway. Narvik, which lies beyond the Arctic Circle, is perhaps one of them, as the warm waters of the Gulf Stream keep its harbour ice-free throughout the winter; Bergen, 700 miles to the south, is certainly amongst them. Since it was seized by the Nazis on that April morning of treachery it has been visited time and again by the bombers of our Coastal Command and the Air Arm of the Fleet. Reports have come to hand from time to time of troop assemblies in its neighbourhood; and though the Nazi army of occupation in Norway has been much reduced in numbers of late months, we may be sure that a very considerable proportion is still kept in or near Bergen—ready for a dash on the Orkneys or Scotland, if an opportunity should present itself.

On the other side of the Skagerrak lies Denmark, whose principal port in the North Sea, Esbjerg, can hardly be included in our category. But only a few score miles to the south are the great ports of north-western Germany, Kiel and Hamburg, Bremen and Bremerhaven, Emden and Wilhelmshaven. All of these may be counted as invasion ports, and hence all of them have come to know full well the sound of our bombers' engines. The docks at Hamburg in particular, extensive as they are, have been devastated in raid after raid, and the same may be said of the shipbuilding yards on the Weser.

From ports in North Germany to Hull or Newcastle the distance is only some 350 miles; it is even less from the great ports of the Low Countries—Amsterdam and Rotterdam, Flushing and Antwerp—to England's east coast, and less still between Ostend, Dunkirk, Calais and Boulogne, and the coast of Kent. Such a situation never arose in the

From any of the ports of Western Europe included in this map Hitler may (or may not) strike at the British Isles. As will be seen, if distance were the only obstacle it might be readily surmounted.

last war, for although the Belgian ports were captured by the Germans, the invaders never secured Dunkirk, Calais, Boulogne, or Dieppe, not to mention Havre, Cherbourg, and the rest. Many of these, indeed, served as bases of the British Army on the Continent. Being so near to England, Boulogne and Calais in particular might be regarded as being the most obvious invasion ports, and there is plenty of evidence that the Germans think so, too. Large numbers of flat-bottomed boats have been reported there by our air observers, and it is known that many thousands of troops are distributed along the coast of Northern France.

When the invasion threat was first realized, it was the general view that the onslaught would be delivered from just across the Straits of Dover. It was thought that Hitler

would make an effort to decoy away the ships of the British Navy; then when the Straits were left, if only for a few hours, unguarded, he would launch across the narrow seas his armada of barges, crammed to the waterline with men and tanks and guns. At the same time the Luftwaffe operating with overwhelming force would drive the R.A.F. from the skies, and lay Dover and Chatham, Portsmouth and most of London in ruins.

We do not know if this was the plan in Hitler's mind, but if ever he entertained it he may well have come to the conclusion that it involved too many "ifs" for its successful completion. If the British Navy could be decoyed away, if the Luftwaffe could secure supremacy in the air, if the tides were favourable and the sea was not too rough—a boisterous Channel crossing might play havoc with the invaders' insides!—then, Hitler's Armada might sail, his men might land in Kent or Sussex.

Of late months, however, it has been thought more likely that if the invasion comes it will be from more than one direction. Thus while an attack on Scotland—up the Firth of Forth maybe, or against the Orkneys and the Western Isles—was delivered from Norway, a second onslaught might be delivered from the Scheldt across the North Sea against the east coast, while a third might have for its objective south-west England, or more likely, Southern Ireland. Hence the centre of interest has now shifted to the more western ports of Hitler's Europe—Havre and Cherbourg, St. Malo and Brest, Lorient, St. Nazaire, and even Bordeaux. At each of these places there have been reported troop concentrations and fleet assemblies, and so each has received innumerable visits from our bombing 'planes, while the ocean that links them is watched unceasingly by ships of the Royal Navy. From the ports of Brittany it would be a matter of a few hours' sailing to

Cork Harbour is one of the ports in Southern Ireland which Britain used extensively in the last war but is forbidden to use in this. This photo is of Spike Island, one of the several fortified islands which are part of the harbour's defences, and it was taken on July 11, 1938—the day on which Eire's flag supplanted the Union Jack in accordance with the Anglo-Irish Agreement of April 25, 1938.

Photo, Wide World

So Near Are They to Britain—and Yet So Far!

BERGEN was one of the Norwegian ports occupied by the Nazis at the beginning of April 1940, stands on a peninsula in a deep bay, has a well-equipped harbour and is an important industrial centre.

BOULOGNE, so familiar to people travelling to the Continent, is memorable in the story of invasion, for on its cliffs in 1804 Napoleon assembled the great army which he hoped to land on the Kentish coast.

OSTEND, an important Belgian port, was in German hands from Oct. 16, 1914, until Oct. 17, 1918. British warships on April 23 and May 9, 1918, attempted to block the harbour.

Éire, that member of the British Commonwealth which still seeks safety in an outmoded neutrality. During the last war Britain enjoyed the use of naval bases in Eire (in particular Berehaven, Lough Swilly, and Queenstown, at the head of Cork Harbour), but since 1938 Eire's defence has been a matter for Eire alone—and how weak she is!—and Britain has been deprived of harbours which would be of inestimable value in fighting the U-boats preying on the ships which feed the people of Britain and of Eire alike. Lorient has been in the news of recent weeks as a base for Germany's submarines, and even from Bordeaux there have come stories of invasion manoeuvres on the broad sands of the Gironde estuary. At Merignac airport, still nearer the open sea, large assemblies of troop-carrying aircraft have been reported—assemblies which were countered immediately by our bombers.

These, then, are Hitler's invasion ports—the places where at this very moment are assembled the men and ships and 'planes with which the Fuehrer, in the blindness of his pride and illimitable ambition, intends to bring Britain to her knees.

ANTWERP, Belgium's greatest port lies on the river Scheldt. In the photograph is the tower of its fine cathedral. The city was in German hands from 1914 until 1918.

BREST, one of France's chief naval bases, lies at the extreme west of Brittany, and has great naval shipbuilding yards, docks, magazines and barracks, while Brest Roads form a safe anchorage for big ships.

LORIENT, another important naval base, lies on the south coast of Brittany, near the junction of the rivers Scorff and Blavet. In addition to the dockyards it has important naval armament factories.

Photos, Fox, M. O. Henchoz, Dorien Leigh, Fauchois, and E.N.A.

Canada's White-hot Stream of Help for Britain

NICKEL is of supreme importance in the production of nickel steel for armaments, and more than 90 per cent of the world's supply comes from Canada. Here one of the great Canadian smelting furnaces in which nickel is extracted from its ore is disgorging its molten contents to help Britain. Canada's huge war industry is sending Britain Bren guns, trucks, shells, bombs, depth-charges and aeroplane frames in ever-increasing numbers. Soon the Dominion will be ready to send A.A. guns, naval guns, rifles and tanks.

Photo, Central Press

Americans Are Helping Us Here in Britain

One of the hundred mobile canteens given by American sympathizers to Britain.

This smiling woman ambulance driver is a member of the Allied Relief Fund's American Hospital Unit, the second contingent of which arrived in Britain in October, 1940.

Photo, Fox

'Our Purpose and Our Pledge'

OUR most useful role is to act as an arsenal for those nations which are now in actual war with aggressor nations as well as for ourselves. We cannot and will not tell them they must surrender because of their present inability to pay for weapons which we know they must have.

Let us say to the democracies : "We Americans are vitally concerned in your defence of freedom. . . . We shall send you in ever-increasing numbers ships, aeroplanes, tanks and guns. This is our purpose and our pledge." In fulfilment of this purpose we will not be intimidated by the threats of the dictators. Freedom means the supremacy of man's rights. Everywhere our support goes to those who struggle to gain those rights or keep them. Our strength is in our unity of purpose. To that high conception there can be no end save victory.

President Roosevelt addressing the Congress of the U.S.A. on Jan. 6, 1941

General W. H. Hayes, who commands an American mobile defence unit in Britain, was a member of General Pershing's staff in the Great War of 1914-18.

Photos, Planet News

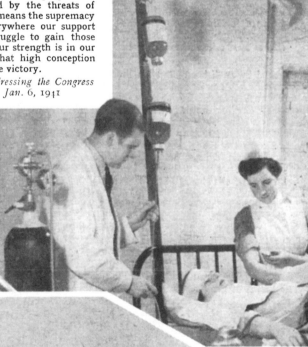

An American ambulance station was hit during a severe air raid, and women ambulance drivers are seen above examining the damage.

Americans living in this country have formed their own Home Guard and work in conjunction with British units. They train under realistic conditions, and are seen advancing through a smoke screen, right.

Photos, Planet News and Wide World

One of the many ways in which the citizens of the U.S.A. have shown practical sympathy with Britain has been by voluntarily giving their blood for transfusions. The blood, specially treated, has been sent to Britain in bottles. A patient (above) is seen at St. Thomas's Hospital, London, receiving a transfusion.

Photo, Associated Press

The 'Terror' Lived Up to Her Name off Libya

As the Army of the Nile rumbled and roared across the Western Desert, ships of the Mediterranean Fleet demoralized and destroyed the Italian forces which lay in its path. Among the ships which took part in the bombardment were the monitor " Terror " and the gunboats " Aphis " and " Ladybird " ; it is their contribution to the great victory which is described below.

Six times the Rome wireless claimed to have sunk the British monitor " Terror," as during the operations along the North African coast between Sidi Barrani and Bardia she and her two accompanying gunboats, " Aphis " and " Ladybird," came close inshore and sprayed the Italian positions and columns of marching troops with their guns. Bombers and torpedo-carrying aircraft swept down upon them night after night, and once they

day," said a lieutenant when the " Terror " had returned to port, " we were off the coast near Bardia. We spotted a big column of troops and lorries, so we loaded up. We sprayed that road for five miles and we smashed up the whole convoy, which, prisoners told us later, was a vital food convoy for Bardia. After that rations were short and the men said they got no food for five days."

" On another occasion," went on the lieutenant, " we spotted whole clusters of

described what the " Terror's " bombardment looked like from the air. " I could see a mechanized column moving up towards the cross-roads. There were tanks among them and troop carriers. Our 15-inchers were so terrific that I could hear them above the noise of the engine. The first few ranging shots threw up great mushrooms of earth and smoke. Still there were rifts through which I could see the column moving. When I had given my directions a salvo arrived smack on the column. I signalled O.K. and another and another came. Nine successive salvos found that column. Before the Wadi became a mass of turbulent smoke and dust, I had seen tanks and lorries flung into the air like straw in the wind. Then I could not see anything more, not even the shape of the Wadi."

Time after time, as mentioned above, the three ships were attacked by Italian 'planes and torpedo-bombers. " Once the torpedoes were so thick in the water that we could almost knit them," said an officer of the " Terror ", " we were constantly forced to swerve to right and left. Even so, one torpedo passed 20 feet from the stern." On one occasion 10 bombers escorted by about 40 fighters bombed the ships heavily, seeing that they were unprotected by fighters ; next about five came over, then three delivered an attack, and finally four. " There were some near misses, one load of bombs straddling our stern, others sending huge columns of water up either side of us. But fortunately we escaped a direct hit. No fewer than 12 times have these fellows tried to get us." Yet the only casualties were in the " Aphis," caused by a near miss from the land batteries.

On the day before the big ships of the Mediterranean Fleet smashed Bardia's defences into pulp, the " Terror " and the two gunboats bombarded the town and the roads which led into it. The Italian shore batteries replied, but they were soon silenced by the " Terror's " heavy guns, so enabling the " Aphis " and " Ladybird " to get close into shore, creating havoc among the shipping in the harbour. But throughout the attack the " Terror's " gunner took good care not to hit the lighthouse at Bardia since "it was so handy for getting our range ! "

TWO RIVER GUNBOATS came from Chinese waters to take part in the bombardment of Bardia. They were the " Ladybird," above, and the " Aphis," belonging to a class of nine 625-ton river gunboats built in 1915 for operations in Chinese waters. Their draught of less than 4 ft. enables them to come close enough inshore to bring their two 6-in. guns into action.
Photo, Associated Press

were attacked by an E-boat. But the little ships survived every assault and they arrived back safely at their base in Egypt when they had seen the Union Jack hoisted over Government House in Bardia.

Beginning with the attack on Fort Maktila early in December, the three ships were almost continuously engaged until the surrender of Bardia. While the main battle fleet was occupied elsewhere, these shallow-draft vessels were able to keep up a continuous harassing of the Italian positions. The " Terror " alone poured nearly 600 tons of 15-inch high explosive shells into Bardia while the place was still resisting. She also sprayed the coast road with devastating results : " Hellfire Corner " was blown away with a direct hit, and so, too, was a 150-yard stretch of the escarpment. " One

motor transport moving across open country towards the port. We fired and saw them turn in another direction. We kept chasing them round and round, getting hit after hit until the whole lot had stopped. Then the dust haze hid them."

The story was taken up by a gunnery officer. " One day off Sollum," he said, " we picked on the coast road, zigzagging up an escarpment. Our first shell tore out a piece at least 200 yards long. The whole road, zigzags and all, crumbled down the cliff side. Prisoners told us that our 15-inchers often cleared an area of 600 yards radius, making a terrific shower of splinters of rock and iron."

One day they found a target in a mass of motor transport in Wadi Rahab, near Bardia. An observer in a spotting 'plane

H.M.S. " TERROR," veteran monitor of the last war, was also amongst the ships that took part in the bombardment of Bardia. She was completed in August 1916, and, with many other monitors, was employed in the shallow waters of the North Sea against the German positions on the Belgian coast. With a draught of only 11 feet, yet carrying two 15-in. and eight 4-in. guns, this 7,200-ton monitor was able to come close inshore off Bardia, as twenty-three years ago she had done off the sand dunes around Ostend, and helped to plaster the Italian stronghold with a rain of high explosives.
Photo, Topical

Watch and Ward O'er the Seven Seas

CEASELESS PATROL of the high seas is kept up, day in, day out, by ships of the Royal Navy which guard our shores, strive to make the seas safe for our merchant shipping, escort convoys and maintain a constant watch and ward. These warships on patrol, anti-aircraft guns manned against the ever likely threat of air attack, are performing one of the routine, but none the less vital, tasks of the Silent Service.

Photo, Fox

More Laurels for the Amazing Greeks

" We begin 1941 resolved to fight to the last breath until the enemy has been exterminated."
In these words General Metaxas addressed the Greek people in a New Year message.
" Victories to us ! Victories to our great Ally ! And more than victories—heroism
and glory ! "

JOY-BELLS rang in Athens on January 10 when shortly after noon it was announced that Klisura had been captured by the Greeks. The people poured into the streets and gave a tremendous reception to King George and General Metaxas, who acknowledged their greetings from a balcony at the Palace. In the hospitals, too, men who had been wounded in the war, men who had lost their limbs through frostbite, raised themselves in their beds and cheered. They knew what conditions were like on the mountain battlefield ; they knew, as only they could know, what difficulties had had to be overcome before the joy bells could be set a-ringing.

Klisura had been the Greeks' objective for many weeks—since, indeed, the fall of Argyrokastro in early December. It was a key town, a bastion of the defence line which the Italians had painfully constructed across mountain and gorge to bar the way to Valona and the heart of Albania. Lying in a defile and surrounded by steep cliffs it was insignificant enough as a town, but the Italians had ringed it with a threefold line of trenches and concrete emplacements, liberally provided with positions for artillery and machine-guns. Then in front of all had been arranged belts of barbed wire. Everything possible, indeed, had been done by the Italians to make the place impregnable, and the local commander issued an order which said that in view of Klisura's strategic importance any retreat would be considered as desertion, so that out of every ten men retreating one would be shot.

For weeks the Greeks battled vainly against the Italian positions in the mountains, and they had to fight, too, in the most bitter

weather. Blizzards were frequent and everywhere the snow lay several feet deep, while the mountain streams were swollen into roaring torrents. Again and again the Greeks charged the Italian lines with fixed bayonets, and one by one they subdued the strong points, the machine-gun posts, the gun emplacements. The Italians fought hard, but they were fighting a losing battle—and knew it. The day came when the Greeks stormed the remaining heights and Klisura lay revealed beneath them. It was this engagement which was referred to in the communiqué issued by the Greek High Command on the night of January 9 :
" During local engagements today important heights were captured at the bayonet point. About 200 prisoners fell into our hands as well as much material, including twenty 81 mm. mortars." The next day the Greeks carefully made their way down the mountainside and entered the town hard on the heels of the Italians. The Albanian population swarmed out of their houses and refuges and welcomed them as liberators.

Italian Retreat on Tepelini

As for the Italians, they were making their way as best they could down the Viosa valley to Tepelini, which was now, as the result of Klisura's fall, elevated into the position of the Greeks' main objective. Their retreat was hampered by the fire of the Greek patrols, who took advantage of every bend in the tortuous road, of every crag of overhanging rock which might afford cover for a sniper's rifle. Then from time to time the retreating column was bombed and machine-gunned by Allied 'planes. Another hundred or so prisoners were taken,

together with much material, including mortars, machine-guns, and automatic rifles.

Tepelini, like Klisura, was one of the principal points in the new defence lines which the Italians had hoped to hold in Central Albania. Strategically, perhaps, it was of even greater importance, for the town —village, rather—is situated at the junction of the Viosa with the Drinos, along whose valley from Argyrokastro other detachments of Greeks had been pushing for some time past. Thus Tepelini was now threatened from two directions, from south and east, and only a day or two after Klisura's fall it was reported that it, too, had been captured by the Greeks. And between Tepelini and Valona there is no place where the Italians might hope to make a stand.

About this time the Italians issued their casualty list for December. It gave the number of dead in the fighting in Albania as 1,301, of whom 97 were officers, 65 N.C.O.s, and 19 Albanians. The total number of wounded was 4,598, of whom 10 were Albanians. The missing numbered 3,058, including 88 Albanians. Compared with the losses in the Great War, these figures may seem so small as to appear almost negligible ; but we must have regard to the extraordinarily difficult nature of the country, militating against the use of large bodies of troops, and the terrible weather conditions, which for days at a time halted the war. But at least it may be said for the Italians in Albania that they put up an infinitely better fight than their comrades in Libya.

To the Greeks, then, all the more honour for their amazing performance in driving the Italians— Mussolini's crack troops included—from their mountain fastnesses.

KLISURA and TEPELINI are key-points in the Albanian war. Left is the bridge over the river Viosa at Klisura. Above, the ruined castle at Tepelini of Ali Pasha. Known as the Lion of Janina, he lived from 1741 to 1822 and by his ruthlessness, rose from the brigand he was in his early days to become pasha of Janina.   *Photos, E.N.A.*

Again There Was Rejoicing in Athens

An enthusiastic group of Greek soldiers is seen before leaving for the front. The advance of the Greek Army in all sectors of the Albanian campaign was maintained in the face of tremendous difficulties, reflecting great credit on the men and their leaders.

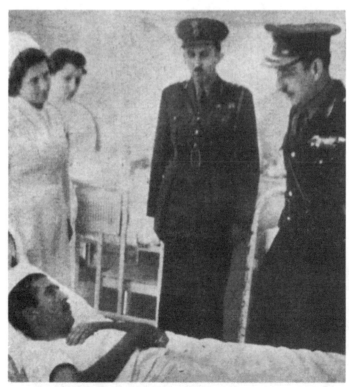

GENERAL PAPAGOS, Greek C.-in-C., talks to a wounded officer in hospital. The officer is a member of the Evzones, the famous kilted Greek soldiers, and was wounded in the battle of Koritza.   A Greek casualty (right) responds to the cheers of his comrades as he is carried on a stretcher.

Photos, British Official: Crown Copyright ; and Black Star

Ye Mariners of England! Whose Flag Has B

OFF THE LIBYAN COAST, seen silhouetted in the distance, the White Ensign, symbol of Britain's naval might, flutters proudly in the breeze as British warships sweep the Mediterranean despite all Mussolini's boastings about "Mare Nostrum." As Thomas Campbell, whose immortal lines are quoted above this page, prophesied : "The meteor flag of England shall yet terrific burn ; till danger's troubled night depart, and the star of peace return." No small part was that played by the British Navy in our successes in the Western Desert, nor was its help to Greece insignificant. The

a Thousand Years the Battle and the Breeze!

Mediterranean Fleet, braving constant attack from the air and from beneath the waters, bombarded Graziani's bases and lines of communication in Libya swept the Italian Navy from the open sea, and even sailed up to the Adriatic under the very noses of the Italians to bombard the port of Valona. Truly, the Royal Navy is living up to its great traditions. On each side of the stern of the destroyer in the foreground are paravanes, an invention of the 1914-1918 war employed as a protection against mines. Paravanes, used in pairs, deflect the mines, cut their mooring cables and render them easy to destroy.

Ack-Ack on Target! How the Gunners Go To It

As a rule the non-gunner knows little of the practice and problems of anti-aircraft gunnery, now of such vital importance to Britain's defence. This article, written by a former member of our staff who is now an Artillery officer, is an attempt to present some of these in clear language, although it is impossible to touch on more than the fringe of so vast and technical a subject.

WITHIN the Anti-Aircraft Command of the Royal Artillery—itself the largest single corps in the British Army—are all the A.A. guns, both of heavy and of light calibre, and all the searchlight units. The latter were at one time under the Engineers, but are now all " Gunners." This A.A. Command, therefore, has charge of everything (on land) that hurls defiance at the raider, from a 4·5-in. to a Lewis gun, and has been expanded and expanded until its ill-equipped nucleus, as it was in the early 'thirties, or even at the time of " Munich," seems a mere plaything. Its G.O.C. is Lt.-Gen. Sir Frederick Pile.

The anti-aircraft gunner has an exceptionally difficult task—far more so than the layman realizes—and a ceaseless one. All over the country, and mostly far from home, are these groups of men who, for over a year, have been on three or four minutes' notice to come into action. The inaction that is the temporary bane of most of our home-based troops can now be the lot of few A.A. units. The gunner's recompense is that his science, unlike some of his weapons, is never static. New theories, new developments, new " drills " arise in a constant flow, with experience of the air war now fluctuating over Britain. Yet the basic principles of what one may call " predicted " shooting (the term will be explained later) remain unaltered.

The essence and the limitation is that the guns are laid and fired on a " future position " in space where the fleeting target will be if it continues on its present course, at the same height and speed. It will be appreciated that, especially with heavy guns, where handling cannot be so rapid, it is most necessary to register a hit with the first salvo. Moreover, everything must be not only ready but steady—including the

nerves of everyone on the gun position. It is truly a case where an ounce of practice is worth a pound of theory.

A typical " heavy " gun site may have an equipment of 3·7-in. guns, placed so as to command as wide a view and field of fire as is practicable, with due thought to concealment of the position with the aid of camouflage.

Let us imagine what will happen here on

ANTI-AIRCRAFT UNITS are being continually called upon to perform extraordinarily difficult tasks, for the enemy is constantly evolving new tactics in his air war against Britain. Changing methods of aerial attack upon our towns and cities are ceaselessly challenged by the A.A. gunners. Here are some of them running to man their gun during an Alert.
Photo, British Official : Crown Copyright

that looks solid and good, has a satisfying bark, and its effectiveness has been proved " to the hilt."

Manning each of these guns and at their post when the No. 1 reports " ready for action " are the detachment, and we may enumerate some of their duties. First, each man is responsible for certain items when equipment is examined—a daily routine—but the No. 1, who is in charge

an alarm being sounded—in clear daylight, for a night " shoot " is a different proposition, with the added complication of the aid afforded by the searchlight men, equipped with their powerful projectors and delicate sound locators.

The alarm is probably broadcast by 'phone to the " signallers," who are always on duty in the Command Post dug-out. This little underground room is the real hub of everything " operational " on the site. Though the G.P.O.—in ack-ack language ; the Gun Position Officer—retains a large measure of initiative (and a responsibility very big for one who may be only a junior " sub "), it is over the Command Post 'phone that instructions and information come from a control operations-room.

A hostile raid, then, is definitely plotted on the large map in the dug-out as approaching our gun-site, and the alarm is sounded. Our guns are 3·7-in. of the mobile or static type—that is to say, some may be bedded down in permanent concrete establishments, while others can be moved. A 3·7-in. does not sound (on paper) a heavy weapon when compared to the 15-and 16-in. weapons of our battleships, but it is a gun

and usually a Sergeant (though he may be a Bombardier, the R.A. equivalent of a Corporal), is responsible to the G.P.O. for his gun.

There are other layers on the right, with the traversing gear, and on the left with the elevating handwheel. Presuming that we have mechanical fuse-setters, the setter also sits in front of a dial, and ensures that the correct fuse length is set at any moment in action. On the platform facing the gun is the gunner who opens or closes the breech as required—though the modern semi-automatic mechanism eliminates this in action—and he actually fires the gun. This he does by pulling the firing lever to the rear.

These duties, as already described, are basically the same on all types of heavy A.A. guns, but the remainder differ in detail. There are also ramming and loading tray numbers, while the rest of the detachment (never " crew " or " team ") are concerned with supplying ammunition either from the recesses round the gun or from magazines. Not that these men are negligible in their duties - very far from it. The weight of a round is itself daunting enough, and " ammo "

Behind the Scenes at a Daytime 'Shoot'

numbers in action have a really responsible " he-man " job.

The ammuntion used consists, of course, of " fixed " rounds—that is, the fuse, the shell and the propellant charge (with the primer in the base) built up together in one piece. The fuse in the nose can be set by hand with a key, to alter the time taken for the powder or clockwork mechanism within to explode the shell after it has been fired.

Our 3·7-in.s, then, have reported " ready for action." On the Command Post the spotters are observing with their telescope, and the men on the other instruments are also waiting, with steel helmets adjusted and respirators at the alert, for the " Jerry " that is their lawful victim.

What are these other instruments? First, the predictor, and, secondly, the height-finder. The predictor, like a box with its side panels crammed with dials and hand-wheels, is one of the most ingenious machines yet devised by military scientists, for though it requires several men of intelligence, who must work as a team to get results, it does predict exactly what we want—the future position of the target ; and these " future " data (Q.E. or quadrant elevation, bearing, and in some cases fuse length) are transmitted electrically direct to dials on the guns.

Though much else—ballistic, human, and mechanical—enters into it, two things only are basically necessary for this *tour de force* : that the layers on the predictor will (unlike those on the guns) follow the target visually with great accuracy and smoothness, and that an accurate height is set in from the heightfinder—a specialized version of the artillery rangefinder, in that the range to the target is calculated first by optical means, and from it an accurate height can be deduced trigonometrically.

Our target is now coming into range, and the Section is ready for action. This report is made by the G.P.O.'s assistant, or " G.P.O. Ack," a functionary who needs quick brains, a voice, and a megaphone. Suddenly a spotter reports " Spotter on Target," and the G.P.O. Ack runs to the telescope and reads off the bearing and angle of sight to the other instruments. The G.P.O. looks in the telescope, identifies the target as hostile,

Enemy 'planes get a lively reception when they attempt to attack Gibraltar. The famous Rock is well protected, for as a British naval base it is of paramount importance. Here an anti-aircraft crew is manning one of the powerful Bofors A.A. guns.   *Photo, Topical*

ensures that there are no friendly aircraft in the vicinity, and decides to engage—not forgetting to report back to the operations-room. The instruments get " on target," and a first height is called from the heightfinder and set in the predictor. The layers and the Nos. 4 on the guns are smoothly following the electrical pointers on their dials, and the predictor is reported steady. The target is swiftly approaching the " crossing point."

" Fire ! " The rounds are put in the fuse-setting machines, these are set and passed like lightning to the loading trays : the trays are over, the rounds are rammed, the trays are back, and the guns fire as one. Simultaneously they recoil, ejecting the spent cartridge cases, and the shells speed at over 2,000 feet per second to the distant target. The G.P.O. observes the burst " on target " —and we hope he gets his Heinkel.

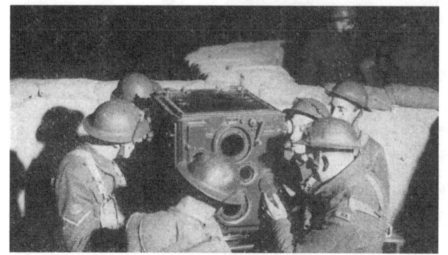

THE PREDICTOR, the box-shaped instrument at which men are seen working in this night photo-graph, is an ingenious machine for estimating the position in space of a hostile aircraft at a given moment. That now used by Britain's defenders is described as being an "absolute killer." The instrument is manned by a team who work in conjunction with the heightfinder and gunlayers, as explained in this page.   *Photo, Fox*

Cardiff and Liverpool Have Their Scars

SEVERAL savage raids were made by enemy bombers on provincial cities and towns in England and Wales during December 1940, and among those to suffer severely were Liverpool and Cardiff. Left is St. Nicholas' Church, Pierhead, Liverpool (known as the Seamen's Church from its dedication to the patron saint of sailors), after it had been burned out during one of the raids ; the interior is shown in the oval below. At Cardiff many bombs fell on working men's homes in the outskirts. In the photograph above a stretcher-party is carrying away a casualty; below is one of Cardiff's burning buildings.

Photos, Topical and " Daily Mirror "

Meet One of the 'Nits': a Pilot in the Making

Broadcast by an Acting Pilot Officer one evening in December 1940, this talk on the training of a "Nit" is printed here as a very human document, describing a phase of experience which cannot but interest deeply all who admire our magnificent airmen.

IT's several months now since a very Junior Acting Pilot Officer first put on, perhaps a bit self-consciously, a very new R.A.F. uniform, and admired himself in a mirror. I remember how naked he thought the uniform looked without the pilot's wings over the left top pocket, and how he wore his greatcoat on every possible occasion to cover up that enormous gap of blue cloth where, one day, he hoped wings would grow.

Well, today that uniform isn't quite so new, and its wearer perhaps not quite so self-conscious; but he still puts on the greatcoat, even on a sunny day, because those wings aren't there yet. In a few weeks maybe—but, at the moment they're—well, shall we call it ?—semi-sprouting.

Discipline is Good for You!

When I first joined the Service I was plunged into something which I didn't think I was going to like very much. It was called a disciplinary course and, being a very un-disciplined sort of person, I approached it in a " nasty medicine " sort of way—with a " I know this is going to do me good but all the same I don't want to take it " sort of attitude. But I must say I rather enjoyed it. I was taught how to march instead of slouch; how to be drilled and to drill, and, very important, how, when, where, and whom to salute. After the first few hours of this I realized that there was a higher art on the barrack square. This surprised me; it was rather like finding out at the age of twelve that rice pudding is really quite palatable. But it was so—as anyone who has ever seen the awful muddles resulting from giving, say, the command " Halt " on the *left* instead of on the *right* foot, will appreciate.

By the time I could get a squad on the move, and halt it again without having everyone falling over everyone else's feet, I was posted to an E.F.T.S. I became, in fact, a pupil pilot—or, in other words, a " Nit "—the derivation of this term is obvious, and, in most cases, I fear—all too justified. It certainly was in mine.

An E.F.T.S. is an Elementary Flying Training School, and there I joined in with a lot of other pupil pilots who had just come from an Initial Training Wing. There they had already had instruction in several useful things like Morse, and navigation and arma-ment—which put them a bit up on me because I did not know a " da " from a " dit " at Morse, or a Browning breech-block from a sewing-machine shuttle.

The main job of the E.F.T.S. was to teach us to fly. But, in the case of people like me, who thought they could fly a bit already, instructors had a double job to do—first showing us that we couldn't fly, and then teaching us the right, proper, official and R.A.F. way. My instructor was a very tough and exceedingly competent Flight Lieutenant, with that odd mixture of patience and ex-plosiveness which forced his pupils to keep on their best performance all the time they were flying with him. I shall not forget his remark to me on my first bit of dual. He told me to do some turns. I pushed the aeroplane round to the right in my most polished manner. Silence from the front cockpit. So I pushed her round to the left. Still silence. I sat and waited. There came, in my earphones, a long, over-patient sigh—and then a gentle voice : " You may call those turns, laddie, but, as far as I'm concerned, they're just changes of direction."

The machines we flew at E.F.T.S. were Tiger Moths—open cockpit biplanes of great stability and little speed. We grew to love them; they were such very forgiving aero-planes. The one I flew mostly (old 84) forgave me many things : crooked loops, bad side-slips, flat turns, bump landings—so much, in

Here is a typical cadet at one of the Flying Training Schools. The examination for physical fitness which future pilots and ob-servers have to undergo is the severest that science can devise.   *Photo, Planet News*

fact, that when my flying got a bit better and 84 had less to put up with, I felt like giving her a lump of sugar or an extra ration of oil in return for past favours.

First Steps in the Air

Most of my fellow " Nits " went solo after about seven or eight hours' dual. The ordinary flying syllabus included slow rolls, stalled turns, rolls of the top of a loop, spinning at least once every two hours, and other gentle means of disturbing one's half-digested lunch; and we had also to do forced landing practices, cross-country flights and one or two other indispensable exercises. In our course only three pupils failed to make the grade, and this involved no shame on the people concerned at all. The R.A.F. is purely voluntary, and if pupils decide that they don't like flying—or that they aren't good enough—then they're at full liberty to say so, and to turn to something else. One of our instructors put it rather well when talking to a pupil who'd just been suspended. This instructor said : " There's

CADETS in the R.A.F. are returning to their quarters at one of the many training schools where thousands of young men who have volunteered for service in the air are learning to be pilots and observers. They go through much the same course of military drill as the Army and are as smart on parade as any crack regiment.   *Photo, L.N.A.*

How an R.A.F. Fledgeling Grows His Wings

MAP READING plays an important part in the airman student's curriculum, and here prospective pilots are seen being given instruction by a pilot officer.   *Photo, Fox*

from the examiners to tell me that the proper answer to " What would you do if your aircraft caught fire in the air ? " is not " Dial ' O.' "

Now a word about the instructors themselves. Someone recently published a bit of verse which summed up their lives. He wrote :

What did you do in the war, daddy ?
How did you help us to win ?
Circuits and bumps and turns, laddie,
And how to get out of a spin.

And very true it is.

These men—experienced pilots all of them —are doing one of the R.A.F.'s greatest and most unpublicized jobs. Hours of circuits and bumps, correcting the same old faults, getting " Nits " off solo— and then seeing them go away— having their places taken by another bunch who're going to do the same silly things in the same silly way all over again. Yet, on the whole, most of them say it isn't too bad, and that they

nothing wrong in not being able to fly. What would seem wrong would be if everyone could."

Our ground work was—at least for me— pretty hard, especially the Morse. I managed to learn the code and get up to about six or seven words a minute, sending and receiving, on the buzzer. But receiving signals on the Aldis lamp foxed me 'completely, and in the examination I failed on the lamp—the only

INTRICATE MECHANISM of a bomb-sight is being minutely examined by these young cadets who have recently arrived at their Training School. Left, absorbed in a navigational course, two cadets are hard at work in a classroom.   *Photos, Sport & General and L.N.A.*

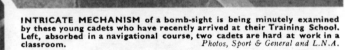

one on the course to do so. I am only just managing to cope with it now, after another spell of work at my present place, but I fear I shall never grow to love it. We had quite a stiff examination on our ground subjects, including navigation, airmanship, rigging, engines and armament. I got through all right, I think, but I'm still waiting for a note

become first-rate psychologists, which probably they do.

But the real joy of an instructor's life is his collection of stories of the things "Nits " have done. There is the instructor who, to give a titled and illustrious but rather nervous pupil some more confidence in landings, held his hands above his head as the 'plane was coming in, so that the pupil could see that he alone was doing the landing. The 'plane came down, bounced, came down, bounced again and finally jolted to rest. The instructor looked angrily round, and there sat the pupil, hands held firmly above his head. " Well," he said, " you told me last time round to watch how you did things and then to do them your way, so I did ! "

Britain's Army is the Best-equipped in Europe

Equipment for the Army is the work of thousands of women and girls in workshops all over the country. Above, in the West Country a battery of power-driven sewing-machines has been installed in a cabinet-makers' factory to produce webbing equipment. Circle, girls are making up anklets.

Raw material and metal fittings for the webbing equipment are being checked off as they are brought into the factory, left. The first haversack made was completed in 45 minutes. Above, a scene in another factory where 16,000 pairs of boots are turned out every week.   *Photos, "Daily Mirror" and Sport & General*

Feeding Those Who Have Lost Their Kitchens

MOBILE CANTEENS presented by the King and Queen serve 1,300 meals to Londoners every day. The canteens go wherever they are required, and hot meals are seen being loaded into one of them at the Amberly School, Harrow Road, London, where the food is assembled for distribution to rest centres and shelters.

This Community Feeding Centre at Stroud Green, London, clearly displays its tariff on the railings, above, and schoolchildren, right, enjoy the two-course lunch provided there at sixpence a head.

Photos, " Evening News"
" Daily Mirror " and Fox

ROYAL INTEREST was shown by the King and Queen in the meals served to homeless victims of air raids, when their Majesties visited Sheffield on January 3, circle. Soldiers and sailors, above, are seen at a Y.M.C.A. canteen at a London station. Ninepenny packet meals consisting of ham sandwiches, sausage roll, cake, and a bar of chocolate are popular.

I WAS THERE!

Eye Witness Stories of Episodes
and Adventures in the
Second Great War

'My Gunner Set Fire to a U-Boat'

The 2,473-ton Welsh collier " Sarastone " arrived in port from Lisbon
at the beginning of January, 1941, following a battle with a U-boat,
which left the latter disabled and on fire. The following account of
this exploit by the " Sarastone's " gunner, Jim O'Neill, was told by
her master, Captain John Herbert.

CAPTAIN John Herbert, of Swansea, the
master of the "Sarastone," told his
story on reaching port. He said :

The chief engineer came to me and
explained that our boilers had blown. " We
shall have to leave the convoy and take a
chance on our own," he added.

Our engines would not carry us faster
than two knots. So while the rest of the
ships steamed on we altered course and headed
for Lisbon.

I was having a nap in my cabin two days
later when the second officer on the bridge
shouted down the voice-pipe beside my bed :
" There is something on the horizon that
I don't like, sir."

When I got to the bridge I saw what
appeared to be a mast about three miles
distant. Then I saw it rise higher, until the
streaming conning-tower of a U-boat emerged.

I put " action stations " on and swung the
ship round to bring the submarine astern.
But while she was still lying on our quarter
she fired, the shot falling off our starboard
quarter. It was a warning to stop. We kept
on. The U-boat's speed was about fifteen
knots, and she overhauled us rapidly for
ten minutes without firing. Then, about
4,000 yards from us, she loosed a further
five shots, but we held our fire. We've only
a twelve-pounder, but I'd talked over with
my naval gunner what we'd do in such a
predicament and our plans were made.

She was getting closer and closer. I held
my breath waiting for the moment when we
could open fire with any hope of damaging
her. Her shells were uncomfortably close.

My gunner, Jim O'Neill, is a naval pen-
sioner who rejoined the Service as a reservist
in September 1939. He was marvellous. The

U-boat was about two thousand yards off
when O'Neill opened fire. His first fell short
but in perfect line. He fired again. A direct
hit.

We all cheered. I shouted, " Go on,
O'Neill, give it to him ! " His second shot
fell at the base of the after gun, putting it
out of action and causing yellow smoke to
rise in a cloud. Our third and fourth shots
were near misses, but the fifth burst 20 feet
abaft the first hit, and the yellow smoke now
turned black. The U-boat was still firing
back, with only one gun.

Then we steamed on. I had orders not
to risk my cargo.—" *Daily Express.*"

Gunner James O'Neill, hero of the collier
" Sarastone," made his first direct hit on the
U-boat with his second shot.
Photo, Associated Press

'We're Sitting On 100 Italians!'

The lighter side of war was amusingly illustrated by the story of how
the Italians lost the only British prisoners they had captured in the
Western Desert battle. This story was recounted by the captain of
an Australian destroyer which took part in the " rescue " of the
British prisoners from an Italian ship off Libya.

A BRITISH sergeant, a corporal and
seven men were captured in Libya
early on Christmas morning while
patrolling a dry river-bed. The captives
belonged to a well-known British regiment
and were apparently much prized, as at least
four Italian generals came to look at them.

Then they were put on the 100-ton schooner
" Zingarella." On December 29 the little
prison ship set sail for Tobruk. Darkness
fell and a storm got up. The schooner, with
100 Italian soldiers and 15 naval ratings, and
their nine precious prisoners in the hold,
hugged the Libyan coast.

An Australian destroyer was patrolling
the enemy coast that night, and at 2 a.m. she
sighted a small vessel directly ahead.

Telling his story later the captain of the
destroyer said :

We immediately eased towards her, being
unable at that time to determine whether
she was a submarine or some other type of
warcraft. We fired a single round over the
top. The vessel stopped her engines, and we
put a searchlight on her.

We were both rolling so heavily that I
kept about 20 yards away, but in the beams
of the searchlight I could see the hold full of
very green-looking Italians. Others were
waving shirts, or anything white they could
find, and shouting in chorus, " Prigionieri
Inglesi " (English prisoners).

I yelled through the megaphone in answer.
The weather was too rough to lower a boat.
Then I saw a British sergeant make a flying
dash through the exit of the hatchway. He
bowled over the Italian guards, and then was
followed by eight other British soldiers.

Apparently he had guessed, on hearing our
shot, that help was at hand, and had nipped
out of the hold with great presence of mind
to turn the tables on his captors. Even as we
were talking he got the 100 Italians battened
down in the hold. They were so completely
seasick that I don't think they cared at
all who won the war.

The destroyer's captain saw the sergeant
take over the schooner from unresisting
deck hands. The captain continued :

I called out, " Sergeant, have you got the
situation in hand ? " and though he could
hardly maintain his feet on the heaving deck,
he replied, " Yes, sir, and 100 Italians are
below. We're sitting on them."

I instructed the sergeant to tell the captain
of the schooner to follow us. He replied,
" I'll see to that, sir."

Then we began our tedious journey back.
In response to anxious inquiries about our
progress I had sent a signal explaining that
the " Zingarella " was no ocean greyhound.

The remarkable escape of the pilot, observer and gunner of an R.A.F. bomber when their 'plane
was damaged during a raid on an Albanian port is told in Vol. III, page 667. This photograph,
recently received in London, shows the pilot, left, with one of the crew after their return to their
base in Greece.   *Photo, British Official ; Crown Copyright*

We Made Quite a Mess of Mannheim

Mannheim, the industrial and commercial centre of south-west
Germany, was raided by the R.A.F. four times in eight nights in
December 1940. An account of one of these raids was broadcast by a
Squadron Leader who took part in it, and his story is given below
in his own words.

THE Squadron Leader in a heavy
bomber squadron who told the
story of a raid on Mannheim holds
the D.F.C. for his work in an attack on
Munich. He said:

The operation against Mannheim in which
I took part was on a pretty big scale; aircraft
from a number of squadrons were operating.
The general idea was to send in the early
ones with incendiaries so as to light up the
target, then for the main force to come along
with heavy stuff. The operations of the main
force incidentally were spread over a period
of six or seven hours. We left at regular
intervals. It was important to keep strictly
to the scheduled take-off times because of
working in with other stations, so as to make
the bombing a more or less non-stop affair
once it started.

Just when we were due to get away it
started raining cats and dogs. One could see
just a few blurs of light indicating the flare-
path and that was all—rather like driving a
car in heavy rain without a windscreen wiper,
only more so. However, we got off all
right. The cloud base was at a thousand
feet, and we had to climb up to get through
it. We were climbing rather slowly, too,
because we were carrying a heavy load.
Once we got above the clouds we were in
bright moonlight and the navigator got his
sextant out and started taking Astro sights to
check up our position. We flew on, keeping
straight and level. Then, 50 miles inside the
Dutch coast the cloud cleared and we saw the
ground for the first time since we'd taken off.

Altogether, it was a very uneventful trip
out. In Germany they'd had a fall of snow,
which was quite a help to navigation. When
you have a light fall, as this was, the important
things—woods and rivers, lakes and towns and
villages—all stand out much clearer, and so,
with the moon very bright, we pin-pointed
ourselves quite easily as we went along.

We were some distance from Mannheim
when the front gunner reported heavy "flak"
ahead. We were then about ten minutes
away, heading straight for it, and we knew it
must be Mannheim. The stuff was coming
up in bursts and then dying away, then
breaking up again, spasmodically.

I told the navigator to prepare for bombing,
and he came up into the bomb-aimer's
position in the nose of the aircraft with his
map. Having done that, he had to check up
on the bomb-switches, select his bombs, and
we determined the length of the stick. One
can drop a widely spaced stick or a close one;
this time I had decided on a very close one.

As we approached I could see fires already
well under way, and it was obvious that the
blitz was in full swing. We picked up the
Rhine, followed the river, and then started to
take avoiding action because there was quite
a lot of "flak," mostly light stuff, coming
up. When it gets like that, one just goes
through it, doing evasive stuff. I don't
think "flak" deters any of the fellows from
carrying out the job.

As we got a bit closer the navigator called
out "Ready," and I levelled out and opened
the bomb doors. You only do that at the
last minute because when they are open it
makes the aircraft drag a bit, so you open the
throttles a little to compensate the slight loss
of speed. You tell the navigator, "Bomb
doors open, master switch on," and he
repeats that back to you. He will probably
make a few corrections to course—"Left,
left, right, right, steady"—and when he's
bombed he calls out "bombs off."

As a matter of fact you can feel the bombs
go. You get a slight lift in the aircraft and
it immediately becomes more lively. On this
occasion everything went normally, and as
soon as the bomb-aimer said "O.K., sir,
bombs burst," I put the aircraft into a steep
turn to let the crew have a look. There were
three groups of huge red fires burning down
below and spirals of heavy black smoke
rising above the town. The fires were increasing in intensity all the time. Then we
set course for home; we could see other
people bombing as we came away. I told
my rear gunner, as I always do, to note the
time when we could no longer see the fires,
and we were about sixty miles away when he
called out and said he'd lost them.

Many times bombed (e.g. on Dec. 16-17, 1940; see page 719, Vol. 3),
Mannheim, a river port and chief centre of trade on the upper Rhine,
stands on a tongue of land at the confluence of the Rhine and Neckar,
top. It has important iron foundries as well as engineering and
chemical works. In the lower photograph night bombers are taking off
for such a raid as is described in this page.   *Photos, E.N.A. and Mrs. Muir*

She 'Mothers' Submarines and Their Crews

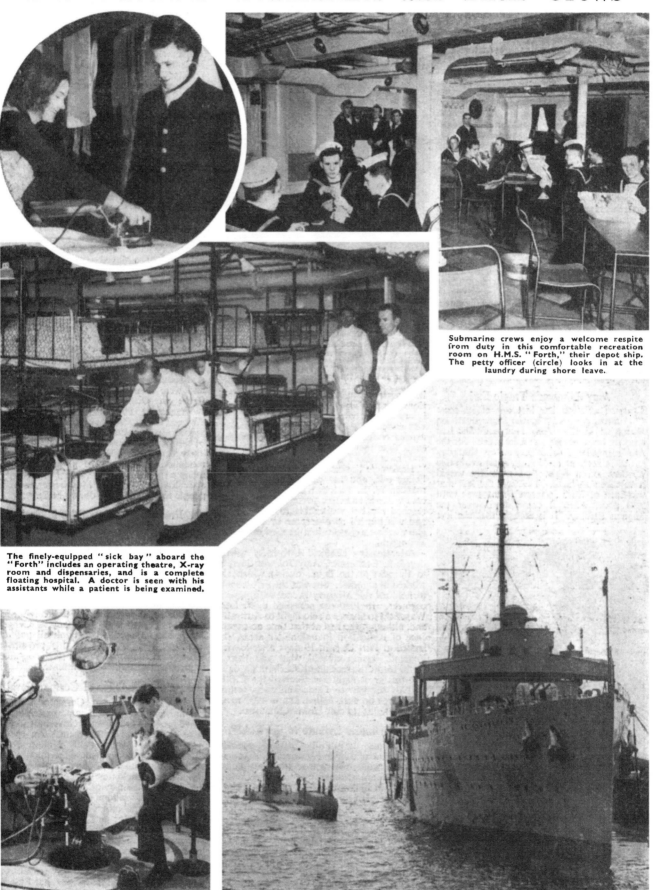

Submarine crews enjoy a welcome respite from duty in this comfortable recreation room on H.M.S. "Forth," their depot ship. The petty officer (circle) looks in at the laundry during shore leave.

The finely-equipped "sick bay" aboard the "Forth" includes an operating theatre, X-ray room and dispensaries, and is a complete floating hospital. A doctor is seen with his assistants while a patient is being examined.

H.M.S. "FORTH," the Navy's latest depot ship for submarines, has accommodation for the crews of twelve vessels. The ship is a miracle of modern equipment, which comprises plant for charging submarine batteries, machine shops, foundry, plate shop and smithy, thus enabling her to undertake repair work while at sea. Submarine crews live in special quarters aboard the parent ship when in port. Left, a patient is seen in the up-to-date dental surgery, and above, a submarine comes alongside the depot ship.

Photos, Central Press and G.P.U.

OUR SEARCHLIGHT ON THE WAR

Incitement to Spying in Norway

FOLLOWING the established practice in Dictator-run countries, the Chief of Police in Oslo, who rejoices in the name of Jonas Lie, is endeavouring to institute a system of universal spying among the civil population in order to trace so-called political offenders. With this end in view he has issued a decree instructing all clergy, doctors, solicitors, telephone and telegraph operators, and postal staffs generally, to disregard their traditional oath of secrecy and inform against any persons expressing views contrary to those of Quisling and of Nazism. If sufficient information is not laid, and sufficient arrests forthcoming, the wretched doctors and others will themselves be liable to imprisonment. But it is unlikely that the Norwegians will fall into line with this new order, so repugnant to all sense of decency. They are skilful at evasion, tough at resisting enslavement, and very fertile in devising means of holding up their persecutors to ridicule. One apparently innocent accident was found recently to have occurred in the pages of Quisling's official organ " Fritt Folk." A eulogistic New Year's greeting to him—" Norway's symbol, standing erect and free as our cross, warm and bright as our sun, proud and strong as our eagle "—was headed by the Quislingist emblem of an eagle, but by some mischance the block had been put in upside down and the eagle was lying helplessly on its back, with the cross rising triumphantly above it.

Amy Johnson's Tragic End

BRITISH aviation has lost one of its most daring exponents by the tragic death on January 5 of Miss Amy Johnson. She had recently been working as a ferry pilot for the Air Transport Auxiliary, and on that day left the airfield at 10.45 a.m., in unfavourable weather, on a flight that normally would have taken an hour. That was the last that was seen of Miss Johnson's aeroplane until 3.30 p.m., when it came down over the Thames Estuary. It is thought that she lost

SQUADRON-LEADER A. G. MALAN, D.S.O., D.F.C. and bar, with his dog and the mascot sent from Batavia referred to in this page. Batavia is a far cry from England, but there is no part of the freedom-loving world which has not followed with admiration the epic story of the R.A.F.
Photo, British Official: Crown Copyright

AMY JOHNSON, photographed in 1937 when she was flying as a commercial pilot, is seen alighting from the cockpit of an aeroplane on the Portsmouth-Isle of Wight service. She began to fly in 1928.   *Photo, Planet News*

her course owing to the bad weather conditions, and after flying round for several hours crashed owing to lack of petrol. It was stated at the airfield that the machine carried enough for a flight of 4¾ hours, the exact time that elapsed between the take-off and the crash. The crew of the naval trawler " Haslemere " saw the figure of the pilot baling out, and her commander, Lt.-Commander W. E. Fletcher, dived into the ice-cold water in an heroic attempt at rescue. He reached her, but was unable to support her, and was himself so overcome by exhaustion and extreme exposure that he died on arrival at hospital.

After leaving Sheffield University with a degree in Economics, Amy Johnson learned to fly outside the hours during which she worked in an office. She was the first woman to hold an Air Ministry licence as a ground engineer. In 1930 she prevailed upon Lord Wakefield to finance a solo flight to Australia, and, although she had at that time no experience of navigation in unfamiliar areas, she landed at Port Darwin 19 days after leaving England, having created what was then a world record by reaching Karachi in six days. For this great flight she received the C.B.E. In 1931 she flew to Japan and back, setting up records on both flights, and in 1932 made record flights to and from Capetown.

Dutch Indies Tribute to the R.A.F.

A SMALL beautifully carved wooden statue of a Javanese woman, a specimen of native work, was sent to the Netherlands Spitfire Fund through the British Consul-General in Batavia as a Christmas gift to " A pilot of the R.A.F." The donor, Mr. W. A. de Vos, an elderly merchant of Bandoeng, who hoped that " it will become as dear to the new owner as it has been to me," paid an enthusiastic tribute to the Royal Air Force. " In these days of tears and mourning," he said, " when the whole world is shivering at the idea of what the day of tomorrow may bring over parents, brothers and children, the eyes of all the peoples look out to the one light in the pitch dark sky—the Royal Air Force of Great Britain. When in this war the Germans will be defeated, and

I am sure they will, never in the history of mankind one people will have so much deserved the blessings of hundreds of millions now threatened by oppression and slavery." The statuette has been transmitted by Air Marshal Sholto Douglas to Squadron-Leader A. G. Malan, D.S.O., D.F.C. and bar, a young South African who commands one of London's Spitfire squadrons.

American Food for French Children

THE British Government has acceded to a personal request by President Roosevelt to allow passage through the blockade of limited supplies of concentrated foods and of clothing from America to the children in unoccupied France. These supplies are to be distributed to the most needy by the American Red Cross, who guarantee that none shall benefit the enemy. There has hitherto been opposition on the part of Britain to permit the passage of food ships, for it was felt that to feed the stricken inhabitants of enslaved countries in Europe would merely strengthen Hitler's hand.

Night Life Underground

LONDON Transport officials make a nightly census of the numbers of people who use the Underground and Tube stations and tunnels as air raid shelters. The highest figure recorded—177,500—was on the night of September 27, for Londoners had been made uneasy by heavy raids over both central and suburban areas on the night of the 26th, and were taking no chances. The average figure in October was 138,000, and in November 116,000. On Christmas night it dropped to 75,000. The present figure is 96,000. According to shelter officials, most of their guests are asleep by 10.30. London's Tube stations afford very much better accommodation than the large public shelters in many a provincial town, and Lord Horder, after touring those at Manchester, advised people to stay at home during raids.

Pro-British Sympathies in Syria

GENERAL DENTZ, the new High Commissioner in Syria who succeeded the ill-fated M. Chiappe, is a close friend of General Weygand, under whose direct orders he holds his post. His appointment has therefore been interpreted as part of a plan of the Pétain Government to ensure unity of action in countries of the French Empire in the event of any situation that might arise between France and Germany. General Dentz has imposed a ban upon all political meetings, but in spite of this pro-British feeling is stronger than ever and continues to grow as Italian prestige diminishes.

Insoluble Problem of German Jews

JEWISH refugees from Germany now in unoccupied France are presenting a grave problem to the Vichy Government, who have to feed and house them. An appeal was therefore made to the United States to arrange to receive them, either alone or in conjunction with other American republics. But the United States Government believes that it would be playing into Hitler's hands to receive Jews whom he is driving out of his country, and has refused the appeal on two main grounds : first, that no distinction could be made between refugees on religious and racial considerations ; secondly, that no basic changes could be made in the existing immigration laws, and quota limits were already filled. Another reason for rejecting the French request was that Frenchmen who had been granted the necessary American visa to enter the United States had not been able to do so because Vichy refused exit permits.

What Have *These* Done to Hitler?

ANIMAL VICTIMS of the Nazi raiders have been only too many; here are two of them. A greyhound, while searching for his master, an A.R.P. warden, was wounded by shrapnel and was rescued by the People's Dispensary for Sick Animals. Then here is a pigeon which had its tail shot away and sustained a breast wound in the fire raid on London on Dec. 29, 1940.

"Chum," an Airedale, extricated a woman from her shelter; here she is with her rescuer (right). "Chum" was awarded the "Dogs' V.C."—the Bravery Medal of Our Dumb Friends' League.

Photos, Pix, "Daily Mirror," and Planet News

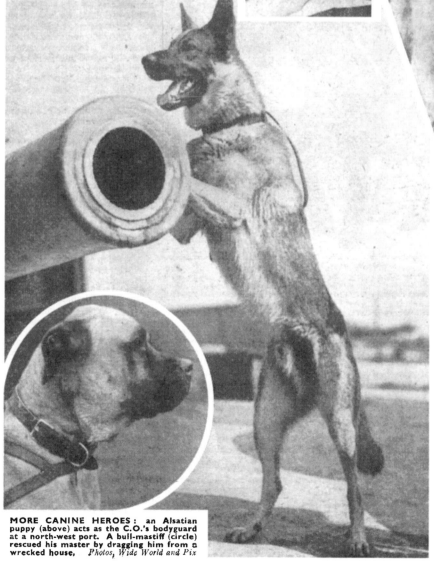

MORE CANINE HEROES: an Alsatian puppy (above) acts as the C.O.'s bodyguard at a north-west port. A bull-mastiff (circle) rescued his master by dragging him from a wrecked house. *Photos, Wide World and Pix*

This horse was rescued, badly frightened, from a blazing stable, and was soon treated by the P.D.S.A. *Photo, Pix*

OUR DIARY OF THE WAR

TUESDAY, JAN. 7, 1941   *493rd day*

War against Italy—Operations towards Tobruk proceeding satisfactorily. Reported that during operations at Bardia three Blackshirt commanders deserted their troops, leaving Regular commanders to fight on.

Home Front—Daylight raids by single aircraft. Bombs fell in a number of places including London and town in Midlands. No enemy activity at night. Enemy aircraft shot down by A.A. fire off East Coast.

Greek War—Greek Admiralty announced that on night of Jan. 5 Greek destroyers, sailing unmolested into Adriatic, heavily bombarded Valona, firing 60 shells.

R.A.F. bombers raided military stores and buildings at Elbasan.

WEDNESDAY, JAN. 8   *494th day*

On the Sea—Admiralty announced that H.M. submarine " Tuna " had reported night engagement on surface with U-boat in enemy waters ; U-boat was damaged by shell-fire and then chased for an hour.

Admiralty stated that H.M. submarine " Regulus " was overdue and must be considered lost.

In the Air—R.A.F. bombers attacked naval dockyards at Wilhelmshaven and Emden. Other aircraft bombed aerodrome on island of Borkum.

War against Italy—Concentration of British forces in Tobruk area continuing. Italian garrison now hemmed in. R.A.F. continued intensive bombing of Italian aerodromes and landing-grounds in Eastern Libya. Benghazi and Tobruk were also raided. Enemy convoys north-west of Jarabub were attacked and damaged.

On nights of Jan. 6-7 and 7-8 Massawa was heavily raided.

Home Front—During day single enemy aircraft dropped bombs in East Anglia and Midlands. No night raids.

Junkers 88 shot down by R.A.F. fighters.

Greek War—Athens reported that during preceding week Greeks had made advances in three sectors—coastal region, Klisura area, where important fortified peaks were captured, and northern region.

Lord Baden-Powell died in Kenya.

THURSDAY, JAN. 9   *495th day*

On the Sea—Reported that British steamer " Shakespear " had been sunk off Azores on Jan. 5 after 3-hour fight with U-boat.

First unit of Free French Navy, submarine " Narval," reported sunk by enemy action.

In the Air—R.A.F. bombers' main target was synthetic oil plant at Gelsenkirchen. Others were inland ports of Duisberg-Ruhrort and Düsseldorf, oil plant at Rotterdam, docks at Flushing, Dunkirk and Calais.

Coastal Command aircraft heavily attacked docks at Brest.

War against Italy—Preparations for reduction of Tobruk proceeding.

R.A.F. carried out heavy raid on Messina during night of 9-10 ; bombs fell across cruisers in harbour and army marshalling yards. Warships, merchant shipping, docks and railway station attacked at Naples. Other aircraft bombed Palermo.

Reported that Abyssinians, with help of R.A.F., forced Italians to abandon Gubba, and were closing in on enemy.

Five Italian 'planes shot down over Malta.

Home Front—Slight enemy activity during day, mostly near East and South-east coasts. At night raids occurred over widely separated areas, including London and Liverpool.

Two German aircraft brought down at night by A.A. fire in North-west.

Greek War—Local engagements, during which Greeks occupied important heights at the bayonet point.

FRIDAY, JAN. 10   *496th day*

On the Sea—Fierce engagement between British warships, escorting convoy with material for Greece, and German and Italian aircraft, after an Italian destroyer had been sunk in Sicilian Channel. H.M. destroyer " Gallant," aircraft-carrier " Illustrious " and cruiser " Southampton " suffered casualties and damage. At least 12 enemy aircraft shot down. Convoy passed through according to plan.

'TWIXT REITH AND WREN

" Charming, Sir Christopher ! And now where shall we put the power stations, the communal restaurants, the airports, the bus depots, the overhead cross-roads, the multiple stores, the municipal baths and the B.B.C. ? "

From the cartoon by Illingworth, by permission of the Proprietors of " Punch "

In the Air—Mass daylight raids by R.A.F. bombers and fighters on aerodromes and military installations in Northern France.

At night R.A.F. attacked Brest U-boat base and shipping in harbour of Le Havre.

War against Italy—Covered by operations to westwards, concentration of British forces around Tobruk continued.

During nights of 9-10 and 10-11 R.A.F. bombers heavily raided aerodromes at Benina and Berca. Benghazi also was attacked.

Aircraft of Fleet Air Arm carried out raid on shipping in Palermo harbour.

On Kenya frontier British troops entered villages of Buna and Turbi unopposed.

In Italian East Africa Caproni workshops at Mai Adaga were bombed. Asmara was also raided.

Defence positions of Berbera, Somaliland, attacked by R.A.F.

Home Front—Enemy made heavy night attack on Portsmouth. Twenty-eight big

fires were caused and there were many casualties. Among buildings destroyed were six churches. Working-class districts were severely damaged.

Two enemy 'planes destroyed, one by night patrols, one by A.A. fire.

Greek War—Klisura taken by Greeks, Italians retreating towards Berat.

SATURDAY, JAN. 11   *497th day*

In the Air—R.A.F. bombers attacked in daylight number of targets on or near Dutch and Belgian coasts.

During night other aircraft bombed ship-building yards at Wilhelmshaven.

War against Italy—Shelling of Tobruk by British forces intensified.

R.A.F. bombed railway and docks at Benghazi, and barracks and defences at Derna.

R.A.F. bombed Royal Arsenal at Turin.

Home Front—Many thousands of incendiaries were dropped during night raid on London. High explosive bombs fell at intervals in several districts. Street subway, where people were sheltering, wrecked.

Greek War—Greeks pushing on from Klisura in direction of Berat. R.A.F. attacked retreating troops and convoys.

SUNDAY, JAN. 12   *498th day*

In the Air—During small hours British fighter patrols attacked from low level troops in trenches near French coast.

During night Bomber Command attacked oil targets in Germany, Belgium and Italy, including refineries at Regensburg, on the Danube, and Porto Marghera, near Venice. Docks at Brest, Le Havre and Lorient were again bombed.

War against Italy—Preparatory activities in Tobruk area still proceeding.

R.A.F. raided aerodromes at Berca and Benina.

During night R.A.F. made series of attacks on aerodrome at Catania, Sicily, causing severe damage.

On Sudan frontier British troops reported to have made successful raids on Italian positions about Metemma.

In Italian East Africa night raids were made on aerodromes at Asmara, Barentu, and Agordat, and on Caproni workshops at Mai Adaga.

Home Front—No air activity during day. After dark bombs fell in London and at several places near Thames Estuary.

Greek War—Athens reported limited mopping-up operations. Greeks occupied positions of cardinal importance north-west of Klisura. In coastal sector they continued to advance and occupy new positions.

MONDAY, JAN. 13   *499th day*

In the Air—Coastal Command aircraft successfully raided submarine base at Lorient. R.A.F. bombers attacked Dunkirk area.

War against Italy—Systematic preparation for capture of Tobruk continued. Italian forces still in Libya remained passive.

Home Front—No daylight activities. At night enemy made heavy attack on Plymouth. Thousands of fire bombs preceded high explosives. Severe damage and casualties.

Greek War—Greeks advanced to considerable depth in Klisura-Tepelini sector, having dislodged enemy from many more points.

General Soddu, in command of Italian forces in Albania, replaced by General Cavallero, Chief of Italian General Staff.

THEIR SHIP ROSE FROM THE GRAVE TO TRIUMPH

The submarine "Thunderbolt," as announced by the Admiralty on January 3, 1941, sunk an Italian submarine which was proceeding under escort to a base in enemy-occupied territory—a very gallant exploit. She returned to port about a fortnight later. Some of her crew are here seen on deck with 1st Lieutenant J. Stevens in the centre. The "Thunderbolt" was launched as the "Thetis" in 1939, and all Britain was deeply stirred by her tragic sinking on her trial trip off Liverpool on June 1 of that year. After desperate efforts at rescue, 99 out of 103 men on board were lost. She lay beneath the sea for five months before being salvaged.

Photo, British Official : Crown Copyright

As Tobruk Falls, Mussolini's Empire Crumbles

When in June 1940 Mussolini declared war on the Allies he did so in the hope of a
speedy victory and one, moreover, secured at little cost. Even before 1940 had passed
into 1941, however, the Italians, so far from having extended their empire, were everywhere on the defensive. In North Africa they had suffered a series of crushing defeats,
and in East Africa they were confronted by a large-scale revolt.

At Tobruk the war was temporarily halted, as in the middle of January a terrific sandstorm burst like a hurricane above the beleaguered town. Besieged and besiegers alike sought what

Wearing an Italian officer's cap and carrying the spoils of victory, this R.A.F. pilot is seen with a fine collection of " souvenirs " left by the enemy in the Western Desert.
Photo, British Official: Crown Copyright

shelter they could find from the biting, blinding winds. Not a 'plane could take the air, not a ship could approach the stormbound coast.

When the hurricane had passed, that other storm beat anew at Tobruk's forts and harbour. Night and day the Italians were shelled

by the British guns, and every day, too, the R.A.F. bombed it mercilessly. With sure step the British forces were brought across the 75 miles of desert which separate Bardia from Tobruk ; the tanks were regimented, and the guns brought into position. At the aerodromes recently captured from the Italians the R.A.F. made ready for the final onslaught.

Early on January 21 the onslaught began, and before noon Imperial troops—British and Australians, supported by tanks and artillery—backed by the Royal Navy and the R.A.F., had penetrated both the outer and inner defences of the place to a depth of over five miles on a broad front. On the next morning there came the news that Tobruk had fallen.

While they awaited zero hour within and without Tobruk, events were moving fast in the other sectors of the vast front under General Wavell's charge. First there came the news of activity in the Sudan. " Our troops have reoccupied Kassala. By intensive patrols over a period of weeks our troops, at low cost to themselves, have inflicted daily casualties on the enemy, who have now been forced to evacuate strongly defended positions in and

around Kassala," it was announced in Cairo on January 18 ; " Italian troops all along this front are retreating, pursued and harassed by our mobile detachments. Active patrolling continues in the Metemma region of Gallabat."

Kassala was captured by the Italians on July 4—the same day on which they took Gallabat, which was recaptured by the British on November 6. Kassala is a much more important place than Gallabat, however, since it is connected by railway with Port Sudan on the Red Sea and with Khartoum. When it was taken by the Italians its loss was recognized as serious, since in view of the overwhelming numerical superiority of the Italians it was considered quite possible, indeed very likely, that it was the prelude to a determined attack on the Sudan. The attack never materialized, however ; and now, so far from the Sudan being invaded from Eritrea, it was Eritrea's turn to be invaded from the Sudan. Following Kassala's capture it was reported that British troops had penetrated some twenty miles into Italian territory (see map, page 91).

Next the curtain was lifted on operations which have been proceeding in Abyssinia for

months past. Some weeks after Italy's entry into the war a British mission, under a Colonel well-versed in African ways and a master of the Amharic tongue, travelling on foot with mule transport, crossed the Sudanese frontier by night and began a trek through the desert and semi-jungle of Western Abyssinia to Jojjam, in the uplands, nearly 400 miles away. Very soon the Italians got wind of their approach and started to comb the country for them. The British officers and N.C.O.s, however, made contact with a band of Ethiopian rebels, led by one of Haile Selassie's loyal lieutenants, and succeeded in establishing their headquarters in an area of wild peaks and rolling parkland. The Italians continued their search for them, and frequently bombed their neighbourhood without knowing it. The work of the mission was unaffected, however, and from time to time officers were detached on special undertakings. Thousands of men in all parts of Abyssinia were rallied anew to the Emperor and the guerilla warfare (see page 91) which had been going on ever since Haile Selassie's

Water is of paramount importance to troops in desert regions, and during the British advance in Cyrenaica the Italians were forced to abandon many precious water points. British water-carts centre, right) are filling at a water point wrested from the enemy at Fort Capuzzo. Above, water sealed in tins is being loaded on to a lorry. *Photos, British Official: Crown Copyright*

Wavell's Mechanized Army Closing in on Bardia

BRITISH MECHANIZED UNITS advancing to attack Bardia, in the first great triumph of mobile armoured forces obtained by the British in this war. Some of the heavy tanks that took part in the final assault are seen crossing the desert. In the lower photograph one of the A.A. guns that gave Italy's Regia Aeronautica a bad time at Bardia is being towed into position. Bardia fell on Jan. 4 ; Tobruk followed on Jan. 22.   *Photos, British Official : Crown Copyright*

Into Kassala and Beyond Pressed the British

KASSALA lies in the Sudan, 18 miles from the frontier with Eritrea. Above is one of the positions that the Italians fortified after it had fallen into their hands. No effort was spared to make Kassala a veritable stronghold, for the Italians were aware of its strategical importance in any attempt they might make to invade the Sudan, as well as in the defence of their own colony of Eritrea.

departure from the country in 1936 was greatly intensified. Everywhere the Italians were harassed by the rebel bands, recruited largely from deserters and armed with the weapons which the Italians had taught them to use and which they had been able to bring away with them.

Today the British officers and N.C.O.s composing the mission are living in the heart of Abyssinia, in a part of Mussolini's empire where Abyssinian courts sit and Abyssinian law runs. There, towards the middle of January, they were visited by a British Staff Officer who flew from the Sudan to a secret landing ground, hundreds of miles inside Abyssinia, where he conferred with the military mission.

It was a flight which ought to be remembered— one in which the Staff Officer, the R.A.F. Flight Lieutenant and the sergeant observer took their lives in their hands. None of them had more than the vaguest notion of the exact position of the mission's headquarters, and they had to seek it in a country of great mountains and deep gorges, clothed with impenetrable forests. A message reaching them from Abyssinian Patriots told them to watch out for signals which would guide them to the landing-ground.

" We could not see the signal for which we were searching," said the officer on his return to Khartoum. " The pilot took the 'plane up and down gorge after gorge, but nothing could be seen. We thought we

should be forced to turn back when, just as dusk was falling, the observer sighted the signal. We made towards it, and as we approached saw a crowd of natives 2,000 feet below us, grouped around an agreed letter signal marked in stones across a tiny patch of ground." The little biplane— specially selected because it could land and take off in a short space of ground—made a rather shaky descent, and the adventurous trio were given a tremendous reception by the British colonel and the Ethiopian chiefs and advisers surrounding him. After delivering his dispatches and receiving news

of the revolt—" the Patriots, I learned," said the officer, " are following up every British bombing raid by attacks on Italian camps, and these are gradually driving the Fascists farther and farther east towards Addis Ababa, the capital "—a great feast was prepared. Bonfires blazed in the clearing and sheep were roasted whole. Then one by one the chieftains announced their loyalty to Haile Selassie and his British allies.

The next morning the plane took off on its return journey ; or, rather, tried to do so, for it was found that the clearing was too short. So the Abyssinian chief summoned his tribesmen ; quickly the jungle was cut down so that the 'plane cleared the trees and winged its way back to Khartoum.

ITALIAN PRISONERS taken during the operations in Libya have been brought to Egypt by tens of thousands. The latest figure given for the number captured up to January 20, 1941, was over 80,000. By lorry, by sea and on foot, they were taken to the railhead at Mersa Matruh, and here some of them have been placed in trucks that are going back to Alexandria to load up with fresh supplies for the troops.   *Photos, E.N.A., British Newsreel Association*

Crashed in the Regia Aeronautica's Graveyard

THIS FIAT C.R.42 BIPLANE crashed in the Western Desert while attempting a landing with one of its wheels shot away. It is but one of the vast numbers of Italian aircraft which now litter the battlefield of Libya, where the Regia Aeronautica has been hopelessly outclassed by the R.A.F. By January 14, 1941, the Italians had lost over 600 aircraft in Africa since they entered the war, the R.A.F. losses in the same theatre amounting to 80.

Photo, British Official: Crown Copyright

At Jarabub an Italian Army Is In Peril

The walled oasis of Jarabub has been the headquarters of the Senussites since 1855, when Mahommed Ben Ali, Sheik es Senussi, founder of the Senussi sect of Mahomedans, moved there from Mecca.

THE operations of the Army of the Nile in Libya now extend far out into the desert. It was reported in Cairo in the middle of January 1941 that an Italian army, estimated to number between 20,000 and 30,000 men, was at Jarabub, in danger of being surrounded, and that British troops had cut its lines of communication with Tobruk and Derna. The R.A.F. had, moreover, successfully bombed Italian convoys making for Jarabub. The force was concentrated at this point by Graziani to make a drive through the Siwa Oasis towards the Nile Valley.

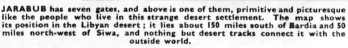

JARABUB has seven gates, and above is one of them, primitive and picturesque like the people who live in this strange desert settlement. The map shows its position in the Libyan desert; it lies about 150 miles south of Bardia and 50 miles north-west of Siwa, and nothing but desert tracks connect it with the outside world.

Mahommed the Senussi, who died about 1859, is buried in the ornate tomb above. The Mahomedan School, which he founded at Jarabub, is one of the most famous in all Islam; right, students are marching through the streets on their way to the school chanting verses of the Koran.

Photos, Wide World. Map by courtesy of the "Daily Telegraph"

Abyssinia on the Verge of Revolt

Long simmering, the Abyssinian cauldron shows every sign of boiling over. The Italians in East Africa are on the defensive, striving desperately to maintain their hold over a country whose people are now within hail of their former Emperor and are receiving arms and armed support from Britain.

A characteristic Ethiopian type, this Abyssinian warrior now in Kenya is waiting his opportunity, along with many of his countrymen, to fight the Italians.
Photo, Movietone News

NIGHT after night the royal war drums of Haile Selassie are being sounded on the hilltops of Western Abyssinia and along the frontier of the Sudan. They tell the native princes and peoples that their Emperor, who was forced to leave them five years ago, is now once again near at hand, ready and eager to lead them in revolt against the hated invader.

not frontal attacks, but ambushes and surprise raids which have succeeded in terrifying the Italians over large areas. At first the guerilla bands had to rely for their arms and ammunition on what they could capture from the enemy, but in due course further supplies were forthcoming from British sources in the Sudan and Kenya.

Assistance in other ways has been rendered by the R.A.F., which sometimes flies over Abyssinia, bombing Italian troops and outposts, and sometimes makes leaflet raids, dropping hundreds of thousands of propaganda leaflets, printed in Amharic, telling the natives the fate of Sidi Barrani and Bardia and inviting them to rally anew to the flag of their former Emperor. Many of these leaflets were distributed by rebel agents; there was one old fellow in particular who was not content with sticking them on tree trunks, but even pushed them under the doors in the Italian officers' quarters!

The first positive sign of revolt in Abyssinia

the plain to fetch water and stores; they dared not leave their retreat at night for fear of ambush, or in full daylight because of the prowling 'planes of the R.A.F.

" Most of the men," wrote the Special Correspondent of the " Daily Telegraph " on the Sudan-Abyssinian border, " were by that time covered in sores as a result of having insufficient food. They had not even medical aid. The doctor had gone mad, and merely sat on the ground gibbering when asked advice. The chief occupation of the garrison's 25 Italian officers and N.C.O.s was shamming sick so that they might have a chance to get away in a 'plane which would come to take away those wounded by Patriots."

Some of the men who got away, but not all of them, succeeded in getting through the circle of the besiegers, now reinforced by

HAILE SELASSIE

THE GHOST WALKS
From the cartoon by Illingworth, by courtesy of the " Daily Mail "

ABYSSINIA is likely soon to be the scene of a rising by the Ethiopians against their conquerors of 1936. Rebellion against the Italians is rapidly mounting in the province of Jojjam, where Ras Mongasha has raised the standard of his Emperor, Haile Selassie.
By courtesy of the " Daily Telegraph "

Since last July Haile Selassie has been at Khartoum, capital of the Anglo-Egyptian Sudan. Shortly after his arrival there he opened up communication with many of his supporters in his former empire, and frequent visits have been paid to him by the chiefs of the neighbouring province of Jojjam—and, indeed, of very many other districts in the heart of the country; some 500 chieftains, in fact, are reported to have made perilous journeys through the Italian lines to welcome their Emperor back to Africa.

Although the war against the Italians in Abyssinia has never ceased, it has blazed up more fiercely than ever since Italy's entry into the war against Britain and Haile Selassie's return to the borders of his former realm. With the spreading of the news of Italy's defeat in North Africa, opposition to the Italians in Abyssinia became more open, and by early in the New Year a guerilla warfare has developed in the mountains. On the one hand are the numerous and well-equipped troops of the Italian army of occupation under the command of the Duke of Aosta, the Viceroy; on the other are large groups of discontented tribesmen, numbering many thousands, under the immediate command of their native chiefs but linked in a confederation which has its directing intelligence and inspiration in Haile Selassie, living under British protection in Khartoum.

Bands of rebels known as " shiftas," and bodies of Amharas, deserters from the Italian army in Abyssinia, have made frequent and ever-increasing attacks on the Italians—

was contained in a communiqué issued by G.H.Q., Cairo, on January 9. " Abyssinia," it read : " Patriots, encouraged by support from the R.A.F., have compelled the Italians to evacuate the post of Gubba. The Patriots are now closing round the fleeing Italian garrison." Gubba lies 25 miles inside Abyssinia from the Sudan frontier, and for many months the Italian garrison had been cut off from their comrades in the interior, save for an occasional 'plane which landed at the aerodrome, three miles distant, bringing with it essential supplies and taking away the wounded. When the rains ended in September the Patriots surrounding the place closed in, so that the garrison were compelled to leave their comfortable bamboo-stockaded quarters in the plain for a hillock on the slopes of Jebel Gubba, the 6,000-ft.-high mountain on which the Commandant's house was placed. There, sheltered only by the huge rocks from the burning sun, they passed their days, while at night the velvety blackness of the sky was split by the fires of the tribesmen who seemed to be drawing ever nearer. At dusk and dawn the Italians ventured down into

The Emperor's War Drums Sound the Call to Arms

Sudanese patrols in addition to the R.A.F., and in reaching the next Italian outpost. At last the Italian commander gave the order to evacuate, and one night the Italians moved out, hoping to make their escape in the darkness. But the rebels were ready for them, lying in ambush on the track which they had to follow through the jungle. Half-way to Wanbera, 40 miles to the south-east, the Abyssinians closed in on the rearguard and inflicted a number of casualties ; the rest succeeded in reaching Wanbera.

So serious did the situation become in Jojjam that the Duke of Aosta himself paid a visit to the Fascist troops in the province so as to learn for himself the actual state of affairs and also to stiffen their morale, weakened as it had been by the ambushes, the surprise raids, and the unending guerilla war. At the same time, General Nasi, who commanded the Italian troops in their successful campaign against the British in Somaliland, was sent from Addis Ababa with strong reinforcements, including two battalions of Savoy Grenadiers with orders to put down the revolt in Jojjam with a stern hand. But the revolt in Jojjam continued, showing every sign of spreading until the whole of Abyssinia becomes aflame.

In their revolt against the Italians the Abyssinians will be far better armed than they were when their country was conquered. The warriors, above, within a few miles of the frontier, have quickly learned to handle their new weapons—trench mortars.

Abyssinians in revolt against the Italians have crossed over the frontier into Kenya to be trained by South African officers. Left, some of them are on the parade ground, and though they could not be called smart, their keenness makes them formidable fighters, while they add to recently acquired military knowledge their own proficiency in guerilla warfare.

Other subjects of Haile Selassie have crossed over into the Sudan and have been armed by the British. Below is a march past of Abyssinian troops before the Emperor, who is taking the salute. He has his headquarters at Khartoum. The Crown Prince of Ethiopia heads the detachment.

Photos, British Official: Crown Copyright; and Movietone News

What They Fight With In the Western Desert

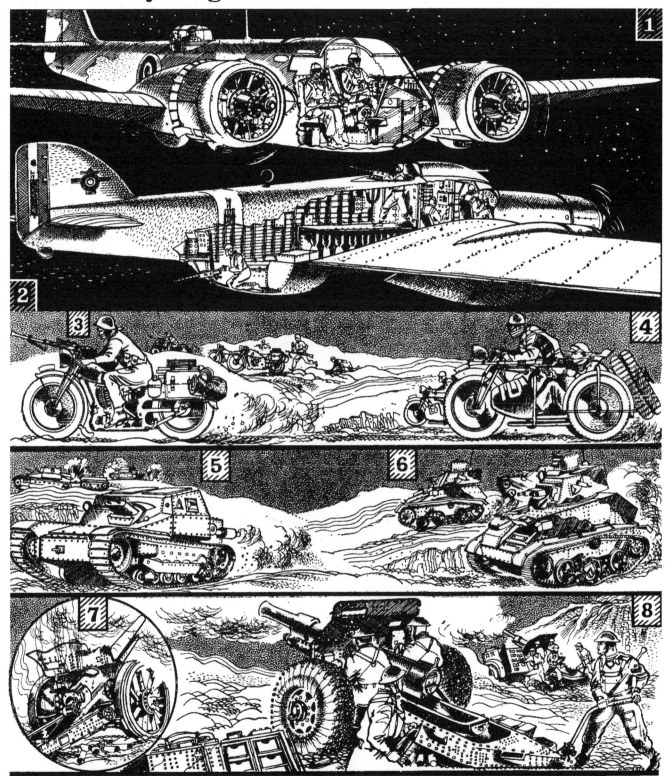

In a struggle such as the present Anglo-Italian war it is always interesting to compare the equipment of the opposing forces. Most of the war material now used in Libya by the Italians seems little different from that used in the Spanish Civil War, and cannot compete with the high-quality equipment which the Army of the Nile is putting to such good use.

AIRCRAFT

(1) The British Blenheim bomber is being used both in Greece and Libya. It has a speed of about 300 m.p.h. and can function as a fighter if so required.
(2) Italian Savoia-Marchetti S.M.-79. Although not of the latest design Italy has built a great number of these planes. They are strong and carry a maximum bomb load of 2,755 lb. at about 250 m.p.h., 2 guns above the fuselage and one beneath are Breda (SAFAT) 12·7-mm.

MOTOR-CYCLE TROOPS

(3) Italian Bersaglieri saw service in Spain in large numbers. The standard Breda machine-gun is mounted in the cycle besides grenades in panniers and full equipment for the soldier.
(4) We have developed the light sidecar combination with Bren gun mounted.

TANKS

(5) The Fiat Tankettes with half-inch armour and twin machine-guns have proved no match for our mechanized cavalry. The high speed does not compensate for the lack of a revolving turret. Light-tracked supply vehicles are sometimes pulled behind.
(6) British cavalry tanks with revolving turrets have proved fast, manoeuvrable and powerful. They also wear well over rough country.

ARTILLERY

(7) This 150-mm. Italian gun is typical—rather old-fashioned but sturdy.
(8) The 25-pounder Gun-How. is typical of the high-quality material now being used against the Italians. It has long range and by varying the charge can be used as a howitzer. It combines the job once done by several guns.

Specially drawn for THE WAR ILLUSTRATED *by Haworth*

One Way or Another Our Airmen Keep Warm

LEATHER HELMET OVER BALACLAVA

TELEPHONE MOUTHPIECE ENCASED IN PADDED LEATHER

COAT AND TROUSERS LINED WITH LAMB'S WOOL

LEATHER GAUNTLETS OVER SILK GLOVES

LEATHER BOOTS OVER WOOLLEN AND SILK SOCKS

SUMMER or winter—the season makes no matter—R.A.F. crews are accustomed to fly at temperatures which may fall to 25 degrees and more below freezing point. Nevertheless, they must keep warm. Numbed and chilly crews are not in a fit state for operations.

Heavy bombers, travelling great distances and expected to stay aloft for eight and nine hours at a stretch, are equipped with central heating. The hot gases from the exhausts are conducted in pipes around the interior of the aircraft before making their final escape—a simple automatic arrangement which ensures some warmth for the crew in the coldest weather.

Medium bombers are for the most part without this device as yet. and precautions against cold and frost-bite must be taken individually by each member of the crew. Good blood-circulation is a chief necessity ; so is cleanliness which keeps the pores open. Then clothing but this is a matter which each man can decide for himself. Airmen look bulky in their flying clothes, but, as far as possible, bulkiness which tends to hamper movements is avoided.

Layers of silk, wool, and leather are found to be the best protection against cold. For instance, silk gloves (three thicknesses round the hand, five round the wrist) may be worn beneath the woollen gloves, both pairs being enclosed within leather gauntlets. Some pilots wear silk socks under their woollen socks and the ordinary leather boots on top.

Clean undergarments are vital a vest slightly damp from perspiration may cause great discomfort and start a chill at minus temperatures. The head is protected by the usual leather helmet, and a silk scarf or a Balaclava may be worn underneath. The face is adequately covered by the oxygen mask and by the mouthpiece of the telephone, which is encased in padded leather. Scarves, either of silk or wool (usually wool), go round the neck, and the outer flying coats and trousers are, of course, of leather and, like the flying boots, are lined with lamb's wool.

In the air, oxygen is an unfailing antidote to cold. It is not strictly reserved, as some imagine, for flying at great heights ; sometimes it is turned on soon after the take-off — not at full strength, however, an unnecessary waste and causes the body to become noticeably warmer.

The air gunner, in his semi-open cockpit, is the one most liable to feel the cold ; but even he, taking these various precautions, can remain fairly comfortable in Arctic conditions.

Protection from cold is of vital importance to airmen. The photographs above, examined in conjunction with the article in this page, show how this is achieved.   *Photos, Fox and Topical*

Flying suits for airmen, which are made of shaped skins, are manufactured in enormous quantities. This airman is seen trying on a completed suit in a fitting-room.

The Air Frontier May Soon Be Over Germany

Opening the New Year with a display of daring initiative, the R.A.F. began a daylight offensive on the German-occupied territory of Northern Europe. By so doing it revealed that Britain cannot be far short of air parity with the Nazi Reich.

EVERY day since the war began the Air Ministry in London has issued its communiqué—on many days more than one—describing the progress of the air war, of its duel to the death with the German Luftwaffe. Of all these hundreds of communiqués, none, perhaps, has been of greater interest or importance than that which was issued on January 10, 1941.

" A strong force of fighters," it stated, " accompanied R.A.F. bombers on an extensive sweep over the Pas de Calais at midday today. Several enemy aircraft were bombed and machine-gunned, and attacks were also made from a low level on the military installations and patrol vessels. Only a few enemy fighters were encountered. Three were shot down and a number damaged on the ground. None of our aircraft is missing from these operations," went on the bulletin, " but one fighter crashed on returning, the pilot being injured."

the last detail—and it is no easy matter to organize a raid of this description in which a host of 'planes are employed. It seems that the Germans were taken completely by surprise, or they would have seen to it that an opposing force of at least equal numbers was ready to take the air. As it was the British formation swept across the ports and aerodromes with virtual impunity. A railway station was set on fire, and fires were started in the woods near Calais. On the return flight a section of the fighter escort carried out a low-level machine-gun attack on gun posts and enemy troops in the neighbourhood of Wissant. A number of Henschel army co-operation aircraft seen on the ground in a corner of Guines la Plage aerodrome were also heavily machine-gunned by the Polish pilot of a Hurricane who flew across the aerodrome at ground level to deliver his attack ; as he climbed away he shot down a Messerschmitt 109, one of two which he

of our pilots who are shot down bale out in safety and arrive back at their aerodromes only an hour or two late for lunch, if they experience the same hard luck over German territory, they will come down to earth in a prisoners-of-war camp. But this is inevitable if the victory is to be won.

Influence on Nazi Morale

Against these losses must be set the enormous effect on German morale. Up to now millions of Germans have heard R.A.F. 'planes, but few have seen one. Before long the slaves of Nazidom will see only too often for their comfort and peace of mind the red, white, and blue rings on a 'plane's underside. Already they must be seriously disturbed, for they cannot but remember Goering's boasts that the German towns, Berlin in particular, and the Ruhr and other industrial areas, would not, could not, be bombed.

For months now they have been driven to

NEW TORPEDO BOMBERS and general reconnaissance 'planes, the Blackburn Bothas, are now in service with the R.A.F. The Bothas are twin-engined, high-wing monoplanes, 50 ft. 11½ in. long, 18 ft. 3 in. high, and have a wing span of 59 ft. They are powered by 890 h.p. Bristol Perseus engines. Since the Bothas are among the latest types of British 'planes, their performance has not yet been disclosed. Here three of the new aircraft are seen flying against a frieze of clouds above snow-capped hills.
Photo, British Official : Crown Copyright

Reading between the lines of this statement it is clear that Britain is now approaching air parity with Germany ; indeed, we are so near to it that the R.A.F. can run the risk of incurring what may be heavy losses. For daylight raids are apt to be expensive, as we discovered in the early weeks of the war when we sent out bombers unescorted across the North Sea to raid Heligoland and Kiel, and as the Germans learnt more forcibly when last autumn they sent over waves of bombers against London and South-east England. In these ventures they lost hundreds of machines, and even when strong forces of fighters were sent to accompany the bombers the losses were still large—so large, indeed, that the mass raids in daylight were given up in favour of nocturnal bombing, with results which, however destructive to life and property, are generally altogether devoid of military value, as the bombing must necessarily be very largely haphazard.

But the R.A.F.'s raid on Northern France on January 10 was carried out without losses, so carefully prepared had it been down to

sighted just below him. Another Hurricane on the return journey sighted four enemy patrol boats off the French coast, came down low and sprayed the ships with machine-gun bullets ; after which he went to the assistance of a Spitfire which was being attacked by a Messerschmitt 109, and sent the Nazi smoking into the sea.

Offensive by Day and by Night

This daring daylight raid was repeated on the following days, and again with remarkable success. For months the R.A.F. had been obliged to confine its offensive to the night hours, ranging hundreds of miles over Germany and German-occupied Europe. Now it was displaying its offensive spirit by daylight—proof positive of its growing power, its increasing confidence. Just as the R.F.C. secured the supremacy of the air over the battlefields of France and Belgium in the Great War, so now the R.A.F. has embarked upon the same great venture. And we may be sure that it will be just as successful. Losses there will be, for whereas now most

take shelter as soon as night falls, and although the damage done to German towns by our 'planes can hardly be as great as that done by the Nazis to ours—for our pilots have instructions to confine themselves to military targets, whereas the Germans are out to do as much damage as they can—neutral observers have told of very considerable material damage done to many places, and of immense damage done to Hamburg and one or two other nerve centres of Germany's war machine.

No doubt, too, many Germans have been killed and wounded, although the number must be small compared with our civilian casualties : in December 1940, 3,793 civilians were killed and 5,044 seriously injured.

Perhaps the developing situation may be most conveniently summed up in the statement that the R.A.F. is now engaged in shifting the air frontier. For some months past that frontier has been over England, and for a few weeks it was even over London ; now it is over Northern France, but is creeping steadily eastwards. Soon it will be over Germany itself.

The Greeks Tore the 'Tuscan Wolves' to Shreds

The New Year brought no respite to the Italians in Albania. Still they retreated before
the steady pressure of the Greeks, and on Jan. 13 their failure was blazoned to the world
when it was announced that General Soddu, the Commander-in-Chief, had resigned
" for health reasons."

ALTHOUGH snow was still falling heavily on the Albanian front the Greeks continued their offensive following their brilliant capture of Klisura—a victory which brought them appreciably nearer to Berat, and, still more important, Valona, the Italian base port on the Adriatic. The Italians made one or two counter-attacks in a desperate endeavour to regain the positions that they had lost, but they were beaten back, leaving behind many wounded and dead, together with a number of prisoners. Several tanks were also captured and straightway employed against their former owners.

For a few days the Greek communiqués referred merely to " limited local activity," but those in Athens who knew how cautiously the Greek G.H.Q. framed its bulletins anticipated another victory. And they were right, for on January 18 it was announced that " during today's successful operations we have captured strong positions. We have taken 1,000 prisoners, among whom are several officers, including Colonel Meneghetti of the 77th Regiment, the ' Wolves of Tuscany,' which has lately arrived in Albania."

The " Wolves of Tuscany " were one of the crack Italian divisions, and not only the 77th but the 78th regiment was badly cut up in the fighting referred to in the communiqué.

That, perhaps, is unfair to the Italians, who on many occasions on the Albanian front and elsewhere have shown that they can fight well enough if only their heart is in the business. But most of them, as may be judged from Colonel Meneghetti's revelations, have little spirit for the war against the Greeks.

From every side came further evidence of the ill-preparedness of the Italians. They had expected a war of waving flags and blaring bands ; they had made little or no preparations for a war of blood and frostbite. The plight of the Italian wounded, who were sent back from the Albanian front to their homes in Northern Italy, was reported to be pitiable. Many of them had seen no fighting whatever, but they had been so severely frozen in the bitter mountain weather that it had been found necessary to amputate their limbs. Italian hospitals in Bari and Brindisi were said to be filled to overflowing, so that many of the wounded had to be taken to ports in the North Adriatic before even their bandages were changed since they left the front line. One case was mentioned of a seriously wounded officer who had been carried for three days on mule-back across the mountains, and then spent a day crossing the Adriatic and two days travelling up the coast by railway, without receiving medical treatment or having his uniform changed. Valona

was reported to be jammed with more than 30,000 Italian troops wounded on the battlefield or suffering from frostbite ; they crowded the hospitals and the houses, waiting for transport to take them back to Italy. But the transport was slow in coming, and the confusion in the little town grew apace.

No wonder the Italians who were taken prisoner congratulated themselves on their fate. As they trudged through the mud and snow on the way to Janina they looked miserable enough, but when they had left the front far behind them they cheered up wonderfully. A Greek officer stood beside the road and watched them pass. "There goes the second Roman Empire," he said sardonically.

Very different was the spirit displayed by the Greek troops, and yet they had to face the same bitter weather. They had to clamber along the same precipitous paths, they trudged through the same mud and floundered in the same deep snowdrifts. Like the Italians, they suffered wounds, endured frostbite, and many of them died. But they struggled on, living on little more than a crust of bread and melted snow. They had no fires and little shelter, their boots were worn out, their clothes were poor, and many of them were even without gloves. Yet theirs was the spirit of the men who would conquer or die.

The Greek war zone has few roads and no railways. It is therefore through mountain defiles or over such undulating plains as this that troops moving up to the front must pass.

Colonel Meneghetti, interviewed after his capture, stated that the division had been decimated in the course of the 10 days' battle which had just concluded. He also confirmed the reports that to an increasing extent Italian soldiers were running away from the front line and so had to be shot down by their officers. Another interesting item of information that he vouchsafed was that a Greek submarine had recently torpedoed two Italian vessels, the " Lombardia " and the " Liguria," one of which was carrying his division's entire artillery.

A little later it was announced that the figure of 1,000 prisoners taken was likely to be exceeded ; so many were the prisoners, indeed, that the wits in the Athenian cafés expressed the opinion that the Tuscan wolves must have been wolves in sheep's clothing !

The young Greek, above, aged 13, captured a number of spies and was promoted lancecorporal on the field. The Greek militiaman, right, claims to be 105.

British Official : Crown Copyright ; Associated Press

See the Conquerors Enter Argyrokastro

ARGYROKASTRO, which the Greeks finally captured on December 8, 1940, paved the way for later Greek victories in the Klisura-Tepelini sector of the Albanian front. The town yielded a great quantity of war material abandoned by the retreating Italians. In these photographs we see Greek mounted troops crossing a bridge on their triumphant entry, and others busily searching some of the ruined buildings.   *Photos, Associated Press*

In Snowbound Newfoundland American Bomber

THA
for
for the
has be
time w
1941,
Hugh
in this
Canadi
all are
cial fl
pilots
the Min
tion fr
Airway
machin
Lockhe
Boeing
Fortr
Ventur

Many American aircraft destined for the R.A.F. are now being flown directly across the Atlantic to aerodromes in Britain. At the top of the page is a line of U.S.-built Lockheed Hudson bombers waiting at Newfoundland Airport to be ferried across to Britain. Wintry conditions now prevail, and above, a Hudson is seen embedded in a snowdrift on the airport. To enable 'planes to take off after a heavy fall of snow special tractor rollers (right) are employed which flatten out and harden the surface snow. In the circle is Captain Pat Eves,

ait Their Turn to be Flown Across the Atlantic

service
destined
Atlantic
or some
Jan. 8,
shal Sir
engaged
an and
sh, and
ommer-
e ferry
ed " by
Produc-
verseas
he chief
are the
er, the
'Flying
kheed
olidated

one of the Atlantic ferry pilots, who recently set up a new time record for the Atlantic crossing while ferrying across a new type of American bomber. He is an experienced British Airways pilot who, before the war, was engaged on air lines in the Middle East and India. Other British Airways pilots engaged on this service are Capt. Sydney Cripps, D.F.C., Capt. D. C. T. Bennett, Capt. A. G. Store, Capt. Ian Ross, Capt. W. L. Stewart and Squadron-Leader R. H. Page. Over 30 types of American aircraft are now supplementing British production.

tures
TRATED
ws

'They're Prisoners-of-War in Germany'

In thousands of homes in this country and in the Empire overseas thoughts turn to a husband or father, son, brother or lover who is "kicking his heels" in a German prisoners-of-war camp. Some account of the camps and of the prevailing conditions is given in the article that follows.

I N Germany and German-occupied territory there are at the present time, it has been estimated, some 2,500,000 prisoners-of-war. Nearly two million of these are French, hundreds of thousands are Polish, tens of thousands are Belgian, Dutch, and Norwegian, while the British number about 44,000.

This vast host is quartered (except for those enlisted in labour gangs) in prison camps, of which there are three types, known officially as Oflag, Stalag, and Dulag, contractions for Offizierslager, Stamlager, and Durchgangslager, respectively. Oflag is a camp used for officer prisoners, while Stalag is one for privates and N.C.O.s. Dulag is a transfer camp, i.e. a camp to which officers and men are taken soon after their capture, and where they are graded before being dispatched to either an Oflag or a Stalag.

The camps are periodically visited by delegates of the International Red Cross, and reports on some of them have been published. Thus a few weeks ago two Swiss doctors, Dr. Marti and Dr. Des Coeudres, reported on Oflag VII C, where there are

1,245 British officers, including a general and five colonels, 31 chaplains, and 39 doctors. It is contained in an old castle in a Bavarian town, and the quarters comprise three floors, the number of prisoners in each room varying from nine to 120. The food, though rather monotonous, is not too bad, and British cooks are employed. Most of the prisoners,

the visitors found, were at that time in need of warm clothes; shirts and so on could be purchased at the canteen, but they were very dear. Four British doctors are on duty in the hospital, and, generally speaking, the health conditions are satisfactory. Hot baths are available once a week and there are facilities for playing games. On Sundays four religious

services are held. Books are scarce, but the supply is being augmented by the Y.M.C.A.

The same two visitors inspected **Stalag XIII**, where there are 1,036 prisoners – not only British, but French, Poles, Belgians, Dutch, and Norwegians. This prison camp was found to be decidedly overcrowded, and the delegates commented unfavourably on the fact that the beds had only one sheet and two blankets, and that the only heating was a small oven in the centre of the room. "This seems inadequate heating," they said, "during a severe winter, and the health conditions seem generally defective."

Dr. Marti also visited some of the camps reserved for R.A.F. prisoners. In one Stalag he found 231 N.C.O.s and 57 privates; the camp leader was Flight-Sergeant Hall, No. 569838. These were housed in three wooden barracks, which Dr. Marti described as comfortable; "food, good; prisoners, satisfied." The men, he went on, "like to work in the labour detachments, in which they receive a minimum of 20.8 marks per month, and are well treated."

In Oflag IX there are 44 naval officers and 17 doctors. Dulag Luft, a transfer camp for airmen, consists of three large, well-heated barracks, with running hot and cold water, accommodating 102 men. Here are Dr. Marti's notes on the place: "Rooms with one to three beds; tables, easy chairs; exceptional comfort; dining-room; whisky every evening; papers; various games; walks outside camp; food excellent, similar to that received by the German officers of

WULZBURG CASTLE, near Weissenburg, Bavaria, where these photographs were taken, is a prisoners-of-war camp in which the majority of the prisoners are British and French. In the upper photograph some of them are seen making articles of clothing under the supervision of a Nazi guard. Lower photo, the organ provides solace, during recreation hours, to those who are fond of music.   *Photos, Fox*

Where the Nazis Hold Our Men in Captivity

P.O.W. CAMPS in Germany and Poland are shown in this map. There are 106 within the boundaries of the Reich (including Poland and Austria) and 62 in France. OFG (" Oflag ") denotes a camp for officer prisoners ; STG (" Stalag "), a camp for other ranks ; " Luftlager," camp for airmen ; " Dulag," a transfer camp. This map, compiled from a list supplied by the Nazi authorities, was published in the French newspaper " Paris Soir," and reproduced in the " Daily Telegraph."

the camp ; well-stocked canteen ; receiving pay ; correspondence received irregularly.''

Another delegate, Dr. Marcel Junod, was commissioned by the International Red Cross to visit prisoner-of-war hospitals in Brussels, Malines, Ghent, Paris, and Rouen, amongst other places. On the whole his report was not unsatisfactory ; thus the wounded at Malines hospital are '' satisfied,'' being under the care of two Army doctors, Major R. W. Ganderson and Major D. N. Stuart. On being passed fit the men are given a complete double set of underclothing by the Belgian Red Cross before being sent to the prison camps in Germany. But warm underclothes were badly needed in some of the hospitals, and the wounded often asked for soap.

Now here is a letter from a British officer who is imprisoned in Oflag VII C/H ; it was dated December 10 and was received by his

BRITISH PRISONERS in Germany lead a monotonous life, and after their day's work, which may be arduous road-making or canal construction, games provide a very welcome diversion and keep their minds occupied. Two prisoners above are keeping their wits alive with a game of chess, while their comrades follow the moves closely.

Photo, Fox

Lives of Toil and Boredom Are Their Lot

wife on January 8 by air mail via Lisbon. "We rise at 7.30 a.m. and have a half-litre of ersatz coffee. Parade or roll-call is at 9.15. Lunch is at 11, and usually consists of soup, sometimes thin and sometimes thick, and potatoes. Twice a week we get a meat and potato mash instead. Next meal is at 4 p.m., of more soup, and potatoes, or on Sunday a 2-oz. Camembert and some jam with coffee, or Red Cross tea if we have any. Two other meals a week in the afternoon are either cheese or sausage, tea or coffee. We get half a litre of milk two or three times a week, which we pay for. Our supper comes out of the above, with 10 oz. of bread which we get every day. Naturally, parcels are we comed for a change of diet!"

Thus it is clear that, while the prisoners may receive rations comparing quite fairly with those issued to their Nazi guards, they may well complain about the quality and monotonous character of their diet.

PARCELS OF FOOD and comforts, dispatched through the British Red Cross, are eagerly awaited by our men who are prisoners-of-war in Germany for the rations of a prisoner are by no means lavish. Small wonder, then, that the arrival of the parcels post at a P.O.W. camp in Germany is a red-letter event in these men's lives. Lower photo, British prisoners are seen clearing away the debris of bombed and shelled buildings in Calais, work that puts a keen edge on the appetite. Centre, parcels are being stamped prior to dispatch at a parcels centre of the British Red Cross.

Photos, Fox, Photopress and Planet News

Packing Parcels of Good Cheer for the Prisoners

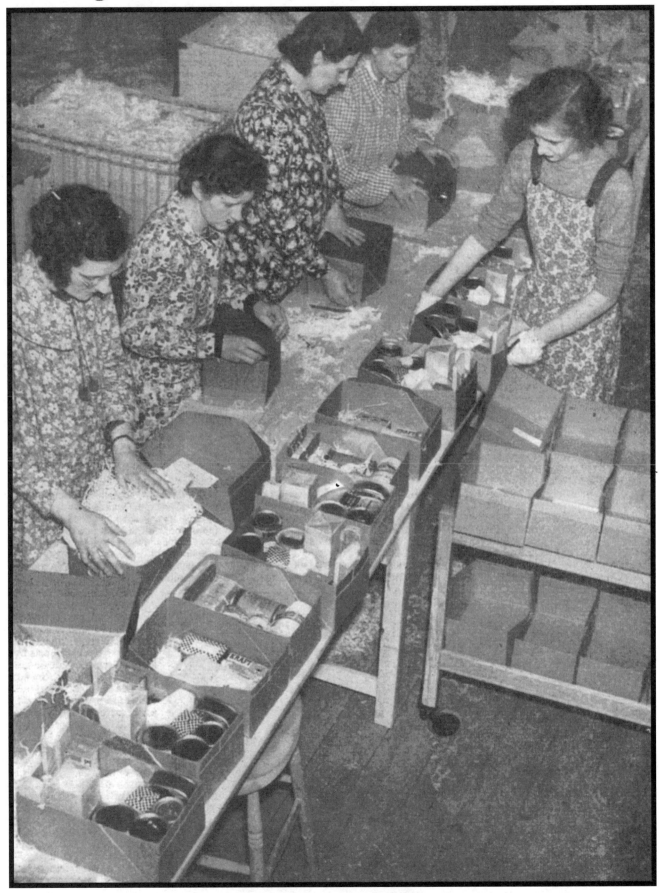

THE RED CROSS organization faced a difficult task after the Battle of France in sending parcels to prisoners of war in Germany. Many of the thousands of men posted as "missing" were prisoners, but for a time the Red Cross had in its possession the names of only a fraction of the total number. Moreover, parcels have to travel from a British port to Lisbon, thence by rail to Barcelona, from Barcelona by sea to Marseilles, and then overland to Geneva. A 10-lb. parcel is sent by the Red Cross every week to each of our 44,000 prisoners of war in Germany.   *Photo, Fox*

Norway's Sons are Fighting at the Side of Ours

This account of the contribution made by Norwegians to the common cause is contributed by Henry Baerlein, who not long since was privileged to visit the Norwegian naval establishment at a certain port in this country.

JUST before Hitler's invasion of Norway he was assured by Quisling that the Norwegians were anxious to become his faithful lieges. By now, however, they both must be disillusioned, for Quisling has been able to enrol only a handful of the ragamuffins who will vanish the moment that the Germans are swept out of Norway.

No one acquainted with the Norwegians could ever have any doubts of their patriotism, and now in Britain they have entered upon the struggle to liberate their native land. The Norwegian Navy is doing excellent work from various British ports; their Army is enthusiastically training; and in Canada large numbers of Norwegian airmen are preparing to emulate over here the exploits of the Poles and the Czechs.

Nor is this by any means the extent of Norway's assistance in the common cause—remember that Norway's population is much less than half that of London, though this has not prevented her producing in the last few decades a series of world-famous men, such as Nansen, Ibsen, Björnson, and Grieg. One of Norway's chief contributions is her extremely large Merchant Navy, which the Germans endeavoured to obtain as soon as they reached Oslo. But the Norwegians are not a people who act in haste, and when soon after the German orders from Oslo there came that from the B.B.C., sent out at the request of the legal Norwegian Government, it was the latter which was obeyed, and all over the world Norwegian vessels made for the nearest Allied port. It is one of Hitler's grievances that Britain possesses far too many ports in different parts of the world.

Navy, Merchant Service and Army: I did not find it an easy matter to visit a unit of the Norwegian Navy operating over here. Most of the ships are at sea with very brief intervals, but ultimately I was told that one of them would put in at a certain port. Armed with the necessary permit from the

Admiralty and with the blessing of the Norwegian naval authorities in London, I set out for that port, arrived only an hour late at the station, drove to the building which is now the naval headquarters and encountered a couple of Vikings, splendid-looking young men. It would be an exaggeration to say that I got much out of them, although they replied that they would be glad to tell me all I wanted.

As a preliminary a drink had to be taken at the bar with them and two or three British officers, and almost at once an alarm was sounded and among the ships required instantly was that of these Norwegians. In less time than it takes to write they had disappeared, arrayed themselves in suitable kit (there was quite a boisterous sea), and off they rushed. It was from their British comrades that I learned how gaily they go out day after day, braving the dangers of mine and torpedo, German coastal guns and dive-bombers. Their one hope is to meet the enemy who has overrun their beloved country. The tougher the job, the better they like it. They are devoted to their work over here because it gives them an opportunity of attacking. Offensive actions are what these modern Vikings look forward to. I was told of several of their outstanding exploits : one, which the British officers characterized as a very gallant affair, occurred when they went to the rescue of a bombed merchant-ship and were themselves heavily bombed ; the top was blown off the Norwegian gunner's binoculars, and he was severely wounded in the stomach, but

this did not prevent him from carrying on. A good many of the crews on the Norwegian warships are men who have seen service in the Merchant Navy, and they have lost little time in adapting themselves to their new conditions. Those who remain in the Merchant Service are assisting the Allied cause

KING HAAKON of Norway, who arrived in Britain on June 15, 1940, is here seen at a Norwegian hospital in England taking leave of the Matron, a Norwegian lady married to a Swedish Count now with the Norwegian Army in England.

all over the world. They number no fewer than 35,000 first-class men, all of them, and when replacements are required they are supplied by the Norwegian Shipping and Trade Mission in London, which has taken over the management of all the Norwegian lines, whose captains and sailors loyally obey their instructions. The ships, of course, have been well armed in Britain.

Enrolled in the Norwegian Army in England is a Swedish Count who fought in Spain and Finland, and who is now married to a Norwegian nurse who is in charge of her country's hospital service. His case is exceptional, for the Norwegian troops, a smallish but very useful body of men, are otherwise 100 per cent Norwegian. They have been fully equipped with all modern weapons, which, like everything they handle, has been paid for from out of their own funds. The officers were all in the Army in Norway, but of the men only 25 per cent, the others having previously served either with the Navy or the Merchant Navy. However, the same spirit prevails among all of them, and there is no doubt as to their efficiency. In Canada, too, a "Little Norway" has arisen, where exiles and Canadian-born Norwegians are training for the battle against Hitler.

NORWEGIANS IN CANADA are eager to fight for their country. The Navy makes a great appeal to this sea-faring race and a special training centre has been erected on the seashore at Lunenburg, Nova Scotia. Here men and officers are standing at attention when the centre, known as Camp Norway, was opened on December 3, 1940.
Photo, Wide World

While Her Princes Share the Honour of Exile

NORWEGIAN WARSHIPS are now serving in comradeship with the British Navy, and Prince Olaf, Crown Prince of Norway, who, like all his countrymen, has the sea in his blood, is seen above in Admiral's uniform leaving a Norwegian destroyer in a British port after an inspection. Norwegians resident in this country have formed an infantry company. Below it is drawn up for inspection by King Haakon. In the circle are three patrol boats of the Norwegian Navy fitted as minesweepers. *Top photo: British Official: Crown Copyright*

Waiting for the Invader at 'Hell Fire Corner'

WHY are German aircraft heard overhead on nights when the weather is reported to be too bad for our bombers to operate over Germany ? One of the reasons is that while the Germans have a large number of alternative bases within easy striking distances of this country, and in the event of bad weather in the Channel or over the French coast they can operate from bases in Holland and Belgium instead, the R.A.F. has not the same wide choice of alternative bases, and, moreover, has much farther to go except for such targets as the "invasion ports." These longer flights involve greater risks, especially in bad flying weather. Then for a flight occupying, say, seven hours, it is harder to forecast changes in the weather than for a short "trip." Our aircraft might set off for Berlin in ideal conditions, only to find on their return that fog had hidden their base.

The policy of the R.A.F. is to attack definite military objectives, hence the weather over the objective is also of great importance to us. To fly 700 miles out, only to find "ten-tenths" cloud, which would prevent the location of any objective, is largely a waste of effort. The Germans, however, appear content to bomb indiscriminately. On some of the nights they have come over they could not have seen anything of the ground, let alone, pick out particular objectives. Many of these aircraft are probably either lost and fail to return, or crash on landing, because the weather has "closed in" over their base.

WATCH AND WARD on the Kentish coast during the cold spell of January 1941 brought considerable hardships to the troops, but these men, ankle deep in snow, have beside them a hint of happier days. The strip of Kentish coast below, with gleams of wintry sunshine lighting up the Channel beyond, is known as " Hell Fire Corner " and at any moment the wayfarers may be under fire.   *Photos, Planet News*

Eye Witness Stories of Episodes
and Adventures in the
Second Great War

We Saw the Battle of the Sicilian Channel

On January 10, 1941, as told in the Admiralty communiqué printed in this page, there was a fierce combined naval and air action in the Sicilian Channel – the stretch of water separating Sicily from Tunis. In these pages we tell the story in the words of eye-witnesses – the first, given below, by a British United Press correspondent who was on board a British warship.

As the first thin streak of grey showed in the eastern sky a star-shell burst to the west of us. It came from a British cruiser which had spotted two Italian destroyers. The battle was on.

Cruisers and destroyers raced after the enemy, who proved to have plenty of speed – in fact one of the Italian destroyers slipped away in the early morning haze and was never seen again.

The other Italian destroyer, however, was caught in a heavy fire from our ships. Two cruisers pumped several salvos into her, crippling her beyond hope, while a British destroyer raced alongside and finished the job.

A huge burst of water, steam and smoke could then be seen rising from the Italian ship at a distance of about 10 miles, indicating that the boiler had burst. She went down almost immediately, presumably with all hands, although some of the crew may have been able to reach the Italian coast, which was only a few miles away.

The Italian vessel fought with courage and determination, but she must have known she was doomed from the very start. Her small guns made a valiant but feeble

return against the heavy British naval guns.

The first retaliation for this action under the very noses of Italy's long-range coast defence guns in the fortress of Pantelleria occurred a few minutes after 11 a.m., when our aircraft spotted enemy aircraft approaching the Fleet and chased them away. But the Italian effort was not futile, for by this flight they learned the position of the Fleet. One hour later two Italian torpedo bombers flew in with the sun behind them for the attack. They met with a tremendous barrage of anti-aircraft guns and pom-poms.

One dropped its torpedo, which passed across the stern of this ship, ran its course, and finally sank harmlessly in the distance. The other torpedo bomber retained its load, and both turned tail and disappeared.

At 1.30 p.m. the Luftwaffe made its Mediterranean debut in a spectacular bombing attack which must have been carried out by some of Germany's best aces. A squadron appeared about 8,000 ft. overhead, and, breaking into groups of three, pointed their noses downward, and in an almost completely vertical dive raced for their targets with throttle wide open.

They met with a barrage of thousands of shells, but manoeuvred with extraordinary skill through the barrage ceiling to let go their deadly cargoes. In some cases they straightened out less than 100 ft. above the water and re-formed for another dive, which was carried out with the same precision and expertness. Fifteen aircraft took part in the attack.

Although it seemed humanly impossible for them to get in and out of the barrage without some of them being hit, none was observed, from our ships, to fall into the sea. Other fighters later intercepted the squadron and shot down a number of them.

At 6 p.m. we had another visit, this time by 11 dive-bombers. So far as one could see in the growing dusk they seemed to be the same squadron that attacked us before. If so, four of the original squadron must have been either shot down or too badly damaged to carry on.

H.M.S. " SOUTHAMPTON," whose tragic fate it was to be sunk by the guns of the British Fleet when it was found impossible to get her to port. This 9,000-ton British cruiser was the first warship in this war to be hit by a bomb from a German aircraft. On October 16, 1939, while she was lying in the Firth of Forth, an enemy bomb glanced off her, causing slight damage to her bow. The map shows the scene of the battle of the Sicilian Channel.
Photo, Wright & Logan ; Map by courtesy of the " Daily Telegraph "

IIIIIIIIIIIIIIIIIIIIIIIIIIIIIIIIIIIIIIIIIIIIIIIIIIIIIIIIIIIIIIII **I WAS THERE!** IIIIIIIIIIIIIIIIIIIIIIIIIIIIIIIIIIIIIIIIIIIIIIIIIIIIIIIIIIIIIIIIIIIIIIII

The " Illustrious," which though hit by bombs got safely back to port, is one of a class of six 23,000-ton aircraft carriers laid down between 1937 and 1939. She can carry 70 'planes.
Photo, Topical

The tactics of this attack were the same as in the previous raid, but a new feature of air warfare at sea was introduced. Many times the machines levelled off after a dive at a dangerously low level—not more than 10 ft. above the water—and continued to fly for several miles like stunt fliers engaged in " hedge hopping." The first time this happened all hands were convinced that the aircraft had been hit. But just as we expected them to plunge into the sea we saw them climb to make another dive a few moments later.

Considering the comparatively short range of the German dive-bombers—about 220 miles with full load—the bombs they dropped round the Fleet were exceptionally heavy. This would indicate that they are operating from bases in Sicily, and presumably from the southern part of the island.

Many of the columns of water blown up by the German bombs near this ship towered scores of feet above the bridge from which I watched the action. It was almost as if the attacking aircraft wanted to leave no doubt of their identity, which in any case could not have been mistaken. But just to make sure, one huge, jagged chunk of bomb fell on the deck of this ship, and was seen to have a swastika painted on it.

As the bombs exploded alongside this ship she seemed to leap from the water like a whippet getting off the mark. But they did nothing but the most superficial kind of

damage, such as knocking off flakes of paint.

Once a piece of bomb, weighing 7 lb., fell among seven men in the control tower of this ship without touching one of them. The piece was from a bomb which exploded harmlessly in the sea near the ship.

Not all the men were so lucky. One sailor on board this ship, who, like all the others, stuck to his gun with traditional British doggedness, was mortally wounded by machine-gun fire from one of the dive bombers. He died a few hours later.

Every Gun in the 'Illustrious' Roared

Here is a second eye-witness account of the Sicilian Channel battle— this time by a special correspondent of Reuters on board the aircraft-carrier "Illustrious." The "Illustrious" was one of the main objectives of German dive-bombers operating from Sicily, but she triumphantly rode through the attack and was brought into port with her ensign flying and her crew undaunted.

WHEN the first attack came, soon after noon, two torpedo-carrying Junkers swooped down from the sky and loosed their torpedoes. They passed harmlessly astern. Then the main assault developed.

Three Junkers 87s approached out of the clouds. Simultaneously the guns of all the British ships opened up a terrific barrage. More 'planes swooped down. The sky was filled with a confused mass of bursting shells and twisting 'planes. The noise was appalling.

As the leading 'plane dived through the inferno I watched a single 1,000-lb. bomb hurtle towards us. It fell in the sea slightly astern.

Then a wave of 15 bombers dived on the Fleet. My attention was divided between watching these and watching our own fighters taking off from the flight deck of the " Illustrious."

A few seconds after our last machine had flown off a tremendous explosion shook the ship. A 1,000-lb. bomb released by one of the Junkers diving very low had scored a direct hit. The next moment the wing of a German 'plane fell across the after lift of the " Illustrious."

The hit was apparently immediately below the bridge. I have a vivid impression of a sudden sheet of flame and choking smoke. I felt a severe blow on my shoulder from blast, and then I was pulled into the wireless cabin and thrown to the floor. We lay coughing and listening to the sudden roar of aeroplane engines close overhead. The diving 'planes swooped so low that they sounded as though they were landing on the flight deck.

Near misses sent shudder after shudder through the ship. The German bombers converged from all sides and then dived one after another in the face of blazing gunfire. They held their bombs until the last minute, then swerved quickly off. After what seemed an eternity gunfire ceased.

We opened the door. Splintered and riddled steel pipes and wires lay where we had been standing a few minutes before. The deck was covered with foam from the fire extinguishers.

The flight deck was covered from end to end with debris from the bomb explosion. Further forward was a twisted crane, a heap of bomb splinters and empty shellcases.

Through all the action the gun crews never eased for a moment. Every man moved with precision.

Spaces below decks, including the church, were cleared for casualty stations. Wounded were tended as fast as possible. During the period of quiet efforts were started to clear the deck.

The " Illustrious " steamed into port unaided. When we anchored the wounded were quickly taken ashore and the work of cleaning up the ship proceeded.

BOMBS rained down on the British warships during the attack by dive bombers in the Sicilian Channel. This photograph, taken during a previous attack, shows enemy bombs falling wide of their mark. The fact that so few of our warships have been sunk by air attack affords proof of the failure of aircraft against warships well handled and defended.   *Photo, Fox*

New Appointments on the Home Front

Miss Verena Holmes, whose appointment as adviser to Mr. Ernest Bevin, Minister of Labour, on the training of women munition workers was announced in December 1940.

Mr. Robert Leitch and Mr. J. Gibson Jarvie (top left and above), were appointed by Col. J. T. Moore-Brabazon, Minister of Transport, on January 11 Regional Port Directors for the North-Western Region and the Clyde Region respectively. Mr. Leitch, lately Assistant General Manager of the Port of London Authority, is responsible for all ports between Stranraer and Oban. Mr. Jarvie, Chairman of the United Dominions Trust, Ltd., deals with the ports between Holyhead and Silloth.

Air Marshal A. G. R. Garrod, C.B.

Air Commodore J. A. Chamier

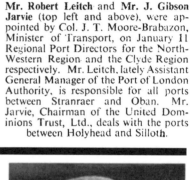

Wing Commander Lord Nigel Douglas Hamilton

Mr. J. F. Wolfenden

Air Vice-Marshal Keith Rodney Park, decorated by the King with the Order of the Bath (Military Div.) on December 10, 1940 for organizing R.A.F. fighters that beat back the violent German air attacks on London and S.E. England during the summer of 1940. He also organized air squadrons to protect Holland, Belgium and France when the enemy invaded the Low Countries. Air Vice-Marshal Park was a leading ace in the last war.

Photos, British Official: Crown Copyright; Associated Press, Fox, Central Press, Planet News and Barratts

THE AIR TRAINING CORPS, inaugurated on Jan. 9, 1941, was formed to meet the growing demand of the R.A.F. and Fleet Air Arm for pilots and air crews. All boys of 16 and upward, physically fit and wishing to serve eventually in either of these Forces, can join. Above are four of the Corps' leaders. Air Marshal A. G. R. Garrod, Air Member for Training on the Air Council, is in charge of this scheme of Pre-Entry training, as it is called. Directly responsible to him is the Director of Pre-Entry Training, Mr. J. F. Wolfenden, previously headmaster of Uppingham School. Air Commodore J. A. Chamier has been appointed Commandant, and Wing Commander Lord Nigel Douglas Hamilton is an Air Member for Training.

OUR SEARCHLIGHT ON THE WAR

Safe-Conduct for Italian Women

WITH the probability of an Italian defeat in East Africa becoming daily more certain, the plight of Italian women and children in that area is extremely hazardous. The Abyssinians are a primitive people and, remembering what their own families have suffered at the hands of the invader, they may lose control and wreak vengeance on helpless victims. The British Government, therefore, is prepared to secure the co-operation of the French authorities at Jibuti and to guarantee the safe-conduct of all Italian women and children if such an evacuation is ordered by Rome. These refugees from Abyssinia, Somaliland, and Eritrea would travel to an agreed port in Italy by way of Jibuti or some other port in East Africa.

Norwegian Regiment against England

PUBLICITY has been given to the report that Quisling's hated "Hirdmen" are to form the nucleus of a special Norwegian regiment which will proceed to Germany, led by Quisling himself, in order to fight against England's despotic yoke. Those who realize the deep and fierce patriotism of Norway, shown every day by some act of defiance against the oppressor, by the cherishing of prohibited photographs of King Haakon, or by the numbers of Norwegians who still contrive to reach these shores, may well accept the interpretation put on this re-cruiting scheme in Scandinavia—that it is a method of " saving face" while getting the unpopular Quisling and his adherents out of Norway.

From Oran in a Stolen 'Plane

GENERAL DE GAULLE has just been pre-sented with an Italian six-passenger monoplane for the use of the Free French air force. The French pilot who landed it at Gibraltar told an exciting story. He was at Oran with a friend whom he had run across at Algiers. Anxious to escape, the two young men hung about the airport, where, in a hangar was this 'plane, the property of the Italian Commission in French North Africa. They tried every expedient they could think of to obtain the key of the hangar so as to get away by night, but in vain. So in broad daylight they boldly entered the air-field and, finding the doors open, slipped undetected into the hangar. Here disappoint-ment awaited them, for the doors of the air-craft were locked. With one eye on a squad of mechanics outside they tried to force back a bolt with a crowbar, but failed. Then the pilot, of slim, lithe build, wriggled himself through a small sliding window and shot back the bolt for his companion. The engines, being cold, took a little time to start, but in a few minutes the machine emerged from the hangar and taxied down the runway for what seemed an interminable time before taking off. Such audacity brought its reward, for they left unmolested and there was no pursuit. Over Gibraltar a British patrol 'plane suddenly appeared above them to inspect, and below they could see A.A. guns trained upon their aircraft. But their friendly intentions were evidently understood, for there was no attack, and on landing they and their booty were given an enthusiastic reception.

President Roosevelt's Special Envoy

MR. HARRY HOPKINS, former U.S. Secretary of Commerce and a close friend of the President, has been sent by him to London as personal representative for a few weeks until a new Ambassador is appointed. He is a man of 50 who has lived at the White House for the past year, and is thus in a position to explain fully to members of the British Government the President's ideas and views on matters of urgent interest to both countries. The day after his arrival he saw Mr. Eden and Lord Halifax, and then had luncheon and a long private conversation with Mr. Churchill. " American Production," said Mr. Hopkins to some Press correspondents, " will reach its peak at the end of this year and early in 1942. There is going to be a united and altogether successful effort in the production of defence materials in the United States to be used by ourselves, by Great Britain, and by Greece and China. We are building up new capacities for production on every front relating to defence. We cannot carry that on and run business as usual. Machines which are normally used for things not necessary for our defence will be used for defence. If that cuts luxuries, then it will cut luxuries—or anything else that gets in the way."

'San Demetrio' Heroes Rewarded

THE amazing story of the "San Demetrio," a motor-tanker belonging to the Eagle Oil and Shipping Company, which was shelled and set on fire by a German raider in the North Atlantic on November 5, 1940, was told in detail in Vol. III, p. 597, of THE WAR ILLUSTRATED. The sequel—aptly de-scribed by Mr. Justice Langton as " a fitting and not unworthy sequel to one of the great English stories of the sea"—took place recently in the Admiralty Court, when sixteen men of the British Merchant Navy shared in salvage awards totalling £14,700. Judge, counsel and owners united in paying great tribute to the gallantry of the crew of the "San Demetrio," who, as experienced seamen, knew well the risks they were running in attempting to save the burning ship and its cargo of oil. Of Mr. Arthur Godfrey Hawkins, the second officer, who for 700 miles navigated the ship without instruments - not even a compass—and brought her safe to port with the aid of a sixpenny school atlas, Counsel said : "Mr. Hawkins is a worthy namesake of the Elizabethan seaman whose name is immor-talized with those of Frobisher and Drake."

Tribute was also paid to John Boyle, a greaser, who died after carrying on in the

MR. HARRY HOPKINS, President Roosevelt's personal envoy to Britain, arrived in London on January 9, 1941. He will act as contact man between Mr. Roosevelt and the British Government. *Photo, G.P.U.*

engine-room for three days despite broken ribs. One incident upon which the Judge dwelt with pleasure was the unanimous request of the crew that the Red Ensign from the "San Demetrio" should be given to Ross Preston, an American who had signed on as member of the crew and did much to help in salvaging the vessel. "I am sure," he said, "that Ross Preston is a man of the quality to treasure this piece of bunting."

"I would not like to leave this case," concluded the Judge, "without thanking everybody concerned for having given me the happiest working day of my life, listening to the very modest recital of two gallant gentlemen concerning a memorable achieve-ment."

Corvettes against U-Boats

WHAT the Admiralty terms " anti-submarine vessels of the whale-catcher type " are becoming better known under the old name " corvette." There are already a large number in commission and more are under construction, for their value as escorts of convoys is being increas-ingly recognized. They are more speedy than trawlers, which are also used for the same purpose, and have an excellent anti-U-boat armament. They are, moreover, thoroughly seaworthy and able to weather the severe winter conditions of the North Atlantic. Rather incongruously, all the tough little members of this class of warship are named after flowers. The crew consists of three officers besides the captain, and about 50 ratings. A number of officers recently decorated earned their awards while serving in corvettes, for their successes against U-boats are many. The old corvettes were small full-rigged ships with flush decks and one tier of guns.

THE CORVETTE has been reintroduced into the British Navy, and a number of anti-submarine vessels, for which the old designation " corvette" has been revived, are now in commission. One of them is seen above. Details of them are given in this page.
Photo, British Official : Crown Copyright

Who Should Help 'Pompey' If Not the Navy?

FRENCH SAILORS from ships of the Free French Navy lying in Portsmouth harbour were among those who helped to clear away the wreckage after the Nazi raid on "Pompey," as the sailors style Portsmouth, on the night of January 10, 1941. Here French ratings are searching for personal belongings of the former occupants.

Naval ratings, always handy men, did at Portsmouth much the same work that the Royal Engineers and Pioneer Corps did in London in clearing up the debris. Wearing steel helmets, these men dealing with a heavy girder gave a fine exhibition of "pully-hauly" to the admiration of the Army onlookers.

PORTSMOUTH felt the full weight of Nazi ruthlessness on the night of January 10, 1941, but it was saved from the worst consequences by the terrific anti-aircraft fire put up by the Royal Navy and by the fine help that the Navy gave to the A.F.S. Left, a bluejacket is still spraying smouldering ruins the day after the raid. Right are the ruins of a church, one of six destroyed on that fateful night. *Photos, Planet News, Keystone and Associated Press*

OUR DIARY OF THE WAR

TUESDAY, JAN. 14, 1941   *500th day*

War against Italy—Pause in military operations in Libya, although reconnaissance and patrol work continued. R.A.F. kept up bombing of communications.

R.A.F. attacked Benghazi during nights of 13-14 and 14-15. Harbour mole heavily bombed and large fires caused among surrounding buildings. Shipping was also attacked. Benina aerodrome was machine-gunned.

Asmara raided during night of 13-14, and Assab during that of 14-15.

Home Front—No enemy activity over Britain.

Greek War—Italians resisting stubbornly in mountains beyond Klisura. Greeks still engaged in mopping-up after retreat of enemy. Local offensive operations round Tepelini.

WEDNESDAY, JAN. 15   *501st day*

In the Air—Coastal Command aircraft carried out raid on Norwegian aerodromes, a railway bridge and a supply ship. Brest harbour was again attacked.

Naval base at Wilhelmshaven was R.A.F.'s chief night target, and extensive fires were caused. Docks at Emden, Bremerhaven, Rotterdam and Flushing were also bombed, as well as aerodromes in north-west Germany and Holland.

War against Italy—All Abyssinia now reported to be in revolt.

Six enemy raids on Malta. Block of flats in Valletta was hit and casualties resulted.

Home Front—Little activity over Britain during day, although bombs fell in west of Scotland, Midlands and Kent. At night enemy raided west Midland town, dropping high explosives. Incendiaries fell in London, but fires were quickly put out. Men's hostel demolished, with many casualties.

German 'planes also reported over Liverpool and East Anglia.

Two enemy bombers shot down by R.A.F. night fighters.

Greek War—Athens reported Greek success in central sector, an important height being captured, as well as much war material. Allied air formations bombed communications round Berat.

General—Sir Gerald Campbell, H.M. High Commissioner in Canada, appointed H.M. Minister in Washington.

Naval promotions included Vice-Admiral Sir Andrew Cunningham, C.-in-C. Mediterranean Fleet, who becomes an Admiral.

Lord Wakefield died.

THURSDAY, JAN. 16   *502nd day*

On the Sea—Admiralty announced that H.M. submarine " Pandora " had sunk two enemy supply ships in central Mediterranean.

Admiralty stated that H.M. cruiser " Southampton " had become a total loss following air attack in Mediterranean on Jan. 10.

In the Air—R.A.F. heavily attacked naval base at Wilhelmshaven. Other aircraft bombed docks at Emden, Boulogne and Calais, railway junction at Ostend, and an aerodrome in occupied France.

War against Italy—Preparations round Tobruk continued without any enemy opposition. During night of 16-17 R.A.F. raided Tobruk and Derna, and aerodrome at Martiza, Rhodes.

During night of 15-16 R.A.F. attacked aerodrome at Catania, German dive-bombing base in Sicily.

Ten enemy aircraft destroyed during raid on Malta.

In Italian East Africa Caproni workshops in Mai Adaga were again attacked. Assab was also raided.

Motor transport near Berbera, British Somaliland, attacked.

Home Front—Bombs fell during day at two places in East Kent.

Another long night raid made on Bristol area, when incendiary and high explosive bombs fell on houses, shops and other premises. Bombs were also dropped at other places in west of England and at widely-separated points in south and south-east.

Greek War—Enemy counter-attacks were repulsed.

FRIDAY, JAN. 17
    503rd day

On the Sea—Reported that two Italian troop-carrying liners had been sunk in the Adriatic.

In the Air—Coastal Command aircraft bombed and machine-gunned enemy shipping off Dutch coast, direct hits being secured on four ships.

Despite bad weather, small-scale attacks were made on docks at Brest and Cherbourg and on two aerodromes in occupied France.

War against Italy—War in Libya held up by violent sandstorm.

Home Front—During day enemy air activity was very slight. Night raids centred on Swansea, where thousands of incendiaries were followed by high explosives. Several stores, a public building, school, church, cinema and houses were hit.

Enemy bomber shot down into sea off north of Scotland.

SATURDAY, JAN. 18   *504th day*

On the Sea—Admiralty announced that H.M. trawlers " Chestnut " and " Desiree " had been sunk.

War against Italy—R.A.F. raided Tobruk during night of 17-18. Large transport yard at Assab was bombed and several direct hits registered. Bombs fell on military buildings at Hargeisa, Somaliland. Asmara again raided during night of 17-18.

Ten Junkers 87 dive-bombers brought down by British fighters and A.A. fire during enemy raids on Malta.

Home Front—During day five bombs were dropped on outskirts of London. Raider machine-gunned a train in East Anglia and several passengers were hurt. No night raids.

Long-range shelling from both sides of Straits of Dover.

Greek War—Greek forces occupied strong enemy positions, capturing 1,000 prisoners, including many officers.

General—Marshal Pétain and Laval had a meeting of reconciliation.

SUNDAY, JAN. 19   *505th day*

War against Italy—Cairo announced that Kassala, in the Sudan, had been re-occupied by British troops.

R.A.F. attacked motor transport and gun positions south-east of Tessenei in Eritrea during the night of 18-19. Massawa was twice raided on the same night, and raids were also made on Assab and Hargeisa.

Reported that British officers and N.C.O.'s are in Abyssinia training and organizing army against Italians.

At least 17 enemy aircraft brought down during raids on Malta.

Home Front—Enemy aircraft dropped bombs in South and South-east England and in the London area, but raids were nowhere on a heavy scale.

Five enemy bombers destroyed during the night, four of them by A.A. fire.

Greek War—The R.A.F. made a successful raid on Berat in Albania.

MONDAY, JAN. 20   *506th day*

On the Sea—Greeks announced destruction of an enemy submarine.

War against Italy—Cairo announced that on the Kassala front fortified positions about Sabderat and Tessenei had been occupied by our troops.

Announced from Nairobi that South African troops had captured prisoners and material in the El Yibo area on the Kenya-Abyssinia front. Neghelli, Abyssinia, was successfully bombed by the South African Air Force during night of 19-20.

Tobruk was heavily raided by R.A.F. during night of 19-20; in spite of intense A.A. fire, direct hits were registered on the military barracks and many bombs fell on a camp.

Home Front—Little activity over Britain during day, though bombs were dropped in Norfolk, Kent, and the Home Counties; these caused only slight damage and no casualties. No night raids.

Greek War—Enemy bomber formations made attacks on the Piraeus, but did no military damage.

During night of 19-20 the R.A.F. made heavy bombing attacks on Valona.

General—Hitler and Mussolini met, supposedly at Berchtesgaden, and had " a thorough exchange of views on the situation."

TROUBLE IN SICILY

" I want you to stop calling it Mare Nostrum, and call it Unsere See."
" Need I call it either ? "

From the cartoon by E. H. Shepard, by permission of the Proprietors of " Punch "

VICTORS OF THE WESTERN DESERT IN CONFERENCE

General Sir Archibald Wavell (right), Commander-in-Chief, Middle East, and Major-General R. N. O'Connor, Officer Commanding operations in the Western Desert, are here in conference before the final assault on Bardia on January 5, 1941. To their perfect planning and bold execution of the plans is due the fact that Sidi Barrani, Sollum, Bardia, " the bastion of Fascism," and the port of Tobruk were taken, together with over 100,000 prisoners, at the cost of only 1,900 casualties—a triumph unique in modern warfare.　　*Photo, British Official : Crown Copyright*

'Come Right On In, Pals, Tobruk is Yours!'

As already reported in an earlier page (see page 86), Tobruk was captured by the Army
of the Nile on January 22, 1941. Below we describe its fall, and in pages 135-136 are
accounts of the fighting as seen by eye-witnesses of the land, air and naval operations.

FOR thirteen days Tobruk had been completely cut off from the outside world. Within its perimeter, crowded in its forts and white-walled houses, were some 20,000 Italian troops—according to the Italian account, " one infantry division, the Sirte division, a battalion of frontier guards, a battalion of Blackshirts, and some detachments of sailors and artillery." On every day of those thirteen they expected the onslaught, as peering above their entrenchments and through the loopholes of their strongpoints they saw the assembling of the British and Australian troops, the tanks rumbling up and the guns brought ever nearer.

All through the night of Monday, January 20 the British guns kept up a continuous fire, while bombers of the R.A.F. came over in an almost incessant stream and dropped on the doomed town their cargoes of death and destruction. Then at dawn on January 21 the men went over the top, preceded by a colossal box barrage dropped on Tobruk and its environs, the biggest of the war to date. According to an Italian account there were three divisions of Australian infantry, two armoured divisions of British tanks, two heavy artillery regiments, and a motorized formation of what were rather quaintly described as " dissident French troops."

First the Australian sappers ran across the desert and cut the wire which was spread so thickly in front of the Italian trenches ; they also dealt with the minefields and put the booby traps out of action. Then the Australian infantry, who during the night had been brought up to within a thousand yards of the wire, sprang up and moved across the desert towards the enemy positions. Resistance was fierce in places and the Australians paid tribute in particular to some of the Italian machine-gunners and artillerymen who kept firing to the last and died at their posts. But, as in the previous battles, great masses of the enemy held up their hands as soon as the Australians drew near. In a few minutes long columns of prisoners were being marched away to the rear of the battle.

Shortly after the battle had begun the outer line of the Italian defences was stormed for a distance of several miles, and through the gap the British tanks and the motorized detachments spread out in all directions, taking in the rear those of the Italians who were still firing. The Italian guns were most active along the high ground on either side of the junction of the El Adem and Bardia-Tobruk roads, but soon the resistance was overcome, and the leading units of the Australians swept on north towards the town of Tobruk, while a second force mopped up the ground which had been won, and a third made steady progress along the coast. Then all their efforts were centred against the three forts, Pilastrino, Solario and Airente, which lay on the high ground west of the road to El Adem. All three were taken late in the afternoon. Solario was the first to fall, being carried by the Australians at the point of the bayonet ; its fellows, seeing its fate, surrendered.

With the fall of these forts the inner defences had been breached, and as night fell the victors looked down on Tobruk, only some two miles away. A great and thick pall of smoke hung over the port as the oil reservoirs were afire ; in the harbour a liner was ablaze from end to end, and the old warship, " San Giorgio," was also burning. Firing continued through the night, and at daybreak the advance was continued. The remaining resistance was speedily overcome, and the fort on top of the cliff overlooking the port was blown to pieces as a British shell hit the magazine. An advance guard of an Australian cavalry regiment dashed up in their Bren-gun carriers, broke down the steel and concrete barrier, and swept into the town, where a couple of bursts of machine-gun fire marked the end of the enemy resistance. At 10.15 a.m. the garrison surrendered; and as a Union Jack was not available at the moment, a " Digger's " hat was promptly hoisted on the flag pole as the signal of victory.

One of the first to meet the Australians as they entered the town was one of their comrades who, a few days before, had been captured when he had lost his way in a car with a British corporal. " Come right on in, pals, the town's yours ! " he shouted. He had been imprisoned in a cell in the military prison, but when the shelling got heavy the Italians took him to a large concrete shelter. There he did his best to undermine their morale by telling them it was simply useless to resist. Soon the Australians' approach reinforced his argument, and the role of captors and captured was reversed.

The streets of the town were almost empty when our troops entered, but there was an impressive little scene when the Brigadier received its surrender. In front of their staffs and a guard of Carabinieri, the Italian commanders stood at attention in full dress with medals—General della Mura, commander of the 61st Metropolitan Division, Admiral Vietina, commander of the naval base, and Major-General Barberis, commander of the garrison troops. The Admiral made a formal speech of. surrender in English : " The town capitulates and all the troops are disarming " ; to which the Brigadier replied, " Please delegate officers immediately to show the position of every minefield in the harbour and the town."

Only some 500 casualties were incurred by the British and Australians, while Italian prisoners alone numbered over 20,000.

TOBRUK, with its fine sheltered harbour, and the adjacent countryside are shown in this contour map, the arrows on which indicate the line of the British advance. The perimeter defences and various strong points mentioned in the text are clearly marked, as well as the roads leading from Bardia and El Adem. Tobruk, capital of the district of Marmarica, had, in 1937, a population of 4,130. In 1939 the Italian residents numbered 822.

Specially modelled for THE WAR ILLUSTRATED, *by Felix Gardon*

There Was No Stopping the 'Aussies' in Libya

The storming of Bardia on January 5, 1941, resulted in few casualties to the attacking forces. Here Australian troops are crouching behind the parapet of an anti-tank ditch constructed by the Italians on the outskirts of the town. Shells can be seen bursting over Bardia itself.

BARDIA had been reduced almost to ruins, before the Australians entered, by the terrific bombardment to which it was subjected by the Navy, the R.A.F., and the big guns of the Army of the Nile. Above, Australian soldiers with fixed bayonets are advancing through the debris during the process of "mopping up" the town. Centre, the crew of one of the tanks that led the advance on Bardia give the photographer a cheery wave while taking part in the exercises that preceded the attack. Similar tanks with the infantry are seen in page 116.　　*Photos, British Official : Crown Copyright*

The War Illustrated

GENERAL WAVELL'S ARMY OF THE NILE swept swiftly forward to overwhelming victory because its leader had learnt and even improved upon the lessons which the Germans had taught in other theatres of war. Every detail and every contingency had been thought out and provided for, and the troops had rehearsed every phase of the battle. Some of the tanks that smashed the defences of Tobruk, with men of the Australian Imperial Forces following, are seen practising the part they were to play in the advance. The combination of light tanks and Australian troops, who, as Mr. Lloyd George remarked of their fathers "were marked out for the grim horror of heading assaults and plunging in wherever the fighting was fiercest," resulted in the fall of Bardia on January 5, 1941, and of Tobruk on January 22.

Photo Australian Official: Crown Copyright

Haile Selassie Is Back Again in Abyssinia

While the Army of the Nile was capturing one by one the Italians' strongholds in North Africa, General Wavell's men on other fronts, 2,000 miles to the south, were inflicting new blows on Italy's prestige and power. As told below, the armies of the British Commonwealth have taken the offensive against the Italians in Eritrea, Abyssinia and Somaliland.

AFTER five years of exile Haile Selassie, "Lion of Judah, King of the Kings of Ethiopia," crossed the frontier from the Sudan into his own country on January 15, 1941.

On a natural clearing in a dried river bed just within the frontier of Abyssinia a number of native chiefs and troops of the new

ITALIAN EAST AFRICA, as this map shows, is being invaded on all sides. The arrows indicate the points at which British and Imperial troops are advancing from the Sudan and Kenya. *Courtesy of the "Daily Telegraph"*

Abyssinian Regular Army were drawn up to greet him. The sun was high in the heavens when shortly before 11 an R.A.F. 'plane was seen approaching, accompanied by an escort of two fighter machines. They came to land just behind a screen of trees, and then, preceded by a tall officer of the British Guards, a little procession made its appearance. It was headed by Bishop Gabri Giorgio, and

behind him came Haile Selassie and his two sons, the Crown Prince and the Duke of Harrar, and representatives of the British Army in the Sudan. As he stepped on to the parade ground, a British officer unrolled a scroll and read out the message of greeting. "A message to his Imperial Majesty, Haile Selassie the First, from the Major-General commanding troops in the Sudan," he began.

The man who not so long ago had been carrying his shopping basket through the streets of Bath—who, more recently, had been referred to in Khartoum as "Mr. Smith" or the "little man"—had come home. Once again he was "his Imperial Majesty."

Upon returning to his country, the Emperor—or Negus, to use the Abyssinian term—issued a proclamation to his former

subjects, calling upon them to rise against the Italian invader, and promising pardon to those who, during his absence, had been compelled to bow the knee to the enemy. "Italy is cornered by the grip of Great Britain," he went on, "by sea, air and land power. The Italians in Ethiopia will not escape my trusted warriors." Then he concluded with an expression of thanks to the Government and people of Great Britain, "for the touching and unforgettable reception and hospitality during my bitter trials. Long live Ethiopia! Long live Britain!"

Then the Emperor reviewed his troops, men of that Abyssinian Army which has been in process of formation for months, and which reflects the greatest credit on the British and Australian officers and N.C.O.s who were entrusted with its training. Some of the men were described by the "Daily Telegraph's" special correspondent in Khartoum when he was present at the start of a convoy of arms, war materials and other supplies - not forgetting a quantity of the great silver dollars, freshly minted most of them, which bear the head of the Empress Maria Theresa of Austria and the date 1780, the dollars which have been Abyssinia's

SOUTH AFRICAN AIR FORCE fighter 'planes on the Abyssinian frontier of Kenya, standing in readiness to take the air as soon as the enemy is sighted (left). Above is a Bren gun section of the South African forces at exercise in the same area. *Photos, Sport & General*

currency for 150 years—which was just setting out to cross the frontier into Abyssinia. "Irregulars, chin-bearded members of the Amhara tribe, with battered trilby hats or squat topees, heavy-featured dark Gallas, and light-skinned members of the Gumuz frontier tribe, were lined up into smiling ranks as if for a Sir Roger de Coverley. Behind them were the 'presents' yet unopened—rows of boxes of English and Italian ammunition. The men had already been given rifles, and they were now filing by to receive rounds of ammunition in canvas

Italian East Africa Invaded

bandoliers and a green canvas satchel, about the size of a girl's large handbag, which is supposed to hold bullets or food. As each got his share he returned to his place in the ranks, gravely telling his comrades the number of rounds with his fingers. Only when he

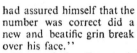

had assured himself that the number was correct did a new and beatific grin break over his face."

News of the Emperor's arrival spread like wildfire through the Abyssinian villages, and soon from every quarter the tribesmen were hastening to his standard. While the Italian empire in East Africa was being thus threatened from within to such a degree that it was soon reported that the Italian authorities were already making plans for the almost complete evacuation of Abyssinia, and the concentration of all their available forces in the uplands of Eritrea, the armies of the British Commonwealth were attacking on every side. Following the recapture of Kassala on January 18, British mobile detachments crossed the frontier into Eritrea, and within a few days were reported to have penetrated 100 miles inside Italy's original colony in East Africa. Biscia, the terminus of the railway to the Red Sea port of Massawa, was abandoned by the Italians with scarcely a fight, 100 prisoners being captured, and Agordat, 25 miles down the line, was threatened by the British advance. More than 1,100 prisoners were taken in these initial operations. In their swift advance British units pierced two Italian lines of resistance: one running from Keru to Aicota, and the other from Biscia to Barentu. Cairo's communiqué remarked that the difficult country afforded good opportunities for defence, but the enemy made little use of it.

As usual the R.A.F. was active, supporting very effectively the advance into Eritrea. The railway line and station at Biscia were heavily bombed and motor transport concentrated west of the town was attacked. Dive attacks were made on enemy fighter aircraft, motor transport vehicles, and the railway at Agordat. A number of fires were started at Umm Hagar, and the railway station at Keren was also bombed. A Rhodesian squadron d r o p p e d bombs near the bridge at Tellina and machine-gunned motor transport at Barentu.

To the south the British Army continued steadily in the Metemma area, near the Sudan frontier. On the Kenya-Abyssinian border active patrolling was continued by South African troops, and two Italian outposts, at

RAS KASSA, one of the Emperor of Abyssinia's most trusted generals. He is now back in his own country with Haile Selassie.
Photo, Central Press

El Yibo and El Sardu, about 75 miles east of Lake Rudolf, were captured, and in encounters with " banda," as the native Italian troops are called, many prisoners were taken. Then another nibble off Mussolini's empire was made in Italian Somaliland, where British forward patrols were reported to have penetrated into hostile territory and to be continuing vigorously in all sectors to extend the area of their drive.

From west and south, then, Italian East Africa was being attacked, and nowhere did the Italians put up anything that might be described as a determined stand. As in the Western Desert far to the north, they seemed to have lost heart even before the battle began.

ABYSSINIANS who have gone over into Kenya to be trained by South African officers are seen in the top photograph ; they have been given modern equipment with which to fight the Italians. Centre, the British C.O. of this Abyssinian unit. British headquarters, above, showing the hut where military conferences take place.
Photos, British Paramount News

Kind Hearts and Skilled Hands Help the Wounded

The great victories in North Africa have been accomplished with extraordinarily few casualties. Preparations had been made to deal with many more, and the wounded were speedily rushed off to hospital. Left, a Medical Officer, himself wounded, is supervising the evacuation of wounded from Sollum during an air raid. Convalescent soldiers, wounded in the taking of Gallabat on the Abyssinian frontier, are seen, below, at a hospital in the Sudan.

Photos, British Official: Crown Copyright

Casualties have been remarkably few in the Battle of Britain as well as on the two fronts in the Middle East. Most of the men who are now in hospital in Britain have sustained their injuries in the air. Centre left, a sergeant masseur is giving treatment to two airmen on Swedish bars. The staff of all the hospitals are bent on their patients having the best possible time, and the nurses at one hospital, above, found time to take part in snowball battles with convalescent men during the cold spell of January 1941.

Photos, Planet News

Australia's 'There' All Right!

Australia has set an example— a magnificent example—to the Commonwealth and the world of liberty-loving peoples. In this war as in the last she is giving of her best freely and without stint. Here we tell of some of the more striking features of her contribution to the Empire's effort.

"FREEDOM produces the best soldiers," said Mr. S. M. Bruce, Australia's one-time Prime Minister and present High Commissioner in London, in a broadcast on Australia Day, January 26. "In the Western Desert," he went on, "the Blackshirts of Fascism, trained for eighteen years in militarism and denuded of liberty of thought and expression, have crumpled before the men of Australia – a country where militarism is abhorred and where freedom is the very breath of life."

Although her total population is only some seven millions, the Australian Common-

Four members of an Australian air crew are seen in front of their 'plane before they set out on a reconnaissance flight.

wealth has raised a great army. Even six months ago the number of men under arms in the Australian Home Defence Force was over 100,000, and it is planned to increase it to 210,000 by March 1941. More than 120,000 have volunteered for overseas service, and tens of thousands of the Australian Imperial Force have proceeded to the United Kingdom, to Egypt and Palestine, and, as the Italians have recently learnt to their cost, to the Western Desert. At Sidi Barrani, Bardia and Tobruk the Diggers of this generation have covered themselves with glory as did those of a generation ago on Gallipoli and the Somme.

Units of the Royal Australian Navy are operating in the Pacific, the Red Sea and in the Mediterranean ; at the outbreak of war the R.A.N. had in commission 2 heavy cruisers, 4 other cruisers, 2 sloops, 5 destroyers and other smaller craft. For a year past a contraband control system has been operating from Australian ports so as to relieve the pressure on the British control bases elsewhere, and Australian ships have taken part in convoying the successive contingents of troops from "down under." Before the war the personnel of the Royal Australian Navy numbered 5,400 ; today it numbers over 15,000 men and is still growing.

The Royal Australian Air Force is on active service in the United Kingdom, Egypt, Palestine and Malaya. Enlistments for the

R.A.A.F. and the Empire Air Training Scheme have been 125,000 and over 30,000 are already in training ; the personnel of the R.A.A.F. has been nearly trebled, and by last autumn nearly 19,000 men were in training. An Australian squadron of the R.A.A.F. has been serving with the Coastal Command of the R.A.F. since December 1939. Then, as regards the Empire Air Training Scheme, Australia's War Cabinet decided that the total of recruits to March 1943 should be 57,473, comprising 14,300 pilots, 16,173 air crews and 27,000 ground personnel. The first of 36 training schools are now in operation, and of the aircraft actually required about one-third are being provided by the factories of the Commonwealth. The total expenditure on Australia's three years' air armament scheme is estimated at £80,000,000.

Practically all ammunition and armaments for the Australian forces are being made in Australia, and many millions of pounds' worth of orders have been executed for the United

Kingdom Ministry of Supply and Admiralty. Recently the Commonwealth embarked on a vast programme for the production of £100,000,000 worth of munitions, which will ultimately involve the employment of 150,000 men and women. Australia is also concentrating on warship construction for the United Kingdom ; every available shipyard is being brought into commission and new yards are being established, while a

The Australian ensign has a large seven-pointed star in the lower canton immediately beneath the Union. It was formerly six-pointed, to represent the six States of the Commonwealth ; a seventh point was added when the Northern Territory came under Commonwealth administration. In the fly are five stars representing the Southern Cross.

graving dock costing £3,000,000 is to be built at Sydney. The vessels under construction include 3 destroyers and 50 patrol craft.

During the next three years Australia has budgeted to spend £55,000,000 on aircraft construction and maintenance. During the present year it is planned to turn out one Bristol Beaufort bomber every day in addition to numbers of Wirraway second-line fighters and trainer 'planes.

The United Kingdom has bought the whole exportable surplus of Australia's copper, zinc, tungsten and tungsten ores, and the whole of the Australian wool clip for the period of the war and one year after at thirty per cent above the pre-war price. Vast purchases of lead, wheat and flour have also been made ; and our Ministry of Food, in conjunction with Canada, made contracts at the beginning of the war with the Queensland sugar producers to buy all the available supplies at pre-war prices. Quite early in the war, too, the United Kingdom agreed to take the Dominion's entire surplus of dairy produce, eggs, meat and dried and canned fruit.

Australia's defence and war expenditure was £55,200,000 for 1939-40, and at least £100,000,000 is being spent on munitions alone in the financial year which is just ending. The money is being raised by taxation and internal loans.

Stacks of bombs, ready for filling, await the assembly of their fins (centre), as Australia's magnificent war effort steadily increases. Members of the Australian Women's Legion (above) march through Sydney's streets on their way to the city's Town Hall in a procession organized in aid of Red Cross war funds.

Photos, Australian Official, Sport & General, Central Press and Topical

Men from 'Down Under' are 'Top Dogs' at Sea

THE ROYAL AUSTRALIAN NAVY, though small, has spared every ship possible to assist the British Fleet. The personnel is highly trained. Gunnery practice is in progress on board this Australian warship in home waters. An Admiralty communiqué issued on January 22, 1941, dealing with the co-operation of the Mediterranean Fleet in the battles of the Libyan desert, said: " Units of the Royal Australian Navy have played a conspicuously successful part in these operations."

Photo, Keystone

What are the Nazis up to in Sicily?

What with Wavell's tanks and Greek bayonets, Mussolini can have little hope nowadays
of that second Roman Empire of which he has boasted so often.   The war—*his* war—
is less than a year old, but his troops have been defeated on every front, and now he has
to submit to the crowning humiliation of appealing to his ally for assistance.

FIRST definite news of the arrival of Germans in Italy was given in an Order of the Day issued by General Pricolo, Chief of the Italian Air Staff, on January 2. "Detachments of the brave German Air Force," it read, "are at present being transferred to some of our

GERMAN AIRCRAFT, drafted into Italy and Sicily with a view to attacking our Mediterranean bases and Fleet from short range, have met with a warm reception both from our fighter aircraft and from our A.A. defences. This Heinkel may have "returned safely to its base," but the bullet holes tell their own story.

bases to collaborate in the bitter air and, naval battle which is now going on in the Mediterranean." Since then more reports have come in telling of the arrival of quite a number of German soldiers and airmen in Italy, and Sicily in particular, would seem to have come under German control.

Why Sicily? it may be asked. Several reasons may be suggested, most of them obvious enough after a few minutes' study of the map. One, however, is independent of geography: Hitler, having become convinced in his own mind that Italy is about to crack and Mussolini about to crash, may be determined to seize all that he wants to seize in

Italy before it is too late. In this case he would probably try to secure Trieste, the great port on the Adriatic which in the last war was the main outlet of the Austrian-Hungarian empire, and the island of Sicily. And this, indeed, is what he is doing, apparently, since not only Sicily but Trieste is reported to be virtually in Nazi hands.

Now let us look at Sicily's place on the map. It lies in the middle of the Mediterranean, dividing the great sea into two parts, a western and an eastern. Up to now, and still today, the Mediterranean is what it has been for centuries, a highway of British naval and commercial power. But if an enemy of Britain were to establish himself in Sicily, then that highway would be threatened—indeed commanded and perhaps completely blocked. Less than 300 miles away is Tripoli, in Italian North Africa; and the Sicilian Channel, which divides Sicily from Tunis, is only about 100 miles in width, and almost half-way is Pantelleria, the islet which Mussolini has converted into a miniature Gibraltar. Malta, Britain's naval stronghold, is only 60 miles from the Sicilian coast, and in theory, at least, it would seem to be at the mercy of the bombing 'planes of an enemy established only a few minutes' flying distance away.

With Sicily in their hands the Germans might well expect to use its many aerodromes and harbours as bases for their dive-bombers and U-boats operating against the hated British. It was from Sicily, indeed, that the Stukas

took off on January 10 for their onslaught on the British Fleet, which resulted in the sinking of the "Southampton" and the damaging of the "Illustrious"; and it was a Sicilian aerodrome—at Catania—which was promptly bombed in retaliation by the R.A.F. From Sicilian aerodromes, too, we may be sure the Nazi 'planes are proceeding to bomb Malta. Many raids on the little island have been delivered since Italy entered the war last June, but of late weeks the air attacks have been greatly intensified. Malta, however, knows how to hit back; and in the raids delivered between January 15 and 19 at least 39 German dive-bombers were shot down.

If the Germans could secure air mastery over the central Mediterranean, if only for a week or two, then they might reinforce Graziani's hard-pressed troops with a strong stiffening of Nazis—hardened veterans of the battles of the Western Front—who might be expected to put up a far better show than Mussolini's Blackshirts and native levies. Graziani's fast-dwindling stores of food, water and petrol might also be replenished.

The Germans in Sicily may see yet another possibility—that of making contact with the great French colony of Tunis. They may have their plans for a seizure of Tunis, or of the French Navy, which, if report speaks true, is concentrated in the harbour of Bizerta.

But there is another side to the picture; it is true that Malta and the ships approaching and leaving it can be easily reached by Nazi dive-bombers operating from aerodromes in Sicily. But just as truly the whole of Sicily, not to mention southern Italy, Sardinia and Pantelleria, are also within range of British bombers taking off from our aircraft carriers or operating from bases in Greece, Crete, or west of Tobruk. And what if Wavell continues to march from triumph to triumph? What if the Italian resistance in North Africa collapses and the Italians at home begin to murmur and riot? Then Sicily might become a trap, like every other piece of land which is surrounded by water, to be sprung in good time by a Britain supreme at sea.

SICILY has now been taken over by the Germans as an aircraft base for dive-bombers operating against our Mediterranean Fleet. This map shows the effective range of Junkers JU87 dive-bombers and twin-engined JU88s. Italian possessions are marked in black.
Photo, Keystone; map, courtesy of the "News Chronicle"

They Carry just One Torpedo—but One's Enough!

TORPEDO-DROPPING AIRCRAFT are used both by the Fleet Air Arm and by units of the Coastal Command, the former employing mostly Fairey Swordfish and Albacores, and the latter Bristol Beauforts. Above, a dummy torpedo is being fixed beneath an Albacore which is about to practise target work.

Some idea of the size of the torpedoes carried may be judged from the one above, which is being wheeled to the aircraft. Right, torpedo-carrying Albacores in flight.
Photos, Central Press and Fox

WHEN the Fleet Air Arm delivered its smashing blow against the Italian Navy at Taranto on November 11, 1940, the air-launched torpedo proved its full worth. The photographs in this page are some of the first to be taken at a Naval Station where pilots of the F.A.A. are instructed in the technical side of their duties. The course includes workshop routine, tactics, the loading of torpedoes on to aircraft, and finally practice with dummy torpedoes against target ships. See also Vol. III, pages 561, 573 and 629.

They Are Making It 'The Glory that *Is* Greece'

Photo, Associated Press

GREECE'S ARMY, a detachment of which is seen entraining for the Albanian front, continues to take heavy toll of the enemy. Despite the many efforts of General Cavallero, the new Italian C.-in-C. in Albania, to regain the Initiative, his over-hastily prepared counter-attacks were smashed with heavy loss towards the end of January. It was estimated in Athens on January 26 that of the 20 Italian divisions employed on the Albanian front since October 28, 1940, seven have been completely broken up.

'Uncle Sam's' Navy of Today and Tomorrow

In the last war the Navy of the U.S.A. shared the burden and heat of the day with the
Navy of Britain. Once again it is a powerful factor in a fast-developing situation,
although as yet its guns have not begun to speak. Below we tell something of its size
and power, actual and potential.

AMERICA—or, to speak more exactly, the United States of America—has the second largest Navy in the world, one that is second only to Britain's. Yet it is not large enough for her security. As Col. Frank Knox, United States Secretary of the Navy, made clear to Congress on January 17, the U.S.A. has been successful in maintaining the Monroe Doctrine, i.e. in keeping America for the Americans, only because the British Navy has been so overwhelmingly strong as to deter and defeat aggressors in Europe.

Outbuilt by the Axis

For 125 years that position has been maintained, but it is now threatened. Figures presented by Col. Knox showed that the United States Navy possessed 322 fighting ships on January 1, 1941, while the navies of the Axis Powers—Germany, Italy and Japan—were estimated to amount to 658 ships. And the situation is steadily worsening. By January 1942 the figures are calculated to be: U.S.A. fleet, 342 ships; Axis fleets, 803 ships. And by January 1943 the ratio is expected to be 422 compared with 962.

For many years, Col. Knox pointed out, the U.S.A. and the British Commonwealth of Nations have possessed what was in effect a two-ocean Navy, operated for a single

Navy will share the fate of the courageous nation that supports it. Should that come to pass our Fleet would necessarily be divided to meet the danger in both oceans. Whether it would be strong enough to protect even the regions nearest to us is a matter that cannot now be foretold. Once we lose the power to control even part of those seas, inevitably the war in Europe and Asia will be transferred to the Americas.''

Fundamentally, the U.S. Secretary of the Navy went on, the present war is an attempt by Germany to seize control of the seas from Great Britain. Since the World War the United States has maintained a one-ocean Navy—in the Pacific. ''That that Navy has proved adequate in both directions is only because the existence and deployment of Britain's Navy gave us security in the Atlantic.''

Such being the position, it is not surprising that the great republic is now taking dramatic steps to increase the power and size of her Navy—not because any responsible section of American opinion anticipates Britain is shortly about to collapse, but because the great mass of Americans now realize that Britain is fighting America's battle as well as her own. At present the U.S.A. is guarded by the British Navy; circumstances may be envisaged in which that protection could no longer be afforded, and it is only

reasonable, therefore, that America should see to her own defence.

Up to now the United States Navy has been organized in two main divisions—the United States Fleet, with its main bases in California and Hawaii, and the Asiatic Fleet. From the former was detached a small force—a training unit comprising four of the oldest battleships, a division of cruisers of the latest type, and a number of destroyers and submarines—which was based on the east coast and known as the Atlantic Squadron. Since the war began this Atlantic Squadron—it was renamed last autumn the Atlantic Patrol Force—has grown until it now includes some 125 ships, and, as Col. Knox says, '' has assumed a dignity which warrants its establishment as a separate fleet.''

America's Three Fleets

Henceforth, then, the U.S.A. is to have three Fleets—Atlantic, Pacific and Asiatic—each with its own Commander-in-Chief. The Pacific Fleet is to remain as the largest and most important, and its Commander-in-Chief, who is also C.-in-C. of the combined Fleets, is Rear Admiral Husband E. Kimmel, who has been in command of the cruisers of the United States Battle Force. The Atlantic Fleet is commanded by Rear-Admiral Ernest J. King, lately in command of the Atlantic Patrol Force, and the Asiatic by Admiral Thomas C. Hart—all these appointments taking effect from February 1, 1941.

In anticipation of the two-ocean Navy, a four thousand million dollar Navy Expansion Bill received the President's signature on July 20, 1940. On that date the American

''MINNEAPOLIS'' is a U.S. cruiser of 9,950 tons armed with nine 8-in. guns and eight 5-in. A.A. guns. She is fitted with two catapults and carries four aircraft.

peaceful purpose. '' We—the U.S.A.—still have a one-ocean Navy,'' he went on. '' We are building a two-ocean Navy, but its structure will not be complete for six years. We need to complete that structure so far as we can because the other part of our two-ocean Navy is now in grave danger.'' That '' other part '' is, of course, the British Navy, which, to quote Col. Knox again, '' can survive only if the British Isles survive. Should the British Isles fall, we can only believe that the British Navy, which never runs from danger, will fall at the same time. I think we can safely assume that the British

'' COLORADO '' is one of a class of three battleships that are the newest in the United States Navy. She has a displacement of 32,500 tons. Her chief armament is eight 16-in. guns, twelve 5-in. guns and eight 5-in. A.A. guns and she has a speed of 21 knots. She has two catapults and carries three aircraft. The ship was completed in August, 1923.   *Photos, Wide World*

American Naval Might in the Pacific: So

the Ships Which Meet Japan's Challenge

THE U.S.A. FLEET is second largest in the world, and sea power of the most formidable kind is exemplified in these photographs taken on manoeuvres. Top left are some of America's great battleships in line ahead. The leading ship is the " New Mexico," while following her are the " Maryland," " Tennessee," " Oklahoma " and " California." Above, U.S.A. ships in line ahead are executing a right turn. Left, the Pacific Fleet, escorted by an imposing array of fighting and bombing 'planes. *Photos, Wide World and Keystone*

America's Fleet the Second Largest in the World

Navy was stated to consist of the following ships :—

Types	Built: 1940	Building 1940
Battleships	15	10
Aircraft Carriers	6	5
Cruisers	37	21
Destroyers	237	60
Submarines	102	40
Total	397	136

In addition to the ships included in the " building " column above, orders have been, or are about to be, given for a very large number of fresh vessels, so that by 1947 it is planned that America's two-ocean Navy shall comprise : 35 battleships, 20 aircraft carriers, 88 cruisers, 378 destroyers, and 180 submarines, a grand total of 701 ships. (Even so, its strength would be considerably below that estimated for the Axis fleets in 1943, estimated above to be 962).

America's Capital Ships

Now let us consider the American Fleet as it exists at the present time. First there are 15 battleships, actually built and in commission, but all are over age (in the American Navy a battleship is estimated to be over age when it is 20 years old). The biggest are " New Mexico" & "Idaho" (33,400 tons), which were laid down in 1915, and next ranks "Mississippi" (33,000 tons). Then there is the "Penn-

sylvania " (33,100 tons), and also " Arizona," " Tennessee," " California," " Maryland," " West Virginia," " Colorado," " Texas," " New York," " Nevada " and " Oklahoma "; and, smallest and oldest,

"SARATOGA," right, was the first aircraft carrier to be completed for the American Navy. She and her sister ship, the " Lexington," have displacement of 33,000 tons, the " Saratoga" carrying 79 aircraft and the " Lexington " 90. Both are to undergo reconstruction. The largest concentration of the U.S. Navy has hitherto been in the Pacific ; top, destroyers are seen in line ahead during manoeuvres in that ocean.

" Arkansas " (26,000 tons), completed in 1912. At the outbreak of war three 35,000-ton battleships were under construction : " North Carolina," " Washington," and " South Dakota "; of these, the first two were launched in June 1940. Three battleships—" Maryland," " West Virginia," and " Colorado "—have eight 16-inch guns ; the others, with the exception of " Arkansas," have ten or twelve 14-inch guns.

Cruisers and Aircraft Carriers

Next we come to cruisers. The U.S.A. possesses 18 of the heavy 8-inch-gun type, displacing 9,000 to 10,000 tons each, viz. Pensacola class, 2 ; Northampton, 6 ; Portland, 2 ; Minneapolis, 7 ; and Wichita. The first-named were completed in 1929-30, and the Wichita in 1939. Then there are 17 light cruisers (Brooklyn class 7, Omaha class 10, armed with 6-inch guns. Two light cruisers still under construction are " Helena " and " St. Louis," both of 10,000 tons with a principal armament of fifteen 6-inch guns.

There are six aircraft carriers : " Ranger," completed in 1934 ; " Enterprise " and " Yorktown," completed in 1938 ; the giants " Lexington " and " Saratoga," completed in 1927 and displacing 33,000 tons ; and " Wasp " (14,700 tons), completed in 1938. " Hornet " (20,000 tons) and a sister ship are under construction.

The destroyer strength is about 160, after allowing for the 50 recently transferred to the British Navy in exchange for bases in the Atlantic. During the last five years some 70 modern destroyers have been built ; the latest, of the Benson class, displace 1,620 tons. Many more are on the stocks. Submarines number just under 100 ; (Col. Knox says that the present underseas fleet of the Axis Powers is 284, and that by 1943 it will be 500.) Mention may be made of the " Argonaut," which with its submerged displacement of 4,080 tons ranks second in size only to the French " Surcouf " (4,300 tons). The " Nautilus " and " Narwhal " are slightly smaller. Then there are many auxiliary vessels of one kind or another ; 280 smaller warships for anti-submarine work and mine-sweeping have just been voted by Congress.

Like Britain the United States has a Naval Air Service. It is stated to be the largest in the world, its " useful " aeroplane strength being not less than 3,000.

With regard to the U.S. Navy's personnel, in 1939 the total number was less than 120,000. Since the war began it has increased to some 190,000, and in January 1941 it was raised to its full war strength of not far short of 300,000 officers and men. The Budget for 1942 allocates £2,897 millions to the Navy.

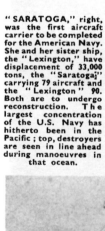

SUBMARINES were first adopted by the American Navy in April 1900, eight months before the British Navy gave its first order for five of these craft. The first practical submarines were called Holland boats, after their designer, John P. Holland, who also gave his name to the submarine tender above. The " Holland " is here lying at San Diego, California, with some of her charges around her.

Photos, Wide World

Keeping Watch for the 'Deathly Glow Lamps'

FIRE WATCHERS, whose vigilance through the dark winter nights should never be relaxed, wait at their post, ready to deal with any emergency. These three men in their steel helmets and oilskins are part of the great civilian army of Britain which is now in the "front line." On January 16, 1941, Mr. Herbert Morrison, Minister of Home Security, signed an order which made it obligatory for all persons between 16 and 60 not in Government service to register for fire-watching duty and so defeat the "deathly glow lamps"—to use his pregnant phrase. Stirrup-pump, axe, buckets and sand form the necessary equipment of the fire watcher.

Photo, "Daily Mirror"

Saved from Terror, Perhaps from Death

EVACUATION OF CHILDREN from danger zones, especially from London, has again and again been urged upon parents, but the two photographs in this page present the argument in favour of it far more forcibly than any words could do. Top is a scene in the neighbourhood of Blackfriars Road, London, bombed at the end of 1940. Many children whose parents had taken advantage of the Government's scheme were spared the nights of terror that bring such devastation in their train. In the lower photograph are some of the kiddies who had been evacuated from Blackfriars, smiling and carefree at their wartime home, a Dorsetshire village.
Photo, Central Press

Above War's Storms Broods Eternal Britain

FAR FROM THE WAR-SCORCHED TOWNS are thousands of square miles of peaceful countryside where the eternal spirit of Britain still reigns supreme. The winter sun shines down on hills and dales unscarred save by the kindly hand of Nature, giving promise, like the first snowdrops of spring, of better days to come. Here are two scenes, one in Scotland, one in England, such as must have given treasured and inspiring memories to millions in the stress of war. In the top photograph the plough is at work on Tweedside, at Manorfoot Bridge, near Peebles ; the lower one shows a winter pastoral on the Westmorland coast. with Whitbarrow Scar in the background.

Photos, " The Scotsman" and Fox

Britain's New Fighters in the Night Sky

In this article Grenville Manton discusses the problem of the night bomber—the problem to whose solution the best brains in aeronautics are devoting their attention in this country as (we may well believe) in Germany. The most effective answer, it is suggested, is likely to be the night fighter.

IN this war no problem of defence has been more difficult to solve than the combating of the night bomber. Goering's Luftwaffe, baulked, battered and beaten in all its daylight assaults against this country, has for many weeks carried out raids under cover of darkness and, by flying at great heights, has managed to return to its bases with negligible losses. How best to meet this menace has been a matter which has engaged the minds of many. While ground defences from time to time are successful in bringing down one, two or more enemy aircraft, results have shown that some new departure or development is required to counter successfully massed night raids.

the duties of night patrol and combat. Such a machine must have an exceptional rate of climb, it must have a top speed well in excess of that of the enemy bombers, it must have a long duration and it must have a reasonably slow landing speed. Here one thing counteracts another. If an aircraft is to remain in the air for many hours at a stretch it must carry a big load of fuel, and the bigger the load the slower the rate of climb, so that a compromise has to be made. Other qualities, too, tend to cancel out each other ; a high top speed is usually obtained at the expense of control in the lower regions of the air speed indicator. It is all a matter of weight, power, size and

a crew of three and, besides a gun turret on top of the fuselage, a battery of four fixed machine-guns is arranged under the fuselage. The initial rate of climb of this multi-seat night fighter is 1,540 feet per minute, and it has a service ceiling of well over 27,000 feet. Tried and trusty, the Blenheim, which as a type is now five years old, drones in our skies with its steady two-motor throb, heard, but for the most part unseen, by the millions it seeks to protect in these long winter nights.

Sharing with the Blenheim this grim and hazardous task of seeking battle with the bomber in the cold and darkness is the Boulton Paul Defiant, that fine two-seater fighter which wrought havoc amongst the enemy at Dunkirk. Since then little has been heard of this machine, but, unknown to the public, it has been carrying on, its role changed from day-fighter to night-fighter ; and when the full story can be told the Defiant's name will rank high amongst those 'planes which tore the German threat from the sky. At present no performance figures have been released ; its speed, rate of climb, its useful load and duration and range— these are still secret. But it can be said that it is a low-wing monoplane with a Rolls-Royce 1,030 h.p. Merlin engine. Its span is 39 feet 6 inches ; it has a wing area of 250 sq. ft., and its length is 30 feet. Behind the pilot's enclosed cockpit, the gunner is housed in a Boulton Paul electrically-operated gun turret. This turret is fitted with four Browning machine-guns which are so arranged that the gunner has a tremendous sweep of fire.

These are the machines which, augmented by other new types, will settle accounts with the Luftwaffe's night bombers. It will not be accomplished suddenly, any more than the Gotha in the last war was vanquished in a night, but methods and equipment of which nothing must be disclosed – for defence against the night bomber is as much a problem for the Nazis as for ourselves—are being evolved, tried and developed.

On a night in January, one of our fighter-pilots, single-handed, destroyed two raiders during a night patrol. He was Flight-Lieutenant John Cunningham, and he received for his exploit the first D.F.C. awarded in respect of night flying. His first successful action was over the South Coast. After following an enemy bomber for ten minutes and climbing to nearly 20,000 feet (the temperature was 50 degrees below freezing point) he put in a single, well-directed burst of fire lasting only four seconds. The raider, struck amidships, blew up with an explosion like a " firework display."

A few minutes later he sighted another enemy bomber flying above him. Undetected, he manoeuvred himself into position and then, easing up the nose of his aircraft, opened fire. Streams of tracer bullets could be seen striking the engines and cutting into the port wing. Both gunners were apparently killed or wounded with the first long burst, as there was no return fire. For about thirty seconds the enemy bomber flew on an even course ; then, with engines almost stopped and streaming vapour, it turned slowly to port and dived towards the sea.

THIS R.A.F. TRIO are waiting light-heartedly in their quarters " somewhere in England " for the order to take off. They hope most fervently that they may contact a Nazi night bomber, then open fire with their deadly Browning machine-guns and so down yet another enemy. For hours they will be aloft, these cheerful and courageous comrades, partners in a grim drama of the night.

Photo, British Official : Crown Copyright

The most promising way of combating the night bomber is to be found in the development of the night fighter patrol. In this there have been many difficulties, the greatest of which is the lack of visibility. Only those who have flown at night can appreciate the task which faces a pilot who, flying in the darkness, seeks another aircraft— what one pilot has described as " like trying to swat a wasp in a blacked-out room." Without the light of the moon, with no navigation lights to aid him, he can only scan the blackness with the hope that he may discern the tell-tale glow from the exhaust manifolds of the enemy machine. Even then it is impossible for him to tell friend from enemy by this means alone. Detecting the enemy—that has been problem No. 1.

Another difficulty which, though not insurmountable, has not been easy to overcome, is the evolution of a 'plane suited for

speed. But baffling as these problems have been, British designers, whose genius has provided the R.A.F. with the world's finest day fighters, long-range bombers, torpedo-'planes and dive-bombers, have tackled the task of producing machines which will in the end take the sting out of the Nazi night attacks.

Meanwhile, our night-fighter pilots are growing in numbers, gaining more and more experience in a new technique of night interception which has now been evolved, and the toll they are taking is rising. In this work, which calls for a courage, skill and endurance of the highest order, the R.A.F. are using various types of 'planes. One is the Bristol Blenheim Mk.1 fighter-bomber, a mid-wing cantilever monoplane built throughout of metal. Two Bristol Mercury engines of 840 h.p. each give it a speed of nearly 300 m.p.h., and it has a range of 1,125 miles when flying at 200 m.p.h. It carries

Finding the Answer to Goering's Murderers

THIS DORNIER 17 set out from the other side of the Channel on its errand of destruction. Flying high to evade the British searchlights and shells from A.A. guns, it was nevertheless doomed never to return to its base. Its dark form was spotted by a vigilant night-fighter pilot of the R.A.F.; machine-guns snapped, and the enemy plunged earthwards. Here two soldiers are seen viewing the burnt-out wreckage.

NIGHT-FLYING practice was in full swing, out under the stars ; a flickering line of naphtha flares marked the runway. At a signal from the control officer pupils were taking off into the inky darkness, doing their flights and landing again down the flare-paths, their landing lights stabbing the darkness like an angry luminous eye. A dozen or more aircraft were up there somewhere in the dark sky or lying out on the flying field.

Suddenly the "flap" arose. A lorry rumbled up to the Control Officer. A sergeant jumped down and passed over a message. By the light of the torch slung round his neck the officer hastily read the message. The word was passed round : "All flying to cease, uncover the flares."

From nowhere running figures appeared ; the line of flares sprang into greater brilliance as the lid from each was uncovered. The waiting machines were swung around and taxied to the edge of the field, coloured rockets soared into the sky.

"There are two fighters from 'X' trying to get down - think they may be landing here," said the control officer. Then a moment later : "What's that light, is that a star ? I believe it's one of the Hurricanes ! "

Sure enough, the "star" rapidly assumed the appearance of a meteor flying straight towards us. Then another navigation light could be seen. It was a fighter coming down to land. A few moments later it had "touched down " and was being taxied out of harm's way. "Well, that's one, anyway—I wonder where the other man is ? "

Over in the Nissen hut, the sketchy night quarters for the pupils and instructors on night flying, there was subdued excitement. At the field telephone a duty pilot was busy. Messages were passed to the parent fighter station, Observer Corps, and the police. For miles around the countryside was on the watch for the missing fighter. Half-an-hour passed. Then came the news that the fighter had come down safely a few miles away. Night-flying practice resumed its normal routine. The "flap" was over.

PILOT AND GUNNER of a Bristol Blenheim fighter go aboard their 'plane. Messages have been flashed to the night fighter squadrons, orders have been given, and air crews who have been standing-by promptly set out to patrol the sky to locate and destroy the prowling enemy. So begins one more gallant attempt to check Goering's night raiders.

Photos, British Official : Crown Copyright ; and Planet News

For Nazi Flyers Who Fail to Get Home

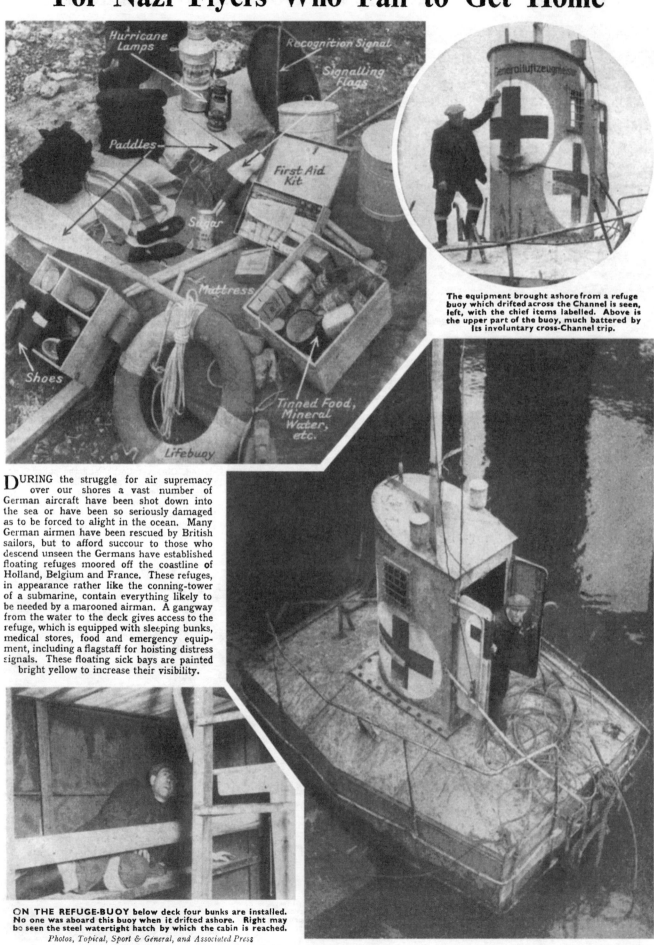

The equipment brought ashore from a refuge buoy which drifted across the Channel is seen, left, with the chief items labelled. Above is the upper part of the buoy, much battered by its involuntary cross-Channel trip.

DURING the struggle for air supremacy over our shores a vast number of German aircraft have been shot down into the sea or have been so seriously damaged as to be forced to alight in the ocean. Many German airmen have been rescued by British sailors, but to afford succour to those who descend unseen the Germans have established floating refuges moored off the coastline of Holland, Belgium and France. These refuges, in appearance rather like the conning-tower of a submarine, contain everything likely to be needed by a marooned airman. A gangway from the water to the deck gives access to the refuge, which is equipped with sleeping bunks, medical stores, food and emergency equipment, including a flagstaff for hoisting distress signals. These floating sick bays are painted bright yellow to increase their visibility.

ON THE REFUGE-BUOY below deck four bunks are installed. No one was aboard this buoy when it drifted ashore. Right may be seen the steel watertight hatch by which the cabin is reached.

Photos, Topical, Sport & General, and Associated Press

Near Tobruk I Saw a Terrible Sight

The final advance of our troops on Tobruk was so rapid that the war correspondents were able to follow in the wake of supply columns half an hour after the attack opened. One of them was Reuters' special correspondent, whose vivid account of the scene is given below.

THE battle began for me on Sunday morning (Jan. 19) when I took up quarters at the deserted El Adem airfield behind Tobruk. Amid more than eighty wrecked 'planes—the ghost of Graziani's air force—we were shelled periodically by " Tobruk Tom," the big gun of the " San Giorgio." I lay flat in a silt trench as shells plugged the field.

That night the Royal Navy poured broadsides into Tobruk, and the ground shook to the crashing of 15-inch shells. Throughout the night, too, the R.A.F. rained bombs on the port.

When this terrific air onslaught ceased a sinister silence hung over Tobruk. Then I heard the low rumbling of tanks and lorries. The " big show " was on.

I moved up to our advanced positions. After another intensive R.A.F. bombardment lasting two and a half hours the full force of the British artillery barrage opened up. Tanks and infantry went into action. . . .

Half an hour after the attack started I followed in the wake of supply columns and Red Cross units over the broken defences. In the growing light of dawn I met the first batch of Italian prisoners coming out.

Some Australian wounded walking past shouted : " Look out, mate. You'll cop it farther down the track."

They were right. Half a mile farther on we narrowly escaped a barrage from enemy gun positions still firing frantically.

Then I saw a terrible sight. Thousands of Italian prisoners streaming back were caught in the barrage from their own guns. Shells burst among them, killing many and wounding others. The remainder dashed panic-stricken in all directions.

When I reached the gun positions which had been our first objective I found the Australians—true to type—had got there ahead of schedule. They had taken the positions in two hours instead of the four allowed for by the staff.

Many of the guns there had received direct hits from our covering artillery. Red Cross men were already attending the wounded crews.

I spoke to the crew of a British tank christened the Caterpillar, which had broken a gap in the perimeter wire. The sergeant was modest about it. He said : " We did nothing. We take our hats off to the sappers for cutting the wire. Those blokes are superb."

Stretched below was a sandy plain extending to the final escarpment dropping down to Tobruk. Over the port itself black smoke came from oil dumps and barracks set ablaze by our bombers.

I took up a position next to a gun observation post. While the commanding officer was giving crisp telephonic instructions to the batteries stationed in the rear I saw the Imperial Army moving across the plain to attack the Solario and Airente forts.

It was an astounding sight. Like ants on the vast desert, the troops moved methodically without hurry towards their objective. Bren-gun carriers, infantry, tanks, and armoured cars and infantry went forward in perfect order.

The battery behind me was giving the foremost fort a terrific drubbing. Columns of jet black smoke hung over its walls.

Throughout the attack I was most impressed by the skill and accuracy of the British artillery. Before the capture of this strategic ridge all firing had been " blind," but its effects were deadly. There was something uncanny about its accuracy.

Towards sunset the roar of battle went on. We decided to dash down the road direct to Tobruk. A staff car went ahead with an officer of the Ordnance Corps on board.

From the top of the final escarpment we saw Tobruk for the first time. Below us lay the white houses of the town, with the setting sun glinting off the still waters of the harbour.

A large liner lay at anchor—ablaze from stem to stern. Smaller craft which were tied up alongside were also in flames. Masts and funnels of sunken vessels showed above the surface. The " San Giorgio " lay in the harbour mouth.

A few men wandering through the town were the only signs of life, but a formidable battery of at least six guns, posted on a headland, was blazing away on the advancing British forces . . .

We of the 'Terror' Pounded Tobruk

The veteran monitor " Terror " (see page 66) was prominent in the naval bombardment that preceded the attack on Tobruk. For nearly two hours her 15-inch guns lobbed tons of high explosive into the Italian lines, as described here by W. F. Hartin, " Daily Mail " special correspondent, who was on board the " Terror " at the time.

WE on board the " Terror " were part of a now famous flotilla which includes gunboats built for Chinese rivers—incongruous craft which, because of their shallow draught and indomitable crews, can skate over minefields and are always popping up where the Italians least expect them.

Yet as we waited in the early hours of darkness to take up our positions we were not without misgivings. Tobruk had the reputation of being a well-defended port, with two heavy shore batteries apart from an old cruiser, the " San Giorgio."

This vessel, torpedoed and bombed at the outbreak of war, and partially sunk in Tobruk Harbour, was still able to fire her 10-in. and 7·5-in. armament.

We were anxious to test these possibilities before the hardy little gunboats, prowling right under the Italian defences, were exposed to outranging fire.

For this reason, steering a course carefully plotted against the possible range of these batteries, we went into action first

Zero hour had arrived, and we crossed the line where our chart showed we must open fire. The fire-bell rang with an inconsequential ting-ting, like the bell of a London 'bus.

A second later and the darkness and everything else were lost in that first terrific and vivid flash of death. The old ship shuddered as the roar swept around us.

Somewhere in that sandy ravine known as Wadi Sehel, west of Tobruk, we knew that shell would spread wreckage and destruction

THE HAUL OF PRISONERS at Tobruk, the siege of which is graphically described by an eye-witness in this page, was as colossal as it had been a fortnight before at Bardia, where this photograph of surrendering Italians was taken. Over 100,000 Italians have so far been captured during the swift Libyan campaign. *Photo, British Official: Crown Copyright*

among the dense concentration of Italian reserves waiting there to meet and counter-attack the first onrush of the Imperial forces.

Far away we could see lights winking momentarily. "The shore batteries," we said to one another in a silence which hung heavily by contrast with the roar of the guns.

We waited to hear the whine of shells seeking us out, but none came ; and we took up our solo song of destruction again.

If the shore batteries are not replying, we thought, at least we may expect an attack from some E-boats which the Italians were known to have in the harbour. Look-outs, muffled to the ears, scanned with night glasses the placid waters now growing more luminous as the hour of moonrise approached.

Still, there seemed no response from doomed Tobruk, and between us and the faintly discernible shore we now saw new winks of light which meant that the other gunboats were also in action.

With monotonous regularity we pounded away, the gunnery officer shifting his range so that our shells would fall first in one area and then in another.

Thus he brought the camps, transport, vital junction where five roads meet, and the area in which were the Italian headquarters, under harassing fire.

Finally came the order to cease fire, and none of us was really sorry, for we were all tired. At times we had been firing very near our own troops, and only the most accurate calculations had avoided a margin of error which might have flung the shell wide by just those few hundred yards separating our forces from the Italians.

A thin crescent moon stole into the sky to guide us on our course seawards. Our consorts joined us, and as we rolled home like the three jolly huntsmen we saw that the Air Force were taking up the job where we had left it . . .

Back we turned, and plunged again into the fantastic blaze of bursting shells. Another flare was burning, and Tobruk's bay and promontory showed up like a gigantic thumb sticking out into the sea.

We made a straight run for the target, but showers of tracers met us and barred the way. The pilot swerved momentarily and tried again from another angle. Again I heard, " Bombs gone ! " and this time I saw flames belch up straight across the road junction we were aiming at.

Two blinding flashes to our left made me jump, and I reported to the pilot, " A.A. shells close behind." For a couple of seconds we swerved and twisted, eluding the gunners. Then we jockeyed into position for a third run.

This took us slap through the thickest barrage. The grounded cruiser " San Giorgio " in the harbour was pumping up stream after stream of tracers. I saw a white one coming straight at me—a diamond necklace this time. Then it veered off slowly and missed.

Right in the middle of the barrage our bombs fell, and flares with them. This time the result was spectacular. A large barnlike building flashed into orange flame, and its roof soared gently upwards, then fell back in fragments. Swirls of white smoke spiralled up, and as we swung away out to sea I saw two more explosions shatter the flaming walls.

Those were our last bombs, and once more we passed Tobruk and watched other people's bombs crash down against the fantastic background of A.A. fire. The Italian gunners were certainly standing up to their job well.

Dawn was glimmering on the eastern horizon as we raced back to our base. But other slim black shapes sped past us invisible in the darkness. They would be over Tobruk as dawn broke . . . .

I Saw the R.A.F.'s Bombs Rock Tobruk

The final assault on Tobruk was heralded by tremendous bombing attacks by the R.A.F. which started at 3 a.m. on January 21. The " Daily Mail " Special War Correspondent, Alexander Clifford, took part in one of these raids, which he describes in the following graphic dispatch.

EARLY on the morning of January 21, by the light of the dying moon, I saw the R.A.F. unleash a cyclonic blitz that opened the British Army's attack on beleaguered Tobruk. The rear-gunner's turret of a British long-range bomber was my front-row seat for the most thrilling show I have ever witnessed.

For the Italians the offensive began soon after three in the morning. For me it started 12 hours earlier in a sandy fly-haunted shack beside a desert airfield. The squadron leader had summoned the pilots to hear instructions.

" Blitz on Tobruk tonight," he told them, " Take off after midnight. There will be five targets. You can take your choice."

All knew they would be duelling with the enemy in a few hours and that gave a zest to the conversation.

For those few intervening hours we dozed on straw mattresses. Then, booted, helmeted and warmly overalled, we were walking out to dimly silhouetted 'planes.

The moon, like a luminous slice of melon, was topping the horizon as we screamed down the flare-path, and lifted gently into the night.

There was nothing to see. I crouched down, trying to keep warm and watching spangles of stars slide past the little glass bubble above me. Vaguely in my earphones I heard the crew chatting about heights, courses, clouds, and navigation signals. I fell asleep.

Somebody wakened me and yelled " Tobruk ! " I fumbled my way forward and peered out of the 'plane's transparent nose to see earth and sky slashed with flame.

Groups of big yellow flashes were bombs landing. Clusters of incendiaries wove crazy patterns of dazzling white flame athwart the landscape.

To my unaccustomed eyes the A.A. barrage seemed terrific. It was our turn to go in. For a second there was icy panic inside me and I wished I had not come. Then I grew too excited to be afraid.

I raced back through the 'plane's darkened belly, past the bomb-aimer lying flat on his stomach, and over racks of sleek, yellow bombs waiting to be released. Fumblingly, I eased myself into the rear-gunner's turret. Through earphones I heard the bomb-aimer's steady monologue :

" Bomb-doors open . . . left . . . left . . . steady . . . right . . . steady." Then a pause. Then, sharply, " Bombs gone ! "

I swivelled my turret round, manoeuvring to see the bombs land. I had almost given them up when the earth below me erupted in five flaming volcanoes. " Plumb in the target area," came the bomb-aimer's voice.

Stuff was coming up all around us. The sky seemed filled with coloured tracers, and A.A. guns were going flat out.

DESERT AIRMEN have just landed with their Blenheims after an intensive raid on beleaguered Tobruk and are enjoying welcome refreshment, mugs of tea and sandwiches, in the Western Desert. Tobruk was bombed again and again by the R.A.F. before it was finally captured on January 22.
Photo, British Official: Crown Copyright

Cartoon Commentary on the War

"I MUST HAVE A SCREW LOOSE SOMEWHERE"
From the "Salt Lake Tribune"

'DIGGERS' FOR VICTORY!
By Illingworth, courtesy of the "Daily Mail"

WAR and political upheaval provide grist for the mills of those modern-day lampooners, the cartoonists. In a world increasingly used to the visual image the cartoonist, by skilful exaggeration of his theme, lays bare before mankind the essential weaknesses of those things or persons against which he tilts, pricking bombast with the stroke of a pen and pointing a moral in Indian ink.

"A LITTLE BIT OF HEAVEN"

"SAY SOMETHING!—SO THAT MY PATIENCE CAN BE EXHAUSTED!"

"AND WHEN THE ANGELS FOUND IT, SURE IT LOOKED SO PEACEFUL THERE"
By Moon, courtesy of the "Sunday Dispatch"

By Zec, courtesy of the "Daily Mirror"

OUR SEARCHLIGHT ON THE WAR

How America Helps the Axis

RECENTLY Mr. Martin Dies remarked that in some ways the United States were aiding the Axis countries more than the Allies. The way that this is possible is an indirect one. American goods, more particularly cotton and plant for oil-fields, may reach Germany through Russia. In the course of two months – October 15 to December 15 – the Soviet purchased from American exporters more cotton than her normal imports from all sources in one year. This fact is illuminating when it is also revealed that in 1940 Germany imported from Russia 100,000 tons of cotton, and that it is proposed to increase this amount in the future. The economic pact signed between the two countries at Moscow on January 10 lends significance to a report that has reached London from Buenos Aires to the effect that Russia intends to create a merchant fleet of some 200 vessels solely to bring her imports from North and South America and later re-export them to her European customers.

New Czechoslovak Centre in London

AT 18, Grosvenor Place, London, S.W., a social and cultural centre for Czechoslovaks in this country was opened by Mr. Eden, the Foreign Secretary, on January 21, 1941. The Czechoslovak Institute, as it is called, will co-ordinate the work of Czechoslovak communities in various parts of the country and will also provide a link between the Czechoslovak peoples in this country and those in other parts of the Empire. The Institute will be the headquarters of Czechoslovak writers and dramatists, and there will be frequent exhibitions by Czechoslovak painters as well as concerts and other social functions.

Badge for R.A.F. Bomb Disposal Units

THE special badge worn by Royal Engineers engaged on bomb disposal has been illustrated in page 722, Vol. III. Now we illustrate the distinctive badge which has just been approved for personnel of the bomb disposal squads of the R.A.F. The badge depicts a bomb with the

letters B and D on either side of it within a laurel wreath. When worn with the blue home service dress of the R.A.F. the badge is in light blue silk on a dark blue background. For wear with tropical dress the badge is in red on a khaki background. Personnel of the R.A.F. bomb disposal squads will wear

R.A.F. BOMB DISPOSAL SQUADS BADGE
Photo, British Official : Crown Copyright

the badge on the right upper sleeve of the service dress jacket.

Portable Canteens on Railway

PORTABLE canteens on railway trains were inaugurated on January 20, 1941, by the L.M.S., acting in co-operation with the Army Welfare, Y.M.C.A., and Salvation Army authorities, to enable members of the Forces travelling by train to obtain light refreshments at prices similar to those charged in their own canteens. By means of special portable equipment, an ordinary third-class compartment can speedily be fitted up as a canteen. The carriage next can be used for stores or fitted with a portable draining board for washing-up. The first train to leave Euston with one of these canteens on board carried sufficient tea for 800 cups, and a plentiful supply of meat pies, sausage rolls, fruit tarts and buns.

Britain's New Ambassador in U.S.A.

LORD HALIFAX was personally welcomed to America on January 24 by President Roosevelt who, in an unprecedented gesture of friendship towards Great Britain, boarded his yacht, the " Potamac," and sailed down Chesapeake Bay to meet the new Ambassador at Annapolis. Lord and Lady Halifax and their suite had crossed the Atlantic in Britain's newest battleship, H.M.S. " King George V," having been seen off from a northern British base by the Prime Minister and Mrs. Churchill, and Mr. Harry Hopkins, the President's personal envoy in Britain (see photo, p. 140). Soon after reaching Washington Lord Halifax paid his first visit to the Secretary of State, Mr. Cordel Hull, and, after an hour's conference with him, told the reporters : " We see things very much alike." He added : " We have no illusions about Germany's strength or plans, but we know they will not succeed. England is in good heart."

Poles' Gift Towards a New Guildhall

GENERAL SIKORSKI, Prime Minister of Poland, has sent to Mr. Winston Churchill a cheque for £450, contributed by Polish serving officers and men and civilians now resident in this country, towards the rebuilding of Guildhall, " as a token of our lasting admiration of the gallant-hearted men and women of London." Thanking General Sikorski for this generous gift, Mr. Churchill wrote : " This is a moving token which will stir the hearts of everyone in this city and Empire. We see in it a symbol of the friendship of the great Polish nation, whose homes have been broken and whose monuments have been shattered, but whose free spirit will never crumble like bricks or stone."

Hostel for Working Boys

A HOSTEL for young lads working in London whose mothers and families have been evacuated has just been opened in Camberwell by the Cambridge University Settlement. If it is a success other similar hostels will be set up in London and big provincial cities. Accommodation is provided for 40 boys who will be selected by various welfare organizations. They must be between the ages of 14 and 20, and they pay £1 a week, or, if they cannot afford it, two-thirds of their wages. A lunch is packed ready for them when they leave for work in the morning, and a hot meal awaits them when they arrive home at night.

Collapse of Iron Guard Revolt

DISORDERS in Rumania, said to have been fomented by Germany for her own ends, reached their climax on January 22. The revolt originated in a split in the Iron Guards, the minority being opposed to General Antonescu and blaming him for shortage of food, general conditions of hardship, and mass executions. On Jan. 22 reports filtered through from Bucharest that the rebels were in control of police headquarters, the Ministry of the Interior, and the radio station, and that troops were firing upon them with machine-guns. By the next day, 1,000 people having been killed in Bucharest alone, the revolt was reported to be dwindling. The rounding-up of the rebels continued and their leader, M. Horia Sima, Deputy Premier of Rumania, was stated to have been arrested and to be " awaiting his destiny" before a court martial. The former Ministers of the Interior and of Propaganda have also been arrested for their part in the organization of the revolt. A new military Cabinet was formed on January 27.

The first canteen for Servicemen on a Scotch express of the L.M.S. was inspected by a party of distinguished visitors at Euston on January 20, 1941. Left to right are Princess Helena Victoria, Lieut.-Col. Moore-Brabazon, Minister of Transport, Lord Croft, Under-Secretary of State for War, and Lord Stamp, Chairman of the L.M.S., at the inauguration.   *Photo, Topical*

'Miss Ack-Ack' Had a Date with Jerry!

They were in the middle of a rehearsal when an Alert sounded. "Jerry," like Time, waits for no man, so the rehearsal was called off while contact was made with the battery.

MAKE-BELIEVE is a fine antidote for boredom, as soldiers well know ; hence the popularity of concert parties in this war as well as the last. These "ladies," in reality men of the R.A. from a Coastal Defence Battery, were to give a show at a local town hall, and are here posing for the cameraman in their stage costumes. What happened next is shown in the photograph top right.

Then, still wearing their dresses, the dancers rushed to their action stations—wolves in sheep's clothing, so to speak. But " it will be all right on the night "—and on "Der Tag," as well!

Photos, John Topham

OUR DIARY OF THE WAR

TUESDAY, JAN. 21, 1941   *507th day*

On the Sea—Admiralty announced loss of H.M. trawlers " Manx Prince " and " Refundo."

War against Italy—Imperial troops, supported by Royal Navy and R.A.F., penetrated defences of Tobruk to depth of 5 miles on a broad front. Italian cruiser " San Giorgio " in harbour set on fire.

During night of 20-21 R.A.F. carried out heavy raids on Catania (Sicily) and Derna (Libya).

East of Kassala British troops in pursuit of retreating Italian forces reached point 30 miles inside Eritrea.

Assab and Massawa raided by R.A.F. and Neghelli and Javello by S. African Air Force.

Home Front—Considerable enemy activity over eastern part of England during daylight. Bombs fell in outskirts of London and in Home and Eastern Counties. No night raids.

Enemy bomber shot down in Channel.

Home Front—Enemy aircraft dropped bombs at places in Yorks and Kent during daylight. After dark a few bombs fell in Eastern Counties.

Two German bombers destroyed by R.A.F. fighters.

Greek War—Greeks reported to have achieved important advance in Klisura sector. Intensification of aerial warfare reported. Allied air forces again attacked Valona and Berat. Enemy aircraft raided Salonika and other ports.

THURSDAY, JAN. 23   *509th day*

War against Italy—British troops reached coast near Derna, and Mekili, 50 miles inland. R.A.F. bombers attacked Apollonia, Derna and Maraua. During night of 23-24 aerodrome of Maritza, Rhodes, was raided.

In Eritrea British troops were in contact with Italian forces withdrawn from Kassala

THE PRIME MINISTER AND LORD HALIFAX stood watching with interest the great new British battleship "King George V" in the dim light of a January day as they approached her in a tender at a northern port. The "King George V" is the first of five ships of her class to be commissioned. These 35,000-ton ships represent the latest practice in naval architecture.
Photo, British Official : Crown Copyright

Greek War—Athens reported that successful local operations had been carried out.

Reported that R.A.F. had carried out heavy raids on Valona during night of 19-20 and by daylight on January 20. Military objectives at Elbasan were also raided.

WEDNESDAY, JAN. 22   *508th day*

On the Sea—Admiralty announced that H.M. destroyer " Hyperion " had been sunk by our forces after being severely damaged by torpedo or mine.

In the Air—Two small fighter sweeps carried out by Polish pilots over enemy-occupied territory between Straits of Dover and R. Somme. Low-level attacks made on aerodromes, troops and ground defences.

At night R.A.F. bombers attacked targets at Düsseldorf and other parts of the Ruhr.

War against Italy—Tobruk captured by Australians. Mopping-up operations in western section of perimeter proceeding. R.A.F. raided barracks at Apollonia.

Aerodromes in Sicily heavily raided by British bombers during night of 22-23, including Comiso, Augusta, Syracuse, and Catania.

In Kassala sector Italian forces reported to have withdrawn 40 miles into Eritrea, pursued by British. On Kenya front enemy was being driven out of British territory.

area and holding defensive positions covering Biscia and Barentu.

In Abyssinia pressure on enemy east of Metemma was maintained. S. African Air Force successfully bombed Sciasciamanna, 120 miles south of Addis Ababa, destroying four enemy aircraft and damaging others.

Home Front—Slight daylight enemy activity. Bombs fell at three places on coast of East Anglia. No night raids.

Greek War—Athens reported successful local operations. Capture of 250 prisoners and much war material.

FRIDAY, JAN. 24   *510th day*

On the Sea—Admiralty announced that H.M. submarine " Parthian " had sunk Italian supply ship south of Italy.

War against Italy—British troops in Libya continuing advance westwards. R.A.F. heavily raided Italian bases in Sicily.

In Eritrea Italians evacuated Keru and Aicota and were still in retreat.

Stated that Haile Selassie had arrived in Abyssinia from Khartoum to place himself at head of patriot army.

Home Front—Very little enemy activity in daylight. No night raids.

Greek War—Athens announced capture of new enemy positions and 200 prisoners.

Rumania—Gen. Antonescu succeeded in quelling Iron Guard revolt in Bucharest.

General—Lord Halifax was personally welcomed by President Roosevelt on arrival in U.S.A., having crossed Atlantic in battleship " King George V."

Marshal Pétain appointed advisory Council of nearly 200 members.

SATURDAY, JAN. 25   *511th day*

On the Sea—H.M. trawlers "Strathrannock," "Galvani " and "Philippe " engaged enemy aircraft and set it on fire.

In the Air—During night of 24-25 Coastal Command aircraft bombed submarine base at Lorient.

War against Italy—Advanced British elements reported to have been in contact with enemy 3 miles east of Derna. Column of enemy medium tanks engaged and dispersed.

R.A.F. bombed landing-ground at Maraua and aerodrome at Barce.

In Eritrea operations east of Keru and Aicota progressing satisfactorily. About 600 prisoners taken. Numerous supporting raids carried out by R.A.F.

East of Metemma (Abyssinia) pressure on enemy increased. Large portion of country now stated to be in hands of Patriots.

In Kenya ejection of enemy detachments from British side of frontier continued.

Home Front—Day activity by enemy aircraft was on small scale. Bombs fell at two points in East Anglia. During night bombs were dropped on a coastal town in Cornwall.

Greek War—Greeks forced Italians to withdraw their advanced outposts around key town of Tepelini to positions behind original lines. R.A.F. made successful attack on Boulsar, near Elbasan.

SUNDAY, JAN. 26   *512th day*

On the Sea—H.M. trawler " Galvani " was attacked by bomber which she so damaged that it crashed on Norfolk coast.

H.M.S. "Wallace " and H.M. drifters "Fisher Boy " and "Reids " were in action against enemy aircraft and destroyed at least two.

War against Italy—British troops in contact with enemy near Derna being reinforced.

In Eritrea, Biscia now in British hands. Operations proceeding in direction of Agordat. Enemy evacuated Umm Hagar.

R.A.F. bombed aerodrome at Barce and landing grounds at Derna and Apollonia. British fighters shot down five enemy aircraft.

Home Front—During day hostile aircraft dropped bomb on N.E. coast. At night enemy were reported near inland town in East Anglia.

Greek War—Italian counter-attacks foiled by Greek forces. Six enemy bombers destroyed, three over the front and three in flames at Salonika.

MONDAY, JAN. 27   *513th day*

In the Air—R.A.F. bombed Hanover in early hours of morning.

War against Italy—Operations in Derna area developing satisfactorily. Stated that prisoners taken at Tobruk number 25,000.

Marshal Graziani reported dismissed.

In Eritrea British forces closing in on enemy positions about Agordat and Barentu.

Further Patriot successes reported from interior of Abyssinia.

R.A.F. bombed railway stations at Keren and Aisha, 70 miles south-west of Jibuti, and railway bridge and road east of Adarti. Stores and warehouses at Assab also attacked.

Home Front—German 'plane shot down by A.A. fire at Boston, Lincs, after dropping bombs on one coastal town. Other reports of enemy activity came from East Midlands, N.E. England and E. Scotland.

Greek War—Further Italian counterattacks repelled by Greeks. Fighting along entire front growing in intensity. Greeks attacked between Malina and Hondiste.

THEY WILL BE SAVED FROM THE FATE THEY DESERVE

Such a scene as this has been enacted many times since the Nazis began their intensified " blockade " by submarines.   One more U-boat has been spotted by a British destroyer, and depth charges have sealed its fate.   The crew have jumped overboard, except one man who, fearing to take the plunge, still stands on the stern of the sinking U-boat.   They can be confident that British sailors will observe the chivalry of the sea which they themselves have so shamelessly violated, and send boats to their rescue.   The photo was taken from the destroyer.   *Photo, Exclusive to* THE WAR ILLUSTRATED

Derna: Another Step in Wavell's Victory March

Derna, on the North African coast 100 miles west of Tobruk, was captured by the
Imperial Army of the Nile on January 30. The story of its taking is given below, together
with an account of the attack by Free French forces on the Italian outpost at Murzuk.

EVEN before Tobruk had fallen the British mechanized patrols were reported to be in the neighbourhood of Derna, the little seaport which lies some 100 miles to the west along the coastal road.

MARSHAL GRAZIANI is here seen almost as bemedalled as Marshal Goering. In 1936 he succeeded Marshal Badoglio as Viceroy of Abyssinia, and in 1940 he followed Marshal Balbo as Governor and C.-in-C. in Libya.
Photo, Keystone

Derna is a town of considerable size—its population before the war was in the neighbourhood of 10,000 – but it had next to no defences other than the trenches left by the Arabs of years ago and what Nature has provided in a hilly and rugged countryside. Its garrison, too, was considerably smaller than that which had capitulated so easily at Tobruk. Only some 10,000 men were left in the place by Graziani to receive the onslaught of the Army of the Nile ; and to their credit be it said that they put up a far better show than their comrades in any of the battles of the preceding weeks.

For two or three days they contested a number of minor actions outside the town, thus giving time for many of the inhabitants to be evacuated, to Barce, 100 miles away on the road to Benghazi, and for most of the garrison to be successfully withdrawn to the west. Indeed, for the first time in the Libyan war the Italians launched a counter-attack on a considerable scale, representing a last desperate effort to halt the British advance into Cyrenaica, the really fertile portion of Libya where perhaps as many as 20,000 Italian settlers have their homes, their olive groves and fields of barley.

The counter-attack was speedily crushed, however, by British armoured units and Australian infantry, and the Italians were then driven behind a ridge where they dug themselves in beside their artillery. British forces closed in under heavy fire, while another detachment engaged the enemy at Siret el Chreiba, on the escarpment 10 miles to the south-west. Here again the Italians displayed altogether unusual powers of resistance, using 20 mm. guns mounted on lorries and medium tanks, while their aircraft, which for days had failed to put in an appearance, made dive-bombing and machine-gun attacks on the British forces.

For four days in severe weather and often in blinding sandstorms the artillery duel proceeded, while the infantry and tanks clashed in bitter fighting in the desert, but by January 29 the Imperial troops had made such good progress that they were looking

down on Derna, and on the next day they poured down the hillside and captured the town. There were no dramatic incidents such as had marked the fall of Tobruk and Sidi Barrani ; there was no zero hour, no swift encirclement of the place, no roaring barrage or heavy bombing by the R.A.F.; no spectacular bayonet charges. But first the outposts were captured by Australian and British troops, then the town itself was entered, and those of the garrison who had not made their withdrawal along the road to Barce held up their hands in surrender. The retreating troops were heavily strafed by the R.A.F. as they pressed through the mob of civilian refugees on the way to join what was left of Graziani's army.

Meanwhile, the main body of the Army of the Nile was streaming across the desert, making a short cut to Benghazi, the seat of the Italian administration of Cyrenaica. This, it was admitted, was now Wavell's main objective, but in view of the determined Italian resistance at Derna it was believed that there would be hard fighting before it could be captured.

With Benghazi in their hands the British would have completed the occupation of the most fertile portion of Mussolini's North African empire ; a few miles beyond the town the desert begins again, running for hundreds of miles before another comparatively fertile stretch opens near Tripoli.

DERNA, which was entered by Imperial troops on January 30, 1941, lies to the west of Tobruk. It is not a port of any value, but the little bay on which it stands provides a safe anchorage for small craft. The feature of most importance is its good water supply, which will solve a major difficulty confronting General Wavell's Army.
Photo, E.N.A.

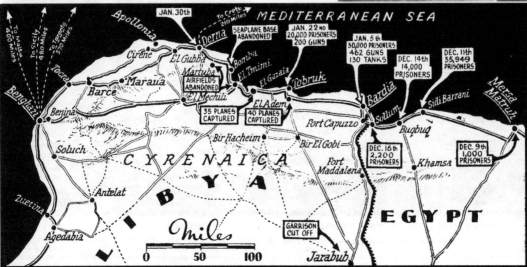

The successive stages of the advance of the Army of the Nile towards Benghazi is shown in the map left, together with the distances of various points on the coast of Libya from British and Italian bases. Double lines show the roads and dotted lines the desert tracks.

Map, " News Chronicle"

In Bardia, One-time 'Bastion of Fascism'

IMPERIAL TROOPS were in high fettle on the memorable January 5, 1941, when they entered Bardia and struck a staggering blow at Mussolini's vaunted African Empire. (1) Australian soldiers are walking very much at ease along a deserted road in the captured town. (2) The barrier across the Capuzzo-Bardia road is eloquent testimony to the eagerness of the troops, for it warns motorized units that this is the point where discretion becomes the better part of valour. Beyond they might run into an enemy barrage with the consequent useless waste of life. (3) Ample proof of their success was afforded the troops by such sights as this mass of Italian prisoners rounded up as in a huge desert corral, photographed from the air.

Photos, British Official: Crown Copyright

'Free France' Strikes at an Italian Outpost

MURZUK against which the Free French Camel Corps of the Chad made its remarkable raid covering four hundred miles, has this old fort to which the Italian troops withdrew when the French entered the town. Right is a map showing the line of the French advance from Chad. *Photo, E.N.A ; Map, courtesy of the " Daily Telegraph"*

After a flight over Bardia, these Australian Air Force pilots are discussing their experiences. An instance of the British superiority in the air was given by a Pilot Officer back from the battle of Sidi Barrani. "My Squadron," he said, "shot down 72 Italian machines. We lost six machines, but three of the pilots were saved." *Photo, British Official: Crown Copyright*

While these operations were proceeding on the Mediterranean coast, Free French forces 600 miles to the south-west made a daring attack on Murzuk, a town in the desert province of Fezzan, in south-west Libya, where the Italians have established an air base. The French force was dispatched from the Chad territory, and was composed of the Free French Camel Corps. During the day they took what cover presented itself, pushing forward on their swift-moving camels at night. The Italian garrison at

Murzuk, though 500 strong and so considerably more numerous than the attackers, were taken completely by surprise. They withdrew into the fort and allowed the French troops, consisting of soldiers from the Tibesti and Tuareg native tribes of the Sahara, under French officers and N.C.O.s, to work havoc in the aerodrome. All the aircraft on the ground were destroyed and the hangars and warehouses burnt. All day long the French carried on their work of destruction, unhindered by the enemy who watched unavailingly from behind the walls of the fort. Unfortunately, the leader of the daring exploit, Lieut.-Col. Colonna d'Ornano, was killed by a sniper's bullet ; he was honoured posthumously by General de Gaulle, Leader of Free France, with the cross of the " Ordre de la Libération." A very small number of the French were wounded, and they took back with them into Chad a score of Italian prisoners. Details of the raid, which took place some time in the middle of January, were given to the world by General Catroux on January 28.

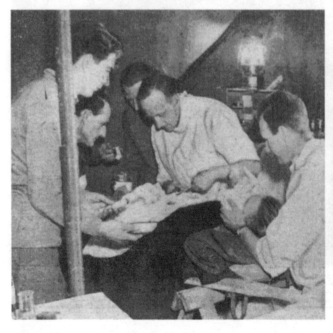

WOUNDED SOLDIERS on the Western Desert are sure of the best and speediest treatment. Above, ambulance men are picking up a stretcher case under shellfire. In a very short time the patient will be treated in a well-equipped hospital tent such as that illustrated in the photograph on the left, where an operation is in progress.

Photos, British Official: Crown Copyright

Bombs for the Italians in the Desert Battle

The R.A.F. is always on the look-out for Italians to bomb in the Libyan desert. This extraordinarily vivid photograph shows the actual bursting of a bomb dropped by a British aircraft among enemy troops. As the great missile came whizzing down the men threw themselves prone on the ground to avoid the blast, which at such close quarters—only 50 yards away—would be death-dealing. The machine-gunner on the left, however has stuck to his post and continues to work his gun.

Photo, Associated Press

Now the War is Carried into Eritrea

Only a few short months ago the Italians occupied British Somaliland and were believed to be about to attempt a drive against Khartoum. Now the situation has been completely reversed, however, and it is Italian East Africa which is invaded, not from one side but from several.

FOLLOWING the recapture of Kassala on January 18, a British army in the Sudan, under the command of Major-General W. Platt, crossed the frontier and invaded the Italian colony of Eritrea. It was largely composed of troops of the Indian Army, but it also included mechanized units which some six weeks before had played their part in the triumph of Sidi Barrani. Now they had been brought to this new front, 1,500 miles to the south, and the fact that General Wavell was able to release them was not the least encouraging sign in an encouraging phase of the war.

Two columns of Imperial troops invaded Eritrea, one making for Agordat, due east from Kassala, while the other had for its objective Barentu, some 50 miles to the south. At the same time other columns still farther to the south invaded Abyssinia, striking through Metemma in the direction of Gondar and Lake Tana. These moves coincided with yet other attacks made by the Imperial Army in East Africa (South Africans, Indians, and Rhodesians) under Major-General A. Cunningham, delivered in a northerly direction from the Kenya frontier. It was not long before it was reported that these troops were nearer Addis Ababa, the Abyssinian capital, than they were to their own headquarters in Nairobi.

General Platt's main drive was in the north, and within a fortnight the invaders were reported to be some 150 miles inside Italian territory—and this though the advance had to be made through difficult bush country and the Italians put up a strong, even fierce resistance. (Eritrea, it must be remembered, is the Italians' oldest and most highly developed colony in East Africa, and the Eritrean troops are in a very different category from the Libyan levies which have put up such a poor show in North Africa; the Eritrean Askaris, indeed, were the troops principally employed by the Italians in their conquest of Abyssinia.)

Much of the credit for General Platt's speedy advance was attributed to the Cape Mechanical Transport Companies, consisting of coloured volunteers and officered by Europeans, raised in the Union of South Africa shortly after the outbreak of war. These men showed remarkable skill in driving their vehicles through the rugged and largely roadless country, and also in maintaining them in a high state of efficiency.

The Italians were holding two strong lines—Keru to Aicota, and Biscia to Barentu —but after several days' fighting they were compelled to withdraw from both. Biscia, terminus of the railway from Massawa on the Red Sea, was reported captured by the British on January 26, and on February 1, Agordat, some 25 miles down the line and one of the most important Eritrean towns, was taken. Many hundreds of prisoners, with guns and mechanical transport, were captured, announced G.H.Q. Cairo. "Six Italian medium tanks, five light tanks, and 15 guns were also destroyed. The enemy sustained heavy casualties during our final attack which was carried out by British and Indian troops with Royal Air Force co-operation. Advanced elements of our forces closely pursued the enemy withdrawing towards Keren."

The road linking Barentu with Agordat was cut on January 31, and so the Italian defenders of the former town lost their

principal line of retreat—and that they would have to retreat was soon obvious. "In the Barentu area," announced G.H.Q. Cairo, in the same communique, "operations are developing well." Barentu, an important Italian base and airport, was reported to be defended by at least 7,000 and possibly 12,000 men. Imperial troops had arrived at

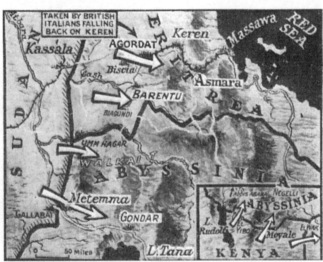

ITALIAN EAST AFRICA is now being invaded. The arrows in this contour map show the direction of the British advance into Eritrea, while the inset map shows the advance of South African forces from Kenya into Abyssinia. *By courtesy of the "Daily Telegraph"*

Aicota, 25 miles west of Barentu, on January 23, and proceeded to envelop the town in a pincers movement from north and west. The Special Correspondent of the "Daily Telegraph" was present during the operations which decided the town's fate.

"At the moment our medium artillery took up positions behind lorries which looked like vast removal vans," he said " an orange flash signal appeared for a split second a few feet in front of the squat snouts of our guns. Then, with a crash that echoed like a thunderstorm round the encircling hills, the medium and lighter guns opened up. Our troops moved up to the first objective as soon as the barrage lifted—a hill surmounted by a brown and white painted mission church. I heard the rattle of machine-gun fire, like coals tumbling out of infernal scuttles . . . next came occasional bursts of artillery as our gunners were told to blot out this or that outstanding enemy machine-gun post. So it went on until the sounds of battle died in the early morning when the Italians finally decided to retire."

On Feb. 2 Barentu was captured, the garrison escaping into the bush. Though the enemy put up a good resistance, the British and Indian casualties were extraordinarily low; in none of the battalions engaged did they exceed 10. In fact, the Italian troops failed to exploit their advance in the matter of ground and cover. An Indian officer who had had experience of fighting in the North-West Frontier, told the Correspondent that 50 Pathans could have held up the entire British brigade for a week, so absolute was the command given by the hillcrest trench positions of the defenders.

AGORDAT, the fall of which was announced on February 2, 1941, is an important town of Eritrea, as it is connected with Massawa, the colony's port on the Red Sea, by a railway running through Asmara, the capital. It lies about 90 miles from the frontier with the Sudan, and about the same distance from Massawa. *Photo, E.N.A.*

How the Germans Plan to Scale Our Cliffs!

A GERMAN INVASION OF BRITAIN would involve the attackers in tremendous difficulties, even supposing that sufficient of the invasion force survived after receiving the attention of the Navy and the R.A.F. to effect a landing, for not only men but guns, tanks, war material and supplies of every kind would have to be put ashore. This German photograph—which, like those in the next page, was received via America, and purports to show German troops rehearsing an invasion somewhere on the Continent—demonstrates the difficulty of hauling even a machine-gun up a few feet of rocky cliff. Moreover, during rehearsals, the Nazis have no opposition ; they would find the real thing much more complicated.

Photo, Exclusive to The War Illustrated

The Nazis Think the Invasion Will Be Like This

Left, a German soldier is hauling himself up the cliff side with the aid of a rope. Above, two members of a machine-gun team are making a climb that puts their gun temporarily out of action. Below, a landing-party is taking up a position among the rocks, evidently not an easy task even when there is no enemy about.

Photos, Exclusive to THE WAR ILLUSTRATED

THE unique photographs in this and the preceding page arrived in England through American sources. The German censor has allowed only the barest descriptions to accompany them, but they no doubt show rehearsals for the invasion of Britain. Somewhere in Germany or Norway stretches of coast have been selected to resemble points on the British shore at which a landing may be attempted. In the opposite page are just a few of the millions of men the invaders would meet in making their invasion attempt.

And So it Might Be—If it Were Not for These!

Our mobile army will move swiftly to any part of the country threatened by invasion. Motor-coaches now provide transport for the erstwhile "foot-slogger."

Nazi invaders will find themselves up against ubiquitous and well-armed motor-cyclists, like this man of the London Irish, who, with eyes protected by a visor, is eager to demonstrate the rate of fire of his sub machine-gun.

Photos, British Official: Crown Copyright; Fox and Keystone

THEY MET THE NAZI, these men of the Welsh Guards, at Arras and elsewhere, and know they are his match. They are now preparing for the next bout, should the enemy land on our coast. But first he will have to face the fire of guns like the 6-in. seen (right) in action at a West-coast battery.

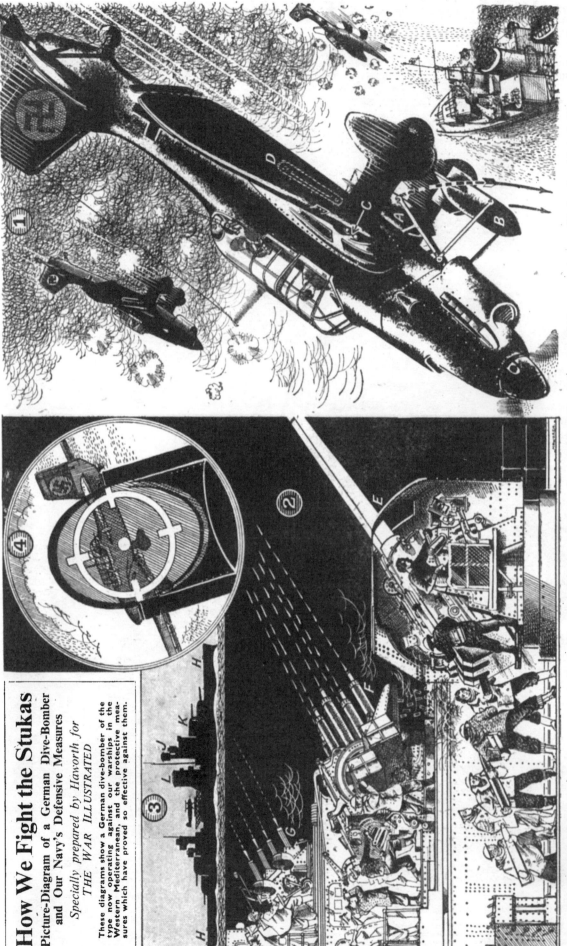

How We Fight the Stukas

Picture-Diagram of a German Dive-Bomber and Our Navy's Defensive Measures

Specially prepared by Haworth for
THE WAR ILLUSTRATED

These diagrams show a German dive-bomber of the type now operating against our warships in the Western Mediterranean, and the protective measures which have proved so effective against them.

JUNKERS JU.87 DIVE-BOMBERS, popularly known as "Stukas," are being used from Axis bases in Sicily against our naval craft in the Western Mediterranean.

The Ju.87 (Diagram 1) is an all metal two-seater, easily identified in front elevation by its cranked wings and sharp dihedral angle, and by its spatted non-retractable undercarriage legs. The main bomb-load —one 500 lb. or 1,000 lb. bomb (A)—is carried externally on two arms which at the end of the dive swing the released bomb (B) clear of the airscrew. Smaller bombs may be carried under each wing, but sometimes,

as in the Norwegian campaign, their place is taken by extra petrol tanks to increase the range.

Although powered by a Junkers Jumo 211 engine of 1,150 h.p., the whole craft is so heavily built to withstand diving strain that it is comparatively slow. In either wing is a machine-gun (C) and the observer-wireless operator has a rear-firing swivel-mounted m.g. The dive attack is normally made from about 10,000 feet and carried out almost vertically. To limit the diving speed so as to improve the aim, the Stuka is fitted with special air-brakes (D), metal strips under

the leading edge of the wings which are turned to oppose the air-stream, as the 'plane dives.

Long before the war experts realized the menace of air attack, and warships were provided with means of defence (Diagram 2). The twin 4-in. guns (E) tackle the approaching bomber while it is still at a great height, but should the pilot evade these he finds himself faced by a wall of fire from the 2-pdr. pom-poms (F)—nicknamed the "Chicago piano"—which cover a very wide area with their deadly fire. Against low-flying aircraft similar batteries of heavy machine-guns (G)

fill the air with lead. Diagram 3 shows the vulnerable points of a battleship attacked by dive-bombers : damage to lightly-armoured bow or stern (H) might reduce speed or impair manoeuvrability. (J) Control tower. (K) Main gun turrets. (L) A bomb down the funnel is a real nightmare to sailors.

Whenever ship-borne fighters such, for instance, as the Fairey Fulmar, are in the vicinity, the Ju.87, here seen through the modern reflection sighting apparatus (Diagram 4), will receive short shrift.

Many Fine New Ships for the Royal Navy

Rightly enough, a veil of secrecy shrouds the new ships which have been, or are being, added to Britain's Navy. Occasionally, however, the veil is lifted, as when we were shown H.M.S. King George V arriving in an American harbour, and many more of the ships mentioned below are no doubt in commission.

ALTHOUGH she has been in service for some time—for just how long has not been revealed—H.M.S. King George V made her debut before the world when she arrived at Annapolis, U.S.A., on January 24, with Lord Halifax, Britain's new Ambassador to the United States, on board.

H.M.S. King George V is one of five ships of her class, which together will form the first complete squadron of new capital ships to be added to the Royal Navy since the end of the Great War. With her sister ship, Prince of Wales, she was provided for in the Naval Estimates of 1936, and was laid down on January 1, 1937. The three other vessels, Duke of York, Jellicoe and Beatty, were also laid down in the same year—on May 5, July 20 and June 1 respectively, and it was stated at the time that all five ships would be completed in 1940 or 1941. They were actually launched in 1939 : King George V on February 21, Prince of Wales on May 3, Duke of York on September 16, and Jellicoe and Beatty on November 11.

Each of the ships displaces 35,000 tons. They are driven by Parsons geared turbines developing 130,000 horse-power, giving a speed of over 30 knots. They are oil-fuelled with two funnels.

As regards armament, they have a main battery of ten 14-inch guns mounted in two quadruple and one double turrets. It is stated that these 14-inch guns are built on a new model and have an effective range greater than the 15-inch mounted in earlier battleships. The 14-inch shell weighs only 1,500 pounds compared with the 2,000 pounds shell of the 16-inch gun, but it is claimed that its penetrative power is as great and its power of destruction very little below that of the larger shell. Moreover, the 14-inch gun fires nearly three rounds a minute, which is more than the 16-inch can do. Thus in practice it is anticipated that the weight of metal discharged from the King George V's ten 14-inch guns would practically equal that from, say, the Rodney's nine 16-inch. Then each ship carries as secondary armament a battery of sixteen 5·25-inch guns, weapons which have only recently been introduced into the Royal Navy, being first mounted in

cruisers of the Bonaventure class which were launched in 1939. They are also provided with a battery of 4·5-inch quick-firing guns, as well as a number of pom-poms and multiple machine-guns. No torpedo tubes are mounted, but there is accommodation for three aircraft. The fire control installation in each ship cost £213,000.

All the ships have been designed to meet intensive air attack, such as battleships of the last war never had to encounter. It has been stated that the weight of armour is over 14,000 tons, with a thickness at the water-line of 16 inches ; and the distribution of deck and side armour and the system of underwater protection also represent a marked advance beyond previous practice.

King George V and each of her consorts has cost about £8,000,000 ; she carries a complement of 1,500.

In addition to the ships of the King George V class, Britain has four other battleships under construction—the Lion,

Téméraire, and two others unnamed as yet of the same class. Their displacement will be about 40,000 tons, and their primary armament will be 16-inch guns. Then there are a number of cruisers in a more or less advanced stage of construction. Under the 1936-37 estimates provision was made for five cruisers of 5,450 tons (Dido, Euryalus, Naiad, Phoebe, Sirius) ; another five of 8,000 tons were provided for in the estimates of 1937-38 (Fiji, Kenya, Mauritius, Nigeria, Trinidad), and two of 5,450 tons (Bonaventure and Hermione) ; while under the 1938-39 estimates provision was made for four cruisers of 8,000 tons (Ceylon, Gambia, Jamaica and Uganda) and three of 5,450 tons (Charybdis, Cleopatra and Scylla). Under the 1939-40 estimates there are building or completing two more battleships of 40,000 tons, and four cruisers of 8,000 tons.

The construction of many other warships has been put in hand since the war, but naturally details have not been published.

H.M.S. KING GEORGE V. is seen, top, as she arrived in Chesapeake Bay on January 24, 1941, with Lord Halifax on board. The photograph was radioed from America. The lower photograph is the first to be released for publication.
Photos, British Official: Crown Copyright; Planet News

Canada 'Full Out' in the Air

In the last war Canada's greatest effort was made in the military field, and today her Army is the largest of the three services. But she has also a Navy of considerable size, while, as is told below, her effort in the air is already assuming tremendous proportions.

BEFORE the war the Royal Canadian Air Force had a permanent establishment of 635 officers and 5,500 airmen. Even by last November, however, it had increased to over 31,000 officers and men, and it gets larger every day. Squadrons of the R.C.A.F. have been serving in the United Kingdom for some time past, and more than 1,000 Canadians have enlisted in the R.A.F.

But although Canada is sending all available help eastwards across the Atlantic, she is by no means neglecting the security of her own seaboard. Both the Atlantic and the Pacific shores of the great Dominion are regularly patrolled by aircraft of the Canadian Air Force, which for this purpose is divided into two air commands, a Western and an Eastern.

The Western Air Command has under its close supervision the 600 miles of British Columbia coast ; including the inlets, fiords, and the thousand islands which fringe the coast, the shore line to be patrolled extends more than 6,000 miles.

Giant flying-boats and seaplanes fly hundreds of miles out over the Pacific on patrol duty or guarding convoys. The pilots selected for this work are specially trained at the seaplane training school at Jericho Beach. The training includes practice patrols over 400 or 500 miles of ocean, during which the men take part in anti-submarine operations and convoy protection, and are taught the methods of ship recognition and sea reconnaissance.

From the ice-bound waters of Newfoundland to the United States border a constant patrol is maintained by the aircraft of the Eastern Command of the R.C.A.F. They have to watch and guard the vital sea lanes between Canada and the British Isles ; and although for the most part their work is unseen, they rapidly make their presence

known to every ship which appears within 700 miles or so of the Canadian coast. Every convoy which puts to sea to England is protected by a squadron of the Eastern Command, and before the ships leave harbour the waters outside are subjected to a search from the air.

The aircraft used are mainly land 'planes, although they may have to spend a day at sea, at times, hundreds of miles from land. A report from a fishing boat of a suspicious-looking craft may entail a flight of thousands of miles. At the Command headquarters the pilots and observers are trained most carefully in the art of ship identification, and the men employed are well-seasoned fellows of long service, qualified naval officers, and gunnery and armament experts.

'Host' of the Empire's Airmen

Canada is the home, or, as Mr. Vincent Massey, Canada's High Commissioner for London, has put it, the host, of the great Empire Air Training Scheme—that plan which was first announced in the House of Commons by Sir Kingsley Wood on December 10, 1939, and is now far ahead of schedule. "The buildings and aerodromes which were due to be completed in 1941 were all finished last year," said Mr. Massey on January 22. "Instead of 33 training schools, scheduled to be operating last month, there are 48. The large number of officers and airmen in training at the end of the year exceeded by over a third the strength anticipated at that time."

Canada is bearing most of the initial cost, but will be reimbursed by Britain, Australia and New Zealand on the basis of the number of airmen trained. Most of the latter will be trained in Canada—the instructors coming for the most part from the United Kingdom —but contingents are arriving in Canada from Great Britain and the two Dominions. New Zealand gives elementary training to her men, but Australia provides both elementary and advanced training; in both cases, however, the finishing touches are given in Canada.

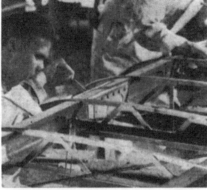

" Canada is now 'full out' in her war programme," said the Hon. Vincent Massey on January 22. Students from Canadian technical schools are here seen assembling wings.
Photo, Planet News

The Scheme in Canada has four commands, at Toronto, Winnipeg, Montreal, and Regina. Each command has an initial flying school and observers' school, and others for bombing, radio, gunnery, navigation and engineering. At Trenton, Ontario, is the central training school for flying, where instructors are turned out. When the Scheme is in full swing 4,000 aeroplanes, it is estimated, will be in constant use, and of these 1,282 are being manufactured in Canada except for the engines, and 593 in the United States. The aircraft are being standardized on six types of machines—the fleet trainers, the De Havilland Tiger Moth, the Avro Anson, the North American Harvard, the Fairey Battle, and the Noorduyn Norseman. When fully working the Empire Air Training Scheme will produce no fewer than 20,000 pilots and 3,000 air crews a year.

Not all the men Canada is training to win supremacy in the air for the British Commonwealth are British citizens. Just before Christmas Mr. L. Brockington, Counsellor to the War Committee of the Canadian Cabinet, told an audience of New York business men that 10,000 citizens of the U.S.A. had volunteered for training with the R.A.F. in Canada since last May, and that 2,520 of them had so far been accepted. "They have come," said Mr. Brockington, "to help us as volunteers of their own free will, from all over the country."

Air Marshal Sir Cyril Newall, passing through Ottawa at the end of January, 1941, said that "what we want in Britain are vast numbers of your highly-trained airmen." The response had already begun when he spoke, and below are some of the men trained in Canada under the Empire Air Training Scheme arriving at a British port. They are wearing their winter forage caps.
Photo, British Official : Crown Copyright

In the Home of the Empire Air Training Scheme

Canada is the home or host of the Empire Training Scheme now producing great results. Top, pilots in training at Borden, Canada, are marching past a line of Yale intermediate training 'planes after the presentation of wings to a group of non-commissioned pilots. Left centre, mechanics are at work assembling one of the Fairey Battle 'planes shipped from England for training purposes. Centre right, recruits are learning the working of an engine. Above, a class of ground wireless operators is drawn up at No. I Wireless School, Montreal.

Photos, Exclusive to THE WAR ILLUSTRATED

Behind an Actual Barrage of Bursting Shells

BRITAIN'S SOLDIERS are busily engaged in learning new ways of war, and Army training today incorporates many a lesson learnt in the light of recent campaigns abroad. The art of warfare is not static: new conceptions have arisen, exemplified by the Nazi "blitzkrieg." That we can learn to counter these methods and improve on them General Wavell has shown in North Africa, and the Home Army is only awaiting the opportunity of putting the new precepts into practice. One experience to which all troops have to get accustomed is shell fire. Although only

'n's New Army Develops the Offensive Spirit

a small proportion of Britain's huge new Army at home has actually received its "baptism of fire" on active service abroad, the remainder are now being trained under conditions as similar as possible to those experienced by the first B.E.F. Part of their field training is carried out under actual shell fire ; and above, infantry are seen advancing under cover of a heavy barrage. Our new Army is now battle-worthy and thanks to its training and indomitable spirit there is " no doubt whatever," as Mr. Churchill remarked at Portsmouth, " that we shall come through to triumph."

'Rat-Catching Terriers' on the U-Boat Trail

Much has been written of the "greyhounds of the Fleet," as the motor torpedo-boats, destroyers and light cruisers have all been called at one time or another. But now meet the "rat-catching terriers" of the Navy—the trawlers—the little ships that the U-boats most certainly do not like.

ALL around the coast of Britain, and way out into the stormy winter Atlantic, the trawlers are busy today—small, squat-looking craft, doing one of the biggest jobs of the present phase of the war. Every day, in all kinds of weather, you will find them sweeping the mines, hunting the U-boat and guarding the convoys which bring home Britain's bacon. On them falls much of the responsibility of seeing that the people of these Islands are fed, that the raw materials reach the war machine, and that British trade carries on.

By Necessity out of Fishing Fleet is the humble pedigree of the Anti-Submarine Trawlers, but to Britain today they are almost worth their weight in gold. Along all the sea lanes of the Empire plod these terriers of the sea, "sniffing" with their amazing super-hydrophones for the lurking U-boat, and when they find him, smashing at him relentlessly with their depth charges.

To the casual eye the anti-submarine trawler is much the same ship as she was in times of peace, when fish instead of U-boats were in the catch. But now there is a steel platform carrying the main gun forward, with light anti-aircraft guns aft and beside the bridge to fight off attacking 'planes; and, most important of all, the rows of depth charges right aft forming the sting in the tail which the U-boats have learned to fear. Below decks there are similar changes. Where once the cargoes of fish were stored there have been built the quarters for the officers and men and the fitting of the anti-submarine gear.

The crews, too, are changed. These small craft are now mainly commanded by lieutenants of the Royal Naval Reserve and Royal Naval Volunteer Reserve, some of them men who have come recently from the Merchant Service, but many of them men who "swallowed the anchor" years ago and started life anew on shore, or else have been yachtsmen who devoted their leisure hours in the years of peace to training themselves for the Navy in the R.N.V.R. These are the men with the wavy bands of gold braid on their sleeves. These trawler commanding officers are in turn training up to command their junior officers who come from all walks of life, but all with the common bond of the sea in their blood. In the ward-rooms of the trawler fleets are to be found officers who have been architects, journalists, engineers, advertising experts, business managers; men whose ages range from 19 to 40.

Here are youngsters who talk casually of the dive-bombers which strafed them in the Norwegian fiords or at Dunkirk, men already wise in the ways of the sea and confident in the exercise of authority and initiative. For it is in these small ships that initiative and the power of decision are at a premium. On the lower deck it is much the same story. Here, likewise, are men from the shore, though with a good leavening of men who were seamen and fishermen in the days of peace.

Hunting submarines is their job, and they like it. Their talk is constantly about past hunts and hunts to come, of U-boats which their ship has attacked and U-boats they are convinced they have sunk, even though

the imprimatur of the Admiralty experts, who study the evidence, may not have been placed on some of the victories claimed. Champion of the trawler fleet at present is a ship which has two U-boats to her credit; soon she may be seen sporting a couple of proud though, strictly speaking, unorthodox gold stars on her funnel.

Competition is keen. Every man is on his toes for that report from the upper bridge that a U-boat has been located, and the ship swings round to go into the attack. Up goes the flag which signals that a U-boat is in the trap. Round swing other trawlers, straining to be in at the kill.

Like terriers running eagerly round a rat hole they jockey for position and make their run in to drop their depth charges on the U-boat. Should such encouraging signs as oil and air bubbles rising to the surface

appear, there is as likely as not a terrific argument between the crews of the trawlers taking part in the attack as to who struck the probable deathblow.

Such is the hour for which these men of the trawler fleet live, though, for the main, their life is one of dull and hard hours, days and weeks of hunting or escort duty around the coasts of Britain or out into wide waters of the Atlantic.

Occasionally the monotony may be broken by a fine feat of rescue or salvage, should a U-boat slip through the cordon and strike home against a merchantman; or a bombing attack with the trawlermen standing to their light anti-aircraft guns and hoping that those German 'planes overhead will come low enough to collect a packet. Without much limelight and with little kudos, these sea-terriers are carrying on one of the most vital jobs of the day—and liking it.

HUNTING NAZI SUBMARINES and sweeping mines are among the tasks of many of the trawlers that in peacetime brought their catches of herrings to the East Coast ports. Above, a trawler is leaving port for patrol duty. Top right: the scene in the engine-room, the danger spot in any ship in wartime and, in one of these small craft, always very cramped quarters.   *Photos, Fox*

Overboard Goes a Present for the Enemy Below

DEPTH CHARGES are the deadly offensive weapons of the U-Boat hunting trawlers. Here one of the crew is standing by to release the charge after an enemy submarine has been located. When depth charges are dropped the utmost speed must be got out of the ship in order that it may get clear of the explosion. It is then that the men in the engine-room (see opposite) get more power out of their engines than they were ever meant to achieve.

Photo, 1 ov

After Fire Bombs Were Rained on Plymouth

There were many lucky escapes during the air raid on Plymouth on the night of January 13, 1941.　Above, the owner of a house stands in a hole made in the front room when a high explosive bomb dropped near by. He was in the room at the time but did not receive a scratch.

Plymouth school children, top right, are watching, not perhaps with unmixed feelings, workmen clearing debris from their bombed school. Below, some of the bombed-out children are being amused so as to keep their minds off their terrible experience.　　*Photos, L.N.A.*

This Is the Way to Deal With 'Incendiaries'

Sandbags on the kerb are now common objects in the streets of London. Here is one in a Westminster street ready for any passer-by to use if he spots an incendiary bomb.

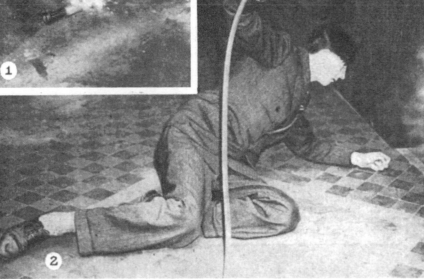

ALL able-bodied men who are not in the Forces, and boys too, may be called upon to deal with incendiary bombs. As with many ailments, so with incendiaries, the important point is that they should be "taken in time." Three of the photographs in this page show how to do it with sandbag or stirrup-pump.

(1) Approach a fire-bomb holding a half-filled sandbag to protect the face and body. When within reach throw the sandbag on the bomb. (2) This is how the nozzle of a stirrup-pump should be held to spray a bomb. Smoke can be avoided by keeping close to the ground. (3) If a fire has started in a room open the door gradually. Smoke and flame may rush out. Keep close to the ground; the air is fresher there.

Photos, Ministry of Information

Boy Scouts (left), trained as fire watchers and fighters, live up to their motto: "Be prepared." Above, a spotter Scout sounds the alarm on a dust-bin lid.

Photos, Keystone and Planet News

Their Bravery Has Not Gone Unrecognized

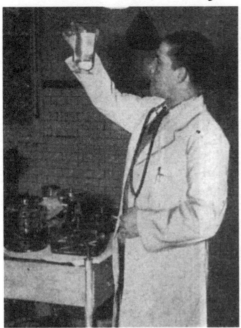

MISS C. McGOVERN

George Medal for devotion to duty when a heavy bomb hit the Royal Chest Hospital, London, while she was acting for the matron. Badly cut and injured by falling debris, Miss McGovern, altogether oblivious to her own wounds, continued to help in the removal of injured patients and staff. Then, supported by a police constable, she went through the ruined building to make certain that nobody had been left behind.

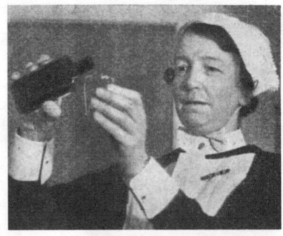

PETER DEREK WILLERINGHAUS

Mentioned in dispatches for gallantry under enemy action, is a 16-year-old member of the Home Guard. In October, 1940, Willeringhaus was carrying an important dispatch between the H.Q.s of two Home Guard units during an air raid, when a bomb fell about 10 yards from his motor-cycle, lifting machine and rider into the air. Despite wounds in the head, legs and hands, the young dispatch-rider delivered his message on foot before going to a first-aid post to have his wounds seen to.

DR. ANDRE BATHFIELD

George Medal for gallantry and devotion to duty when the Royal Chest Hospital, London, of which he is resident M.O., was bombed. The in-patient block was almost demolished, patients and staff being covered with debris; but though Dr. Bathfield had been badly cut and was bleeding profusely, he joined in the rescue work and refused to have his own injuries attended to until every injured person in the building had been treated and removed.

MISS EVELYN HARMER

O.B.E. (Civil Division) for staying at her switchboard and transmitting messages for three hours during a raid on Southampton, though fully aware that delayed-action bombs had fallen in the vicinity. One exploded within 100 yards of the office. Miss Harmer, who stated : " All I was concerned about was doing the job I had been asked to do," is only 16.

NORMAN TUNNA

George Cross for gallantry during a raid on the Liverpool port area. Tunna, a 32-year-old railway shunter, of Birkenhead, saw two incendiaries burning on an open wagonload of 250-lb. bombs, which were covered only by a waterproof sheet. With a total disregard of danger, he tore off the waterproof sheet and sprayed water over the bombs to cool them. Then he extinguished the incendiaries and removed them from the truck. " We really had no time to feel scared," he modestly explained, " because of the excitement."

Photos: "Daily Mirror," Associated Press, Planet News, Topical Press, Fox, G.P.U.

WILLIAM PENDLE

George Medal for devotion to duty when the Hospital for Sick Children, Gt. Ormond Street, London, was bombed. The explosion shattered the furnaces and burst gas and water mains. Pendle, who is the stoker, calmly proceeded to draw his fires, shut off steam, and made everything as safe as possible, although bombs were falling and water was swirling up to his waist.

At Dead of Night the Greeks Charged to Victory

Defeated in battle after battle in North Africa ; defeated in Eritrea, their oldest colony, and defeated, too, in the war of outposts on the Abyssinian frontier—the Italians continued to be defeated in that war zone where the bubble of their military reputation was pricked. Below we tell of some further remarkable successes by the Greeks on the Albanian front.

ATHENS was filled with sad faces on January 29, when the news spread through the streets and cafés that General Metaxas, Greece's Prime Minister, had died at 6.20 that morning. He had been indisposed, it transpired, for some weeks, but even when it was announced that he was about to have an operation for throat trouble, it was confidently expected that his strong constitution would carry him through. Indeed, only a few days before he died, he had a consultation in Athens with General Wavell, who found him apparently his old self.

So on a bitterly cold January day the streets of the Greek capital were lined with silent crowds and members of the Neolaia, the Metaxas youth movement, as the body of the old statesman was taken on a gun-carriage to lie in state at the cathedral. Metaxas was dead, but his fame will endure as the captain of Greece when the little country took the tremendous decision to stand up to Mussolini. A few hours after the Premier's death a successor was found in the person of M. Alexander Korizis, Governor of the National Bank of Greece and formerly Minister of Social Welfare in several of General Metaxas' cabinets. M. Korizis pledged himself to continue his old leader's policy of victory over the foreign aggressor and of social progress. The rest of General Metaxas' cabinet continued in office.

Both Rome and Berlin would have liked to believe that the death of the great Greek leader would have its repercussion in a slackening of Greece's fighting spirit. From Rome, indeed, there was broadcast the story that General Metaxas had died in the midst of a revolt of the infuriated Athenian population ! In fact, however, Greece was united as she had never been before in her history as a kingdom. Spokesmen of the

GENERAL METAXAS, Prime Minister of Greece since 1936, whose death on January 29 deprived his country of a great leader. M. Alexander Korizis (inset) succeeds him.

Axis renewed their suggestions that Greece might now seize the opportunity of seeking peace with Italy, but such suggestions were scouted amongst the Greeks themselves. Their war aim remained what it had always been—to remove completely the menace of Italian aggression. And that, indeed, was what the Greek troops were engaged in doing in the snowbound mountains of Albania.

In the belief that the death of Metaxas had dispirited the Greeks, General Cavallero, who had just succeeded the unsuccessful General Soddu as commander of the Italian army in Albania, launched a number of heavy counter-attacks in the central area of the front. "The Italian counter-attacks," said the war correspondent of the Greek newspaper "Estia," quoted by Reuter, "were very severe, being supported by huge reinforcements of troops, heavy artillery, large mortars and many tanks. The Greeks smashed them all, and then

This general map of Albania shows the various towns and villages mentioned in the communiqués telling of hard fighting near Tepelini. *By courtesy of " The Times "*

launched their counter-offensive. I followed this magnificent feat of arms and saw detachments climbing up those dangerous mountains in the dead of night, dragging their artillery with them up on to the seemingly unscalable peaks."

" One of the Greek attacks," went on the correspondent, " against a particular height was made before dawn in a fog, with snow falling heavily. The thunder of guns rolling into the night took the Italians completely by surprise, for they never imagined heavy artillery could have been hauled up so high and with such secrecy. The mist was transformed into a flaming cloud. Then our infantry charged with their resounding war cry through the fire of Italian mortars, and swept across every obstacle, carrying one height by storm and rushing on to the next. On the other side of the mountain fresh Greek detachments were coming up and threatening the rear of the enemy. The Italians then broke and ran in great confusion down the western slopes of the range, leaving in our hands 200 prisoners, guns, mortars, rifles and much valuable war material."

About the same time the Greek army scored another considerable success in the coastal area, where, as on the Tepelini front, the Italians threw their strong forces into a large-scale counter-attack. They received what was described as being the severest thrashing they had had since General Cavallero assumed command. Having suffered terrible losses—reported to be twenty to one as compared with the Greeks—they retreated in disorder, and were quite unable to re-form their broken ranks. After pursuing the enemy beyond their original positions the Greeks seized a line of peaks, 5,000 feet high, from which they dominated the whole area to the north.

WINTER IN ALBANIA has made the passes and roads extremely difficult for Greek transport. In spite of the heavy snow the Greeks have inexorably pushed on, and their latest gains have been achieved in the Klisura sector, where Italian counter-attacks have been crushed. These Greek women of the Epirus have swept the road free for their countrymen to advance.
Photos, British Official: Crown Copyright ; and Planet News

OUR SEARCHLIGHT ON THE WAR

Australia's Aircraft Proposals

A SCHEME is on foot in Australia to submit plans for transferring from the " old country " to the Commonwealth a large part of the plant for manufacturing aeroplanes. together with staff, workmen and perhaps the wives and families. The object of this transference would be threefold : (1) to prevent interruption of manufacture due to enemy activity ; (2) to relieve Britain of the problem of feeding workers in one of the great vital industries ; and (3) to enable Australia to produce many more varieties of aircraft, instead of the two or three to which she is at present limited. Were heavy long-range types produced, such as bombers and reconnaissance machines, they could be flown to the war area. Mr. Menzies, Prime Minister,

COUNT CIANO, Mussolini's son-in-law and Italy's Foreign Minister, is a Lieut-Colonel of the Italian Air Force. On January 27 Rome announced that he had resumed command of the " Disperata " (" Do or Die ") bomber unit. It was in command of this squadron that he gained a reputation for bombing Abyssinian natives.
Photo, Planet News

who sponsors the scheme, takes the view that the war is going to be a protracted affair, and that even if all aircraft factories were transferred to Australia, the Empire output would, in the long run, be enormously augmented.

Diamond Smuggling Up-to-Date

B RAZIL is the setting for the large-scale activities of a diamond-running organization said to be directed by the German ambassador, Herr Kurt Pruefer. The British ambassador, Sir Geoffrey Knox, is reported to have made representations to the Brazilian Government to the effect that Nazi agents are paying very high prices for the entire output of the diamond mines, and Pruefer is causing the stones to be smuggled out of the country in the German diplomatic bag, which is then flown to Rome in Italian 'planes of the Lati service, and thence reaches Germany. It has been stated that were Germany prevented from cornering the Brazilian market— South African supplies are naturally cut off— the Nazi war machine would come to a stop in a matter of a few months. The British Ministry of Economic Warfare has long been aware of the illegal traffic and is said to have the matter well in hand.

Measure to Prevent Speculation

L ORD REITH, Minister of Works and Buildings, has taken the wise and far-seeing precaution of setting up a committee of experts, headed by Mr. Justice Uthwatt, whose job it will be to examine the question of compensation for sites in bombed areas. The intention is to prevent post-war reconstruction being hampered or held up by land speculation, and the Committee will make it a matter of urgency to advise upon steps to be taken perhaps immediately, at any rate before the end of the war. From the Minister's statement to the House of Lords it would appear that unscrupulous speculators have already been at work buying up bombed land in order to re-sell later at a large profit to themselves, and so to penalize still further an already suffering community.

Rioting Reported in Italy

U NCONFIRMED reports of disturbances in Milan, Turin and other towns of Northern Italy were first sent out from Belgrade on January 26. German soldiers, it was said, were being forced to patrol the streets to prevent or suppress demonstrations. According to one report three Italian officers had been shot by these troops, and there were many other dead and hundreds wounded. Agents of the Gestapo were supposed to have seized the Post Office, telephone and telegraph buildings at Milan, as well as similar important centres in other cities. On January 28 serious rioting was reported from Trieste, following anti-Fascist and anti-German demonstrations made by factory workers. Travellers who reached Yugoslavia gave accounts of fights between strikers at the Lloyd Triestino workshops and Fascist militia, the workers shouting " Down with Germany ! Down with the war ! " One who guyed Mussolini in speech and attitude was shot by a soldier, who himself was promptly lynched by the infuriated workers. Thereupon the soldiers fired upon the crowd, and there were hundreds of casualties and arrests.

Britain Will Win, says America

C OLONEL LINDBERGH's implied conviction that Britain cannot defeat Germany, and that anyhow it would be better if neither side won, has roused a storm of protest from Americans both on the far side of the Atlantic and elsewhere. Mr. Thomas W. Lamont, famous New York banker, derides Nazi invincibility. " I am impatient with all this talk that Great Britain at best can never defeat Germany," he told the Merchants' Association. " I say that Germany can be beaten, that she is being beaten, and that she will be beaten." Admiral Leahy, United States ambassador to France, addressed American Press representatives at Vichy in the following terms : " I have noted that a certain Belgian newspaper published a statement to the effect that the American ambassador to France is of the opinion that the British will be defeated in the present war. In the interests of truth and accuracy, I should like to take this opportunity to say that the aforesaid Belgian report is completely false. My personal opinion is that the British Government can and will prosecute the present war to a successful conclusion." Mr. Henry Stimson, U.S. Secretary for War, declared before the Senate Foreign Relations Committee on January 29. that the probability of victory for Great Britain would be " overwhelming " if she were able to withstand the crisis of the spring and summer of 1941. General George Marshall, U.S. Chief of Staff,. expressed his firm belief that Great Britain can and will withstand it.

American 'Live Wire' in London

M R. WENDELL WILLKIE, unsuccessful candidate for the American Presidency, arrived in London on January 16 on a visit to " find out for himself." He declined to answer any questions or to discuss the relations of America and Britain. " I have come over to look and not to talk, and I have not had an opportunity of looking

MR. WENDELL WILLKIE arrived in this country on January 26 for a personal investigation of wartime Britain. He is seen at the Home Office preparing for a visit to London shelters during a night raid. " I have come to get all the information I can," Mr. Willkie declared.
Photo, " Daily Herald "

yet," he said. Since that day Mr. Willkie has had a very busy time " looking " and meeting Britain's most prominent leaders of thought and action. On his first day, January 27, he visited the Ministry of Information, had an interview with Mr. Anthony Eden, toured the City, lunched with the Prime Minister, had a long talk with Mr. Bevin at the Ministry of Labour, and dined with Lord and Lady Stamp. Since then he has experienced his first air raid, visited the Bank of England and had a talk with Mr. Montagu Norman, listened to debates in the House of Commons, called on Cardinal Hinsley, made a tour of London's shelters, attended a meeting of the T.U.C., and met a number of Ministers and General Sikorski. Mr. Willkie was received by King George after visiting some of the provincial centres and Eire—and so home to America to tell them how Britain is facing critical days.

We Flew Round Padua's Spires & Chimneys

On January 12, 1941, a "small force" of aircraft of the Bomber Command was dispatched to bomb the oil refineries at Porto Marghera, near Venice. The Wing Commander who led the attack brought back a remarkable story of low-level flying over enemy territory, which we give below in his own words.

BY the time we got to the Alps the valleys were just beginning to fill with fog, but the peaks stood out in the moonlight as clear as though it were day. The plains of Lombardy also were covered by fog. Then as we neared the Adriatic coast the fog disappeared, and when we got to Venice it was again like day.

I had more or less made up my mind all along to go down low, and the moment we got over the Alps I had started losing height. Over Venice we circled round to draw their fire and see how much there was. They had quite a. lot of light stuff. Some of it was getting pretty accurate towards the end. Having seen how much there was I decided to go right down. We flew over Mestre, whistling among the chimneys. There was a sort of fort or citadel outside Mestre, and two sentries standing on the ramparts had a crack at us. We could see them standing up with levelled rifles. I had given orders to the front and rear gunners that they were to fire back at anybody who fired at us, and they opened up on the sentries.

The time now was round about 2 a.m., yet it was so light that one could see people in the street. I heaved the aircraft over a couple of factory chimney stacks; then we started to climb to do the bombing. We went up to 700 feet. We were carrying one of our heaviest bombs; and when it burst it very nearly blew us out of the air. The bomb landed either on or beside a large building with a lot of pipes all round it. There was a colossal belt of smoke and flame which shot up almost level with the aircraft. The smoke died away, but the flames persisted. Then there were a couple of great explosions. We went round again and dropped the other bomb in the middle of the flame, adding to it by half as much again.

I knew of an aerodrome about 20 miles away at Padua, so we went whistling along the railway tracks at about "nought" feet to find it. We passed three trains on the way. We were flying right alongside them.

We flew over Padua itself, again doing tight turns round the chimneys and church spires, and having dropped our leaflets there we flew on to Padua Aerodrome, where the front and rear gunners let fly, left, right, and centre at the hangars.

We streaked across the aerodrome at 20 ft. We could see there were no aircraft dispersed around the aerodrome, so we assumed that they were in the hangars.

Immediately we came on to the scene the aerodrome defences opened up on us. Tracer was flying alongside almost parallel with us. I was dodging behind the trees to get cover.

I had wanted to have a crack at another aerodrome, but there was not much time left and we'd got the Alps to cross again, so we left it at that and came away.

I hadn't given any instructions to the others in my squadron about going down low, but I had dropped a few hints, and they all went down over the Porto Marghera.

One of them made three bombing runs, the first at 9,000 ft. But he got tired of that and came down to 1,500, and on the third run he was down to 1,000. He said that he was using the smoke from fires already burning as cover from the ground defences.

He got direct hits on a refinery building, and one of his crew said that the whole place seemed to go up in smoke. They were so low that the smoke got inside the aircraft and made some of them splutter.

Altogether, we reckoned it was worth going almost 1,500 miles to do the job.

Nineteen of My Men Died of Exposure

The conferment of the O.B.E. on Capt. R. G. Hammett and the award of the George Medal to his second officer, Mr. E. L. Barnes, announced on January 7, 1941, were in recognition of their "high courage and endurance" after their ship had been torpedoed and sunk in the Atlantic. Capt. Hammett's own story is given below.

WHEN the announcement of his award was made Capt. Hammett was still recovering from his ordeal of thirteen days' sailing in an open boat. He said:

The Germans torpedoed us and then put twelve shells into us.

One boat, an open eighteen-footer with sail, was left for the twenty-nine of us. I reckoned we had to cover about 150 miles to land. I had sent out an S O S before the ship sank, but there was no reply. So we could only sail for it.

I had seen that there was plenty of food. The water would have been enough for the normal number the boat should have carried, but I had extra men and the supply ran short.

For the first five days we had to live "on our constitutions," the water just serving to moisten our lips and tongues.

Then we ran into a gale which continued for the rest of the trip. We got waterlogged, and during the whole time everybody was wet through.

Altogether nineteen of my men died. They had died from exposure and lack of water.

For the whole trip I had just to let the boat go with the wind, and I reckon the distance we covered in those thirteen and a half days was about 1,300 miles.

When we reached shore we still had on board 28 lb. of biscuits, a 7 lb. tin of beef, and six tins out of twenty-six tins of condensed milk. We had used the milk to eke out the water. Every day I used to get the men to take a lick from a wooden spoon.

Two days after we were torpedoed we sighted a steamer, but she took no notice of us. Then, after nine days, when we were all feeling pretty down, another steamer passed quite close, but did not see us.

On the twelfth day I made land early in the morning, after lying to in a gale. All went to take a pull at the oars, but we were too weak, and I lost sight of the land.

But on the thirteenth day I made it again, and we at last beached at a little place called Northton in the Hebrides. Crofters found us and took care of us.

I can't describe the fortitude of my men. They were a fine lot.—"*Sunday Express*"

PADUA, twenty-two miles west of Venice, was recently "visited" by the R.A.F. when the aerodrome was attacked and leaflets dropped on the city. An account of the flight is given in this page. Taken from the Observatory, this view of the city shows the Cathedral on the right. Padua has a population of over 100,000.   *Photo. E.N.A.*

My Nightmare Climb near Tepelini

Difficulties of terrain and weather in the mountainous Greek front line above Tepelini would seem to make fighting almost impossible. The feats performed daily by muleteers and ambulance parties serving the troops are described in the following dispatch by Ronald Monson, of the Australian Consolidated Press.

AFTER arriving in the foothills above Tepelini via the valley road from Argyrokastro I rode a captured Italian motor-cycle over a shell-torn road to a point where further progress was impossible and then procured a mule and rode with a supply train up the mountain side in darkness.

The way was soon so steep I had to dismount and urge the mule upwards. Fifty other muleteers in single file ahead strove throughout the night to assist their burdened beasts up the backbreaking slopes which at times seemed almost sheer walls of rock.

Intense cold sleet and Italian shells screaming overhead did not make the job easier. But the Greek muleteers, seemingly untiring, did not pause for breath that long night, and I had to toil along lest I should be left behind. The rate of the climb was phenomenal and my lungs seemed as if they would burst. Even the sides of the mules were heaving like bellows before we were halfway.

We reached a rough track after climbing over rocks, and we followed this upward for a 200-foot rock wall. When we got to the top I saw dark shapes preparing to climb down the way we had come. They were stretcher-bearers carrying wounded. They had been carrying wounded from the snow-line since the previous day and were now preparing to go down into the valley.

We loaded off at a deserted Albanian village on top of that mountain, which just reached the snowline. Next morning we reloaded fresh mules and our real job began —a climb up through the snow. The path was now even steeper. Snow was falling steadily ; a cold wind was blowing.

At 5,000 feet a blizzard struck us. Our greatcoats became sheets of ice ; our eyebrows, weighted down with snow, froze to our eyelids. Hands and feet were numb. Still the awful climb continued.

For hours we went on through the awesome cloud wrack from which the merging snow created a phantom world, wherein only the sting of driving sleet in the eyes and aching muscles seemed real. Another 500 feet and we reached the artillery positions. A little farther on was a line of tiny tents just showing above the snow. We had reached the front line.

Greeks Carried Me over the Mountains

Onlookers who saw a British bomber in flames over the Italian lines in Southern Albania gave up the entire crew as lost, but twelve days later the pilot and observer turned up at their base. Here we give the story in the words of the pilot, a 23-year-old Flight Lieutenant.

SITTING up in bed, his leg and arm in splints, the Flight Lieutenant said :

"We had dropped our bombs and then Italian fighters were after us. A Macchi 200 got a good burst in and suddenly the fuselage between the cockpit and the air-

IN SOUTHERN ALBANIA few roads are now as passable as this, but the untiring Greek muleteers can get supplies up the trackless mountain-sides even in darkness.
Photo. Sport & General

hours. Occasionally we stumbled over a dead mule which had fallen in one of the earlier trips and lay across the path. One of our mules fell dead from exhaustion. We divided its load among the others.

Finally the nightmare was ended by climbing what seemed in the darkness to be

gunner's turret burst into a blazing furnace. I told the crew to jump out, but the air-gunner must have been killed, for his gun had stopped and I could get no reply from him.

The observer climbed out first, and was gone, but the hatch on my side stuck, so I moved over to follow the observer. Jolly

fortunate I did so, for just as I was squeezing through to the hatch, an enemy fighter let another burst into our aircraft, this time destroying my seat and the instrument panel.

When I did bale out part of my parachute harness, which I discovered afterwards had been nicked by a bullet, caught round my leg, and as the parachute opened it jerked my leg up behind my neck and broke the leg just above the knee.

I was not in too good a shape because previously I had received a bullet through the elbow. Even while I was sailing down an Italian fighter came after me and put 20 bullets through my parachute—we counted the holes later. Because of the punctured parachute and broken harness I landed pretty heavily. My observer came down at a village farther away in the valley. I lay down on the ground for about half an hour. Then Greek soldiers found me—we had landed just inside the Greek lines.

Soldiers bandaged me up as best they could ; then they found a stretcher. They were absolutely splendid. For four days they carried me cheerfully over the mountains, often through deep snow and along narrow mountain tracks with precipitous edges. Looking over one side of my stretcher I saw nothing but a horrifying chasm. Yet they were surefooted and never slipped or slithered about.

At last we reached Koritza ; then on to Florina, where my leg and arm were put into splints, and my observer, who was O.K. except for burns, was attended to.

R.A.F. IN GREECE are giving the Greek Army substantial help by bombing the Italian bases in Albania. This bomber crew is just going to take off on another raid
Photo. British Official: Crown Copyright

What had *They* to do with 'Peace and Goodwill'?

ADOLF HITLER spent Christmas with Hess, his deputy, and von Brauchitsch, Commander-in-Chief, inspecting the army in the West. On Christmas Eve he was amongst the soldiers and labourers at a coastal defence station where Dr. Todt, constructor of the Siegfried Line, was superintending the installation of more heavy batteries. Here Hitler and Todt are seen dining in the mess-room of the unit.

BENITO MUSSOLINI began his Christmas celebrations on December 22, 1940, by distributing money prizes to Italian mothers of large families at the Palazzo Venezia, his luxurious home in Rome. He is seen above handing the awards to the women. Previous to the ceremony, the recipients had been marched past the tomb of Italy's Unknown Warrior—which may have reminded some of the purpose for which Mussolini needs more young Italians. Both the photographs in this page arrived in London via the United States and were over a month on the journey.

Photos, Associated Press

The Belgians Here are a 'Happy Band of Brothers'

Here is another article from the pen of Henry Baerlein, one of a series he is contributing to our pages on the subject of Allied troops now in Britain. This time he writes of the Belgians and reports some of the stories told him by Belgian refugees who have escaped here from Hitler-ridden Europe.

AFTER days of heroic resistance against overwhelming numbers and machines, the Belgian army was ordered by King Leopold. to cease fighting and lay down its arms. Many Belgians, however, managed to escape to Britain with a view to continuing the war, although the Nazi propagandists worked overtime in trying to impress upon such folk that if they succeeded they would not merely starve, but arrive just in time to see Hitler's triumphal entry.

It was no easy matter for Belgian soldiers to make their way to these shores, yet hundreds of them have arrived and many more from all over the world are on the way. Those in groups A and B came back with the assistance of Belgian consuls as soon as France was at war with Germany : those in groups C and D came when the danger to Belgium was more imminent, and those in group E when general mobilization, which now prevails, was declared. The " lettre de service," as it is called, of an officer enables him to return with the least delay, as his services are the more valuable. In a visit the other day to the Belgian troops over here I found them extremely well organized, and quite ready to make the best use of all their compatriots who will now be joining them.

Comradeship in Exile

Fully re-armed and equipped for the war, the morale of the Belgians is remarkably high. An excellent spirit of comradeship is found among them—Walloon and Fleming, Conservative, Liberal, and Socialist, young and elderly men, they are united in the resolve to liberate their country and their king. Some who are in this country will never fight again on account of their wounds, but these are being absorbed into war work of other kinds ; many of them, experts in wireless or in electrical trades, are giving perfect satisfaction with the R.A.F. or in aeroplane factories. And when the Belgian air force is large enough to have squadrons of its own it is hoped that some of these skilled artisans will be released for service with their countrymen.

One has heard little of the Belgian airmen ; the French were almost as determined as the Germans to prevent them bringing their 'planes over here, but a certain number of fighter pilots managed to get through, and some of these have scored notable successes. Among these we may mention Lieutenant Philippart, who came to England before Belgium was in the war for training as an instructor ; he brought down six German 'planes in a single day before he was killed. A good many young men will soon have finished their training, and students who were not old enough for the army at home are asking to be enrolled in the air force.

One of the best of the Allied newspapers now being published here is that of the Belgian troops. It is called " Vers l'Avenir " (Towards the Future), and there is, of course, an identical edition printed in Flemish. It contains the latest news brought out of Belgium, interesting political articles, and domestic items of interest to the troops, and there is no lack of humour, sardonic and

otherwise. " We are," it says, " a happy band of brothers and there are still a few vacancies." In calling upon all Belgians to join the army in Britain, it recommends those who cannot make up their minds to stay at home and join them after the victory. There is an announcement of a new secret Italian 'plane which moves silently at a tremendous rate ; it is manned by a pilot, an observer, a gunner and twenty men, for the purpose of dropping parachutists behind the enemy's lines. One man is the parachutist ; it is the duty of the other nineteen to push him out !

BELGIUM IN BRITAIN is symbolized by this Belgian soldier mounting guard at a Catholic church when General van Strydonck, commanding the Free Belgian Forces, attended Mass.
Photo, Keystone

As one associated with these Belgians, one is told, very modestly and humorously, of the obstacles they had to overcome on their way to England. Two brothers, of whom one had served in the army for about a year, dressed themselves as boy scouts and got over the frontier into France with the help of the father of a friend of theirs who, being a professional smuggler, was well acquainted with the secondary roads. They cycled through occupied and unoccupied France with innumerable adventures on the way, sold their machines before entering Spain, and when they were being taken to a concentration camp in that country they managed to mingle with a crowd of Spanish refugees arriving from France. For eight days they were concealed by some kind women at Valencia, and, becoming engaged in an altercation with a

Portuguese police-official, near Badajos, one of our friends thought it would be a good plan to box his ears and be lodged in prison, as they would then have the right to get into touch with a Belgian consul. The Portuguese pushed them back into Spain, and there—the Spanish and Portuguese appearing anxious to annoy each other—the two refugees were given the option of three months in prison or getting back into Portugal within two hours. They chose the latter alternative, and were shown by the Spaniards how they could go by unfrequented paths. In Lisbon they were lodged at the British Club, and all was well.

How they Eluded the Nazis

One who in civilian life is a magistrate and who was helped on his way by false documents, almost fell a victim to the German Gestapo in Madrid, where, as elsewhere in Spain, they collaborate, of course in mufti, with the local police. But the children of the hotel proprietor had been generously treated in Belgium during the Spanish civil war ; he helped the magistrate to escape by 'plane.

Then there is the tale of a sergeant who with two friends constructed a raft near the mouth of the river Somme. With his beautiful sheep-dog they embarked, and for six days, in rough seas and with scarcely any food, they suffered a great deal. The dog was in a worse plight than the men, so that the sergeant was forced at last to shoot him. He turned away and wept when the two others started to eat the dog. Then the raft began to disintegrate, and they repaired it as best they could with six handkerchiefs. More dead than alive they drifted over to England, their sail a curtain and army shovels their only oars.

My last story shall be that of a monk who, being an artillery officer of the reserve, is now once more a gunner. As second-in-command of a battery he took part in continuous and desperate fighting, and not one shell was left with which to blow up the guns. (By the way, on the night before Belgium's collapse all the regimental flags were collected and burned.) The former monk made use of his wits in having his papers and those of fifty others stamped as being demobilized. He stayed for a while in Brussels, where the German soldiers made up for what they had previously lacked by acquiring underclothes and eating quantities of butter unaccompanied by bread. They had orders to be polite, so that the Belgians—vain hope !—should become reconciled to being for evermore in Germany's Lebensraum.

'Nothing against the Belgians'!

The Germans explained that they had nothing against the Belgians, and they regretted having been obliged to kill so many thousands of refugees on the roads ; it was Belgium's misfortune, they said, to be in Germany's way—they were geographical victims. When the monk set out in a car to travel through France, he found the general morale so bad that by giving a good dinner to a man in charge of a petrol store he could usually obtain as much petrol as he wanted, while tires were offered to him at half-price.

On the other hand, the latest news of the morale of the people in Belgium is excellent.

'Gallant Little Belgium' Lives Again in Britain

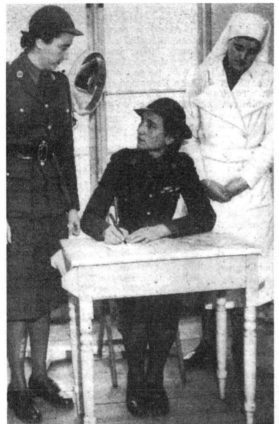

FREE BELGIANS are our allies still, and a considerable force of them are in training in the United Kingdom. Above, a British officer standing between two Belgian N.C.O.s bears witness to the alliance.

Left, a Belgian woman doctor, who wears the medals she won in the last war, is giving instructions to members of her staff. She is with the Belgian troops training in the Western Command.

General van Strydonck, who is in command of the Free Belgian Forces in Britain, is here seen inspecting a parade of light tanks "somewhere in the Western Command." All able-bodied Belgians of military age beyond Hitler's clutches were called up to serve with the Belgian Army in Britain on December 14, 1940.

Photos, Keystone

OUR DIARY OF THE WAR

TUESDAY, JAN. 28, 1941   *514th day*
On the Sea—Admiralty announced that H.M. submarine Triton was overdue and must be considered lost.

In the Air—During night of 27-28 R.A.F. bombers carried out heavy raid on Capodichino (Naples) aerodrome. Railway junction and marshalling yard at Naples were also attacked. Catania aerodrome and Comiso raided same night.

War against Italy—Concentration of British forces on Derna area continuing. Fighter patrols supported advancing troops.

In Eritrea operations progressed in Agordat-Barentu area and mobile troops continued to press Italian forces retreating from Umm Hagar. Prisoners now totalled 1,200.

Cairo announced that a Free French force from Chad territory had advanced 400 miles and raided Murzuk in south-west Libya.

Home Front—During day enemy aircraft dropped bombs through clouds in Eastern Counties and over South-east England. Incendiaries and several high explosives fell in London area.

Greek War—Athens announced capture of enemy positions and more prisoners and material.

WEDNESDAY, JAN. 29   *515th day*
In the Air—R.A.F. made night attacks on Wilhelmshaven and elsewhere in Germany.

War against Italy—Pressure on enemy forces in Derna area increasing.

Operations in Agordat-Barentu sector developing. Enemy in retreat from Umm Hagar and being closely pursued.

Vigorous patrol activity across frontier on Italian Somaliland.

Home Front—Three bombs dropped in Thames Estuary district in daylight. In early evening bombs fell on a town in the north-east and on one in the west.

Night raiders attacked London first time for 10 nights. Flares and fire bombs were dropped, but were quickly put out. High explosives also fell. Scores of incendiaries showered over an East Anglian district, and heavy bombs on a south-east town and one in Thames Estuary.

Greek War—Athens reported that during last 24 hours Italians continued desperate efforts to initiate offensive, but all attacks were repulsed with heavy enemy losses.

General—General Metaxas, Prime Minister of Greece, died. M. Alexander Korizis, Governor of National Bank of Greece, was appointed his successor.

THURSDAY, JAN. 30   *516th day*
War against Italy—Derna captured by Imperial forces after sharp fighting. R.A.F. made heavy attacks on aerodrome at Barce.

In Eritrea concentration of British forces in Agordat - Barentu sector proceeded smoothly.

R.A.F. bombed bridge on Mega-Neghelli road. In Moyale area dive attacks were made on Italian artillery and infantry positions.

Home Front—During day single enemy aircraft dropped bombs in London area and in parts of S.E. England, East Anglia and East Midlands. No night raids.

German bomber shot down by fighters near Clacton-on-Sea.

German fighters made concentrated attack on Dover balloon barrage.

Greek War—Athens reported limited but successful activity at the front. Enemy still endeavouring to launch counter-offensive.

FRIDAY, JAN. 31   *517th day*
War against Italy—Italians trying to stop British advance west of Derna towards Apollonia and Benghazi.

In Eritrea pressure continued towards Agordat and Barentu. Some British patrols penetrated 40 miles into Italian Somaliland.

R.A.F. carried out heavy night raid on docks at Tripoli ; one ship set on fire, two others damaged.

Aerodrome at Barce again heavily raided.

R.A.F. fighters destroyed three aircraft on ground at Teramni, Italian East Africa.

Home Front—During day single enemy aircraft dropped bombs through clouds on several points in London area and few places in Southern and Eastern England. Three London hospitals hit by high explosives. Slight activity at night, but no bombs fell.

Two German bombers destroyed, one off Cornwall, the other at Plumpton, Sussex.

Greek War—Athens announced successful local operations. Some enemy positions taken and about 200 prisoners captured. R.A.F. bombed Dukaj, 7 miles north-west of Tepelini.

SATURDAY, FEB. 1   *518th day*
In the Air—Coastal Command aircraft made night attack on docks at Brest.

War against Italy—British troops maintained offensive west of Derna.

Agordat, Eritrea, was captured, with many hundreds of prisoners, guns and tanks. By dusk advanced elements were in pursuit of enemy towards Keren.

R.A.F. bombed number of targets in Italian East Africa.

Two enemy aircraft shot down over Malta.

Home Front—Bombs fell during day in East Anglia, causing slight damage and some casualties. No night raids.

Greek War—Entire Tepelini area reported to be under Greek domination. Italians retreating down road to Valona. North of Klisura Greeks still retained initiative. In central sector height of 5,700 feet was captured. Valona bombed and machine-gunned by R.A.F.

SUNDAY, FEB. 2   *519th day*
On the Sea—Announced that Greek submarine Papanikolis had torpedoed large enemy transport off Brindisi on night of Jan. 28-29.

In the Air—Shortly before dawn R.A.F. bombed docks at Boulogne and Ostend. During daylight large formations of fighters and bombers carried out offensive sweeps over Straits of Dover and enemy-occupied territory. Three enemy fighters destroyed.

Other attacks made by Coastal Command on aerodromes at Ostend and Berck.

War against Italy—Concentration of forces in area west of Derna proceeding.

In Barentu sector operations developing well. Farther south Biacundi was captured.

In Abyssinia enemy in full retreat on Metemma-Gondar road.

Enemy falling back before pressure of British patrols in Italian Somaliland.

R.A.F. fighters and bombers very active between Derna and Benghazi.

Naval Swordfish aircraft carried out successful attack on power plant in Sardinia.

Home Front—Slight enemy activity over Eastern England. Bombs fell in few places in East Anglia and Kent.

Greek War—Athens reported further local successes. More territory was occupied, and 260 prisoners taken much war material.

MONDAY, FEB. 3   *520th day*
On the Sea—Admiralty announced that German aircraft had bombed ship containing Italian war prisoners, causing many casualties.

In the Air—R.A.F. bombed Brest docks and other targets before dawn.

War against Italy—Advanced elements captured Cyrene, west of Derna.

British troops captured Barentu, Eritrea. Mechanized forces continued to press upon Italians retreating towards Keren.

In Abyssinia pursuit of enemy forces towards Gondar continued.

South African forces occupied two Italian frontier posts on Dukana front, 10 miles inside Abyssinian border.

On night of 2-3 R.A.F. bombed Castel Benito aerodrome of Tripoli, and surrounding districts.

R.A.F. bombers raided Berka aerodrome and Barce. Fighters made machine-gun attacks on troops between Slonta and Tecnis.

S. African bombers attacked Gobwen aerodrome, near Kismayu, destroying 5 aircraft.

Home Front—Single aircraft made number of daylight raids over East and South-east coast. Bombs fell in London area and in East Anglia and Kent.

At night raiders were reported over London outskirts and from widely-separated places in England.

German bomber shot down by fighters into Thames estuary.

Greek War—Athens announced further successful local operations and more prisoners taken.

On the Way Back from Bombing Tobruk

WHILE over the sea on the return journey from a raid on Tobruk an R.A.F. bomber's starboard engine burst into flames. The aircraft crashed into the sea.

The rear-gunner and another member of the crew were at the time standing amidships. The next thing the rear-gunner knew was that he was lying on top of the fuselage with his legs in the water. He had been thrown out of the aircraft and knocked unconscious, but had fortunately landed on the fuselage instead of in the sea. Another member of the crew had released the rubber dinghy and was attempting to right it.

There was no sign of life from inside the aircraft, which suddenly sank, leaving the two airmen with the dinghy they were unable to right. The sergeant was suffering from a deep head cut sustained when he was thrown safely through the top of the fuselage, and one arm was practically useless. He decided that, despite the nasty swell running at the time, his best course was to attempt to swim to the shore half a mile away. His colleague elected to stay with the dinghy, as he knew he could not swim the distance. The rear-gunner made the trip successfully, but collapsed on the beach and lost consciousness.

When he recovered he searched frantically for the dinghy but could find no trace of it. His one obsession was to find help, so he began to walk inland.

Throughout the night he plodded on, but to his dismay found himself two or three hours before daybreak back at approximately the same spot on the coast from which he had started. Again he searched for the dinghy, and this time he found it, with the dead body of his colleague lashed to it.

Once more the sergeant set off to search for assistance, maintaining his direction by the wind, which was blowing off the sea. All day he staggered on without meeting a soul, and just before nightfall he found a stone enclosure with a number of small rooms, one of which was partly filled with straw. It had apparently been occupied by Italian or British troops. He slept during the night in the straw, and set out again in the morning in a last desperate effort to find help, as he had had neither food nor water. Some faint car tracks gave him renewed hope and he stuck grimly to these until at last he came upon a road. His trials were over, for he was picked up by a passing convoy and rushed to the nearest casualty clearing station.

HAILED BY THE NEW MEN OF HIS OLD REGIMENT

MR. CHURCHILL began life as a soldier. Passing through Sandhurst he was gazetted to the 4th Hussars, and after serving on the North-west Frontier fought in the Sudan campaign of 1897-1898 that led to the fall of Khartoum ; as an officer attached to the 21st Lancers he rode in the charge at Omdurman. In the Boer War he saw active service with the South African Light Horse, and after resigning his post as First Lord of the Admiralty in November 1915 he went to France, and was for a while in the front line in command of a battalion of the Royal Scots Fusiliers. The Premier recently paid a visit to his old command during a tour of the Eastern Counties, and is here acknowledging the vociferous cheers of officers and men after he had addressed them.

Photo, British Official : Crown Copyright

Benghazi: Crowning Triumph of the Libyan War

" The capture of Benghazi," said the King in a message of congratulation to General Wavell, G.O.C.-in-C. Middle East, " is a notable landmark in the campaign in North Africa which has been carried on with such brilliance by you and the Imperial troops under your command, in conjunction with the Royal Navy and the Royal Air Force. I warmly congratulate all ranks . . . on this further success which will rank high in the military annals of the British Empire."

"**B**ENGHAZI is in our hands." This five-word message from G.H.Q., Cairo, issued on the afternoon of February 7, gave the first news of the latest, greatest, and most astounding victory of General Wavell's Army of the Nile.

After the capture of Tobruk, Mussolini's principal naval base in Libya, on January 22, that truly Imperial host, composed of British, Dominion and Indian troops, valiantly supported by their Free French allies, pushed on into Cyrenaica, the most fertile region of Italy's Northern African colony. Derna, 100 miles to the west along the coastal road, was captured on January 30, and four days later Cyrene, which not long before had been Graziani's headquarters, shared its fate. Most of its garrison escaped in the direction of Barce. They were pursued by O'Connor's

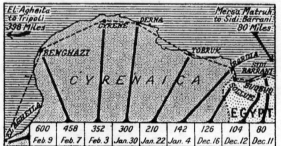

The remarkable advance of the Army of the Nile from Sidi Barrani to El Agheila is shown above diagrammatically with distances in miles and dates at which each point was reached.

men along the parallel roads which link Derna with Barce and so on to Benghazi.

Although the country is, militarily speaking, far more difficult than the flat desert across which the invaders had come, it was reported to be completely unfortified, and the British maintained a progress of 20 to 30 miles a day. Town after town in Italy's most prized over-

seas dominion was abandoned, often without a shot being fired. Again and again it was believed that here Graziani would make a stand, here he would endeavour to repair his shattered fortunes, or at least do something to retrieve his reputation as a military commander. But day after day went by and still the Marshal did not give battle. Very likely he could not, even if he would, for of the 250,000 men who were reported to be under his command in Libya when the war began, nearly half were now interned in Egypt and India, and the rest were strung out in numerous garrisons all the way back to Tripoli.

Now let us quote the communiqué which gave in some details the story of Benghazi's capture. " By brilliant operations the British armoured forces moved south of the Jebel Akhdar (the range of mountains running westward from Derna) and established themselves astride the Italian lines of communications leading southward from Benghazi. At the same time Australian troops advancing from Derna gave the retreating enemy forces no respite. Demoralized and out-manoeuvred the enemy were unable to put into effect plans for the defence of Benghazi."

These brief sentences describe one of the most brilliantly planned and skilfully executed strokes in the history of modern war. The Italians had expected, as Wavell intended them to expect, that the main attack on Benghazi, Cyrenaica's capital, would be along the road which follows the coast through fertile, well-watered country north of Jebel Akhdar. This road and the one which parallels it some distance inland were indeed taken by

the Australians, but at the same time a strong force of British armoured troops swept from Tobruk, south through Bomba and El Mechili, and then straight across 130 miles of barren and waterless desert along a road, or rather track used by only an occasional caravan, to Soluk, south of Benghazi.

Through frequent dust-storms the British armoured formation roared on, if not silently at least secretly, for they refrained even from using their radio. As the communiqué put it, " they made a forced march of 150 miles in 30 hours, brushing aside resistance en route to close the enemy's last line of retreat." Their arrival east and south of Benghazi had been timed to coincide with that of the Australians attacking from the north. The time-table was kept to the minute. At the same hour Australians and British tanks delivered a combined onslaught on Benghazi. " Surprised by the speed of this brilliant exploit the enemy, endeavouring to withdraw from Benghazi, found themselves finally hemmed in. Numerically superior enemy armoured forces, supported by infantry and artillery, then made determined efforts to break through our cordon. Every attempt was repulsed with heavy losses to the enemy. After 60 of their tanks had become battle casualties the enemy finally ceased fighting." Thousands of prisoners were taken, including an Army Commander, a Corps Commander (" Electric Whiskers " Berganzoli), and five other senior generals, together with vast quantities of war material of all descriptions.

With the capture of Benghazi the whole of Cyrenaica, apart from a few isolated posts to the south, was in British hands. These pockets of resistance were soon overwhelmed, and the Imperial avalanche swept on. By February 9 advanced elements had occupied El Agheila, 175 west of Benghazi.

BENGHAZI, which fell to the Imperial Forces on February 7, 1941, has a population of 65,000. Its excellent harbour is seen above, and on the town centres the whole of Cyrenaica's road system, while it has first-rate airfields. Its importance can be judged from the comment of the famous German newspaper, the " Frankfurter Zeitung," after the fall of Sidi Barrani on December 11, 1940: " The British cannot speak of this as a decisive action," that journal said; " before using the word decisive they would have to have advanced as far as Benghazi and to have secured an air base for attacks upon Italy itself."

Photo, Dorien Leigh

Smoke-Wreathed Tobruk Awaits the Assault

Tobruk's fall was heralded by clouds of smoke rising from the oil stores which, like other parts of the town had. been set alight by the concentrated fire of the Fleet, the bombers of the R.A.F. and the artillery. In the foreground is massed together an imposing array of the enemy's captured motor transport.

Left, troops leaving cover with fixed bayonets to take part in the final assault on Tobruk. Above is one of the British field guns that joined in the bombardment.

Photos, British Official : Crown Copyright

Wavell's Five-Front Attack on Italian Africa

Often has Mussolini boasted of the new Roman Empire which Fascist Italy was to create.
After 18 years of his dictatorial rule, however, Italy is losing not only her conquests of
the last few years but those colonies which were acquired before the Great War.

FROM his headquarters in Cairo General Sir Archibald Wavell is directing an offensive against the Italians in Africa, not on one front but on five. Libya and Eritrea, Abyssinia from two sides, and Italian Somaliland—all are threatened, indeed are actually invaded, by the armies under his command.

Libya is the main battleground where the fate of Italy's colonial empire, and perhaps of Italy herself, is being decided. Only as recently as September 1940 Marshal Graziani invaded Egypt with a great blowing of propaganda trumpets. He reached Sidi Barrani, some 50 miles across the frontier into Egypt, and there he dug himself in, making no further advance and not even attempting one. Then, on December 9, General Wavell struck at the invader, and in a few days the Italians were driven helter-skelter out of Egypt and the invader became the invaded. In the battle honours of the Army of the Nile are the names of Sidi Barrani and Sollum, Bardia and Tobruk—smashing victories every one of them, and all achieved at a cost of less than 2,000 casualties. But the Italians did not get off so lightly. We do not know how many they lost in killed and wounded, but we do know that more than 100,000 Italian prisoners have taken the road into Egypt. They have, indeed, reached

Cairo ; not as conquerors, however, but as captives.

Then, to crown all, came that master-stroke of Wavell's strategy, the two-pronged advance on Benghazi. As we tell in another page (see page 170), while the Australians advanced along the coast strong forces of British armoured troops swept straight across the desert and took the Italian defenders in the rear. Before this double assault Benghazi capitulated after a brief stand on February 7.

War in Torrid Eritrea

Very different from the Libyan war zone is the second of Wavell's fronts. In Libya our men have been shivering with cold, and have gone into battle wearing their greatcoats and with their tin hats perched above Balaclava helmets. In Eritrea, 1,500 miles to the south, the troops of General W. Platt's army of invasion—British (Highlanders and Midland troops were mentioned particularly in the communiqués), African regiments and Indians with experience of fighting on the North-west Frontier—are in the tropics. True, it is still winter there, but spring comes in March, bringing with it day temperatures of well over 100 degrees—heat which is oppressive enough for the soldier on the ground, but well-nigh unendurable for the man in a tank. Then close on the heels of spring comes the rainy season of summer, when the tracks through the bush, up the hillsides and across the mountains are turned into quagmires or washed away by boiling torrents. No wonder, then, that General Platt struck hard and fast, for soon the time must come when no man can fight in that tropic war zone—when even living is a torment.

Within a fortnight of crossing the frontier from the Sudan General Platt had occupied one fifth of Eritrea's area, and there was no staying his advance. Agordat fell on

February 1, and Barentu the next day. More than 1,500 prisoners and much equipment were taken, and the retreating Italians were closely pursued as they fled towards Asmara, and as they fled they abandoned lorries and guns, food, water and ammunition. Not until they arrived at Keren, some 50 miles east of Agordat, did they make a stand.

Where the Italians fought, they fought well ; and their Askaris (native troops) in particular reflected credit on their leadership and training. But in Eritrea as in Libya they were outmanoeuvred and then outfought. Platt's drive went on ; he was bent, it was clear, on chasing the enemy into the Red Sea at Massawa and on cutting off the retreat of the Italian garrison now increasingly hard pressed by the Patriots in Abyssinia.

Abyssinia provides General Wavell with fronts three and four. Number three takes its direction from the Sudan-Abyssinian frontier, where Gallabat faces Metemma. Its objective, apparently, is Gondar, an ancient city which for several centuries was the capital of the Abyssinian empire and is today a centre of local industry and trade with the tribesfolk of the Blue Nile regions of the Sudan. Here the war resolves itself into the capture of isolated posts, as the country is too difficult for large-scale operations, and, besides, Gondar is next door to nowhere.

Into Abyssinia from the South

For the fourth front we turn to Kenya, whose northern border runs with that of Abyssinia. On this frontier there have been clashes between patrols for weeks past, and small detachments drawn from the army of Major-General A. Cunningham—who has under his command African troops, drawn not only from the Union and Rhodesia, but from East and West Africa—have made considerable progress into the interior. They

THE AFRICAN WAR ZONE comprises many fronts, as shown on this map. Indian troops have played an important and gallant part in the victories of the Army of the Nile, and are fighting both in Libya and Eritrea. In the latter colony they have found conditions which are by no means new to them, for the highlands are in many respects similar to the country on the North-west Frontier of India. **Right,** a patrol of Indian infantry holding a post on the Eritrean frontier is moving through the bush.

Photo, British Official: Crown Copyright. Map by courtesy of " The Times"

They Covered 150 Miles in 30 Hours

CAVALRY TODAY is represented by light motorized units, and famous regiments that had their horses in the last war now go into action on petrol-propelled steeds, though they still bear the old names of Dragoons, Lancers and Hussars. Along the roads of the Western Desert during General Wavell's lightning advance through Bardia and Tobruk to Benghazi passed many hundreds of such light cavalry cars as this one, whose smiling crew have paused to be snapped, together with their dog mascot—a stray picked up during the advance.

Photo, British Official : Crown Copyright

Tearing Italy's Empire to 'Shreds and Tatters'

EAST AFRICA has been deeply impressed by the British successes, evidence of which was given recently at Nairobi when a number of captured guns were shown near the town hall, proudly guarded by native soldiers.

difficult, often desert, country. Then 450 miles separate Kenya from British Somaliland, which fell to the Italians in their one successful offensive in August 1940. One would suppose, however, that any attempt to reconquer this territory would be not from the land, across that great tract of rugged waste, but from the sea. In spite of the Italian hold on so many hundreds of miles of the coast of the Red Sea and the Gulf of Aden, the British have remained masters of the vital Straits of Bab el Mandeb; and it may well be that not only Berbera but

Abyssinia in particular, has been precarious; now, following the risings of the Patriots, guided and armed by Britain and inspired by Haile Selassie, their situation is becoming definitely dangerous. Thus it was hardly surprising that on February 6 it was reported that Mussolini had sent Count Volpi, his former Finance Minister, to negotiate with British interests for the evacuation of Italian colonists who had settled in Abyssinia since the Italian conquest in 1935. At the same time it was stated that the French managers of the railway which runs from Addis Ababa to Jibuti in French Somaliland had been asked to reopen the line—closed since Italy's entry into the war in June 1940—to facilitate the evacuation of the threatened Italians. If these reports were true, then no stronger confirmation could be required of the utter hopelessness of the Italian position in East Africa. So soon was Mr. Churchill's prophecy of December 23, made in the course of his broadcast to the Italian people, being brought to fruition: "Our armies are tearing and will tear your African Empire to shreds and tatters."

Command of the air is one of the main factors in the victories won by the Army of the Nile. How complete it was may be gauged from this photograph of the attack on Tobruk. Artillery is shelling the objective from the open desert without any protection, and is easily open to aerial attack. Yet the Italian Air Force failed to put them out of action.

are moving in the direction of Addis Ababa, i.e. about due north, but the country they have to traverse is almost trackless, although there is a road from Addis Ababa to Moyale passing through Javello and Mega. Moyale was captured by the South Africans on January 25.

Operations on the fifth front are also being carried out by Cunningham's men. Here the attack is being directed from Kenya eastwards against Italian Somaliland. A successful raid was made on the Italian frontier post of El-Wak, during which it was destroyed and made unusable for the Italians on December 16. About a month later the Italians were ejected from their slight gains on the Kenya side of the frontier, and were promptly chased across the border. By the end of January British patrols were reported to have penetrated some 46 miles into enemy territory, and the advance was continuing as the Italians fell back before the increasing British pressure. The enemy post of Beles Gugani, 45 miles inside Somaliland, was captured by strong native African patrols, it was announced in a communiqué issued from G.H.Q. Cairo on February 5. The advance was taking the direction of the Italian port of Mogadishu, but even as the crow flies this is some 300 miles across

Assab and Massawa may soon be brought within reach of the long and strong arm of Britain's sea power.

On every side, then, the Italians in East Africa are surrounded. For many months—certainly since last June and very likely since the outbreak of war in September 1939—the Italian garrison (reported to comprise 50,000 tribal levies, 100,000 Metropolitan and Blackshirt troops, and 100,000 natives: 250,000 in all) has been living on such supplies and resources as were theirs when the war began. Next to nothing can have reached them overland, and very little through their ports, although it is only to be expected that swift-sailing dhows have managed to land a few cargoes of guns and ammunition and other stores. For months the position of the Italians in East Africa, and in

TRANSPORT IN ABYSSINIA presents a difficult problem, but trains of pack camels have carried the necessary supplies and munitions over mountain tracks to the fighting men.

Photos, British Official: Crown Copyright

The Heroic Greek Army Hurled Back Mussolini

ALBANIA has experienced an exceptionally hard winter, and the Greek troops fighting in the mountains have felt the full rigour of it. Right, a column of pack mules, often the only possible transport, is moving forward. The Arctic conditions brought about heavy mortality among these indispensable beasts of burden.

The women of Greece have shown equal heroism with the men in the battle, and there has been no lack of nurses to follow the men in their pursuit of the invader. Below, two of them are helping a wounded soldier back to an advanced dressing station.

GREEK SOLDIERS have remained indomitably cheerful in the face of hardships, and have shown the old campaigner's readiness to shift for himself. Right centre, one of them, outside his small tent, uses the butt of his rifle as a writing desk. The photograph above shows that when it comes to armaments there is no makeshift. Greek soldiers, actually in action, are loading an anti-tank gun.

IN his broadcast on February 9, 1941, the Prime Minister, speaking of the misdeeds of the Duce, said : "Without the slightest provocation, spurred on by the lust of power and brutish greed, Mussolini—the crafty, cold-blooded, black-hearted Italian who had sought to gain an Empire on the cheap—attacked and invaded Greece, only to be hurled back ignominiously by the heroic Greek Army who have revived before our eyes the glories that from the classic age have gilded their native land."

The Italians still maintain a precarious hold in Albania, but it is only exceptionally bad weather that has saved them from being driven into the sea ; all their counter-attacks have been repulsed. On February 7, 1941, one on a large scale was made north-west of Klisura. Some 15,000 men, regular troops and Blackshirts, were massed for the attack. It was met by withering artillery fire from the Greeks. The Italian vanguard was practically wiped out, and then the Greeks made a bayonet charge which put the Italians to flight. When the fighting was over more than a thousand dead Italians were left on the field.

THEIR CANNONADE AT GENOA TOLD THE FRENCH "THAT FRIENDS ARE NEAR, THAT BRITANNIA RULES THE WAVES"

Britain's Western Mediterranean Squadron gave the great Italian port of Genoa a tremendous pounding at dawn on Sunday, February 9, 1941. "Our forces," read the Admiralty statement, "under the command of Vice-Admiral Sir James Somerville, consisted of the battle cruiser Renown, the battleship Malaya, the aircraft carrier Ark Royal [these three vessels are shown in our lower photograph, right to left, passing the Rock of Gibraltar] and the cruiser Sheffield, with light forces in company. Military targets in and around the port of Genoa [seen in our upper photo] were subjected to a bombardment in which over 300 tons of shells were fired." "If the cannonade of Genoa," said Mr. Churchill on February 9, "reached the ears of our French comrades in their grief and misery, it might cheer them with the feeling that friends, active friends, are near, and that Britannia rules the waves."

Photos, British Official: Crown Copyright; Topical.

The Sea Effort of the Empire's Navies

Addressing the Royal Empire Society in London on January 20, Admiral of the Fleet
Lord Chatfield gave an impressive survey of " Our Empire's Sea Effort." By courtesy
of the Royal Empire Society we are permitted to reproduce here the most informing and
important passages of the address. Lord Chatfield, it need hardly be said, speaks with
exceptional authority, derived from his long experience at sea and at the Admiralty.

WHY is it that the Empire's sea effort
is so important in this as in all our
wars that it overshadows even more
than most minds conceive all other fighting
factors ? It is because our Empire was
founded by sea power ; founded by our
merchants and soldiers under the shelter
of sea command and all the advantage that
command gave and still gives.

Let us consider for a moment what the
Naval forces of the Empire have accomplished in the last sixteen or seventeen
months. We are faced with a very different

shipping are correspondingly lessened. The
causes of our recent heavier losses are therefore understandable. Despite this the flow
of imports vital to the prosecution of the
war continues.

Let me say a word about our cruisers—
they have swept the seas of enemy ships.
Those cruisers are ever too few. It was the
same in Nelson's time. Only four years ago
we were only permitted to have 50, thanks to
international agreements ! When these hampering agreements ended in 1937 we started
to build feverishly, and when war broke out

we had a large number under construction.
Many of these are now at sea, but so great
is our cruiser task, we have had to augment
them by armed merchant ships. These
combined cruiser and armed merchant
cruiser forces have established the blockade
of our two enemies. Always they are at
sea, ever on watch and ward ; no daily
bulletin records their labours, for they work
unseen and unheard guarding our convoys,
denying enemy waters to world shipping,
protecting our supply ships, carrying troops,
arms, air supplies to our army in Africa.

What of our destroyers, again all too few
in numbers ? They have to fulfil innumerable tasks—submarine hunting, for instance.
Until Germany occupied French ports they
had mastered the submarine menace. Now
their task is more strenuous, more exacting.
Nevertheless, they will assuredly again do so.
Then they have hunted German destroyers
in the North Sea, fought them at Narvik,
and the Italian ships in the Mediterranean
and Red Sea. They are one of our important
defences in the Channel against invasion.
Individual destroyers have been bombed in
the narrow waters as many as forty or fifty
times in one day ; some have sacrificed
themselves in their duty. Then our submarines ; no brave bomb-disposal squad
takes on greater risks than do daily our
submarine crews.

'Full-Back of the British Empire'

Behind all this effort stands the battlefleet,
the final arbiter on the sea. The battlefleet
is old, built for the most part twenty-five
years ago. Yet it truly controls the seas
and the war ; it is the queen on the chess
board, the full-back of the British Empire.
Now our new ships are putting to sea. Laid
down in 1937, they have been built with
great rapidity, thanks to our shipyards, our
armour and gun-mounting firms, and their

situation from that which obtained in the
last war. Then we had the assistance of the
Navies of France, Japan and Italy and, in
the latter part, of the United States. The
United Kingdom stood in a commanding
position across the sea routes along which
attacks could be launched on our merchant
shipping Aerial attack was negligible. In
this war, since the fall of France we have
had to reckon with a hostile coastline extending from the Bay of Biscay to the North Cape.
U-boats are based on the Norwegian and
Biscay ports, and their passage to their hunting grounds is therefore shorter and less
hazardous than during the last war. Long-
range aircraft are operating from aerodromes
in Western France to attack our shipping.
The entrance channels to our Western ports
are subjected to continuous mining activity.
Our forces disposable for the protection of

IN ALL WEATHERS the Royal Navy carries on. The lower photograph was taken on a destroyer
during a very cold spell. Top, is a very different scene in the Mediterranean. The 16-in. guns of
a battleship, such as bombarded Libya, are being sponged out. The Marines are wearing topees,
their head-dress in warm climates.   *Photos, British Official : Crown Copyright ; and Sport & General*

Britain's Bulwarks Both Royal and Imperial

An Australian cruiser is putting to sea from her base for a cruise in home waters. The main repair base and depot of the Royal Australian Navy are at Sydney.

The New Zealand Naval Force has a number of ships for home defence, among them being minesweeping trawlers. Above is one of these ships.   *Photos, Keystone and Planet News*

skilled labour and their skilled leaders of industry. With the aid of the destroyers obtained from America (and let us hope to be further obtained) and our own new construction the sea situation is showing continual improvement.

The Admiralty, looking far ahead, have always encouraged the building of naval forces by our Dominions. We had accumulated so many enemies under the system of Collective Security that the British Navy's responsibilities became too great, and the defence of the coasts and waters of our Empire everywhere became a duty that devolved on each part of it. The Empire has on the whole responded wonderfully to its increased responsibilities.

The **Royal Canadian Navy** consisted in 1939 of 13 ships. In 1940 it consisted of 155 ships. Canada is doing a great deal of shipbuilding. At fifteen shipyards along the coasts and inland waters thousands of men are working day and night, and their numbers are ever increasing. The present programme calls for the construction of over a hundred vessels for various naval and air force purposes, including 64 patrol ships and 26 minesweepers. The construction of most of these larger ships is far advanced; many were delivered last year and others will be this year.

In 1939 the personnel, including reserves, was just over 3,000; in 1940 it rose to over 13,000. Men from the shores of the inland lakes have hastened to join, and recruits from the prairie provinces are now training alongside natives of the Atlantic seaboard and British Columbia. 250 officers and men of the Canadian Navy have given their lives; over 3,500 ships have been successfully convoyed, excluding troop convoys. No Canadian troops have been lost in transit. Six U.S. destroyers, part of the first batch of fifty, are in the Canadian Navy.

The **Royal Australian Navy** consisted before the war of five cruisers, five destroyers, two escort vessels, and one surveying ship. In a broadcast on defence Mr. Playford, South Australian Premier, has said: " The Australian Navy is now two and a half times as large as it was in June last year. In fourteen months there has been a 250 per cent increase in the number of officers and ratings, and ten naval vessels have been laid down, including destroyers and patrol vessels. In a few months the output will be two vessels a month. Since the outbreak of war Australia has equipped five armed merchant cruisers and 30 auxiliary war vessels. More than 150 merchant ships have been defensively equipped."

New Zealand has also played a brave part for so comparatively small a Dominion in increasing our Naval strength. We have built for her Navy valuable cruisers which she has paid for and manned. We remember that H.M.S. Achilles took part in the defeat of the Admiral Graf Spee; she was a unit of the New Zealand division. A number of additional trawlers have been also commissioned as minesweepers, and others have been also fitted out. Three specially designed training-vessels have been built for minesweeping and anti-submarine work. The Naval base at Auckland have equipped over 20 merchant ships for defence in case of attack on the high seas and have provided gun crews from the R.N.V.R. of New

Zealand. These activities are supplementary to the setting-up of the necessary organization for the defence of the New Zealand ports.

Newfoundland. Through the foresight of the British Admiralty, a fine body of sailors known as the Royal Newfoundland Naval Reserve was kept in being during the peace, with the result that when the war broke out Newfoundland was able to send a body of trained seamen over to England to take their part with the Fleet. They are splendid boatmen, in great demand when small boats have to be launched for inspection purposes in rough seas. Beatty described them as " the best boatmen in the Grand Fleet." It is a sad yet glorious fact that a contingent of Newfoundlanders was serving in H.M.S. Jervis Bay at the time of her loss.

South Africa. South Africa has created a local seaward defence corps, and three companies, allocated under the Cape, the Eastern Province and the Natal Command, have been established. The decision to create these new units was taken shortly before the war.

India. In 1939 the personnel of the Royal Indian Navy consisted of just over 1,500 officers and men. In that year the Royal Indian Naval Reserve and Royal Indian Volunteer Reserve were established. By April 1940 these reserves produced more than two hundred officers and about 1,250 ratings. The expansion both on the active list and in the reserves continues. The sloops and other vessels of the Royal Indian Navy are doing invaluable work in patrolling the Indian Ocean and Bay of Bengal.

The Mercantile Marine. Unopposed by any great fleet worthy of its steel, our Navy has once again as its main task the protection of our island base and its supplies, as well as of carrying our armies and air forces to the scenes of action and maintaining their communications. These vital supplies have, as ever, to be carried in merchant ships. On those merchant ships and their gallant seamen everything therefore depends. We are inclined to think of our merchant ships as material things, just to count how many tons have been lost each week. But those ships really represent a great army of merchant seamen, marching in their ships great and small across the Seven Seas. No danger the human being faces is greater than theirs; the nearest analogy is that of explorers trekking through forests with Red Indians lurking in ambush. In them is summarized our sea effort. If they failed the Navy would be of no avail, nor our soldiers or airmen. Yet if the Navy failed to guard them all their courage would not save them. Combined work again. The story of the Mercantile Marine teems with gallantry of individuals and men in the mass.

The Admiralty. Let me finally remind you of the vast responsibility that ever rests on the Admiralty. In that building are the brains that control our Naval dispositions, the plan of campaign, the security of our merchant ships. It is their planning that defeats the submarine, in the Atlantic, the organization of our convoys, the sweeping of mines of ever-changing type continuously being laid off our coasts. We are lucky indeed therefore to know that in the Naval staff and its chiefs we have that high ability, that expert imagination and organization the country needs.

Comrades of the Seven Seas

SOUTH AFRICA has an efficient minesweeping flotilla, among the most important of its sea defences. This seaman in one of the sweepers is using an Aldis signalling lamp.

MALAYANS are men of a seafaring race, and have made a fine response to the call of the Straits Settlements R.N.V.R. for recruits. Their training ship is H.M.S. Palandok, and above some of the men are seen at gun practice on board her. Those who have gone through the three-months' training in seamanship, gunnery and signals are now manning patrol boats off the coast.

CANADA has embarked on a great new shipbuilding programme, included in which are submarine chasers to work with convoys ; above, one of these vessels is being launched. Canadian destroyers are operating in the Atlantic, and, right, one of them is rescuing survivors from a torpedoed merchantman.

Photos, South African Official, Ministry of Information, Paul Popper, and Fox

What Germany Holds on the Continent Today

UNOCCUPIED FRANCE lives in constant dread that it will in turn be overrun by the detested "Boche." Above, at a march past of cadets on the Quai des Belges, Marseilles, Marshal Pétain is taking the salute. He is accompanied by Admiral Darlan, who has been acting as envoy between the Vichy Government and Abetz, the German ambassador in Paris.

IN BELGIUM, as in all the countries they occupy, the Nazis have continued their savage campaign against the Jews. This notice on the door of business premises in Belgium tells passers-by in German, Flemish and French that it is a Jewish concern.
Photos, Associated Press and Sport & General

HITLER OVER EUROPE 1939–1941

WHEN war broke out in September 1939 the German Reich had already extended its boundaries by the forcible incorporation of Austria on March 12, 1938, and the piecemeal annexation of Czechoslovakia in 1938-1939. Then in September 1939 came the lightning campaign against Poland, followed by the partition of that country between Germany and the U.S.S.R. Beginning on April 9, 1940, the flood-tide of Nazi invasion swept over Scandinavia and the Low Countries, and one by one Denmark, Norway, Luxembourg, Holland and Belgium were carried into the Nazi maw. Then came the turn of France, which, compelled to capitulate in June, 1940, saw half its land occupied by the conqueror. Hungary and Rumania retained a nominal and precarious independence, but had to submit to what, to all intents and purposes, amounted to a German occupation. Even Italy came more and more under the heel of Hitler, for following her calamitous defeats at the hands of Britain and Greece in N. Africa and Albania, German troops were dispatched to Italy in increasing numbers. Of the remaining Balkan states, Yugoslavia and Bulgaria so far remain uneasy neutrals. The map, left, shows the territory in Europe which at the beginning of 1941 was under Nazi occupation or domination.

Now the Nazis Are 'Taking Over' Italy

MUSSOLINI'S first admission of the sore straits in which he found himself in Libya and the Mediterranean came on January 2, 1941, when it was announced from Rome that a section of the German Air Force had arrived in Italy "to take part in the air and naval struggle in the Mediterranean."

In order to soothe the feelings of the Italian people, who might not unnaturally be depressed by the news that the Duce had had to send an S O S to Hitler on behalf of his vaunted Regia Aeronautica, it was added that the Nazi squadrons would be considered as "an Italian striking unit." The photographs in this page show the arrival of the Nazi airmen in Italy, that at the bottom having been radioed from New York. The first activities of the German airmen were recorded on January 10, 1941, when they took part in the attack on a British convoy bound for Greece, eye-witness accounts of which appear in pages 107-8 of this volume. At least 12 of the German and Italian 'planes engaged were destroyed by the British and others were damaged. On other occasions Nazi dive bombers made attacks on Malta, but met with strong opposition from fighters and A.A. guns.

In two or three days, Mr. Churchill revealed in the course of his broadcast on February 9, the Germans lost in these operations, out of 150 dive-bombers, upwards of 90, 50 of which were destroyed in the air and 40 on the ground.

German police and Storm Troopers were sent to Rome some time ago for instruction in police duties in Africa. Here the visitors are being presented with " daggers of honour."

Germans in Italy have been instructed to be pleasant to the Italian people and make themselves acceptable by their winning ways. Centre right, two Nazi airmen are chatting with members of " Piccole italiane," the Fascist organization for little girls. Above, another of the Nazi "invaders" is talking to Italian youths in Rome.

Neither Nazi nor Fascist propaganda admits that any Germans other than airmen have entered Italy. That the Luftwaffe has sent many men to help the Regia Aeronautica is shown by this photograph of a detachment of Nazi aircraftmen marching through the streets of a city in Southern Italy. It may well have occurred to the watching crowds that they are but the forerunners of a German army of occupation.

Photos, Associated Press

'We Shall Not Fail or Falter   We Shall No

"None of our plans would have succeeded had not our pilots, under Air Chief Marshal Longmore, wrested the control of the air from a far more numerous enemy." This Gladiator of the R.A.A.F. patrols the skies above Bardia.

" They remind me of the British squares at Wa coats ; they are just ordinary English, Scottis together. But their spirit is the same . . ." He

I VENTURED to draw Gen. Wavell's attention to the seventh chapter of the Gospel of St. Matthew, at the seventh verse, where it is written, "Ask, and it shall be given you ; seek, and ye shall find ; knock, and it shall be opened unto you.". The Army of the Nile has asked and it was given. They sought and they have found. They knocked and it has been opened unto them.

In barely eight weeks, by a campaign which will long be studied as a model of the military art, an advance of over 150,000 miles has been made. The whole Italian army in the East of Libya, an army which was reputed to exceed 150,000 men, has been captured or destroyed.

The entire province of Cyrenaica, nearly as big as England and Wales, has been conquered. The unhappy Arab tribes who have for 30 years suffered from the cruelty of the Italian rule have at last seen their oppressors in disorderly flight or led off in endless droves as prisoners of war.

Egypt and the Suez Canal are safe, and the port, the base and the air fields of Benghazi constitute a strategic point of high consequence to the war in the Eastern Mediterranean.

" That series of victories in Lib tary power in the African

The quotations in this page are

Photos, British Official: Crown C

Weaken or Tire   We Will Finish the Job'

...t squares of soldiers ; they do not wear scarlet ...men, women and children standing steadfastly ...s his sympathy with the bombed folk of Bristol.

" Nor would the campaign have been possible if the British Mediterranean Fleet under Admiral Cunningham had not chased the Italian Navy into its harbours and sustained every forward surge of the Army with all the flexible resources of sea power."

...ken irretrievably the Italian mili-...ry about to assault Tobruk.

...'s broadcast of February 9, 1941.

...ssociation and the " Daily Mirror"

THE other day President Roosevelt gave his opponent in the late Presidential election a letter of introduction to me, and in it he wrote out a verse in his own handwriting from Longfellow, which he said applies to you people as it does to us.   Here is the verse :

Sail on, O ship of state!
Sail on, O Union, strong and great!
Humanity with all its fears,
With all the hopes of future years,
Is hanging breathless on thy fate !

What is the answer that I shall give in your name to this great man, the thrice chosen head of a nation of 130,000,000 ?

Here is the answer which I shall give to President Roosevelt. Put your confidence in us : give us your faith and your blessing and under Providence all will be well.

We shall not fail or falter. We shall not weaken or tire. Neither the sudden shock of battle nor the long-drawn trials of vigilance and exertion will wear us down. Give us the tools and we will finish the job.

Eritrea : Key to Italian East Africa

In invading Eritrea, General Wavell is thrusting at the strongest and most highly-developed section of Italy's empire in East Africa. Below we tell something of the country, its people, and its history since it became an Italian colony.

ERITREA is the oldest of the Italian colonies. Italian influence in the district dates from 1869, when the Rubattino Shipping Company, an Italian concern, sought to establish a coaling station on the western shores of the Straits of Bab el Mandeb, where the Red Sea joins the Gulf

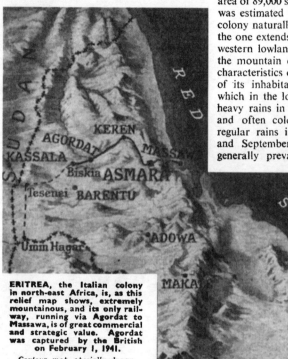

ERITREA, the Italian colony in north-east Africa, is, as this relief map shows, extremely mountainous, and its only railway, running via Agordat to Massawa, is of great commercial and strategic value. Agordat was captured by the British on February 1, 1941.

Contour map specially drawn for THE WAR ILLUSTRATED *by Felix Gardon*

of Aden. A suitable site was found on the Bay of Assab, and it was purchased from the local sultans for £1,800.

Hardly had the deal been concluded when objections were raised, not only by the Sultan of Turkey, overlord of the territory involved, but by Britain and Egypt, who were distinctly averse from the Italians establishing themselves by what was, in effect, the gateway to the Suez Canal. These objections came to nothing, however ; the Sultan was too far away to exercise any real influence, and Britain was no longer nervous since she had secured a commanding position at Aden. Ten years after the original concession a small Italian force occupied Assab, and in 1882 the territory was formally ceded to Italy, and in 1890 it was put on a permanent basis as a crown colony.

During the next few years the Italians endeavoured to expand to the south and west. Their advance into Abyssinia was ended following the crushing defeat inflicted on the Italian invaders at Adowa by the Abyssinians in 1896. At about the same time the activities of the Mahdi in the Sudan induced them to restore Kassala, which they had occupied, to the Anglo-Egyptian Sudan ; it was not again in Italian hands until the autumn of 1940, and then only for a few weeks. Some additions—the cession of a corner of French Somaliland and the island of Doumeirah in the Red Sea—were made to Eritrea in 1935 by the agreement concluded

in Rome between Laval and Mussolini. Then in 1936, following the Italian conquest of Abyssinia, Eritrea was incorporated as a state or government of Italian East Africa, certain former Abyssinian territories being added to it.

As at present constituted Eritrea has an area of 89,000 square miles, and its population was estimated in 1939 to be 1,500,000. The colony naturally divides itself into two parts : the one extends along the coast and over the western lowlands, while the other comprises the mountain districts of the interior. The characteristics of each region and of the lives of its inhabitants are dictated by climate, which in the low-lying area is tropical, with heavy rains in the winter, while in the cool and often cold mountain areas there are regular rains in the summer between June and September, and temperate conditions generally prevail. This latter region, an extension of the Abyssinian Plateau, is largely agricultural, grain, tobacco, cotton and coffee being cultivated. In the low-lying western plains irrigation schemes are preparing the ground for intensive cultivation of cotton and other tropical produce. In the extreme south the country is wild and largely desert interspersed with a few fertile oases. Here durra and maize are grown, but the people are mainly nomads at a low stage of culture, living in tents and pasturing large herds of cattle, sheep, goats and camels.

For the most part the Eritreans, like most of the natives of Italian East Africa, belong to the Hamitic and Semitic races, but on the coast the Arab strain predominates, while on the Sudanese frontier negroes are in evidence. Although for the most part they are slimly built and of no great muscular development, the tribesmen are capable of bearing fatigue to an almost unlimited extent. From them are drawn the Italian Askaris, the native soldiers who under good leadership make excellent fighters—as, indeed, recent experience against our

troops has confirmed. They are generally loyal to the Italian regime, and it was largely through their aid that the Italians were able to extend their sway over Abyssinia.

In religion the natives are either Christians of the Coptic variety, or Mahomedans, although there are also some Roman Catholics and a few pagans. The Italians have established separate schools for Coptic Christians, Gallas and Moslems. The people speak Tigrine and Tigré, two derivatives from the ancient language of Ethiopia, but there are many other languages and dialects in use ; in the ports and lowlands Arabic is spoken.

Since the Italians have been established in Eritrea for more than half a century, communications are far better than in other portions of the Italian overseas empire. There is a railway from Massawa, on the Red Sea, to Asmara, the capital, and thence north and west to Agordat and Biskia, though this last stretch has not been worked. Both these last-mentioned towns have been captured recently by the British. Asmara—set in the hill country, 7,765 feet above sea level, with some 80,000 inhabitants—is also the centre of the country's road system, as from it first-class motor roads run east to Massawa, south to Addis Ababa and Gondar, and west to the Sudan frontier, opposite Kassala. The Italians have done much to develop agriculture in Eritrea by way of irrigation works, and gold and salt are amongst the country's principal exports. Every effort, indeed, is being made to develop the colony and make it suitable for the settling of Italian emigrants. But the financial cost has been heavy, and the Italian people who have endeavoured to make their homes there do not take kindly to the climate.

Lifeline of Eritrea is this single-track railway, the only one in the colony, which runs across mountainous country through Agordat via Keren and Asmara (the capital) to the port of Massawa on the Red Sea—a distance of about 200 miles—as shown in the map in this page. *Photo, Associated Press*

Abyssinia's Emperor Reviews His New Army

HAILE SELASSIE is once more Emperor of Abyssinia, and somewhere well inside the frontiers of his realm he is encouraging his army to fight and his people to rebel against the Italian usurper. Above, the "Lion of Judah," as he is called, is addressing Abyssinian troops that have been led into their native land, fully-trained and equipped, by British officers. Their part in the war is to harass the retreating Italians and cut their communications, a role for which their knowledge of the country makes them particularly suitable.

Photo. British Official : Crown Copyright.

This Is how I Felt When I Was 'Blitzed'

Many of our readers have passed through such an experience as is here related, but
few of us could describe it in terms so simple yet so moving. Hence we publish it here,
as a kind of footnote to Mr. George Godwin's previous tale, and in the hope and belief
that his philosophy may be a help and comfort to those who read it.

IN this sort of war a day will do to date a
writer's record. For example, since I
wrote in these pages an account of the
condition of the Temple (see Vol. III, p. 690)
new misfortunes have befallen it. Today
libraries, Halls, courts and blocks of chambers,
and even what were once lawns and noble
trees, stand in varying degrees of tragic ruin.
I occupied then a small set of chambers at
lawn level, and, despite one " blitzing," still
preserved intact the illusion of personal
immunity that is deep-rooted and almost
universal in human nature.

You know how it is. We say : " Ah, that
happened to poor old Jones, but it would

but its windows, long since blasted out, were
stoutly shuttered and screwed up. In that
little setting I enjoyed the illusion of safety
that is almost as important, psychologically,
as the reality—almost as important and
much more convenient, since it enables one
to dispense with the troglodyte existence of
the deep shelter.

When precautions become the parents of
fear (the " anxiety states ") they are not
worth taking. That everything has a price
beyond which it is never economic to go is
true of safety first, as it is of that charming
house with all modern conveniences. But I
digress . . .

I was truly alive, but I was not feeling very
well. My head felt queer, and my face as
though it had been dealt the most terrific of
punches. I got up slowly and thoughtfully
and made my way like a man newly blind
into my neighbours' quarters.

Sitting beside a warm fire that I must, alas,
soon exchange once more for the surgical
ward of a hospital, I see the subsequent
events of that night in mental images that are
etched on the tablets of my mind for ever.

I see a group of men in a setting that
might be a coal mine at the moment of
disaster. They are black and bloody and
immobilized by shock. Presently both black
and blood are to be washed away. Wits will
return when the horrific moment has slid
into the kaleidoscopic pattern of life to
become a theme to set off the pint pot.

I see, too, another room whose occupant
so short a time before sat chatting there with
me. Now he lies groaning under the wreckage
that has fallen on him. I ease him, take his
hand, talk comfort, not realizing that he is
far beyond all hearing. I see myself groping
in the dark of my own rooms again for the
carefully-preserved big first-aid kit, and myself
opening up that kit beside the injured man
and then spilling the whole lot into the foul
filth of the wreck-strewn floor. I see the entry
of the Rescue Squad. They come out of the
night, through where the windows were, and
in their shiny oilskins and tin hats they look
like infantrymen going over the top.

All this and much more I see, sitting here.
And I hear a voice which tells me that the
most prominent feature of my face has come
adrift and is flapping on my cheek. And I
suffer myself to be led away.

'We Will Build Again'

Does it sound very horrible ? Granted,
the experience is not nice. But it has a
certain compensation. At fifty-one, one
knows, the ordinary Londoner—you, I—
" can take it." And that means that London
can take it—that the blitz can never succeed.

There exists a law that assures and
guarantees to all that has intrinsic worth and
value the power of re-birth and self-renewal.
Aerial bombardment and fire might, conceivably, raze London. But that would not
be London's end. For a great city is the
casket wrought by the genius and spirit of
long generations of her people. Destruction,
by Act of God or act of man, may overwhelm
it, its stones may be shattered, its storied
treasures scattered until no more remains
than was left of the city of King Ozimandias.

But even that would not be the end. For
a great city perishes only when the spirit of
its people perishes ; when the courage that
endures fails, and the vision that quickens is
quenched. This terrible destruction we must
lament only in terms of the personal
tragedies involved in it. Otherwise we must
see it as the essential preliminary to the
re-creation of a new and finer land. Out of
the warm ashes of the old—and often bad—
we will build again, better and more wisely.

These are the things I tell myself even as
(being human) I pipe my eye for those wrecks,
the Temple, my chambers and my face.

DESTRUCTION IN THE TEMPLE is one of the tragedies of the air raids on London, for many
irreplaceable and storied treasures were destroyed. Here Mr. Wendell Willkie, on his brief visit
from the States, is viewing the ruins of the Inner Temple Library, together with Viscount Simon,
the Lord Chancellor, himself a Bencher of the Inner Temple. *Photo, Wide World*

never happen to me." The catastrophe which
befalls our neighbour is as far from our own
door, we feel, as floods in China.

Now, queerly enough, this infantile conviction of a personal immunity exists in
most of us side by side with an anxious
preoccupation about how we would behave
if it *did* happen to us. We ask ourselves :
How would I stand up to it if I did get a
packet ? But only events can supply the
right answer.

I had wondered about this myself, as, no
doubt, the reader has done. A very large
bomb provided the right answer.

A Londoner's chances of becoming a
casualty are, it has been calculated, 750 to
one against—fairly long odds, but not too
long to eliminate personal interest.

It was as No. 750 that a few weeks ago I
stood warming myself about midnight before
a gas fire preparatory to turning in. The
room in which I stood looks out over a lawn,

It had been a fairly quiet night, and I had
spent the immediately previous half-hour
chatting with some young fellows living
opposite me. We had suffered one blitzing
in common, and that experience, from which
we all emerged with nothing worse than a
good shake-up, had engendered a feeling of
comradeship.

Afterwards, I was told that the detonation
had shaken buildings some distance away ;
but I heard nothing of it though no more
than the length of a cricket pitch distant.

Quite simply I was blotted out, extinguished as completely as though struck by
lightning. Full consciousness returned almost
as swiftly. But I shall never know how long I
lay on the floor by the glass-panelled door
against which blast had catapulted me.

Hidden by the darkness of a sooty fog lay
the wreckage of my room. But a little voice
spoke to me at once and said : " Well,
you're alive, Old Cock, anyway."

Bombed—But Still the Village Smithy Stands!

THE UNDEFEATABLE SPIRIT of the British people is typified by the two photographs in this page. This blacksmith's forge, which has stood for over a hundred years in a town of South-east England, was badly shattered by a bomb (top). In spite of the complete destruction of his forge the blacksmith was not defeated. With true British doggedness he set to work to rebuild, and from a hopeless ruin has emerged a new forge (lower photograph), a faithful reproduction of the old building.

Photos, John Topham

OUR SEARCHLIGHT ON THE WAR

First Ethiopian Patriot Regiment

MILITARY authorities at Nairobi revealed on February 2 that an Abyssinian refugee regiment had been formed in Kenya as far back as June 1940 and had several times been in action against Italian forces. The original intention had been to raise an all-Ethiopian unit which, under its own guerilla leaders, would cross the frontier, make contact with friends and patriots in the Shifta country and, with their help, promote unrest amongst the native population. This plan failed because the battalion could not get into touch with sympathizers nor obtain food. So after the loss of many killed or wounded by Italian bombers, the straggling and exhausted remainder returned to Kenya. Their spirit, however, was undaunted, and with new recruits they reorganized their unit and were given proper military training by British officers. Since then they have cooperated with the King's African Rifles and fought several successful actions against the Banda (Italian native levies), the most important resulting in the capture of Dukana, a frontier post in north-west Kenya.

Passing of a Great Empire Servant

THE State has lost one of its most able and energetic Ministers by the death, at the early age of 61, of Lord Lloyd, Colonial Secretary and Leader of the House of Lords. The latter office he never exercised, for, although appointed on January 10, in succession to Lord Halifax, his illness prevented him from attending any sittings. Lord Lloyd began to acquire his unrivalled knowledge of Eastern manners and politics at an early age, for after leaving Cambridge he made a long caravan journey from Turkey to Tibet, the first of many such travels. In 1905 he was

LORD LLOYD, Colonial Secretary, whose death occurred on February 5, is seen inspecting Auxiliary Military Pioneers. Lord Lloyd represented the Crown as Governor of Bombay and as High Commissioner in Egypt during two long and critical periods.   *Photo, Fox*

attached to our Embassy in Constantinople, and in 1908 was given his first Government mission, that of examining the prospects of British trade in the Near East. His first duty in the Great War was to organize an intelligence service in Egypt, and here he met Lawrence of Arabia, with whom he was to form an enduring friendship and, passing as an Arab, to help in raising the revolt in the desert. In 1918 he was appointed Governor of Bombay, and dealt in masterly fashion with the disaffection that was rife, and later with the " civil disobedience " movement promoted by Gandhi. Liberal social reforms and many great public works, such as the

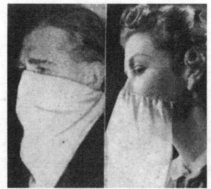

GERM MASKS for shelters, two types of which are here shown, are simple and effective. An improvised mask (left) is a folded handkerchief, and a " yashmak " (right) consists of a georgette handkerchief treated with transparent cellulose lacquer.
Photos, by courtesy of the Ministry of Health

Lloyd Dam, constitute an enduring memorial to Lord Lloyd's sagacious five years' Governorship. In 1925 he succeeded Lord Allenby as High Commissioner for Egypt and the Sudan, but he could not see eye to eye with the democratic school of Imperialism, and when Labour came into power in 1929 he resigned office. In 1930 he became president of the Navy League, and in 1937 Chairman of the British Council. Three years later Mr. Churchill made him Secretary of State for the Colonies.

American Observer in Near East

COLONEL DONOVAN, President Roosevelt's special envoy, has recently been touring the Balkans and having talks with the leaders of these countries. On January 22 he was received by King Boris at Sofia, and also saw the Prime Minister, the Foreign Minister, and several Bulgarian generals. Later he went to Belgrade and Athens, and on January 31 was flown to Istanbul by Lord Forbes, Assistant Air Attaché in Athens. Here M. Sarajoglu, the Turkish Foreign Minister, received him, he met the British Ambassador and later attended an official dinner given in his honour by the Government. Colonel Donovan intended to travel through Syria to Palestine, Egypt and Libya, but Vichy, presumably by Hitler's order, refused a visa for Syria, so he reached Palestine in Lord Forbes' aeroplane. Judging from radio fulminations in Berlin and Rome the Dictators are annoyed and considerably disquieted over this tour, not so much because of what Colonel Donovan may have learnt in its course, but on account of the information that he has been freely imparting on American views about the war, and Mr. Roosevelt's undertaking to assist with military material all countries standing up to Axis aggression. He has removed any possible doubt as to the significance of the American policy of giving aid to Britain, and it is said that the result of his visits to Bulgaria and Yugoslavia has been to stimulate and strengthen the national spirit of independence in these countries.

Free Issue of Shelter Masks

HALF a million germ masks are being supplied by the Ministry of Health to public air-raid shelters. The standard type consists of a transparent piece of non-inflammable material, cellulose acetate, 5½ inches square, which is placed across the bridge of the nose and held in position by an elastic band over the head. The authorities hope that the public will take kindly to these masks and wear them during periods of flu danger. Occasions for which they should be donned are the first few minutes after entering a shelter, and again when leaving it, as the abrupt change of temperature is apt to bring on coughing and sneezing, with the consequent spread of droplet infection. In spite of the favourable breeding-ground for germs afforded by the crowded deep shelters, no outbreak of infectious disease has been reported from any one of them. Sir Wilson Jameson, Chief Medical Officer of the Ministry of Health, maintains that the best preventive of infectious diseases is dispersal—dispersal from overcrowded areas to less populated parts of the country;' dispersal from overcrowded shelters by the provision of new and better ones: dispersal within a given shelter by the spacing out of the occupants and the use of the new masks.

Belgian Gold for Germany

GOLD to the value of about £65,000,000, the property of the Bank of Belgium but unfortunately in French custody, is being handed over to Germany by the helpless Vichy Government. Before the invasion of Belgium two-thirds of her gold was safely transferred to England, Canada, the United States, and South Africa. The remaining third, which was still in the hands of the Government when the country was invaded, was hastily removed to Tournai and later to Paris. When France was overrun the Belgian Government asked that the gold should be sent through Brittany to England on board a British cruiser, but the French Government shipped it instead from Bordeaux to Dakar, in West Africa. It is now being brought back in instalments for transfer to Germany. Since diplomatic relations no longer exist between France and Belgium the only course open to the Belgian Government has been to issue a writ of attachment against the funds of the Bank of France in the United States.

Parting Words to Britain and Germany

MR. WENDELL WILLKIE, before he left England on February 5, after ten strenuous days, gave a final message to this country. " I have not seen quite everything in Britain I wanted to see because of having to cut short my visit, but I have certainly seen plenty. What I said when I arrived over here still goes. Anything I can do in America to help Britain in her fight for freedom I certainly shall do. Your people have shown magnificent courage. Keep your chins up." He also left a longer and severe message to be broadcast in German by the B.B.C. on medium- and short-wave lengths. In this he said : " I am of purely German descent. My family name is not Willkie, but Willicke. My grandparents left Germany 90 years ago because they were protestants against autocracy and demanded the right to live as free men. I, too, claim that right. I am proud of my German blood, but I hate aggression and tyranny. Tell the German people that my convictions are shared to the full by the overwhelming majority of my fellow-countrymen of German descent. They, too, believe in freedom and in human rights. Tell the German people that we German-Americans reject and hate the aggression and lust for power of the present German Government."

Now the Munitions Drive Gets into Its Stride

Small parts for bombers are here being made by girls. A jig with holes in the position of those to be bored is clamped over the metal plate. By pulling a lever the drill, revolved by compressed air, is brought in contact. *Photo, Fox*

NEW factories on which work was begun only after the commencement of the war are now coming into operation, and to meet the need for men and women workers to staff them the registration and call-up of civilian workers has been announced by the Government. In the meantime thousands of men and women who volunteered as munition workers are either being trained or are already at work. Mr. Ernest Bevin, Minister of Labour and National Service, said on November 14, 1940, that at nearly 40 Government training centres, in technical colleges and factories, women would be trained in skilled work side by side with men and that employers were being asked to train more men than their particular factories needed in order to provide workers for new factories.

For men qualifying for skilled work as fitters and tool-makers lectures are given by fully-qualified instructors. Above, in a munitions factory in North-east England some of the 600 men training there are taking notes. *Photo, Keystone*

Front Line Women When the Bombs Are Falling

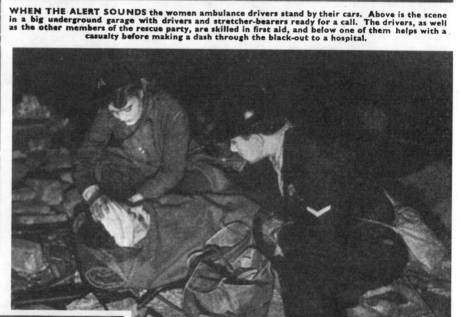

WHEN THE ALERT SOUNDS the women ambulance drivers stand by their cars. Above is the scene in a big underground garage with drivers and stretcher-bearers ready for a call. The drivers, as well as the other members of the rescue party, are skilled in first aid, and below one of them helps with a casualty before making a dash through the black-out to a hospital.

Ordinary cars as well as ambulances are used in the rescue of casualties who are not stretcher-cases. Here at a London ambulance station an attendant is sitting in one of the cars awaiting a call.

STRETCHER-PARTIES are quickly on the scene when bombs fall. Often their work of carrying the casualties over the debris while bombs are dropping is arduous and dangerous. Back in the garage (right) the ambulances are overhauled and made ready for another call.   *Photos, Topical*

I WAS THERE !

Eye Witness Stories of Episodes
and Adventures in the
Second Great War

We Watched the Air Fight over Derna

Derna was captured by the British on January 30, 1941. The Special Correspondent of the Air Ministry News Service arrived on the heels of advance infantry units, and here describes the final air operations over the town, together with some sidelights—dramatic and humorous—on the war in the Libyan Desert.

THREE of us arrived at Derna aerodrome three hours after advance infantry units had driven the enemy out. All was quiet. A shed was smouldering, otherwise there were little signs of battle.

There is a big thrill on entering a captured town. Everyone wants to be there first. In this case we knew it would be additionally exciting, for Derna is different from Bardia or Tobruk. There are trees, hills and signs of ordinary life. There was no knowing too what the place could offer in the way of billets. That is an important item when you have been shaving in what was left of morning tea and sleeping in a car drawn up in a wadi for wind protection.

We counted 19 gutted Italian aircraft. This was no novelty after seeing 22 at Gazala, a dozen or so at Gumbut, 30 at Bardia and 87 at El Adem, in addition to lots wrecked by the wayside. We decided on lunch, so crawled back to the car after looking at Italians through field glasses. The Air Ministry official photographer who was with me had biscuits, an American war correspondent fancied bully beef, and I had a can of beetroot. We were seeking a spot for lunch when suddenly—boom, and a cloud of dust burst no more than 50 yards away. We looked at each other in amazement. Then shells began bursting all over the aerodrome, bangs and crashes all round us.

We all thought of the same thing at the same time and dived for a hole 20 yards away.

Then the show started properly. We lay in that hole until 3.30 in the afternoon. I spilt the can of beetroot and was dripping gory juice. The American mislaid his helmet and wore an Italian one picked off the battlefield. The photographer, who had been in the desert for just three weeks, spent his time between taking pictures in having his hair cut by a tough Australian who had never cut hair before.

A hail of earth and chips of rock fell all around us. The Yank got a superficial wound in the hand. When at last things subsided we got to the hangar. I found one lad lying on a bench with a deep wound in his leg but smoking and joking as if it was a lark.

Then we saw the gladdening sight of a formation of Hurricanes coming zooming overhead to attack enemy bombers and fighters. We watched enthralled. One enemy aircraft crashed in flames less than half a mile away. It was smashed to smithereens when we dashed up. We guessed which squadron had done the damage and drove as fast as we could to its landing ground. We were lucky. The pilots had just landed when we got there.

It had been a grand victory. That afternoon no fewer than five enemy fighters had been shot down, two G50s by a Canadian pilot from Toronto and three CR42s by the inimitable " Imshi." This is the nickname of a flying officer who hails from Blackpool and who had just been awarded the Distinguished Flying Cross. This last three brought " Imshi's " total bag up to 13 since December 9. He was still in his flying suit when I saw him. He had been obliged to force-land after shooting down the third

AIR WARFARE IN LIBYA has been one long record of the supremacy of the R.A.F. over the Regia Aeronautica. A typical episode, fought out in the skies over Derna, is described by an eye-witness in this page. Above, the gutted skeleton of a Fiat CR 42 lies in the sand. The upper photograph shows one of our Wellington bombers having a punctured wheel changed.

Photo, British Official: Crown Copyright.

Italian and had been brought in by Australians. " Imshi " loves fighters ; he loves speed in almost anything. Some time ago he acquired an Italian tank. This he guards jealously and calls it his car.

We dined with a reconnaissance squadron. Dinner was bully beef and dry biscuits washed down with neat whisky as there was no water. Suddenly the flap of the tent opened and a head poked in. " Have you a doctor here ? " said a Cockney voice. It was an ambulance driver who had lost his way in the dark and had a full load in his car, among them six wounded Italians.

In a few minutes the patients were receiving attention from the Royal Air Force doctor. Four men were put to bed with sedatives, others had their wounds dressed. There had been a tank battle and the Italians were picked up after the fray. One, who came from Carmona, was badly injured, with a gashed hip, and when the doctor took a pair of scissors to cut away the fellow's trousers, he screamed. It was, I think, the most dramatic

192　　　　　　　　　　　　　　*The War Illustrated*　　　　　　　　　　　*February 21st,* 1941

IIIIIIIIIIIIIIIIIIIIIIIIIIIIIIIIIIIIIIIIIIIIIIIIIIIIIIIIIIIIIIIIIIIIIIIIIII **I WAS THERE!** IIIIIIIIIIIIIIIIIIIIIIIIIIIIIIIIIIIIIIIIIIIIIIIIIIIIIIIIIIIIIIIIIIIIIIIII

scene I have ever witnessed. We were in semi-darkness, just the flickering light of a hurricane lamp. The Italian was given morphia and he lay muttering and glistening with sweat. The doctor sat with him throughout the night, giving him oxygen. He seemed to revive a little and repeated the name " Ricci, Ricci." Perhaps that was his brother, or best friend. At dawn he died.

It is not all drama here in the desert ; there are often some amusing scenes. On one occasion a motor cyclist arrived—a grubby, tousled and cheery signaller. On the pillion was an Italian prisoner. The signaller explained that he had been sent forward with

telephone wire when the prisoner came innocently towards him. It took him a split second to knock the Italian off his bike, mount it himself and compel the Italian to jump on behind. Then he rode back triumphantly with his spoils.

How can I picture this amazing war in the Libyan Desert where simple human episodes blend with great military strategy : where our airmen camp on sandy wastes making tea with salty water and for days eating nothing but biscuits and bully, and where a loaf of bread baked a week ago is luxury ? It's got to be seen and lived to be fully appreciated, but my, it's good !

essential, however, that the main forces should proceed unmolested, as they were still within easy range of E-boats. One destroyer was detached as protection, and not until these main forces were well clear of any harm was the wireless signal sent out recalling us to her assistance.

While we were going all out to reach the scene of the disaster the protecting destroyer came alongside her crippled companion, transferred the casualties (together with some of the officers and crew), and endeavoured to tow her. The effort was at first successful; but unfortunately the tow rope later parted and the Hyperion, with cabins and wardroom flooded, lay motionless on the water with the attendant destroyer looming a cable's length distance away.

Our Captain Had to Sink the Hyperion

The Admiralty issued on January 22, 1941, a brief statement that " H.M. destroyer Hyperion sustained damage by torpedo or mine, and had subsequently to be sunk by our forces." Here, told by eye-witnesses on accompanying destroyers, is the full story of that incident—a story worthy of the highest traditions of the British Navy.

BEHIND the Admiralty's announcement of the loss of the Hyperion there is the story of how a small destroyer, protected by one other destroyer, lay crippled in the sea almost under the very guns of the Italians for nearly two hours before the call for assistance was sent out in order that the operation on which she was employed should not be detected. Finally, responding to the call, three destroyers rushed to the rescue of her crew, and, working against time, made their getaway from under the lee of powerfully fortified enemy territory.

The following account was given by men from other destroyers :

The Hyperion formed part of the light forces which, sweeping the Adriatic as far as Durazzo three nights previously (see Vol. 4, p. 7), were detailed to carry out a sweep some miles ahead in order to deal with any E-boats or submarines which might appear. Our sweep proved uneventful, and eventually turning back in the small hours of the morning we went full speed ahead for home.

We did not know for some two and a quarter hours afterwards that one of the escort had struck a mine half an hour after passing us. The Hyperion, investigating the possible presence of a submarine, had struck a mine and was badly holed aft. It was

Our captain had made a quick decision. His small destroyer force was in a vulnerable position with only two more hours of darkness in which to get clear. Under the circumstances the idea of towing had to be rejected, and, calling the signalman, the captain said, " Send this to Hyperion : ' Prepare to abandon ship. Am going to sink you.' "

Slowly in eerie silence we were skilfully manoeuvred alongside the stricken ship, while other destroyers formed a slow circling screen. Although her afterdeck was awash the smooth sea enabled the men, with the utmost calm and discipline, to clamber over the sides with the scanty belongings some of them had been able to retrieve. We then withdrew a short distance and the signal was given to one of the circling destroyers to sink her.

Nobody spoke a word as we stood on the bridge waiting for the end, together with some of the Hyperion's officers. There followed a flash from the torpedo tubes, a few seconds' pause, and then a deep, muffled explosion. The shock of the explosion broke off the after-funnel, a column of water and smoke shot skywards from amidships, and the Hyperion slowly rolled over.

There were no flames or subsequent explosions—very gently she sank—and one of her officers quietly remarked, " How gracefully she goes down ; she was a graceful ship."

It was a moment of great sadness. As the ship heeled over her gaping wound could be seen. Then only the keel was visible as she gradually disappeared from view. When we thought she had gone for good her bows suddenly again broke surface and she remained thus perpendicular for some minutes, presumably owing to an air pocket, before the waters finally closed over her.—*Reuter.*

H.M.S. HYPERION, seen in the lower photograph, is of the same class as the five destroyers that took part in the gallant action fought in Narvik on April 11, 1940. She and her seven sister ships were all completed in 1936. They have a displacement of 1,340 tons and a main armament of four 4·7-in. guns and eight 21-in. torpedo tubes. Their speed is 36 knots and their normal complement 145. In the top photograph two destroyers, while at full speed, are making sharp turns to avoid bombs dropped by enemy aircraft.　　　　*Photos, British Official : Crown Copyright ; and Wright & Logan*

On Him May Depend the Aircraft's Safety

THERE is hardly a more interesting job in the R.A.F. than that of wireless operator. When he signs on he may know little about wireless, but after a course in fundamentals and another in operational duties, he goes into the air ready for any emergency. Those emergencies are sometimes exacting and often exciting. He is trusted with valuable secrets, and he may be the one to bring the aircraft back through dirty weather by the signals he receives and sends.

The heavy bomber radio operator's day starts with the careful inspection of his instruments. Any major fault is reported to the flight sergeant, who details a mechanic to correct the defect. Active duty begins with a test of the set while the aircraft is still on the aerodrome. Then, if the operator is taking part in an operational flight, with the other members of the crew he goes for "briefing"—the final instruction before going out on a raid. This takes place generally in the early evening, and the signals officer brushes up procedure with the operator and gives him such details as he will require on the journey. After the evening meal the wireless operator is at his aircraft about half-an-hour before the take-off for a final check-up.

ONCE the aircraft has taken off it is a lone unit, if things go smoothly, until well on the way home. The wireless operator, however, maintains a listening watch. In the early part of the journey he takes action to ensure that the home stations can maintain full contact and facilitate speedy rescue should the aircraft be forced down into the sea. On returning he is interrogated with the rest of the crew by the intelligence officer, who seeks to build up a complete picture of the trip—what has been experienced, and what has been done. Then follows an interview with the signals officer, who goes through the log and the evening's work. Errors are corrected and difficulties straightened out.

A good wireless operator is invaluable. When landmarks or other navigational aids fail he can frequently be of the greatest assistance to the navigator. That is not the whole of his job. In certain types of aircraft he releases flares over the target area, to enable the observer to pin-point his position, and, should it be a pamphlet raid, he assists with unloading the cargo. He also sees that the electrical bomb gear is functioning, that the batteries are properly charged, and the fuses

WIRELESS OPERATORS receive intensive training at Cranwell, Lincolnshire, which is also the college where cadets are trained for permanent commissions in the R.A.F. Part of the instruction is given in aeroplanes on the ground, the students attending in full flying kit. Top left, a lesson in " tuning in " ; above, instruction in the cockpit of a grounded 'plane. *Photos, Keystone*

in order. Some bomber aircraft carry two wireless operator-gunners, who are interchangeable. The second operator is the rear gunner. Each, however, can handle the wireless instruments and the guns.

MANY operators have a long record of flights—some are nearing their fortieth raid—but generally after they have become highly proficient in operational work they are transferred, and in their turn take over the instruction of new operators. Many outstanding feats are to their credit, and more than one crew that has come down in the sea owes its rescue to the cool competence of the wireless operator who got his signal through in spite of the misadventure.

Some Lesser-Knowns of the Luftwaffe

In earlier pages we have described and pictured most of the types of aircraft which Goering
has employed in his raids against this country. Now Mr. Grenville Manton writes of
some other types which the Nazis have employed not quite so frequently, and which,
therefore, have not been so prominently in the public eye

HITLER'S fighter aeroplanes, the Messerschmitt Me 109, and those ugly
bombers, the Junkers Ju 88, the
Dornier Do 17 and the Heinkel He 111, are
familiar to all people in Britain by name.
Night after night we have heard these enemy
'planes mentioned in radio news bulletins,
and many of us have seen their battered

weighs 20,020 lb., while empty the weight
is 11,670 lb.

The He 115 has been developed from the
Heinkel mailplane which in March 1938
created a record by flying for 1,240 miles
with a load of 4,400 lb. at 204 m.p.h. It has
a maximum speed of 220 m.p.h. when
operating at 11,150 feet and cruises at about

Another Nazi aircraft which has been
caught prowling about over the North Sea
is the Dornier 18 flying-boat. It is an all-
metal parasol monoplane-type with two
engines placed in tandem above the centre
section of the wing. These motors are
Junkers Jumos developing 600 h.p. each and
they run on heavy oil. The hull from stem
to stern has a length of 63 feet and is equipped
with machine-gun positions in the bow and
near the tail. The wing, which has rounded
tips, is braced on each side of the hull by
struts, and is fitted with flaps which assist
the take-off and help to maintain control
at reduced speeds on the glide.

Record-breaking Dornier

The main purpose of this flying-boat is
long-distance sea reconnaissance, but it has
also been employed in bombing attacks on
shipping. Like the Heinkel He 115, its
prototype was a record-breaker. In 1938 it
flew 5,200 miles non-stop and so set up a
record for its class. But achievements of
three years ago do not mean much in this
air war of ever-rising speeds, ever-length-
ening distances and growing striking power.
The Dornier 18, which weighs 22,000 lb.,
can top a mere 161 m.p.h. and falls far short
of the needs of today.

Another of the smaller fry of the German
Air Force is the Henschel Hs 126, a general
reconnaissance monoplane intended for
artillery spotting duties and photography.
It has a single 880 h.p. B.M.W. motor and
at 10,000 feet it can attain a maximum speed
of 220 m.p.h. It has a high wing which is
strut-braced, an enclosed tandem cockpit

FOCKE-WULF FW 187 two-seater fighter is a twin-engined 'plane of the German "Zerstörer"
(destroyer) type, built on lines similar to the Messerschmitt ME 110. It has two Daimler-
Benz engines of 1,150 h.p., and is armed with four guns mounted in pairs on each side of the
pilot's cockpit. One of Germany's latest types, it now forms the equipment of various squadrons,
but so far has yet to make its debut against the R.A.F. in action.

By courtesy of "Flight"

remains being carried away to their last
inglorious resting-place after being downed
by the R.A.F. and our A.A. guns. These are
the machines which the Nazis have used
with such reckless abandon in their vain
endeavour to beat us in the skies. But
they have many other aircraft of different
types : they are the lesser-knowns of
Goering's Luftwaffe.

In their efforts to smash our
ocean links the Germans are
employing mine-laying seaplanes. One of these is of
the Heinkel breed—the He
115. More than one specimen
has fallen into our hands, and
post-mortems have revealed
its secrets. It is a mid-wing
monoplane with a wing-spread
of 72 feet 10 inches and a
length of 56 feet 9 inches. It
is powered with two B.M.W.
radial engines of 880 h.p. and
has two 34-foot-long floats
of light alloy construction.
Right in the nose of the fuselage there is a glass-panelled
compartment which accom-
modates the front gunner, and
behind him the pilot and the
rest of the crew are housed in
a long, covered cockpit. Like
most of the German bombers,
the He 115 is poorly armed,
and, being devoid of any form
of turret, is ill-equipped for
defence against rear and
beam attacks. The 'plane is
designed to carry a torpedo
weighing 1,760 lb., as well
as mines, and, as an alternative, it can carry 4,400 lb.
of bombs. With full load it

180 m.p.h. Its duration is 7¼ hours and it
has a range of 1,300 miles. In workmanship
and finish this minelayer, which is one of the
newer types of German 'plane, is good. But
its slow speed, its meagre gun-power and
clumsiness in manoeuvre make it a vulnerable
machine in any combat. It is "easy meat,"
in fact, for almost any R.A.F. 'plane.

HENSCHEL HS 126 is the Luftwaffe's "opposite number" to the famous Westland Lysander army cooperation 'plane which did fine work in France and has also been successfully employed in the Middle East. The
HS 126 is designed as a reconnaissance machine, but up to the present it has not played a conspicuous part in the
war. Hurricanes engaged on a recent "sweep" over Northern France discovered an aerodrome where many
of these craft were based, and with bombs and machine-gun fire played havoc with them.   *Photo, Planet News*

'Planes on Which the Nazis Build Their Hopes

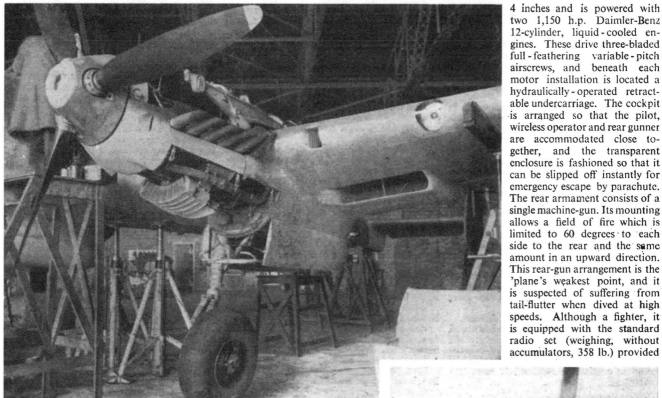

THIS MESSERSCHMITT ME 110 has been partially dismantled at an R.A.F. station. with a view to probing enemy secrets. Note how the radiator is housed in the under side of the wing. The undercarriage is of unusually simple design and retracts into the engine nacelle through the flaps which are seen in open position. The three-bladed airscrew is of the controllable-pitch type.
Photo, courtesy of "Flight"

4 inches and is powered with two 1,150 h.p. Daimler-Benz 12-cylinder, liquid-cooled engines. These drive three-bladed full-feathering variable-pitch airscrews, and beneath each motor installation is located a hydraulically-operated retractable undercarriage. The cockpit is arranged so that the pilot, wireless operator and rear gunner are accommodated close together, and the transparent enclosure is fashioned so that it can be slipped off instantly for emergency escape by parachute. The rear armament consists of a single machine-gun. Its mounting allows a field of fire which is limited to 60 degrees to each side to the rear and the same amount in an upward direction. This rear-gun arrangement is the 'plane's weakest point, and it is suspected of suffering from tail-flutter when dived at high speeds. Although a fighter, it is equipped with the standard radio set (weighing, without accumulators, 358 lb.) provided

and fixed undercarriage. Superficially it resembles our Westland Lysander. Henschel Hs 126 machines have probably been used by the Nazis in spotting for their long-range guns which sporadically shell Dover from the French coast. They will not fare well if any R.A.F. fighter catches them in the act.

Of all the German aeroplanes which have been shot down in this country, the most formidable is undoubtedly the Messerschmitt Me 110 three-seater fighter. It is fast, well-armed, and has a long range. At 19,000 feet its maximum speed is 365 m.p.h., and it is equipped with four forward-firing Rheinmetall-Borsig machine-guns of 7·92 calibre and two 20 mm. cannon. Metal construction is employed throughout and the wings are covered with a flush-riveted metal skin. A low-wing monoplane, it has a span of 53 feet

for German bombers. This includes short and long wave transmitter and receiver and blind approach equipment.

One of the latest types to be placed in service with the Luftwaffe is the Focke-Wulf Fw 187 "Zerstörer." Like the Me 110, it is a twin-engined fighter and is powered with Daimler-Benz 1,150 h.p. engines. With a long fuselage of exceptionally small cross-section and with its wings set at a pronounced dihedral angle it has an ugly, if ferocious, aspect. It is known to carry cannon as well as machine-guns, and at a height of 20,000 feet this enemy fighter does 362 m.p.h. Or so the Nazis say.

DORNIER AIRCRAFT have been famous in the past when they were used for mail-carrying duties and other peaceful pursuits. Here is seen the Dornier DO 18 civil flying-boat, the armed version of which has been used by the Nazis in attacks on our shipping. It is powered with two Junkers Jumo engines which run on heavy oil and are installed tandem-wise in the centre section of the wing (centre, right). It has a top speed of only 161 m.p.h.

Photo, courtesy of "Flight"

OUR DIARY OF THE WAR

TUESDAY, FEB. 4, 1941   *521st day*
On the Sea—Admiralty announced that H.M. trawlers Relonzo and Luda Lady had been sunk.

In the Air—R.A.F. made successful night raids on Düsseldorf, docks at Brest, Dunkirk, Dieppe, Ostend and Bordeaux, and aerodromes at Vannes and other places.

Coastal Command aircraft raided Cherbourg twice.

War against Italy—Advance westwards in Libya continued. R.A.F. made repeated raids on Barce, Berca and Benina.

In Eritrea Italian retirement from Agordat continued. British troops nearing Keren. From Barentu enemy being pursued in southerly direction. Many enemy aircraft destroyed by R.A.F.

In Abyssinia British advance on Metemma-Gondar road continued. Advance patrols from Kenya now 60 miles inside frontier.

British patrols captured Beles Gugani, post 45 miles inside Italian Somaliland.

R.A.F. raided Maritza (Rhodes) aerodrome during night. At least three enemy aircraft destroyed over Malta.

Home Front—Slight enemy activity during day over Suffolk coast and Kent. Night raiders dropped bombs in London area, Midlands and elsewhere.

Four Nazi aircraft destroyed by fighters.

Greek War—Athens reported limited and successful patrol and artillery action. Big fires burning at Tepelini, indicating evacuation. Beyond Himara Greek troops captured mountain pass which Italians had made into stronghold.

WEDNESDAY, FEB. 5   *522nd day*
On the Sea—H.M. trawler Lady Philomena shot down dive bomber attacking convoy off S.E. coast. H.M. trawler Tourmaline, escorting vessel, was sunk.

Unconfirmed report that British Battle Fleet in Mediterranean had made another sweep, but neither Italian ships nor German dive bombers were sighted.

In the Air—R.A.F. very active over Channel and N.W. France. During offensive sweep by our fighters and bombers aerodrome at St. Omer was attacked. Four enemy aircraft destroyed. Seven British fighters lost.

War against Italy—Italian retreat towards Benghazi quickening.

In Eritrea operations round Keren developing successfully.

Home Front—During day bombs fell in S.E. Scotland and in Kent. At night raiders were over London area, a south-east coastal district and two towns in East Anglia.

Greek War—Athens reported capture of important positions north of Klisura.

THURSDAY, FEB. 6   *523rd day*
In the Air—R.A.F. made night raids on docks at invasion ports in Northern France.

War against Italy—Benghazi surrendered after twofold attack from Australian troops pressing along coast and British armoured units from south.

In Eritrea British closing in on Keren.

During night of 5-6 R.A.F. raided Benghazi, Berca and Jedabia.

Home Front—No enemy day activity over Britain. At night raiders were reported from S. Wales, West of England and Liverpool.

Greek War—Athens reported limited patrol and artillery activity. R.A.F. bombed military targets west of Tepelini.

General—Mr. John G. Winant appointed American Ambassador to Britain.

FRIDAY, FEB. 7   *524th day*
On the Sea—Admiralty announced that H.M. destroyer Vanity shot down a Dornier.

In the Air—During night waves of R.A.F. bombers attacked German invasion ports.

War against Italy—General Wavell's forces now sweeping southwards round Gulf of Sidra. Situation round Keren, Eritrea, developing satisfactorily.

Free French force from Chad captured Italian air base at Kufra, S. Libya.

In Abyssinia, advance along Gondar road progressing. Area of penetration into British Somaliland being continually enlarged.

Home Front—Single enemy aircraft dropped bombs on town on N.E. coast of Scotland. Town on East Anglian coast attacked.

Greek War—Heavy shelling of Tepelini area continued.

SATURDAY, FEB. 8   *525th day*
In the Air—R.A.F. bombers attacked industrial targets at Mannheim. Other aircraft bombed Rotterdam and Flushing, and attacked convoy off coast of Norway.

War against Italy—Operations south of Benghazi proceeding.

In Keren area British pressure increased. Farther south troops continued pursuit of enemy retreating towards Arresa.

Enemy raided Malta during nights of 7-8 and 8-9, causing damage and casualties.

On night of 8-9 R.A.F. raided aerodromes at Calato and Maritza (Rhodes). Fleet Air Arm attacked Tripoli.

Home Front—Very little daylight enemy activity reported. At night bombs fell in Yorks, and raiders were also reported over West Coast. Three enemy aircraft shot down.

Greek War—Tepelini said to have been evacuated after 2-months' siege.

SUNDAY, FEB. 9   *526th day*
On the Sea—British naval forces carried out heavy bombardment of Italian naval base at Genoa, inflicting much damage.

Admiralty announced that H.M. trawlers Almond and Arctic Trapper had been sunk.

In the Air—Two Spitfires carried out offensive patrol over Calais area.

Coastal Command aircraft made torpedo attacks on enemy destroyers off Norwegian coast, hitting one amidships.

Other aircraft bombed oil tanks at Flushing and docks at Antwerp.

War against Italy—Advanced British armoured units occupied El Agheila, on Gulf of Sidra.

Despite enemy reinforcements, operations round Keren proceeding satisfactorily.

Naval aircraft attacked aerodrome and railway junction at Pisa and refineries at Leghorn.

Home Front—Enemy daylight activity near South-east and East coasts, but no bombs.

At night bombs fell in East Anglia, Essex, Home Counties and one place in west of Scotland. Two German bombers destroyed.

Greek War—Enemy counter-attacks repulsed, but Greeks held up by bad weather.

R.A.F. shot down seven Italian fighters in Klisura area.

General—M. Flandin resigned from Foreign Ministry. Marshal Pétain appointed Admiral Darlan, Minister of Marine, to be Vice-Premier and Foreign Minister.

MONDAY, FEB. 10   *527th day*
In the Air—In early hours Bomber Command aircraft attacked enemy bases on coast of N.W. Germany.

Large R.A.F. forces made offensive sweeps over Northern France, bombing targets at Boulogne, Calais and Dunkirk.

Strong bomber force made heavy 6-hour night raid on Hanover. Other aircraft attacked docks at Rotterdam, Boulogne, Cherbourg and Ostend, and several aerodromes.

War against Italy—In Libya clearance of areas up to El Agheila proceeded. General Wilson appointed C.-in-C. and Governor of Cyrenaica. British troops in Eritrea occupied Mersa Taclai and Karora.

R.A.F. again raided Calato (Rhodes).

Home Front—Slight enemy activity during day. At night bombs fell on two East Anglian towns. Our night fighters damaged, probably destroyed, two Heinkels.

General—British Government broke off diplomatic relations with Rumania.

H.M.S. MANCHESTER, a 9,400-ton cruiser of the same class as the ill-fated Southampton, was commissioned in 1938, and since then has seen war service in many seas, from the Indian Ocean to beyond the Arctic Circle. In the spring of 1940 she was promoted to be flagship of Vice-Admiral Sir Geoffrey Layton, second in command of the Home Fleet, and took part in the Namsos, Aandalsnes and Molde operations off the Norwegian coast. In November of last year she was sent to reinforce Admiral Sir James Somerville's squadron in the Western Mediterranean and led the line when that force chased an Italian Fleet sighted off Sardinia on November 27, 1940. The big silk ensign presented to the ship by the Corporation of Manchester to be flown in action was hoisted for the first time, and cheers broke out from the crew as it was broken at the masthead. But the Italian squadron, despite immense superiority in numbers, refused battle and made for their home base. The Manchester set one enemy cruiser ablaze aft and then hit (and probably sank) a destroyer before the greater speed of the Italian vessels enabled them to get away. Prior to this action the Manchester, which has no ancestors in the Navy List, had therefore no battle honours. Today her honours' board bears the name of her first victory: "Spartivento, 1940." In a year she has steamed 55,000 miles.   *Photo, Topical*

SHE FIGHTS FOR BRITAIN AT A MUNITIONS BENCH

Women munition workers—we have not yet called them Munitionettes as in the last war—can already be counted by thousands, but, as Mr. Ernest Bevin, Minister of Labour, has announced, industry will have to utilize women far more than it is doing at present, and it is expected that compulsory registration of the female population will soon be instituted. Our photograph shows one of the great army of young women who have already found their wartime vocation. Her husband is a prisoner of war in Germany, but she, who when she last went out to work made medicinal capsules, has now learnt to operate a lathe in a great munitions factory.

Photo, Planet News

Behind the Scenes of the Abyssinian Revolt

Leader of the British Military Mission which encouraged the Abyssinian Patriots in the province of Gojjam to revolt against the Italian invader is a British colonel who, with a heavy price on his head, has been operating in enemy territory for the past six months. Here we have his own story, as told to Reuter's Special Correspondent.

To obtain an eye-witness account of the revolt in Gojjam, Reuter's Special Correspondent travelled for many days from an advanced base, driving the first motor vehicle over the territory into the heart of the Western Abyssinian lowlands. Finally he had to abandon the car in a ravine before an uncrossable mountain range, and then he continued on foot for many miles through uninhabited bush and bamboo woods. At last he arrived, exhausted and in rags, at the meeting-place, where he was met by a British officer who greeted him with : " Good morning. Would you like a glass of beer ? " Then in a small hut made of grass and tree branches he interviewed the head of the mission, a bald and bespectacled colonel.

After describing the situation in Abyssinia following the Italian conquest in 1936, the colonel went on to tell how on the outbreak of war with Italy, Britain recognized Haile Selassie as Emperor and promised full support for the Ethiopian cause. Two months later the British military mission trekked in the rainy season through the fever-infested western Abyssinian lowlands, swimming swollen rivers, and succeeded in establishing themselves behind the fortified Italian line

covering the Gojjam escarpment, with the object of making contact with the Ethiopian chiefs, advising them in the conduct of the war and arranging for the supply of arms and munitions.

After they had scaled the top of the mountain barrier and within two hours of the beginning of their first conference with Abyssinian chiefs, a large enemy force which was waiting for them behind a neighbouring hill began an encircling drive, whereupon the mission scrambled down the mountainside for safety.

Italian aircraft repeatedly swooped down and Italian troops machine-gunned them from the cliff above. However, the mission succeeded in getting through the Italian cordon and, although continually pursued, established its headquarters in the heart of the highlands, which resembled Scottish moors created by a giant hand, where cool winds rustled between heather ten feet high and 12-foot thistles grew like small trees, their purple blooms the size of prize chrysanthemums.

The first task of the mission was the distribution of Haile Selassie's proclamation calling on Abyssinians to unite against the Italians. Next they had to bring about a

public reconciliation between dissident chiefs. The first two chiefs met in a coppice in the centre of a large plain, concealed from observation from the air, and embraced each other. This example led to a general sinking of differences between chiefs all over the province. They accepted the Emperor's proclamation, which was read out before assembled troops and the British mission, and the chieftains expressed their loyalty by kneeling and kissing the ground and celebrated by firing machine-guns.

The mission got into contact with leading chiefs in the east, who stirred up trouble for the Italians to such an extent that the eastern troops were not only contained there but had to be reinforced by troops from the west. But the Italian operations proved entirely lacking in thrust and drive ; all movement along the road was harassed by Patriot guerillas, and at the same time the R.A.F. bombed the Italian positions in Western Gojjam with the greatest effect. Finally, the speed of the Italian retreat from the Sudan frontier and the auspicious start of the British offensive brought home to the Ethiopians the realization that the moment when liberty might be restored was at hand.

ABYSSINIA and Italian East Africa as a whole are being assailed from every side. This contour map shows those parts in which the British and South African Forces with Abyssinian Patriots are taking the offensive. The white arrows indicate the direction of the advances by the British troops, and the broken white arrows, attacks on Italian aerodromes. In Eritrea Keren is invested ; on the west, Kurmuk, last of the Sudanese outposts captured by the Italians some months ago, was retaken on February 14 ; in the south the South Africans have invaded not only Abyssinia but Italian Somaliland, and by February 17 they were nearing the line of the Juba river.

Italy's First Victim Fights for Freedom

After the Italians conquered Abyssinia in 1936 they constructed over 2,000 miles of motor roads, but most of them are still in Italian hands. Such heavy lorries as these, with British crews and native guides, have, however, been able to make their way over the old tracks.

The first Ethiopian troops to enter Abyssinia, trained on British territory and officered by Australians, depended on camel transport for supplies. Above are some of the camels with their native guard and white officers during their trek of 200 miles. Centre, the O.C. studies a map of the route.   *Photos, British Official: Crown Copyright*

'X.O.-6' Was the Greatest Battle of All

Some have called it "X.O.-6" because it took place in a blank space on the map ; to others it is the Battle of Soluk. But all agree that the last stand made by the Italians just after they had evacuated Benghazi was the greatest battle of the Libyan War. Below we give the story of the desperate struggle in the words of Alan Moorehead, "Daily Express" staff reporter at the front.

WHILE the Australians were marching into Benghazi, British armoured units, then lying nearly 200 miles away, south of Derna, were ordered to make a forced march straight across the desert, south of the "Green Mountains," to cut off the mass retreat of the Italians to Tripoli.

No army had ever crossed that wasteland before. Even Beduins seldom attempt it. Camel tracks lead nowhere. The British commanders set a compass course and led their convoys into action. They cut down their men's water ration to one glass daily. Everything was sacrificed to speed—even halts for sleep and food. There was only one Order of the Day, " Get to the coast."

"LIKE A BLOOMING RED INDIAN, EH?"
Cartoon by Zec, by courtesy of the "Daily Mirror"

A storm of full gale force sprang up against them. First it blew powder-fine sand into their faces, cutting down visibility to three yards. Then frozen rain streamed down in the wind.

And so they bumped hour after hour. They travelled bonnet to tailboard in darkness, spaced out again as protection against air raiders in daylight.

The Commanding General's own car broke down trying to keep pace with the great column. Even so, at places it was impossible to do more than six or seven miles per hour. The drivers, muffled up to their ears and strapped in leather jackets and goggles, became unrecognizable under the caking of mud. Yet they did it in thirty-six hours. Two hours later it would have been too late. The Italians would have slipped through.

At midday on Wednesday (February 5) British mechanized cavalry travelling ahead tapped out in Morse the message : " We've reached the coast and contacted the enemy thirty-five miles south of Benghazi. They're packed along the road. Hurry."

It was the last of Graziani's force escaping, with all his senior generals, with 125 tanks, over 100 guns of all calibres, many hundreds of vehicles, and more than 16,000 men. The British were outnumbered five to one in

tanks, five to one in men, and three to one in guns. They were up against a fresh, desperate enemy.

At one p.m. Wednesday British tanks swept in over sticky, sodden ground. British guns deployed and shot.

For the last time the Italians turned and fought—fought out of desperation more fiercely than they have done since the war began. This, in fact, was the only time they have honestly given battle, complete battle to the death or surrender.

The British commanders, hastily meeting under shellfire, made their plan. There were several hours of daylight left. Under heavy shelling British tanks crept up to the coast mile by mile.

British artillery got the range of the coastal road from which the enemy were operating. By nightfall over forty Italian tanks were out of action, just smoking steel carcasses lying in the mud. Twice the British tanks exhausted their ammunition and had to go back for more.

All Wednesday night the shelling continued, while one after another the Italian field guns were registered by their flashes, straddled with shot and finally hit.

The Italian general in command (General Tellera) turned, as every Italian general has done before him, and looked for some

loophole to escape. " I cannot believe," he told his staff, before he died, " that the full strength of the British have got here so soon or that they can have cut our road to the south."

But he was wrong. In the darkness one section of the British forces spun fanwise round his north flank and reached the sea. Another raced to the south and mined the road along the line of the Italians' retreat.

Caught Between Two Fires

On Thursday morning (February 6) these two jaws began to close. The Italians lost all hope of escape then. They counter-attacked. The attack was fought to a standstill. Some thirty enemy medium tanks, pursued by twenty British, fled down the coastal road on to our minefield, where more British tanks were awaiting them. The enemy gave up.

There was carnage in the centre of the battlefield. British machine-gunners and light units went into support of the artillery. They picked off one enemy vehicle after another until for ten miles the road was littered with upturned, smashed vehicles that crashed into one another or up-ended themselves grotesquely in the air.

Yet again the Italians tried to attack early on Friday morning (February 7). But it was far too late. White handkerchiefs began appearing, waved by men who came out of hiding in the rocks from every direction.

General Tellera, struck by a bullet, died on the field, and General Cona took over. He had a more forlorn hope than ever General Weygand had in France.

Soon the fighting was carried into the sand-dunes. It was there the Tommies found

As step by step the Army of the Nile pushed along the Libyan coast, not only over 100,000 prisoners fell into its hands, but many Italian wounded. These were given the best of treatment; and here a British officer is helping an Italian to carry one of them to an ambulance, while a second Italian awaits his turn.
Photo, British Official ; Crown Copyright

Italian Wounded Tended by the R.A.M.C.

AROUND BARDIA underground hospitals were arranged by the Italians in the rock formations, for, hemmed in by sea and land, it was impossible to remove the wounded out of the range of the Briitsh bombardment. When the town surrendered the wounded were in the charge of Italian doctors, but parties of stretcher-bearers of the R.A.M.C. soon carried them away to the ambulances waiting to take them to more comfortable quarters at the base.

Photo, British Official: Crown Copyright

They Were 'Just Too Quick' for the Italians

IN LIBYA **Beduins** welcomed the arrival of the Imperial troops and often proved ready to give information about enemy movements. Above, a British officer makes friends with the help of a packet of cigarettes. Below is the spot on the Capuzzo-Bardia road seen photographed a few weeks earlier in page 143 of this volume. Now it is no longer closed ; most of the enemy are captives, and British cars move freely along it.   *Photos, British Official : Crown Copyright*

Berganzoli and many other staff officers, and a rejoicing message went back to headquarters, " Berganzoli's in the bag."

By Friday midday it was all over. Only one or two tanks and a few score vehicles are known to have escaped.

The day after the battle General Berganzoli, wearing a private soldier's uniform, gave me his story in a redstone farmhouse at Soluk.

" Yes, I supposed you would want to know how I have kept eluding you since last December," he began.

" Well, I walked out of Bardia on the third day of the battle. I saw it was hopeless, and with several of my officers set off, walking by night and hiding in caves by day.

" It took five days to reach Tobruk. We passed right through the British lines. We were so close we heard your troops talking, saw their watch fires, and smelt their cooking.

" After Tobruk fell I flew out on board the last 'plane to Derna. Derna, I think, was our best stand of all. But when at last many of our guns were put out of action and we had no more ammunition, I got my troops away at night, and with them drove off in a baby car down the coastal road to Benghazi.

" We had no time to prepare defences outside Benghazi.' In any case, it was an open town. We had no wish to expose women and children to more misery.

" We decided to leave with all our remaining forces for Tripoli. You were just too quick, that is all. Your forward units found us on the coast on Wednesday morning and we gave battle.

" Our artillery, tanks, and men, tired though they were and at a disadvantage on the coast, came quickly into position and gave battle magnificently.

" We launched two counter-attacks. Our tanks pushed forward against superior numbers right up to a British battalion headquarters.

" Our second attack was made when our forces were largely decimated and our ammunition almost exhausted. When that failed we had no choice but to make honourable surrender."

These Are the Men Who Conquered Cyrenaica

General SIR ARCHIBALD WAVELL, K.C.B.
" a master of war—sage, painstaking, daring and tireless "

"THIS is the time, I think," said Mr. Churchill in his broadcast oration of February 9, "to speak of the leaders who at the head of their brave troops have rendered distinguished service to the King.

" First and foremost, General Wavell, Commander-in-Chief of all the Armies in the Middle East, has proved himself a master of war—sage, painstaking, daring, and tireless. But General Wavell has repeatedly asked that others should share his fame. General Wilson, who actually commands the Army of the Nile, was reputed to be one of our finest tacticians, and few will now deny him that quality. General O'Connor, commanding the Thirteenth Corps, with General Mackay, commanding the splendid Australians, and General Creagh, who trained and commanded the various armoured divisions which were employed—these three men executed the complicated and astoundingly rapid movements which were made and fought the actions which occurred. I have just seen a telegram from General Wavell in which he says that the success of Benghazi was due to the outstanding leadership and resolution of O'Connor and Creagh, ably backed by Wilson."

Then the Premier paid those tributes to Air Marshal Longmore and Admiral Cunningham already quoted in pages 182-183.

Lt.-Gen. SIR H. M. WILSON
" one of our finest tacticians "

Maj.-Gen. M. CREAGH   **Maj.-Gen. R. N. O'CONNOR**
" outstanding leadership and resolution "

Maj.-Gen. I. G. MACKAY
" commanding the splendid Australians "

Air Marshal SIR A. LONGMORE
" wrested the control of the air from the enemy "

Admiral SIR A. CUNNINGHAM
" chased the Italian Navy into its harbours "

Photos, British Official : Crown Copyright ; Wide World, " Daily Mirror." Associated Press, Sport & General, Elliott & Fry

Darlan Stands at Pétain's Right Hand

Never very clear, the situation in Unoccupied France has become ever more confused as Laval, Hitler's puppet, strives to oust the veteran Marshal Pétain, if not from the supreme place, at least from supreme power. Now Laval seems to be eclipsed, and it is Admiral Darlan's star which is in the ascendant.

Not "the French Quisling, commonly called Laval"—as Mr. Churchill has described him—but Admiral Darlan is now Number Two in the French State. On the evening of Sunday, February 9, Marshal Pétain announced that he had appointed Admiral Darlan Vice-Premier and Secretary of State for Foreign Affairs, while still retaining his post as Minister of Marine. Furthermore, a few hours later, by a Constitutional Act, the Marshal named the Admiral his successor as Head of the State should the Marshal be prevented from carrying out his duties.

Jean François Darlan was born in 1881 near Bordeaux, and comes from a family which for generations has given its sons to

direction of Admiral Darlan, France has set about the creation of a really first-class Navy. The ports—Lorient and Dunkirk in particular—have been modernized under his guidance, and a number of fine vessels have been laid down; many, indeed, are already in service, in particular the battleships Strasbourg and Dunkerque. Two other battleships have been launched, the Richelieu and the Jean Bart. These ships are amongst the finest and most powerful in the world, and we may well believe that they are the apple of Darlan's eye. This being so, we can also imagine the chagrin and grief with which he heard of the battering to which they had been subjected by the Navy of Britain, so recently France's ally: the Dunkerque badly damaged at Oran on July 3,

Armistice between France and Germany provided that the French Fleet, "except that part left free for safeguarding French interests in the colonial empire," was to be collected in certain ports, demobilized and disarmed under German or Italian control. This demobilization and disarmament, however, has (so far as we can judge) never been carried out, but in July last there was a very real fear that the ships were shortly to come under Hitler's control: hence the "melancholy action" of Oran and the hardly less melancholy operation at Dakar.

A month before these blows, at his beautiful ships Admiral Darlan was prominent amongst those at Bordeaux who had urged an immediate armistice with Germany; and as the summer months passed he was reported to be ever more anti-British, until there came a time when he was said to be pro-Hitler.

Rivalry with Laval

But then there developed a struggle behind old Marshal Pétain's coat-tails, one that became more and more a tussle between Pierre Laval, the wily politician, and Darlan, the bluff but shrewd sailor. For a long time Laval seemed to have the ball at his feet. On July 20 he was nominated by Marshal Pétain Vice-Premier and successor. But on December 16 he suddenly fell from office. According to report he was willing to serve Hitler too well, and Pétain was unwilling to pay the price demanded of him. Hitler could offer France a place in his "new Europe," he could restore the two million French prisoners of war to their homes, he could lift the financial burdens of the German occupation; he could do all these things, but he would do them only at a price, and that price, there could be little doubt, included the transference to German control of France's warships. Pétain, that old soldier of rigid honour, stuck to the terms of the Armistice; never would the French ships be handed over, he declared. Laval had outplayed his hand, and, driven from office, he strove in vain for his reinstatement. Not even Hitler could persuade or compel Pétain to restore Laval to his former office and greatness, although the Marshal did offer him a seat in the Government as a Minister of State and as a Member of a Committee of Direction. The swarthy little fellow with a white tie wanted much more than this, however; he wanted to be Premier, first man in the French State so far as power was concerned, though he was willing to let Pétain keep the trappings of office.

As Laval chafed in the wilderness, Darlan grew in greatness. He held in his hands the French fleet; the ships at Toulon and Bizerta, at Dakar and Casablanca, were all under his orders, their officers and crews followed his star unhesitatingly. And early in February 1941 he gave an interview to the "Journal" in which he is reported to have said, "The French Fleet, at present and in the future, will remain under complete French control, and will defend itself and the Empire against any challenge whatsoever, and against any attack from any quarter." Only a few days after that statement Darlan became Number Two to Pétain's Number One.

GENERAL WEYGAND, as Commander-in-Chief of France's colonial army, holds one of the trump cards which has helped the Vichy government to prolong its resistance to Hitler's demands. On Feb. 12, 1941, General Weygand left Algiers for a tour of West Africa. He is here seen during a previous visit being greeted by ex-service men in Senegal. *Photo, Associated Press*

the French Navy; his great-grandfather was on board the Redoubtable at Trafalgar. Darlan entered the Navy in 1899, and during the Great War commanded naval guns in France and at Salonika. After the war he saw service in Chinese waters, and was for some years instructor and commander in the training cruiser Jeanne D'Arc—hence in large measure his unrivalled influence with the present officers of the Fleet. Then he became Chief of Staff of the Second Division, Rear-Admiral commanding the First Light Cruiser Squadron and Vice-Admiral commanding the Second Squadron, until in December 1936 he was appointed Chief of the French Naval General Staff.

Following the conclusion of the Great War in 1918, there set in a period of decline for the French Navy, furthered by the decision of the Washington Naval Conference of 1921 which allowed France naval parity with Italy—far below Britain, the U.S.A. and Japan. But of late years, largely through the vigorous

1940; the Strasbourg torpedoed and bombed while racing from Oran to Toulon; and the Richelieu severely damaged at Dakar, on July 8.

Shortly before the outbreak of the present war—on June 6, 1939, to be precise—Darlan was promoted Admiral—a rank new to the French naval hierarchy—which made him, in effect, Commander-in-Chief of the Navy. His first consideration was for the reorganization of the French Admiralty, and when the war began the Navy under his command was supposed to be as good as any which has sailed under the French flag. For the first months of the war there was cordial cooperation between Darlan and Pound, between the French Navy and the British, and the comradeship of the last war was revived in the common experiences of Channel convoys, the campaign in Norwegian waters, and finally the epic of Dunkirk. Then came France's collapse, and comradeship was converted into rancour, even hostility. Article 8 of the

France's Men of Destiny Meet at Toulon

MARSHAL PETAIN AND ADMIRAL DARLAN, the men on whom the hopes of France and the eyes of the world are centred today, are here meeting for a conference on board the battleship Strasbourg in Toulon harbour. Strasbourg was at Oran during the " melancholy action " of July 3, 1940, and only with difficulty managed to run the gauntlet of the British squadron and reach Toulon. The memory must have been fresh in the minds of both France's " No. 1 " and " No. 2 " as they met on the great ship's deck. In the background is another French warship.　　*Photo, Associated Press*

The Battle of Nerves in the Balkans

Once again all eyes are centred on the Balkans—that south-eastern corner of Europe which for so many centuries has been the scene of so many wars. This article tells of the increasing success of Hitler's policy of penetration in what until recently Italy boasted was her sphere of influence.

A PATCHWORK of political divisions, a jumble of geographical features, a medley of peoples, a cauldron of trouble never far from boiling-point—that is the Balkans.

Five countries are included within its bounds. The largest and most important is Yugoslavia, which came into being on December 1, 1918, as the Kingdom of the Serbs, Croats and Slovenes, although since 1929 it has been more simply known as the Kingdom of Yugoslavia. It is the pre-war Serbia, swollen by the addition of Montenegro and vast areas of the Slavic regions of the old Austro-Hungarian Empire. Its present sovereign is King Peter II, a boy of 17 ; power rests in the Regency Council, presided over by the King's uncle, Prince Paul.

To the east is Rumania, now but the shadow of its former greatness. After 1918 it was at least a second-rate power, but now, following the exile of King Carol, the coming into office of General Antonescu, followed by what is in fact, if not in name, a German invasion, it is one of Hitler's puppet states, hardly more independent than Norway or Holland. There is still a king in Bucharest— Michael, a youth of 19—but Antonescu is the real ruler, and Hitler pulls Antonescu's strings.

Then there is Bulgaria, over which reigns King Boris in Sofia. Along her southern frontier run that little corner which is all that is left to the Turks in Europe and the kingdom of Greece. To complete the jigsaw, we have only to drop little Albania into its place on the western coast.

Of these, Albania and Greece are involved in the war, the one as an Italian possession and the other as Britain's ally against Mussolini. For the rest, they are all threatened, even if they have not been actually strangled, by the tentacles of the Nazi octopus.

Rumania, as we said above, is one of Hitler's puppet states. Its king has no power ; its premier, its corps of officers, its press, its chief political faction, the Black Guards, its newspapers and its wireless, its

oilfields and its railways, are all under Nazi domination. For weeks past a great German army has been assembling on the Rumanian plains ; one estimate gives its number as a quarter of a million men, another as half a million. For a surety it is a formidable force, well supplied with armoured divisions, that has now been mustered on the northern banks of the Danube and waits to cross, perhaps for Hitler to give the word, perhaps for the melting of the ice in springtime. Small wonder, then, that on February 10 it was announced that Sir Reginald Hoare, British Minister in Rumania, had been recalled. " Some months ago," to quote from Mr. Eden's Note addressed on his instructions by Sir Reginald to General Antonescu, " you informed me that a small number of German troops were arriving in Rumania in order to instruct the Rumanian Army in modern methods of warfare and that the necessary equipment was likewise being dispatched from Germany for the rearmament of the Rumanian troops. Some instruction has no doubt been imparted, but the essential development is that the German High Command is building up in Rumania all the elements of an expeditionary force and is concentrating at strategic points large supplies of munitions and oil fuel. Rumanian territory is thus being used by Germany as a military base in furtherance of her plans for prosecuting the war."

If and when the Nazis cross the Danube, Bulgaria will be Hitler's next victim. She has an army of a war strength of some 500,000 men, and in many a war the Bulgars have shown themselves to be splendid fighters. But the sight of those German troops and tanks just across the river has affected the morale of the governing class. In his broadcast on February 9 Mr. Churchill stated that, supposedly with the acquiescence of the Bulgarian Government, airfields were being occupied by thousands of German ground personnel so as to enable the German Air Force to go into action from Bulgaria. Mr. Churchill went on to remind the Bulgarians

King Boris of Bulgaria, whose country lies across Hitler's path to the Near East, succeeded to the throne on the abdication of his father, King Ferdinand, in 1918. He is 46 and married Princess Giovanna of Savoy, daughter of the King of Italy, in 1930.
Photo, Planet News

of the mistake they made in 1915 when they threw in their lot with the Central Powers. " I asked the Bulgarian Minister to dinner," he said, " to explain to him what a fool King Ferdinand would make of himself if he were to go in on the losing side. It was no use. The poor man simply could not believe it, or make his Government believe it. So Bulgaria, against the wishes of her peasant population, and against all her interests, fell in at the Kaiser's tail and got steadily carved up and punished when the victory was won. I trust that Bulgaria is not going to make the same mistake again."

But the Bulgarian Army is pro-German, and so, too, is the Bulgarian press. The politicians are also inclined to look to Hitler, for they believe that it was through his influence that Rumania was persuaded to hand back Southern Dobruja to Bulgaria on August 31, 1940, and they hope that the same influence will be brought to bear to force Greece to restore that corridor to the Aegean Sea at Dedeagatch which was lost in 1919. As for the peasants, they tend to be pro-Russian, still regarding Russia as the big brother of the Slavs ; but politically the peasants do not count for much.

Perhaps it was because he anticipated Hitler's drive into the Balkans that Mussolini attacked Greece in October, 1940 ; he wanted to seize what he could while there was still something left to seize. But his men met nothing but disaster, and now there is talk of Hitler undertaking a Balkan expedition to rescue the Italians from the Greeks they had so wantonly attacked. If Hitler indeed decides to invade Greece, then he would probably do so via the Struma Pass, which lies on the direct route from Sofia to Salonika. But before he does so he must make sure of Yugoslavia, for it would never do to expose his flank to so considerable a power. So now Yugoslavia is being taken in hand. As reported on February 13 her Premier and

Saluting Iron Guards at a celebration parade in Bucharest are seen (left to right) General Antonescu, Rumanian Prime Minister, whose counter-measures broke the Iron Guard revolt early in 1941; Signor Pellegrino Ghigi, Italian Minister; Herr von Fabricius, German Minister; and Horia Sima, notorious Iron Guard leader who became a fugitive.
Photo. Keystone

They Came to 'Teach' but Stayed to Conquer

RUMANIA'S " peaceful penetration " by the Nazis was admitted by the Rumanian Legation in Berlin on October 7, 1940, when it was announced that German troops had arrived there to " reorganize the Rumanian Army." In the top photograph some of them are goose-stepping through the streets of Bucharest. By the middle of February 1941 the number of German troops in the country was estimated at between 250,000 and 500,000. Lower photo, lorries loaded with Nazis and towing light guns are streaming through the streets of the capital.　　*Photos, Associated Press and Keystone*

War Clouds Loom above Europe's Cockpit

Foreign Minister, Tsvetkovitch and Markovitch, were " invited " to Berchtesgaden and there, after a conference with Ribbentrop on the way, they met the Fuehrer and heard his will. Report has it that Yugoslavia must give up some little pieces of territory to Hungary and Bulgaria and submit to German military and economic penetration, in return for which she would receive—from Greece !— some territory round Lake Ochrida, and a corridor to Salonika ; she would also receive

(so it was said) Northern Albania—this time from Italy.

" Of course," to quote Mr. Churchill's Sunday evening oration again, " if all the Balkan peoples stood together and acted together, aided by Britain and Turkey, it would be many months before a German army and air force of sufficient strength to overcome them could be assembled in the south-east of Europe, and in these months much might happen ; it will certainly happen

as American aid becomes effective and as our air power grows, and as we become a well-armed nation, and as our armies in the East increase in strength.

" But," the Premier went on, " nothing is more certain than that if the countries of south-eastern Europe allow themselves to be pulled to pieces one by one, they will share the fate of Holland, Denmark and Belgium, and none can tell how long it will be before the hour of their deliverance strikes."

SOUTH-EASTERN EUROPE, or the Balkans as it is frequently styled (after the mountains of that name which form its rocky frame), is a mass of complications, physical, political and racial. As this map shows, Hitler dominates the northern lands, and he is now reaching out across the Danube to Yugoslavia and Bulgaria. If these fall into his clutches, then a drive against Salonika and another at Turkey, guardian of the Straits, may be expected. All the principal railways and road routes are indicated, and the mountain heights give some indication of the natural difficulties that must be faced by an invader.

Map by courtesy of " Free Europe"

Another Loss Made Good in Our Merchant Navy

NON-STOP SHIPBUILDING is the order of the day at all British shipbuilding yards.　A remarkable illustration of the push being made is afforded by this photograph.　A big tanker has just taken the water from the slipway.　Before she was towed away to dock for fitting out the workmen, who had paused for a moment to give her a cheer, were again busy getting the keel plate of the next ship into position.　*Photo, Topical*

BRITAIN needs ships—many ships and of many different types. This has been made clear by Sir Arthur Salter, Parliamentary Secretary to the Ministry of Shipping, in a recent statement. Till last June the average weekly toll exacted by the enemy was 41,000 tons (Allied and neutral as well as British tonnage). Since then it has averaged some 90,000 tons, but up to date our losses have been nearly balanced by new building, transfer and capture. We still have more than 97 per cent of the total seagoing tonnage under the British flag in 1939. A reduction of less than three per cent would not be serious in itself, since we have cut down on the civilian peace consumption of imported goods about ten times that percentage, but our losses have increased since the enemy has been able to use French ports.

Moreover, our opportunities of replacement are in some respect, e.g. by capture, less than they were. Many of our ships have also been needed to carry troops or military supplies to the Army in Africa, or to serve as armed cruisers, and are not therefore available to bring imports. We have chartered much neutral and allied tonnage and have requisitioned all ocean-going British vessels. We are building, buying and chartering all we can ; we have, for example, chartered four million tons of neutral and allied shipping, and have bought over 500,000 tons, mainly from the U.S.A. We are hoping that the U.S.A. will make an even greater contribution in this way.

FROM our own yards we have ordered many ships of a definite type (cargo tramps), but we also want tankers, some fast cargo vessels, fast passenger ships, as well as the bread-and-butter ships and tramp steamers which constitute the greater part of the building in this country. We are increasing the rate of shipbuilding here, but we have not yet surpassed the peak figure attained in the course of the last war, when in 1918 we produced 1,348,000 tons gross.

OUR losses in the course of 1940, said Mr. Ronald Cross, Minister of Shipping, on February 5, amounted to 4,300,000 tons, and our losses in the worst year we have ever known, namely 1917, amounted to 6,000,000 tons. In the last war the submarine menace was only overcome by new building on a huge scale. That new building came mainly from the United States, and although it is not possible to say what shipping contribution the U.S.A., Democracy's arsenal, proposes to make, that there will be a contribution is beyond doubt, for it would indeed be inconsistent for the U.S.A. to make her present great efforts to provide this country with aircraft, tanks and many other munitions of war, if it were not paralleled by assistance to our vital communications.

Down this Ravine of Blistered Rock, Strew

UP THE HILL ABOVE BARDIA roars a dispatch rider of the Australian forces—those splendid Australians, as Mr. Churchill has called them. On the far hillside are the whitewashed houses and the church of the little town, and from them a road leads down to the Wadi Gerfan, that ravine through which the Australians and the British tanks made their victorious onslaught (see page 30 of this volume). At the foot of the wadi lies the harbour with that jetty by reason of which Bardia is entitled to be described as a port. In the foreground are two Italian tanks—two of the many

Italian Tanks, Swept the Army of the Nile

which were abandoned in the débâcle. Interesting in itself as showing one of the places whose names are included in the battle-honours of the Army of the Nile, the photograph gives an excellent impression of the kind of country through which that Imperial force moved and is moving to victory. Brown and barren, sun-bitten and arid ; only at the bottom of the wadi, reached by occasional rains from the Mediterranean, whose smooth expanse forms the background of the photograph, a few trees struggle to keep alive.

Photo, British Official: Crown Copyright

Over Germany's Aerodromes with a Camera

Written by an Intelligence Officer of the R.A.F., this article describes a reconnaissance flight over Germany—just such a flight as has now become a matter of ordinary, every-day routine. Yet, as he makes clear, however ordinary the flight may be—indeed, usually is—it is adventurous and charged with danger.

A VAN, its headlights shielded, moves quickly across the aerodrome towards the heavy outline of an aircraft from which engine and cockpit covers are being removed. In the van are men with cameras and drums of ammunition. It is still some thirty minutes before dawn, and, though it is damp and cold, the men work with unhurried haste, concentrating on the job in hand to the exclusion of everything else. Theirs is the responsibility of seeing that the now silent bomber is fully prepared for its task —a photographic reconnaissance of aerodromes and other military objectives in Germany and German-occupied territory.

Under the watchful eye of the squadron's photographic corporal, the observer unloads the two cameras from the van, while at his side the air gunners are collecting the drums of ammunition for their guns. Inside the aircraft the wireless operator and the two pilots are checking their instruments.

The observer, with his single wing and sergeant's stripes dimly visible on his tunic, carries the vertical camera across to the aircraft. He screws it firmly into place, removes the lens cap, and satisfies himself that it is ready for action. Then, while he is placing the oblique camera into its position inside the fuselage, the corporal inspects the vertical camera once more. All the necessary adjustments have been made, but no care is too great to ensure complete efficiency.

The two cameras weigh only twenty-eight pounds, some sixty pounds less than their German counterparts. They are compact, boxlike cameras, simple and robust in design, and constructed to work in the worst conditions with the minimum attention. They are equipped with interchangeable magazines, containing enough films for one hundred and twenty-five exposures. The vertical camera is worked electrically and is mounted in the middle of the aircraft with its lens pointing through a hole in the floor. The oblique camera, which is manually operated and hand-held, can, of course, be adjusted in the air, but the vertical has to remain at its original focal setting.

As soon as the installation has been completed and the electrical leads to the controls in the cockpit have been connected, the observer gets in the seat beside the pilot and operates the remote control to make sure that everything is working properly. In the meantime, the first pilot has started up his engines and the crew now clamber aboard. The observer follows, clad like the others in electrically-heated clothing, with radio-telephone and oxygen-leads dangling from his helmet. Around his neck hangs the thirty-five millimetre camera. His parachute harness and life-saving jacket are part and parcel of the flying suit.

Maps and instruments are laid on the chart table, the observer takes his seat, and the aircraft speeds across the aerodrome on its way to Germany. The pilot sets his course and the observer works out the strength of the wind and levels the vertical camera. Together the crew form a well-trained and well-tried team, each knowing something of the other man's job and each realizing the full value of cooperation.

AERIAL RECONNAISSANCE CAMERAS are of two types. One for taking vertical photographs is worked electrically from a fixed position in the floor of the aircraft : one for oblique photographs, as shown above, is manually operated. For an example of a vertical air photograph see Vol. 3, page 590, and for an oblique view, Vol. 4, page 127.   *Photo, British Official : Crown Copyright*

The great waters of the North Sea pass quickly beneath them, and landfall is made. The air gunners are at their posts, with loaded guns and ready, their eyes quartering the sky unceasingly. The altimeter records a height of five thousand feet; actually, the aircraft is flying just above the cloud bank which now hides the ground below. Carefully and seemingly casually the pilot and the observer check their course to make certain that they are near their first objective. Assured of this, the engines are throttled back to allow the pilot to make a gentle glide downwards through the clouds, which grow thinner as the land begins to come in view. Away on the left a semicircle of hangars discloses the exact position of the first target, and the aircraft swings over towards it, while the observer takes hold of the remote control in readiness to operate the camera.

Over the centre of the aerodrome the pilot flies a straight and level course. The observer presses the control button and the

camera begins to do its work. Two thousand feet below lies a German air force station with twenty or thirty aircraft of varying types lined up on the centre of the tarmac and dispersed round the boundary. Within a minute or two the solitary raider, with his record complete, has passed, flying just below the clouds towards his next objective.

Suddenly the pilot turns the aircraft and signals to the observer to start the camera again. He has seen an alternative landing ground and that, too, is photographed.

At last they reach the southern-most point of their flight and prepare to photograph another aerodrome. Ahead there are signs of activity, but the bomber flies on at a set speed, height and course, while the observer works out the time intervals between exposures necessary for the required overlap of sixty per cent. Apparently the Messerschmitts are unaware of the intruder's identity, for from the British bomber they can be seen lowering their wheels as they approach the aerodrome to land.

With these new photographic records taken, the British machine turns homewards, travelling north so as to get a further record of activity on yet another aerodrome. And again the same procedure is adopted. A steady course is kept as they approach their objective. The time interval is set on the automatic control and the release is pressed. This time as they pass over the centre of the aerodrome the observer takes one or two photographs of the aircraft and hangars with his thirty-five millimetre camera. To make matters more exciting, there are fighters diving on their tail, but the air gunners hold their fire until the Messerschmitts close in. Then they let them have it, good and hard.

All the time the vertical camera continues to run. This time to make certain of good results the pilot also brings his aircraft down to a thousand feet. At this height they get a warm reception from both pom-poms and machine-guns, but the further record, taken by the hand-held oblique camera, is well worth it.

At last their task is finished and the bomber slips into the clouds above. Homeward once again, they hurry over the sea and finally land at their base, where the magazines are removed without delay and rushed to the photographic section for development. The observer also hands in his report.

In a matter of two or three hours copies of the prints will be in the hands of the experts at the command. Stereoscope and magnifiers will tell the trained eyes and mind as much as the aircraft ever really saw—and a great deal more. Aircraft types will be recognized, unusual activities will be noted, and a detailed report will soon be on its way to the operational staff.

Tomahawk Is the Hurricane's American Cousin

CURTISS TOMAHAWK is one of the many types of aircraft now being sent to us from the United States. Fighter machines of this kind are brought over by sea, the fuselage and engine in one crate and the wing assembly in another. Here a Tomahawk (Curtiss Hawk 81) is seen in the assembling shop at an R.A.F. station, where mechanics are adjusting the three-bladed, electrically-controlled, variable-pitch, propeller. Beneath the crankcase can be seen the radiators, and six exhaust tubes jut from the engine cowling. The Tomahawk, which is the United States' equivalent of the Hawker Hurricane, has a 12-cylinder Allison engine of the " V " liquid-cooled type, developing 1,090 h.p. Each machine goes through a flying test before being sent to its operational station. American 'planes flown direct to Britain are shown in pages 98—99 of this volume.

Photo, Topical

Tugs Are Now Men-o'-War

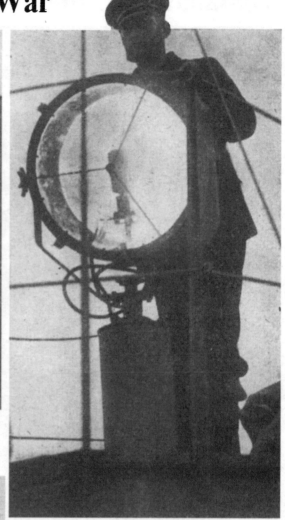

Tugs, those small craft that in peacetime plied on rivers and at the great ports, now fly the White Ensign, and, equipped with guns and searchlights, serve with the Royal Naval Auxiliary Patrol watching the coast for enemy activity. Right, one of a tug's crew is at his post with the searchlight. Above, the paymaster calls to hand the men's pay to the Captain. Below, the gunners are at their stations with the two machine-guns.
Photos, Fox and Associated Press

'On Our Merchant Ships Everything Depends'

THE success of the convoy system in countering U-boats depends largely on the seamanship of the masters of the merchant ships. The two photographs in this page show the preliminaries to a convoy setting out for its home port. Top : Ships from many different ports have assembled at the rendezvous, where their escort will pick them up. A tug, in the foreground, is bringing the skippers ashore for a conference at which they will receive their final instructions. In the lower photograph they are being given verbal instructions by a Captain in the R.N.R. in what was once a pavilion where entertainments were given for holiday-makers. The Masters are told what their ships' positions in the convoy will be, and their ships' papers are examined. Any extra armaments they ask for will be supplied. "On our merchant ships and their gallant seamen," Lord Chatfield has said, "everything depends." *Photos, G.P.U.*

OUR SEARCHLIGHT ON THE WAR

Captured " Wolves " and " Demi-Gods "

How unassuming, to the point of dullness, are the names of British regiments compared with the sonorous titles given by Italy to her units ! Even when we apply an affectionate nickname it is modest and non-committal, like " The Buffs." By contrast Italy has—or had—her famous " Wolves of Tuscany." Through mis-adventure they were routed in mid-January, soon after they set foot in Albania, and their commander, Colonel Meneghetti, was taken prisoner (see page 96). So great was the dejection of this " Wolf " that, when the Greek officer escorting him to Athens apologised for the staring crowds, explaining that they were not used to seeing a captured officer of such high rank, the Colonel rejoined disconsolately : " They must get used to it ; they will soon be seeing generals." But the " Wolves of Tuscany," plodding along to their prison camps, are not alone. They are in the company of " Red Devils of Piedmont," " Eagles of the Alps," " Demi-gods of Julia," " Green Flames of the Alps," " Veterans of the Mud and Torrential Rains of Pusteria," and " Hercules of Ferrara."

Safety in a Steel Cage

An air-raid shelter for use within the home has been designed, tested and found satisfactory, and will soon be available to the public. According to Mr. Herbert Morrison, " it achieves not only dispersal but warmth and dryness, and it avoids the discomfort of leaving home at night and the dislocation of family life." The new shelter, which is in the form of a table with removable sides, is not proof against a direct hit, but, installed on the lowest floor, it will afford protection against the debris caused by the collapse of a two- or three-storeyed house from a nearby explosion. The sheet of steel which forms

INDOOR SHELTER beds are 6 ft. 6 in. long and 4 ft. wide and weigh 5 cwt., about the weight of a grand piano. The shelters will be supplied in parts and must be put together by the house-holder. Their adoption by the Ministry of Home Security followed upon the discovery that houses form a better protection against bomb than it was originally supposed they would do.
Photo, courtesy of the Ministry of Information

the top has been tested by having a heavy weight dropped upon it, and also by a blow similar to that of a collapsing floor. The steel mesh sides also protect the inmates from debris. Two average-sized adults and a child, two adults and two infants, or even four thin adults can be accommodated inside the cage, the floor of which is sprung to take a mattress. When not in use as a shelter

the sides can be removed and the top utilized as a table. Mr. Morrison stated that dis-tribution would be limited at first to certain areas more vulnerable than others, and, within those areas, to householders as yet unprovided with an Anderson shelter. To

Lord Moyne, left, now Colonial Secretary, sat in the House of Commons as Hon. Walter Guinness, from 1907-1931. Mr. J. G. Winant, the new American Ambassador in London, centre, is a Republican appointed to the most important diplomatic post by a Democrat president. Mr. Malcolm MacDonald, who goes to Canada as High Commissioner, has been successively Dominions and Colonial Secretary and Minister of Health.   *Photos, Sport & General, Topical and Lafayette*

such it will be free, provided that the house-hold's income does not exceed £350 a year. To others the cost will be about £8.

Diplomatic and Ministerial Appointments

President Roosevelt's nomination of Mr. John G. Winant to be the new American Ambassador to Great Britain was officially announced on February 6, although it had long been surmised. Mr. Winant has seen much public service in the States, and his knowledge of European problems acquired while head of the International Labour Office in Geneva will stand him in good stead in his new post. Another American diplomatic appointment is that of Mr. A. D. Biddle, Ambassador to Poland and formerly in Warsaw, who is now named in addition Minister to the Governments in London of Belgium, Norway and the Netherlands. There have been several recent changes in the British Cabinet. Mr. Malcolm MacDonald

has been selected to fill the post of High Commissioner in Canada, left vacant by the appointment of Sir Gerald Campbell as additional Minister to Washington. He is succeeded at the Ministry of Health by Mr. Ernest Brown. Lord Moyne has been made Secretary of State for the Colonies in succession to the late Lord Lloyd, and will also be Leader of the House of Lords. He undertook a financial mission to Kenya in 1932, and was chairman of the West Indies Royal Commission which started work in 1938. His former post at the Ministry of Agriculture is being taken over by the Duke of Norfolk. Another new appointment is that of Mr. Thomas Johnston as Secretary of State for Scotland, the post relinquished by Mr. Ernest Brown.

Belgium's Quisling Gets Busy

Léon Degrelle, leader of the Rexist (Fascist) party in occupied Belgium, is stated by the Italian Press to be working on the creation of an air force to be under the control of Germany. The Belgian Govern-ment in London has heard nothing as yet of this scheme. Degrelle has already organized several units, the purpose of which would appear to be that of protecting Rexist meet-ings rather than taking any active part in the war. This Fascist party is exceedingly unpopular in Belgium and, despite German repression, clashes are apt to occur when Degrelle's followers gather together. The Rexists have a party organ—" Le Pays Réel "—which, after being suspended at the time of the invasion, resumed publication under German patronage in August 1940. Meanwhile, the clandestine newspaper " La Libre Belgique " pursues its secret way.

New Severe Laws in Rumania

Some of the most drastic laws ever intro-duced into any European country were announced in Bucharest on February 6 by General Antonescu. Death is now the penalty for possessing, using or acquiring firearms ; for writing, publishing or dis-tributing literature against the Government ; for sedition or incitement ; for looting ; for sabotage and any form of interference with transport and communications. Member-ship of any organization, whether social, political or religious, which does not see eye to eye with the present regime is punish-able with life imprisonment. These laws apply to everyone over 15, and special penal-ties are devised for offenders in positions of authority, such as teachers and priests. On February 12 further restrictions were imposed upon the populace, one being that military and police patrols were instructed to shoot at sight any person who refused to halt.

Not All the Parachutists Are Nazis!

BRITISH PARATROOPS IN ITALY!

A Story (*Unfinished*) in Six Chapters

CHAPTER 1

Minsk, 1936. At the Russian military manoeuvres there was a remarkable display of parachutists dropped from 'planes. Amongst the onlookers was a British Military Mission, headed by a certain Maj.-Gen. Wavell, who said : " We greatly admired the work of the parachutists. They demonstrated a brilliant spectacle of courage and good training."

CHAPTER 2

Rome, Feb. 11, 1941. The " New York Times " correspondent wired to his paper, " It is not permitted to write a word from Rome tonight about the big story [passage censored]."

CHAPTER 3

Rome, Feb. 14. The Italian High Command issued a warning to the Italian public that during the night of February 10-11 enemy parachutists had descended in Calabria and Lucania . . .

CHAPTER 4

Rome, same date. The Italian News Agency, giving further details of the raid, states :

The parachutists, who carried automatic arms and explosives, certainly intended to damage the regional water-supply system, a magnificent achievement of the Fascist regime which made possible an agricultural revival throughout the district, together with railway lines, bridges, and roads.

Having landed in a clearing surrounded by forests, the parachutists occupied some farms and immobilized the peasants. One parachutist who had broken a leg was left in one of these farms, where he was later arrested by guards. The British parachutists deceived the peasant farmers by shouting " Duce !" and so inducing them to open their doors to them.

After abandoning their injured companion the British made their way to the springs which feed the irrigation system, guiding themselves by means of maps with which they were provided. But the alarm had been given in the region, and guards, cooperating with the military, police and the military organizations of the Fascist party, drew a cordon round the area. A search was instituted, making the position of the parachutists very precarious.

Speedily surrounded, they were unable to execute their plans and had to hide in the woods to avoid capture. To make capture more difficult they divided up into several groups, hoping that some at least would be able to break through the cordon and carry out a part of their plans.

Their plans failed, for while eleven parachutists were seized in one place seven others were arrested at the same time a mile or two away. The latter attempted to put up a resistance, turning a tommy gun on the patrol, consisting of one guard, one police constable, and a shepherd who was guiding them over the mountain paths. Shots from the British officer's gun put the policeman and the shepherd out of action.

The guard, left alone, defended himself with his rifle, forcing the parachutists to remain behind a rock until other guards, hearing the shots, came up. Seeing that all resistance was hopeless, the parachutists surrendered.

Another group, which had taken to the scrubland, remained to be found. The search went on and the rest of the parachutists, including a captain, were seized without trouble. All of them were clothed in khaki-overalls and had Air Force caps. They were armed with tommy guns and automatic pistols and were provided with Italian money. They have been handed over to the regional defence command.

CHAPTER 5

London, Feb. 15. The Ministry of Information announced: " Soldiers dressed in recognized military uniforms have recently been dropped by parachute in Southern Italy. Their instructions were to demolish certain objectives connected with ports in that area. No statement can be made at present about the results of the operations, but some of the men have not returned to their base."

CHAPTER 6

Rome, Feb. 15. " The British parachutists captured will be treated as prisoners of war in the honourable and chivalrous manner which is characteristic of the Italian people. They will be lodged in a concentration camp, where representatives of the International Red Cross will be allowed to visit them."

LANDING is one of the chief perils that paratroops must face. This photograph, taken when Nazi parachute troops were in training, shows one of them just after coming to ground, but his parachute, caught by the wind, is still a source of danger. As told in the adjoining column, one of the British parachutists who dropped in Southern Italy broke his leg.   *Photo, Pictorial Press*

Cartoon Commentary on the War

AUTHENTIC GREEK MASTERPIECE (CIRCA 1940-1)
Fitzpatrick in the "St. Louis Post-Dispatch"

"DON'T YOU RECOGNIZE ME, DUCE? THE BRITISH DID!"
Vicky in "Time and Tide"

"I DISAGREE"
Vicky in the "News Chronicle"

CROCODILE TEARS
Armstrong in the "Melbourne Argus"

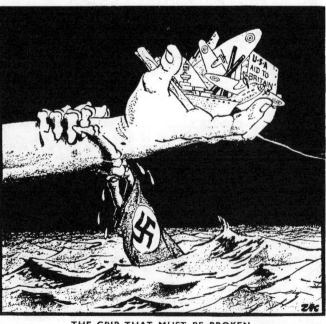

THE GRIP THAT MUST BE BROKEN
Zec in the "Daily Mirror"

I Saw Our Shells Pour into Genoa

"At dawn this morning," said Mr. Churchill on February 9, " our Western Mediterranean Fleet bombarded in a shattering manner the naval base from which a German expedition might soon have sailed to attack Gen. Weygand." Here is a vivid eye-witness account of the sea and air operations off Genoa by a Press Association correspondent on board the battleship Malaya.

WHEN the Malaya left harbour and turned east into the Mediterranean with the Renown, the Sheffield and the Ark Royal, only a handful of people on board the ships knew the Admiral's intentions, though we guessed that something unusual was afoot. Later the thrilling words, " There is a possibility that the ship may be in action tomorrow morning," appeared in the daily orders. It looked like business too when pictures, glass light shades, and anything likely to be smashed by concussion from the guns were taken down and laid on settees, chairs, or tables.

Throughout the night we steamed at full speed. Not until the stand-to at 6 a.m. the next morning was the secret revealed . . . . A young fresh-faced midshipman told me without the faintest flicker of excitement in his voice, " We are going to bombard Genoa."

We were steaming up the Gulf of Genoa towards our target. The first gleams of day were beginning to lighten the sky and ahead I saw the big blurred outline of the Renown and the smaller dim shape of the Sheffield. Between us and the shore destroyers raced through the water guarding the bombarding ships from submarines or possible attacks from 60-knot E-boats.

Over the still invisible Italian coastline flashes of bursting A.A. shells, vividly red against the pale primrose sky, told us that the Italians were putting up a barrage against the Swordfish bombers attacking targets at Leghorn and Pisa. Then, in the growing daylight, the high snow-capped peaks of the mountain range behind Genoa appeared suddenly out of the thick white mist which blanketed the coastline.

Our 'plane was catapulted away with others from the Sheffield and the Ark Royal to act as spotters. There was no sign from the shore that our presence had been detected. The coast looked pleasantly peaceful.

The Renown turned into position. Silently we and the Sheffield turned with her. Battle pennants were run up to the mastheads. We flew the same Malay Union flag that had been hoisted when the Malaya fought in the Battle of Jutland.

A few minutes before the bombardment began we were sighted from the shore. White and green lights flickered out a challenge, " Who are you ? " In a matter of seconds we sent our reply. A great spurt of red flame shot from the Renown's side as the first salvo of 15-inch shells travelled towards the distant targets. Flames flashed from the Sheffield as her 12-inch guns began to pour shells into the important Ansaldo electrical and boiler works.

The huge 31,100-ton bulk of our ship shuddered from stem to stern as two guns of one of the forward turrets opened up. Again came the nerve-racking explosions as one of the rear turrets belched out two more ton shells. We strained our eyes towards the shore to see the bursts, and though the distance was great we twice thought we could spot a faint red glow. It was left to the 'planes to see the damage.

The Sheffield's side was almost continu-ously aflame as her quick-firing guns pounded the works. Our own guns were now firing regularly. The Renown, sharing with us the important objectives in the inner harbour, was firing at the same rate. We were then steaming parallel with the coast. High above the targets our spotters, dodging a hail of A.A. fire, were constantly signalling directions to the guns.

For fifteen minutes the Italian batteries failed to reply. Then came a red flash from the shore to south of the city and a white column of water shot up from the sea 1,000 yards short of the ships. More shells were fired from the shore, but the aim was so bad that the escorting destroyers abandoned the smoke screen they had started to lay.

As we steamed on our guns slewed round until towards the end of the shelling they were firing on an after bearing. With the muzzles much nearer the superstructure choking clouds of smoke and cordite fumes swept over us. Doors were blown off and cabins were wrecked. The stout tarpaulid protecting the bridge from bad weather was ripped like paper. The Malaya's share in the bombardment had been nearly half the total weight of metal fired.

The Italian reply consisted at the most of 20 shells, mostly of small calibre, and not one of which fell nearer than 500 yards. Our returning aircraft joyfully signalled the success of the bombardment as they swooped past, the observers leaning out and waving their hands above their heads . . . .

We Were 'Shot Up' in an Italian Ambush

In a desperate attempt to hold up the British advance on Benghazi, Italian troops laid an ambush on the main road outside Barce. Into this ambush ran a car containing a War Office photographer and two Press correspondents, Alan Moorehead of the " Daily Express " and Alexander Clifford of the " Daily Mail," who tells the following dramatic story of their escape.

IT was about 5.30 in the evening of February 5 when our foremost armoured cars swung round the corner 12 miles from Barce and found Italian engineers actually laying mines across the road.

Our truck was following close behind, and I saw the enemy scattering headlong into the bushes. In a couple of minutes our engineers were there neutralizing the mines, and we stood watching while they made the road safe.

Suddenly we saw some of the Italians racing up the tree-clad hillside, and the first armoured car nosed forward to pursue them.

Then it all began. Without warning tracer bullets were flashing all around us. Machine-gun fire zinged through the air above our heads, and heavy Breda anti-tank shells screamed down the road to explode with a deafening crack.

I flung myself into the bushes, with Moorehead beside me. Machine-guns, rifles, and heavier guns seemed to be chattering from all around us. Half a dozen Arabs laden with sacks, who had somehow got mixed up in the fight, went screaming up the hillside. I heard hobnail boots of men from the armoured cars clattering along the road.

I got to my feet and began to run. As I skirted the blazing truck I turned back and saw the driver lying in the road and the conducting officer running back to him. Another burst of fire scattered us again for a minute, but finally we got to him and pulled him into the side of the road.

Moorehead was there first, and he pulled the bandage off his own sore knee to tie up the driver's arm. Then the conducting officer arrived with first-aid kit from one of the armoured cars. We cut off the wounded man's sleeves and bound his great gaping wound.

The Italians could still see us plainly, though it was growing dusk. They must have been able to see what we were doing and they knew we were not armed. They

H.M.S. MALAYA played an important part in the bombardment of Genoa on February 9, an account of which is given in this page. This 31,100-ton battleship, belonging to the Queen Elizabeth class, was completed in 1915, and was given by the Federated Malay States. She has a normal complement of 1,184, and her main armament is eight 15-inch guns. (See also page 176.) *Photo, Wide World*

were so close that I could hear them chattering excitedly among the trees and I could feel the blast of their heavy weapons on my face.

They shelled us unmercifully. As we tore the ground with our hands to get cover, Breda shells were again screaming down and bursting just beside us.

For a little while a British machine-gun poured reddish tracer bullets over our heads, but it soon stopped. Then the conducting officer gave a little gasp, and I knew he had been hit.

We were the only target left, and they were concentrating everything on us. Suddenly something bit the back of my right thigh with a sharp blow, and I waited for a wave of pain to flood over me. But it did not hurt much. It obviously was not bad.

Along the road vehicle after vehicle spurted flame. Our own 15-cwt. truck rocked and shuddered as bullets of every description crashed through it.

" God have mercy on us," somebody said. We knew the Italians had only to walk down the road and we were prisoners. But they never stopped firing. It was obvious that we were all going to be wiped out very soon. The only thing to do was to run for it.

Moorehead and I dragged the driver by his heels deeper into cover. Then, in the darkness, we began a crazy dash for safety. Every now and then the Italians spotted us among the trees and another murderous burst of accurate fire threw us to the ground. They pursued us mercilessly, and I do not know how they managed to keep sight of us in the gathering dusk.

At last we reached a newly-dug ditch and there we paused to bind up wounds. We spent something like 20 minutes crouching by the road. The driver had lost plenty of blood. He behaved magnificently, but he could not walk without assistance.

I undid the conducting officer's wrist-watch and found a neat hole where a bullet had gone in and had not come out. We poured a phial of iodine on it and bound it up with wound dressing and hoped for the best.

The firing had died to almost nothing and we pushed on into the night. Dodging among bushes, careful not to get too near the road and not too far away, we made the eerie journey. We talked in low voices in case enemy patrols were near, and we did not light cigarettes.

The driver got cold, and I gave him my greatcoat. We wondered how far we would have to go. The photographer revealed that he had been hit slightly in the leg, and the driver was now very weak.

Suddenly we heard voices, and they were English. We hailed them, and we were safe. A Bren-gun carrier took us aboard and back to a field dressing station. All our wounds were attended to. We got hot tea.

All was quiet behind us, and we knew the ambush had finished with our departure. Australian infantry were creeping round the hills, but the Italians had undoubtedly cleared off when their job was finished.

An officer and the driver were taken off in an ambulance. Moorehead and I slept in the dressing station. The army moved on.

'I Headed My Machine for the Marshes'

Although diving at a speed which he estimated at " round about 700 m.p.h.," the pilot of a Spitfire managed to head his blazing machine away from a Thames Estuary village and baled out over the marshes. This story, which had an interesting sequel, is told below in the pilot's own words.

THE pilot who " saved " the village returned to his station after a spell in hospital to have a piece of bullet extracted from his leg. He then told the following story :

Our squadron had chased a few Messerschmitts across the Channel to the French coast, and over there we got split up. We decided to return climbing back over the English Channel until we were all together again at 26,000 feet over the Thames Estuary.

Suddenly I was " jumped on " from out of the sun by a few Messerschmitts. First they hit my tail, and my controls went all sloppy. That, I think, was a cannon shell. I immediately tried to get away, but a moment later incendiary bullets hit my engine. Then a bullet came through the side of the cockpit and went through my left boot, and a split second afterwards another bullet crashed through the side, struck the metal under my seat, and split into two parts. One piece went harmlessly away, the other went into my right leg just above the ankle.

Then I was adjusting my compass when a hail of machine-gun bullets came through my hood and shattered my instrument panel, and a second after I had taken my hand away from the compass it was shattered by further bullets. The only instruments left O.K. were my altimeter and my air speed indicator. There were more bullets still to come in. One lot tore my hood completely away. One bullet came from the side and across my stomach, lodging in the release clasp of my parachute. Then another bullet took my left earphone away, bruising my helmet and taking away my goggles.

I rolled over on my back, headed my machine for the marshes and went into a steep, inverted dive. I saw my airspeed indicator leaping up, and it got between 650 m.p.h. and 700 m.p.h. with the throttle wide open. At about 6,000 feet the aircraft caught fire, and then she straightened out on her side and went in a slight dive, almost horizontal, in a sort of fluttering way. This gave me a chance to free myself from the machine, and at about 4,000 feet I baled out.

It was pleasant when I got out, but it wasn't pleasant watching my Spitfire going down. Just as I pulled the rip cord, she hit the mud. There was a blinding flash, and a cloud of black smoke hung like a pall over the spot. The Spitfire had disappeared. Soon I had to think about myself, for I was right over the mud of the Thames. I came down, and the parachute dragged me, face downwards, through the mud until it finally collapsed. While it was dragging me along I must have looked like a porpoise going up and down through the mud.

A man who is a Home Guard in his spare time came in gumboots to my rescue. He helped me out, and then there arose the problem of how to get me clean. I went into a yard and they threw buckets of water over me—warm water, luckily. They also got a stirrup-pump and squirted me with that. Then I took all my clothes off and was washed a bit more, and put on a suit of clothes lent to me by the Home Guard.

I had my leg patched up, and after a few hours was driven back to my home station. I arrived there at 10.30 at night, and all the boys got a good laugh, seeing me in a suit which was too small for me, with the trousers half way up my calves !

Thanks from the Villagers He Had Saved

A FEW days later, the officer commanding the fighter station to which this pilot belonged, received the following letter :

Dear Sir, The people of a very small village in north-east Kent would very much like to thank the pilot of a fighter 'plane who baled out over some marshes, for staying at his controls and steering his damaged 'plane away from the village and a factory which is in the vicinity before baling out. Hearty congratulations and good luck always !

As a further sequel to the incident, the pilot while in hospital wrote to the member of the Home Guard who had dragged him from the mud, thanking him for his help. In reply he received this letter :

Dear Sir, I hardly know how to reply to your very nice letter. It gives the people of the village and myself the greatest pleasure to know you are recovering from your wounds. . . . Now, sir, I am going to write : it is not myself who wants thanking for so small a deed, but you and your fellow pals who show such splendid courage above our heads from dawn till dusk."

Then the letter concluded : " Please believe me when I say : you and your pals will always find a pair of willing hands down here if any of you ever again have to bale out, whether in mud, water or fire."

Out of the clouds comes a Messerschmitt to attack a British fighter, an incident such as that described in this page. The photograph was taken from a German 'plane and was published to show the Luftwaffe's superiority over the R.A.F. The actual figures of fighters brought down show that it is very seldom that the tables are thus turned.   *Photo, Associated Press*

Italian Generals—and an Admiral—'In the Bag'

"BERGANZOLI'S in the bag !" was the dramatic message sent back from the tanks which smashed their way into the heart of the Italian forces retreating from Benghazi. But "Electric Whiskers" was not the only general to become a prisoner-of-war in the Battle of Soluk.

"There is a little brown villa in this dreary village," wrote the Special Correspondent of the "Daily Telegraph" from Soluk on February 11. "It houses almost more Italian officers than it can hold. I found six Italian generals together in a room. Squat, grey-bearded Cona, an army commander, stood apart, silent and pensive. Bignani, a Bersaglieri commander, talked in undertones with Megroni, chief of the technical services. Giuliano, Tellera's chief-of-staff, was looking out of the window with Bardini, commander of the motorized forces. Villani, artillery commander, was writing busily in a note-book.

They told me that Berganzoli was outside, sitting in a car in the muddy courtyard ; but it was not the same brisk, dynamic figure whom I had seen continue directing the battle after he had been wounded in an Aragon village during the Spanish civil war. It was a kindly, rather gentle old man. The old fire was gone. He seemed older, more bowed, and even his ginger-coloured 'electric whiskers' did not seem to bristle so fiercely. He remembered me, and the old light came back into his eyes for a moment ; but it faded when I asked him about Bardia. 'It was a miracle,' he said, and when I suggested that he had blundered at Benghazi and left too late, he said swiftly, 'I had to obey orders. The British had superior forces.' " Soon Berganzoli and his generals were on their way to Egypt.

When Tobruk fell on January 22, 1941, Admiral Vietina, commander of the naval base, was among the prisoners. Above the Admiral, centre, and an Italian naval captain, right, are being interrogated by a British staff officer in battle dress, left. Below three Italian generals taken prisoner at Sidi Barrani are arriving at Cairo with their staffs.

Photos, British Official: Crown Copyright

'We Shall Fight in the Fields, In the Streets'

Every night, all night, turn and turn about, the headquarters sentry keeps watch over the sleeping village. In sudden emergency his comrades of the guard are within instant call. Nine months of eager training have gone far in teaching them the art of modern warfare.

IT was after midnight when we left the village to climb the hill. It is a stiff climb, and the wind pierced the thickest greatcoat.

Only men with a set purpose would climb the hill on such a night as this.

Our purpose had been set for us. I was out with a patrol of the Aston Clinton platoon of the Home Guard, fulfilling an instruction to go up to " High Point " and see if all was well there.

There were four men in this patrol, including the section leader, who told me he had worn the Queen's—that is, Queen Victoria's — uniform. All four knew the ground well, for this was the platoon's fixed observation post

last summer when parachute-spotting was the chief preoccupation of the L.D.V.

We tramped the windswept hilltop, back and forth, our boots crunching the frozen crust of snow, and, finding nothing untoward, returned to Platoon H.Q. to report all well.

Returning the challenge of the sentry outside H.Q., we passed into the warmth and light of the hut. Sausages were sizzling in a pan on the stove. The teapot waited for the kettle to boil.

Counting the sentry, eight men were on duty : a sub-section of the platoon. There are eight sub-sections, and all take in rotation a night of " lying-in " duty. Hours : 8 p.m. to 6 a.m. It doesn't seem much, one night

The post is inspected inside and out, and a member of the patrol left on guard with his automatic rifle. Well-equipped and armed, ready to meet any emergency, these men of the Aston Clinton platoon of the Buckinghamshire Home Guard are typical of those who answered the call for a citizen army throughout the country.

Without warning orders come through for a special midnight patrol of an outlying area. In less than five minutes half the guard turn out and set off for the distant defence post.

Photographs specially taken for
THE WAR ILLUSTRATED
by John Heddon

Night In, Night Out, the H.G. Never Sleeps

in eight ; but there are drills or lectures every Wednesday night as well, and on Sunday mornings there is always something on—field operations, musketry practice or a full-dress rehearsal of an invasion alarm.

Captain de L. Leach, Acting Platoon Commander, was busy with plans for such a rehearsal when I returned with the patrol. He spoke enthusiastically of all his men : " I couldn't have wished for a better lot of chaps."

A YEAR ago many of these men, although living in the same parish, were strangers to each other. Came that memorable evening in May when Mr. Eden, then War Minister, broadcast his appeal for Local Defence Volunteers in every town and village.

The three neighbouring parishes of Aston Clinton, Buckland and Drayton Beauchamp made the same ready response as everywhere else. The volunteers were asked to report at the house of Air Commodore P. F. M. Fellowes.

They met in the garden : farmers and farm labourers, grocers, building workers, stockbrokers and solicitors, publicans, insurance agents. With Air Commodore Fellowes as commander the platoon was formed. The district was divided into eight sectors, to be patrolled at dawn and dusk.

The volunteers had no uniform. Their weapons were any they could lay their hands on. During those anxious days and nights that followed Dunkirk, the patrols were out, morning and evening, always in pairs. Cars were stopped during Alerts. Suspicious-looking strangers were challenged. Mysterious lights were tracked down.

And all this time the work of fortifying Aston Clinton was pressed with feverish haste. The danger that threatened villa and cottage alike was enough to break down all conventional reserve and to found friendships

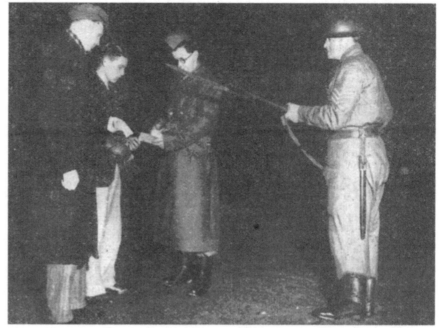

Meanwhile, his companions make a rapid tour of the surrounding district, immediately challenging anyone unknown to them and examining identification cards. Everything is found in order and the patrol returns to headquarters to report. Before turning in again, tea and sausages claim their active attention, below.

that will long outlive this war. The platoon is now at full strength, with ample reserves of eager youths to fill the gaps as members are called up for the Army; and it is well equipped.

As I drank my tea a hefty printing worker, who is in charge of the armoury, fondled an automatic rifle as if it were a pet. A journalist

buttoned up his greatcoat and went out to relieve the garage worker who had completed his two hours' sentry go. I went out with my brother-journalist. " The Home Guard," he said, as he took up his post, " was a stroke of genius, don't you think ? Men will fight to the last for their own homes."

Story by William Forrest, retold here by courtesy of the " News Chronicle "

OUR DIARY OF THE WAR

TUESDAY, FEB. 11, 1941   *528th day*
On the Sea—British warships bombarded port of Ostend in early hours, causing much damage and many destructive fires.

In the Air—Fighter Command aircraft made offensive sweep over Northern France.

Aircraft of Bomber and Coastal Commands made night attacks on targets in N.W. Germany, Holland, Norway and Denmark, including seaplane base at Thisted, Jutland.

War against Italy—Operations on all African fronts proceeding satisfactorily. In East Africa R.A.F. bombed aerodrome at Addis Ababa and raided Keren-Asmara area.

King's African Rifles took Afmadu, 100 miles inside Italian Somaliland.

During nights of 10-11 and 11-12 R.A.F. bombers heavily attacked aerodromes on island of Rhodes.

Five-hour raid on aerodromes at Comiso and Catania (Sicily) during night of 11-12.

Home Front—Nazi aircraft reported over East Midlands and East Anglia. At night few bombs fell in East and S.E. England.

Greek War—Athens reported successful local operations and more 'planes shot down.

WEDNESDAY, FEB. 12   *529th day*
On the Sea—H.M. drifter Eager shot down a Junkers bomber.

War against Italy—In Eritrea British forces occupied Elghena. Operations about Keren developing. R.A.F. very active in support. No change on other African fronts.

Home Front—No day raids reported over Britain. At night there was slight activity near western coasts, but few bombs fell. Some casualties occurred in South Wales.

Enemy bomber destroyed in East Scotland.

Greek War—North-west of Trebesina Greeks reported to have captured new heights and also to have occupied important positions north-east of Himara.

General—Mussolini and Franco met and conferred together at Bordighera.

THURSDAY, FEB. 13   *530th day*
On the Sea—Six ships in British convoy between Madeira and Azores sunk by German surface raider.

War against Italy—British troops about Keren improved their positions in hills covering the town. Farther south advance towards Arresa progressed satisfactorily.

In Hobok district, Abyssinia, S. African troops extended area of penetration.

On night of 12-13 heavy bombers of R.A.F. attacked harbour of Rhodes. Enemy aircraft bombed Malta.

Home Front—During day bombs fell in East Anglia and north of Scotland. At night bombs were dropped in London residential district, causing many casualties.

Messerschmitt attacking Dover balloon barrage was damaged by Spitfire.

Greek War—Athens reported successful local operations against heights of more than 6,000 feet, enemy being expelled from their positions. R.A.F. made repeated attacks in Tepelini area and on Elbasan.

During night of 12-13 aerodromes at Tirana and Durazzo were bombed.

General—Marshal Pétain received and conferred with Gen. Franco at Montpellier.

FRIDAY, FEB. 14   *531st day*
On the Sea—On night of 13-14 aircraft of Fleet Air Arm attacked convoy in Central Mediterranean, sinking one merchant vessel.

In the Air—R.A.F. made daylight sweep over German invasion ports and at night bomber formations again attacked them.

Night attacks made on Gelsenkirchen, inland port of Duisberg-Ruhrort and docks at Ostend. German oil tanker hit by Blenheim off Bergen.

War against Italy—Operations for reduction of Keren, Eritrea, proceeding. British reoccupied Kurmuk, Abyssinia. S. African Air Force bombed Bardera.

On night of 13-14 R.A.F. bombed aerodromes in Dodecanese.

Rome reported that during night of Feb. 10-11 British parachute detachments had landed in Lucania district of Calabria, but had been captured.

Home Front—British fighters drove back strong German formations from S.E. coast and air battle took place over Channel. One Messerschmitt shot down.

Single enemy aircraft dropped bombs in N.E. Scotland and in Kent. At night incendiaries fell over London, but fires were prevented. Raiders also reported from East Anglia and elsewhere. Enemy bomber shot down off East Coast by A.A. fire.

Greek War—New Greek offensive along 80-mile front ; over 7,000 prisoners captured. R.A.F. bombers maintained attacks north of Tepelini.

General—Hitler had 3-hours' talk with Yugoslav Premier and Foreign Minister.

SATURDAY, FEB. 15   *532nd day*
In the Air—R.A.F. made night attacks on targets in Western Ruhr. Other aircraft raided Channel ports, Boulogne being main point of attack. Calais docks bombed by aircraft of Coastal Command.

War against Italy—Concentration of troops about Keren proceeding.

Cairo announced that South African troops had occupied Kismayu, It. Somaliland, and that Queissan, Abyssinia, had been captured by units of Sudan Defence Force.

On night of 14-15 R.A.F. bombed Lindos harbour (Rhodes).

Ministry of Information confirmed that parachute troops had landed in S. Italy.

Home Front—Single enemy aircraft made daylight raids on Britain. Large formation crossing Kent coast beaten back by Spitfires. Two enemy bombers destroyed.

At night few bombs fell in London area, and incendiaries in Liverpool district. Three enemy bombers brought down at night.

Greek War—Italian Eleventh Army routed in Moskopoli-Tepelini sector. R.A.F. carried out raids in Buzi area and offensive patrols north of Tepelini.

SUNDAY, FEB. 16   *533rd day*
In the Air—Leaflets dropped over Cracow and Katovice areas of Poland by R.A.F. during night of 15-16.

Bomber Command made daylight attacks on harbour at Hellevoetsluis, shipping off Dutch coast, and targets at Zeebrugge, Middelburg and Den Helder.

War against Italy—Continued support by R.A.F. in Keren region. Heavy damage done at Mai Adaga. Dive bombers attacked Italian posts on east bank of Juba river, Abyssinia.

R.A.F. bombed aerodromes at Brindisi and in Sicily on night of 15-16. Malta raided ten times.

Home Front—Some enemy day activity by single aircraft. Bombs fell in London area and at some places in eastern and S.E. England and Home Counties. At night bombs fell in E. Anglia and N.E. coast town.

Enemy bomber shot down at Shoreham.

Greek War—R.A.F. attacked enemy positions in Buzi area, north of Tepelini.

MONDAY, FEB. 17   *534th day*
War against Italy—Cairo reported situation unchanged in Libya and Eritrea. In Italian Somaliland enemy now driven back to line of Juba river.

Home Front—During day few bombs fell in East and South-east England and north of Scotland. At night incendiaries and high explosives caused casualties and damage in London and an East Anglian town. London shelter received direct hit.

Two German bombers destroyed off Norfolk coast by British fighters, and another damaged. At night three were shot down, one by a fighter, the others by A.A. fire.

Greek War—Athens reported successful local attacks in which enemy were driven back at several points.

General—Turkey and Bulgaria issued joint statement reaffirming policy of non-aggression.

OUR EAST AFRICAN GAZETTEER

Addis Ababa. Cap. of Abyssinia ; pop. 150,000 ; founded in 1885, it was made the capital by Menelek II in 1892 ; lies among mountains in Shoa ; connected by railway with Jibuti in Fr. Somaliland. A motor road runs to Asmara.

Agordat. Eritrea ; captured by British on February 2, 1941 ; 55 miles west of Keren ; terminus of Eritrea's only railway, which runs 193 miles east to the coast at Massawa.

Asmara. Cap. of Eritrea ; 74 miles south-west of Massawa ; contains fine public buildings and Governor's residence. Occupied by Italians in 1889. Pop. about 80,000.

Barentu. Italian base in Eritrea, 40 miles south-west of Agordat, and about 50 miles north-west of Abyssinian frontier. Captured by British on February 3, 1941 ; was important air base.

Berbera. British Somaliland ; chief town and port ; 155 miles south of Aden ; fine harbour. Pop. about 20,000 ; became British in 1884 and was occupied by Italians in August 1940.

Gallabat. Fortified village on Sudan-Abyssinian frontier ; taken by Italians in July 1940, it was recaptured by British in November. About 100 miles south from Kassala.

Gondar. Abyssinia ; cap. of Province of Amhara, 24 miles north-east of Lake Tsana ; built on a hill at an altitude of 6,000 ft. Pop. about 22,000.

Harar. Abyssinia ; ancient walled city, 200 miles west of Berbera ; stands at an elevation of 6,000 ft. ; formerly a large trading centre and noted for coffee. Pop. about 30,000, which includes many Italian colonists.

Jibuti (Djibouti). Capital of French Somaliland ; seaport on African coast opposite Aden ; terminus of railway to Addis Ababa (496 miles) ; extensive harbour works and of strategic importance. Pop. about 20,000.

Kassala. Anglo-Egyptian Sudan ; on R. Gash, 260 miles south-east of Khartoum ; at foot of Abyssinian highlands, 15 miles west of Eritrean frontier. Founded by Egyptians in 1840 and taken by Italians in July 1940, it was recaptured by British in January 1941.

Keren. Eritrea ; on railway between Agordat and Massawa ; 70 miles north-west of Asmara ; strongly defended by Italians who withdrew here after their defeat at Agordat in Feb. 1941 ; of considerable strategic importance, since it guards Asmara and route to coast.

Massawa (Massura). Chief port of Eritrea ; built on small coral island in Red Sea, it is joined to coast by a causeway, one mile in length ; occupied by Italians in 1885. Pop. 20,000.

Mogadishu (Mogadiscio). Capital of Italian Somaliland (Somalia Italiana) ; chief port ; acquired by Italy in 1905. Pop. about 50,000 (8,000 Italians).

AUSTRALIA'S 'UNSUNG SOLDIERS OF THE LINE' ENTER BENGHAZI

With bayonets fixed, the Australian troops, who had played a great part in the taking of Benghazi, marched into the town on Feb. 7.   They passed in front of substantial buildings, far different from the ramshackle conglomeration of houses that compose most of the Libyan towns.   Arches in the background are bricked up in anticipation of air raids, but it is significant that the R.A.F. had never bombed the residential part of the town, it being left to the Luftwaffe to give their Italian allies, as well as the harmless Arabs, who form a large part of the population, their first experience of that form of warfare.   For other illustrations of the fall of the capital of Cyrenaica, see pages 227, 238, and 239

Photo, British Official : Crown Copyright

Into Benghazi Marched the Army of the Nile

As we have told in page 170, Benghazi was entered by the Army of the Nile on the morning of February 7, and we have also described the Battle of Soluk or " X.O.-6 " (see page 200), in which the retreating Italian Army was completely destroyed. Now we give a picture of the city's actual fall, and of its occupation by the Imperial forces.

WHILE the Italian tanks and infantry that had fled from Benghazi were fighting desperately but all unavailingly to escape from the trap which had been set for them a few miles to the south, the City Fathers decided that the time had come to capitulate. So at 6 p.m. on Thursday, February 6, Nicola Epifani, Mayor of Benghazi, accompanied by a priest and one or two Italian officers, drove out to the aerodrome at Benina, and there in the draughty barracks handed over to the Australian brigadier the keys of the capital of Cyrenaica, of Mussolini's principal naval base in North Africa. The Brigadier—" Red Robbie " as he is called by the " Aussies "—accepted the submission, assured the Italians of his protection, and sent them back to the city with instructions to maintain order and, in particular, to prevent looting.

Early on the next day the Army of the Nile marched into Benghazi. It was the unsung soldiers of the line, wrote Alan Moorehead, " Daily Express " staff reporter, who finally had the honour of completing the great thousand-mile march from the Nile and taking the town. " In the grey, cold early morning light they got down from their trucks in the streets—just one company— and marched into the square before the Town Hall. They were unkempt, dirty, stained head to foot with mud. They had their steel helmets down over their eyes to break the force of the wind. Some had their hands botched with desert sores, all of them had rents in their greatcoats and webbing. They had fought three battles and a dozen skirmishes. They had lost some of their comrades, dead and wounded, on the way. They had often been hungry, cold and wet through in these two months of campaigning

Benghazi—the town itself, its environs and harbour—is shown in this map with the roads and railways that radiate from the town.   *By courtesy of " The Times "*

in bitter weather. . . . The townspeople swarming round the square had half sullenly expected brass bands and a streamlined military parade. Instead they got this little ragged group of muddy men. They hesitated. Then a wave of clapping broke down from the housetops, along the pavements and across the whole of the massed square. I felt like clapping myself in that one highly-charged moment."

At nine o'clock the Brigadier drove into the square in his cream-coloured limousine, and as he stepped out on to the Town Hall steps the troops " swept out with fine snap and swung round to full parade-ground salute." Mayor Epifani, distinguished by a tricolour sash across his shoulders, stood waiting nervously, wiping his spectacles. Beside him stood Bishop Vescovo, and in the background was a group of municipal councillors, police and Carabinieri in their full-dress uniforms. Every window, every doorway, that looked on to the square was filled with Italians, and the women held up their children to get a better view.

As the Brigadier alighted from his car the Mayor stepped forward. The representatives of the conquerors and the conquered shook hands, and with that handclasp Benghazi passed into British possession. Then through an interpreter the Brigadier

issued his orders. " I reappoint you," he said, " and all civil officers in their present positions. You will continue with your normal work. Get your people to reopen their shops and businesses. Your civil guard will act in conjunction with my own garrison troops." No sooner had the interpreter finished when the enthusiasm broke out afresh. The whole throng of onlookers—Italian men in felt hats and overcoats, pretty girls in fashionable dresses, smartly-uniformed officials and police, and grinning Arabs who had already learnt to salute the British way—they all clapped and cheered. It was a dramatic moment, a moment as astonishing as dramatic.

Swiftly the townspeople set themselves to obey the Brigadier's order. Down came the shutters from many of the shops, and the cafés and the hotels were soon doing the best business they had done for weeks. Although many of the houses had been scarred by shellfire the town was practically intact. The water supply was still functioning, and so too was the electricity for lighting and heating—much to the delight of the soldiers who for weeks past had been marching and fighting in the dust and dirt of the desert, and who only a few hours before had been plunging through an ocean of red mud, whipped by the sand-laden wind. For the first time in many weeks, too, they were able to drink their fill of water, not to mention the other more tasty beverages which were to be obtained in the town's " pubs."

Before many days had passed Benghazi had settled down under the British occupation. Most of its wealthier citizens had fled to the supposedly safer towns along the coast to the west, and the banks, the chief shops and offices remained closed. But the smaller shops and hotels were open.

Cyrenaica Under British Rule

On February 10 it was announced in Cairo that Lieut.-Gen. Sir Maitland Wilson, Commander-in-Chief of the conquering Army of the Nile, had been appointed Military Governor and General Officer C.-in-C. Cyrenaica, and in his administration of the province he was assisted by a number of military and civil officers. But so far as possible the Italian functionaries were retained in office, and in the streets the traffic was directed by British military police standing side by side with Italian police and Bersaglieri. As conditions became more settled, numbers of the population who had fled trickled back steadily to their houses and farms. But their homecoming was not always happy and peaceful. It was soon made plain to the British that there was no love lost between the Italians and the Arabs whom they or their fathers had dispossessed. In large measure the cordial welcome given to the troops by the Italian population might be attributed to their relief at finding themselves under such strong protection. Without that protection the lot of the Italian settlers would have been uncomfortable, if not dangerous, for the Arabs who had been so sorely maltreated by Graziani looked forward eagerly to wiping off old scores.

The people of Benghazi welcomed, even with enthusiasm, the British and Australian troops when they marched into the town. These children were among the large crowd in the streets when the place was formally surrendered.   *Photo, British Official : Crown Copyright*

Cheers and Smiles Greeted the Victors

The formalities for the surrender of Benghazi were accomplished without any great military parade. Above left, the Italian Mayor, Nicola Epifani, with Bishop Vescovo on his right, hands over his authority to the Brigadier in command of Australian troops. Right, the Brigadier is seen outside the civic building.

AUSTRALIANS ENTERING BENGHAZI were greeted rather as deliverers than as conquerors, and from the crowds that witnessed their passage through the streets came smiles, friendly words, and even hand-clapping. No great precautions were taken, and above is a typical scene when Australian artillery entered the main square passing through crowds of townspeople who still moved freely about.

Photos, Australian Official: Crown Copyright

In Jubaland They 'Hit Them—and Hit Them Hard'

From July until December 1940 there was a gap of some 100 miles between Italians and British on the Kenya-Italian Somaliland front. But on Dec. 16 General Cunningham opened an offensive which in two months carried the Imperial forces beyond the Juba.

"HIT them; hit them hard, and hit them again." This was the injunction given by the G.O.C., Lt.-Gen. A. G. Cunningham, to the East African Imperial Force on the eve of their invasion of Jubaland—that south-western corner of Italian Somaliland that was part of Britain's Kenya Colony before 1925 and is now once again in British occupation.

Composed of troops drawn from the Union of South Africa, from West Africa and from East, General Cunningham's force delivered its first attack against El Wak, a frontier post set in the heart of the bush and defended in considerable strength. The attack was launched on December 16 by South African troops—it was the first action in which the South Africans were officially stated to have taken part—supported by an East African armoured car unit and a Gold Coast battalion with tanks. Two South African units which particularly distinguished themselves were the Natal battalion which captured a burning village—they went over the top, so it was reported, singing a Zulu war song—and a Transvaal battalion which captured the Italian Brigade Headquarters; and the South African Air Force, which plastered the Italian defences with bombs at the opening of the attack, also calls for special mention.

After El Wak had been put out of action General Cunningham organized and made his preparations for an invasion of Italian

than wait for the British onslaught which was timed for dawn on February 12. In this action the King's African Rifles particularly distinguished themselves.

From Afmadu the invaders moved on through the dense thorn and scrub, across a largely waterless and almost roadless

BRIGADIER DAN PIENAAR, in command of the South African Forces operating in East Africa, has just been awarded the D.S.O. for his brilliant leadership at El Wak. Below is a private of the Gold Coast Regiment, Royal West African Frontier Force, on the look-out.

'planes of the S.A.A.F. subjected Kismayu to severe bombing. The Italians did not make much of a stand, and at 2 o'clock on February 14 the King's African Rifles marched into Kismayu and hoisted the

WHAT THE G.O.C. SAID

Lt.-Gen. A. G. Cunningham's Order of the Day to the East African Imperial Force

The victory of the Imperial troops farther north has filled us in East Africa with pride and excited thought. No doubt the ensuing period has touched us with envy and there has been a strong desire to emulate their achievement.

The chance is now here. This force is no whit behind in dash, courage, and endurance. Confident in this, I send to the South African and West African troops taking part in the operations a message of good luck.

Hit them; hit them hard, and hit them again.

Union Jack in the main square. The Italian garrison, two battalions with some artillery, had evacuated the place two days before, after having destroyed everything that might be of military value. The natives, who thronged the streets of the little town with its thatched, whitewashed houses, gave the Imperial troops a perfervid reception and expressed no little pleasure at being, after 15 years of Italian rule, once more under the British flag.

General Cunningham now pressed on across the Juba towards Mogadishu, and on February 25 this, the capital of Italian Somaliland, was taken by Empire troops.

Somaliland from points far to the south; and in view of the success which has crowned his arms there can be little doubt that he laid his plans and executed them with that same careful precision and masterly generalship that is so characteristic of General Wavell's operations in Libya. First a number of frontier posts were subdued, Liboi on January 24, Haweina on January 27, and Beles Gugani on February 4. General Cunningham's men pressed on into the interior until, 100 miles from the frontier, they came up against the Italians at Afmadu on February 8. The place was held by an Italian battalion, supported by field artillery and considerable numbers of *Banda* (native levies). But after the South African Air Force had bombed the place, the Italians quitted on the night of February 10 rather

wilderness to Kismayu, the Italian port at the mouth of the Juba river. They encountered little resistance in their advance, and what little there was was overcome by the Gold Coast Regiment, supported by an Indian mountain battery, who seized the bridgeheads on the river. At the same time units of the Royal Navy harassed the Italians who were moving along the road between Kismayu and Mogadishu, while

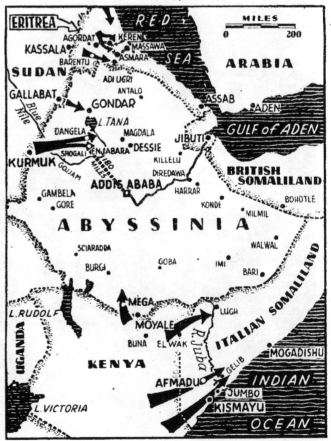

The lines of advance of the British troops and Abyssinian Patriots against the Italians in Eritrea, Abyssinia and Italian Somaliland are indicated by the arrows in this map. *Photos, South African Official, and British Movietone News; Map, "News Chronicle"*

'Alert' and 'Raiders Passed' at Addis Ababa

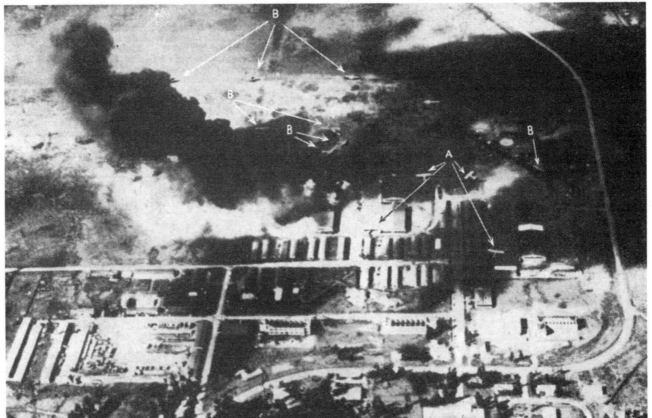

Bombs have already fallen on the aerodrome of Addis Ababa, seat of Mussolini's Government in Abyssinia, as the two unique photographs in this page show. That on the top of the page was taken by one of the reconnaissance 'planes that preceded the bombers. Dispersed on the landing field are (A) Caproni bombers, (B) Savoia-Marchetti bombers. The lower photograph shows the same scene when the raiders had passed. Direct hits on hangars had been made and, as they burned fiercely, clouds of dense smoke cast deep shadows over the aerodrome.　　*Photos, British Official: Crown Copyright*

Smiters of the Regia Aeronautica

Once a formidable Savoia-Marchetti S.M.79 bomber, this heap of burnt and buckled metal was found by our troops on the aerodrome at El Adem.

Air Commodore Raymond Collishaw, who commands the R.A.F. in the Western Desert, started his career as an airman with the Royal Naval Air Service in 1915. He is 47.

Men of the R.A.F. show a keenness and audacity which have compelled the admiration of the world. Here are six gallant fellows serving with a bomber squadron in Libya.

COMMANDING the squadrons of the R.A.F. in the Western Desert is one of the most inspiring personalities serving Britain today. He is Air Commodore Raymond Collishaw, D.S.O., O.B.E., D.S.C., D.F.C. Born in Canada on November 22, 1893, he has crowded into his 47 years high adventure and grand achievement on land, sea and in the air. After studying at the Canadian Naval College he joined the Canadian Navy in the Fishery Protection Service. Then he went on Scott's ill-fated Polar expedition. When the war of 1914-1918 came Collishaw, of course, was in it. In 1915 he forsook the sea and joined the Royal Naval Air Service. It was not long before he began to show that dash, initiative and superb skill in markmanship and flying, which, by the time the war had drawn to a close, raised him to second place in the long list of British air "aces." Altogether this tough, smiling Canadian shot down sixty German machines and, when the Armistice came, he had won the D.S.O. and Bar, the D.S.C. and the D.F.C. Still serving with the R.A.F., he went to North Persia in 1920, and later to Iraq, where he remained until 1923. For three years from 1929 he served in H.M. aircraft carrier Courageous as Senior R.A.F. Officer, and then he commanded various R.A.F. stations in England. Time passed and once again Collishaw was posted abroad, first to the Sudan and then Heliopolis. Now as Air Officer Commanding the Egypt Group, Middle East Command, he is proving his worth in Libya.

ON EL ADEM AERODROME, the largest air base in Libya, no fewer than eighty-seven Italian aircraft were found smashed and ruined as a result of the intensive bombing by the R.A.F. A portion of one of the wrecked enemy machines is shown in the circle. Italian aircraft, whether they met the R.A.F. in the sky or remained grounded at their bases in the desert, could not escape destruction in the mighty British offensive. Above is another scene on the aerodrome at El Adem. The machines are, or rather were, twin-engined bombers.

Photos, British Official : Crown Copyright

'It Caught Fire and Crashed in Flames'

FIRE FIGHTING is such an important duty of the R.A.F. that a special school gives instruction in it. When a 'plane crashes and bursts into flames the fire parties, who must be of first-rate physique and strong nerve, may have to go right into the blaze to save the crew. Here one of them, clothed from head to foot in an asbestos suit, is spraying a foam mixture on a burning wreck. On most aerodromes fire fighters with their equipment are ready for all emergencies.

Photo, Topical

How Aircraft Are De-Iced

Picture-Diagram illustrating the Methods adopted in the Royal Air Force and the German Luftwaffe to defeat Ice

Specially drawn by Haworth for THE WAR ILLUSTRATED

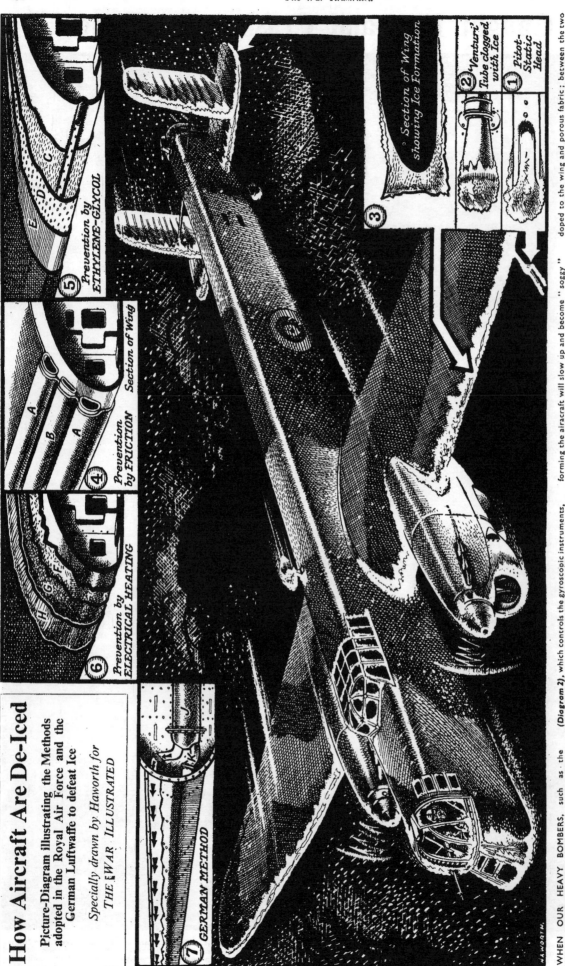

① GERMAN METHOD

④ Prevention by FRICTION   Section of Wing

⑤ Prevention by ETHYLENE-GLYCOL

⑥ Prevention by ELECTRICAL HEATING

③ Section of Wing showing Ice Formation

② 'Venturi' Tube clogged with Ice

① Pilot-Static Head

WHEN OUR HEAVY BOMBERS, such as the "Whitley" here shown, make trips deep into Germany or over the Alps to Italy, they often encounter weather conditions which cause ice to form on the aircraft.

Under such conditions the hinges of the ailerons, rudders and elevators have a tendency to become locked, the guns in the revolving turret may freeze up, the airscrews become coated, flinging off sharp pieces of ice which are a danger to the crew, and, more serious still, the pitot-static head (Diagram 1), which controls the airspeed indicator, and the "Venturi tube"

(Diagram 2), which controls the gyroscopic instruments, may become clogged with ice and refuse to function. Both of these are outside the plane, but actuate instruments inside the cockpit on which the pilot relies. On some types of aircraft, too, the bomb-release gear tends to become jammed by ice unless treated beforehand.

Diagram 3 is a section of the aircraft's wing showing how ice will completely alter the shape of the leading edge; the same applies in the case of tail and rudders. The shape of these lifting and directing surfaces has been carefully designed, and if the ice is not prevented from

forming the aircraft will slow up and become "soggy" and unmanageable.

All modern aircraft carry instruments which warn the pilot when ice formation is beginning, and there are several methods of prevention, some of which are shown in the remaining diagrams.

Diagram 4 shows a method similar to that used by the R.A.F. Rubber tubing is fixed on all leading edges and by alternately inflating and deflating the ice is cracked off. Tubes A A are inflated, B deflated. C and D are respectively rubbered fabric

doped to the wing and porous fabric; between the two runs a perforated tube carrying ethylene-glycol which seeps through the outer cover of leather E and prevents ice accretion.

Diagram 6: F is a layer of cork, G one of asbestos and H a special dope which conducts electrical warmth, to prevent ice formation.

Diagram 7 shows the method used by the German Luftwaffe. Hot air from the engine is conducted through a reservoir J along the leading edge of the wing. It can be by-passed through valve K when not required.

The Way the Ground Staff Beat the Winter

Despite the extra work which winter conditions impose upon R.A.F. ground crews, the men, as we see, can still find time for recreation. Their charge is a Vickers Wellington bomber.

THOUGH modern instruments and efficient training enable the R.A.F. to fly even in appalling weather conditions, throughout the winter snow, ice, frost and sleet are still the greatest enemies of our bomber squadrons.

But a severe winter not only adds to the difficulties of the bomber pilots ; active service conditions necessitate the aircraft being kept out in the open and this greatly increases the work of the ground personnel. Hard weather conditions entail much extra work for those responsible for the maintenance of the machines.

Whether it rains or snows, constant inspection of all aircraft has to be carried out minutely at regular intervals. The great engines of the bombers must be kept warm by shrouding them with heating devices and taking steps to ensure that they will start up at a second's notice. So that the bomb-aimer's sight shall not be obscured by frost and misting up, the windows from which he scans his target must be regularly wiped over with glycerine. Even such routine work as greasing and cleaning is no sinecure when carried out in bitter weather which numbs the fingers and chaps the hands.

Many components and accessories of the aircraft's equipment have to be specially treated to prevent trouble developing in the air through ice formation (see diagram opposite), and landing-grounds themselves have to be kept in good condition. And while all this regular maintenance work is going on, engine overhauls, repairs to the airframe, to the retractable undercarriage, the wireless equipment, the armament, etc., have to be carried out swiftly and thoroughly. A hundred and one small details, which, though small, are vital, have to be attended to, and all this requires patient devotion to duty on the part of the riggers and fitters.

EACH man attached to the ground staff of an R.A.F. station must be a highly skilled technical expert, trained to a high pitch of efficiency. Although considerably less spectacular than that of the flying branches of the R.A.F., the work of the maintenance crews is every bit as essential, if the efficiency of the Service as a whole is not to be impaired. They are " key " men, and without their skill and steadfast devotion to duty, by day and by night, all the courage of the pilots and aircrews who man the machines to raid and fight the enemy would be of little avail.

MAINTENANCE OF AIRCRAFT during a hard winter entails hard work. Though snow covers its wings and fuselage the Wellington bomber (oval) is ready to take off at a moment's notice, for its engines are enclosed in a special tent in which a heating device keeps them at a working temperature. Above, maintenance staff are wheeling out a Handley Page Hampden from its hangar to the repair shop.   *Photos, Planet News and Fox*

See the 'Stuka' Dive Screaming Down

DIVE BOMBING, in its different stages, is well illustrated by this series of photographs (from German sources) of the way "Stukas" attack shipping. Note how the machine, a Junkers JU 87, from level flight (1) goes into a dive by executing a half-roll (2 and 3) and is then followed down by its companion (4). The "Stuka" is next seen (5) and (6) swooping down the target, and the final photograph shows the attacker pulling out of the dive after releasing its bomb. The last three photographs were taken from a German steamer, an attack having been staged by request, so that photographs might be taken.

Photos, E.N.A.

Men of the 'Old Dozen' Ready for Anything

THE SUFFOLK REGIMENT was represented amongst those who waited amidst a rain of bombs on the sands of Dunkirk on the memorable days of early June 1940, when the British Expeditionary Force snatched triumph out of defeat. Now, the Suffolks who got safely home are training to fight again. The regiment was established as the 12th Foot in 1685, and it took part in the last siege of Gibraltar 1779-83, commemorated in the regimental badge (top left) by a castle and key, the arms of Gibraltar.

Photo, British Official : Crown Copyright

War & Threat of War in the Far East

Since 1937, when the Japanese invaded China, there has been war in the Far East. The
"Chinese Incident," as the Japanese have called it, is by no means ended, yet such are
her imperialistic ambitions (stimulated, no doubt, by Germany) that possibly Japan may
ere long stir up against her a fresh host of enemies.

SINGAPORE has been reinforced. On February 18 a strong force of Australian troops, some thousands in number and officially described as the largest ever to land in Malaya from a single convoy, stepped ashore at Singapore. The men were drawn from every state in the Australian Commonwealth, and the units comprised infantry, artillery, transport and signallers. Their howitzers and field guns were of the most modern type, all produced in Australian arsenals, and the anti-tank regiments were similarly equipped with home-made weapons. At the same time it was revealed that this was not by any means the first landing, although it was the largest; for weeks past our garrisons in Singapore and Malaya have been steadily strengthened. Moreover, there have been large reinforcements of the R.A.F. and the Australian Air Force in the Peninsula.

Following the announcement of the expeditionary force's arrival, Vice-Admiral Sir Geoffrey Layton, C.-in-C. of the China Station, stated that "the safe arrival of these strong reinforcements is viewed with satisfaction. It is yet another demonstration of power, given by the British command of the sea, which enables us to station our forces, as and when they complete their training, in areas where they are most needed. It is also a clear indication of the growing strength of the Empire forces, which now need leave no part of the Empire inadequately defended." The Governor of the Straits Settlements, Sir Shenton Thomas, for his part said that the reinforcements were "one more proof of the unity of the Empire, one more recognition of the fact that we all stand or fall together"; while Major-General Gordon Bennett, G.O.C. Australian Forces, who had arrived in Singapore some days earlier, stated that his men were "as efficient and fit a lot as ever left Australia," and that they were even better equipped than earlier troops to leave the Commonwealth because of the great strides which had been made in the development of Australian war industries.

British spokesmen were careful to emphasize that the expeditionary force had arrived solely to defend Singapore and Malaya and not to attack anyone. None could doubt, however, that the move was a reply to Japan's distinctly bellicose words and acts of recent months. For ten years and more Japan has been engaged in a campaign of imperialistic aggression; first she invaded Manchuria in 1931; in 1937 she attacked China; and since the collapse of Holland and

France she has made no secret of the fact that she regards the Dutch East Indies and Indo-China as being within her legitimate sphere of influence. Even Siam, or Thailand as it is now officially styled, has been penetrated by Japanese emissaries, and Thailand is next door to Burma and Malaya. Particularly since the conclusion of the Tripartite Pact with Germany and Italy on September 27, 1940, has Japanese intransigence been most marked, for it was concluded when Japan thought that Germany was bound to win. But now things are not going too well with Italy; and the future, we may suppose, is not quite so clear to Hitler as he would like it to be. Hence Japan has been prodded into action by her partners with a view (we may presume) to diverting some of Britain's naval and military strength, and also to persuade the Americans to go slow in their policy of utmost aid for the democracies, since their ships and 'planes and munitions might be required for a war of their own.

Reactions to Japan's Aggression

If these, indeed, are the motives which lie behind some of Japan's recent activities, then the results have been far other than might have been anticipated. Faced with the possibility of a Japanese offensive by sea, land and air, aimed at British Malaya and

the Dutch East Indies, and possibly, too, at Australia, both the U.S.A. and the Australian Commonwealth reacted strongly and at once. From America came the news that the Pacific Fleet would be immediately reinforced with a large number of dive-bombers and the latest types of fighter 'planes, so that the complements of the aircraft carriers would be brought up to wartime strength; the garrison at Manila in the Philippines was strengthened, and there were reports of fresh Anglo-American collaboration in the Far East. Thus it was stated that Britain had suggested that Japan should be prevented from building up strategic reserves of oil and other war materials—a suggestion with which the American Government might be expected to concur, since they had already banned the export of metals and scrap metals to Japan. Then the House of Representatives at Washington on February 19 authorized the expenditure of about £60,000,000 on the development of the U.S.A. naval bases.

Then in Australia there was immediate reaction to news of recent developments in the Pacific. The sitting of the War Advisory Council, presided over by Mr. A. W. Fadden, Acting Prime Minister in the absence of Mr. Menzies, who was on his way to England, was suddenly adjourned on February 13, and in a statement issued by Mr. Fadden and Mr. Curtin, the Labour leader, it was stated that "we think we should tell the people that in the considered opinion of the War Council the war has moved into a new stage, involving the utmost gravity." On the next day the Chiefs of Staffs, together with Sir Robert Brooke Popham, Commander-in-Chief in the Far East, were called into consultation, but no details were given of the news which had been regarded as so portentous. In any case, Australia was not really in need of any reminder of the seriousness of the war situation. As Mr. Menzies said on his arrival in England on February 20, "We are on your side, we are all in this together, and you will never be beaten while there are any of us left on the surface."

Australia's preparedness, demonstrated so obviously and forcibly by the dispatch of the expeditionary force to Singapore, and America's determined stand against the mere threat of further Japanese aggression in the Pacific, together combined to counsel a more moderate policy in Tokyo, and Mr. Matsuoka, Japanese Foreign Minister, sent a conciliatory message to London. So for the present at least it was peace, albeit a strongly armed peace, and not war in the Pacific.

SINGAPORE—the Gibraltar of the Orient—is a powerful bulwark against a possible Japanese threat, not only to India but to the Dutch East Indies and Australasia. This map, illustrating recent developments, shows the distances between strategic points; the lighter-shaded portions represent Dutch possessions.   *By courtesy of the "News Chronicle"*

China's Gateway that the Japanese Cannot Close

CHINA'S NORTH-WEST ROAD, shown in the map below, runs for the most part through primitive country. One big town stands upon it—Lanchow, with a population of about 200,000 ; above is the city wall. Near Lanchow the road runs for some distance beside the Great Wall of China. Below right is a soldier on guard on the road ; he carries a German Bergmann sub-machine gun.

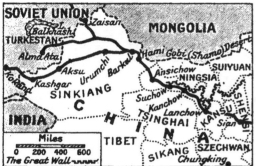

Many inhabitants of the Shensi and Kansu provinces through which the road runs live in caves cut in the loess cliffs of the R. Hwangho ; above is the entrance to one of them.

OF the three roads which connect China with the wider world, the Burma Road is frequently bombed by Japanese airmen, while that which runs through Indo-China has been closed by the Japanese occupation of Southern China. The third road, however, remains open—that which leads from Sianfu, in the heart of China, between the Gobi Desert and the highlands of Tibet, into Sinkiang and so on into Asiatic Russia. This is the great North-West Road, the road which in the Middle Ages was travelled by Marco Polo and along which for centuries have passed the silk caravans. Now it is thronged with motor-lorries and trains of coolies bringing to Chiang Kai-Shek's armies those munitions of war which the Soviet supplies.

The defences of the road would be useless in modern warfare, for they consist of blockhouses, such as that above left, built of mud, which is liable to crumble under stress of weather, making repairs an interminable process. Mud walls are the only protection of the villages, like that above. On the other hand, the difficult nature of the terrain, seen clearly in the photograph, would form a natural defence.

Wide World Photos : Exclusive to WAR ILLUSTRATED

On the Steps of Benghazi's Town Hall the A

ON FEBRUARY 7, 1941, there was no goose-stepping parade and arrogant display of armed might in the Nazi manner when a detachment of the victorious troops of General Wavell arrived in Benghazi. Just one company of Australian infantry, in greatcoats and steel helmets, marched into the square before the Town Hall. And, what is truly remarkable, far from being greeted in sullen silence by the assembled townspeople, they were clapped and cheered more as liberators than as conquerors. Perhaps, indeed, it is as liberators that a people weary of Totalitarian oppression

ian Brigadier Receives the Town's Surrender

looked upon them. Then, as the Brigadier of these Australian troops stepped from his car, the troops saluted, representative of conquerors and conquered shook hands, the Brigadier issued a proclamation through the medium of an interpreter, and in a typical British and unostentatious manner Benghazi, capital of Cyrenaica, passed into our possession. The Australian Brigadier is seen in the centre, between the two cars, taking tha salute. Other pictures of the entry into Benghazi of the troops of the Imperial Army of the Nile are given in pages 225 and 227.

Mighty Men of Valour Are the Greeks

Fighting in some of the most difficult country in Europe, often in the most appalling
winter weather, the Greeks are steadily thrusting back the Italians, who had the temerity
to invade their land.   Here we tell something of their recent successes, but more of the
Greek Army itself.

"MAGNIFICENT" is not too strong a word to apply to the Greeks who for so many weeks past have been battling in the Albanian mountains.   Even during the height of winter—and the winter in the Balkans has been terrible indeed with its blizzards and heavy rains, its biting cold —the Greeks have maintained their pressure. True, there was a general slackening in the operations when the weather turned for the worse on December 13 and for six weeks the battle was immobilized by the snow ; but as soon as conditions were a little more favourable the struggle was resumed.   Now it was the Italians who intensified their effort, and in 25 days General Cavellero ordered his men over the top in 46 counter-attacks.   Not one of the 46 was successful ; each was smashed by the Greek artillery and riflemen, blown to pieces by the bombers of the R.A.F., or slithered to disaster in the snow-filled gorges.

Fighters with the Bayonet

Six months ago, even three months, it would have seemed improbable, if not impossible, that the Greeks could have put up so splendid a show.   Even the most optimistic of their admirers and wellwishers have been astounded by what they have actually accomplished.   They have proved themselves to be more than masters of the Italians ; before the war the Greek soldier had the reputation of being the best marcher in Europe, but now he has won recognition as a master-fighter with the bayonet.   Time and again the communiqués have described the fierce bayonet charges of the Greeks, and time and again the Italians have fled rather than face that glittering line of bared steel.

During the Balkan wars of 1912-1913 the Greeks distinguished themselves against the Turks, and in the Great War they proved themselves of value as the allies of Britain and France on the Salonika front.   But their invasion of Turkey ended in complete disaster in 1922, and following the Treaty of Lausanne in the next year the Greek Army was neglected. The politicians were too busy squabbling amongst themselves to see that the soldiers had the war material they needed.   What equipment the Army possessed was old and out of date ; there was practically no artillery and no anti-aircraft guns, engineering equipment was similarly conspicuous by its absence, the only bridge-train being one dating from the Balkan wars ; fortifications, roads, and railways were alike neglected ; the intake of conscripts was diminished consequent upon the reduction in the period of military service, and particularly in officers the Army was sadly deficient.

Following the outbreak of the Italo-Abyssinian war in 1935 there began to be manifested a demand for the Army's modernization and extension, as it seemed clear that war might soon spread to the Mediterranean. Little was done, however, until the advent to power in 1936 of General Metaxas, and then much was done, speedily and well.   Large sums of money were voted for the Army, for the improvement of communications and the strengthening of the country's fortifications. The Metaxas Line, with its 3,000 concrete strong-points, was planned and constructed along the country's northern frontier.   Some hundreds of field, anti-aircraft, and light mountain guns—especially the last, so that today Greece's light mountain artillery, transported by mules, has particularly distinguished itself—were purchased, as well as quantities of trench mortars, anti-tank guns and anti-tank rifles.   Tanks, armoured cars, and modern automatic weapons were also added, together with bridge trains and other sappers' equipment of the latest type, transport animals, stocks of clothing, spare parts, and medical stores.   Thirty new barracks were

constructed, as well as many depots, hospitals and warehouses.

Up to the time of the Balkan wars of a generation ago, the Greek Army was inclined to model itself upon that of Austria-Hungary, but after 1918 the influence of the French Military Mission made itself felt, and uniforms and equipment were based very largely on French models.   Early in the thirties, however, French influence began to wane, and when King George returned to the throne in 1935 from his exile in England, it was but to be expected that the English touch should become ever more apparent. The Air Force, too, is organized on English lines, while the Navy has always striven to follow the English tradition.

Boys in the Front Line

Military service in Greece is compulsory and universal ; normally the conscript serves for 24 months, followed by 19 years in the First Reserve and eight years in the Second. The annual batches of conscripts are called up for service in March and September, and the normal annual intake is 50,000 recruits (although in wartime young men under conscription age can volunteer for service, which accounts for the number of young boys who are now serving at the front).

Only the officers of the Army are professional soldiers ; they are trained at a college in Athens which corresponds to our Sandhurst and the French St. Cyr.   The cadet, who wears a blue uniform with brass buttons and yellow ornaments, follows a three or four year course and is known as a "Euelpis" ("Good Hope Boy," from the fact that his country puts its trust and confidence in him). That that trust is not misplaced has been more than made clear by the splendid way in which the officers of today have captained their men in the hard and bitter fighting on the Albanian front.

FIGHTING IN ALBANIA is proceeding approximately along the dotted line in this map.   Above, two Greek airmen stand triumphantly on the wreckage of an Italian heavy bomber just brought down.   Deep snow on the ground gives an indication of the exceptionally severe weather experienced in Albania early in 1941, rendering air operations difficult.   *Map, " News Chronicle" ; photo, by courtesy of the Royal Greek Legation*

Soldiers of Our Ally Ready for Action

Greece has no great munition works, and her Army's equipment has come largely from foreign sources. Many of her field guns, one of which is seen above in Albania, were supplied by Krupps, the great German armament firm.

The Greek sentry, left, standing on guard at cross-roads eight miles from Koritza, wears the usual uniform of the Greek infantry, not very different from that of a British infantry-man.　His helmet is of more individual type. Below, a field-telephone unit using imported apparatus is at work on the Albanian front.

Photos by courtesy of the Royal Greek Legation

A Turn for the Better in the Shipping War

Continuing his series of chapters describing the course of the war directed by the enemy against our mercantile shipping, D. E. Maxwell describes below that comparative " bright patch " which overlapped Christmas and the New Year, when, though it could not be claimed that the enemy attack at sea had been mastered, at least the figures of sinkings were encouraging after the dreary record of the previous months.

EARLY in December 1940 the losses of British and Allied shipping fell abruptly from the high toll the enemies had succeeded in taking week by week since the beginning of the previous June. At the time it was thought that the better record might be due to chance, the weather, or some other temporary swing in the pendulum in our favour. But as weeks passed and the losses remained comparatively—but only comparatively—low, it became apparent that the downward movement was of a significant character.

This significance derives from the fact that in previous months not only had losses been high but they had been *consistently* and depressingly high. The question now being asked was, How much longer is this to continue ? In every one of the six months from June to December the enemy succeeded in sinking an average of more than 55,000 tons of British shipping per week and more than 80,000 tons of British, Allied and neutral ships combined. Over the whole of this period of six months the average weekly rate of loss was of the order of 65,000

But by themselves weekly figures are deceptive because they do not show the trend of losses and may be disproportionately swelled by the inclusion, for example, of a vessel of 30,000 tons sunk perhaps a few minutes before the time limit set to each week. The trend is, therefore, better illustrated either by monthly totals or average weekly figures over periods of four or five weeks.

A loss of nearly 100,000 tons of British, Allied and neutral shipping per week, such as was sustained during June-November 1940, corresponds to an annual loss of over 5 million tons gross. This is nearly six times the tonnage launched annually during the five pre-war years by Great Britain, the British Empire, and the United States together. It was for this reason that the Prime Minister declared in the House of Commons on December 19, 1940 that we must regard the keeping open of the Atlantic channel to the world " as the first of the military tasks which lie before us at the present time." He did not repeat the error made by other members of the Government, notably Mr. Arthur Greenwood, who sug-

THE TREND OF SHIPPING LOSSES
(Average Weekly Losses)

	British	British, Allied & Neutral
	Tons Gross	Tons Gross
Sept. 3, 1939—May 27, 1940	20,000	41,000
June 1940 ...	63,000	100,000
July 1940 ...	57,000	83,000
August 1940 ...	65,000	82,000
September 1940 ...	76,000	101,000
October 1940 ...	64,000	88,000
November 1940 ...	68,000	89,000
Average, June—Nov. 1940	**65,000**	**94,000**
December 1940 ...	52,000	68,000
January 1941 ...	32,000	47,000
Average, 9 weeks ended Feb. 9, 1941	**31,000**	**44,000**

But, potentially, the situation was one of the utmost gravity, since we could look for no more assistance from neutral European countries—assistance, that is, such as we received as a result of Hitler's violation of the neutrality of one European nation after another in the spring of 1940—and little more from two other previous avenues of supply, namely, capture and purchase ; while the losses, as has been shown, were at a rate considerably in excess of the capacity during the next eighteen months of British, Empire and American shipyards.

The extent by which these high losses were arrested in December and January is shown in the accompanying table giving the average weekly losses during the eight months following the German occupation of the French ports along the English Channel—a strategic advantage which had a profound effect on the war of blockade and counter-blockade, and one of which the Nazis made full and immediate use. The sudden fall in sinkings during December would be more apparent if the first week of that month—a bad patch —were excluded. In this case the average for the remaining three weeks of December would be 34,000 and 48,000 tons respectively; and the fact that the trend of losses broke at this period is taken into account in the last of the figures in the table, which show the rate of loss since the better record was first established. The table also illustrates the point that the steady rate of sinkings was broken for the first time in six months.

Stronger Naval Escorts

No single factor will suffice to explain the satisfactory reduction in sinkings, but of the several causes there is little doubt that the most important was the stronger naval escorts provided for the Atlantic convoys. Mr. Churchill stated, in the speech referred to above, that " from now on we shall steadily increase our resources in flotillas and other methods of defence." The increase in the naval escorts was brought about not only by the new vessels being turned out from British and Empire shipyards, but by the destroyers transferred from America and by the improvement in the Mediterranean situation following the British advance in Africa and the crippling of an important part of the Italian Fleet at Taranto.

Among the other factors are the weather and the strengthening of the defensive patrol of the Coastal Command of the R.A.F.

CORVETTES are the latest type of ship evolved by the Royal Navy to escort convoys. In this photograph, taken on board one of them escorting a large convoy in the Atlantic, the crew of the 4-in. gun is going to action stations when a U-boat is believed to be near. Corvettes present but a small target to dive bombers, against which also they are armed. See also page 110 of this volume. Canada has built at least 45 of these craft. *Photo, Central Press*

tons of British and 94,000 tons total shipping sunk ; in the former case more than three times the average up to the time of the collapse of France, and in the latter more than double the corresponding rate.

The sustained success the enemy was achieving at that time is shown by the fact that there was a difference of less than 10,000 tons in the record for the best of those months compared with the average for the period as a whole. The weekly totals issued by the Admiralty necessarily showed greater fluctuations, rising in one week to over 150,000 tons of British shipping sunk.

gested that the shipping situation was as perilous as it had been in the spring of 1917, but he stressed that the losses continued " at a disquieting level."

In fact, the seriousness of the immediate shipping position could not be compared to the worst period of the war of 1914-18, owing mainly to the tonnage contributions of our Allies, Norway, Holland and Greece, and to the fact that British losses had largely been made good by building, capture and purchase—the net British losses, indeed, amounted to less than 3 per cent of the tonnage owned at the outbreak of the war.

They Were Marooned in the South Seas

EMIRAU ISLAND with its palm-fringed beach was not an altogether inhospitable spot on which to be marooned. Right are some of the huts in which the victims made their homes until rescue came; the natives lent a willing hand in building them. The island lies north of Bismarck Archipelago, off New Guinea.

Residents in Emirau provided the motor-launch with a Kanaka crew, seen below, in which a small party of the survivors went to Kavieng, a port in New Ireland, 40 miles away, whence the news of the marooning was flashed to Australia.

TRAGEDY and drama were the lot of the passengers and crews of six British ships and one Norwegian that were caught by German raiders in the South Pacific in the last four months of 1940. Eventually, as we have told in pages 38 and 52 of this volume, some 500 survivors were crowded into one of the raiders, where their treatment was fairly good. Then, on December 21, 1940, the prisoners were landed on the little South Seas island of Emirau. Before leaving them, the commander of the German·ship made sure that there was a plentiful supply of fresh water, but as there are only a little over two hundred inhabitants on the island, food and shelter were hardly adequate. Fortunately, the news of their marooning soon reached friendly ears and on Christmas Day they were rescued and taken to an Australian port. On the rescue ship they enjoyed the "best Christmas dinner of their lives"—bread and butter, cheese and coffee.

Rescued survivors are seen in the photograph above being towed in boats to the rescue ship. They were landed at a Northern Australian port and taken thence by special train to Sydney, where they were met by the Governor-General, Lord Gowrie, Lady Gowrie, and Federal and State Ministers. Right are two injured women leaving the station.   *Photos, Sport & General*

OUR SEARCHLIGHT ON THE WAR

Costliest War in History

BRITAIN's daily expenditure on the war effort is now over £10,500,000. This is more than twice what it was a year ago, and one and a half millions more than the daily cost in October. Sir Kingsley Wood, quoting figures from the Great War, told the House of Commons that the highest annual expenditure then was £2,432,000,000 in 1917. In the current financial year we shall have spent £3,300,000,000. Of our present daily ten and a half millions, eight millions are for the fighting services and two and a half millions for war services such as the Ministries of Shipping, Food and Home Security. "But," said the Chancellor, "the tremendous figures I have given are, indeed, striking proof of the country's determination to prosecute the war with all its might and with all energy and speed." He asked for, and readily obtained, two Votes of Credit—£600,000,000 for the current and £1,000,000,000 for the coming year.

Germany Raises the Wind in America

FOR some years Germany has been selling works of art, chiefly Italian, in order to increase her credit overseas. At first these were mainly Italian bronzes, objects of high value and comparatively small bulk, which were shipped to the States under the cloak of Italian trade. She has now sent a number of Old Masters for sale in America, and because of the British blockade they were dispatched via Siberia and the Pacific Ocean. There are fourteen of these pictures, drawn from the smaller treasures of the Kaiser Friedrich Museum in Berlin. They comprise three Rembrandts, three Van Eycks, and one each of Botticelli, Fouquet, Vermeer, Velazquez, Raphael, Giorgione, Fra Lippo Lippi and Domenico Veneziano. The picture by Lippi is of the Nativity and is stated to have been painted as the altarpiece in the Medici Chapel in Florence. Italy possesses merely a copy of it. There are few examples extant of the works of Fouquet and Giorgione. With the sale of the three Van Eyeks only one important example by either of the brothers will be left in Berlin. It has been surmised that Hitler

intends to draw upon the art galleries of Holland, Belgium and France to replenish Germany's depleted collections. With the large sum of money raised by the sale of these pictures Nazi propaganda and espionage in America will doubtless receive a very useful subsidy.

New Life-Raft

MR. R. S. CHIPCHASE, a ship repairer, has invented a reversible life-raft, and has passed over to the Ministry of Shipping all royalties and patents concerning it. Having watched a public demonstration of the raft, officials of the Ministry warmly recommended its use to the Merchant Navy. It is kept slung across the bulwarks of the ship. A kick will release it, or if there is no time even for that, it will free itself by an automatic floating release. One novel and important feature about the new design is that it is immaterial which side up it falls on the water. It has great manoeuvring power and cannot be sunk by machine-gun fire. Mr. Chipchase maintains that his invention can be cheaply mass-produced. "If you give our lads a sporting chance they will go anywhere," he said. "This raft will give them that chance in all weathers and whatever the circumstances." And the captain and crew who tried it out emphatically agreed.

Medical Aid Posts Underground

LONDON Transport, with the cooperation of the Ministry of Health, Lord Horder and his Committee, the British Red Cross Society, the St. John Ambulance Brigade, and the Metropolitan Borough Councils, has erected medical aid posts at all of the eighty Tube stations which are used as air-

LIFE-SAVING RAFT which, no matter how it enters the water, is right way up. Both sides of this new raft have provision for the storage of equipment ; it is bullet-proof, and can float off a sinking ship. After the sail has been set, the lee-boards are erected.   *Photo, Topical Press*

raid shelters. The first, which was used as a model, was opened at Kensington. Most of the posts are on the platforms. They are extraordinarily compact, the enclosed space being only 18½ feet long by 7½ feet wide. Within these limits are a space for consultation, five bunks in an isolation bay for the temporary accommodation of infectious cases, cupboards for medical supplies, surgical instruments and dressings, water supply, electric sterilizer, and bunks for the nurses. The medical officer in charge of each post—he is appointed by the local Borough Council—makes a nightly inspection of the entire shelter population. In some stations a routine medical examination has been started of every child under fourteen. Inoculations against diphtheria are also carried out.

Abyssinia's National Newspaper

ACCORDING to a Reuter special correspondent, there has been established in the heart of the Gojjam Forest, in Western Abyssinia, a publishing office from which every week copies of a newspaper entitled "Bandarachen" (Our Flag) are distributed free to the Ethiopian fighting forces and civilian population by native newsboys armed with spears or rifles. It is the first national newspaper to appear in the country for the last five years, and its production has been made possible through the enterprise of a propaganda unit which, under the command of a young British officer, made a fantastic journey across the Abyssinian lowlands, passing within a few miles of the Italian positions, to the place in the forest chosen for the newspaper's headquarters. The convoy consisted of 60 camels carrying a printing press, bundles of newsprint, boxes of Amharic type, other varied equipment, and a complete newspaper staff. "Bandarachen" has a decorative border in the Ethiopian colours, topped by the Lion of Judah, symbol of the Emperor Haile Selassie.

MEDICAL AID POSTS have been set up at the 80 London Tube stations used as air-raid shelters. Each post is a miracle of compression, containing the equipment normally found in a doctor's surgery. These children appear to be enjoying their medical examination at South Kensington.
Photo, Wide World

But for Their Masks They Would Have Wept!

BRIGHTON gas-mask rehearsal was a great day for the children, left. Putting on their masks they walked happily to school, proudly conscious of the fact that they passed through real gas, while the policeman in his Service mask who shepherded them across the road was an amusing part of the new game.

The milkman, below, on his rounds wore his gas mask and his customers wore theirs. In sealed bottles the milk escaped contamination and a supreme example of "business as usual" was given.

Photos, Fox, Planet News and Keystone

EXERCISE DANGER TEAR GAS

Warning of the presence of gas was given in the prescribed official way by wardens sounding their rattles—an unmistakable and penetrating noise. Above, pedestrians are putting on their gas masks at the first sound of the rattles. The warning lasted 30 minutes and then the "all clear" was given.

Throughout the gas alert there was no appreciable difference in Brighton's traffic, and here during the warning a policeman on traffic duty directs a coach-driver, both wearing their gas masks.

REALISM in a gas-mask test can teach useful lessons to those who are apt to neglect the simple injunction : " Carry your gas mask." On Feb. 17 Brighton had a realistic rehearsal of a gas raid. For two days the inhabitants had been warned that mild tear gas would be released over a certain area of the town, and that everyone entering this area when the warning had been given must wear a gas mask. The gas was released outside a cinema in which a first-aid station had been prepared. The response was excellent. Those in shops and offices worked on in their masks ; policemen, postmen, omnibus conductors and tradesmen on their rounds set a good example, and only a few civilians forgot their masks and wept copiously as a result !

MIDDLESBROUGH, Yorkshire, has another way with gas masks. As an example to the public, policemen wear gas masks for two periods of 10 minutes every day, at noon and 5 p.m.

Honoured for Gallant Conduct

S./Ldr. G. R. McGREGOR

D.F.C., for gallantry in air battle. Squadron Leader McGregor (left), of No. 2 Canadian Squadron, who is a native of West Mount, Quebec, led his squadron with great gallantry on several occasions, and has himself been responsible for the destruction of three enemy machines. He is seen receiving his decoration, and congratulations, from the King.

F.Lt. J. CUNNINGHAM

D.F.C., for carrying out 25 night sorties, during which he destroyed two enemy bombers and made seven interceptions. This 23-year-old pilot (right) gained his wings at the age of 18 and is a member of No. 604 Squadron (County of Middlesex) Auxiliary Air Force. He is known to his comrades as "Cat's Eyes." The official record states that he "has operated with confidence and success in extremely bad weather."

Mrs. Goodbody (below), a Lambeth A.R.P. driver, awarded the O.B.E. for courage displayed during an air raid. Regardless of falling bombs and a heavy barrage, she helped to dig a tunnel with her hands and free 14 trapped people, although an old tower was liable to fall and bury her at any minute.

Below : Warrant Officer J. McDonald (left) was awarded the D.C.M. for exceptional bravery during dive bombing and shelling attacks on Dover. Gunner Bennett (right) gained the M.M. for bringing down an enemy 'plane with his A.A. gun. Though he fired without orders he was exonerated by a court of inquiry.

C.S.M. J. McDONALD　　　**Gnr. A. E. BENNETT**

A/Cpl. JOAN HEARN

M.M., for gallant conduct under fire. Throughout a heavy air raid, when bombs were falling alongside, Acting Corporal Avis Joan Hearn of the W.A.A.F. stuck to her post where she was controlling telephones.

Mrs. MARY GOODBODY

Able Seaman K. F. BOYNE

Able Seaman F. Houghton (left) was awarded the D.S.M. for gallantry in fighting the submarine menace. He was one of several members of the crew of a former Hull trawler, the St. Loman, who were honoured by the Admiralty. Able Seaman K. F. Boyne (above) received the Royal Humane Society testimonial for rescue work at sea. When the lifeboat of H.M. Trawler Brimnes capsized and the crew were flung into the water, Able Seaman Boyne, seeing one man drifting astern of the ship in difficulties, jumped into the sea and took a lifebelt to him. Vice Admiral Sir C. G. Ramsey, C.-in-C., Rosyth, is seen presenting the testimonial.

A.B. F. HOUGHTON

Photos, British Official: Crown Copyright; G.P.U., Associated Press, Planet News, "Daily Mirror"

I WAS THERE!

Eye Witness Stories of Episodes and Adventures in the Second Great War

I Was Six Months Escaping from France

Called up with the " twenties " in November 1939 and sent to the Western Front in the following spring, Sapper John Garbett had a remarkable series of adventures before reaching England in December 1940. The story he told to Bernard Drew of the " Kentish Times " is exclusive to " The War Illustrated."

WITH other British soldiers I was taken prisoner at St. Valery-en-Caux on June 12, 1940, and, after marching about 200 kilometres towards Germany, decided I did not like the idea of going any farther. While we were being marched from one camp to another a friend and I took advantage of a chance to escape and ran around the back of a barn, diving into a bed of nettles. This was easily managed as there were about 200 prisoners in the column, and there was a commotion at the back over some food which a French-woman was offering. As we were all in a starving condition the boys at the back made a dive for it, regardless of the German guards, who freely used their bayonets. This was when we did the vanishing trick.

After lying in the nettles until the column had passed, we crept into some bushes and stayed there till nightfall. That night we started off to get to the coast and came upon a deserted house. We went in and changed into French peasant clothes and also had a good meal, as there were plenty of vegetables in the garden. Next day we set out for the coast again and, after four days' hard going, during which we lived on chickens and potatoes, which we obtained illegally, we reached the coast near Boulogne.

There we were in an extraordinary position, for our bombers were overhead and were " knocking hell " out of the place.

We started searching for a boat, but were spotted by a German sentry who shouted something, and, as we did not like the idea of speaking to him, we made a run for it. This must have surprised him because although he shot at us he missed and we reached some trees, and again did the disappearing trick.

After this we decided to make for Spain, and away we went. We came right through the big towns and down the main roads, mixing with the Jerries all the time. When we were asked for identity papers at bridges and the entrances to towns, I told them we were Belgian refugees looking for work. I had picked up a little French, and as the Jerries couldn't speak Flemish, we were fortunate and got away with it. Each time we played this trick we were told to report to the local French police and get identity cards. We would have done this, only the French police would have recognized us, and probably have turned us over to Jerry.

During this time we were sometimes helped by French people who gave us money and food, although we often went hungry and had to sleep in woods and ditches. The route we took was Boulogne, Amiens, Beauvais, Gisors, Vernon, Nantes, Chartres, Vendôme and Tours. There we discovered about " unoccupied France," so we decided to head for Marseilles instead of Spain. We managed to cross the frontier just outside Tours, and jumped on a train going to Marseilles. When we arrived there we were arrested by the French police, who sent us to an old military prison called Fort St. Jean, where we were interned, but after a few days were allowed to go out to the town by day. We were not allowed outside Marseilles, and it was here I lost my friend, who decided to go to Spain. I wanted to try to stow away to North Africa on a boat.

I stayed in Marseilles for six weeks, during which time I stowed away twice, but was discovered each time just before the boat

Sapper John Garbett, of Belvedere, Kent, whose astonishing adventures are told in this page, is now back in Britain with the troops who are training to have "another go at Hitler."

sailed, and handed over to the police. After these failures, I decided to follow my friend's example and try to get to Spain. Incidentally, except for the spells I did in prison, I thoroughly enjoyed myself in Marseilles—as I made friends with a Corsican family who gave me clothes and money.

After I decided to make for Spain, I eluded the French police and caught an express as it was moving out of the station. After a few adventures I reached the Pyrenees. It took me two days to climb the mountains and get through the frontier guards into Spain. Here I was again arrested, by the Spaniards. I served a month's imprisonment for illegally entering the country, and was then turned over to the British Embassy at Madrid. From there I was sent to Gibraltar, and came home by liner—in a first-class cabin ! All this took me about six months and about ten tons of luck to accomplish.

We Bombed Brest with Our Engines Frozen

The following story of a night raid on Brest was broadcast by the pilot of a Coastal Command Blenheim Bomber. A vivid description of the difficulties and dangers caused by the icing-up of aircraft engines, it is also a tribute to the quality of the 'planes which can survive such difficulties and of the crews who bring them safely home.

ONE night we were just making an ordinary night attack on Brest harbour. We'd been there before, and we knew roughly what to expect. There was a bright moon when we got near the place, and the flak—the anti-aircraft fire—was coming up in much the usual sort of way. There were curtains of fire here and there, cones of fire over the more important spots and search-lights wandering all over the place.

It was pretty cold, but you expect it to be

cold at the height at which we were flying. Then suddenly the port engine stopped. My observer, who was in the nose of the aircraft, switched on the inter-communication telephone and asked : " What's happened?"

" Port engine stopped," I told him. Then, just as I said it, most of the noise died out of the aeroplane, and I said : " Gosh, starboard engine stopped, too."

" Well, here we go," said the observer, and that was all you *could* say about it

The frontier between Occupied and Un-occupied France, seen here, is now far more closely guarded than it was at the time when Sapper Garbett and his companions crossed en route for Marseilles. *Photo, E.N.A.*

I WAS THERE !

Effects of R.A.F. raids on the French invasion ports are seen in this photograph, taken more than 20 miles away. Huge fires blaze on the horizon ; above, searchlights cluster and white blobs show where A.A. shells are bursting. The glow of fires is seen high in the sky. A vivid description of a raid on Brest is given in this page.
Photo, Keystone

Both engines had iced up and stopped, and we were gliding, without any power, slowly downwards.

I was not particularly worried at first. Engines do sometimes ice up and stop, and when you come down into warmer air, with any luck they pick up again. My only worry was to travel as slowly as possible, so that the glide would last as long as possible. The observer and I had a chat about it and decided that, as we were already over Brest, we might as well have a smack at the target, even without any engines. The flak had died away for the moment, so we started our first run in. By then we had lost about a thousand feet in height.

We made a run across the target area, but we couldn't see the exact target we wanted, so we came round again and started another run, a few hundred feet lower. And we kept on doing that, a bit lower each time, for what seemed about ten years—although really our whole glide lasted for less than a quarter of an hour.

By this time, of course, the German gunners knew we were there, and now and then they seemed to have a pretty good idea exactly where we were. There was one particularly nasty burst of flak all round us when we were about half-way down, and it shook the aircraft a bit, but we weren't hit. Every now and then a searchlight picked us up and I had to take avoiding action to get out of it. I didn't want to do that more than I could help, because every time I did it we lost a little more height, and shortened the length of the glide.

Once I called to the air gunner to ask him if everything was all right. "Sure," he said. "May I shoot out some of those searchlights ?" But I couldn't let him do that for fear of giving our position away completely. He was disappointed, and every now and then he came on the 'phone and said hopefully : "There's a searchlight on us now, sir."

By the time we were down to about 4,000 feet, still without any engines, things began to look rather nasty. We were still gliding, and still making our runs over the target area, with the observer doing his best to get the primary target into his bomb sight— and, of course, we were still losing height. To add to our worries, another Blenheim high above us, without the slightest idea

that we were below, was dropping flares and lighting the place up.

When we had lost another thousand feet we ran slap into the middle of trouble. The flak came up like a hailstorm going the wrong way. But even then, by a stroke of luck, nothing hit us. A little lower, however, our luck broke. The port wing stopped an explosive shell, which tore a hole two feet square in it. I called to the observer to get

r'.d of the bombs on something useful, because we hadn't got enough height to go round again. The observer released the bombs, and they fell near the entrance to the Port Militaire—and still we were gliding downwards.

By now we were so low that we could see almost everything on the ground and in the harbour. I took one quick look over the side, but one look was enough. The tracer fire was coming up so quickly at us that I had to rely on the observer to direct me through the various streams of it. I had no time to watch it myself. The gunner got the dinghy ready in case we came down in the water, and he afterwards swore that he could see the black shapes of men by the guns on the ground, but I think it was probably the gun emplacements that he saw.

Right over the middle of the harbour, at just about 1,000 feet, we were caught in a strong blue searchlight—and almost simultaneously both our engines picked up again. I raced out of the harbour, through even more violent flak, fortunately without being hit again.

All the way home I had to keep the control wheel hard over to the right, to hold the damaged wing up, and several times the observer had to come back to help me hang on to the wheel, the pull was so heavy. We made for the nearest aerodrome in England, where they did everything they could to help us down. But directly I lowered the undercarriage the aircraft started to drop out of the sky like a brick.

The only thing to do was to land fast, so the crew braced themselves on the straps, opened all the hatches, and we came in 60 miles an hour faster than the Blenheim's usual landing speed. Luckily, the undercarriage was undamaged and we landed safely.

I Spent a Wintry Night in a Destroyer

Even on a " quiet " night there is ceaseless activity on board the destroyers escorting convoys, and the rigours of winter add to the trials of the crews. This account of a night in a destroyer, told by the Australian broadcaster Colin Wills, is published by arrangement with " The Listener."

WHEN I went aboard, the crew, in thick, buff-coloured coats with hoods, were hoisting in the boats, heaving up the ladder, and getting ready to slip the moorings. The ship hummed as the engine revved up. Then sailing orders were signalled, cables were slipped, and she moved to sea as easily as a train. As soon as we were moving, the bo'sun's mate shouted, " Action Stations ! " Men ran up from below and doubled to their stations—at the guns fore and aft, at the anti-aircraft pom-poms, at the machine-guns, torpedo tubes and depth-charge throwers. (Even cooks and stewards have action stations and take part in fighting the ship.) The guns swung precisely to one side and there were small explosions as charges were fired to test the electric firing-circuits. When we had cleared the harbour the ship was ready for anything.

That was in the late afternoon. Then night fell. Everywhere doors slammed, curtains fell into place, ports were clamped close, gun-crews huddled beside their guns and tried to sleep. I can't describe how cold the wind was. Seamen—many of them had been miners, clerks, salesmen before the war—were hauling on ropes and frozen wires. The decks were covered with a slush of ice and water.

When I got on the bridge the wind simply froze my face, made it ache. The bridge is the fighting headquarters of the ship as well as the navigating centre. All the time officers were speaking, giving commands, messengers appeared and went away, signals flashed by lamp from other ships

in the darkness were received and de-coded, telephones, telegraphs and speaking-tubes brought news and took away orders. The masthead man kept calling out : " White flashing light on port bow, Masthead " . . . " Darkened ship to starboard, Masthead " . . . " Red light ahead, Masthead."

I left the bridge and prowled about the ship. I was aft with a gun-crew, watching the flicker of our wake, when an alarm gong sounded. I stumbled forward over the iced decks and clambered up to the bridge again. A radio message had come saying that a convoy was being attacked to the eastward. The destroyer was already heeling over as she turned.

I could just hear the thud of gunfire from somewhere ahead. " Bombers ? " I asked. " No," said an officer. " E-boats. We thought there might be some about with the sea so calm." The gunfire ahead became louder. The vibration of the ship increased and our bows kept plunging into the sea, throwing up clouds of spray that turned to ice as it settled. A star-shell burst far away, then another, and then a shower of them. The convoy was trying to see the E-boats so that it could keep them out of torpedo-distance with gunfire.

We seemed simply to roar towards the battle, but we were out of luck. Before we got there the message came, " Enemy retiring to eastward." We circled round until the moon rose, expecting another attack, but none came, and in the morning we steamed into port.

1915~After the Battle a Dip for the Anzacs~1941

Fighting is a dusty, dirty business, and soldiers become boys again when they get an opportunity for a plunge in the sea. It was the same twenty-five years ago as it is today. The top photograph was taken below the Red Cross Station at Helles, Gallipoli, in the spring of 1915. Men of the Anzacs, away for the moment from enemy fire, took on the holiday spirit. After the fall of Bardia in 1941 a similar scene took place, and in the lower photograph men of General Wavell's victorious army enjoy the luxury of a bath in the shallow waters of the harbour, smiling, no doubt, because Mussolini has said so often that it is his sea!

Photos, British Official : Crown Copyright ; and Central News

In Poland the Nazi Brute Still Rages

Poland under the Nazis is a land of darkness and the shadow of death. It is a vast prison-house in which the Poles are treated as criminals and something worse. It is a huge torture chamber, a monster concentration camp. It is a lesson in Nazi brutality, a demonstration of what Hitler's gangsters can do and will do, given the opportunity.

I N spite of the savage treatment to which the Poles have been subjected for some 18 months, they still refuse to abandon hope, and so far as in them lies they keep up the struggle. Sabotage against the Germans is an everyday occurrence, and as Moder, Commander of the S.S. troops in the Warsaw region, complained not long ago, there are still many Poles who have not lost all hope in the resurrection of an independent Poland. Polish saboteurs and those in possessions of firearms are sure of the death sentence from the Nazi tribunals, but resistance and secret arming continue. For the most part, however, the resistance is passive.

Thus on the first anniversary of the outbreak of war between Poland and Germany there was a huge passive demonstration in Warsaw, details of which have only recently arrived in this country. September 1 was a Sunday, and after attending morning church the Poles returned to their homes. The city, gay with German flags, was completely deserted save for the Nazi troops and officials ; the Poles refrained from travelling in trams and trains, they deserted their usual seats in the cafés and restaurants, and even kept away from the cigarette stands and newspaper kiosks. Then at about 6 p.m., when the German military parade had ended and the loudspeakers set up on the street corners were silent and the platforms deserted, great crowds of Poles poured into the streets and made their way to the Tomb of the Unknown Soldier and other of their national monuments. There they heaped red and white flowers on the plinths and sang their national hymns. At once the Gestapo got busy, arresting many of the demonstrators and removing the flowers, but as soon as the Germans had gone the Poles again flocked round the monuments

INTO LUBLIN'S GHETTO the Nazis herded every Jew of this Polish city, once famed for its university. Behind these five little boys, two Jews are seen raising their hats to a German officer who was with the photographer when this photograph was taken. The men wear arm-bands designed to stigmatize them as Jews.

and piled fresh heaps of flowers round their bases. Again the crowds were dispersed, this time by German troops ; many, including women and children, were cruelly handled, while many others were arrested and sent off to the labour camps in Germany.

Many hundreds of thousands of Poles, both men and women, have been deported to Germany to work on the land for German farmers. In the Reich they are paid very low wages, and that payment is dependent upon their "physical abilities" and "psychological attitude," as to which the employer is the sole judge. Theoretically, Polish agricultural labourers are allowed to send

home to their families 600 marks per annum, but the procedure for arranging the transmission is so complicated as to be almost prohibitive.

Not payment, indeed, or even persuasion, but brute force is employed in filling the ranks of these agricultural slaves. A local authority is given an order to supply a given number of workers, and if fines and threats do not produce the required quota, then regular man-hunts are organized by the Nazis, with rifle and whip in hand. Streets and fields, woods and marshes, are systematically combed, until at last a pitiable convoy of captives is ready to be taken away to Germany like cattle. It is stated that the number of Polish slaves in Germany is nearly a million and a half, including 650,000 Polish prisoners of war who have been "released" on condition that they stay in or go to Germany as "voluntary" workers.

In Poland itself the condition of the people is deplorable. In the country districts food may be sufficient, if not plentiful, but in Warsaw and the other big towns there is a definite shortage of foodstuffs. And all the time the country is being systematically and thoroughly looted. Even the animals from the Warsaw zoo have been removed to Germany, while the zoo itself is being used for breeding pigs—for German consumption.

STREET CARS IN CRACOW, ancient city of Poland, have been divided into two compartments—not "smoking" or "non-smoking" as in many European cities, but "Jews" and "non-Jews." With Teutonic thoroughnesss, the Germans have subjected Polish Jews to every conceivable form of humiliation and insult.   *Photos, Associated Press*

Tyranny Walks Abroad in Unhappy Warsaw

To convince the Poles that they have come to stay and to give them a constant reminder that they are a conquered people, the Nazis have renamed one of the principal streets of the city, Siegesstrasse (Victory Street).

Round Warsaw's Jewish quarter a concrete wall has been erected, and all Jews must live within it. Some of the streets are closed altogether to Jews. The notice below states that no Jew must set foot in it.

IN POLAND, as in the other Nazi-occupied territories, oil shortage is most marked. Thus in Warsaw cars other than those used by the invaders are rare. As a result the old horse-drawn cabs have been brought out once more, and here a few of them, in the centre of the city, await fares. Above them is a grim reminder of the days of the siege.

Photos, E.N.A., Associated Press

OUR DIARY OF THE WAR

TUESDAY, FEB. 18, 1941   *535th day*

On the Sea—Admiralty announced that naval aircraft had sunk two enemy supply ships in Central Mediterranean.

H. M. trawler Stella Rigel shot down enemy aircraft in North Sea.

H. M. minesweeper Huntly reported sunk.

War against Italy—Cairo reported that in Abyssinia Italians had evacuated Danghila and other posts in Gojjam area. Mega, S. Abyssinia, surrendered.

Operations on line of R. Juba, Italian Somaliland, continuing.

R.A.F. raided aerodromes on Dodecanese Islands on nights of 16-17 and 17-18.

Enemy aircraft raided Benghazi. Three shot down and others damaged.

Home Front—During day bombs fell in East Anglia and few places in south and south-east England. Train in East Anglia machine-gunned.

German bomber destroyed by A.A. fire in Norfolk.

Greek War—Athens reported violent local engagements and new positions captured. R.A.F. maintained concentrated attacks on Tepelini area.

General—U.S.A. created number of defence zones in Pacific and Caribbean Sea, from which foreign ships and aircraft without permits will be excluded.

WEDNESDAY, FEB. 19   *536th day*

In the Air—Coastal Command aircraft attacked enemy naval bases at Brest and docks at Calais.

War against Italy—Cairo stated that Patriot situation in Gojjam, Abyssinia, was developing satisfactorily. Enjabara had been captured, and post of Piccolo Abbai occupied.

R.A.F. carried out repeated attacks supporting Army offensive in East Africa.

S. African Air Force very active over Italian Somaliland. Attacks made on Bardera, positions north of Jelib, targets at Iscia Baidoa and Dinsor.

Enemy aircraft again raided Benghazi. One destroyed and one damaged.

Home Front—Enemy raiders dropped bombs at two places on N.E. coast of Scotland, near East Anglian coast and over Yorks and Lincs.

At night heavy attack was made on Swansea, thousands of incendiaries and high explosives being dropped. London also raided, and bombs fell in southern England and in east Scotland.

During air fight in snowstorm over Straits of Dover, two Spitfires came down in flames, both pilots baling out.

Greek War—Athens reported that further strong positions had been won, 300 prisoners captured and more material taken. Greek Air Force made bombing attacks on battlefields.

General—Announced that British defences in Far East had been strengthened by R.A.F. reinforcements and landing of Australians at Singapore.

THURSDAY, FEB. 20   *537th day*

On the Sea—Admiralty announced that H.M. Sealion had sunk enemy ship by gunfire off Norwegian coast.

H.M. minesweeper Bramble destroyed a Messerschmitt by gunfire.

H.M. armed auxiliary Crispin reported sunk.

In the Air—R.A.F. bombed docks at Ymuiden, Holland, by daylight. At night offensive patrol was made over aerodromes in Northern France.

War against Italy—Cairo announced that British troops had crossed R. Juba, Italian Somaliland, driving off counter-attacks.

Enemy aircraft raided Benghazi ; one was destroyed.

Home Front—Few bombs fell by day in East Anglia. At night another attack was made on Swansea. Many fires started, but quickly controlled. Extensive damage by high explosives to dwelling-houses. Bombs also fell in south of England, London area, S.E. England and eastern counties.

Greek War—Athens reported restricted local mopping-up operations.

General—Mr. Eden, Foreign Minister, arrived in Cairo for consultations with military chiefs.

Mr. Menzies, Australian Premier, arrived in England.

THE POETS & THE WAR

XLII

THE FLOWER

By Christmas Humphreys

Now England's moat is manned ;
On every tower
The yeomen of an island country stand
And wait the hour.
Now wonder dies away and through the land
Fair mistress pleasure sleeps within her bower.
With sword in hand, all leisure laid aside,
Heart fortified with olden memories and older pride.
We wait, serene. Ours is the final power,
The will to freedom still to bonds unknown
That waits the enemy with laughing eyes, alone.

All must be offered now, of toil
Or splendour, all that England's soil
Has need of, all that life endears ;
The wisdom of the years
And youth's abounding still unravished dower.

Let there be neither doubting now, nor tears ;
He nothing fears
Who life itself wears lightly, as a flower.

FRIDAY, FEB. 21   *538th day*

In the Air—R.A.F. made night raids on Wilhelmshaven, industrial targets in the Western Ruhr and many aerodromes in France and Holland.

War against Italy—Announced that British troops had forced R. Juba north of original crossing. Operations from both bridgeheads developing.

Reported that King's African Rifles had seized islands near Kismayu.

R.A.F. bombed aerodromes at Catania and Comiso, Sicily on night of 20-21.

Home Front—Slight enemy activity during day, mainly over eastern England and east Scotland. At night third successive attack made on Swansea, considerable damage being done.

Heinkel shot down by A.A. fire at night near Bristol.

Greek War—Athens reported that strong enemy positions had been occupied and 200 prisoners and much material captured. Greeks shot down five enemy aircraft and R.A.F. destroyed seven. Bombing raids made by R.A.F. on Berat and Tepelini.

Balkans—German troops massing on Rumanian-Bulgarian frontier ; advance units said to have crossed Danube.

General—Lord Harlech appointed High Commissioner to Union of South Africa for duration of war.

SATURDAY, FEB. 22   *539th day*

In the Air—R.A.F. bombers made night attack on Brest.

War against Italy—Nairobi announced that South African troops had captured port of Jumbo, at mouth of R. Juba. Brigade staff and other prisoners and much material taken. S. African bombers attacked troops on river banks and motor transport in Jelib area and west of Mogadishu.

Operations in Eritrea and Abyssinia proceeding. R.A.F. raided aerodromes at Chinele and Diredawa. Fighters of S. African Air Force attacked aircraft on ground at Massawa.

Announced that German airmen had twice bombed hospital ship Dorsetshire and also a hospital at Malta.

Home Front—Some bombs fell during day, mainly in East Kent and town in S.W. England. Unconfirmed reports of great air battle over Straits of Dover.

At dusk coastal town in N.E. Scotland was attacked. Raids during night were slight.

Enemy bomber destroyed near Bristol Channel and a fighter near S.E. coast.

Greek War—Athens reported renewal of Greek offensive, mainly in central sector. R.A.F. bombers active, especially in Buzi area, near Tepelini. In Preveza area three enemy aircraft shot down.

General—Reported that Vichy had rejected compromise plan put forward by Japan for settlement of dispute between French Indo-China and Thailand.

SUNDAY, FEB. 23   *540th day*

On the Sea—Admiralty announced sinking of at least seven enemy supply ships by H.M. submarines in Mediterranean.

H.M. trawler Ormonde reported sunk.

War against Italy—Cairo reported that British troops, reinforced by Free French forces, were advancing in Eritrea along Red Sea coast.

In Abyssinia, Shogali had been occupied by British and Patriot units. Enemy counter-attacks repulsed.

Following capture of Margherita and important post of Jelib, It. Somaliland, advance east of R. Juba was progressing.

S. African aircraft destroyed eight enemy 'planes on landing ground at Makale, Eritrea. Targets at Neghelli, Abyssinia, were bombed. In Brava area, Italian Somaliland, six motor-transports were destroyed.

Home Front—Slight enemy activity during day, mainly off east and south-east coasts. At night high explosive and incendiary bombs damaged a north-east England town. Raiders were also over Home Counties, a London district, south-eastern area and east coast.

Greek War—R.A.F. supported Greek Army operations by raiding Dukaj.

MONDAY, FEB. 24   *541st day*

In the Air—Aircraft of Bomber and Coastal Commands attacked Brest, dropping bombs in area where cruiser of Hipper class was lying.

War against Italy—Cairo reported that in Eritrea British forces advancing southwards had dispersed Italian troops holding positions about Cubcub, making many prisoners.

In Abyssinia British advanced elements had reached Amanit.

West African troops captured Brava, port 160 miles north of Kismayu.

Home Front—During day bombs fell at a place in north Scotland. At night raiders were reported from East Anglia, Merseyside and a Home Counties area, but casualties were few and damage slight.

IN TURKEY'S CAPITAL THEY ARE PRACTISING 'A.R.P.'

THE TURKS are prepared for all eventualities. While war was still a far-off possibility air-raid precautions in Ankara were perfected, and the police were trained in rescue work. During all the practices gas masks were worn. Above, police are carrying a casualty to a dressing-station. One of the men wears an armlet with a red crescent on it, for the Crescent, as the religious symbol of Islam, is there the equivalent of our Red Cross.

Photo, Associated Press

The Battle of the Western Approaches

After threatening us for months with an invasion, Hitler now promises a war of extermination on the high seas. Certainly we may expect in the near future an intensification of the U-boat campaign in our Western Approaches—those Atlantic traffic lanes along which the life-sustaining ships reach British ports.

WHERE can Hitler "get us down"? Not in the Western Desert, not in the wastes and jungles of East Africa; not in the Balkans or the Aegean; not in Palestine or at Suez. Not anywhere, indeed, save within sight of our own shores. Only by a tremendous onslaught against the British fortress could Hitler perhaps win the war; only in that way—or by starving us out.

Of the two alternatives we may well suppose that the Fuehrer would prefer the second. If he can turn the sea approaches to this island into one vast graveyard of British ships then there will be no need for the sacrifice of hundreds of thousands of German lives. The fortress would have to surrender —brought low not by the guns of the enemy but by the grim spectre of famine. Thus the really decisive battle of the war may have to be fought—perhaps it is even now being fought —in the Western Approaches, in the traffic lanes to our ports that face the Atlantic. We may trace them in a huge semicircle enclosing our western coasts, stretching from the Bay of Biscay to where the Atlantic joins the Arctic. The English Channel, the Irish Sea, St. George's Channel, the waterways of the Atlantic between Iceland and the Faroes, the Faroes and the Orkneys, between the Orkneys and Norway, the North Sea—these together constitute one great battlefield in which even now Hitler's U-boats are waging deadly war against our ships.

A time of crisis is approaching; Mr. Stimson, America's Secretary of War, has declared that he is "apprehensive as to the possibility of a crisis within the next 60 or at least 90 days." He was speaking on Jan. 17, so he had in mind the end of March and April. Many other indications go to suggest that these weeks of spring will be indeed critical.

'We Have Not Been Asleep this Winter'

Certainly Hitler will do his best to make them so. "Now our sea warfare can begin in earnest," he declared in his speech in the Munich beer cellar on Feb. 24. "We have been waiting for our new U-boats, but in March and April a naval warfare will start such as the enemy has never expected. Wherever Britain touches the Continent we shall face her. Wherever British ships cruise, our U-boats will be sent against them until the hour of decision arrives." Then, after boasting that the German Naval High Seas forces and U-boats had sunk 215,000 tons of shipping in two days, including a convoy with a tonnage of 125,000, he went on: "they will then see whether we have been asleep this winter, and who has made use of time." The Fuehrer's figures were ludicrously false, but his boasts about his U-boats are in a different case. A year ago it was being said that "Hitler had missed the bus," but in a very short time it was

proved beyond a doubt that he had caught it with plenty of time to spare. We may be sure that he has not missed this bus either, and that all during the winter the shipping yards under his control—and what a collection they make, not only in Germany at the ports on the seas and rivers, but in Occupied France and Belgium, Holland and Denmark and Norway, Italy and Rumania, and, maybe, Japan !—have been working overtime in producing those U-boats which, though smaller than their predecessors, may well prove just as dangerous because they will be operating at only short distances from their home ports. "There is no doubt," said Lord Beaverbrook in his broadcast to Canada on February 23, "that the enemy intends to attack us in our ocean pathways— above all in the North-Western Approaches. We shall be subjected to constant raids on our shipping. There will be ceaseless attacks under and over the seas. The battle will be long and bloody. The toll of tonnage will be heavy, too."

In the last war the Kaiser's U-boats had to be ocean-going ships, for their bases were hundreds of miles from the principal shipping lanes which were the scene of their activities; but in this war Admiral Raeder has control of the Channel ports, of Brest and Bergen, and many more. One advantage accruing to the Nazis from their occupation of the Channel ports is that the U-boat crews do

ANSWERING HITLER'S CHALLENGE of Feb. 24 when, speaking at Munich, he threatened a new U-boat campaign of unparalleled intensity, the shipyards of Britain and the Empire are turning out new ships at a rate never before approached. The work of the Royal Navy is one reply to Hitler's threats; another is the scene above, typical of many similar ones elsewhere, in a British shipyard. The merchantman on the left is being rapidly completed, while that on the right is ready for launching. In the approaching ocean struggle, as Lord Beaverbrook warned the Empire, "the toll of tonnage will be heavy." We must be ready to replace it.   *Photo, Central Press*

From His U-Boats Hitler Expects Our Downfall

Admiral Lothar Arnauld de la Periere, O.C. German Naval forces in Occupied France, was killed, say the Nazis, at Le Bourget aerodrome on Feb. 24.

GERMAN COMMERCE RAIDERS which are making strenuous attempts to sink British shipping include such huge ocean-going submarines as the one here seen returning to its home port. Note the naval gun and the anti-aircraft gun on the superstructure.

The crew of a Nazi U-boat are seen above, grouped around a gun on the conning tower, on their return to a home port. Below, a Nazi submarine, the craft on which the Germans are concentrating all their energies in the hope of cutting off Britain's supplies from overseas, is seen in course of construction.

Photos, E.N.A., Wide World, Topical and Associated Press

NAZIS' ACE SUBMARINE is seen arriving at a German-occupied port in France to refuel. Her captain, Lt.-Commander Gunther Prien, who it is claimed sank the Royal Oak in Scapa Flow on October 14, 1939, is hailed as one of Germany's most successful U-boat commanders.

'We Shall Make our Way through All Right'

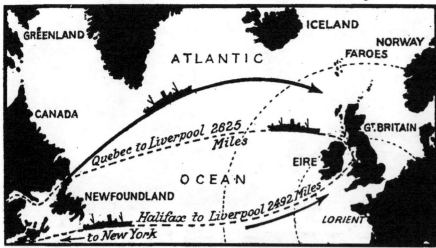

Here we show the Western Approaches to the British Isles where Hitler's U-boats are striving to cut our life-line with America. The dotted circles denote a radius of 500 and 1,000 miles respectively from the Nazi U-boat base at Lorient.

not require so long a training as would be necessary if their craft had to make long journeys under water and to remain many days, or even weeks, at sea. At the height of the U-boat campaign in the last war it was estimated that Admiral von Tirpitz had a hundred U-boats in commission, though probably only some fifty were ever at sea together ; at the present time Hitler is estimated to have perhaps 150 submarines.

True, some estimates put the figure very much higher, at 600 or even 1,000 craft. Such figures are certainly exaggerated, however, being out of all proportion to the capacity of the German shipyards, supply of skilled workers and the raw materials available. Moreover, submarines are masterpieces of intricate mechanism and cannot be mass produced. Then we must deduct from the number of boats actually in commission perhaps twenty required for training purposes at the Submarine School at Kiel, while of the remainder, experience shows that only about a third are available for

active service in any one week, since a third are usually resting and the other third undergoing repairs.

If Raeder is better placed than was " old Turps," Britain is labouring under many disadvantages that were not hers a generation ago. True, Admiral Tovey has to take account of no such powerful German fleet as confronted Jellicoe ; but the Royal Navy is today doing work which in the last war it shared with the navies of France, Italy, Japan and the U.S.A. In capital ships, in the ships which decide battles such as Jutland or Tsushima, Britain is enormously strong now that George V and her consorts have come, or are coming, into service ; but the Admiralty could do with more, many more, of the smaller craft such as are most useful against submarines. Since the war began we have put into service a number of destroyers, corvettes, armed trawlers, and other submarine-hunting ships, and we have received 50 destroyers—a first instalment ?—from the United States Navy. But we shall want many more such vessels if the U-boats are to be beaten, and we must get them somehow, by purchase or grant, by seizure from the enemy or from the shipyards. Whatever the strain, the danger and difficulties, we may be sure with Mr. Churchill that " we shall make our way through all right."

This remarkable photograph (centre) shows depth charges ready for action on the stern of a corvette. Corvettes are built to withstand the roughest weather, and the ship below is seen on patrol amid the swirling seas of the Atlantic. (See also page 110 of this volume.)

A BRITISH CONVOY is seen from an accompanying ship in mid-Atlantic on its way from a Canadian port to this country. Food and war supplies are both vital necessities, and Britain's command of the seas is shown by the regularity with which convoys reach the home ports.

Photos, Planet News, Associated Press

Only Practice—but It May Save Their Lives

SUBMARINE CREWS are trained not only in the handling of the very complicated piece of machinery which is their home at sea, but also in the use of the Davis escape apparatus, which gives them their one chance of escaping with their lives if their vessel cannot surface. For training, a special tank is built with an escape hatch beneath it similar to that in a submarine. Before passing through the hatch the men don the apparatus, consisting of a bag containing a mouthpiece and tube connected to a small oxygen cylinder and provided with a pad to absorb the exhaled carbon dioxide. Above, a class that has just surfaced listens to the instructors' criticisms.

Photo, " Daily Mirror "

Britain's Submarines on the War Path

"OUR submarines in the Mediterranean," read an Admiralty communiqué issued on Feb. 23, 1941, "continue to operate against Italy's communications with her overseas armies, and several successes have recently been achieved.

"H.M.S. Upholder has sunk two enemy supply ships. One of these was a vessel of about 8,000 tons and the other was about 5,000 tons. H.M.S. Rover has sunk an Italian oil tanker. H.M.S. Regent has sunk an Italian supply ship which was almost certainly the 2,472-ton Citta di Messina. H.M.S. Utmost attacked an escorted convoy and hit a supply ship of about 8,000 tons with a torpedo. This ship was later seen to be in a sinking condition with her stern awash and she had been deserted by the convoy escort. H.M.S. Truant attacked an enemy convoy by gunfire and obtained shell hits on one of the enemy supply ships. In another attack H.M.S. Truant sank the largest ship of a convoy, a vessel of about 3,500 tons, by torpedo.

"It has now been established that H.M.S. Triton, the loss of which was announced on Jan. 28, had previously accounted for two Italian supply ships, one of which was a vessel of about 8,000 tons." H.M.S. Truant was the submarine which braved the German minefields in the Skaggerak last year and torpedoed the German cruiser Karlsruhe off Oslo

Above, a submarine is in the act of surfacing; her bow only being visible. When she is once more above water the hatchway, left, is opened and the crew come on deck for a breath of fresh air.

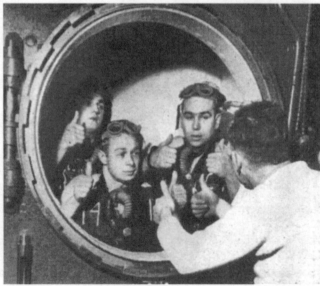

BELOW DECK in a submarine there is not always even room to stand upright. Left, the Chief Petty Officer making his way through one of the bulkheads. It is in this part of submarines that the Davis escape apparatus is situated; a photograph of the tank in which the men are taught to use it is in page 257. Right is the practice escape hatch used in training. After a test the men are told by the instructor to put their thumbs up if they are "O.K."

Photos, G.P.U., " Daily Mirror " and Topical

Poland's Jack Tars Are Smart and Keen

Smartness has been as much inculcated on the crews of ships of the Polish Navy as on those of British ships. On the efficiency of the engine-room staff much depends. Above, a petty officer is at the telephone by which orders are transmitted from the bridge while one of the men stands by for signals from the bridge on the engine-room telegraph.

GENERAL SIKORSKI, Commander-in-Chief of the Polish Forces, is here seen on board one of the ships of the Polish Navy in British waters during a recent visit. With the ship's Captain he is watching a gun crew.

POLAND was never a sea power, and when war broke out her Navy consisted of only four destroyers, five submarines, two small gunboats, five small torpedo boats, a 2,200-ton minelayer, and a few auxiliary vessels. But what the Polish Navy lacked in numbers it made up in spirit. Some of the ships escaped to British waters, including the submarines Zbik and Orzel, which, after an adventurous voyage through the Baltic, succeeded in joining the British Navy. The stories of these gallant little ships are told in our Vol. 1, pages 132 and 511. Since then a new submarine to replace the Orzel—which, after doing good work in the Skagerrak during the Nazi invasion of Norway, was lost in June 1940—has been built in a British shipyard. Named Sokol (Falcon), it is seen below. At the naming ceremony General Sikorski, Polish Prime Minister and Commander-in-Chief, expressed his satisfaction that Polish ships should be fighting by the side of the British, since it gave them unrivalled opportunities of gaining experience. Similarly a new destroyer, Piorun (Thunderbolt), was given by Britain to the Polish Government to replace Grom (Thunder), a Polish destroyer sunk in the North Sea. Today the Polish Fleet, commanded by Vice-Admiral Swirski, is cooperating most efficiently with the British Navy.

A signaller of the Polish Navy is flag signalling to another vessel. This method of conveying messages is used chiefly when ships are in port. Flag signals may be given by the semaphore method, employed by the Polish rating above, or a flag may be "wagged" to correspond to the dots and dashes of the Morse code.

SOKOL is the British-built but now Polish submarine which replaces the lost Orzel; she is operating with the British Fleet, and on the right we have a glimpse of her and of her crew. Polish submarine crews have shown all the enterprise and indifference to danger essential in the most hazardous of all naval services.

Photos, Keystone

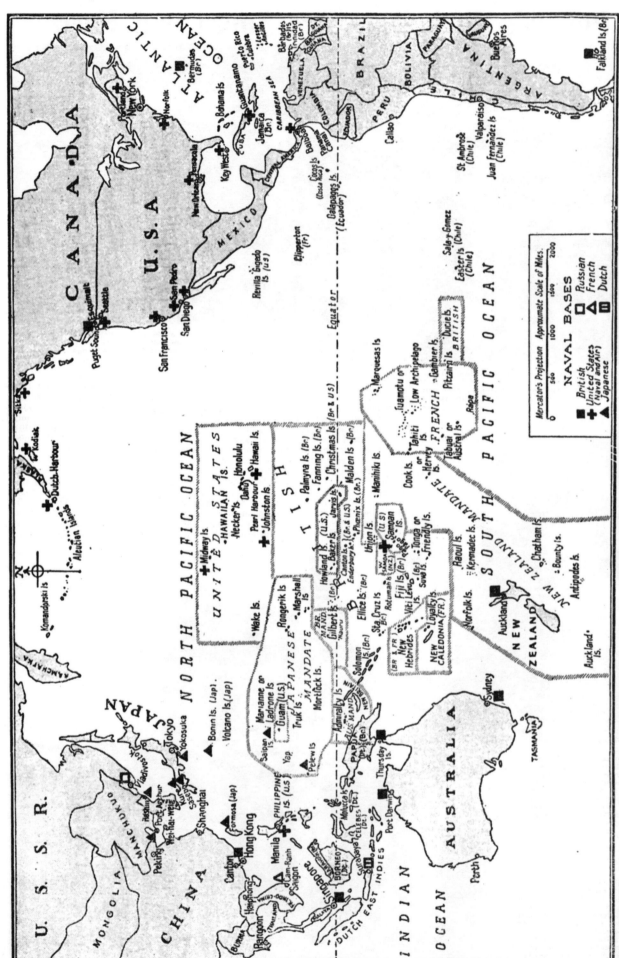

WAR IN THE PACIFIC, should it come, would centre about the bases of the Great Powers which are scattered along the ocean's shores and on its vast expanse. The most important of these—British and U.S.A., Japanese, Russian, French and Dutch—are clearly shown on this map. It will be seen that the Japanese bases are situated in the ocean's western portion, while those of the U.S.A. are in two chains—the one stretching from Panama to the Aleutian Islands in the far north, while the other constitutes a "strategic bridge" across the centre of the ocean. It should be pointed out that the map is on Mercator's Projection, so that the distances are magnified the farther they are removed from the Equator.

By courtesy of "The Manchester Guardian"

Where Would they Fight in the Pacific?

If war comes to the Pacific Japan may find herself confronted by a coalition of the British Commonwealth, the U.S.A. and the Dutch Indies (not to mention China). In such a war bases will be all-important, and here we have a study of the strategic points—a subject which we have already dealt with in Vol. 3, page 424. The article should be read in conjunction with the map given in the opposite page.

So vast is the Pacific—it covers a quarter of the entire surface of the globe—that in the case of war it may prove exceedingly difficult for the fleets of the rival powers to get to grips. Pearl Harbour, Hawaii, for instance, where the main force of the United States Pacific Fleet is based, is 3,379 miles from Yokohama, and Yokohama is nearly 3,000 miles from Singapore, Britain's naval stronghold in the Far East. Such distances are too great for battle fleets to cover unless they are sure of being able to refuel at the other end. If instead of arriving at a friendly base there is a prospect of having to fight a large-scale naval action, then they would face almost certain disaster. It is because of the immense distances involved that the question of island bases in the Pacific is all-important.

As already stated, America's principal naval base in the Pacific is at Pearl Harbour, Hawaii. Pearl Harbour is situated seven miles from Honolulu, on the island of Oahu; it is a military station as well as a naval, and its large, land-locked harbour is provided with extensive facilities for the repair and revictualling of America's entire Pacific fleet. There are also air fields in the vicinity, and huge oil storage tanks. But Pearl Harbour itself has to be supplied from bases on the American mainland, the nearest of which—Mare Island, San Francisco, and San Diego—are over 2,000 miles away. That at Puget Sound is 2,339 miles distant, while to Balboa on the Panama Canal it is a little jump of 4,711 miles.

From Pearl Harbour stretches right across the Pacific to the west America's " strategic bridge," composed of Johnston Island, Midway Island, and Wake Island. At Midway and Johnston Islands air bases have been constructed and a naval base is under construction at Wake Island. Then, in the very middle of the groups of islands mandated to Japan after the Great War is the little island of Guam, which for some time past has been used by the U.S.A. as a refuelling station and is now about to be made a naval base. Hitherto America has refrained from carrying out naval works at Guam for fear of hurting Japanese susceptibilities, but that fear is no longer an all-important consideration; as Admiral Stark stated in a letter to Congress on February 19, if Japan should complain against the strengthening of Guam's defences, then her protest would be " unwarranted, unmerited, and should be totally disregarded." Still farther to the west is Manila in the Philippines (American until 1946), where an American naval squadron is stationed. Then in the South Seas there is Pago Pago on the Samoan Island of Tutuila. In the far north of the Pacific there is

another chain of American naval bases, extending from Sitka on the Alaskan mainland, where a naval aircraft base was established in 1937, through Kodiak Island to Dutch Harbour on the island of Unalaska in the Aleutians. Still farther to the west is Kiska, which possesses a harbour capable of development; this is only 1,700 miles from the most northern point of Japan, and not more than 1,400 miles from the Japanese Kurile Islands.

Britain's bases in the Pacific are Hongkong, where there is an advanced naval base;

PEARL HARBOUR, HAWAII, is the U.S.A.'s principal naval base in the Pacific, lying midway between America and Japan. It is also a seaplane station, and seen here are Consolidated PBY-I Patrol flying-boats. On Jan. 28, 1937, 12 of these flew non-stop from San Diego to Pearl Harbour, over 2,000 miles. *Photo, Dorien Leigh*

Singapore, reputed to be the most strongly defended of all the bases in the Pacific, though Americans claim that Pearl Harbour is its close rival in this respect; Port Darwin in Northern Australia; Thursday Island in the Torres Straits, between Papua and Australia; Auckland in New Zealand, and Sydney.

Soviet Russia has a base in the Pacific at Vladivostok, France has one in Indo-China at Cam-Ranh, Holland one on the island of Java at Surabaya, and we may also mention the Canadian base at Esquimalt.

Japan's Muster of Bases

Now we come to Japan, and, as might be expected, her bases are many. In the Japanese islands proper there are Yokosuka, Sasebo, and Kure; in Manchukuo there is Port Arthur; and in Korea, Rashin; one has been established in Formosa. Then there is a chain of bases running through the widely separated islands to the south of Japan—at Bonin, Saipan, and Pelew.

These, then, are the bases of the Great Powers in the Pacific, and of these only a mere handful—Singapore, Pearl Harbour, and Yokosuka in particular—can be classified as first-class naval bases, homes-from-home for the most powerful battle fleets. How, then, can the antagonists come to grips in the case of war?

Obviously, they can do so easily enough in the air, and quite a number of the bases, it will be realized, are air bases rather than naval. But we may rule out those more fanciful pictures of great navies battling in the midst of the Pacific wastes. Generally speaking, a battle fleet cannot operate effectively at a distance of more than 2,000 miles from its main base, or remain at sea for more than four or five days without refuelling. These facts severely limit the possibilities of naval war in the Pacific. Far more likely than these large-scale actions on the high seas are raids by light forces and by submarines against the enemy's lines of communication.

Against such raids Japan—and we may presume that Japan would be on the offensive in the case of war—would be exceedingly vulnerable if she should decide to send her fleet against the British, Dutch, or American possessions in the southwestern corner of the ocean. We have been told little of the defences of Honkong, but at least it is known that these defences are very much stronger than they were only a few months ago. If the objective were the Philippines, then the Japanese raiders would have to encounter a United States fleet of three cruisers, 13 destroyers, and some 20 submarines, not to mention two squadrons of flying-boats—a force powerful enough in itself and capable of being immensely reinforced from Pearl Harbour. If they should decide to make the Dutch East Indies their target, then, again, they would have to meet large land, sea and air forces.

If, finally, the objective were Singapore—and without Singapore the Japanese cannot secure that supremacy in the Pacific which is their aim—their troops would have to penetrate a thousand miles of jungle, not to mention the little difficulty of securing Siam and Indo-China in their rear. Presuming that they delivered their onslaught by land, sea and air together, their forces would encounter the determined resistance of a great fortress, a navy of a strength at which we can only guess, although we know that it is far more powerful than it was in peacetime, an army which has recently been reinforced by men constituting the very cream of our Dominion troops, and an Air Force much more than a match for Japan's.

Can the Japanese embark on such a venture when, as the " New York Herald Tribune " said a few weeks ago, " their army is third-rate and more than waist-deep in the Chinese bog. Their navy's worth is untried and it is short of fuel. Finally, they are down to the population's jewelry "? Can they risk it, even if they would?

Just How Strong Is the Japanese Navy?

When war in the Pacific is regarded as a possibility, if not probability, the strength of the Japanese Navy is a matter of extreme importance. Here we pass the Mikado's Fleet in review so far as Tokyo permits us to see it. Comparison may be made with the articles on the Navies of the United States and Britain given in pages 125 and 151 of this volume.

IN the reference books Japan's Navy is ranked third, next to the navies of Britain and the U.S.A. At the Washington Naval Conference in 1922 the ratio as to capital ships of the three leading naval powers, Great Britain, the U.S.A., and Japan, was laid down as 5—5—3; but towards the end of 1934 Japan gave the required two years' notice of denunciation of the Treaty, and the Naval Conference held in London a year later came to nothing because of Japan's insistence on nothing less than parity with the strongest naval power—a demand which was firmly resisted by both America and Britain. Since December 31, 1936, there has been no naval limitation in the Pacific, but though Japan has claimed parity she has not made (it would seem) any determined effort to attain it. As likely as not the demand was made because Japan felt that nothing less than parity implied an inferiority incompatible with her declared role of leader in the establishment of a new order in East Asia.

True, Japan was reported at the end of 1937 to have under construction in Japanese yards three 46,000-ton battleships, while sixty-three other men-of-war were building or projected. It was then stated that the Japanese Fleet consisted of about 200 ships with a total displacement of 756,798 tons, and that by 1941 it would have been increased to 289 ships, displacing 1,109,130 tons. Then in 1939 a six-year naval building programme was approved by the Japanese Cabinet, when Admiral Yonai, the Navy Minister, stated that the new programme was based on the determination that Japan's Navy must be equal to that of the strongest naval power, and of sufficient strength to deal with any international friction arising out of the construction of the new order in Eastern Asia. In its preparation, said Admiral Yonai, account had been taken of the new naval programme of Britain and the U.S.A., and if these powers were to make any further increase in their fleets, then the Japanese plans would have to be revised accordingly.

To what extent this new programme has been carried into effect is uncertain, for the Japanese naval authorities have nothing to learn in the matter of secrecy. All details concerning Japan's Navy are so closely guarded that there is a story of a newspaper correspondent who once called at the Tokyo Admiralty and inquired with seeming innocence whether it was a fact that Japan *had* a Navy! Financially, Japan is in a very bad way; and it may be doubted whether in view of the running sore of the "Chinese Incident" she has been able to do more than keep her fleet reasonably up to date. It is reported, however, that she has not only three but four or five 16-in.-gun battleships of over 40,000 tons under construction in Japanese yards, and that two of these, Missin and Takamatu, were launched in November 1939 and April 1940 respectively, and so may be expected to be ready for sea this year.

Pride of the Mikado's Fleet

At the present time Japan has in service 10 battleships. The most powerful are Nagato and Mutu, completed in 1920-21; their displacement is 32,720 tons and their main armament is eight 16-in. guns. Then come four completed between 1915 and 1918: Huso and Yamasiro, with displacements of 29,330 tons, armed with twelve 14-in. and sixteen 6-in. guns, and Ise and Hyuga, which have a displacement of 29,990 tons and a primary armament of twelve 14-in. and eighteen 5·5-in. guns. Next there are three ships of the Kongo class, completed 1913-15: Kongo, Haruna and Kirisima. They have a standard displacement of 29,330 tons, and are armed with eight 14-in. and sixteen 6-in. guns. There is a fourth ship of this class, Hiei, which was demilitarized in 1930, but has probably now been rearmed.

Japan's heavy cruisers comprise 12 ships, all armed with 8-in. guns. They are divided into four classes, called after the first ship mentioned in each: Atago, Takao, Tyokai, and Maya, displacing 9,850 tons apiece, and carrying ten 8-in. guns, completed in 1932; Nati, Myoko, Asigara, and Haguro, 10,000 tons with ten 8-inch guns, completed in 1929; and Kako, Hurutaka, Kinugasa, and Aoba, displacing 7,100 tons, carrying six 8-in. guns, and completed in 1926-27. There are also five old cruisers which are now used as coast defence ships: Yakumo (9,010 tons), Idumo and Iwate (9,180 tons), Aduma (8,640 tons), and Kasuga (7,080 tons).

Coming now to second-class cruisers, the newest are those of the Mogami class, all of 8,500 tons and armed with fifteen 6·1-in. guns. They are Mogami, Mikuma, Suzuya, and Kumano, all completed between 1935 and 1937. These ships on their trials have shown themselves to be distinctly top-heavy, so in the two latest ships of the class, Tone and Tikuma, the armament has been reduced and only twelve 6·1-in. guns are mounted instead of fifteen; it is not certain whether these two ships are yet in service. (Nearly all Japan's warships, by the way, are built to Japanese designs, with not altogether happy results at times.) Then there are three ships of the Zintu class (Zintu, Naka, and Sendai), six of the Natori class (Natori, Isuzu, Kinu, Nagara, Yura, and Abukuma), five Kuma class (Kuma, Tama, Oi, Kitakami, and Kiso), two Tenryu class (Tenryu and Tatuta), and Yubari. These range from 5,195 tons in the Sendai class to Yubari's 2,890 tons. They have 5·5-in. guns.

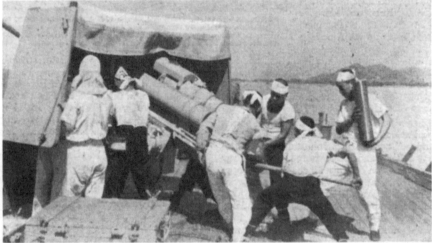

JAPAN'S NAVY is one of the most powerful in the world on paper, but its fighting qualities are so far unknown. Above, a Japanese gun crew in action against the Chinese in the estuary of the Yangtse river.

ASIGARA (left) is a 10,000-ton cruiser armed with ten 8-in. guns, anti-aircraft batteries and 8 torpedo tubes. She was completed in 1929, one of four ships of the Nati class.

Photos, Black Star, Wright & Logan

Ships that Make an Impressive Showing

OUTSIDE YOKOHAMA HARBOUR a Japanese naval review provided this striking photograph of some of the 100 warships which took part. Top centre can be seen the aircraft carrier Kaga.

Japan has seven aircraft carriers. The newest are three of the Soryu class—Soryu, Hiryu, and Syokaku—displacing 10,050 tons ; the remainder are Ryuzyo, 7,100 tons, Hosyo, 7,470 tons, and two of far larger size, Kaga and Akagi, both displacing 26,900 tons. Two more aircraft carriers are under construction.

Of smaller ships the Japanese have some 130 destroyers (12 Kagero class, 10 of them completing ; 10 Asasio, 10 Sigure, 6 Hatu-haru, 23 Hubuki, 12 Mutuki, 9 Kamikaze, 15 Akikaze, 7 Wakatake, 19 Kaya, and 3 Momo). There are 12 torpedo-boats with others building. Japan's submarines are divided into four groups, ocean-going, sea-going, minelaying, and coastal, displacing respectively when submerged 2,500, 1,470, 1,400, and 1,000 tons. They number some 72 with others building.

All these ships make an impressive showing enough, but the United States Pacific Fleet, not to mention her Asiatic Fleet, is as powerful as the whole Japanese Navy, and America's building programme far surpasses that of Japan. Moreover, it may be doubted whether the Japanese fleet would prove as formidable in action as it would appear to be on paper. " Independent experts," Hessell Tiltman, " Free Europe's " correspondent in Washington, wrote a few weeks ago, " consider the Japanese fleet ship for ship about 20 per cent inferior in marksmanship, protection, and manoeuvrability, to the British or American fleet. At Hawaii American naval officers have told me that any American destroyer flotilla leader would be willing to ' take on ' any Japanese cruiser, or any American cruiser a Japanese battle-ship. There is also a wide-spread impression in the Orient that the Japanese personnel does not compare in quality with the blue-jackets of the two great white navies." Yet, went on Mr. Tiltman, the Japanese are a very brave people, and " it would be unwise to minimize the punch packed by the sailors of Nippon."

JAPAN'S BATTLESHIPS Mutu and Nagato are seen in the photograph above, which shows the bow of the Nagato in the foreground, with one of her 16-in.-gun turrets. These two battleships were completed 1920-1921, but extensively reconstructed 1934-36. They have a displacement of 32,720 tons, a speed of 26 knots, and their main armament consists of eight 16-in. and twenty 5·5-in. guns. Each has six torpedo tubes.　　　　*Photos, Wide World, E.N.A.*

In Somaliland 'All Over Bar the Shouting'

In an earlier page (see page 228) we have given some account of the operations on the Kenya-Italian Somaliland front which resulted in the overrunning by General Cunningham's army of Jubaland and the capture of Mogadishu. Now we are able to give further details of this brilliant little campaign which has brought the Italians in East Africa even nearer to complete collapse.

"IT is all over bar the shouting," said a staff officer at British G.H.Q. in Cairo on Feb. 27, just after the news had been given out of the capture by Lt.-Gen. A. G. Cunningham's East African Imperial Force of Mogadishu, capital of Italian Somaliland. Completely defeated in the field, the Italians were reported to be giving themselves up in thousands, and only a remnant of their once considerable army was endeavouring to escape along the road to Harar and Addis Ababa, far to the north in Abyssinia.

When the campaign started in the middle of January the Italians had four or five, perhaps six, colonial brigades occupying strong positions, particularly on the line of the Juba River. Opposed to them General Cunningham had a force of Imperial troops, probably inferior to them in numbers but far superior in spirit.

After capturing a number of frontier posts General Cunningham crossed the frontier into Jubaland, and pushed out patrols in all directions. On Feb. 11 the King's African Rifles occupied Afmadu, 100 miles from the border. Here the British split into two columns. The first sped to the south, and the K.A.R.s captured Kismayu on Feb. 14, with the assistance of a naval bombardment from the sea. A number of ships were captured in the bay, together with a considerable haul of prisoners and large quantities of transport vehicles, ammunition and stores. Then crossing the Juba near its mouth the column (South Africans in the van) captured Gobwen and Jumbo on Feb. 22.

Meanwhile, the second column cut eastward straight through the bush and arrived at the Juba nearly 100 miles north of its mouth. The retreating Italians destroyed what bridges they could, but the river was forded by the South Africans, who waded across the stream holding their rifles above their heads, and the enemy resistance on the

Lt.-General ALAN G. CUNNINGHAM, D.S.O., G.O.C. the East African Imperial Force, whose brilliant operations in Italian Somaliland were crowned by the taking of Mogadishu on February 25. He is a brother of Admiral Sir A. Cunningham, C.-in-C. of the Mediterranean Fleet.
Photo, British Official: Crown Copyright

farther bank was soon overcome. Then pontoon bridges were constructed, and across these poured the British cars and trucks.

Now the two columns converged along the east bank. The South Africans moving up the river captured Margherita and Jelib on Feb. 23, after what was officially described in Nairobi as "an exceedingly vigorous and rapid march for 60 miles, clearing enemy opposition all the way." Then "East African formations," said a communiqué issued in Nairobi on Feb. 26, "having crossed the bridgehead seized by

Gold Coast regiments, carried out a night march through the desert country and cut the only road communication between Jelib and Brava, thus preventing the escape of the main body. The Gold Coast brigade, which had borne the brunt of the early fighting across the Juba, completed the operation and cut off all avenues of escape to the north. A conservative estimate of the number of prisoners is 3,000, while in addition many of the enemy who escaped to the bush are now returning and giving themselves up. An aeroplane reported that the enemy retreating along the beach 30 miles from the Juba immediately waved white flags in token of their desire to surrender. Large quantities of guns and ammunition of all kinds have

ITALIAN SOMALILAND, the south-west region of which is shown in this map, was overrun by the Imperial East African Force in a campaign of five weeks. Towns and villages are shown with the dates of their surrender.

been captured. The South African Air Force cooperated in the capture of Jelib, machine-gunning enemy transport which was trying to escape. The bombardment of the enemy positions and dumps farther along the coast was successfully carried out by the Navy."

With the east bank of the Juba cleaned up, the British columns reunited, swept eastward and on Feb. 24 Brava, 160 miles from Kismayu, was captured by the Gold Coast regiment.

Then the last burst along the coast began. This push was the swiftest of the campaign—indeed, of the war to date. Brava was captured on the Monday, and on the following Tuesday evening the first of General Cunningham's men entered Mogadishu, having covered in sweltering heat 120 miles of difficult country in a day, evidence not only of their own superb quality but of the demoralization of the enemy. Indeed, the main Italian force had fallen into Cunningham's trap at Jelib and had been forced to surrender, so that the capital—the strategical centre of the colony, as well as its most important port—was left very largely undefended. With Mogadishu in his hands General Cunningham is, in fact, master of Italian Somaliland.

MOGADISHU, capital of Italian Somaliland, captured on February 25, is the colony's capital and principal port. It has a population of about 50,000, eight thousand of whom are Italians. With its capture the whole of Italian Somaliland was imperilled. This general view of the town shows the triumphal arch, the cathedral, and the minaret of the Mosque.   *Photo, E.N.A.*

Blowing Up for a Gale in the Balkans

SOFIA, capital of Bulgaria, was very much in the news during the days when it was still undecided whether or not that little kingdom would succumb to the Axis wiles and threats. It stands on a plateau surrounded by mountains, but is on the main line between Vienna and Belgrade on the one hand, and Istanbul on the other. This photograph shows the Maria Louisa Boulevard and the Banya-Bashi Mosque, a relic of Turkish rule.

Below: **Mr. ANTHONY EDEN,** British Foreign Secretary, who arrived in Ankara on Feb. 25 for talks with Turkish leaders.
Photos, Central Press, Topical, and Paul Popper

BULGARIA went the way of all those little neutrals which have refused to stand together against the Nazi aggressor. On Saturday, March 1, 1941, the Bulgarian Premier, M. Filoff, flew from Sofia to Vienna and there signed the Tripartite Pact whereby his country became a satellite of the Axis Powers. On the same day German troops, which had been assembled in readiness on the north bank of the Danube, crossed into Bulgaria at several points, and in a few hours the country was under German control. Meanwhile, in Turkey, Mr. Anthony Eden, Britain's Foreign Secretary, and General Sir John Dill, Chief of the Imperial General Staff, had been holding conversations with Turkey's leaders, and, as announced in a communiqué issued in Ankara on Feb. 28, "there was complete accord in the policy of the two Governments on all subjects." On March 5 Mr. George W. Rendal, British Minister in Sofia, presented a Note to Professor Filoff, Bulgarian Premier, announcing Britain's decision to break off diplomatic relations, and asked for his passports.

Centre : **SIR STAFFORD CRIPPS,** British Ambassador to Soviet Russia, who flew to Turkey on Feb. 28 to consult with Mr. Eden.

Above : **General SIR JOHN DILL,** Chief of the Imperial General Staff, who accompanied Mr. Eden to the Near East.

ANKARA, capital of Turkey, is still often referred to as Angora. Situated in the centre of the Anatolian Plateau, it is far less exposed to enemy assault than Istanbul. Modern Ankara is a monument to Mustapha Kemal—Ataturk—whose statue (left) is one of the sights of the place.

'Before Our Eyes they Have Revived the Glories

This unusual photograph from the Albanian front shows a formation of light tanks captured fro Italians and now being used by the Greeks against their former owners. Oval right, Greek soldi the way to the front with a mule-borne machine-gun. Below left, Greek soldiers, returning outpost duty amid the snows of the Albanian front, thaw out over a cheery brazier.

from the Classic Age Gilded their Native Land'

THIS GREEK SOLDIER on a sure-footed mule wends his solitary way over snowy roads in Albania. Left, an Italian colonel, who once proudly commanded a crack Alpini regiment, now sits dejectedly with his A.D.C. in the side-car of a motor-cycle on his way to Greek Army H.Q. Ironically enough, the motor-cycle is a German one, acquired by the Greeks before the war. The quotation forming the heading is from Mr. Churchill's broadcast of February 9.

Bottom left and right-hand photos by Bosshard, exclusive to THE WAR ILLUSTRATED. *Others by courtesy of the Royal Greek Legation*

How Hitler Formed his Corps of Parachutists

Although it was the Russians who " invented " the military parachutists, it was Hitler who first employed them in actual warfare—in the spring of 1940, in Norway, and, far more effectively, in Holland. This remarkable inside story of how the Nazi Parachutist Force came into being has been specially written for THE WAR ILLUSTRATED by a reliable authority on Central European affairs.

ONE month before Hitler reintroduced compulsory military service in Germany—to be exact, on February 16, 1935—a most extraordinary meeting took place at Professor von Noorden's Vienna sanatorium. The then supreme commander of the German Army, General Baron von Fritsch, who was staying at the sanatorium on short sick-leave, met " by chance " the Soviet Russian Army Commander, First Class (General) Jankir, who was seeking to recover his health at the same time and the same place.

Open Russo-German military cooperation having ceased, of course, as soon as Hitler had assumed power, this chance meeting marked the beginning of a new era : that of fresh, intensified collaboration of Russian and German staff officers in secret. It brought about, in particular, the creation of a new German force, the Parachutist Battalions. Indeed, like so many other aspects of a regime supposed to have been erected for the world's protection against the " Red Plague " of Bolshevism, this new German weapon is of purely Muscovite origin. In consequence of the above-mentioned chance meeting a certain Herr Sperling, director of a department in the obviously quite harmless " German School for Commercial Pilots," obtained an extensive leave of absence.

That school was the camouflage for the secret building up of a German Air Force, and Sperling, strangely enough, spent his leave in Soviet Russia. After three months he returned to Berlin and assembled, at his office on the corner of Voss Street and Hermann-Goering Street, just behind Hitler's Chancellery, thirty carefully selected " commercial air pilots." With these he withdrew to the Staacken aerodrome, between Spandau and Potsdam, where secret and most uncommon activities began. A sector of the aerodrome was walled in ; unauthorized access thereto was forbidden under death penalty, and the thirty men stayed there for months in complete seclusion. The only thing that could be witnessed by outsiders was the erection of several curious scaffolds. Then, once in a while, a few 'planes swept over the walled-in part of the aerodrome early in the mornings, and something appeared to be dropped from them.

First ' Drops ' at Staacken

Nobody knew anything for certain. But a car-driver who once passed the Staacken Aerodrome, where the great Berlin-Hamburg motor road touches it, at the break of the day got a shock—he saw one, two, three men with parachutes dropping from a 'plane. They came from such a low height that he was sure there would be an accident that would cost them their lives. Aghast, he shouted to the two guards at the entrance of the aerodrome : " Parachutes—look over there ! " The guards did not even lift their eyes. " You are day-dreaming ! " one of them observed.

When the traveller insisted that he *had* seen the parachutes, and was quite awake and in possession of his senses, he got a

WE ALSO HAVE PARACHUTE TROOPS

THAT Britain had used parachute troops in Southern Italy came as a surprise to the Italians and the British public alike. A corner of the veil of secrecy has now been lifted, and it has been officially announced that the British Army has a force of parachutists in training.

All the British parachutists are volunteers and come from various branches of the Army. Needless to say, they are picked for their physique and daring, and because of the extra risk involved they receive extra pay. Their training is rigorous, and every man must be able to swim in uniform as well as to undertake the most arduous tasks without fatigue. The parachutists wear goggles over their eyes and crash helmets. Jackets are shaped to the hips and their trousers fit into the tops of their boots, which are similar to the German pattern. Their parachutes are fitted with a special release gear which operates instantaneously, ensuring quicker action than is possible by a man himself pulling at the ripcord. Another parachute descends with them carrying a kit-bag containing their equipment.

No details of the men's training have been divulged, but exercises recently carried out in the presence of General Sir John Dill, Chief of the Imperial General Staff, and many of Britain's war leaders were most impressive ; not only did they clearly demonstrate the potentialities of this form of attack, but they showed the efficiency of the co-operation between the R.A.F. and the Army. As Lieut.-General Sir Douglas Brownrigg, the " Sunday Times " Military Correspondent, puts it : " The Germans may yet regret having started the use of this new instrument of war."

Sq.-Leader LOUIS STRANGE, D.S.O., D.F.C., holds an important position in connexion with the training of British paratroops. Fifty years of age, he is the only pilot still flying who went to France with the original R.F.C. in August 1914. Top, badge of British paratroops.

sharply emphasized " You were dreaming—*understand* ? " He understood, and put his foot on the accelerator for all he was worth.

That happened at about the moment when Herr Sperling had taught his disciples all he had learnt himself in Moscow. With true Teutonic efficiency, however, he was not satisfied with that, and set about the task of improving the procedure. Scientific help was called in ; the " Office for the Research of Defence Psychology," directed by Councillor Grigoreit, in a wing of—an unintentional joke—the Hospital for Disabled Soldiers in Scharnhorst Street, submitted to the thirty men extensive questionnaires, the answers to which yielded valuable conclusions as to a man's psychological reactions during a jump. The Medical Officer for the Forces had to make detailed investigations as to the physical effects of a parachute drop. And a combination of the findings of both sources brought about, in January 1936, the publication of the first " Instructions for the Setting-up of Parachute Troops."

A school for parachutists was established at Spandau, recruiting its pupils exclusively from volunteers. Herr Sperling (his name, appropriately enough, means " sparrow ") suddenly became a colonel, and not long afterwards a general of the Air Force ; 24 of his first pupils were " Troop Leaders " with the rank of lieutenant.

Training the Leaders

At first no regiments were formed ; but 50 men were included in the " Condor Legion "—the body of German "volunteers" who fought in the Spanish Civil War in order to gain practical experience. Only 23 of them came back ; the others lost their lives in a number of daring enterprises. Upon the knowledge gained from their experiences was based the creation of an " Academy for Parachutist-Leaders," a department of the " Academy for Aerial Warfare " at Gatow, near Berlin. Only men with a particularly high standard of education, intelligence, technical qualification and physical fitness are admitted. They have to undergo, in the Spandau " school " as well as in the Gatow " academy," the most intricate and complete training imaginable : jumping with parachutes, of course—but at night, and in unknown surroundings, too ; normal military training with rifle and machine-gun ; engineer's work, such as blowing up bridges, crossing rivers, and so forth ; Morse code and wireless, map-reading, special technical training—for instance, destruction of motor-cars and machinery, and foreign languages.

By 1938 there were two regiments of parachutists, of two battalions each ; every battalion comprised 500 men, but not all of them were parachutists—the staff, 'plane personnel and technicians being included. A third regiment seems to have been ready at the beginning of the war. That troop suffered heavy losses when utilized for the first time in Holland and Belgium. In view of those losses, and of the length of time taken in the special training, the Nazis should not at present have more than six regiments of "jumpers."

Where the Nazis Learn to Drop from the Clouds

ON STENDAL AERODROME a parachute is still fully spread just after landing. Below, a combined descent is being practised. The machine from which the men have dropped is seen on the left of the photograph.

FOLDING PARACHUTES is a delicate operation, and airmen and paratroops are entirely dependent for their lives on the ground staff that folds and packs the apparatus. Here is the German training school at Stendal. Skilled hands are arranging the gear of parachutes used in training beginners.

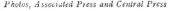

Photos, Associated Press and Central Press

Swansea's Three Nights of Brutal Battering

ONE OF THESE DAYS THEY WILL BE DROPPING PARACHUTE TROOPS

SWANSEA

SWANSEA WILL REMEMBER
Cartoon by J. C. Walker.   Courtesy of the " South Wales Echo "

After the great raids on Swansea those who were engaged in the work of rescue and salvage, such as these two Salvation Army officers, walked through streets covered with the debris of fallen buildings.

GUTTED BUILDINGS OF SWANSEA bore witness to the thousands of fire bombs which wrought havoc such as is seen above in the raids of February 19, 20 and 21, 1941. Those who were rendered homeless found what accommodation they could. Right are some of the women and children in the crypt of a church used as a rest centre.
Photos, Planet News

'Fiery Warriors Fight Upon the Clouds'

ABOVE THE STRAITS OF DOVER there was great aerial activity during daylight on February 22, 1941, when British fighters intercepted many formations of the German Luftwaffe. This photograph was taken while the battle was in progress. By the use of plates sensitive to infra-red light waves, which can penetrate haze and mist, and a telephoto lens, the cliffs of France have been brought apparently close to England, and the white trails left by the swift-moving 'planes, trails familiar to all who witnessed the aerial battles of the summer of 1940, stand out clearly in the sky.

Photo, " Keystone"

OUR SEARCHLIGHT ON THE WAR

'Love and Kisses' in Code

So sympathetic is the attitude of the Post Office towards the wives and sweethearts of men serving in H.M. forces in the Near East that a code system has been devised for a large variety of messages, each having a distinctive number, divided into groups such as " Greetings," " Health," " Money," etc. In the first-named group every degree of affection is included, from simple " Kisses " to " Fondest love and kisses." Number 61, " You are more than ever in my thoughts at this time," may well hearten a lover bumping along in an armoured car over a dry, waterless desert. Number 69, " All well ; children evacuated," will bring peace to the mind of an anxious father whose heart is in London while his body is contending with a sandstorm. A young husband receiving No. 85, " Son born ; both well," may bless the Postmaster-General more than he who receives No. 113, " Glad if you could send me some money." But almost certainly it will be the romantic " Greetings " group of numbers which will most often be consulted by operators decoding these messages sent out East.

£10,000 Well Spent !

A WIRELESS invitation by the German Government to Americans to send, at its expense, messages of not more than 21 words suggesting items for the German broadcasts to the United States met with an exuberant response. So enthusiastic indeed was the desire to take advantage of these facilities that a new organization, calling itself " United Americans " was hastily formed with the object of sending 30,000 to 40,000 cables, for which the collecting charges

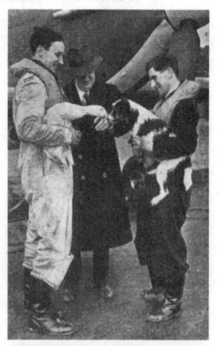

R.A.F. MASCOTS are often live ones, given by well-wishers. Above, Commander Milo Warner, of the American Legion, is seen making friends with Wilfred, the duck mascot of an R.A.F. fighter-squadron he was visiting.
Photo, British Official : Crown Copyright

cancelled by the short-wave announcer in Berlin, who complained that " the senders of some of the messages do not seem to be among our most ardent admirers." For once he spoke the truth. Here are a few sample cables. " Broadcasts of R.A.F. bombings of Germany would be most welcome to Americans. We want especially a description of bombings of the German Chancellery, of Berchtesgaden, and of the Brown House in Munich." " Give me a six-hour talk on the ways and means to exterminate Adolf Schickelgrube." " We request a graphic description of a British invasion of Germany." " Why is Goering so fat when the Germans are so lean ? "

Dog Mascots in the R.A.F.

In January the R.A.F. Comforts Committee rashly made public that a fine Alsatian dog had been received from an admirer with the suggestion that it should be given to a fighter squadron as a mascot. No sooner had this been done than the Committee found another Alsatian waiting on its doorstep, anxious to join the R.A.F. He went to a squadron of the Bomber Command. Since then two more Alsatians have arrived at the Committee's headquarters in Berkeley Square—as well as two mongrels, ready and eager to serve wherever they might be sent, a bull terrier, a bloodhound, a golden cocker and a Manchester terrier. All are now officially attached to bases of the R.A.F., but the Committee has had to announce that no more dogs are wanted for the moment (though musical instruments suitable for an R.A.F. station band would be very welcome). Mascots of the R.A.F. are not, however, all canine. There is one fighter squadron which is apt to attribute its immunity to the tame duck attached to its mess.

Life-Saving Drug for Greece

One million tablets of the sulphanilamide compound, discovered after years of research by chemists in the laboratories of Messrs. May and Baker, and popularly known as "M & B 693," have been presented by this firm to the Lord Mayor's Greek Relief Fund. This drug has effected thousands of dramatic cures in many germ diseases, particularly pneumonia, and will be a boon to Greek doctors in the field. The generous gift, which is valued at £5,000, was accepted on behalf of the Fund by the Duchess of Kent. Already 20,000 of the tablets have been sent by air mail to the British Minister in Athens, who had cabled an urgent request for the drug, with the suggestion that £1,000 of the Lord Mayor's Fund should be used in this way to combat the scourge of pneumonia in the Greek Army.

What Airmen Read

Their tastes are varied, and it is a mistake to imagine that only thrillers are in demand. It may well be that the thrills in a pilot's personal experience explain his frequent preference, on returning to his base, for novels such as " Pride and Prejudice," " Vanity Fair," and " David Copperfield." Incidentally, men who have seen the film versions of these and other classics are indignant when they differ from the original

story, and inclined to be critical of the casting. But not every man in the R.A.F. has the wish or ability to concentrate on a long book for what are inevitably short periods, so that P. G. Wodehouse is a prime favourite. " Pickwick Papers," which can be opened anywhere to while away ten minutes or half an hour, is also very popular, as are the short stories of O. Henry. Periodicals of every type are found on the table, many catering for serious minds. In every mess there may well be a Tolstoy enthusiast ; a man who dips for refreshment into anthologies of poetry ; a pilot who—perhaps after bombing Den Helder—becomes immersed in Motley's " Rise of the Dutch Republic " ; and another deeply absorbed in a mathematical treatise. One shrewd observation has been made ; most modern novels hailed by critics as " masterpieces," even those which become best-sellers, are turned over—and left unread.

Death of a Famous Scientist

Sir Frederick Banting, discoverer of insulin, was killed in an air crash at Trinity Bay, Newfoundland, on Feb. 21. He was flying to England on a mission of high scientific importance, rumoured to be the demonstration of a new method of nullifying the effects of poison gas on the human body. Sir Frederick, who was Professor of Medical Research at Toronto University, had also been engaged recently on special work in what may be described as aviation medicine. Dean C. J. Mackenzie, President of the Canadian National Research Council, describing the thoroughness with which he carried this out, said : " He would go up in an airplane as high as it could go to discover the effect of lack of oxygen on the blood. He insisted on diving to see the effect divebombing had on bomber crews. He made his pilots do everything an airplane can do in the air in his study to discover means to counteract the heavy strains on human beings in these unusual circumstances." Sir Frederick had also taken part in tank manoeuvres to study the reactions of the body to this drastic method of making war.

THE DUCHESS OF KENT is here seen at the presentation by Messrs. May and Baker, the well-known chemists, at the Mansion House, London, of a million tablets of their sulphanilamide compound ("M & B 693") to the Lord Mayor's Greek Relief Fund. This drug has proved most valuable in the treatment of pneumonia.
Photo, " The Times "

would be not far short of £20,000. The Radio Corporation of America, authorized by Germany to accept the messages, actually handled about 15,000, at a cost to Dr. Goebbels' propaganda fund of about £10,000, before the offer was prematurely

'Australia's Messenger Brings No Empty Words'

Rt. Hon. ROBERT GORDON MENZIES, Premier of the Australian Commonwealth, is seen inspecting a Guard of Honour of Australian infantrymen when he visited the Ministry of Information in London ; he arrived in England on February 20, 1941, by flying-boat, having flown 21,000 miles. Below we have a photograph of him congratulating a fellow-countryman at Benghazi during his tour of the Middle East.
Photos, British Official: Crown Copyright ; G.P.U.

MY greeting to you comes from the whole of the Australian people of all creeds and political parties. On the issue of this war we are not divided. You and we are of the one blood, and we are not to be put down by ambitious adventurers or predatory rogues. You must never even be tempted to think that your fight is a lonely one. Speaking, I am sure, not only for Australia but for the whole of the British Empire beyond the seas, I say to you : We are in this most holy war with you ; everything that we have of man-power or treasure or skill or determination is pledged to work and fight for and with you until victory is attained and a better and juster day dawns for the world in which our children are to live. This is not a mere expression of sentiment. It is supported by every deed of which we are capable.

The total population of Australia is considerably less than the population of London. But the Australian Imperial Force, our expeditionary force, is already an Army Corps of four divisions and corps troops, thousands of the personnel of which have already made

their blows, their just blows, heard in Rome, and desire only to deliver them at Berlin itself. I have visited in the Mediterranean ships of the Royal Australian Navy, which from the day war broke out have cooperated with yours in the Seven Seas and have, by their skill and fighting qualities, not subtracted from the glories of the Royal Navy. I have seen Royal Australian Air Force men in Libya clad in strange garments and sometimes " bearded like the pard," but always attacking, attacking, attacking. Add to these things our munitions effort, which already produces 20 times our volume of production when war began, and you will see that Australia's messenger brings no empty words . . .

WE are not shrinking from the burden either of men or of money. And why should we ? As I said recently at home, every bomb that falls on London or Coventry is a bomb dropped upon the security of Australia. We are in this danger together, and by faith and work we shall triumph over it.

From the Australian Premier's broadcast from London, Feb. 23, 1941

At Derna They Even Left the Duce's Picture!

DERNA fell to the Imperial Forces on Jan. 30, 1941, in the course of the ever-memorable dash to Benghazi. So precipitate was the Italians' retreat that they omitted to destroy vital bridges of great value to the pursuers. Above is one intact, with Imperial troops standing in front of it.

Among the " booty " that fell to the victorious Army was a grim-looking portrait of Mussolini that inspired in these men of the Army of the Nile only contemptuous amusement.

" BELIEVE, OBEY AND FIGHT " were the words inscribed in big letters on this wall in Derna to encourage the Italian troops. The latter may once have believed they had an easy task; they certainly obeyed the order to retreat—even to run ; but as for fighting, neither they nor their generals had much stomach for it.

The capture of Derna was important, for there it was possible to sink wells and get an adequate supply of water. Above, a British well-boring unit is at work. Left, a British machine-gun in action near the town just before its fall.

Photos, British Official: Crown Copyright

Here's My Log When We Were Torpedoed

When his ship was torpedoed, Able-Seaman Sydney Light, G.M., took charge of one of the boats, and by his "courage, leadership, self-sacrifice and stout heart" saved not only his own crew of eight, but 16 men in another boat which he towed. Here we publish the log which he kept during ten days of privation, weariness and danger.

FIRST DAY (midnight). Torpedoed on starboard side. Wind N.E. Force 6, heavy seas, shipping heavy sprays starboard side. Mean course 93 degrees true. Standing by on main deck when struck, reported immediately to third mate, Mr. Craze (officer on watch), for orders.

He instructed me to call all hands on deck and abandon ship. This I carried out and reported to my boat station No. 4 boat.

The second mate, Mr. Garner, had not appeared at the boat. I therefore inquired of Mr. Parr, fourth mate, if I should prepare to swing out the boat. He told me to carry on. This was done with the very able assistance of the stewards.

The boat having been swung out on the davits, the second mate, lamp trimmer, and A.B. Fish arrived. The second mate ordered me into the boat to see the plug was secure and stand by the forward fall and painter.

The stewards and engineers then got into the boat and Mr. Garner ordered "Lower away aft," after which "Lower away together." A very heavy sea lifted the stern and unhooked the after fall, with the result that all hands except Jeffries, greaser (caught in a thwart) and myself, hanging on the forward fall (on which the boat was then hanging vertically), fell out.

Another sea then lifted the boat and swamped the boat. I released the forward fall, and gave orders to Jeffries to hold her off. I then ran aft and pulled aboard the rest of the survivors.

During this time the boat had several nasty bumps against the ship's side, and in consequence I pulled the toggle of the forward painter (it was impossible to keep the boat off the side because the rudder was not shipped).

We then drifted away, and I ordered "Out oars," and tried to row to the lee side to pick up other survivors. This proved to be impossible as the men were exhausted. We then drifted away from the ship in the heavy seas, which we tried to keep head on. This also was impossible. I then gave instructions to bale out, the water then being up to the thwarts.

As we lay broadside on the seas were breaking on the port side and rolling off the starboard. A searchlight was then shone round, which I presumed was from the submarine, but owing to us being so low in the water we could not see it.

Second Day. Morning came, sea and wind abated to force 2, we then baled out and squared up the boat, stepped the mast, and set sails. At 11 o'clock another lifeboat with sails set was sighted. After conversation with them we learned they were survivors of another torpedoed ship.

They informed us that they had seen a boat which they believed was one of ours without sails or oars; we sailed around in the hope of picking them up, but all without avail. I informed them to steer a course by compass S.E., gave them some cigarettes, and they proceeded on.

At one o'clock, p.m., we sighted two steam vessels to the south. We hoped they would pick us up, but, unfortunately, they missed us. I then suggested to the others we had better get on our course and proceed. They were unanimous, and this was done.

Wind was N.E. 2, swell heavy, and then the wind veered to west, increasing to south. We shortened sail and steered south-east. All hands then had physical exercise to keep them warm.

We reset the mainsail and continued until 19 hours, and lay to on the sea anchor, covering ourselves over with the boat cover. A look-out was kept during the night.

A.B. Sydney H. LIGHT, whose heroic action in the story described in this page (taken from his log), has won him the G.M. Before the war he was landlord of the "Southborough Arms," Kingston By-pass. *Photo, Associated Press*

Nothing to report. Heavy rain squalls all night which abated at 5 a.m. Wind and rain then moderated.

Third Day. We got under way at 7.30 a.m. after having something to eat (one dipper of water, a biscuit, a small portion of corned mutton, and condensed milk), under mainsail and jib with one reef in mainsail.

At 9.30 a.m. shook out reef and continued under steady breeze 4. Estimated speed 3 knots. 11 a.m. sighted flying-boat in northerly direction about fifteen miles to eastward of us; we hope to see him later so that he reports us.

12 noon. All hands except Mr. Clay, chief electrician (who is suffering from pains in the legs and stomach) are happy and well. Mr. Clay we have made as comfortable as possible forward; proceeded on our course south-east. All hands in good spirits, had something to eat, all disappointed did not

see flying-boat again, downed sails, put out sea anchor at 19 hours and settled down for the night.

Fourth Day. Sea breeze had eased down, under way at 7.30 a.m., with jib and mainsail all set, wind northerly, estimated speed 3½ knots, course S.E. Navigation very difficult not knowing position of ship when torpedoed, only knowledge had was course (true) and distance to port from noon on Friday.

12.00 noon. Wind and sea freshened considerably, but continued under all sail. Mr. Clay has for first time come out of his position forward, looking rather pale and weak, but bright and in good spirits; all hands bright and hopeful; had community singing and physical jerks, which we have done since Saturday. All hands soaking wet, which they have been since leaving the ship.

16.00 hours. Captain's steward Rolf at the tiller sighted a lifeboat without oars, sails or any sign of life at all, except a canvas tent fitted amidships. Altered course to N., and all hands shouted with gusto, and out came chief officer of another torpedoed ship, who came on deck.

I shouted him and told him to stand by to take a line from me. We unfastened the ground anchor warp, came about, and he picked up the line and made fast; and we took them under tow at 16.30 hours.

We now learned there are sixteen men in the boat. The chief officer asked me what course I was steering, and I told him S.E.

We then gave him a tin of corned mutton and a lighted cigarette, which unfortunately went out, downed sails and lay to on sea anchor at 19.00 hours. Wind and sea increased, and heavy rain fell, shipped a lot of water; second steward and myself baled out twenty-six buckets of water during the night.

Fifth Day. All hands soaking wet and very stiff, got under way at 7.45 a.m. and did physical jerks, agreed with mate of the other ship to steer new course. Speed reduced considerably since towing other lifeboat. All hands in boat in good spirits, ate well. Speed approximately 2½ knots.

Thought to have sighted land about 17.30 hours, and kept going until 19.00 hours. Suggested to other boat we lay to all night, as we did not want to go in not knowing the condition of the coast.

I did not want to hit a rock or shoal, as some of the men in the other boat had been injured when torpedoed, and, further, most of them were without lifebelts.

We lay to on the sea anchor all night, gave the other boat two tins of corned mutton and half pound of tobacco and cigarette papers, also some matches. Have arranged to keep two look-out men in each boat throughout the night.

Sixth Day. Wind dropped to 1, sea dropped to big land swell. Was up at five o'clock, it was dead calm, but there were zephyrs, counted six to the minute. I hope this will turn into a light breeze by sunrise.

Gave the other boat four oars, keeping three ourselves, have now learned we lost one while rowing away from the ship. Have set sail in hope of getting a little breeze, but seems of no avail at the moment, but we will keep them up as a passing vessel might see them.

Torpedoed 700 miles off Lisbon by an enemy submarine, the captain and crew of the British freighter St. Agnes were rescued by the U.S. liner Exochorda. Here are the rescued men coming alongside the American ship.

Photo, Associated Press

Continued rowing all day until 16.00 hours, and considered it foolish to fatigue the men any more, so stretched out boat cover and all hands turned in for the night.

Seventh Day. Mate of other boat called and we came alongside, by this time a light breeze, N.W. 2, had sprung up. He informed me two of his men had bad feet (similar to trench feet). I went aboard, massaged them, and gave them my seaboot stockings, and left them quite comfortable. I then got the first-aid kit cleaned, and dressed the thigh wound of Mr. Lane, chief steward, and the hand and ankle of carpenter.

The mate of the other boat, Mr. Fiddler, Mr. Graham, third mate, and myself unanimously agreed, as a slight breeze had sprung up, we would sail all night. Mr. Graham volunteered to come on board and do watch with me.

At midnight Pyner, deckboy, complained of terrific pain in his feet. I had him on deck and massaged the feet and got the blood back into circulation, and tore up a blanket in strips and bound his feet.

Mr. Graham and Rolf relieved us at midnight, and a heavy rainstorm beat the wind out between 01.00 and 02.00 hours, when it freshened again.

Eighth Day. I came out on deck at 05.00 hours in brilliant moonlight, wind and sea calm. Mate of other boat on deck at 06.30 hours, hauled alongside, and went on board and found galley-boy with trench feet, massaged them, and gave him relief.

Wind has now dropped to dead calm, mate and I decided to row during day; wind freshened at 10.00. Mr. Graham and I decided to fit jib to an oar and make a mizzen of it and cut up boat-cover and make foresail.

Continued to sail through night. This was the first opportunity I had to take a bearing of the North Star to find compass error.

Ninth Day. Light breeze 2 southerly, same routine as before. 15.00 hours wind and sea increased violently. Chief officer of other boat hailed me and we decided to transfer men, provisions and water into our boat so that we could make better headway.

This I put to the members of the boat, who agreed, but that we should wait until the weather abated. Under a double reefed

mainsail, wind from the S.E. and heavy rain, we continued to make slow headway.

Tenth Day. Wind and sea eased considerably by 09.00 hours. We then transhipped crew and provisions from towed boat and continued our course. Owing to wind veering S.E. it was decided we should break into three watches.

Food and physical exercises continued.

Eleventh Day. Relieved Mr. Fiddler, four o'clock. Wind S.E. 3. Sighted ship at 07.15 B.S.T. Lit one flare with no answer ; another five minutes later, to which he answered our signal.

Called all hands, cleared away tent, shipped rowlocks, out oars and rowed towards the ship. A nasty choppy sea running went ahead of her and round to portside. All hands boarded without mishap or injury at 08.00 hours B.S.T. After being served with hot tea, reported to captain.

I will take this opportunity to express appreciation on behalf of the survivors and myself for the kind consideration and generosity afforded to us by the officers and men of our rescue ship.

S. H. LIGHT, A.B.

Read and confirmed—
R. CLAY, Chief Electrician.
A. J. D'AGORNE, Chief Certificate Engineer.

'Night Flying is Rather Terrifying at First!'

The thrill of night fighting—of being one of the cat's eyes of the R.A.F.—has been described by Flying Officer D. A. Willans, who was recently awarded the D.F.C. for his successes in night fighter operations in Britain's skies. Below we tell his experiences in his own words.

"IT was rather terrifying at first," said Flying Officer Willans, "but now I would not change my job." He speaks from experience, for he has been with a Night Fighter Squadron since the war began.

"It is a grand feeling to be up there at night," he went on. "When it is a moonlight night you can see almost everything on the ground, and it is not too difficult to spot a Hun. But, on dark nights, it's a different matter and you have to rely principally on searchlights. Some of our fellows are better than others are at seeing in the dark. Diet helps to develop one's power to see in the darkness, and we also carry out special training in the daytime. Combat is not easy unless the enemy is held by searchlights because the rear-gunner can open his vision panel and have a crack at you, while you have to keep your screen closed."

The first bomber Flying Officer Willans caught at night was an He. 111 which he encountered over Norwich. He probably destroyed it. "I first saw the Hun held in a concentration of searchlights," he said, "and chased him for five minutes. He

dodged the lights and I lost him, but picked him up again after I had seen incendiaries burst below. One beam caught him again and I saw clearly that he was an He. 111. I made one attack which met with a certain amount of return fire from the upper and lower guns, and then had another crack at him. All at once his firing ceased. To make sure, I let him have another burst and went underneath him. He made for the sea and an observer reported that one of his engines was ' not working so good.' "

On another occasion Flying Officer Willans damaged a Do. 17 in a night combat over France. He saw the Do. attempting to land at an aerodrome and attacked at 2,000 feet with short bursts from 30 yards range. His bullets went wide and he dived again, attacking on the port side with incendiary bullets. "I saw a flash from the enemy machine as I broke away," he reported, "he went down and crashed well short of the aerodrome flare-path. One engine of my machine cut out just then so I concentrated on getting back. There was no cloud, no moon and it was very dark, but I just managed to make it."

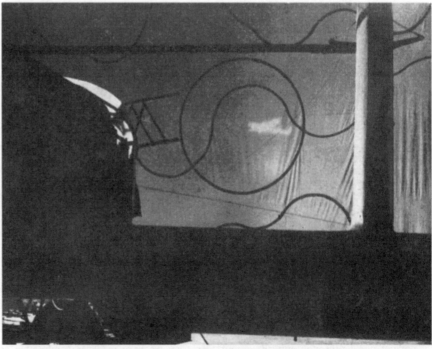

BRITAIN'S NIGHT FIGHTERS, as described in this page, receive a thorough and intensive training before they are ready to play their part in the air battles in the dark sky. This photo shows a rear gunner being trained by means of an ingenious device : his machine-gun is pointed at a representation of an enemy 'plane which is moved rapidly across a screen. *Photo, Planet News*

'Spanner, Spade & Saucepan' Take the Offensive

Potatoes are now sold in grades, and (top) on a Sussex farm a hand-driven machine sorts them out with ingenious mechanism into the grades to which they belong. Immediately above is a land girl who did the same job in the last war and likes it now just as she did then.

BRITAIN'S OFFENSIVE, said Captain Harold Balfour, Under-Secretary of State for Air, in a speech at Stockport on February 23, cannot be confined to bomb, tank and ship, but must embrace the spanner, spade and saucepan. Here in this page we have illustrations of these latter types of offensive action. Two of the photographs have an agricultural appeal. Two were taken in war factories—one showing the hardening of caterpillar track links on a Bren gun carrier, and the other, two Belgian refugees at work on reconditioning machine tools. Finally, as an illustration of the "saucepan" we have a glimpse of one of the Liverpool Corporation's central kitchens.

Photos, L.N.A., Associated Press, "Daily Mirror," Fox and Planet News

Our Czech Allies Are Training for 'The Day'

In an earlier article (see p. 352, Vol. 3) Henry Baerlein has told us something of the Czech airmen in this country. Now he writes of the army formed by the Czechs over here—a truly democratic army, an army worthy of the people's great past.

WHAT adventures they had on their travels, the Czechs and Slovaks who have managed to elude their Nazi " protectors " ! To leave their own stricken Republic by legal means was nearly always impossible, for the fangs of the Gestapo gripped all those who possessed any fortune or whose political past displeased them. It is true that many a Gestapo man would be amenable to a little financial persuasion ; but Himmler is aware of this weakness, and each of his agents is watched by one or two others.

THESE CZECH SOLDIERS are seen marching along a country road during the Battle of France in the summer of 1940, when they fought fiercely against the Germans. Men of the reorganized Czech Army now in Britain are highly trained and splendidly equipped, ready once more to continue the fight. Here are some of them on parade (right).

Sometimes a Czech would succeed in getting across the German frontier into another country and then find that the guards of that land were on friendly terms with the Nazi guards. This happened to a man who was a State employee in Prague, a man of forty-one who during the last war was a member of the Czech Legions which for years were the sole organized body in Siberia. In August 1939 this man left Czechoslovakia without an exit visa, travelling among a trainload of workers who had been allocated to the Ruhr. At Hanover he left that train, went on alone, got into Holland, was sent back to Germany and spent four months in prison at Münster—where the treatment, he says, was not too bad because that region is profoundly Catholic and the wardens were not of the young fanatic type. However, his money was confiscated ; and when he was allowed to go to Prague he would have had to walk there if one of the warders had not been willing to buy his gold watch. From Prague he turned south and crossed to Hungary on the way to Yugoslavia, where he knew that all would be well ; but in spite of the assistance he received from the French consul in Budapest, from the Polish Red Cross and from a bribable Hungarian official, he was sentenced on three occasions to terms in Hungarian prisons.

But the Czechs never lost hope, and when

one sees them here one realizes what grim determination they possess and that they will play a splendid part in the liberation of their Republic. True warriors that they are, they have a profound love for children ; now and then a children's edition of their army paper *Naše Noviny* (Our News) is published, of course, in English. It is delightfully written. No wonder these men are popular among the children in their present winter quarters ; as I went with one or other of them through the streets there was a continuous cry of *Nazdar ! Nazdar !* (the Czech word that is a combination of Good Luck ! and Hullo!). And among the adult and the military part of the population I found that these troops are highly appreciated; they are men of initiative, as one would expect from the people in whose country lies the Skoda factory, men who gave the world the Bren gun, which the British army values so much.

As an example of the injustice they had to suffer in their own country, let me describe the experiences of one of their soldiers now over here, a sensitive-looking young man who smiles when he talks of the past, but who is dreaming, like all of them, of the vengeance they will exact when their turn comes. He used to live in the Sudeten region, where he owned a door-handle factory. This was seized by the Germans after Munich, whereupon he started a similar factory in the " rump " of Czechoslovakia. This factory was eventually also seized after a lawsuit had been brought against him by the manager of his original place, who complained of the competition of the second factory. Having bribed the Gestapo, the young man was allowed to go to Yugoslavia, ostensibly for

medical treatment ; and although other minions of Himmler's police asked for him to be delivered to them, the Yugoslav authorities refused, and our friend took the road which so many of his countrymen have trod— to Greece, Turkey, Palestine, Egypt and France.

Thus they have followed the great example of their fathers who in the last war managed to escape from their hated Hapsburg masters and form in Russia the Legions, the ever-famous Seventy Thousand, whose exploits, fighting their way round the world, are so well known. One of the differences between those men and the Czech army now in Britain is that the Czechs and Slovaks of those days had served in the Austro-Hungarian army, whereas those of today have behind them more than twenty years of a Republic with, of course, its own army. Very few Czechs had the ambition to serve as Austrian officers, and when the Legions were established in Russia they were officered by men who, after serving for a year or so, had left the army as officers of the reserve and had settled down in Russia, where the language resembles their own, as engineers, doctors, chemists and so forth. These improvized commanders, such as General Sirovy, their chief, who had been,

I believe, a brewer, gave an excellent account of themselves, for the average Czech is a highly intelligent person ; but now the Czech Army has the advantage of being officered by men who have chosen the military career. Such, for instance, is their commander, General Ingr, a quiet, youngish man who gives one the impression of being a military student. He possesses the confidence of his entire army. One of its outstanding figures is Col. Kalla, the military attaché, a dapper little man with a genius for organization. In his own country he was an aviator, and many are the prizes he has won in air races.

The colour of the Czech uniforms at home was very like that of our own khaki, so that now the Czech troops have no feeling of even temporary strangeness in the British uniforms with which they have been provided. Of course, these uniforms have certain distinguishing marks—Czechoslovakia " on the left shoulder and the rampant lion of the Czech arms in their headgear.

President Benes Reviews His Men in Britain

CZECHOSLOVAKIA and Poland affirmed on Nov. 11, 1940, their intention to collaborate in post-war Europe. Dr. Benes, President of the Czech Republic, is seen above with General Sikorski, the Polish Prime Minister, during an inspection of Czech troops in Britain. Undergoing intensive training in this country, Czech soldiers man a machine-gun (circle); an important part of their training is physical drill, and the men seem to like it.

Photos, Planet News, Central Press, Sport & General

OUR DIARY OF THE WAR

TUESDAY, FEB. 25, 1941   *542nd day*

On the Sea—H.M. destroyer Exmoor, escorting convoy in North Sea, was sunk during attack by German E-boats.

In the Air—R.A.F. made offensive sweep over Channel by day and shipping off French coast was also attacked. Three enemy fighters destroyed. Submarine depot at Flushing bombed.

At night Bomber Command attacked industrial targets in the Ruhr and aerodromes in occupied France. Separate raids made on ports of Boulogne, Dunkirk and Calais.

War against Italy—Cairo reported further advance south of Cubcub, Eritrea. S.A.A.F. bombed targets at Nefasit, east of Asmara.

Advanced elements of East and West African troops captured Mogadishu.

Nairobi announced that Abyssinian irregulars had captured both British and Italian Moyale and area had been occupied by S. African troops.

During night of 24-25, R.A.F. raided Tripoli, heavily damaging power station.

Castellorizo, small Italian island with seaplane base in eastern Mediterranean, occupied by British forces.

Two Dorniers shot down off Malta.

Home Front—No daylight raids. At night incendiaries and high explosives fell over a S.E. coast town and a N.E. town. German night bomber shot down in East Anglia.

Balkans—Mr. Eden and Gen. Sir John Dill arrived in Ankara for military talks.

WEDNESDAY, FEB. 26   *543rd day*

In the Air—R.A.F. made daylight sweep over Northern France. Calais docks attacked.

Short but fierce air battle over south-east coast during afternoon, British fighters driving raiders back over Channel.

Bomber Command carried out heavy night attack on industrial targets in Cologne. Fires started at Boulogne and Flushing. Air bases in Northern France bombed and machine-gunned by fighter patrols.

War against Italy—Following capture of Mogadishu enemy forces surrendering in large numbers. Bardera occupied.

Malta raided by dive-bombers, seven of which were shot down and others damaged.

Home Front—Few bombs dropped during day in Kent and East Anglia. At night there were widespread raids. Many houses wrecked in south-east town. Welsh coastal town and one in S. Wales suffered heavy attacks.

Nazi bomber shot down over S. Wales by A.A. fire. Two others damaged, probably destroyed, by night fighters.

THURSDAY, FEB. 27   *544th day*

On the Sea—Heinkel hit by small naval units in North Sea.

War against Italy—Cairo announced that advanced elements of British mechanized forces had driven back German armoured units west of Agheila, Libya.

In Eritrea British forces had occupied Kelemit, 30 miles north of Keren. R.A.F. bombed Keren area and targets at Assab.

Home Front—Many daylight attacks made by single aircraft, chiefly along East Coast, causing considerable damage and some casualties. No night raids.

Greek War—Athens reported lively artillery action in certain areas. R.A.F. attacked aerodrome at Valona and shot down seven Italian aircraft. Greek A.A. fire destroyed two more.

FRIDAY, FEB. 28   *545th day*

In the Air—During night R.A.F. heavily attacked Wilhelmshaven, Emden, naval barracks near Lorient, and Boulogne.

War against Italy—German bomber shot down near Benghazi, Libya. Cairo announced that in Eritrea British troops were in contact with enemy north of Keren.

Admiralty and War Office issued joint statement that British forces which landed on island of Castellorizo had been withdrawn, having accomplished their object.

Enemy raided Malta, causing some casualties and considerable damage to property.

Home Front—Few bombs fell at Dover. At night raiders were over London and number of flats were damaged.

Greek War—R.A.F. shot down 27 Italian aircraft over Albania and damaged nine more.

Balkans—Communiqué issued at Ankara stated that there was complete Anglo-Turkish accord.

General—King Alfonso died at Rome.

SATURDAY, MARCH 1   *546th day*

In the Air—Fighter Command destroyed three enemy fighters during offensive sweep over Northern France. German bomber shot down in Channel.

Bomber Command made heavy night attack on Cologne, and on docks, railway targets and oil installations in the Ruhr, Rotterdam and Boulogne.

War against Italy—Kufra, S. Libyan oasis, surrendered to Free French Forces.

In Eritrea British captured important pass covering approach to Keren.

R.A.F. bombed targets at Valona and Berat. One fighter pilot shot down three enemy machines.

Home Front—Night raiders attacked a town on East Coast. Considerable enemy activity over other parts of the country. Night bomber shot down off Scottish coast.

Balkans—Bulgaria signed Tri-partite Pact at Vienna. German troops marched into Sofia and occupied Black Sea port of Varna.

General—Mr. John G. Winant, new U.S. Ambassador to Britain, arrived in England.

SUNDAY, MARCH 2   *547th day*

In the Air—Aircraft of Coastal Command bombed aerodromes at Borkum and Haamstede and port of Harlingen.

Enemy convoy in North Sea was attacked and one vessel torpedoed amidships. Aircraft of Bomber Command raided seaplane base at List and enemy shipping off Dutch Islands.

At night Brest was heavily bombed, particularly dock where cruiser of Hipper class was berthed. Other aircraft attacked enemy aerodromes.

War against Italy—Cairo stated that Gojjam Patriot forces had inflicted losses on Italian garrison of Burye, Abyssinia.

Enemy positions in and around Keren attacked by R.A.F. and S.A.A.F.

Village of Abruzzi, 80 miles north of Mogadishu, was occupied.

Home Front—Slight enemy activity by day. Bombs fell on north Scottish coastal town and at a place in East Anglia. Nazi bomber shot down off east coast. At night short but sharp raid made on small south-west town.

Greek War—R.A.F. heavily bombed aerodrome at Berat.

Balkans—Mr. Eden and Sir John Dill arrived in Athens for military talks.

MONDAY, MARCH 3   *548th day*

On the Sea—Admiralty reported that H.M. trawler Ouse had been sunk.

In the Air—Heavy night raid on Cologne. Other targets were docks at Calais, Ostend and Brest, and many aerodromes.

War against Italy—Advance in Italian Somaliland proceeding. Isha Baidoa and Bulo Burti, 130 miles from Mogadishu, occupied.

R.A.F. shot down five Italian bombers near Corfu.

Home Front—During day bombs fell on town in Kent. At night Cardiff was heavily attacked. Many casualties and considerable damage. Three towns on N.E. coast were raided and bombs fell over S.E. Scotland. Enemy aircraft also reported from west Midland town, S.E. coast town, East Anglia and London. Bomber shot down by A.A. fire near Cardiff.

Enemy fighter destroyed near Kent coast. German bomber crashed in Co. Wexford.

Balkans—German troops, spreading through Bulgaria, reached Greek frontier.

OUR BALKANS WAR GAZETTEER

Adrianople (Edirne). Turkey; on R. Maritsa at its confluence with the Tunja; 137 miles west north-west of Istanbul; captured by Bulgarians in 1913, but restored to Turkey in same year. Pop. about 40,000.

Ankara (Angora). Cap. of Turkey; on Angora river, about 220 miles from Istanbul. Created capital in 1923 and contains Government buildings and fine modern streets. Pop. about 120,000.

Athens. Cap. of Greece; built on and around a group of hills, about 4 miles from its port, the Piraeus (pop. about 200,000); situated in an extensive plain watered by the Ilissus and Cephissus. Pop. about 400,000.

Bucharest (Bukarest). Cap. of Rumania; on R. Dombovitza, a tributary of the Danube; centre of the country's road and railway system. Pop. 650,000.

Constanza. Rumania; in the Dobruja, (Southern Dobruja was ceded to Bulgaria by Rumania on August 21, 1940); on Black Sea, 140 miles east of Bucharest and principal Rumanian port; docks cover over 150 acres; exports grain and petroleum. Pop. about 60,000.

Istanbul (Constantinople). Former cap. of Turkey; lies on shores of the Bosphorus; the Golden Horn, an inlet of the Sea of Marmora which divides the city into two parts (Stamboul and Galata), forms a fine harbour. Pop. 750,000.

Philippopolis (Plovdiv). Bulgaria; on R. Maritsa, about 100 miles west of Adrianople; junction on railway from Sofia to Istanbul; manufactures textiles and is a busy commercial centre. Pop. about 100,000.

Salonica (Thessalonica). Greece; at head of Gulf of Salonica, has a magnificent harbour and is a busy railway junction; about 140 miles south-west of Sofia; one of the most important ports of south-eastern Europe; founded from Corinth in 315 B.C. The town and surrounding country was turned into a vast fortified camp when the French and British landed an expeditionary force in 1915. Pop. about 250,000.

Sofia (Sophia). Cap. of Bulgaria; situated on a plain below the Rhodope Mountains, 407 miles north-west of Istanbul; seat of Government and a Greek metropolitan; created cap. in 1878. Pop. about 300,000.

Smyrna (Izmir). Turkey; on west coast of Asia Minor at the head of the Gulf of Smyrna; great commercial centre; built partly on the slopes of Mount Pagus; chief seaport of Asiatic Turkey; exports include carpets, tobacco, silk, wool and hides; connected with Ankara and Istanbul by railway. Pop. about 170,000.

Varna. Bulgaria; fortified seaport on Black Sea; good harbour; 325 miles by railway from Sofia. Pop. about 70,000.

FLAMES OVER NORWAY: LOFOTEN'S OIL TANKS FIRED BY THE BRITISH

During the brilliant raid on the Lofoten Islands carried out by British forces on March 4, 1941, 26 oil plants in the islands were completely wrecked. British soldiers are here standing by while some of the storage tanks burn furiously. The fish oil plant on the Lofoten Islands was one of the Nazis' biggest sources of glycerine for making explosives, for more than half of Norway's annual output of eight million gallons were produced there. The raid, which took the Nazis completely by surprise, robbed them of 50,000 barrels of oil, and the wrecked plant will take a long time to replace.

Photo, British Official: Crown Copyright

Once Again Bulgaria Takes the Wrong Turning

Only a few weeks after Rumania had been occupied by German troops, her southern neighbour, the kingdom of Bulgaria, fell into Hitler's clutches. So soon was Mr. Churchill's warning, made on February 9, that if the Balkan countries did not stand together they would be pulled to pieces, one by one, justified by the event.

"UNDULY confident of victory." That was the phrase used by Mr. Rendel, British Minister in Sofia, to describe the attitude of M. Filoff, the Bulgarian Premier, when the latter accepted from his hands the Note in which Britain announced her decision to break off diplomatic relations with Bulgaria. "I reminded him," went on Mr. Rendel, "that Mussolini was also confident of German victory, but had suffered

"INDEPENDENCE DAY"
(March 3 is celebrated as Bulgaria's Independence Day)
Cartoon by George Whitelaw in the "Daily Herald"

severely as a result. I told him that others might suffer, too."

Perhaps there was very little that M. Filoff could say, for he had already burned his boats behind him. When he saw Mr. Rendel on March 5 there were still fresh in his memory the scenes of his visit to Vienna, four days before, when on behalf of his government he signed the Tripartite Pact, formally linking Bulgaria with the fortunes of Britain's enemies. Perhaps he was still bemused by the splendid reception which had been given him. Maybe he recalled the scene in the Yellow Hall of the Belvedere Palace, ablaze with lights and glittering with be-medalled uniforms . . . his signing of the impress-

IN THE BALKANS the situation changes from day to day as Hitler's aggressive designs take shape, but this map shows the position following the seizure of Bulgaria. *By courtesy of the "Daily Telegraph"*

ive-looking document lying on the table before him, and how 63 others had put their signatures after his . . . how he, the representative of one of Europe's smaller countries, had mixed on terms of equality—at least, so it seemed—with the representatives of powerful Germany and Japan, even of Italy and Hungary. (Though perhaps coming events cast just a shadow before them as he watched the delegates of Rumania and Slovakia signing in their turn, for not so long ago Rumania and Czechoslovakia were sovereign states of Europe, whereas now they numbered among Hitler's vassals. And Bulgaria was about to share their vassaldom.)

In his speech to his hosts, the Bulgarian Premier made much of what he described as the hard conditions of the Peace Treaty, and paid tribute to "the Axis Powers and their great leaders, Adolf Hitler and Benito Mussolini," to whom Bulgaria owed the return of Southern Dobruja. He did not

say what Hitler had offered Bulgaria in return for her allegiance, but it was generally understood that, lavish as always in the distribution of other people's property, the Fuehrer had promised her most of the Greek coast on the Aegean. In reply, the German Foreign Minister, von Ribbentrop, waxed eloquent concerning the policy pursued by the States of the Three-Power Pact. Always it had been their aim, he said, and always it would remain so, to fulfil and to safeguard the vital claims of their nations for territories which ought to be theirs by Nature—claims against those powers " who are living in an abundance of territory, and while too sterile and incapable of using them are grudging them to the young nations."

All these European peoples, he went on, now realized that " instead of their former insecure life in a conglomeration of European states constantly fighting each other and dependent on Great Britain's mercy, they will in future be able to live in the safety of a continent independent of Great Britain, and made secure by the powerful Axis states." Which must have sounded a little strange in Filoff's ears, than whom none could know better that Britain had next to no interest in Bulgaria ; even our trade with Bulgaria, never very great, has dwindled to nothing. Unfortunately, let us add, for if our economic links with Bulgaria and the other Balkan states had been more and stronger, then Germany would not have

Over the Balkans Spread the German Hordes

THE MARCH INTO BULGARIA was in full swing by the beginning of March, 1941, and it was reported from Sofia that about 200,000 men had crossed the German-Bulgarian frontier on one day, while tanks, lorries and military cars streamed along the roads towards the Greek and Turkish frontiers.

Right, a German armoured car is crossing a bridge in Bulgaria on March 2; the photograph was radioed from Berlin to New York and thence to London.

NAZIS IN RUMANIA explained their presence by the necessity to defend the Rumanian oilfields against attacks from Britain! Centre, a Nazi light anti-aircraft gun is in position near oil-storage tanks. Left, a hangar on a Rumanian airfield with German mechanics overhauling one of the 'planes. The rings on the wing of the right-hand machine are the identification mark of Rumanian Air Force 'planes — red, yellow and blue concentric circles, with the red on the outside.

Photos, Associated Press

In the Balkan Ferment Turkey Stands Fast

PRINCE PAUL of Yugoslavia, who is said to have met Ribbentrop, and Ciano following the Nazi seizure of Bulgaria, when pressure was put upon him to join the Axis, is here talking to Hitler during an earlier meeting.

MR. G. W. RENDEL, British Minister at Sofia, who conveyed to M. Filoff, Bulgarian Premier, on March 5, Britain's formal announcement of her breaking off relations with Bulgaria.   *Photos, Fox; "The Times"*

be spared visitations by British bombers. A few hours later the German detachments moving down the Struma Valley had arrived at Bulgaria's southern frontier, only 65 miles from the great Greek port of Salonika, and they were not far from the Turkish.

Not all the Bulgarians, however, were so pleased with the Pact as M. Filoff professed to be, and the critics were encouraged by Russia's attitude. In its reply to a Bulgarian note, stating that the Bulgarian government had given its consent to the entry of German troops into Bulgaria so as to preserve peace in the Balkans, the Soviet Government remarked that the step " will lead not to the preservation of peace, but to an extension of the conflict, and to the involvement of Bulgaria therein." The Turks, too, were scornful of the Bulgarian plea. In Ankara the news of Bulgaria's adhesion to the Axis was received with a shrug of the shoulders. But it made not an atom of difference to Turkey's attitude. Her alliance was with Britain, and so far from recent events changing her attitude, she was now more than ever resolved to stand by her Ally until victory be won.

THE BRITISH MILITARY MISSION made a tour of Turkish military zones early in February. On February 15 Lt.-Gen. Sir J. H. Marshall-Cornwall, D.S.O., and Air Vice-Marshal Elmhirst, of the Middle East Command, left Ankara after highly successful staff talks. This photo shows Lt.-Gen. Sir J. H. Marshall-Cornwall inspecting Turkish troops at Ankara station.   *Photo, Associated Press*

Field-Marshal LIST, German blitzkrieg expert, who commands the German forces on the Bulgarian-Greek frontier, is seen during the Nazi occupation of Czechoslovakia in 1939.   *Photo, Associated Press*

been able to secure that economic predominance which has proved the prelude to political domination.

But Britain is far away, and Germany is very near. In the circumstances in which he found himself, M. Filoff, like Mr. Chamberlain at Munich, could perhaps do no other than he did. He knew full well that, while he was in the Belvedere, German troops, who for weeks past had been massing on the north bank of the Danube, were actually crossing the stream into his country. About eight o'clock on the preceding evening the electricity supply was cut off in Ruschuk, the town on the Bulgarian side of the Danube opposite Giurgiu, the centre of German assembly. Under cover of the darkness a pontoon bridge, which had been run down stream, was floated into position, and shortly before midnight the first uniformed German soldiers went across it and toiled up the

slope to Ruschuk, to join their comrades not in uniform who were already in Bulgaria.

Certainly these forerunners had done their work well. Air-raid listening posts, food dumps and barracks had been arranged and were already under Nazi control. Underground hangars were reported to be under construction, radio stations had been established, the military telephone system was in full working order, and headquarters had been chosen for the German Staff at Chamkuria, 43 miles from Sofia.

Crossing the Danube not only at Ruschuk but at Nikopol and Vidin, the German forces, mechanized units in the main, poured across Bulgaria in the direction of the Greek and Turkish frontiers. Varna, Bulgaria's most important Black Sea port, was occupied on Sunday, March 2, and so, too, was Sofia, although the capital itself was declared an open city in the hope that thereby it would

Were the Italians *Really* Glad to See Them?

Nazi anti-aircraft guns as well as 'planes have made their appearance in Italy. Here a caterpillar tractor is pulling one of the guns over rough ground, a German officer superintending.

NAZI AIRMEN IN ITALY first arrived there in December 1940 and a friendly reception for this " new Italian striking unit," as it was officially called, was carefully engineered. Circle left, the commander of a squadron in a town of South Italy thanks the people for their cordial welcome. Above, bombs made in Germany are being unloaded by German armourers on an Italian airfield. Circle right, a Nazi bomber is heading for Malta, but the Nazi attacks on the island have been no more successful than those of the Regia Aeronautica.

Photos, Associated Press

The Navy Knocks at Hitler's Back Door

Swooping out of the blue on the Lofoten Islands, a joint British and Norwegian force delivered a lightning thrust at Hitler's power in this northern extremity of his realm. Below we tell the story of the raid of March 4, as it has been revealed in a joint Admiralty and Norwegian Naval communiqué, supplemented by the eye-witness account by Reuter's Special Correspondent.

EARLY on the morning of Tuesday, March 4, in cold so intense that the spray froze as it broke over the boats, an Anglo-Norwegian raiding force made its appearance off the Lofoten Islands in the channel leading to Narvik, on what has been described as "Hitler's back doorstep."

The raid was planned with a threefold object. In the first place it was desired to destroy the plant used for the production of fish oil. This is the season in the Lofoten area in which the production of fish oil takes place, and the whole of the fishery products, like all other Norwegian products required by Germany, are entirely absorbed by the enemy; the fish oil produced was of particular importance to Germany, as it is used as glycerine in the making of explosives. The second object was to destroy any German ships or ships under German control found in the locality. Thirdly, it was desired to take prisoner Germans concerned in the control of the fishing industries, and such local "Quislings" who were aiding and abetting the enemy.

THE LOFOTEN ISLANDS, scene of the daring Anglo-Norwegian raid of March 4. They cover the entrance to Narvik fjord.

The raiders were composed of hand-picked and specially-trained British troops and Norwegian marines armed with Tommy-guns and accompanied by Norwegian guides. Arrived off their objectives—Svolvær and three other principal fishing ports of the islands—the landing-parties were put ashore before anyone there had time to discover what was happening.

"Within ten minutes of landing," said Reuter's Special Correspondent, who accompanied one of the parties, "the troops had taken control of the telegraph station, post office, and police office. Next they turned their attention to the oil, cod liver oil, and cod-fishing factories known to be working for the Germans, and soon six of these had been destroyed. The English manager of one factory was rescued and brought back to Britain. Three petrol storage tanks were also destroyed by this group, one going up in flames."

Explosions, intermittent gunfire and clouds of smoke told of the progress of the raiding-parties. Fish-oil factories and a power station were destroyed and the oil storage tanks set on fire. One of the parties sank a 10,000-ton floating fish-oil factory after taking from the ship a number of prisoners. Altogether, nine German vessels and one Norwegian merchant vessel under German control were sent to the bottom, and also a German armed trawler. Losses inflicted upon enemy shipping totalled approximately 18,000 tons.

Every care was taken to safeguard the lives and property of the local people, and the opportunity was taken to supply them with "comforts" such as chocolate, cocoa, tobacco, cigarettes, flannel, leather and knitting-wool—all things which they had been robbed of since the German occupation. Some of the fishermen bartered their fish with the men in the warships for English cigarettes and bully-beef.

Having achieved all their objects, the Allied forces withdrew. But they went back more numerous than when they came, for they took with them 215 German prisoners—mostly seamen, but including several naval officers, two of high rank, and 20 German airmen—and ten of the local "Quislings." They were also accompanied by a number of Norwegian Loyalists, for powerful loud-speakers had been used to state that the crews would be willing to take on board any volunteers for the Norwegian Free Forces. Hundreds of young men immediately responded, and as the ships were there for several hours they had time to get their best clothes and pack up all they wanted.

Practically no opposition was encountered, the little there was coming from the German armed trawler, which returned the fire of one of the warships, but was quickly disposed of. One German naval officer and six ratings were killed, but no damage or casualties were sustained by our forces.

When, after hours of unmolested activity, the raiders withdrew they glanced back at a dense black column of smoke billowing out far above the clouds, while another enveloped the mountains for miles in a thick foglike pall. Only when the ships had left the islands behind them did a solitary German aeroplane make its appearance. But before it could drop a single bomb it was driven off by fire from the warships.

Swiftly the warships returned to Britain, where the prisoners were sent to a prison-camp and the patriots proceeded to London. There they had the intense gratification of being congratulated by King Haakon.

Their task completed, the raiders prepare to leave Stansund, one of the ports visited, while the wrecked oil plant burns furiously.
Photo, British Official: Crown Copyright

Snatched from Norway, the Prisoners Come Aboard

THE LOFOTEN RAID yielded a " bag " of 215 German prisoners—soldiers, sailors and airmen. When the British squadron was at sea the captives were brought up on deck and transferred, blindfolded so that they should see nothing of what was happening, to another ship. They are here formed up on the deck of the first ship, each man with his hands on the shoulders of the man in front of him, ready to follow their leader on board the other vessel. With them were ten " Quislings " who, with the prisoners, were sent to a British prison-camp, while the 300 Norwegian patriots who were taken off the islands entrained for London.

Photo, British Official: Crown Copyright

Pages from the Prison Diary of a British Officer

How British prisoners fare in Germany is a subject of anxious interest to the relatives and friends of more than 40,000 of our soldiers, sailors and airmen. Here we give a first-hand account of everyday life in an officers' prison camp, in the shape of extracts from the diary of Captain C. A. Hood, R.A., of Oxshott, Surrey. For permission to reproduce the extracts we are indebted to the courtesy of the " Surrey Comet."

O N May 29, 1940, Captain Hood's battery was part of the British Expeditionary Force which was fighting its way towards the coast after the collapse of the Allied line in Belgium. " Spiked everything and walked out of Cassel, 9.30 p.m." is the laconic but pregnant entry in his diary for that day. Next on May 30 we read, " Held up by machine-gun fire at 5.30 a.m. Captured 10 a.m. after being chased by tanks and machine-gun fire . . ." Then came days of marching or travel by car or truck until eventually he found himself one of the 1,400 officers and orderlies confined in Oflag VII C/H at Laufen, a small village in Bavaria on the Salzach, about 10 miles north-west of Salzburg (*see* map in page 101). There he continued to keep his diary, from which the following entries are extracted.

July 9. Weather broken a bit now, but has been good. Usual sort of day is coffee at 7 a.m., roll call parade 9.15, walk or sit in the field till lunch at 11. Then sleep for an hour, and then there are usually three lectures of about three-quarters of an hour up to 4.15. Tea, soup, and potatoes, with cheese as an extra on Sundays, is at 5. We usually stay in the garden till about 7, and then play bridge or some other cards till bed at about 10.

July 16. Have had a pullover from Red Cross parcel, so don't send one. Small excitement last week sharing Red Cross food, one parcel to eight. Made a change, and small pieces of luxury were very welcome.

August 13. Red Cross have guaranteed delivery of this, so will repeat some of previous letters in case they haven't arrived. " Rowley" (Second-Lieutenant M. Rowland) and seven others are here. Am very well indeed, but am in need of a few things, which please try to have sent. Parcels are allowed up to 10 pounds. Any sort of tinned food is welcome as diet is plain. Would like chocolate, golden syrup, barley sugar, bully

RED CROSS PARCELS for British prisoners of war are now delivered with minimum delay. The parcels section of the British Red Cross is now under the direction of Mr. Stanley Adams, above, who as a former general manager of Messrs. Thomas Cook & Son has unrivalled experience of Continental traffic routes.   *Photo, Associated Press*

beef fortnightly, and tobacco. We have lovely views of mountain and woodland scenery, and there is a garden running down to river. Two beds of antirrhinums and dahlias are very fine.

September 9. We get some food in bulk from Red Cross, but when divided doesn't come to much. Tails well up here.

Sept. 17. Weather is colder now, snow is staying on some of the higher mountain tops, looks grand in the sunlight, colours especially marvellous at sunset. Great doings today, delivery of Red Cross parcels. Shared one between four, most we have had so far. It is wonderful what a difference even a small portion of bully beef or sausage makes to a rather monotonous soup diet.

Oct. 1. Hooray ! Your letter of August 13 arrived September 24. So glad to get news. Well done for sticking out. It was greatest concern when realized that notification was taking a long time. Tails still up. We can take it.

Oct. 15. News is the most important thing here. This is a large camp, very full, 27 in my room. Manage to keep occupied all day. Have two piano recitals (range from Handel to swing duets), and one concert weekly. Orchestra of 20 is rehearsing and will be performing shortly. During the week, there are about 140 talks, lectures, etc., on subjects from metaphysics to bee keeping and fly fishing in New Zealand or tiger hunting in India. Also we have a good library. Weather at the moment fine, very warm in the sun ; can sit out to read or for lectures. Trees about are a grand sight. Your letter of August 14-17 received. Red Cross parcels still very scarce. Am on list for British Legion, but no luck yet.

Oct. 29. Letters of September 19, 23 and 27 arrived last week. Concerts are going well, one piano, one orchestral and one variety each week. Plenty of talent, pianists especially good. There were 12,500 letters in over week-end, so I should get something. No clothes or baccy arrived yet, but have had three parcels from Legion, Red Cross still sparse, only about one to four each week. Weather now cold, snowed on Sunday. My bed, if a bit hard, is warm. There are 27 in my room, which is about 15 by 30. Beds in tiers of three round the walls, tables and stools for reading, writing and eating in the middle. We have coffee at 7.30. Soup and potatoes at 11 and 4. On three days a week we have tea or coffee in lieu of soup at 4. Tea is the best " do " of the week. We also get a loaf for five days, and cheese, jam and dripping twice a week. For breakfast and supper we eat what we can save during the day. Thank all for messages sent.

TITTMONING CASTLE, UPPER BAVARIA, is now Oflag VII C/Z—Oflag being an abbreviation of Offizierslager (German for camp in which officer prisoners are confined). Right are British prisoners who have been put to work in a coal mine near their camp.   *Right-hand photo, Keystone*

Though in Enemy Hands They're in Good Heart

November 8. Have a battle dress and mac, also uniform which was luckily in my pack when I was captured on May 30. Still very well, legs and arms a bit thin, but tummy and chin are still there.

Nov. 12. Letters of August 24 and September 2 and 6 arrived. Clothes parcel is here, but have not got it yet.

Nov. 19. Clothes parcel grand. Was not allowed to keep tooth paste, windcheater or trousers, having the latter dyed. Have just had fourth British Legion parcel, and total of about four Red Cross, which have stopped now. Enjoy yourselves at Christmas. Don't worry about us ; we will make the best of it here.

Nov. 26. Since we started fires, have been having some good suppers of toasted cheese and fried or roast potatoes, and toast, rather at the expense of a few burnt fingers. Have just been issued with a peacock blue overcoat. No letters arrived for a fortnight. Please ask someone to write. Any odd news is welcome.

BRITISH PRISONERS in the hands of the Italians are very few compared with our 150,000 Italian prisoners. The photographs in this page, sent from Italy via a neutral country, purport to show, according to the Italian captions : top, British prisoners in Addis Ababa ; centre, British prisoners working in an orchard in Italy ; above, British airmen in a concentration camp in Italy.

Photos, Keystone and Associated Press

December 3. Weather grand. Frost after snow. Rather like a school. Bell goes for getting up at 7.30. Have a cold shower, and then go on parade at 9.20, usually lasts till about 10. Quarter-hour's p.t. and walk round before lunch. Have hot shower once a week, and hot water is now on tap for our washing. Makes a difference after using cold. Vests are now almost white. Had two more Legion parcels. V. good.

Dec. 10. Yours of October 31 by air mail here December 9. We have big programmes of Christmas games, etc. Ping pong, deck tennis, deck race meetings, darts and bridge. Latest theatre, Galsworthy's " Escape." Orchestra and dance band twice weekly. Pantomime for four nights. Everyone settled down now, but first three months very grim.

Dec. 17. Very cold. 32 deg. frost. Lovely snow, dry and packed hard. We hope to be able to skate in the field soon. 1,700 Red Cross parcels about one and a half each, arrived on Sunday. These are the ones which you have been told we were getting weekly, in August, I expect. Lost in second round of ping pong.

'Pages of Glory' Written by Men of Free France

France was defeated in the great battle of last summer, but French soldiers are still carrying on the war. Here we tell of some of the exploits of the Free French Army, of the men who have rallied and are rallying in ever-increasing numbers to the standard raised by General de Gaulle.

MARCHING and fighting side by side with the British and Australians in the Army of the Nile, sharing to the full the ardours and the glories of the campaign, are contingents of the Free French forces. In all the battles which have marked that triumphal campaign the French volunteers have played a most gallant and worthy part. They were in the van at the storming of Sidi Barrani, the First Battalion of French Marines being specially mentioned in an Army Order by General de Gaulle. They were hard on the heels of the Italians as they fled from Egypt into Libya, and they held a vital stretch of the front line at Bardia. They were at Tobruk and Benghazi, and still in the front line somewhere in the Libyan desert they are maintaining those traditions of gallantry and endurance which have ever characterized the French soldier.

All the French troops included in the Army of the Nile are volunteers, drawn from those under the leadership of General Catroux, High Commissioner of Free France in the Near East. Some escaped from Syria with Colonel (now General) de Larminat when that great territory was involved in the collapse of Metropolitan France, among them being detachments of the Foreign Legion, colonial infantry, and Spahis. Some have come from the Free French Army which has been established at Ismailia on the Suez Canal, and some are colonial troops which had been stationed in Cyprus, by agreement with Britain, since the beginning of the war. Yet others have come from all parts of the world, men resolved to do what in them lies to wipe out the stain of the surrender at Compiègne.

Raiding the Oases

But De Gaulle's men are fighting on several other fronts in Africa—wherever, indeed, they can come to grips with the Italians who " defeated " them last June. In the middle of January one little force of Free French troops made a daring and highly successful raid on the Italian positions in Murzuk, in the Fezzan oasis (see page 144). Another little detachment of General de Larminat's Free French forces in Chad—it consisted of a motorized column, just a handful of officers and perhaps 100 Senegalese soldiers under the command of Col. Leclerc—besieged the Italian garrison in the oasis of Kufra from Feb. 7 until March 1, when it surrendered. A thousand prisoners and much war material were taken by the French.

While Kufra was being besieged, there came from Vichy a curious report that General de Larminat's troops had attacked and captured the Italian garrison at Ghadames, on the southern border of Tunisia, about 250 miles south-west of Tripoli. As Ghadames is separated by some 600 miles of desert from the Free French base in Equatorial Africa, it seems much more likely that it was captured by another body of French troops—by men who, though not professing open allegiance to Free France, yet are patriots who could not resist an opportunity of striking a blow against the enemy who had so foully stabbed their country in the back. " Bravo, my comrades," broadcast

General de Larminat to North Africa ; " Tomorrow you will be with us ! "

Yet another detachment of General de Larminat's Free French Army left Fort Lamy, in the heart of Equatorial Africa, early in December, and crossed some thousands of miles of the jungle, desert and mountain in their lorries until they made contact two months later with the British in the Sudan. They carried their own equipment—rifles, machine-guns, ammunition and trench mortars—and arrived on the other side of Africa without losing a single vehicle ; they wanted only artillery to be ready for action, and that was soon supplied them by the British. Then with their guns and lorries they were taken to Port Sudan on the Red Sea, whence they were carried by British transports to the Italian port of Marsa Taklai, just captured by the British. They were landed under cover of darkness on February 22— hundreds of fine fighting men, Senegalese all save for their officers and N.C.O.s. Commanding them was a colonel who was in the French secret service, and a member of the Franco-German Armistice Commission until his escape from France at the end of last November. Another battalion left Chad territory on January 1, and at the beginning of March was engaged in the operations directed against Keren in Eritrea ; this battalion towards the end of February took

General Catroux, who was Governor of French Indo - China before he came to England to join General de Gaulle's Free French Force in the Near East, is seen left at Alexandria in January 1941. With him is a representative of Free France with whom he had been in conference. Above, a trumpeter of the Free French Force in the Western Desert stands beneath the tricolor and sounds the " reveille."

Photos, British Official : Crown Copyright ; and Wide World

The battle-fronts in Africa on which a French Army is still maintaining its great traditions and winning new glory for France.

a brilliant part in the capture of Cub Cub. Then the French Foreign Legion is also amongst the comrades of the British Army in East Africa. They were landed at Port Sudan towards the end of February, thousands of laughing, singing légionnaires. Forty-six nationalities are represented among

them—French, Poles and Belgians, Dutch and Greeks, Americans, Spaniards, even Italians and Germans. Less than a year ago they were in the front line at Narvik, where they were bombed day and night ; then they were evacuated to Brest, and held the line around Rennes in Brittany. After the French Army collapsed, their C.O. managed somehow to get them transported to England, whence they went to Libreville via Dakar.

These, then, are some, but only some, of the exploits of the soldiers of Free France, of the men whose emblem is the Cross of Lorraine. " I as their leader "—it is General de Gaulle speaking—" say that the heroic deeds of our soldiers at Tobruk, Murzuk and Kassala, of our sailors of the submarine Narval [whose loss through enemy action was announced on January 9], of our airmen in the skies of Libya and Abyssinia, are pages of glory which our children's children will read with pride. But I also say that these magnificent episodes will soon be followed by even greater action."

They March to War in the Middle East

PATRIOTIC FRENCHMEN in France's African Empire found the Armistice with the Nazis little to their liking, and after General de Gaulle's clarion call to Frenchmen on June 23, 1940, many began to slip across the frontiers and take service under the banner of Free France. Here, near their desert outpost, men of the Free French Colonial Infantry are marching past at an inspection in the autumn of 1940. It was to such men that General de Gaulle referred on January 31, 1941, when in a broadcast he said: " the feats of our soldiers at Tobruk, Murzuk and Kassala . . . are pages of glory which our children's children will read with pride."

Photo, British Official : Crown Copyright

Now the Watchword is: 'On To Addis Ababa!'

While there was little to report from the Libyan war zone, from East Africa there continued to come news of fresh Italian losses, of fresh victories won by the armies of General Cunningham and the Abyssinian Patriots. Below we give some further account of the progress of that campaign which is being waged so successfully and at so small a cost.

AFTER the capture of Mogadishu on February 25, General Cunningham's troops drove the enemy northwards along the road which links Mogadishu with Jigiga, a town of considerable importance just east of Harar, on the railway from Jibuti to Addis Ababa. As their drive continued the situation of the Italians to the east and in British Somaliland became ever more precarious, for Harar is the key. to the communications between these regions and Central Abyssinia. If Harar fell, then their doom would be sealed.

Little fight, indeed, was left in the Italians, who in a campaign of three weeks had been forced to cede a territory as large as the British Isles and had lost 21,000 men in casualties and prisoners. So many were the prisoners, indeed, that at Mogadishu the conquerors were unable to deal with them all at once, so that several officers and 1,100 men of the shattered Italian Army when they expressed their desire to surrender were told by the British that " they couldn't be bothered," so " come back again to-morrow ! " Thus the Italians who so wanted to be prisoners were compelled to spend a night on the beach with not even one British soldier to look after them. The next morning they came back as instructed, and this time their surrender was accepted.

The great haul of prisoners, as well as huge quantities of arms, fuel, food and stores—not to mention five Italian merchant ships captured in the harbour of Kismayu—were secured at the cost of a mere handful of casualties. Up to February 27 the total British casualties in the Somaliland campaign were stated to be 205—95 East and West African and 110 South African. The figures are proof

positive of the overwhelming superiority of the Imperial troops in the field of battle, but they are also proof of fine staff work and splendid leadership. Time after time in East Africa, as in the Western Desert, the enemy found themselves surrounded or outflanked and gave themselves up knowing their position to be hopeless.

Following General Cunningham's victory, the occupied territories, " formerly ruled, claimed, or occupied by the Italian Government in Ethiopia and Somaliland," were placed under his military jurisdiction. After issuing a stern warning that actions against the public peace or the British forces would be punishable by death, or lesser penalties, the General in his proclamation declared that " all existing laws, customs, rights and properties in the said territories will be fully respected in so far as they are consistent with my proclamations. So long as the inhabitants remain peaceable and comply with my orders they will be subjected to no more interference than I consider essential to the performance of my duties. And they need have no fear." General Cunningham's authority was exercised through officers of the Kenya Administration well versed in native laws and ways.

Abyssinian 'Robin Hoods'

Meanwhile in Abyssinia the revolt of the Patriots against the Italian invader was growing day by day in strength. The great north-western province of Gojjam and the district of Wolkait, bordering the Sudan, were practically abandoned by the Italians and the revolt swept through the key central province of Shoa to the very gates of Addis Ababa. The capital, according to refugees' accounts, was by now an armed camp

surrounded by barbed-wire defences through which no one could pass without a permit. The city was virtually besieged by bands of guerillas under Arregai, who commanded a battalion of the Imperial Guard under Haile Selassie and just before his country's fall was the city's police chief. He had never been more than 100 miles away from Addis Ababa, and as head of the secret league of Abyssinian Robin Hoods known as the Society of Ethiopian Braves had kept up constant communication with the Emperor and his representatives.

Capture of Burye

The first major success of the reborn Imperial Army was the capture of the Italian stronghold of Burye, 160 miles north-west of Addis Ababa. After standing a week's siege, the Italian garrison, unnerved by the R.A.F.'s relentless bombing, weakened by desertions of the native conscripts, and having just heard the news of the fall of the small fort of Mankusa, 10 miles away, decided on evacuation, and under cover of darkness made its escape by mountain tracks. On March 5 Haile Selassie's standard, the crowned lion on a green, gold and red tricolor, floated proudly over the Italian commander's headquarters. The Patriots pursued the enemy along the road through the rolling parkland in the direction of Debra Markos, 40 miles to the south-east. With them, never far from the front line, was their Emperor, who cheered them by his words and was greeted with the most fervent enthusiasm. With the province of Gojjam practically cleared of the enemy, the Patriots and their British allies had a new watchword : " On to Addis Ababa !."

General Sir Archibald Wavell (centre), commanding Britain's Army in the Middle East, is here seen making an inspection, accompanied by Major-General W. Platt, commander of the British Army in the Sudan. The map, right, is a guide to distances in Italian East Africa, where British troops are operating on so many fronts.   *Photo, British Official:* *Crown Copyright. Map by courtesy of the " Manchester Guardian"*

How a Filter Beat the Libyan Sands

Mr. C. G. Vokes, inventor of the Vokes Aero filter, is seen studying plans of his ingenious device, described in this page; a factory worker (right) drills the casing for the filter.

Photographs specially taken for The War Illustrated *by John Heddon*

HUNDREDS of men and women worked day and night and gave up their holidays to enable the Army of the Nile to advance to the capture of Cyrenaica. Their unceasing toil, backing the inventive genius of Mr. Cecil Gordon Vokes, an engineer who has never failed to solve any problem of filtration set before him, enabled British tanks and aeroplanes to be fitted with filters to beat a more persistent and dangerous enemy than the Italians—sand.

Sand very quickly chokes the engines of tanks and aeroplanes operating in the desert. It gets into the bearings, rapidly wearing out good engines, shortening the life of valuable mechanized vehicles. Some time ago it was realized that something would have to be done if our forces were to advance across the desert with any chance of success.

In ten days Mr. Vokes designed and made a filter that would enable our tanks and other vehicles to travel 150 miles a day without the least trouble from sand. Tests on machines in this country occupied another fortnight. Then factories buckled to, working day and night so that the filters could be flown out to Egypt in time for General Wavell to launch his great attack.

And everybody knows the wonderful sweeps and drives our armoured vehicles have made out there, and the vitally essential part they have played in the victory.

At one factory engaged on filters, after it had been decided to give all workers two hours off just before Christmas to do their shopping, a deputation said : " We don't want the time off. We'll shop later on. We've a job of work to do."

Mr. Vokes not only designs these filters which have contributed so much to our victories, he is the driving force behind the workers. He gives them talks on their job and the part they play in making victory secure. Recently he arranged for an airman to tell them how the filters had enabled him and his comrades to sweep the Italians from the skies.—*Story retold by courtesy of the* " *Daily Mirror.*"

The Vokes Aero filter enabled British mechanized transport to travel through sandstorms (centre) and our tank columns, like the one above, to advance unchecked across the Western Desert.
E.N.A. & British Official : Crown Copyright

H.M.S. King George V~Most Recent Symbol of

Seen from the air, Britain's great new battleship presents an even more imposing appearance than from sea level. In the photograph above the guns visible are the four 14-in. guns of the quarter-deck turret, which, top centre, are in action. In the foreground are some of her anti-aircraft guns. Top right, look-outs at action stations on the bridge. An impressive photograph of the ship is that (right) taken by an American airman when she was steaming up Chesapeake Bay carrying Lord Halifax to Washington (see also Vol. 4, p. 151).
                        Photos, British Official : Crown Copyright ; Fox and Keystone

n's 'Great, Majestic and Unrelenting Sea Power'

MR. A. V. ALEXANDER, First Lord of the Admiralty, speaking in the House of Commons on the Navy Estimates on March 5, 1941, called for "more ships, very solid ships," and for "great numbers of men, very solid men, to man them."

"The great body of the Fleet of August, 1939, remains intact," he went on ; "the number of ships in most classes, and especially in the destroyer class, now at sea or instantly ready for sea, is at the moment greater than at any time since the war began. The ships that will come into service during 1941 of themselves make up a formidable force judged by almost any other Naval Power's standards."

"The main actions of the Fleet during the past year unfold a story of great, majestic and unrelenting sea power. . . . . In our solemn hour of national testing the Royal Navy is bearing an immense responsibility, but this is no new thing in our history. The spirit of the Royal Navy is the same as ever, and the leadership in no way inferior to that of the past."

When the Captain Orders: 'Make Smoke Screen!'

Often we read of ships-of-war putting down a smoke screen to baffle the pursuing enemy
or to veil their attacking manoeuvres. Here we have an account of the operation,
written by one who has a behind-the-scenes knowledge of how it is done.

WISPS of smoke besmirching the horizon may betray the presence of unseen ships beyond the brink. So naval engineering has devoted great attention to the science of fuel burning, enabling warships to steam economically with a clear funnel. The use of oil fuel has simplified the problem. Whatever the speed

The engine-room receives the message and immediately roars its own version of the message through the voice-pipe to the indiscreet boiler-room.

But naval strategy often demands that they should produce heavy black smoke that lies on the water to form a smoke screen. Destroyers enjoy it. They are experts! They hustle around the convoy or battlefleet with gusto, thick black smoke belching from their funnels and billowing in their wake.

Clouds of Blackness to Order

Smoke screens are made to protect a convoy, or to conceal the movements of a manoeuvring fleet, and therefore are needed in the height of action. When the captain wants a smoke screen to be made he just presses a button on the bridge. This flickers a warning light in the engine-room and gives a signal on a loud rattler. The watch-keepers are on their toes, knowing that some sort of action is pending. The artificer on watch rings the boiler-room telegraph to "Make Smoke Screen." Stokehold watch-keepers immediately switch on the special smoke-making sprayer which admits cold unvaporized oil into the blazing furnaces. Instantly, owing to incomplete combustion

of oil-fuel, huge clouds of dense black smoke roll from the funnel. This heavy smoke lies on the water forming an impenetrable barrier, blocking the enemy's view.

Prolonged smoke-making may have a harmful effect on the boilers and so recently another method has been developed. A container for smoke-making gas is mounted on the stern of the vessel. The gas is conveyed over the side of the ship by a small-diameter pipe, and when it comes in contact with the water thick white vapour is given off, which also lies solidly on the water.

The most effective smoke screens are produced when these two methods are combined. The results are perfect, and the screen lingers for a long time.

Warships also carry smoke floats in the form of drum-shaped containers, fitted so that they can be quickly dropped over the side. They give off white smoke and are dropped to mark a spot in the sea for easy manoeuvring, or perhaps to indicate precisely to another ship where a suspected U-boat is lurking.

Smoke certainly has its uses, although at times it may be "cussed most hearty" by the captain, especially when he has a convoy of coal-burning merchant ships.

The chief stoker of a destroyer just about to put to sea prepares the white smoke apparatus at the stern of the ship.

of acceleration, a warship should always steam with no trace of smoke issuing from its funnels. Those who have their daily job down below in the stokeholds are nurtured in this art; to them, steaming with a clear funnel is an inherent consideration.

And woe betide them if a pernicious puff of smoke wafts from the funnel. Long before it has dispersed an irate officer of the watch will yell down the phone: "Stop making that damn smoke!"

BY FLAG SIGNAL a destroyer leader of the Tribal class is ordering the other ships of the flotilla to make a smoke screen. As soon as the order to make a black smoke screen is received in the engine-room the petty officer on watch signals through to the boiler room, right centre, and the chief stoker "gets busy" on the job.   *Photos, L. C. Roling*

Black or White, They're Excellent Cover Both

MAKING A SMOKE SCREEN—this is the explanation of the oily cloud belching from the funnel (above). Right, both black and white smoke screens are being used simultaneously ; while below, a completed smoke screen lies between the destroyers that have made it and the enemy.

Photos, L. C. Roling

They Would Have Preferred Turtle Soup!

THE PIONEER CORPS in clearing up London, have given rise to strange scenes in the City and West End. In historic Guildhall, now damaged and roofless, some of the men are seen making their own banquet among monuments of the past that once looked down upon crowned heads and famous men as they partook of the City's hospitality manifested in turtle soup and baron of beef. The lower photograph presents an equally strange contrast. Outside a famous London hotel that had been bombed a sedate waiter serves tea to the Pioneer Corps among the debris in the roadway.

Photos, "Daily Mirror," G.P.U.

Of Course, the 'Shiny Seventh' Will Be There

THE ROYAL FUSILIERS (City of London Regiment), whose nickname is the "Shiny Seventh" (because of their smart appearance), are here taking up positions beside a flood-filled dyke in England during exercises. This famous regiment was raised in 1685 under its old name of the 7th Foot. Between 1914 and 1918 forty-seven battalions were raised ; 235,476 Royal Fusiliers fought in every theatre of war except Mesopotamia, and 21,941 died for their country. The regimental badge is the united white and red rose, with the Garter and Crown above it.

Photo, Planet News

OUR SEARCHLIGHT ON THE WAR

Welcomed by the King

B Y personally meeting Mr. John G. Winant, the new American envoy, at a station during the journey to London on March 1, King George created a precedent, for this was the first time a British monarch had made such a gesture in welcoming a new Ambassador. In so doing he reciprocated the friendly act of President Roosevelt who, on January 24, sailed down Chesapeake Bay

NEW U.S. AMBASSADOR to Britain, Mr. J. G. Winant, who arrived in this country on March 1, is seen with the Duke of Kent, being greeted by the King at a railway station en route for London. The Duke met Mr. Winant at Bristol airport when the latter arrived from Lisbon.
Photo, Keystone

to greet Lord Halifax on his arrival as Ambassador to the United States. Mr. Winant, who had crossed the Atlantic to Lisbon by Clipper, flew on from there to Bristol airport, where he was welcomed by the Duke of Kent, members of the staff of the American Embassy, and many other dignitaries. " There is no place I would rather be at this time than in England," said Mr. Winant shyly into the inevitable microphone, and then drove with the Duke through the bomb-damaged streets of Bristol to the special train awaiting them. After presenting to the King his Letters of Credence, the new Ambassador had tea with their Majesties. On arrival in London, Mr. Winant went straight to the Embassy where, the following morning, his first engagement was to receive and answer the questions of over 50 British and foreign journalists. Drawing this to a close he explained : " I have come here to do a job, and I want to get to work right away."

Greek Earthquake Victims Bombed

O N March 1 the Greek town of Larissa was devastated by an earthquake. Virtually all public buildings and private houses suffered either complete or partial destruction or the cracking of their walls. Immediate help was forthcoming from detachments of the R.A.F. already in the area, first-aid squads being sent out to help in the treatment of victims who survived being buried under the debris. In addition, British bombers were flown from headquarters carrying medical supplies and a contingent of the R.A.M.C. The number of casualties has twice been increased by Italian 'planes which have dropped bombs on the stricken town. The second time this outrage was committed retribution overtook the five returning

bombers, for they were intercepted by fighters and four were brought down near Larissa. The fifth machine had to make a forced landing, and the crew were captured.

Growing Resentment in Holland

S O great is the unrest caused in Amsterdam and elsewhere by harsh treatment under the German occupation that military control was imposed upon North Holland on February 27. Jews have been, as usual, targets for special persecution by the authorities. Jewish professors at the universities of Leyden and Delft have been dismissed, and, as the result of indignant demonstrations by students and staff, these universities have been closed. Jewish businesses have had to be " Aryanized." Repeated patrols have been made in Jewish quarters by storm troopers who punished ruthlessly any disturbance created by their own provocative behaviour. Heavy fines have been imposed upon the population. Amsterdam has had to pay 15 million guilders, the equivalent of £2,000,000, following riots in that city. Because a German soldier had been shot at Hilversum, 35 citizens were imprisoned and a fine of £350,000 was levied. Many towns have been similarly penalized. Dutch mayors and other municipal officers have been superseded by German Commissioners directly responsible to the military authorities for maintaining order in their districts.

A Wavell on the Home Front

W HILE General Sir Archibald Wavell sweeps with his victorious armies through North Africa, his sister, Miss Mollie Wavell, personally sees to the creature comforts of troops in Hampshire. She is head of the Y.M.C.A. Mobile Canteen Service in that county. Her first tea car was lent to Southampton when the city was raided, and while on service there was so damaged by enemy bombs that it was rendered useless. So another was provided, and from this Miss Wavell cheers the men at nine isolated stations with hot tea and cocoa, sandwiches and biscuits, and her own heartening smile. The voluntary staff of these mobile canteens have to be women of courage, resource and pertinacity. In a bombed area, where the need is greatest, they have to cope with conditions that may include lack of water, gas and electricity, and no evident means of replenishing their supplies. They may have to cajole a road repair squad into loaning them a brazier on which to boil water – and every drop, even for washing up, may need to be boiled ; they certainly have to be able to deal with any mechanical trouble developed by the car towing the canteen trailer. All honour to the cheerfulness which they bring to their job.

Another Nazi Lie Scotched

F LYING the British flag, a German raider joined a British convoy off the Azores during the night of February 12. Early the next morning she manoeuvred into position, hoisted the German flag and opened fire, hurling salvos of shells into the ships for half an hour before vanishing over the horizon. All the vessels returned the fire and after the action was over cruised around picking up survivors. About 100 of these were landed at Funchal on February 14. The official German version of this exploit claimed that the raider had sunk 14 out of the 19 ships in the convoy, representing a displacement of 82,000 tons. The actual facts are as follows : five vessels are known to have been sunk ; eleven are safe ; the remaining three were, on March 11, not yet overdue at the ports for which they were bound.

Graziani a Prisoner in Rome ?

T HE former Italian Commander-in-Chief, Marshal Rodolfo Graziani, of great but somewhat sinister military fame, was reported to have been under house arrest in Rome after his dismissal on January 27, following the fall of Tobruk. When disaster overtook his armies the Marshal was recalled by Mussolini and, at a meeting of the Supreme War Council, is said to have disclaimed all responsibility for the defeats in North Africa and to have made some dramatic disclosures regarding his reluctance to undertake the campaign at all. According to Graziani, it was Mussolini who devised the invasion of Egypt and planned its conduct. To confirm this he laid before the Council the actual orders received from the Duce, together with copies of his own dispatches in which he most strongly opposed both the expedition and the strategy laid down for him to follow. His reasons were cogent and included the obvious difficulties of ensuring supplies of food, water, petrol and other war materials, and the danger of being encircled. Mussolini's replies to these objections, which were also laid upon the table, ignored the adverse arguments and again ordered the advance. Having submitted his defence, the Marshal formally resigned from the Fascist party and said that henceforth he would serve his country merely as a professional soldier. But the angry Duce, all for hushing up the scandal, put him secretly under arrest. Since then Graziani is reported to have been reinstated.

GEN. WAVELL'S SISTER, Miss M. Wavell, is seen in her canteen, busily serving soldiers. The Y.M.C.A. has now 510 mobile canteens on the road in Britain, and 200 more are under construction.
Photo, L.N.A.

Still the Greeks Are On Top in Albania

Greek Red Cross ambulances are seen amid the deep snows of the Albanian mountains, where a peasant woman is plodding in front of her mules—the surest means of transport in that country in winter.

A group of Greek soldiers charge with fixed bayonets through the snow-covered ruins of a mountain fort, three miles from Tepelini. It was from this mountain that the Greeks forces dislodged an Italian detachment.

RESUMING their offensive in the central sector of the Albanian front on March 7, the Greeks stormed position after position in a veritable labyrinth of trenches, artillery posts, and machine-gun nests. In three days they took nearly 2,500 prisoners, the 9th regiment of the Julia Division and the 7th Blackshirt Battalion being practically wiped out. Italian losses in killed and wounded were also extremely heavy ; ravines were said to be strewn with Italian bodies, while the pitiful groans and cries of the wounded filled the air. On the body of an unidentified major was found a personal message from Mussolini, exhorting him to do his utmost to check the Greeks. " Fascist Italy bases her last hope on your defence," it read ; " save her ! "

Circle, a Greek soldier lights a candle over the rough grave of his comrade who fell in battle on the mountain side. Above, a Greek Army tractor is seen hauling material for bridge-building along an Albanian road.

EVZONES, highlanders of the famous kilted Greek infantry regiment which corresponds roughly to the British Brigade of Guards, make friends with Albanian children (right). The King of the Hellenes' bodyguard is drawn from this regiment. (See Vol. 3, p. 620.)

Photos, Bosshard, Exclusive to THE WAR ILLUSTRATED, *Planet News, and courtesy of the Royal Greek Legation*

In Skirts or Trousers, Good Soldiers All!

Army lorries need careful handling. A.T.S. girls, such as those top, are not only quite at home at the wheels of these vehicles, but, as seen above, can carry out their own running repairs.

Speed and efficiency are demanded of the A.T.S. telephone girls. Here a corporal, who has specialized in this work, is instructing a class.

NEARLY 40,000 women and girls have joined the A.T.S., but, as the Countess of Carlisle, the Chief Commandant, said on March 3, at least 25,000 more are needed for new jobs and in new places in the Army. Some are wanted for anti-aircraft centres, where "the nimbleness of woman's mind and fingers" are of great value in the assembly of predictors, and others are required for special work with General Wavell's armies in the Middle East. Women photographers and girls who are good at figures are wanted in the Army Pay Offices and for secret work in connexion with the artillery. Recruits are most welcome between 20 and 30.

Physical fitness in the A.T.S. is helped by "physical jerks." The girl in front is French, and hopes to join General de Gaulle's Army.
Photos, " Daily Mirror," L.N.A., and Fox

Eye Witness Stories of Episodes
and Adventures in the
Second Great War.

'Our Boys of the Grom Behaved Splendidly'

Bombed by a German 'plane off Narvik in May, 1940, the Polish destroyer Grom sank in less than two minutes, and 59 of the crew lost their lives. This moving story by a Polish officer (received through the Polish Ministry of Information) tells of the sinking of his ship and the rescue of the survivors by British vessels.

ON the evening of May 2, 1940, the Grom received the order to relieve our sister-ship, Blyskawica, on a patrol off Narvik. The Blyskawica had been damaged by four hits from a German land battery and needed slight repairs. We received an additional task—to locate and to destroy the battery of guns which had damaged the Blyskawica.

The rising day, May 3, was Poland's National Day, and we of the Grom resolved to celebrate it appropriately. At 4 a.m. the Grom received her first wound. A shell fired from land pierced the starboard side and hit the boiler No. 1. That was for us the signal to begin, and the whole day long the guns of the Grom went on firing and destroying everything within range in the German positions on the shore.

In the afternoon we discovered the German battery which the day before was most probably responsible for damaging the Blyskawica. When the wind blew away the smoke of explosions and uncovered the cleverly camouflaged positions, I remember seeing the debris of German guns littered about by the tremendous force of our guns.

The morning watch on May 4 passed equally busily. The sun was just coming out from behind the mountains, and in this slanting light we could see interesting details on the German shore—two new guns, a few barbed-wire entanglements and farther to the left machine-gun emplacements on an innocent-looking hill. The commander decided that after 8 a.m. we should receive the battle order and begin with all our guns to pound the newly-discovered objectives.

While I was being relieved from my watch, one of those bright British boys who acted as signallers on the Grom, after his usual "Good-morning, sir!" said: "It's a fine day for air attacks—the sky is unusually clear."

I looked round and thought: Well, just the same as yesterday, the sun is uncannily, incredibly beautiful, the mountains as white as ever, the water in the fjord just as calm as always. And I descended into the mess for breakfast.

We hurried on with breakfast, eager for the new day, which promised to be exciting. The air-raid alarm blaring out just then did not make any impression on us. Why, someone said, they won't trouble to bomb us, if close by they can have a battleship and two cruisers as a tasty bit! And immediately afterwards the whole ship was shaken by a terrible shock, or rather, a series of rapidly following quivers.

I tried to leave the mess by the normal door leading amidships. But the gangway was full of steam, smoke and flames. I rushed through the sailors' quarters towards the prow, where men were already jumping into the water. I did not realize that things were so bad as they really were. One had such a strong, unshakable faith in the ship which for so long had been our home, our country,

everything we had. Nevertheless something terrible must have happened to our Grom, because she was listing on the port side.

The list was increasing and the wound must have been terrible. The stern became invisible; everything was covered with smoke and steam. From under the clouds of steam, from a hopelessly burning lifeboat bleeding men were crawling away.

I made my way towards the stern on the port side, climbing rather than running, for the ship was more and more turning on her side. And then I remember only the frantic effort to move away in the icy water, to swim away from the ship and not to get stiff to the bone.

The stern was now standing up vertically—the huge red and elegant stern of the Grom. The stem, completely separated, also stood out of the water. The decks of the stem and the stern were approaching each other with uncanny rapidity, like the arms of some monstrous pincers. They closed with a terrifying crash, and after a second everything disappeared under the water.

On the surface our men were struggling in the water. From the shore the Germans were firing at us with machine-guns, while away in the distance, from the end of Rombaksfjord, appeared the tiny outlines of British ships hastening to our rescue. The swimming would have been quite comfortable if it were not for that foul oil, the smell of burning, and some gas which threatened to poison one. But it was quite jolly in the water. The boys of the Grom behaved splendidly. They were offering each other lifebelts and were prodigious with mutual advice. One could hear the men in the water whistling, while those swimming close to each other were having a friendly chat.

But the groans of the wounded could also be heard, though both of us, wounded and unhurt, all believed in the brotherhood-in-arms which united us with the British Navy. And the whole world knows that no British ship has ever left sinking comrades on the sea of battle. The cruiser Aurora and the destroyers Faulknor and Bedouin pulled us out of the water.

It wasn't an easy matter. The engines had to stop in order that the boats could be launched. The whole work of rescue takes a long time, and the rescuing ship gives up its most important anti-air-raid defence: rapidity of manoeuvre. From the sunlit skies bombs might have hit them as they hit us. But the commanders, the officers and sailors of H.M. Ships Aurora, Faulknor and Bedouin did not, I am sure, think for a moment that their labour of mercy was an act of heroism.

During our long peregrinations before reaching England we met everywhere, on each British ship, warmth, care, and fore-thought that it is difficult to describe. From our wandering from ship to ship, during which we were bombed almost uninterruptedly, one great picture remained in my mind:

THE POLISH DESTROYER GROM (1) off Narvik just before she was bombed. (2) The boats of a British destroyer putting off to rescue the survivors. (3) One of the boats with rescued Polish sailors coming alongside a British ship. (4) Some of the survivors, still wearing their lifebelts, on board a British transport. *Photos, Gaumont-British Newsreel*

We were just being transferred from the battleship Resolution to our Polish Burza. The entire British crew with the officers at their head crowded the deck. Under the muzzles of the gigantic guns the ship's band took its position. The Burza moved away. We were standing on the deck, feeling rather miserable, uncertain of the future, when suddenly the crew of H.M.S. Resolution stiffened in salute as the orchestra struck up the mighty anthem : " As Long as We Live Poland Shall Not Perish ! "

As the tune of the anthem was played, I seemed to hear its words which, on the lips of the British sailors, standing upright against the might of the naval colossus, sounded like an oath : As long as we live Poland shall not perish !

We Left Norway to Fight Beside You!

When the raiders returned from the Lofoten Islands (see pages 281, 286-7), they brought with them not only a number of German prisoners but several hundreds of young Norwegians. When the latter arrived in London they had vivid tales to tell of the arrival of the raiding parties, and some of these are given below.

MORE than 300 blue-eyed and fair-haired Norwegian volunteers arrived in London on March 7. They were dressed just as they had left the Lofoten Islands four days before, some in skiing suits, others in gaily coloured jerseys and caps. The majority are fishermen or workers in the fish-oil factories.

" I was in the town when I heard a great commotion," said one six-foot-tall Norwegian in quite good English. " Then the voice of the loud-speakers coming over the water. Again and again in Norwegian they said : ' The English are here. We are your friends.'

" There was a wild burst of cheering as we rushed madly down to the water front, and we went on cheering as the British came ashore.

" At first some people had been terrified when the little British ships were seen in the distance. They were afraid more Germans were coming, but when the loud-speakers gave us their message many of the women cried with joy.

" Nearly all the young men on the island volunteered to go to England to fight. Most of them had no time to go home, but left messages for their families. Others rushed back to their homes, gathered up a few things they needed, and said good-bye to their families. Some young fellows knelt to receive their fathers' blessing before they embarked.

" Our greatest delight was seeing our local Quislings, whom we all detested, rounded up and taken under guard to the ships. There are so many Quislings that it was good to see even some of them taken prisoner.

Another fair-haired, 19-year-old giant, Tora by name, said : " I was skiing when I heard shots and rushed down to see what was going on. I found the British Navy were in the fiord. I didn't wait. I just rushed up and said to them : ' Can I get back to England to fight with you ? ' "

Another youth was on the mountainside when he heard shots far below. He thought it was the Germans attacking his friends in the village, but rushing down the slope to take his part in the fray, he recognized the raiders at once. " I can't describe my feelings at seeing British uniforms," he said. " You've no idea what it means to be in England. I am going into the Navy, and I am going to fight the Germans until they are beaten. I know, and we all know in Norway, that the Germans will be beaten."

Another of the volunteers was wearing Norwegian Army uniform when he arrived amongst those who had come to cheer King Haakon in London. It transpired that as a sergeant he had fought side by side with the British at Tromsoe and Narvik, and though after the Germans had overrun Norway he found it advisable to change into mufti, he had carried his uniform with him ever since, hoping for the day when he could put it on again. " We have come to fight," said the sergeant, " and I know there are thousands more at home wanting to come, too. They are jealous of us who were brought away."

One of the volunteers was a 36-year-old fisherman who had been out of a job since the German invasion of Norway, because he refused to work for them. " I arrived at the smallest town in the island to take a job on the very day that the English landed," he said. " I was standing near the factory when I saw an English soldier. He stopped me going into the factory, and when I questioned him, he said, ' You can't go in there. We are going to blow it up.'

The Polish destroyer Piorun was given by Britain to the Polish Government to replace the ill-fated Grom, the story of whose sinking is recounted in page 303. A running repair is being carried out on the paravane derrick aboard the new ship.
Photo, British Official : Crown Copyright

" I said to him, ' Well, if you are blowing it up, you had better take me to England and find me a job.' The soldier said, ' Sure. Go with the rest.'

" I joined the other patriots. As we stood on the deck of the boat, we saw every one of the factories in that part of the island, most of them fish oil factories, blown up."

Among the Norwegians who were brought to England there were eight women ; seven unmarried girls and one widow. " Why have we come to England ? " repeated one of them when questioned. " We heard that they were asking our menfolk to go. We saw the boats. We asked your Navy to take us. They agreed, and here we are.

" My family don't know that I have left them," she went on. " I was in bed when the ships came in and my people were out. People were shouting, ' The English soldiers are here ! ' I jumped out of bed and went into the street in my dressing-gown. Then I dressed and went to the ship.

" I work in a shop," she concluded. " We don't like the Germans. We love to listen to the B.B.C. news, for, though it is prohibited in cafes, most of us manage to hear it somehow."

KING HAAKON OF NORWAY is seen above talking to one of the Norwegian sailors who was engaged in the raid on the Lofoten Islands. Left, some of the women who were taken off. A Norwegian officer (right) is talking to young fishermen from the islands who intend to join the Free Norwegian Navy.
Photos, G.P.U., Keystone and Fox

Then as Now in the Empire's Service

GENERAL J. C. SMUTS, South African Premier and Minister of Defence, who at the end of February and the beginning of March, 1941, visited the South African troops now fighting in East Africa, was on familiar ground, since he commanded the Imperial troops fighting against the Germans in East Africa in 1916-17. He is seen, left, in the front line during his visit. The photograph below was taken during the last war, when in 1917-18 he was South Africa's representative in the Imperial War Cabinet. It shows him inspecting City of London Volunteers outside London Guildhall ; with him is the Maharajah of Bikaner.   *Photos, South African Official and Topical*

LORD BEAVERBROOK, as Sir Max Aitken, did valuable work with the Canadian Army during the last war. He acted as war correspondent with the Canadian Expeditionary Force in 1915; he was Canadian Representative at the Front in 1916 and Officer-in-charge of Canadian Records in 1917. Above, he is seen during his service with the Canadian Army. Oval, as Minister for Aircraft Production in the present war, he is receiving a cheque for £100,000 for aircraft from M. Gutt, the Belgian Minister of Finance, who is on his left.

Photos, Topical and Fox

FIELD-MARSHAL LORD MILNE is almost the only survivor of our military chiefs of the last war. He was appointed to command the British Salonika Force in May 1916 and, under the supreme direction of the French Commander, first General Sarrail and later General Guillaumat, was responsible for the operations that ended in the defeat of the Bulgarians in 1918. Left, he is seen with the Serbian General Mishich inspecting a guard of honour at Salonika in January, 1917. In this war he is Colonel Commandant of the Pioneer Corps, and, above, he is seen chatting to a member of the Corps.

Photos, Imperial War Museum and Planet News

'Tell Us What It's Like to Bale Out!'

Five fighter pilots of the R.A.F., who have baled out and lived to fight again another day,
called at one of our factories recently to thank the men and women who had made the
parachutes which saved their lives. Here is an account of their visit and of some of the
stories which were dragged out of them.

WHEN the five young fighter pilots entered the factory they received a great reception. Then one by one they were invited—or, rather, compelled, for they all seemed to be decidedly nervous —to climb upon a table to describe what it felt like when they jumped. Each started off his story with the words, " Thank you for saving my life ! "

Two of the officers had baled out twice. A Squadron-Leader, besides making a jump, had also escaped from a Hurricane by lifting the hatch and climbing out when his machine had already dived 30 feet under water on its way to the bottom of the North Sea. Another pilot who jumped from a blazing fighter still had burn marks on his face and hands.

The pilots came from two fighter squadrons

above me. I had to creep up behind him, and he soon started banging away at me. However, I gave him a good squirt. Then suddenly there was a tremendous explosion just in front of my tummy, and I felt to see if it was still there.

" I could not believe that I had been shot down ; you see I was not used to that sort of thing. I was twelve miles out at sea, and I turned round rather hoping in a futile way that I would get back to the coast. My 'plane began to smoke. I thought of the night before when I said I should not have the guts to bale out. It was that or a forced landing on the sea. I counted three and stepped over the side. Another three, in the approved fashion, and pulled the plug. So I began to float down, and the sensation is absolutely wonderful. There was the North

which we call ' June Bees.' I singled out a nice fat pig—that's a 110—who was trying to catch up with his pals. Down came the 109s and absolutely smothered us. This went on for a bit, then suddenly I saw a lot of balls of fire in front of me. There was a terrific bonk on the floor of the 'plane and a deluge of petrol in front of me. I tried to get back, but the engine would not go. So I thought, Well, here we are again ; I have done it before, it is easy this time. I duly landed quite comfortably in a blackberry bush. I picked myself up and found a rifle muzzle levelled at my head. I put my hands up and said, ' For God's sake don't shoot me ! ' The chap was very decent and said, ' All right.' They took me to hospital, but I am afraid nurses did not give me the drinks the sailors did."

So each pilot told his story. One described how he fell into a hop field and was mobbed by 300 excited children. Another how he kept afloat by his parachute for 1½ hours in the sea before he was picked up.

All the pilots are members of the Caterpillar Club (see page 20, Vol. 2), membership of which is confined to those whose lives have been saved by parachute. They wear a little golden caterpillar brooch. At lunch each pilot was presented with a caterpillar tie by Mr. Irvin, maker of the parachutes.

They saw many letters from airmen shot down over Germany and now prisoners, who had written applying to become members of the club. One letter was from an officer who belonged to the squadron of two of the pilots. They were presented with his prison camp application to hang in the mess-room at their station.

Later, when the officers made a tour of the factory, they saw every stage of parachute making. They learned how it takes 60 square yards of purest white silk (enough for 30 women's garments) to make one parachute, and the cost is £20.

At one sewing machine they talked to pretty 19-year-old Irene Britchford, who a few months ago was a parlour-maid in Sloane Square. " You mind those stitches," chaffed one officer.

PARACHUTE WORKERS, seen at their factory, form an appreciative audience as they listen intently to a fighter pilot describing how his life had been saved by means of a parachute when his 'plane was shot down. His story will give them an added incentive to " go to it."
Photo, British Official : Crown Copyright

who have already shot down 226 Nazi 'planes.

" Tell us what it's like ! " shouted a bunch of smiling girls, who had been singing away at their work.

A tall, wavy-haired, 26-year-old Squadron-Leader jumped on to the table ; he said : " We do thank you very much indeed for all the work you are doing. I hear you go on working in spite of air-raid sirens. I am absolutely terrified when the sirens go myself, and think it wonderful of you. Without your help, and others in the aircraft industry, we would not be where we are today."

" Tell us about your jumps," the girls persisted, stamping and clapping their hands. The pilot said he felt nervous, but they would not let him get down. " All right," he said, " here goes. One night last year I was talking to one of my Flight Commanders about baling out, and I said how terrified I should be to have to do it, and that I should not have the guts. Next morning at 6 a.m. three of us were sent off over the North Sea. The weather was bad and it was raining a little, but soon I saw a Dornier 5,000 feet

Sea below and a little ship. I saw my 'plane crash into the sea, and I was very sorry, because I had my best hat in it.

" I began to breathe very deeply as I reached the sea, in case I went under. As I hit the water I pressed a button which threw off my parachute harness, and in a couple of seconds I was swimming round, and enjoying myself. I was just set for a nice sea bathe, which I had for about 20 minutes. Then a little boat came out from the ship, and I heard someone say, ' Gawd, he is a Jerry ! ' I shouted, ' No, please, I am not, I am English.' They picked me up and put me on board, and then I began to feel very frightened, as I knew there were a lot of mines in the North Sea. They gave me a pint glass full of rum. When the mate's back was turned I poured some of it down the sink. They took me round a dozen ships, and on each one I had to have a drink.

" The second time I had to jump," went on the pilot, " was when over London. My squadron ran into a whole lot of ME 110s heavily protected by Messerschmitt 109s,

" You won't mind how many times you jump now you have seen how we make the 'chutes," said brunette Sybil Iley, who has thrown up her job of bookbinding to make parachutes.

There were girls at work in the factory who had formerly been engaged making corsets, in the printing trade, making handbags, shop girls and many other varied jobs.

At a testing bench the pilots talked to Mrs. Doris Williams, who has inspected every parachute the factory has made for years past. " We've never had a failure," she said. " We hear of our parachutes being pulled inside out, but they still work. I've passed out tens of thousands, and that meant inspecting millions and millions of yards of stitching."

At almost every bench the girls had pasted up pictures of airmen who had jumped or had been decorated for bravery. Many left their work as the officers went round, and begged for their autographs.

One Day He May Have a Much Longer Jump!

BALING OUT is an unpleasant experience which a bomber's crew may have to go through at any time, and so the men have to practise, as shown above, the correct method of leaving the escape-hatch of the 'plane, for, as can be seen, the exit does not provide much space for a fully equipped man with a parachute. After leaving the aircraft the airman baling out must allow a certain time to elapse before pulling the ripcord, for if he is not well clear of the machine his opening parachute might get entangled in it.

Photo, Topical

OUR DIARY OF THE WAR

TUESDAY, MARCH 4, 1941   *549th day*

On the Sea—British naval raid carried out against German interests in Lofoten Islands, off Norway. Eleven enemy ships sunk. Landings made at four principal fishing ports. Fish oil factories and a power station destroyed, and oil storage tanks burned. Forces withdrew bringing 215 German prisoners, 10 Quislings, and a large number of Norwegian patriots.

In the Air—Coastal Command aircraft on patrol attacked aerodrome near Brest. At night dock and railway sidings at Calais were bombed.

War against Italy—In the Gojjam, Patriot forces occupied important Italian fort of Burye. Enemy withdrew towards Debra Marcos, on road to Addis Ababa.

Home Front—Slight air activity, but no bombs dropped during day. At night raiders again attacked Cardiff. Bombs also fell in two towns in Home Counties and at other widely separated places.

Three night bombers destroyed by A.A. fire.

Greek War—R.A.F. bombers attacked enemy warships off Himara. Nine of their escorting fighters destroyed. Another attack made on enemy warships off Valona.

General—Government announced that non-essential factories are to be closed and available labour and other resources concentrated on war production.

WEDNESDAY, MARCH 5   *550th day*

In the Air—R.A.F. attacked docks at Boulogne. Other squadrons made offensive sweep over Channel and Northern France.

Coastal Command flying-boat shot down one enemy bomber over Atlantic and severely damaged another.

Home Front—No raids over Britain either by day or night.

War against Italy—Revolt of Abyssinian Patriots now spread to central province of Shoa and as far as Addis Ababa.

Sixteen enemy aircraft destroyed during heavy raid on Malta, and others damaged. One R.A.F. fighter shot down.

Greek War—Athens announced successful local operations in central sector resulting in capture of tanks and 165 prisoners.

Balkans—Great Britain broke off diplomatic relations with Bulgaria.

Mr. Eden and Gen. Sir John Dill left Greece for Cairo, having reached complete agreement with Greek leaders.

THURSDAY, MARCH 6   *551st day*

On the Sea—Italian submarine Anfitrite attempted to attack British convoy in Aegean, but was sunk by escort craft.

War against Italy—Cairo reported that forward elements of mechanized forces in Libya had again driven off enemy armoured fighting vehicles west of Agheila.

In Italian Somaliland Fer-Fer, 100 miles north-west of Bulo Burti, had been occupied.

Considerable R.A.F. activity in Eritrea, particularly in Keren area.

Home Front—Many raids by single enemy aircraft during day. Bombs fell in East Anglia and Kent and at one point in London area. At night raiders were over north-east coast.

Enemy bomber shot down in Channel.

Greek War—Athens reported energetic and successful artillery action. In central area Greeks captured new positions which had been well fortified by the enemy.

FRIDAY, MARCH 7   *552nd day*

On the Sea—Admiralty announced that H.M. destroyer Dainty had been sunk.

In the Air—Aircraft of Coastal Command sank enemy supply ship off Dutch coast. They also bombed naval harbour at Den Helder and aerodrome at Ockenburg.

War against Italy—Cairo stated that in Abyssinia Patriots on Gondar road were now operating east of Amanit. In Italian Somaliland advance progressed along main Mogadishu-Jijiga road.

Announced that five Italian merchant ships were seized when Kismayu was captured.

During night R.A.F. bombed harbour at Tripoli and several aerodromes. In Eritrea considerable damage done in Keren area.

Home Front—Single enemy aircraft were active over various parts of England. Many casualties and buildings destroyed at one Midlands town.

Two Nazi bombers shot down, one by machine-gun fire off Gorleston, the other by H.M.S. Guillemot, escorting a convoy. Another destroyed at night by colliding with mast of trawler it was attacking.

Greek War—Athens reported that successful action in central sector had led to occupation of new positions and capture of 1,000 prisoners.

In support of Greek Army operations R.A.F. bombed big troop concentrations at villages of Besist and Dragoti in Tepelini area.

General—Gen. Smuts, who had flown from Kenya, joined conference of Mr. Eden and Gen. Sir John Dill with Gen. Sir Archibald Wavell at Cairo.

SATURDAY, MARCH 8   *553rd day*

On the Sea—H.M. trawler Nadine hit, and probably destroyed, a Heinkel.

War against Italy—Cairo stated that in Italian Somaliland operations continued to develop satisfactorily. Air support was given by R.A.F. on all fronts, particularly near Keren, Eritrea.

Home Front—Heavy night raid on London. Much damage done to houses, shops, a block of L.C.C. flats, police, ambulance and fire stations. Casualties were many in a West-End restaurant wrecked by a bomb.

Three enemy bombers destroyed off East Coast.

Greek War—Athens announced that after stubborn struggle still more positions had been captured and 1,000 prisoners taken. R.A.F. attacked troop and transport concentrations in Tepelini and on Glave-Buzi road.

During the night of 8-9, R.A.F. heavily bombed harbour installation at Durazzo.

General—U.S. Senate passed Lease-and-Lend Bill by 60 votes to 31.

SUNDAY, MARCH 9   *554th day*

On the Sea—Admiralty announced that Italian commerce raider Ramb I had been destroyed in Indian Ocean by H.M. cruiser Leander.

H.M. trawlers Remillo and Cobbers reported sunk.

War against Italy—Cairo announced that our troops have occupied Gabre Darre on Mogadishu-Harar road.

Home Front—Slight enemy activity during daylight. Bombs fell at few points in south-east and eastern England.

At night London was again main objective, fire and high explosive bombs being dropped in many districts. Heavy attack made on Portsmouth; much damage done to property, but casualties light. Raiders were also over number of coast towns from north-east Scotland to South Wales.

General—Ministry of Labour made an order under which Admiralty is to control labour in the shipyards.

MONDAY, MARCH 10   *555th day*

On the Sea—Admiralty announced that Italian cruiser of Condottieri A class had been torpedoed and almost certainly sunk.

In the Air—Three offensive sweeps made by aircraft of Fighter Command over Channel and occupied France.

At night R.A.F. launched heavy attack on Boulogne, Cherbourg and Brest. Targets in Western Germany were also bombed, among them being Cologne.

War against Italy—In Abyssinia, Italians retreating from Burye were driven out of Dambacha by British and Patriot forces advancing from Sudan.

British column now over half-way on road from Mogadishu to Harar.

R.A.F. bombers had attacked aerodrome at Diredawa and positions in Keren area.

Three enemy formations attacked Malta from different sides, but were driven off.

Home Front—During daylight enemy activity was mainly over Channel and south-east England.

Portsmouth again suffered severe night attack. Many buildings were demolished and fires started, and there were casualties. Bombs also fell at widely separated points elsewhere, including area of Thames Estuary, but without much effect.

Eight Nazi night bombers destroyed.

Greek War—Athens reported that fresh positions had been taken. Italians attempted strong counter-attacks which were repulsed with enemy losses; 300 prisoners taken.

" HONEST JOE."

" If only I dared——"

From the cartoon by E. H. Shephard, by permission of the Proprietors of " Punch "

H.M.S. RENOWN RETURNS FROM 'A FIRST-CLASS SHOOT'

One of the British naval units which took part in the shelling of Genoa on February 9, 1941, was the battle-cruiser Renown. She is here seen steaming into a Mediterranean harbour after her successful action, cheered by ratings on board another British warship. The Renown, whose 15-in. guns wrought havoc among the objectives in Genoa harbour, is a battle-cruiser of 32,000 tons. Completed in 1916, she underwent extensive reconstruction from 1936 to 1939, when her armour protection was considerably increased. After the action Vice-Admiral Somerville signalled his congratulations on what he described as 'a first-class shoot' (see pages 176 and 219).

Photo, "Daily Mirror"

If War Should Spread in the Middle East

After Bulgaria, what next? What will be the contents of the next chapter in the story of Nazi aggression? Many signs go to suggest that Turkey, and beyond Turkey, the Middle East countries of Iraq and Iran, are about to be drawn into the field of the war of nerves—perhaps of actual military operations.

WHEN, on the morning after the Nazi rape of Bulgaria, Hitler sent President Inonu a special letter expressing his regard for the country which was Germany's ally in the Great War, and accompanied his message with a gift of his portrait, the Turks —sensible fellows that they are—took down their guns. They know only too well that the countries which the Fuehrer fawns upon are destined soon to be confronted by the choice of, Surrender or fight.

Since Hitler started to collect countries as other men collect postage-stamps or old coins, the German troops have penetrated ever deeper into south-eastern Europe. One state after another has been "bagged." Slovakia, Hungary, Rumania—and now with the fall of Bulgaria German troops are again on the frontier of Turkey as they were in 1918. The Turks realize full well what these moves mean. They remember that in the Kaiser's day the Germans were lured on by the dream of Berlin to Baghdad, of reaching out to the rich oil deposits of Mesopotamia and Persia. They are convinced that Hitler, too, has dreamed the same dream. Mesopotamia has become Iraq and Persia is Iran today. But only the names have been changed; the oil is still there, and Hitler needs oil far more

than "Kaiser Bill" ever did. No modern state can exist without that rich mineral substance born of the rotting vegetation of millions of years ago; certainly no war can be carried on without it. Germany produces some oil, she has more under her control in Rumania, she is receiving some from Russia (although the Soviet now has less and less to export as her agriculture is mechanized and her industries grow and grow). But all these sources supply Germany with far less than enough of what she needs to drive and lubricate her war machine. No wonder Hitler looks out with greedy eyes on those enormously rich deposits which lie beyond Turkey in the Middle East.

Turkey Stands on Guard

But how to get to them? The way might be open if Turkey could be induced to surrender, as Bulgaria and Rumania have surrendered. But across the Dardanelles he sees two million Turkish bayonets flashing in the sun. The Turks will fight; and even before the German troops could reach the Dardanelles they would have to destroy the great Turkish fortress of Adrianople and smash through the Chatalja Lines which, stretching for 25 miles from the Black Sea to the Sea of

Marmara, defend Istanbul. Supposing these to be overcome, supposing the Straits to be crossed—no easy matter, surely, in face of the opposition of British and Turkish sea power, operating from bases on the Gallipoli Peninsula and the islands of Lemnos and Imbros – the invaders would then plunge into the heart of a country which has proved the grave of many a military reputation. The nearest of the great oilfields is at Mosul, in the north of Iraq; but between the Dardanelles and Mosul stretch 900 miles of largely mountainous country—a vast, hostile territory defended by millions of the soldiery who in the last war inflicted severe defeats on the British and today are ranked amongst the finest and best-equipped of modern armies.

But let us suppose that Turkey has been conquered, that Asia Minor has been overrun, and from its passes the Nazi hordes now debouch on to the plains of the Middle East. The first country to be attacked would be Iraq, one of the new states carved out of the Turkish Empire at the end of the last war. Iraq owes her independence to Great Britain, which until 1932 exercised a League of Nations mandate over her territory. Since that year Iraq has enjoyed her independence, but by the Treaty of Alliance signed in 1930

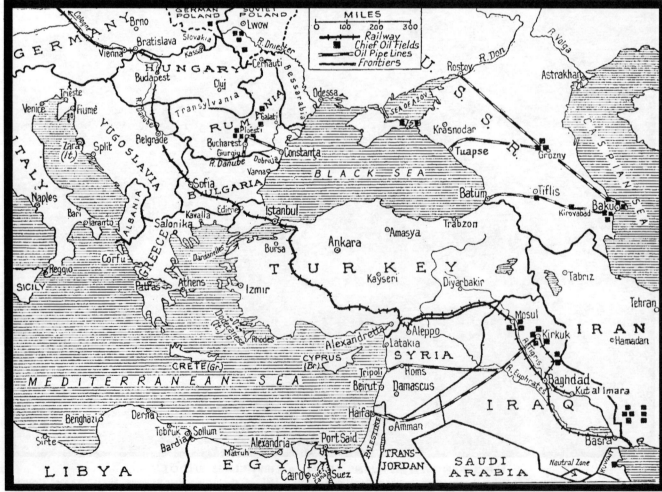

This map of the Balkans and Asia Minor shows the Berlin-Baghdad railway, completed in July, 1940, the chief oilfields, and the pipelines. It will be seen that Turkey forms the chief obstacle lying between the German troops in Rumania and Bulgaria and the rich oilfields of Iraq and Iran. Russia also has many valuable oil deposits in the territory between the Caspian Sea and the Black Sea.
By courtesy of "The Manchester Guardian"

Hard to Recognize Old Persia in Modern Iran

IN IRAN military service is compulsory, and the Iranian army, though small, is well organized and includes a mechanized brigade. Its peacetime strength is about 120,000, but there is a large army reserve. On the left, Iranian cavalry are seen on parade. Below is the modern building which houses the National Bank of Iran at Teheran. This bank has branches all over Iran, and since 1930 has had the sole right to issue notes in the country.

RIZA KHAN PAHLEVI, above, was in 1925 elected Shah of Iran after the overthrow of the Kajar dynasty. Iran's chief export is oil, and at Abadan, near the entrance to the Persian Gulf, on the eastern side of the Shatt-al-Arab, are large refineries (right), machine shops, storage tanks and shipping facilities for dealing with the oil brought by pipeline from the interior.

Photos Black Star, E.N.A., Dorien Leigh

Iraq Is Britain's Ally in Time of War

THE OIL WELLS OF IRAQ lie around Kirkuk, a town of 30,000 inhabitants lying 90 miles south-east of Mosul. This is what one of the fields looks like by night. Iraq is potentially very rich in oil, but at present production is limited by the capacity of the pipelines

Iraq is pledged to give Britain in peacetime the right to maintain air bases in the country, and in wartime to grant her the use of Iraq's communications, airports and waterways. In the event of invasion, then, the Iraqui Army (peacetime strength, 28,000 officers and men) would have the support of the British Army, which would have behind it the almost inexhaustible resources of men and material of the Empire in India and the Antipodes.

Iran's Debt to the Shah

Beyond Iraq lies Iran, another of the great oil-producing countries of the world. Iran is the Persia of yesterday, and it is difficult to recognize in the strongly nationalist and independent state of today the country which only a quarter of a century ago was parcelled out into spheres of influence by Tsarist Russia and Britain. If modern Turkey is the creation of Mustapha Kemal, modern Iran owes its being to Riza Khan Pahlevi, who was once a trooper in the Persian Cossacks, who in 1921 became Commander-in-Chief of the Persian Army, in 1923 Premier, and in 1925 deposed Sultan Ahmad and ruled as Shah in his stead. The last 15 years have been years of far-reaching change, inspired and directed by this rough but highly capable soldier-statesman. Iranian men wear European dress, and their womenfolk have been banned the veil; the Moslem clergy have been deprived of their power, and the bribery of government

FAISAL II, King of Iraq, was born in 1935 and succeeded to the throne when his father King Ghazi died as the result of an accident in 1939. Until the king comes of age the country is under the regency of his uncle, Emir Abdul Ilah.

officials is no longer the best, even the only, way to get things done. The Shah is a dictator, but his is a benevolent dictatorship. He has breathed a new spirit into a people who for long have lived in subjection; he has established his country's independence and developed its strength. Not the least of his many achievements is the completion of the Trans-Iran Railway, linking the Caspian Sea with the Persian Gulf.

Iran has an army of some 120,000 officers and men, including a number of anti-aircraft, tank, and mechanized infantry regiments, while its air force has been equipped with modern machines, mostly of British make. In the event of war it might be expected to give an excellent account of itself.

If it comes to fighting in the Middle East, Iran would probably be ranged beside Turkey, Iraq, and Afghanistan, for by the Saadabad Pact of 1937 all these powers are pledged to close cooperation in the face of common danger. Moreover, they would, of course, rely on the powerful support of Britain, whose interests in the Middle East, strategical, political, and economic, are so important.

BAGHDAD, storied city of the east, a picturesque square in which is seen above, is the capital of Iraq, with a population of some 500,000. It stands on both sides of the Tigris about 300 miles from the Persian Gulf, and recent developments in communications have made it the great distributing centre of the country, restoring to some extent its former greatness.
Photos, Mrs. T. Muir, W. Bosshard

The Young Iraqi Guards His Country's Wealth

WATCHING OVER THE OIL OF IRAQ, this sentry stands at a well in the Kirkuk oilfields. A pipe, two hand-wheels and a few square yards of trellis fencing are all that is visible, but along that pipe travels the oil without which modern armies cannot move. At present the extraction of oil in Iraq is limited by the capacity of the pipelines to Tripoli and Haifa, and by no means all the wells are in active operation. But new pipelines and another refinery are under construction, which will enable greater advantage to be taken of the abundant oil supplies of the region. *Photo, Mrs. T. Muir*

Britain's Railways Still Beating the Bombers

KEEPING THE RAILWAYS RUNNING, the staffs responsible for traffic arrangements have special emergency control centres underground for use during severe air raids. Here they can carry on as usual.

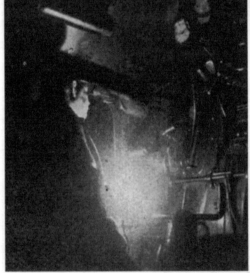

No such cover protects this driver of the L.N.E.R. "Night Scotsman" on his 500-mile journey through the black-out. But he, too, carries on.

BOMB DAMAGE on the line is made good with the minimum delay. Left, a repair gang is hard at work on a badly damaged section of the line. While one party fills in the bomb crater other workers remove damaged sleepers and rails. Above, the line has been restored and a railway inspector is signalling "Halt" to the driver of the heavily laden goods train which has been making a test run over it.

Photos, Topical, "Daily Mirror" and Fox

Theirs Is the Growl of the British Bulldog!

GIANT HOWITZERS are among the many big guns which now protect our island fortress. This 12-inch howitzer on a railway mounting fires a shell weighing a third of a ton, and guns of this type would deal death and destruction on a large scale to the enemy should he attempt the invasion of our shores. A camouflage netting is spread over the gun and its carriage to hide them from aerial observation, for German reconnaissance 'planes are constantly trying to probe our secrets.

Photo, British Official: Crown Copyright

On Both Sides of the Line in France

At this German aerodrome in Occupied France a Nazi mechanic is bringing a flare for a German bomber— according to the caption on this Nazi photograph.

NEW U.S. AMBASSADOR to Vichy, Admiral William Leahy, is seen above after presenting his credentials to Marshal Pétain (left). The admiral, by stressing his country's determination to give full aid to the Democracies, undoubtedly stiffened Vichy's resistance to further Nazi demands.

This charcoal-burning motor cycle is a French invention designed to cope with the shortage of motor fuel in that country, most of which has been commandeered by the Nazis.

FRENCH NORTH AFRICAN TROOPS, repatriated after seven months' internment in Switzerland, are here seen returning to France. The French Government has decreed that Jewish stores must be labelled ; right, a Jewish-owned shop in Bordeaux.

Photos, Associated Press, Wide World

What the Lease and Lend Act Means to Us

Since the beginning of the year the newspapers on both sides of the Atlantic have been filled with reports of the progress of the Lease and Lend Bill through the U.S.A. Congress. It became law on March 11—the measure which, as Lt. Com. R. Fletcher, M.P., has said, " is sentence of death for Hitler."

WHEN on the afternoon of March 11 the President wrote the words *Franklin D. Roosevelt* to the Lease and Lend Bill, the United States of America became in effect an active partner of Britain and her allies in the war against the Dictators.

Think what the Act does, or rather what it empowers the President to do. When it was introduced on January 10 in the Senate and the House of Representatives as the " Act to promote the defence of the United States," its sponsors declared that it translated " into legislative form the policy of making this country an Arsenal for the Democracies, and seeks to carry out President Roosevelt's pledge to send to these countries in ever-increasing numbers, ships, aeroplanes, tanks, and guns."

Under the Act the President is empowered, " when he deems it in the interest of national defence," to " manufacture in arsenals, factories and shipyards under American jurisdiction, or otherwise procure any defence article for the government of any country whose defence the President deems vital to the defence of the United States." It enables him to " sell, transfer, exchange, lease, lend, or otherwise dispose of, to any such government any defence article . . . To test, inspect, prove, repair, fit out, recondition, or otherwise to place in good working order any defence article for any such government." (" Any defence article " includes any such articles, whether manufactured in the U.S.A. or not ; thus the British battle-cruiser Renown could be repaired in Brooklyn Navy Yard if the President considered it in the interest of American national defence to do so. Moreover, any of the American military, naval, or air bases can fit out or repair weapons of countries whose defence is deemed vital to the defence of the U.S.A.) Then the President may " communicate to

any such government any defence information pertaining to any defence article furnished to such government."

" Now a new era of United States history begins," wrote Robert Waithman, " News Chronicle " New York correspondent, " for the Bill empowers President Roosevelt to send to Britain and her allies war supplies made by American workmen in American factories, and *owned and paid for by the Government of the United States*. The Bill means that what Britain will receive from America in future will be directly sent, not by United States manufacturers, but by the United States Government, and that the funds to build these arms will be provided, not by the British taxpayers, but by the American taxpayers. The United States— its Government and the people behind the

Government—will now be working without subterfuge or camouflage for the defeat of the Axis."

For two months the Bill was fiercely assailed in Congress. Some opposed it because of their personal hostility to the President, others because they shrank from giving him such unprecedented powers. The Pacifists were against it, and the Communists, a section of the Irish Americans and the American Nazis. Then there was the great body of Isolationists who urged that America should not again become entangled in a European quarrel ; why should the sons of American mothers die on foreign battle-fields ? they demanded. At least it is not difficult to understand their attitude. To Senator Nye the war must seem a long way away from N. Dakota in the Middle West.

'A NEW MAGNA CARTA' was how Mr. Churchill described the Lease and Lend Bill, which President Roosevelt is seen signing, left, on March 11. Above, Senator Barkley, Senator Wheeler (an Isolationist opponent) and Senator George are indulging in mutual congratulations after the passing of the Bill.

Radio photos from New York, Planet News

Yet if the opposition was vociferous, the support forthcoming for the Bill was nothing less than amazing. All the critics' sound and fury came to nothing. Some of the amendments proposed were accepted by the Roosevelt Administration ; thus it was decreed that the President must not dispose of any defence articles without first consulting the U.S. Army Chief of Staff and the U.S. Chief of Naval Operations. A time limit, June 30, 1943, was fixed for the duration of the Bill ; the value of arms, etc., belonging to the American military forces that may be supplied is limited to £385 millions ; and the President must report to Congress regularly on the operations under the Bill, unless it be incompatible with public interest for such information to be issued. More important was the amendment which declared that the Bill should neither authorize nor permit the use of American warships for convoy duties,

'This Monument of Far-Seeing Statesmanship'

SUPPORTERS OF THE LEASE AND LEND BILL are here seen giving their testimony before the Foreign Relations Committee of the American Senate. Left to right they are Miss Dorothy Thompson (Mrs. Sinclair Lewis), the columnist whose writings are read by millions of readers ; Mr. Fiorello La Guardia, Mayor of New York since 1934, famous for his able administration of the city's affairs ; Mr. William S. Knudsen, U.S. Minister of Defence Production, who spoke with authority on America's ability both to defend herself and aid the Allies ; and Mr. Cordell Hull, Sécretary of State, who is America's Foreign Minister.   *Photos, Wide World, Planet News, and Associated Press*

but an amendment to impose an outright ban on the use of warships was rejected by the Foreign Affairs Committee. It is seemingly an open question whether under the American constitution the President, as Commander-in-Chief of the Army and Navy, has authority to authorize the use of American warships for convoy duties. Certainly if the President has that power then, as Mr. Sol Bloom, Chairman of the House of Representatives Foreign Affairs Committee, told the press, " We can't, and we won't, take it away from him." As the " New York Times " has put it, " In responsible quarters is now heard the candid opinion that if American convoys are needed to deliver the products of the Arsenal of the Democracies to the British war machine, they should be furnished. And some officials are beginning to say that in this event they will be furnished.'" It is inconceivable that America, once having undertaken the job of supporting the Democracies to the utmost

of her power, will not go through with it. Somehow the products of the American factories will be got across the Atlantic.

In the House of Representatives the debate began on February 3, and five days later the Bill was passed by 260 votes to 165. It then went to the Senate, who began their debate on February 13. The discussion was prolonged, for it is in the Senate that the Isolationists are most strong. Scores of amendments were proposed, and the time came when President Roosevelt had to issue a warning that if the Bill were further delayed, then the delivery of war materials to the Democracies would inevitably be slowed down. The Administration leaders were loath to apply what we should call the closure, and at last all the Isolationists had said all they had to say. On March 6 Senator George, Chairman of the Senate Foreign Relations Committee, made an eloquent appeal that pettifogging argument and narrow quibbling should be thrust aside.

" If we are realists," he said, " we should know that every hour and every moment wasted here counts in the Battle for Britain. We profess that her survival is in our own national interests." Then turning on the Isolationist leaders who for two weeks had carried on a filibuster—the American term to describe the method adopted by a minority to delay legislation indefinitely by talking interminably, and so prevent its being voted on—Senator George thundered, " The collapse of the British Empire would mean chaos in this world." Stirred by his words, the Senators decided to hold a night session, and on March 8 the Bill, with some minor amendments, was passed by 60 votes to 31. When it came back to the House of Representatives on March 11, it was finally passed by 317 votes to 71, after a debate of only two hours. A few minutes later a copy was rushed to President Roosevelt at the White House, and only 15 minutes after it had left the Capitol his signature made it law.

Less than a quarter of an hour after signing the President met reporters and declared, " Immediately after I signed the Bill, authorities of the Army and Navy considered a list of United States Army and Navy war material, and approved it being sent overseas. Part goes to Britain, and part to Greece. What is involved must be kept secret for military reasons." A few hours afterwards President Roosevelt sent Congress a request for the House to vote seven thousand million dollars (£1,750,000,000), " to carry out the fixed policy of this Government, to make for the Democracies every gun, 'plane, and munition that we possibly can."

In Britain the news of the passing of the Lease and Lend Act was received with the utmost enthusiasm. Rising in the House of Commons on the afternoon of March 12, Mr. Churchill said that he was sure that the House would wish him to express on their behalf, and on behalf of the nation, " our deep and respectful appreciation of this monument of generous and far-seeing statesmanship. . . . The Government and people of the United States have in fact written a new Magna Carta, which not only has regard to the rights and laws upon which a healthy and advancing civilization can alone be erected, but also proclaims by precept and example the duty of free men and free nations, wherever they may be, to share the responsibility and the burden of enforcing them."

MR. WENDELL WILLKIE, the centre figure before the microphone, is addressing the Foreign Relations Committee of the Senate within a few hours of his arrival by 'plane after his whirlwind tour of investigation in Britain. So great was the interest in his speech that crowds had fought all the morning to gain admission to the room, and his arrival was delayed 25 minutes by the press of people. When he arrived it took a number of policemen to force a way for him round the committee table to his place at the microphone.   *Photo, Wide World*

American Ships and 'Planes to Beat the U-Boats

'MOSQUITO BOATS'— motor torpedo-boats, that is—are amongst the 99 U.S. warships which, it was stated in Washington on the morrow of President Roosevelt's signing of the Lease and Lend Bill, would be transferred to Britain before the end of the year. The one seen right has four torpedo tubes visible at the sides, and four machine-guns in turrets. The boats are also equipped with smoke-screen pots.

Among other vessels stated as being included in the transfer are 17 over-age destroyers, nine over-age submarines, and 55 patrol boats — submarine chasers. The ships will be handed over as new vessels to take their place are added to the U.S. Navy. In this way, as in the probable transfer of a great tonnage of merchant ships for carrying war supplies, the U.S.A. will be granting us immense assistance in meeting and defeating the Nazi U-boat menace in Atlantic.

U.S. AIRCRAFT PRODUCTION, with the passing of the Lease and Lend Bill, will increase enormously its output to Britain, for, as President Roosevelt stated in a letter to the Speaker of the House of Representatives : " it is the fixed policy of this Government to make for the Democracies every gun, plane and manition of war we possibly can." Above, engines and fuselages of Curtiss P.40 pursuit 'planes for the U.S. Air Corps and Curtiss Tomahawk fighters for Great Britain under production at the Buffalo plant of the Curtiss-Wright Corporation

Photos, Associated Press, Wide World

Who Will Win the Race to Addis Ababa?

From every side the Italian Empire in East Africa—Africa Orientale Italiana, as the Italians call it—is being invaded by General Cunningham's East African Imperial Force, supported from within by bands of Abyssinian Patriots. This article continues the story from page 292.

How many columns of General Cunningham's men are invading Italian East Africa? Some commentators say twelve, others nine, but we may distinguish five as being the most important, most spectacular in their progress.

First we have the troops who have invaded Eritrea from the north. They comprise British, Indian, and a number of Free French (see page 290), and have for their main objective the Italian stronghold of Keren, which is situated on the railway between Asmara, the Eritrean capital, and Agordat, the fall of which was announced on February 2.

Agordat was captured by Column No. 2, which has invaded Eritrea from the west. This column is based on the Sudan, and is composed of British, Indian, and Sudanese troops, under the command of Major-General W. Platt. Probably it has the most difficult task of any of the invading forces, for not only is the country it has to traverse formidable in the extreme, with its mountainous heights and deep gorges, but at Keren the Italians have assembled an army estimated to number at least 40,000 men, comprising some of the best Eritrean regiments, stiffened by a division of Savoy Grenadiers, rushed up from Addis Ababa. Keren is the key to the Italian defences in the northern part of their realm, and for some weeks past it has been practically invested by the columns approaching from north and west, and has also been subjected to intensive bombing by the R.A.F.

Now we come to the third column, or perhaps we should say group of columns, for the most part operating in Western Abyssinia. In large measure this force consists of Abyssinian Patriots, partly irregulars operating under their own chiefs and partly regular Abyssinian troops, trained in the Sudan before the invasion began. But, in addition, this western force includes large numbers of Rhodesian, Kenya, Australian, and British officers and N.C.O.s, who direct the activities of the Patriots, as well as some Belgian troops and units of the Sudan Defence Force. By the end of February practically the whole of the province of Gojjam and the Lake Tana region had been wrested from the Italians, who were in full retreat to Addis Ababa. Deserters reported that the Italians were quite panic-stricken, incapable of making a stand, intent only on reaching the comparative safety of the capital. As they fled down the road they were sniped by Abyssinian irregulars and ambushed at every turn.

Many hundreds of miles to the south is operating the fourth of the invading columns. Composed of South Africans, it crossed the frontier from Kenya at Moyale, and is now somewhere in the neighbourhood of Neghelli (the town from which Graziani takes his title

LAND MINES IN ERITREA were strewn about in profusion by the Italians during their retreat, but Indian sappers have done excellent work in the hazardous business of locating and removing them.
Photo, British Paramount News

of Marquis). Little more than 200 miles separates this force from the fifth portion of General Cunningham's army, which after overrunning the western region of Italian Somaliland is invading Abyssinia from the south-east. This is a purely African force, composed of troops drawn from the Union and from East and West Africa.

Of the five columns it seems that this has the best chance of winning the race to Addis Ababa. In the middle of March the British and Patriot forces round Lake Tana had not so far to go, but between them and Addis Ababa lay the formidable barrier of the great canyon of the Blue Nile; and the South Africans operating from Moyale and Lake Rudolf were confronted by a tangled mass of almost trackless bush and jungle. Column No. 5, however, had its feet well planted on a good, modern tarmac road—one of the achievements of the Italian occupation—and was making astounding progress.

In speed it was breaking even the records established by the Army of the Nile. For a fortnight, following the capture of Mogadishu, the columns averaged 40 miles a day across the rising uplands. They were heading up the Farfan valley to Jijiga, separated by only 50 miles of sun-baked tableland from the frontier of the Somaliland that, until last August, was British. Fifty miles on the other side lies Harar, where the Italians were reported to be feverishly occupied in switching round the fortifications, so that they should not face north-east—when they were constructed the only danger that was anticipated was from Jibuti—but south-east. But it was not at all certain that a stand would be made at Harar, for not only were the Italians showing plentiful signs of demoralization, but it was doubtful whether the Duke of Aosta would be able to spare any considerable force for the town's defence. When the war in East Africa started, the Duke was said to have under his command some 200,000 men, but these were scattered over a vast territory: 40,000 are now believed to be behind the walls of Keren, and more than 30,000 are certainly in the British prison camps.

GENERAL WAVELL watches through a monocular glass—he lost the sight of his left eye during the last war—an aspect of the campaign on the Eritrean front, where the hard-pressed Italians are being threatened by a pincers movement around Keren. *Photo, Associated Press*

Where the War is Raging in East Africa

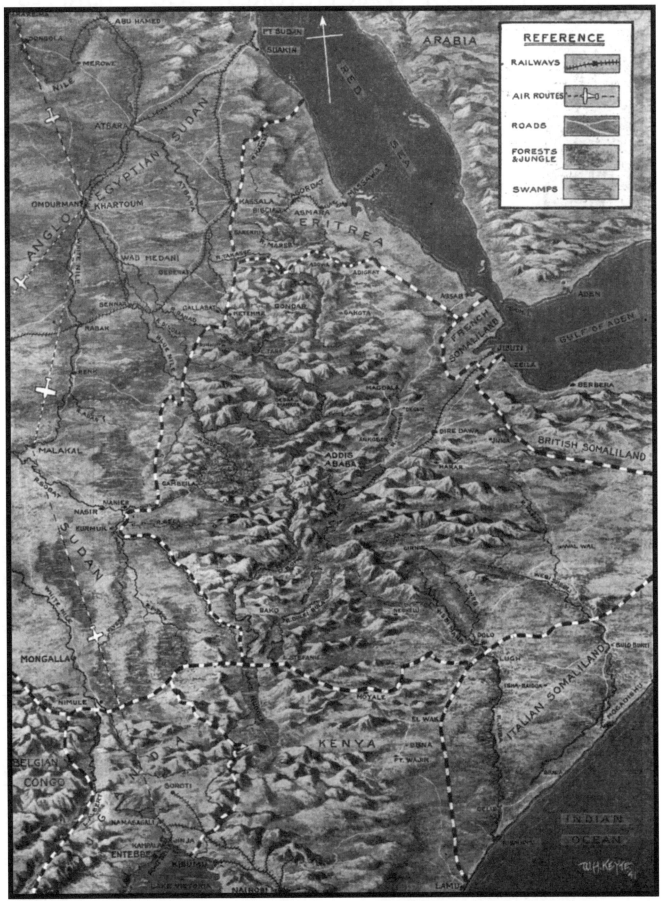

THE CAMPAIGN IN ABYSSINIA and its adjoining territories may be followed on this map, which covers the theatre of operations in Eritrea, Abyssinia and Italian Somaliland. The boundaries shown are those which existed prior to the Italo-Abyssinian war.   *By Courtesy of " The Crown Colonist"*

OUR GALLERY OF WAR PICTURES: GOD'S TEMPLES A[

'COVENTRY CATHEDRAL, November 1940'   *Randolph Schwabe*

'THE TUBE, Oc[

'SILVERTOWN, September 7, 1940'   *P. Gillett*   'A FARM IN W[

...MES OF MEN SWEPT BY THE FURY OF FIRE AND BOMB

Feliks Topolski

John Armstrong

'ST. MARY LE BOW, March 1941'   *Dennis Flanders*

WAR, as seen through the artist's eye, has an interest and an appeal such as no photograph can give. In earlier pages (see pp. 545-548, Vol. 3) we have given a selection of officially commissioned pictures reflecting the struggle as it has involved the Fighting Services. By way of contrast, we now reproduce some striking artists' impressions of the results of Germany's determined onslaught on the civil life of Britain. It is interesting to note the many different ways in which the artists have reacted to difficult and distressing subjects.

Mr. Schwabe's "Coventry Cathedral" shares with Mr. Flanders' "St. Mary le Bow" the purely architectural approach : thrusting aside feelings of sadness and horror, these draughtsmen have faithfully recorded for posterity the simple material details of wanton destruction. Mr. Flanders, indeed, sees good out of evil, for he obviously delights in revealing the beauty of Wren's lovely spire. Drama, design and depression are the keynotes of the other three works. The flare of great fires, the blank stare of blasted windows, and the hurrying figures of the rescue squad dominate Mr. Gillett's powerful "Silvertown." In his "Farm in Wales," Mr. Armstrong has perceived a grim pattern in the bomber's handiwork ; while Mr. Topolski's "Tube Shelter" is redolent of the drab weariness of nights spent underground.

FIGHTING THE FIRES

Paintings for the Nation by Firemen Artists

'Fireman Resting'   *Norman Hepple*

'Rescuing a trapped comrade from a bombed fire station, Streatham, October 1940'   *Rudolph Haybrook*

'Auxiliary Firemen working from a roof'   *Matvyn Wright*

NO more dramatic subject for the artist's brush could well be imagined than the heroic exploits of Britain's fearless firemen during the air raids. Amateur and professional alike have performed deeds of bravery comparable with the most notable in military history. It is peculiarly fitting that such devotion to duty should have been permanently recorded for the nation by actual members of the Fire Services. Both Mr. Rudolph Haybrook and Mr. Matvyn Wright, whose spirited paintings are shown here, are themselves auxiliary firemen.

In peaceful contrast to the virile action of their canvases is Mr. Norman Hepple's vivid little water-colour of a fireman resting. This, with the pictures in the preceding pages, was recently on exhibition at the National Gallery, London.

No, It Didn't Occur to You, Frau Hilda!

Below we print a translation of a talk given by Mr. Stronski, Minister of Information
in the Polish Government in London, broadcast to Poland by the B.B.C. in the course
of a Polish News Bulletin.   It forms an interesting commentary on the present state
of affairs in Nazi-occupied Poland.

LOOKING through the latest batch of
German newspapers to reach us in
the " Hamburger Fremdenblatt " of
February 1, I noticed the title of an article
describing a visit to the German so-called
Kreisleiter, or regional leader, in the German
East, as they call it in German—in other
words, in Poland.   The title read : " *Wir
wollen immer hierbleiben !* " (We wish to
remain here for ever.)

I read the article.   And I learned that the
Kreisleiter's wife, with whom the journalist
of the " Hamburger Fremdenblatt " had a
talk, is a charming blonde rejoicing in the
name of Frau Hilda.   May I also, Frau
Hilda, also have a little talk with you ?

You say that you were very reluctant to
go with your husband to Poland because you
were very comfortable in Westphalia.   The
journalist hastens to agree with you : " Why,
of course, what sort of life can you have in
such a little town where at every turn you come
upon the disorder of the Polish times ? "

Did it not occur to you, Frau Hilda, to ask
why this gentleman of the " Hamburger
Fremdenblatt " had chosen to visit this
" disorderly East ? "   I will tell you why it
did not.   As can be judged from the context,
this happened about the middle of last
January.   And it was just then that the
British Air Force, in revenge for the attack on
the ancient City of London, was fearfully
bombing old Bremen and giving old Hamburg
also a little unpleasantness.   And the energetic
journalist of the " Hamburger Fremdenblatt " at that moment suddenly had an
urgent desire to acquaint himself with the
" disorderly Polish East," as he said con-
temptuously.   You will at least admit, Frau
Hilda, that this German coward who scoffed
at Poland was also a bit of a skunk.

But we will not bother ourselves any more
with that idiot, who for that matter, as
appears, answered very ineptly, for you interrupted him energetically, exclaiming :
" But now, after a year, I tell you that
voluntarily I never shall leave the East, nor

my husband either.   We've settled down
splendidly here.   Tell me yourself, could I be
anywhere better off than here in this little
house of ours with its large garden ?   We've
got enough Polish servants for all the rough
work, and I've got a very nice *Volksdeutsch*
(local German) girl for our child and the
rooms.   It is so easy to run the house here that
all the housewives in the old Reich must envy
me, and our two guest rooms are never empty.
And I have a comfort even for my loneliness."

At this, Frau Hilda opened the door to the
next room, and the gentleman who is so fond
of visiting the untidy East while Hamburg
is being bombed tells us what he saw : " At
the window there was a great fat baby boy
in a cradle, well fed and satisfiedly sucking his
little finger."

How can we thank you, charming Frau
Hilda, for this picture of a German idyll in
Poland ?   A fine little house, with guest
rooms, in its large garden . . . .

But whose little house, whose garden, and
for what guests were those rooms ?   It was
not you who built that house and cared for
that garden, Frau Hilda and Herr Kreisleiter,
and the guest rooms were prepared neither
for yourselves nor for your friends from the
Gestapo.   Why should we hide the fact, Frau
Hilda, that you and your worthy husband and
contented offspring are able to luxuriate in
that pleasant little house in a large garden
only by driving a Polish family out of it ?
Possibly the Polish husband was shot without
trial as one of the hundreds who have been
murdered, or possibly he has been shut away
with thousands of others in a hellish concentration camp ; maybe his wife has died
of a broken heart, and their children are
roaming in misery somewhere.   Or maybe they
were all simply evicted from their house and
today are taking shelter where they can.   And
you three, Frau Hilda, are lolling on others'
property and at the cost of others' wrongs.

Frau Hilda, everything you have all around
you and which makes you so happy is stolen.

You are a common thief.   Your Kreisleiter
husband is an experienced burglar of others'
goods, your infant in the stolen cradle looks
around at the walls of a stolen house, and
your guests in those guest rooms are thieves
from the same band of international robbers
as you, who work under the same ringleader,
or, as you call him now, Fuehrer.

PERSECUTION in Poland does not even spare the children.   While German children such as
those below enjoy the best of everything, such little slaves as those above must act as scavengers,
sweeping the streets and chlorinating the gutters, simply because they are Poles and Jews.
Photo, Fox

You also say, Frau Hilda, that not only do
you not have any difficulties in carrying on
the house, but that all the housewives in
Germany should be envious of you.   I
believe it.   To ensure that you should lack
nothing, there are orders in the spirit of
German law to the effect that only when the
Germans in Poland have bought all they
want are Poles allowed into the empty shops.
So you have heaven on earth.   But while your
house, Frau Hilda, is crammed with good
things for you and your German guests, all
around you the Polish people are starving.
And from his birth your son, that fat little
fellow, has on his conscience the thousands
of Polish infants who have died of under-
nourishment.

So you say : " Voluntarily I never shall
leave this place."   It seems to me, Frau
Hilda, that some, half-conscious thought
must have passed through your blonde little
head, when you said " Voluntarily."

Why, yes, Frau Hilda, your journey back to
Westphalia will be involuntary, and assuredly unpleasant, and then those Polish
servants for rough work, whom you spoke of
with such contempt, may well use the rougher
end of the roughest of shovels by no means
respectfully on the Westphalian hams of the
good lady from the Herrenvolk.

I will vouch for the Polish men, Frau Hilda
—though undoubtedly they will then be very
occupied with taking leave of your Kreisleiter
husband and your friends of the Gestapo in
both the guest rooms—but the Polish women
servants for rough work also will not want to
be idle at that (as you so beautifully expressed
it) involuntary moment.

German children in Poland, whose parents,
like Frau Hilda and her husband, are " in possession of stolen goods," are here seen at
school.   Happy, well fed, well clothed, their
lot in comparison with those above needs no
comment.   *Photo. E.N.A.*

On a Floating Aerodrome of the Fleet Air Arm

AIRCRAFT CARRIERS, though not prepossessing to a sailor's eye, are as spick and span as any other ships of the Royal Navy. Right, the quarter-deck gets its morning scrub. In the background are two of the 4-in. A.A. guns which are always kept manned.

'Planes, below, are lined up on the flight-deck of an aircraft carrier. That nearest the camera has just returned from a patrol. In the centre is one that has been hoisted from the well. The wings, which are folded back when it is lowered into the well, are being spread.

A Supermarine Walrus amphibian reconnaissance 'plane takes off from the aircraft carrier at dawn. On the extreme left of the photograph can be seen the officer known as "Wings," who gives the O.K. to pilots as they take off and signals them back to the ship.

OFFICERS AND RATINGS of the Fleet Air Arm are drawn up on the quarter-deck of an aircraft carrier to be congratulated on the work they have done. The First Lord of the Admiralty and the First Sea Lord made special mention of the Fleet Air Arm in their congratulatory message to Sir Andrew Cunningham, C.-in-C. of the Mediterranean Fleet, at the conclusion of the first stage of the Libyan campaign in mid-December 1940.

Photos, British Official : Crown Copyright

Another Good Ship Saved by a Sunderland

SUNDERLAND FLYING BOATS of the Coastal Command have played a great part in helping home the "lame ducks" of convoys after enemy attacks. Early in 1941 news was received at a Coastal Command station that a merchant ship, disabled by enemy action, was drifting in the worst of Atlantic winter weather 300 miles west of the Shetlands. The crew of a Sunderland were given the position of the ship and instructions to find her. Visibility was only two miles; clouds were down almost to sea level, and a gale was blowing. Yet by skilful navigation the Sunderland found herself within two hours right over the crippled ship. After staying as long as fuel allowed, the Sunderland started for home, but relays of the same type of aircraft were sent to escort the merchantman, and eventually she was shepherded safe home. Left is the crippled ship as first seen from the flying boat and, above, a close-up view of her.

COMFORT FOR THE CREW is one of the considerations that the designers of the Sunderland flying boats did not neglect. A mess room, above, and a galley, right, enable the crew of six to be well fed during the 10 hours that they may be in the air.

Photos, British Official: Crown Copyright; and "Daily Mirror"

OUR SEARCHLIGHT ON THE WAR

'Robin Hood' of the Balkans

Now that Bulgaria has thrown in her lot with the Axis, the Macedonian leader, Mihailoff, has emerged from hiding. He is the head of a widespread secret organization known as the Imro, a revolutionary Macedonian movement which has long been a thorn in the side of Bulgaria and has also caused watchful anxiety in Yugoslavia. Parts of Macedonia are included in both these countries, the rest being in Greece. Bands of Macedonian Comitadjis (independent hillmen) are escaping over the Bulgarian frontier and offering their services to the Greek Army. Others are organizing themselves into guerilla bands with the object of harassing any invasion of Greece from the north.

Italians to Fight Against Italy

INCLUDED among many thousands of men of the famous French Foreign Legion who disembarked recently from a British troopship at an East African port was a large contingent of Italians. Their comrades were Frenchmen, Poles, Belgians, Dutchmen, Greeks, Spaniards who had seen service in the Civil War—and two Germans. All were ardent anti-Fascists on their way to join the British Army in Eritrea. Now that Great Britain is giving sanctuary to so many refugees from all over Europe, it has been proposed that an English Foreign Legion should be formed.

Nazis Say Lofoten Raid Was 'Unfair'!

AFTER complaining that the British Fleet took unfair advantage of Germany's difficulty in fortifying the long Norwegian coastline, Quisling's newspaper " Fritt Folk " suggested that raids similar to the one on the Lofoten Islands might be prevented in future by the system of hostages—" a number of persons well chosen from suitable circles, and with their names duly published, would work wonders." Already the islanders have been well punished. About 100 were arrested within an hour or two of the arrival, after the raid, of Terboven, Reich Commissar in Norway. A fine of 100,000 kroner has been levied ; the maintenance of the families of the Germans and Quislings taken to England

based on " an exaggerated feeling of justice which has nothing in common with real life."

Swedish Verdict on Lofoten Reprisals

THE consensus of opinion among a large number of Scandinavians on the vindictive German reprisals after the Lofoten raid is reflected in an article in the newspaper " Handelstidning," published at Gothenburg. Among other things the writer observed : " The Germans say we have succumbed to propaganda. Yes, perhaps we have. When we hear that German airmen who have crashed or are shot down in England are buried by the British with the same military honours as their own who have fallen, inspite of the fact that they were dropping bombs on English towns, killing women and children, we doff our hats to the British. When just afterwards the radio tells us about the houses and homes burnt because some Norwegians have gone to England to fight for their country's liberation, and others, allegedly, have helped them to go, comparisons are forced upon us."

German Refugees' Newspaper

ON March 12 there appeared in London the first issue of the only free and independent German newspaper in Europe. It is entitled " Die Zeitung," and its editors, Dr. Lothar and Dr. Haffner, are anti-Nazi journalists of distinction, the latter being also the author of two books, " Offensive against Germany " and " Germany—Jekyll and Hyde." The aim of the newspaper, as set out in its leading article, is to aid in rallying all the resources, physical and moral, of the Free Germans on behalf of Britain. It calls upon them to join the Czechs, Poles, Dutch, Belgians, French and Norwegians who are fighting for the liberation of their countries by the side of Britain, for " the British Isles have become the bastion not only of the Free British Commonwealth, but of European freedom."

R.A.F. Rest House in Cairo

HURRICANE House, recently opened in Cairo, appears a dream of home fulfilled to the R.A.F. air crews who reach its cool portals from the heat and dust of the desert. It owes its existence to the sympathetic initiative of Air Chief Marshal Sir Arthur Longmore, C.-in-C. of Air Forces in the Middle East. Knowing only too well the strain undergone by sergeant pilots, observers and air gunners during long periods of duty over the arid wastes of North Africa, he instituted this rest house to which tired men can be sent for a month of sleep and recuperation. Breakfast in bed, followed by a leisurely bath and shave, are as great a treat as the weekly dances ; sit-

Overseas Gifts for Bomb Victims

GOODS to the value of more than £2,000,000 have been distributed to areas suffering from enemy action through the agency of Mrs. Elsa Dunbar, head of the Purchasing and Overseas department of the Women's Voluntary Services. Most of the articles are gifts from Canada, the United States and

MRS. ELSA DUNBAR, head of the Purchasing and Overseas Dept. of the W.V.S., is pinning on her map another flag denoting a further substantial gift for British bomb victims.
Photo, Planet News

friendly neutrals in South America. They include such items as babies' layettes, sent by Uruguay, small children's clothes and toys from children in British Columbia, and a recent gift of twelve delivery vans from the American Red Cross. Mrs. Dunbar told an interviewer that wherever there is a British Embassy or Legation a W.V.S. party gets to work and sends goods to Britain. " We are on such good terms with our suppliers," she said, " that we tell them what we need most." Stores are established in widespread towns and villages in order to minimize loss through enemy action, and to facilitate the dispatch of goods to areas stricken suddenly by enemy raids.

£10,000,000 in Gifts for Aircraft

FROM time to time the Ministry of Aircraft Production has acknowledged the receipt from the public of sums of money, large and small, for the provision of more bombers and fighters. These contributions have included both individual gifts and the combined result of little amounts saved with difficulty, but good-will by humble citizens who recognize in this way their debt of gratitude to the Royal Air Force. On March 7 Lord Beaverbrook issued the following statement : Through the generosity of the public, through the gifts we have received from warm-hearted people at home and abroad, we have been able to carry out a splendid enterprise. Without any appeal by the Government, more than £10,000,000 has been sent to us for the provision of aircraft for the defence of this island and for our offensive operations oversea. We propose, therefore, to devote to the benevolent funds or Service charities of the three fighting Services and the Merchant Navy 10 per cent of the money sent us after the end of March. It is our belief that by doing so we shall interpret the desire of the public to unite their gratitude to the valiant defenders of freedom with their determination to strengthen the squadrons of the Royal Air Force.

HURRICANE HOUSE, new R.A.F. rest centre in Cairo, was recently opened by Air Chief Marshal Sir Arthur Longmore. Here the padre is seen surrounded by smiling sergeant pilots and observers.
Photo, British Official : Crown Copyright

is to be paid by the islanders ; the houses of those who helped the British and those who left voluntarily have been burnt down. A semi-official explanation and a warning have been issued through the Norwegian Telegram Bureau. In this the imputation that the German measures against the inhabitants of Lofoten are hard and unjust is described as

ting about doing nothing in the surrounding green gardens is probably more of a refreshment than shopping and sightseeing tours made available by the central situation of the rest house. In any case, the improvement in the health of the first batch of guests has been such that the scheme is to be expanded.

Mountain Warfare in Albanian Heights

THE GALLANT GREEKS, fighting as they are often at heights of 6,000 ft., make extensive use of mule transport, not only for food and other needs, but for the hauling of guns and ammunition. Many of these guns have to be transported in sections by the pack mules, and laboriously carried up narrow winding paths to the mountain crags above, where they can be assembled and brought into action.

In the warfare now being carried on in the mountainous districts of Albania the Greeks are making extensive use of small mountain howitzers, almost the only type of artillery which can be transported and used to good effect in this difficult terrain. The high trajectory of its shell makes it possible for the Greeks to fire over peaks and high ridges and dislodge an enemy entrenched beyond. In this manner even strongly held machine-gun posts can be dislodged before the infantry storm the position.

To haul the guns into position a lengthy train of mules is needed, each animal carrying a weight of about 200 lbs. The drawing gives an idea of how the guns are taken in sections up the mountain sides, and shows : A, the gun-wheels ; B, part of the breech mechanism ; C, the gun-shield ; D, part of the trail ; E, the barrel. On other mules are loaded the recoil mechanism, sighting apparatus, ammunition and other essentials.

In the foreground a small mountain howitzer is seen being trained on to its objective by means of the telescopic sighting apparatus F, and is about to be fired by means of the lever, G. Each gun is manned by a crew of six.

Specially drawn for THE WAR ILLUSTRATED *by Haworth*

Cartoon Commentary on the War

OPENING THE FLOOD-GATES
Illingworth in the " Daily Mail "

FLOWERS THAT BLOOM IN THE SPRING, TRA LA!
George Whitelaw in the " Daily Herald "

GERMANY'S INVASION CHANCES
From " Het Bataviaasch Nieuwsblad "

" ALL RIGHT—YOU CAN PUSH THE NEXT ONE IN
Neb in the " Daily Mail "

" HISTORY TOOK US BY THE THROAT . . . ."—Mussolini
Vicky in " Time and Tide "

" WHO'S BEEN EATING MY PORRIDGE ? "
Zec in the " Daily Mirror "

I WAS THERE!

Greek Islanders Treated Me Like a King

Here is another first-hand story of the R.A.F. units who are cooperating with the Greeks on the Albanian front. It depicts the difficult climatic conditions under which they work and, like earlier stories in this section, tells of the warm hospitality shown by the Greek peasants to wounded British airmen.

IN torrential rain and thick cloud, which reduced visibility to zero, an R.A.F. bomber returning from a raid in Albania sought vainly for a landmark on the mountainous west coast of Greece. Lightning had put the radio out of action. Gusts of wind made control and navigation almost impossible. The young Flying Officer decided that the only chance of survival was to put the aircraft on the sea.

Tersely he told the crew. They prepared calmly for an emergency as he circled 400 feet above some shadowy islands near which he proposed to surface his craft.

" On my way down," said the pilot, " we opened the top hatches and undid our parachute harness while the air gunner got the rubber dinghy ready. The aircraft struck the water about a quarter of a mile from the beach of a small island. The nose went down immediately and the bottom was ripped off by the impact."

After a short struggle with the safety belt the pilot and observer came to the surface and swam round looking for the air gunner. They found him dead.

A few seconds later the bomber sank. With great difficulty they released the dinghy, but could not fully inflate it. Lying across it on their stomachs they tried to paddle it with their feet towards the shore. Repeatedly the exhausted observer fell off the

water-filled frail craft and the steadily weakening pilot hauled him back. Finally the observer released his hold on the dinghy and floated away on his lifebelt. Desperately the pilot swam after him to find him lifeless.

" We drifted apart," he said, " and I saw him no more. I was almost in a state of coma from the extreme cold. I actually prayed I too might die of exposure rather than drown.

" Quite suddenly I realized that the wind was taking me perceptibly nearer the island.

I made final efforts to swim the 300 yards to shore and I was tiring rapidly when I saw a shepherd appear over the brow of the hill. I shouted with all my might until he saw me, and, after what seemed a long time, a motor-boat came alongside.

" They seemed to be taking me for an Italian, so I yelled frantically that I was English. I was lifted on board and collapsed. The simple islanders treated me like a king and overwhelmed me with their kindness.

" Two days later, when I had recovered, I got some stones and marked out my name in three-foot letters on the top of the island in the hope that some passing aircraft would see it. None did apparently, but after some days the weather became calm enough for me to be taken to the mainland, where the English wife of a Greek doctor acted as an interpreter and I was able to 'phone my base."

This Is My Life in a German Factory

What are conditions *really* like in Germany? Here we have first-hand evidence in the shape of a report by a member of one of the illegal organizations engaged in rebuilding the German Trade Union movement. It dates from just before the war; if it were written today its gloom would be even more apparent.

UNDER the Nazis we have all become hypocrites. It begins on the way to work. In the tramcar or train compartment sits a parrot-minded person who ruminates on yesterday's leading article in the Nazi paper. You disagree, of course, but can't say so. If you are directly addressed you must at least express vague assent, because the person may be a *provocateur*. Even if he is only one of the herd your answer is certainly overheard by other

passengers. You never know whom you are dealing with. Upon entering the washroom you look around to see who is there and what kind of morning greeting is indicated. The (Nazi) agent must not be given a chance of even reproaching you with half-heartedness. Those marked as half-hearted are suspect, suspect of hostility to the State. Those hostile to the State end in a concentration camp.

The whistle goes, and the conveyor-belt claims us again. When this system was introduced from America fifteen years ago the Nazis howled that it killed the soul of the worker. But now a " German soul " has been breathed into the conveyor, and its speed has been greatly increased. Conveyor and piece work have undergone changes. The humiliating stop-watch has disappeared, but what does that matter if the times allowed are reduced more and more ?

Silence is Golden!

Repair work also has its problems. Where should one begin and where is the material to be obtained ? Pressure from above : manager and foreman, time recorder and ganger—all links in the chain, handing on the stick which beats the hindmost. There is many a quarrel. Those who dare speak back do so in cautious language. Everything is couched, more or less, in technical terms. You pretend to be concerned because the methods employed are not conducive to efficiency. No exception can be taken to that. *You* are not an enemy of the State ; no, you just want to do your job as well as possible . . .

At one time—how long ago is it ?—it was possible to speak your mind if it seemed necessary, even to the boss. Today you hardly dare approach him. If you talk to him in official language he is either better at it than yourself or he falls back on the " interest of the nation "—and who dares to argue about that ? Since the employer

R.A.F. IN GREECE continue to give valuable support to the Greek Army and Air Force. Here a bomber crew on a Greek airfield are just about to enter their aircraft on their way to bomb more Italian military objectives in Albania.   *Photo, British Official: Crown Copyright*

has been made the head of the staff he is in absolute charge. The works council is his faithful assistant, its members are grateful for the comfortable jobs with which they have been bought. They receive the pay of skilled workers although lacking all the qualifications. They are afraid of losing their jobs. To count upon them for protection would be foolish.

The mates cannot help you. You cannot speak frankly with them unless you are among intimate friends, for one traitor can land a whole workshop in a concentration

peace. Meanwhile the wife, at home with the children, must manage with the few shillings you are able to send her.

Formerly, when we were still workers and not mere machines, the evenings enabled you to forget much of the worry of your job. Today you are too tired and run-down to try to spend your spare time in an enjoyable way. A book? You hardly read any more, lack the peace of mind for it. Those fond of tinkering and able to get the material still do a little of it. But for the rest you sit and brood. All there is is the radio—the

least something to eat. Formerly many of us always had fried potatoes with our evening meal, and often also with our breakfast. Today there is no fat for fried potatoes. If the fat is used for potatoes there is none for the bread, and you cannot always take bread-and-jam to work.

The family, that much-praised primary unit of society, in reality exists no more. While the children are very young things are not too bad. But when, because the wife must go out to work, they have to be taken to the kindergarten, they come under the influence of the Nazi welfare organization.

Nazis and the Children

This continues at school, and reaches its climax in the youth organizations. It is no longer possible to talk openly with the children; in their innocence they may repeat what you have said and get you into serious trouble, which is terribly hard also on the children. One must just watch them and try to protect them against evil influences without talking about them. This is to some extent possible as long as the children are at home, but the real troubles come when they have to go to the youth camps or land service. The Nazis want them to live wildly, to get into difficulties, for then they have them in their power. Then come the dangers we know so well and against which no warnings can be given. Only parents who can rely upon the discretion of their children and have no neighbours in the house to spy upon them are in a somewhat better position. But upon the children it imposes the burden of a double life.

You want to give the children the benefit of what you have learnt and acquired in your own life. But you cannot anticipate. You must just watch. This anxiety about the children is for many an even greater worry than the difficulties of everyday life.

In the morning you again go joylessly to your work. In the tramcar or train compartment sits a parrot-minded person who ruminates on yesterday's leading article in the Nazi paper. And so the days pass by. (*International Transport Workers' Federation.*)

GERMAN SCHOOLCHILDREN from the large cities, like the children of our own vulnerable areas, have been evacuated to country districts, and here a class is seen listening to its teacher in a farmyard. The pernicious influence of Nazi teaching upon the youth of Germany is stressed in the article in this page.　　　　　　　　　　　　　　　　　　*Photo, Associated Press*

camp. You cannot speak aloud. In every workshop prowls a spy; even when alone you feel his presence. You are safest if you hold your tongue. However skilled you are, if your views are not exactly what they should be, i.e. if you do not rank 100 per cent loyal to the State, then you may go on devoting yourself to your job, but promotion is confined to those officially recognized as loyal to the Nazi Party. There are many other things which embitter life in the workshops, from little vexations to deliberate victimization such as the allocation of the worst work. You are (even in peacetime) liable to be placed at the disposal of the labour exchange, which sends you to a job in some forsaken place.

Deportation under existing conditions often means separation from one's family for months at a stretch and the loss of one's last bit of private life. The fine-sounding phrase "community life in the barracks" cannot conceal that. In fact, this community life, after a day's hard work for a famine wage, is perhaps the worst feature of all. You must join the others in listening to radio programmes, "Strength through Joy" talks telling the old, old story. You have not an hour to yourself; every minute is looked after. Only when you collapse on your straw mattress do you get a few hours'

foreign radio, to listen to which is a crime. Occasionally you meet a good friend with whom you can talk openly. But he is as tired and run-down as you are.

Then there is the poor food. You know with what difficulty the wife gets it, to what trouble she goes to give at least such savour as it has. Are you to tell her about the worries of your work, adding to a burden which perhaps is already bigger than your own? All the time she is wondering where to find the food to fill all the hungry mouths. Hans' shoes are wearing out, when can I have them soled? How can I get a new pair for Grete? Where can I get the material for some patches? If I buy wool for darning stockings, I shall not have enough ration coupons for a shirt.

The dinner-carrier is coming into fashion again—no wonder, with all the overtime. Mother does her best to give you something nourishing, but then there is nothing left for her and the children. You will not have it, and insist that she and the children must also have some meat and fat. Formerly the wife saw to it that you had sausage on your bread, preferring to eat dry bread at home, for what would your workmates think? Today it is different; and just as in the war of 1914-18 we take bread-and-jam to work, so that those at home may have at

A NAZI WORKMAN busy with a shell-case on the lathe. The deplorable conditions in German factories are described in the article above.　　　　　　　*Photo, Wide World*

Good Food and Plenty of It for the Army

TROOPS' RATIONS are still plentiful and of excellent quality. Judging by this well-stocked Army larder every soldier is amply provided with meat.

Roast beef, Yorkshire pudding, mashed potatoes and turnips, followed by baked jam roll and custard, form the substantial midday meal of the men stationed at the Divisional Headquarters, where these photographs were taken.

THIS ARMY COOK is making baked jam roll — exceedingly popular with members of the Forces, just as it was with the men who served a generation ago.

The two men seen right are enjoying their midday meal out of doors. Soldiers have four good meals a day — breakfast, dinner, tea and supper.

Photos, Sport & General, War Office Official

Queen Wilhelmina Has an Army in Britain

Concluding his series of articles describing the military forces of our Allies which have
their stations in this country, Henry Baerlein below tells us something of the Dutch troops
in Britain.   In addition to these forces Queen Wilhelmina has, of course, a very considerable army, not to mention navy and air force, in the Netherlands Indies.

WHEN Holland was bludgeoned into
submission a number of her soldiers, drawn for the most part from
the southern army, managed to reach Zealand
and subsequently made their way to this
country. Their adventures, as may be
imagined, were many ; one or two of them
will show the determination of these gallant
fellows to continue the struggle.

"Our little party," a lieutenant told me,
"made its way across the north and west of
France. We arrived at Brest : four officers,
a hundred men and forty-two lorries. France
was by that time in a pitiable state, and we
were informed that it was foolish to hope for
a vessel that would carry us to England.
Then, however, a Dutch cargo ship from
South America sailed in with 10,000 tons of
grain, and the captain—a big, broad-shoul-
dered, slow-speaking person from Rotterdam,
who was particularly anxious to do all he
could against the Germans (it will be remembered that in Rotterdam the German bombers
killed about 30,000 civilians in twenty
minutes)—said he would be glad to take us to
England. That, said the French, was impossible ; there was no convoy, they wanted
the grain, and, if we sailed without their
permission, they would fire at us. To these
objections the only reply of the captain was
to load the lorries and set sail. We were not
fired at, and the sole affair of that kind on the
trip was when near Lundy Island we had the
pleasure of seeing a U-boat sunk by a British
'plane."

'Rotterdam,' Reply the Dutch

From every little harbour in Belgium and
Northern France, and in any craft they could
borrow, the Dutch came across the sea.
Some are coming still, although the Germans
in Holland keep on pointing out to them that
it is so absurd to make for a country which is
on the verge of being included in the Greater
German Reich ! They might as well, say

**PRINCE BERNARD of the Netherlands has
been appointed chief liaison officer between the
Royal Netherlands Army, Navy and Air Force
and the corresponding British forces. He is
seen (right) with Gen. Van Oorschot of the
Free Netherlands Army.**

the Germans, stay where they are and be on
friendly terms with the good Nazis—to which
the Dutch, as a rule, reply with one word—
"Rotterdam."

The Dutch army in Britain is in excellent
condition. The one object of officers and
men is to make themselves as efficient as
possible, and they have gone about it with the
thoroughness one would expect of them. It
matters not that most of the officers are not
regulars, but men who after the war will
resume their professional careers. Lawyers,
shipowners, chemists, social workers and
others, they are officers of the reserve and
most competent.

With regard to their uniforms, all our Dutch
allies in this country have now been provided
with the same as those of our own troops,
but with the word "Nether-
land" on the left shoulder and
the Dutch lion on their headgear. *Je maintiendrai* ("I will
uphold," as one might say)
is the national motto, and of
that there is no doubt. As for
decorations. I noticed that
even the officers of long standing
are chary of displaying more
than one or two ribbons. It is
of interest, by the way, that the
Dutch Government is paying,
both in Britain and the United
States, for all its requirements,
not only in the matter of
uniforms, etc., but in every
other respect : the Dutch and the
Norwegians are our only active
allies fortunate enough to be in
this satisfactory position. In
their East Indies alone the Dutch
have enormous resources. (It
will be remembered that great
sums have been presented from
those parts for the building of
Spitfires and Hurricanes ; the
latest to us is a luxury liner fitted
out as a hospital ship.)

At a place where I visited the Dutch troops
I found that they had settled down very well
in several disused factory buildings (though
less improvized accommodation will be ready
for them elsewhere very shortly), and where
they are now the officers have to be quartered
in various houses in and around the little
town. The Dutch have a talent for languages, and every officer I met was quite
fluent in English, which is one reason why
they have become so popular in that neighbourhood. But they do not allow anything
to interfere with their military duties : every
morning the wide space between the buildings
is a scene of activity. A considerable array
of motor vehicles is at their disposal, and
more and more tanks are being acquired.

A typical officer whom I met is in civilian
life a publisher. His job in the war was to
hold the famous Moerdyk Bridge that joins
North Holland to Brabant. He had been
mobilized for eight months, and I would as
soon be with him in a dangerous spot, which
that bridge certainly was, as give him a book
to publish. "Responsibility," he said,
"makes you calm—you know that they depend on you." No wonder that the British
army authorities who have been brought into
contact with such men have the highest
opinion of their morale.

"The morale of the men is good," said a
South African corporal who left his 6,000-
acre farm and came back to fight in Holland,
where he had been born. "We Dutch," he
said, "have a saying that a soldier who does
not grumble is no good. We don't grumble
much, I think, because we recognize that this
is not an ordinary affair and we are so glad to
be with the British who will go on shoulder
to shoulder with us." This South African, a
giant of a man, helped for a time in the
recruiting office over here ; the age limits for
applicants, by the way, are twenty to thirty-
six, although men both younger and older
have been accepted if they have passed the
medical test. One man who had, temporarily
at all events, to be rejected was a Dutchman
who had lived in the Hebrides, his mother's
home, and could speak only Gaelic ; he was
invited to learn either English or Dutch.
Quite a number of young fellows born in this
country, but of Dutch parentage, have joined
this Dutch army in Britain, and some of them
have now had to learn the language of their
ancestors ; they pick it up pretty soon.

The Price of Popularity

There is so much that the Dutch and ourselves have in common, e.g. the administration of a vast Oriental empire, and we are
getting to know them well in this country.
Everywhere the Dutch soldiers have troops of
friends, some of whom are optimistic enough
to believe that a Dutch soldier is always ready
to shed his buttons on the altar of friendship.
"Any knoops today ?" is the cry that often
greets them. It is reported that English girls
have been charming the gilded lion from
Dutch uniforms, and a captain is even said
to have yielded his three stars, thus reducing
himself for the time being to the ranks ! To
imagine that the Dutch are always dour is
quite a mistake ; that quality they are keeping in reserve for the Nazis.

**'VRIJ NEDERLAND' (Free Netherlands) is a Dutch news-
paper produced in Britain and eagerly read by members of
the Dutch fighting forces stationed here. "Je maintiendrai"
(I will uphold), the words seen underneath the title, is the
motto of the Royal House of Orange.**
Photos, Keystone

Doughty Dutchmen Among Our Allies

ENGLISH-SPEAKING DUTCHMEN, who cannot speak their mother tongue because they have lived all their lives in Great Britain, are now busily engaged in learning Dutch, or in some instances perfecting a meagre knowledge, assisted by instructors and records.

FIELD TELEGRAPHY, an important part of army training, is here being studied by a party of Dutch soldiers in Britain. There are many fighting men of the Netherlands now in Britain, awaiting the day which shall release their country from Nazi tyranny.

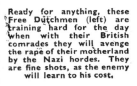

This gigantic Dutchman, W. J. Vanderberg, of S. Africa, left his 6,000-acre farm to fight in Holland's cause. No battle-dress in stock could be found to fit him, for he weighs over 17 stone and stands 6 ft. 6 ins. Inset, the Dutch lion that is worn by the troops as their badge.

Ready for anything, these Free Dutchmen (left) are training hard for the day when with their British comrades they will avenge the rape of their motherland by the Nazi hordes. They are fine shots, as the enemy will learn to his cost.

Photos, G.P.U., Keystone

OUR DIARY OF THE WAR

TUESDAY, MARCH 11, 1941   *556th day*

On the Sea—Admiralty announced that British submarine had sunk heavily laden troopship in Mediterranean.

In the Air—Single R.A.F. aircraft bombed oil storage plant at Rotterdam and factory near Utrecht. At night attacks were made on naval base at Kiel, docks at Bremerhaven and two aerodromes.

War against Italy—Cairo reported that Imperial forces in Abyssinia had captured Afodu escarpment south-east of Kurmuk and were advancing towards Asosa.

On night of 10-11 R.A.F. made heavy bombing raid on Tripoli, damaging harbour buildings and shipping. Other aircraft raided aerodrome in Tripolitania.

Two bombing attacks on Rhodes during nights of 10-11 and 11-12. Large fires started at Maritza and Calato.

Enemy made night attack on Malta, causing some damage. Two raiders destroyed. Other aircraft reported to have attacked R.A.F. aerodromes at Port Said and Ismailia, but without causing damage.

Home Front—Enemy activity during day slight except in Kent coastal area. At night raids were chiefly directed against south coast, a town in Midlands and a north-west town. Few raiders were also over Liverpool and in other areas.

Enemy aircraft shot down by fighters off south coast. Coastal Command destroyed two Heinkels, one off east coast of Scotland, other off Danish coast.

Greek War—Athens reported that enemy continued his attempted attacks, but all had been repulsed with considerable losses. In Greek counter-attacks 450 prisoners taken.

R.A.F. bombed troop movements and motor transport on Glava-Buzi road. Seven Italian fighters shot down.

Balkans—Attempt on life of Mr. Rendel, former Minister in Sofia, by explosion of two bombs in his hotel at Istanbul.

General—Lease and Lend Bill was passed by U.S. House of Representatives, signed by President Roosevelt, and became law.

WEDNESDAY, MARCH 12   *557th day*

In the Air—Heaviest raid of war on Germany when R.A.F. made night attack on Berlin, Hamburg and Bremen.

Schiphol aerodrome also raided, and single aircraft attacked targets in N.W. Germany and Low Countries. Large fires started at Boulogne.

War against Italy—Cairo reported that on March 10 British troops in Somaliland occupied Dagga Bur, 600 miles north of Mogadishu.

R.A.F. carried out heavy night raid on Rhodes. Tripoli was also attacked.

Home Front—During day few bombs fell in Kent. At night enemy made large-scale raid on Merseyside, but achieved little. Raiders were also reported from many other widely separated parts of England, Wales and Scotland.

Nine night bombers destroyed.

Greek War—Heavy fighting reported in Albania. Since early morning on March 11 Italians had launched six successive attacks at various points. All were repulsed.

Fifteen Italian aircraft shot down and others severely damaged by R.A.F. fighters in Tepelini-Klisura area. At night Valona aerodrome and Saseno Island were attacked.

Balkans—Million men called to colours in Yugoslavia.

THURS., MARCH 13   *558th day*

On the Sea—Greek destroyer Psara reported to have sunk Italian submarine in Aegean Sea.

Dornier hit and probably destroyed by H.M. trawler Milford Queen.

H.M.S. Manistee reported sunk.

In the Air—Coastal Command aircraft torpedoed enemy destroyer off Jutland. Two supply ships hit, one in Ymuiden harbour other off Norwegian coast. Another torpedoed and sunk off Frisian Islands.

Fighters and bombers attacked aerodrome at Calais. At night R.A.F. delivered heaviest attack yet made on Hamburg. Oil storage plants at Rotterdam bombed, also Bremen, Emden, and two Dutch aerodromes.

War against Italy—Nairobi announced that Patriot forces had occupied Yavello, 70 miles north of Mega.

Home Front—In early morning our fighters intercepted formation of enemy fighters and bombers near S.E. coast and shot two down. Night attacks were widespread. Heavy and prolonged raid on Clydeside. Relays of bombers over Merseyside and N.E. town.

Thirteen night bombers destroyed.

FRIDAY, MARCH 14   *559th day*

In the Air—R.A.F. made night raid on oil plants at Gelsenkirchen and on Düsseldorf.

War against Italy—Cairo announced that in Abyssinia Asosa had been occupied and troops now advancing along Mendi road. Patriot forces had reached outskirts of Debra Marcos.

Home Front—No bombs fell during day. Bomber shot down off Welsh coast. Clydeside again attacked at night. Town in N.E.

PERA PALACE HOTEL, Istanbul, where bombs exploded in the baggage of Mr. George Rendel, the British Minister recalled from Sofia, on the night of March 11, 1941, is a substantial modern structure, yet the force of the explosion was so great as to rock the whole building. *Photo, E.N.A.*

England had sharp raid, and other widespread places were also bombed.

Five night bombers destroyed.

Greek War—Repeated violent enemy attacks repulsed. Greeks counter-attacked and captured number of prisoners.

R.A.F. shot down eight Italian aircraft in Klisura area.

SATURDAY, MARCH 15   *560th day*

In the Air—Another night attack on Düsseldorf and on Lorient.

War against Italy—Considerable air activity in Keren region. Fighters of S.A.A.F. destroyed eight Italian aircraft at Diredawa.

Home Front—London was enemy's chief night target. Bombs also fell in other districts, mostly S.E. England and Home Counties.

Greek War—Italian offensive defeated with great loss. R.A.F. bombed aerodromes at Berat and Valona.

H.M.S. LEANDER, which sank the Italian armed merchant cruiser, Ramb I, in the Indian Ocean on March 9, 1941, is a cruiser of 7,270 tons, completed in March 1933, and a sister ship of the Ajax and Achilles of River Plate fame. She carries eight 6-in. guns, eight 4-in. A.A. guns, and one aircraft. *Photo, Wright & Logan*

CYRENAICA'S CONQUEROR INSPECTS AN ENEMY UNIT

Lieut.-General Sir Henry Maitland Wilson, who commanded the Army of the Nile during the operations in the Western Desert, was appointed Military Governor and C.-in-C. of Cyrenaica on February 10, 1941, and was created G.B.E. He is here seen in the most westerly area inspecting a Tripolitan camel corps who with their beasts fell into British hands when the Italians made their hasty retreat. General Wilson is wearing a uniform of his own devising, a jersey with the shoulder badges of his rank. His aide-de-camp following him wears the same unconventional but comfortable attire.

Photo, British Official: Crown Copyright

Again the Greeks Smashed the Italian Hordes

As likely as not the Italian offensive which opened in the mountains of Albania on March 9 was intended to coincide with a German demonstration against Greece and even more against Yugoslavia. But once again the Greeks upset the Axis time-table, since, as we tell below, they completely repelled the Italian onslaught.

TIRED of the months of indecisive war-fare in the Albanian mountains, increasingly resentful of the damage done to his already diminished prestige, Mussolini in March ordered General Cavallero to hack his way through the Greek lines. We can imagine the Duce angrily striding up and down his great room in the Palazzo Venezia, fuming over the news from the front, that news to which not even his pen could give the semblance of victory. Why did not Cavallero advance ? Why did he not smash the Greeks ? Why had he not appeared before the gates of Salonika where his army ought to have been months before ? Why, indeed ! The Greeks gave Mussolini his answer—those once despised but now feared Greeks who have proved more than a match for the crack troops of the Italian Empire.

News of the coming offensive seems to have trickled through to the Greek High Command, for on March 6 General Papagos anticipated it by launching a local offensive, which in a few hours developed so success-fully that his men gained mastery of important heights which the Italians had intended to be their jumping-off ground. Fierce fighting continued for several days, in which the Italians were pressed still farther back, so that when they launched their great offensive on Sunday, March 9, they had to begin it at a great tactical disadvantage.

But Mussolini had given the order, and Cavallero knew better than to disobey. Having brought up large reinforcements and plentiful supplies of ammunition, the Italian C.-in-C. gave the order to advance. From Lake Okhrida to the Adriatic the battle front in mountain and valley blazed into activity after the long rest forced by the bitter winter weather. But the principal zone of oper-ations was a sector barely twenty miles in width facing Tepeline, extending from the valley of the River Aoos (Vijose) to the southern slopes of Mt. Tomori. On this narrow front

seven Italian divisions were hurled into the fight, supported by a special legion of Black-shirts, three independent regiments of picked troops, and eight other battalions. The chief weight of the Italian offensive was concen-trated on a front of 2½ miles wide, on the north of the Trebeshina range, where it was calculated that the Greek resistance would be weakest.

But this calculation was soon disproved. Wave after wave of Italian shock troops – Alpini, Bersaglieri and Blackshirts to the fore —were dashed back with the most bloody loss. The ground in front of the Greek positions was covered with wounded and dead. Though subjected to a heavy bombard-ment from a vastly superior artillery and frequently bombed from the air, the Greeks

GENERAL PAPAGOS
(right), Greek C.-in-C., has just been appointed by the King an Hon. G.B.E.

These houses (below left) in the Greek town of Larissa were destroyed by Italian bombs while their inhabitants were still suffering from a severe earthquake.

On the map below is shown (dotted line) the approximate battle front following the bloody repulse of the Italian offensive of March 9-15.
Photos, Sport & General and Planet News

gave never an inch. Each enemy attack was followed, as a matter of course, by a counter-attack, which drove the enemy headlong down the mountain side. As a result of these counter-attacks the Greeks had taken, even early in the battle, more than 3,000 prisoners, including many senior officers.

For six days the battle raged ; for six days 120,000 Italians were continuously engaged on that twenty-mile front in an endeavour to cut their way through. But all in vain. After suffering horrible losses they retired to lick their wounds. Their casualties in killed and wounded alone were stated to amount to 50,000, and in addition several thousand prisoners were left in Greek hands. Several of the Italian divisions were so shattered that they had to be withdrawn from the line, and many units were reported to have lost forty or fifty per cent of their effectives. Among the casualties were six members of the Fascist Grand Council, including Professor Pellegrini, who was taken prisoner, and Barberini and Bottai, Minister of Education, who were among the slain ; according to report, Bottai was killed while endeavouring to rally his retreating troops with his revolver.

" The enemy has failed to occupy a yard of territory," announced a semi-official statement issued in Athens, " and the offen-sive has been completely checked." It was claimed that " the results of this success are among the most important we have yet won, especially as the enemy's attempt was pre-ceded by long preparations, as immense quantities of ammunition were accumu-lated and large forces en-gaged far in excess of our own." So conclusive was the Greek victory that it was regarded as improbable

(Continued in page 340)

What Did the Duce Think of the Débâcle?

BEHIND THE GREEK LINES the staff at a regimental office are censoring letters to mothers and wives. Family affection is strong among the Greeks, and the soldiers from country districts where compulsory attendance at school is not always strictly enforced manage to find a friendly scribe to write home.

Not least of the many virtues that the Greek Army has displayed is the cheerfulness with which they have endured Arctic conditions in Albania. The sentry, above, standing by a supply wagon in a blizzard, still smiled.

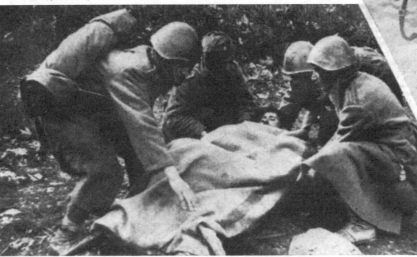

TENDING WOUNDED in Albania was made extremely difficult by the rough roads and the absence of railways. The soldiers themselves, as this photo shows, often gave first-aid to their wounded comrades. Casualties had sometimes to be carried long distances on stretchers to the nearest first aid post.

THE GREEKS have proved themselves a nation of both heroes and heroines, for women have voluntarily undertaken tasks so arduous that only their life of strenuous toil in the fields makes them capable of the exertion. Right, stouthearted and sturdy daughters of Greece are carrying heavy boxes of ammunition towards the front over a mountain track so rough and steep that wheeled transport is impossible.

Photos, Bosshard and Courtesy of the Royal Greek Legation

What Will Be the Next Change in Europe's Map?

that the enemy would be able to renew the offensive for weeks to come.

If report spake true, Mussolini himself was an eye-witness of the débâcle. Perhaps he thought that his presence would suffice almost of itself to give his men the victory. If he indeed were at the front, still more if he were actually directing the offensive and had insisted (as was said) on a decisive victory by March 15, then what must have been his chagrin, his humiliation, when he saw his crack regiments, despite all their frantic efforts, shattered against the granite walls of the Greek resistance ? The soldiers were told that the Duce was with them, that he

was touring that vital central sector in an armoured car or a tank. But none of the prisoners seemed to have actually seen him, although some had been informed that he was " visiting the next unit."

March 15 came, but it brought with it no victory. " The Duce," said Athens radio, " planned to return to Italy on Saturday with a victory, but what he will take back will be one more defeat, the heaviest of all, and the maledictions of the battered Italian army." So beaten, indeed, that deserters who made their appearance in the Greek lines confessed that the Italian army in Albania " was rapidly disintegrating " after the

failure of the great offensive. Many units, they said, were in wild, headlong flight towards the Adriatic, and there was little discipline left anywhere. True, Cavallero and his lieutenant, General Geloso, sent their men over the top in yet another attack, but this, too, was beaten back by the indomitable Greeks, powerfully supported by bombers of the R.A.F. Then came the news that Tepeline, which had been one of the principal Greek objectives since December, had been entered by the Greek troops. The report, as it happened, was premature, but there was nothing uncertain about the Greek triumph.

THIS STRATEGICAL MAP OF WARTIME EUROPE shows as clearly as may be the areas under the control of the belligerent Powers—Britain and her Allies on the one hand and the Axis states on the other. It also has a strategical interest, for on it are indicated the direction of military operations already in progress and even more of the moves which the future may hold in store—in particular the invasion routes which it has been suggested the Nazis might attempt, the zones of the blockade and counter-blockade, and the German thrust into the Balkans and the British into Libya.

Map from " New York Times "

Thirty Is the Burma Squadron's Bag—So Far

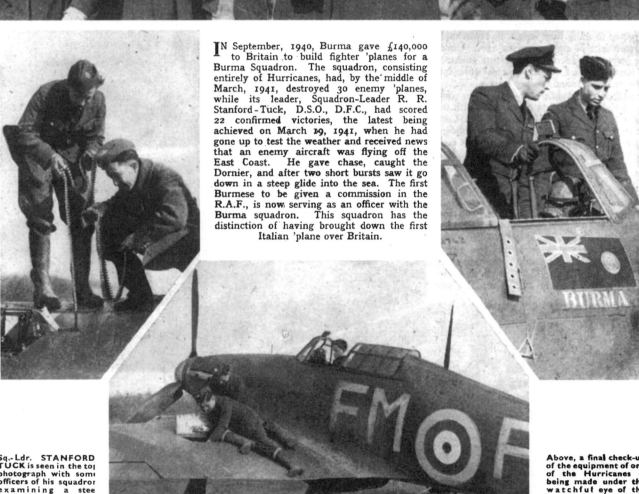

IN September, 1940, Burma gave £140,000 to Britain to build fighter 'planes for a Burma Squadron. The squadron, consisting entirely of Hurricanes, had, by the middle of March, 1941, destroyed 30 enemy 'planes, while its leader, Squadron-Leader R. R. Stanford-Tuck, D.S.O., D.F.C., had scored 22 confirmed victories, the latest being achieved on March 19, 1941, when he had gone up to test the weather and received news that an enemy aircraft was flying off the East Coast. He gave chase, caught the Dornier, and after two short bursts saw it go down in a steep glide into the sea. The first Burmese to be given a commission in the R.A.F., is now serving as an officer with the Burma squadron. This squadron has the distinction of having brought down the first Italian 'plane over Britain.

Sq.-Ldr. STANFORD TUCK is seen in the top photograph with some officers of his squadron examining a steel helmet, a souvenir of the first Italian 'plane brought down over England. Above with the Squadron Leader, the Burmese officer (right) is overhauling the ammunition belt of a Hurricane.

Above, a final check-up of the equipment of one of the Hurricanes is being made under the watchful eye of the Squadron-Leader. Left, the ground staff of the aerodrome are at work on the special wire netting which helps "take-offs" when the ground is greasy with mud.

Photos, Planet News

Well May Turkey be Proud of Her Army

Though with the seizure of Bulgaria the Nazi troops were on their very frontier, the Turks refused to be cowed. " Turkey," declared the. Ankara radio, " stands as a fortress, ready to obey every command of the President. Turkey stands erect, head high, and proud." This article treats of the Army in which our ally so rightly puts her trust.

MANY a resounding page has been written in European military annals by the Turkish Army since that day, some six centuries ago, when the Sultan's hosts crossed the Dardanelles from Asia Minor and embarked on that career of conquest which carried them to the gates of Vienna. Even in the last hundred years, when the Ottoman power was visibly declining, the valour of the Turkish soldiery was never in dispute. On many a hopeless field they have fought just as bravely, just as stubbornly, as did their fathers when the crescent flag was the emblem of victory. Defeated in the Balkan wars, defeated in the Great War, in both Turkey's soldiers more than maintained their reputation as fighting men.

Since 1918 that reputation has been enhanced by the triumphs of the war against Greece, which in 1923 resulted in the Greeks being driven out of Asia Minor ; and in a war today the Turks may be confidently expected to more than repeat the remarkable performance of eighteen years ago. Under the inspiring leadership and expert guidance of Kemal Pasha (Ataturk) and his lieutenant, now President Inonu, Turkey's army is second to none in the Middle East—indeed, in some very important respects it may rank with the finest military establishments of the Continent. To modern Turkey, as to modern Japan, the army is the symbol, as it has been the instrument, of the national renascence.

Two Million Bayonets

Every Turk is liable for military service between the ages of 20 and 46 ; usually he serves 18 months in the infantry or two years in the cavalry, artillery, and air arm. Every year not far short of 100,000 young men are called to the colours, and the peacetime strength of the army is approximately 20,000 officers and 175,000 rank and file. For the past year or two—since the war

clouds began to loom over the Eastern Mediterranean—the army has been put on a war footing, and it is believed that Turkey has at the moment considerably more than a million men under arms. In the event of war she might muster two million bayonets. In peacetime the army was organized in nine army corps, each of which was normally composed of two infantry divisions, a heavy artillery regiment of two to four batteries, a squadron of cavalry, and the usual corps troops. Each infantry division was made up of three regiments of three battalions and three machine-gun companies, one artillery regiment of two field batteries and two mountain batteries, a company of pioneers, and a company of signallers, etc. Considerable forces are stationed at the four great fortresses of Chatalja (the famous Lines which bar the way to Istanbul from the European side), Izmir (as Smyrna is called today), Kars, and Erzerum.

Turkish officers receive their military education at the military college at Ankara. The usual course is for two years, and every cadet has to serve six months in the ranks. All university graduates when called up for service serve six months in the ranks, then six months in an officer cadet training corps, and a third six months in the army as officer cadets, after which they are demobilized, although they are often called up for refresher courses. At the old-established military academy at Istanbul, field officers take specialist courses.

New Material from Overseas

In the matter of equipment the Turkish army is now reasonably up to date. Large numbers of guns of all kinds, tanks, and trucks for the transport of men and material have been purchased from Britain and Canada, and month by month the number of mechanized and motorized units grows.

The infantry are armed chiefly with Mauser rifles, while the artillery have 75mm. field guns and 10·5 and 12 cm. howitzers. Recently heavy batteries have been equipped with guns supplied by Britain and America.

Under the Turkish Constitution the supreme command of the army is vested in and exercised by the President of the Republic, who is also chairman of the Supreme War Council. In time of peace the actual command of the military forces is entrusted to the Chief of the General Staff—at present Field Marshal Fevzi Chakmak, a close friend and comrade of Ataturk. In the present state of near-war, the Marshal is in effect the Commander-in-Chief of the Turkish army. In the event of actual hostilities we may presume that it would be Marshal Chakmak who would lead the Turkish army in the field—and lead it, we may believe in all confidence. to victory.

THE TURKISH ARMY OF TODAY has been extensively mechanized and re-equipped with modern instruments of war. In the upper photograph a column of lorries, each carrying an anti-aircraft gun, is moving through typical Turkish country during manoeuvres. Above, a Turkish officer is using a range-finder.   *Photos, Fox and Press Topics*

They March Under the Banner of the Crescent

TURKISH REGIMENTS, in keeping with the progressive tendencies of modern Turkey, are now provided with modern military equipment. They have been quick to realize the importance of speed in manoeuvre, and in the top photograph a motor-cycle unit is moving off, three men to each outfit, one in the saddle, one on the pillion and one in the sidecar, with their arms slung across their shoulders. In the lower photograph a Turkish infantry battalion is seen marching past at an inspection during manoeuvres with the national flag—white crescent and star on a red ground—flying and the band playing in the background.

Photos, Fox

The Union Jack Flies Again Over Berbera

When Berbera was occupied by the Italians in August, 1940, Rome claimed that a jewel had been taken from His Britannic Majesty's crown. For our part it was admitted that, though it was a rather dusty jewel and of no great price, its loss constituted a blow at British prestige in the East. The Italian triumph was short-lived, however, for on March 16, 1941, Berbera was recaptured by Imperial troops.

FOR seven months Berbera, capital of the British colony in Somaliland, was in the hands of the Italians. They took it in August, 1940, at the close of a brief campaign in which they had been able to oppose battalions to companies or even platoons. They hailed its capture as the first fruits of a campaign which would ere long end with the British being driven out of East Africa ; they claimed that, with Berbera in their hands, the Red Sea would be closed to British trade and the Mediterranean Fleet would be bottled up. This was their claim, their hope, but the one was falsified as they were disappointed in the other. Their tenure of the place proved to be of little advantage to them, and they did next to nothing to consolidate their

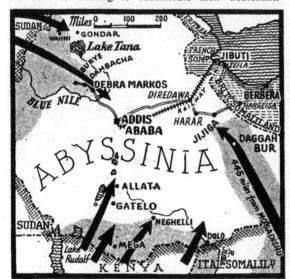

The capture of Berbera gives, as this map shows, a new point of attack for the Imperial and Patriot forces in Abyssinia. The direction of the other advances is shown by arrows, while the territory already taken is shaded.

" conquest." Then, in March, they lost in a few hours what in August they had taken nearly a fortnight to win.

" The British flag again flies over Berbera," read a communiqué issued from British G.H.Q., Cairo, on Monday, March 17, " which was yesterday recaptured after our troops had made a successful landing in cooperation with units of the Royal Navy and the Royal Air Force." The story was given a few hours later in a cable from Aden.

Landings in the Dark

Plans for the assault were prepared with the utmost care and skill. From reports which had been received from friendly natives it was known that the Italians holding the town were in no position to make a prolonged resistance. First our aircraft photographed the whole enemy position, so revealing the Italian plan of defence. Next the bombers of the R.A.F. went into action, heavily raiding the enemy aerodromes. Then, shortly before midnight on Saturday, March 15, a little fleet of British warships and troop-carriers crept silently in the dark towards the Somaliland coast. The night was calm and

the moon, obscured now and again by clouds, showed dimly the long low line of the foreshore with a mass of mountains beyond.

With a view to dividing the already depleted and demoralized Italians, two landings had been planned at places most unfavourable for the defence. The one on the west was entrusted to picked Indian regiments supported by engineers and artillery, while the second on the east was to be carried out by a force of Somalis and Arabs specially raised for the purpose at Aden and under English officers.

Attack from East and West

Just before zero hour one of the warships crept in close to the coast and lowered a tiny skiff in which were three men under a lieutenant. They were the pioneers of the re-occupation, and their job was to mark a landing beach without being detected by the enemy. The little boat slipped away into the dark, and to the anxious watchers it seemed an age before a single flash announced that they had completed their task. Then suddenly the peace of the Gulf of Aden was shattered by the thunder of the naval guns. At once the force on the west wing began their assault, while the Somali force on the other side of the town continued their landing and advanced along the shore towards Berbera, about two miles distant. Later it was learned that the greater part of the Italian forces had left the town under cover of darkness just before our approach, but with a few machine-guns and field guns

those who had been left behind tried to hold up the advance of the Somalis. Their resistance was soon crushed, however, by the naval guns, the accuracy of whose fire in the murky light with only an occasional flash to give them their aim was remarkable.

Swiftly the Somali-Arab force pushed their way along the shore, while to the west the major attack was developing satisfactorily. By 9.20 on Sunday morning the operation was over and Berbera was once more in British hands. As the victors entered the outskirts they were greeted by crowds of natives waving Union Jacks and Somaliland flags which they had kept hidden in their huts in anticipation of this day.

One of the first to enter the town was an officer of the Somaliland administration who during the months of exile at Aden had kept in personal touch with the territory. He strode through the streets as though he were just coming back from his usual morning walk, and from all sides he was greeted by smiling men and women. Within a few hours transport and stores were being landed from the ships and gangs of Somali labourers were repairing the road which the Italians had blown up in their flight.

About 100 prisoners were taken, forlorn fellows enough in ragged clothing and miserably equipped. When the major in command handed over his revolver to a British officer in token of submission, he burst into tears. " I am an old soldier," was all he could say.

So Berbera was recaptured. Our casualties were stated to be negligible, while the R.A.F., whether in the air or on the ground—it was revealed that their armoured cars had played a valuable part in the capture of the town—incurred no casualties whatever.

When this photograph of Italians hoisting their flag over the Fort at Berbera in August, 1940, was published in Italy, it was said to prove that Italians were even better than Germans at blitzkrieg, as they had captured a British Colony in "the remarkably short time of 12 days." They held it for the remarkably short time of seven months.   *Photo, E.N.A.*

Thick Fall the Bombs on Doomed Keren

KEREN, key point of Eritrea, was the first position at which the Italians made a determined stand after General Platt's Army took Agordat on February 1, 1941. It at once became a main objective of the Royal Air Force and was bombed many times. Above is the scene during one of the aerial attacks. A stick of bombs has burst among the buildings of the town and direct hits have been secured on the Asmara-Agordat railway, the curved line in the centre.

Photo, British Official: Crown Copyright

Down Swooped the Nazi~the Convoy Sailed On

In the unique photograph left, two bombs are seen dropping from a Messerschmitt 110 which swooped down to 120 feet above the convoy. They fell in the sea, but one near miss damaged the stern of the ship above.

SHIPS IN CONVOY off the British coasts have frequently been attacked by Nazi bombers. On board one of them recently was a photographer who, though bombs were dropping and the ship was machine-gunned, still carried on. A Messerschmitt 110 made a low dive above the ship he was in, and when one of the escorting destroyers directed a hail of machine-gun fire at it the Nazi 'plane replied with bombs, as seen in the top photographs. In the lower photograph are some of the other ships of the convoy still keeping their stations with precision during the attack.
Photos, Planet News

One of the Most Momentous Battles Ever

Admiral Sir Percy Noble, left, whose appointment as Commander-in-Chief of the Western Approaches was announced on March 14, 1941, is sixty-one years of age. He was in command of the China Station from 1938 to 1940. Above are destroyers in line ahead. These small ships are playing a most important part in the Battle of the Atlantic.

Photo, British Official: Crown Copyright; and Bassano

"THE Battle of the Atlantic," said Mr. Churchill on March 18 in his speech at the luncheon given in London in honour of Mr. John G. Winant, the new American Ambassador, "we must regard as one of the momentous ever fought in all the annals of war. . . . It must be won beyond all doubt if the declared policies of the Government and people of the United States are not to be forcibly frustrated. Not only German U-boats, but German battle cruisers have crossed to the American side of the Atlantic and have already sunk some of our independently routed ships not sailing in convoy. They have sunk these ships as far west as the 42nd meridian.

"Over here upon the approaches to our island an intense and unrelenting struggle is being waged to bring in the endless stream of munitions and food without which our war effort cannot be maintained. Our losses have risen for the time being, and we are applying our fullest strength and resource, and all the skill and science we can command, in order to meet this potentially mortal challenge. But our strength is growing every week. The American destroyers which reached us in the autumn and winter are increasingly coming into action. Our flotillas are growing in number. Our air power over the island and over the seas is growing fast. We are striking back with increasing effect."

Hard by St. Paul's in the City's Storied Heart

LOOKING down from the gallery that surrounds St. Paul's great dome, one sees now just beyond the Churchyard a wilderness of shattered buildings, of streets flanked by ruins, of little squares which now enclose nothing more than heaps of debris. For many years, indeed for centuries, what is now a scene of desolation was the home of those who produced books and sold them, one of the favourite haunts of those who read them. For generations the narrow streets and alleys, the little closes, the shops, the warehouses, the printing rooms, played their part in our intellectual life ; then, on the night of December 29, 1940, there descended upon them a hail of incendiary and high-explosive bombs, so that when morning dawned nothing was left but a heap of smoking ruins. Paternoster Row and Paternoster Square, Ave Maria Lane, Ivy Lane and Warwick Lane and Amen Corner—names which recall the religious and historic associations of this ancient quarter—these are now little more than names. So it has come about that today they stand not for man's literary heritage accumulated through the ages, but constitute a monument to Nazism's unrelenting warfare against the things of the mind and of the spirit.

derness of Shattered Streets and Blackened Ruins

"**A**FTER thirty-one days of ruthless bombing, the old massive capital stands solid and intact": this is what we wrote shortly after London had become the main target of the Nazi bombers, and we published a photograph (see page 434, Vol. 3) to substantiate the claim. But, alas, no such claim can be made today, when another six months of furious war has left all too many scars upon the Empire's capital, although the principal landmarks fortunately remain standing. Above, viewed from the dome in March 1941, is the area, devastated by Nazi bombs and cleared of dangerous structures by our Pioneers, which lies just north of St. Paul's. The chief objects of interest are numbered as follows:

1, St. Paul's Cathedral ; 2, Ludgate Hill ; 3, St. Martin's Church, Ludgate Hill ; 4, Fleet Street ; 5, Memorial Hall, Farringdon Street ; 6, The Fleetway House ; 7, St. Andrew's Church, Holborn ; 8, Old Bailey (Central Criminal Court) ; 9, St. Sepulchre's Church ; 10, General Post Office ; 11, Smithfield Meat Market ; 12, St. Bartholomew's Hospital ; 13, Christ Church ; 14, Newgate Street ; 15, Ivy Lane ; 16, Paternoster Row ; 17, Paternoster Square ; 18, Warwick Lane ; 19, Amen Corner.

By way of comparison we reproduce on the left the photograph taken from almost the same place and showing some of the same area on October 9 last year.

Photos, Central Press, Planet News

They Soon Drove the 'Enemy' Into the Sea

INVASION PRACTICE was carried out by troops of our Eastern and Western Commands in early spring, 1941. The results were highly satisfactory, but not to the "enemy," although the dice was loaded carefully in their favour. The photographs in this page show scenes during these realistic practices. Top, 6-in. howitzers, towed by motor-lorries, are being rushed along a country road to a point where the enemy has landed. Left centre is a small "enemy" armoured car captured by troops with Tommy guns. Two "enemy" Bren gunners, centre circle, are holding the corner of a street in a town of which parachute troops had taken possession. Left is an "enemy" armoured car brought to a standstill by barbed wire and incendiary bombs.

Photos, British Official: Crown Copyright

Britain's Invasion Barges Make Their Début

The general lines of the British invasion barges are clearly shown in the photographs left and that below. Flat-bottomed and broad in the beam they can carry, without fear of capsizing, as large a number of men as can be squeezed on board. They are power-driven with a protective shield over the steersman and engineer. The forward view in the photograph below shows the square bow which, though not conducive to speed, greatly assists speedy landing.

IN THE LOFOTEN ISLANDS RAID of March 4, 1941, invasion barges were used for the first time by the British. The ships of the Royal Navy that took part in it, though described as light forces, could not get alongside the jetty and wharves of the four fishing harbours raided, so the invasion barges were brought into use and took the troops and naval ratings ashore. Above is one of them alongside a wharf loading up for the return journey with troops and Norwegian refugees.

Photos, British Official : Crown Copyright

AMERICA THE ARSENAL OF DEMOCRACY

President Roosevelt's Declaration of Utmost Aid for Britain

'Speed, and Speed Now' is the Watchword

WE American people are just now engaged in a great debate. It was not limited to the halls of Congress. It was argued, argued in every newspaper, on every wavelength, over every cracker barrel in all the land, and it was finally settled and decided by the American people themselves.

Yes, the decisions of our democracy may be slowly arrived at; but when decision is made, it is proclaimed not with the voice of any one man but as the voice of 130,000,000. It is binding on us all and the world is no longer left in doubt.

This decision is the end of any attempt at appeasement in our land, the end of urging us to get along with dictators, the end of compromise with tyranny and the forces of oppression.

The urgency is now. We believe firmly that when our production output is in full swing the democracies of the world will be able to prove that the dictatorships cannot win, but now, now, the time element is of supreme importance. Every 'plane, every other instrument, old and new, every instrument that we can spare now, we will send overseas. That is common-sense strategy.

The great task of this day, which rests upon each and every one of us, is to move products from the assembly lines of our factories to the battle lines of democracy now.

We can have speed, we can have effectiveness, if we maintain our existing unity. We do not have, and never will have, the forced unity of a people browbeaten by threats, misled by propaganda. Ours is a unity that is possible only among free men and women who recognize the truth and face realities with intelligence and courage.

Here in Washington we are thinking in terms of speed, and speed now. I hope that that watchword "Speed, and speed now" will find its way into every home in the nation.

Nothing Short of an All-Out Effort

I MUST tell you in plain language what this undertaking means to you, you in your daily life, whether you are in the armed services, whether you are a steelworker or a stevedore, a machinist or a housewife, a farmer or a banker, a storekeeper or a manufacturer. To all it will mean sacrifice on behalf of your country and your living.

Yes, you will feel it, the impact of this gigantic effort in your daily lives. You will feel it in a way that will cause you many inconveniences.

You will have to contend with lower profits, lower profits from business because obviously your taxes will be higher. You will have to work longer at your bench, or your stores, or your machine, or your desk.

I ask you for an all-out effort because nothing short of an all-out effort will win.

We are dedicated from here on to a constantly increasing tempo of production, a production greater than we now know or have ever known before, a production that does not stop and should not pause.

Tonight, I am appealing to the heart and to the mind of every man and

every woman who, within our borders, loves liberty. I ask you to consider the needs of all nations at this hour, to put aside all personal differences until victory is won.

The light of democracy must be kept burning. In the perpetuation of this light each of us must pool his own strength.

The single effort of one individual may seem small, but there are 130,000,000 individuals over here, and there are many more millions in Britain and elsewhere bravely shielding the great flame of democracy from the black-out of barbarism.

It is not enough for us merely to trim the wick and polish the glass. We must provide the fuel in ever-increasing amounts to keep the flame alight.

Vital Bridge of Ships Across the Ocean

A FEW weeks ago I spoke of freedom—freedom of speech and expression, freedom of every sort to worship God in his own way, freedom from wrong, freedom from fear—they are the ultimate stakes. They may not be immediately attainable throughout the world, but Humanity does move towards those glorious ideals through democratic justice.

If we fail, if democracy is superseded by slavery, then those four freedoms, or even the mention of them, will become forbidden things. Centuries will pass before they can be revived.

By winning now we strengthen the meaning of those freedoms. We increase the stature of mankind. We

MR. ROOSEVELT, seen above delivering his inaugural address after being sworn in for a third term as President, delivered a memorable speech on March 15, 1941, at the annual dinner of the Association of Newspaper Correspondents accredited to the White House. The salient points of his speech are given in this page.   *Photo, Wide World*

strengthen the dignity of human life. Upon the national will to sacrifice and to work depends the outlook of our industry and our agriculture.

Upon that will depends the survival of the vital bridge across the ocean, the bridge of ships that carry the arms and the goods to those who are fighting the good fight.

Upon that will depends our ability to aid other nations which may determine to offer resistance. Upon that will may depend practical assistance to people now living in nations that have been overrun, should they find the opportunity to strike back in an effort to regain their liberty—and may that day come soon.

There is no longer the slightest question or doubt. The American people recognize the supreme seriousness of the present situation. That is why they have demanded, and got, a policy of unqualified, immediate, all-out aid for Britain—for Greece, for China, and for all Governments in exile whose homelands are temporarily occupied by the aggressors.

From now on that aid will be increased and again increased until total victory has been won.

Magnificent Morale of the British

THE British are stronger than ever in the magnificent morale that has enabled them to endure all the dark days and the shattering nights of the past ten months.

They have the full support of Canada, of the other Dominions, of the rest of their Empire, and the full aid and support of some non-British people throughout the world who still think in terms of the great freedoms.

The British people are braced for invasion, whether such an attempt comes tomorrow, next week, or next month.

In this historic crisis, Britain is blest with a brilliant and great leader in Winston Churchill. But, knowing him, no one knows better than Mr. Churchill himself that it is not alone his stirring words and valiant deeds that give the British their superb morale.

The essence of that morale is in the masses of British people, who are completely clear in their minds about the one central fact that they would rather die as free men than live as slaves.

These brave people—civilians as well as soldiers, sailors and airmen, women and girls as well as men and boys—they are fighting in the front line of civilization at this moment. And they are holding that line with a fortitude that is the pride and inspiration of all free men on every continent and every island of the sea.

America Will Play Its Full Part

THE British people and their Grecian allies need assistance, and that they will get. They need ships: from America they will get ships. They need 'planes: from America they will get 'planes. From America they need food: from America they will get food. They need tanks, and guns, and ammunition and supplies of all kinds; from America they will get tanks, and guns and ammunition and supplies of all kinds.

So our country is going to be what our people have proclaimed it to be, the arsenal of democracy. Our country is going to play its full part

Washington Stages a Great Military Parade

President Roosevelt took the oath of office for the third time in the Capitol, Washington, on January 20, 1941. This was followed by a military parade, which was watched by the President from a stand in front of the White House. Above, light tanks are passing along Pennsylvania Avenue with the Capitol in the distance. Over 6,000 troops with mechanized units took part in the parade, while 235 naval and military 'planes flew overhead.

Photo, Keystone

Japan Had a Part in the Thailand Drama

Many a paragraph has appeared of late concerning the territorial dispute between French Indo-China and Thailand—the dispute which has now been settled in somewhat dictatorial fashion by Japan. This article is in the nature of a summary of the course of events.

OVERSHADOWED by the great tragic drama of many scenes now being played in the Old World, a smaller one has recently been performed in the Far East— one on which the curtain is now rung down, at least for the time being. The actors were Thailand (Siam), the French colony of Indo-China, and Japan, who aspired to the position of actor-manager.

Thailand, " Land of the Free People," has an area of 200,148 square miles, about 45,000 of which are in the Malay Peninsula. The boundaries have been subjected to frequent adjustments from 1891 to 1909. Her present king, Ananda Mahidol, succeeded to the throne in 1935 as a boy of nine, following the abdication of his uncle, and during his minority the country is governed by the Council of Regency, headed by the Premier, Luang Bipul. The 286,000 square miles which make up Indo-China comprise five states : the colony of Cochin-China ; the protectorates of Annam, Cambodia, Tongking and Laos ; and Kwang-Chow-Wan, leased from China. The whole country is under the Governor-General, Admiral Decoux, who succeeded General Catroux in July, 1940, when the latter joined General de Gaulle.

What might be termed the Prologue was the announcement in Bangkok on September 8, 1939, that the government of Thailand had officially proclaimed that country's neutrality in the war. Act I opened with the guarantees of this neutrality by Pacts of Non-Aggression signed on June 12, 1940, in Bangkok between the Thai Government and Britain and France, and by a Treaty of Friendship, signed in Tokyo the same day, between Thailand and Japan, to be valid for five years.

Frontier 'Incidents' Point the Way

The fall of France on June 17, only five days after the signing of the Pact of Non-Aggression with Thailand, created a new state of affairs, and Thailand later refused to ratify it on the grounds that her demands for frontier rectifications had not been met by the Pétain Government. By the autumn there was considerable tension on the border. A number of " incidents " arose, and there were mutual recriminations about the violation of frontiers. Early in October Thailand's demands became more ambitious, comprising nothing less than the cession of Cambodia and Laos, which had been annexed by France early in the present century. The Vichy Government repudiated all such claims, but stated that it was ready to submit to arbitration the possible restoration to Thailand of islands in the Mekong River.

By the middle of November spasmodic fighting had broken out at Vientiane and other points on the frontier, and bitter accusations were hurled to and fro on the subject of unprovoked attacks, bombing raids, and the firing of towns and villages. By the end of the year the incidents had developed into what the Thai Command called hostilities on a grand scale, and early in January, 1941, there was fighting along the entire frontier. Thai troops penetrated into Cambodia and advanced towards Angkor. French 'planes bombed several Thai villages as a reprisal for an aerial attack on the Cambodian town

Above are shown the frontier rectifications demanded by Thailand with the support of Japan. Saigon, the capital of Cochin China, is the chief French military and naval base in the Far East.   *Courtesy of " The Times "*

of Sisophon. On January 17 the Navy joined in the fray, and a battle was fought between a French force, consisting of a cruiser and four sloops, and a Thai squadron of two coast-defence cruisers and three torpedo-boats, with the result that the French ships sank two of the torpedo-boats and damaged the third without loss to themselves.

Shortly after this engagement Japan made her entrance upon the stage, offering her services as a mediator. The offer was accepted by both parties. Hostilities ceased on January 28, and an Armistice Commission consisting of seven Japanese, five French and five Thai representatives, under the presidency of Maj.-Gen. Sumita, boarded a Japanese

Admiral Decoux, Governor-General of French Indo-China, centre, is seen receiving the Japanese Vice War Minister, left, when the latter visited Cochin China early in 1941 to confer with the government of the Colony.
Photo, Wide World

warship and started negotiations. The Armistice was signed on January 31.

Although Europe may have felt that these events were of slight moment compared with her own pressing problems, Singapore watched them with profound interest. It was thought by many observers that Japan's offer of mediation was just another step in the Axis scheme for a " new order " ; that by intervening in the affairs of Thailand and Indo-China she could establish herself in so strong a position in the two countries that the southward advance for which she is working would be definitely promoted. It was unlikely that Japan would undertake the task of arbitration merely for the sake of restoring peace and heightening her own prestige. Most certainly she would require good remuneration, and it was conjectured that this might take the form of naval and air bases in Indo-China or Thailand.

Peace Conference in Tokyo

The peace conference between Indo-China and Thailand was opened at Tokyo on February 7 by Mr. Matsuoka, Japanese Foreign Minister, who began by declaring that the " Greater East Asia " policy of his country, which he passionately reaffirmed, was a historical necessity. The leader of the Thai delegates politely interpreted this policy as " Prosperity for each ; stability for all." M. Arsène Henry, French Ambassador in Tokyo and head of the French delegation, merely expressed, with the realism of his race, a desire for a speedy and equitable solution to their differences. That Singapore was aware of what lay behind Japan's seeming disinterestedness was apparent from the strengthening of the garrison (see p. 236).

Soon the peace conference at Tokyo had reached deadlock. It was reported from Singapore that the French were resisting the Thai demands, and that Thailand was firmly refusing all concessions to Japan or " anything inconsistent with strict neutrality." On February 27 it was stated that Thailand's territorial claims had been cut by 60 per cent, but that France was still demanding a further reduction. Thereupon, there began a campaign of vilification in the Japanese newspapers, and the Vichy Government was warned that Japan would stand no interference from a " Third Power "—an obvious reference to Great Britain.

At the end of February there were signs that Japan and Thailand might take action against Indo-China if France did not send an immediate acceptance. On March 2 Vichy yielded to the latest plan, subject to certain conditions, involving some complicated details. Finally, on March 11, 1941, the French and Thai plenipotentiaries signed a draft agreement, the terms of which are to be embodied later in a formal treaty. About 25,000 square miles have been ceded to Thailand.

Thailand is now placed under a considerable obligation to the mediator, and although her Premier, Luang Bipul, has professed his faith in " a just and friendly " attitude to Japan, it remains to be seen in what way Toyko will collect repayment of the debt—and so round off this little drama with an epilogue.

Splendid Already, India's Effort Grows Apace

H.H. THE MAHARAJAH OF PATIALA is seen above at a parade ceremonial, invoking a blessing on members of the Yadavindra Infantry of Patiala State before they proceeded overseas on active service.

A St. John Ambulance Nursing Division war work party busily engaged in making hospital supplies at a Red Cross centre in Lahore.

INDIAN TROOPS IN BRITAIN are shown in these three photographs. Left, men of the R.I.A.S.C., with sabres at the salute, who were among the troops evacuated from Dunkirk. Above, the Duke of Devonshire reviewing Indian naval ratings in Scotland. Below, Mr. L. S. Amery, Secretary of State for India, inspects Indian troops at Aldershot.

MR. L. S. AMERY, Secretary of State for India, broadcast, on February 24, 1941, an account of the part India is playing in the war. Referring to the military strength of India, he told how the Indian Army is expanding rapidly from its peacetime strength of 160,000 Indian and 50,000 British troops to a force of some half a million men of all arms, trained, equipped and mechanized on a modern scale. That, he pointed out, is exclusive of the troops already serving abroad, and was only a first instalment.

The Indian Air Force, also, is being expanded as fast as it can obtain machines, while the Royal Indian Navy has been more than trebled since the outbreak of war and is worthily playing its part in the defence of India's coasts and the task of escorting convoys. India's 40,000 merchant mariners are also giving faithful and efficient service. In the matter of supply and equipment India is far more advanced than she was in 1914. She makes her own rifles, machine-guns, field artillery and ammunition, as well as something like 90 per cent of all the miscellaneous equipment she requires.

INDIA lies centrally between the two gateways into the Indian Ocean—the one the Suez Canal and Red Sea, the gateway from Europe and the West, and the other the narrow strait dominated by Singapore, the gateway from the Far East—and is thus (Mr. Amery went on) able to send to either point reinforcements, whether of troops or aeroplanes, of munitions or supplies, in far less time and with far less danger of enemy interference than they could be sent from England.   *Photos, Fox, Topical, G.P.U., and Sport & General*

OUR SEARCHLIGHT ON THE WAR

Protecting Horses from Gas

RESPIRATORS for horses were recently demonstrated at the Royal Veterinary College in London to a number of owners. Three horses were chosen to act as mannequins and submitted with dignity and good humour when the masks were put into position. Three types were shown. Two

GAS MASKS FOR HORSES are now provided to protect their wearers against the dangers of possible gas attack. This pony is wearing a charcoal-box type of mask and transparent eye-shields. The lower jaw is left free, for a horse breathes only through the nostrils.
Photo, G.P.U.

are composed of layer upon layer of impregnated cotton towelling enclosed in a container rather like a milliner's hat-box. The third, the charcoal-box type, resembles to some extent the human respirator and, because it is stronger and will last longer, is the pattern most likely to be used in the Army. Either type allows the horse, who may consider it a new sort of nosebag, to do light work for a time. Devices for protecting the animal from mustard gas were also demonstrated. These consist of transparent eye shields and a species of suit of white material which can be fitted very quickly by a soldier to his mount.

'Make and Mend' in the Army

MAJOR-GENERAL J. BUCKLEY, Controller-General of Economy, who a month ago took over the job of stopping waste in the Army, thinks that the public outcry was not justified, and that stories of over-lavish supplies ending up in the waste bins were grossly exaggerated. "I have been amazed," he said, "to find how little food is wasted, especially in the fighting formations. Such waste as occurs is usually of unpalatable rations. Drastic steps are now being taken to stop waste of every kind." One way of promoting economy which is to be put into practice is to teach the men to darn their socks and mend their own clothes. This had already been introduced into some units by their C.Os. Senior officers, in overalls, are attending classes where they are taught to repair machines. Other matters receiving attention are transport problems, oil reclamation and hutting schemes.

First ' Kill ' Through a Mistake

ONE of the Free French pilots fighting for Britain and the common cause is a young Frenchman whose instant understanding of the English tongue at one time

lagged behind his flying skill. On a certain morning he was out on patrol with his Spitfire squadron when the order was given to change course.

Through a misinterpretation the Frenchman turned right while the remainder of the squadron went off to the left. By the time he discovered his mistake they were separated by a mile or two. As he was about to set off in pursuit an enemy aircraft came into view. Here was an amazing opportunity, and the young pilot promptly seized it. Flying as close as he dared he gave the enemy machine several bursts from his eight machine-guns and with such good effect that it burst into flames as it went down. Since this first-chance kill the Frenchman has disabled, if not destroyed, two other Nazi aircraft — and has also brushed up his English.

Luxury Shelter

LORD HORDER would surely approve of the underground communal shelter beneath a big transport garage in Westminster which is now nearly completed. It will provide unexampled comfort and safety for the 800 people who take refuge there every night. Its first aid post is probably the largest in London, for it has 40 casualty beds. Near it is an airy bay reserved for shelterers who suffer from asthma or who have weak hearts. One part of the shelter is divided up into " houses " by brick partitions about 10 feet high. Here are the offices of the shelter marshal and of the doctor, the restaurant, the nursery, the hospital, and other centres. The " sleeping houses " are designed for married couples, children, single men, and single women. Finally there is " Victoria Hall," a room 70 feet by 50 feet, devoted to recreation.

Thanks for the Tanks

PAYING a high tribute to the soundness of British workmanship, General Wavell said recently that " weight for class, Italian tanks, many of them newly delivered from manufacturers, proved no match for British products." This verdict was endorsed when two officers of the Royal Armoured Corps visited a munitions factory somewhere in England to thank the shop workers on behalf of the African armies. After describing a tank battle near Benghazi, in which the British force of tanks, seriously outnumbered by the Italian force of seventy, presently reduced these to thirty, one of the officers added ; " We couldn't have done it if you fellows who had been making the tanks and the armour had not been doing your jobs damned well."

New Weapon Against Keren

BY no means a secret weapon, but one which might well wear down the final resistance of an exhausted enemy, was used against the troops defending Keren. It took the form of a powerful broadcasting apparatus, fitted with half-a-dozen megaphones, which was installed at the foot of this natural fortress. Day and night the megaphones bombarded the helpless garrison, sending up to the mountains a barrage of propaganda in two tongues : Italian, and Amharic for the colonial troops. All emerged from a comprehensive collection of gramophone records made specially for the occasion. There were speeches of remonstrance in Italian, arguments on the futility of resistance based upon recent events in East Africa—which may have been news to most of the garrison. There were speeches in Amharic by trained Abyssinian orators, which lacked nothing in drama, and proclamations by the Emperor Haile Selassie. And there were sentimental songs and excerpts from the Italian operas skilfully chosen to rouse acute home-sickness in the white troops. Interspersed with or overlying these appeals would come the additional persuasion of bursts of artillery bombardment.

Ambassador to Four Nations

ANOTHER United States Embassy has been set up in London, and here Mr. Anthony J. Drexel Biddle, who arrived at Bristol airport on March 14, has taken up his appointment as envoy to the four exiled Governments of Poland, Belgium, Holland, and Norway. Mr. Biddle will meet many friends among the Polish colony, for he was formerly U.S. Ambassador to Warsaw, and it was he who first told the world of the German invasion of Poland. On the morning of September 1, 1939, he sent the news to Mr. Bullitt, U.S. Ambassador in Paris, and the latter at once informed the news agencies. With his staff Mr. Biddle made a perilous journey to Rumania, his car being attacked by German bombers fifteen times on the way. With him in his recent flight across the Atlantic by Clipper was Mr. Averell Harriman, President Roosevelt's special envoy, who has come to England to expedite the delivery of all types of war material.

CIVILIAN HELMETS, intended particularly for fire fighters, have caused the Ministry of Supply factories to work at full speed. The new helmet is supplied free to street fire parties working in the fire prevention areas, and is sold for 5s. 6d. to employers. A man is seen at work on one of the 250-ton presses which mould the steel sheets into shape.   *Photo, Sport & General*

'One of Ours' and Their No. 1 Tell the Workers

MUNITION WORKERS, both British and German, are being urged to " go to it," and these two photographs, alike in setting but widely differing in the spirit they display, show how it is done. In the top photograph an anti-aircraft gunnery officer is addressing the workers of a factory under the control of the Ministry of Supply. Speaking on March 11, 1941, he praised their efforts unstintedly and revealed that his battery had shot down 22 'planes, four of them in one day, with guns made in the factory. Near the platform are three Bofors A.A. guns. Great cheers greeted his speech. Just three months before, on December 11, 1940, Hitler addressed 10,000 workpeople in the Borsig works in the northern suburbs of Berlin, above. His speech was merely the usual tirade against Britain.

Photos, Sport & General, E.N.A.

I Had Breakfast with Our Night Fighters

That the night fighters of the R.A.F. are getting the measure of the
enemy is being made clear as their " bag " of 'planes grows. Thus
on the night of March 12 they brought down five Nazis, and on the
next night eight. Here we read of a visit to the crew hut of a Night
Fighter Squadron somewhere in the south of England.

VISUALIZE a metal hut rather like an out-
size Anderson shelter. Add a few beds,
a pile of flying clothes and parachutes,
and a coke stove boiling water for cocoa.
We sat with our feet up. Outside the wind
whistled round the hut and the rain beat
down. " Cloud down to 2,000 feet, sir,"
reported the telephonist to the Squadron
Commander. " Foul night for flying,"
put in a young man with an observer's
wing on his tunic.

A fat spaniel puppy waddled from beneath
a chair—pawed at the Wing Commander's
foot, looking up with appealing eyes. The
spaniel won his point and the next moment his
head disappeared inside a large mug of cocoa.

Two of the pilots had on their flying jackets.
Their names were on the duty board, but in
such weather the Huns were unlikely to
venture out. So we yarned and waited and
listened. What we listened for was word of
two crews out somewhere over England,
the Channel or Occupied France. There was
a gale warning on and no news of them yet.
We, safe and comfortable down below, put
more coke on the fire.

" The navigators will be having a tough
time . . ." A sergeant pilot from the corner
had started to speak, but he stopped abruptly
when a pilot officer with earphones on his
head put up his hand for silence. " So and
so reported over —— 15 minutes ago.
Should have landed by now. Wonder what's
keeping him ? " No one answered the
question. No one, in fact, appeared to take
the slightest interest in it. We were all
pretending not to be concerned. The spaniel
pup, full of cocoa, slept on.

Then, above the noise of the wind, came
the roar of aeroplane engines and at once
there was a change in the atmosphere of the
hut, a hint of relief in the air. " Landing
lights on," called the telephonist. The
aircraft roared overhead once more as it
circled to land.

In a few minutes three young men, looking
like returned Arctic explorers, came stumping
into the room. Their flying boots were caked
with wet mud. As they took off their
helmets the air gunner exclaimed " Warm
as anything upstairs. Down at 6,000 feet
I was as hot as could be." Questioning
brought out the fact that the actual temperature " upstairs " was 4 degrees below
zero—36 degrees of frost. But to those
night fighter boys that was a warm night.

We sat back waiting for their story. " It
was a vile trip," said the pilot. " We went
cruising round and round for what seemed
hours and did not see a single Hun. Finally
we went over to look for him above his own
aerodromes. But he was having a night off.
There wasn't a flare path or a light anywhere. We found three of his aerodromes,
but they weren't worth wasting a bomb on.
It looked as though they had all gone home
to Germany for the night."

" The other machine's been reported.
Will be here any minute," said the

telephonist. A lull in the conversation, and
in came the second machine.

" Hard luck," said the Squadron Commander, as the crew came in to tell almost
the same story as the first lot. " It was a
filthy night any way. That's why I sent out
the recall."

" I'm darned annoyed about it," said the
pilot. " Not one Hun would show his nose.
We saw a beacon light once as we went over
to take a look at the aerodromes in France."

" We saw—— Aerodrome clearly enough,"
said the observer.

" We certainly did," laughed the pilot.
" We came down to 800 feet and dropped a
stick of bombs right along the runway. I
bet that shook them a bit—if there was
anybody there."

By now the cocoa was ready again, and the
Intelligence Officer was wanting to go on with
his reports. " Any ack-ack ? " he asked. " Any
searchlights ? What was your course ? and
your height ? What lights did you see ? "

It was the catechism familiar to every pilot,
but tonight it produced little result. Six
men and two aircraft had flown over parts
of England, over the Channel and over
Nazi-occupied territory without having so
much as a searchlight on their tail.

But after a night of patrolling, even dull,
monotonous patrolling, there is always food
in the mess. We all climbed into the squadron
brake and drove to the mess to eat bacon,
eggs and fried bread. They followed it up
with cold beef and pickles—at four a.m. !

**This group of night fighter pilots wearing their
full equipment are walking on to the landing-
ground on their way to take-off when night
raiders are about.**

Photo, British Official : Crown Copyright

We Kept Our Balloon Up in the Channel

Through rain, snow, ice and fog, through fierce gales and tem-
pestuous winds, the R.A.F. crews of balloon barrage vessels help to
escort our Channel convoys safely to port. Something of what their
job means may be gathered from this first-hand account.

JUST towing a balloon at the end of a
length of cable . . . surely a dull,
monotonous sort of job. But that
there is adventure enough on the Channel
convoys is shown by the log of an R.A.F.
officer on a balloon barrage vessel—one
which has now accompanied and guarded
many convoys up and down the Channel.
Here, to start with, are some extracts in his
own words telling of attacks by motor
torpedo boats and dive-bombers.

0950 hours. Mine sighted on port bow
necessitating sudden change of course. This
was followed by sighting other mines on the
starboard bow until eventually we zigzagged
through 23 of them. Obviously they had
broken loose during the storm.

1105 hours. An Me. 109 made two
machine-gun attacks on " ——." Shooting
bad and no hits. " —— " attacked by four
dive-bombers. Bombs could be seen hitting
the sea beside the ship.

1856 hours. Vivid flashes from French coast.

2143 hours. Enormous flash from French
coast followed some eighty seconds later by
the sound of heavy explosion.

2224 hours. A.A. fire from French coast.
Throughout the night there was a series of
flashes and occasional A.A. fire from both
coasts.

Thursday. 0220 hours. This has been
written subsequently as things moved too
fast to record them at the time. I came below

to call my relief, and as I came on deck again
I was told that a motor-boat had been heard
on our port bow and had disappeared. About
five minutes later there was an explosion
astern followed immediately by another.

Immediately the place seemed to become
like a Brock's firework display. Everybody
who had anything seemed to let it off.
Tracers showing up scarlet in the night were returned
by bullets which appeared green in colour.
We kept dead quiet. The trouble was about,
or appeared to be about, a quarter of a mile
astern and we were in a position that we
could do nothing effective if we did open fire.

What actually happened we shall not know
till we reach port, but the Motor Torpedo
Boat brigade were putting up flares all over
the place. Presently we heard a " phew "—
almost next door it seemed, but whatever
it was it did not find its mark. After what
seemed hours, but was only a few minutes,
it seemed that the firework party was falling
astern. Personally I heaved a sigh of relief.
By the gun flashes and rattle of machine-guns
I knew our escort was doing its stuff. But
suddenly right on our starboard beam two
high flares shot up and came sailing down
lighting " —— " and ourselves as clear as
day. There followed what we all expected
. . . a sickening thud. We thought the
" —— " had got it. Then there was another
lull followed by the usual cries of " There
she is " as machine-guns opened up again
and flares showed us up.

IIIIIIIIIIIIIIIIIIIIIIIIIIIIIIIIIIIIIIIIIIIIIIIIIIIIIIIIIIIIIIIIIIIIIIIII **I WAS THERE!** IIIIIIIIIIIIIIIIIIIIIIIIIIIIIIIIIIIIIIIIIIIIIIIIIIIIIIIIIIIIIIIIIIIIIIIII

Suffice it to say that I think all of us were glad when dawn broke and we could see " where the next one was coming from." One must feel sorry, I think, for anyone who is powerless to help either himself or others, and while the merchantman is worse off, as he is bound to be the first target, my immediate thoughts could only be for our lads.

Our R.A.F. crew, needless to say, are splendid. With all the excitement last night when I went aft, I hardly expected to find anyone at the winch. But there he was— our man who shall be nameless.

1155 hours. This looks bad. About thirty Junker 87s with an escort of Messerschmitt 109s arrived over the convoy. The procedure is simple. The fighters try to put the balloons down in flames and, like one platoon following another on the parade-ground, the dive-bombers follow. Whether they saw something we didn't, I don't know, but the bombers suddenly veered away and that was that. But not before our fighters had got a couple of Junkers and possibly a third.

1845 hours. Alongside quay. Tied up.

Here is another typical entry :

1834 hours. Shelling starts from the French coast. Shelling lasted for approximately three and a half hours, during which upwards of 200 shells were counted. Shells covered the whole convoy ; near misses observed.

1926 hours. Tremendous orange flashes seen over the English coast. This may have been the English long-range guns firing.

1933 hours. Three shells fall well astern. Many sparks observed.

2150 hours. Shelling now much more desultory. Shells falling far astern.

2254 hours. Passed Dungeness . . . the convoy, shelled continuously, had once more successfully run the gauntlet. The ships were safe and the balloons still flew.

Balloon boat crews are in the unusual position of being by turn actors and audience. When the R.A.F. bombers go out to blast the invasion ports, the balloon men have almost a grandstand view. One night at 10.30, when the sky overhead was a blaze of stars, the balloon ships were coming up Channel to an accompaniment of the drone of aero engines as our bombers flew out to the invasion ports. " Many searchlights," says the log entry. " Bomb explosions are continual on the French coast and the flashes can clearly be seen—both of bombs and anti-aircraft shell fire—stretching right along the coast."

BALLOON BARRAGES are one of the means of protecting convoys from low-diving aeroplanes. This photograph, taken from an R.A.F. patrol boat—note the Lewis gun pointed in readiness at the sky—shows a balloon ascending from one of the ships of a convoy. When enemy 'planes are about they are flown at a much greater altitude.
Photo, Fox

The wireless operator whose experiences are described in this page occupied such cramped quarters as those above. The photograph was taken in a Vickers Wellesley bomber.
Photo, Planet News

Our Wireless Operator Read a Thriller

A night bombing raid over Germany would appear to the layman to be a sufficiently exciting, not to say hair-raising, experience. But, as the following story by a bomber pilot shows, familiarity breeds—not perhaps contempt, but at least remarkable indifference to danger and discomfort.

IT has often struck me as an odd fact that the farther one goes into the air the more one has to be shut in ; it is almost as bad as going into the depths of the sea, and anyone who suffers from claustrophobia would be as uncomfortable in a heavy bomber as in a submarine. In fact, when you get into the bomber it is rather like going down into the Tube, except that there is far less room ; you can travel all over Europe in a bomber and see very little except your own immediate and very cramped surroundings.

Naturally, it is exciting enough when we are actually doing the bombing and most of us get the chance to see what we have done to the target, but there are long hours when we are just travelling, and that is all.

I remember one night when I myself thought there was almost too much excitement ; over the target the anti-aircraft fire was very fierce, and we had to go to and fro over the oil plant we were attacking, dropping flares at each end of the factory and finally getting the bombs down in between the flares. The anti-aircraft shells were coming very close, and I was not particularly sorry when we had finished the job, watched a good fire burning down below, and turned for home.

Even then our troubles were by no means over, for on the way back ice began to form in the airscrew, and though we went up and

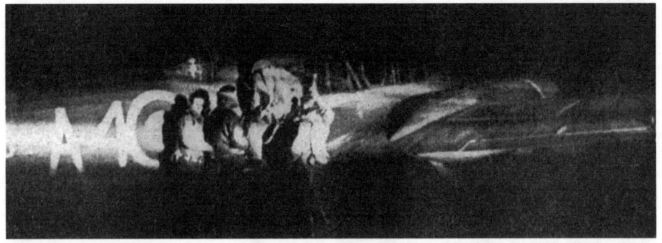

When night bombers take off from aerodromes " somewhere in England " to smash the invasion ports and Hitler's munitions factories, the scene is an eerie one. For a short time the aerodrome is not blacked out and bright beams of light are thrown on the bombers while the pilots and crews take their places. Then when they have whirled away into the night the lights go out.
Photo, Planet News

down to get out of the layer of cold and moisture which is always apt to produce ice, it was not at all easy to find better weather.

The ice was driving back off the airscrew and hitting the fuselage ; some of the largest pieces of ice were making holes in it and letting in the cold. The holes were not very large, but the pieces of ice were driving so hard against us that, when this began, I wondered for a moment if it were shrapnel that was hitting us.

I realized almost at once that it was only ice because, of course, I could not hear the bursts of the anti-aircraft shells, as you always can when they come very close. The shells make, by the way, an extremely queer

sound, not very loud against the roar of the engines, but exactly like the. barking of a dog which is beginning to get suspicious about you. I remember that when I first heard the sound I could hardly believe my ears ; it seemed such an unlikely thing to hear right up among the clouds.

The ice was doing no great harm, but it certainly let in a good deal of cold air ; as second pilot there was not much for me to do at this particular moment, so I thought I would pay a visit to the wireless operator, partly to see if a little exercise would warm me up and partly because I wondered how he was getting on.

I crept along to him, expecting to find him

ready for a mild grumble about the cold, but he was sitting there with his eyes on a book and paying no attention at all to the ice that was cutting up the fuselage or the cold air coming in ; he was reading a Wild West thriller—something about the girl of the something ranch—as though his life depended on it !

He seemed quite disappointed to be dragged back from the adventures of cowboys in Dead Man's Gulch, the cattle rustlers, the six-shooters, and the innocent heroine, to the dull and prosaic reality of a trip over Germany at one o'clock in the morning and the monotony of anti-aircraft fire, electric storms, or ice coming off the airscrew.

OUR DIARY OF THE WAR

SUNDAY, MARCH 16, 1941   *561st day*

On the Sea.—Submarine Snapper overdue and considered lost.

War against Italy.—Berbera recaptured by British. Important 'heights above Keren taken.

R.A.F. bombed aerodromes at Castel Benito and Makina during night of 15-16.

Home Front.—Heavy night raid on Bristol. Fully loaded Junkers crashed in south of England.

Greek War.—Italian offensive in central sector, begun March 9, crushed. R.A.F. dropped 10 tons of bombs on Tirana. Valona also raided.

Enemy 'planes again bombed Larissa.

General.—Mr. Bevin announced new national registration for industry of men and women of certain ages.

MONDAY, MARCH 17   *562nd day*

In the Air.—R.A.F. made night attacks on Bremen, Wilhelmshaven, Rotterdam, Emden and Oldenburg.

Three enemy aircraft destroyed in night combat by our bombers.

War against Italy.—Jijiga (Abyssinia) occupied. Enemy counter-attacked without avail against recently captured positions in Eritrea.

R.A.F. made heavy night attack on Tripoli. Fleet Air Arm attacked shipping at Valona and Durazzo.

Home Front.—Slight activity over East Coast, but no bombs. Raider shot down over Clydeside.

Greek War.—Italians attacked in northern sector, but were repulsed. Heavy fighting reported north of Ostravitza and round Tepelini.

TUESDAY, MARCH 18   *563rd day*

On the Sea.—Mr. Churchill announced destruction of three German submarines.

In the Air.—Coastal Command aircraft sank Nazi supply ship off Frisian Islands. Enemy shipping off Dutch coast bombed.

Heavy night raid on Kiel. Other targets were at Wilhelmshaven, Rotterdam, Emden, Texel and two Dutch aerodromes.

War against Italy.—Further important positions south of Keren captured. Pressure by Patriot forces developing against Debra Marcos.

Home Front.—Two enemy aircraft shot down over sea. Large-scale night attack on Hull.

Greek War.—Further minor attacks in northern and central sectors repulsed.

R.A.F. bombed docks at Durazzo and motor transport and camps on road between Buzi and Glave.

Balkans.—Mr. Eden and M. Sarajoglu, Turkish Premier, conferred in Cyprus.

WEDNESDAY, MARCH 19   *564th day*

In the Air.—Fierce night attack on Cologne. Oil storage tanks at Rotterdam and three Dutch aerodromes bombed. Lorient submarine base raided.

War against Italy.—British steadily advancing on Keren (Eritrea). Patrols in contact with enemy near Marda Pass, 8 miles from Jijiga (Abyssinia).

Home Front.—Slight day activity, but no bombs dropped. Two day raiders destroyed. London heavily raided at night.

Greek War.—Italians attacked with tanks, but were again repulsed.

General.—Government introduced Bill to make civil defence compulsory.

THURSDAY, MARCH 20   *565th day*

On the Sea.—Admiralty announced successes of submarines against Italians. One transport certainly, another probably, sunk. Two supply ships sunk, a third almost certainly destroyed.

German dive-bomber destroyed by H.M. drifter Young Mun and H.M. yacht Chico.

In the Air.—Lorient submarine base bombed. Coastal Command attacked number of E-boats and enemy patrol vessel off Frisian coast.

War against Italy.—Hargeisa occupied.

Home Front.—During day Kent coastal town was bombed and machine-gunned. At night main attack was on Plymouth. Widespread damage from incendiary and high-explosive bombs. Raiders also over South Wales, east and south coasts, and London.

Greek War.—Restricted patrol and artillery activity.

FRIDAY, MARCH 21   *566th day*

On the Sea.—H.M. trawlers Kerryado and Gulfoss reported sunk.

In the Air.—R.A.F. attacked enemy warships and supply vessels off Frisian Islands and in Heligoland Bight, and bombed escorted tanker off Belgian coast.

Night raids on submarine base at Lorient and on docks at Ostend.

War against Italy.—Jarabub surrendered after siege of 15 weeks. Heavy air attacks on Harar and Diredawa.

Home Front.—During day bombs fell in Kent coastal town and at two places in Norfolk. At night Plymouth was again raided.

Greek War.—Enemy launched night attack in central sector, but was driven back.

Balkans.—Crisis in Yugoslavia over proposed pact with Axis. Four Serb Cabinet ministers resigned.

SATURDAY, MARCH 22   *567th day*

On the Sea.—Survivors from five ships of British convoy, said to have been torpedoed 100 miles north of Cape Verde Islands, reached land.

In the Air.—Enemy supply ships in Egersund Harbour, Norway, attacked and left blazing.

War against Italy.—Local successes during incessant fighting around Keren. Asmara heavily bombed by R.A.F.

Enemy raided Malta, but was chased out to sea by British fighters.

Home Front.—Enemy activity slight. Raider shot down near East Coast.

Balkans.—Opposition in Yugoslavia to compromise agreement with Germany increased.

RESCUED AFTER SIX DAYS ADRIFT IN THE WIDE ATLANTIC

Wartime tragedy at its most poignant is exemplified in this photograph. The men are the survivors of a small merchant ship torpedoed in the Atlantic.
Of the crew of twenty, ten managed to get on board a life-saving raft; the rest went down with the ship. The survivors drifted for six days on their
frail craft with only a gallon of water and six tins of condensed milk on board. Two men were washed overboard, and two lost their reason and died.
On the sixth day a British warship sighted the raft and, above, a life-line is being thrown to the men as the rescue ship comes alongside.

Photo Exclusive to THE WAR ILLUSTRATED

Though Betrayed Yugoslavia Was Not Lost

On March 25 Yugoslavia's Premier pledged his country's adhesion to the Tripartite
Pact. Below we give an account of the developments which led up to this momentous
step, and the dramatic events which immediately followed.

WHEN Mr. Tsvetkovitch came to sign the
Pact which bound Yugoslavia to the
Axis, his manner was distinctly
distrait. As he stood at Ribbentrop's side
in the glittering ensemble of the Belvedere
Palace in Vienna he betrayed every sign of
nervousness. His lips were constantly
twitching, and time after time he pulled
out his handkerchief and then hurriedly
thrust it back again into his pocket. When,
after Ribbentrop had signed for Germany,
Ciano for Italy, and General Oshima,
Japanese Ambassador in Berlin, for Japan,
it came to Mr. Tsvetkovitch's turn, he forgot
that he had to sign more than once and after
every signature replaced the top of his pen,
carefully repocketed it, only to take it out
again immediately afterwards to continue to
sign on the dotted line.

Then, when the writing was finished, he
made a nervous little speech. The chief aim
of Yugoslavia's foreign policy, he said, was
the maintenance of peace for her people, the
safeguarding of their security. In joining the
Three Power Pact, Yugoslavia wanted to
ensure her peaceful future in cooperation
with Germany, Italy, and Japan. She
wanted to contribute her share towards the
organization of a new Europe, fulfilling in
this way a supreme obligation both towards
herself and the European community . . .

Prime Minister Tsvetkovitch had good
reason to be nervous ; was he not treading
the path which the premiers of Bulgaria and

**KING PETER II of Yugoslavia is here seen (left)
with the former Regent, his uncle, Prince
Paul, at a review at Belgrade in 1940.**
Photo, Associated Press

Rumania had trodden so recently before
him ? Could he be certain that the fate
which had befallen Yugoslavia's neighbours
would not also be hers ? True, the document

which he had just signed seemed not too
dangerous, at least on the surface. It merely
stated that Yugoslavia joined the Three
Power Pact, concluded in Berlin on September
27, 1940, by Germany, Italy, and Japan, and
that any discussions of the joint technical
commissions provided for in Article 4 of that
Pact should be attended by Yugoslav representatives when any of Yugoslavia's interests
were concerned. To this Protocol—which was
almost identical with the Protocols signed by
Slovakia, Hungary, Rumania, and Bulgaria,
and was drawn up in German, Italian,
Japanese and Serb—was attached the text of
the Three Power Pact, by subscribing to
which Mr. Tsvetkovitch and his Foreign
Minister, Mr. Cincar Markovitch, agreed
that Yugoslavia " recognizes and respects the
leadership of Germany and Italy in the
establishment of a new order in Europe, and
of Japan in Eastern Asia " and, still more
important, undertakes with them " to assist
one another with all political, economic, and
military means if one of the contracting
parties should be attacked by a power at
present not involved in the European war, or
in the Sino-Japanese conflict."

After the Pact had been signed, Mr.
Tsvetkovitch was handed two Notes bearing
the signature of Joachim von Ribbentrop.
In the first Germany's Foreign Minister
declared that " the German Government re-
affirms its determination to respect at all
times the sovereignty and territorial integrity

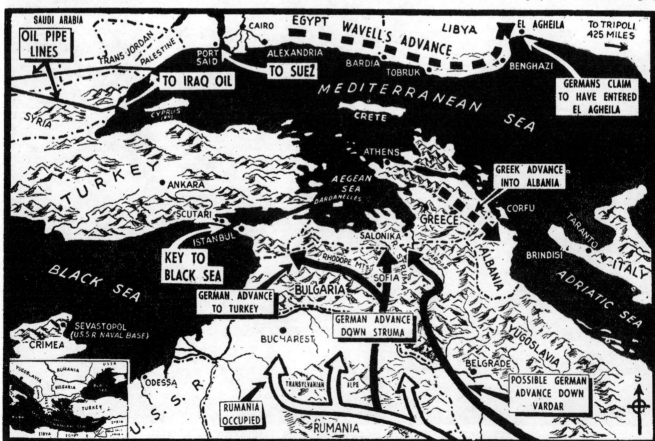

We are not accustomed to looking at a map of the Near East from this angle, but this is how Hitler sees it as he plans the next moves in his Balkan
campaign. Open arrows show where German troops have occupied Rumania, while the black arrows show the directions of possible German advances
against Greece through the Struma valley in Bulgaria and the Vardar valley in Yugoslavia. The importance of Turkey's attitude in the event of a German
drive forward is shown by her position athwart the direct route to the Iraq oilfields. Inset, normal map of the area.   *Courtesy of the "Daily Mail"*

Dramatic Reactions to the Pact with Hitler

of Yugoslavia ''; and in the second that " during the war the Governments of the Axis Powers will not make any demands on Yugoslavia to allow the passage or the transit of troops through Yugoslav territory."

From an unguarded reference in this second Note to " conversations '' it was apparent that not everything which had been concluded between Yugoslavia and her new partners had been made public. There were secret clauses beyond a doubt ; and in Belgrade it was openly declared what these clauses were believed to be. Thus it was said that one stated that after the war Yugoslavia's aspirations for an outlet on the Aegean Sea would be sympathetically considered. Another was alleged to be that Yugoslavia had agreed to allow the passage of war material and hospital supplies over her railways, without any right of control and without hindrance. Furthermore, it was stated that Yugoslavia had agreed to check all anti-Axis activity within her bounds, and that her national economy should be brought into harmony with the economic system of the German Reich.

Ribbentrop Talks of 'Intrigue'

Herr Joachim accompanied the gift of his two bits of paper with a speech in which he displayed even more than his customary Pecksniffian unctuousness. He declared— and none would gainsay him here—that " this event will be of a special importance to the future of Yugoslavia and the welfare of the Yugoslav people." The new order in Europe and East Asia was being carried through, he said ; and then he went on to denounce a " crooked intrigue '' of England's destined to mobilize Yugoslavia against this new order. " Even in the last few days," he plaintively declared, " so I am told, attempts at interference have been made by English and American quarters in the politics of Yugoslavia—attempts which can only be described as unheard of, and which can in no way be reconciled with the respect due to the sovereignty of a free European state."

When the Yugoslav Premier heard that, did he give a thought to Schuschnigg, the last Premier of free Austria, who for three

years had been a prisoner of Hitler, confined within a few hundred yards of where he sat on his gilded chair ? But Mr. Tsvetkovitch can surely have needed no such reminder that whoever sups with Hitler needs a long spoon.

Before he left Belgrade for his trip to Vienna he had had to overcome a series of Cabinet crises. Several of his ministers had resigned by way of protest against the proposal to link Yugoslavia with the Axis ; the newspapers—practically all of them save those which were under his Government's control —were strong in their condemnation ; the Army was against it, the students, the great mass of the Serbian people, if not of the Croats. Several times it was stated that the Premier's train would leave Belgrade at a certain hour, only for the arrangements to be cancelled at the last minute ; and even when the " betrayal train '' was just about to start at 10 p.m. on March 24, one of his ministers, Mr. Pantitch, Minister of Physical Education, thrust his letter of resignation into the Prime Minister's hands.

From abroad, too, came appeals to

MR. RONALD CAMPBELL has been British Minister in Belgrade since 1939, and, to quote Mr. R. A. Butler, Under-Secretary for Foreign Affairs, handled the Yugoslav crisis "with the utmost discretion and the greatest skill."

Rumania has already experienced what it means to bow the knee to the Axis. The long stretch of the Danube which forms the greater part of the frontier between that country and Bulgaria is now completely under Nazi control. This Nazi anti-aircraft battery is guarding one of the bridges across the river. *Photos, Planet News, Keystone, and Associated Press*

MR. DRAGISHA TSVETKOVITCH, who signed the pact with the Axis in Vienna on March 25, 1941, and was arrested two days later, became Prime Minister of Yugoslavia on February 5, 1939.

Yugoslavia to think not once but twice before she took a step which would certainly be fatal to her independence. The Greeks appealed to their old comrades in arms " never to let their glorious history be blackened by a stab in the back for an ally." The Turks uttered a strong warning ; and Britain's Minister in Belgrade, Mr. Ronald Campbell, handed Mr. Tsvetkovitch a note in which it was stated that His Majesty's Government had been shocked to learn that Yugoslavia contemplated the signature of an agreement by which she not only abandoned her neutral attitude but apparently entered the system of Britain's enemies.

But the Yugoslav Government turned a deaf ear to every warning as to every entreaty. The plenipotentiaries signed, and on the morrow of their signature returned to a country seething with unrest. When their train drew up at the station platform in Belgrade at 9.4 a.m. on March 26, the

station was empty save for pro-Nazis, and the ministers on their way to a long conference with Prince Paul, the Senior Regent, drove through silent streets—silent, although not empty. The mood of the people was tense, increasingly dangerous. The news was of meetings of angry protest, of rioting, of shootings. They had signed their country's capitulation to Hitler, and how the country regarded their action was soon seen.

At 2.30 on the morning of March 27 there was a dramatic coup d'état in Belgrade. The men who signed Yugoslavia's surrender were thrown out of office and placed under arrest, and the three Regents—Prince Paul, Dr. Stankovitch, and Dr. Petrovitch—resigned. Young King Peter assumed the direction of affairs, with General Dusan Simovitch, Chief of Air Force Staff, as his Prime Minister. The Yugoslav nation had, as Mr. Churchill said when he announced the news in London, found its soul.

Long Live Greece, Free and Immortal!

A hundred and twenty years have passed since Greece threw off the Turkish yoke and declared her independence. In 1941 the anniversary was celebrated with much more than usual fervour, and in every country where men still love liberty and are prepared to defend it tribute was paid to the valour of the little country which is holding the pass against the Fascist hordes.

IN a mood of ardent enthusiasm coupled with stern resolution the Greeks celebrated on March 25 the 120th anniversary of their country's independence. In Athens the streets were gay with flags, but there were no soldiers to parade in the spring sunshine. The crowds on the pavements who watched the King and his sister, Princess Catherine, drive to the Cathedral were composed almost entirely of old men, women and children. The young men were all at the front, far away in the snowbound heights of Albania, keeping the pass as their fathers of long, long ago held the pass at Thermopylae.

But even in the front line Independence Day was honoured. The Greek soldiers roared out their National Anthem so that the Italians could not fail to hear, and followed it with a rendering of their favourite folk songs. They made little blue and white rosettes and stuck them in their rifles and machine-guns, and for their midday meal they had a double ration of meat. When the Italians delivered their usual attack they were repelled again as usual, but with even more than usual vigour, for the Greek soldiers knew, and the Greek people knew, that they were facing a crisis, what might be a supreme crisis, in their history. Bulgaria had fallen into the Nazi trap; Yugoslavia had just succumbed (or so it seemed) to Hitler's wiles; on Greece's frontier a great German Army was massed, and the drive to Salonika might start at any moment.

But on that day, at least, no great attack was delivered. The Germans still marked time; and as for the Italians, they were licking the wounds incurred in yet another ill-fated attempt. Following the complete repulse of the offensive of March 9-16—that offensive which was said to have been delivered under Mussolini's own eye, indeed to have been actually directed by him— General Cavallero had sent his men once again over the top. The story of the battle was given over the Athens radio on March 20. "The attack was as great in intensity as those of last week," said the announcer, "with the difference that it was not over such a wide front. Whatever hopes the Italians may have placed in this new move they were doomed to disappointment, for the offensive was completely crushed.

"The Greek forces stood up to this mechanized assault with the same cool determination as that which characterized their victorious resistance to the violent attacks a week ago. The tanks came forward first to open the way for the Italian infantry. Our anti-tank batteries immediately opened an intense and rapid fire. After the first few rounds one tank received a direct hit, which broke its chain and caused it to overturn. A few seconds later a second tank was shattered by another hit from our batteries. A third followed soon. All the other tanks turned about and fled.

"Then came the turn of the Italian infantrymen, who had the courage not to imitate the ignominious example of their mechanized brothers. They came under the concentrated fire of the Greek artillery and the cross-fire of Greek machine-gunners. The losses of the Italians were terrific. As they came on in waves they were mown down in masses and the field was strewn with dead."

The announcer concluded with a comment on the part played by the R.A.F. "Another day of Mussolini's spring," he said, "has added more victory posies to Greek and British buttonholes."

Upholding the Sacred Flame

In this critical hour there was never a sign of wavering in Greece. In an address to members of the Metaxas Youth Movement, the Premier, M. Koryzis, expressed himself in terms of the most forthright patriotism. Just as the Greek revolt in 1821 began the emancipation of Europe from the rule of the Turkish Sultans, so today, he declared, the Greeks believed that the present war meant the dawn of Europe's liberation from a mechanized tyranny. As it was in 1821, so it is in 1941. "The same divine spirit moves us," said M. Koryzis, "the same high moral ideals and faith in freedom and honour. At this hour, when new threats are discerned on the horizon, you shall swear to uphold the sacred flame."

In Britain, too, the anniversary of Greek Independence was celebrated with pride in the exploits of a most gallant ally. At a mass meeting in London, Mr. Amery, Secretary of State for India, paid tribute to the troops who had fought month after month with such grim resolution. "We are in this conflict with you to the end," he said, "and that end will be the assured victory of freedom and civilization." "On this day of proud memories," said Mr. Churchill in a special message, "I would add one brief tribute to those which the whole civilized world is paying to the valour of the Greek nation. One hundred and twenty years ago all that was noblest in England strove in the cause of Greek independence and rejoiced in its achievement. Today that epic struggle is being repeated against greater odds but with equal courage and with no less certainty of success. We in England know that the cause for which Byron died is a sacred cause; we are resolved to sustain it."

Again the German invasion of Greece was reported to be imminent. The Greeks replied by moving a large part of their army into Thrace. But Yugoslavia refused to be inveigled into the camp of her enemies.

WINTER IN ALBANIA imposed very severe conditions upon the Greek troops. The rough roads were frequently blocked by snowdrifts, and in the mountains ponies and mules were used as the surest means of transport. This pony is loaded with water barrels. A Greek soldier (inset) shelters in his tent.   *Photos, Bosshard, Exclusive to* THE WAR ILLUSTRATED

Her Warriors Write in Blood a Glorious Epic

'I THANK YOU, GREEK WARRIORS'

King George of the Hellenes' Order of the Day to the Greek Fighting Forces

AFTER more than four months of fierce fighting against a numerically superior enemy, your heroic struggles with men and the elements have not only failed to exhaust you but have steeled your determination and endurance to an admirable degree. When the enemy for a week, after long and careful preparation, thought himself ready to break you and launched the violent offensive on which he based so many hopes, not only did you hold him, but you dealt him a severe blow, gave him a fitting answer, and taught him one more lesson of what Greek gallantry and courage are capable.

You Greek warriors won because the blood of the fighters of Marathon and Thermopylae flows in your veins. You have won because right is on your side and God and the Virgin have protected you. You are victorious because you have opposed the enemy's tanks and machines with breasts of steel and a will of granite. While you are writing in blood the glorious epic of the newer Greece on the snow-covered mountains of Epirus and Albania, your brothers of the Royal Navy and Air Force are also adding golden pages to Greek history by sea and air. The whole civilized world is watching with amazement the achievements of Greek arms.

Deeply moved by your feats of gallantry and full of fatherly pride, I thank you, brave Greek warriors, in the name of the Motherland. You may rest assured that every Greek conscience is inspired and guided by the unshaken determination to guard the honour and freedom of Greece at all costs.—*Athens, March 18, 1941*

ARCTIC WEATHER hampered the movements of the Greek troops during the winter of 1940-41 as the three photographs in this page show. In that at the top of the page, Greek troops are moving forward over wooded hills in which the trees are bowed down with snow. Centre, soldiers are in front of their fragile shelter, yet they make the best of it and have hung out their washing on a line to dry—or freeze. Despite the weather the wounded were well looked after, and, above, motor ambulances are seen on a snow-clad road.

Photos, Bosshard, Exclusive to THE WAR ILLUSTRATED

Yugoslavia's Army in the Hour of Crisis

When the Yugoslav Cabinet decided to hitch their country to Hitler's star the Army was particularly loud in its condemnations, and it was with its ardent support that young King Peter assumed the Royal power. As this article reveals, the Yugoslav Army is not only intensely patriotic but has an efficiency and fighting spirit which combine to rank it next to Turkey's in the Balkans.

FOR many hundreds of years the South Slavs—the people who under the names of Serbs, Croats, Slovenes, make up the population of present-day Yugoslavia (Yugo: South)—have ranked amongst the finest and fiercest fighters in the Balkans. Theirs is a spirit which ages of Turkish domination proved unable to tame. They are men of high courage and of an intense patriotism. Their fighting capacity was proved beyond a doubt in the Balkan wars of 1912-13, when they defeated the Turks and Bulgarians. Still more was it shown in that disastrous retreat across the Albanian mountains in the autumn of 1915, when, already overwhelmed by the Austrians in the north, they were suddenly attacked from the right rear by the Bulgarians. After enduring terrible hardships and suffering enormous losses, a remnant of the Serbian army reached Salonika, where it soon took its place in the Allied front. In October 1918 it was again on the offensive, and in a few weeks it had recaptured all and more of the territory which had been lost. At that time it numbered some 65,000 combatants, but its battle casualties had exceeded 331,000, including 45,000 killed and over 133,000 wounded. It was a war record, indeed, of which any country might well be proud.

Serbia became Yugoslavia or, as it was called in those early days, the Triune Kingdom

fit is liable for military service between the ages of 21 and 50, although he spends only eighteen months with the colours—those months dating from the year in which his 21st birthday falls. In times of emergency men fit to carry arms may be called up for service between the ages of 17 and 21 and 50 and 55. The peacetime strength of the Yugoslav Army is about 130,000 men, though at the present time it is estimated that some million are under arms. With reserves,

For military purposes Yugoslavia is divided into five army areas, each of which is subdivided into divisional areas and military districts. The first and most important army is centred about Belgrade, with its headquarters at Novisad. The second army is stationed in Bosnia and Dalmatia, and its H.Q. is at Sarajevo, where on that July day in 1914 Gavrilo Princip fired the shots which precipitated the first Great War. The third army is in the south, occupying the territory

YUGOSLAV INFANTRY advancing down a slope during large-scale manoeuvres. The leaves in their helmets provide an effective camouflage. Below, a machine-gun unit is ready for action.   *Photos, Keystone*

between Albania, Greece, and Bulgaria: its headquarters are at Skoplje. The fourth army is in the opposite corner of the country facing the frontiers of Italy and Germany, with its headquarters at Zagreb in Croatia. Then the fifth army, with its H.Q. at Nish, faces the Bulgarian frontier. The vitally important valleys of the Morava and Vardar are included in the zones of the fifth and third armies. The Army as a whole consists of 56 regiments, plus a regiment of guards in Belgrade, and another of fortress troops.

Under Yugoslavia's constitution the King is the supreme head of the Army, and the Army's loyalty to the Throne was shown beyond a doubt on March 27 when young King Peter deposed his uncle Prince Paul, and dismissed the pro-Axis Cabinet. The executive power is wielded by the Chief of the General Staff, who is at present General Peter Kositch, who is also tutor to young King Peter. General Milan Neditch has been called the Iron Man of the Army; he is a former Chief of the General Staff and resigned his office as Defence Minister last November because of the strong stand he had taken against the pro-Axis policy of the Government. He was succeeded by General Petar Peshitch, who, like Kositch and Neditch, is a veteran of the Great War. None of the Yugoslav war leaders is, indeed, a young man; Kositch is 60, Neditch is 59, and Peshitch close on 70.

of Serbs, Croats and Slovenes, and the Serbian regiments found themselves grouped in the Yugoslav Army with regiments which in the late war had been fighting on the opposite side. They settled down well together, however, and the Croats in particular represented a considerable increase in military strength, for they had long been counted among the most efficient and hard-fighting of the troops under the command of the old Emperor Francis Joseph.

Every young Yugoslav who is physically

Yugoslavia could put, it is estimated, two million men into the field. In addition to the regular Army there is a body something akin to our Home Guard, but primarily a physical culture organization—the Sokols—whose membership numbers some 300,000. The total population of Yugoslavia, it may be mentioned, approaches 16,000,000—about 8,000,000 Serbs, 5,000,000 Croats, and a million and a half Slovenes, with Germans, Magyars and Macedonians making up the balance.

King Peter's Men Ready for Battle

A MILLION YUGOSLAVS were called up during the early part of March, and as the crisis developed took up their battle positions on the frontiers. Above, is seen a well-equipped motor-cycle detachment.

Photo, Keystone

The calling to the colours of Yugoslavs was described by the authorities as " Army manoeuvres." The driver of a light tank (circle) is seen receiving instructions. A heavy field gun (below) is being hauled by a motor tractor.

Photos, L.N.A. and Keystone

Here Are Some of 'the Boys in the Back Room'

AIR COMDRE. PATRICK HUSKINSON, Director of Armament Development, was formerly vice-president of the Ordnance Board at Woolwich Arsenal. He gained the M.C. while serving with the R.F.C. in 1916.

MR. W. S. FARREN, who has done great work in the design of the new 'planes, was an experimental engineer and pilot in the last war. In 1937, he became Deputy Director of Scientific Research at the Air Ministry.

MR. G. P. BULMAN, who "fastened on to" the Sabre engine, is a Civil Servant who before the war dealt with engine production for the Air Ministry. He is now with the Ministry of Aircraft Production.

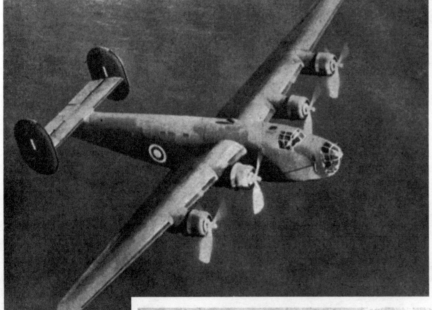

LORD BEAVERBROOK, Minister of Aircraft Production, broadcasting on March 23, 1941, spoke of the new types of 'planes and engines either in manufacture or development. Then he went on :

" Now who is responsible for this work of development on which so much depends ? I will tell you. It is the boys in the back room. They do not sit in the limelight, but they are men who do the work. Many of them are Civil Servants. There is Bulman, and there is Farren. But a long list of names could be given, and one day must be given. It is in connexion with one of our new engines, the Sabre, that Bulman should have our praise. For this Civil Servant fastened on to the Sabre. He took all the chances, certain of condemnation if he failed and with no great expectation of praise if he succeeded. Well, he has succeeded, so let us praise Bulman. I know that the designer is entitled to the highest credit ; history will give it to him. The manufacturer must be taken into account also, but it is the courage and foresight of Bulman that I wish to record now.... Air Commodore Huskinson is one of our leaders. He designs bombs. Big bombs, fat bombs, thin bombs, beautiful bombs. And he puts his heart into the job.''

Amongst the first American bombers to be released for use in Great Britain are Giant Consolidated B 24s, one of which is seen above in flight in America, while right is one that has just arrived on a British aerodrome after delivery from America. Both they and the Boeing B 17 (Flying Fortress) are equipped with the famous Sperry bomb sight, an American invention. The Consolidated has a full working range of 3,000 miles and a speed of 335 m.p.h. The range of the Boeing is slightly less.

Photos, Planet News, Central Press, and British Official : Crown Copyright

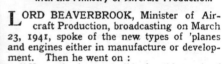

Soon They Will Need a New Score Board

A TALLY OF VICTIMS destroyed by one redoubtable R.A.F. fighter squadron is kept on the propeller of a wrecked German aircraft and, as can be seen, takes the form of miniature swastikas. The bottom section shows the squadron's score in France; the centre shows the total shot down in daylight over this country. The squadron has recently taken over night fighting operations and its first "bag"—a Nazi bomber—is recorded in the top section. Two men in this group are wearing the new R.A.F. battle dress.

Photo, British Official : Crown Copyright

Of Course, the British People 'Can Take It'

PLYMOUTH was given a severe battering by Nazi bombers on the nights of March 20 and 21, 1941, as part of Hitler's campaign to put our principal ports out of action. But the spirit of Plymouth's people was undaunted, finding expression in a Union Jack fluttering above the ruins (right) and the oft-repeated wish : " Let the R.A.F. give the Germans what the Germans have given us." Mr. R. G. Menzies, who was in Plymouth during the raid, also bore witness to the growing tide of anger and wish that the Nazis should be given a dose of their own medicine. Below, at an Emergency Post in Plymouth the police are dealing with inquiries from those who have lost their all.

Photos, " News Chronicle"

THE King has sent the following message to Viscountess Astor, Lady Mayoress of Plymouth, who was hostess to their Majesties when they visited Plymouth on Thursday, March 20, just before the first great raid : " After our happy day the Queen and I are deeply distressed to hear what you have all been through last night. Whatever the people of Plymouth may be called upon to suffer we feel quite certain the spirit of the West Country will rise above it all. God bless you all."

ON CLYDESIDE, as at Plymouth, the worst ruthlessness of the Nazi bombers fell upon working-class districts, where there were many such pitiful scenes as this. These women (above), bombed out, have collected a few of their belongings, but their only home for the moment is the street. The one bright spot is that they have managed to boil a kettle and make a cup of tea. Left, is one of the destroyed tenement houses. The next morning some of the former occupants stood by gazing at the smouldering ruins of their former homes. On Clydeside, as at Plymouth, the chief reaction was one of fierce determination to pay the Nazis back in their own coin.   *Photos, Keystone*

But It's Full Time the Germans Took It Too!

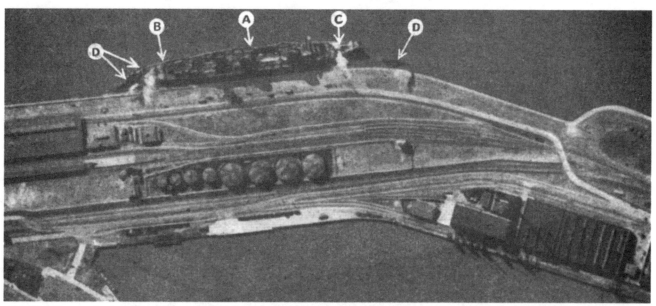

BREMEN, Germany's crack liner, is now a burned-out hulk. On March 17, 1941, a Nazi news agency announced that fire had broken out on board the ship lying at Bremerhaven, her home port. The origin of the fire was said to be unknown, but the extent of the damage was verified by the R.A.F. in the photograph above. A, the waist burned out. B, the stern still smoking. C, the bow on fire. D, small ships presumably pumping water on the flames. It is significant that on March 13-14 a single British 'plane bombed the docks at Bremerhaven as an alternative target.

OSTEND is one of the most important of the so-called invasion ports on the coasts of Belgium and France at which the Nazis have assembled barges and other small craft for the long-threatened but oft-postponed invasion of Britain. It has therefore been the object of particular attention from the bombers of the R.A.F. This photograph, taken from a reconnaissance 'plane, shows the Bassin de la Marine with its rows of warehouses completely gutted after the visits of the R.A.F.

Photos, British Official : Crown Copyright

Not All Hitler's Might and Malice Will Succeed

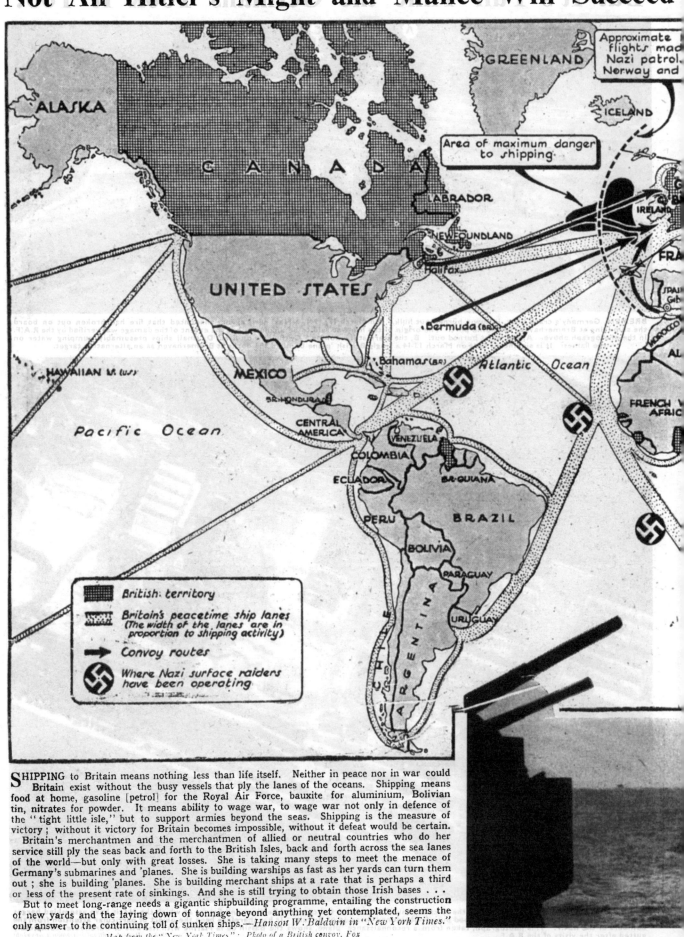

GREENLAND

Approximate flights mad[e] Nazi patrol. Norway and

ICELAND

Area of maximum danger to shipping

ALASKA

C A N A D A

LABRADOR

NEWFOUNDLAND

IRELAND

UNITED STATES

Halifax

FR[ANCE]

Bermuda (BR.)

SPAIN Gib.

MOROCCO

HAWAIIAN Is. (U.S.)

MEXICO

Bahamas (BR.)

Atlantic Ocean

AL[GERIA]

BR. HONDURAS

FRENCH W. AFRIC[A]

Pacific Ocean

CENTRAL AMERICA

VENEZUELA

COLOMBIA

ECUADOR

BR. GUIANA

PERU

B R A Z I L

BOLIVIA

PARAGUAY

A R G E N T I N A

URUGUAY

Legend:

British territory

Britain's peacetime ship lanes (The width of the lanes are in proportion to shipping activity)

Convoy routes

Where Nazi surface raiders have been operating

SHIPPING to Britain means nothing less than life itself. Neither in peace nor in war could Britain exist without the busy vessels that ply the lanes of the oceans. Shipping means food at home, gasoline [petrol] for the Royal Air Force, bauxite for aluminium, Bolivian tin, nitrates for powder. It means ability to wage war, to wage war not only in defence of the "tight little isle," but to support armies beyond the seas. Shipping is the measure of victory; without it victory for Britain becomes impossible, without it defeat would be certain.

Britain's merchantmen and the merchantmen of allied or neutral countries who do her service still ply the seas back and forth to the British Isles, back and forth across the sea lanes of the world—but only with great losses. She is taking many steps to meet the menace of Germany's submarines and 'planes. She is building warships as fast as her yards can turn them out; she is building 'planes. She is building merchant ships at a rate that is perhaps a third or less of the present rate of sinkings. And she is still trying to obtain those Irish bases . . .

But to meet long-range needs a gigantic shipbuilding programme, entailing the construction of new yards and the laying down of tonnage beyond anything yet contemplated, seems the only answer to the continuing toll of sunken ships.—*Hanson W. Baldwin in "New York Times."*

Map from the "New York Times"; Photo of a British convoy, Fox

tting the Life-lines of Britain's Imperial Commerce

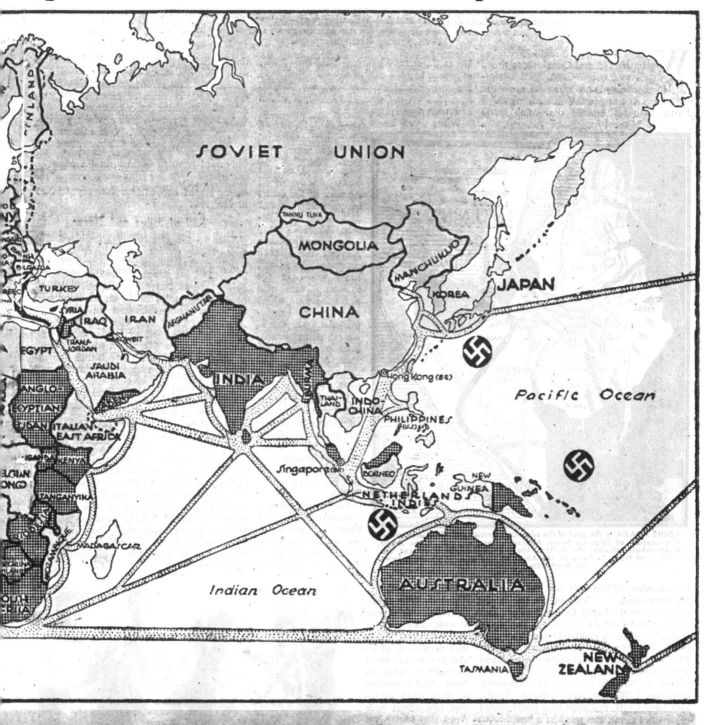

Closing in On the Italians in Abyssinia

Steady progress all along the line at a fast-increasing pace—that was the position in the East African war zone as the rainy season drew near. Below we review the outstanding developments of the campaign.

WHERE will General Cunningham spend Easter? Lord Croft, Joint Under-Secretary for War, in his speech in the House of Lords on March 25, suggested that the General seemed anxious to spend Easter with his brother the Admiral, the

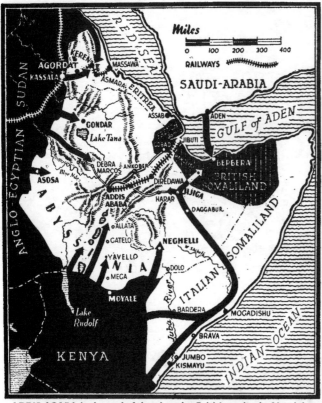

ADDIS ABABA is the goal of the advancing British armies in Abyssinia. The capture of Jijiga by South African troops threatened the Addis Ababa-Jibuti railway, the Italians' life-line to the coast, and cut the main road from Berbera to the Abyssinian capital. This map shows the British lines of advance.

Up to February 23 they totalled only 2,966, of whom happily only 604 were killed. On the other hand, we had inflicted over 200,000 casualties on the enemy, 180,000 of whom had been taken prisoners.

While from Libya there was practically nothing of importance to report—the only news was a story from Berlin of the occupation of El Agheila, in the desert between Benghazi and Tripoli, by a "German Africa Corps"—on other fronts in Africa the battle continued, always with heavy losses to the Italians. There was not a front on which they were not retreating—not one, save at Keren, their stronghold in Eritrea, which they defended with desperate valour. But even at Keren the British columns were drawing ever nearer to the central fortress, creeping up the frowning precipices, storming one by one the beetling pinnacles, and on March 27 Keren, too, was taken by the British.

Far to the south a column of General Platt's men was heading straight for Gondar, the ancient Abyssinian city in which

tinued their march towards Addis Ababa, some 200 miles to the east.

From the Kenya front the news was equally good. Four columns of Imperial troops—African units from the colonies of East and West—were pressing north across a practically trackless wilderness. One column was reported to have reached Allata, another was at Yavello; yet another captured the important town of Neghelli and pressed on northward. On this front the morale of the enemy troops encountered was reported to be very low.

Fall of Jijiga and Harar

Then to the east Italian Somaliland was now under British control. After their triumphs at Kismayu and Mogadishu the South Africans struck northwards along the desert road to Daggabur, and on March 17 occupied the town of Jijiga, an important centre of communications in south-east Abyssinia. From here one column turned west along the road to Harar, whose fall was reported on March 27, while a second marched north-eastward into British Somaliland, reaching Hargeisa on March 20, and sped onwards to join up with their comrades advancing from the newly retaken Berbera. Soon the whole of British Somaliland was once again in British hands.

Thus from every side the Italians in Abyssinia were now being attacked day by day; the country under their control grew ever more narrow as the British columns pressed on and the tide of rebellion rose higher and higher. Militarily they were in an impossible position, and if the Duke of Aosta continued the war it was probably because he hoped that the April rains would bring a period of respite. That may well have been his hope. General Cunningham's intention was that that hope should be disappointed.

Commander-in-Chief of our fleet in the Mediterranean. "Starting with high velocity from the Indian Ocean," his columns of West and East African troops had swept through Italian Somaliland, and were now nearly 300 miles over the Abyssinian border. They were already approaching Harar and threatening the Jibuti railway. They had advanced 770 miles from the Kenya frontier, and some 1,100 miles from railhead. Surely, said Lord Croft, this must be a world record of distance covered in so short a time.

Then, referring to the campaigns in Africa as a whole, he spoke of the "glorious succession of victories" on so many fronts. "The astonishing story of the comradeship in arms of free citizens of the British Empire, drawn from all contingents and fighting with such fixity of purpose, such wonderful valour, skill and cooperation, is the vindication of British, Dominion and Empire rule. Hitler and Mussolini thought that they had only to hit us below the belt and the Empire would fall to pieces; instead, the whole British Empire has fallen upon its enemies like one man in a phalanx of freedom and faith."

Still referring to the fighting in both North Africa and East, Lord Croft announced that our casualties had been surprisingly small.

the Italians had congregated their women and children from over a wide area; about the middle of March they deemed it advisable to withdraw them hurriedly by 'plane to Addis Ababa, another of these cities of refuge (the others were Asmara in the north and Jimmu in the south). Another hundred miles or so to the south a third column of Imperial troops, allied with large contingents of Abyssinian Patriots, was struggling to enter Debra Marcos. Here Italian resistance was stubborn, and their positions seemed to be fairly strongly held. To the south-west, Anglo-Belgian troops captured Asosa and continued

ABYSSINIAN PATRIOTS, who were trained in Kenya by a British Military Mission in their revolt against the Italians, were led into Abyssinia by British officers. Here an officer is seen talking to Patriots.
See also Vol. 4, page 118. *Photo, British Official: Crown Copyright*

'Flaming Onions' Flung Against the R.A.F.

Like a sheaf of rockets these " flaming onions " are going up into the German sky. They are part of Germany's air defences and were photographed from a raiding British 'plane. They are not new, for they were used in the last war, primarily with a view to setting fire to aircraft. Two projectiles strung together go hurtling into the air leaving a trail of fire, but though at first sight they seem alarming they are not as deadly as they appear to be, for they do not reach to any great height and are erratic in aim.

Photo, Keystone

Stills from the Nazi 'Bogey Bogey' Film

FORT EBEN EYMAEL, most powerful and modern of the Belgian forts, considered before the war to be almost impregnable, is blasted by fire from shells and mines while shock troops paddle furiously across the Albert Canal under cover of heavy protective fire.

A party of Germans is here seen landing on the farther bank of the Albert Canal, while a protective smoke screen hides their movements from the defenders. So thoroughly had the attack been planned that the fortress was obliged to capitulate on May 11, 1940.

Nazi engineers are using flame-throwers, preparing the way for the German infantry to capture pill-boxes and blockhouses in the system of enemy fortifications.

"SIEG IM WESTEN" (Victory in the West), the Nazis' new propaganda film, stills from which are here reproduced, is designed to hearten the German people and impress whatever neutrals are left to be impressed. A sequel to "Campaign in Poland," which was widely shown in neutral countries to persuade those reluctant to side with the Nazis how all-powerful was German might, the new film depicts the "blitzkrieg" of 1940 in Western Europe. Von Papen showed it to Turkish politicians at the German Embassy on the day Mr. Eden arrived in Ankara, but it failed to cow representatives of a race renowned for their fighting qualities, and the success of Mr. Eden's mission was in no way jeopardized.

One of the many army cameramen detailed to make this film is here seen following up the fighting. More than twenty of these soldier-cameramen were killed at their work.

A GERMAN ASSAULT GUN is firing a 4-inch shell at point-blank range against a house in which soldiers have been defending a road. The heavy armoured shield enables the crew of the gun, which is mounted on caterpillar tracks, to advance heedless of rifle and machine-gun fire.

The assault is then carried forward. The gun rumbles ahead, supported by Nazi assault troops armed with light machine-guns, to go into action once again at the next centre of resistance, which, in turn, will be blasted out of existence by point-blank shell fire.

Hitler's 'O.T.' Men On the Job

DR. FRITZ TODT, who has designed the Nazi forts on the French coast, was born in 1891 and became Inspector-General of Roads in the Reich in 1933.

Batteries of guns along the coast of occupied France are preceded by batteries of machines such as this, a series of giant concrete mixers which daily pour out hundreds of tons of concrete—a material in great demand for modern fortifications.

GERMANY has a great body of labourers, military in everything but name, known as the "Organization Todt," generally shortened to O.T. The name comes from its head, Dr. Todt, who is the Nazis' Concrete Engineer Number One, for he built the great German motor roads and the Siegfried Line, which, he boasted, was impregnable, When the great Nazi push of May 1940 came the O.T. was called upon for strenuous labour with and behind the fighting men. As the French retreated it had to clear up the damage done, re-open the roads for the streams of military traffic, rebuild bridges, fill in shell and bomb craters, clear away masses of rubble and get works and factories going again. It is proudly boasted by the Nazi propagandists that between May 10 and June 10, 1941, a single Front Labour O.T. Command maintained some 1,000 miles of roads, repaired 22 bridges, constructed 5 new bridges, and filled 58 large craters and many smaller ones. A bridge in Northern France 55 feet long and 20 feet wide is said to have been built by 35 men of the O.T. in 45 hours. Their most recent work has been the construction of forts along the French coast.

Machinery of all sorts plays a vital part in the work of the "Organization Todt." After the concrete mixers come the giant cranes, such as that above, to lower the guns and other equipment into position. A few days later the brown-clad workers, such as those right, seen using an excavator, disappear and leave only an inconspicuous mound covering a new fort.

These particulars of the O.T. and the photographs in this page are from "Facts in Review," a magazine of Nazi propaganda published by a German agency in New York

British Tanks Are as Tough as Their Crews!

Originally a British invention and first used by the British Army with devastating effect
in the last war, the tank has now become part of the equipment of every modern army.
Yet still today British tanks take the lead—in spite of all Nazi trumpetings to the contrary
—because of their fine quality and the splendid spirit of the men who man them.

FROM Libya, from Eritrea, from Somaliland—from all the fronts on which the British land forces have been in action—come heartening reports of the fine qualities of the British tanks ; qualities made the most of by the skill and endurance of their crews. Through terrific Italian fire, such as no infantry could have penetrated, over sandy wastes and across boulder-strewn country covered with outcrops of rock, these British tanks have pressed forward relentlessly, smashing their way to victory and pulverizing the defences of Italy's crumbling empire.

That British tanks are tough a few incidents of the recent campaign will show. One tank, which received a direct hit from an Italian field gun, showed only a short crack in the armour plating ; another was immobilized for a few minutes with clutch trouble in the middle of a battle right in front of the Italian lines. Machine-gun bullets drummed a tattoo upon its sides, grenades blew off the searchlights, and a 65 mm. gun was trained upon it, yet the only part penetrated was where a bullet smashed the tough glass in the aperture in front of the driver.

Two army officers, members of the Royal Armoured Corps who had shortly before been engaged in the Libyan fighting, recently visited a British tank factory. Then they knew why their tanks were so tough. Every tank made in this great Ministry of Supply factory—and this applies, of course, to all our tank factories—has to undergo various and stringent tests. This, British workmanship aiding, has enabled our tanks to pass the most stringent test of all—the battering of enemy guns.

One of the officers, describing a great tank battle near Benghazi, told how our tank forces were outnumbered by an Italian force which included seventy heavy tanks. The battle continued throughout the day, and the Italian heavy tanks were reduced to about thirty effectives. Then reinforcements arrived to complete the Italian defeat. In that fierce engagement the British casualties amounted to only two killed and five injured. "But," continued the officer, "we couldn't have done it if you fellows who had been making the tanks and the armour had not been doing your jobs damned well . . . it was by using British tanks made of British steel that we got the better of them." As one factory worker commented : "It makes you feel you're doing something worth while when you hear that the blooming tank you worked on helped to win a battle."

Six Thousand Separate Parts

Moreover, the making of a tank is a highly complicated job. As many as 6,200 separate parts go into the completed structure of some of them, and these parts require about 50,000 different machining and assembling operations. In this one factory over 500 different machine tools are used in the course of these operations, for some of which an accuracy of one ten-thousandth of an inch may be necessary.

In this sphere, as indeed in every sphere of Britain's colossal factory effort, British workmanship has shown itself to be in a class apart, and General Wavell's own words are sufficient proof : "Weight for class," he has written, "Italian tanks, many of them newly delivered from manufacturers, proved no match for British products." He added : "As a further tribute to British workmanship it is noteworthy that our long-range desert patrols have now covered a total distance of half a million miles without loss of a single vehicle from mechanical breakdown."

One of the officers visiting the factory described three types of Italian tanks he had encountered, two medium and one light. The first Italian medium tank had a good gun, but owing to its short traverse its fire was largely ineffective ; also the sides of the tank were thinly armoured. The second medium type was, he said, an excellent armoured fighting vehicle with an all-round traverse. But the Italian light tank he described as a miserable little affair which stood no chance against even our lightest tank.

Then one of the workmen wanted to know whether our British tanks had proved superior to German tanks. Swift came the reply from one of the officers, who had taken part in the fighting in France. "Definitely, yes," he said.

Heavy tanks for assault, light tanks for reconnaissance and patrol work, armoured cars and Bren gun carriers ; all our mechanized equipment has been made by an army of British workmen who are determined that those who are using the weapons they forge shall never be let down by their comrades in the factories of Britain.

ARMAMENT WORKERS in many factories have recently had visits from the men who have been in action with the 'planes, tanks and guns they have produced, and have been encouraged to greater efforts by the stirring stories told to them. The officer above is talking to a worker in a tank factory in the Midlands. He had been in action against the Italians in Libya and praised highly the superiority of British tanks, due to British workmanship. As he put it : "A split pin may mean the difference between standing up and going down."

Photo, G.P.U.

At Home and At the Front They Show Their Paces

Many a picturesque village in East Anglia has become accustomed to strange and noisy visitors disturbing its ancient peace when army training is in progress, and streams of tanks, lorries and cars thunder along the narrow lanes. Left, a medium tank of the type that is being turned out in an incessant stream from factories such as that seen in page 378 has drawn up by the roadside with a scout car behind it.

A factor which has enabled British tanks in action to stand up to heavy fire is the quality of their armour plating.

Right, a tank of a slightly different type from that shown in the top photograph has drawn up in a small town in the South of England, where it was engaged in rounding up parachute troops supposed to have landed on the downs. In the Western Desert light tanks, performing the task once allotted to cavalry, have dashed forward at an almost incredible speed. Above, a squadron of them, each with a place name beginning with an A, is on patrol. A searchlight can be seen mounted on each of these tanks.

Photos, British Official : Crown Copyright

OUR SEARCHLIGHT ON THE WAR

What Nazi Slavery Costs

THE German occupation in western Europe is costing the territories in question the gigantic sum of £1,050,000,000 per year by direct levy, the greater part being exacted not in money but in kind. Details of how this total is apportioned were recently given in Parliament by Mr. Butler, Under-Secretary for Foreign Affairs, and are shown in the following table, where the sterling equivalents are based on rates of exchange obtaining before the occupation.

	Total	Per head of population
	£	£
Norway	68,000,000	25
Denmark	26,000,000	8
Belgium	75,000,000	8
Holland	54,000,000	6
France	827,000,000	20

There is also a great deal of widespread unofficial looting, of both produce and livestock, which the inhabitants are helpless to prevent lest a worse fate befall them. But this is not the whole of the burden laid upon the hapless people. The amount of goods sent to Germany is greater than what is received in return, and this surplus is paid for in blocked marks, from which no credit is ever likely to be derived. Although smaller now that there is so much less to export, the annual loss from this source is still about £100,000,000 a year. The estimated burden upon the western occupied territories thus reaches a grand total of £1,150,000,000.

Germany Returns to Tangier

ON March 15 the Spanish authorities gave notice that they were about to eject the Mendoub of Tangier, and the following day this was done. By the Convention of 1923, signed by the Governments of Britain, France and Spain, Tangier was created a permanently neutralized international port, under the sovereignty of the Sultan of Morocco. The Mendoub was the Sultan's representative. Even when, last December, the Spanish Government suddenly took over the administration of Tangier from the International Committee of Control, the Mendoub's authority was not challenged. On March 17, the day after the ejection, his official residence,

the Mendoubia, was handed over to the German Consul with a good deal of ceremony. General Asensio, High Commissioner for Spanish Morocco, inspected the guard of honour in which were included a few Italian Blackshirts, and then made a flowery speech in which he said that the handing-over was not only a gesture of friendship towards Germany but an act of justice as well. The Swastika flag was hoisted, the German and Spanish national anthems played, and then the company proceeded to a banquet at the Rif Hotel, given by Herr Heberlein, Counsellor of the German Ambassador in Madrid. An inspired report from La Linea that the British Consulate in Tangier was to be closed, and that British residents had been ordered to leave Morocco, was denied in London on March 24.

'Vilna' Squadron Takes the Air

A NEW unit of the R.A.F. Fighter Command made its first patrol at dawn on March 24. It is a large squadron and its entire personnel, both flying and ground staff, is Polish, with the exception of the British commanding officer and two British flight-commanders. The average age is 23, the average keenness 100 per cent. Many of the pilots have had between 2,000 and 3,000 hours of flying experience. As members of British squadrons, with whom they have been completing their training, these Polish airmen have already accounted for 25 German aircraft, and one sergeant pilot was recently awarded the D.F.M. The name of the new Hurricane squadron is " Vilna."

Boats Built to be Bombed

HIGH-SPEED armoured target boats, in use by the R.A.F., have been built for this purpose by a famous British constructor of racing craft. He was faced with the problem of combining a very high turn of speed with such armouring as would protect the crew and vital parts from the impact of light bombs. The result is an ingenious

WOMEN OF THE A.T.S. now wear a coloured field service cap with walking-out dress. The new headgear, two examples of which are seen here, has replaced the peaked cap. It is beech brown with leaf green piping. *Photo, Planet News*

compromise. The three members of the crew and the controls are placed amidships, and are hooded with stout armour plate mounted on rubber buffers. The rest of the hull, which is left without protection, is packed with a special buoyant substance called onazate, which is only one-fifth the weight of cork. Practice bombs, even though dropped from a height of several miles, strike harmlessly against the armour plate. If they hit the hull they pass right through it without making the boat unseaworthy. The crew are safeguarded by masks against the fumes of bursting bombs. The target boat is driven by triple 100 h.p. engines, each actuating a separate propeller.

Let Bullying be Unconfined!

NORWAY's Quisling Government has given the Nasjonal Samling Party carte blanche to make whatever reprisals they like against anti-Quisling Norwegians, with the assurance that no legal proceedings will be taken against them. Members of the Party complained that they were constantly being subjected to abuse and assault. Quisling's " Hirdmen " also harboured a grievance in that they had no authority to make arrests. Now both grievances are removed, for vengeance may be taken on the population without interference by the police. But the Norwegians are a spirited race in spite of incessant bullying. The authorities of Oslo University have threatened to close it if the Quisling Commissar for Education does not put an end to interference with university teaching.

Fortune Smiles on the Trawlers

GONE are the days when the herring-fishers of our coasts were unable to dispose of their hardly won catch because nobody wanted it. Today trawlermen are making so much money that they are not only refurnishing their homes, but contributing liberally to the Red Cross and putting thousands of pounds into war savings. This prosperity is not due to a spectacular rise in wages, but to the present demand for fish, which has altered to an unprecedented degree the value of their individual shares in the catch. The lowest paid member of a trawler's crew can now make a sum during one trip that works out at over £1 a day. A mate's daily earnings average £5, while those of a skipper may equal the salary of some Cabinet Ministers. One boat fishing in home waters recently disposed of its mixed catch for the record sum of £4,824. A big Iceland trawler, with the enormous catch of 36,000 stones, sold it for £19,000. No wonder that the " penny herring " now sounds like a myth

R.A.F. TARGET SPEEDBOATS are 40 feet in length and are armoured so that hits by light bombs will not inflict damage to crew or vital parts. Here is one of them travelling swiftly through the water. It carries a radio to enable the crew to communicate with the " enemy " attacker.
Photo, British Official : Crown Copyright

Honours for Lion-hearted Civilians

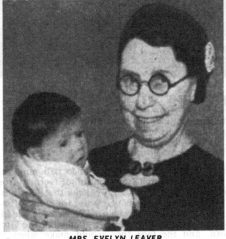

MRS. EVELYN LEAVER

British Empire Medal for bravery during an air raid on Manchester. Mrs. Leaver, a midwife, was attending a patient when the doors, windows and staircase of the house were shattered by a bomb. She moved the patient to a cellar and attended her in the confinement. Mrs. Leaver is seen above with the baby.

DAVID WILEMAN

Awarded the R.S.P.C.A.'s bronze medal for tunnelling alone through the debris of a bombed house to rescue a Scotch terrier. Mr. Wileman, aged 24, Chief Animal Guard for Southgate, Middlesex, under the national A.R.P. scheme for animals, holds a rescued cat.

MISS M. E. WHITE

Given the British Empire Medal for remaining alone at her post at the village telephone exchange of Kirby Muxloe, near Leicester, when it was heavily bombed. Doors and windows were blown in and Miss White was showered with glass. This happened at 8 p.m., but at 7 a.m. next day she was still on duty dealing with emergency calls.

SAMUEL DONNER

The British Empire Medal was awarded to Air Warden Samuel Donner for an act of gallantry at Stepney on September 7, 1940, when the greatest daylight raid of the war on London was made. Mr. Donner was one of the earliest London A.R.P. workers to be decorated, and he is seen above when he returned to his home after receiving his medal in March, 1941.

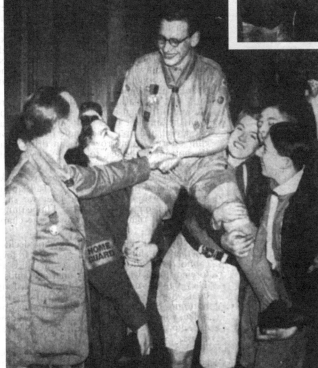

SCOUT ANTHONY BONE

Anthony Bone, a member of the Holborn (London) Scout troop, receives the Scout Gilt Cross for gallantry. Scout Bone did valuable work during the great fire bomb raid on London, December 29, 1940. When not on duty in the A.R.P. control room he has gone out into the streets during raids to give what help he could.

GEORGE W. PAVELEY

Awarded the George Medal for assisting on two occasions in the removal of unexploded bombs, Mr. George William Paveley is a steam-roller driver at Chelmsford. On the first occasion he excavated down to a depth of 10 feet with a pneumatic drill to reach the bomb and drove the steam roller that dragged it out.

Photos, British Official : Crown Copyright; G.P.U., Fox, Planet News, " Daily Mirror "

I WAS THERE!

Eye Witness Stories of Episodes
and Adventures in the
Second Great War

We Didn't Laugh Long at the Greeks!

The tragic conditions on the Italian front in Albania, and the consequent deep depression prevailing among the troops, were revealingly told in a diary kept by a captured Italian officer, typical extracts from which are given below.

BITTER resentment at the incompetence and ignorance which brought the Italians into such straits on the Albanian front is expressed by the officer, himself a Fascist, in his diary. He complains that the Italians were told the Greeks were cowards who could only fight when doped with brandy. His troops were physically depressed as a result of the bad distribution of food, which '' disappeared in a strange fashion '' on its way up to the line. He wrote :

'' I was twenty days on a snow-covered height with nine men without our command sending us even a scrap of bread.'' Another reason for discontent was that the postal service was set up as much as fifty miles to the rear. '' Letters were often lost and Christmas parcels were distributed in a scandalous manner.''

The troops were kept in ignorance of the real situation. The ''soldiers' wireless '' announced that the Army of the Po had entered Yugoslavia and was marching on Salonika and revolution had broken out in Greece. '' Finally, it gave the great news which electrified our troubled minds, news confirmed by the generals—the Duce had announced the immediate intervention of German troops on condition that we held the positions at Klisura. It was of no use for some of us to grumble at this help. We were delighted to save our own lives, we laughed at the Greeks and the face they would make when they found themselves struck in the back.

'' All this happened on January 3 and 4. Then Colonel de Bensi rang up General Dave to ask him when the Germans were coming. The reply was that nothing was known of the matter. The first dreadful doubt began to creep into our minds. It was a terrible disappointment.

'' Then we heard over the wireless that we had lost Cyrenaica. As if that was not enough we learned that the Julia Division had been completely cut up by the Greeks. Little by little the fatal feeling grew that we were inferior to the enemy and that it would be impossible to resist him.

'' Why did the Duce not understand ? '' asked the officer in conclusion. '' Our war was based on the mistaken conception that our entry into Greek territory would suffice to bring down the whole Greek military and political structure and to bring about a revolution. We ought to ask whether this was treason or exaggerated levity on the part of our diplomacy.''—*Press Association*.

The British Navy Is Waiting for Us !

In many a neutral harbour, in the ports of Spain and of all the Americas, skulks what is left of Hitler's Merchant Navy. On board are thousands of German seamen whose life, as the following extracts from a letter written by one of them to his wife at home show, is far from a happy one.

WHAT sort of life is that of the German seamen who are kicking their heels on the German merchantmen laid up in many a neutral port ? There are thousands of them, seamen who are kept going at useless work, sometimes persecuted by malicious officers, living in fear of having to put to sea and run the gauntlet of the British Navy. The boredom, anxiety and anger of these unhappy men is revealed in this letter, written to his wife by one of the crew of a ship lying in a tropical harbour.

"**Tuesday.** Another day is over. They are cleaning the hull of the Martha as though they are paid for it. Yet no one is the least interested in the job. For weeks there have been rumours that we are to weigh anchor. Probably some toff wants to distinguish himself at our expense. All the ships have fuel, water and provisions on board. This equipment must have cost a lot. But 10 marks a month is all we are allowed in foreign money. None of us, not even the simplest boy, wants to put to sea. We are all fed up. The whole day long we chip off rust, tomorrow we can drink it at the bottom of the sea, for if we sail we shall not get farther than 10 miles.

"**Wednesday.** You should see us work. Two at it and three looking on. Talk about good fellowship. Sooner or later we shall finish up in some British camp. I hope things turn out all right without any of the chaps being lost.

'' I should like to know who decides whether the ships shall sail or not. If they cannot even afford to keep a few ships in foreign ports, why send out unarmed ships ? They cannot do anything, for any fishing boat with a small gun can send us to the bottom. So if you hear of our ships having sailed, you know what it means. You know my ship, and can trace me through the Red Cross.

'' Soon after the New Year (1940) strict economy was ordered. All of us, from the skipper to the boy, had to take their meals on the Martha. The ships are berthed in a row, at distances of 200 metres. Quite a procession every day. Meals were taken in the first, second, and third class quarters, ordinary folk below deck, of course, the better-class comrade citizens above. Above all, no undue familiarity between the ranks. The

Italian prisoners captured in Albania have, like those above, shown symptoms of low morale. The Italian diary quoted in this page shows why. *Photo. Sport & General*

food was usually adequate, even good. But it did not last long, by the end of March the collective catering ceased.

"Certain people probably missed their pickings. Now that each ship again does its own catering they are no doubt faring better. The outfitting of six ships certainly also proved lucrative. A few days ago three ships weighed anchor. They were spotted before they had been gone for more than a few hours. Only the X, a brand-new ship, was, thanks to its speed, able to get as far as A by nightfall.

"**Thursday.** You will be wondering how I am. Fairly well as far as health is concerned. Though you cannot expect a cart-horse to become a racehorse. The officers are upset at the apathy. The other day I was called on the carpet. But if you put your foot down things are quiet again for a while. For the past few months we have had autumn weather. The mosquitoes had disappeared, so life was bearable. It was time the weather changed, for we were all covered with insect bites, and some suffered from malaria fever. Besides there were women, and the usual consequences. Patients are attended to on the Martha, which has a doctor. That's all for today. I hope you get my letter."

Such has been the life of thousands of German seamen for many months past. Day after day the same boredom, no pocket-money, and the constant fear that the captain will suddenly receive orders to run the gauntlet of the British Navy.-- *International Transport Workers Federation.*

What I Saw of London's A.F.S. in Action

At the Central Fire Station they seemed to think that an A.F.S. officer from the North was a little mad to want to be attached to the London Brigade for the night. But the matter was soon arranged, and here is the visitor's account of his experiences on a typical night of Nazi attempts at fire-raising.

As soon as I arrived at the A.F.S. station the sub-officer showed me round. Upstairs there was a recreation-room with a three-quarter size billiards table hired on a weekly basis by the men. There was also a small canteen run by the men themselves. The regulars had their own quarters, and for the auxiliaries there were a large messroom, kitchen and scullery, two bath-rooms, and a dormitory with thirty-six beds. Although there were only enough beds for the men actually on duty, each man is supplied with two blankets and a pillow. Every man not actually " standing to " was lying down resting. They have realized the importance in London of taking every available opportunity to rest ; otherwise they could not keep going night after night in the magnificent way they do . . .

Well, the sirens have gone and I am on the roof with the sub-officer. The anti-aircraft barrage is thundering all round. To the east a German bomber drops a flare and half London seems to be lit up. The whistle of a bomb is heard and we duck behind a chimney, but the crash is not near enough to worry us. Suddenly the white glare is broken by a deep red glow. " Looks as if they have got something with an oil bomb," says the sub-officer ; " it's in our district, too." The glow spreads as we make our way downstairs.

The telephone in the duty-room rings. " Stand by with three machines for —— in —— street." Another two minutes, then another ring—" Turn out ! "

The Steeple a Glowing Pyramid

It is as light as day as we approach the fire. The building is well alight, and the flames are using the hole made by the oil bomb as a chimney. A church next door has caught, and soon the steeple is a glowing pyramid. The building is doomed, and all jets are concentrated on saving surrounding property. There are several jets in the church and more in the business premises at the back. Auxiliaries with their backs to the fire, are making a curtain of water to protect the shops on the other side of the street. These premises have started to catch fire although the street is sixty feet wide. Two or three more pairs of auxiliaries are in the middle of the street using their jets to drive the flames back through the warehouse windows.

In what seems an incredibly short time the fire is under control. Two-thirds of the church has been saved and the fire stopped everywhere else. I have time to look where the water has come from and find that the only static supply has been a swimming-bath where suction hose is kept permanently installed ready to be attached to a stirrup pump. Jets are now being knocked off and machines sent back to their stations.

But this is only the beginning of the night. A senior officer takes me under his wing, and we drive back to Main Fire Control to see what is happening elsewhere. We are told of another " twenty-pump job " farther along in the same district and off we go again. It is going well, but the buildings are isolated and there is no risk of the fire spreading. There are aeroplanes overhead and the whistle of two or three bombs makes us get down flat for a moment. Rather too near to be comfortable this time ! Two of them seem to be time bombs, as there is only one explosion.

Encircled by a Ring of Fires

These aeroplanes have evidently dropped a load of oil bombs, and soon we seem to be encircled in a ring of fires. The senior officer sends a messenger back for fifty more pumps to be sent, to approach the rendezvous from different directions. He also sends for his control car, which will mark the rendezvous by its flashing red lamp and will contain necessary maps and locations of water supplies. Motor-cyclist messengers are summoned as well.

Motor-cyclists are sent round to find what the fires are, who is in charge, and what appliances are there already. When the convoys of pumps arrive they are distributed to the various fires as they are required. The organization seems to be faultless ; everybody knows his job. There is no excitement, no shouting, no hesitation, and in a short time every fire is surrounded and under control.

Two more churches are blazing, a school, some industrial buildings, and a small timber yard. The smoke from the two buildings is producing strange smells. I find myself on a flat roof with an L-shaped warehouse burning round me ; the roof beside me is catching alight. There is no jet up here, but I find, and use, some fire extinguishers.

But everything is well in hand now. The " All Clear " is sounding. Our driver covers the seats of the car with waterproof sheets and back we go to Main Control. Before I leave the sirens go again and control prepares once more for action. But all the fires are doused before the next raiders arrive and there are no flames to guide them. —" *Manchester Guardian.*"

HOSES IN ACTION at one of the fires caused by a heavy raid on London. How London's A.F.S. thwarts the designs of the Nazi fire-raisers is vividly described by an eye-witness in this page.
Photo, Fox

OUR DIARY OF THE WAR

SUNDAY, MARCH 23   *568th day*

ON THE SEA.—H.M. trawler Rubens reported overdue and considered lost.

IN THE AIR.—Coastal Command aircraft destroyed German barrack block at Quiberon and scored hit on escort vessel near Brest.

Heavy night raids on Berlin, Kiel and Hanover. Smaller-scale attacks on coastal targets in N.W. Germany and Holland, including naval base of Den Helder.

WAR AGAINST ITALY.—Cairo announced capture of Negelli. Enemy troop positions at Keren bombed continuously by R.A.F. Addis Ababa-Jibuti railway attacked by S.A.A.F. At night R.A.F. raided aerodrome at Tamet and shipping at Sirte (Tripolitania).

Thirteen Stukas destroyed over Malta.

HOME FRONT.—Bombs fell during day near Channel coast and at one point in N. Scotland. Three enemy aircraft destroyed. At night few bombs fell in eastern England.

GREEK WAR.—R.A.F. raided Berat. Six enemy aircraft destroyed, others damaged.

MONDAY, MARCH 24   *569th day*

IN THE AIR.—Bomber Command aircraft sank enemy vessel off Dutch coast. Coastal Command bombed Cherbourg docks.

WAR AGAINST ITALY.—Cairo reported that after beating off seven counter-attacks British troops at Karen were advancing.

Nairobi stated that our advanced troops successfully attacked strong enemy positions holding Marda Pass, west of Jijiga.

Enemy force occupied El Agheila, Libya, from which British had been withdrawn.

During night R.A.F. raided Tripoli.

HOME FRONT.—Bombs fell in S.E. Kent and S. Wales during day. Two enemy aircraft shot down.

GREEK WAR.—Italians launched unsuccessful local attack in region of Aoos River.

TUESDAY, MARCH 25   *570th day*

ON THE SEA.—Announced that Mediterranean Fleet had been operating during period March 21-24, covering convoy movements.

German merchant ship Oder, trying to escape from Massawa, reported captured by H.M. sloop Shoreham.

IN THE AIR.—Bomber Command aircraft attacked small enemy convoy off Dutch coast. A.A. ship damaged off Ameland and naval patrol vessel near Borkum bombed.

WAR AGAINST ITALY.—Imperial forces approaching Harar. Operations north-west of Negelli developing successfully.

Further positions covering Keren gained. R.A.F. carried out numerous raids supporting land operations in Eritrea and Abyssinia.

R.A.F. bombed aerodromes at Scarpanto and Calato and shipping at Astropalia island (Dodecanese).

HOME FRONT.—Enemy aircraft active round coast. Bombs fell on town on south coast and at place in West of England.

BALKANS.—Yugoslav Premier and Foreign Minister signed Axis Pact in Vienna.

WEDNESDAY, MARCH 26   *571st day*

ON THE SEA.—Admiralty stated that in operations by light forces in North Sea during last few nights German E-boats attacking our convoys were hit and driven off.

H.M. submarine Sturgeon reported to have sunk enemy tanker off Norway.

IN THE AIR.—Beaufort bomber torpedoed and sank enemy supply ship off Dutch coast.

WAR AGAINST ITALY.—Pressure on Keren increasing. Heavy and incessant air attacks.

R.A.F. and S.A.A.F. carried out severe raids on Addis Ababa-Jibuti railway.

HOME FRONT.—Single enemy aircraft active during day. Bombs fell in two places in West of England and at two in southern England. Two raiders destroyed.

THURSDAY, MARCH 27   *572nd day*

ON THE SEA.—Admiralty announced that H.M. yacht Mollusc and H.M. trawler Lady Lilian had been sunk.

H.M.S. Leith, escorting convoy in Bristol Channel, shot down one Heinkel and damaged another.

WAR AGAINST ITALY.—Keren captured, with 1,500 prisoners. Remainder of Italian troops retreating to Asmara.

Harar occupied by British.

HOME FRONT.—Some activity by enemy aircraft during daylight. Bombs fell on towns on S.E. and S. coasts.

BALKANS.—Yugoslav Army deposed and arrested Prince Paul and members of his Government. King Peter assumed power and Gen. Simovitch formed new Cabinet.

GENERAL.—Agreement for lease to U.S. of naval and air bases in Atlantic signed in London.

FRIDAY, MARCH 28   *573rd day*

ON THE SEA.—Big naval battle in Eastern Mediterranean. Italy lost three 10,000-ton cruisers and two destroyers, and battleship of Littorio class was damaged.

Submarine Parthian reported to have torpedoed two ships in convoy south of Italy.

IN THE AIR.—R.A.F. attacked enemy shipping, operations extending from Frisian Islands to La Rochelle in Brittany. Supply ship in Alderney harbour hit. Brest naval base attacked.

WAR AGAINST ITALY.—Italian troops being pursued towards Asmara. R.A.F. bombed motor transport and troops, and targets near Asmara.

HOME FRONT.—Small-scale enemy activity during daylight. Bombs fell on S.E. coastal town. Enemy bomber shot down by fighters near Beachy Head.

BALKANS.—Nazis demanded written statement of Yugoslav policy.

BALKANS.—Riots in Yugoslavia following signing of Pact with Axis.

FREE FRENCH 'A.T.S.'

THE Corps Féminin Français, an organization which bears the same relationship to the Free French Forces of General de Gaulle as the A.T.S. does to the British Army, was formed on November 7, 1940. Its commandant is Mme. Simone Mathieu, the world-famous tennis champion. As soon as news of its formation was made public numbers of Frenchwomen residing in England hastened to join, and it was not long before the first contingent was sent for training to an A.T.S. camp.

After a period of initial training, mostly devoted to drill and the inculcation of military discipline, members are selected for special duties according to their aptitude. Those already trained in office and secretarial work are sent where there is most need of their services. Those who wish to train as nurses can follow special courses ; others, with a mechanical bent, can serve as motor drivers and mechanics. There are instructional courses for those who wish to perfect their knowledge of the English language. Then there is always a need of cooks in the army, and what Frenchwoman does not know how to cook ?

All sorts and conditions of women have joined the Corps Féminin Français. One woman, now a corporal, once directed a

FRENCHWOMEN in the Corps Féminin Français wear a uniform only slightly different from that of the A.T.S. Here some of them are seen on parade being inspected by their commandant, Mme. Simone Mathieu, when nearing the completion of their training.
Photo, L.N.A.

famous fashion house, employing many hands, which was destroyed in the autumn " blitz." Another was among the last of the refugees to leave Saint Jean-de-Luz. Some of them have lived in England for many years ; others might never have seen

England but for the war. But one and all are doing their bit, as Free Frenchwomen, to uphold the honour of their country and to play their part in the fight for Freedom by the side of those Frenchmen who refused to accept the bondage of Vichy.

SHE BLEW THE DUCE'S WARSHIPS OUT OF 'MARE NOSTRUM'

H.M.S. WARSPITE, flagship of Admiral Sir Andrew Cunningham (Flag Captain D. B. Fisher), played a most important part in the great naval victory off Crete on the night of March 28.   A whole broadside from her 15-inch guns blasted the Italian cruiser Fiume, and further salvos from the Warspite, Valiant and Barham destroyed her, together with the Zara, flagship of Admiral Cantoni.   The Warspite, whose impressive armament is shown in this aerial view, is a 30,000-ton battleship of the Queen Elizabeth class.   She was completed in 1915, in time to take part in the Battle of Jutland in the next year, but she was extensively reconstructed between 1934 and 1937.   In April 1940 she distinguished herself as leader of the raid on Narvik.

Photo, Associated Press

How the Yugoslav Nation Found Its Soul

The first news of the Yugoslav revolution was given to the world by Mr. Churchill in a speech in London on the morning of March 28. " I have great news for you and the whole country," the Prime Minister told his audience of Conservative delegates ; " early this morning the Yugoslav nation found its soul." Below we give a description of the principal events of that day which may well mark a turning-point in the war.

Premier Tsvetkovitch, tired no doubt after his excursion to Vienna in which he had signed away his country's freedom, had gone to bed—to sleep or not to sleep, we do not know. The hours passed. Midnight struck, and with its striking ushered in Friday, March 28. Yugoslavia's day of revolution had begun.

Shortly after midnight some 40 officers of the Yugoslav Air Force surrounded Tsvetkovitch's villa in a Belgrade suburb. Their commander was Captain Rakotchevitch,

The broken black lines show the line of advance of the German troops through the Balkans, and the arrow heads indicate the points at which they were massed. The danger of the position if Yugoslavia were actively hostile is obvious.   *Courtesy of the " Daily Telegraph"*

GEN. DUSAN SIMOVITCH, Yugoslavia's new patriot Premier, was born in 1882 and entered the army in 1900. He is Chief of the Yugoslav Air Force Staff.   *Photo, " Daily Mirror"*

who entered the house, made his way to the Prime Minister's bedroom, and told him curtly to " Please follow me." Tsvetkovitch went pale. " What right have you to give me such an order ? " he demanded. " I shall certainly not obey." Rakotchevitch drew his revolver and said, " March, or I fire." Tsvetkovitch was taken away to the War Office under close arrest. There he arrogantly demanded of General Simovitch, " In whose name have you assumed power ? " " In the name of those whom you never represented," flashed back the General in reply.

At the War Office the men who had planned the coup, all Air Force officers under the leadership of General Dusan Simovitch, Chief of the Air Force Staff, had assembled at midnight. Soon they learnt that certain other Cabinet Ministers had been arrested, and that the Belgrade police headquarters, the Foreign Office, the Ministry of the Interior, the telephone exchange and the broadcasting station were also in the hands

of their men. " We have done the job allotted " was the message telephoned as each building was occupied and each minister was taken into custody. In every case the men concerned were Air Force officers, pilots being given the job of seizing the buildings, while officers of high rank were charged with the arrest of the ministers.

When these preliminaries had been completed, General Simovitch drove to the royal palace shortly after 2 o'clock and requested that the young king should be roused. The royal servants protested, but the General insisted. So after a few minutes King Peter, wearing a dressing-gown and with his eyes still heavy with sleep, entered one of the Palace drawing-rooms. "Your Majesty," said General Simovitch, " from now on you are King of Yugoslavia, exercising full sovereign rights." At 7 o'clock all the Yugoslav radio stations broadcast King Peter's first proclamation to his people.

BELGRADE was the scene of street fighting when hostility to the signing of the Axis Pact reached fever point. After the Regent, Prince Paul, had left and King Peter had assumed full sovereign powers the principal streets of the city, including Belgrade's main artery, the Kralmilanova, seen above, were thronged with cheering crowds.   *Photo, Keystone*

The Nazis Seem Quite at Home in Bulgaria

FIELD MARSHAL WILHELM LIST, who arrived in Bulgaria from Rumania at the end of February 1941 to take command of the German troops who were then pouring into the country, is seen on the extreme right of the top photograph in conversation with the German minister at Bucharest, Baron Manfred Von Killinger. On the left are members of his staff. Right, Nazi motor-cycle troops and lorries are passing along a snow-clad road in the uplands of Bulgaria, while below motorized units are seen in a village in Bulgaria driving over a road much the worse for wear.   *Photos, Presse Diffusion*

Theirs the Honour of Saying No to Hitler

**PATRIARCH GAVRILOV, head of the Ortho-
dox Church in Yugoslavia administered the
oath to the young King Peter II in Belgrade
Cathedral on March 28, 1941.**
Photo, British Official : Crown Copyright

Serbs, Croats and Slovenes [it read], at this
moment so grave in the history of our people
I have decided to take the royal power into
my own hands.

The members of the Regency Council appreciated the correctness of the reasons for my
action and immediately resigned of their own
accord.

My loyal Army and Navy have at once
placed themselves at my disposal and are
already carrying out my orders. I appeal to
all Serbs, Croats and Slovenes to rally round
the Throne. In the present grave circumstances this is the surest way of preserving
internal order and external peace.

I have charged Army Corps General Dusan
Simovitch with the formation of a new Government. With trust in God and the future of
Yugoslavia, I appeal to all citizens and all
authorities of the country to fulfil their duties
to King and country.   (Signed)
                                        PETER II

Belgrade was electrified by the news, and
at once the streets were filled with a surging
crowd who for hours paraded up and down,
waving flags and singing patriotic songs.
There was a tremendous demonstration
outside the British Legation, and at the
Greek Legation the Minister was carried
shoulder high. On the other hand, the
German Travel Bureau, headquarters of
Nazi propaganda, and the Italian Travel
Bureau were wrecked by the mob. Anyone
who looked like a Briton or American was
enthusiastically hailed ; pictures of Hitler
and Mussolini were trampled under foot,
while those of Mr. Churchill and President
Roosevelt were carried in jubilant procession.

At 11 o'clock there was a solemn service
of thanksgiving in Belgrade Cathedral, and

again the King was given a tremendous
ovation. Wearing the uniform of a Marshal
in the Yugoslav Air Force, he lit a candle
beside the great Bible. Then, standing before
Patriarch Gavrilov, who had made no secret
of his detestation of Tsvetkovitch's policy,
King Peter took the oath.

I, Peter II, ascending the Throne of the
Kingdom of Yugoslavia and taking over the
Royal power, swear by God Almighty that I
will guard above all the unity of the nation,
the independence of the State and the integrity
of its territory, that I will rule according to
its laws and constitution, and that in all my
endeavours I will ever keep before me the
welfare of the nation. So help me God.

Then, having formally congratulated the
King on his accession, the Patriarch rejoined,
" You take over royal powers at a difficult
moment. There are dark clouds all around
us, but the Yugoslav heaven is bright."

On his return to the Palace the King was
again given a tremendous reception. All
Belgrade's population marched past the Royal
Palace, cheering and waving the national

**YUGOSLAVIA has one town, Sarajevo, that conjures up poignant memories, for it was here that
the Archduke Francis Ferdinand of Austria was assassinated on June 28, 1914. Centre, Yugoslav
peasants in a street in Sarajevo are discussing the political situation. Yugoslavia is an agricultural
country, and in peacetime soldiers, as seen above, help with the harvest.**   *Photos, G. P. U.*

flags. Young people joined hands and
danced in the streets. Peasants drove in
from the country and overhead roared the
warplanes of the Yugoslav Air Force.

While the crowds were rejoicing General
Simovitch was presiding over the first
meeting of his Cabinet. He himself assumed
the office of Prime Minister, while Dr.
Matchek, leader of the Croats, was reap-
pointed to the position of Vice-Premier which
he had held in the Tsvetkovitch Cabinet.
The vital post of Foreign Minister was
given to Mr. Nintchitch, a former Foreign
Minister, who was reputed to be of pro-
British sympathies. All the other ministers
were members of the opposition parties or
had opposed the Tsvetkovitch policy of
subservience to the Axis. Following the
Cabinet meeting a proclamation of Government policy was issued, of which the keynote
was struck in the words, " Let us look after
our own interests—let us be independent and
respected." The General made it clear
that Yugoslavia wanted to maintain a strict
neutrality ; in other words, she wanted to
go back to the position she had occupied
before the signing of the Vienna Pact.

But would she be permitted to do so ?

They Hobnobbed with Hitler—So They Fell

On Feb. 14, 1941, the then Prime Minister of Yugoslavia, Dr. Dragisha Tsvetkovitch and his Foreign Minister, Dr. Cincar-Markovitch, arrived at Berchtesgaden in reply to a summons from Hitler. There they presumably discussed the details of Yugoslavia's adherence to the Axis Pact, so shortly to be signed but destined never to be ratified. Hitler is here seen ushering Dr. Tsvetkovitch into his mountain retreat. Just behind him is Dr. Cincar-Markovitch, while on the right is von Ribbentrop with the interpreter, Herr Schmidt. After the Yugoslav revolution of March 27 the two Yugoslav signatories to the Axis Pact were arrested.

Photo, Sport & General

Peter II King of Sixteen Million Yugoslavs

THE BOY KING TAKES OVER

KING PETER II of Yugoslavia, who assumed the Royal power on March 27, 1941, following the revolution led by General Simovitch, would normally have done so on his eighteenth birthday, on September 6, 1941. Eldest of the three sons of Alexander I, assassinated at Marseilles on October 9, 1934, and Queen Marie, sister of ex-King Carol of Rumania, he succeeded to the throne on the death of his father, but during his minority the Royal power was vested in a Council of Regency headed by his uncle, Prince Paul. This Council resigned on March 27, following the revolution, and Prince Paul left the country.

The young king, who has received the full support of the Yugoslav army and people, speaks English almost as fluently as his mother tongue. He was at school in Surrey when he was recalled to be the king of 16,000,000 people. For six years he has been sedulously preparing himself for the day when he should take over the reins of government, and endowed as he is with the fighting blood of the Karageorgevitch house it is hardly likely that he will allow himself or his country to be coerced.

Born at Belgrade on Sept. 6, 1923, King Peter of Yugoslavia is not yet eighteen. Above he is seen in naval attire at the age of about two and a half.

Always intensely interested in everything appertaining to his country, he is here seen studying a map of his future kingdom at his private school in Yugoslavia. *Photo, Keystone*

For a while King Peter, then eleven, was educated at Sandroyd School, Cobham, Surrey, where this photograph was taken. He returned to his country in 1934. *Photos, Fox*

The young king shakes hands with officers of the Royal Cavalry Guard at a national festival; behind him is Prince Paul. Left, a recent portrait of the King. *Photo, Wide World*

Britain's Night Fighters Have 'Cat's Eyes'

One of the night fighters that the Nazis fear so much is taking off from an aerodrome by the light of flares. On the tips of the wings are the navigation lights used only when the 'plane is taking off or landing, or for recognition purposes.

These two Sergeant-Pilots of the R.A.F. have just returned from a night flight over Britain in search of enemy raiders. They are taking a well-earned meal before turning in for a few hours' rest.

DURING the night raids over Britain in the first half of March, 1941, twenty-two Nazi night raiders were brought down—some of them, it was officially announced, by secret devices. What those devices are has not been disclosed, but it is known that night fighter pilots now undergo special training to enable them to see in the dark. They sit in a dimly-lit room wearing green goggles before going up on patrol, and by this means they acquire an extraordinary aptitude for noticing the faintest changes in illumination. Quickness of sight and clearness of vision are of great importance, for both the pilot and his quarry are moving fast. One pilot relates that on a night of shifting cloud recently he saw what he thought was the flicker of an enemy exhaust. He gave chase, the light flickering and vanishing in front of him. Just as he fancied he was coming within range a wider gap in the clouds revealed the light to be nothing more than that of a rising star!

The scene above is in a rest-room at an aerodrome somewhere in Britain. Night fighter pilots are sitting round the stove wearing the green glasses that cause the eyes to adjust themselves to darkness. Right centre is one of the pilots photographed in the cockpit of his 'plane after his return to the aerodrome, when for a time he can let his eyes go back to normal.

Photos, British Official: Crown Copyright

They Fight in the Air above the Atlantic

Not only on the Atlantic but above it deadly war is being waged as Hitler's 'planes contend
with those of Britain's Coastal Command for the mastery. Some of the principal types
of machines used on both sides are the subject of this article by Grenville Manton.

ONE of our Sunderland flying-boats of
the Coastal Command—one of those
four-engined giants which have
patrolled the skies far from land, day in day
out, since the first hour of this war—has
lately encountered and completely worsted
two long-range bombers of the Luftwaffe
above the Atlantic.

The Nazis, working in cooperation with
the U-boats, were prowling round seeking

sea to meet its end. Meanwhile its fellow
with engines running at full throttle sought
to escape and find a hiding-place in clouds.
But he was not to get away without a wound;
it was with smoke streaming from an engine
nacelle that he started the desperate run for
home.

Such was an episode which will be
repeated again and again as the Battle of the
Atlantic surges and bubbles to its peak. As

war on land, a patch of oil, a rubber dinghy,
a strip of tattered fabric, a petrol tank floating in the waves—these will be the only signs
that the red, white and blue cockade has met
the white-edged swastika.

The Nazis, their plans set all awry by the
thrashing their air force received in the Battle
of Britain, by the unending failure of their
Fascist ally, and by the united and unquenchable spirit of the British Empire, have been
working with frantic haste in preparation for
the Atlantic struggle. U-boats are being
mass-produced, crews are being trained in the
Baltic, and the Luftwaffe, bruised and smarting still from the hammering given it by the
R.A.F. last summer, is being re-equipped
with long-range aircraft.

Goering's New Models

We know something of these new machines
—the four-engined *Focke-Wulf Kurier* and
others. We know where they are being built,
we know their constructional features and
their performance. Like several other
German bombers, the Kurier is a military
version of a commercial machine. It is a
strengthened and modified edition of the
Kondor air-liner. It has four B.M.W. 14-
cylinder radial engines of 1,300 h.p. and its
wing span is 108 ft. 3 ins. It is of all-metal
construction and carries a crew of six. Its
armament is formidable; it has a gun turret
which is electrically operated and houses
four machine-guns, and guns are mounted
in the nose and under the fuselage facing to
the rear. At 18,000 feet its maximum speed
is 280 m.p.h. and it can carry a bomb load of
6,000 lb. The range is 2.300 miles. Of the
Junkers 88 and the *Heinkel He*.111K we know
everything, for many specimens have fallen
into our hands, shot down in raids over this
country. Each has been modified for work
in the Battle of the Atlantic.

COASTAL COMMAND FLYING-BOATS, operating in all weathers and all the year round, range
the vast expanses beyond Britain's shores to frustrate the U-boat and preserve the country's life-
lines. Here is a Saro London II general reconnaissance flying-boat. The machine has a range of
1,700 miles and carries a crew of six.   *Photo, British Official : Crown Copyright*

out our merchantmen as they ploughed their
way in convoy *en route* for England. Sharp
eyes, peering through the windows of the
commander's cabin, spotted the marauders;
control wheel and rudder-bar were swung
over to put the 22-ton aircraft in a turn, and
as the first German came into range the
Brownings in the turrets snapped. At once
the *Junkers Ju*.88 dropped a wing, lifted its
nose, stalled and plunged down towards the

the days lengthen the struggle between ship
and U-boat and bomber will be mingled with
protracted combats in the sky. High above
the immense Atlantic, where but a decade
ago only the most adventurous dared to fly,
the R.A.F. will meet the enemy. The clash
will be unprecedented in the whole history
of air warfare. In place of shattered buildings,
piles of rubble, bomb craters and smouldering
heaps of twisted metal that mark the trail of

The use of these machines for long-distance
flights over the sea, by the way, means that
Hitler has had to improvise in his air plans
for the Atlantic blockade, for the Junkers and
Heinkel were never intended for such work.

THIS FOCKE-WULF KURIER lost its way in a fog and crashed at Moura, in Southern Portugal, on the Spanish frontier. The crew attempted to get
into Spain, but when they were arrested they were found to be in civilian clothes, though there can be little doubt that the giant bomber was
making a short cut after being used to attack British convoys in the Atlantic. As is stated in this page, the Focke-Wulf Kurier is a long-range bomber
aircraft, a military version of a commercial machine, which is being largely employed by the Germans in their desperate attempt to close the
Atlantic to our shipping.   *Photo, Central Press*

New Machines for a New Kind of War

OUR MERCHANTMEN PRESS ON in convoy to bring precious cargoes into port, while the R.A.F. keeps watch and ward with far-seeing eyes above them. Hour after hour the great flying-boats cruise to and fro on patrol ready to pounce should a U-boat surface to make an attack. This impressive photograph was taken from a Short Sunderland as it flew above a convoy in the Atlantic. *Photo, British Official : Crown Copyright*

In contrast, our Coastal Command is equipped with aircraft specially designed for this air war over the sea. The *Short Sunderland* has already proved itself to be one of the finest flying-boats ever built. It has a great range—2,880 miles—a high cruising speed, and, with gun turrets in the nose and tail and gun positions amidships, it can fight anything it meets in the air. Moreover, unlike the Nazis flying in the Junkers and the Heinkels, the crew can live, eat and sleep aboard in comfort, and if necessary the flying-boat can fly non-stop for more than 16 hours. The *Saro Lerwick* is another flying-boat now in service with Coastal Command squadrons.

It is employed on similar duties to those of the Sunderland, but because it is one of our latest types, performance figures cannot be disclosed. It is powered with two Bristol Hercules 11 motors, which give a combined horse-power of 2,750. The construction is all-metal throughout and with three power-operated gun-turrets it is powerfully armed.

These two British stalwarts are the mainstay of the squadrons engaged on long-range duties from England's shores, but already new American craft are coming into service. Amongst them is the *Consolidated Model 31* patrol flying-boat, a high-wing twin-engined machine which can fly at 285 m.p.h.

and cover great distances. The *Consolidated Catalina* is another U.S.-built flying-boat which is being supplied to Britain. It carries a crew of six and can fly no less than 4,000 miles non-stop. These are the vanguards of a great fleet which will come from the U.S.A.

With the Sunderlands, the Lerwicks and other great flying-boats and long-range fighters they will fly out to meet the enemy in the limitless arena hundreds of miles from land. No crowds will watch with bated breath as they wheel and turn in battle, but we shall hear their story when the Battle of the Atlantic is won, and the remnants of the Luftwaffe lie at the bottom of the sea.

Matapan Was a Great and Glorious Victory

In what was described as the most overwhelming and most momentous naval victory achieved since Trafalgar, Admiral Cunningham and his Mediterranean Fleet met Italy's much-vaunted Navy off Cape Matapan, Greece's most southerly point, on Friday, March 28, and literally blew it to pieces. Below is the full story of the action which put *finis* to Italy's naval power.

O^N the very day that the Yugoslavs rose in wrath against their betrayers the Italian battle fleet left the safety of its harbours and sailed eastwards across the Ionian Sea in the direction of Crete. Maybe they were hoping to intercept a British convoy between Egypt and Greece, or perhaps they had been ordered to attack Greece from the sea, their attack being timed to coincide with a German onslaught by land. Whatever their objective, they were sailing to their doom.

Hardly had they passed Cape Passero in Sicily when they were spotted by British reconnaissance 'planes. The news was signalled to Admiral Cunningham in Alexandria, and at once the Commander-in-Chief put to sea with his battle fleet.

At 7.49 a.m. the next day the Italians were spotted by our reconnaissance 'planes—a battleship, six cruisers and seven destroyers —and soon they were joined by two more cruisers and at least two destroyers. At 8.2 a.m. contact with enemy cruisers was made by the British cruiser Orion, flying the flag of Vice-Admiral H. D. Pridham-Wippell, off the coast of Crete. Pridham-Wippell, who had with him the cruisers Ajax, Perth and Gloucester, and some destroyers, at once decided to do as Beatty did at the Battle of Jutland. Deliberately he trailed his coat before the Italians with a view to luring them on until they came within range of Admiral Cunningham's main battle fleet, then about 120 miles to the east.

About 9 a.m. the enemy cruisers turned north-westward and the British followed suit, in order to keep in touch. Then at 10.58 a.m. the Vice-Admiral sighted the Vittorio Veneto, 16 miles to the northward, and he again turned south-east so as to lure the Italian battleship to where Cunningham, flogging his engines to the utmost,

THE ADMIRAL'S 'WELL DONE!'

T^{HE} operations just concluded have given us a notable success over the enemy.

The skilful handling of our cruisers and the untiring efforts of the Fleet Air Arm kept me well informed of enemy movements, and the well-pressed-home attacks of torpedo-bomber aircraft on the Littorio so reduced the speed of the enemy fleet that we were able to gain contact during the night and inflict heavy damage.

The devastating results of our battleships' gunfire are an ample reward for months of patient training.

This work was completed by the destroyers in the admirable way we have come to expect of them.

The contribution of the engine-room departments to this success cannot be over-emphasized. Their work, not only in keeping their ships steaming at high speed for long periods, but in the work of maintenance under very difficult conditions, has been most praiseworthy.

I am very grateful to all in the Fleet for their support on this and all other occasions.

Well done !

was speeding westwards to meet them. Riccardi fell into the trap, and for hours kept up the chase, firing from a range of

some 16 miles. "The firing of the Italian battleship," said Pridham-Wippell later, "was exceptionally good, but that of the Italian cruisers was only mediocre. A number of 15-inch shells fell close to us, but we, like all the other British ships engaged in the action, escaped without chipping our paint."

Meanwhile, the Fleet Air Arm carried out a fierce bombing raid on Lecce, the enemy's air base in southern Italy, grounding dive bombers and reconnaissance 'planes which might otherwise have come into action against our fleet ; and a squadron of Greek destroyers put to sea and raced south at full speed in the hope of playing their part in the battle. Then, at about noon, the Vittorio Veneto began to be attacked by bomb and torpedo-carrying dive-bombers of the Fleet Air Arm launched from H.M.S. Formidable. Some of the bombs found their target in the great ship, and several torpedoes struck home. The enemy cruiser Pola was also torpedoed, a direct hit being made on the engine-room, which dislocated all the electric controls, rendering the gun turrets useless. By now it was afternoon, and the Italian admiral had turned for home.

Just as the ships were turning a number of R.A.F. bombers joined the naval 'planes, and several hits were obtained, not only on Italian cruisers and destroyers but on the Vittorio Veneto, which was so severely damaged that her speed was reduced from well over 30 knots to less than 15. The Italian ships put up a terrific barrage, but the British 'planes bore down to within 200 yards of their target before letting go their "fish" only ten feet above the water. From that moment the Vittorio Veneto and her accompanying ships were given no rest, as wave after wave of bombers entered the battle. When last seen by the British 'planes she was listing heavily and badly down by the stern.

While the Vittorio Veneto made her way westward three Italian heavy cruisers, the Fiume, Zara and another, went back to give what aid they could to the cruiser Pola, which had been bombed to a complete standstill. It was now dark and the night was moonless, so that there was no horizon. Thus the Italian ships had no warning of the imminent approach of Cunningham's battleships. Pridham-Wippell reported to Cunningham the exact position of the Pola, and at 9 p.m. the admiral, who was aboard the veteran battleship Warspite, with the battleships Barham, Valiant, the aircraft-carrier Formidable and a destroyer screen steaming in echelon, made for where the stricken ship lay. They reached her at almost the same moment as the Italian cruisers. At 10.26 a number of darkened ships, steaming at right angles to them, were reported on the starboard bow. Three cruisers and two or three destroyers could be distinguished steaming in line ahead. Then the British ships were challenged by the Pola from the port beam. Admiral Cunningham at once turned his fleet to starboard, so bringing his ships parallel to, but steaming

CUNNINGHAM'S GREAT VICTORY over the Italian battle fleet was fought out in the night of March 28 to the south of Cape Matapan. The map above illustrates the course of the action. Admiral Sir Andrew Cunningham, Commander-in-Chief of British naval forces in the Mediterranean, whose signal after the battle is reproduced, centre, is seen in the photograph at the top of the page. *Photo, Planet News ; Map, courtesy of the " Daily Telegraph "*

How Cunningham Smashed the Italian Fleet

H.M.S. HAVOCK, 1,340-ton destroyer of the Hero class, was the only one of the five destroyers which the late Captain Warburton-Lee led into Narvik on April 10, 1940, to escape undamaged. Lieut. G. R. G. Watkins, inset, was in command of the Havock at the battle off Cape Matapan when she hung on to the Italian cruiser Pola after all her torpedoes had been fired.
Photos, Universal and Topical

and as no British ships were reported in that quarter it seemed clear that in the darkness and confusion the Italians were firing at each other. For hours the firing went on.

On the morning of Saturday, March 29, nearly 1,000 Italian survivors were picked up by British ships, but many hundreds more, clinging to rafts in the sea, had to be left to their fate as German dive-bombers attacked the rescuing ships. In addition to the 1,000 prisoners, at least 3,000 officers and seamen of Mussolini's navy perished when five—three cruisers and two destroyers—probably seven, of his ships were sent to the bottom. Yet on our side there was not a casualty beyond one 'plane lost, and not a ship suffered the slightest damage.

in the opposite direction to, the Italians. Still the enemy apparently had not spotted our ships' approach.

Then suddenly one of the British destroyers, Greyhound, switched its searchlights on the third of the Italian ships, the heavy cruiser Fiume, and at once, without wasting a second, the Warspite's 15-inch guns, firing from a range of only two miles, flung a salvo into the Fiume with devastating effect. The Italian had not time even to swing her gun turrets into position. The after-turret was blown clean over the side, and the whole ship burst into flames. A second broadside converted her into a blazing furnace. Then the British guns were turned on to the Zara, Admiral Cantoni's flagship, with the same result. A third heavy cruiser, probably the Giovanni delle Bande Nere, was very badly damaged and probably, sunk as well. Then two enemy destroyers, caught in our searchlights, fired torpedoes at the British warships, but the battleships turned in time and opened fire on the destroyers. These laid down a smoke screen, but the shells pounded through the murk and two destroyers, the Vincento Gioberti and Maestrale, were sunk, and possibly a third.

Now Admiral Cunningham ordered the British destroyers to come in and finish off the burning cruisers. Already the Havock (Lieutenant G. Watkins) had signalled to the flagship, "Am hanging on to the stern of cruiser Pola. Shall I board her or blow her stern up with depth charges? Have no torpedoes left." That was at 10.30, and Watkins was told to abandon his prize, which was soon after-

wards torpedoed by the Jervis. The Pola had not struck her flag, but a large white sheet was displayed over the quarterdeck rail, and the crew were drawn up on the quarter-deck in readiness to surrender. A gangplank was thrown between the quarter-decks of the Pola and the Jervis, and across this the Italians clambered aboard the victor. While this was going on other British destroyers were circling around, picking up survivors from the Italian destroyers which had been sunk. The Zara was then also torpedoed and sunk.

Then firing was heard in the distance,

H.M.S. ORION, the "decoy" ship of Admiral Cunningham's fleet, is a cruiser of 7,215 tons, completed in January 1934. She carries eight 6-in. guns and has a speed of 32·5 knots. Inset is Vice-Admiral D. H. Pridham-Wippell, Commanding Light Forces, who flew his flag in the Orion (Flag Captain G. R. B. Back). *Photos, Topical and C. E. Brown*

The three Italian cruisers sunk in the action off Cape Matapan are here seen in harbour. They are, left to right, the Pola, Zara and Fiume, 10,000-ton cruisers completed in 1931-32, armed with eight 8-inch guns and carrying a normal complement of 705. They had a speed of 32 knots.
Photo, L.N.A.

They Spoke~and Speaking, Made of the Duce's

SALVOS FROM THE BIG GUNS of three of the battleships of the Royal Navy struck a staggering blow at cruisers of the Italian fleet on March 28, 1941. Here are some of those guns. H.M.S. Valiant is firing a broadside while steaming in line ahead with the other two capital ships which took part in the action off Cape Matapan, the Barham and Sir Andrew Cunningham's flagship the Warspite. Captain C. E. Morgan of the Valiant has told how his 15-inch guns opened fire within seven seconds of the first broadsides from the Warspite striking the Fiume, making her burst out amidships.

Ships Flaming Hulks, Plunging to Their Doom

Warspite, Valiant and Barham belong to the Queen Elizabeth class and were completed in 1915-16. The reconstruction of this class between 1925 and 1933 involved an expenditure of about a million pounds per ship, and in 1934 the Warspite underwent further extensive alterations at a cost of £2,362,000. Later the Valiant underwent similar renovations to the Warspite. The main armament of these ships is eight 15-inch guns. Each gun weighs nearly 100 tons and fires a 1,920 lb. projectile with a muzzle velocity of about 1,700 m.p.h. It can hit a hostile ship 15 miles away.

See the British Army Take to the Water!

The two men above are crossing a river in a rubber reconnaissance boat which is none too easy to handle. Accidents may happen, so the Sergeant-Major, left, cruises round in a motor boat to pick up anyone who may happen to fall in !

AN army in retreat, unless it is so utterly routed that it is in hopeless confusion, blows up the bridges over every river and stream that it has crossed. The pursuing army must use its own devices to cross them and continue its advance, so at training centres in England and Northern Ireland soldiers are taught to become amphibious. The training includes swimming with full equipment, which includes Tommy guns, specially protected to withstand a wetting. The troops are given intensive training in the handling of assault boats that carry a number of troops and reconnaissance boats that carry only two. The latter are a small edition of the Navy's Carley boats and are entirely of rubber. They are black and are so low in the water that they are practically invisible at night. Large numbers of the rubber boats, when deflated, and the collapsible boats, when folded up, can be carried on a single lorry.

Collapsible boats of wood and canvas, known as assault boats, much larger than the rubber boats, are used when a number of troops are to be carried across water. Above, a number of them are being launched, while right, one that has received its load is being pushed off. All the men wear life-jackets.

Photos, British Official : Crown Copyright ; and Fox

They Are Helping Their Men to Win in the Air

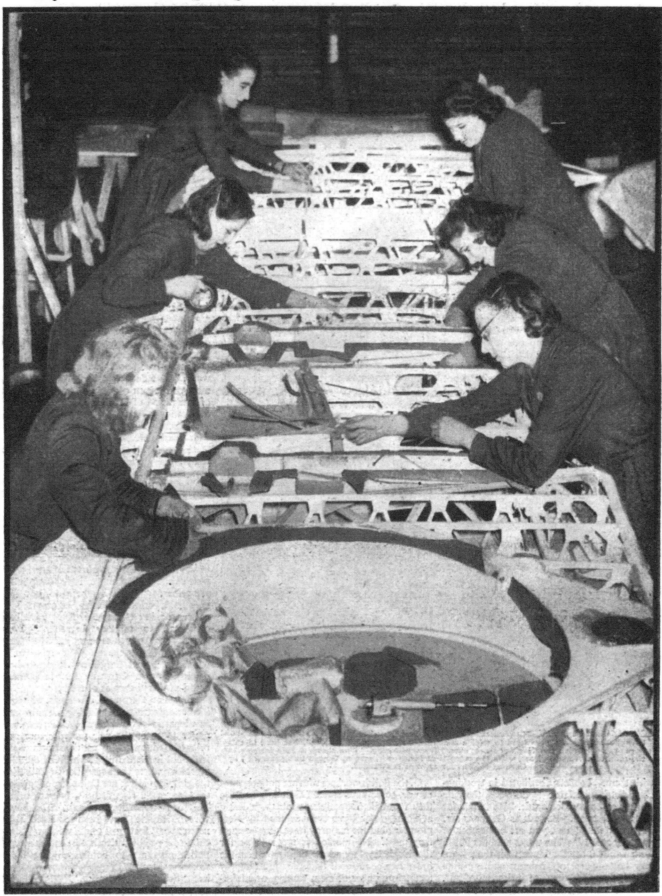

While men of the R.A.F. and the F.A.A. fight for freedom in the air with a courage and skill unrivalled in history, their womenfolk lend invaluable aid in a multitude of ways in our aircraft factories. Deft, swiftly-moving hands operate machines to make and assemble parts that go into 'planes—the 'planes which are giving us superiority in the air against the Luftwaffe and the Regia Aeronautica. The girls in this picture are fixing fabric to the ribs of an aircraft's wing in a works " somewhere in England."

Photo, Fox

Good Nazis Mustn't Be Kind to Polish Slaves!

In Poland the Nazis have unloosed a reign of barbarity which is without precedent in the written history of the white races. The most horribly spectacular of their brutalities is the judicial murder of patriotic Poles (see, e.g., the photographs opposite), but it may well be that their greatest contribution to human misery is their treatment of their Polish slaves. This article is based on information obtained by the International Transport Workers Federation from informants on the Continent.

OF the two and a half or three million foreign slaves employed in Germany—men and women who at Hitler's orders have been dragged from their homes and families to work in a foreign land for the profit of the conqueror—it is estimated that at least a million are Poles. Of these about 650,000 are prisoners of war who have been "released," that is, let out of the prison camps on condition that they stayed in or went to Germany as "voluntary" workers. This release from captivity has been quoted by the German Ministry of Information as a proof of Hitler's magnanimity, but actually the motive was to save the German Army the trouble and expense of keeping watch over a large number of prisoners scattered all over the country.

In Germany the Polish workers are regarded as no better than convicts. They are required to wear the "Polish mark"—a large P in a violet-edged, two-inch yellow square—on the right-hand side of the breast of jacket, pullover or shirt. The German men and women farm workers are forbidden to treat the Poles as equals; they must not eat with them at the same table, or fraternize with them in any way, or even go to church

sufficient numbers then the Gestapo and the Nazi soldiery round up their victims themselves. The word "branka" goes from mouth to mouth, and there is a veritable panic among the population eligible for seizure. The whole district is searched for fugitives, until at last a sufficient number of unhappy workers have been rounded up in the market-place, ready to be driven off like cattle from the homes which they are unlikely ever to see again.

One of the many hundreds of thousands of Poles who have been compulsorily transferred from Poland to work in Germany described his life in a letter sent home last summer. " I am employed on the building of a factory," he wrote. " My wage when all the deductions have been made amounts to 44 marks a month, out of which I must pay one mark a day for food ; what remains is for tobacco. As to the barrack routine, at 4.30 in the morning the daily ration of bread, sausage and margarine is issued, and work begins at 6. It is nearly one-and-a-half hours' walk to the place of work, and I don't get back for the evening meal until seven o'clock. The meal consists of some kind of broth, often unpeeled potatoes, and cabbage. Then we turn in for the night in dirty, vermin-infested quarters, with three blankets per head. The men are tired out, but it is almost impossible to sleep. Nearly every night you awake with a start just as you have fallen asleep owing to the noise of aircraft overhead, and you think you are back in Warsaw during the siege, and must go through it all again."

Tens of thousands of Polish girls and young women are amongst those who have been carried off to compulsory labour in Germany. Many work on the big estates in East Germany, many in the households of Nazi dignitaries, and many more have disappeared altogether. " What happens to our girls here is a crime," Polish labourers have written home ; " many of them have been consigned to military barracks." From time to time women are sent back to Poland ill and often pregnant. The relatives of women and girls transferred to compulsory employment in Germany live in constant dread of what becomes of them.

In Eastern Germany Polish girls, who to an increasing extent are obtaining employment as domestic servants since the German girls prefer to enter the war factories, are as a rule treated as badly as the Nazis would wish, but in German towns west of the Elbe, especially where the population is Catholic—the girls themselves are Catholics, of course—they are still regarded as human beings. This does not suit the Nazis. The housewives in Munich have been reminded in the newspapers that a Polish woman " is a child of a people which is destined to serve." Polish girls are to be treated like Polish workers, who "so to speak, always work and live ' behind barbed wire.' " Polish girls are not " to eat at the same table and share the joys and sorrows of the family." Even children must be taught by their parents to see in Polish servants something alien.

Few photographs are permitted to trickle out from German-occupied Poland, but here in this page are two which the Nazis are not averse from releasing. One shows a Pole begging in the snow of a Warsaw street, while the other is of Polish workmen at Gdynia being searched by German soldiers for arms or contraband.

with them. Leaflets distributed in working-class districts declare : " Germans, the Pole can never be your comrade. He is inferior to every German. Be just, as Germans are, but never forget that you are a member of a master race ! " The wages paid the Polish farm workers are far lower than those—not very large—paid to Germans, and are little higher than the pay of prisoners-of-war. There is the same discrimination in the matter of allowances in kind ; the non-Germans get neither wheat nor milk and a much reduced allowance of cereals and coal.

Of the Polish workers who are not prisoners of war, some have entered Germany because they found it impossible to obtain a living at home, some have been deluded by Nazi promises, but the majority have gone because they must. No method is too ruthless for the Nazis in Poland to employ when the order has gone forth that they must supply a certain number of men, women, or adolescents for the German labour market. The town and village councils are simply told their quota, and it is up to them to obtain it. If the workers are not forthcoming in

Poles They May Kill but Poland—Never!

Typical of German methods in the occupied countries is the scene right. A number of male Polish civilians have been rounded up by the military police and are being marched off—perhaps to internment, perhaps to be put to forced labour, while possibly an even worse fate awaits them. They have apparently been forced to wave their caps as a mark of respect to their captors ; or maybe they are waving farewell to the friends they are leaving probably for ever.

The photograph above is not unusual, for left is another similar scene, this time in a town in Silesia. Again the brutal methods of the Nazis are noticeable, for the prisoners are compelled to march with their hands clasped behind their heads in order that any movement, save marching on to an unknown fate, should be impossible. What would happen if they made the least show of resistance is indicated by the way the guards carry their rifles with bayonets fixed.

Below is the last tragic scene in this tale of horror. Polish civilians who have incurred the Nazis' wrath have been lined up like those right and shot with their hands' tied behind their backs. A touch of brutality is added to this act by the fact that other Polish prisoners are being forced to dig a common grave for their martyred compatriots under the eyes of an armed Nazi guard (below).

Three men who are offenders in the sight of their Nazi masters have been lined up at a lonely spot to face a firing-party of German military police armed with Czech Mauser rifles.   *Photos, Keystone*

"WE are living in hell." This is the incessant refrain of the letters which have been smuggled out of Nazi-occupied Poland. The photographs in this page, which have recently reached Britain, go to prove that such words are no exaggeration. It is stated on good authority that during the first four months of the German occupation an average of 12 to 14 Poles were executed every day in Warsaw alone, while the executions in the rest of Poland during the same period have been estimated at 25,000. Moreover, many hundreds of thousands of Poles who have not been shot or imprisoned have been enslaved. As the Polish Minister of Justice said, "Poland's sacrifice is in the nature of a holocaust."

Singapore Is Now Strong Beyond Compare

The Singapore Volunteer Corps, part of the Straits Settlements Volunteer Force, before the war included infantry, artillery and signal and engineer sections. Now an armoured-car section (seen above) has been added to it.

BRITISH SUBMARINES are based at Singapore, and above are a few of them alongside H.M.S. Medway, a depot and repair ship of 14,650 tons which can mother 18 submarines.

ON March 30, 1941, it was announced from Singapore that further large reinforcements from Britain and India had arrived there. Air Marshal Sir Robert Brooke-Popham, speaking of the arrivals, said : " Our greatly increased strength in the Far East is a threat to none, but, on the contrary, a great stabilizing force and influence for peace. Already India and Australia have sent strong forces to this area, and they are continuing to play a most important part in maintaining the status quo in the Far East. It is a cause of considerable satisfaction to be able to record that the situation in other theatres of war is so favourable that forces from so far distant as the United Kingdom can not only be spared for this area, but can be transported safely in spite of the enemy's concentrated sea and air campaign." The majority of these reinforcements consists of famous Indian regiments, but also includes units from the British army ; artillery, infantry and mechanized units, as well as R.A.F.

MALAYA has also a regular native regiment, the Malay Regiment, for which there has been no lack of recruits since the outbreak of war. Here a detachment of the regiment, marching through the streets of Singapore on its way to Mosque parade, is saluting—" eyes left."

R.A.F. REINFORCEMENTS arrived in Singapore during March, together with artillery and infantry. Among the personnel coming from Britain were crack pilots, some of whom had brought down many enemy 'planes. The R.A.F. material included Blenheim bombers, some of which have long been operating in Eastern waters, for Singapore has for some considerable time been an Air base as well as a Naval and Military base.

Photos, Press Topics, Associated Press

The Battle for Keren Is Fought and Won

For six weeks the fate of Keren, stronghold of the Italian power in Eritrea, hung in the balance, as the garrison strove against the stranglehold exercised by General Platt and his Free French allies. Then on March 27 the British and Indians carried the last mountain ramparts by storm and entered the town in triumph. So ended what will always be regarded by the men of both sides as a great feat of arms.

IN peacetime Keren, or Cheren as it is sometimes spelt, is a pleasant place enough, one of the pleasantest towns in East Africa. Of its 10,000 inhabitants all are natives save about 700 Italians, who for a few hours a day work in the government offices or in the Italian banks, and then go home to spend the evenings on their verandas, looking out on their tropic gardens. It is an important trade centre, and from its market-place large quantities of tobacco, coffee, sisal, and bananas have passed by road or rail to Massawa, the Red Sea port 85 miles away, and thence to Italy. But Keren's days of pleasantness and peaceful prosperity came to an end when Italy entered the war; and early in February it found itself in the very front line—the principal objective of General Platt's victorious army, pressing on to the east from its capture of Agordat.

Defended by a garrison reported to number at least 40,000 men, including Savoy Grenadiers —the Guards of Italy—with nearly 200 guns, it put up a determined resistance. Indeed, it was at Keren that there was witnessed the hardest fighting of any on all the African fronts. It was recognized as a key point of the defence of Eritrea, and months of preparation had made it a veritable stronghold. Nature, indeed, had intended it for that from the very beginning, for, set at the top of a plateau rising 6,000 feet above the plain, surrounded by precipices and jagged peaks, and approached by way of a steep gorge, it was in itself a natural fortress.

Early in February the British force glimpsed only four miles away the white houses and mosques gleaming in the sun, but high up, and divided from them by great slopes of rock; on February 6 the siege was begun. Up these formidable and grimly forbidding slopes General Platt now prepared to battle his way. By day and night streams of armoured cars, tanks, Bren-gun carriers, and long convoys of motor lorries moved to the foot of the plateau, while in front of them the way was blasted by the British and Indian sappers, and line after line, outpost after outpost, was carried by storm, or laboriously nibbled by the infantry.

For about a month these preliminary operations continued. Then the attack began in real earnest on both sides of the road and railway which links Keren with Agordat. One column gradually edged its way up the slopes so as to attack Keren from the north, while a second, operating on the other side of the valley, approached it from the south. Then a third column, principally composed of Free French troops, fought their way along the road from Cub Cub in an attempt to cut the Italian communications with Asmara.

The real battle for Keren began at dawn on March 15, when Imperial troops—men from Clydeside and the Highlands, England's

home counties and the Midlands, and of famous Indian regiments, Punjabis, Mahrattas, and Rajputs—fought their way up the almost sheer sides of three of the peaks commanding Keren, and carried them by assault. Their advance was preceded by a tremendous barrage, which for hours covered the peaks in a thick fog of smoke and dust, while 'planes of the R.A.F. and South

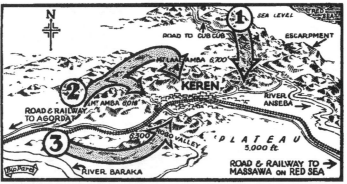

ADVANCES ON KEREN took place in the three directions indicated by the arrows in this map. 1, line of advance of the Free French troops along the coastal plain from the north-east. 2 and 3, lines of advance of the Imperial troops from the west.　　　*Courtesy of the "Daily Express"*

African Air Force bombed and machine-gunned the Italian positions. A week passed, and the battle was still proceeding with ever rising fury. Tons of bombs were dropped on the Italians from the air, and on the ground the infantry were ever at grips with hand grenades and bayonets.

So fierce was the enemy resistance that several of the peaks which had been captured by the British and Indians had to be captured for a second time, and time and again the Italians delivered furious counter-attacks. One of the fiercest of these was hurled at the bare, forbidding heights of Fort Dologorodoc, just after it had been captured by the British. There was one moment when the charging Italians swept right through the British line and reached the headquarters of the brigade defending the fort, and by the light of the moon the Brigadier and his staff went into action with their revolvers in the hand-to-hand battle. Then with the Brigadier at their head the little garrison swept

the Italians out of the fort and hurled them back far beyond their starting point, taking most of their mortars and guns and inflicting very heavy casualties.

Sunday, March 23, was the ninth day of the great battle, and still it raged furiously. In the sky the R.A.F. and their South African comrades fought the Italian 'planes which had now been flung into the battle, and on the ground British and Indian infantry toiled up the bullet-swept slopes, dodging here and there among the rocks, fighting an enemy who was ensconced on the heights far above, from which he dropped a deadly rain of hand grenades and small bombs.

Then the fighting reached its zenith in fury. While an Italian counter-attack was in progress against Fort Dologorodoc, a British force delivered a sudden and overwhelming onslaught on the foothills of the vital Sanchil peak, while an Indian unit wiped out the Italian battalion attacking Dologorodoc. After twelve counter-attacks delivered in 48 hours the Italians were sick and tired, and all around them the mountain-side was littered with their dead and wounded. On the night of March 26 General Platt—with whom was the Commander-in-Chief, General Sir Archibald Wavell, who was paying a flying visit to the front—decided that the moment had come for the final attack. First the sappers, British and Indian were sent along the road which had been blown up by the Italians, and after hours of work under heavy fire from the enemy they cleared the track, so that by the first light of morning the British mechanized columns surged forward and charged the Italian positions. Arrived at the top of the plateau, the British and Indian infantry, shouting and cheering, swept forward and rushed the town, from which the Italians were already in full retreat down the road to Asmara. So at 7 o'clock on the morning of March 27 Keren fell. Four days later Asmara, too, capitulated.

THE KEY TOWN OF ERITREA, Keren, whose fall finally sealed the fate of the Italian colony, lies on a plateau 6,000 feet above sea level and is surrounded by hills which were the scene of desperate fighting. In the twelve days preceding its fall on March 27, over 120 tons of bombs were dropped in the Keren area by the R.A.F. and S.A.F.　　　*Photo, E.N.A.*

OUR SEARCHLIGHT ON THE WAR

Brazilian Ship Bombed by Nazis

CAPTAIN MARIO TINOCO, master of the 7,000-ton Brazilian steamer Taubate, arrived at Alexandria on March 26 complaining that four days earlier his ship was attacked by a German aeroplane, despite the fact that she was flying two large Brazilian flags. One of his crew was killed and twelve were injured. The Captain's dog received a bullet in the shoulder, but this had been extracted and the animal now appeared quite well. The Nazi first released four bombs, swooping down to within 200 yards of the vessel. None scored a direct hit, but the nearest, 50 yards away, caused some damage below the water line. The enemy then flew repeatedly over the ship firing machine-guns and shells from small cannon. The crew frantically waved white sheets, but without avail, so, having no defences, prepared to abandon their ship. The aeroplane then concentrated its fire on the life-boats, which were badly damaged. Only when the raider had exhausted all his ammunition did he make off. The radio operator of the Taubate, who had been slightly wounded when his wireless cabin was shelled, at last got out a signal, with the result that British fighters arrived. "It was a grand sight," said Captain Tinoco, "but though we sent them off in the direction we had last seen the German, I doubt if they were in time to catch him."

Food Convoys for Bombed Towns

WITH the consent of H.M. the Queen the new Ministry of Food convoys for carrying food and comforts to badly bombed towns are to be called "Queen's Messengers." These units will consist of a water tanker holding 300 gallons, two food lorries, each containing 6,000 meals, two kitchen lorries equipped with soup boilers, fuel and utensils, and three mobile canteens to distribute the food. Each of these canteens has six containers for six gallons of vegetable stew, which will keep hot for four hours. Five motor cyclists to make and maintain contact with local authorities complete the convoy. There will be a fleet of eighteen Queen's Messengers. The first is the gift of Her Majesty; the remainder are being presented by the American Allied War Relief Organization. Each convoy costs about £5,000. They will be attached to the headquarters of each divisional food area and will stand ready to rush (at a speed of about 40 m.p.h.) to succour the homeless people of a bombed town.

Railings into Tanks

THE railings which for two hundred years preserved the gardens of Berkeley Square from contamination by the lower classes were recently removed and are now suffering a transformation in order to take part in the battle for democracy. Old metal collected by the Iron and Steel Control of the Ministry of Supply is sent to an ironworks to be turned into raw material for war purposes. Here scrap such as the Berkeley Square railings is cut by a species of enormous shears into lengths of a convenient size, which are then passed into drums to have the paint removed, an operation known as "rumbling." After this the pieces are packed into iron boxes and heated in furnaces to a temperature of 1,300 degrees Centigrade. Hefty workmen, well protected from the heat and wielding pairs of tongs, seize the great chunks of red-hot metal and toss them to and fro through rollers, which so shape them that eventually what emerges is a new bar of iron measuring anything up to 80 feet in length. This is the raw material which goes to the armament works and may eventually become part of a tank, a destroyer, or a Bren gun.

Polish School of Medicine

OPENED at Edinburgh on March 22, the Polish School of Medicine was described as "the first demonstration by the scientific world against Hitler's 'new order.'" The inaugural ceremony took place in the McEwan Hall, the Vice-Chancellor, Sir Thomas Holland, presiding. The School has been provided for the Polish Government by the Senatus of Edinburgh University and the first to benefit by its establishment will be doctors who, although they had completed their studies in Poland, were unable, owing to the war, to sit for their final examination. The President of Poland, Dr. Raczkiewicz, was presented for the honorary degree of Doctor of Laws in the University.

WROUGHT-IRON RAILINGS, which have stood in Berkeley Square, London, for two centuries, have been removed from their aristocratic quarters to serve democracy as raw material for war purposes.

Photo, Keystone

Two Britons Take a Town

AN episode that occurred during the conquest of Italian Somaliland, in which the town and district of Roccolittorio surrendered to two British officials, was recently revealed by Nairobi G.H.Q. It appears that one morning a South African Air Force machine flew over the town dropping not bombs but leaflets. These informed the stricken populace that the following day the aircraft would land with supplies and would evacuate the sick and women and children. Next day the bomber punctually made its appearance and effected a landing. Out of it stepped a British political officer and an interpreter. They were greeted by the chief Italian officials, who agreed to the surrender of the town and the district. Supplies brought by the aircraft were unloaded for distribution, and arrangements made for the evacuation of invalids and children to the hospital at Mogadishu.

Children in Uniform

STANDARDIZED clothes make for economy, and women advisers to the Board of Trade have recommended that, particularly in the case of children's clothes, manufacturers should introduce standard sizes, styles and colours. Fewer styles would demand fewer types of cloth, and this would prevent wastage of yarn. Standard sizes would result in conservation of stocks and in economies in manufacture, distribution and consumption. If these proposals take effect children will probably not object, for the average boy, at any rate, hates to be made conspicuous, his aim being to look as much like his contemporaries as possible. But women may not take so kindly to the plan if it is applied to their own clothes, despite its success in the U.S.A.

'QUEEN'S MESSENGERS' is the title given to these mobile canteens which Her Majesty, accompanied by Lord Woolton, is seen inspecting at Buckingham Palace. They are intended to drive straight to bombed streets during a raid and serve food to the homeless.

Photo, P.N.A.

They Have Won Honours in Freedom's Cause

Gnr. D. J. E. Roberts, Royal Artillery, G.M., for rescuing one of the crew of a burning Wellington bomber.

L.-Sergt. E. A. Provins, R.A., G.M., for leading the rescue party of which Gnr. Roberts was a member.

R.Q.M.S. David Borthwick, M.M., for rescuing victims trapped in a Bristol shelter which suffered a direct hit.

Major R. J. Williams, of Toronto, M.C., for gallantry. He is the first Canadian to receive the M.C. in this war.

C.Q.M.S. A. J. Mitchell, Grenadier Guards, D.C.M., for conspicuous bravery and fine leadership at Dunkirk.

Sgt. David Lorimer, D.F.M., for shooting down an Me.109 during a raid on Hamburg, thus saving the aircraft in which he was gunner.

Pilot Officer E. S. Lock, D.F.C., D.S.O., for landing his 'plane safely with both legs injured and an arm broken.

Assist. Sect. Officer F. H. Hanbury, O.B.E., Military Div. for service in operational commands of R.A.F.

Sqn. Ldr. N. G. Mulholland, D.F.C., for taking photographs of Kiel and the results of Mannheim raids.

Pilot-Sgt. R. N. Stubbs, of the R.A.F. Volunteer Reserve, D.F.M., for gallantry and devotion to duty during air operations.

Stoker J. J. Collins, of Belfast, D.S.M., for displaying outstanding courage and daring at Dunkirk.

Second-Hand P. J. Green, D.S.M., for rescuing two injured men on a trawler during attack by enemy 'planes.

Ldg. Wren N. Williams, telephone operator, B.E.M., for remaining at her post at aerodrome during raids.

C.P.O. Charles M. Felcey, D.S.M., for courage and enterprise and resource during patrols by H.M. submarines.

Seaman U. Peters, R.N.R., D.S.M. for displaying conspicuous courage against the enemy and devotion to duty.

Chief Constable Bolt, of Dover, O.B.E., for displaying courage and devotion to duty during air attacks.

Chief Inspector Stacy, of Southampton, M.B.E., for conspicuous gallantry and initiative during air raids.

Chief Supt. P. Chatfield, of Southampton, M.B.E., for outstanding qualities of leadership and courage.

Stn. Sergt. W. E. Douglas, Metropolitan Police, G.M., for rescuing two girls imprisoned in wrecked house.

P.-C. J. P. James, Metropolitan Police, G.M., for rescuing people trapped under wreckage of bombed flats.

Dispatch Rider S. E. G. Bradford, London A.F.S., G.M., for clearing away wreckage until he was overcome by gas fumes.

Miss G. Tanner, London A.F.S., G.M., for driving a lorry through burning streets to refuel fire pumps during raids on the city.

Sect. Officer J. C. Sargent, of Tottenham Fire Brigade, O.B.E., for displaying outstanding courage in fighting oil fires.

A.F.S. Driver W. Eustace, O.B.E., for displaying great coolness and courage in driving an A.F.S. canteen among falling bombs.

Sect. Officer S. A. Wright, of Luton A.F.S., G.M., for assisting to save 20,000 tons of oil from a fire blazing among oil tanks.

We Spotted and Sank Two Italian Boats

The story of how the British submarine Parthian attacked an
escorted convoy of Italian ships bound for Albania, and sank two of
them, was told by her captain when the Parthian reached port. Here
is Commander Rimington's story in his own words.

COMMANDER M. G. RIMINGTON, D.S.O.,
captain of the Parthian, said that he
encountered a convoy, probably
bound for Albania, off the toe of Italy, and
after sinking two ships, managed to get away
despite a six-hours hot chase by Italian anti-
submarine vessels.

He continued : " We spotted a convoy of
three vessels escorted by a small warship. I
drew a bead on the first and second vessels—
a 6,000-ton cargo steamer and a 10,000-ton
tanker—and fired a salvo of three torpedoes
at each.

"Although we submerged immediately, I
heard four explosions of terrific force. This
led me to believe that each vessel had been
hit by two torpedoes."

Within twenty minutes anti-submarine
vessels had arrived from the Italian coast.
Prior to their arrival the submarine's instruments showed that the engines of only two of
the four Italian ships were turning.

" That made it a certainty that the steamer
and tanker had been sunk," Commander
Rimington said.

" Then the first depth charges—a series of
five—dropped very close to the submarine,
shaking the ship severely. They kept on
dropping them for about six hours."

CDR. M. G. RIMINGTON, D.S.O., R.N., who
recently sank two enemy transports in an
escorted convoy, has had three previous successes with his submarine, H.M.S. Parthian.
Photo, G.P.U.

What My Day on the Farm Is Like

Farm work is hard and monotonous, but its regular rhythm as the
seasons go round forms part of its attraction. So, at least, found
the writer of the following article—one of the many town-dwelling
women with a love of country life who have joined up in the Land Army.

MY working day begins at seven, and
I was glad when, for the first time
this year, I was able to finish my
breakfast with the curtains drawn back and
by daylight. A cold, rather raw daylight,
but daylight, nevertheless.

I go to work by a footpath alongside
a straggling hedge, and as I went a gleaming
yellowhammer flirted and darted ahead of
me. His chant about a little bit of bread and
no cheese seemed more than usually poignant.
I sympathized ; it is many weeks now that
honey has taken the place of cheese in my
lunch-basket.

As I turned into the farmyard I noticed
a van down the lane by the rickyard, and
two men and our foreman and one of our
horses. We have talked of selling one for
some time, so I paid little attention, except
to wonder idly that they had brought an
open van instead of a horse-box. I let the
cows out from the lodge into the yard, then
thought I might as well step through the
hay barn to see what they had decided about
Prince.

I slipped the latch, and as I stepped over
the threshold I saw the two strangers, one
holding the horse's halter, the other apparently fondling his muzzle. There was a
sudden, not very loud crack, and the great
horse crumpled, toppled over and lay still,
without a quiver. Our foreman called out
something to me about being " too late,"
and as I walked toward them I found myself
bewilderedly saying, " But ... but ... why ? "
He was not so young, I knew, but he had
been a useful horse, and nothing wrong with
him but a maddening habit of backing
erratically, so that I renamed him " Waltzing
Matilda." " 'Cos he's worth more to 'un
dead nor alive," said our foreman baldly,
but I could see he, too, was shaken. And there
it was, and the horse lay still in the cold, raw
morning air. One learns to accept death
on a farm, but I admit that Prince's haunted
me all day. . . .

The calves were clamouring for their

breakfast. I have ten on hand at the moment,
all under a month old and two of them
in the weaning stage, where they have to be
taught to drink from the pail. They are
clumsy, foolish pupils. At first the pail
means nothing to them, and they nuzzle me
or even send me flying head over heels.
Then they suck furiously at the finger I half-
submerge in the warm milk and gruel.
After a day or two they need only the
tip of a finger at their lips, and within a
week they are greedily drinking without any
help, tails wagging furiously as the warm
drink disappears.

Then the usual round of littering, foddering

H.M.S. PARTHIAN, which so far has damaged
one enemy cruiser, sunk one submarine and
sunk two merchantmen and a tanker, was
completed in 1930. She has eight 21-inch
torpedo tubes and carries a complement of 50.
Photo, Wright & Logan

In this page a member of the Women's Land
Army describes her working day. Here a
member, stationed at the Northamptonshire
Institute of Agriculture, is seen mothering an
orphan lamb. *Photo, Keystone*

April 18th, 1941   *The War Illustrated*   407

IIIIIIIIIIIIIIIIIIIIIIIIIIIIIIIIIIIIIIIIIIIIIIIIIIIIIIIIIIIIIIIIIIIIIIIIIIIIIII **I WAS THERE !** IIIIIIIIIIIIIIIIIIIIIIIIIIIIIIIIIIIIIIIIIIIIIIIIIIIIIIIIIIIIIIIIIIIIIIIIIIIIIII

the cows, putting out their tea ration, bulk and concentrates, clearing up the cow lodge, feeding the hens.

And so at last to the real job of the day. At present we are laboriously engaged in draining a nasty two-acre bit with almost no fall in it, so that every spit has to be considered carefully to get the most out of it. The boss and the foreman are doing the digging. My job is to put in the tiles, and then bush up with hedge trimmings to within nine inches of the top, and finally throw back the sodden clay heaped on the edge—yard after heavy, back-breaking yard of it, almost every forkful having to be dragged off the fork with my boot and then prodded off my boot with the fork ! For the first day or two one's mind rebels at the apparently insensate, monotonous drudgery of it, and then it becomes almost second nature, and one just goes on and on, sticking the fork in, levering and prising, jerking and shaking, scraping and kicking and stamping and plodding on.

The Farmer's Work Never Done !

I used to think, as many town-dwelling " country lovers " have thought, that farm work was so gloriously various. Six weeks of muck-carting gave me a sort of idea I might be mistaken. Now I know that, bar the occasionally erupting odd jobs, hardly any farm work is done in a day : most of it just goes on and on. But after the first shock of realizing this one accepts it not merely as inevitable, but as right and proper and enjoyable.

There has not been one job that I have not liked, nor one—except hedging and ditching—of which I have not been heartily sick and tired, and yet when it comes round again next season, one goes at it with zest. I think it is the sense of continuity that exalts one. A curious, fascinating, fatal, enduring exaltation which probably does much to explain why farmers so seldom give up the life despite all their grumbling, most of which is so thoroughly justified.

These thoughts and others were running round my mind as I plodded and floundered all day, with just the half-hour break for " beaver " and the hour for dinner. I stick to my townee habits of evening dinner, as I have no time to cook as well as eat, and at one o'clock I merely heat some stock and

THE WOMEN'S LAND ARMY has been joined by women and girls from many different walks of life, but it has not taken long for them to become proficient in their new duties. The land girl above was formerly a nurse ; now she attends to newly born calves with the same skill she once showed in attending her human patients.   *Photo, ' Daily Mirror "*

This woman, an expert tractor driver and instructor, now working at the Sparsholt Agricultural Institute, near Winchester, was formerly a commercial artist. Her machine is drawing both a disk harrow and an ordinary harrow.   *Photo, L.N.A.*

drop an egg in at the last minute, or fry up some cold potatoes or rice or lentils.

At last it was four o'clock, and I unstuck my fork for the last time and went up to the farm to milk, and feed my calves again, and do all the other routine stockyard jobs which take an hour and a half at the end of every day.—" *Manchester Guardian.* "

Our Squadron Had a Busy 45 Minutes

R.A.F. fighter squadrons scouting over the Channel and the coast of occupied France sometimes return from their patrols without seeing a unit of the Luftwaffe ; sometimes, as told in the following eye-witness story, a squadron has a short but lively encounter with the enemy.

A T 4 o'clock one day a pilot officer, out with his Spitfire squadron over occupied France, was hoping the Luftwaffe would answer the challenge.

For 20 minutes the Spitfires flew up the French coast. Suddenly three Me.109s streaked over, and seven more came from almost straight ahead.

Here, in the words of the pilot officer, is what happened :

" I pulled straight up and opened fire on the leader. Almost instantaneously there was a great burst of flame aft of the pilot.

" My machine stalled and I let her spin until I had lost about 5,000 feet. I then climbed again after the enemy formation, which had turned north. There were only five machines now, and they were descending.

" I opened fire on the rearmost aircraft and got in three bursts. The enemy aircraft turned right and half rolled. Faint white mist came from under the starboard wing root.

I was forced to break contact when the remainder interfered.

" As I was flying back over the Channel I saw an Me. 109 stalk and shoot at the squadron leader's Spitfire, and then do a climbing turn to the left. The enemy aircraft had not observed me, and I opened fire when some way off, closing to point-blank range. This Me. 109 had large black numerals and a bright green nose.

" I turned to continue the engagement, but broke away on seeing the enemy aircraft emitting dense clouds of black smoke and flames from its starboard side."

It was 4.45 p.m. when the pilot officer landed, 45 minutes from the time his adventures began.

After landing he learned that a sergeant in his squadron had shot down another of the Me. 109s, that his squadron leader had made a forced landing on the coast and was safe, though wounded.

408   *The War Illustrated*   April 18th, 1941

IIIIIIIIIIIIIIIIIIIIIIIIIIIIIIIIIIIIIIIIIIIIIIIIIIIIIIIIIII I WAS THERE ! IIIIIIIIIIIIIIIIIIIIIIIIIIIIIIIIIIIIIIIIIIIIIIIIIIIIIIII

I Flew Back on the Other Pilot's Lap

An amazing feat was performed by a South African airman who landed a single-seater fighter 'plane on an enemy aerodrome under heavy fire, picked up a shot-down fellow pilot, and flew him safely home. The-rescued pilot tells the story here in his own words.

THE airman who showed such remarkable pluck and resource was Lieutenant R. H. Kershaw, No. 3 Squadron, South African Air Force, who was awarded the D.S.O. for his gallantry.

While a flight of Hurricanes was operating over Diredawa aerodrome, the Flight Commander was compelled to make a forced landing. Describing the incident he said :

" When the shot hit my aircraft, smoke began to pour into the cockpit and blinded me. I was forced to land and was just going to set fire to my machine and run into the bush when I noticed another of the pilots of my flight circling around and firing at enemy troops to keep them away from me.

" I never dreamed he would land, for anti-aircraft guns were firing at him continuously, and I was just about to rush for the bush when I heard him shouting to me.

" When I saw he had landed I ran as fast as I could and climbed on to one of his wings, but his engine was revving so hard that I was blown off again by blast from the airscrew. I then tried to climb on to the pilot's back and shoulders as he was taxying back to the end of the aerodrome with the Italians firing at us all the time.

" We realized, however, that I should not be able to stay on clinging to his shoulders, so I climbed over his head on to his lap and got my feet on to the rudder bar. So, with enemy guns still bombarding the aerodrome we got off. It was a pretty good take-off. I worked the stick and rudder, and the pilot from underneath me operated the flap and undercarriage levers. We flew quite normally back to our base and made a successful landing."

Other pilots in the squadron who had seen their leader with smoke pouring from his aircraft were amazed when they returned to find him safely back at the aerodrome.

Lieutenant Kershaw himself was reluctant to discuss the gallant rescue of his commander. All he had to say was, " It wasn't very comfortable with two of us in the cockpit.''

DIREDAWA, here viewed from the air, was occupied by South African troops on March 29. Diredawa is the third city of Abyssinia, and in capturing it the British cut the Addis-Ababa-Jibuti railway and closed the net around the Abyssinian capital.   *Photo, Associated Press*

OUR DIARY OF THE WAR

SATURDAY, MARCH 29   *574th day*

IN THE AIR.—Bomber and Coastal Command aircraft attacked enemy shipping off Dutch and French coasts.

WAR AGAINST ITALY.—Diredawa (Abyssinia) captured.

Advance towards · Asmara progressing ; prisoners total 3,775. R.A.F. heavily bombed Asmara. Other targets were encampment near Gondar ; transport north of Dessie and in Awash area ; railway station at Meta Hari.

R.A.F. raided Tripoli during nights of 23-29 and 29-30.

HOME FRONT.—Train in East Anglia machine-gunned. Night raid on place in Bristol Channel area. Junkers destroyed over North Sea.

GREEK WAR.—Athens reported violent artillery and patrol activity. R.A.F. made offensive reconnaissances against villages of Berat, Dukai and Dukati.

BALKANS.—Yugoslav reservists called up.

SUNDAY, MARCH 30   *575th day*

ON THE SEA.—French shore batteries in Algeria fired on British light naval forces intercepting French convoy suspected of carrying German war material. H.M. ships returned fire, but allowed convoy to proceed to Nemours.

IN THE AIR.—Coastal Command aircraft sank anti-submarine vessel off mouth of Loire.

Heavy night attack on Brest, where warships Scharnhorst and Gneisenau were sheltering. Channel invasion ports, particularly Calais, bombed.

WAR AGAINST ITALY.—R.A.F. attacked transport concentrations in Dessie and Alomata areas. Harbour at Astropalia (Dodecanese) raided.

Enemy attempted to raid Malta during nights of 29-30 and 30-31.

HOME FRONT.—Some activity off E. and W. coasts. Bombs fell in N. Scotland and S. England. Junkers shot down near Middlesbrough.

GREEK WAR.—R.A.F. bombed military targets at Elbasan.

GENERAL.—All Italian, German and Danish ships in U.S.A. ports seized to prevent sabotage.

MONDAY, MARCH 31   *576th day*

IN THE AIR.—Two tankers fired off Le Havre by Bomber Command. Destroyer off Frisian Islands twice hit. Troops and gun-emplacements on islands of Terschelling and Ameland bombed and machine-gunned. Direct hit scored on supply ship in convoy.

Night attacks on Emden, where powerful new bomb was used, Bremen, Bremerhaven, Oldenburg, and on petroleum harbour at Rotterdam.

WAR AGAINST ITALY.—Advance towards Asmara continuing. Troops progressing westwards beyond Diredawa. Operations proceeding in Negelli and Yavello areas.

In Libya British were in contact with enemy infantry and mechanized units in Mersa Brega area.

R.A.F. attacked targets in Dessie-Assab sector. During night of 30-31 shipping and docks at Tripoli were heavily raided.

HOME FRONT.—Sharp night raid on N.E. coast town causing severe damage. Bombs also fell in S. and S.W. England and S. Wales.

GREEK WAR.—Athens reported that Italian fortified height had been occupied and 200 prisoners taken.

Successful R.A.F. raid on troops and motor transport moving on Buzi-Glave road.

BALKANS.—German Note to Yugoslavia demanded apology, ratification of Pact and demobilization.

GENERAL.—Six Axis ships scuttled by their crews in S. American ports.

TUESDAY, APRIL 1   *577th day*

IN THE AIR.—R.A.F. attacked German shipping and coastal gun emplacements in course of patrols of French and Dutch coasts. Enemy merchant vessel torpedoed off Denmark.

WAR AGAINST ITALY.—Asmara, capital of Eritrea, surrendered.

Cairo reported that penetration into southern Abyssinia was enlarging particularly north of Lake Rudolf.

R.A.F. bombed aerodromes in Tripolitania.

HOME FRONT.—Bombs dropped by single aircraft at points near south and east coasts. Raiders attempted number of small attacks on aerodromes. Most were ineffective but at one station there were casualties and some damage done to buildings.

Five enemy bombers destroyed. German aircraft crashed in Eire.

WEDNESDAY, APRIL 2   *578th day*

ON THE SEA.—Admiralty announced that Italian destroyer of Pantera class, attempting to escape from Massawa, had been sunk by naval aircraft. German merchant ship Bertram Rickmers, which had left Massawa, was intercepted by H.M.S. Kandahar.

British submarine in Mediterranean reported having sunk Italian U-boat and tanker.

H.M. paddle minesweeper Lorna Doone, attacked by three Dorniers, shot down one and damaged another.

IN THE AIR.—During patrols off Dutch coast, Blenheim bomber scored four hits on armed merchant ship, leaving her sinking.

Bomber and Coastal Command aircraft attacked enemy patrol vessels and aerodromes at Haamstede, Maupertuis and Caen.

WAR AGAINST ITALY.—Cairo reported that in Libya operations north-east of Mersa Brega were continuing and our advanced elements were withdrawing.

In Eritrea enemy retreating from Asmara in south and south-easterly direction.

Operations in Abyssinia developing successfully.

HOME FRONT.—Bombs fell during day at place in East Anglia and village on N.E. coast of Scotland. One enemy aircraft destroyed.

GREEK WAR.—Athens reported that enemy attempted to regain redoubt captured on Monday, but were repulsed with loss.

Three out of four Italian bombers attempting to raid Volos destroyed by R.A.F.

VICTORY IS WAITING FOR THEM AT THE END OF THE ROAD

Not for a moment were the Greeks daunted when Germany, without the shadow of provocation, was numbered amongst her foes. The army in Thrace entered the battle with proud enthusiasm, showing that splendid courage, that indomitable spirit, which their brothers have displayed in the bitter campaigning in the Albanian heights—conditions of which this photograph is eloquent indeed. In words of passionate patriotism King George of the Hellenes inspired and encouraged his soldiers : " All together, Greeks ! " he said ; " Victory is waiting at the end of the road ! "

Photo, Bosshard, Exclusive to THE WAR ILLUSTRATED

How Hitler Struck at Greece and Yugoslavia

Beyond a doubt Hitler hoped, perhaps expected, that Greece and Yugoslavia would succumb to his threats, just as Bulgaria and Rumania had done. But the two countries, small and weak though they are compared with the Axis Powers, refused to be bullied, preferring to fight rather than surrender. So on April 6 the Fuehrer launched his armies against them; the great campaign of 1941 had begun.

WITHOUT troubling to declare war, the Germans invaded Yugoslavia and Greece at dawn on Sunday, April 6, 1941.

"At 5.15 this morning the German Army in Bulgaria perpetrated an unprovoked attack against Greek frontier guards. Our forces are defending their national territory." So read the first communiqué issued by the Greek High Command on that momentous day. A few hours afterwards a second communiqué stated that the attack was being delivered by powerful German forces abundantly equipped with tanks, heavy artillery and aircraft, against which the Greeks could oppose only very small forces. A very violent struggle was in progress, and though the Greek fortifications resisted strongly, one at least of the frontier forts was blasted into surrender and some areas of the national territory had to be evacuated. But along the front as a whole the Germans were held up with heavy losses.

Yugoslavia's first experience of Nazi savagery was when at 3.30 on that Sunday morning the first of many waves of German bombers appeared over Belgrade's roofs. The capital had been declared an open city by the Yugoslav authorities, but the claim was brushed aside, and soon the German radio was gloating over the destruction caused by the Nazi 'planes. "Our target was the military and moral nerve centre of Yugoslavia." In a short time the Stukas had turned the city into a mass of ruins, and the streets were littered with the dead bodies of women and children and old men. After the attacks had been launched,

Ribbentrop in Berlin handed Notes to the Greek and Yugoslav ministers, "explaining" the German aggression. Germany and Italy had never asked more of Greece, he protested, than that she should preserve real neutrality, but she had more and more openly ranged herself with the enemies of Germany, and in particular with England. "Within the last few days Greece has openly become a theatre of operations for British forces. Large-scale operational landings and troop movements of British troops are now being carried out, and American reports confirm that a British army of 200,000 men is standing ready in Greece." So the German government had given orders to their forces to drive the British from Greek territory. Any opposition would be ruthlessly crushed, but "the German troops are not coming as enemies of the Greek people . . . the blow which Germany is forced to deal on Greek soil is intended for Britain."

In the Note to Yugoslavia reference was made to the Three-Power Pact signed in Vienna on March 25—"an agreement which granted lasting security for the Yugoslav State, and a happy future for its people." Yet the Yugoslav ministers who had put their signatures to the agreement were arrested on their return to Belgrade by order of "a clique of conspirators." So, to quote the concluding sentence from Hitler's proclamation to the German people broadcast by Goebbels at 5 a.m. that same morning, "I have decided to entrust the further representation of German interests to that force which it has again been proved is alone able to protect right and reason."

Although Hitler had known it for some weeks—the German Consul in Salonika kept him well informed of every development—the British public were surprised to hear that a British Expeditionary Force had already gone to Greece. The news was given in an official statement issued in London on the night of April 6.

"After the entry of German troops into Bulgaria had brought to a head the long threatened German invasion of the Balkans, his Majesty's Government in the United Kingdom, in full consultation with the Dominion Governments concerned, have sent an Army to Greece, comprising troops from Great Britain, Australia, and New Zealand, to stand in the line with the soldiers of our brave Ally in defence of their native soil. The British Air Force, which has for some time been operating in Greece against the Italians, has been strongly reinforced."

A little later it was revealed that the new B.E.F. had reached Greece losing not a ship or a man on the way. German and Italian aircraft had altogether failed to interrupt the flow of convoys; and as for the Italian fleet — it too had made the attempt, only to permit Cape Matapan to be inscribed on

The map shows the peacetime disposition of the Yugoslav Armies. Following the German invasion of April 6 the Third Army was soon in difficulties, while the First, Fourth, and Fifth were compelled to fall back.
Courtesy of " News Chronicle "

the roll of Britain's victories. The expeditionary force included Australians, New Zealanders, and other veterans of the Libyan campaign, and their reception in Greece was enthusiastic beyond description.

The German masses which crossed the Greek frontier from Bulgaria met with the most determined resistance from the Greek troops, particularly in the Struma valley. Here and there the Greek forts were over-

Where the New Balkan War Is Being Fought

SKOPLJE (Uskub in Yugoslavia is 130 miles from Salonika. Here is a scene in the Turkish quarter.

ZAGREB, capital of Croatia-Slavonia, on the River Sava, is famous for its cathedral and university. A general view shows the city roofs stretching towards the long line of the mountains.

BELGRADE, although previously declared an open town, was ruthlessly bombed by the Nazis.

THE BALKANS WAR ZONE : opening moves in the campaign, Yugoslav (small arrows) and German (heavy black arrows.)

STRUMA VALLEY, scene of the powerful Nazi drive towards Salonika, runs from Bulgaria into Greece, some sixty miles to the north of the great Greek port. By her invasion of two more countries (Yugoslavia and Greece) Germany created a new front of almost 700 miles—from the Adriatic to the Aegean Sea. **SALONIKA,** right, was captured by German mechanized forces, after fierce fighting with Greek covering troops, on April 9 ; this view shows the large harbour.

Map, " Daily Sketch" ; Photos, Dorien Leigh, Associated Press, Wide World, Fox

Salonika Fell After Three Days of War

whelmed by the German armoured hordes and fell, having resisted to the last ; but others managed to beat off every attack. Elsewhere, however, the battle was not going so well for the defenders. In order to avoid unnecessary sacrifice, western Thrace was evacuated according to plan, with the result

repulsed with the greatest vigour. The Germans were invading the country from Hungary, Rumania and Bulgaria, the principal thrust being the third, aimed at separating the Yugoslavs from their Greek allies, and by April 9 the Germans claimed that with both Nish and Skoplje (Usküb)

THE YUGOSLAV ARMY had to face Nazi thrusts in force from Austria, Hungary, Rumania and Bulgaria, as the Germans attempted to encircle them and cut them off from their Allies. Yugoslav infantry are seen above during manoeuvres. *Photo, Press Topics*

in their hands and the Albanian frontier reached, this had been accomplished.

But the principal struggle was between the Greeks and Germans at the Struma Pass. Even the German official spokesman was constrained to admit that the Greeks were fighting courageously, but the weight of men and metal soon began to tell. Greek resistance was thrust aside and a German mechanized division thundered into Salonika at 4 a.m. on April 9.

that the Germans on April 7 reached the Aegean, thus cutting off Greece from land communication with Turkey. Then just west of the Struma Valley where the frontiers of Yugoslavia, Greece and Bulgaria meet, the Yugoslav army was forced to withdraw in front of great German pressure, thus leaving the Greek left flank uncovered. Seizing their advantage a German mechanized division penetrated the mountainous region to the east of the Vardar and swooped down on the Greek town of Doiran. For many hours a small Greek mechanized formation strove heroically to slow down the enemy advance, but finally the Germans succeeded in advancing dangerously far down the Vardar valley in the direction of Salonika.

Meanwhile, what of the war in Yugoslavia ? The first communiqué of the Yugoslav High Command, broadcast over the Belgrade wireless on April 8, said that on all fronts the situation was in the Yugoslavs' favour and that the enemy attacks were being

GREECE'S GREATEST PORT, Salonika, was raided by Italian aircraft many times, and among the buildings damaged was the church of St. Sophia, seen in the centre photograph ; on April 9 the great port was captured by the Germans. Above, British anti-aircraft guns parked in a Greek town.   *Photos, British Official ; Crown Copyright ; and Wide World*

Eden and Dill Acclaimed in Athens

BRITAIN'S FOREIGN SECRETARY, Mr. Anthony Eden, accompanied by General Sir John Dill, Chief of the Imperial General Staff, arrived in the Greek capital on March 2, 1941, on an official visit which lasted until March 5 ; they paid another visit at the end of the month. They had long discussions with the King of the Hellenes and the Prime Minister (M. Korizis), but in the intervals visited some of the glorious ruins of ancient Athens. They are here seen leaving the Acropolis amidst an admiring crowd. General Dill is thoroughly familiar with the Near and Middle East, for after serving on the General Staff in India, 1929-30, he commanded the British forces in Palestine, 1936-37.

Photo, Keystone

British Soldiers Are No Strangers to Greece

THE B.E.F. IN GREECE is following in the footsteps of the men who took part in the Salonika campaign against the Bulgarians in 1915-1918. The two photographs in this page show scenes during that campaign. Top is a mule-drawn "travois," a litter with one end trailing on the ground used for conveying wounded to the dressing stations. Lower photograph, British troops on a rough road in Macedonia have discarded their tunics to march in the baking sun. The Balkans B.E.F. of those days was commanded by Lord Milne.

Photos, Imperial War Museum, L.N.A.

THE MARVEL OF CAPE MATAPAN
Admiral Cunningham's Victory Hour by Hour

ABOUT midday on March 27, 1941, air reconnaissance reported that enemy cruisers were at sea to the south-eastward of Sicily. Commander-in-Chief Mediterranean was then at Alexandria with the main body of his fleet. It was immediately clear to him that these enemy cruisers could not be up to any good and he concluded that their probable intentions were to attack our convoys between Egypt and Greece.

Acting on this supposition he made the following dispositions of the forces at his disposal : The Vice-Admiral Commanding Light Forces, Vice-Admiral H. D. Pridham-Wippell, C.B., C.V.O., R.N., with his flag flying in H.M.S. Orion (Flag-Captain G. R. B. Back, R.N.) had with him the cruisers Ajax (Captain E. D. B. McCarthy, R.N.), Perth of the Royal Australian Navy (Captain Sir P. W. Bowyer-Smyth, Bt.), and Gloucester (Flag-Captain H. A. Rowley, R.N.) and some destroyers. This force the Commander-in-Chief Mediterranean ordered to proceed to a position south of Crete in which it would be strongly placed to intercept any enemy forces attempting to interfere with our traffic with Greece.

The Commander-in-Chief, whose flag was flying in H.M.S. Warspite (Flag-Captain D. B. Fisher, C.B.E., R.N.), had with him the battleships Valiant (Captain C. E. Morgan, D.S.O., R.N.) and Barham (Flag Captain G. C. Cooke, R.N.), the aircraft carrier Formidable (Flag-Captain A. W. La T. Bissett, R.N.) and some destroyers. This force was ordered to raise steam with all dispatch.

As soon as it became possible that a fleet action might take place, a force of Greek destroyers steamed out to the westward in the hope of intercepting enemy forces endeavouring to escape into the Adriatic. Unfortunately the line of the enemy retreat did not give them an opportunity to attack.

March 27. P.M. The Commander-in-Chief took his main fleet to sea from Alexandria and steamed to the north-eastward in the hope of intercepting enemy forces and bringing them to action.

March 28. 07.49. Air reconnaissance reported enemy force consisting of one Littorio class battleship (later stated to be the Vittorio Veneto), six cruisers and seven destroyers about 35 miles south of Gavdo Island. This enemy force was steering to the south-eastwards, and soon after being sighted it was seen to be joined by two more cruisers and at least two more destroyers. At the time of this sighting V.A.L.F. with the cruiser force was about 40 miles to the south-eastward of the enemy. The Commander-in-Chief with the main fleet was then about 95 miles to the south-eastward of the cruiser force and steaming to the north-westward.

08.02. Acting on the aircraft report of

Some account of the great naval victory off Cape Matapan has been given in page 394. Now we are able to give a more detailed account issued by the Ministry of Information, supported by first-hand stories of the action by officers of the ships engaged, and with the Italian communiqué as an interesting, if hardly factual, conclusion.
24 hours time : 07.49 = 7.49 A.M. ; 17.00 = 5 P.M.

sighting the enemy, our cruiser force altered course to the northward and made contact with enemy cruisers. Having made contact, V.A.L.F. turned his cruisers to the south-eastward to draw the enemy on towards the battle fleet.

About 09.00. The enemy cruisers turned 16 points and began to steer to the north-westward. The British cruiser force followed suit in order to keep in touch.

10.58. V.A.L.F. sighted the Littorio class battleship 16 miles to the northward. On sighting the enemy battleship V.A.L.F. turned his cruisers once again to the south-eastward in order to keep outside range of the heavy guns of the enemy battleship and to draw the enemy forces towards his Commander-in-Chief.

11.30. A torpedo bomber attack launched from H.M.S. Formidable developed on the Littorio class battleship. One possible hit was claimed in this attack. Either this attack or the knowledge of the presence of an aircraft carrier caused the Littorio class battleship and her accompanying cruisers to turn to the north-westward. The enemy was thus again heading for his bases. This abrupt turn by the enemy caused V.A.L.F. to lose touch, but our cruiser force almost immediately came in sight of our own battle fleet and the whole of our forces pressed on after the enemy.

11.35. Our aircraft sighted and reported a second enemy force about 80 miles west of Gavdo Island. This force consisted of two Cavour class battleships, three cruisers and four destroyers. At about this time another torpedo bomber attack by naval aircraft was launched against the enemy force, which included the Littorio class battleship. One hit was claimed in this attack.

Early afternoon. Naval aircraft again carried out a search for the enemy, with whom touch

had been temporarily lost. The enemy was again located. A further torpedo bombing attack was launched, and three torpedo hits on the Littorio class battleship were claimed.

Between 15.00 and 17.00. Blenheim bombers of the R.A.F. attacked the enemy with bombs. In these attacks it was claimed that two direct hits were scored on one cruiser, one on a destroyer, and two probable hits on another cruiser.

16.00. The Commander-in-Chief received a report from aircraft that the speed of the Littorio class battleship had been drastically reduced. He at once ordered V.A.L.F. to press on with his four cruisers to regain touch.

Dusk. Two further torpedo bombing attacks were launched by naval aircraft. One enemy cruiser was definitely hit by a torpedo. The

This Admiralty plan of the naval Battle of Cape Matapan shows the approximate courses followed by the British and Italian ships. The solid black line, bottom right, shows the attempt by Vice-Admiral H. D. Pridham-Wippell, Commanding the Light Forces, to draw the main Italian force towards the battleships of the Commander-in-Chief.   *Map, British Official : Crown Copyright*

Vice Admiral Commanding Light Forces regained touch with the enemy just after dusk, and some destroyers were ordered to attack, others being retained with the battle fleet for screening duties. Having led the destroyers to the position from which they were to commence their attack, V.A.L.F. led his cruisers clear of his destroyers to the north-eastward.

22.10. It was reported to the Commander-in-Chief that an enemy vessel was lying damaged and stopped three miles to port of the battle fleet's course. The Commander-in-Chief at once turned the battle fleet to engage this unit, revealed as the Italian cruiser Pola.

While approaching the Pola three enemy cruisers were sighted on the starboard bow. This enemy force consisted of two Zara class cruisers led by a smaller cruiser of the Colleone class. This enemy force was crossing the bows of our battle fleet from starboard to port. As the enemy cruisers passed ahead of the screen H.M.S. Greyhound illuminated the leading heavy cruiser. Our battle fleet at once opened fire. The enemy must have been taken completely by surprise. The first salvos hit at a range of about 4,000 yards and practically wrecked both the heavy cruisers of the Zara class as far as fighting was concerned. Enemy destroyers which were astern of the cruisers were then seen to turn and fire torpedoes and our battle fleet turned away to avoid them.

Exactly what followed is still obscure, but H.M.A.S. Stuart (Captain H. M. L. Waller, D.S.O., R.A.N.) and H.M.S. Havock (Lieutenant

H.M.S. GREYHOUND (Commander W. R. Marshall-A'Deane) was the destroyer which turned her searchlights on the enemy cruisers as they crossed the bows of our battle fleet from starboard to port. Greyhound was completed in 1936, has a displacement of 1,335 tons, and is armed with four 4·7-inch guns and eight 21-inch torpedo tubes.   *Photo, Wright & Logan*

Victors of Cape Matapan

Outstanding Features of a Cruiser and an Aircraft Carrier which shared the Glory of Admiral Cunningham's Great Victory of March 28, 1941.

Specially drawn by Howarth for THE WAR ILLUSTRATED

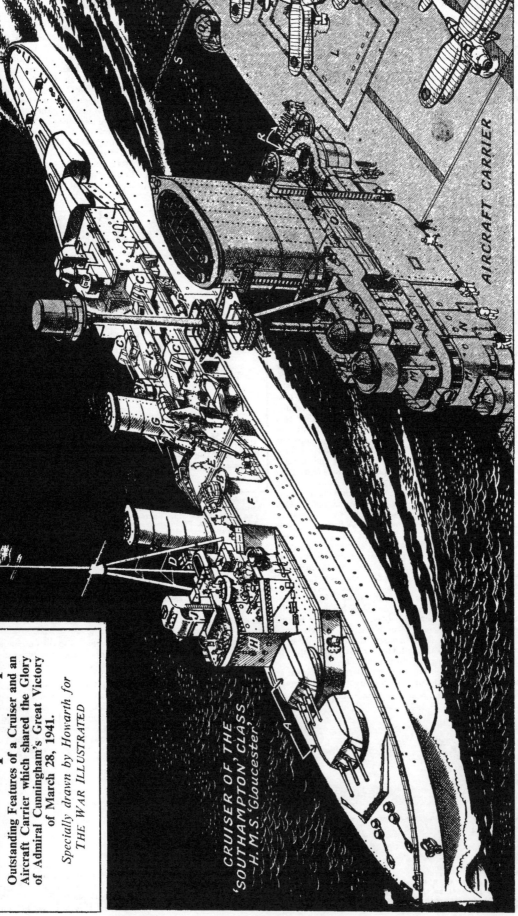

CRUISER OF THE 'SOUTHAMPTON' CLASS.—H.M.S. 'Gloucester.'

AIRCRAFT CARRIER

CRUISERS AND FLEET AIR ARM were largely responsible for the victory off Cape Matapan.

Seen in this drawing is a cruiser of the Southampton class, one of which, H.M.S. Gloucester, was operating under the flag of Vice-Admiral H. D. Pridham-Wippell when the Italians were intercepted. She displaces 9,400 tons, has an overall length of 591½ feet, and turbines of 82,500 s.h.p. give her a speed of nearly 33 knots. The twelve new pattern 6-inch guns (A) can be elevated to 60 degrees (the centre gun in each turret is set slightly back to allow for ease of working). Against aircraft the multiple pom-poms (B) and twin batteries of high-

angle 4-inch guns (C) are deadly. Two sets of triple 21-inch torpedo tubes (D) are also included in the armament. An aircraft catapult (E) is permanently fixed athwart the vessel, and three aircraft are housed in the hangars (F) either side the funnel. Two cranes, in stowed position, for lifting the aircraft back on to the ship, are seen at (G). The navigating and directing of the ship is all carried out in the large armoured superstructure (H) on top of which is fitted the revolving tower (J) which directs the fire of the 6-inch guns. Amidships at (K) can be seen the ship's motor-boats. Accommodation for the crew of 700 in these ships is well planned.

In the foreground of the drawing is shown the superstructure and part of the 100-feet-wide deck of a modern aircraft carrier. This is a very similar vessel to H.M.S. Formidable.

The Albacore torpedo-bombers (6 squadrons of varied types of aircraft are carried) have been brought up from the hangars below by means of the large lift (L) and are now closely packed in echelon on the after part of the flight deck, waiting to follow the leading plane into the air.

The navigating of the ship is carried out at (M) and inside the superstructure (N) are the chartroom and

meteorological office from which pilots and observers obtain data for their flights. The bridge (O) can be slung out over the flight deck, giving better control over the aircraft during certain operations. Twin 4.5-inch A.A. guns (P), of which there are usually 16. (Q) shows the fire-directing tower for these guns (one tower for each set of guns). Multiple pom-poms (R) and aerial mast (S) in lowered position.

The modern aircraft carrier displaces about 23,000 tons, and has a length of 700 feet. The 110,000 s.h.p. engines give a speed of over 30 knots. The great ship has a complement of 1,600.

'Planes and Ships in Victorious Combination

G. R. G. Watkins, R.N.) certainly did considerable execution. The destroyer attacking force which was searching for the damaged Littorio class battleship failed to locate her and it seems probable that she moved off during the action between our battle fleet and the enemy cruisers. Some of the destroyers from this attacking force subsequently made touch with the destroyers sent in by the Commander-in-Chief to mop up, and they assisted in sinking Zara and Pola.

Night. March 28-29. It appears probable that the Littorio class battleship became heavily engaged with her own forces as heavy gunfire was heard at a time and from a direction which made it impossible for any of our forces to be engaged.

March 29. A.M. Extensive air search failed to disclose any of the remaining Italian ships, who must have made their escape under cover of darkness.

Some 55 officers and 850 men from the Italian vessels which had been sunk were picked up by our forces, and by Greek destroyers which were now actively cooperating. The survivors included Captain Despini of the Pola ; Admiral Cantoni, commanding the Italian heavy cruiser squadron, is thought to have been lost in the Zara. Some hundreds more Italian survivors would have been picked up by the Allied forces had not the lifesaving operations of our ships been interrupted by dive-bombing attacks delivered by the German Air Force. These dive-bombing attacks, although ineffective, caused the abandonment of our rescue operations. One JU 88 was shot down during these attacks. One JU 88 which had attempted to interfere with our operations on the previous day had also been shot down.

When the Commander-in-Chief reluctantly decided to abandon the rescue of Italian seamen in order to avoid exposing his ships and incidentally the Italian survivors to danger from the German aircraft, he made a signal *enclair* to the Chief of the Italian Naval Staff, stating that over 350 Italian survivors were believed to be on rafts, giving their positions, and stating that a fast hospital ship would be needed to pick up such survivors as he had been unable to rescue. He received the following reply from the Commander-in-Chief of the Italian Navy : " Thank you for your communication. Hospital ship Gradisca already left Taranto yesterday evening at 17.00."

Admiral Cunningham also made a signal thanking the Greek Navy for its very prompt and valuable co-operation.

Seen from the Gloucester's Bridge

O NE *of the light cruisers composing Vice-Admiral Pridham-Wippell's squadron was H.M.S. Gloucester. She maintained contact with the fast enemy squadron through March 28, and a vivid picture of the battle was given by her Gunnery Officer, whose position 70 feet up in the cruiser's control tower gave him an unsurpassed view of the whole action.*

We had contacted about three enemy heavy cruisers shortly after 8 a.m. We turned away and they followed, lobbing salvos in the direction of our squadron while keeping out of range of our lighter armament.

After about an hour of this, during which time we were steaming south-eastwards in the direction of our own fleet, they had closed the

H.M.S. BARHAM'S 6-in. guns are here firing a salvo. The destruction of the three Italian cruisers at Matapan was achieved by the eight 15-in. guns of each of the three capital ships engaged. The Barham carries twelve 6-in. guns.
Photo, Sport & General

range to about 23,000 yards—13 miles—which gave us some chance. We let go several salvos which were falling pretty close when the Italian cruisers suddenly turned off.

That was the signal for us to turn again, and we kept them in sight until shortly before 11 a.m., when there was a series of terrific explosions which many of us thought at first were salvos of bombs.

I swept the horizon with my director, and there, far on our starboard bow, was this Italian warship. It took my breath away.

There she was, just in her ordinary battleship grey, without a scrap of camouflage, about three-quarters on to us, so that her fighting tower and two funnels made a solid mass of upperworks. She was at an angle which enabled all her guns to bear on our squadron. From time to time she was hidden in gigantic puffs of smoke and flashes, and her 15-in. "bricks" began to sing all round.

We turned off so that we brought her on our port quarter, and the squadron was ordered to put out a smoke screen. Unfortunately for us we were the windward ship, with the result that our smoke covered the others but left the poor old fighting Gloucester outside it.

The battleship at once shifted her range and began to pump shells at us in earnest. Splinters from some of her 15-in. shells actually fell aboard us, but they did not even scratch the paint-work.

We were going all out while she was keeping course which would enable her after-guns to bear on us still. After half an hour of this, during which time some of her salvos fell within 50 yards of us, we were very relieved to find the range was opening.

By this time the battleship was hull below the horizon, but even so you could still see her bow wave.

Then I saw some of our torpedo-machines circling round her.

Towards dusk we sighted the Italians. As the light failed it was impossible to maintain sight of their ships, but I clearly saw through my glasses our own aircraft silhouetted like blobs against the remaining bit of light in the west.

Then " Brocks' Benefit " started from all the Italian ships. I have never seen anything like the barrage those pilots of ours were going through.

Our fellows must have torpedoed the battleship then, because we heard a number of distant explosions under water.

Formidable's 'Planes in Action

B RITAIN'S *new aircraft carrier the Formidable played a vital part in bringing the Italian fleet to action. Indeed, the battle was the first occasion in history in which skilful coordination of naval operations with attacks launched by aircraft have resulted in the enemy's speeds being so reduced that the Fleet's main units were able to force action upon a reluctant combatant.*

Arrived back in Alexandria, Rear-Admiral Denis Boyd, who flies his flag in the Formidable, and her commander, Captain La Touche Bissett, told in an interview of their great ship's part in the battle. Formation attacks by Formidable's aircraft were carried out at 11.45 a.m., 2.30 p.m., and dusk (March 28).

Captain Bissett. We are certain of three hits on the battleship. One in a morning attack and two during the afternoon attack.

I think our first attack was of great assistance to our cruiser force. When we launched it our cruisers were being fired on heavily at long range by the Italian battleship. As our machines came down to launch their torpedoes the battleship turned right round to avoid them and at once abandoned firing on the cruisers.

We claim one hit in that attack, after which the Italian battleship started away at 25 knots in a westerly direction. One Junkers 88, which came to attack us, was shot down.

In that first attack the Italian squadron was about 100 miles west of the main Battle Fleet and some 50 miles south-west of Crete. At about 12.15 we sent off our second striking force.

Soon after doing that and rejoining the fleet, we were attacked by two torpedo-carrying aircraft ourselves, but avoided them easily. They must have been Italians.

Our second striking force remained in the vicinity of the fleet until 2 p.m., when we sent them off to attack the Italians, which they did half an hour later. They were able to come down low before being seen by one of the battleship's escorting destroyers.

Behind the first group of our machines were two others and above them two of our fighters.

These fighters immediately dived on the destroyer, which was firing, and " shot her up " so that she turned away.

Meanwhile the first lot of our machines manoeuvred into the sun, somewhat ahead of the Italian squadron

CAPTAIN H. A. ROWLEY, in command of H.M.S. Gloucester at Matapan, is here seen as a lieutenant after the last war.
Photo, Topical

and dived to launch their torpedoes at the same moment as the battleship began turning away with the intention of avoiding them. They scored at least one hit.

In turning, however, the battleship exposed her flanks, unprotected by her covering craft, to our other two machines which were following behind.

These found themselves in perfect position for attack and loosed off their torpedoes. At least one of these was seen to hit, but in turning away machines may have missed seeing others that hit.

How the Navies Grappled in the Dark

After the attack the Italian battleship was seen to be considerably slowed down.

Admiral Boyd. One of the most outstanding points of the observers' reports lay in the battleship's erratic speed. She kept slowing down, then going ahead, her speed varying between 12 and 14 knots.

I want to emphasize the amazing courage of our pilots. They must have pressed home their attacks fiercely, especially in view of the fact that it was broad

REAR-AD. D. BOYD, appointed to command aircraft-carrier squadron March 22, 1941. He flew his flag in Formidable.
Photo, Associated Press

daylight and the ship was awake to the menace of them.

Captain Bissett. Furthermore, these were the men who had been out in the early morning search which had located the Italian squadron.

At 2 p.m. we had no contact with the enemy, so we at once sent up two machines to maintain contact. These reconnaissance machines remained with the enemy until after dusk. One crew spent five and three-quarter hours in the air that afternoon alone.

At 4.15 in the afternoon we received the report from these observers that the Italian battleship was slowed down to a speed of about eight knots.

As soon as possible we assembled the third striking force, which went off and kept the enemy fleet in sight until the light began to fail.

Then, as they started their attack in formation, they were met by such a terrific barrage from the enemy ships that temporarily they turned back.

CAPT. A. BISSETT, who at Matapan was in command of the Formidable, flagship of the aircraft-carrier squadron.
Photo, Vandyk

I believe that the Italian barrage with the tracer shells showing red, presented a firework-like display which flabbergasted the officers in our cruiser Orion watching it.

It spurted out in all directions. This was because our machines, after turning away, split up and made a number of individual attacks from all quarters.

It is well known now, of course, that one 10,000-ton cruiser, which proved to be the Pola, was hit, but in the fast failing light it was impossible to see what other results were obtained. Anyhow, all our aircraft returned safely from this attack.

Contact was maintained until after 8.30 p.m. and the Vittorio Veneto was reported to be practically stopped with her quarterdeck awash.

Although, in all, there only remained one aircraft unaccounted for as a result of a gruelling day, every man had been put to the utmost strain.

Admiral Boyd. As the Italian battleship still had four hundred miles to go before reaching Messina, I think she would have the greatest difficulty in getting there if she was so down by her stern.

However, it is possible that our reconnaissance machines mistook the stopped Pola for the Littorio class ship. It was after dark when a mistake could easily have been made, for both ships have similarities. It is about a 50-50 chance that she went down.

Now Warspite's Guns Fired

WHILE *our light cruisers had been leading the enemy on, while our aircraft were delivering their successive attacks on the Italian ships, Admiral Cunningham with the British battle fleet was drawing ever nearer to the scene of action. Night had fallen when Warspite, Valiant, Barham, and their destroyer screen, came within range. Here is the story of the battle as told by the Gunnery Officer of Warspite; from the battleship's control tower he had a grandstand view.*

Shortly after nine o'clock on Friday night—a night then moonless, with a flat calm, so that there was no horizon—the battle fleet was ordered to close on a position where an unknown vessel had been reported by the Vice-Admiral commanding our light forces.

At 10 o'clock we were approximately in position, and at 10.26 we sighted a number of

Our fleet turned to starboard, bringing our ships in line ahead on an opposite course from the enemy cruisers.

All our armament was brought to the ready and a few seconds later one of our destroyers, the Greyhound, switched her searchlights on to the third ship. We recognized her as one of the 8-in. gunned, 10,000-ton Italian cruisers of the Zara class. She proved subsequently to be the Fiume.

The Warspite's 15-in. guns opened fire from the closest range. Our whole broadside appeared to strike the Fiume with devastating effect.

From the foremost funnel to her after-gun turret the Fiume burst into a mass of red flames. One observer reported that the after-turret was blown clean over the side, while another described the effect of our broadside as making the vessel look like a "factory lit up by night."

H.M.S. WARSPITE, Admiral Sir Andrew Cunningham's flagship at the Battle of Cape Matapan, fired the first salvos from the 15-in. guns (seen above) at only 4,000 yards range. Inset, Captain D. B. Fisher, C.B.E., R.N., who was in command of H.M.S. Warspite. *Photos, Central Press, Topical*

darkened ships fine on our starboard bow. They appeared to be three cruisers and two or four destroyers.

Almost simultaneously we were challenged by another ship on our port beam. This proved to be the Pola, crippled by the Fleet Air Arm attacks during the day.

An aircraft of the Fleet Air Arm, which played such an important part in the victory of Cape Matapan, is here seen taking off from the deck of an aircraft carrier in the Mediterranean.
Photo, Central Press

After the second broadside, which caused another gigantic outburst of fire and left the Fiume hopelessly crippled, we swung our turrets on the Zara, the next ship in the Italian line.

Our first broadside on her produced another of these incredible effects. For part of this time our other battleships were also firing into the Italian line, and the destruction of the Pola was completed in the general crash of broadsides from all our ships.

The third cruiser was a 6-in.-gun cruiser of the Bande Nere class, but in the darkness and mêlée we do not yet know what her exact fate was. She must, however, have suffered heavy damage. I think these three cruisers had been hurrying to the aid of the damaged Pola.

While the battle fleet was in action our searchlights picked up two enemy destroyers, which were ideally placed for torpedo attack on us. We think they carried it out, for observers reported seeing torpedo tracks in the darkness. In any case we at once turned and avoided them.

We immediately engaged the destroyers, which hid behind a smoke screen through which we continued to pound them with our main and secondary armament.

At the same time the C.-in-C. ordered our destroyers to come in and finish off the two burning cruisers with torpedoes—which they did.

Vivid Pen-Pictures of the Great Battle

Valiant's Withering Fire

NEARLY 40 tons of high explosive shells were poured by H.M.S. Valiant's big guns into the Italian cruisers, Fiume and Zara ; at least 75 per cent of her shells scored direct hits.

Captain Morgan said that the Fiume seemed just to burst out amidships only four minutes and six seconds after the first shot had been fired. "It was the

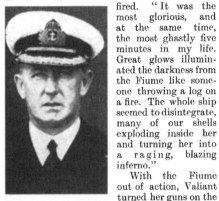

most glorious, and at the same time, the most ghastly five minutes in my life. Great glows illuminated the darkness from the Fiume like someone throwing a log on a fire. The whole ship seemed to disintegrate, many of our shells exploding inside her and turning her into a raging, blazing inferno."

With the Fiume out of action, Valiant turned her guns on the Zara, and again there was a tremendous, reddish glow as the Italian cruiser burst into flames and seemed

CAPT. C. E. MORGAN, of H.M.S. Valiant, is a descendant of Sir Henry Morgan, famous buccaneer.
Photo, Wide World

about to break in two. Said Captain Morgan :

"There was no replying fire from either the Fiume or Zara. We fired some star shells to help light up the targets, and the cruisers apparently thought they were flares from aircraft, for they let go some of their guns in the direction of the falling star shells."

As Our Bombers Saw It

SQUADRONS from the R.A.F. Middle East Command played an important part in the battle. Some of their bombs scored direct hits and crippled one cruiser, probably another, and hit a destroyer, while sea reconnaissance aircraft located the enemy's forces and shadowed them. All the R.A.F. aircraft taking part in the action returned undamaged. The following account was given by R.A.F. Headquarters in Cairo.

R.A.F. bomber pilots were setting off on normal raids on military objectives in Tripolitania when they received news that a large part of the Italian Navy was at sea.

The squadron leader who led one of the attacks said, "The weather was very hazy over the sea, but we soon found the Italian navy in two groups, steaming like billy-ho for home. They began to zigzag as soon as they saw us and their anti-aircraft guns opened up. We made a dive attack and fairly plastered them. Pilots in my squadron registered hits on one big ship, and we think other vessels must have been damaged or delayed by near misses."

A sergeant-pilot who secured two direct hits with heavy-calibre bombs on a very big ship said, "Though they changed formation and zigzagged quite a lot, we spent some time taking aim and made a low-level attack. I saw two of my biggest bombs hit the largest ship amidships. Clouds of black and yellow smoke issued from her for a long time and then she stopped."

It is no secret that to hit a warship travelling at high speed is one of the most difficult bombing feats there is. The sergeant-pilot said, "It was a hefty but agreeable surprise when I saw those bombs hit the ship in just the places aimed for, right amidships. First there was the normal white smoke of the bomb bursting, and then columns of black and yellow smoke shot into the air to about 200 ft. For 15 minutes after we made off the rear gunner had a good view of the ship and gave us a running commentary. It had stopped, and he thought that it had begun to list before he lost sight of it."

Another formation, led by a D.F.C. flight lieutenant, discovered an enemy battleship, escorted by three cruisers and its destroyers, fleeing for home. The flight lieutenant said, "The enemy fleet appeared to be in great confusion, zigzagging violently, and now and again one ship would get in another's way. We bombed and added to the confusion, but though we saw no hits there were plenty of near misses, and when we left the enemy was busy laying a smoke-screen."

How The Italians Described It

THE official communiqué issued in Rome on April 2 ran as follows :

For some time past the growing intensification of the enemy traffic between Egyptian and Greek ports has been remarked. Against this traffic our destroyers and aircraft had often taken action, inflicting losses which were announced in bulletins. Nevertheless, it was necessary to attempt a bigger offensive action in order to force the enemy to adopt stronger method of protection so as to avoid losses. The offensive began on the night of March 25-26 with a brilliant action by shock units which penetrated into Suda Bay. The next night, after an extensive air reconnaissance, eight Italian cruisers, escorted by destroyers, left their bases supported by a battleship.

ADML.A. RICCARDI, the Italian commander, who flew his flag in the battleship Vittorio Veneto.
Photo, E.N.A.

On the morning of March 28 this force reached a position south of Crete, and opened fire on a detachment of enemy cruisers, which at once evaded contact. While our ships were returning, sweeping the sea, our aircraft made torpedo attacks and succeeded in hitting two cruisers and an aircraft-carrier, as well as several merchant ships. In the afternoon of March 28 the enemy aircraft also made torpedo attacks, and towards evening hit a cruiser, which was obliged to slow down by the damage received.

A detachment which included one cruiser, while acting as a screen some distance from the main body, encountered in the night enemy forces which included, according to British statements, several battleships. A violent battle ensued. Our ships at once opened fire and made a destroyer attack which, according to enemy accounts, was pressed home to short range from the enemy ships. Many torpedoes were fired.

Our losses were three cruisers and two destroyers. Next day squadrons of our Air Force on offensive reconnaissance hit another cruiser with torpedoes and an aircraft-carrier with bombs. "The Daily Telegraph," Reuter, etc.

H.M.S. AJAX, one of the immortal trio which chased the Admiral Graf Spee into the humiliating refuge of Montevideo harbour, again won distinction at the Battle of Cape Matapan when, under the command of Capt. E. D. B. McCarthy, she formed part of Vice-Adml. Pridham-Wippell's squadron. She is a light cruiser of 6,958 tons, completed in 1935.
Photo. Wright & Logan

As in the Last War So in This Greeks and Yugos:

YUGOSLAVIA AND GREECE were invaded by Hitler's armies early on the morning of Sunday, April 6, 1941. For some six months Greece had been counted amongst our Allies, and now the British Government hastened to range the British Empire upon the side of the Southern Slavs. " We welcome them as a resolute and powerful Ally. We renew the comradeship which in the Great War carried us through tribulation to victory. We will conduct the war in common, and we will make peace only when right has been vindicated and law and order are again enthroned.''

Are Our Comrades-in-Arms in the Fight for Freedom

Here in these pages we have photographs of our Balkan allies. In the upper photograph in the opposite page detachments of Yugoslav infantry are seen on parade; while beneath, some of King Peter's men are manhandling a gun into position. Then in this page one photograph shows a cheerful group of Greek soldiers proudly displaying Italian machine-guns and ammunition that they have captured in Albania, while in the other a little group of British gunners are giving a demonstration of the working of an A.A. gun to a deeply-interested audience of Greek soldiers.

Now It Was the Germans Who Took Benghazi

Occupied by the Imperial troops on February 7, Benghazi, capital of the Italian province of Cyrenaica, has been evacuated in face of a thrust by a strong German-Italian force. The news, announced on April 4, came as a surprise; but when the Germans invaded Yugoslavia and Greece two days later it was clear that the advance in Libya was closely connected with the new Balkan campaign.

FOR some weeks after the Australians entered Benghazi in triumph there was little to report from the front in Libya. A great Italian army had been completely annihilated, and the most fertile region of Italy's North African empire had been completely overrun. General Maitland Wilson continued his advance as far as El Agheila, some 100 miles to the south, but there, on the edge of the great Sirte Desert, the Imperial troops were halted. Beyond lay

The coast of North Africa from Tripoli to Derna, which Rome claimed on April 8 was retaken by Axis forces. The long line of their communications runs close to the sea.

hundreds of miles of wilderness, and General Wavell decided that an advance across this inhospitable waste was not required by his strategic plan. So Libya passed out of the news.

But towards the end of March it began to be mentioned once again in the communiqués. First there came a report from Berlin that a "German African Corps" had occupied El Agheila, and this was confirmed on March 26 by Cairo. A small enemy detachment, it was revealed, had occupied El Agheila from which our standing patrols had previously been withdrawn. The enemy force was stated to consist of mechanized units of Italians and Germans, whose vanguard was composed of tanks supported by infantry and dive-bombing aircraft. Apparently the Germans had been landed at Tripoli, or at points in the Gulf of Sirte, where they had been joined to the four Italian divisions left to General Italo Gariboldi, Graziani's successor in North Africa. Gariboldi was believed to be in supreme command; but the German African Corps, said to be composed of four divisions of crack troops, was under General Rommel.

Even as early as March 23 the R.A.F. had bombed shipping at Sirte—amongst their targets were the transports which had brought over the Germans from Sicily—and from the night of March 24 Tripoli was bombed night after night. On the night of April 1 the R.A.F. delivered a heavy attack on enemy motor transport at Ras Lanuf in Tripolitania, many of the vehicles being destroyed. On the following night a heavy attack was made on convoys in the Mersa Brega area. Contact was established by the British forces with the enemy infantry and mechanized units in this area on April 1, and on the next day operations continued as our advance elements withdrew before very heavy enemy pressure. Then on April 3 it was officially announced in Cairo that Benghazi itself had been evacuated by the British.

"In the face of a determined advance by strong Italo-German forces," read the communiqué issued in the early hours of the next morning, "and in pursuance of the policy so successfully adopted at Sidi Barrani of waiting to choose our own battlefield, our light covering detachments have been withdrawn to selected concentrated areas. In the course of this withdrawal the town of Benghazi has been evacuated after all captured military stores and equipment had been destroyed. Benghazi is indefensible from the military point of view, and it has not been used by us as a port. As in the autumn of 1940, the enemy is evidently seeking a propaganda success at the expense of stretching still farther an already extended line of communication. In their withdrawal our troops have already inflicted on the enemy considerable casualties in personnel and in tanks."

The fall of Benghazi was a nasty pill for the British public to swallow, but as Lord Moyne made clear in the House of Lords on April 9, it was the direct consequence of the new Balkan campaign. Many of the armoured units which conquered the Italians had been withdrawn from Libya when operations there came to an end, and so the Germans were able to make their swift stroke at a moment when we were not in full strength. But after their 600 miles advance from their bases at Tripoli and Benghazi they were now probably right at the end of their reach and facing growing difficulties of fuel, water, and the supply of munitions, without the sea power which enabled our spectacular advance to get over those difficulties. "Our tanks and reinforcements are now returning, and by means of our sea power they have re-established themselves in force in the strong fortifications of Tobruk."

First support by the Nazis for the Italians in the Western Desert came from the air. On February 16, 1941, Benghazi was attacked by the Luftwaffe eight days after it had fallen into British hands, and further attacks followed during the British occupation, but Australian fighter aircraft soon proved their superiority over the Germans. Right, is a Nazi machine ready to take off in the desert; and above is another completely burnt out in front of a wrecked hangar at Benghazi.

Photos, British Official: Crown Copyright; and Wide World.

Hitler's Troops Arrive to Fight in Africa

The Nazi forces operating in North Africa consist largely of mechanized units brought from Italy to Tripoli. Left are some of the men in tropical kit and pith helmets drawn up for inspection soon after their arrival.

Other Nazi troops have "volunteered" to stiffen the Duce's troops in East Africa. Below, a flag symbolizing the complete unity of the Axis Powers is being presented to volunteers on their arrival. On one side it has the Nazi symbol and on the other the Fascist standard.

Photos, Planet News and Keystone

The forward striking force of the Nazis in North Africa consists of tanks supported by infantry and aircraft. Above is a Nazi armoured car in the Libyan desert. Many of them were used in the enemy advance from El Agheila to beyond Benghazi.

The Italian Army in North Africa, broken by the Army of the Nile, had its last humiliation thrust upon it when it witnessed the march of Hitler's men through the streets of Tripoli, seen right. All the photographs in this page were radioed from Berlin to New York and thence to London.

Photos, Associated Press and Keystone

South Africans Won the Race to Addis Ababa

With dramatic suddenness, Addis Ababa, Haile Selassie's former capital and since 1936 the capital of the Italian Empire in East Africa, capitulated to the British on April 5. The story of its fall is given below, together with some account of other successes won by our armies in that tropical war zone.

ADDIS ABABA has fallen! The world heard the news in a communiqué issued from Cairo, but long before it appeared on the tape it was spread by word of mouth through all the towns and villages of Abyssinia. Again the Emperor's war drums throbbed, but now they sounded in triumph.

It was the South Africans who won the race to the capital—those South Africans who, following their triumphs on the Juba and at Mogadishu, swept over the border from Italian Somaliland into Abyssinia on March 7. Exactly four weeks passed; and in those four weeks they covered 700 miles of most difficult country in face of an enemy resistance which, though altogether ineffective, was by no means negligible. The Italians' last stand was at the Awash gorge, 90 miles from Addis Ababa, where they had destroyed the great steel bridge that hung dizzily above the canyon, 200 feet deep. But the South Africans got across the gorge and stormed the Italian positions, though they were strongly defended by artillery and machine-guns. That last 90 miles was covered in two days, and the South Africans never stopped, but hour by hour drew nearer the doomed city, driving the Italians helter-skelter before them.

Some days before the end British 'planes dropped messages on the city, pointing out the hopelessness of the Italian position and demanding their surrender; and as a result an envoy from the Viceroy of Italian East Africa, the Duke of Aosta, flew to our lines on April 3, when conditions were presented to him to ensure the safety of the civil population of Addis Ababa in the event of fighting round the city. The Italians hummed and hawed, obviously to gain time for the evacuation of the garrison; and so General Cunningham sent the South African Air Force once more over Addis Ababa. In a few minutes the approaches to the city, transport columns and parks, aeroplane hangars, barracks and gun emplacements were smashed by bombs and swept by machine-gun fire. The argument was a convincing one, and no further resistance was encountered.

At two o'clock on the afternoon of April 5 the South African armoured cars reported their position 20 miles east of Addis Ababa. They pushed on through misty rain and quagmires of red mud until that same evening they swept into the city and marched triumphantly into the main square. The Duke of Aosta, General Nasi, Chief of the General Staff, and General de Simons, Commander of the Eastern Sector, had already left the city, retreating northwards with the great majority of their forces. Only armed police had been left in charge of the city, and they were hard put to it to ensure the safety of the 38,000 Italian women and children who had been left behind, since the native tribesmen rioted as soon as they had seen the Italian garrison march away. But with the entry of the British forces order was quickly restored in accordance with the promise which

Cunningham by the Italian envoy before the entry of the British troops into Addis Ababa. "His Royal Highness the Duke of Aosta," he said, "wishes to express his appreciation of the initiative taken by General Wavell and General Cunningham regarding the protection of women and children in Addis Ababa, demonstrating the strong bonds of humanity and race still existing between the nations."

At 10.45 on the morning of Sunday, April 6, the Italian flag was hauled down and the Union Jack hoisted on what had been the Viceroy's official residence and not long before the palace of Emperor Haile Selassie.

Meanwhile, in the north General Platt's army, having stormed Keren on March 27, swept along the road to Asmara, which surrendered without a fight on April 1, 5,000 prisoners being taken. Then the march was continued to the gates of Massawa, the port on the Red Sea, which hoisted the white flag on April 8. Adowa, 100 miles south of Asmara, had been captured two days before.

In Western Abyssinia the Imperial troops and their Patriot allies were also making good progress. General Martini was in danger of being surrounded at Gondar; Debra Markos was reported to be in our hands on April 7.

The fall of Addis Ababa occurred on April 6, 1941. Above are some of the Ethiopian Patriots who took part in the march on their former capital. Right, the Duke of Aosta, C.-in-C. in Italian East Africa, who was in supreme command of the forces defending the town. The map shows the rapid advance of British and Imperial Forces through Italian territory in East Africa.
Photos, British Official: Crown Copyright; and Keystone. Map, Courtesy of the "Daily Telegraph"

General Cunningham had given the Italian envoy some hours before.

This gesture on the General's part was received in the proper spirit by the Duke of Aosta, as is seen by the message which was given verbally to General

Two African Capitals Lost by the Italians

ADDIS ABABA, capital of Abyssinia and of the Italian Empire in East Africa, was formally surrendered to the British on April 6, 1941. During the five years of Italian occupation the airfield seen in the top photograph had been constructed, while the centre of the town itself had been entirely Italianized. In the lower photograph is the main street during the occupation, with Italian pedestrians, Italian motor-cars, Italian shops and Italian methods of traffic control, while not one of the native inhabitants whose city it was, is to be seen.

ASMARA, the capital of Eritrea, fell to General Platt's army on April 1, 1941, thus opening up the road to Massawa. Above, left, is a street scene in the town with natives in the flowing white robes that are their usual wear. The normal population of Asmara is 85,000, and trades mainly in agricultural produce. Right, is the market-place, where the crops from the surrounding country are handled. There are a number of good modern buildings in Asmara, while its amenities include a wireless station.

Photos, Sport & General and Wide World

Not All the 'Vives' Are for the Nazis!

General Weygand is here taking the salute at a parade of North African Légionnaires at Algiers. With him, left, is Admiral Abrial, Gov.-General of Algeria.   *Photo, Wide World*

All over Occupied France the Nazis have given very convincing evidence of their domination. Below is a traffic centre near Dunkirk with German traffic signs.   *Photo, E.N.A.*

In a small hotel across the Channel Goebbels has housed journalists and others of his minions to report the invasion of Britain. All they have to do so far is to wait.   *Photo, E.N.A.*

SINCE Paris was occupied by the Germans, anti-Nazi feeling has been steadily rising. In shops and cafés Nazis are treated with cold disdain, while the poster propaganda of Goebbels is countered by such announcements as that below, a small "sticky-back" that has appeared all over Paris. It reads : "Long live De Gaulle ! Long live England ! For them there is but one aim : to beat Germany, a nation that preys upon others, that has lived and lives only by robbery, rapine, pillage and murder. Then the whole world will breathe again."

VIVE DE GAULLE
VIVE L'ANGLETERRE

Avec eux un seul but abattre l'Allemagne, nation de proie qui n'a vécu et ne vit que de vols, de rapines, de pillages et d'assassinats.

Alors le monde entier respirera.

Below, General Studt, head of the German control of French war industries, is leaving the French War Ministry at Vichy after seeing General Huntziger.   *Photo, Associated Press*

Australia Joins the Imperial Guard at Singapore

POWERFUL REINFORCEMENTS of Australian troops arrived at Singapore on February 18, 1941, when the crisis in the Far East became once more acute (see page 236). Here some of them are on board a transport before disembarkation. The troops numbered some thousands trained as shock troops and having the latest mechanical equipment. Major-General H. Gordon Bennett, the Australian G.O.C., stated in a broadcast from Singapore that these soldiers were even better equipped than the first members of the A.I.F. who went to the Middle East. *Photo, Associated Press*

OUR SEARCHLIGHT ON THE WAR

B.B.C. Organ Burnt Out

ON April 4 it was revealed that the famous B.B.C. theatre organ had been destroyed when St George's Hall was set on fire during a night raid on London.

ST. GEORGE'S HALL, so long associated with the magic names of Maskelyne and Devant before becoming a studio of the B.B.C., was completely gutted after a recent air raid on London. Above, looking towards the stage that was. *Photo, P.N.A.*

Although not the largest organ in the world it had the most complicated and luxurious equipment. There were 260 stops connected to four rooms at the sides of the Hall. In these were from 2,000 to 3,000 pipes, a grand piano, apparatus for producing a great number of "effects," and a pipeless instrument, the electrone, which was responsible for the carillon. Recitals by Reginald Foort and later by Sandy Macpherson became very popular with many wireless listeners.

Fellowship of the Bellows

FOUNDED in Argentina in October, 1940, to raise money for the purchase of aircraft for the R.A.F., the "Fellowship of the Bellows" now boasts 25,000 members in that country and 5,000 in Uruguay. Already it has raised the cost of its first "Whirlwind" fighter. The organizing committee, known as the Servants of the Bellows, comprise High Wind (President), Whirlwind (Secretary), Receiver of Windfalls (Treasurer), Keeper of the Windbag (Assistant Treasurer) and Bearer of the Bellows (Master of Ritual). The Committee's stratagem of holding out promotion in the hierarchy of fellowship as a reward for an unbroken sequence of contributions is extremely ingenious. A member pays one cent for every enemy aeroplane brought down since he became a Fellow. When 1,000 aeroplanes have been destroyed and he has paid 10 pesos he becomes a "Puff." He is promoted to be a "Gust" when he has paid 25 pesos (2,500 aeroplanes), and a "Hurricane" when his subscription reaches 50 pesos, the equivalent of 5,000 enemy aircraft. When 10,000 'planes have been destroyed, and he has not missed paying one single cent of 100 pesos, he will be invested with the Order of the Bellows. The scheme has so amused Latin America that other countries are taking it up, and the United States are launching their own branch of the Fellowship.

New Ambassador

MR. WELLINGTON KOO—Ku Wei-Chun in his own country—is succeeding Dr. Quo Tai-Chi at the Chinese Embassy. He is not unknown to London, for after serving as China's plenipotentiary at the Peace Conference of 1919 he was Minister to Great Britain from 1920 to 1922, when he returned to China to become Foreign Minister and later Prime Minister. He has since been Ambassador to the United States and then from 1932 Ambassador to France, and it was from Paris that he came to London in 1939 to give the annual Richard Cobden lecture. At Geneva and The Hague Dr. Koo was a prominent figure, being Chinese representative on the Council of the League of Nations and also at the International Court of Arbitration from 1927. Dr. Quo, who has been in London for nearly nine years, leaves to take up his appointment as Foreign Minister in the administration of General Chiang Kai-Shek.

Death Before Betrayal

COUNT PAUL TELEKI, Hungarian Prime Minister, was found dead in his bed on April 3. He had shot himself at the moment when Hitler was demanding the passage of German troops through Hungary, because, according to a letter left behind, he did not feel able to carry on his "difficult and unhappy task." Count Teleki was an authority on every branch of geography, physical, political and economic, and spent many years in geographical research, the results of which were published in a number of erudite volumes, more particularly his famous "Cartography of the Japanese Islands." During the Great War he served on the Italian and Balkan fronts. Later he became Foreign Minister in the anti-Communist Government which overthrew Bela Kun, and after the Peace Treaty he was appointed Prime Minister. But he became weary of politics and in 1921 returned for many years to his geographical researches and lectures at the University. In February 1939 he succeeded Dr. Bela Imredy as Premier, and after war broke out, and the Germans overran Europe, he became more and more entangled in the web of Axis intrigue, although his own personal sympathies were said to be with the British. The new Hungarian Prime Minister is M. Laszlo de Bardossy, who succeeded Count Csaky as Foreign Minister on the latter's death in January, 1941.

Britain's War Bill

THE national accounts for the year April 1, 1940 to March 31, 1941, although showing a substantial surplus in ordinary revenue, bear little relation to the actual expenditure on the war effort. This increased so gigantically in the course of the year that at the end of March the total expenditure for the twelve months was £3,867,000,000 and the daily cost had reached an average of well over 14½ million pounds. The following table shows the course of this expenditure as it expanded month after month.

Period	Total as it increased £	Daily in the period £
April 1 to April 27	186,300,000	6,900,000
„ „ May 25	369,400,000	6,540,000
„ „ June 30	715,100,000	9,600,000
„ „ Oct. 26	1,942,600,000	10,400,000
„ „ Nov. 30	2,736,400,000	12,400,000
„ „ Dec. 31	2,774,200,000	12,800,000
„ „ Jan. 25	3,095,200,000	12,800,000
„ „ Feb. 22	3,424,100,000	11,740,000
„ „ Mar. 22	3,813,800,000	14,700,000

Restaurants for Bombed Areas

MANY have been the criticisms of the name "Community Feeding Centre" for the attractive eating-houses that are springing up all over the country to provide cheap and good meals in bombed areas. So they are to be renamed "British Restaurants." Towns which have them total over 100, and in the London area there are 147. Stocks of food placed at the disposal of the local authorities are of considerable magnitude. There are 2,000,000 cans of Ministry of Food soup, with eight portions to each can; 1,800 tons of biscuits; 2,500,000 cans of baked beans; 750 tons of canned beef, hash and meat roll; and 750,000 cans of unsweetened condensed milk for children.

HUNGARY'S NEW PREMIER, M. Laszlo de Bardossy (left) succeeds Count Teleki (right), who committed suicide on April 3, his health undermined by constant Nazi demands. M. de Bardossy, formerly Hungary's Foreign Minister, is a pro-Nazi and was Counsellor of the Hungarian Legation in London, 1930-34. *Wide World, Keystone*

Cartoon Commentary on the War

MATAPAN, KEREN . . .

Strube in the "Daily Express"

FRIENDSHIP CAN GO NO FURTHER!

Zec in the "Daily Mirror"

THE VOICE OF THE PEOPLE

Clive Upton in the "Daily Sketch"

LEND A HAND, FRIEND!
Sir Kingsley Wood introduces his " 10/- in £ " Budget
Zec in the "Daily Mirror"

TOURIST MATSUOKA: "WHAT DID THAT, HERMANN?"
HERMANN: "MICE!"
(Acknowledgements to Bruce Bairnsfather)   *Strube in the "Daily Express"*

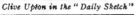

I Was There! .... Eye Witness Stories of the War

We Learned a Lot on Our Iceland Trip

The crew of a Sunderland flying-boat of the Coastal Command which had to make a forced landing in Iceland declared that "we learned a lot that trip." Here is the story of how they surmounted difficulties in taking-off, refuelling, and de-icing their aircraft.

BAD weather forced the pilot to seek refuge in Iceland. He had encountered severe snow-storms and clouds of grey lava-dust from the Icelandic mountains which stuck to the windows. It was getting dark when he decided to land in a fairly sheltered fjord, but there was a strong tide running and he could not accurately gauge the depth of water. The aircraft landed safely, but grounded on a shoal before finishing its run. It struck the shoal at about 60 miles an hour, but, thanks to the strength of its construction, it suffered no damage.

Fishermen from a whaling station rowed out to the stranded flying-boat and greeted the crew with their best and only English phrase—" Velcome to Eeceland." Fortunately, an Icelander who had been in the

The second pilot said : " We had to use petrol tins out of an old barge. We formed a human chain and sent them up by hand. It was bitterly cold and sometimes chips of ice would fall into the tanks. There was water in the bottom of the barge and it looked as if some of the tins were leaking. We were afraid we might have trouble—and we did. When we started up next day, the engines ran for a little while, and then stopped. There was nothing for it but to empty and clean out the entire petrol system.

" Our wing commander, who was with us, had helped in the refuelling, and now he got busy with the rest of us in taking out the big tanks. He spent hours on the wings with screw-drivers and other tools covered with grease and dirt. It took four days to complete the clean-out, and then we refuelled with

FERRYING PETROL, a few cans at a time, in their rubber dinghy from an old barge to their aircraft, was one of the trials of the crew of a Sunderland flying-boat which made the forced landing described in this page.
Photo, British Official : Crown Copyright

A complete clean-out of the entire petrol system, a job which lasted four days, was one of the tasks of these men of the Coastal Command who made a forced landing in Iceland. Water got into the petrol they found for refuelling and caused engine trouble. Above, one of the huge tanks has been taken out for cleaning.
Photo, British Official : Crown Copyright

some petrol which we took good care to see was free from dirt or water.

" The next day off we went, only to run into a severe electrical storm with visibility nil and ice-forming conditions. Back again to Iceland. That night we had 27 degrees of frost, and the next morning the Sunderland was completely covered in a layer of snow on top of ice. We brushed off the snow and tried to chip off the ice with axes, screw-drivers, and anything handy. Then I managed to get help from a trawler with a steam hose-pipe. That melted the ice where we could not reach to chip, and the water ran down and formed icicles where we could get at them. The temperature rose that night, and the next day we flew to Scotland. We learned a lot that trip."

United States Air Force in the last war turned up and acted as interpreter. The bombs were made safe, lifted out by the crew, and taken ashore in the fishermen's dinghy.

That night the crew remained on board, and in the early hours, when the tide rose, the flying-boat went afloat. By using the port and starboard engines alternately, she yawed off the shoal into deeper water. When daylight came the pilots surveyed the take-off area. They had a run of approximately 400 yards, but at one part the fjord was little more than 50 yards wide. The span of a Sunderland is nearly 38 yards.

In the afternoon the pilot made his attempt. With the help of a strong wind and a full throttle he got the flying-boat off the water after a run of only 150 yards, and cleared the narrow part of the fjord with a few yards to spare on each side. The Sunderland went to another part of the Iceland coast to seek fuel.

I Was A Nazi Parachute Trooper

Written by Erich Weber, a former member of the " Col. Beck Force," Germany's first parachute regiment, this article gives many details of the life and training of these Nazi desperados. As a sequel to his story, Weber says that he jumped a train on its way to Switzerland and, by an extraordinary piece of luck, managed to get away.

I WAS trained to be one of Hitler's " Luftschützertruppen." I thought it was a great stroke of luck when I was drafted to the Col. Beck Greenshirts—Goering's private regiment, one of the most historic in all Germany.

Like a million other youngsters I was proud to be a German ; proud to be a soldier. When we began parachute training (" Fallschirm Landen ") I was proud to risk my neck. . . .

It took three months to turn me into a good Fallschirm trooper—three months of iron

discipline, technical training, practice on the bomb-sighting machines used by Luftwaffe pilots, and 10-hour-a-day training.

They taught us parachute-dropping by easy stages—beginning with the technical stuff and routine work of folding the silk (not so easy, when you consider that a Fallschirm consists of at least 850 square feet of silk) and ending with the real thing.

Between those extreme stages it is easy to break a few bones. We had to do special parachute exercises—climbing up a steel stairway and jumping through a spring-loaded door ten feet high. The spring gives the same effect as the great rush of air in actual flying, and you must learn how to poise yourself for the jump so that the parachute harness doesn't get caught.

So that we should be able to allow for drift, and pull the strings of our parachutes to guide them in falling, we were sent, often late at night, to practise on the bomb-sighting machines used for training Luftwaffe pilots.

You sit on a balcony, peering down at the moving strip on which is painted a realistic picture of the earth as it appears from the cockpit of a bomber. By an ingenious system of lenses it gives the impression of being 2,000, 5,000 or 8,000 feet away, while change of lighting gives the effect of " dawn " and " twilight." You sight the apparatus and endeavour to register a " hit " on the moving canvas. The sheet is moved electrically at speeds representing 200 and 300 m.p.h. and the exact position of each hit is shown by the flash of an electric light.

Intriguing and interesting ? It might have been, but for the *Oberst*. His idea was that as most bombing raids take place at dawn or at night, practice must be done at those times. After a hard 10-hour day of marching, drilling, engineering instruction, book study and exams, we were suddenly dragged from our bunks and ordered to be on duty in six minutes.

In the Nazi 'Chamber of Horrors'

Hungry, because rations were small at Braunschweig, tired, bullied and dispirited, we assembled in what came to be nicknamed the "Chamber of Horrors."

In turn we climbed the gallery, took our seat at the bomb-sighter and tried to register direct hits as the *Oberst* or an *Unterleutnant* bawled " Zielen " (" Aim ").

Month after month of this discipline helped to break us in ; but it meant that we were often working over 14 hours a day. There were language classes, in French and Dutch, there were technical classes in the operation of the 88-mm. light machine-guns that we were to carry on a parachute descent, and more than 200 things to learn by heart before we made our first " Versuch " (trial).

If we thought discipline was firm at our training camp, we got a rude shock when we were transferred for final training to the Col. Beck barracks at Charlottenburg, near Berlin.

Of course I was " raw." Now I tremble to think what most of the officers must have thought of me. I'd just scraped in, and they

knew it. They gave me a hell of a time. I was always in fatigue parties. All the dirty jobs found their way to me.

But the time came when I had to rebel. There was a Swastika and Death's-head flag in a niche by our parade ground, and like everybody else I always dutifully clicked my heels and saluted it on passing—a ritual of the Col. Beck Force. One sweltering hot afternoon an officer, having had more dunkel beer for lunch than was his ration, thought he'd have a bit of fun. " Floh (You flea)," he grinned when we met on the parade ground, " You didn't salute the flag."

Mechanically I repeated I had, but he was determined to have his sport, and ordered me to do solitary sentry duty by the flag for two hours, saluting it each time I passed it. In the blazing hot sun I began my pacing, but it wasn't my time for duty and I was hungry

and faint. Spots grew before my eyes, and while the bully was still gaping at me the earth suddenly came up to meet me. I had fainted.

He wasn't finished yet. He dragged me to my feet, ordered me once more to march past the flag and salute. Sick, weak, I managed to stand. As I saluted he kicked me to the ground, and once more dragged me up. Again I saluted, and again I bit the dust. Then everything went black.

When I awoke I was in the hospital ward, and a kindly-faced military surgeon was gazing down at me, and offering me a cigarette. I was sick—not only with physical pain but at the shock of my first encounter with a brutal officer of the old Junkers class. From that very moment something within me changed. I had wanted to be a good soldier. I had wanted to be an obedient Nazi. But from now on I'd look after No. 1 first.

We Are Standing Up to the Raids in Malta

By the first week in March 1941 Malta had already been bombed on 114 occasions, it was revealed by Sir Archibald Sinclair on March 11. The manner in which the defenders and the civil population of the island reacted to these raids is vividly described in this letter.

S PEAKING in the House of Commons, Sir Archibald Sinclair paid tribute to the " gallantry and efficiency of the defenders of Malta and to the courage and high morale which the civil population had throughout displayed." In a letter to a friend in England, a young Maltese said :

The Luftwaffe has taken over the central Mediterranean area from the Italians. It's only German 'planes we now see. Anyhow we are giving a very good account of ourselves, and the Jerries know that too well.

The first time they raided they came over in the afternoon in two waves. There was quite a good number of 'planes, too, and they kept diving over the Grand Harbour for half an hour. Then came an interval of about quarter of an hour and then they started all over again.

It was a good sight to watch ; and I stayed in the open somewhere very near the targets engaged and utterly enjoyed it. It was

the first big-scale warlike action I have ever witnessed. But although the Jerries had guts to come down, yet they were terribly shaken. 'Plane after 'plane zoomed over me very low indeed with engine sparking and smoke coming out from wings and tail.

Every imaginable A.A. shell was used and the barrage was simply grand. The sky was ablaze and I got nearly deaf with bomb and shell explosions. Anyhow I was one of the first that collected souvenirs ; bits of shirts and wings. During that engagement the

RAIDS ON MALTA have proved costly to the Italians. Below, bombs are being prepared in the ancient quarries of Syracuse, used by the enemy as workshops. Above, two Italian pilots are returning in their bomber from a raid. A description of an attack on Malta is given in this page. *Photos, E.N.A.*

Jerries left behind them 11 'planes, while I suppose the others took back to Sicily loads and loads of wounded and dead.

They then visited us on Saturday, losing nine 'planes certain, and on Sunday losing 19 certain. Those were the three most hectic days, but we won. The number of civilians lost must be about one-third the number of pilots the Germans lost.

The spirit of the people cheered me up and warmed my heart. You remember when Italy joined the war you told me to stand fast and fling the invaders back in the sea. The chaps out here did not need any encouragement ; they are out for it. I should like the Jerries or Ities to try a landing. They would never go back.—*The Times.*

Our Diary of the War

THURSDAY, APRIL 3, 1941　　579th day

Sea.—Admiralty announced destruction by naval aircraft of two Italian destroyers.

Three raiders attacked convoy in Thames Estuary. One destroyed and two damaged by H.M.S. Locust.

Air.—Heavy night raid on Brest. Small-scale attacks on oil tanks at Rotterdam and docks at Ostend.

War against Italy.—British evacuation of Benghazi announced. R.A.F. bombed Tripoli and Mersa Brega area.

Cairo announced capture of Miesso on railway to Addis Ababa.

Home.—Four-hour night raid on Bristol. Bombs also fell in East England and elsewhere. Two raiders destroyed.

Greek War.—R.A.F. bombed military targets at Berat.

Balkans.—German Legation ordered by Berlin to leave Belgrade.

Count Teleki, Hungarian Prime Minister, committed suicide. M. Laszlo Bardossy appointed his successor.

FRIDAY, APRIL 4　　580th day

Sea.—Two Italian destroyers, Pantera and Tigre, reported scuttled off Saudi Arabia.

Air.—R.A.F. fighters attacked by day aerodromes in N. France and Belgium. Heavy night bombing of battle cruisers Scharnhorst and Gneisenau at Brest.

War against Italy.—In Harar sector troops reported near R. Awash. Offensive in Negelli-Yavello area progressing.

Six enemy machines shot down in Western Cyrenaica. Tripoli raided.

Home.—Bristol raided again at night. Four bombers brought down. Enemy activity also in S.W. England.

SATURDAY, APRIL 5　　581st day

War against Italy.—Imperial forces entered Addis Ababa. General advance farther south.

Adowa and Adigrat reported captured.

Road block between Asmara and Massawa cleared and advance continued.

Home.—Day attack on coast town in N.E. Scotland. Small-scale enemy activity at night over S.W. England.

SUNDAY, APRIL 6　　582nd day

Air.—Single Spitfires made machine-gun attacks on targets in N. France. Daylight attacks on enemy destroyers, supply vessels, troop concentrations and aerodromes.

Brest again bombed at night. Other aircraft attacked docks at Calais and Ostend and aerodromes in Low Countries.

Home.—Daylight raid on S. Coast town.

Balkan War.—Germany invaded Greece and Yugoslavia.

Belgrade heavily raided. R.A.F. replied by bombing military targets in Sofia and German transport in Struma valley. Five Messerschmitts shot down without loss.

MONDAY, APRIL 7　　583rd day

Air.—Nine relays of R.A.F. heavy bombers raided Kiel. Emden and Bremerhaven also attacked.

War against Italy.—Operations around Massawa developing. Advance towards Dessie and Gondar progressing. Debra Marcos in British hands.

Enemy recaptured Derna, Libya.

Home.—Considerable night raids over Liverpool area, East Anglia, S.W. and central Scotland, London, and elsewhere. Bombs fell for first time in Northern Ireland.

Six enemy aircraft destroyed.

Balkan War.—Germans continued violent attack in Struma valley and in heights of Nevrokop. Nazi mechanized division captured Doiran, on Greek-Bulgarian-Yugoslav frontier.

Reported that Yugoslavs had occupied Italian port of Zara, Dalmatia.

R.A.F. attacked motor transport near Strumitsa, Yugoslavia. Another German raid on Belgrade.

TUESDAY, APRIL 8　　584th day

Air.—R.A.F. made daylight attacks on shipping in North Sea and objectives in Denmark, Low Countries, and Northern France.

Kiel heavily bombed at night. Other targets were Bremerhaven, Emden and oil targets at Rotterdam.

War against Italy.—Massawa surrendered and was occupied. Hard rearguard action in Libya.

Home.—Heavy double night attack on Coventry. Hospital repeatedly hit. Hostile aircraft also reported from other areas.

Seven enemy aircraft destroyed.

Balkan War.—From Doiran German mechanized division advanced into Greece east of R. Vardar in direction of Salonika. In Struma valley enemy was still held by forts of Rupel, Usita and others.

Yugoslavs forced to withdraw in South, leaving Greek left flank uncovered.

WEDNESDAY, APRIL 9　　585th day

Sea.—H.M. trawlers Lord Selborne and Cramond Island reported sunk.

Air.—R.A.F. bombed railway traffic and wireless station in Denmark, aluminium works at Hoyanger and naval unit at Brest.

Heavy three-hour night raid on Berlin. Opera House destroyed, other famous buildings severely damaged.

Home.—Night bombers again over west Midlands, including Birmingham. Bombs also fell in N.E. district, East Anglia and elsewhere. Twelve enemy aircraft destroyed.

Balkan War.—Germans occupied Salonika, cutting off Greek forces east of R. Vardar. Enemy also captured Skoplje and Nish, Yugoslavia.

In Albania Yugoslav troops, having crossed R. Drin, advanced towards interior.

THURSDAY, APRIL 10　　586th day

Air.—R.A.F. bombed cruisers Scharnhorst and Gneisenau at Brest and aerodrome at Merignac. Düsseldorf and Borkum also attacked.

War against Italy.—Ceaseless air attacks on enemy troops in Libya. Advance into S. Abyssinia from Italian Somaliland developing.

Home.—Night raids on Birmingham and Coventry, causing heavy damage and casualties. Ten German raiders shot down.

Balkan War.—British and Imperial forces made contact with Germans in northern Greece.

German forces reported to have reached Monastir and Yannitsa. R.A.F. made great onslaught on enemy.

OUR WAR GAZETTEER : YUGOSLAVIA

Belgrade. Cap. Yugoslavia ; at confluence of R. Danube and Sava ; greatly modernized during last twenty years ; cathedral, royal palace ; university ; name means " white city." Pop. about 270,000.

Bitolj. (Monastir). 130 miles N.W. of Salonika ; of strategic importance ; became Serbian in 1913. Pop. about 20,000.

Dubrovnik. (Ragusa). Dalmatia ; on Adriatic ; 105 miles S.E. of Split ; the harbour being partly closed by sand, large ships use Gravosa, 4 miles distant ; oil refineries. Pop. about 15,000.

Kotor. (Cattaro). Seaport at head of gulf of Cattaro ; 35 miles E. by S. of Dubrovnik ; naval base. Pop. about 6,000.

Lyublyana. (Laibach). Former capital of Austrian province of Carniola ; 40 miles N.E. of Trieste ; university, episc. see ; manufactures textiles ; large trade in leather and chemicals. Pop. about 60,000.

Maribor. (Marburg). Slovenia ; stands on both banks of the R. Drave ; 40 miles from Graz ; 16th-century cathedral ; manufactures railway stock, boots and shoes ; large wine trade. Pop. about 30,000.

Monastir. See Bitolj.

Nish. On R. Nisava, trib. of R. Morava ; 130 miles S.E. of Belgrade ; important railway junction. Pop. about 40,000.

Novi Sad. 50 miles N.W. of Belgrade ; pottery and cotton works. Pop. 50,000.

Sarajevo. Cap. of Bosnia ; on R. Miljacka, 122 miles S.W. of Belgrade ; scene of the murder of Archduke Francis Ferdinand, June 28, 1914, event which precipitated the Great War ; manufactures pottery, silk, flour, sugar. Pop. 80,000.

Skoplje. (Usküb). On R. Vardar, 130 miles N.W. of Salonika ; large trade in tobacco, grain and agricultural products ; taken by Bulgarians in 1915. Pop. 60,000.

Sombor. Voivodina ; 94 miles N.W. of Belgrade ; trading centre for corn and cattle. Pop. about 30,000.

Split. (Spalato). Dalmatia ; seaport and naval base ; on the Adriatic, 74 miles S.E. of Zara ; contains Palace of Diocletian ; extensive trade in wine, oil, wheat, figs and leather ; fisheries. Pop. 40,000.

Struma River. Rising in Bulgaria, about 20 miles S. of Sofia, flows west and south-east through Bulgaria and Macedonia to enter Aegean Sea. Length 150 miles.

Subotica. (Szabadka). Voivodina ; near Hungarian frontier ; centre of agricultural and cattle-rearing district ; manufactures boots, railway trucks and furniture. Pop. about 100,000.

NOTE.—That most of the above-mentioned places have two names points to the fact that at some period they have been under the sway of Turkey, Austria, Hungary, Italy, etc. The first name given is the Yugoslav (Serb, Croat or Slovene) name, and that in brackets the original. Thus Laibach was the capital of the Austrian duchy of Carniola. Marburg was in Austria, Usküb in Turkey. After Macedonia passed from Turkish rule in 1913, Monastir became Bitolj. Cattaro and Spalato are Italian forms. The name Ragusa reminds us that the place called Dubrovnik was colonized by Latin settlers.

BINOCULARS FROM JAMAICA to the value of £1,000 have been sent by the Boy Scouts of that country, who are here seen examining them prior to dispatch.
Photo, Topical Press

Usküb. Turkish for Skoplje, q.v.

Vrsac. (Versecz). Voivodina ; in agricultural region, 40 miles N.E. of Belgrade ; flour milling and distilling. Pop. 30,000.

Zagreb. (Agram). Capital of Croatia-Slovonia ; on R. Sava ; cathedral, university ; manufactures linen, carpets, leather and tobacco. Pop. about 190,000.

IN BOMBED, BLASTED AND BURNT LONDON THE DOCTOR STANDS BY

After the great air raid of the night of April 16-17 many of the victims were pinned beneath the wreckage. When daybreak came the A.R.P. workers were still making heroic efforts to reach them and deeds of remarkable bravery were performed by both men and women. Here in a bomb-stricken district in London a woman doctor in her white coat and white-painted helmet bearing the letters M.O. (Medical Officer) waits while the workers tunnel through the ruins of a block of flats to reach people buried beneath them. Finally, a way was hacked to where a woman lay seriously injured and the doctor crept along it to give first aid.

Photo, " News Chronicle." Exclusive to THE WAR ILLUSTRATED

Into Battle Went the 'Forces of the Empire'

The Forces of the Empire, as the British Expeditionary Force in the Balkans has been officially styled by British G.H.Q. in Cairo, began its landings in March, and first made contact with the German enemy on April 10, 1941. Below we tell something of its passage and of the opening brush on the new field of battle.

WEEKS before it was officially released in London, the news of the safe arrival in Greece of the " Forces of the Empire " had spread far and wide. The Greeks knew it ; how could they do otherwise when they saw arriving at the Piraeus, the port of Athens, the great stream of transports, packed with troops and with war material of all kinds ? The Bulgarians knew it, for on March 20 it was announced over the Sofia wireless that 300,000 British troops—a fantastically large figure, of course —had landed at Salonika. The Yugoslavs knew it, too ; as early as March 11 it was reported in Belgrade that British troops were landing in large numbers, and perhaps the knowledge determined them to make that last desperate bid for freedom which began when they threw over Tsvetkovitch and his pro-Nazis, and decided to fight before surrendering.

All the troops were convoyed to the ports of disembarkation by Admiral Cunningham's

Then the Australians and New Zealanders constituted a corps which as from midday, April 12, was known as the Anzac Corps. " The G.O.C.," read a message sent by Lt.-Gen. Sir Thomas Blamey to the Australian and New Zealand Commands, " desires to say that the reunion of the Australian and New Zealand divisions gives all ranks the greatest uplift. The task ahead, although difficult, is not nearly so hard as that which faced our fathers in April, 26 years ago (a reference to the

This map shows the line occupied by the Imperial and Greek troops from Mount Olympus to a point on the coast opposite Corfu when the great German and Italian attempt thrust into Central Greece began in mid-April 1941.　　*By courtesy of the " Daily Express "*

landing of the Anzacs at Gallipoli in 1915). We go to it together with stout hearts."

So after a lapse of more than 20 years British and Imperial troops once again marched along the Balkan roads. To begin with, they were given positions somewhat behind the Greeks, who were now fiercely engaged with the German invaders, but on April 10 the first clash occurred between men of the Forces of the Empire and the Nazis. A German column halted on the road was shot up by some British tanks, and a number of our armoured cars which, while escorting demolition parties somewhere near the Yugoslav border, had been outflanked by a German column, fought their way back through 800 German infantrymen. From then onwards our troops were more or less constantly in action, doing their utmost to support their allies, the Greeks, whose line was now bending dangerously before the German onslaught. In mountainous country, and in the most bitter weather—snow was still falling on the heights and the wind was cruel—the British and the men from " down under " took up their positions. So rough was the country in which the troops were deployed that motor transport had to be supplemented by mules and donkeys, on whose backs were brought up food, ammunition, and other supplies.

The War Office communiqués told little of what was going on, but it was learnt that our forces were withdrawing to new positions. On April 14 the communiqué read, " Our covering troops inflicted severe casualties on the enemy, who maintained continuous pressure on our eastern sector during this withdrawal. Marked activity on the right of our line, but no serious clashes." The German High Command declared that motorized units and S.S. troops had thrown back British infantry and armoured forces. Then on April 16 Cairo announced that " our troops are now in contact with the enemy along the whole of our front." A big battle was in progress in Western Macedonia, and British and Imperial forces clashed long and often with German mechanized units.

MOUNT OLYMPUS, close to the coast on the western side of the Gulf of Salonika, formed the right bastion of the line of the Allied armies shown on the map. *Photo, Dorien Leigh*

ships, and in spite of the Italian submarines and Nazi aircraft not a ship, not a man was lost in the passage across the Aegean Sea. Some of the units had come from far across the sea ; others, veterans of the Libyan campaign, only from Alexandria. They comprised British and Australians, New Zealanders and men from Cyprus ; all were in good heart, fit as fiddles, ready and eager to go into action immediately. At the bases great Ordnance and R.A.S.C. establishments came into being, and the R.A.M.C. units assembled—amongst them an ambulance unit of Quaker volunteers, who though their consciences forbade them to take up arms found nothing in their religion to forbid them the work of mercy.

This new British army in Greece was under the command of Lt.-Gen. Sir Henry Maitland Wilson, who himself was stated to be under the direction of General Papagos, Commander-in-Chief of the Greek Army.

LT.-GEN. SIR H. MAITLAND-WILSON, D.S.O., in command of the Forces of the Empire in the Balkans, commanded the troops who defeated the Italians in the Western Desert. *Photo, British Official: Crown Copyright*

Belgrade: Tragic Capital of the Yugoslavs

BELGRADE'S NATIONAL LIBRARY and Technical Faculty are housed in the modern structure above. Yugoslavia's capital, bombarded by the Austrians in the last war, was devastated by mass Nazi air raids on April 6, 1941. There was an efficient A.F.S., which included many women, who worked heroically. Right, some of them are "manning" a fire engine.

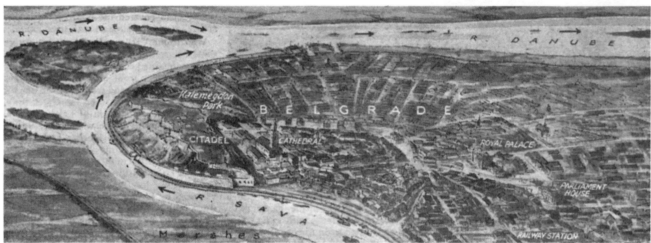

The drawing above shows the main features of Belgrade. The city stands on the south shore of the Danube at its junction with the River Sava.

YUGOSLAVIA'S INDICTMENT OF GERMANY

WE inform all civilized peoples of the frightful crimes committed by the German armed force in the war imposed upon us.

Belgrade, the capital of our country, which in good time was proclaimed an open and undefended city, was bombed by German aircraft without a declaration of war.

On Sunday morning, while the sound of church bells was calling the faithful to church for Divine Service, a bombardment eclipsing in horror all imagination was launched by German aeroplanes. A veritable deluge of incendiary and explosive bombs turned the city into a mass of ruins and gutted homes, while all the streets of Belgrade were covered with the bodies of children, women, and old men.

Never during the long history of this martyr city were such cruelties committed even by the most primitive invaders. This devastation of a defenceless and open city was executed by aircraft of that nation which claimed for itself the first place among cultured peoples.

All the precepts of international right and human considerations were set aside by the German aeroplanes, which destroyed most of the hospitals, churches, schools, and cultural institutions of Belgrade in broad daylight.

The royal palace at Dedinje [a suburb of Belgrade] was completely destroyed by 30 direct hits during the mass air raids on the city on Sunday. The German aeroplanes even bombed isolated houses . . . Horrible scenes occurred during the bombardment, when German aeroplanes machine-gunned women and children fleeing from their burning homes. Flying low, the German bombers turned houses into hecatombs.—*Message addressed by the Yugoslav Government to "All Civilized Peoples."*

Prior to the Nazi air raids, Belgrade was fast becoming the finest capital city in the Balkans, with many modern office buildings and tall apartment houses often in quaint juxtaposition with the old houses built under the Turkish regime.
Drawing, courtesy of "The Sphere." Photos, Dorien Leigh, G.P.U., and Fox

When Greek Met German in Macedonia

Below we give an account of the opening phase of the invasion of Greece by the German armies operating from Bulgarian soil. It is based on a statement issued by Colonel Contoleon, Liaison Officer and Acting Military Attaché at the Greek Legation in London.

WHEN it first seemed probable that Hitler would shortly order an invasion of Greece, the Greek General Staff prepared its plan of defence on the assumption that Yugoslavia would be favourably disposed towards the Axis Powers ; and this assumption seemed to be well grounded when on March 25 Mr. Tsvetkovitch put his signature to the Tripartite Pact at Vienna.

Believing then that the attack would be developed or delivered through Yugoslavia, the main Greek line of defence, which aimed

the Greek Army ; the routes across the Greco-Serbian frontier were guarded by the Yugoslav Army ; and Eastern Macedonia was protected by the main Greek Army. The Forces of the Empire, composed of British and Anzac troops, were farther south.

Although the German attack was launched with all the customary violence and the technical equipment of " blitzkrieg "—with tanks, abundant heavy artillery and considerable air forces—along the whole Greek line during the first two days the Germans

Skoplje (Uskub), a German mechanized column succeeded on the morning of April 8 in capturing the Serbian town of Doiran, thus reaching the Greco-Serbian frontier 22 miles to the rear of the extreme edge of the Greek lines, and entered Greek territory by the flat corridor east of the Vardar. The very small Greek mechanized formations put up a hard fight against an enemy whose equipment was incomparably superior, both in quantity and in quality, but the battle was too unequal. At dawn on April 9 the German forces entered Salonika. Fortunately the delaying action of the Greek mechanized units had permitted the great port to be stripped of anything that might have proved useful to the enemy, while all military installations had been destroyed.

After the capture of Salonika the Greek units holding the frontier of Eastern Macedonia were cut off. Their position was hopeless, but there was not a sign of weakening in their resistance. For days they maintained their lines intact, and the forts in the Rupel pass at the mouth of the Struma valley still continued to blaze defiance at the enemy whose dead covered the floor of the ravine and reddened the streams with their blood.

West of the Vardar valley the Greek forces slowly moved back, resisting all the way. They maintained contact with their comrades on the Albanian front, but when the Germans occupied Monastir and reinforced the Italians in Albania, the pressure on the Greek lines, particularly in the region of Lake Ochrida, became too great to be withstood. So the Greeks fell back from Koritza and Florina and then, still fighting hard all the way, crossed the hilly country in the neighbourhood of Lake Kastoria to the foothills of the great massif of Pindus. From the river Vistritza to Mount Olympus, close to the shore of the Aegean, the front was held by Greek units and the Forces of the Empire. Thus, since the Greeks had also fallen back from their advanced positions in Albania, the line of battle now stretched from the mountains of South Albania on the west to Mount Olympus on the east.

THESE GERMAN ALPINE TROOPS white-coated and cowled as camouflage against the background of snow, are operating on a mountainside in the Balkans. These troops were used by the Nazis during the Norway campaign. Camouflage of this kind is very effective when the men are lying on the ground, but when upright they are betrayed by their shadows.   *Photo, Keystone*

at the preservation of the territory won in Albania and the covering of its eastern flank, was to be concentrated in Central Macedonia, i.e. that portion of Greece lying to the north-west of Salonika. Eastern Macedonia, i.e. the area south of Bulgaria as far as the port of Kavalla, would also be defended, but its defence was entrusted in the main to the forts covering the principal passes from Bulgaria. Western Thrace, lying between Kavalla and the Turkish frontier, was deemed to be indefensible, and before the war began it was evacuated, not only of its garrison but of the greater part of its civilian population. Its defence would have been advisable only in the event of a concerted action with Turkey.

Then on March 27 came the revolution in Belgrade, when Yugoslavia, from being a friend of the Axis, declared herself as an ally of Greece. The Yugoslav Army was already mobilized and had on the whole completed its dispositions. Substantial forces had been mustered in Southern Serbia, so that the routes into Greece seemed to be adequately covered. Consequently the Greek divisions were transferred from this part of the front to the Bulgarian frontier, with a view to making the defence of Eastern Macedonia more effective. This transfer, though dictated by logic, proved fatal.

When at 5 a.m. on April 6 the Germans delivered their onslaught on Greece and Yugoslavia, the Albanian front was held by

made no progress anywhere. They destroyed it is true, the two advanced fortified positions of Istimbey and Kelkaya in the Rupel pass, but their persistent attacks with tanks, dive bombers, on the two main forts of Rupel and Ussita were completely repulsed. The next day, April 8, Perithori was temporarily captured by the enemy, but immediately afterwards was recaptured by a Greek counter-attack. Similarly the Dassavli fort was recaptured after it had fallen to the enemy. At the same time Greek troops operating outside the forts succeeded in recovering other points where the enemy had temporarily established a foothold.

So far, so good. But Yugoslav forces defending the Strumnitsa pass, which leads westward from the Struma valley in Bulgaria, were forced to withdraw. Swiftly the Germans developed their advantage. While the Yugoslavs were retreating up the Vardar valley toward

In this radioed photograph a German supply column is seen making its way along one of the mountain roads in Yugoslavia. Many such motorized columns poured over that country's frontiers following Germany's invasion, and many were destroyed by Allied aircraft.

Photo, Associated Press

Britain v. Germany : the Strategy of the War

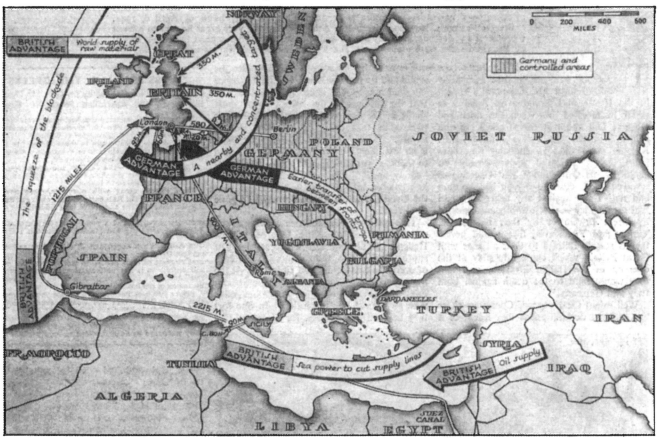

THE CAMPAIGN OF 1941 is being fought over a vast battlefield stretching from the Atlantic to the Black Sea, from the North Atlantic to the Suez
Canal. How advantageous in some respects is Germany's position will be apparent from this map ; but it shows, too, the strength that Britain
derives from her sea power.   *From " The New York Times Magazine "*

A Note on Strategy

FROM the Pyrenees to North Cape, from
the English Channel to the Black Sea,
Hitler's legions march with none to
say them nay. Not even Napoleon at the
height of his greatness ruled over so many
countries, chained so many peoples to his war
machine. The swastika flag waves over
regions into which the Roman eagles never
penetrated. Never was Europe so " united "
as today, when, with the exception of only two
or three comparatively minor states, the whole
family of continental countries makes up
Hitler's empire.

Great have been the victories won by the
generals and the soldiers of the man who was
a company runner on the Western Front in
the last war. Great victories and many, but
still the war is not over. Just beyond the
rim of Hitler's Europe sail the ships of
Britain's Navy. If the land is Germany's the
sea is still what it has been for centuries—
Britain's. As in Napoleon's day so in this,
the mighty struggle is one between a whale
and an elephant.

Germany's Supremacy on Land

The elephant's strength is based on what
are called the interior lines. He occupies the
inside of the circle, and it is an easy matter
for him to transfer his troops and his trains
from one sector to another. His communications are magnificent, consisting as they do
of the network of railways and roads with
which generations of enterprise have equipped
the continent. He has enormous populations
—his own and the races he has enslaved—on
which to draw for his cannon fodder and his
industrial serfs. Then for years he prepared
for war, and he did not make the mistake of
thinking that this new war would be fought
on the same lines as that of 1914-1918 ; in
other words, he thought not of trenches and

barbed wire and concrete, but of tanks and
motor lorries, of dive bombers and troop-
carrying 'planes, of spies and Fifth Columnists.
It is not really surprising that with all these
advantages, to which may be added the
tradition of discipline of Europe's greatest
militarist nation, the Germans should have
proved able to crush all their foes within reach
of their armoured columns.

Britain's Mastery of the Sea

Against this continent in arms Britain flings
into the balance her Islands, her Commonwealth, her Mercantile Marine and incomparable Navy, the resources of a quarter of the
globe, the products of the labour of one fifth
of the human race. All that might tends to
be concentrated in the waters that surround
the Fuehrer's Reich. To the British Isles a
great stream of ships brings food and raw
materials without which our millions could not
live, the war supplies without which we could
not continue the fight. At the same time our
fleets have swept from the seas Hitler's ships,
and hold the Continent in the relentless grip
of the blockade. No doubt there are many
leaks in the blockade ; in our impatience its
operation seems all too slow. But there is not
a home, not a factory, not a fort or camp in
Hitler's Germany which is not the poorer
because of our patrolling Navy.

Sea-power, then, is Britain's great advantage. Because of it she can feed her own
people and (eventually, at least) make the
Germans go hungry. Her fighting line can
be supplied from America, democracy's inexhaustible arsenal. She can tap the world's
oil supplies, whereas the Germans have to " go
easy " on petrol, and if they want to replenish
their stocks must make a drive against Iraq
or the Russian oil fields in the Caucasus.

But the sea is no obstacle to the aeroplane,
and Hitler's air power is still greater than

Britain's. Far out over the Atlantic rove his
bombers, seeking whom they may devour
of our merchant ships, and night after night
there descend from the skies on our cities
loads of death-dealing metal. True, Britain
too has a great Air Force, one which is growing
daily in numbers and might ; but in the air
war the Germans have the advantage of a
concentrated target, whereas the British
offensive has to be distributed over a vast
area, many of the most vital spots being
almost out of range of even our long-distance
'planes. Already there is discernible a shift of
industry from the much-bombed Rhineland
and Ruhr to Czechoslovakia and even to
Poland ; and as our air strength grows, as
our bombers multiply and grow in range, more
and more of Germany's factories will be transferred to the more distant parts of Nazi-controlled Europe. But in Britain no such transfer
is possible ; war workers, her civilian population, are in the front line in very deed. They
must fight where they stand ; they can do no
other.

Whale or Elephant : Which ?

This, then, is the strategical setting of the
battle of 1941. Already the curtain has gone
up on the terrific drama ; already the issue
is joined between the hordes of Hitler's
slaves and the armies of free men put into the
field by the British Commonwealth and its
Allies. In the passes of Greece, on the sun-
blistered desert of North Africa, the
mechanized Attila is struggling furiously, with
an utter disregard for human life, to pierce the
ranks of those—oh ! so few and none too
well equipped—who alone stand between him
and the domination of the world.

Before the year ends the issue will have
been decided. Whale or elephant ; which will
win ? By the time the leaves now forming
in the spring sunshine have withered and
fallen we shall know.

We Simply Had to Help the Greeks!

After more than holding their own against the Italians, the Greeks were suddenly
attacked by a new and even more powerful foe in the early hours of April 6, 1941.
" Greece," said Mr. Kotzias, Governor of Athens, " has the very great honour to affront
a people of 135,000,000, perfectly armed and showing its hatred against the Greek race."
Yet the Greeks were undismayed, and for the second time they answered " No."

THOSE amazing Greeks ! Just how
amazing was not perhaps generally
realized until Mr. Churchill's speech
in the House of Commons on April 9 in
which he revealed that when Mr. Eden and
General Dill had met the Greek King and
Prime Minister, the Prime Minister, Mr.
Koryzis (who died so suddenly nine days
later), had " declared spontaneously on
behalf of his Government that Greece was
resolved at all costs to defend her freedom
and native soil against any aggressor ; and
that even if they were left wholly unsupported
by Great Britain or by their neighbours,
Turkey and Yugoslavia, they would nevertheless remain faithful to their alliance with
Great Britain which came into play at the
opening of the Italian invasion, and that
they would fight to the death against both
Italy and Germany."

Well might the House of Commons cheer
that spirited declaration as they learnt of it

our power. If they were resolved to face the
might and fury of the Huns, we had no choice
but that we should share their ordeal and
that the soldiers of the British Army must
stand in the line with them." There was
hazard in that decision, indeed a double
hazard. " But," averred the Premier, " there
is no less likely way of winning the war than
to adhere pedantically to the maxim of
' safety first.' " So early in March Britain
had entered into a military agreement with
the Greeks, and an Imperial army had gone
to Greece.

That spirit of independence which marked
every utterance of King George of the
Hellenes and his ministers in Greece's hour of
supreme crisis was soon evinced by Greeks
of every rank and class and situation. At the
front, particularly in the forts of the Struma
Pass, the soldiers took on enormous odds
with an almost gay resolution. In one fort
they beat off every attack for 36 hours, and

either flank and had occupied Salonika far
to the rear. Against artillery and dive-
bombers, against flame-throwers and the
assaults of Hitler's shock troops, those little
groups of Greeks kept up the fight isolated
and alone, hopeless of succour, yet resolved
to keep their flag flying to the last. Then
behind the lines the civilian population
laboured untiringly, while women toiled in
repairing roads broken by shell-fire and
building new.

Speaking in London on April 16, when
there was no information nor indication
that the main forts had yet fallen, Colonel
Contoleon, Acting Military Attaché at the
Greek Legation in London, said : " The self-
sacrifice of their brave defenders has not
been in vain. Not only have they written one
of the most brilliant pages of Greek military
history, but they have also for many days
blocked the routes into Eastern Macedonia,
thus making possible the rescue, smooth embarkation, and transportation of substantial
numbers of the Greek forces of Eastern
Macdonia. When these numbers are revealed
they will cause amazement and relief."

In common with many other 'planes of the Regia Aeronautica operating in Albania, this Savoia-
Marchetti bomber, which Allied soldiers are intently examining, bears traces of the damage
inflicted upon it by Greek or British bullets before it was forced down. On the underside of the
wing are the three fasces—symbol of Italian Fascism.   *Photo, Bosshard*

' Nothing More than Chauffeurs !'

When at last the forts fell it was because
they were literally overwhelmed by the
weight of the German mechanized armament.
" We thought we would have to fight against
soldiers," said one of the Greeks wounded as
he lay in his bed in an Athens hospital,
" but we found we had to fight machines.
We knew we could not survive such an
onslaught, but we felt we must kill as many
as possible before dying. Yet when we got
the Germans out of their machines and away
from their steering-wheels we found them no
better than the Italians."

from Mr. Churchill's lips. Amongst the
countries of the Continent, Greece is one of
the least consequence in size, population and
material resources. If any country might be
excused for bowing the knee to Hitler, then
that country might be Greece. But in the
Greeks of today there is more than a suggestion of that fine spirit which was seen in the
Greeks of old—in, say, that little force who
held the pass of Thermopylae against the
Persian hordes, and who on the eve of that
never-to-be-forgotten fight were observed by
the wondering enemy nonchalantly combing
their hair in complete disregard of the death
which was so soon to come upon them.

" This being so," went on Mr. Churchill,
" it seemed that our duty was clear. We were
bound in honour to give them all the aid in

the defenders were almost overwhelmed
when the Germans managed to enter the fort's
underground passages. But the little garrison
were undaunted, and after a tremendous
struggle the intruders were driven out. One
advanced detachment fought so heroically
that the German commander, when the
battle was over, saluted the Greek dead by
way of tribute to their bravery.

Then there was the " Battalion of Death,"
which lived up to its name—a special force of
crack troops formed to fight rearguard
actions to cover the withdrawal of the main
forces ; when the commanders of the frontier
units called for volunteers for the battalion,
every soldier stepped forward. For days the
fight went on in those frontier regions, long
after the Germans had thundered past on

Then a note of contempt entered his voice
and he almost spat. " They didn't like our
bayonets," he said ; " they are nothing
more than chauffeurs." And his comrades
in the beds around him grinned their assent

Not Winter Nor the Italians Beat Our Allies

GENERAL PAPAGOS' MEN had weather as well as the enemy to fight against. Deep snow and extreme cold were an ally of the Italians, hampering the Greeks' pursuit when victory seemed almost within their grasp. Top, troops are marching to the front in conditions that made mechanized transport impossible. In the lower photograph a long line of ambulances wends its way over snowy roads to the base. Now that the Italians have Nazi allies spring has come, the snow has melted and made the use of German mechanized forces possible where it would have been impossible but a month or two ago.

Photos, Bosshard

Prelude to the Battle of Cape Matapan

H.M.S. Hasty, one of the destroyers that took part in the battle of Cape Matapan, is seen in the top photograph steaming full speed ahead. Four enemy shells have just missed her. Left, the officer of the watch of the Hasty is observing the movements of the ships, while on the horizon is H.M.S. Gloucester.

First photographs of the Battle of March 28 to be published are reproduced in this page. They show the earlier stages of the battle, which took place in daylight, when Vice-Admiral Pridham-Wippell succeeded in decoying the Italian ships towards the big guns of Admiral Cunningham's battleships. Above, destroyers are laying a smoke screen to cover the approach of the British Fleet. While doing it they were shelled by the Italian battleship, Vittorio Veneto. H.M.S. Gloucester, which joined with the destroyers in making the smoke screen, is seen below.   *Photos, " The Times"*

'Her March Is O'er the Mountain Wave'

H.M.S. RENOWN, flagship of Vice-Admiral Sir James Somerville, in command of the Western Mediterranean Fleet, is here seen ploughing through a heavy sea during one of those recent sweeps of the Mediterranean that have had such dire results for the Italian Navy. In rough weather such a great battleship presents a most imposing spectacle. Her huge bulk of 37,400 tons full load, driven forward at a speed of 29 knots by engines of 120,000 horse-power, cuts through all but the biggest rollers and sends clouds of spray over her fo'c'sle.

Photo, Central Press

Last Flickers of War in East Africa

Following the fall of Addis Ababa, the fighting in East Africa rapidly drew to its close.
Hardly a town of any consequence was left to the Italians ; and, as for their army, it
had been so mauled in battle and guerilla combat, so weakened by desertions, that it was
incapable of further resistance. So, as we tell below, the stage was set for surrender.

"KEREN has been stormed and the main resistance of the Italian Army overcome. Asmara has surrendered. The port of Massawa is in our hands. The Red Sea has been virtually cleared of enemy warships. Harar has fallen and our troops have entered and taken charge of Addis Ababa itself. The Duke of Aosta's army is retreating into the mountains, where it is being attended upon by the Patriot forces of Ethiopia. The complete destruction and capture of all Italian forces in Abyssinia may be reasonably expected." In these words Mr. Churchill summed up the most recent achievements of our armies in East Africa when in the House of Commons on April 9 he reviewed the progress of the war.

Massawa, capital of Eritrea, Italy's oldest colony, and Mussolini's sole remaining port on the Red Sea, was entered by Imperial troops on April 8. Before the final battle began an 18 hours' truce was accorded the Italians so that they might consider the British terms for surrender. The Italian commander, Admiral Bonnetti, realized full well the hopelessness of his position and so, if left to himself, would probably have decided upon capitulation, but he received— so it is believed—an order from Rome to keep the British troops engaged as long as possible. So after one of his staff officers, blindfolded during his passage through the British lines, had conveyed his decision to " fight to the last," the truce was ended and the final battle began.

From the air the R.A.F. heavily bombed the Italian positions, while on the ground a prolonged artillery bombardment prepared

Following the fall of Addis Ababa and Asmara,
the survivors of the once great Italian Army
were herded into the Gondar and Dessie
regions, shown in the centre of this map.
Courtesy, "The Times"

the way for the assault. The attack was pressed home by the infantry led by Free French troops, and very shortly the Admiral decided that further resistance would be futile and hoisted the white flag.

Following Massawa's capture large numbers of Italian troops and naval ratings surrendered, and the number grew hour by hour as they streamed in from the surrounding countryside. Even before the fall of the port the number of prisoners taken in

Eritrea was stated to be 41,000—1,000 Italian officers, 14,000 Italian other ranks, and 26,000 colonial troops. Nothing was left, in fact, of the Eritrean army which had put up such a good show at Keren save straggling columns and isolated units of beaten and disorganized soldiery, quite incapable of making any further prolonged stand. The same was true, indeed, of the Duke of Aosta's army as a whole. Only a few weeks before it was reported to number 250,000 men ; now it numbered—just how many or how few none could say.

Every day that passed saw an extension of the Italian rot. A thousand prisoners a day were passing through Addis Ababa as the country within 100 miles of the city was mopped up. General Santini, one of the ablest of the Italian divisional generals and who had been on the run since the battle of the Jelib river, was brought in on April 13, having surrendered with a brigadier, three colonels, 40 other officers, 120 white troops and 160 Eritreans—all that was left of his once considerable force—to a handful of South African officers. Close-pressed by the Imperial troops, harassed by the Abys-

Above are a gunner and a gun-carrier of the
Nigeria Regiment of the Royal West African
Frontier Force, which has added to its fame
as a fighting regiment in the East African
campaign.   *Photo, E.N.A.*

sinian Patriots, cold and tired and utterly depressed, the General and his men had reached the limit of endurance—and admitted it. Colonel Rolle, leader of a detachment of some 700 irregulars, soon followed.

Everywhere the Italians were in the utmost confusion, and there were many such absurd incidents as when an Italian sentry rushed into the Italian headquarters in a certain town to give warning of the approach of the British, only to find a British officer seated at the table to receive his tidings : the place had been captured several days before ! Then there was the case of the Italian dispatch-rider who suddenly found himself in the midst of a British supply column. The lorry drivers were probably as surprised as he was !

The Duke of Aosta, Viceroy of Abyssinia, with part of the garrison of Addis Ababa, had left the city before its fall, and endeavoured to reach Gondar or Dessie, which, with Jimma, were the only Italian strongholds still remaining. But even these were on the verge of collapse. The end was inevitable.

MASSAWA was captured by the Imperial troops on April 8. Its fall sealed the fate of
Italy's oldest colony, since it meant Mussolini had lost his last port on the Red Sea. Above is
the main street of the town with its bars and cafés, all deserted in the intense midday heat of that
latitude.   *Photo, Paul Popper*

Their Gallant Deeds Stirred All the Empire

INDIAN TROOPS operating in Eritrea were the subject of a message of congratulation from Mr. Winston Churchill to the Viceroy of India which was published in Delhi on April 9, 1941. " The whole Empire has been stirred by the achievement of the Indian forces in Eritrea," said the Premier. . . . " I ask your Excellency to convey to them and to the whole Indian Army the pride and admiration with which we have followed their exploits." The two photographs in this page give an idea of the arduous conditions the Indians faced. In the top photograph troops are advancing over rocky, mountainous country in Eritrea. In the lower photograph are Garhwalis, troops of one of the Punjab states, on a mountain ridge.

Photos, British Official : Crown Copyright

WHERE THE BATTLE OF BRITAIN W.
History's First Mass Air Struggle Show

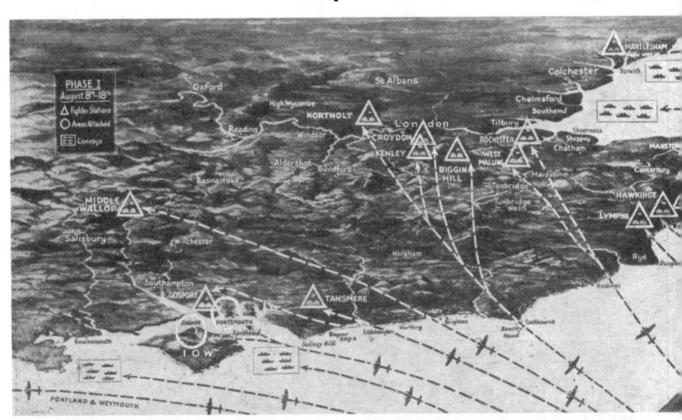

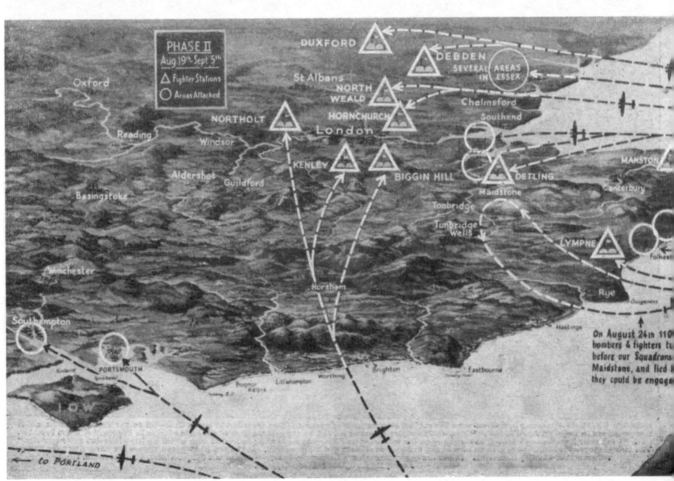

UGHT AND WON

by Phase

THE air Battle of Britain, in which British airmen "undaunted by odds, unwearied in their constant challenge and mortal danger," to quote Mr. Churchill, flung back the might of the German Luftwaffe, may be divided into three stages.

Phase I, lasting from August 8-18, 1940, consisted of twenty-six attacks directed mainly against shipping, coastal towns and fighter aerodromes in the South and South-East of England (map, left). A certain amount of damage was done, but at a cost of 697 German aircraft. Our own losses were 153, but sixty pilots were saved. Phase II, from August 19-Sept. 5 was made up of some thirty-five major attacks delivered against inland fighter aerodromes and aircraft factories (map below, left). They cost the Nazis 562 aircraft known to have been destroyed, while our own losses amounted to 219, with a hundred and thirty-two pilots saved. The heavy task of the defence is shown in the fact that during these first two phases no fewer than 4,523 Fighter Patrols, of varying strength in aircraft, were flown in daylight. Phase III, Sept. 6-Oct. 5 was characterized by the hurling of the main strength of the Luftwaffe against London and the Thames Estuary, with subsidiary and diversion attacks against the South and South-East Coasts (map below).

It was on September 15 that the Germans launched their greatest attack against Britain ; 500 aircraft, 250 in the morning and 250 in the afternoon, made a desperate attempt to smash a way through the British defences. They failed, and their attempt cost them 185 aircraft known to have been destroyed. This final phase of the Battle of Britain cost the Nazis in all 883 aircraft. The R.A.F. had gained the greatest victory in its history. Never again did the Germans come in daylight in such numbers. The day raids continued for a time, but on a much smaller scale ; and the night raids, with less danger of interception for the enemy, took their place.

The maps in this page, reproduced from the Ministry of Information booklet " The Battle of Britain," show for the first time the actual targets of Goering's Luftwaffe.

THE CONTROL SYSTEM of the British air defences is shown, right, in diagram form. Britain's coastline is divided into Sectors, each with its own Fighter aerodromes and H.Q. These sectors are grouped together under a Group H.Q., which in turn comes under the control of Headquarters, Fighter Command. In the Operations Room of each H.Q. is a large map table upon which, by means of various symbols, is shown every available item of information which can be gleaned concerning the strength and disposition of the enemy and his direction of flight. The Controllers also have all possible information before them as to the location and state of their own Squadrons, as well as meteorological reports.

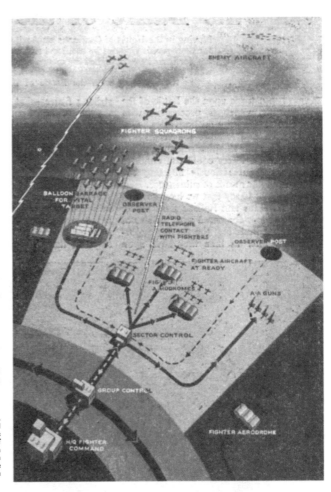

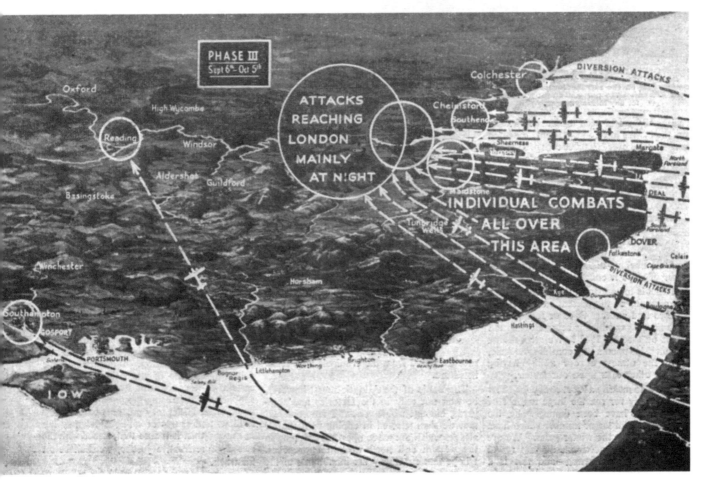

Why the Battle of the Atlantic Must Be Won

Moving in the House of Commons on April 9 a resolution of thanks to his Majesty's forces for their recent victories by sea, land and air, and to those at home who " by their labours and fortitude have furnished the means which made those successes possible," Mr. Churchill went on to describe the progress of the war. Perhaps the most important passages were those dealing with the Battle of the Atlantic which we reproduce below.

EVERYTHING turns upon the Battle of the Atlantic, which is proceeding with growing intensity on both sides. Our losses in ships and tonnage are very heavy, and, vast as are our shipping resources which we control, these losses could not continue indefinitely without seriously affecting our war effort and our means of subsistence.

It is no answer to say that we have inflicted upon the Germans and Italians a far higher proportion of loss compared with the size of their merchant fleets and the fleeting opportunities they offer us than they have upon

ON CONVOY DUTY, the navigating officer of this destroyer keeps a watchful eye on his charges and on the surrounding sea and sky. Guns are trained to port and starboard ready for any lurking danger.

us with our world-wide traffic continually maintained. We have, in fact, sunk, captured or seen scuttled over 2,300,000 tons of German and Italian shipping. But we have ourselves lost since the beginning of the war nearly 4,000,000 tons of British shipping. As against that we have gained under the British flag over 3,000,000 tons of foreign or newly constructed tonnage, not counting the considerable foreign tonnage which has also come under our control. Therefore, at the moment our enormous fleets sail the seas without any serious or obvious diminution so far as the number of ships is concerned.

But what is to happen in the future if these losses continue at the present rate? Where are we to find another three or four million tons to fill the gap which is being created, and carry us on through 1942? We are building merchant ships upon a very considerable scale, and to the utmost of our ability having regard to other calls upon our labour.

We are also making a most strenuous effort to make ready for sea the large number of vessels which have been damaged by the enemy, and a still larger number which have been damaged by the winter gales. We are doing our utmost to accelerate the turn round of our ships, remembering—and this is a

striking figure—that even 10 days saved on the turn round of our immense fleets is equal to a reinforcement of 5,000,000 tons of imports in a single year. All the energy and contrivance of which we are capable has been and will continue to be devoted to these purposes, and we are already conscious of substantial results.

But when all is said and done, the only way in which we can get through 1942 without a very sensible contraction of our war effort is by another gigantic building of merchant ships in the United States similar to that prodigy of output accomplished by the Americans in 1918. All this has been in train in the United States for many months past. There has now been a very large extension of the programme, and we have the assurance that several millions of tons of American newbuilt shipping will be available for the common struggle during the course of the next year. Here, then, is the assurance upon which we may count for the staying power without which it will not be possible to

Unceasing vigilance is needed on convoy duty. The "look-out" keeps careful watch and the crew of the A.A. machine-guns are at their station, for death comes quickly whether from sea or sky. The searchlight, just behind the look-out, is ready to train on any suspicious object at night.
Photos, Planet News

save the world from the criminals who assail its future.

The Battle of the Atlantic must, however, be won not only in the factories and shipyards, but upon blue water. I am confident that we shall succeed in coping with the air attacks which are made upon the shipping in the western and north-western approaches. I hope that eventually the inhabitants of the

sister island may realize that it is as much in their interest as in ours that their ports and air fields should be available for the naval and air forces which must operate ever farther into the Atlantic. But while I am hopeful that we shall gain mastery over the air attack upon our shipping, the U-boats and the surface raiders ranging ever farther to the westward, ever nearer to the shores of the United States, constitute a menace which must be overcome if the life of Britain is not to be endangered, and if the purposes for which the Government and people of the United States have devoted themselves are not to be frustrated.

We shall, of course, make every effort in our power. The defeat of the U-boats and of the surface raiders has been proved to be entirely a question of adequate escorts for our convoys. It will be indeed disastrous if the great masses of weapons, munitions and instruments of war of all kinds, made with the toil and skill of American hands, at the cost of the United States, and loaned to us under the Aid-to-Britain Bill, were to sink into the depths of the ocean and never reach the hard-pressed fighting line. That would be a result lamentable to us over here, and I cannot believe that it would be found acceptable to the proud and resolute people of the United States. Indeed, I am today authorized to state that 10 United States revenue cutters, fast vessels of about 2,000 tons displacement, with a fine armament and a very wide range of endurance, have already been placed at our disposal by the United States Government and will soon be in action. . .

Hitler may at any time attempt an invasion of this island. This is an ordeal from which we shall not shrink.

At the present moment he is driving south and south-east through the Balkans, and at any moment may turn upon Turkey. But there are many signs which point to a Nazi attempt to secure the granary of the Ukraine and the oil fields of the Caucasus as a German means of gaining the resources wherewith to wear down the English speaking world.

All this is speculation. But once we have gained the Battle of the Atlantic, and are certain of the constant flow of American supplies which is being prepared for us, then, however far Hitler may go, or whatever new millions and scores of millions he may lap in misery, then it is sure that, armed with the sword of retributive justice, we shall be on his track.

'Delectable Tidings' of the U-Boat War

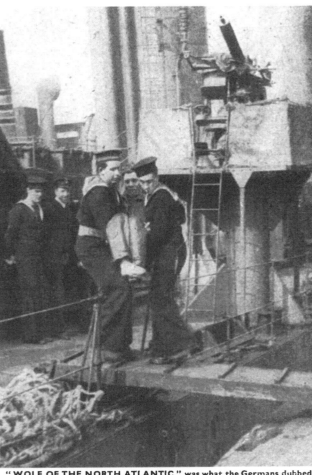

"WOLF OF THE NORTH ATLANTIC" was what the Germans dubbed Commander Otto Kretschmer, captain of U99, and one of Germany's most successful U-boat commanders. His capture was announced on April 9, 1941. Left, Commander Kretschmer lands as a prisoner from a British destroyer. Above, a member of a U-boat crew being carried ashore.

U-BOAT PRISONERS are lined up on the deck of a British destroyer which sank two enemy submarines out of the three which the Prime Minister alluded to in the House of Commons on March 18 when he referred to the certain destruction of three enemy submarines in one day as " delectable tidings of a triple event." The British Navy considers that it takes eight years' training and experience to make a first-class " submariner," so the loss of these men to Germany will be keenly felt.

Photos, Associated Press

Wellingtons & Tomahawks in the Middle East

Below is one type of American aircraft which has already arrived in the Middle East— the Tomahawk single-seater fighter, built by the Curtiss Wright Corporation. It is interesting, being the first American machine to be used by the R.A.F. powered with the Allison 1,090 h.p. twelve-cylinder liquid-cooled engine.

For some time past Wellington heavy bombers have been reinforcing our bomber squadrons in the Middle East. Circle, a wireless operator, with the navigator behind him, in a Wellington. Top, a long line of bombs ready for storage in the bomber's capacious racks.

The crew of this Wellington bomber operating in the Middle East have rather different kit from those who fly in colder regions. Their mascot is a " Santa Claus " Winston Churchill, complete with the inevitable cigar.

Photos, British Official : Crown Copyright ; and Topical

They're Turning Out Spitfires by the Hundred

THAT marvellous British fighter aircraft, the Supermarine Spitfire, is being produced in our factories in ever-increasing numbers. The latest model, the Spitfire Mark 3, has been re-powered with a new Rolls-Royce Merlin engine, has clipped wings, and is faster and more powerful than the original Spitfire. Some of them are now armed with shell-firing cannon. Many interesting operations are involved in the construction of a Spitfire. For instance, the metal skin of plated light alloy sheeting, after being rust-proofed and heat-treated, is subjected to an electric " stretching " of 600 tons, which " irons out " surface wrinkles too small to be seen by the eye. It is afterwards drilled and riveted into position by electric tools. In the sub-assembly shops the Spitfire begins to assume its familiar appearance. From the machine shops and press shops comes a continuous flow of finished parts, while from the fabricated parts store come the numerous accessories such as windscreens, self-sealing tanks, parachute-flare releases, etc. Hundreds of different machine-tools are needed for making the 90,000 components of a Spitfire.

SPITFIRES are being constructed in this vast assembly shop of a British factory, left ; men are busy working on fuselages, an interior view of one of which, showing the metal framework, is seen above.

THE ROLLS-ROYCE MERLIN, above, is a twelve-cylinder, liquid-cooled Vee engine, developing over 1,000 h.p. Right, a line of completed Spitfires waiting to undergo their tests.
Photos, P.N.A.; Ministry of Aircraft Production, Planet News, G.P.U.

Our Searchlight on the War

Twenty-four Million Trouser Buttons

PROBLEMS of supply in the Army range from tanks and 15-inch guns to stockings for the A.T.S. and buttons for battle dress, of which 24,000,000 (14 per pair of trousers) were demanded early in the war from the Quartermaster-General's department. Lt.-Gen. Sir Wilfred Lindsell, who is in charge of the Administration of the Home Forces, says that every soldier, whether at home or abroad, requires one-third of a ton of supplies per month, this ration including food, equipment, ammunition, transport, and petrol. Incidentally, it has been found that the Army uses only two-thirds of the amount of petrol consumed by private motor-cars. General Lindsell feels that it is high time that the civilian allowance was reconsidered.

U.S.A. Moves in the Battle of the Atlantic

ON April 11 President Roosevelt made two proclamations which will have a far-reaching effect on the transmission of supplies from U.S.A. to Britain. The first was that an agreement had been signed with the Danish Minister in Washington, M. Henrik Kauffmann, acting in the name of the King of Denmark, to take Greenland under American protection and to establish there naval, military and air bases. This agreement will be of immediate benefit to Britain because Canada will have free use of the bases. The ferrying of short-range warplanes across the Atlantic will now become a practical proposition. American plans for making the Western Hemisphere free from belligerent activities will be immensely helped by securing the safety of an area already threatened by Germany—as was shown by the recent flights over Greenland of enemy reconnaissance 'planes. The President's second announcement was to proclaim that the Red Sea and Gulf of Aden are no longer combat zones since British troops have wiped out all Italian resistance

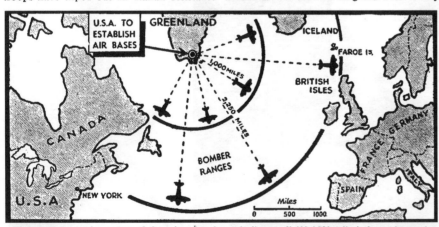

The map shows the ranges of American bombers of all types (2,000-4,500 miles), from the newly acquired U.S.A. bases in Greenland. With their aid American merchantmen could be convoyed from the air and, as British practice has proved, the bomber can be a most serious menace to U-boats when the days are long and visibility good.   *Courtesy of the "Daily Mail"*

in East Africa. This means that these waters are now open to American shipping and that war supplies can be carried to a non-belligerent country such as Egypt round the Cape of Good Hope and up the Red Sea as far as the mouth of the Suez Canal.

Changes in the Budget

IN a recent page (p. 428) we showed in a table how the cost of the war had so increased that by the end of March, 1941, the daily expenditure—over 14 millions—was more than twice that of a year earlier. In an attempt to meet this

gigantic figure the Chancellor of the Exchequer made some drastic proposals when presenting his fourth War Budget on April 7. The changes that most concern the average man and woman have to do with income tax. They are : Increase of the tax by 1s. 6d. to 10/- in the £, with reduced reliefs in personal and earned income allowances ; the extra tax payable owing to these reductions to be refunded after the war ; exemption limit reduced from £120 to £110. Two points of interest arise out of these proposals. First, the reduction in the allowances and in the exemption limit will increase by over 2,000,000 the number of persons liable to pay income tax. Second, as a result of the increases the rate of income tax and surtax will reach a maximum of 19s. 6d. in the £ on the highest incomes, a figure, as Sir Kingsley Wood remarked, " approaching the sphere of limit of taxation. In order to enjoy a tax-free income of £5,000 a year, it would be necessary to have a gross income of £66,000 a year, and very few today have an income approaching that size."

Italian Waiter's Heroism

FORTUNATO PICCHI, former Soho waiter and later assistant banqueting manager of the Savoy Hotel, has been hailed as the first Free Italian to be martyred for freedom's sake. In the last war he served as a sergeant in the Italian army and was wounded at Salonika. He came to England over twenty years ago and had not visited Italy for fourteen years. Picchi was a declared opponent of Mussolini's regime and during his recent internment in the Isle of Man he led the anti-Fascist group there. When released by a tribunal he decided to take an active part in the war, and joined the Pioneer Corps. Then he turned parachutist and, because of his familiarity with the district, he went with the British paratroops as guide in their famous descent into Calabria on February 10. But he was captured, arraigned on a charge of sabotage and shot at a place near Rome on Palm Sunday.

Kent's Mobile Library

KENT COUNTY COUNCIL, by combining imaginative sympathy with generosity, has evolved a method of brightening the lives of soldiers stationed in remote districts. It has rounded up more than 20,000 books discarded from the county libraries' shelves, and with this collection as a nucleus 33 special centres have been established from which books are distributed by a library van to out-of-the-way places where men of the fighting services are billeted. In the course

A mobile library of the Kent Education Committee used to reach Servicemen billeted in remote districts is here seen pulled up by the wayside. It supplies not only fiction and light reading, but a large variety of educational books as well.   *Photo, M. White*

of a day the van arrives at ten or twelve villages, remaining in each for anything up to one hour. Realizing how impracticable it would be to expect the return of books handed to a constantly shifting population, the Council is giving instead of lending them.

Terboven to Leave Norway

HITLER has, it is reported, approved a new plan for governing Norway by which Terboven, the Reich Commissioner, will be withdrawn, together with the whole personnel and apparatus of the German civil administration. The army of occupation will remain and, with this support, the quislingist authorities are to organize a Norwegian Riksting, or National Congress, to supersede the Storting. Quisling himself will be proclaimed head of the State and will be authorized to join the Axis Pact. Following the two recent successful naval raids on coastal centres of war industries, the German authorities intend to remove all such factories from the Norwegian islands to the mainland, where they will be less easy to invade.

Heinkel Destroyed by Ship's Mast

BY clever seamanship the captain of the British merchant vessel Jamaica Producer not only saved his ship but brought down the aggressor. It was on the evening of March 11 that a German bomber was seen to be approaching in a long low glide. When he was about 400 yards away the pilot opened his throttle, but to the watchers on the bridge of the Jamaica Producer it appeared that he might have misjudged the height of their mast. Promptly the captain put the helm hard over and the ship swung round directly in the path of the enemy. The Nazi opened fire, which was returned, and then began to climb steeply. But he was not quick enough, and his machine fouled the fore topmast, a result for which the captain had manoeuvred. Down came the wireless aerial and the topmast backstay, together with pieces of the tail of the aircraft. A moment later the Heinkel, now completely out of control, crashed into the sea. Having effected repairs, the Jamaica Producer resumed her course.

How 'Lorna Doone' Celebrated Her Jubilee

THE LORNA DOONE is a paddle-steamer, built in 1891, that plied before the war as a pleasure steamer. Right, she is seen in the days of peace. Above is the anti-aircraft gun now mounted on the decks once crowded with happy passengers.

There are still smiles on board, and above some of her crew are standing on one of the paddle-boxes and making the sign of victory after their exploit. On the fore deck the Lorna Doone carried a bigger gun, right, which was also in action against the enemy aircraft.

In command of the stout little ship at the time of the Lorna Doone's victory was Temporary Lieut. T. W. Sherrin, R.N.V.R. In peacetime he had often been a passenger on board her.

ON April 3, 1941, the Admiralty announced that a "spirited and successful action" was fought between H.M.S. Paddle Mine sweeper, Lorna Doone, and three Dornier 215s. The Nazis delivered machine-gun and bombing attacks from low-lying clouds. Shells from the Lorna Doone's guns were seen bursting round them. One of the Dorniers was seen to be on fire and losing height rapidly. A coastguard station in the neighbourhood of the action reported that large pieces were seen falling from another of the Dorniers. The third made good its escape in low visibility. By skilful manoeuvring the Lorna Doone avoided four large bombs dropped by the enemy and only two of the crew were wounded, while the only damage sustained by the little ship was superficial damage to the deck and deck-houses from machine-gun bullets. And that is the story of how a Victorian paddle steamer, built in 1891 for pleasure jaunts, kept her end up against the apparently overwhelming force of three modern Dornier bombers.

After the ship had returned to port the ratings assembled in their mess and were joined by the officers. Mugs of beer were passed round, and Lieutenant T. W. Sherrin, R.N.V.R. (her captain), spoke a few words to the crew and read out some of the many messages of congratulation received. In an interview he said : "Little did I think, when I sailed in her as a tripper between Bournemouth and Southampton, that I should ever live to command the old Lorna Doone. Why, I used to look up at that bridge and wonder what it was like. I know now."

Able Seaman G. Bee, the gunner who hit one of the 'planes, is a Welshman nicknamed "Buzzer." He carried on his steel helmet a reminder that he would rather be called "Taff."

Photos. " News Chronicle" and G.P.U.

What Healthy Young Woman *Wants* to Be Idle?

Chimney sweeping is one of the hard tasks in which women are lending a hand. This woman sweeps chimneys with her sister.

Street lamps must still be kept in order. In Sheffield some of this work is done by a former mannequin in a London store.

Here a girl on a farm near Marlborough, Wilts, is using a "fiddle drill," the "bow" of which is drawn backwards and forwards to scatter seed.

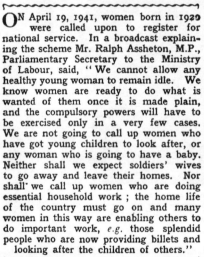

ON April 19, 1941, women born in 1920 were called upon to register for national service. In a broadcast explaining the scheme Mr. Ralph Assheton, M.P., Parliamentary Secretary to the Ministry of Labour, said, "We cannot allow any healthy young woman to remain idle. We know women are ready to do what is wanted of them once it is made plain, and the compulsory powers will have to be exercised only in a very few cases. We are not going to call up women who have got young children to look after, or any woman who is going to have a baby. Neither shall we expect soldiers' wives to go away and leave their homes. Nor shall we call up women who are doing essential household work ; the home life of the country must go on and many women in this way are enabling others to do important work, *e.g.* those splendid people who are now providing billets and looking after the children of others."

The village blacksmith at Norton-on-Tees near Stockton can get no male assistant, so his 16-year-old daughter is following in her father's footsteps.

The morning milk is handled by milkmaids at both ends of its journey to the breakfast-table. This girl pushes her truck on a long round in the City of London.

On the railway platforms women are doing porters' and ticket collectors' work. This portress (left) is a married woman, but after doing her housework in the morning she goes on duty at a Birmingham station for a long spell, seven days a week. Ilford has tried the experiment of employing women to collect salvage. Right, a squad are loading up a corporation dustcart.

Photos, Planet News, "Daily Mirror," Keystone and Topical

I Was There! . . . . *Eye Witness Stories of the War*

I Was Nearly Caught in Salonika

The Greek withdrawal by sea from Macedonia and Thrace of scores of officers and hundreds of men was an achievement ranking as a smaller "Dunkirk." Here is the eye-witness story of the correspondent of the "Chicago Daily News," who was the only foreign correspondent in northern Greece at the time of the German advance.

MOST of the Greek army holding the northern frontier against the Germans were able to withdraw from around Salonika Bay. They blew up bridges as they went.

But to save the heavy equipment of the artillery and the invaluable technical heads of the General Staff of the Eastern campaign and to accomplish thoroughly the work of sabotage, relatively small Greek forces had to hold the breach during the withdrawal.

When the surrender of Salonika was imminent these men, having loyally done their job as a stopgap, were given the choice of yielding to the Germans or making their way to the sea, where a motley assortment of vessels of all sizes awaited them. Some refused both alternatives and went on fighting.

Being the only foreign correspondent in northern Greece during the German occupation, I was able to choose between going southward by motor-car or railway with the General Staff's equipment and the majority of the troops, and taking the chance of embarking with the ragamuffin flotilla.

This began leaving Macedonian and Thracian seaports 48 hours after the last bridge over the Cestos had been blown up and mobile retreat westward voluntarily cut off.

Luckily I chose the latter and slower course. I was accompanied throughout the three and a half days' journey by Mrs. Ray Brock, the wife of the "New York Times" correspondent, who had arrived from Belgrade aboard the last train before the Nazi invasion overran the Vardar Valley.

Caiques, as the Greeks call their small fishing boats, were the principal conveyances from the burning Salonika waterfront, which we reached by taxi at the moment when the fiercest night raid by the Germans was directed against the port.

The first left Salonika Bay three hours before the Germans arrived, with firing already audible in the suburbs, and with an unearthly glare from the oil tanks fired by the British demolition experts reddening the sea. Two large buildings topping the peninsular cliff were walls of flame as the caique passed.

As the sun rose the horizon ahead bulked heavy with the outline of Cassandra, the first of the three peninsulas extending south-eastward from Chalcidici. The skipper's intention was to pass through the canal bisecting Cassandra at Potiri.

The sergeant in charge at Potiri insisted that the boat must leave immediately without pausing for provisions. Mrs. Brock and I here bade adieu to the first caique, whose captain, in his anxiety to obey the sergeant, quickly sailed for a remote island in the middle Aegean, taking all our luggage as well as our overcoats and food.

About an hour after the caique left another was found at the canal's eastern end. Finally sail was hoisted, the engine panted, and the vessel began clipping the waves southward, barely half an hour, as it was ascertained from the following craft, before the German squads reached Potiri.

When another lumbering caique overtook our boat the colonel commanding ordered

contact to be made, and the ships were brought together.

Many soldiers, federal constabulary, and troopers in blue-green uniforms were ordered overside, and, learning that the new caique was bound for an island a few hours from our baggage destination, we also clambered from one bucking vessel to the other.

The sea retreat was organized upon the waves. Majors and colonels upon poops of dozens of craft, most of them less than 40 ft. long, talked over the situation with old island salts. Meals consisting of soft black bread and oranges, with hard tack as dessert, were served by passengers tossing food from hand to hand.

On the second night the sea grew rough, and the cold was too great for sleep upon the rainswept crowded decks. Before dawn came the craft had picked her way into the harbour of a land-locked island far to the south.

The harbour was crowded by dozens of caiques, and a worried portmaster was pacing the stony quay endeavouring to persuade the skippers to leave promptly so as to eliminate the danger of air raids.

A terrific wind was blowing, but eventually the craft began to slip out, and we found a fourth vessel bound for a near-by island where our luggage had been deposited.

Embarking again, we finally reached the white-walled town where we rejoined the original transport squad and spent the night in relative comfort on a wooden bench.

In the starlit morning we set out in a tiny motor-boat for a small bay on the island of Euboea, which we reached about noon, and after a two-mile hike to the nearest village a motor-car was procured which brought the entire company to one of the principal towns in central Greece. After the mayor himself had turned out the constabulary to find a taxi, I set forth on the long drive to Athens.

SALONIKA HARBOUR, from which the small Greek force that held the town so gallantly escaped, is here seen with some of the "motley assortment of vessels" that is always to be found there, including caiques, picturesque sailing vessels that trade round the coast and between the Greek islands. Before the town fell to the Germans everything that could have been of use to them, including all the public utilities, was destroyed.   *Photo, E.N.A.*

We 'Roof-Hopped' Over Hamburg

During a recent raid on Hamburg one of our heavy bombers came down to 3,000 feet in the teeth of a heavy barrage, bombed the target, and swooped down to within 20 feet of the rooftops to baffle the search-lights and A.A. fire. Here is a first-hand account of this exploit.

DESCRIBING his adventurous night, the sergeant-pilot said : Over Hamburg we were getting near to our target and thought we were unobserved when suddenly one searchlight picked us up and immediately 20 more came up and held us in a cone of light. We got clear by coming down in a screaming dive and from 3,000 feet we released our bombs.

The bomb aimer said he could clearly distinguish through the slight haze and smoke from factory chimneys the block of buildings we wanted to hit. Then we could see our bombs explode right on the dot. The buildings went up in flames, first white and then red, which showed that the fire had got a complete hold. But again we were caught in the searchlights and flak was weaving around us.

The rear gunner was temporarily disabled by a hunk of shrapnel which tore through his turrets, pierced his Irvin jacket, and without drawing blood raised a hell of a lump on his arm. The hydraulic system in the rear turret was damaged, and the front gunner also reported that for the time being his guns wouldn't work. I found it very difficult to get away from the searchlights and flak, and the second pilot called out that if we didn't get out of it we should have to hit the deck.

I went down to 20 feet and then the rear gunner called out that he had got one gun going again and asked me if he could use it. He tried it out on a row of buildings we were passing and reported that it was doing fine. I could see everything beautifully and I was doing some quite pretty tree-hopping when, not more than 200 yards ahead, a new light suddenly shone right in our eyes and we were almost blinded. I yelled to the front gunner to shoot it out, and out it went.

Above is a Wellington bomber returning to an aerodrome at dawn after a raid over Germany. The photograph was taken by infra-red ray methods. Top, a flare with which the target is lit up is being placed in the chute of one of our bombers.

All at once I saw a wood only 20 yards in front of us ; the tops of the trees were standing up ten feet above us. I hauled back the control column to clear the branches and just then I saw with a gasp of relief some high tension cables below us which we had just missed by no more than six feet.

This wasn't the end of our adventures. When we had got away from Hamburg and were over Holland, my rear gunner called out : " There's a Me.110 tailing us."

We watched the enemy, looking very confident and rakish as he sailed gaily along 50 feet above us. He never fired, I can only imagine because he was searching the sky above him, and couldn't have expected to find a heavy bomber skimming along so near the ground. But the gunners on the ground knew where we were, and were firing red tracer bullets just above us to give the enemy fighter our position. The front gunner turned his turret round and I saw his tracer going right into the enemy's fuselage. The Me. did a steep dive and we never saw him again. I think he was finished.

After it was all over my second pilot told me that he thought I was trying to knock people over on the roads, I was flying so low. I don't know whether we knocked anyone over, but we certainly gave the people in Hamburg a nasty shock.

Anti-aircraft gunfire of the most intense severity is directed against British airmen when they raid German towns. This photograph, from a German source, is stated to show the barrage over a North German town while a raid is in progress. It was through such a screen of shells that our airmen, as described in the stirring narrative in this page, dived down to within 20 feet of the rooftops.
Photos, British Official ; Crown Copyright ; and Associated Press

This Is How We Entered Asmara

Asmara, capital of Eritrea, surrendered with dramatic suddenness on April 1. A Special Correspondent of the "Daily Herald" rode with the vanguard of Imperial troops who occupied the town, and his story of the scenes of surrender is told below.

LONG before dawn I had started in an Army truck to see the tanks go through in what everyone imagined would be merely the latest of our attacks on the Keren-Asmara road. An attack by Indian infantry during the night had bought us to a road block outside the village of Teclesan, some 25 miles from the capital.

In the half-light I paused to watch the tank assault on the position. Suddenly a civilian car came round a corner towards us.

It was a small open brown Fiat. In it were two khaki-clad Italian officers and one British. On the left side of the windscreen was a large white flag. Bruno, of the Asmara police, was driving to advanced divisional headquarters to arrange the bloodless surrender of Asmara.

I waited in the village for the result. The scenery might have been that of a Cornish moor—rolling hills with savage outcrops of stone grey, a watery light, and a high, cool breeze.

The sexton of the church was just sounding the bell for mass when the order came to move on. For the next 20 miles I might have been the centre of a Royal procession. Almost all along the road we met groups of Italian soldiers straggling back to be made prisoners, with the weary air of schoolboys released from a stiff day's work, or recumbent by the roadside like picnickers waiting to be picked up. Soldiers all saluted us; some even cried "Viva."

We were also greeted by natives, who ran to the roadside to clap hands at our passage, while women hailed us with shrill cries of "Lulubu."

Over the horizon at last the tall latticed towers of Asmara radio loomed, and in a great amphitheatre of low stony hills the negotiators confronted each other. Our side of the road and the slopes beside it were crammed with tanks, Bren carriers, lorries and troops. On the Italian side there was a procession of three small cars and a big green-grey bus.

Before the negotiators stepped into the bus for their talks I got an outline of the events leading to the collapse from an Italian officer.

On the Eve of Surrender

Eritrea had been having a hard time. Foods were severely rationed and wine almost unobtainable. Bus services were running on charcoal. But, even after Keren s fall, optimists believed that resistance might be prolonged for another month or two till the saving rains came and the Germans could help. Then came news that our tanks had broken through and that an entire battalion of Savoy Grenadiers sent from Addis had surrendered to a man. The R.A.F. raids were becoming unendurable. Military and civil chiefs were in almost constant conference. Finally two Abyssinian conscript battalions mutinied in Asmara barracks, shot their officers and started to loot the town.

It was evident that safety lay only in surrender. A proclamation issued by the police chief was posted on every wall in the city. "British troops, despite the heroic resistance of our officers and men, have finally broken our lines." It said, "Asmara is an open city. Nobody must resist the adversary when he enters."

Just half an hour was taken over the discussions in the bus. The brigadier commanding the British advanced column inquired about the functioning of police and municipal services, and the whereabouts of British prisoners, who had to be surrendered at once. The Italians were told they must put their clocks back an hour to Sudan time, though the brigadier called it "B.B.C. time," hand over arms and material undestroyed, continue the curfew, and hand over the barracks. They were informed that we would try to continue a postal service to Italy, under British censorship.

This 9 a.m. meeting was strangely matter-of-fact. Every now and then the sound of a distant explosion would be heard through the windows, and an Italian officer would throw his hands in the air. "That's a mutinous battalion throwing grenades," he would say. "We need your help quickly."

But for the most part Gen. Barile, Chief Secretary of the Government, and the police chief, Pasquinale, replied as briskly and unemotionally as the brigadier asked questions.

And so we moved on past the rusty bins of the municipal dump to the eucalyptus-lined avenues of Asmara with their blocks of modern flats. Dark-haired girls who pretended not to be looking at us stared from behind every closed window. Saluting policemen lined the road at 50-yard intervals.

As we reached the central square a convoy of British fighters roared down over the roofs to salute the arrival of the Imperial force.

Then I witnessed the memorable scene outside the new and red-brick Governor's Palace.

At exactly 11 o'clock an Italian guard of honour in khaki and topees sprang to the "Present." At the same moment the British brigadier alighted from the first of a procession of cinnamon- and coffee-coloured army trucks.

Italian officers standing on the palace steps saluted him. Indian soldiers, seated with rifle or machine-gun in hand in a long train of vehicles, gazed in wonder at brick-red geraniums, purple bougainvillaeas and splashing fountains in the little public garden before the palace.

Up and down the broad Via Benito Mussolini rifle-bearing policemen and civilian vigilantes shouted "Sinistra, Sinistra" (Left) to puzzled cyclists, who wove the oddest patterns in the streets till they realized that under British occupation the rule of "Keep left" must apply. The Imperial forces had arrived in Asmara.

ASMARA, administrative capital of Eritrea, was entered by the Imperial Forces on April 1, 1941. Above is a photograph taken on February 19, 1941, during one of the R.A.F. attacks on the aerodrome there. 2, Hangars with holes in the roofs. 3, Demolished buildings. 4, Damaged hangars. 5, Large devastated area. 6, Damaged motor transport buildings. 7, Bombs bursting. 8, Aircraft on fire.

Photo, British Official : Crown Copyright

Our Diary of the War

FRIDAY, APRIL 11, 1941   587th day

Air.—R.A.F. carried out extensive sweep of North Sea. Patrol ships hit. Fortified buildings on North Frisian coast bombed.

War against Italy.—British troops fighting west of Tobruk. R.A.F. harassing enemy by intense bombing attacks. R.A.F. raid on Calato aerodrome at night.

Home.—Heavy night raid on Bristol. South-coast town suffered sharp attack. Six raiders destroyed.

Balkan War.—Empire Forces drove Germans back near Florina after all-day fighting. R.A.F. made widespread attacks on motor transport and tank columns between Monastir and Prilep.

German troops in Zagreb. Croatia declared independent State. Hungarian troops occupied area between Drava and Tisza rivers.

German bombers raided Piraeus. Two shot down. Enemy sank hospital ship Attiki.

SATURDAY, APRIL 12   588th day

Sea.—Norwegian destroyer made night raid on Oksfjord, near Hammerfest, N. Norway, and destroyed large fish oil factory.

Air.—Day attacks on shipping off Dutch coast, docks and petrol stores at Flushing, targets north of the Ruhr.

Two enemy supply ships bombed near Fécamp. Fighter Command attacked aerodrome at Le Touquet and storage tanks at Hazebrouck.

Night attacks on Brest, Lorient and aerodrome at Merignac.

War against Italy.—Bardia occupied by enemy, British troops having withdrawn. Fighting reported from Tobruk and Sollum.

Home.—No daylight raids. At night bombs fell near South Coast.

Balkan War.—Germany claimed that units of tank division entered Belgrade during night of 12-13.

Yugoslavs said to have captured Durazzo.

SUNDAY, APRIL 13   589th day

Air.—R.A.F. bombed shipping off Dutch and German coasts. At night raids were made on Merignac and docks at Bordeaux.

War against Italy.—R.A.F. attacked enemy concentrations in various areas of Cyrenaica. At night Tripoli was bombed.

Home.—Slight day activity over S. and E. coasts. At night bombs damaged a N.W. town. Enemy bomber shot down off Cornwall.

Balkan War.—During night of 12-13 Empire Forces in Greece withdrew to new positions south of R. Vistritsa.

Yugoslavs reported to have counter-attacked near Nish.

During night of 13-14 R.A.F. bombed Sofia.

Many enemy convoys attacked in regions of Yannitsa, Ptolemais and Koziani.

General.—Soviet Union and Japan signed neutrality pact.

MONDAY, APRIL 14   590th day

Air.—Day attacks on enemy shipping off Dutch coast and many targets inland. Heavy night raid on Brest.

War against Italy.—German attack on Tobruk completely repulsed. Reported that B.E.F. had withdrawn to Mersa Matruh.

Germany claimed capture of Sollum and Fort Capuzzo.

R.A.F. shot down 22 enemy aircraft near Tobruk. Heavy night raid on Tripoli, and on aerodromes at Derna, El Adem and Menastir.

Retreating Italian army hemmed in north-west of Addis Ababa.

Home.—During day bombs fell in various districts. Sharp evening raid on two N.E. coast towns. Two enemy aircraft destroyed, one by naval trawler.

Balkan War.—Fleet Air Arm destroyed two large ships in Valona harbour. R.A.F. bombed bridge over R. Vardar at Veles. Motor transport on Veles-Prilep road attacked.

Yugoslav counter-attacks at Topola and Barberin, in Morava Valley.

Italians claimed recapture of Koritza.

Athens suffered first daylight raid. Preveza and Yannina also bombed.

TUESDAY, APRIL 15   591st day

Sea.—Enemy convoy of five transports and three escort vessels sunk by Navy off Tripoli. H.M. destroyer Mohawk lost during action.

H.M. submarine Tigris reported to have sunk heavily laden tanker.

Loss of H.M.S. Bonaventure while escorting convoy reported.

Air.—R.A.F. sank two supply vessels off French coast. Borkum bombed. Offensive patrols over Channel and Northern France.

At night Kiel was heavily bombed. Other targets in N. Germany and docks at Boulogne also attacked.

War against Italy.—Duke of Aosta sent envoy to Diredawa to parley with British.

R.A.F. heavily damaged troops and transport in El Adem—Tobruk—Bardia area.

A.A.F. destroyed four Junkers over Capuzzo.

Home.—Main night raid on Belfast and elsewhere in Northern Ireland. Eight enemy aircraft destroyed.

Balkan War.—Cairo reported that British right sector had repulsed several attacks.

Violent enemy air attacks against Larissa,

Volo, Trikkala and Karditza. Five German dive-bombers shot down over Piraeus area.

WEDNESDAY, APRIL 16   592nd day

Air.—Blenheim bombers attacked Heligoland and aerodrome at Berck-sur-Mer. Heavy night attack on Bremen, other N. German towns and on Brest docks.

War against Italy.—Enemy attacks on Tobruk repulsed. British patrol made successful sorties, capturing many prisoners and destroying 20 tanks.

Fort Capuzzo bombarded by Navy.

Punishing attacks by R.A.F. on enemy troops and landing grounds in Cyrenaica. Heavy night raid on Tripoli shipping and harbour buildings.

Home.—Great force of raiders made 7-hour indiscriminate attack on London. Heavy casualties and much damage. Six enemy aircraft destroyed.

Balkan War.—Big battle in Macedonia. German units crossed Vistritsa at two points. Servia occupied. Advance continued towards Kalabaka.

THURSDAY, APRIL 17   593rd day

Air.—Day attack on Cherbourg and enemy merchant shipping. Severest night raid yet made on Berlin, new heavy bombs being used. Attacks on Rotterdam, Cologne and elsewhere.

War against Italy.—British patrols engaged in hard fighting near Tobruk and Sollum. R.A.F. attacked Derna and continued to harass enemy transport.

In Abyssinia British forces were in contact with enemy 14 miles south of Dessie. Troops advancing south and south-west of Addis Ababa and north from Negelli and Yavello.

Home.—Bombs fell on town in N.E. Scotland. Portsmouth heavily raided at night. Three enemy bombers destroyed.

Balkan War.—Allies holding firm against increased German pressure. Many successful counter-attacks. R.A.F. ceaselessly attacked enemy supply lines.

Germany stated Yugoslavia had capitulated. Greeks evacuating positions in Albania.

FRIDAY, APRIL 18   594th day

Air.—Two merchant ships and one escort vessel set on fire off Heligoland by R.A.F. Two supply ships hit and left sinking off Norway.

War against Italy.—British patrols again active outside Tobruk and Sollum.

In East Africa S.A.A.F. bombed aerodromes at Kombolcha and Sciasciamanna.

Balkan War.—Greek and Imperial Forces gradually withdrawing to shorter line of defence, under cover of fierce rearguard action. Germans advanced both sides of Mt. Olympus, evacuated by British, and occupied Larissa.

General.—Mr. Koryzis, Greek Premier, died.

APRIL 12. MR. CHURCHILL VISITED SWANSEA during his tour of bombed areas in South Wales and Bristol. " I go about the country," said the Premier, " whenever I can escape from my duty at headquarters, and I see the damage done by the enemy's attacks, but I also see, side by side with the devastation and amid the ruins, glad, confident, bright and smiling eyes . . . . I see the spirit of an unconquerable people."
                                                                                                            Photo, Associated Press

AN ANZAC OF THE LAST WAR, HE LLEADS THE ANZACS IN THIS

LIEUT. GENERAL SIR THOMAS BLAMEY, who has been appointed Deputy Commander-in-Chief for the Middle East, was Chief of Staff of the Australian Corps in 1918, at the youthful age of 34. During his four years' service in the last war he was mentioned seven times in dispatches and won the D.S.O. in 1917. In 1938 he was Controller General of Recruiting in Australia; two years later he was in command of the Australian Forces in Egypt and his men formed the spearhead of Wavell's attack across the Western Desert. In announcing General Blamey's new appointment in a broadcast to Australia, Mr. Menzies, the Commonwealth Premier, spoke of his " very skilled and gallant services."

Photo, Associated Press

How Britons and Anzacs Fought in Greece

Driven ever backward by the overwhelming hordes of Hitler's war machine, the Forces of the Empire gave most gallant and resolute support to their Greek allies. Below we give an account of the fierce rearguard actions in which Anzacs and Britons, fighting side by side, wrote fresh and never-to-be-forgotten pages in the Empire's annals.

WHEN the Germans, taking advantage of the fatal gap which had developed between the Yugoslavs and the Greeks, pushed south from Monastir across the frontier into Greece, they were opposed by a British armoured force. Although the British were outnumbered by 20 to one, they put up a resolute defence and inflicted the most severe punishment on the Adolf Hitler Division, which constituted the Nazi van. Retreating in good order, they reached a mountain pass to the south of Florina ; here the defence was taken over by British infantry while the armoured units passed through to the rear. For 27 hours a furious battle raged as the Germans strove to eject the British from their positions. At length, after a tremendous artillery bombardment—the Germans were now using a new gun of 105 cm.—supported by incessant dive-bombing attacks and an almost continuous onslaught by wave after wave of

in battle across the one flat strip of land in World War style, and all the time the German infantry were being mown down in wave after wave, until the Flanders poppies in the field looked dull beside the red earth which these men embraced now." For four hours the battle raged at the entrance to the Kozani pass, and it continued as the Australians fell back, bitterly contesting every foot of the way. One Australian unit, we are told, hung on to their position in the heights until they were 20 miles behind the German lines ; yet they fought their way back to their comrades.

Then a fresh stand was made on a bridge over the Haliakmon (Vistritsa), to the west of Mount Olympus. "I would not have believed it," said a young Australian machine-gunner to "The Times" correspondent. "They came up the side of the road like flies, shouting something. We were giving it to them from all sides, and they went down

like you see in the movies. It was just like a movie."

For some days it had been realized that it was impossible to hold the line which rested on the Pindus mountains and Mount Olympus —more particularly when the Germans thrust through the Metsovo pass and took the Greeks holding the left flank in the rear. "In face of increasing pressure by German forces which are daily being reinforced," said a communiqué issued by British G.H.Q. in the Middle East on April 18, "Greek and Imperial forces on the northern front are gradually withdrawing to a shorter line of defence." More detailed was the story given in a bulletin issued by the Greek Press Ministry on April 20. After stating that along the whole line of the British and Greek fronts the Germans were still attacking fiercely, the bulletin went on to say that the Allied line, although it had been modified at some points at the initiative of the defenders, remained unbroken, and all the violent efforts by the enemy to force a decisive and immediate issue had failed.

"The German losses are enormous. The Nazis are bringing up more and more reinforcements of mechanized units, infantry, and aircraft. But in spite of all their efforts, the British and Greeks fight like lions, still holding their positions." Advancing in waves, the Germans attempted to force the passes at all costs. They failed, and paid dearly for their failure. In the Olympus area the Germans continued to sacrifice the lives of their soldiers by the thousand, without being able to break through. "The heroic exploits of our allies," went on the bulletin, "the Australians and New Zealanders, are weaving new legends round the slopes of Mount Olympus."

But at length the line which pivoted on Olympus had to be abandoned, and the Allies fell back across the plain of Thessaly, and took up new positions south of Larisa. The new line was shorter and easier to hold,

Volo, above, which the Germans claimed to have reached on April 22, 1941, stands on an inlet of the Aegean Sea and is the chief port of Thessaly. Right, is the pass of Thermopylae, around which Imperial troops put up a heroic resistance.
Photos, Fox and E.N.A.

infantry, the British were compelled to withdraw as far as Kozani, where they again turned at bay.

Here the Australians came into action, and from their gun pits cut in the side of the mountain played havoc with the enemy hordes. "From the mountains covering the pass," wrote an Australian correspondent in "The Times," "Australian big guns pounded day and night at the German troops' transport positions below. Machine-guns were

'They Wove New Legends Round Mt. Olympus'

This map shows the approximate lines held by the Allied forces in Greece on April 17, 18, 21 and 23, 1941, during the masterly withdrawal from the Mt. Olympus line to the new position near Thermopylae. This line was in turn abandoned, and the Nazis entered Athens on April 27.
Specially drawn for THE WAR ILLUSTRATED *by Felix Gardon*

GERMAN LANDING 21ST APRIL

GREEK EPIRUS ARMY SURRENDERS 23RD APRIL

APPROX. LINE	
APRIL 17TH	▪▪▪▪▪▪▪
„ 18TH	▬●▬●▬
„ 21ST	+ + + +
„ 23RD	▬▬▬▬

stretching across the mountain ranges where our big guns were already in position. To it struggled back the Australians and New Zealanders, closely followed by the enemy tanks. At Larisa a body of the Anzacs was surrounded by the German mechanized forces. Some of the enemy strove to cut them off, but the British and Imperial troops turned and fought their way through the streets out of the town. "The fighting was terrific," said a B.U.P. war correspondent. "Not only were the Germans using their tanks where they could, but their infantry were roaming the town with tommy-guns, lying in wait for the British and Imperial troops at the street corners. All round the defenders the town was burning, having been set on fire through the repeated bombings from the air, and through this a few of our troops fought their way out."

Of German origin, this photograph purports to show a German anti-tank gun in action in the Balkans. Enemy tanks are approaching under cover of smoke. *Photo, Keystone*

Here is another picture of the retreat drawn by the same correspondent. "I watched lines of British infantry and artillery and munitions manoeuvre along the mountain roads or along tracks by the sea shore. Every path of the convoys wound along like a snake as far as I could see, throwing up dust which covered the steel-helmeted Aussies and New Zealanders with grey powder. Many of the troops had just left the line after bitter fighting. They lay sprawled out on top of their kit, piled on the lorries. When they could they slept under the warm sun. By them flashed dispatch riders and staff cars, taking 'brass hats' up the line. Tanks lumbered along at a fair speed, while the more nippy Bren-gun carriers moved quickly over the mountain terrain."

Only too often the enemy pilots had it all their own way. If only we had a hundred more Hurricanes, cabled the B.U.P. correspondent, they would give us a margin to break the enemy's domination of the air. But not only in the air were the enemy numerically superior. "The British forces are outnumbered," wrote "The Times" Australian correspondent. "It has been the same since the German push started. More tanks, guns, aeroplanes, men. If the British had equal, or even half, their strength here in men and aeroplanes, this would have been a different story."

Now it was that Lieut.-Gen. Sir Thomas. Blamey, General Wavell's deputy and the Anzac G.O.C., issued an Order of the Day, in which, after a reference to the magnificent way in which the Anzac corps and attached troops had carried out the withdrawal, he declared that "with strong hearts, energy and determination on the part of every officer and man, we can hold this position. I call on every Anzac to set his teeth and to be worthy of his fathers." But it was not to be. Against the thin khaki line the Germans flung fresh masses of infantry, dive bombers, tanks. . . . On April 25—Anzac Day, anniversary of the landing of the first Anzacs on Gallipoli in 1915 — the Germans were able to claim that the pass of Thermopylae had been taken by a pincer attack. Nor had it been intended that the new line should be held for more than a brief space, just sufficient space to enable the main body of British and Imperial troops to complete their withdrawal from the Greek mainland. The Greek army on the left had been crushed into capitulation. The German bombers, operating from aerodromes only 20 minutes' flying time away, were smashing the Greek towns and ports. At 9.25 on the following morning (Sunday, April 27) the last British resistance was brushed aside or overcome by Hitler's mechanized hordes, and the swastika, floating above the Acropolis, looked down on the German tanks thundering through the streets of Athens.

The Greeks Fought Nobly to the End

After putting up a tremendous fight against odds which might well have appalled a people far more numerous, far more powerful, gallant little Greece was at last overwhelmed by the armies sent against her by the two empires of the Axis. Here is an account of the concluding phase of a campaign which may well rank in history as amongst the most glorious ever fought by a little nation.

FOLLOWING the collapse of the Yugoslav resistance in South Serbia, the Germans poured through the Monastir Gap into Greece in a flood of men and mechanized armament hardly to be withstood. The Greeks put up a hard and bitter resistance, but every effort was made by strong German mechanized forces to break through their defences and to separate them from their allies, the Forces of the Empire, who were holding the right flank of a line pivoted on Mount Olympus. Again and again the Greeks managed to extricate themselves, but only at the price of retreat all along the line.

During the week-end that followed the German pressure increased. British rearguards were driven from Mount Olympus, and the Nazi tanks broke through to the plain of Thessaly. West of the Pindus mountains the Greeks continued their withdrawal; and in Albania, too, the Italians were able to claim a considerable advance—although in this case it was achieved not by hard fighting but because the Greeks had made a strategic withdrawal. Then on April 21 German forces pushed their way across the Pindus, through the pass of Metsovo, thus threatening to take in the rear the Greek divisions still holding on tenaciously to the

thrust separated them from their allies to the south and east, and made their position hazardous in the extreme. Moreover, the

retreating columns were also exposed to constant assault from the air. " We were bombed continuously throughout the day," said a Greek soldier. " We had only one or two roads on which to withdraw to our new positions. Waves of German bombers ranged up and down, machine-gunning and bombing until the roads were unusable." At last the Greeks could endure no more, and what was left of the army in Epirus and Macedonia opened up negotiations for an armistice.

" In the course of attacks by German forces deep into the flank of the Greek Northern Army," read an announcement made by the German High Command on April 23, " capitulations of a local character and offers for an armistice were addressed to the Commander of the 12th German Army. Yesterday a Greek deputation submitted an offer to lay down arms to the Commander of the Italian 11th Army in the Epirus sector. The entire Greek Northern and Epirus Army, hemmed in by the Italian armed forces from the north and by the German troops from the east, and cut off from its rear communications, has capitulated."

The armistice was concluded in the mountain villa near Salonika which had been made the headquarters of Field-Marshal von List's staff. It was signed for the Greeks by General Tsolakoglu, for the Germans by General Jodl, and for the Italians by Lieut.-General Ferrero ; it came into force at 6 p.m. on April 23. Though their surrender was unconditional, the valour of the Greek troops was recognized by the Germans, who agreed to their officers keeping their swords and equipment. It was also stated that, as soon as military operations in continental Greece and the Ionian Islands had been concluded, the question of releasing the prisoners would be taken in hand.

News of the capitulation was given by the King of the Hellenes to his people in a message telling them of his decision to leave Athens—with his brother, the heir to the throne, and the lawful Government—and proceed to Crete, which henceforth would contain the nation's capital (*see* inset).

On the same day M. Tsouderos, the Greek Premier, attributed the capitulation of the Epirus Army to " fatigue brought about by six months' unequal but victorious struggle."

But surely no excuse was needed for the Greek surrender ; no shadow of reproach could rest upon that gallant little people. Right to the end the voice of liberty spoke from Athens. " Greeks, stand firm," came the broadcast on Saturday night, April 26, " be each one proud and dignified . . . have Greece in your hearts ; live inspired with the fire of her latest triumph and the glory of her army. Greece will live again and will be great because she fought honestly for a just cause and for freedom. Brothers ! Have courage and patience. Be stouthearted. We will overcome these hardships. We have been an honest nation and brave soldiers." Only a few hours later the Germans marched in.

Here are men of the Greek Army on the march in Albania, their capes wound around them as protection against the icy wind. Many of them, cut off from their rear communications by the Germans' eastward thrust, were forced to surrender.   *Photo, Keystone*

Albanian front. Attacked from two sides, the Greeks again withdrew ; yet even now they turned time and again and bloodily repulsed Mussolini's troops. Italian war correspondents described the Greek resistance as exceptionally stubborn. The Greeks, they said, made clever use of the ground and their well-prepared defences. Furthermore, their rearguards systematically destroyed the roads and bridges as they withdrew, so that the Italian triumph was won only by tremendous efforts and sacrifices.

The passage of the Metsovo Pass proved to be decisive. Till then the Greek armies of Epirus and Western Macedonia were withdrawing in quite good order before the Italians. Now, however, this new German

Following the sudden death of M. Koryzis, the Greek premier (left), on April 18, 1941, King George called upon M. Tsouderos, the Greek Foreign Secretary (right), to take over the office.
Photos, Keystone and Associated Press

The Lion of Judah Rampant Once More

A FTER the fall of Addis Ababa the Italian northern army retreated among the hills in face of the steady advance of Imperial forces and Abyssinian Patriots, and it was not until April 18 that they turned and made a stand before Dessie, in a strong defensive position astride the mountains where a semicircular mountain ridge commands the main motor road. In a battle described as the fiercest of the entire Abyssinian campaign, the Italians were completely routed by the South Africans; and from Nairobi on April 28 came the news that Dessie was ours.

Meanwhile General Wavell urged the Duke of Aosta to surrender, since he could accept no responsibility for protecting and succouring Italian nationals except in places already occupied by British forces. General Wavell's plea was made in the interests of humanity, for reports reached London that in the Jimma area of Abyssinia Italian native troops had got out of hand and were burning houses and looting ; in this area there were at that time no British troops.

HAILE SELASSIE, Emperor of Ethiopia, who was an exile for over five years after the Fascists overran his country in 1935, once more trod the soil of his native land when he crossed the frontier on January 15, 1941. After an arduous trek of two weeks from the Sudan with a train of camels, he made his headquarters 200 miles beyond the frontier. He is seen in the top photograph, at his camp, where he had a guard of a few officers and Patriot troops, some of whom, in the lower photograph, proudly display the Emperor's standard emblazoned with the Lion of Judah.

Photos, British Official : Crown Copyright

Now the Germans Swept on to Egypt

With disconcerting suddenness the situation in Libya was transformed when in a few days German mechanized formations recaptured what the Army of the Nile had taken as many weeks to capture. An account of the German advance to the frontier of Egypt follows below, together with some details of the British counter-measures.

WHEN Benghazi was captured on February 6, the Imperial Army of the Nile moved on beyond it to take El Agheila, some 130 miles to the south-west. There the advance was halted. The campaign in Libya was finished—and a very satisfactory conclusion it seemed to be from the British point of view, since the most fertile region of the Italian Empire in North Africa had been seized at a trifling cost and the Italian army of 150,000 men had been completely destroyed.

True, there were some who argued that General Wavell should have pushed on to Tripoli. But General Wavell's critics did not know what he knew—that the clouds of war were gathering thick and heavy above the mountains of the Balkans. Bulgaria signed a pact with Germany on March 2, and her adhesion to the Axis was considered to be a prelude to a German attack on Greece. The Greeks had deserved well of their allies ; and so some of the finest regiments from the Army of the Nile and much of its armoured strength were conveyed across the sea to Greece. Others of General Wavell's men were dispatched to East Africa, there to aid General Cunningham in overcoming the stubborn resistance of the Italians at Keren and so bring the war to a conclusion before the April rains put a stop to military operations. Moreover, it may be argued that even if Wavell had pushed on to Tripoli, the situation might have been worse in North Africa, instead of better, when, as soon transpired, the Germans began to take a hand in the game.

First news of the arrival of German units in North Africa was contained in a message from Berlin stating that a German African Corps was in action. The military spokesmen in Cairo were inclined to dismiss the matter in a rather light-hearted way ; it was not thought possible that the Nazis could have shipped across from Sicily any considerable number of troops, let alone armoured formations. Just a few light units—that was all that the military voice would allow the Nazis to have in Libya.

Soon, however, it was made plain that not just a few units but three divisions, and perhaps four, of German mechanized troops had been got across into Libya. *How* they got across was not too clear, but it was suggested that the transports had crossed

MAJ.-GEN. ROMMEL, in command of the Nazi troops in Libya, is a personal friend of Hitler, with whom he is seen here. He rose from the ranks, became an officer in the last war, was on Hitler's staff during the invasion of Czechoslovakia and Poland and commanded a division in France. He is 49.   *Photo, Keystone*

from Sicily to Tunis at night, and then had voyaged through Tunisian waters, hugging the coast all the way.

Soon after they arrived in Africa the Germans demonstrated their strength. Benghazi was evacuated by the British on April 3. Four days later Derna was occupied by the Germans ; on April 12 they claimed to have occupied Bardia, and on April 14 they marched triumphantly into Fort Capuzzo and Sollum. Shortly afterwards their advanced units could claim that they were actually on Egyptian soil (see map below).

So swift, indeed, was the Nazi advance, so determined and so heavy, that the British seemed to have been caught unawares. Most of the conquerors of a few weeks before were in Greece or Abyssinia ; apparently only a handful of troops and of mechanized units were available to meet the new onslaught. Very early the Germans had claimed that they had taken 2,000 prisoners, and Cairo admitted that the claim might well be true. Still more ominous was the fact that three British generals were among the prisoners— Neame, O'Connor and Gambier-Parry. The Germans also claimed to have put out of action a considerable number of our tanks and motor vehicles. Fortunately, the R.A.F.,

valiantly supported by their comrades in the South African Air Force, were able to maintain air supremacy over the African desert, and so the advancing Germans were made to pay heavily for their successes.

For a time things looked black, very black indeed ; and it was generally realized that this was no mere diversion, intended to dissuade Wavell from dispatching his divisions to the Balkan front, but a large-scale offensive designed to cut the life-line of the British Empire which runs through Egypt and the Suez Canal. If Alexandria fell, then where in the Mediterranean would Admiral Cunningham's ships find harbour ? The fall of Egypt and the evacuation of the Mediterranean suddenly loomed up as grim possibilities.

Then the situation became, if not better, at least no worse. Tobruk was invested by the Germans, but attempts to take it by storm were repulsed with heavy loss. A convoy of ships taking supplies and reinforcements to Libya was wiped out by the Navy between Sicily and Tripoli on April 15 ; Fort Capuzzo was heavily bombarded by the Navy's guns on April 16, and on April 21 Tripoli was fiercely bombarded from both the sea and the air. On the night of April 19-20 a British force landed near Bardia, and blew up an important bridge and destroyed a quantity of stores, particularly valuable to the enemy, although some 60 men were left behind as prisoners.

Meanwhile at Sollum the main German advance was halted. The Germans themselves said that the check was due more to natural difficulties than to British resistance ; they pointed out the difficulty of supplying their troops when war material had first to be got to Libya, and then sent across the desert for hundreds of miles. Special tires had to be fitted on to the lorries carrying not only ammunition but fresh water, fuel for field kitchens, and enormous quantities of oil for 'planes, tanks, and other mechanized equipment. The Junkers 52s, it was stated, were maintaining rapid communication between the German G.H.Q. and the troops at the front, and the machines were stated to be standing up well to the sandstorms and the torrid climate. But, be the reason what it may, the Germans did not cross the Egyptian frontier in force until the evening of April 26.

FROM TOBRUK TO SUEZ   *Courtesy of the " News Chronicle"*

General Rommel's Men Arrive in Libya

Much of the material that the Germans under General Rommel are using in Libya was transported by Junkers Ju 52/3 transport monoplanes. Above, one of them is being unloaded on its arrival. Reinforcements of men have also been sent to Libya by air. Diagrams of a troop-carrying 'plane are given in page 491, Vol. II, of this work.

Right, the crew of a tank in Libya are taking their midday meal sitting on the top of their landship. As the German lines lengthen food for the men and petrol for the machines will become an increasingly pressing problem.

Above, is one of the many barbed-wire entanglements erected by the Germans on the Libyan coast. Below, is a Nazi staff car bearing on the bonnet the sign of the Nazi African Corps.

In Libya the German airmen will have to meet conditions far different from those which they encounter in Europe, and it has been necessary to give them a course of instruction in the new tactics that the different climate renders necessary. Above, an officer is giving a lecture to some of the pilots on a Libyan airfield. Right, newly-arrived bombs are being examined.

Photos, Keystone

BOMBS FOR BERLIN are about to be loaded up on one of the great Wellington bombers with which the Royal Air Force has shown the Nazis that the British can give it as well as take it. The bombs are carried on to the airfield in trains of four-wheeled trucks drawn by a tractor, and it is not until they are close to the aircraft that the fuses are attached. Here the ground staff are giving that last deadly touch to the missiles. Recent raids on Berlin are believed to have surprised both officials and civilians by their effectiveness and severity. Berlin is far less well prepared than London in the matter of A.R.P., and great efforts are now being made to make up deficiencies in equipment and shelters, for it is recognized that as the R.A.F. reaches parity with the Luftwaffe the attacks will become more and more intense.

Photo, Fox

They're *Most* Unpopular in Berlin!

WHEN the Battle of Britain was raging in the autumn of 1940 and the R.A.F. was taking an almost incredible toll of enemy machines, independent and impartial observers from the United States verified the British claims and declared that they were if anything an understatement. The same caution is observed by the R.A.F. in reporting its raids upon Germany. The crews of aircraft returning from bombing expeditions give their own accounts of their achievements, and must be prepared with substantial evidence of their claims before they can be officially recognized. That they have never over-estimated them is proved by the fact that information now filtering through from Germany tends to show that Berlin has suffered almost as much as London, while the new bombs which the R.A.F. has recently used in the raids have added a new terror to the lives of the Berliners.

Top photo : As the sun sets on an evening when visibility is good a Wellington bomber, is loading up for its night flight over military objectives in Germany and German-occupied countries. The Vickers-Wellington, a long range heavy bomber, is largely used for bombing distant targets.

The Nazis have been reluctant to release photographs showing the damage done to Berlin and other German cities by the R.A.F. That centre left has been received in Britain via America, and it is certain that what it shows might be repeated many hundreds of times.

Photos, Fox and Keystone

British bombers have been met over Germany by such intensive A.A. gunfire as is seen in page 375 as well as by night fighters. Above, a Wellington bomber shows the scars of battle on its wing and rudder. Its rear gunner shot down an enemy night fighter.

Pilots and crews of British bombers who have just returned from bombing military objectives in enemy territory are here giving an account of their achievements. They still wear their flying kit, but when they have given full details of their night's work they will go to a well-earned rest.

Photos, British Official : Crown Copyright

Twice in a Week They Rode the Storm

London's firemen and A.R.P. workers had their second gruelling test within a week on the night of April 19-20, 1941. Above, firemen who had been on duty all night enjoying a cup of tea. Right, a 65-year-old man rescued after being buried for 15 hours.
Photos, Keystone, and "News Chronicle." Exclusive to "THE WAR ILLUSTRATED."

After the two great raids on London of the week-ending April 19, many streets were littered with glass. Next morning unofficial workers were busy sweeping the pavements.

ON the nights of April 16-17 and April 19-20, 1941, London suffered raids worse than any since that of Dec. 29, 1940. Both lasted practically from dusk to dawn, and all night long Londoners heard the roar of enemy 'planes and the thunder of a terrific barrage punctuated by the sound of high explosive bombs. In the first raid eight hospitals, including Guy's and Chelsea Royal Hospital, were hit ; St. George's (R.C.) Cathedral, Southwark, the City Temple, St. Andrew's, Holborn, and Chelsea Old Church were destroyed, and St. Paul's was damaged. Office buildings, blocks of flats, shops, restaurants and public houses were wrecked ; cinemas and theatres were struck, and many streets were rendered impassable. In the second raid four hospitals, two museums, a town hall and a grammar school were among the buildings damaged or destroyed. In addition a great deal of destruction was done in residential districts. Among the many casualties were A.R.P. workers and members of the A.F.S.

During the raid of April 16-17 six enemy bombers were brought down by night fighters and A.A. fire; one fell in Kensington and another at Wimbledon. Above, a soldier is examining the wreckage of one of them.

Left, two fire watchers are silhouetted against the sky, lit by the flames of many fires. Right, is the scene outside a famous London tobacco and pipe shop. Trade was carried on at a small table outside the wrecked premises and no one went away unsatisfied.
Photos, Associated Press, L.N.A., Planet News and G.P.U.

London Again a City of Dreadful Night

LONDON'S SKY was flame-lit on the night of April 16-17, 1941, when waves of Nazi bombers, estimated to number between 450 and 500, swept over the metropolis for many hours. This awe-inspiring photograph was taken from a high building at a time when several fires were raging in a comparatively small area. Thousands of high-explosive and more than 100,000 incendiary bombs were dropped, but London's defence services rose heroically to the occasion and none of the fires got out of control.

Photo, Keystone

London's Greatest Blitz : Famous Features of

The Royal Hospital, Chelsea, that beautiful Wren b
of the red-coated military pensioners, received a
of April 16-17.   Above are the ruins of the infirm
Left, the forecourt before the

Guy's Hospital was set
April 16.   Above, one of
Left, the front of the
wing is on the right.
Wide World. Topical, C

oried Streets As They Are and As They Were

Two famous London places of worship, St. Andrew's, Holborn,
and the City Temple, standing close together near Holborn Viaduct, were burnt out during the raid of April 16-17. Above and
left are the two churches as they were. Below is the scene the
morning after the raid, when only the shells remained.

Yugoslavia Crushed in 12 Days' Total War

Although resistance is still being offered by isolated bands of soldiery in the valleys of the interior, Yugoslavia is now in the Nazis' hands, and young King Peter has found a refuge in Jerusalem. The story of the 12 days' campaign is given below. A map showing the disposition of the Yugoslav armies when the battle opened will be found in page 410.

WHEN at dawn on April 6 Field-Marshal von List began his invasion of Yugoslavia he had at his disposal 25 divisions—perhaps a million men—including two *Panzer Divisionen*, each of some 6,000 men, with 500 tanks and a brigade of motorized infantry. This enormous host marched into Yugoslavia from every frontier at once, from Germany and Hungary, from Rumania and Bulgaria, until the Yugoslav armies were faced by a vast semicircle of battle.

Before the war clouds actually broke it had been generally assumed that the main weight of the Nazi onslaught would fall on Yugoslavia's northern provinces; and it was in this region accordingly that the greater part of the Yugoslav armies had been assembled. But the Germans seldom do what is expected of them; they prefer what seems to be a difficult and unlikely path to one which to other eyes than theirs has the appearance of being more easy and obvious. So it was now.

Not in the north but in the south List made his principal attack, through the passes that lead from Bulgaria into the heart of Old Serbia. Each thrust was a punch packed with terrific power, of men and 'planes and mechanized armament. Dive-bombers led the way, coming over in wave after wave, pounding every village, every line of resistance, every gun emplacement and fort. They were followed by troop-carrying 'planes, again in their hundreds, that dropped behind the Yugoslav lines walking arsenals of determined men. Most of the paratroops were wiped out, but not before they had blasted into ruin the forts that constituted the Yugoslavs' main line of defence. Then up and down the valleys, over mountain tracks which heretofore had seen hardly any traffic beyond flocks and herds and lumbering ox-carts, great columns of tanks and motorized infantry made extraordinarily rapid progress. The light detachments, which were all that the Yugoslavs could muster to oppose them in this region of rugged glens, were crushed or swept away in hopeless rout.

At least four thrusts were delivered from Bulgaria. The most strikingly successful was that up the Strumitza valley to the highlands which had been granted to Yugoslavia after the last war because they dominated Bulgarian territory, but which were now overrun by the German troops in a few hours. Then, swiftly developing their advantage, the invaders swept to the left, some down the road to Doiran and others, somewhat farther to the west, down the Vardar valley, but both converging on Salonika. The great port fell on April 9; but even more important strategically was the outflanking of the Greek army which was making such a magnificent stand at the head of the Struma pass. At the same time some of the units which had made their way along the Strumitza turned *up* the Vardar valley and made straight for Skoplje (Uskub). At Veles, stormed by 200 tanks, they made contact with the units which had thrust their way from Bulgaria through the Bregalnitza pass. Yet a third thrust at Skoplje was delivered from Kyustendil, to the south-west of Sofia. Along these three roads poured a vast mass of German might, which shortly overwhelmed the Serbs in Skoplje, although the town was taken and retaken several times before the defenders' resistance was finally overcome. From Skoplje one German column rushed westward along the road to Tetovo with the object of linking up with the Italians in Albania, who were now being attacked by the Yugoslavs from the north as well as being contained by the Greeks in the south. Contact with the Italians was soon established; but even more important was the isolation of the Yugoslavs from their allies, the Greeks and British, operating in Greece to the south. In these operations the Germans claimed already to have taken 20,000 prisoners, including

six generals, and a large number of guns and other war material.

Uskub, Veles and Tetovo were all occupied by the Germans on April 9, and on that same disastrous day Nish, too, fell to General von Kleist, whose divisions attacked it not only from the south but from the direction of Sofia, through Pirot on the east. Then from Nish a column plunged westwards across the mountains into Albania, to the rescue of the Italians who had been driven from Scutari.

On the next day, April 10, the German advance through South Serbia reached Bitolj (Monastir), and continued onwards through the Monastir Gap against the Greek positions at Florina. This advance was referred to in the first communiqué from British G.H.Q. in Greece, issued on the afternoon of April 11; it briefly stated that German forces advancing into northern Greece came into contact with the British and Imperial forces on April 10 (Thursday).

Peter II, above, accompanied by General Dusan Simovitch, Prime Minister and General Ilitch, Minister of War, leaves the Cathedral in Belgrade after attending a service of thanksgiving for his accession to the throne on March 28, 1941. The young King's grandfather, Peter I, was forced to retreat with his army in 1915, when the Serbs were overwhelmed by Austro-Hungarian forces; he is seen, left, seated dejectedly on an ox-drawn gun-carriage.
Photos, Ministry of Information, E.N.A.

With Nish, Uskub and Monastir, all three, in their hands, the Germans controlled all the lines of communication in southern Yugoslavia, and the Yugoslavs' third, fifth and sixth armies had been practically destroyed. Their comrades elsewhere had had no better fortune. The main (First) Yugoslav army, which had taken up its position behind and on either side of Belgrade, was outflanked by the Nazi columns which raced through Nish to Kragujevats, and was forced to fall back into the mountains. A special communiqué issued by the German High Command on

How Marshal List's Tanks Thrust to Victory

The photographs in this page are the result of a remarkable journalistic enterprise. They were taken during the Nazi advance into Yugoslavia, which began on April 6, 1941; they were then radioed to New York and brought by Clipper 'plane to England, where they arrived on April 24. Above, a Yugoslav outpost taken by a Panzer division has been set on fire by the troops holding it. Left, a Yugoslav soldier, taken prisoner, still bears himself proudly. Right, other prisoners, overwhelmed by huge odds, lay down their arms. Below, German tanks advancing. The map shows the principal stages of the campaign.

Map by courtesy of " Time & Tide ";
photos, Keystone

Sunday, April 13, stated that " German troops, commanded by General von Kleist, occupied the Serbian capital and fortress of Belgrade from the south at dawn today." This followed the penetration of the city from the north across the Danube on Saturday afternoon by a small detachment of the S.S. division, commanded by Captain Klingenberger. The Yugoslav Government retired to Sarajevo, capital of the province of Bosnia and the headquarters of the Yugoslavs' Second Army, which was now flung into the battle. To little avail, however. Sarajevo itself was mercilessly bombed by the Luftwaffe, and on April 16 the Germans claimed

the fall of the town and the capitulation of what was left of the Second Army. Some 50,000 men and eight generals had been taken by one German division, boasted Berlin radio; " the roads," it went on, " present a picture of a complete military rout. They are strewn with abandoned and broken-down tanks, as well as rifles and machine-guns."

Sarajevo's fall in effect marked the end of organized resistance in Yugoslavia. All the northern parts of the country, which had been evacuated since they were so obviously indefensible, had been overrun. The Italians, attacking from the west, had occupied Ljubljana, and, pushing down the Dal-

matian coast, had seized town after town in an almost uninterrupted progress; Split fell to them on April 16. On April 11 German troops under Colonel Baron von Weichs forced the passage of the river Drava, and armoured troops captured the Croat capital of Zagreb; so rapid and overwhelming was the German advance that the Serbian Fourth Army was soon broken. On the same day Hungarian troops marched into the territory between the Danube and the Tisza, and on April 12 occupied Novisad.

In a communiqué issued on April 16 the Germans declared that the remnants of the Yugoslav Army were on the verge of disintegration. Then at 11 o'clock on the night of April 17 the official German news agency issued this statement: " All the Yugoslav armed forces which have not been disarmed before laid down their arms unconditionally at nine o'clock tonight. The capitulation comes into force at 12 noon tomorrow."

Ups and Downs in the Battle of the Atlantic

Against the deadly U-boat menace our destroyers, which are among the hardest worked of any class of vessel afloat, do magnificent work. Above, depth charges ready for release over the stern of a destroyer. Left, the deck of a destroyer seen from the crow's nest.

Captain Schepke, German U-boat ace (above), went down with the U 100 when she was sunk by our Navy. The map, right, shows the threat to our communications in N. and S. Atlantic should Hitler gain control in Spain and at Dakar.

DESCRIBING in a speech at Tottenham on April 20, 1941, the progress of the Battle of the Atlantic, Mr. A. V. Alexander, First Lord of the Admiralty, said :

" This battle has its ups and downs, but I can assure you that neither the U-boats nor the Germans' long-range aircraft are having it all their own way.   We continue to take a toll of both, and as the strength of cooperation of the Navy with the Coastal Command increases, and as the number of escorting destroyers and corvettes expands, that toll of the enemy will increase until the Battle of the Atlantic is won."

Members of the crews of British ships sunk by the German battleships Gneisenau and Scharnhorst are seen after landing at Brest.
Photos, Planet News, Associated Press and G.P.U.

America Knows How to Deal with Sabotage

A lieutenant of the U.S.A. Coast Guard, left, is examining the propeller shaft of the 5,000-ton Italian liner Ada O., which was partially sawn through. Right, a coast-guard is investigating damage done to the Italian S.S. Alberta, lying at Port Newark, New Jersey. Below are three Italian ships seized in Philadelphia harbour to prevent sabotage. Top, the Mar Glauco ; bottom, left to right, the Santa Rosa and the Antoinetta.   *Photos, Wide World, Planet News and Associated Press*

A T the end of March 1941 the U.S.A. Government discovered that the crews of five Italian ships lying at New Orleans and Newark had attempted to damage the machinery. Mr. Morgenthau, Secretary to the Treasury, immediately ordered the Coast Guard to seize and examine 27 Italian ships in American ports to prevent any further acts of this nature. The motive of the sabotage was not clear, but it was probably due either to instructions from Rome or to the fear of the crews that they might be ordered to put to sea. The Axis Powers made a protest to the U.S.A. Government against the seizures, but this did not affect in the slightest the American attitude. The lead of the United States in this matter was soon followed by other American nations.

Strikes at U.S.A. armament factories have caused delay in arms output. Above, outside a plant in Milwaukee a disturbance has arisen and a motor-car has been overturned and wrecked by the strikers as they clashed with the police.

Our Searchlight on the War

Eyes and Ears of the R.A.F.

In future, by approval of the King, the Observer Corps is to be known as the Royal Observer Corps, in recognition of valuable services rendered over a number of years. The Corps is a civilian organization consisting of some 30,000 watchers, all volunteers, most of whom do this work of 'plane-spotting in their spare time. There are observer centres over the entire country, each

THE CHIEF OBSERVER at an outlying post of the Observer Corps telephones to Headquarters news of the arrival and course of a hostile 'plane. *Sport & General*

controlling a number of posts, some in very isolated parts of the area. At these posts a day and night watch is kept for sight or sound of aircraft. Every aeroplane, whether hostile or not, is subjected to careful scrutiny. If it is an enemy the alarm is quickly given by telephone to headquarters, and the course of the aircraft is plotted by means of a special instrument. The Fighter Command, acting on this information, sends up its 'planes to meet the raider. If the night shift of Observers are made aware by their sound locator of the presence of an aircraft they determine its position and inform the searchlight unit, which speedily picks it up. Then the A.A. batteries come into action, and one more raider has run the gauntlet of Britain's defences all set in motion by the lonely and devoted civilian watchers in their far-flung outposts.

Salvage Great and Small

Bombed buildings are furnishing many tons of steel scrap which will be melted down to provide new war weapons. But minor raid debris is also being put to good use by at least one group of workers whose skill and ingenuity are only equalled by their sympathetic understanding. The staff of Fulham A.R.P. depot have become toymakers in their spare time. Answering an appeal made some six weeks ago by the Nursery Schools Association on behalf of evacuated children who have nothing to play with, they set to work to convert valueless odds and ends from the dumps into dolls' cradles, horses and carts, trains, ships and aircraft, as well as small-size chairs and tables for the children who would otherwise have nothing but the floor on which to sit and to play. Nurses at the First Aid Post attached to the depot have scrounged bomb-damaged bed linen, and with this have equipped the toy beds that will soon delight the eyes of little children in the reception areas.

Help from U.S. Doctors

The British Red Cross recently sent a telegram to the sister society in America pleading for 1,000 doctors to serve in Britain with the R.A.M.C. and the Civilian Emergency Medical Service. Mr. Roosevelt, as President of the American Red Cross, launched the appeal, which had an instant response. Within 24 hours 200 doctors had applied. One flew to Washington to be among the first to volunteer. Another wired, " Bags packed. Ready to leave. When and where shall I report ? " For service with the R.A.M.C. the Red Cross asked for doctors under 40 years of age. Doctors up to 45 will be taken for Emergency Medical Service. Applicants are asked to serve for a minimum of one year and will retain their status as American citizens. They will be given British registration and parity with British medical men. It has been pointed out how vastly greater are the demands on the medical services in Britain today than in the last war.

The Nazis May Miss It

One more London landmark, the single remaining tower of the Crystal Palace, disappeared on April 16. The Palace, a glittering monument of the Victorian Age, constructed mainly of glass and iron, was originally the habitation of the Great Exhibition in Hyde Park, opened by Queen Victoria on May Day, 1851. It was designed by Joseph Paxton, gardener and architect, who used as model the conservatory he had designed for Chatsworth. The great water towers at either end were built by Isambard Kingdom Brunel. Removed and rebuilt on Sydenham Hill in 1852, the Palace became the home of great musical festivals, animal shows and educational exhibitions of many kinds, including a permanent one depicting the architecture of all ages and countries. There were rare plants in the indoor gardens, and in the elaborately laid out grounds, where the startled visitor encountered antediluvian monsters, the firework displays originated by Brock became famous. In 1914 the Palace was taken over by the Admiralty as a recruiting centre for the R.N.V.R. and other units, and over 125,000 men were trained there. In June, 1920, it became the property of the nation, and here, on June 9, King George V opened the Imperial War Museum, later removed to South Kensington. In 1936 the Palace caught fire, and all but the North Tower was burnt out. Now, because this was a prominent landmark for enemy airmen, and also on account of the valuable metal it will furnish, this gaunt survival of a peaceful and prosperous epoch was brought crashing down to earth in a matter of some ten seconds.

Girls in the Firing Line

Girls of the A.T.S. are now to be found behind the A.A. guns helping to fight the Battle of Britain. In their charge are the range-finders and predictor calculating machines, on the skilled use of which the accuracy of the gunfire largely depends. All these girls are mathematical experts who have taken a special course in range-finding and other scientific observations relating to predicted fire. Women may also be taking over the balloons, and the North Midlands area is to make the first experiment in this scheme. If it is successful large numbers of men will be released and replaced by girls of the W.A.A.F. As the work is arduous—it will include driving the winches and trailers and hauling on the ropes—only the strongest and fittest recruits will be accepted.

Bombs Ready for Rome

His Majesty's Government announced on April 18 that, in view of the German threats to bomb Athens and Cairo, it must be clearly understood that if either of these two cities were molested a systematic bombing of Rome would begin. Moreover, the Government was perfectly well aware that an Italian squadron was being held in readiness to drop captured British bombs upon the Vatican City should a British raid take place. As the strictest orders had been given that the utmost care must be taken to avoid any damage to the Vatican City, it was necessary to expose in advance this characteristic trick of the Italian Government. Rome's reaction to this disclosure was one of great annoyance, and the whole of the Axis radio and press embarked on a new campaign of vilification against Mr. Churchill.

A mighty crash marked the fall of the last of the famous towers of the Crystal Palace. Above, the collapse begins ; inset, a cloud of dust marks the end. The tower was 250 feet high, weighed 1,500 tons, and is expected to yield about 840 tons of metal for munitions.
Photos, Wide World and Topical

Tangier (Now Spanish) Greets the Nazis

A NOTHER blow at French prestige in North Africa was struck by the Nazis when the swastika was run up over the Mendoubia, formerly the official residence of the Sultan of Morocco's representative in Tangier. The authority of the Mendoub was abrogated, and Dr. H. Noehring, who arrived with no fewer than 200 "assistants," took up his abode, as German Consul-General, in the ancient residence of the Sherifian representative evicted by the Spaniards under Axis pressure. More "assistants" will soon be on their way from Germany, and Nazi penetration of France's vast North African domain will thus be facilitated.

Axis Pressure on Spain manifested itself at the end of March when Germans in Tangier, the Spanish-dominated "international zone" in N. Africa opposite Gibraltar, took over the Mendoubia. Above, the new consul, Dr. H. Noehring (photo inset), entering the Consulate.

Posters hurriedly put up after the Nazis had entered the Mendoubia, from which the Mendoub, representative of the Sultan of Morocco in Tangier, had been evicted.

No enthusiasm can be seen on the faces of this crowd of Spaniards and Moors as they watch the Nazis' theatrical display outside the Mendoubia. Right, Dr. Heberlein, Counsellor at the German Embassy in Madrid, shakes hands with Gen. Ponte, Commander of the Spanish troops in Morocco. *Photos, Associated Press*

They Have Won Honours in Freedom's Cause

Sig. E. R. Savidge, R.N.V.R., **D.S.M.**, for displaying outstanding courage and devotion to duty on active service.

Lieut. H. West, bar to his **D.S.C.**, for great courage and conspicuous bravery on active service against the enemy.

Skipper Lieut. Grace, **D.S.C.**, for displaying great courage in successfully bringing down enemy aircraft at sea.

Cmmdr. J. Bull, D.S.M., **D.S.C.**, for fine leadership and recovering from the sea an enemy mine for examination.

Capt. N. Rice, **O.B.E.**, for saving his ship containing valuable cargo from attack by enemy submarine.

A.B. N. Stringer, **D.S.M.**, for displaying outstanding courage and untiring devotion to duty on active service.

C.S.M. Davies, Cheshire Regt., **D.C.M.**, for displaying conspicuous courage and devotion to duty.

Mr. T. H. Newton, Home Guard, **B.E.M.**, for securing a mine and rendering it safe. Served with distinction in last war.

Pte. Goodwin, Gordon Highlanders, **M.M.**, for displaying outstanding courage, initiative and devotion to duty.

C.S.M. Shaw, Seaforth Highlanders, **D.C.M.**, for displaying conspicuous courage and fine leadership on active service.

Lieut. J. M. Muir, M.B., R.A.M.C., **D.S.O.**, for saving the lives of wounded at Sidi Barrani, though badly hurt himself.

Troop Sgt.-Maj. Shelton, Royal Artillery, **D.C.M.**, for displaying great courage and devotion to duty.

Sgt. A. Halfpenny, **D.F.M.**, for successful flights over Germany and enemy-occupied country.

Sqdn.-Ldr. J. N. Dowland, **G.C.**, for removing an enemy bomb from a steamship, and performing similar duty on a trawler.

Sgt. E. Barker, bar to his **D.F.M.**, for helping to destroy 12 enemy aeroplanes in a single afternoon.

Flight-Sgt. E. Thorn, bar to his **D.F.M.**, for destroying enemy aircraft. Sgt. Barker was his air gunner.

Sgt. D. McKay, **D.F.M.**, for having shot down enemy 'planes. Credited with having destroyed 12-15 aircraft.

Pilot-Officer R. P. Stevens, **D.F.C.**, for having shot down 2 Nazi night raiders in the London area.

Miss D. M. White, **G.M.**, for rescuing an injured nurse from a first-aid post which had been badly bombed.

Mrs. M. Farr, of Portsmouth, **O.B.E.**, for protecting a patient at risk of her own life during an air raid.

Miss Meikle, R.A.F. Nursing Service, **R.R.C.**, for displaying great courage, gallantry and devotion to duty during raid.

Miss Wilson, R.A.F. Nursing Service, **R.R.C.**, for conspicuous bravery and outstanding qualities as a nurse in grave danger.

Sister I. Jones, of Swansea, **A.R.R.C.**, for displaying courage, gallantry and devotion to duty during enemy action.

Miss M. F. Thomas, Woolwich A.R.P. Casualty Service, **G.M.** for rescuing workers and 2 people in bombed house.

Aux. Fireman C. A. Reeves, **G.M.**, for displaying coolness and conspicuous bravery in performance of his duties.

Commdr. A. N. G. Firebrace, R.N. (retd.), Chief Officer London Fire Brigade, **C.B.E.**, for leadership and devotion to duty.

Chief Officer W. Woods, Twickenham Fire Brigade, **G.M.**, for conspicuous courage during violent raids.

Maj. F. Jackson, London Fire Brigade, **M.B.E.**, for great courage and leadership in the course of severe raids.

Dist. Officer R. W. Greene, London Fire Service, **M.B.E.**, for courage, daring and devotion to duty in raids

Fireman B. Evans, **O.B.E.**, for rescuing a comrade from blazing building in the course of a bombing attack.

Mr. G. Williams, Chelsea A.R.P., **O.B.E.**, for rescues from shelter menaced by fire.

Mr. H. F. Shimmings, Supt. Twickenham A.R.P., **G.M.**, for rescuing a woman trapped by debris.

Mr. G. W. Whitehurst, L.N.E.R., Hull, **G.M.**, for helping to rescue a wounded soldier.

Mr. A. Harrison, L.N.E.R., Hull, **G.M.**, for his work in assisting Mr. Whitehurst.

Air Cadet H. R. Smith, **C.G.M.**, for rescuing a woman from bombed house.

Miss M. B. Haldane, of Glasgow, **M.B.E.**, for rescuing people from her ambulance in heavy raid.

I Was There! .... Eye Witness Stories of the War

I Saw the Germans Well Beaten at Tobruk

On April 12 German and Italian forces besieging Tobruk launched a series of attacks by tanks, aircraft and infantry, which were all beaten off. The following graphic account of some of these attacks was sent from inside Tobruk by John Yindrich, special correspondent of the British United Press.

UNDER cover of darkness on April 14 about 30 German tanks penetrated the wire defences of Tobruk from the direction of El Adem and advanced about a mile and a quarter inside the perimeter defences. Lorries carrying about 200 infantrymen followed them.

British tanks dashed across to meet the advancing German and Italian tanks. Firing started about 4 a.m., and an intelligence officer told me later that he had seen about 12 burning tanks.

Then, about 8.30 a.m., 30 big black German Junkers dive-bombers, escorted by Messerschmitts, staged the biggest raid on the perimeter defences as well as the town itself.

For over an hour they were flying over the semicircle of Tobruk and its defences. I saw eight in line dive-bomb the harbour and then swoop over the outer line of defences with their machine-guns blazing.

The infantrymen manning the machine-guns and Bren guns stood up to the attack wonderfully and brought down three of them. Hurricanes brought down two others in a series of whirling dogfights.

Two days ago German troops launched their first infantry attack against Tobruk in a duststorm so thick it was difficult to see a yard in front of your eyes.

Australian infantry and British artillerymen and machine-gunners, wearing celluloid eye shields to protect them from the grains that pierce every conceivable opening, strained their eyes to try and spot the enemy's movements. They remembered how a dust storm helped the British at Sidi Barrani.

While the dust storm was blowing not a single thing could be seen, but about 5 p.m. the wind dropped and the dust fog fell.

Then I saw about 800 German infantrymen get out of about 30 trucks and advance in close formation on the outer semicircle of defences from the direction of El Adem.

Our artillery laid down a heavy barrage to prevent their retreating, while machine-gunners opened a withering fire. In the words of a gunner: " We just mowed 'em down."

At the same time Blenheim bombers observed about 60 German tanks making formation about five miles to the south of the defences. The 'planes dive-bombed and machine-gunned them until they withdrew.

Twelve tanks moving towards the defences a little farther around the perimeter were dispersed by British artillery fire, while two other tanks sitting on the barbed wire near two machine-gun posts were also forced to withdraw.

I saw two wounded German pilots with bandages on their heads being taken to hospital in a lorry. Then lorry-loads of German prisoners, wearing the grey-green peaked cap with the German eagle, went by.

An Australian, a former commercial traveller from Sydney, told how he and five others of a patrol had routed 40 Germans and brought back one prisoner.

" We had repulsed the fifth attack on our post by 300 German infantrymen, supported by tanks, who got within 1,000 yards of our position," he said. " Then, about 10.30 p.m. we got word that about 40 Germans were inside the wire.

" I took about six men, so as not to weaken the post too much. We were under machine-gun fire all the time, so we went at the ' double ' and then lay down about 100 yards from where they were.

" Our people behind us were blazing away over our heads when we tore into them with our bayonets. I got the shock of my life, because not one of them wanted to fight.

" It was only when I came to the fifth one that I found them showing any fight. He grabbed my rifle and pulled me down on top of him. There was another German coming up behind him, but my corporal saved my life.

" I used my rifle on several other German heads until it broke. Then I picked up a stone. The rest of the Germans, probably thinking it was a hand grenade, grovelled there, one shouting, '' I'm a soldier of Germany, don't kill me ! '

" Another was shouting, ' Peace, it is peace, s'il vous plaît ! '

" I must have accounted for about 12 Germans. My opinion now is that when it comes to hand fighting the Germans are about on a par with the Italians.

" In a scrap where it's every man for himself they go to pieces. Perhaps it's because they're so well trained."

My Men Got Sick of Killing the Germans

German shock troops attempting to force a passage in a vital sector of the Mount Olympus front were beaten back with heavy losses by Anzac troops. These eye-witness stories was told by Australians and New Zealanders to a British United Press correspondent.

DESCRIBING how his small unit of machine-gunners and anti-tank gunners fought off repeated attacks by German shock troops, who used rubber boats, armoured cars and parachutists, the New Zealand officer said :

We thought we had a " cushy " post, defending a pass flanked by mountains, through which ran a river, skirted by a small road.

The Germans sent armoured cars to reconnoitre. Then at dawn next day they launched an attack with boats, which we could see dimly in the half-light.

We sank one boat after another, in spite of a barrage of covering fire from German armoured cars. After two hours the river was teeming with sunken boats, from which men were swimming.

Amazement at the absolute disregard of the Germans for their losses was expressed by the New Zealander, who continued :

My men got sick of killing. It was mass slaughter. We mowed down the boats as fast as they came, each with eight men.

Seeing they could not succeed in penetrating the sector along the river, the Germans next attacked from the west, using what appeared to be parachutists. They wore grey shorts and heavy grey jackets, and carried tommy-guns with terrific fire power.

Our position appeared to be in danger until my captain drew a bead on the leader of the enemy with an anti-tank machine-gun. He was a six-footer. He was struck fair in the chest, and went down like a ninepin.

Seeing their leader disintegrate from the waist up, the rest of the attackers, after hurling a barrage of grenades, withdrew, and we continued holding the position.

I was hit by a grenade splinter in the hand, which cut a tendon. I couldn't fire a gun, so I came in for treatment, but I told the boys I'd hurry back.

Australians who fought at Mount Olympus said :

We were walking and fighting for four days and nights. When the order came to withdraw, we obtained mules and loaded our guns on them.

We were often lost in the tracks of the

GERMAN LIGHT TANKS in this photograph, published in Germany on March 30, 1941, are returning to barracks in Libya. The Nazis are reported to have two armoured divisions in Libya, but, as the eye-witness's narrative in this page shows, heavy toll of them has been taken by British artillery and bombers of the R.A.F.

desolate fastnesses of Mount Olympus, and we slept for an hour or two in the snow when we were too tired to go on. And we had just come from the desert.

We reached the pass near the railway by the sea to the east of Mount Olympus and fought with the Germans until nearly midnight the next night. Then we took up our position with New Zealanders.

We used our tommy-guns, while our anti-tank guns pumped at the Panzers. The enemy infantry were picked mountain troops. They crept along with tanks and tried to cross the river to our left, but got a terrific plastering from our machine-guns. Whenever one of the tanks was hit the infantry behind it hopped off pretty quickly.

In the afternoon we heard the rumble of tanks on our left flank. German engineers had blasted a way for the tanks over the wreck of a railway tunnel which our engineers had demolished.

The fighting went on all the afternoon and evening until we pulled out about 11 that night. We swung to the right and then to the left in an effort to stop the tanks. The New Zealanders manning the field guns and anti-tank guns did their stuff marvellously.

One tank went up like a foundry explosion. It seemed as if our shells went through their armour like cheese.

The mountain troops scrambled up the hillsides and we gave them everything we had. The blazing went on through the night. There was a hell of a din as the artillery on both sides smashed at each other.

The tanks were blowing up like small volcanoes, the machine-guns crackling and the other guns pouring a continuous chain of flame. The path was strewn with dead and dying, but the Australians and New Zealanders picked their way through. We carried the wounded to lorries, but most of our fellows had to keep marching.

In the Balkan war, as in the Battle of France, the Nazis made good use of their inflatable assault boats for the rapid crossing of streams and rivers. Above, German sappers are shown training with one of these boats; a pontoon can be seen behind them. *Photo, Fox*

One lorry-load got bogged, so we moved the wounded to another lorry. That got bogged, too, and we lost our tracks in the darkness. A Greek, then a New Zealand colonel, led us out eventually.

Finally we made our way to Larissa. But we found the enemy had already taken it. We made a detour round the town, and began trekking south again. In the last part of the trek we saw three Hurricanes meet eighteen German 'planes. They shot down seven of them.

Another Australian said:

We thought Larissa was still in our hands. Suddenly we ran into an ambush. The streets were strewn with wreckage, the place was blazing and Germans seemed to be everywhere. Luckily we had our tommy-guns, and we blasted our way through as we advanced single file, sheltering in the ruins.

We Chased Nazis Over the Fields on My Tractor

A motor-tractor can be put to many uses, and here is the story of one which, while sedately engaged in ploughing, turned into a kind of tank and engaged in offensive operations against the enemy. It was told by J. Paterson of the Women's Land Army in " The Land Girl."

So often people ask me if it is not dull going up and down the same field all day long, and it is no use trying to explain. But last week adventure dropped on me out of the sky.

I was on the ground setting my plough, when a 'plane rushed into sight, coming at me over trees, very low and on fire. I just started, and then suddenly I saw the black crosses and realized it was a German, and that the cracklings I had heard a few seconds earlier were machine-guns; and I remembered our old ploughman, who had been shot up the day before when ploughing with his team of white Polish horses. I wanted to creep under my friendly little red tractor, but instead of coming down in my fields the pilot must have seen the electricity pylons in it and lifted his 'plane on southwards.

I felt I must do something, so I unhitched the plough, put the tractor into top gear, and went as hard as I could across the next three fields; as exciting as any fox hunt and nearly as fast. I was lucky in knowing gaps and gateways, and there were no queues! I knew I must get to a lane which crossed

our little railway line, and on the way I picked up a special constable and a Home Guard with his rifle, who perched on the tractor as best they could, holding on to me rather like the Gordon Highlanders holding the stirrups of the Scots Greys at Waterloo.

At the railway bridge we sighted our quarry down in a field just over the boundary of " our " land; and on we chased, passing several other men on their way. We heard a big explosion, and when we got to the field there was the 'plane—a Junkers 88—blazing. Four A.F.S. men were already there, and other people came from all sides. Many Home Guards arrived, but not all fully uniformed; and quite soon police, who quietly took charge and kept people away from the temptation of picking and stealing souvenirs.

But the Germans had disappeared—a woman had seen them—four men in uniform. Two small coverts were searched by the Home Guard without success, and then some of us were formed up in line to beat the big covert—armed and unarmed alternately—when suddenly we heard a whistle and a shout, and running round to the far side of the wood we saw the Germans, who had surrendered themselves to two farm hands: four fair boys rather like Norwegians, dazed by their own narrow escape from the death they were trying to bring to our people, and unsure of the treatment in store for them, but dignified and calm.

By this time we were quite a large crowd, about fifty people, and the police took their prisoners as quickly as possible to the road and their cars. I was sent back to guard the wreckage, shutting a lot of gates on the way, and when soldiers arrived I was saluted and dismissed. I started up my tractor and drove back at a more sedate pace and went on with my job. All that day and the next we were pestered by people wishful to see the wreckage; apparently they had no jobs to do, and did not mind what harm they did to fences and crops in satisfying their idle curiosity.

Few Land Girls are likely to experience such an adventure as befell the one who describes her experiences in this page, but all lead a healthy life and are doing war work of vital importance. This one, once a commercial artist, now drives a tractor. *Photo, L.N.A.*

May 9th, 1941   *The War Illustrated*   479

IIIIIIIIIIIIIIIIIIIIIIIIIIIIIIIIIIIIIIIIIIIIIIIIIIIIIIIIIIIIIIIIIIIIIIIIIIII **I WAS THERE!** IIIIIIIIIIIIIIIIIIIIIIIIIIIIIIIIIIIIIIIIIIIIIIIIIIIIIIIIIIIIIIIIIIIIIIIIIII

I Was with London's A.R.P. that April Night

London was the objective of the German air raiders on April 16, when the capital suffered the heaviest bombing it had so far endured. Here are some extracts from the dramatic article in the "Daily Express" by William Hickey, who visited the scene of a big "incident" during the night.

"WE hear they've hit the ——," said the news editor, naming a Big Building. "Could you hurry along there ? It's apparently a pretty big incident."

They hadn't hit the Big Building. But it was certainly a big "incident." A hundred or more yards from it the air smelt charred ; drifts of dark smoke began to obscure the tiaras of flares that hovered above us, as in some hellish pantomime or firework pageant.

As usual, all the burglar alarms had been set ringing ; nothing would stop them for the rest of the night. Scores of shops were wrecked ; as I got near the incident I had to step over doors and window-frames that had been hurled bodily into the road.

Wading through an ankle-deep porridge of glass and water, I looked at the slag heap that had, an hour earlier, been a block of —fortunately—empty offices. Less fortunately, one corner of it had been a pub : "there was usually 20 or 30 of 'em in there about that time," said a copper.

I was glad of living human company— glad when the A.R.P. people stopped me, took me to see their Incident Officer.

Half-sheltering in a ruined shop that was his office-for-the-moment (two blue lamps and a wooden flag mark it), he was a shadowy, lean, quickly-moving figure under a white tin hat. Henry, they called him. He used to make Savile Row suits. Decision and a clear head are needed. Henry had them. In the half-light of flame and smoke there were even forms to be filled up and signed.

Stretcher-parties were waiting. It would be many hours, perhaps daylight, before they could be used.

The men waiting made the usual simple cracks—"Just like old times " . . . " He ain't half cross with us tonight." They coughed a good deal in the acrid smoke. One had been gassed in the last war. " You all right, chum ? " they 'asked him. " All right," he would gasp. " It's only me old complaint."

All this time, intermittently, more bombs were swishing down. As each fell, or as a 'plane sounded like diving, we stepped back a pace or two into the gaping shop, crouching instinctively, in unison, hardly needing to say, " Here's another." Again instinctively, with a protectiveness that might have been pathetically futile, the men would shield each others' bent shoulders with their arms. Twice, as we crouched, the blast—a foul, hot giant's breath—swept sighing through the shop, tore its way through glass at the far end.

A rosy, judgement-day glow shone down on us. Some of the men moved over the road to a darker place. " It's funny," said Henry, " when it's bright moonlight and they're overhead, you instinctively walk in the shadow. . . ."

It was time for the Incident Officer to go and look at some other incidents ; wardens, sometimes girls, had turned up, panting but collected, to say, " Incident in —— St., between —— and —— Sts.," or " They want help badly round at —— Buildings."

His blue lamps, his flag, were moved to another street. We set off swiftly but circumspectly, skirting the buildings to dodge the tinkling shrapnel, pausing in doorways when we heard the death-whistle.

We looked in at several public shelters. None of these had been hit, nobody in them was worse than shaken. They all seemed to know Henry ; the sight of him reassured them. " What's it like outside ? " they would ask. " Oh, not so bad," he would lie.

For the raid's ferocity had been suddenly intensified.

Fires that had seemed quenched flared up again. New fires began in every quarter of the sky ; they even lit up pinkly the balloons floating high above.

We turned a corner. Henry ran on quickly. Ahead was a tall house, nearly every window alight with a cosy, crackling, Christmasy flame.

His face was drawn, agonized, in the leaping light. " God ! " he said. " That makes me feel bad. There's a lot of old ladies live in these chambers—retired nurses and such."

As good wardens do, the wardens of this district know pretty accurately how many people are sleeping in a building each night. Henry reckoned there would have been 63 here.

" About 30," we learned, had been brought out alive, taken to hospital, some able to walk. Two, still in there, had been certified dead by a doctor.

Arguing fiercely that it *must* be possible to reach *that* room or *that*, where the fire didn't yet show, Henry dived straight into the house. The sparks danced about him ; he vanished behind fallen, flickering timbers.

It was five anxious minutes before we saw him again, on the stairs, helping two firemen undo a knot in the hose they were playing up the liftshaft. Their figures stood up darkly against the evil red light—three men walking unharmed in the midst of the burning fiery furnace . . .

Before we had begun to think that this night could be nearly done—so timeless seemed its incidents, so endless the treadmill of its grim routine—we looked up . . . and the light in the sky was not all from the fires.

The chill dawn wind fluttered burned paper in our faces. Already men were sweeping up the crunching glass. A big lorry switched off its lights as it stole past us : " That's the street-barriers arriving," said Henry.

As thousands have said after a bad raid night, Henry said, " It doesn't seem so bad by daylight, does it ? "

There was time to visit his snug post, where a kitten played perilously with the iodine that was being dabbed on a warden's cut hands ; time to relax in a canteen over a cup of tea . . .

London experienced one of the worst air raids of the war on the night of April 16, when an indiscriminate bombing attack was made on the city. As usual the Civil Defence services worked magnificently ; above, a party of A.R.P. workers are seen bringing a casualty out of the debris of a wrecked block of flats.

Photo, Sport & General

Our Diary of the War

SATURDAY, APRIL 19, 1941   595th day

Air.—R.A.F. successfully attacked enemy shipping off Dutch coast. Brest bombed.

War against Italy.—R.A.F. made heavy attacks on enemy troops and material in Cyrenaica and Tripolitania. Benghazi and Tripoli raided during night of 18–19, and on 19–20 Derna, Benghazi and Gazala.

Home.—London suffered heavy night attack, casualties and damage being severe. Two raiders destroyed.

Over 300,000 women of 1920 class registered for service under the Employment Order.

Balkan War.—Greek and Imperial troops continued planned withdrawal, covered by rearguard action. Despite enormous losses, Germans pushed up reinforcements.

Athens stated that in Kalabaka area Germans failed to force passes.

General.—Announced in London that Imperial forces have arrived in Basra to open up lines of communication through Iraq.

SUNDAY, APRIL 20   596th day

Sea.—H.M. minesweeper Bassett destroyed two Messerschmitts. H.M. yacht Torrent reported lost.

Air.—Daylight attacks on shipping off Dutch coast. Supply ship sunk off Norway.

Night raids on Cologne, Düsseldorf, Aachen and several aerodromes. Oil stores at Rotterdam and docks at Dunkirk, Ostend and Brest were also bombed.

War against Italy.—Further enemy tank attack against Tobruk repulsed. R.A.F. bombed Tripoli during night of 20–21.

Reported that columns advancing on Dessie had fought with enemy holding covering positions.

Home.—Enemy day activity over coasts of Kent and N.E. Scotland.

Balkan War.—During night of 20–21 R.A.F. heavily attacked enemy-occupied aerodromes in northern Greece.

At least 22 enemy aircraft shot down in air battle over Athens.

Greek forces in the Epirus and Macedonia began negotiations for capitulation.

MONDAY, APRIL 21   597th day

Sea.—Navy heavily bombarded Tripoli while R.A.F. supported with bombing attacks. Great damage done to port and shipping.

Admiralty announced that H.M. submarine Tetrarch had sunk fully laden tanker bound for Tripoli.

Air.—Coastal Command aircraft attacked docks at Le Havre.

War against Italy.—Patrol activity reported at Sollum. R.A.F. made heavy attacks on aerodromes at Derna and Gazala.

Motor transport at Bardia and Capuzzo bombed and machine-gunned.

In Abyssinia British troops occupied important position covering Dessie.

Home.—Small-scale day activity over S.E. England. Heavy night attack on Plymouth. Bombs also fell in East Anglia. Two raiders destroyed over Plymouth and two others near French coast.

Balkan War.—Withdrawal of Imperial and Greek forces to new positions almost completed. Movement covered by brilliant delaying action of Anzac troops. Enemy suffered heavy losses.

Athens reported bombing of two Greek Red Cross ships, Hesperus, which was sunk, and Ellenis, damaged.

TUESDAY, APRIL 22   598th day

Sea.—Admiralty announced torpedoing of three enemy ships in Mediterranean.

Free French naval H.Q. announced that submarine Minerve had torpedoed large tanker off Norway.

Air.—Daylight attack on supply ship off Norway and a minesweeper. Two night raids on Brest.

War against Italy.—During night of 21–22 Australian troops made two successful raids on Tobruk, capturing about 450 prisoners.

Air battle over Tobruk in which enemy lost four 'planes.

Malta had its worst night raid; heavy damage but few casualties.

Home.—Some daylight activity, mainly in S.E. England. Another heavy night raid on Plymouth. South coast town and other places also bombed. Enemy machine destroyed in Channel.

Balkan War.—Empire Forces now occupying new defensive positions south of Lamia. Contact maintained with Greeks whose left flank is in danger from German thrust across Pindus Mts.

German aircraft repeatedly raided the Piraeus, Eleusis, Megara and district of Attika. Hospital ship Ponikos attacked.

WEDNESDAY, APRIL 23   599th day

Sea.—Admiralty announced that H.M. armed merchant cruiser Rajputana had been sunk by torpedo.

Air.—Daylight attacks on targets in N.W. Germany and shipping off Dutch coast. At night heavy bombs on sea raiders in Brest docks. Le Havre attacked.

War against Italy.—R.A.F. attacked Derna and other targets. Eight enemy aircraft destroyed over Tobruk.

Heavy raids on Benghazi and Tripoli during night of 22-23, and on aerodrome at Calato (Rhodes).

Reported that Italians defending Dessie had been routed. Maji, near Sudan border, occupied.

Home.—Daylight activity mainly near East Coast. Night bombers again attacked Plymouth. Two raiders destroyed.

Balkan War.—Empire Forces consolidating new defensive positions at Thermopylae. Announced that King of the Hellenes and Government had gone to Crete.

THURSDAY, APRIL 24   600th day

Sea.—Admiralty announced that H.M. submarine Urge had sunk 10,000-ton tanker.

Air.—Enemy tanker set on fire off Norway. Night attacks on Kiel and Wilhelmshaven.

War against Italy.—Attack on Tobruk repulsed with heavy enemy losses. R.A.F. bombed mechanized units and aerodromes in Cyrenaica. Night raids on Tripoli and Benghazi.

Home.—Bombs fell during day in Kent. Night raids on southern England and East Anglia. Two enemy aircraft destroyed.

Balkan War.—German aircraft raided districts of the Piraeus, Aegina, Eleusis and Megara. Two hospital ships, Polikros and Andros, sunk. Corinth bombed.

Empire Forces continuing ordered withdrawal.

FRIDAY, APRIL 25   601st day

Air.—Daylight sweep over Holland. Supply ship hit, railways damaged, iron and steel works at Ymuiden bombed. At night raids centred on Kiel. Berlin, Bremerhaven, Rotterdam and many other targets also attacked.

War against Italy.—R.A.F. bombed oil tanker and other vehicles between Derna and Barce. Night raid on Benghazi.

Home.—Night attacks on towns in N.E. England and on one in Northern Ireland.

Balkan War.—Germans claimed that Pass of Thermopylae had been captured; also that troops had crossed from Thessaly on to island of Euboea, and thence to mainland.

General.—British troops reported in Mosul. Lord Gort appointed Governor and C.-in-C. Gibraltar, succeeding Sir Clive Liddell.

SATURDAY APRIL 26   602nd day

Air.—Three supply ships off Norway attacked. Big night attack on Hamburg. Emden, Bremerhaven and Cuxhaven, and docks at Le Havre and Ymuiden.

War against Italy.—In Sollum area enemy crossed frontier at several points. In Abyssinia British captured Dessie.

Home.—Merseyside attacked at night.

Balkan War.—Empire troops fighting tenacious rearguard action N.W. of Athens. German parachutists captured Corinth.

REGISTRATION OF WOMEN for war service began on Saturday, April 19, 1941. Above are some of those born in 1920 waiting to register at a Westminster Labour Exchange. Over 300,000 women registered, and some of them were married on that morning and went on to the exchange to register. A large number of young women in later categories did not wait to be called up but enlisted in one of the uniformed services, the W.R.N.S., the A.T.S. and the W.A.A.F., during the week-end.

    Photo, Central Press

THE PREMIER'S GRAND TOUR OF THE PEOPLE'S PLUCK

As a tonic to defeatists, Mr. Churchill, in his broadcast of April 27, recommended a tour of those British towns which have been the most savagely bombed—since, as he said, " it is just in those very places . . . that I have found the morale most high and splendid." That the country is solidly behind its fighting Premier is evident from many photographs like that above taken during a recent visit to Liverpool. It was scenes of such loyal affection, oft-repeated, on the part of common folk, which made him exclaim : " Of their kindness to me I cannot speak, because I never sought it or dreamt of it, and can never deserve it."

Photo, " Daily Mirror," Exclusive to THE WAR ILLUSTRATED

Bitter Indeed Were the Last Hours in Greece

After putting up a magnificent stand against tremendous odds, the British and Anzac troops composing the Forces of the Empire were evacuated from Greece. Here we tell something of the end of a campaign which, given reasonable odds in the air, might have had a very different conclusion.

WHEN the Greeks could fight no more—when their troops were utterly exhausted by the days and weeks of continuous battle, when their ammunition and their supplies had been used up, their transport blown to pieces, their planes (few, so very few, even at the beginning) driven from the skies—then, outflanked, surrounded, and overwhelmed by the enemy masses, they sent a message to their allies.

" This state of things," read this note from the Greek Premier communicated to the British Minister at Athens on April 21, " makes it impossible for the Greeks to continue the struggle with any chance of success, and deprives them of all hope of being able to lend some assistance to their valiant allies." The continuation of the struggle, while incapable of producing any useful effect, would have no other result than to bring about the collapse of the Greek Army, and bloodshed useless to the Allied forces. " Consequently the Royal Government is obliged to state that further sacrifice by the British Expeditionary Force would be in vain, and that its withdrawal in time seems to be rendered necessary by circumstances and by interests common to the struggle."

First definite news that the Imperial troops were leaving the Greek mainland was given by Mr. P. C. Spender, Acting Australian Treasurer, when at Sydney, on April 28, he

stated that " the evacuation of certain of our troops from Greece has begun. As far as this has proceeded, it has been successful." The withdrawal was by no means easy, for the Empire troops were in close contact with the enemy in the Thermopylae position. Moreover, the Nazis had obtained complete command of the air, and by repeated attacks had made the one good port available, the Piraeus at Athens, unusable. " Consequently "—we are quoting from the special communiqué issued by G.H.Q., Middle East, on May 1—" a re-embarkation had to take

place from open beaches, against continual enemy pressure on land and heavy and repeated attacks from the air. In such circumstances the withdrawal of large numbers of troops can be effected only at the cost of heavy losses of vehicles and equipment, while rearguards which cover this withdrawal may have to sacrifice themselves to secure re-embarkation of the others." The British and Anzacs who composed the rearguard put up a tremendous fight against the Germans, displaying almost reckless bravery, sacrificing their own lives in order

to enable their comrades to get away. At the same time Greek infantry, who knew well that they had never a chance of escaping from the country, strove to cover the British flank—a last splendid service rendered by our most gallant ally.

Grim pictures of the withdrawal were painted by German spokesmen. " The remnants of the fleeing British troops are now trying to escape from various harbours in Greece, in barges, fishing boats, and all sorts of vessels, leaving behind arms, war material, and equipment of all kinds. A large number of vessels have been sunk, and many others damaged. Many sailing boats and other vessels have been bombed and machine-gunned, some on the beaches and some at sea." Remnants of the British forces were stated by Berlin to be arriving at Alexandria in small fishing smacks ; " the condition of the soldiers is pitiful." A broadcaster from Berlin said that the formidable effect of the German air attacks on British transports was indicated in reports from Athens that " innumerable bodies " had been washed ashore. This time the B.E.F. (he went on) had not had the advantage of persistent fog as at Dunkirk, and the journey to Crete was much farther than across the English Channel. The Luftwaffe was resolved not to allow the repetition of " glorious Dunkirk,"

THE NEAR EAST is now the principal war zone. Greece has been evacuated by the Allies, and the Greek Government moved to Crete on April 23 ; the photo shows King George of the Hellenes making one of his last appearances in Athens when he spoke to his people from a balcony at Army H.Q. Note in the map the chain of Greek Islands off Asia Minor, which are being snapped up one by one by the Nazis.   *Map, Courtesy of " The Times "; Photo, Keystone*

Once Again the 'Few' Did Heroic Work

Greek liaison officer explaining point of next attack to R.A.F. bomber-pilots. Top: Fighter pilots enjoying a moment's respite from their bitter struggle against heavy odds. Full figures of enemy 'plane losses over Greece are not available, but 16 German destroyed as against our 7 on April 20 is indicative of British aerial efficiency.

R.A.F.—R.I.P. Wreckage of the 'plane, the cross, and Greek soldiers who dug this grave compose a poignant symbol of the Anglo-Greek alliance; here is the resting-place of the first two British airmen to die in Greece. Right: Air-gunner in rear turret of an R.A.F. bomber. Though all too few the R.A.F. played a vital part in the successful evacuation of the Forces of the Empire, in spite of the fact that towards the end of this operation the Germans were using no fewer than 860 aircraft.

Photos, British Official : Crown Copyright ; and Planet News

All Greece Overrun by the Nazi Hordes

and so the position of the armed forces was represented as being "quite desperate."

Hardly less grim was the statement by Mr. A. W. Fadden, Acting Australian Premier. "The Imperial forces are conducting themselves with great heroism in the face of heavy enemy pressure. The task entrusted to our forces has been carried out with fidelity. Many of our troops have now left Greece after stubbornly contesting the enemy's advance, even to the last few inches of Greek soil. Unfortunately, we cannot hope to avoid casualties . . ."

Here is a description of the final fighting by a German war correspondent, quoted by Berlin radio on April 29. "Behind Thermopylae German tanks were unable to take the main road to Athens because of its destruction by British troops. They had to take the mountain passes and tracks which had never seen motor vehicles before, and moved slowly along the coast in a south-easterly direction. The road was frightful, and there was not a second's rest. All night long the German column moved ahead. Nowhere were the English to be seen, but caution had to be exercised as we did not know where they might suddenly jump on us.

"As the morning lengthened we reached Thebes. South of the town the British rearguard opened fire on us, while the British batteries, which had been well concealed, began firing. This obstacle had to be by-passed, and since the main road and all bridges ahead were destroyed, we again made a detour into the mountains towards the east. German scouting tanks suddenly reported by radio that British troops had been sighted. But we did not want to meet and engage them, so we again turned north-east, away from this area, into the mountains. In this way the outskirts of Athens were reached."

German troops approached the Greek capital from three directions, from Thebes to the north, from Corinth (which was captured on April 26 by German parachutists, together with 900 British troops, "some of whom were so taken by surprise that they had to be hauled out of houses"—so the German account), and from the island of Euboea on the east. Every precaution had been taken to prevent German planes from landing on the Athens airfield; it had been mined and vehicles were strewn all over the landing ground. "German parachute troops, however, overcame these difficulties, and the air-

German troops entered Salonika, which was not defended and from which all stores had been either withdrawn or destroyed, on April 9, 1941. Here is the first photograph to reach this country of Nazi mechanized units in the town. Numerical superiority in machines again enabled the Nazis to advance with great rapidity.

port was quickly cleared." Besides mining the airfield, the British, so the Germans reported, offered a last-minute resistance ; but so that there should be no excuse for the destruction of the beautiful city, the Imperial troops withdrew just before the Germans entered. As the last British soldiers left, they were cheered by large crowds who bade them not good-bye but au revoir.

"The surrender of Athens," said a German account, "took place in a small dark café at the edge of the inner city. The Greek general, Kamenos, the Police Chief of Athens, and the two mayors of Athens and the Piraeus, surrendered the Greek capital." One of the first actions of the conquerors was to impose a curfew at 11 p.m. and 6 a.m. They also set up a Quisling government under a certain General Tsolakoglu.

While the evacuation of the Imperial troops was still in progress, Mr. Churchill made a statement to the House of Commons in

London. Up to the time when evacuation was seen to be inevitable, he said, we had landed about 60,000 men in Greece, including one New Zealand and one Australian division. Of these, at least 45,000 had been already evacuated—a remarkable feat when it was considered that our Air Force had had to abandon the air fields from which alone it could effectively cover the retreat of the troops, and that only a small portion of it could cover the ports of embarkation.

"The conduct of our troops," went on the Premier, "especially the rearguard, in fighting their way through many miles to the sea, merits the highest praise. This is the first instance where air-bombing, prolonged day after day, has failed to break the discipline and order of the marching columns, who, besides being thus assailed from the air, were pursued by no less than three German armoured divisions, as well as by the whole strength of the German mechanized forces which could be brought to bear.

"In the actual fighting," the Premier continued, "principally on Mount Olympus, around Grevena, and at Thermopylae, about 3,000 casualties, killed and wounded, are reported to have been suffered by our troops. This is a very small part of the losses inflicted on the Germans, who on several occasions, sometimes for two days at a time, were brought to a standstill by forces one-fifth of their number."

"At least 80 per cent of the original force," said the statement issued by G.H.Q., Middle East, to which we have already referred, "has been safely conveyed to areas where it can undertake further active employment." This operation, the statement went on, had been made possible only as the result of great skill and devotion by all three arms of the services, in particular of the rearguards, and by the Royal Navy and the Merchant Service, the Royal Air Force and the Fleet Air Arm.

"It is noteworthy that in spite of the heavy fighting they have been through, and the trying experiences of re-embarkation under such conditions, troops which have returned from Greece are entirely unperturbed by their struggle against such odds, and are convinced of their superiority over the Germans, both as individuals and as units and as formations. The successful withdrawal of so large a proportion of these invaluable troops is a noteworthy achievement.

"The troops have all retained their fighting equipment as well as their fighting spirit, and the heavy equipment and transport which have been lost will soon be replaced."

GREEK REFUGEES are seen in this photograph (transmitted by radio) walking behind their belongings, piled on a horse-drawn cart, through a line of halted Nazi tanks. As in France and the Low Countries, so in Greece, the homes of poor peasants were wrecked by the swarms of Nazi dive-bombers.

Photo, Associated Press

Bigger and Better Bombs to Bring Victory

An idea of the size and power of our newest bombs may be gathered from this monster weighing 2,000 lb. It is being loaded into a Whitley heavy bomber.

BRITAIN'S growing strength in the air is the most hopeful factor in the present stage of the war. Our new bombs are not only causing havoc in Germany, but giving the Nazi leaders more than a headache. We hold the record for the biggest and most powerful bomb yet, one designed by Squadron Leader R. H. Garner. Having created this weapon, he flew with it to Germany and dropped it on Emden. "He had gone," said Lord Beaverbrook on April 23, "in pursuit of aviation, to see the bomb straight through to its final destination. That was the bomb which created so much interest in Germany and this country.

It was the biggest bomb ever flung out of a bomber."

Members of the R.A.F. get ready to "give it to them back." They will soon be over enemy territory with another load.

Squadron Leader R. H. Garner, the bomb-designer, one of the "boys in the back room," is an officer in the Development branch of the Royal Air Force.

Photos, British Official: Crown Copyright; Central Press, Associated Press and Keystone

IN BERLIN, columns of smoke are seen pouring from the State Opera House after a heavy raid by the R.A.F. on April 9. The attack was the heaviest so far, all the fire-brigades being called into operation. Yet Goering told the German people that the war would never reach their capital!

The Nazis Just a Little Nearer the Nile

After their spectacular career through Cyrenaica, General Rommel's armoured columns have crossed into Egypt. There, however, they are making much slower progress. Maybe the natural difficulties in their path are proving unexpectedly strong, or maybe some new move, even more daring, is under way.

Not until Mr. Churchill gave the figure in his broadcast on April 27 was it realized how small were the forces with which General Sir Archibald Wavell—"that fine commander whom we cheered in good days, and whom we will back through the bad"—smashed Mussolini's power in North Africa and took an Italian army of 180,000 men captive. "In none of his successive victories," said the Premier, "could Wavell maintain in the desert or bring into action at one time more than two divisions, or about 30,000 men."

No wonder, then, that when the call came to us from Greece—when "Hitler, who had been creeping and worming his way steadily forward, doping and poisoning and pinioning, one after the other, Hungary, Rumania, and Bulgaria, suddenly made up his mind to come to the rescue of his fellow criminal"—the British force in Libya was seriously weakened by the loss of those troops which were sent across the sea to the aid of our supremely valiant ally, now assailed by the two empires of the Axis. Moreover, the bulk of our armoured forces, which had played so decisive a part in defeating the Italians, were withdrawn from the line to be refitted, and only a single armoured brigade was left to hold the frontier.

Then came the German invasion of Libya. The Nazis' advance was made sooner and in greater strength than our generals had expected. The armoured brigade was worsted; tanks were captured or destroyed, supplies had to be burnt, and considerable casualties were suffered—quite early in the push the Germans claimed 2,000 prisoners. The British infantry, which did not exceed one division, had to fall back, said Mr. Churchill, "upon the very large Imperial force that had been assembled and had to be nourished and maintained in the fertile delta of the Nile." Day by day the German

columns drew ever nearer to Egypt, and on April 27 they were reported to have crossed the frontier. On the next day they occupied Sollum. Only Tobruk, far to the rear, maintained a stubborn resistance. If the British had not suffered a really serious military defeat, at least they had experienced a psychological reverse.

Having crossed into Egypt, the Germans

made slow progress across the desert which lies between Sollum and Mersa Matruh, the main centre of British resistance on the road to Alexandria. The town was reported to be strongly fortified, with the sea on one side

Control of the Nile is part of Hitler's mega-lomaniac dream of world-conquest. Advancing from Libya he may attempt several routes across the desert : (1) from Jarabub to Cairo ; (2) the line to Asyut ; (3) from Kufra to Isna. Route (4) branches from (3) leading to Aswan, the town famous for its great Nile dam.
Courtesy of the "Daily Express"

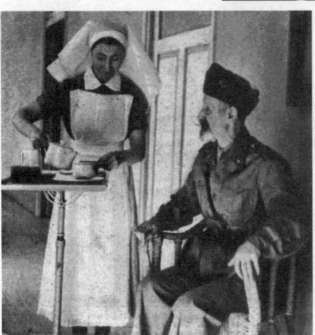

After taking many thousands of Italians prisoner, the British army loses a handful of soldiers to Mussolini's fellow-dictator. Lined up under armed guard they were among the 2,000 claimed to have been captured on the Libyan front by the Nazi Tank Corps.
Photo, Associated Press

General Annabile Bergonzoli, who commanded Italian forces at Bardia and was taken prisoner by us at Agedabia, convalescing in a military hospital. When captured he was in poor health, suffering from incipient appendicitis.
Photo, British Official: Crown Copyright

and on the other the huge Qattara depression, which—at least, it was hoped—would prove an impenetrable barrier to the German tanks. As the fortress of Tobruk was strongly resisting—it could hardly be regarded as beleaguered, since access to it was open by way of the sea—General Rommel, the Nazi commander, had to detach considerable forces to mask it and, if possible, to effect its capture. One great tank assault on the place was completely defeated on April 17, and a second, launched on May 1, was similarly unsuccessful. Then far to the south German tanks were reported to have arrived in the Kufra oasis ; there was talk of a German armoured division which had been "lost" in the desert, and which, it was suspected, might be making its way across the sands to the Nile valley, hundreds of miles to the south of Cairo. Such a dash across the desert is what we have learnt to expect from our experiences of Hitler's strategy ; true, some

'Hellish Struggle' in the Western Desert

The Curtiss Tomahawk, known in America as the Hawk 81-A, is already in service with the R.A.F. in the Middle East (see page 448). Three Tomahawks, low-wing cantilever monoplanes of the single-seater fighter type, are seen, right, in formation.

Below, General Sir A. Wavell is seen with General de Gaulle, who arrived in Cairo during April after visiting Free French units in the Middle East.
Photos, British Official: Crown Copyright

suggested that it would be impossible for the Nazis to maintain their lines of communication, but (it may be asked) what have lines of communication to do with a column of tanks which carry with them their own fuel, water and munitions ?

All the same, conditions in Libya are now distinctly unpleasant, and are becoming increasingly so.

" It is getting terribly hot now in the Libyan desert," wrote Mrs. M. G. Beadnell, wife of an official of the Egyptian Desert Survey Department, who has spent much time in the Western Desert, in the " Daily Telegraph " on April 24 ; " and sand storms are blowing up with ever greater frequency and violence. The enemy tanks and armoured cars will be subject to incessant delays from the penetration of the sand into every particle of machinery, with more sand blowing into the engines as one lot is dealt with. The

The Egyptian army has been expanded and modernized of late years. Below, Egyptian mobile artillery is exercising in the desert.
Photo, Keystone

wheels will plunge into pockets of soft clay and sand. When heat and thirst are very great it becomes increasingly difficult to swallow food. The sun beats down on the back of the neck and makes head and eyes ache—then sunstroke."

One German radio reporter has described the " hellish struggle " experienced by Rommel's advanced units, after the guns of the British garrison in Tobruk had forced them to abandon the coastal road and make a bypass to the south. " Many vehicles were lost in the desert," he said. " Many men rejoined their units after spending several days and nights in the desert, without food and drink—subjected to sweltering heat by day, to frost by night, to attacks by low-flying British aircraft and raiding motorized forces, and to the 'death hail' of British naval guns." His description ended with the

words, " Compared with conditions of that coastal road, the worst fields of Poland seemed paths of paradise to old campaigners."

That, perhaps, is a picture painted deliberately in sombre colours. The Germans have long prepared for the conditions which their troops are now experiencing in the Western Desert—have not their soldiers, wearing full equipment, been exercised for hours in hothouses ? And if accounts speak true, many of the natural difficulties are being overcome by the use of the Junkers 52. At the end of April a Canadian pilot spotted at Benina aerodrome, near Benghazi, 100 of these giant troop-carriers, lined up wing-tip to wing-tip.

" It seemed as if they had just landed," he said, " for there were groups of soldiers stepping out." Diving to 50 feet from about two and a half miles up, the Canadian flashed along a line of

Tanks of the German Afrika Korps are here moving along a road in Libya. Profiting by the Royal Navy's preoccupation with convoying troops to Greece, the Nazis landed many tanks in Africa.   *Photo, Keystone*

German aircraft, while his gunner " gave them all he had." One of the aircraft burst into flames, and smoke poured from others. " The soldiers were, apparently, too startled to raise their tommy-guns. They just closed up like penknives and toppled to the ground."

" I should be very sorry to see General Wavell's armies to be in the position of the German invaders," said Mr. Churchill in his broadcast. But as yet the Nazi threat to Egypt and the Canal is a very real one.

Just What Are These 'Panzer' Divisions?

What is this mighty instrument of war that the Germans, if they have not invented at least have developed to an unprecedented degree—this armoured force which smashed its way across Poland, France and the Balkans, which drove the British out of Libya, and is now feeling its way across the Egyptian deserts? Below we give some details of Hitler's Panzerdivisionen, and of the counter-measures designed to halt their progress.

A PANZER division—Panzer is the German word for " armoured "—comprises 400 tanks, divided into two brigades of two battalions each, but in addition to the tanks, each division contains a brigade of infantry carried on motor lorries; a reconnaissance unit of motor cyclists; a regiment of field artillery; an anti-tank battalion; a heavy machine-gun battalion; an engineer battalion, equipped for bridge and road construction and repair; and a mobile repair and supply unit. Furthermore, it has attached to it a squadron of aircraft for reconnaisssance and dive-bombing operations. Altogether, the number of vehicles is about 3,000, all motor-driven, and the number of men is some 14,000. But perhaps the most important fact about a Panzer division is that it is *a self-contained unit*, it is

When going into action the Panzer division seeks to outflank, rather than to make a frontal attack. If, however, it is not possible to work round the enemy the motor cyclists and the light motorized unit probe the opposing defences, searching everywhere for a soft spot. As soon as this is found a wedge is driven in by dive-bombers and heavy tanks.

Once the line is penetrated, then the tanks spread out like an opening fan; and behind them, through the gap which they have caused, pour the rest of the Panzer division. Far and wide throughout the countryside speed the motor cyclists and the light tanks, the heavies, the flying artillery, spreading confusion and destruction. The enemy communications are first threatened, then disrupted, severed, smashed. The

Not to be withstood—at least, not by lines of defence, by trenches and concrete positions, such as are the delight of the military engineer, who thinks still in the terms of the battles of the last war, of the Somme and of Arras, of Cambrai and Ypres. Nor are they to be withstood by those masses of infantry which still, to most people, constitute an army. It has been said that if the Yugoslavs had mobilized their millions, if Wavell had been able to send hundreds of thousands of men into the Balkans—then Greece would not have been overborne; there is still talk of the million Turkish bayonets which bar Hitler's way to the oil-fields of the Middle East. But such suggestions, such talk, belong to yesterday. Millions of men armed with rifles and bayonets cannot stop Hitler's Panzerdivisionen; if they are flung into the battle against these armoured hordes they are doomed to be ground beneath the tractors into a bloody pulp. Even if they were supplied with masses of artillery, with thousands of anti-tank guns, even if they were supported by armadas of aircraft—still there is every reason to believe that the tanks, moving in unison under the direction of one audacious brain, would cut their way through to victory. Only one thing can beat the tank divisions—tanks, more tanks, directed with yet more skilful generalship, moved by a supremer audacity. Thus it is not too wide of the mark to say that the battle against Hitler's Panzerdivisionen will be won in Britain's workshops.

capable of acting on its own and does act as an individual army, receiving its direction from the divisional commander, who rides with his staff in the H.Q. armoured vehicle.

Germany has 15, or perhaps 16, of these armoured divisions, representing a total strength of more than 6,000 tanks. Three of the divisions are reported to be in Libya, and seven are believed to have been engaged in the fighting in the Balkans. Four sufficed to crush Poland, and ten triumphed in the Battle of France.

In each division there are usually heavy, medium, and light tanks. The fast light and medium models range from 18 to 20 tons; each is equipped with a 37-mm. gun (100 mm. are a little short of 4 ins.), and 2 machine-guns, and its armour is about 30 mm. in thickness. It carries a crew of three. The heavy tank, which the Germans seemingly are coming to prefer, is a cruiser with a road speed of about 30 miles per hour. It weighs about 36 tons, but there has been talk of monsters of between 70 and 100 tons. Its armour is some 50 mm. thick, and it carries a 75-mm. gun and two machine-guns. It has a crew of five, and can carry a heavy load of ammunition. A model PZWK 6 shown in Berlin in 1939 had armour 50 to 60 mm. thick and carried two guns of 75 mm. or 105 mm. and a 47-mm. anti-tank gun; its crew numbered eight.

The rapid advance of the German forces in North Africa was due mainly to the fact that they had succeeded in transporting vast quantities of tanks to Libya. Above, German tanks being shipped from an Italian port. Right, Nazi tanks in a Tripoli street.
Photos, Associated Press and " Berliner Illustrierte Zeitung "

civilian population are driven from their homes and become panic-stricken mobs. The opposing troops are cut off into isolated pockets of resistance, which may continue firing hours after the main battle has swept past and beyond them; they are left to be dealt with by the motorized infantry. So what was once a nibble has become a thrust; what was once a crack is now a breach, through which rushes a flood of armoured troops not to be withstood.

Britain Has Tanks as Good as Hitler's !

BRITISH TANKS are playing a big part and will play an ever-growing part in the war. Our Armoured Divisions have lately been reorganized, and now form one of the most powerful instruments of war. In the light of experience changes have been made in the types of vehicles used, and both in gun-power and armour our mechanized forces are believed to be equal to anything Germany can put in the field. In a recent mock invasion test more than ten thousand vehicles of every kind were used.

Photo, Fox

Yet Another to 'Make Her Mightier Yet'

H.M.S. PRINCE OF WALES, sister ship of H.M.S. King George V (see pp. 294-5 in this vol.), is already in commission and hard at work. She is seen, top, with a crane hoisting one of her three 'planes out of the water. Above, her Captain is inspecting some of the ship's company during " Divisions." The Prince of Wales, laid down in January 1937, has a displacement of 35,000 tons, a speed of about 30 knots, and a main armament of ten 14-inch guns. These guns are of a new model with an effective range greater than that of the 15-inch guns mounted in earlier ships.

Photos, British Official : Crown Copyright

America Has Her Part in the Atlantic Battle

THE CHELAN is one of ten similar U.S. cutter-destroyers sent to the aid of Britain; she displaces 1,983 tons. Below, British freighter, Empire Attendant, arrives battle-scarred at New York.

Between fire and water, menaced by mines and bombs, stokers aboard a minesweeper do their bit to keep the Atlantic "lane" open for our shipping.

How the United States could maintain a "safety zone" for shipping as far as Greenland, and thus help to guarantee our vital war supplies almost half-way across, this map shows.

THE PRESIDENT'S TREMENDOUS DECISION.

IT is the Battle of the Atlantic which holds the first place in the thoughts of those upon whom rests the responsibility for procuring victory. It was therefore with indescribable relief that I learned of the tremendous decision lately taken by the President and people of the United States. The American Fleet and flying-boats have been ordered to patrol the wide waters of the Western Hemisphere and to warn the peaceful shipping of all nations outside the combat zone of the presence of lurking U-boats or raiding cruisers belonging to the two aggressor nations. We British will, therefore, be able to concentrate our protecting forces far more upon the routes nearer home, and take a far heavier toll of the U-boats there. *From Mr. Winston Churchill's broadcast of April 27, 1941.*

H.M.S. MALAYA, British battleship of Queen Elizabeth class, of 31,100 tons displacement, reaches New York for attention in the U.S. Navy Yard.
Map, "Daily Express"; Photos, Keystone, Associated Press

Battling Across East Africa's Barren Uplands, Ben

INDIAN TROOPS IN ERITREA have fought their way across hundreds of miles of mountainous country and, side by side with British troops, have written a glorious new chapter in the history of the Indian Army. Indian mechanized cavalry, infantry and engineers have been in the van of operations in Italian East Africa, and above some of them are seen clearing a village. On the right an armoured car finds the going difficult in the country around Keren. Bottom right, Indian troops stationed at a road junction where an Italian lorry lies on its side.

SOUTH AFRICAN TROOPS were among the Imperial force which routed the enemy in Italian East Africa, and some of them are seen above examining with in front of the fort of Mega in Southern Abyssinia. In the circle, General Smuts, South Africa's Prime Minister and Commander-in-Chief, is seen with Lieu forces in North-East Africa, at Government House, Nairobi. In a message to the South African troops, Gen. Smuts congratulated them on the shatterin of arms," he said, " and especially of endurance, has been remarkable, and is one rivalling in its way the brilliant performances of the Army of the Nile in Lib

Pitiless Sun, Theirs Was a Mighty Feat of Arms

IN a series of brilliant actions against the enemy in Eritrea and in Abyssinia Indian troops have displayed the greatest prowess. Indeed, the campaign in Eritrea may be described as one of the biggest triumphs in the history of the Indian Army. Kassala and Gallabat, Barentu and Agordat, the epic siege of Keren—such were the successive stages in an advance in which fierce sieges and lightning advances alternated. The Indian troops took kindly to the country over which they were fighting, for large stretches of it bore more than a passing resemblance to their own North-West Frontier region. The occupation of Barentu was the culmination of a five-day battle fought by an Indian Brigade through a narrow gorge, and in the great struggle for Keren Indian infantry fought their way up fantastic peaks and ridges. A special word of praise, too, is due to the Indian sappers. In the advance towards Keren, when the Italians attempted to delay the British advance by destroying roads and strewing landmines over the countryside, these men did heroic and invaluable work. Many instances of initiative and gallantry have been recorded, and the Indian soldiers were specially congratulated by General Platt.

red Italian guns and material
ingham, G.O.C. the Imperial
truck the enemy. " This feat
British Official : Crown Copyright

Britain Forced to Take Action in Iraq

In an earlier page (see page 310 of this volume) we have written of the great strategic
and economic importance of Iraq and Iran at the present stage of the war. Since then
events in Iraq have moved swiftly, as will be seen from what is told below.

To London on April 4 came the news that German intrigue had succeeded in engineering a coup d'état in Iraq through the agency of Sayid Rashid el Gailani, former premier of pro-Axis sympathies, supported by four senior officers of the Baghdad garrison, all fervent Pan-Arabists, and almost certainly assisted by the Mufti

FAISAL II, the boy king of Iraq, gardening with the assistance of an aide-de-camp.
Photo, Black Star

of Jerusalem, Haj Amin el Husseini, who, since his expulsion from Palestine, has been deeply engaged in political intrigue in both Iraq and Syria.

By one sudden stroke, choosing a moment when Parliament was in recess and the Regent, Emir Abdul Ilah, absent from the capital, this cunning politician turned out the Prime Minister, General Taha el Hashimi, deposed the Regent, and seized power. He then re-established himself as Premier and installed a new Regent to govern the country in the name of the little six-year-old King Faisal II. In language somewhat reminiscent of the Nazi dictator, Sayid Rashid stated in a broadcast that the army had entrusted him with the responsibility for the preservation of peace and order and the safeguarding of the Constitution against any excesses.

The deposed Regent, who is an uncle of the young King, protested vehemently in a broadcast from Basra. "Heedless of Iraqi public opinion," said he, "Sayid Rashid has seized power by instigating rebellious elements, who have adopted falsehood as a weapon, and who are an instrument in the hands of foreigners who, in order to enjoy the benefits of the country, seek the destruction of its independence."

From Damascus, through Vichy, came reports that Sayid Rashid had formed a military cabinet, in which he is the only civilian, while his colleagues include the Chief of the General Staff, the Commander of the Mechanized Brigade, the Commander of the Iraqi Air Force, and the Director of National Defence.

The situation remained obscure and gave rise to considerable uneasiness until April 19, when it was announced in London that strong Imperial forces had arrived in Basra "to open up lines of communication through Iraq." This is in accordance with Article 4 of the 1930 Treaty of Alliance, which provided that if Great Britain should be involved in war the King of Iraq would undertake to furnish "all facilities and assistance in his power, including the use of railways, rivers, ports, aerodromes and means of communication," and authorized the British Government to maintain air bases and troops in his territory in order to protect lines of communication.

The landing of British forces made the situation less disquieting, but mystery was deepened by the announcement that "the new Iraqi Administration, true to the initial assurance given by Sayid Rashid, are affording full facilities, and have sent a high officer to Basra to welcome the British Officer Commanding and to collaborate with him in making all arrangements."

It was to be expected that the local population, "who have happy memories of British and Indian soldiers from the last war," would give our troops the warm welcome that is reported, for they have little to do with the

Emir Abdul Ilah, Regent of Iraq (left), was deposed recently through the machinations of Sayid Rashid el Gailani (right), a cunning politician with pro-Axis sympathies. *Photos, E.N.A.*

political intrigues of their rulers. But the final smooth paragraph of the official announcement carried a suggestion of the iron hand within the velvet glove : " The co-operation of the Iraqi authorities in the execution of this movement has made a favourable impression in London and leads to the hope that more normal relations between the two countries may soon be established."

The landing of British troops was received in Ankara with the greatest satisfaction, and in Germany with deep chagrin. Authorities in Berlin characterized the move as a breach of international law. A commentator on the German radio said : " Great Britain has selected Iraq and the Persian Gulf as a further region for the extension of the war." The Berlin " Borsen Zeitung " was even more bitter : " This is quite in accordance with the century-old British practice. An independent Arab State is militarily raped to achieve what could not be attained by the intrigues of London diplomacy—namely, the recruitment of a new blood donor for the British war and new support for the tottering Empire."

Later the official attitude in Baghdad became less cordial, and, when informed by the British Ambassador, Sir Kinahan Cornwallis, that further British troops were to arrive in Basra, the Iraqi Government took the line that this would not be permitted until those previously landed had passed through and out of the country. Britain refused to accept this strange interpretation of the terms of the Treaty, and the troops reached Basra without difficulty. Moreover, the Iraqi Government was requested to remove concentrations of mechanized forces from around the aerodrome and R.A.F. training school at Habbaniya, 60 miles west of Baghdad.

This request was not only ignored but the Iraqi troops were reinforced, and early on May 1 they opened fire on the cantonment, compelling British forces to take counter action. It was later reported that Sayid Rashid had appealed to Germany for help against a British " invasion."

OIL-FIELDS AROUND KIRKUK have long attracted covetous glances from Germany, whose oil problem is a real one. British troops have gone to guard them.
Photo, E.N.A.

They Went to Greece to Honour Our Bond

SIXTY thousand men who could ill be spared from other theatres of war were, thanks to the Royal Navy, taken safely across the Mediterranean that we might honour our pledge to the gallant Greeks. In this page we have glimpses of life aboard a British troopship. Top, troops keeping fit with physical drill ; right, a party parading for lifeboat drill ; above, men disembarking on Greek soil with the customary British smile.

Photos, British Official: Crown Copyright

Is There Any Need to Worry about Gibraltar?

As Hitler's grandiose scheme for the ejection of Britain and Britain's Fleet from the Mediterranean takes shape, it is becoming ever more likely that an attempt will be made on Gibraltar—if Franco's Spain can be induced to grant free passage to the German troops. In this event, what sort of stand would "Gib" make?

As night falls on Gibraltar it brings with it the military ritual of the Ceremony of the Keys. Through the steep and narrow streets of the old town tramp the soldiers with bayonets fixed, to the music of fife and drum or perhaps the skirl of the pipes; down to the gates they go, and there the ponderous portal is locked and the key carried back by the Key Sergeant to the Government House, where it is laid beside the Governor's plate at dinner.

So it has been for more than two hundred years, and so it will continue to be, for the fortress of Gibraltar—we have every reason to believe—is impregnable, with its gun emplacements carved out of its rocky face, its magazines far underground, its storehouses and deep shelters, its miles of galleries, and its bristling defences of every kind. Months of bombing and bombardment could do little more than chip and scar the Rock's surface; its heart would remain undented. New guns, we are told by Moscow radio, have recently been mounted, and—so the same source says—the Rock is now an island, a deep trench, impassable by tanks, having been cut across the isthmus by Canadian soldiers. Nor could its garrison be starved out, since stocks of food to last two years and more have been accumulated, and the great "catchment areas" provide a sufficiency of fresh water.

Once in its history the Rock stood a three years' siege, from 1779 until 1782, when General Eliott, with 5,000 men, successfully beat off every attack delivered by a combined

GEN. LORD GORT, V.C., who, it was announced on April 26, has been appointed Commander-in-Chief of Gibraltar in succession to Lieut.-Gen. Sir Clive Liddell. *Photo, L.N.A.*

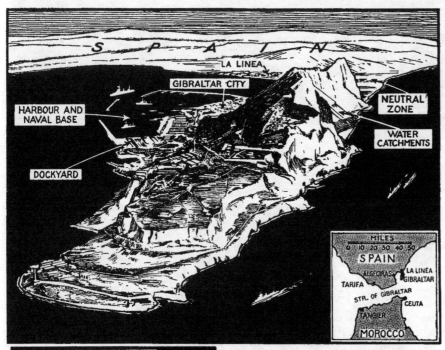

'THE ROCK,' whose salient features are marked in this map and plan, may be attacked at any moment. Its power of resistance has been much strengthened recently by detachments of Royal Canadian Engineers' tunnelling companies, many of the men being expert diamond drillers. *Diagram specially drawn for* THE WAR ILLUSTRATED *by Felix Gardon. Plan by courtesy of the "Daily Express"*

army of French and Spaniards. Perchance "Gib" is destined to be besieged again; then Hitler's tanks and dive bombers, his parachutists armed with flame-throwers and tommy-guns and demolition charges, will be beaten off just as the floating batteries employed in the siege of long ago were destroyed by Eliott's red-hot cannon balls and incendiary shells.

But Gibraltar is more than a fortress; it is also a great naval base, and it can hardly be maintained that the harbour, which lies on the western side of the Rock looking across the Bay of Algeciras to the Spanish shore, is invulnerable. Theoretically, at least, it would be an easy matter for guns mounted on the Campo, as that shore is called, to make the harbour untenable for our warships and

to destroy the town which lies above its quays. Big guns have been reported to have been established on the Campo, seven or eight miles distant; and aerodromes in Spain are only a few minutes' flying-time away. But if the harbour could be attacked—and it can be—the guns of the fortress could also hit back. Gibraltar's armament, ranging from 9·2-inch guns to the latest 3·7-inch A.A. guns, can put up a terrific fire; and the hostile artillery across the bay would provide an easy target. It might well prove, then, that the harbour could be and would be kept open as a base for Cunningham's ships.

Whether the Straits of Gibraltar could be kept open is another matter. Between the Rock and Ceuta, immediately to the south in Africa, the Straits are 15 miles wide, but opposite Tarifa, some 20 miles to the west on the Spanish coast, they are only eight miles wide. The guns of Gibraltar, then, can hardly be said to control the Straits any more than the German guns at Calais control the Straits of Dover; in the one case as in the other it would be possible for convoys to slip through under cover of the opposite coast, with the added protection of smoke screens. The most they could do would be to harass passing shipping. Heavy guns mounted near Tarifa, however, firing in conjunction with guns on the Moroccan side of the Straits, *might* close the waterway, since they would not have to fire at a maximum range of more than 8,000 yards—say, four and a half miles. But, even so, ships might run the gauntlet, particularly at night.

At the worst, the fortress of Gibraltar might be invested and its garrison contained or bottled up, while its harbour was denied to our fleet. More likely, perhaps, is it that the Rock's big guns could cast over the base a protecting mantle of fire. And if the harbour remained in service, then the ships which use it would be able to sally forth to the protection of our convoys, moving east or west through the Straits. Moreover, land power might come to the aid of sea power; in other words, territory on both sides of the Straits would be occupied by our military forces, so as to ensure that the narrows should remain open to our ships.

Whatever Storms May Blow, Ready Aye Ready!

GIBRALTAR AND BRITISH SEA POWER are almost synonymous terms, for while our ships can be based on the great fortress harbour we hold the western entrance to the Mediterranean. Small wonder, therefore, that Axis policy should envisage an attack upon this vital position. The Rock of Gibraltar, here seen from the deck of a British battleship, is connected with the Spanish mainland by an isthmus 1½ miles long and ¼ mile broad. The harbour of 260 acres can accommodate the British Mediterranean fleet.

Photo, L.N.

Our Searchlight on the War

Chelsea Old Church No More

ALL SAINTS, Chelsea, better known as Chelsea Old Church, now laid in ruins by German bombs, dated in part from the early 14th century, although the tower and west end were not built until 1667-70. Up to 1824 it was the parish church of Chelsea ; in that year it became a chapel of ease to the new parish church, St. Luke's. Chelsea Old Church was closely associated with Sir Thomas More, who lived near by, and it contained the More Chapel, and also, in the chancel, a monument which he caused to be erected in his lifetime and for which he wrote the inscription. Tradition states that after his execution in 1535 his headless body, buried first at the Tower, was re-interred here. The Church was partly restored in 1910. In 1922 there was discovered, behind the monument of Sarah Colville, the earliest painted glass window in London, its preservation from the 14th century being due to the bricking-up of the window containing it. Chelsea Old Church contained some interesting chained books, including a "Vinegar"

Bible. A canopied tomb at the south-east corner of the churchyard is a monument to Sir Hans Sloane, the physician (died 1753), who gave his name to Hans Place and Sloane Street. It is still standing, and is shown in both the photographs above.

Lindbergh Resigns

PRESIDENT ROOSEVELT's recent attack on Mr. Lindbergh as an "appeaser," in which he referred to him as a "copperhead," the name of a deadly viper, has resulted in Lindbergh resigning his commission as colonel in the United States Army Air Corps Reserve, and in the announcement later that the War Department had accepted the resignation. In his letter, which was sent to the Press some time before it reached White House, Lindbergh said he had hoped to be able to express his point of view to the American people in time of peace without giving up the privilege of serving his country as an Air Corps officer in time of war. But, since the President had implied that he was no longer of use as a reserve officer, and in view of the imputations on his loyalty, character and motives, he could see no other honourable course open to him than to resign. It was in 1927, a month after his famous flight from New York to Paris, that Lindbergh received his commission. It

remains to be seen whether he will return the Order of the German Eagle with which he was decorated by Goering in 1938 at Berlin.

R.A.F. Grow More Vegetables

MANY R.A.F. stations have for some time been growing much of their own food in adjoining spare ground. This admirable activity has now been intensified and made more widespread through the appointment by the Air Council of a technical adviser on

CHELSEA OLD CHURCH, here seen before and after its destruction in the German air raid of April 16-17, was built early in the 14th century and contained many ancient monuments.
Photos, Will F. Taylor and Sport & General

horticulture. The first Air Ministry Gardening Officer is Mr. A. H. Whyte, a former student of the Royal Botanic Gardens, Edinburgh, late Horticultural Adviser to the Shropshire County Council, and himself a practical gardener. He will tour the R.A.F. stations, studying and solving their individual problems of vegetable production. He will advise units how to obtain grants for ploughing up new land and for the purchase of tools, seeds and fertilizers. He will work in liaison with catering inspectors and station welfare officers of the R.A.F., and will co-ordinate the gardening activities of the Service with the Ministry of Agriculture and Fisheries and other relevant bodies. Produce will be sold direct to the station messes at cut prices, a constant supply of fresh vegetables being ensured.

Interned Nazis Escape

ON April 18 twenty-eight German airmen, prisoners of war in an internment camp set in the wilds north of Lake Superior, escaped by tunnelling under the fences. The region is without roads or habitations, so it was not surprising that sixteen of these were quickly recaptured. Of these one was shot and wounded by a patrol, while three surrendered to a foreman employed by the C.P.R. who was armed only with a shovel. After a few days all but six had been rounded up. Most of the men were glad to be retaken, for bitter weather and lack of food had reduced them to a condition of great wretchedness. There was reason to believe that the escape, which had been carefully planned, was by way of being a "dress

rehearsal " for goal-breaking on a large scale in celebration of Hitler's birthday on April 20, but that the vigilance of the camp guards prevented this.

Three Days in a Dinghy

FIVE airmen, the crew of a bomber, recently spent three days and two nights in their dinghy in the North Sea. They had dropped bombs on their allotted targets in Germany and been hit by A.A. gunfire. Over the enemy coast the 'plane caught fire and the crew had to abandon it. The dinghy was flung out, the five scrambled on to it and began to paddle furiously westwards. Dawn broke. All that day aircraft flew near and one even saw them, but could not find them again as the sea was rough. Those who were not using the paddles had to keep bailing the water out of the rubber dinghy with their leather caps. Suddenly " we noticed black objects on the water and others just under the surface." They had entered a minefield.

Later on the third day they were spotted by a Hudson aircraft. Flying low, it dropped a bag containing brandy, biscuits and cigarettes. Soon afterwards there arrived a Hampden, which dropped a sound dinghy into which the exhausted crew scrambled with thankfulness. " Then," said the pilot, " we heard the pleasantest sound of all. It was the chug-chug of a motor, and just before it got dark we saw a naval cutter coming up. Directly it got to us the sailors threw down a rope ladder, but we had to be hauled aboard like seaweed."

ENEMY AND BRITISH AIR LOSSES
From the Beginning of the War
September 1939—March 1941
(Air Ministry revised figures)

	Enemy	British	Pilots saved	
Over Britain				
Sep.-Dec., 1939	23			35 by A.A. first
Jan.-Dec., 1940	3038	847	427	year.
Jan.-March, 1941	133	13	2	
	3194	860	429	
West Front Campaign				
Sep.-Dec., 1939	14	5		
Jan.-June, 1940	943	374	—	Includes Dunkirk.
	957	379		
Scandinavia				
Apl.-June, 1940	56	55	—	
At Sea				
Sep. 1939-Dec. 1940	33	37	—	
Jan.-Mar., 1941	4	Nil		
Enemy and Occupied Countries				
Sep.-Dec., 1939	20	26		
Jan.-Dec., 1940	45	349		Figures for pilots
Jan.-March, 1941	23	115		saved unknown.
	88	490	—	
Middle East				
June-Dec., 1940	421	78		Mainly Italian; 114 destd. on ground or captured.
Jan.-March, 1941	792	64	4	Mainly Italian; 411 destd. on ground or captured.
	1213	142	4	
Totals : Europe				
and Middle East	5545	1963		

Germans have admitted the loss over Britain of 3,100 machines and 7,000 airmen up to March 1941.
From April 1-30 German aircraft shot down over Britain numbered 112, 87 at night.

The Nazis Can't Beat the Spirit of Drake!

A heavy death roll was the result of German raids on Plymouth, which had five severe attacks in nine days. Above, Lady Astor, M.P., Lady Mayoress of Plymouth, leads mourners at a mass funeral for the victims. Centre is Admiral Sir M. E. Dunbar-Nasmith, V.C., C.-in-C., Plymouth.

Voluntary helpers are seen outside the temporary offices of the Lord Mayor's Fund and W.V.S. at Plymouth with gifts sent to air-raid sufferers from all parts of the kingdom.

PLYMOUTH bears many honourable scars following the intensive bombing of the city by the Nazis. Here is a scene in an industrial thoroughfare following one of Plymouth's heavy raids.

DRAKE was once Mayor of the city with which his name is for ever associated, and there, as we see, his spirit lives on; witness the undaunted morale of these elderly folk and children, waiting to be moved from a bombed district, and the sailor lending a helping hand.   *Photos. " News Chronicle," L.N.A. and Associated Press*

U.S. 'Plane Production Getting Into High Gear

Right: Maurice Summers, one of our chief test pilots, who recently flew back from the U.S.A. in a new American machine in the amazing time of seven and a half hours.

Below : Messerschmitt 110, shot down over Britain undamaged and sent to the U.S. for examination by the Vultee Aircraft Corporation, at moment of disembarkation.

Mechanic at Boeing factory, Seattle, explaining adjustments on bomber destined for Britain to R.A.F. pilots. Top photo : Boeing aircraft with R.A.F. symbols already painted on them.

Photos, Associated Press, Keystone and G.P.U.

AEROPLANES are first among the "tools" that are coming in increasing numbers from the United States. In spite of German denials the ferrying system is highly successful, only one aeroplane so far having been lost. Every effort is being made to improve on existing types, and it is a notable fact that the Vultee Aircraft Corporation, after careful study of a Messerschmitt 110 sent to the U.S.A. for inspection, report that at least four American-made fighter- planes are equal to, and in some respects superior to, Nazi aircraft. The four British pilots seen in the above photograph are 'flying bombers back to this country. Left to right, they are W. Brown, A Sherwood, A. Buckton and Bert Unwin.

I Was There! .... Eye Witness Stories of the War

I Did the Transatlantic 'Hop' with American Bombers

Lord Beaverbrook announced on April 23, 1941, that of the stream of bombers ferried across the Atlantic since the autumn, only one aircraft had been lost. The story of one of the American pilots engaged in this arduous service is reprinted here by arrangement with " Life " magazine.

These British ferry pilots at Seattle, Washington, headquarters of the Boeing Aircraft Company, are about to ferry over huge four-engined Boeing " Flying Fortresses," travelling first to Canada before crossing the ocean.   *Photo, Wide World*

OUR job since November 1940 has been to fly Lockheed Hudson bombers across the Atlantic. Recently we have begun flying even bigger four-engined Consolidated B 24s.

We pilots hail from the United States, England, Canada, Australia, New Zealand, Norway and Egypt.

I was in the first flight of Lockheeds to England (*see* pp. 98, 99 of this vol.). It had few of the trappings of an historic event. It had snowed earlier that day and we spent part of the morning clearing ice and snow from our planes while ploughs swept the great macadam surface of the main runways clean.

torial tastes. Some of the men wore business suits, others tweed sports jackets ! One Australian wore a beaver hat, and many of the men had skiing outfits. We looked as though we were heading for a costume ball instead of a Transatlantic hop.

Bennett flashed a signal light and took off. At minute intervals the rest of us followed. At a pre-arranged height we levelled off, flying in wide echelon formation. It was a relief to be off at last across the Big Pond.

" George," the automatic Sperry Gyro pilot, flies us, but we were kept busy watching Bennett's tail lights, checking and logging our instruments every half-hour and keeping

that have appeared, we did not fly in the stratosphere. At high altitudes we inhaled oxygen through rubber tubes in our mouths. The taste of the rubber was sickening, and on the first trip I vomited three times. Now we use Mayo oxygen masks.

Five hours out we ran into heavy clouds and everyone lost track of Bennett. It was every plane for itself the rest of the way and our plane crossed the ocean first.

Although we made bad time after land was sighted, we set an over-water Transatlantic record of 8 hours 57 minutes.

After delivering the bomber to Britain I came back to Canada by boat. Soon we will be ferried back on transport planes and by the summer, with better weather and more planes, each of us should be flying the Big Pond three or four times a month.

My second Transatlantic flight began about Christmas. When we were out six and a half hours everyone lost sight of Bennett in a cloudbank. Each pilot flew the rest of the way alone, and as this was the second time the flight group had become separated we now always make the entire trip solo.

After losing sight of Bennett our plane cruised, sometimes at a great height, and at other times skimmed the tops of the waves at 50 ft. When we were two hours from one of the spots toward which we were heading we received a radio report that Germans were bombing the neighbourhood. Accordingly we changed destination and soon were taxiing down at a British base. The ground crew had not been told to expect us, but these Transatlantic hops have already become so uneventful that when I stepped out the ground staff just said " Hallo." Then they rolled the plane away and I sent my wife the customary cable : " One hundred per cent crossing." Flying bombers across is done almost as nonchalantly as this.

THE LOCKHEED HUDSON, an American twin-engined general reconnaissance bomber, fitted with two Wright Cyclone engines, is being flown across the Atlantic in large numbers. In the opposite page are other photographs relating to America's aeroplane effort on behalf of Britain.

Ground crews scurried around the planes, checked the 1,200 horse-power engines and filled the two extra fuel tanks which each plane carried.

Then Captain Donald C. T. Bennett, R.A.F., in command of our flight, in plane No. 1, called us together. He handed each pilot the latest weather reports. Flight plans and route were discussed and agreed upon. To identify ourselves as British to each other, to other planes and ships, each crew was handed a Verey pistol with a combination of variously coloured flares to be changed at hourly intervals. Each plane, likewise, received its secret code number, which was also changed hourly. As a result it is almost impossible for a German plane, ship, or radio station to pass itself off as British by code or flare.

In a last word, Bennett cautioned us against flying over ships or towns lest we were fired on by mistake. Then, with a crisp " Thumbs up, good luck," he ordered us into our planes.

Comic relief was afforded by the sight of the pilots coming out to enplane. Our woollined flying suits had not yet arrived, so each man was dressed according to his own sar-

radio and navigation logs in minute detail. A constant worry is checking to make certain that the remaining gasoline in our tanks is equally distributed to help to balance the plane. About midway across we had a midnight snack of tomato soup, coffee and chocolate bars. Occasionally we rested on our cots. Contrary to some fanciful accounts

In Greece We Got Our Revenge for Calais

One British tank unit in Greece fought day and night for over ten days in the northern passes, wrecking 15 German tanks and bringing down 11 planes without loss to themselves. Here are some of the officers' experiences as told to a British United Press correspondent.

THE tank unit which distinguished itself in Greece was one which came out of Calais in the summer of 1940 with only seven officers and 15 men surviving. Telling of his experiences in Greece, one of the officers remarked, " We got some of our revenge for last year."

They first met the brunt of the German push in the Florina region after the German break through at Monastir. Later, when the German planes attacked, they stood their

ground and met the oncoming armoured forces with concentrated fire from their guns.

The officers, worn out, were enthusiastic about the way their unit had come through.

" You must have had a close shave, Jim," said one major to a captain. " Wasn't it your tank barring the way at that little bridge near Grevena when the Germans rushed it ? "

Captain Jim grinned, and said it was.

" But I'd had the bridge well taped for hours," he said. " My gunner had probably

502　　　　　　　*The War Illustrated*　　　　　　　*May 16th, 1941*

IIIIIIIIIIIIIIIIIIIIIIIIIIIIIIIIIIIIIIIIIIIIIIIIIIIIIIIIIIIIIIIIIII **I WAS THERE !** IIIIIIIIIIIIIIIIIIIIIIIIIIIIIIIIIIIIIIIIIIIIIIIIIIIIIIIIIIIIIIIIIII

never fired more than a dozen rounds, but I trained the gun myself square on the centre of the bridge.

" I held my fire until Jerry was so close that if he had fired he would have blown me back to Blighty. Then I ordered the gunner to fire. He pulled the trigger and the shell went through the leading tank, then pierced the second. There was a terrific explosion, the bridge collapsed and the other Huns pulled out quickly."

Another officer said : " Dive-bombers made it pretty hot for us. One bomb went off a few feet from my machine and nearly capsized it ; but that wasn't half the trouble. We fired our guns so fast that my brain began to feel like a scrambled egg.

" My tanks brought down two German 'planes with Bren-gun fire. The gunners were firing continuously, not only at the tanks but at other auxiliary machines, too.

" I spoke to one private whose gun was red-hot and congratulated him on winging a low-flying fighter," said the officer. " He answered, ' Thanks, sir. I'm pretty tired and I can't shoot as I'd like to, but there's so many of them and they're coming so low that I just can't help hitting them.' "

Another officer described how he had seen German shock troops advancing with arms locked behind the tanks which were coming down the snake-like road under heavy gunfire.

" Our tanks squatting on the plain looked like toads in the setting sun," he said. " But the guns were pointed the right way. When Jerry came up we let drive together with rapid fire. It played hell with Jerry. Then we pulled out, because we knew we were outnumbered."

'The British Did a Good Job at Bardia'

A remarkable tribute to the British landing-party who, on the night of April 19-20, did invaluable demolition work at Bardia, was paid by a German war correspondent who witnessed the capture of those of the British who failed to re-embark. Both his and the British official stories are given below.

A BRITISH statement issued on April 23 announced that " on the night of April 19-20 a British force with special demolition materials was landed near Bardia. They had a definite plan to carry out : to destroy an important bridge, a dump of stores, and to do the maximum amount of damage possible to the coastal defence guns.

The bridge was blown up, the dump consisted of stores particularly valuable to the enemy and was left burning fiercely, and four coast defence guns were made useless.

The Italians claim to have captured the whole of the raiding party. This statement is untrue. The major part of the raiding party embarked safely and returned to their base, but about 60 of its members failed to re-embark, and their capture has been claimed by the enemy."

In a broadcast from Berlin, a German war correspondent said :

On the night following April 19 about midnight, a radio call for help was received at headquarters from a German mobile radio unit somewhere near the beach. " British troops are landing," said the S O S. " The radio station is encircled. Send help." Shock battalions were formed at once.

The British had done their work magnificently. Their boots were soled with rubber, and they had moved on to the beach and cliffs so silently that nothing betrayed their presence. These noiseless and in-

visible British soldiers were somewhere in the fog within reach, but they could not be found.

German troops were searching everywhere in every corner, but nothing could they find. They became anxious for their comrades at the mobile radio unit, for they found the unit empty.

Then suddenly heavy detonations were heard and red flames leapt up in the night. Later it was discovered that the British had succeeded in reaching their own munition dump and had blown it up.

They had done it quickly and noiselessly. It was a really good piece of work. But the dumps were quite useless to us, for the ammunition was British and we could not have used it.

Still the hours passed, while the search went on, and we achieved no results until there were a few bursts of fire. A soldier shouted in the darkness, " I think I have got them,"

and a German lieutenant raced to the entrance of a cave.

The lieutenant shouted in English, " Come out," but no one answered from the cave. A hand grenade was thrown in, and then, one after another, the British soldiers came out, with their tin hats nonchalantly tilted. They were holding up their hands, but they were big, strong fellows, and they were magnificently equipped.

The search then went on in the same area, and British soldiers came out of many caves and surrendered. In the morning the work was finished, and the British landing force had been captured.

We captured a major, two captains, three lieutenants and 65 men.

BARDIA, showing some of the objectives which a British landing-party destroyed under cover of fog, the Nazis being taken completely by surprise. *Courtesy of the " News Chronicle "*

We Know We Made Vital Hits at Tripoli

So sudden was the devastating naval attack on Tripoli just before dawn on April 21 that it was 15 minutes before the first shore battery opened in reply. A special correspondent of the " Daily Telegraph " watched the bombardment from one of our warships, and here is his story of the scene.

A THIN sickle late moon lit the sea, but Tripoli, some six or eight miles away, gleamed eerily in the light of dozens of descending flares. I have never seen such a display of fireworks. With their quick-firing Breda guns the Italian harbour defences sent up a frantic blaze of green, red and white tracers which weaved patterns round the flares that hung like baleful lanterns in the sky.

Yet, despite the fact that it looked like one of Brock's set pieces over the town, I did not see a single flare shot down. As they burnt out, Fleet Air Arm machines, droning overhead, dropped ever-fresh clusters.

The harbour defences had already been harassed throughout the night by R.A.F. bombers, and there is little doubt that the whole defence was concentrated on the possibility of fresh air attack to the exclusion of other forms of offensive.

As I stood in darkness on the bridge of my ship, my eyes got sufficiently accustomed to the conditions to pick out other huge shapes like ours carefully checking their course through the minefields. That done, intricate calculations of range, already worked out, were themselves checked and re-checked, for each ship had specific target areas where the maximum amount of damage could be done.

As 5 a.m. approached on Monday, April 21, I knew from previous experience of similar operations that Tripoli was going to suffer an inferno of fire such as it had never before known. At 5 to the second our battleships opened with broadsides which echoed angrily

ON GUARD IN BARDIA after General Wavell's Libyan victory. The fortune of war has, however, put Bardia again in possession of the enemy—but only precariously, for a British force landed in the neighbourhood on the night of April 19-20 and destroyed a bridge, in addition to doing other important damage. *Photo, British Official : Crown Copyright*

TRIPOLI, the waterfront of which is seen above, is the main Italian supply base in Northern Africa. At dawn on April 21 it was heavily bombarded by units of the British Mediterranean Fleet, as related in this page. Extensive damage was done to military objectives shown in the plan, right, by 530 tons of shells. Several enemy ships were sunk and hits were made on the Spanish Quay and the Karamanli Mole.　　　　*Photo, Topical. Plan, Courtesy of " Daily Mail "*

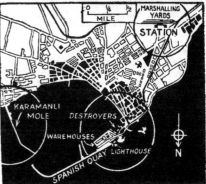

back and forth between the folds of the distant coast. Splashes of fire, springing up on the illuminated horizon that was Tripoli, told their own grim story of bursting 15-in. shells. Then the remainder of the fleet joined in.

Precisely four minutes after the beginning of the bombardment my ship crossed the line, and our first salvo rocked us from stem to stern.

I have tried to tell before of the awe-inspiring, even frightening, majesty of night bombardment as experienced from the right end of these monstrous guns. Let it suffice to say, then, that our gunnery officer described it as the finest " shoot " he had ever done.

We knew we were hitting the enemy vitally, for after the first few salvos the brilliance began to die out of the display of tracer shells patterning the sky around our flares. They got ragged and only came in short spurts.

It was obvious that those who retained the courage to man their guns on shore were ducking between their shelters and their posts amid the showers of our projectiles.

Bigger anti-aircraft guns were equally uncertain, and the sparkle of their bursting shells high in the sky stopped altogether at times when things began to get too hot for them.

The procession of our big battleships steaming unperturbed along the enemy coast, pouring in their broadsides, had proceeded without interruption for a quarter of an hour before the enemy shore batteries appeared to wake up. Then a noise like a cartload of bricks being dropped suddenly behind me warned us of their counter-fire.

Now and again the whine of shell splinters seemed unpleasantly close as they sang their mournful chorus through us in the dark night, but more often the shells hummed high overhead ; and that, if you can command sufficient presence of mind, assures you they are well past.

Now, as we turned to steam back on our course, the great guns swung silently to starboard and a new deluge of death began to fall towards Tripoli.

Soon the pall of smoke and dust, hanging like a solid wall between our flares and the town below, began to be tinged underneath with a lurid glow. Fires were taking hold of shipping in the harbour. Soon these fires brightened like an angry dawn over the town.

Light tracer shell-fire faded away altogether, and only here and there did the forlorn spark of a heavier anti-aircraft gun flash for a second skywards. We seemed to have cracked the morale of the defenders.

Even the fire of the shore batteries became incidental. We, meanwhile, pounded away like giants forging some new destiny, oblivious of the protests of a mere midget race of men.

At the end of fifty minutes the " Cease fire " came, but there was unceasing tension. We expected the enemy would now give us his portion, but not a single shot came back to answer us and the leviathans of the Fleet were allowed to proceed uninterrupted.

What I Saw of India's Great New Arsenal

Impressive evidence of India's ever-growing war resources was gathered by Reuters' special correspondent who paid a visit to the site of India's latest and most up-to-date arsenal, set among hills and encircled by block-houses.

I HAVE just paid a visit to the site of India's latest and most up-to-date arsenal which a year ago was part of a vast rolling countryside. As I passed through the closely guarded gates, protected by a double line of high steel railings, I saw 20,000 coolies at work completing the construction of new buildings and roads.

I was first of all taken to a high vantage-point in the middle of the grounds to obtain a general view of the arsenal. Like a huge, sinuous snake the surrounding metal railings, some 12 feet high, curved up the hills and down the valleys which are a feature of the local countryside, completely encircling the arsenal and guarding it from unauthorized intruders. Squat block-houses, from which a constant watch is kept, could be seen at strategic points on hilltops overlooking the arsenal.

The magazines themselves were cunningly recessed in the hillsides. When the grass and foliage, removed at the time of their construction, has had time to grow again, they should be almost invisible from the air, and I was told that they are virtually bomb-proof.

Elsewhere were small buildings designed for fusing ammunition. This is done at some distance from the magazines to avoid the possibility of accidents. All are connected with an elaborate system of roads and railway sidings.

I was then shown one of the magazines. Massively constructed of reinforced concrete, it has heavy steel doors opening into a long, low room painted in gleaming white and brilliantly lighted. Strong pillars support the roof, on which automatic fire-extinguishing devices are fitted.

Before me were rows upon rows of neatly stacked bombs, painted a dull yellow. Most of them were heavy calibre bombs, and with their tapering noses pointing to the ceiling they seemed full of silent menace. The other magazines, I was told, contain various types of munitions, and each has its own railway platform and siding.

Our Diary of the War

SUNDAY, APRIL 27, 1941   603rd day

Air.—Daylight attacks on factory and camp near Cologne, docks at Ymuiden and aerodrome at De Kooy. Enemy patrol vessel off Brittany hit.

War against Italy.—Enemy troops which had penetrated five miles across Egyptian frontier were halted by British tanks.

Sudan Defence Corps captured Socota, Abyssinia. R.A.F. damaged motor transport and fired petrol dump at Alomata.

Home.—Slight day activity over S.E. coast. Heavy bombs fell at night on Portsmouth. One raider destroyed.

Balkan War.— German forces entered Athens. British withdrawal continuing.

MONDAY, APRIL 28   604th day

Sea.—H.M. minesweeper Elgin destroyed a Heinkel without casualty or damage.

Air.—Coastal Command attacked two enemy destroyers escorting supply ships off Dutch coast. Day raids on Emden, shipping off France and Holland, factories, docks, and aerodromes in Holland.

Night attacks on Scharnhorst and Gneisenau lying at Brest.

War against Italy.—R.A.F. attacked number of Junkers embarking troops at Benina. One aircraft destroyed, seven others damaged, and many casualties. Heavy night raids on aerodromes at Benina and Derna, and on Benghazi.

Home.—Day raid on coastal district in N.E. Scotland. Bombs also fell on E. and N.E. coasts of England. Heavy night attack on Plymouth. Enemy also over East Anglia. Four raiders destroyed.

Balkan War.—Announced in Sydney that evacuation of Australian troops from Greece had begun.

TUESDAY, APRIL 29   605th day

Air.—Fighter command made offensive sweeps over coast of northern France. Bombers attacked enemy shipping off coasts of France, Belgium and Norway. One supply ship set on fire and four others damaged.

Night attack in force on Mannheim. Oil stores at Rotterdam bombed.

War against Italy.—In Sollum area enemy invaders being harassed by our patrols.

Home.—Enemy day activity in areas near S.E. coast and other points. Another severe night attack on Plymouth. Eight raiders destroyed. Dover shelled for five hours.

Balkan War.—Evacuation of Greece proceeding.

WEDNESDAY, APRIL 30   606th day

Air.—Daylight harassing of enemy shipping off Dutch coast. Norwegian radio station bombed. Main night attack on Kiel. Other targets were in Berlin area, industrial centre of Hamburg and port of Emden.

War against Italy.—Enemy penetrated outer defences of Tobruk. British patrols active in Sollum area. R.A.F. heavily bombed transport in Cyrenaica.

In Abyssinia operations aim at linking up northern and southern columns converging on Amba Alagi, where enemy holds defensive positions.

Balkan War.—Withdrawal from Greece continuing.

THURSDAY, MAY 1   607th day

Air.—Day attacks on submarine base at Den Helder, oil tanks at Vlaardingen and shipping off Dutch coast.

War against Italy.—C.-in-C. Mediterranean announced that naval units had bombarded troops and supplies at El Gazala, Libya.

Enemy continued to attack outer defences of Tobruk. British counter-attacked, supported by R.A.F., and destroyed 11 tanks.

R.A.F. bombed Benghazi, aerodrome at Benina, transport at Acroma.

In Abyssinia British occupied Bahrbar and Debub. Heavy R.A.F. attack on enemy positions at Amba Alagi, Alomata and fort in Falaga Pass.

Home.—Small-scale daylight activity; bombs fell at one point on South Coast. At night raiders were over Merseyside and other areas. One shot down.

Iraq.—More British troops reported to have landed in Basra.

FRIDAY, MAY 2   608th day

Air.—R.A.F. bombed Hamburg, Emden and oil stores at Rotterdam.

War against Italy.—Tobruk holding out against violent all-day attacks. Two enemy bombers shot down. R.A.F. made night attack on Benina, destroying two troop-carriers and damaging others.

In Abyssinia British occupied Fike.

R.A.F. attacked convoy of merchant vessels in Mediterranean, scoring hits on three and on escorting destroyers.

Home.—Another large-scale night raid on Merseyside. Six enemy aircraft destroyed.

Balkans.—Announced that evacuation from Greece was over, and that 43,000 men had been withdrawn.

Iraq.—Cantonment at Habbaniya attacked by Iraqi troops, forcing British to take counter action. Iraqi Air Force tried unsuccessfully to raid aerodrome. Rutbar, near Haifa pipeline, occupied by Iraqis.

British forces occupied airport, dock area and power station at Basra.

SATURDAY, MAY 3   609th day

Sea.—Admiralty announced that after evacuation from Greece two destroyers, Diamond and Wryneck, had been sunk. Armed merchant cruiser Voltaire overdue and considered lost.

Air.—R.A.F. heavily bombed industrial centre of Cologne. Smaller attacks made on Essen, Düsseldorf and oil tanks at Rotterdam. Scharnhorst and Gneisenau in Brest docks were again attacked ; also docks at Cherbourg and Boulogne and aerodrome at Le Touquet. Other forces bombed oil tanks and aerodrome in southern Norway.

War against Italy.— Enemy attack on Tobruk brought to standstill by artillery fire. In Sollum area British mechanized forces carried out successful raid. R.A.F. raided Benina and Benghazi.

In Debub sector, Abyssinia, Indian troops occupied Emadani and Ulethert.

Reported that R.A.F. had sunk enemy destroyer and a freighter in Mediterranean.

Home.—Third successive night attack on Merseyside. Many casualties and much damage done. Bombs fell at many other points of Britain. Sixteen raiders destroyed.

Iraq.—Fighting in progress between British and Iraqis at Habbaniya. Pipe-line to Haifa reported to have been cut.

R.A.F. heavily attacked petrol dumps and magazines at Moascar Rashid, Iraqi aerodrome outside Baghdad.

FROM ONE GREAT DEMOCRAT TO ANOTHER

ROOSEVELT
to CHURCHILL

FORTUNATE indeed is it that in this supreme hour Britain and the U.S.A. should be captained by democrats cast in heroic mould. President Roosevelt echoed our Premier's mood when he concluded his personal letter to Mr. Churchill with a quotation from Longfellow. The document, brought over by Mr. Wendell Willkie last January, has been issued by the Ministry of Information, and a facsimile is reproduced on the right. "I think this verse applies to your people as it does to us," wrote the President.

Sail on, Oh Ship of State!
Sail on, Oh Union strong and great.
Humanity with all its fears,
With all the hope of future years
Is hanging breathless on thy fate.

CHURCHILL
to the NATION

THE Premier, broadcasting to the nation on the evening of Sunday, April 27, on the war situation, concluded with an extract from the poem by Arthur Hugh Clough, " Say not the struggle nought availeth," which, Mr. Churchill might have added, applies equally to America and to us.

For while the tired waves, vainly breaking,
Seem here no painful inch to gain,
Far back, through creeks and inlets making,
Comes silent, flooding in, the main,

And not by eastern windows only
When daylight comes, comes in the light
In front, the sun climbs slow, how slowly,
But westward, look, the land is bright.

UNHAPPY FRANCE! WHERE ST. JOAN'S BANNER IS FLOWN NEXT TO HITLER'S

General de Gaulle appealed to all Frenchmen to observe an hour's silence on May 11 in memory of St. Joan of Arc. It cannot be doubted that many responded, the fact that their country is under the Nazi heel making the patriotic symbolism of St. Joan all the more poignant. France will rise again, and when she does this German picture will become just a historic curiosity. It shows a statue of the Maid of Orleans erected twenty-five miles south of Verdun in memory of soldiers who fell in 1914-18. Now beside St. Joan's banner floats the swastika. *From the "Berliner Illustrierte Zeitung"*

At Tobruk Britain Stands at Bay

On May 7 the House of Commons, by 447 votes to 3, approved "the policy of His Majesty's Government in sending help to Greece, and declares its confidence that our operations in the Middle East and in all other theatres of war will be pursued by the Government with the utmost vigour." The two days' debate was wound up by the Prime Minister in a speech whose principal topic is reviewed below.

A YEAR ago not one Englishman in a thousand had ever heard of Tobruk, and to those few who knew of its existence it was just an Italian harbour of little interest and of less importance. Italy had not then entered the war, and even for some time after Mussolini had taken the plunge, Tobruk remained a backwater. Not until Graziani took the road into Egypt, not until in December the Italian mass was ripe for the sickle—Mr. Churchill's phrase—did Tobruk's name appear more and more often in the newspapers. For a few days in the New Year it achieved headline prominence, but after its capture by the Australians of the Army of the Nile on January 22 it sank back into obscurity. So far as it was concerned, the war was over : that was the general belief.

But it was not so. Only a few weeks more and there was a swift reversal of fortune in the Western Desert. Tactical mistakes were committed, said Mr. Churchill in his review of May 7 ; missed chances occurred ; our armoured force became disorganized. Our generals on the spot believed that no superior German force could advance effectively across the desert towards Egypt as soon as or as quickly as they did ; or if they did advance, then they would not be able to nourish themselves.

Even the Germans had no expectation of proceeding beyond Agedabia, 100 miles or so along the coast road west of Benghazi. "But when they won their surprising success, they exploited it with that enterprising and organizing audacity which ranks so high in the military sphere. They pushed on into the blue, or might I say the yellow ochre, of the desert, profiting by their easy victory, as they have done in so many cases, and they took in this case little thought of what they should eat, or what they should drink ; but they pushed on until they came up against Tobruk."

"There," continued the Premier, "they met their prop . . . A hard and heavy prop, none the less important because, like all

these desert operations, it was on a small scale." Warfare as is now being waged in the Western Desert can be conducted, the Premier pointed out, by only small numbers of highly equipped troops ; 30,000 or 40,000 men are the most that can be fed or supplied in the desert. Here the fortunes of war are subject to violent oscillations and mere numbers do not count.

Now the Nazis have come up against the large forces which guard the frontier of Egypt ; and although they have the superiority in armoured vehicles and the air forces are about equal, they are confronted by problems far more difficult, since they are on a far larger scale, than any General Rommel has yet solved in Africa. For the invasion of Egypt great supplies must be built up, magazines provided, pipe-lines made to carry an artificial river forward with the troops, and so on. On the other hand, we are now "lying back on our fertile delta, which incidentally is the worst ground in the world for mechanized vehicles, and enjoying the command of the sea." Moreover, General Wavell (Mr. Churchill revealed) has now under his orders nearly half a million men. "A continuous flow of equipment has been in progress from this country during the last 10 months, and now that Italian resistance in Abyssinia and Africa and Somaliland is collapsing, the steady concentration northwards of all these forces is possible and, indeed, has for many weeks been rapidly proceeding, and General Smuts has ordered the splendid South African Army forward to the Mediterreanean shore."

While Tobruk stands, a large-scale invasion of Egypt would seem to be a temerarious venture ; and it is for this reason that the place has been, and is being, most fiercely assailed by the enemy. And it is being as fiercely defended. "Tobruk," to quote Mr. Churchill again, "has already been the centre of a most stubborn and spirited defence by the Australian and British troops gathered in this widespread

fortified land, under the command of the Australian general, General Morshead."

Behind its iron ring of defences, the little garrison is making a tremendous stand. The heat is terrific ; the sky from dawn to dusk is a vast brazen bowl ; the wind is heavily charged with particles of grit which fill men's eyes and mouths and nostrils, their clothes and food ; rifle barrels are so hot that they

GENERAL L. J. MORSHEAD, D.S.O., defender of Tobruk, here seen with Mr. P. C. Spender, Australian Army Minister, led the famous 33rd Australian battalion in the last war.
Photo, Courtesy of the Australian Government

blister the hands that touch them. But at least the British defenders have shady bungalows in the town itself, while in the front line their refuges down below ground are heavenly cool compared with the hellish heat prevailing in the world above.

German prisoners—about 3,000 have been taken since the siege began—have described the conditions in which they are forced to fight as hellish. Their tanks are not air-conditioned, and the crews are reported to have fainted from the terrific heat. And what of the hooded infantrymen with flame throwers, who are reported to be employed by the enemy in an attempt to smoke out the Australian infantry from their dug-outs and underground concrete posts ? Theirs must be a hot job, indeed !

Both the one side and the other know the issues that are at stake. "Loss of the Suez Canal, loss of our position in the Mediterranean, loss of Malta," said Mr. Churchill, "would be among the heaviest blows which we could sustain. . . . We intend to defend to the death and without thought of retirement, the valuable and highly defensive outposts of Crete and Tobruk."

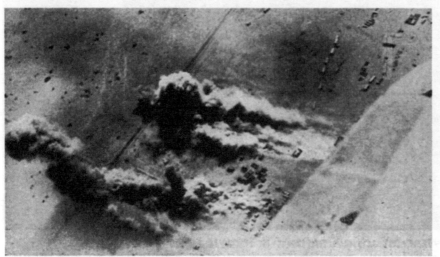

TOBRUK UNDER FIRE, as in this dive-bombing attack by Nazi Stukas, remains solidly in British hands. German air activity has been considerably reduced recently as a result of intensive R.A.F. raids on German airfields in Cyrenaica. *Photo, From German source, Associated Press*

In These the Nazi Army Wings to War

JUNKERS JU 52/3m TRANSPORT MONOPLANES are extensively used by the Germans for troop and freight carrying. The Ju 52 was brought out about 1932 as a commercial air liner (see top photograph) for 15-17 passengers. In 1935 the Ju 52 was produced as a bomber for the Luftwaffe, but more recently has been produced in large numbers as a troop-carrier. One such is seen above.

The pilot of a German troop-carrying aircraft is here seen receiving a message from his radio operator.

BY PLANE TO LIBYA came much of the war material needed by the German Afrika Korps for their advance towards Tobruk. Here the Nazis are unloading equipment flown, probably from Sicily, to one of their bases in Cyrenaica.
Photos, Keystone and Planet News

VAST numbers of troop-carrying aircraft have been used by the Nazis since the beginning of the war, particularly in Norway and now in North Africa, where the attackers of Tobruk and Egypt are being " fed " by this means. It is, of course, a matter of common knowledge that many of Germany's commercial air-liners in peacetime were designed and constructed in such a way that they could easily be converted into military machines. Prominent among such aircraft is the Junkers Ju 52/3m, photographs of which are given in this page. Similarly the Ju 86 and Ju 90 can be used either as civil or military machines. The Ju 52, still extensively used, is a three-engined monoplane with a cruising speed of about 175 m.p.h. The Ju 89 (the military version of the Ju 90) is a four-engined monoplane with a cruising speed of about 200 m.p.h. The Focke-Wulf Fw 200 Condor, a four-engined troop-carrier, is also being extensively used by the Germans, and this aircraft, which can carry a large load, has a cruising speed of some 210 m.p.h. As a troop-carrier it has accommodation for about 30 fully-armed men in one long cabin.

The Campaign in Greece: A Factual Survey

What follows is the first official account of the campaign in Greece, which has now come to an end with the evacuation of the Forces of the Empire and the withdrawal of the Greek Government to Crete. Although the account overlaps in some measure what we have already published, it is reproduced here in its entirety because of the importance and historic interest of its subject.

At 5.45 a.m. on April 6 the Germans crossed the Bulgarian-Greek frontier. There was no warning or ultimatum; but the German attack had been awaited for some time and the Metaxas Line which runs along this frontier was manned by three Greek divisions.

The Germans came across the frontier at five points; down the Struma valley to the Rupel pass, over the Nevrokop plateau towards Drama, towards Xante, towards Komotine, and from Svilengrad down the Maritsa valley. The last line of advance was not seriously opposed, nor was it intended to be, and the enemy reached the sea at Dedeagatch on April 9. Elsewhere the Greeks successfully withheld the initial German attacks, and inflicted heavy casualties. At the Rupel pass the Germans employed parachute troops, dropping 150 behind the Greek lines; of these 100 were quickly killed and the remainder captured.

Our plan was to make the high ground west of the Vardar valley our main defensive position, and to delay the Germans on the Metaxas Line. We intended to inflict the maximum damage on the enemy in Eastern Macedonia and Greek Thrace, but, if necessary, to withdraw from that part of Greece which lay east of our main defensive line.

Simultaneously with an attack on Greece, the Germans also invaded Yugoslavia, which, though partly mobilized, was not ready for war. Although the Tsvetkovitch Government

had been overthrown, the adherence to the Tripartite Pact had not been repudiated by the Simovitch Government; and, as was the case with Greece, no ultimatum or other warning was given. The disposal of the Yugoslav forces appears to have been governed not alone by military but also by political considerations, and inadequate forces had been allotted to the south of the country where the real threat lay. This disposal had been planned by the Tsvetkovitch Government, and General Simovitch had no time to revise the plans. Consequently the Germans were able to advance rapidly up the

Strumitza valley, past both sides of Lake Doiran and down the Vardar valley. They reached Salonika on the evening of April 8. The three Greek divisions in the east were cut off from the main body of the allies.

But the rapidity of the German advance in Yugoslavia held a yet more serious threat. Skoplje (Uskub) and Veles were reached on April 8, and it was evident that the Monastir Gap was threatened. How serious this was is seen when we consider the disposal of our and the Greek forces. By far the greater part of the Greek Army was in Albania, some 30 to 40 miles away from the Greek frontier, and with its left flank on the sea and its right flank on the Yugoslav frontier. Two Greek divisions and Imperial troops, all under the command of General Wilson, who was, in his turn, under the command of the Greek Commander-in-Chief, General Papagos, had taken up a strong natural line of defence running from the sea near Katerini through Veria and Edessa to the Yugoslav frontier. A British armoured force was out to the east of this line, engaged in demolition work and similar activities. The force under General Wilson, therefore, was opposing the Germans along a front of 60 to 70 miles on the east, while to the west the main bulk of the Greek army was opposing the Italians along a front of similar length; between the two mountains of Southern Yugoslavia formed a barrier pierced by the Monastir Gap, and manned only by mountain guards.

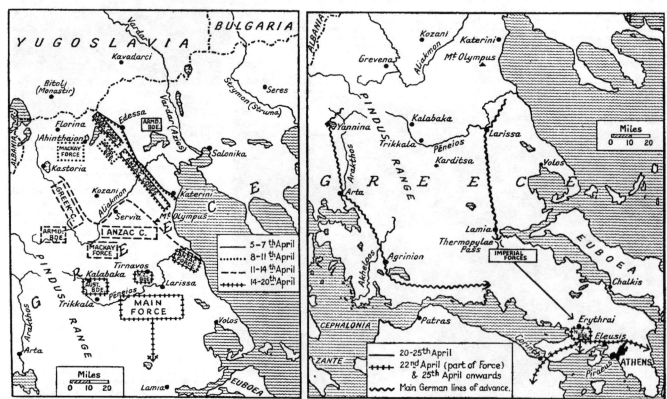

APRIL 6-25, 1941. These maps show successive stages in the development of the campaign in Greece, from the time when German forces crossed the Bulgarian-Greek frontier until the evacuation. The first main line of resistance of the Allied forces was, as shown in the left-hand map, from the Aegean Sea near Katerini through Veria and Edessa to the Yugoslav frontier. A British armoured force remained to the eastward of this line, engaged on reconnaissance and demolition work. But the disaster to the Yugoslav forces led to the loss of the Monastir Gap and threatened the Allied left flank. Other stands were made at positions indicated on the map, but the superiority of the Germans in numbers and in aircraft compelled the Allied forces to make a fighting withdrawal. Magnificent rearguard actions by Imperial forces at Peneios Gorge and later at Thermopylae (right-hand map) enabled the main forces to be withdrawn to the evacuation beaches.

Maps, Courtesy of Ministry of Information

Twenty Days of Fierce Fighting All the Way

AUSTRALIAN SOLDIERS, captured at Larissa, are here seen under supervision of German guards. The fighting round about Larissa was among the fiercest in the retreat from Mount Olympus. Right: a Greek prisoner (so the German caption runs) obeys his captors and helps to smash Greek rifles—not the least humiliating order inflicted upon a valiant people who defied Nazi brutality and fought for honour and freedom.
Photos, Associated Press

By the evening of April 7 the disaster to the Yugoslav forces was apparent, and the threat to the Monastir Gap had become a reality. A small reserve, under a Brigadier, consisting of a machine-gun battalion and some medium artillery, was formed near Ahinthaion, south of Florina. Next morning General MacKay was sent with his Divisional headquarters, some artillery, one anti-tank regiment, and an Australian brigade (less one battalion), to augment this force, which remained in the Ahinthaion neighbourhood to await the Germans. Meanwhile the armoured force was ordered to blow up its demolitions, and withdrew to Edessa behind the Australian division, under whose orders it was placed.

Withdrawal to Mt. Olympus

Preparations to meet the threat through the Monastir Gap were made only just in time. On April 9 the Germans appeared south of Florina and hotly engaged General MacKay's force during this and the next day. The Imperial Force inflicted heavy casualties on the enemy, but it became apparent that a stand could not be made indefinitely against the greatly superior German numbers. If the enemy could not be held at Ahinthaion it was clear that the whole line on this front would have to be withdrawn; otherwise it would be outflanked. On April 11, therefore, the Imperial and Greek forces began to withdraw to a new line which ran from the sea south-east of Mount Olympus north-west to Servia, thence south-west along the River Aliakmon, and finally north-west again, along the high ground to the west of the plain of Kozani. At the same time General MacKay's mixed British and Anzac force, which had suffered considerable losses, withdrew down the Kozani valley and behind the new line; and the armoured force moved to Grevena.

The line from the sea to Servia and along the Aliakmon was held by Imperial troops, while the high ground along the Kozani plain was held by the two Greek divisions. These two divisions were heavily engaged by the enemy. Meanwhile, enemy forces advancing down the Kozani valley were engaged by our forces at Servia and suffered heavy losses.

The Greek divisions, having fought valiantly under overwhelming conditions and suffered very severe casualties, had now almost ceased to exist as a fighting force. The flank and rear of the Imperial Force were accordingly threatened and a further withdrawal was necessary. Therefore, withdrawal to the Thermopylae Line south of Lamia was ordered.

The Imperial Force now had to withdraw without further aid from the Greek Army; the corps which had been fighting with our troops could do no more, and the rest of the Greek Army was away beyond the Pindus mountains.

On April 14 an Australian brigade was ordered to Kalabaka at the head of the railway from the south in order to cover our left flank of withdrawal. On April 15 a New Zealand brigade took up a covering position north of Tirnavos, and a small New Zealand force which held the eastern entrance to the Peneios gorge south of Mount Olympus was heavily engaged by a greatly superior enemy force and driven back. Next day two battalions of an Australian brigade went to its support. This small Anzac force, now

about the strength of a brigade group, fought two German divisions in the Peneios gorge; its losses were heavy, but withdrawal was secured on our right flank.

During the following days our forces withdrew to the Thermopylae position under very heavy enemy bombing, and by April 20 we were in our new positions. The New Zealand division held the right to the sea, while the Australians held the pass on the left.

Artillery of both the British Army and the Anzac forces played an important part in the campaign. Undoubtedly it inflicted very heavy casualties, and the Germans themselves have testified to the accuracy of our shooting.

By this time it was obvious that the Greek Army could fight no longer. The Greek Government, recognizing this, requested on April 21 that the U.K. and Empire Contingent which had been sent to its help should be withdrawn from Greece. The German forces which had been held up for some time by the gallant rearguard action at the Peneios gorge had passed through Larissa and Lamia and were in contact with our forces on the Thermopylae position; meanwhile, other German forces, freed from any threat to their rear by the capitulation of the Greek Epirus army, were rapidly coming south from Yannina through Arta and Agrinion, and constituted a threat to the rear of our position. On April 22 a New Zealand brigade had accordingly been withdrawn to a position on the pass south of Erythrai to cover the withdrawal of the remainder of our forces to embarkation areas; and on April 25 the last of the forces on the Thermopylae position withdrew behind Erythrai and began to embark in warships and transports from various beaches in Attica, Argolis, and Peloponnese.

How the Navy Got Our Men Away from Greece

Although full details have not yet been given, it is now possible to describe in some
measure the great part played by the Royal Navy in the evacuation of the British Army
—not to mention a large number of Greek and Yugoslav troops and civilian refugees—
from Greece. What follows has been supplied by the Admiralty.

THE withdrawal of the Imperial troops from Greece began on the night of April 24-25. It was known that this would be an operation of extreme difficulty and danger owing to the enemy's command of the air, the configuration of the Greek coast, and the fact that enemy air attacks had already made most of the major Greek ports unusable. During that night about 13,500 men of the Imperial Forces were withdrawn from the Rapthis and Nauplia areas. One empty transport ran aground; she was bombed and burned out.

On April 25 it was reported that enemy forces had landed on Euboea in order to attack Khalkis, from which port it had been intended to withdraw a large number of Imperial troops.

On the night of April 25-26 about 5,500 men of the Imperial Forces were withdrawn from the Megara area. One transport was bombed and sunk by enemy aircraft; fortunately she had not embarked troops and was empty. The same night an empty transport was damaged by enemy air attack; she was taken in tow by a destroyer but afterwards became a total loss.

During the night of April 26-27 about 16,000 men of the Imperial Forces were withdrawn from Greece—over 8,000 from the Kalamata area, over 4,000 from Nauplia, and 3,500 from the Raphina and Rapthis areas.

While troops were being withdrawn from Nauplia a transport was bombed and set on fire after having embarked troops. A destroyer, H.M.S. Diamond (Lt.-Cdr. P. A. Cartwright, R.N.), at once went to the rescue of the troops from this transport. Although H.M.S. Diamond and the boats from the transport were continuously attacked from the air, the destroyer picked up about 600 men. On leaving Nauplia H.M.S. Diamond was joined by H.M.S. Wryneck (Commander R. H. D. Lane, R.N.), and both destroyers returned to Nauplia to search for further survivors from the transport. H.M.S. Wryneck rescued a further 100 men, and the burning wreck of the transport was sunk by torpedo from H.M.S. Diamond, since it was a danger to navigation and was providing the enemy with light by which to deliver his air attacks. H.M.S. Diamond and H.M.S. Wryneck then left Nauplia.

Next morning both these ships were attacked by German dive bombers and sunk. It is feared that the casualties were heavy,

although some fifty survivors were picked up by another of our destroyers sent to search the area, and at least one boat may have reached the Greek shore. The survivors from the destroyers reported that they were repeatedly attacked by machine-gun fire by the German aircraft while they were struggling in the water.

During the night of April 27-28 about 4,200 men were withdrawn from the Rapthis area by warships. It was then hoped to carry out the final embarkation on the night of April 28-29. It was estimated that there were about 8,000 troops and a number of Yugoslav refugees to be embarked from the

Kalamata area, about 4,000 troops to be embarked from Monemvasia, and about 750 R.A.F. personnel from Kithera. Arrangements were made for the withdrawal of all these forces by warships.

Soon after midnight on April 29 our forces which had proceeded to the Kalamata area reported that it had already been occupied by the enemy, and so the plan to embark 8,000 men and the Yugoslav refugees had had to be abandoned. General Wilson was at once consulted. He gave it as his view that the only possibility of embarking further troops from this area was to pick up stragglers in destroyers' boats from the east side of the Gulf. As it was, despite the enemy's occupa-

---

ADMIRAL CUNNINGHAM'S MESSAGE

I WISH to convey my appreciation and admiration of their work, to the masters, officers and men of the Merchant Navy and of all the allied merchant vessels who took part in the movement of the Imperial Forces into Greece and in the recent operations when they were withdrawn. Throughout these operations under conditions of considerable danger and difficulty there was no faltering, and the determined way in which ships fought back against the aircraft attacks with their defensive armament was magnificent. We of the Royal Navy and the officers and men of the Imperial Forces realize the extent of the service rendered and of the debt owed to the Merchant Navy for their devoted work during these past weeks.

---

tion nearly 500 men were withdrawn by our naval units from the Kalamata area during this night. At the same time, 3,750 men of the Imperial forces were withdrawn from the Monemvasia area and 750 R.A.F. personnel from the Kithera.

On the night of April 29-30 our destroyers again operated in the Kalamata area in the hope of picking up survivors, but only 33 officers and men were found and embarked. On the next night, however, our destroyers carried out another search of the Kalamata area, and succeeded in rescuing a further 23 officers and 179 men.

Soon after midnight on April 30-May 1

DIAMOND and WRYNECK were the only British warships sunk during the withdrawal from Greece. H.M.S. Diamond was a sister ship of H.M.S. Dainty, above, and was a vessel of 1,375 tons provided for in the 1930 programme. H.M.S. Wryneck (left) was a destroyer of 900 tons dating from 1918.
Photos, Wright & Logan

the Commander-in-Chief, Mediterranean, reported that about 45,000 Imperial troops and R.A.F. personnel had been withdrawn from Greece, and also a large number of refugees. Admiral Cunningham stated that the bearing of all concerned under continuous air attack and heavy enemy pressure had been splendid throughout. At the same time he reported that after consultation with the military authorities it had been decided that no further withdrawal of troops or refugees could take place, and that our naval forces were consequently being withdrawn from the vicinity of the Greek coast.

On the morning of May 1 one of our large convoys carrying troops was repeatedly attacked by E-boats when in the Kaso Strait; these attacks were all driven off without loss to the convoy or to its escorts.

By way of footnote to the official story just given, it may be added that, in the words of the First Lord of the Admiralty, "it was almost a miracle" that only two destroyers were lost during the withdrawal. H.M.S. Diamond was hit twice when attacked by six Junkers 88 dive-bombers. She turned over and sank in a few minutes. Large numbers of the personnel and soldiers aboard her were able to scramble aboard floats, but none of the Diamond's officers was seen again. H.M.S. Wryneck was also hit, but launched a whaler and several floats, before sinking. Her captain, Commander Douglas Lane, was last seen hanging on to a float. During the bitterly cold night he was supported by a wounded seaman, but in the morning both had vanished.

Snatched from Hitler's Balkan Pincers

A BRITISH SOLDIER heartens his comrades from Greece with the appropriate note, whether "Tipperary," or "There'll Always Be an England." Right : Tired troops, having disembarked, have left their kit temporarily on the quayside. Beneath : Crowded scene just after the troops had landed. The safe withdrawal of between 40,000 and 50,000 British and Imperial soldiers from open beaches against continual enemy pressure on land and repeated attacks from the air was a remarkable achievement. *Photos, British Official : Crown Copyright*

Haile Selassie Has Come Home Again

On May 2, 1936, the Negus (Emperor) of Abyssinia left Addis Ababa as a fugitive, and four days later Marshal Badoglio entered the capital in triumph. Time passed, and on the fifth anniversary of that very day, on May 5, 1941, Haile Selassie was welcomed back to Addis Ababa with traditional pomp and ceremony. So the wheel of fortune turned the full circle, and the first victim of Axis aggression was righted by Britain's sword.

INTO Addis Ababa he rode—" Conquering Lion of Judah, Elect of God, King of Kings of Ethiopia." He rode in an open car with one of his commanders, escorted by police in khaki uniforms with white gloves, mounted on white chargers. Before him marched a great procession of Ethiopian soldiers and South Africans, headed by armoured cars of our East African army and a British colonel on a prancing white arab. In his entourage rode his sons, the Crown Prince and the Duke of Harar, the ever-faithful Ras Kassa and Ras Abeba Aragi, and the British brigadier who had played so notable a part in the organizing of the Patriot revolt. Members of the Sudan Frontier Defence Force were there, too ; and along the route South African, East African and West African troops were mounted as guards of honour. The streets were packed with dark-hued natives ; they crowded the roof tops and perched precariously in the trees.

" The procession passed under a gay cloud of green, gold and red Ethiopian flags," wrote " The Times" correspondent, who was among the throng. " The trilling voices

palace which he had left as a fugitive five years before—and there he was welcomed by General Cunningham, the British generalissimo, while a vast crowd cheered and cheered again, a forest of British and Ethiopian flags waved in the sultry air, and Britain's African artillery fired a royal salute of 21 guns—with captured Italian ammunition.

This was a day of rejoicing and triumph, he went on. " Let us therefore rejoice, but in the spirit of Christ. Do not reward evil for evil. Do not indulge in the untimely atrocities which the enemy, even in these last days, has been accustomed to practise against us. Do not shame Ethiopia by acts worthy of our enemies. I shall see they are disarmed

HAILE SELASSIE is seen here riding home to Addis Ababa, which he re-entered on May 5, exactly five years to a day after the Italians took possession of the capital of Abyssinia. Left, The Emperor going to divine service at St. Gorgis Cathedral, Addis Ababa, to pray for peace just before Mussolini attacked his country in the autumn of 1935.
Photos, British Official : Crown Copyright ; and Keystone

Then he stepped forward to deliver his speech. He spoke in Amharic, and his first words were to recall that it was five years since the Fascist troops had entered the city, that very square. " It is with a sense of deep thankfulness," he said, " to Almighty God that I stand today in my palace from which the Fascist forces have fled. It is my firm purpose to merit the blessings I have received : first, by showing my gratitude to my allies, the British, for my return, and for the benefits I have received, by the release of Imperial troops for warfare on other fronts, and by my supplying them with armed forces wherever they may need them ; secondly, by establishing in Ethiopia Christian ethics in Government, liberty of conscience, and democratic institutions."

and given a safe passage to the place from which they came."

Now the Emperor urged forbearance towards the Italian enemy, and the treatment of the British ally with the kindness shown to a brother. The Ethiopians must unite in everlasting friendship with Great Britain to oppose the dragon of godless brutality which was assailing mankind.

So the Emperor spoke ; and, having finished, turned back into the palace, where in the throne-room, seated on a resplendent throne of green, gold and red—not the " Alga," the famous bed-throne of the Abyssinian emperors, which had been his aforetime but which has now probably a place in a Rome museum—he gave audience to the British officers. And there General Cunningham gave the toast of peace, prosperity and health to the Emperor.

Then the Negus received his soldiers and his people. Bowing low they approached him eagerly, and joyfully kissed each other and their Emperor's feet. That night the hills around were lit with the fires of the Patriot troops, who feasted joyfully on raw meat ; and in every native home in the city they made merry. Only the Italians behind their barred and shuttered windows maintained a silence as complete as it was discreet.

of the women and the deep boom of drums, storms of hand-clapping, and the notes of flutes and zithers filled the air, while flowers were dropped into the Emperor's car from those at the roadside."

Arrived in Addis Ababa, the Negus passed on to the balcony of the royal palace—the

Where the Springboks Crossed to Victory

JUBA RIVER, which flows from the mountains of Southern Abyssinia in a southerly direction to the Indian Ocean, furnished the Italians in Italian Somaliland with a strong defensive position against the British troops advancing from Kenya. But the Italians could not hold it against General Cunningham's drive, and its loss led to the fall of Mogadishu and opened up the way for a general advance by the British forces. This fine pontoon bridge over the river Juba was constructed by South African engineers.

Photo, British Official ; Crown Copyright

First Blood in the Fight for Iraq's Oilfields

The coup d'état in Iraq, engineered by Hitler's intrigues and carried out, perhaps prematurely, by the usurper Rashid Ali, has been described in page 494. Now we go on to give an account of the measures taken by the British to control a distinctly menacing situation.

WHEN at dawn on May 2, 1941, the Iraqi guns which had been trained on the British aerodrome at Habbaniya suddenly opened fire, it seemed that the long foreseen battle for Iraq and its oilfields had begun.

Habbaniya, about 60 miles west of Baghdad, is a Royal Air Force training centre of some years' standing. It has facilities for both land and water craft, and the cantonment includes a general R.A.F. hospital and a number of dwellings for the ground staff and the small guard of native levies. In time of peace it was an important centre, being not only the headquarters of British Forces in Iraq but serving also as a civilian airport. When war broke out five squadrons, mostly in training, were quartered there, as well as a mechanized unit used for "police" patrol work.

During the few days preceding the outbreak of hostilities the Iraqi Government concentrated troops around the aerodrome, trenches were dug, and guns mounted on the edge of the desert plateau overlooking it. The bombardment of May 2 destroyed some of our machines on the ground and caused a small number of casualties. At once British aircraft replied to the challenge, bombing some of the guns into silence and frustrating an attempt on the part of the Iraqi air force to raid the aerodrome. The same day, after presenting an ultimatum which was ignored, our forces occupied the airport, dock-area and power station at Basra.

Later it was learnt that, also on May 2, Iraqi forces took possession of Rutbah, an important station 70 miles south of the Syrian frontier and near the oil pipe-line, after attacking an unarmed British construction party working in the vicinity. In the meantime Rashid Ali had caused the Diesel engines which pump the oil from the wells into the pipe-line at Kirkuk to be stopped. On May 3 and 4, R.A.F. bombers carried out three raids on Moascar Raschid aerodrome, the large military station south-east of Baghdad, wrecking 23 aeroplanes—about

Here are the vital pipe-lines, running from the oil-fields of Iraq to Tripoli and Haifa, which Hitler may attempt to seize.
Courtesy of the "Daily Telegraph"

half the estimated strength of the Iraqi air force—and scoring hits on petrol dumps, magazines and aircraft sheds.

Then Emir Abdul Ilah, the deposed Regent, who had retired to Amman as the guest of his uncle, Emir Abdullah of Transjordan, issued from there a proclamation to the Iraqis :

"A group of military tyrants, aided and abetted by Rashid Ali and other ill-disposed persons bought by foreign gold, have by force thrust me from my sacred duties as guardian of my nephew, your beloved young King. Under their evil sway the noble land of Iraq has been poisoned by falsehood and lies and brought from the blessings of peace to the horrors of a venomous war.

"My duty is plain. I am returning to restore the tarnished honour of our native land and to lead it back again to peaceful prosperity under a lawfully-constituted Government.

"I call upon all true sons of Iraq to drive out this band of traitors and restore to our beloved country true liberty and independence. Recall your sons and brothers from this war, brought upon your heads by the lies and intrigues of foreigners thinking only of their own selfish interests. O soldiers, go peacefully to your stations and there peaceably await my restoration of an independent Iraqi constitutional Government. Long live King Faisal II ! "

By May 4 shelling of the Habbaniya aerodrome had become slight, intermittent and inaccurate, owing to vigorous offensive

patrols by the R.A.F. Two days later the rebels were ejected from the plateau, one of the contributory factors being the arrival by air from Basra of a number of howitzers with which the Iraqi positions were bombarded. Enemy casualties were heavy ; 300 prisoners were taken, and the remainder of the troops retreated towards Baghdad. On May 8 Rashid Ali was reported to have fled from Baghdad, following hostile demonstrations. Then on May 11 Rutbah was captured

Rumours that the usurper had appealed to Hitler for military aid against what he termed the "British invasion," received, for the time being, at least, neither confirmation nor response. As Mr. Churchill commented on May 7: "It may be that the Germans will arrive there before we have crushed the revolt, in which case our task will be greater ; or it may be that the revolt went off at half-cock in consequence of our landing troops at Basra." But further "underground" aid was already within Rashid Ali's reach, for Nazi agents abound both in Syria, where there is a powerful German Armistice Commission, and in Iran, into which thousands of Nazi "tourists" and "technical experts" have been steadily penetrating for some time. If Hitler decided to reinforce the Iraqi opposition he would have to proceed either through Turkey or Syria. Of the first, Mr. Eden said on May 6 that fidelity to the British alliance remains "as ever the basis of Turkish foreign policy." Syria has excellent ports and landing-grounds which must cause the Fuehrer's covetous paw to tingle, but the British Navy could prevent any considerable landings, and powerful land and air contingents will soon be released from Abyssinia to strengthen our forces in the Middle East. In any case, as has been pointed out, even if the Nazis were to obtain temporary possession of the oilfields, they would still have to transport the oil to wherever in Europe they most need it. Nevertheless, the annual yield of some $4\frac{1}{2}$ million tons of petroleum is a prize for which Hitler may be willing to take grave risks

IRAQ TROOPS—a Kurdish company—mounting guard at an Iraq aerodrome. Capture of aerodromes in Iraq, as elsewhere in this war, is one of the main military objectives. Our success at Habbaniya was a heavy blow to the rebels, who were by no means supported by the bulk of the army of Iraq.
Photo, Fox

More and More 'Planes from U.S.A.

LT.-COL. J. T. C. MOORE-BRABAZON (above), appointed Minister of Aircraft Production in succession to Lord Beaverbrook, is a pioneer of aviation, holding the first certificate granted by the Royal Aero Club for pilots. Right, a consignment of Lockheed Hudson bombers on the Floyd Bennett aerodrome, New York, ready for shipment to Britain. Below, U.S. planes on their way to this country are seen in mid-Atlantic.

Photos, Bassano, Planet News, J. Hall

Where Next Will the Nazi Octopus Thrust

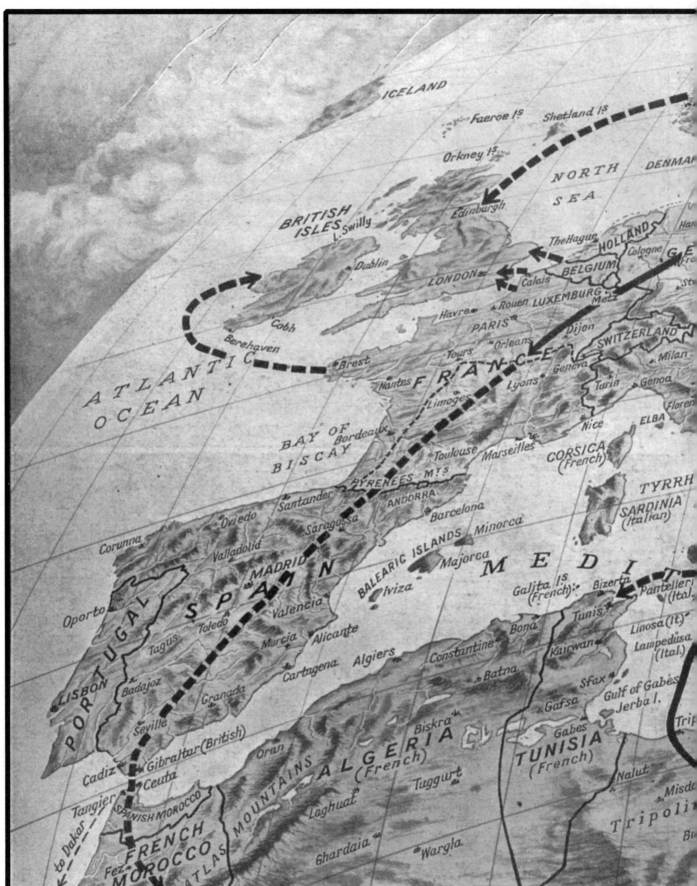

Like a vast and malignant octopus, Nazi Germany stretches out her tentacles over an enslaved Europe. Where will she strike next? This map shows poten[t]
developments with all of which our leaders have to reckon. To the west, Germany may put into practice her oft-repeated threat of the invasion of our Islan[d]
To the east she may decide upon that " Drang nach Osten," which for so many years has loomed large in Germany's foreign policy. The rich wheat belt of [t]

Its Tentacles in a Stranglehold of Slavery?

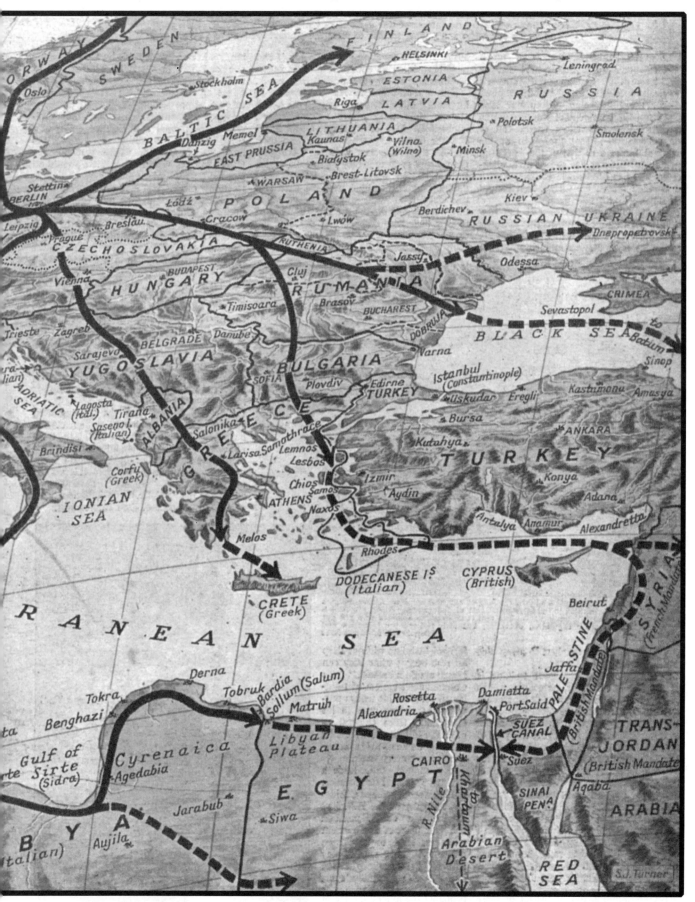

Ukraine lies near to her hand, a tempting prey. The oil wells of the Caucasus, like those of Iraq, are coveted booty in a war wherein the internal-combustion engine plays so large a part. The Suez Canal, too, that vital link between Britain and her Empire in the Orient, is a military objective of the first magnitude towards which the German thrust in North Africa may be ultimately directed. With Gibraltar and Suez in German hands the Mediterranean Sea would become an Axis ocean.

The British Army Gets Tougher Every Day

Very different is the Army of today from that of yesterday. The spirit of the men is the same, true ; but new instruments of war demand new methods. Something of the way in which our soldiers are being trained to meet the guileful Nazis is told below.

THAT the British soldier is a tough customer the Germans have already learned. Though the enemy's numerical superiority in men and machines has—for the time being—driven our land forces from the continent of Europe, it was not before they had taken terrific toll of their adversaries. From the stand of the Guards at Louvain to that of the Anzacs at Thermopylae the war has shown that, whenever contact has been made between British and German forces, the former have proved their superiority man for man.

New methods of warfare call for new methods of training, and recent exercises carried out by our armies in Britain indicate that the Nazis, if they *do* attempt to invade

job is " to do anything under the sun," and toughness allied to enterprise are the qualifications needed for enrolment in their ranks.

During recent manoeuvres " somewhere in England," operations were carried out which at one time might have seemed almost impossible. Men of the Royal Ulster Rifles and the South Lancashire Regt. who took part in these exercises were so thoroughly trained and so fit that they carried on, says a British United Press correspondent, from the morning of the attack until the afternoon two days afterwards without sleep, going through the next day on the small amount of food in their haversacks. " That," said the Corps Commander, " is the only way to train men nowadays—so that they can go

rendered the more difficult by a considerable rise and fall in the tide, mud banks of unequal height, and the continual necessity of taking out the centre raft, in a six-knot current, to provide for the normal traffic.

One correspondent has told of the development of mental and physical agility at a corps school for young officers in the Southern Command, where students are taught to fight with steel helmets should all else fail ! The point of this new training is to endow officers and men alike with a sense of initiative so that they may make quick decisions and take instant action in any emergency.

And here is an interesting sidelight on modern army training. One would never imagine that the British Army contained a large number of " fifth-columnists " ; but seemingly it does ! Fortunately they are only pseudo-fifth-columnists, and their work is to train all ranks in the Army, from the top to the bottom, not to indulge in careless talk. Paul Bewsher has related in the " Daily Mail " how one of these, a young lieutenant, disguised himself as a butler, served dinner to a general while he was staying at a country house during manoeuvres, and afterwards placed a " contact bomb " in the general's bed !

To such a pitch has the training been carried, that A.T.S. girls in civilian clothes have been employed to try to glean, from officers and men, valuable information about troop movements during large-scale manoeuvres. All news garnered in this way is passed back to " enemy " headquarters, and after the " battle " the indiscreet ones are bluntly warned of their carelessness.

Hardening courses are a feature in the training of our new armies. Above, officers and N.C.O.s are swimming in full kit, a great test of endurance. Right, climbing a high wall, also with full equipment. The aim is to produce soldiers who are not only efficient in their regulation exercises, but also trained for initiative and endurance.   *Photos, British Movietone News*

us, will meet the " toughest " army this country has ever turned out.

Some of the most strenuous training is that carried out by our parachute troops (see page 268 of this volume), but for reasons of policy details cannot be divulged. However, these troops have been seen in action during tactical exercises, playing the part of saboteurs with roving commissions, or seizing aerodromes and landing-grounds for air-borne troops ; and in the opinion of competent witnesses the German parachute troops, to use an Americanism, " have nothing on them." One example may be quoted. During a four-days' mock battle in Southern England an officer found himself suddenly confronted by three " enemy " parachutists. He tried to resist, but received a staggering blow, and the next thing he knew was that the parachutists were driving away in his car !

Arduous training, too, is the lot of those platoons of the Guards known as the " S.S." (special service) platoons. Put briefly, their

forty-eight hours without sleep or rest except what they can snatch at odd moments." This Commander's system of training to toughen his troops provides that every man in his Command, from General to private, shall ensure fitness by doing a seven-mile cross-country run every week.

The sapper, too, leads a strenuous life. For instance, during recent exercises a bridging company of the R.E. had to build a 600-ft. pontoon bridge in place of a permanent structure, held to have been destroyed. They worked day and night in six-hour shifts, and in a remarkably short time had completed what was probably the longest bridge of the kind ever made in this country. Their task was

'Old Sweats' Will Remember the Bangalore

Many men who served on the Western Front during the last war will remember the Bangalore torpedo, so named because it was invented by an R.E. officer at Bangalore, Mysore. First introduced in 1915, it was used extensively for cutting gaps in barbed wire entanglements, and has been recently used by British troops during their advances into Italian territory. The torpedo, seen above, is a sheet iron cylinder, the conical head of which holds a charge of high explosive. A fuse is inserted in the trailing end. The cylinder is made in sections, so as to be extensible: if the defences are deep several tubes can be joined together.

Photo, Topical Press

They're Out to Beat Hitler's Minelayers

THE OROPESA FLOAT enables a ship to sweep mines single-handed. Seen left, it is shaped like a torpedo and streams out at an angle from the ship towing it on a wire cable. The wire is kept down to the required depth by a multiplane kite (here seen being lowered by crane). Having put out the float with kite line and sweep wire attached, the vessel, herself remaining outside the mined area, can clean up "lanes" in the minefield rather like a reaper cuts swathes from the side of a cornfield. The name Oropesa was that of the trawler in the last war in which this form of sweeping was first tried out. Above, the Officer of the Watch on the bridge of a minesweeper.

MULTIPLE MACHINE-GUNS are installed on minesweepers to afford them protection from the air menace which constantly threatens them; while barrage balloons, right, afford a further measure of protection from enemy dive-bombers.

Photos, Fox

'The Lifeline of Britain Is Threatened'

THE RAJPUTANA, a 16,644-ton armed merchant cruiser, formerly a P. & O. liner, was torpedoed in the North Atlantic while on patrol duty. Here she is seen settling down in the water, while (in the circle inset) survivors pull away from the doomed ship. A Sunderland guided warships to their rescue.

THE lifeline of Great Britain is threatened. The high-water mark of Nazi effort is at hand in the shape of an attack on the shipping which furnishes Britain with the means and the nourishment to maintain her battle.

Not only does blockade imperil the delivery to Britain of the munitions we are sending her, but the supplies of food necessary for her population are already becoming gradually impaired.

Right now, at this cross-roads of history it is within our power to turn the tide of darkness back from the Atlantic world . . . If today our Navy should make secure the seas for the delivery of our munitions to Britain it will render as great a service to our own country and to the preservation of freedom as it has ever rendered in all its glorious history.—*Mr. Stimson, May 6, 1941.*

Sombrely impressive is this photograph of a ship taking her death-plunge—another triumph for Hitler in the Battle of the Atlantic. The scene in the circle speaks of yet another blow aimed at what Mr. H. L. Stimson, U.S. Secretary of War, has well described as Britain's lifeline.

Photos, Associated Press and Keystone

Our Searchlight on the War

German Troops in Finland

THROUGH "Pravda," the Communist Party newspaper, came the first intimation that German troops had arrived in Finland. The announcement was definite : " According to reliable sources, four German transports arrived on April 26 at the Finnish port of Abo (Turku). About 12,000 troops, fully equipped and with tanks and artillery, landed there and began to move off to Tampere on April 28." It has long been known that Helsinki had made an arrangement by which German troops were to be allowed to pass through Finland, provided that they were simply going on leave from, or returning to, northern Norway, and that the numbers engaged in this cross-traffic were equal. Speculation has been rife as to the significance of the " Pravda " report, if it is true. In Sweden it has been suggested that certain Finnish elements are maintaining

definitely shot down in the British Isles, others in Malta and the Middle East. The A.A. gunners responsible for this achievement have received most, if not all, of their training since the outbreak of war.

Government Changes

A NUMBER of changes in the Cabinet were announced on May 1. Two Ministries—those of Shipping and of Transport—have been merged into one, which will be held by a newcomer to Westminster, Mr. F. J. Leathers. This amalgamation is an important wartime development which, by doing away with divided authority, will expedite the " turn round" of vessels. Lord Beaverbrook, relieved at his own wish of the arduous duties of Minister of Aircraft Production, becomes the head of a newly created Ministry of State, and will devote himself to general questions of policy in the War Cabinet. He is succeeded by Colonel Moore-Brabazon, Minister of Transport since last year, whose great experience in the world of aviation—he is one of the pioneers of flying in this country—will be of definite value in his new post. Mr. Frederick Montague has been made Parliamentary Secretary to this Ministry. The fifth appointment is that of Colonel J. J. Llewellin to be Parliamentary Secretary to the Ministry of Transport. Mr. Leathers is a prominent figure in industry who has been concerned all his life with transport and shipping.

War Dogs

BRITISH dogs have been invited by the War Office to register for national service. Only those of certain breeds and with natural qualifications of a high order will be recruited. Airedales, Collies (both rough and smooth), Hill Collies, Crossbreds, Lurchers and Retrievers (Labrador and Golden) are the most suitable kinds, but members of other breeds will be considered provided that their intelligence and natural ability are of a superior standard. It may be presumed that friendly aliens, such as the Alsatian, will not be turned down through prejudice. Accepted candidates will be given an intensive course of training at Willems Barracks, Aldershot. Those which fail to pass the tests will immediately return home. Successful dogs will serve in the Army for the duration of the war, and receive skilled care and attention.

Bottle-Scarred Warriors

FROM the Middle East H.Q. of the R.A.F. comes a light-hearted story about a certain bombing squadron operating over Albania. They were faced with the problem of disposing of the empty bottles which increasingly cluttered up their mess. At length one young pilot suggested that they should be dumped over the enemy's lines during future expeditions. The following morning, therefore, an aircraft added a cargo of " empties " to the usual complement of bombs and dropped the lot on an Italian camp. One curious result of this manoeuvre was revealed when a prisoner, captured a few days later, complained bitterly that the airmen had been trying to break Italian morale

by dropping whistling bombs. It would seem that an empty bottle, hurtling through the air, gives out a crescendo whistle calculated to add to the terror of the high-explosive bomb accompanying it.

Stalin in Control

MOSCOW radio announced on May 6 that Molotov had, at his own request, been relieved of his duties as Chairman of the Council of People's Commissars, and that Stalin had taken over the post. It is equivalent to that of Prime Minister. Molotov retains his post as People's Commissar for Foreign Affairs, and becomes in addition Vice-Chairman of the Council of People's Commissars. The changes were announced in the form of three decrees signed by Kalinin, whose office corresponds to that of President of the Republic. This is the first time that Stalin has taken any Government post other than that of a member of the Supreme Council. He has been content, as General Secretary of the Communist Party to be the power behind the Kremlin.

AMERICAN MOBILE KITCHENS, presented by the U.S.A. to the Ministry of Food, have done valuable work in feeding the homeless of our "blitzed" cities. This sailor at Plymouth is helping to feed the victims of a raid with food from one of these kitchens. *Photo, L.N.A.*

close touch with the Germans in the hope of recovering the territory annexed last year by Russia. On the other hand, the arrival of the troops may be part of Germany's " war of nerves " now being directed against the Soviet Union along a frontier of 1,500 miles.

One Thousand Not Out

SINCE the beginning of the war British Army anti-aircraft guns have destroyed over 1,000 enemy aircraft in all theatres of operations. This figure comprises only the certainties, and takes no account of machines so damaged that it is extremely unlikely that they were able to reach their base. For example, should a plane be hit while flying at a great height over London, it probably clears the coastline and falls into the sea. But such a casualty is not included in the total of 1,000. Five hundred have been

WHAT OUR WEAPONS COST

The Army	£	Royal Air Force	£
Medium Tank ...	15,000	Bomber Aircraft ...	20,000
Heavy A.A. Gun ...	6,000	Fighter Aircraft ...	5,000
25-Pounder Field		Barrage Balloon ...	700
Gun	3,000	Fighter Airscrew...	350
Light A.A. Gun ...	3,000	Heavy Bomb ...	120
Anti-Tank Gun ...	1,500	Browning Machine-	
Small Gun	1,500	Gun	100
Bren Gun Carrier	1,500	Fighter Radio Set	50
Searchlight Projector	1,000	General Purpose Bomb	45
		Fighter Petrol Tank	40
Spare Gun Barrel		Fighter Compass ...	5
(Large)	500		
Heavy Machine-Gun	350	**Royal Navy**	£
Spare Gun Barrel		Battleship ...	8,000,000
(Small)	200	Aircraft Carrier	3,300,000
Vickers Machine-Gun	150	Cruiser ...	2,000,000
Machine-Gun ...	100	Large Destroyer ...	450,000
3-inch Mortar ...	80	Submarine	350,000
Bren Gun	50	Small Destroyer ...	320,000
Anti-Tank Rifle ...	45	Motor Torpedo Boat	55,000
Mortar	40	Torpedo	2,000
Two-inch Mortar...	25	**Miscellaneous**	£
Tommy-Gun	20	Fully Equipped Am-	
Rifle	8	bulance	500
Rifle	7	Light Ambulance...	300
Heavy A.A. Shell...	4	Equipping an Infantry	
Pistol	4	Soldier	20
		Keeping a Soldier—	
		Pay, Rations, etc.,	
		per annum ...	100

Make Your Money Fight !

What War Has Brought to the Isle of Man

RECENTLY a re-arrangement of the internment camps in the Isle of Man has been made with a view to providing accommodation for the thousand British Fascists who, as was announced in Parliament, are to be interned there. The Fascists, it is stated, will be subjected to the same kind of internment as the aliens already there, but it is considered that the numbers of their military guards will be increased. The interned Blackshirts will have to perform some kind of service, but they will not be permitted to make contact with the alien internees, who are doing land work.

Another new feature is the establishment at Port St. Mary on May 8 of a "camp" for alien married couples interned in the Island ; a selected group of some 170 men were allowed to make their homes with their wives and children in hotels and houses where the women had been interned separately.

DOUGLAS, I.O.M., was before the war the favourite holiday resort of thousands. Along its fine promenade, seen above in peacetime thronged with holiday makers, now stretch barbed wire enclosures, cutting off the hotels and houses accommodating the internees.

The internees on the Isle of Man are under strict military supervision. When off duty their military guards take a little relaxation, sometimes by playing Soccer on the deserted beaches (above), or perhaps by having a tug-of-war. Right, some of the thousands of internees returning to their camp under supervision.

Photos, Topical Press

They Have Won Honours in Freedom's Cause

Sub-Lieutenant R. E. Scammell, R.N., **D.S.M.**, for great bravery in the execution of his duties.

Able Seaman W. Cooper, R.N.V.R., **D.C.M.**, for conspicuous bravery in action aboard Jervis Bay.

Capt. R. McClean, **D.S.C.**, for displaying outstanding skill and courage while on active service.

Capt. Hughes of the Merchant Navy, **D.S.C.**, for gallant conduct during the Dunkirk operations.

Ldg. Stoker D. T. Banks, **D.S.M.**, for bravery at Dunkirk. His father won D.S.M. in last war.

Lieut. Bill, R.N., **D.S.O.**, for setting a fine example of courage when engaged on war service.

Lieut. Q. M. E. Goodrich, R.A.M.C., **D.S.O.**, for devotion to duty. He is the first of this rank to receive this decoration.

Tpr. William G. Hunt, of Northall, **M.M.**, for gallantry while driving a tank in the Somme Valley in May 1940.

Major Robinson, **M.C.**, for displaying great courage and devotion to duty in the course of Dunkirk operations.

Capt. T. V. Somerville, R.A.M.C., **D.S.O.**, for driving " baby car " into front line at Sidi Barrani and tending wounded.

Cpl. B. Wareham, Royal Warwickshire Regt., **M.M.**, for great gallantry in the execution of his duties at Dunkirk.

Lieut. Patrick K. Mayhew, R.A.M.C., **M.M.**, for volunteering to remain and help the wounded away from Dunkirk.

Squad.-Leader Hugh Maxwell, **D.S.O.**, for gallantry and devotion in the execution of his air duties.

Squad.-Leader M. F. Anderson, A.A.F., **D.F.C.**, for night operational flying and destroying enemy aircraft.

Asst. Sec. Officer E. C. Henderson, W.A.A.F., **M.M.**, for devotion to telephone duty in a burning building.

Sgt. Pilot E. E. F. Hewett, **D.F.M.**, for shooting down three enemy aircraft over Tepelini and destroying others.

Sgt. C. R. Frost, R.A.F. (vol. Reserve 144 Squad.), of Beverley, **D.F.M.**, for conspicuous bravery in execution of his air duties.

Flt. Lt. C. F. Currant, **Bar to D.F.C.**, for personally destroying six enemy aircraft and damaging a number of others.

Matron G. C. Ball, **R.R.C.**, for displaying a fine courage and outstanding abilities.

Sister K. B. Davies, **R.R.C.**, for great courage and devotion to her duties during air raid on Hull.

Sister Tomlinson, **R.R.C.**, for setting a fine example of duty and skill in her work as nurse.

Miss Jessie Jackson, Matron of Princess Mary R.A.F. Nursing Service, **R.R.C.**, for bravery.

Miss K. H. Jones, Matron-in-Chief Princess Mary's Nursing Assn., **R.R.C.**, for courage.

Miss Wane, Princess Mary's Nursing Association, **R.R.C.**, for untiring devotion to duty.

Mr. John William Booth, L.M.S. railway porter, **O.B.E.**, for displaying presence of mind in a Sheffield raid.

Vol. W. E. Whybrow (Home Guard), **M.B.E.**, for clambering into collapsing ruins and rescuing a badly injured man.

Mrs. Hilda McGreevy, A.R.P., ambulance driver, of Maghull, near Liverpool, **O.B.E.**, for conspicuous courage in an air raid.

Mrs. Freda Dykins, A.R.P. ambulance driver, **O.B.E.**, for devotion to duty under rain of enemy bombs at Liverpool.

Sec.-Ldr. S. W. Anthony (Home Guard), **M.B.E.**, for crawling through dangerous debris and rescuing man and child at Bromley.

Patrol-Ldr. G. Collins, 12th Shoreditch Group, **Scout Silver Cross** for saving three children injured in an air raid.

Patrol Officer F. C. Revelle, A.F.S., **G.M.**, for devotion to duty under bombs at Bristol.

Patrol Officer M. C. Day, A.F.S., **G.M.**, in recognition of gallant conduct in a Bristol blitz.

Miss R. Gassman, A.F.S., first woman to receive **B.E.M.**, for courage in Hornsey raid.

Mrs. B. M. Plimmer, A.F.S., **B.E.M.**, for maintaining communications and first-aid work in raid.

Fireman B. C. E. Arkell, **G.M.**, for courage under bomb and machine-gun attack in Bristol raid.

Fireman L. J. Watts, **G.M.**, for conspicuous bravery during a continuous raid on Bristol.

I Was There! .... Eye Witness Stories of the War

I Alone of British Journalists Escaped from Belgrade

Four weeks after he left shattered Belgrade, Mr. Terence Atherton, special correspondent of the " Daily Mail," was taken off by a British destroyer with a number of British troops from Argos, after nightmare voyages in open boat and trawler. He pays high tribute to naval efficiency.

TODAY, nearly four weeks after I escaped from bombed and shattered Belgrade, I write this dispatch safe aboard a British ship, the Red Ensign of sanity flying comfortably from her stern. My fellow-passengers include thousands of Imperial troops, Italian prisoners, and Greek volunteers for our Middle East Army.

I regret to record that of the British journalists trapped in Yugoslavia I alone escaped.

With three American newspapermen and a Yugoslav sailor I was able to seize a tiny open boat on the Yugoslav coast. Our equipment consisted of a single sail and a small outboard motor. We had no compass.

Yet we succeeded in running the gauntlet of Italy's Navy, Army, and Air Force down the Adriatic Sea from Montenegro, past the coast of Albania, and through the narrow, mine-infested Strait of Otranto to Corfu.

We passed through part of the Italian Navy convoying troopships near Durazzo.

We were hailed by and exchanged friendly shouts and waves of the hand with Italian minesweeping trawlers, who took us for Albanian fishermen ; we were nearly wrecked one night in a storm on the island of Saseno, Italy's Gibraltar of the Adriatic. We were soaked with spray and exhausted with rowing when sail and motor failed us.

Yet we got through, making our first landfall in Greek territory on the northern tip of the island of Corfu.

Greek naval authorities there greeted us at first with astonishment and suspicion. It is not surprising that they doubted the story of the five unshaven, haggard-eyed Argonauts that we appeared. But, once convinced, they spared us nothing in hospitality.

Even then our dangers were only half over. German and Italian troops were heading us off down the western coasts of Greece, as we sailed south, with a lucky wind, towards Ithaca Island, home of Ulysses, and for Patras.

Off Parga, on the Greek coast—already, unknown to us, in enemy hands—we were machine-gunned by an Italian seaplane, then taken in tow by a Greek naval trawler.

But our gallant little boat, the Makedonka, was swamped and sank in the night with all our belongings, a few miles north of Ithaca.

Aboard the Greek trawler, we were dive-bombed and machine-gunned outside Patras by seven German Stukas, and our Yugoslav comrade, " Mike," was shot dead by bullets which tore through the wooden decks as if they were paper. I myself, three feet away from him, was wounded in the knee-cap by a splinter.

The coat I am still wearing as I write this is stained with his blood.

Next morning our train from Patras to Corinth was raked, outside Agrion, by a Messerschmitt 110, and two more of my comrades were wounded—one, Leigh White, the " New York Post " correspondent, crippled by two bullets in the thigh ; another, Robert St. John, hit in the leg by a glancing bullet from the same burst.

Too badly wounded to be moved farther, Leigh White was carried by us up the cliffs from the coastal railway line to the road.

There, by incredible luck, a British Army lorry passed. We loaded all the wounded from the train into the lorry and reached Corinth hospital in the middle of an air raid which filled the wards and courtyard with the dying and wounded.

The broken line on this map shows the route taken by Terence Atherton in the nightmare journey from Belgrade which he describes in this page.   Courtesy of the " Daily Mail "

Unable to leave White there, and with the Corinth-Athens road now impassable, we reached Argos, on the South Peloponnesus coast, in a night journey along a road down which the Germans had dropped a hundred parachutists to impede the retreat of the Imperial troops.

One New Zealand brigade cleaned up these parachutists to the last man, save for a few who fell into the ruthless hands of Greek villagers whose homes had been savagely bombed that day.

In sight of the sea, British naval units were expected the same night, and arrived to take off some of the last of the Imperial Army contingents with their lightly wounded.

We endured a day of unceasing bombing, when a hospital where we had taken White was singled out for a continuous attack and had to be evacuated.

Lending a hand in carrying out British and Australian wounded, we took White to a near-by sanatorium for his bullets to be extracted, and there we left him with the doctors.

That night we reached a tiny port where, unknown to the German Air Force, thousands of the last Imperial troops, with all their light equipment, were waiting in the pitch darkness for the arrival of the British naval units.

It was touch and go, but the Navy did not let the Army down.

Half an hour after midnight a British destroyer, whose name is famous the world over since the battles of Narvik Fjord, Matapan, and many other engagements, signalled that she was about to enter the harbour.

An hour later all had been got aboard—to the last man, the last machine-gun—in perfect order, methodically, calmly.

To the British Navy must go the chief laurels of this evacuation.

Imperturbably, in conditions utterly unlike Dunkirk—with only small air forces to defend the roads and ports of retreat from the unceasing German attacks, with only limited ships, and only under cover of darkness, from scattered ports along an unfamiliar coast—the Navy took away from certain destruction 45,000 troops and a large part of valuable equipment of all kinds.

I saw, for instance, more than £20,000 worth of irreplaceable optical instruments and invaluable sets of listening and detector apparatus being shipped off the tiny quay where I embarked.

When we moved out that quay was left clean as a whistle.

Only farther ashore, under olive groves skirting the shore, dozens of cars and lorries whose engines had been run to a white heat after the sumps had been drained of oil, were filling the night air with an overpowering smell of hot, burning metal.

Nothing of value was left for the enemy—even medical stores were given, before we left, to the local Greek hospital, where only a few of our wounded—too seriously hurt to be moved—were left.

Crammed into the past three weeks of a nightmare experience, I have seen two Balkan kingdoms and armies overwhelmed by sudden concentrated land and air assault.

How We Turned Our Plane Into a Sailing Ship

One of the war's strangest stories is of three young airmen who, forced down far out in the Atlantic, attempted to reach Africa by converting their Walrus into a sailing boat. Reuter's correspondent at Freetown sent the story.

H.M.S. BIRMINGHAM was off the African coast when her Walrus amphibian aircraft was catapulted off at dawn to carry out a patrol. In it were a pilot, observer and air gunner ; and this, in their own words, is what happened.

We spotted a ship and investigated it, but when we returned our ship wasn't there. We made signals, but got no reply, owing, we believe, to the fault of our wireless,

We were then some hundreds of miles from land and decided to get as close in as possible before our petrol ran out. We kept in the air for some time. Then we made a good landing in the Atlantic about 100 miles from the coast.

All we knew was that Africa was somewhere to the east. There seemed nothing we could do about getting there.

Later in the day we had a brainwave. We got out our parachutes—a £120 worth of silk—and rigged them as sails. For the rest of the afternoon we sailed broadside on towards land.

We took it in turn to keep watch with field-glasses on top of the machine, while others kept below out of the sun. The pilot was incapacitated by seasickness, but our most serious trouble was that we only had seven cigarettes between the three of us.

When night fell everything seemed much worse. The darkness and silence was like a blanket. . . . Here Sub-Lieut. W.——another of the trio, took up the story :

I WAS THERE!

I had the morning watch, and as it grew light I saw land. We suspected that it might be a cloud at first, but after a bit there was no doubt.

We decided to remove the plane's wheels, make a truck with them, and try to walk down to Freetown. But at 11 o'clock the wind changed and again taking us off-shore.

We downed sail and tried towing a bucket as a drogue (a buoy at the end of a harpoon), but could not check our way. In the end we decided to take to our rubber dinghy.

We loaded it with distress flares, emergency flying rations, three pints of water, an axe, and floor-boards from the plane as paddles.

Then we opened the camera hatch of the Walrus to make it sink. We hadn't gone very far in the dinghy when Petty Officer F— thought he saw a shark.

All day and night we paddled on, steering by compass.

During the night two of us sat in the stern and paddled, while one took it in turn to sit in the bows and steer, but we became very sleepy. First, I fell asleep and lost my paddle. Then portside fell asleep. Bows woke up and announced we were 180 degrees off our course. That happened again and again.

Next morning, to our surprise we could see land seven miles away. We opened a tin of bully beef and each took a pinch. Then we closed the tin and put it away. We didn't touch our water, though we had had none since we had flown off the " Birmingham."

The dinghy began to lose air and after four or five hours we were up to our knees in water.

Suddenly we sighted something which looked like a destroyer, so we fired off distress signals. It sheered away and we realized that it was really a native fishing boat.

Then another fishing boat came from the shore and picked us up. The first boat then came alongside. Both contained Negroes wearing odds and ends of clothing. One had a loin cloth, old jumper and sun helmet.

When we said we were British, one named Richard Graham replied in English : " We British, too. All in British Empire are one big brotherhood."

He promised to take us to Freetown in his boat. And he did.

A SUPERMARINE WALRUS amphibian flying boat is seen about to be hoisted on to its parent cruiser. This aircraft, in service in the Fleet Air Arm since 1935, is used for general reconnaissance and submarine spotting, and is carried by all naval vessels equipped with catapult launching gear. The amazing adventure of the crew of one of these machines is described here.   *Photo, Fox*

First they gave us water to wash the salt off our bodies. Then they cooked fish on a brazier in the boat and we ate it with rice. Then Richard Graham went ashore and got provisions for the voyage to Freetown.

We sailed on in his boat all that night and next day. There were five natives in the boat, three of whom could speak English. They talked about everything and were very interested to know about Britain. The second night we anchored for a bit, and at noon on the third day reached Freetown.

Asked what they would like as a reward the leader said he wished to have a certificate to show his friends he had helped in the war.

We wrote out a certificate, and also gave them canvas for new sails, rope, and £20. A small fortune for them.

We Were Surrounded by Parachutists Near Corinth

The first eye-witness story of the operations of German parachute troops in Greece was told by a gunnery major who, with other officers and a handful of men, fought his way through to an embarkation port.

WE were manning anti-aircraft guns on the road south of Corinth in an attempt to protect the last remnants of a convoy, said the major. When the parachutists dropped we found ourselves completely surrounded in about 30 minutes. Ahead of us the Corinth bridge was being grimly held by a company of Australian infantry.

First came an aerial blitz. For three hours planes dive-bombed and machine-gunned our men continuously, zipping over the road at less than thirty feet.

Then I saw thirty-five troop-carrying planes circling overhead. They flew down in line to a height of about 200 feet, then their hatches opened and the parachutists dropped out, fluttering like leaves to the ground at intervals of about 25 feet.

From each machine came one man with a red parachute—presumably a section leader—and several with white parachutes. Occasionally a large bundle, obviously containing mortars and ammunition, crashed to the ground. Many parachutes failed to open. Their owners bounced in the air, then lay still. Several planes flew off with half-open parachutes hanging to their tail.

I knew the position was hopeless. I called on my men to hurry and fight a way out. Many of them were unable to do so. Our small party rushed through before the Germans had time to collect together and take up firing positions. I estimate it takes a parachutist a good five minutes to undo his harness, pull out his machine-gun and go into action.

Making our way across the mountains, we struck a road and jumped on a lone lorry. Along came a yellow-nosed Messerschmitt and smashed up the lorry.

We continued walking until another lorry, carrying a rearguard party of Aussies, picked us up. We eventually reached the port of embarkation after terrific machine-gunning the entire way. I got all my party

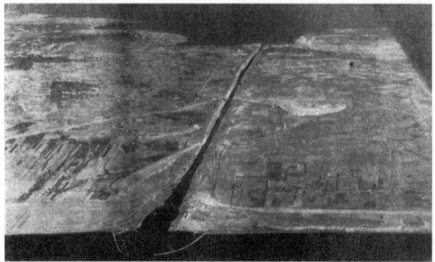

CORINTH CANAL, the fighting around which is described in this page, is here seen from the air. The canal, which provides a passage for ships through the Isthmus of Corinth, is four miles long and seventy feet wide, and most of it has been cut through solid rock. It was opened in 1893.
Photo, G.P.A.

BRITISH PARATROOPS practising descents at a secret R.A.F. station The aeroplane has just released a parachutist and he can be seen immediately before his 'chute has opened. Each plane carries about ten parachutists, and they are "decanted" at intervals of a second and land within a small area, no more than forty yards apart. Light on German parachute methods is given in the story in this page.
Photo, British Official: Crown Copyright

have hopes of promotion Every one of us is just longing to get at the controls of a big bomber or new fighter, for no matter how long you've been a pilot, there is no thrill in the world like flying faster than you have ever done before.

We report for duty every morning at nine. By that time Pauline Gower, chief of the women's unit, is already receiving instructions for the day's work. from Central Control.

Planes are waiting to be picked up from a factory in the north of Scotland, from another in the west of England. They have to be delivered to, say, the Midlands or the South Coast.

Do not imagine because we have all been flying for years that we did not need any training when we joined the A.T.A. Every member goes through a course, for the bigger the machine the more complicated are the controls.

When you first come across the panel of an Anson or a Magister after the simple dashboard of a Puss Moth, you think you've walked straight into a nightmare. Yet in a day or two you find you know all the knobs and handles, the wheels and clocks and gauges, more or less by heart.

There is one thing of which we are justly proud. It is not the excitement and the glamour, but the simple fact that we have delivered hundreds of new planes to the R.A.F. in the last fifteen months—delivered them safely and on time.—"*Daily Herald,*" *copyright Cecil Brooks, Ltd.*

safely on board, including several wounded. The rest of my men and that gallant party of Aussies holding the bridge must be finished, the major concluded. They hadn't an earthly chance. In addition to those dropped south of Corinth, the Nazis were dropping parachutists along the northern coast of the Pelopponese in hundreds. Others who saw German parachutists fall say that each parachutist was followed by two smaller parachutes, carrying arms and ammunition and possibly a machine-gun. Many of the men dropped at Corinth fell in the canal and were drowned.—*Reuter.*

They Call Us 'Ancient and Tattered Airmen'

Some of the Air Transport Auxiliary pilots who ferry aircraft from factories to R.A.F. stations are women—it was on this service that Amy Johnson lost her life—and here one of them describes her work in detail.

"**W**ELCOME to an Ancient and Tattered Airman," shouted one of the R.A.F. men as the new trainer plane touched down on the airfield.

The pilot smiled, bulky and shapeless in flying suit, with helmet and parachute. Out on the ground he came in for a lot of hearty slaps on the back and a good rowdy R.A.F. welcome. At last, in desperation, and to the confusion of the unofficial reception committee, the pilot pulled off his helmet.

The "Ancient and Tattered Airman" was a woman—and very far from being either ancient or tattered. I should know, because she is one of my colleagues, one of the first women members of Air Transport Auxiliary, recruited to help the men in this big job of ferrying new aircraft from factories to R.A.F. stations.

Don't blame the R.A.F. for the title "Ancient and Tattered Airmen." The men pilots of A.T.A. themselves decided that this is what A.T.A. stands for. The reason is that they are all airmen debarred from service with the R.A.F. for reasons of health or age.

And the way to recognize a ferry pilot's sex has become an important part of the R.A.F.'s unofficial training. I gather there is one infallible rule—wait till the pilot takes off his helmet, and if it's a woman—even with a closely-cropped head—she will shake her hair loose !

Although we are the only women in this country whose war work takes them up into the air (even the W.A.A.F. are still earth-

bound), we do not regard ourselves as heroines and our lives are not one great adventure.

Flying may sound very exciting, but long before the war most of us were earning a living in civil aviation, with the result that piloting a warplane is no more unusual to us than driving a car.

And as to adventure—well, our job is to keep out of it. When you are delivering a brand new plane worth several thousands of pounds you don't dawdle about in the sky on the look-out for a Messerschmitt.

On the other hand, flying in wartime is a very different proposition from peacetime aviation. We have none of the usual aids to navigation to help us. We can't pore over meteorological reports and postpone a flight for a day or two if we don't fancy the weather. We were "delivering the goods" right through the winter of 1939-40. And that was one of the severest winters for fifty years.

We have to keep an eye out for prohibited areas, balloon barrages and other devices, and it is advisable to make quite sure before touching down that we have been recognized and are expected ! R.A.F. stations have their own kind of welcome waiting for unrecognized planes in wartime . . .

So far the women's unit of the A.T.A., which is attached to an aerodrome quite near London, ferries only trainer planes.

Spitfires and Hurricanes, heavy bombers, and all the new planes now in production are still delivered by the men, though we

WOMEN PILOTS OF THE A.T.A., Mrs. Gabrielle Patterson and Mrs. Grace Brown (right), who, as described in this page, are doing valuable work in ferrying aircraft. The number of women pilots is being gradually increased.
Photo, Fox

Our Diary of the War

SUNDAY, MAY 4, 1941   610th day

Air.—R.A.F. made heavy attack on battle cruisers at Brest. Other forces bombed docks and shipping at Rotterdam, Antwerp, Le Havre, Cherbourg and St. Nazaire.

Africa.—British troops in Tobruk launched counter-attack, foiling new enemy preparations. R.A.F. made night raids on aerodromes at Benina and Derna.

Advance upon Amba Alagi, Abyssinia, progressing. S.A.A.F. raided Italian H.Q.

Near East.—R.A.F. raided aerodrome at Calato, Rhodes. Four enemy aircraft shot down when attacking Crete.

German troops occupied islands of Mytilene and Chios.

Iraq.—Shelling of Habbaniya aerodrome resumed, but R.A.F. soon silenced guns. R.A.F. also attacked mechanized troops and transport and again raided aerodrome at Moascar Rashid, wrecking 23 planes.

Home.—Fourth successive night raid on Merseyside. Attacks also made on East Anglian town and N.W. seaside district. Heavy sustained raid on Belfast.

Ten raiders destroyed.

MONDAY, MAY 5   611th day

Air.—Day attacks on enemy coastal shipping. Heavy night raid on industrial towns in Middle Rhine, particularly Mannheim. Docks at Boulogne and Cherbourg, and port of St. Nazaire, also bombed.

Africa.—British troops at Tobruk attacked forward enemy posts, taking many prisoners.

R.A.F. made many attacks on mechanized units in Bardia, El Adem, Capuzzo and Sollum areas. During nights of 4-5 and 5-6 they made heavy raids on Benghazi harbour and a number of aerodromes.

Iraq.—R.A.F. maintained constant offensive patrols over Iraqi positions outside Habbaniya.

Home.—Minor day attacks in S.E. England. Large-scale night raids on Clydeside, Merseyside and Belfast.

Two day and nine night raiders shot down.

General.—Maj.-Gen. Freyberg appointed Allied C.-in-C. in Crete.

Haile Selassie made triumphant entry into Addis Ababa.

TUESDAY, MAY 6   612th day

Air.—Attacks on shipping off Dutch and German coasts. One patrol vessel sunk, another set on fire.

Hamburg was main night objective. Le Havre docks also attacked.

Near East.—Italy announced occupation of six islands in Cyclades group.

Enemy carried out heavy raid on Malta.

Iraq.—British ejected Iraqi rebels from plateau overlooking Habbaniya, reinforcements having arrived by air from Basra.

Home.—During day bombs fell on Kent coast. At night raiders attacked N.E. and N.W. England and coastal town in south-west.

Four day and nine night raiders destroyed.

WEDNESDAY, MAY 7   613th day

Sea.—Admiralty announced that naval auxiliary Patia had sunk after combat with enemy aircraft which she shot down.

Air.—Heavy night attack on Scharnhorst and Gneisenau at Brest. Other aircraft attacked submarine base at St. Nazaire, docks at Bremen, shipping off Dutch coast, oil refineries at Donges, and docks and shipping at Bergen.

Africa.—Further raids on targets in Cyrenaica. R.A.F. also attacked enemy convoy in Mediterranean.

Cairo announced that Empire troops had occupied Quoram, Abyssinia, 30 miles south of main Italian position.

On N.E. coastal sector of Italian Somaliland British captured Bender Kassim.

Iraq.—Rashid Ali fled from Baghdad after public demonstrations against his Government. R.A.F. bombed Baghdad airport, magazine at Washash and aircraft at Hanaidi.

Home.—Considerable day activity off S.E. coast and many air combats. Widespread night attacks. Bombs fell in S.E. coastal district, in Humber area, on Merseyside and on West of England town.

Eight day and 24 night raiders destroyed.

THURSDAY, MAY 8   614th day

Sea.—British naval forces in Western Mediterranean, attacked by Axis planes,

destroyed seven, seriously damaged five. No ship was damaged.

Air.—R.A.F.'s heaviest raid yet directed mainly on Hamburg and Bremen. Other aircraft attacked Berlin, Emden and submarine base at St. Nazaire.

Africa.—Enemy reported to have evacuated Debereeh, 44 miles N.E. of Gondar. Further positions near Amba Alagi captured.

Naval forces attacked harbour at Benghazi. Two supply ships sunk.

Iraq.—R.A.F. bombed aerodromes at Sharaban, Baquba and Hanaida.

Home.—Enemy air activity off south and S.E. coasts. Several combats took place. At night Humber area and two districts in North Midlands were heavily attacked.

Fourteen night raiders destroyed.

FRIDAY, MAY 9   615th day

Sea.—Announced that German commerce raider had been sunk in Indian Ocean by H.M.S. Cornwall.

Air.—Destructive night raid on Mannheim and Ludwigshaven. Docks in occupied territory and aerodromes in Norway and North France also bombed.

Africa.—R.A.F. attacked aerodromes at Derna, Jedabia and Gazala.

Iraq.—Revolt collapsing. Rutbah aerodrome occupied by British.

Home.—Night raiders over West of England, Midlands and North-east England. Enemy fighter destroyed in South-east England. Three night bombers shot down.

SATURDAY, MAY 10   616th day

Air.—Bomber Command raided Hamburg, doing immense damage. Smaller forces attacked Bremen, Emden, Rotterdam, objectives in Berlin, and enemy shipping.

Coastal Command bombed supply ships, docks and oil stores at La Pallice.

Iraq.—British captured Majara. R.A.F. bombed military objectives at Mosul.

Home.—Very heavy night raid on London. Westminster Abbey, Houses of Parliament and British Museum hit.

Thirty-three night raiders destroyed.

THE CATALINA LIMPS HOME

TWO Canadians who had joined the R.A.F., Flight-Lieutenant J. G. Fleming, D.F.C., and Flying Officer J. J. Meikle, were recently given the task of flying one of the famous Catalina P.B.Y. flying-boats from Bermuda to Britain. This American aircraft, built by the Consolidated Aircraft Corporation, carried a crew of six : the two pilots, two radio operators, and two flight engineers, and fully loaded the machine weighed about fifteen tons.

The journey started under perfect conditions, but suddenly, when the aircraft was flying at a height of 18,500 feet, the automatic pilot jammed. When this happened the starboard aileron was full down and the effect was to throw the machine into a spiral dive. Both ailerons thereupon began to flutter badly owing to the steep angle at which they were opposing the airflow. The aircraft spun until barely 800 feet above sea level, with both pilots doing their utmost to regain stability.

But the pressure on the ailerons was so great that one of them broke away com-

Flying Officer J. J. Meikle (left) and Flt-. Lieut. J. G. Fleming performed an almost incredible feat when they flew home to Britain a 15-ton Catalina P.B.Y. flying-boat (above) after it had lost both ailerons.
Photos, Ministry of Aircraft Production

pletely. That was the critical moment for the pilots. When the second aileron broke away a few minutes later they found out that it helped to restore the balance of the machine. An S O S was sent out by radio, but was never received, for the good reason that, as was found out afterwards, the fixed wireless aerial had been carried away with the ailerons.

For a time the position of the aircraft seemed desperate. Smoke flares, spares, and tool kit were jettisoned in an effort to save the flying-boat. But their luck held ; when it looked as though the Catalina would hit the water, the pilots regained control.

Then a message was sent out by means of the trailing aerial saying " Both ailerons gone." The signal was duly received, but its recipients were sceptical. It seemed impossible that an enormous machine like the Catalina could still be flying without lateral control. Indeed, to remain air-borne Fleming and Meikle were compelled to sit side by side exerting all their strength on the controls. They had to fly straight ahead, for use of the rudder without ailerons might have sent the machine into a fatal flat spin.

But with amazing fortitude the pilots carried on. To make matters worse they flew into a storm as they approached the British coast. Nevertheless, they succeeded in making a safe landing at last outside a British harbour.

They still had some miles to taxi, and the sea was very rough. Fearing that taxi-ing on such waves would make both themselves and the rest of the crew seasick, this amazing pair actually took off again and skimmed over the surface for three miles to their moorings.

Photo, Fox

BEAUTY LENDS THE BRAVE A HELPING HAND

An injured flying-officer finds progress on earth somewhat halting, but with the aid of two sticks and the helping hand of V.A.D. Nurse Sheila Annesley he will surely arrive at his destination without a forced landing! The procedure with a wounded R.A.F. officer is to send him first to hospital, and then, if his case calls for special treatment, he is transferred, when well enough, to a luxury hotel converted into a convalescent home. Here he recuperates under ideal conditions before returning to battle.

The Strange Case of Rudolf Hess

Filled with surprises as it has been, the war has provided no more strange, indeed amazing,
occurrence than the arrival in Scotland of Rudolf Hess, Nazi Germany's Deputy Fuehrer.
Below we give the bare outline of a series of events hardly to be paralleled in history—
a chapter which we have many reasons to suppose is not yet ended.

RUDOLF HESS—"Nazi No. 3," as he is called, since he held the position of Deputy Fuehrer and had been designated by Herr Hitler as his successor after Goering—baled out from a Messerschmitt and descended by parachute on to a field some eight miles south-west of Glasgow soon after dark on the evening of Saturday, May 10. His plane crashed in flames 200 yards away and was burnt out ; he himself suffered nothing worse than a broken ankle, and was already disentangling himself from his parachute harness when he was hailed by a Scottish peasant, David McLean, who helped him into his cottage (see page 549).

"I have been in the air for four hours," he told his captors. "I left Germany in a Messerschmitt. Although I am a skilled pilot I am really a German military officer."

Then he produced a map on which was drawn a thick blue line, showing his course from Augsburg, in Southern Germany, across the North Sea to Dungavel, which was ringed round in blue. He had followed his course with such accuracy that he actually landed within 12 miles from what was apparently his destination—the seat of the Duke of Hamilton, and Hess told his captors that he had come with a special message for the Duke. He was thereupon removed to hospital under escort, and the Duke, who has been serving with the R.A.F. since the outbreak of war, flew to Scotland and identified the prisoner. Later it was announced that Hess had met the Duke in Berlin in 1936, when as the Marquess of Clydesdale he was attending the Olympic Games. During the past few months he had addressed letters to the Duke, which the Duke had not answered, but handed over immediately to the Security Department of the Government. After the identification, the Duke made a report to the Air Officer Commanding-in-Chief Fighter Command, Air Marshal W. Sholto Douglas, and was instructed to come south to London to give a personal account of the interview.

By now the Prime Minister had been informed, and although, as he himself confessed later, he did not at first believe the story, he ordered an official of the Foreign Office—Mr. Ivone Kirkpatrick, who had known Hess when he was Counsellor of the British Embassy in Berlin, to proceed to Scotland to interview the prisoner. He identified him at once beyond a doubt. This was on the Sunday.

Early in the evening of the next day there came an enigmatic announcement over the German wireless.

"It is officially announced by the National-Socialist Party" (reported Reuter), "that Party

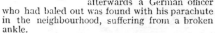

The route taken by Hess on his 800-mile journey from Augsburg to Scotland suggests how he tried to avoid possible contact with British fighters.

Member Rudolf Hess, who, as he was suffering from an illness of some years' standing had been strictly forbidden to embark on any further flying activity, was able, contrary to this command, again to come into possession of an aeroplane. On Saturday, May 10, at about 6 p.m., Rudolf Hess again set off on a flight from Augsburg, from which he has not so far returned.

"A letter which he left behind unfortunately shows by its distractedness traces of a mental disorder, and it is feared that he was a victim of hallucinations . . . In these circumstances it must be considered that Party Member Hess either jumped out of his aeroplane or has met with an accident."

This was the first news of the occurrence which had as yet reached the wider world. A few hours later—at 11.20 p.m.—there came a statement from No. 10 Downing Street.

"Rudolf Hess, the Deputy Fuehrer of Germany, and Party Leader of the National-Socialist Party, has landed in Scotland in the following circumstances.

"On the night of Saturday, the 10th inst., a Messerschmitt 110 was reported by our patrols to have crossed the coast of Scotland and to be flying in the direction of Glasgow. Since an Me 110 would not have the fuel to return to Germany this report was at first disbelieved. However, later on an Me 110 crashed near Glasgow, with its guns unloaded. Shortly afterwards a German officer who had baled out was found with his parachute in the neighbourhood, suffering from a broken ankle.

"He was taken to hospital in Glasgow, where he at first gave his name as Horn, but later on declared that he was Rudolf Hess. He brought with him various photographs of himself at different ages, apparently in order to establish his identity. These photographs were deemed to be photographs of Hess by several people who knew him personally. Accordingly an officer of the Foreign Office who was closely acquainted with Hess before the war has been sent up by aeroplane to see him in hospital."

At 2 a.m. the next morning, Tuesday, May 13, it was stated that the identification had been established beyond all doubt.

The news of the Deputy Fuehrer's arrival in Scotland was received with amazement in Britain and, indeed, throughout the world ; but in Germany with something more—with consternation and dread, as is proved by the succession of "explanations" which followed during the next few days. On the Monday night, as we have seen, the Fuehrer's Deputy was reported to be suffering from hallucinations, and was believed to have lost his life. When the British Government announced that Hess was in Scotland the German story changed. On May 13 the Nazis announced that perusal of the papers left behind by Rudolf Hess revealed that he laboured under the delusion that a step taken on his personal initiative with Englishmen whom he knew would lead to an understanding between Germany and Britain.

That same night it was evident that Goebbels had thought again. Over the wireless, Hans Fritsche, leading Nazi radio commentator, declared that there was hardly

a German who was not deeply shocked by the news concerning the tragic fate of a man who, "thanks to his tremendous energy and will-power, succeeded in postponing for a number of years the consequences of a wound he sustained in the last war." Providing he had not fallen into a British trap, Hess was obviously a victim of his idealism and hallucinations when he boarded the plane to impress on the English that the war was as good as lost for Britain, and that its continuation could only result in increasing British losses. "It was really madness to think that it would be possible to convince that clique of warmongers who have been preparing an assault on Germany for a long time. They cannot be persuaded by any logical reasoning, but only by the hard blows of German arms. It is to be regretted that Party Member Hess fell into the hands of that pitiless, despicable band . . ."

Goebbels Changes the Tune

Wednesday came, and once again Goebbels changed his tune. Now it was declared that Hess was a comparatively unimportant person ; his title of Deputy Fuehrer was only a courtesy one, Goering being Hitler's real deputy. For long Minister Rudolf Hess had been suffering from a disease, and the limitations of his working capacity had been recognized by Hitler, who relieved him progressively from his extensive duties. "Notwithstanding all this, the gradual disruption of his organisms has now led to an open outbreak of mental disturbance, as is always the case with such diseases."

Meanwhile in Britain it was made known that Hess was recovering in body and cheerful in mind, and was "talking freely." That last phrase sounded ominous in Nazi ears—as well it might—and so there came a statement that Hess was not informed of the plans of the High Command, although he knew enough to know that an extension of the German-British war would only bring about the complete destruction of Britain . . .

The state of mind of the German public can well be imagined. On Monday they were told that Hess, the Fuehrer's agent, friend and comrade, the "seagreen incorruptible" of the Nazi Revolution, had suddenly taken off into the blue, and was presumed a suicide. On Tuesday he was revealed as a man who had long been suffering from mental trouble and was getting madder and madder, and had been dabbling in astrology—yet as recently as April 20 he was chosen to broadcast birthday greetings to the Fuehrer, and on May 1 had given a stirringly patriotic address to the workers in the Messerschmitt factory at Augsburg ! On Wednesday he was a deluded pacifist who wanted to save not Germany but Britain from the results of her own warmongering !

Meanwhile Britain's propagandists, after a feeble start, had now taken off the gloves.

"We treat Hess merely as a Nazi who saw the writing on the wall and got out while the going was good," the Germans were told. "*If you knew as much as Hess knows, you would probably also get out if you could.*"

Has Nazi No. 3 Seen the Red Light?

RUDOLF HESS, in the plane, with his wife and Herr Loerzer, President of the Flying Sport Association. The three photographs above are of Hess, seated next to Goebbels and Hitler at a meeting of Nazi leaders; Hess with his master at another Nazi Party gathering; and Hess with Hitler in prison at Landsberg in 1923 (left centre). From the origin of Nazism Hess and Hitler have been inseparable friends, and closely associated with all the activities of their evil regime.

Photos, Keystone, Associated Press, Topical, Planet News

What a Task Was the R.A.F.'s in Greece!

With only a limited number of planes and very few landing-fields, the R.A.F. were severely handicapped from the very start of the campaign in the Balkans. Yet they put up a most gallant fight against tremendous odds. It would make a thrilling tale, but as yet only a little can be said.

WHEN, without the slightest provocation, Mussolini attacked the Greeks in October 1940, some R.A.F. squadrons, which had been fighting for six months past in the Western Desert of Egypt, moved at once to Greece. It was only a small force, but even so it was too big for the few aerodromes that were available. As new bases were built the R.A.F. in Greece gradually increased, but it never approached anything like the strength of either of the air forces which Italy and Germany flung into the fight.

Our airmen quickly settled down, and carried out their first bombing raid only six days after the Italians began their invasion.

ive enemy formations, and in a battle that raged over the whole length of Albania shot down 28 Italians. Towards the end of the campaign there was a great air battle over Athens, in which the same squadron sent 20 Nazis hurtling to destruction.

After six months' arduous fighting the R.A.F. bombers in Greece had carried out more than 300 raids, and had destroyed in the air nearly 300 enemy aircraft, besides damaging a huge number in the air and on the ground.

For months the R.A.F. and their allies of the Greek Air Force maintained their supremacy over the Italians—whose air force was, indeed, literally beaten to the ground.

Larissa flying field, smashing it up and destroying many grounded planes ; and on one day alone wave after wave of Nazi fighters swooped down and machine-gunned the airfields at Niamata, Volos, Almeros, and Paramyathe, and put them out of action.

The R.A.F. carried on, although the enemy hammered continuously our few remaining bases and it became impossible to obtain a replacement of aircraft shot down. Those that did arrive were shot up on the ground. All the same, aircraft—even planes officially described as unserviceable—took off all the time, and inflicted great damage on the advancing enemy.

BRITISH AIRMEN IN GREECE with an Italian trophy outside their mess. The photograph is a reminder of the days when our airmen completely worsted Mussolini's air force. In more than 300 raids, during the first six months of the Italian campaign against Greece, the R.A.F. brought down about 300 Fascist planes. When Germany came to her ally's aid our men and machines, vastly outnumbered, were forced to withdraw; but they did splendid work in making the British evacuation the success it was.
Photo, British Official : Crown Copyright

Then came the order for the Forces of the Empire to be withdrawn, and the R.A.F. rose to the emergency, playing an outstanding part in getting the Imperial troops safely away from Greece. Although heavily outnumbered, the British fighters guarded a continuous stream of ships that came back and forth to Greece, and by day and by night aircraft of every type, bombers and flying-boats, even training machines and civil planes, were packed to capacity with human cargoes, which they flew to safety and returned again for more.

R.A.F. personnel suffered the greatest hardships on their way to the embarkation points. "I saw many of them," said Reuter's Special Correspondent, "tramping along the roadside carrying what kit they could, still wearing their flying uniforms and boots. Most of their transport had been smashed up by the Luftwaffe and made unusable.

"While I was waiting in the woods for embarkation, I found a batch of some 30 aircraftmen. They were without rations and worn out—sleeping on the ground. They had marched about 150 miles across the mountains and valleys to contact the main British forces. While they were hiding in this spot, German bombers came over and unloaded sticks of bombs, one of which dropped in the middle of the R.A.F. party, killing four and wounding many others. Their comrades helped to carry the wounded on board ship. One died at sea."

Many were the lone, heroic deeds of our airmen, fighting against such terrible odds. They paid heavily for their service to their comrades of the ground, but to the end their spirit was unbroken. At the end of the campaign they had only one cry : "Give us the planes and we can really do something."

It was a hard winter, and the flying conditions experienced by our pilots were almost beyond description. Nevertheless, the ports and aerodromes occupied by the Italians were consistently hammered with a view to relieving the pressure on the Greek Army holding their line high up in the mountains.

Early in November the first British fighter squadron arrived, and though it was equipped only with Gladiators, they immediately made their presence felt. On the very day of their arrival in Greece the squadron carried out offensive patrols, and, discovering the enemy in great force, shot down eight, as well as damaging many others. Altogether this squadron accounted for more than 100 Italian and German aircraft before they left Greece. February 28 was their greatest day, when a small force encountered success-

Then, in April, Germany came to her partner's rescue, and once again our pilots met the enemy in the air. When Yugoslavia went down before the German onslaught, our bombers and big Sunderland flying-boats were given the job of rescuing important personages, including young King Peter, from the stricken kingdom, soon after.

When the Nazis turned the Allied flank and the British had to withdraw to a new line, the R.A.F. suffered the most severe blow of the campaign. They were forced back to only two or three bases and a few odd temporary landing-grounds that they had used at the opening of the campaign. All the new aerodromes which had been built at such labour and expense were lost, or were too close to the enemy lines to be used. The Luftwaffe concentrated in particular on the

Hitlerism Pollutes the Fount of Freedom

GERMAN ALPINE TROOPS about to plant the swastika on Mount Olympus in cold and bleak weather. So came the flag of bestial terrorism to the mythical throne of the gods and the cradle of human civilization.

THE ERECHTHEION'S CARYATIDES on the famous Acropolis in Athens look down impassively on Hitler's robots. The Germans entered the Greek capital on April 27, the first troops to arrive being a contingent of motor-cyclists at 9.35 in the morning.

The Mayor of Athens, on the left, and the Commander of the city's forces (centre) surrender the Greek capital to a German army officer, seen on the right. The Gestapo has already begun its sinister work in Greece.

Fighting against overwhelming odds in men and machines, these Greek soldiers were captured by German Alpine troops in the mountains. Under a Nazi guard they await the prison camp, there to remain until Hellas rises free once more.

Photos, Keystone, Associated Press

Hitler's 'Living Room' Was Holland's Dying Space

CENTRAL ROTTERDAM after the week of German bombing which began on May 10, 1940. Whole streets were obliterated in this attack on peaceful Dutch citizens. Beneath : General view of what was a residential district. It is computed that 30,000 men, women and children were massacred in this holocaust.

HOLLAND'S PREMIER, Prof. Gerbrandy, speaking from amid the ruins of the bombed Dutch church, Austin Friars, London, on May 11, 1941—the first anniversary of the Nazi invasion of Holland. His voice was carried across the seas to the Dutch East Indies. Queen Wilhelmina and Prince Bernhard were present at the ceremony, and in the evening the Queen broadcast to the Dutch people. " Hitler has succeeded in invading Dutch territory; he has never succeeded in invading the Dutch spirit," she said.

Photos, Wide World, Keystone

Trophy of Victory Brings No Peace to Germany

THE COMPIÈGNE SALOON CAR in which the Armistice of November 1918 was signed, and which was used theatrically by Hitler for imposing the humiliating terms on France on June 21, 1940, is now being exhibited in Berlin's Lustgarten to aid the War Winter Help Fund. As they pay their marks Berliners must be wondering why the war that was to be over in 1940 is to be prolonged yet another winter. The trophy of Hitler's temporary destruction of France is seen against the banners of paganism and the modern Renaissance cathedral built between 1894 and 1905.

Photo, Associated Press

Britain's Sky-Soldiers Learn Their Job

Britain's Parachute Force first went into action on February 10, 1941, when a number of parachutists were dropped in Southern Italy (see page 217), but for long beforehand they were in training. At first the Force was shrouded in official secrecy, but recently a number of interesting details have been revealed.

ONE, two, three, four . . . one after the other the parachutists sit dangling their legs on the edge of the hatch, then, with a second or so to separate them, drop into space to meet the earth, which seems to be hurtling towards them with terrifying speed. Hardly have they left the plane when their parachutes open—automatically—and the men hit the ground. In a second they have disengaged themselves, struggled to their feet, rushed towards the container carrying their equipment which another parachute, not white like theirs but coloured, has dropped close by, and in a trice they are on the warpath armed to the teeth with Tommy-guns and Brens, pistols and rifles.

They are tough fellows, these men of Britain's Parachute Force—tough, but not " toughs." They are all volunteers and of all ages from 19 to 30, though 24 to 25 is the most favoured, as then, while they have lost the foolhardiness of youth, their bodies are still supple and full of spring. For the most part they are small and wiry in physique, and they must be quick in thought as well as quick on the trigger. They must be utterly and completely reckless, filled with courage and inspired by a cold-blooded resolution. They must be able to work as individuals, as well as members of a team. All are soldiers of the British Army, although quite a number are Australians and New Zealanders by birth. In civilian life they followed a variety of occupations. Some were big-game shots and explorers, others were racing motorists and dirt-track riders; some were steeplejacks, athletes, boxers; some were miners, clerks, salesmen, or youngsters of independent means.

To become a parachutist a man has to be very carefully " vetted " before he is selected. Physical training is the first essential, and this training is rigorous. All the normal work found in Army P.T. is done, but special emphasis is laid on exercises which demand dash and boldness and cultivate an aptitude for rough and tumble. The men have already learnt how to use a soldier's weapons, and now they are taught how to fight unarmed, ju-jitsu and the rest. They are taught how to read maps and find their way by the stars and through strange country by eye and ear without asking questions which might betray them (although linguists are welcome, and the recruits are eager to study modern languages—German in particular). Then, of course, they learn how to jump—first from a tower, next through a dummy fuselage set up in a hangar, then from a cradle attached to a barrage balloon, and finally from a plane.

The " team " have to learn to make their exit as quickly and with as small an interval as possible, and when this has been mastered they learn the drill of entering the aircraft, taking up

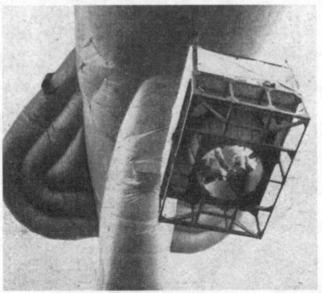

Paratroops about to descend from a captive balloon, and, top, a soldier is seen dropping from a dummy fuselage. So gradual is their training that they are able to face the first " jump " from an aeroplane as a matter of course.

Photos, British Official : Crown Copyright

position, acting on signals, and the packing and unpacking of containers.

Then they have to learn not only how to jump but how to land safely, without breaking a limb. The art of rolling backwards and forwards is studied and practised, so that, given reasonable conditions, a trained man need have no fear of twists and sprains. When doing the real thing the jump will probably have to be made from less than 500 feet.

Equipped for Emergency

Our parachutists wear ordinary infantry uniform, with a gabardine jacket and short trunks to prevent their equipment fouling the hatch through which they have to drop ; they have flying helmets equipped with rubber protection for the neck and back of the head, and they also have rubber knee caps and anklets. Their boots are laced, with rubber soles and heels, and the latter are reinforced with a special rubber strip to take the shock in landing. The heels do not contain springs, as is sometimes supposed. The men also carry emergency rations, packed in two waterproof packages which fit neatly into the two halves of the mess-tin.

The parachutist must be an expert on his own parachute equipment, on its fitting, adjustment and operation, since a badly fitted harness may cause injury when the parachute opens. He must be able to release himself from it quickly, and learn how it may best be concealed. He must also be able to operate his chute in the air ; he can, to some extent, direct it and prevent it from swinging in a gusty wind. This needs skill and practice ; and the elementary stages are done in a hangar, the pupil swinging from beams and going through the motions under the eye of an instructor. A " stick " of parachutists are required to come down within 40 yards from each other.

Troop-carrying aeroplanes from which the men are decanted are Armstrong-Whitworth Whitleys, Vickers Wellingtons and Avro Ansons, each type carrying about 10 parachutists. The Whitleys and Wellingtons are long-range heavy bombers and the Anson is used largely for coastal reconnaissance.

What is it that makes a man want to be a parachutist ? It can hardly be the pay, although by British Army standards this is quite good—from 8s. a day when in training, and £1 a day when fully qualified. Rather it is the exciting life which appeals to them after the m o n o t o n o u s routine of the parade ground and barrack life. Many of them went through Dunkirk, and have been " a bit fed up " since. Now that they wear that badge of a white parachute between light blue wings on a khaki background, they've got excitement and plenty of it.

Beating the Nazis at Their Own Game

The parachute fully open, a soldier is floating gracefully to earth. In the top photograph, paratroops leaving a flight of aeroplanes. Sitting for a moment with their legs dangling in space, they drop through a hole in the fuselage, their parachutes opening automatically.

PARATROOPS still attached to their "silks" on the ground. Centre left, eight parachutists are coming down, looking like giant mushrooms spread over the fields. Training for this branch of modern warfare is very arduous and exacting. The men have to be 100 per cent fit, expert at map-reading and resourceful in finding their way about unknown country. Landing within a comparatively small area, they must form themselves into an efficient fighting unit within ten minutes.

Photos, British Official : Crown Copyright

Bombers Make Ready for the War by Night

GAINS IN THE NIGHT AIR WAR

| Night of May | Nazi Bombers Brought Down | | | | Total |
| | By Fighters | | By A.A. | By B'loon | |
	Over B'tn	Over France			
1/2	1	—	—	—	1
2/3	2	1	3	—	6
3/4	11	2	2	1	16
4/5	8	—	1	—	9
5/6	7	1	1	—	9
6/7	8	—	1	—	9
7/8	17	3	3	1	24
8/9	10	1	3	—	14
9/10	3	—	—	—	3
10/11	29	—	4	—	33
11/12	8	—	4	—	12
12/13	1	—	—	—	1
Totals 12 Days	105	8	22	2	137

Earlier Night Successes

Jan., 15.   Feb., 15.   March, 47.   April, 90.
Total 4 months : 167.   Total to May 12 (Night only) 304.
Probable German loss of aircrew : about 1,216.
Note.—In future totals only, without details, will be given for night successes.

Bombers, British and German, are the subject of these photographs. Top, a Wellington taxies up to the run-way in the moonlight. Centre : British bomber crew entering their plane at moonrise. Right, pilot and crew of German bomber studying their course and targets before taking off for a raid over Britain. Above, German pilot setting out from an aerodrome in Occupied France.

Photos, British Official : Crown Copyright; and Keystone

HISTORIC WESTMINSTER AFTER ONE NIGHT IN MAY

ON the night of May 10, 1941, London was once again exposed to the fire and fury of the Nazi raiders, and some of the marks of the Teutonic beast are illustrated in these pages. Above, the Dean of Westminster inspecting remnants of the medieval Deanery. On the right, Mr. Churchill among the ruins of the Debating Chamber of the House of Commons. Beneath, another photograph of the wrecked Chamber.   *Photos, Topical Press, G.P.U.*

Above, the House of Commons as it was : the drawing shows a debate of the Asquith era. Right and below, as it is today. Only one wall remains of the Chamber, which, after a few hours' intense fire, now looks like an old Roman ruin. Centre, the Speaker's Chair, which was also burned.

...he splendid roof of **Westminster**
...dating from the 14th century,
...en to the sky ; and below right,
...tern on the roof of this building
...ediately after incendiaries fell.

...German High Command, refer-
...g to the blitz on London during
...t of May 10, which it cynically
...a "reprisal raid," admitted
...,000 incendiaries were dropped.
...sult of this savagery several of
...s famous buildings, many fine
...s of Georgian domestic archi-
...and a host of humbler dwell-
...re destroyed. The House of
...s Debating Chamber was
...and the Speaker's Chair, that
...of parliamentary discipline,
...perished in the flames.

G.P.U., Topical, Associated Press

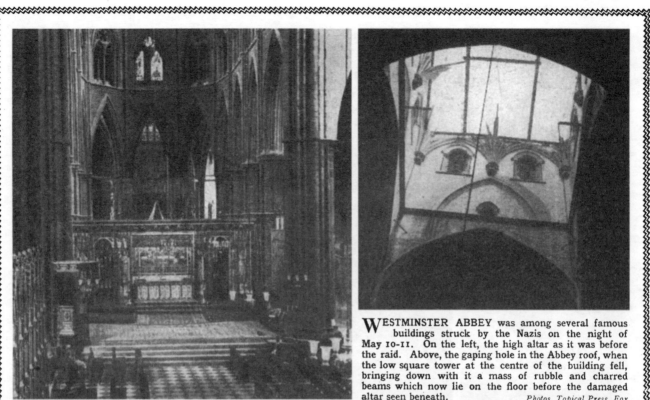

WESTMINSTER ABBEY was among several famous
buildings struck by the Nazis on the night of
May 10-11. On the left, the high altar as it was before
the raid. Above, the gaping hole in the Abbey roof, when
the low square tower at the centre of the building fell,
bringing down with it a mass of rubble and charred
beams which now lie on the floor before the damaged
altar seen beneath.   *Photos, Topical Press, Fox*

Hitler and Nature Make a Morning in Spring

The beauty of spring goes on, and not all the ingenuity of German frightfulness can retard its creative message. An idyllic scene of cherry blossom and sheep in an orchard at Shinglewell, Kent. The photograph is in poignant contrast to the one of a London street wrecked by Hitler's frenzy of destruction, a sight which confronted Londoners on the morning of May 11, when a brilliant sun revealed the hideous work of the Luftwaffe.
Photos, Fox, G.P.U.

Grim Is the Battle in the Vast Atlantic

BATTLE OF THE ATLANTIC: 1941
Shipping Losses—British, Allied and Neutral

Month	British		Allied and Neutral		Totals	
	Ships	Thousand Tons	Ships	Thousand Tons	Ships	Thousand Tons
Jan.	41	205½	17	100½	58	306
Feb.	68	264½	17	69½	85	334
March	81	326½	38	162½	119	489
April	60	293	46	195*	106	488
Totals	250	1,089½	118	527½	368	1,617

*April losses included 187 thousand tons sunk in Mediterranean operations, largely Greek. March and April figures are about 52 thousand tons higher than September, 1940, which was worst month in 1940 (excluding Dunkirk losses, June). **Total British, Allied and Neutral losses since war began 6,127,673 tons.**

TWO EX-UNITED STATES DESTROYERS helping to guard a convoy which includes tankers, munition and food ships. It came safely to port, thanks to the courage of its escort, and thus another point was won in this Atlantic battle of attrition. On the left, two gunners are ready should the enemy put in an appearance.

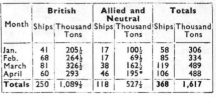

Three bombs on target was the result of an R.A.F. attack on an enemy tanker off Le Havre, though protected by flak-ships. Diving to within two hundred feet, our bombers made sure that their weapons would take effect.

This enemy bomb fell just wide enough to do no damage. Left : mother and child, after being torpedoed and in an open boat for twenty-two hours, safely aboard a British warship.

Photos, British Official: Crown Copyright; Fox, Keystone, L.N.A.

They Don't Want to Fight, But by Jingo—!

THE NEW AMERICAN BATTLESHIP, North Carolina, being placed in commission at the New York Navy Yard. She is one of the Washington class of six ships of 35,000 tons displacement (about 41,000 tons full load). Behind the serried ranks of her crew are three of her nine 16-inch guns. This ship, the largest and most formidable ever built in the United States, will take her place in the fleet's battle line at midsummer. The Washington herself was commissioned at Philadelphia Navy Yard on May 15, and a sister ship, the South Dakota, is expected to be ready early next year.

Photo, Wide World

TODAY the American Navy has in all about 800 ships. With the new battleship North Carolina it has 16 battleships [17 with the Washington], 12 in battle line; it has 6 aircraft carriers; 18 heavy cruisers, 19 light; 159 destroyers, half of which have been built in the past nine years; 40-odd old last-war destroyers, and 105 submarines. The test of the Navy's quality is in its cruisers and destroyers. It is generally admitted that the light—that is, the 6-inch-gun cruisers—are the best of their type in existence; they fire a hundred 6-inch shells every minute. The new destroyers, says one neutral naval expert who recently looked over them, " are the best destroyers I've seen, and they are also A.A. ships."

This Navy operates from bases on the east coast, going from north to south, at now Greenland, and then Boston, New York, Philadelphia, Hampton Roads and Florida; on the west coast, from Puget Sound to San Francisco, San Pedro and San Diego, and far out in the mid-Pacific to Pearl Harbor, which is being equipped to handle a whole fleet. Since the historic agreement with Great Britain last autumn it now has supplementary bases in the East, all the way from Newfoundland to Bermuda, to the Bahamas, to Trinidad and British Guiana.

When the United States woke up with a jump after the fall of France there were two main problems facing the Navy Department. One was to modernize the fighting craft; the other to strengthen the Fleet Auxiliary. During this last year the Navy has not merely managed to do what it wanted; it is ahead of time. Since Colonel Frank Knox became Secretary of the Navy, the Government has bought up every available tug, oiler, cargo boat and ammunition ship, and has now 2,600 merchant vessels on hand. It is rushing the construction of every type of auxiliary from corvettes to long-range patrol planes.

—*Alistair Cooke's American Commentary, May 10, 1941*

Our Searchlight on the War

Enemy Base in Antarctic

OFFICERS of the Norwegian whaler Harpon II, sailing under the Argentine flag, reported on their arrival at Montevideo on May 1 that while in the Antarctic the whaling fleet had received a wireless call to return to the depot ship. Here they found a large vessel which they took to be a raider. The fleet scattered quickly, but two whalers were later reported to be missing, and the crew of the Harpon assumed that they had been captured. This strange tale received some degree of confirmation at Boston on May 5, when a member of the U.S. Antarctic Expedition, Dr. Paul Siple, who had been in charge of one of the Expedition's bases in Little America, stated that Germany had until recently been maintaining naval repair shops at Deception Island, one of the South Shetlands. The island is an extinct volcano, the cone of which rises about 1,800 feet above sea level. On the south-east side the cone wall is broken by an opening about 600 feet wide, forming a circular lake harbour, five miles in diameter, called Port Foster. Dr. Siple, whose information was derived from a Chilean officer, said that the shops had been built in 1938, but were blown up a few months ago. Who had blown them up was not revealed. It was suggested that the Graf Spee might at one time have used Deception Island as a raiding base. The South Shetlands are a group of uninhabited islands in British possession, and form a dependency of the Falkland Islands.

Recruit Every 37 Minutes

SO rapid has been the expansion of the Royal Australian Air Force that at the beginning of the year the number of men being enrolled as air crew or ground staff was equivalent to one every 37 minutes, all round the clock. At Point Cook, on the shore of Port Phillip Bay, outside Melbourne, is No. 1 Service Flying School. Many of the men training here will later be posted to seaplane and flying-boat squadrons. A mental and physical tonic is provided by a regatta held in the Bay every Wednesday afternoon. The men sail 12-foot dinghies or " sharpies " against each other, and as seamanship as well as airmanship is necessary in this branch of the Service, such racing is a pleasant way of acquiring it. Australians training in Canada under the Empire Air Training Scheme have surprised the authorities by the high standard they achieved. The first contingent completed their course at the end of 1940, about the time that the third party was arriving from the Commonwealth.

National Fire Brigade

MR. HERBERT MORRISON has decided that the whole of the fire brigade resources of the country should be put under the control of the Home Secretary and the Secretary of State for Scotland, and is seeking Parliamentary powers to do so. At present there are more than 1,400 local fire authorities in England and Wales, some of them small and with limited equipment. In transferring their control to a central administrative authority the Exchequer would bear the cost of the service, less a contribution from local funds, this amount to be based on 75 per cent of the cost of the service in a standard year. " Local authorities, generally, have done their work well," said Mr. Morrison, " and it is not a reflection on them that the task itself has now grown altogether beyond local resources." Mr. William Mabane, joint Parliamentary Secretary to the Ministry of Home Security, will take charge of this all-Britain Fire Brigade, which will also include

the A.F.S. The other Parliamentary Secretary, Miss Ellen Wilkinson, has been entrusted with the enormous job of organizing Britain's fire-watchers. She will be responsible for the coordination of all schemes, both voluntary and compulsory, in London and the provinces, a task calculated to challenge the abilities of even this competent, dauntless personality.

Heroic Belgians

AMONG the Belgians sentenced by a German court-martial in Brussels on April 14 to various penalties were two, Edgard Lefebre and Marie Guerin, who were condemned to death for sheltering British subjects. During last summer and part of the autumn they helped the Britons to remain concealed in the woods at Flobecque, shared with them their limited rations, took them into their houses when the weather became cold, and finally made easy their escape to Brussels. In addition to the death sentence passed on these two devoted Belgians, eight men and two women received terms of imprisonment as accessaries. The arrest of the British refugees has not yet been reported.

Secret Nazi Orders Captured

WHEN the British raided the Lofoten Islands in March they obtained possession of a remarkable collection of enemy documents, all marked " secret," which were discovered in the military harbour control post at Svolvaer. These papers, facsimiles of which were published on May 8 in a White Paper, had been circulated by the German High Command to local officers. They all show that the invaders are finding the Norwegian people " unhelpful and pro-English." The Nazi C.-in-C. is very anxious

that the Army should try to be on good terms with the population, and some outward display of moderation is urged. Military intervention, therefore, must only occur when there are threats to the troops or army property, or demonstrations against the Fuehrer, when " military force should be brought into action in its full severity." But the Gestapo is given very wide executive powers. It can summarily prohibit a man from practising his trade or profession, it can impose fines, confiscations or imprisonment. It must take action in cases such as the boycotting of pro-German Norwegians, distribution of anti-German leaflets, sending of chain letters of anti-German content. Another

document complains that " neither the Executive Council nor other political group is in a position, or even desirous, to assume in a responsible way the government of Norway . . . In spite of repeated proffered opportunities . . . they are pursuing a deliberate policy of hold-back and wait-and-see, to gain time." Truly a stiff-necked people, whose fortitude is disconcerting to the German bullies.

Assault Against Malta

BOMBING attacks on Malta are increasing both in number and in violence, for nobody realizes better than Hitler how vital to British defence is this island. Malta was first raided a few hours after Italy's entry into the war. By the time the Luftwaffe appeared over the island, taking over a job in which the Italians had shown characteristic incompetence, the total raids numbered well over 200. By now this figure is rising towards 400. But, despite considerable damage to their homes and to historic monuments and beautiful buildings, the Maltese people are standing firm. Warned of an impending raid, the prudent among them resort to the deep shelters with which their

A mother and baby leaving a shelter after the 234th raid on Malta. Left, an old Maltese surveys the ruins of his bombed home.
Photos, British Movietone News

island is honeycombed—underground galleries cut out of the limestone rock by the Knights of St. John to serve as storehouses. Others disobey regulations and stand about to watch the thrilling air battles between the R.A.F. and the enemy, or the successful challenge of A.A. gunners—second to none for superb marksmanship. And when an Axis plane crashes they cheer and rejoice. Otherwise life in Malta goes on as usual, and cafés and cinemas do a brisk business. General Dobbie, lion-hearted C.-in-C., is a practical soldier of high reputation. His deep sense of religion has won for him, an ardent Protestant (he is a Plymouth Brother), the devotion and respect of the Catholic population. He does not mince matters in his demands of the islanders: " I say Malta must stand firm and do its part to maintain the security and integrity of this fortress, so important to Imperial strategy. There must be, and will be, no weakening."

Poland's Naval Cadets in Britain

Among the Polish institutions which have found their refuge and legal domicile on British soil is the Naval School for the training of officers of the Polish Mercantile Marine. We are indebted to a young Polish correspondent for this account of the School's origin and present state.

Typical Polish cadet attached to the Gdynia Naval School, now re-formed in England. He served in the Polish submarine Orzel.

A T a university college somewhere in Britain—we will call it X—the Polish Ministry of Trade, in conjunction with the Polish Shipowners' Association, and with the full support of the British authorities, have established a naval school for the training of Second Mates of the Polish Mercantile Marine.

The Polish boys are somewhat older than their British comrades ; they are not just " prospective cadets," but real young sailors with at least a year of seagoing experience behind them. All except one have been torpedoed—on the liner Pilsudski, or the Polish submarine O.R.P. Wilk, or M/S. Chrobry. Some of them were in the firing-line at Narvik, and others were at Dunkirk. Before the war broke out they had already completed a year's course of theoretical and practical training at the Nautical College in Gdynia, Poland's port in the Baltic. This institution was founded in 1920, and the Polish professors were all well-known specialists ; the College, indeed, achieved a high standard, and had a great reputation even outside Poland, so that many Rumanians, Bulgarians, Yugoslavs and Hungarians came to study there. The average number of students was about 120, and there were 16 professors and instructors on the staff. The last Commander and Headmaster, Captain Boleslaw Kosko, fell in the heroic defence of Gdynia in September 1939.

When the war broke out practically all the students were at sea on board their school-

waters. Subsequently the boys crossed to Britain, whenever and wherever it was possible, on board various merchantmen. Then from Britain the older boys went to France to join the Polish Army which General Sikorski was organizing. About 30 joined the Polish Navy, some got into British naval units, while the last, a batch of 30, decided on a career in the Polish Merchant Fleet.

These began to arrive at the college at X in August 1940, and started their studies with preparatory lessons in English, prior to the opening of their proper course on September 18. They have their own Polish lecturer in the person of an experienced sailor, Captain A. Z., who lectures on several subjects in Polish and also acts as Liaison Officer. The full course lasts for about a

refectory. Next comes the roll-call, which they call " Division," and the hoisting of the British and Polish flags. The first lectures begin at about 9 a.m., and last until about half-past twelve ; then comes inspection— " Quarters," as it is called — followed by lunch. Then, again, four hours of lectures. The rest of the day is taken up by preparation for the following day's lessons, dinner, " Evening Quarters," and a short breathing space, after which there is supper at 9.30. The Last Post is sounded separately for British and Poles ; then come prayers, and at 10 o'clock " Lights Out."

When the first course opened on September 18 last year, there was the inspiring ceremony of hoisting alongside the Red Ensign the school flag which Mr. M., Director of the Polish Naval Department, had rescued from Gdynia. Mass was celebrated, the ensign was blessed and the boys sang a Polish national hymn, *Boze, cos Polske.* " It was a moving experience," says Stanislaw S., " *Znowu razem* ! (Together once more.) After all we have lived through, so far from our country, without news of home, here is this little handful from the Gdynia Naval School, snatched from the torpedoes and the seas."

When I asked them, " What is your greatest wish ? " they answered, " Several things at once ! We want Poland to regain her independence, we want to pass our exams, we want to go back to Poland and to our families, and we want any amount of ships for the Polish Merchant Marine." Thus they revealed themselves as real spiritual brothers of that great sea captain and poet, the English novelist, Joseph Conrad, who was a Pole by birth (his real surname was rather a mouthful—Korzeniowski). They prove that Poland is indeed a maritime nation. They are proving, too, splendid comrades and promoters of closer relations, now and after the war, between Poland and the country which is temporarily their home.

POLISH NAVAL CADETS learning how to steer and navigate. They are members of the Polish Nautical College which has been reorganized in Britain. Most of the students there have already been on active service in the Baltic, at Narvik and Dunkirk. Above : Standards of our Ally's Naval College brought to Britain by cadets who escaped after the German invasion of Poland.

ship, the Dar Pomorza (Gift of Pomerania) —a lovely white full-rigged sailing ship which had twice navigated the globe under the Polish flag. Besides the Dar Pomorza, the young Polish sailors had two smaller school ships, the Lvov and the Zawisza Czarny, the latter being under the command of a well-known poet-sailor and army general, Captain Marius Zaruski.

The Dar Pomorza was homebound in the Baltic in August 1939, when her Commander, Captain Kowalski, received by wireless the alarming order to seek shelter in Swedish

year, and under the guidance of eight professors the Polish cadets study navigation, seamanship, astronomy, chartwork, ship construction, mathematics, signals, mercantile engineering and mercantile law. They are also taught English, as only roughly a third of the instruction is in Polish.

The order of the day begins with " Call " at 6.30 a.m. The boys leap out of their bunks in their bright, clean dormitories, say their morning prayers—all the Polish cadets are Catholics—tidy up their dormitories, and within an hour are having breakfast in the

Hitler's Juggernaut

A German Panzer Division of the Type Used in the Campaigns on the Continent, Shown Going into Action Against a British Tank Unit.

Specially drawn by Haworth for
THE WAR ILLUSTRATED

A GERMAN "PANZER" DIVISION is seen in action on the right of this drawing. The Germans are reported to possess at least 15 such divisions, each one consisting of 400 fighting vehicles plus ancillary units. These divisions are self-contained and have attached to them several squadrons of aircraft, as well as engineers, bridge-building and road-maintenance units, and extensive mobile repair and supply outfits. The dive-bombers smash all the heaviest opposition and strong points. Once this is done the rest of the division can roll forward confident that they will not be menaced by heavier metal than they themselves possess. A "Panzer" division is organized as follows: **The Reconnaissance Section.** (1) Troops of motor-cyclists with machine-guns mounted on side-cars. These are also armed with tommy-guns and hand-grenades and range far in advance, acting as sensitive "feelers." (2) Light armoured cars equipped with a light anti-tank gun and machine-guns. (3) Heavy armoured cars with a heavier armament mounted in a revolving turret. The object of all these is to find and "exploit" any gap or weakness in the opposition. (4) Light 6-wheeled cars which draw mobile anti-tank guns. (5) Mobile infantry in heavy lorries. (6) Lighter types of artillery and gun crews.

The Fighting Section. (7) Light tanks weighing about 5 or 6 tons with a crew of three, two machine-guns and a 200 h.p. engine giving a speed of 30 m.p.h. (8) Heavier tanks, 10 to 12 tons, armed with anti-tank and machine-guns carrying a crew of three and a 250 h.p. engine. (9) Medium (Cruiser tanks) of about 15 to 20 tons armed with a 37 mm. gun and 2 machineguns. A crew of four operate the vehicle, whose speed is 23 m.p.h. (10) Heavy tank weighing 25 to 30 tons worked by a crew of seven. The commander sits at his periscope and directs the gunners who are firing the large 75 mm. gun and heavy calibre machine-gun from the main turret, as well as the machine-gunners in the revolving fore and aft turrets. The power unit develops 350 h.p. and the speed is about 20 m.p.h.

Details of a British Tank and Crew, seen on the left of the drawing. The commander (A) is directing his crew by telephone. The gunner (B) has his eye pressed to the telescopic sighting apparatus, and his left hand holds the lever which swings the whole turret round. With the right he grasps the lever which fires the 2-pound gun (C) and the machine-gun (D). The wire-less operator (E) is also the gun-loader and he is seen about to ram a shell into the breech. The driver sits in front and his look-out position is at (F). This tank is typical of those which have done so well in Libya.

I Was There! .... Eye Witness Stories of the War

I Captured a Nazi Parachutist—It Was Hess!

When Rudolf Hess, Hitler's Deputy, landed by parachute near Glasgow on the night of May 10, he was first encountered at Newton Mearns, 8 miles from Glasgow, by a Scottish ploughman, David McLean, whose story of his sensational " bag " is told below in his own words.

THIS is the story David McLean told after the parachutist he had captured had been identified as Rudolf Hess.

I was in the house that night and everyone else was in bed, for it was late, when I heard a plane roaring overhead. As I ran to the back of the farm I heard a crash and saw the plane burst into flames in a field about 200 yards away.

I was amazed and a bit frightened when I saw a parachute dropping slowly downwards through the dark.

Peering upwards I could see a man swinging from the harness. I thought it must be a German airman baling out, and raced back to the house for help. But they were all asleep.

I looked round for a weapon. All I could find was a hayfork. Fearing I might lose the airman, I hurried round by myself again to the back of the house. There in the field I saw the man lying on the ground, with his parachute near by.

He smiled. As I assisted him to his feet he thanked me in perfect English. But I could see he had injured his foot in some way.

I helped him into the house. By this time my old mother and my sister had got out of bed and made tea.

The stranger declined tea and smiled when we told him we were very fond of it in this country. Then he said, " I never drink tea as late as this. I'll only have a glass of water."

We sent word to the military authorities. Meantime our visitor chatted freely to us and showed us pictures of his little boy, of whom he spoke very proudly.

He told us he had left Germany about four hours earlier, and had landed because nightfall was approaching.

I could see from the way he spoke that he was a man of culture. His English, though he had a foreign accent, was very clear, and he understood every word we said.

He was a striking-looking man, more than six feet tall, and he wore a very magnificent flying suit. His watch and identity bracelet were both gold.

He didn't discuss his journey and, indeed, appeared to treat what seemed to us a most hazardous flight as a pleasure flip.

He seemed quite confident that he'd be well treated, and repeatedly said how lucky he'd been in landing without mishap.

He was most gentlemanly in his attitude to my old mother and my sister. He bowed stiffly to them when he came in, and before he left he thanked us profusely for what we had done for him.

He was anxious about only one thing— his parachute. He said to me, " I should like to keep that parachute, for I think I owe my life to it."

He wouldn't tell me who he was and we didn't like to press the question. We assumed he was just another German airman who had been brought down.

When officials came on the scene he greeted them with a smile, assured them he was unarmed, stood up and held his arms out to let them see for themselves. Then he was taken away.

Mrs. McLean, the ploughman's 64-year-old mother, asked the parachutist at the door if he was a German. She said :

I didn't feel too friendly when he said he was, but he was so pale and tired, and his ankle was so swollen that I had to do what I could for him. He spoke like a gentleman, and had fine manners. He didn't want us to do anything for him except get him in touch with the authorities.

DAVID McLEAN and his mother, Scottish peasants who have become famous by reason of the fact that (as told in this page) they took charge of Hess. *Photo, " Daily Mirror "*

We felt he was someone of importance because of his clothes and his gold wristlet watch and identity disk. His boots were magnificent. They were as fine as a pair of gloves.

Although he looked between 40 and 50 years old I felt I had to mother him—especially after he showed us his little boy's picture.

He wouldn't tell us why he had left Germany and come here, but he seemed glad to be sitting in my cottage beside a good fire.

How We Brought Three Night Raiders Down

Some impressions of the work of the anti-aircraft batteries that line our coast were given in a racy broadcast by a sergeant in a light battery, which is reproduced below by arrangement with " The Listener."

WE have our own method with our searchlights, said the sergeant. We hold them until Jerry's quite close and then snap them on, so it blinds him, and we get in three or four bursts with the Lewis and Bofors before he has time to do anything. By this method we've spotted as many as eighteen targets at night, some of them three of four planes at a time.

I myself have seen three brought down at night recently. One of these we followed with the lights after we'd hit him, and he seemed to be breaking to pieces in the sky as though tracer bullets were coming off him all over his body. One day we sank one and crippled another within a quarter of an hour, and the heavies finished off the crippled one.

Something ought to be said about the searchlight men. Our light guns couldn't do anything without them at night, and they're always on the job. One night our lights got a plane that was coming from the west, and the chaps were holding him till we had him in range. While they were doing that another plane came in from the east and dropped a bomb within 50 yards of the light. It didn't half whistle down. But the men on the lights never worried ; they held Jerry, because they knew we were waiting for him.

They often drop stuff around us, of course. One night they came after us about fifteen times ; but in spite of all the stuff they've dropped, they haven't done a bit of damage ; in fact, they sometimes do us a bit of good. Once when one of their mines came drifting down, we popped it off with a Lewis gun. There was a lot of fish about when that went off—we got a conger 6 foot long—that kept the Sergeants' Mess going for a whole day.

One night they dropped a lot of those Molotov bread-basket things, and some of the little ones went into the sand and didn't go off. When I got in that morning all the rest were asleep ; I'd brought one of the

HESS'S WRECKED PLANE, which crashed with its guns unloaded near Glasgow after Nazi No. 3 had baled out. The bullet-riddled tail and shattered engine, in the case of so important a pilot, may be said to symbolize the ultimate fall of Nazidom. Hess brought with him several photographs of himself at different ages in order to establish his identity. *Photo, G.P.U.*

PROBING THE NIGHT SKY for enemy aircraft, the searchlight is an essential part of Britain's defences, and works in conjunction with our night-fighters and anti-aircraft guns. This photograph, taken at a searchlight station in the London area, shows a projector operating in its pit behind a ring of sandbags and corrugated iron.   *Photo, Central News*

little bombs with me, and I put it into the stove : " That'll sizzle in a bit," I said to myself and, by gum ! it did ; it didn't half shift the chaps out of bed.

When Jerry comes by day he's often too high for us unless he's minelaying. But one chap did catch us on the hop. It was a dewy sort of day, pretty thick. He dropped a couple, but he was too high ; then he went south a bit, dropped another couple and came back flying very low. We were all waiting, and we were so sure we were going to get him, we held our fire till he was too damn close and we missed him. Very annoying it was for us with our record.

There's a lot of back-chat between us and the heavies and the coast defence chaps, especially when we tell them that we're the top scorers in our part of the world and fetched down the first plane in the division —and got three barrels of beer for doing it, too. The coast defence chaps will have a pot at anything they see ; they believe in shooting first and arguing after. When summer comes they'll be firing at the butterflies.

I'd like to say this. I've told you how we hold our fire till the last minute ; if we had one misfire doing that, we should be meat for him. But we've never had one faulty round in all our engagements.

My Diary of Eleven Days in the Libyan Desert

One of the many heroes of the Libyan campaign was Dr. Marchant Kelsey of the R.A.M.C., who made an eleven-day trek over the desert from Derna to Tobruk to avoid capture by the Germans. Here is his story recorded in his own words.

D<small>R.</small> K<small>ELSEY</small> recorded his adventures in the following diary :

First Day.—I believe it is April 7. Approaching a still steeper hill leading eastward out of the town (Derna), we were informed by the colonel that an enemy force was barring our way. We went forward with the tanks. On the top of the escarpment fighting soon began, with much shrapnel whistling round us most unpleasantly. About six wounded, but no ambulances at hand.

One of the wounded was at the back of my truck, shot through the right arm—compound fracture of the humerus. His stretcher was held on by the men on the truck. The vehicles were ordered to make a rush for it, with myself well last. The rest got through. A hidden sniper hit our accumulator at the third shot.

I had previously planned to make off on foot in such circumstances, and had some supplies ready, including water.

The time was 3 p.m. I could not locate the sniper. Later I found him in some trenches, but he seemed afraid of coming to locate me or thought I was dead owing to the speed with which I fell off the top of the truck when he shot at us.

The wounded man " D." was quite helpless and hopeless. Darkness came, and I lay on the ground to watch for any enemy approaching who would be visible against the sky. None came. Made " D." comfortable and we lay down for the night. Very tired.

Second Day.—In morning all seemed quiet. Surveyed damage to truck—only accumulator gone—bad luck !

Later saw enemy searching battlefield about a mile away. Dressed " D." again, who was extremely brave. Later got him on the ground. Hard wind all day and dust storm for two to three hours in the middle of day. " D." would only drink. Eased him with morphia.

Longest day in my life ; no one came. By evening " D." much weaker, and I started to collect stores in case of the possibility of escape. " D." had a fairly peaceful night, but died early in the morning.

Third Day.—Towards dusk some German planes landed near my bush, the nearest one about 150 yards away. I could hear the voices of the Germans. Half an hour later it was dark enough to bolt from the far side of the bush at 8.30 p.m.

I set off on a bearing of 143 degrees across country. After a mile or two the water can started to leak badly, and it became so bad that I had to abandon it. I now had only two bottles of water. The stores carried were ten tins of condensed milk, five packets of biscuits, two tins of cheese, about two and a half quarts of water, one iron ration, vitamin C tablets, sleeping bag, blanket, glasses and compass.

Fourth Day.—Two-thirty a.m. 12 miles from the start. Passed a white-domed minaret on my left shining in the moonlight just beyond the remains of an ordnance camp. Found a few ounces of water at the bottom of a can ; much refreshed. At 3.15 a.m. found about five abandoned vehicles, with food and a little rusty-coloured water and some blankets. Woke about 7 a.m. and found a canyon to the right of the track. The track ended in front of the vehicles and through a cleft the sea was visible. It was the wrong road.

Fifth Day.—Awoke perishing cold. Stayed all day in sight of the road. Trouble starting : paronychia (septic inflammation of the base of the nail) on the right hand. Hands much knocked about these last few days. My right boot nearly worn through. Tried to mend it. Started on my carried rations today.

Sixth Day.—Just before 8 a.m. reached the Wadi el Tmimi. Sixteen miles, but hard going.

After lunch I was at my ease, when I was approached by two Indian soldiers, who led me off to the shore, where there were 12 more of them with two English officers.

They had come so far after escaping from Mecheli. They had no maps and we decided to go on together.

Seventh Day.—We moved on for about a mile to a more remote bit of shore farther from the busy main road. One officer decided to go no farther, but to make for the main road and give himself up. He was no walker and his feet were giving out. The Indians called a conference and decided to give themselves up with him.

The other officer and I were both keen to continue. We said farewell.

Eighth Day.—We stayed in the bushes near the inlet and had a cautious bathe and attempted to mend my failing boot. As dusk came we started cautiously towards the " narrows." We passed the danger point in the darkness, then made a circuit round an aerodrome.

Suddenly there was a loud explosion, and we found ourselves in the middle of a naval bombardment. It lasted some half an hour.

DR. MARCHANT KELSEY, R.A.M.C., who escaped from the Germans in Libya. The story of his trek across the desert is told in this page.   *Photo, " News Chronicle"*

Our objective was the road. Towards 3 a.m. we found a deserted Australian camp. We found good water in metal drums, one tin of bully beef and a ground sheet.

Ninth Day.—Further search of the camp and we replenished our water supplies.

Set off about 4 p.m. while still rather hot. Emerging from sand dunes, we found enemy camp within 200 yards.

Tenth Day.—Up before sunrise and on over the quiet going, following the shore. Our position was half a mile from the sea and 20 miles west of Tobruk.

Eleventh Day.—Moved off at the first glimmer of daybreak.

The doctor's diary ends shortly before he reached safety and British-occupied Tobruk. —(*British United Press.*)

Our Life in Iceland is Too Peaceful

Life for the British troops stationed in Iceland is peaceful, if somewhat monotonous, as described by a former member of the "Surrey Comet" staff who came home on leave after eleven months in the "land of the midnight sun."

" ICELAND is an interesting country, but, naturally, most of the boys would like to be nearer their families, a lot of whom have had to stand up to air raids." So said a soldier on leave from his unit in Iceland, and he confessed that he himself had not enjoyed his first experience of a night raid.

When the troops landed in Iceland, he went on, the Icelanders were very shy about contacting the British soldiers. They obviously resented what they looked upon as an invasion of their territory, although the necessity for it they did not dispute.

With that good humour and adaptability for which the British soldier is renowned in the four corners of the earth the troops soon broke down the barriers, and ere long the natives were challenging them to a soccer match. The British soldiers soon found out that talent for the game was not confined to the United Kingdom. The natives, playing on a sort of gravel pitch, beat a soldier eleven, which included Bryn Evans, former Epsom forward.

"When we got used to the new style of soccer pitch," he continued, "we were able to teach them a few tricks. Nevertheless, they play a fast and good game and the matches were very enjoyable.

"A surprisingly large number of the natives speak and understand English, and one of the results has been that many of them have picked up those pert and often vividly picturesque phrases sometimes used by soldiers. On one occasion one of the natives, greeted by a passing British officer, got rather mixed up with his slang and, in effect, hurled at the embarrassed officer a rather impolite injunction to go about his business !

"There is not a lot one can do in spare time there, but many of the troops have become expert skaters by practice on the frozen

fields and lakes. I noticed that English cigarettes, of which we received fairly ample supplies from home, were in great demand by the Icelanders. It was quite common for the troops to be accosted in the street and asked to sell English cigarettes—but it is against regulations to make a sale.

"There is a rationing system in force in the country and from our point of view meals ' out ' are a bit costly. Egg and chips were an unknown quantity to the café proprietors until we arrived on the scene, but it was not long before the electric signs appeared outside the shops bearing the cheering words ' Egg and chips,' but plus two pieces of bread and butter and a cup of tea it knocked you back 1s. 6d.

"It is almost impossible to describe with justice the beauties of the Northern Lights or the setting of the sun. Green, yellow, purple appear and reappear as the lights seem to glide across the sky. It really is a marvellous sight. As a contrast, I ought to

There is nothing frigid or shy about this little Icelander. He is quite pleased to make friends with the big soldiers from England who have come to protect his home.
Photo, British Official : Crown Copyright

mention one of the chief side-shows in Iceland. This is a trip to some of the huts on the mountain side where fish are hung up to dry. When dried the Icelanders chew them raw—and they seem to like it—but the smell!"

The soldier had one grumble to make. There was a serious shortage of English beer and the Icelanders' substitute for it was below par !

I Was Bombed in a Valley Under Parnassus

" Enemy transport and troops were bombed and machine-gunned behind the lines." The phrase is common enough in war communiqués from both sides, but what it really means is told in the following sketch from the Greek front by Alexander Clifford of the " Daily Mail."

WE were breakfasting beneath the cloud-capped heights of Parnassus, which glowed rosily in the dawn. To the right and left stretched a valley, with its patchwork of fields and its sides covered with wild flowers and rock plants that would make English gardeners burst with envy.

The noise of frizzling sausages drowned the faint hum in the sky. Then someone saw an ugly black Dornier slipping over the hilltop.

I raced for the gully 50 yards away from the road as the bombs screamed down behind me. They fell too close, and I raced another 50 yards to the river bank. There, among

the alder trees, an Australian private gave me a running commentary.

" The whole valley's full of them now . . . There's one coming straight at us . . . Here come the bombs—duck quickly . . . Hell, that was too near . . . Look at the shrapnel splashing in the river. . . . Now he's machine-gunning . . . see those explosive bullets fizzing round us . . . Here comes another . . ."

For an hour and a half it went on like that. Up there the Nazi pilots were having a fine time taking pot-shots at the bridges and level-crossings, diving on the empty trucks and machine-gunning in a haphazard way in the hopes of hitting somebody.

When they disappeared we packed up and drove off to another sector to have the whole thing happen again. Driving under these conditions you've no time to admire some of the loveliest scenery in Europe. You watch steadily a certain slice of sky, and when you see those sinister black shapes you stop the truck and race across the fields to get away from the roads.

Sometimes the scream from the bombs flings you flat on your face. Sometimes someone shouts, " It's a Hurricane," and you give a cheer and go back, laughing, to the trucks.

It's a full-time job. But don't forget to reverse the picture. Our planes were doing that to the Germans all day long, and they are finding better targets, for the enemy were more numerous and slower on the roads, which had already been ruined by our transport and our engineers.

So next time you read that communiqué remember it is not an empty phrase. It's a new feature of warfare which has become part of the modern soldier's daily life.

PEACE OVER PARNASSUS is the spirit of this pre-war photograph of the Greek mountain famed for legend, religious rites and poetry. Mussolini and Hitler brought war to this tranquil scene, and in an article in this page a British correspondent describes his exciting experiences dodging German bombs in a Parnassian valley.
Photo, E.N.A.

Our Diary of the War

SUNDAY, MAY 11, 1941   617th day

Sea.—Admiralty announced that Australian cruiser Canberra and New Zealand cruiser Leander had captured in Indian Ocean German supply ship Coburg and Norwegian tanker Ketty Brovig with German naval prize crew aboard.

Air.—Heavy night raids on Hamburg and Bremen. Smaller attacks on Emden and on docks at Rotterdam. Coastal Command raided docks at Ymuiden and seaplane base at Texel.

Africa.—Mechanized forces at Tobruk made surprise sortie, inflicting casualties and taking prisoners. Heavy R.A.F. raids on Benghazi and aerodromes in Cyrenaica.

Light naval forces bombarded Benghazi during night of 10–11, damaging shipping and military objectives. Heavy R.A.F. bombers attacked Tripoli harbour on night of 11–12.

In Abyssinia, Indian troops captured Gumsa, north of Amba Alagi. Enemy rearguard cut off near Wadala.

Mediterranean.—R.A.F. raided aerodromes at Catania and Comiso (Sicily), and those at Maritza and Calato (Dodecanese).

Iraq.—R.A.F. armoured cars occupied Fort of Rutbah.

Home.—Enemy aircraft driven off from coasts of Dorset, East Kent and Thames Estuary. At night bombs fell in widely separated areas.

Six day and 12 night raiders destroyed.

MONDAY, MAY 12   618th day

Sea.—H.M. trawlers Rochebonne and Kopanes reported sunk.

Air.—Heavy night attacks on Mannheim, Cologne and Coblenz. Other aircraft attacked docks at Ostend, Dunkirk and St. Nazaire.

Africa.—Five enemy mechanized columns advanced from near Sollum but were checked by our forces near Sofafi and bombed by R.A.F. as they retreated. R.A.F. attacked Gambut landing-ground. S.A.A.F. in action for first time in Cyrenaica.

In Abyssinia many air attacks made on forts at Amba Alagi and on enemy camps and troops.

Near East.—Suez Canal zone raided for third successive night.

Iraq.—R.A.F. engaged in punitive operations against rebels.

Home.—Slight enemy air activity by day and night.

General.—Announced that Rudolf Hess, Hitler's Deputy, had flown from Germany to Scotland on May 10.

TUESDAY, MAY 13   619th day

Sea.—Admiralty stated that during period May 6–12 our naval forces in Mediterranean destroyed 16 enemy aircraft and damaged six others.

Indian warship Parvati reported lost.

Air.—R.A.F. bombers made successful daylight raid on Heligoland. Shipping and docks at St. Nazaire attacked. Two supply ships hit.

Africa.—Nine light tanks captured in lakes area south of Addis Ababa.

During night of 12–13 Fleet Air Arm attacked convoy in Mediterranean, hitting merchant ship and destroyer. R.A.F. raided Benghazi and landing-ground at Kattavia (Rhodes).

Iraq.—Fleet Air Arm attacked Amara barracks and other targets.

Home.—Slight enemy air activity by day and night in coastal areas. One day and one night raider destroyed.

WEDNESDAY, MAY 14   620th day

Air.—Coastal Command aircraft torpedoed German supply ship off Dutch coast.

Ostend aerodrome attacked by Hurricanes.

Africa.—Two forces, converging on Amba Alagi, making good progress.

Iraq.—R.A.F. continued to attack rebel positions and military targets.

Home.—Bombs fell by day at points on south coast, east Midlands and eastern England. One night raider destroyed.

THURSDAY, MAY 15   621st day

Air.—Bomber Command attacked escorted convoy off Friesian Islands. Three supply ships hit and left burning. Fighter Command carried out offensive sweeps over Channel and Northern France.

Big night raid on Hanover. Other bombers attacked Berlin, Hamburg, Cuxhaven, shipping and docks at Channel ports.

Africa.—British retook Sollum. In Abyssinia, pass of Shashamanna, south of Amba Alagi, was occupied.

Near East.—R.A.F. attacked German aircraft on three Syrian aerodromes. Malta, Crete and Cyprus bombed by Axis aircraft. Nazi-occupied aerodromes in Greece raided.

Iraq.—Announced that German aircraft had landed in Iraq from Syrian airfields. Fleet Air Arm attacked barracks at Amara.

Home.—Enemy air activity in coastal areas. One day and one night raider destroyed.

FRIDAY, MAY 16   622nd day

Air.—R.A.F. bombed shipping off Norwegian coast. Supply ship sunk. Heavy night attack on Cologne. Shipping in French and Dutch harbours and many aerodromes also raided. Small force attacked docks at Boulogne.

Africa.—Mechanized troops continued pressure against enemy in Capuzzo area. Successful counter-attack in Tobruk area. Heavy night raid on Benghazi, Derna and Gazala.

British troops captured Dalle, important road junction 35 miles south of Shashamanna, taking 800 prisoners and much war material.

Our troops occupied Dante, It. Somaliland.

Near East.—Heavy night raids on enemy-occupied aerodromes in Greece.

Iraq.—R.A.F. attacked German aircraft on aerodrome at Mosul. Nazis raided Habbaniya.

Home.—Enemy made vain attacks on S.E. airfields. At night west Midlands town was main target. Bombs also fell in area in Southern England. Several R.A.F. aerodromes attacked, but damage and casualties were slight.

Eight day and three night raiders destroyed.

SATURDAY, MAY 17   623rd day

Sea.—Announced that H.M. trawler Susarion and drifter Liberty had been sunk.

Air.—Big night raids on French coast from Dunkirk to Boulogne. Heavy bombers again raided Cologne. Smaller-scale attack on Rotterdam.

Africa.—Australians recaptured strong points outside Tobruk. Germans claimed that Sollum and Fort Capuzzo were again in their hands. During night of 16–17 aerodromes at Menastir and Bir Chleta were raided.

Duke of Aosta asked for terms of surrender of his forces in northern Abyssinia.

Near East.—Day raids by fighters and night onslaughts by bombers continued on enemy-occupied aerodromes in Greece, particularly those at Argos, Menidi and Malaoi.

During night of 17–18 R.A.F. raided Calato aerodrome (Rhodes), causing many fires.

Home.—Small-scale activity over Britain. One day raider destroyed.

SHE SANK A NAZI PIRATE IN THE INDIAN OCEAN

H.M.S. CORNWALL (Capt. P. C. W. Mainwaring, R.N.), which sank a German armed merchant cruiser preying upon ships in the Indian Ocean. Twenty-seven British merchant seamen held prisoner aboard the raider were rescued and 53 of the German crew who survived were captured. The Cornwall, a cruiser of the Kent class, displaces 10,000 tons and has a complement of 679.

Photo, Topical Press

'The War Illustrated,' June 6th, 1941

Registered at the G.P.O. as a Newspaper

Vol 4 · *The War Illustrated* · Nº 92

Edited by Sir John Hammerton

FOURPENCE

WEEKLY

A DEPTH-CHARGE has just been hurled overboard from this ex-American destroyer, a German submarine being in the vicinity. The depth-charge is one of our most formidable weapons in the Atlantic battle.   It can be detonated at a predetermined depth of 20, 100 or 200 feet, and can exert such pressure on the submerged vessel as to crush it.   Its shock can open seams and paralyse a U-boat at a considerable distance from the scene of the explosion.

Photo, Fox

Our Searchlight on the War

Axis King of Croatia

THE new Italian puppet state of Croatia has been offered to the Crown as a sort of consolation prize for the loss of Abyssinia. Heading a delegation to Rome came Anton Pavelitch of ill fame—for it was he who was tried by default and condemned to death for the murder in 1934 of King Alexander of Yugoslavia—and made formal request that King Victor Emmanuel should select a ruler for Croatia. The royal choice fell upon the Duke of Spoleto, younger brother of the Duke of Aosta and second cousin to the King himself, and he was duly proclaimed

THE DUKE OF SPOLETO, Hitler's latest puppet, has been appointed King of Croatia, which formed part of Yugoslavia. He is a second cousin of the King of Italy and brother of the Duke of Aosta. This photograph was taken at his marriage to Princess Irene, sister of King George of Greece.
Photo, Keystone

king on May 18. After this ceremony, which was held in the throne-room of the Quirinal, the Croat Quisling was presented to Mussolini, and later a political and economic pact was signed. "The Italian Government and nation," thundered Mussolini at a banquet afterwards, "cordially greet the restoration of the kingdom of Zvonimir (King of Croatia in the 11th century). The dynastic links between Italy and Croatia will create a solidarity between the two countries." That same day the Duke of Aosta, surrounded by his exhausted and half-starved troops at Amba Alagi, accepted the British terms of surrender. But Mussolini feels that what he has lost upon the roundabouts he has gained upon the swings—even though, as some reports suggest, he may also lose Trieste to Hitler as a "free (German) port."

America and Foreign Ships

U.S.A. Senate passed the Ship Seizure Bill on May 15 by 59 votes to 20. By this Bill the Government is empowered to take over by purchase, charter, requisition or condemnation any or all of the foreign vessels now lying in American harbours. There are some eighty of these, of which two are German and twenty-eight Italian. An amendment put forward to prohibit the President from transferring any such vessels from one belligerent country to another was defeated by a vote of 43 to 38. That same night the coastguard, under orders from the Treasury, took into protective custody the 83,423-ton liner Normandie, which has been in New York harbour since August 28, 1940, and twelve French cargo vessels in American ports. These ships were not actually seized, and their crews were allowed to remain aboard, as it was not thought there was any risk of their being scuttled. French ships now at sea will be taken into custody when they arrive in port.

Scandal in Slovakia

VANISHING jewels which reappeared in the wrong place have involved Tuka, the Slovak Premier, and other Slovak Quislings in a political scandal, news of which reached London on May 19. It appears that a short time ago members of the Slovak Government received mysterious information that high officials of the Slovak National Bank, conspiring with other persons, had smuggled part of the foreign currency held at the Bank to London, to help the Czechoslovak Government there. Upon investigation by the Bratislava police it was found that the currency was intact, but that valuable jewels, forming part of the cover of the national currency, were missing. These jewels had been collected when the Slovak State was set up in 1939; some had been given voluntarily, others were expropriated from the Jews. Since no trace of them could be discovered twenty-one high officials of the National Bank and thirty-nine other prominent citizens of Bratislava were taken into custody. Then came a startling development. Women members of the families of Cabinet Ministers were observed to be wearing some of the jewels. Among them were Mme. Tuka and Mme. Mach, wife of the Minister of Propaganda. At this point the report stops short. A member of the Czechoslovak Government in London stated that they had not received a farthing from the Slovak National Bank.

CIVILIAN LOSSES IN THE AIR BATTLE OF BRITAIN		
Casualties for 8 Months		
	Killed	Injured	Total
Sept. 1940 ...	6,954	10,615	17,569
Oct.	6,334	8,695	15,029
Nov.	4,588	6,202	10,790
Dec.	3,793	5,044	8,837
Jan. 1941	1,502	2,012	3,514
Feb.	789	1,068	1,857
March	4,259	5,557	9,816
April	6,065	6,926	12,991
Totals	34,284	46,119	80,403

Of the 6,065 killed in April (third highest total of the Air War) : Men, 2,912 ; Women, 2,418 ; Under 16, 680 ; Unclassified, 55. Missing (in addition), 61.

LONDON'S WAR WEAPONS WEEK, which ended on May 24, was a huge success. An A.T.S. officer standing beside an imitation bomb mounted on a car in Westminster.
Photo, Wide World

London's Answer to Hitler

SIXTY-TWO local savings committees co-operated in the Greater London War Weapons Week, inaugurated on Saturday, May 17. Their aim was to reach a total of £100,000,000, and by May 22 this sum had already been subscribed, so that the King's expressed wish for "an outstanding achievement" was fulfilled. The first day the president of the National Savings Committee, Lord Kindersley, and the chairman, Lord Mottistone, inspected a long procession of decorated vehicles which had come to Constitution Hill from all parts of Greater London. On Sunday massed bands of the Brigade of Guards played in Hyde Park for the first time since the outbreak of war, delighting a crowded audience assembled in the sunshine. Tanks trundled noisily along the streets, local parades of the Home Guard and other defence workers exerted the magnetic attraction of all processions, mobile cinema vans showed special films, the London Fire Brigade gave a display of fire-fighting, crashed enemy machines were on show, gaudy posters and banners enlivened the drab background of the bombed areas, and Londoners, rejoicing in even this sober bit of pageantry, queued up outside the savings centres before they were opened, eager to take their share in "hitting back" at Hitler.

Dutch Strive to Reach England

A RUMOUR that spread with incredible speed through Amsterdam that it was possible to enrol for the Dutch Legion in Britain by applying through the American Consulate, caused the Consulate to be besieged by an army of eager volunteers. All affirmed that they wanted to go to England and that this could be done by making the journey via U.S.A. The embarrassed officials, overwhelmed by sheer numbers, eventually posted the following notice on the door: "This Consulate of the United States of America is not able to give pensions to former members of the Netherlands Army under any arrangement with the authorities in London, and, further, this Consulate does not know of any possibility of persons getting to England or of the consequences which might arise from requests on this subject."

The Way of the War

WHICH OF THE ARABS ARE OUR FRIENDS?

An Analysis of the Moslem East in Ferment

NOT every Arab wears sandals and a burnous, plods the desert sand beside his camel, says farewell to his dying steed, or folds his tent and silently steals away. There are other Arabs than the poets are aware of; in the world today there are fifty millions who bear the Arab name and speak the tongue Muhammad spake. Some, it is true, roam the uncharted wastes of the Sahara and Arabia, but others—and by far the greater number—are to be found in the bazaars or on the feudal estates of the Arab world that stretches from the mountains of Morocco to the great rivers of Iraq, from Damascus, most ancient of the world's cities, to the squalid hamlets lapped by the Indian Ocean. And quite a number of them wear soft felt hats and ready-made suits and shoes of a startling brown.

Altogether they represent a very considerable chunk of present-day humanity, and what they think and what they do are matters of moment not only to themselves. Not that the Arab world has any real unity. Once it was politically one, when the successors of the Prophet ruled from Baghdad to Gibraltar; those days are long past, however. It still is bound by the common faith of Islam, but today all organized religions are in decline and Mahomedanism is no exception. Then if in Arabic it has a common language, this is true only in respect of the written form.

GREATEST of the Arab states in size but not in population is Saudi Arabia, the kingdom which Ibn Saud has erected in the heart of the Arabian peninsula. It is a vast area of 800,000 square miles, but most of it is desert and unpeopled, so that the old king—by far the greatest personality in the Arab world—rules over only some 4,500,000 tribesfolk. Here in the Hedjaz are Mecca and Medina, where the Prophet of Islam was born and buried, the holy cities of two hundred millions. When Lawrence of Arabia was organizing that revolt in the desert which became the basis of a legend and a cult, the Sherif of Mecca was Emir Hussein, a direct descendant of the Prophet. He was driven from Mecca in 1925 by Ibn Saud; but one son secured a throne, first Damascus and then Baghdad, while another, Emir Abdullah, sits by the grace of Britain on that of Transjordan. Today, for the first time for centuries, Arabia forms one great kingdom, with the exception of the sultanates of Oman and Yemen and a cluster of adjacent states enjoying a conditional independence in the south. Save for these, Arabia is the footstool of a Moslem Cromwell who has prohibited alcohol and tobacco and

even coffee. In the present struggle Ibn Saud is usually ranked as a sympathizer with Britain.

Far smaller than Ibn Saud's realm, but far more populous, is the kingdom of Egypt. Young Farouk I can claim a territory less than half his in size, but his subjects number some sixteen millions. Perhaps their right to be included in the Arab fold may be contested; but if Egypt's races are mixed, she is incontestably the leading Arabic-speaking nation, her Press is the most vigorous, her people the most democratic, and she has by far the largest literate, even educated and politically-conscious class. Her sovereignty was fully recognized by the Anglo-Egyptian Treaty and Alliance of 1936. But British troops within her boundaries are a constant reminder of her inability to maintain her freedom in a world which also has to find room for dictators on the prowl.

NEXT to Egypt beyond the Canal lie Palestine and Transjordan. The one is a mandated territory, where until recently Jews strove to create a National Home in a land which nearly two thousand years ago had belonged to their fathers. Only with the outbreak of war did Zionists and Arabs stop their sniping and offer their services to the Power which, whatever its

vacillations in policy, was at least ready and able to defend them against Hitler.

Transjordan is likewise mandated territory. In everything that matters this largely desert country, inhabited by some 300,000 Arabs, chiefly Beduin, is British. Emir Abdullah plays chess at Amman, but Major Glubb and his policemen are the power behind the throne.

To the north of Transjordan is Syria, mandated to France in 1920, although the Syrian people—that is, such of them as cared for these things—agitated strongly for " complete independence, without any form of foreign interference." But words were unavailing when matched against French guns. Rebellion was crushed, but the spirit of nationalism was unsubdued. The war came before a French promise of independence had been implemented, and so today Syria is the setting of an act in the unpleasant drama of French decline.

Iraq, too, started her post-war existence as a mandate, but in 1932 it was announced that henceforth she was an independent state in alliance with Britain. With an area somewhat larger than England, she has a population about half the size of London's. Her independence is a precarious thing enough, although the rebel troops of Raschid Ali have recently put up a surprisingly strong resistance to the British; and she has few of the things that go to the making of a modern state. Iraq's whole prosperity depends on the oil which is drawn from beneath her surface; of the national revenue nearly half is received in the shape of royalties paid by the oil companies, and it is illuminating that not much more is spent on education than on police.

THIS, then, is the Arab world (but not all of it, for to complete our survey we should include the Maghreb—Tunisia, Algeria and Morocco, all under the control of France—and the Italian provinces of Libya). It is a collection of countries which are not real states, a group of peoples fumbling after a union based on a common tongue and a shared religious faith. For years it has lain stagnant; now, however, the waters are troubled by the breath of nationalism. Many there are who dream and talk of an Arabic federation which will include Arabia, Iraq, Syria, Palestine and Transjordan; of these is our old enemy the Mufti of Jerusalem. Others go further and aspire after a revived Arab Empire stretching from Morocco to the Persian Gulf. These dreamers, many of them, have been made into plotters by Nazi and Fascist gold.

E. ROYSTON PIKE

IBN SAUD, King of Saudi Arabia, known as "the Cromwell of the Hedjaz," was recently approached by Nāgi el Sequdi, who sought his support for the cause of Raschid Ali. To him Ibn Saud is reported to have said that if he had agreed with Raschid Ali's movement he would have supported him already   *Photo, Keystone*

'The Superb Women of Great Britain'

Shortly before his departure for America in a Clipper plane Mr. R. G. Menzies, Prime Minister of the Australian Commonwealth, recorded a message to the British people which was broadcast as a Postscript to the news on Sunday, May 4. As will be seen from the passages reproduced below, it took the shape of an eloquent and richly deserved tribute to Britain's Womanhood.

IF some questioner were to say to me quickly, "What is your outstanding impression of Britain today?" I should think of many things. I should think of Winston Churchill, the resolute and supremely eloquent embodiment of the British fighting spirit. I should think of the craft of the Royal Air Force : the boys in blue uniforms questing among the clouds or groping in the dark empyrean for the invading bomber. I should think of the factories with wounded roofs and walls, with shattered homes about them, roaring out their busy answer to the enemy. I should think of the strange new life in Tube shelters and basements, often grimy and drab, always hideously uncomfortable and dangerous—and yet a life accepted philosophically as part of the price of a just war. I should think of the men of the Fire Service toiling in a bombardment at the heart of the incendiary fire and therefore in the centre of the target. I should think of the Bomb Disposal Squads. I should even think of that frequently forgotten man, the London taxi-driver, always, as it seems, old, whiskered, casually humorous, cap on head, battered pipe in mouth, plying his humane trade while bombs fall. I should think of many things, all of them great and moving.

But my answer to the question would still unhesitatingly be : the courage, the action, the endurance of Britain's women. Wherever I go I see them and I marvel at them. Is it possible to believe that not long ago we called them " the weaker sex "? . . . Women conducting vast organizations ; women in the uniform of the Navy, the Army and the Air Force ; women at fire brigade stations in blue overalls, always ready ; women driving great vehicles ; women digging in the fields ; women wielding hammers, and riveters in factories ; women at their gentle work of nursing the sick soldier ; women working in the hospitals in the middle of air raids ; women doing their turn of fire-watching in their own suburban streets as the incendiary bombs rain down ; and, last but not least, that forgotten but splendid woman, the house-wife, who copes with rationing, with shortage of foodstuffs, and who not infrequently goes short herself so that her man and her children may be fed. The vast movement of women into the service of the nation, doing these things and a hundred others, is spectacular. It marks the beginning of a new era. It will usher in enormous social and other changes about which one can only speculate.

My only desire is to record. I confess myself an enthusiast about the superb women of Great Britain. And when I say that, I am not thinking of any one class. From Her Most Gracious Majesty the Queen, whose cheerful and brave smile has brought comfort to thousands of people the wreckage of whose homes she has visited, to the humblest women of the East End, the breed runs true. Palace and slum tenement have alike brought forth the flower of endurance. In some of the great industrial cities where many hundreds of bombs had fallen, where literally thousands of houses had been wiped out, where vast community funerals had been held and human anguish must have been supportable only because it was so widely shared, the quickest recognition and the brightest smiles were seen on the faces of toil-worn middle-aged women ; the faces transformed from homeliness to a sort of radiant beauty by sheer courage.

Words Born of Bitter Experience

At Sheffield a little speech was made to me by a woman who is now a director of a large factory in which thirty years ago she was a simple unlettered manual worker. She had battled with life and knew it at close quarters. And her speech was simply this : " They may bomb our factories, they may bomb our homes. But while we have life, they can't take from us the skill of our hands or the spirit that we have in us," These were not the mock-heroics of the stage or of the platform ; they were born of bitter experience of sudden and surrounding death. I thank God for such people. A few days ago I was speaking to a young professional woman. Her work— important work—occupies her all day and almost every day. I saw that she was carrying some ugly bruises. "How did you get those?" " Oh, it's nothing. I got them climbing into a house to get rid of some incendiary bombs." The " weaker sex," indeed ! Three nights a week that girl serves at a fire station down in the East End where after every raid the fires rage most fiercely.

In any war factory you may see hundreds of women not merely doing the fine precision work of testing and gauging, but wielding the hammer, operating machines, riveting metal sheets ; all in trousers and overalls ; some slim and tall, looking like men ; others not so slim, bulging too much for deception. And everywhere I heard the same story : the morning after the blitz the women are on time ; they are on the job. If they have tears to shed, they shed them privately. They are among the great soldiers of this war.

The next generation in Britain may have mothers who have forgotten how to swoon at times of crisis ; who no longer cling to the male as ivy clings to the wall ; who commit the immodesty of wearing those hideous garments which have long been the gloomy prerogative of men ; who will find no inconsistency between lipstick on the face and axle grease on the hands ; who will in the cant phrase " make their Victorian grandmothers squirm in their graves " ; but they will be mothers of real men.

MR. R. G. MENZIES, Prime Minister of Australia, reviewing women civil defence workers. With soldierly courage British women, from housewives to women in the various services, have taken their places in the battle line. Whatever they are doing, wherever they are, each and all are now proudly a part of the indomitable garrison of the fortress of Britain. *Photo, Sport & General*

Woman-Power in Britain's 'Finest Hour'

Two Red Cross nurses hurrying to the scene of a daylight bomb explosion. Note the practical way in which first-aid requisites are carried round the waist.

The Alert sounded, some of the A.T.S. girls who are now helping to man anti-aircraft gun-posts running to their action stations.

DISTRICT

Girl cleaners are taking the place of men on London's Underground railways. Here are two in their neat dungarees keeping a train spick and span; while, on the right, the first woman to drive a Post Office mail van is seen at the wheel, with parcels for delivery

Photos, Wide World, Fox and Keystone

Life or Death in the Great Atlantic War

The white smoke rising over the Frisian island of Norderney indicates the destruction of three German patrol vessels after British bombers had scored direct hits on them. The Frisian Islands are a nest of U-boats.

Awaiting her clothing of steel plates, this new ship will soon be taking part in the contest. Left: an old British windjammer meets her doom in the South Atlantic.

BRITISH MERCHANTMEN destined for Britain awaiting convoy in an East Canadian port. Honour the brave men who will navigate these ships across the Atlantic in the teeth of German U-boats and aeroplanes. Right, in a cradle snatched from the deep this tiny survivor of German brutality is brought ashore at a northern port by a leading stoker from H.M.S. Hurricane.

Photos, British Official : Crown Copyright ; Associated Press, Topical, and J. Hall

Picturesque Guardian of the Iraq Frontier

AN ARAB LEGIONARY is here on sentry duty at an R.A.F. aerodrome in Transjordan. The R.A.F. stations on the Iraq-Transjordan frontier are guarded to a large extent by the famous Arab Legion of the Emir of Transjordan. Safeguarding the Empire's interests in Transjordan are three remarkable forces—the Arab Legion, the Transjordan Frontier Force and the Desert Patrol. These forces are composed mainly of Arabs under the command of British officers, one of the most celebrated of whom is Major John Bagot Glubb (see p. 562), a mystery man of the desert who has the popular reputation of a second "Lawrence of Arabia."

Photo. British Official : Crown Copyright

Exit 'Sawdust Caesar' from East Africa

British tank removing Mussolini's symbol of Fascism at Kismayu, Italian Somaliland. All over North and East Africa the Italian tyrant erected these signs of his perverted power. They are being " mopped up " in the so-called year **XIX** of the sinister Machiavellian system of Fascism.

WITH the surrender of the Duke of Aosta at Amba Alagi on May 20 the conquest of Abyssinia by British and native soldiers is an accomplished fact. Looking at the campaign as a whole we can see how the enemy, attacked from Kenya in the south, from Mogadishu in the east, from Asmara in the north, and from Sudan in the west, were skilfully hemmed in. The British forces, under Lt.-General A. G. Cunningham and Lt.-General William Platt, carried out an ingenious plan with great courage and fortitude. The longest distance covered was 1,500 miles of most difficult terrain against an army ably commanded by the Duke of Aosta. The Italian position in East Africa, cut off from its home base, was by reason of our sea-power an unenviable one. Over 18,000 prisoners were captured in this area. *Photos, British Official : Crown Copyright ; and E.N.A.*

AMBA ALAGI lies east of the Eritrean border, not far from Magdala, and this photograph gives a good idea of the harsh, rocky terrain. On the left, members of the Transvaal Regiment, the first to enter Addis Ababa, in happy fighting fettle celebrate their victory with cheers and laughter.

Germans Say: 'The Drive on Suez Has Begun'

The Nazi "Drang nach Osten," which began in the Balkans, has developed into a German bid for control of the Suez Canal and the oil of Iraq. The Nazis decided to strike through Syria, but first they must drive the Allies from the important base of Crete. With the landing of German planes in Syria and the attack on Crete, Germany announced: "the drive on Suez has begun."

To avoid an attack upon Turkey, Syria is a necessary stepping-stone in Hitler's march to the Middle East, and reports that the Vichy representatives there had been helping the Germans were officially confirmed by Mr. Eden on May 15. Replying to a question in the House of Commons, he said: "Detailed information at the disposal of His Majesty's Government shows that the French authorities in Syria are allowing German aircraft to use Syrian aerodromes as staging posts for flights to Iraq. His Majesty's Government have in consequence given full authority for action to be taken against these German aircraft on Syrian aerodromes. The French Government cannot escape responsibility for this situation. Their action under German orders in permitting these flights is a clear breach of the Armistice terms and is inconsistent with undertakings given by the French Government."

For once Britain acted swiftly. The next day's official communiqué from the Middle East announced that the R.A.F. had successfully attacked German planes on the Syrian aerodromes at Damascus, Rayak, east of Beirut, and Palmyra, on the Tripoli-Iraq pipe-line. As might have been expected, General Dentz, the French High Commissioner of Syria, protested vehemently over the Beirut radio

Major-Gen. B. C. Freyberg, V.C., in command of the British, New Zealand and Greek forces in Crete, which was attacked by the Nazis on May 20. *Photo, Planet News*

against what he called "flagrant acts of hostility against France." But, as M. Maurice Dejean, head of the political and diplomatic services at the De Gaulle headquarters, rightly pointed out, General Dentz is only "another of these 'good Frenchmen' who show themselves 'good Frenchmen' by blindly obeying Marshal Pétain's orders." M. Dejean said that General Dentz was just an ordinary general who got quick promotion and failed to do much during the early part of the war. "His most brilliant feat," he added, "was when, as General in command of the Paris garrison, he handed the city to the Germans and afterwards went to have dinner—with champagne—with the German General in command of the troops of occupation."

According to reports from Damascus a large number of German bombers had landed at Damascus aerodrome and several transport planes at Rayak, while Nazi tanks and other war material were being moved across the country towards Iraq. But though it was difficult to prevent air-borne troops and material from being landed in Syria from German-occupied Greece, the Navy immediately took steps to see that Nazi reinforcements should not reach that country by sea, and new minefields were laid as far as Turkish territorial waters.

A further violent attack on the British was made by General Dentz on May 19, in which he declared, "we are prepared to meet force by force." This was countered by a vigorous appeal by General Catroux, High Commissioner for Free France in the Middle East, to all French soldiers in Syria, not to be deluded by the specious arguments of the Vichy government nor to associate themselves with a policy of premeditated treason which would cause their name to be reviled.

General de Gaulle likewise made a stirring speech from the radio station at Brazzaville, in the course of which he said: "Free Frenchmen have found the means of reforming an army, a fleet and a fighting air force, and all is not lost for a nation so long as its flag still flies over the battlefield. To all Frenchmen I declare that their duty consists in opposing those traitors who would hand over the Empire after having handed over the Motherland. In all parts of our invaded Empire Frenchmen can and should take up arms against the enemy and against every act of treason." Propaganda leaflets were dropped in large quantities by R.A.F. and Free French planes over Syria, from

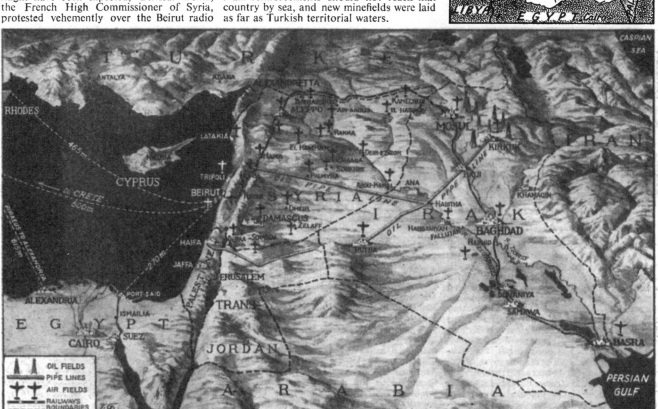

SYRIA AND IRAQ, the German objectives in the Middle East. The French having connived at Nazi plans, the R.A.F. have been striking hard at the Syrian aerodromes now being used by the Germans. The diagram indicates the number and importance of these airfields, and the relative positions of Alexandria, Suez, Baghdad and Basra. Oil-fields and pipe-lines are also shown. The small map illustrates the vital strategic position of Crete in these operations. Hence the desperate efforts of the enemy to possess themselves of the island by throwing all possible resources into the fight with complete disregard for losses. The Allied forces resisting the invasion have received invaluable help from the sturdy Cretan villagers.

The 'Drang nach Osten' is Now Under Way

MAJOR J. B. GLUBB, commander of Arab forces in Transjordan, the Berlin report of whose death has been authoritatively denied, is a 44-year-old Cornishman who carries on the "Lawrence" tradition. *Photo, Planet News*

whence it has been reported that many of the rank and file of the French army are disgusted at the continual truckling to German demands.

Meanwhile, in Iraq itself the besieged garrison at Habbaniyah received fresh reinforcements by air, including men of several famous units of the Indian Army,

aerodrome, was captured without casualties by British forces on May 19. The importance of Fallujah lies in the fact that it controls the crossing of the Euphrates to Habbaniyah, and opens the road to Baghdad.

This occupation was not left uncontested. A counter-attack by Iraqi rebels with infantry and tanks drove back our outposts and penetrated the town, but after heavy

From the cartoon by Illingworth by courtesy of the "Daily Mail"

Minister, stating that he believed the only course open to the Arab nations was to support Great Britain.

One factor which interfered with German plans for sending a full expedition to Syria was the occupation by Allied forces of the important island bases of Crete and Cyprus. When, therefore, aerial reconnaissance had established the fact that the Nazis were con-

Troop-carrying aircraft, like the plane shown with a guard of Arab legionaries in the foreground, were used to rush reinforcements to the beleaguered garrison at Habbaniyah. These reinforcements included many Indian troops. *Photo, British Official : Crown Copyright*

centrating large bodies of troops in the Salonika area and in the Greek islands in the Aegean, it became clear that an attack on one or both of these islands was imminent.

And so it did not come as any great surprise to learn that an air-borne attack on Crete had been launched on May 20. The attack began early in the morning with an intense bombardment of Suda Bay and aerodromes in the neighbourhood. Following this, parachute troops, carried in troop-carriers and gliders, began to land, their main object apparently being the capture of Maleme, an aerodrome on the Bay of Canea

and the situation there, as at Basra, continued calm, the former besiegers remaining for the time being on the defensive, hoping for the arrival of German reinforcements. At the moment the Nazis can send troops to Iraq only by air, and in order to cooperate successfully with Rashid Ali's army they are bound to rely to a large extent on a large-scale Arab revolt against the British. But, as the "Daily Telegraph" correspondent in Jerusalem has pointed out, one indication of Rashid Ali's failure to rally the whole body of his countrymen behind him is that the Arab tribes of the Euphrates Valley, who in every previous anti-foreign trouble have been among the fiercest participants, have so far shown no signs of joining the movement.

The town of Fallujah, to which Iraqui forces had withdrawn after being ejected from the plateau overlooking Habbaniyah

bombing by the R.A.F. British forces recaptured the position.

Irrefutable evidence in British hands shows that every move by Rashid Ali has been made with the avowed object of betraying the Moslem nations in the Middle East and their British and Indian allies into the hands of the Axis. But the British action in Iraq was strongly defended by the Nizam of Hyderabad, who, in a strongly worded manifesto, said : "I am fully convinced and wish it to be known and realized by all Moslems and others who may be interested in Iraq, that the British Government have no other desire than to maintain the most friendly relations with that kingdom, in the creation of which they took a prominent part." Nor did Rashid Ali obtain the support he had hoped for from Ibn Saud, King of Saudi Arabia, who is said to have rebuffed him in an interview with his Finance

GENERAL DENTZ, High Commissioner in Syria, who raged against the R.A.F. bombing of German aircraft in Syria, handed over Paris to the Germans in 1940. *Photo, E.N.A.*

And in Mesopotamia Britain Fights Once Again

RUTBAH WELLS, IRAQ, from the air, showing the fort and aerodrome in the heart of the desert. It is an important point on the Kirkuk-Haifa pipe-line, and was surrendered to the British forces on May 9.

HABBANIYAH R.A.F. Station, Iraq. The rebels who besieged it have been pushed back several miles and the aerodrome has been in constant use throughout operations. On the left, R.A.F. armoured car, one of a number which raised such a screen of dust on the airfield that a British bomber, repaired quickly at night, was able to get away unseen by hostile artillery shelling the position. Circle, an Iraq pipe-line in a cleft between rocks and boulders.

Photos, E.N.A., Keystone, Charles E. Brown, and British Official: Crown Copyright

After Five Years of Italian Rule the Skirl of S

THIS TRANSVAAL REGIMENT entered Addis Ababa in April 1941, soon after the Italian defenders had left the Abyssinian capital. Advance units of South African troops belonging to General Cunningham's forces covered 700 miles from the south in one month, an operation conspicuous in military history. Notwithstanding the difficult country, destroyed and blocked roads and strong enemy opposition, our men moved at the rate of twenty-five miles a day. Addis Ababa was taken on April 5 without resistance, the Italian Viceroy, the Duke of Aosta, having fled by plane, his army

African Pipes Brings Freedom to Addis Ababa

retreating immediately before the arrival of the South Africans. Prior to the occupation of the city South African pilots made continuous raids on the aerodrome, destroying the Italian air arm in this area and making counter-attacks from the air impossible. On the right of this photograph are typical natives to whom the fortune of war has restored their rightful ruler, the Emperor Haile Selassie. Thus Mussolini's infamous adventure in this Biblical land has come to an inglorious end in five years, and Fascism is swept away. (Other photos of the East African Campaign in p. 560).

THIS IS NOT BRITAIN'S FIGHT ALONE

The American Ambassador's Clarion Call to the Democracies

THE English-Speaking Union was formed in the summer of 1918, just before the last World War came to an end. That was the first year in which all English-speaking peoples united to preserve their common ideals.

It is because of this fact that I am particularly happy to speak to you with Anthony Eden, the Secretary of State for Foreign Affairs. We worked in the pre-war days to preserve the rule of law and social justice among nations. We served in the last War in the Allied Armies. Many of our friends fell in France. There they died, and many are buried, that we and our children might live in a free and peaceful world. But now across the Western Front an invader holds sway, and over the free France of La Fayette and Foch waves the swastika.

The common ideals of the English-speaking peoples of this world are not ideals from which other peoples of the world are excluded. They are ideals which are common to all men and women of this earth who do justice, who love mercy, and who walk humbly with God.

The English-speaking countries of the world are peopled by men and women of diverse nationalities and different religions. Our strength comes from diversity and our freedom is born of tolerance—tolerance of other people's origins, other people's religions, and other people's ideas.

And that is true of England no less than the English-speaking countries oversea. It was in this little island that the Angles, the Saxons, and the Normans learned to live together and call themselves Englishmen. Even the English language is a mixture of diverse tongues, and the book—the Bible—which has had a greater influence on English life and literature than any other is a book translated from tongues never spoken in this island.

In past centuries England, like other English-speaking countries, has offered sanctuary to the oppressed, persecuted, and rejected of other lands. It is, therefore, no accident that, in our own century, among her Prime Ministers have been those of Welsh, Scot, and American descent.

It is probably the crowning virtue of English-speaking countries that they recognize and respect virtue wherever they find it, and are not inclined to beguile themselves with the primitive and barbaric idea that they themselves have a monopoly of it. That is the reason that today the common people of all races and of all religions are hoping and praying, and, wherever given a chance, fighting, for victory for Britain and for the English-speaking countries which are rallying to Britain's aid.

For today the English-speaking peoples are again being drawn together in a struggle to preserve not only their common heritage but the common ideals of civilized men everywhere.

Only this week in London, in the early morning hours of the Sabbath Day, enemy bombs destroyed the House of Commons room of the Parliament and smashed the altar of Westminster Abbey. These two hits seemed to me to symbolize the objectives of the dictator and the pagan. Across the street from the wreckage of these two great historic buildings of State and Church,

Saint-Gaudens's statue of Abraham Lincoln was still standing.

As I looked at the bowed figure of the Great Emancipator and thought of his life, I could not help but remember that he loved God, that he had defined and represented democratic government, and that he hated slavery. And, as an American, I was proud that he was there in all that wreckage as a friend and sentinel of gallant days that have gone by, and a reminder that in this great battle for freedom he waited quietly for support for those things for which he lived and died.

With Machiavellian cunning, totalitarian tyranny has sought to divide and conquer peoples and nations that should stand together. By blackmail and terror, by intrigue and deceit, they have sought to weaken and undermine national unity in these countries whose freedom they would destroy. They have sought to revive and inflame old and discredited class and racial hatreds. They have missed no chance to make bad blood between friendly nations in order to delay and frustrate common action against international banditry and aggression which threaten the freedom of all nations.

But make no mistake. So far the totalitarians have been appallingly successful. Experience has proved that they have a way of keeping their threats and breaking their promises. They have destroyed, one by one, one free nation after another. While a few short years ago these lawless men could have been put down by a few simple police measures, had the

then free nations of the world had the will and wisdom to act together, now the forces and resources of all the remaining free nations of the world must be employed if we are to look forward to a world freed from the domination of fear and force.

For men and women of good will there is only one choice. When dictators conspire together, men and women of good will everywhere must act together.

This is no time for vain regrets or futile recriminations. We have all slept while wicked and evil men plotted destruction. We have all thought that we might save ourselves from the holocaust, and that what happened to far distant countries could never happen to us. We have all tried to make ourselves believe that we are not our brother's keeper. But we now are beginning to realize that we need our brothers as much as our brothers need us.

The freedom-loving, peace-loving peoples of this earth are coming to realize that this is not Britain's fight alone. When clever, cunning dictators are striking with lightning speed at any and every free nation that dares stand in their way, the time has come for democratic nations to prove that while they are free to debate they have the power and the will to act.

On the wise use of the navies of the world may hang the destinies of the free peoples of the world. A kindly Providence at this time of stress and danger has placed at the heads of the two great English-speaking peoples two men whose knowledge of the sea is probably greater than that of any statesmen of any time. The problems that are before them in the defence of their countries are not simple problems but complicated problems.

In the controversy that has arisen in regard to sinkings of goods manufactured in the United States, I hope that the people here and at home realize that a mere statement of the sinkings of ships from America does not tell the whole story. It only proves, as does the successful transport of troops to the Middle East, the protective power of an adequate convoy. Such figures do not show the necessity of selection. They do not disclose what food may have to be taken from the children of Britain to give her soldiers arms. They tell only a small part of the Battle of the Atlantic and of the shipping problem to be faced in the prosecution of the total war. In total war it is total strength that counts.

We are engaged in the greatest struggle in all history to preserve freedom in the modern world. We have made our tasks infinitely more difficult because we failed to do yesterday what we gladly do today. Much that we must do today would not have been necessary had we done enough yesterday. The longer the delay the more protracted will be the war and the greater the sacrifices which will be required for victory.

Let us stop asking ourselves if it is really necessary to do more today. Let us, all of us, ask ourselves what more we can do today, so that we may have less to do and sacrifice tomorrow. If we, all of us, will only not put off for tomorrow what can be done today, victory for freedom will come sooner than we dare to hope.

LINCOLN'S STATUE, which stands in Parliament Square, hard by the Hun-ravaged Houses of Parliament and Westminster Abbey, was alluded to by Mr. Winant in his address to the English-speaking Union on May 14 in which he made the striking reaffirmation of democratic principles and call to all freedom-loving peoples to unite in their defence quoted in this page. "As I looked at the bowed figure of the great emancipator," he said, "I could not help but remember that he loved God, that he had defined and represented democratic government and that he hated slavery." **This photograph was taken after the destruction of the House of Commons.** *Photo,* THE WAR ILLUSTRATED

They Have Won Honours in Freedom's Cause

Paymaster Captain P. S. Stuckland, C.B.E., for services rendered in the Country's cause.

Lieut. Valling, R.N.R., D.S.C., for gallantry shown in the execution of his duties.

Capt. Fraser, R.N., O.B.E., for conspicuous services rendered in the Country's cause.

Chief Engineer J. W. Coulthard, R.N., D.S.C., for bravery during the evacuation from Dunkirk.

Skipper Lieutenant Inglis, R.N.R., M.B.E., for services rendered while on active service.

Petty Officer Flattery, D.C.M., for gallant conduct and devotion to duty while on active service.

Sqdn. - Ldr. Barrie Heath, D.F.C., won his award fighting Nazis in a Spitfire paid for by his father.

Flight-Lt. J. C. Dundas, D.F.C. and bar, accounted for at least 13 Nazis, including the German ace Major Wieck.

Flight-Lt. R. M. B. Duke Woolley, D.F.C., for destroying at least three enemy aircraft and damaging several more.

Flight-Sgt. Eric Smith, D.F.M., for displaying great gallantry and devotion to duty in the execution of his air duties.

Flight-Lt. W. W. Campbell, D.F.C., for brilliant bombing successes which included sinking two Italian submarines.

Flying Officer W. D. Brown, D.F.C., for his outstanding performance in raids on the Gneisenau and Scharnhorst at Brest.

Nurse Ruby Rosser, G.M., for shielding and remaining with a helpless patient in a bombed and collapsing hospital.

Miss Sharnaud, D.B.E., for services rendered in connexion with the Women's Voluntary Services for Civil Defence.

Lady Reading, Chairman of the W.V.S., **D.B.E.,** for services rendered in connexion with the Women's Voluntary Services.

Miss Fenno, D.B.E., for services rendered in connexion with the Women's Voluntary Services for Civil Defence.

Senr.Asst. Nurse Aileen Turner, G.M., for rescuing patients and carrying them to the window of a ward as the floor collapsed.

Staff Nurse Mary Fleming, G.M., for the same gallant action as her colleague, Nurse Turner, whom she helped.

David Lazarus, Home Guard, G.M., for rescuing flat dwellers in a demolished tenement until a wall collapsed and buried him. He is only 17.

Albert Bailey, Home Guard, G.M., for risking his life in helping to save eleven people from a badly bombed factory at Birmingham

Miss P. Baxter, A.F.S., M.B.E., for heroic conduct during a night raid on Portsmouth, assisting trapped people and cutting off escaping gas.

Miss H. Taylor, A.F.S., M.B.E., for heroic conduct during a heavy night raid on Portsmouth, together with Miss. Baxter and Miss Whitcher.

Miss M. Whitcher, A.F.S., M.B.E., for heroic conduct during raid on Portsmouth. These three girls helped remove lorries and put out incendiaries.

Mr. D. Moseley, East Ham A.R.P. Warden, **M.B.E.,** for devotion to duty during heavy air attacks, rescuing people and extinguishing fires.

Ambulance-Driver B. Matthewman, G.M., for courage and devotion to duty in driving through fierce air raids with casualties.

Mr. Ernest Biggs, A.R.P. worker, **O.B.E.,** for gallantry and devotion to duty during a fierce raid which took place at Southampton.

Mr. E. C. Channing, A.R.P. Warden, **M.B.E.,** for rescue work though wounded in the foot and handicapped by an artificial arm.

Mrs. Gwendolyn Park, A.R.P. Warden, **M.B.E.,** for rescue work. She bandaged Mr. Channing's wound and together they freed a woman and baby.

John Thomas Cain, G.M., for helping to save people trapped under a blazing factory. This Hackney costermonger is only 15.

Attendant G. Goshwark, Greenwich Aux. Ambulance Service, **G.M.,** for coolness and courage in accompanying Driver Matthewman (left).

Lt.-Com. Jan Van Olm, Royal Dutch Naval Air Service, **O.B.E.,** for rescuing a flying unit from Holland and France.

Sergeant Ligoticky, Czech pilot, **Czechoslovak War Cross and Medal,** for destroying German planes at night.

Officer Air-Gunner Morian Hansen, R.A.F., D.F.C. Mr. Hansen was a popular Danish speedway rider before the war.

Count Czernin, R.A.F., D.F.C. for gallant conduct. Count Czernin is a Czechoslovakian serving with the R.A.F.

Sergeant Krat, Czech pilot, **Czechoslovak War Cross,** for shooting down a Nazi plane during a night raid on London

Flt.-Lieut. G. Jankiewicz, Polish pilot, **Polish Military Cross** (twice) for gallant conduct during air operations

Our Diary of the War

SUNDAY, MAY 18, 1941   *624th day*

Air.—Heavy bombing attacks made on Kiel, Emden and Cherbourg.

Africa.—Duke of Aosta accepted British terms of surrender.

British aircraft damaged convoy of enemy tanks between Capuzzo and Halfaya. Three Junkers shot down over Tobruk. Heavy night raid on Benghazi.

Near East.—R.A.F. bombed Syrian aerodromes, including Palmyra, Damascus and Rayak. Heavy night raids on German-occupied aerodromes in Greece.

Iraq.—Garrison at Habbaniyah reinforced. R.A.F. raided Rashid aerodrome.

Home.—Slight enemy activity round coastal regions. During night bombs fell at two points in south-west. One day and two night raiders destroyed.

General.—Duke of Spoleto designated King of Croatia by King of Italy.

MONDAY, MAY 19   *625th day*

Sea.—Reported that Egyptian liner Zamzam, carrying full unit of British-American Ambulance Corps, had been sunk in S. Atlantic.

Africa.—Formal surrender of Duke of Aosta's forces at Amba Alagi.

Stated that British still hold Sollum, but Germans had recaptured Capuzzo.

Near East.—Enemy aircraft made sustained attacks on aerodromes in Crete. Hospital at Canea bombed and machine-gunned.

R.A.F. attacked Palmyra aerodrome.

Iraq.—Falluja, east of Habbaniyah, occupied by British.

Home.—Enemy activity mainly over south-east and south coasts. Five Messerschmitts destroyed over Channel. Heinkel shot down by four trawlers off east coast.

TUESDAY, MAY 20   *626th day*

Sea.—Stated that survivors of Egyptian liner Zamzam had been landed at St. Jean de Luz.

Admiralty announced that naval auxiliary Camito had been sunk.

Africa.—Duke of Aosta and staff made personal surrender. Torrential rains delaying operations in southern Abyssinia.

Near East.—German parachutists and airborne troops, numbering 1,500, landed before dawn in Canea-Maleka area of Crete, but met with strong resistance. In afternoon 3,000 more air-borne troops dropped in Suda Bay and Heraklion (Candia) areas.

R.A.F. heavily bombed aerodromes in Greece, and at Palmyra and Damascus in Syria. Five enemy raids on Malta.

Iraq.—Rashid aerodrome heavily raided. German aircraft attacked Habbaniyah.

Home.—Very slight enemy activity during day. At night raiders were reported over South Wales and East Anglia.

General.—Announced that Iceland has severed union with Denmark.

WEDNESDAY, MAY 21   *627th day*

Air.—British bombers made surprise attack on Heligoland. Another force raided power-station and oil refinery near Béthune.

Africa.—During night of 20-21 advanced mechanized troops destroyed enemy post on Sollum hill. Benghazi raided during night.

In battle of the Lakes, two enemy divisions now trapped between forces advancing from north and south. Italian counter-attack repulsed with heavy loss. Farther south Italian brigade H.Q. and three colonial battalions captured.

Near East.—Situation in Crete reported to be well in hand. Landings of air-borne troops

continued. Enemy occupied aerodrome at Maleme. Attempts at sea-borne landings frustrated by Navy. Large German convoy sunk.

Iraq.—Round-up of rebels in Faliuja area proceeding.

Home.—Some activity by enemy aircraft in coastal areas.

THURSDAY, MAY 22   *628th day*

Sea.—Auxiliary vessel Queenworth reported sunk.

Africa.—Benghazi raided during night.

Near East.—Further German landings and bomber attacks in Crete. Enemy driven out of Heraklion (Candia) and Retimo after hand-to-hand fighting. Counter-attack at Maleme.

Iraq.—Rebel forces attacked Falluja, but after heavy bombing British retook the town.

Home.—Few single enemy aircraft dropped bombs in Sussex and elsewhere. Two raiders shot down.

FRIDAY, MAY 23   *629th day*

Sea.—Admiralty announced that British submarine had sunk troopship, tanker, Italian destroyer and other ships off Libya.

Air.—Vigorous night attack on Cologne and on aerodromes and ports in occupied territory.

Africa.—Capture of Gelute, Soddu and Uondo, Abyssinia, reported.

Near East.—R.A.F. caused extensive damage to aircraft and troops at Maleme, Crete. Germans continued efforts to reinforce troops on island. Paratroops being mopped up.

Home.—Few bombs fell during day near coast.

THE PASSING OF QUEEN'S HALL will be felt as a personal blow by many thousands of music-lovers, and especially by those who, year after year, were faithful attendants of the popular seasons of promenade concerts for so long conducted by Sir Henry Wood. The Queen's Hall was opened in 1893 and consisted of two halls, the larger of which had accommodation for more than 3,000. Although the London Philharmonic Orchestra lost all its instruments when the Hall was bombed by the Nazis, thanks to the generosity of the music-loving public they were at once replaced by private gifts and loans from all over the country.

Photo, Fox

Here Lie the Bells that Bred a Nursery Rhyme

THE BELLS OF ST. CLEMENT'S may yet ring again, for of its twelve bells made famous in the nursery rhyme " Oranges and Lemons " only two were badly cracked when St. Clement Danes Church was destroyed by Nazi raiders. Of Wren's church, however, nothing now is left but the fire-scorched walls and tower. The remains of the works of the clock and carillon are seen on the right of the photograph. Among the irreplaceable treasures of this church, where Dr. Johnson regularly attended service, was the pulpit carved by Grinling Gibbons.   *Photo, Sport & General*

The Home Guard's First Birthday

On May 14, 1941, the Home Guard was one year old. How a great army of enthusiastic
but untrained and ill-equipped volunteers was transformed into a formidable defence
force within a twelvemonth is here briefly outlined by J. R. Fawcett Thompson, himself
among the first L.D.V.s

"WE are going to ask you to help us. . . .
We want large numbers of men in
Great Britain, between the ages of
17 and 65, to come forward now. . . . The
name of the new force which is to be raised
is the Local Defence Volunteers. . . . Here,
then, is the opportunity for which so many
of you have been waiting. Your loyal help . . .
will make and keep our country safe."

Opportunity had no need to knock a
second time. Scarcely had the voice of Mr.
Eden, newly appointed War Minister, faded
from countless loudspeakers when thousands
of those " men between the ages of 17 and
65 " were out of their homes making hotfoot
for the nearest police station through that
evening of May 14, 1940. No broadcast
appeal can surely have had a greater response
for, as if by magic, a force of 250,000 eager
volunteers was at once enrolled.

The size of the new citizen army was,
perhaps, its greatest embarrassment, and the
capacity for improvization of even the
average Briton was severely tried in rapidly
organizing such a huge number of men for
immediate action. But it was done, and done
quickly, for within a week local patrols were
out all over the country carrying out their
primary function of " watching, observing,
reporting and guarding."

Paramount a m o n g the
reasons which prompted the
Government to establish the
Local Defence Volunteers was
the vital necessity for combating the possible activities of
enemy parachute troops in the
event of invasion. The conquest of Norway and, to a far
greater extent, the lightning
overthrow of Holland were
object-lessons in the destruction, confusion and general
demoralization that could be
caused by the skilful use of
this new form of warfare.

So it was that the early
L.D.V.s earned their nickname
of " Parashots." All through
the wonderful summer months
of 1940, at dusk, at dawn and
in the dark hours of the night
they were ever on the lookout
for the invader from the skies.
From stout cudgels and shot-
guns their weapons at long last
progressed to rifles and bombs
—civilian clothes and armlets
slowly gave place to denim
overalls—the clumsiness of
inexperience was succeeded by
the expertness born of keen
and organized training.

On June 20 Gen. H. R. Pownall, an able
soldier, was appointed Inspector-General of
the new force, proof that the War Office was
taking a lively interest in its protege. Then
in August, at the instigation of the Prime
Minister, it became known as the Home
Guard—a change of title which found ready
welcome among the volunteers themselves.
By now the total strength had swollen to
1,500,000—a truly amazing vindication of
the voluntary system of recruiting.

The days of extempore planning had gone
by and the placing of the whole organization
on an established basis was obviously an
urgent need. The good offices of the Territorial Army Association were enlisted, and
the definite military status of the Home Guard
was made officially manifest when on September 11 Mr. Churchill told the House of
Commons : " We have more than one and a
half million men of the Home Guard, who
are just as much soldiers of the regular army
in status as the Grenadier Guards, and who
are determined to fight for every inch of the
ground in every village and in every street."

Since the Battle of France the crucial
importance of " defence in depth " had at
last been realized. How better could such
defence be effected than by utilizing the
inter-connected network of Home Guard
units covering the whole of
Great Britain ? The defence,
in fact. of each locality by the
men who knew it best.

So, as autumn passed in
to winter, the training policy
of the Home Guard developed
on these lines. The issue of
American automatic rifles
greatly strengthened the fire-
power of sections and platoons
throughout the country, while

intensive courses of field training at such
schools as Osterley Park and its successors
under War Office supervision imparted the
principles and practice of modern warfare to
over 2,600 men who were able to attend.

By the close of 1940 the Home Guard
had acquired an admirable Director-General
in Maj.-Gen. T. R. Eastwood, its leaders were
scheduled to receive the King's commission,
and its personnel, now in regulation serge
battle-dress, constituted 1,200 battalions,
5,000 companies (or 25,000 platoons). During
the heavy and constant air raids of this
period, also, certain units found further
valuable scope for their activities in giving
assistance to civil defence. Especially helpful
was their cooperation with the police, and
in one London borough it was generously
said of the local unit that it worked so well
with the police that the two forces were
well-nigh interchangeable. While carrying
out their work under fire many Home
Guards showed such courage and devotion
to duty that they were honoured by H.M.
the King.

A feature worthy of record was the formation of their own units by various Government Departments and Public Utility con-
cerns such as the Ministry of Information,
the G.P.O., the L.P.T.B. and the railway
groups, each being trained to fulfil the
specialized needs of its respective organization. In certain areas, also, such as the
moors and river reaches, the Home Guard
met local conditions by maintaining mounted
and water-borne patrols.

It is now generally held that the bulk of
future recruits must be looked for among
lads of 17. One of the latest and most
interesting developments, therefore, was the
scheme for affiliating 25,000 members of the
Cadet Force to the Home Guard. Each
cadet unit is to have a " godfather " in it
local Home Guard, and the hope has been
expressed that every cadet on reaching his
17th birthday will make a point of honour
of joining his parent force.

And so, by May 14, 1941, the Home
Guard attained its first birthday without
having come to that close grip with the
enemy for which it had trained so hard and
eagerly. Now being armed with tommy
guns and new anti-tank weapons in increasing
numbers, and beginning to feel immense
confidence in its cooperation with the Field
Army, each unit of this great citizen army
might be likened to " a small active but
fierce dog on a reasonably long chain " only
waiting for the robber to pluck up courage
to come within its reach. It may be that he
never will, and if so the Home Guard has
largely its own enthusiasm and efficiency to
thank for the disappointment.

YOUTH AND AGE work hand-in-hand in the Home Guard.
Here two village stalwarts inspect their makeshift weapons
in the early days, while above, a youngster goes through
special training with the latest type of tommy gun.

Photos, Keystone

From Village Patrol To Palace Guard

Special Home Guard Patrols in outboard motor-boats armed with Lewis guns aid in protecting Britain's waterways.

Camouflage was an important feature of the intensive training courses given at the Osterley Park School, Middlesex.

BUCKINGHAM PALACE GUARD DUTY was the signal honour granted the Home Guard on the occasion of its first birthday, on May 14, 1941. A fruitful source of new recruits will soon be furnished by 25,000 members of Cadet Force units now to be affiliated to their local Home Guard : some of these lads are seen receiving machine-gun instruction in the centre oval. In large areas such as Exmoor, where foot patrols are impracticable, mounted Home Guards keep watch and ward over the countryside.

Photos, British Official : Crown Copyright ; P.N.A., Fox

New U.S. Eagles for Our Embattled Skies

NEW AIRCRAFT IN SERVICE WITH THE R.A.F.

Name	Type	Engines and Speed	Armament
BRITISH FIGHTERS AND BOMBERS			
Hawker **Typhoon**	Fighter, s.s.	Napier Sabre 2,400 h.p. ; over 400 m.p.h.	Cannon and m.g.
Hawker **Tornado**	Fighter, s.s.	Rolls Royce Vulture : over 2,000 h.p. ; 425 m.p.h. Two engines.	Eight m.g. and three 20-mm. cannon
Westland **Whirlwind**	Fighter	—	—
Bristol **Beaufighter**	Fighter (long range ; night)	Two engines	Very heavy
Short **Stirling**	Heavy Bomber	Four engines	—
Avro **Manchester**	Heavy Bomber	Two engines	—
Halifax	Heavy Bomber	—	—
RECENT AMERICAN AIRCRAFT			
Curtiss **Tomahawk**	Fighter, s.s.	Allison 1,100 h.p. ; 360 m.p.h.	Two ·5 m.g. and four rifle-calib. m.g.
North Amer **Mustang**	Fighter, s.s.	Allison 1,100 h.p. ; 400 m.p.h.	—
Grumman **Martlet (2)**	Fighter, s.s. (F.A.A.)	Wright Cyclone 1,200 h.p. ; 350 m.p.h.	Two m.g. in wings and four in fuselage
Brewster **Buffalo**	Fighter, s.s.	Wright Cyclone 1,200 h.p. ; 330 m.p.h.	Two ·5 m.g. in fus. and two ·303 m.g. in wings
Vultee **Vengeance**	Fighter	1 engine ; 350 m.p.h.	—
Havoc (3) (D.B. 7)	Fighter (night interceptor)	A " fighter version " of Douglas Boston bomber (see below); 380 m.p.h.	Four fixed m.g. in nose
Martin **Maryland**	Medium Bomber	2 Pratt & Whitney 1,050 h.p. Twin Wasps ; 305 m.p.h.	Four fixed and two free m.g.
Douglas **Boston**	Med. Bomber and Night Fighter	2 P. & W. 1,050 h.p. Twin Wasps or 2 1,600 h.p. Wright Dble.-row Cyclones; 320 or 370 m.p.h.	Four fixed and two free m.g.
Consolidated **Liberator**	Bomber	4 P. & W. 1,200 h.p. Twin Wasps ; 320 m.p.h.	Turrets in nose, tail and fuselage
Consolidated **Catalina (1)**	Flying Boat	2 P. & W. 1,200 h.p. Twin Wasps ; 199 m.p.h.	Turrets in nose ; gun blisters in hull

Note. The above statements are official. Items omitted are on secret list. An American aeronautical writer has given his impressions of some of Britain's new aircraft which are neither confirmed nor denied by the Air Ministry.
Tornado. 400 said to be ready for service early in 1941.
Whirlwind. Said to have power-operated gun turret, Rolls-Royce Merlin engines giving just over 400 m.p.h.
Stirling. Based on Transatlantic liner designed before war ; stated to weigh about 31 tons.
Manchester. Said to have speed of about 325 m.p.h. and to weigh about 13½ tons.

Nos. in brackets (1, 2, 3) refer to illustrations

Photos, British Official : Crown Copyright ; and Central Press

I Was There! .... Eye Witness Stories of the War

Our Pilots Fought in London's Heaviest Blitz

May 10—the night of one of London's severest air raids—was a record night for R.A.F. night fighters, who shot down no fewer than 29 bombers. The following account of the night's operations was broadcast by a Flight-Lieutenant on duty at a fighter station.

REPORTS began to come in of enemy bombers streaming towards London. In the distance bursting anti-aircraft shells showed that some of them had arrived already. Grim-looking night fighters taxied into position and took off at a signal from the duty pilot. Up they went and in a few moments they were lost to sight.

I was standing just outside the Watch Office when suddenly someone shouted " There goes the first," and I saw a flame in the distance diving to earth. For a moment the horizon was lit up by a great flash when it hit the ground.

Presently the first of the night fighters returned. A tousle-headed pilot came into the Intelligence Officer's room rubbing his hands to get them warm. He told his story in short jerky sentences. " I saw a dark shape—in front. I gave him several squirts with my gun. He went down in a steep dive ; I followed. All the time I kept pumping more bullets. I definitely filled that Hun full of holes, but he got away in the end. He went down so low I nearly hit a tree trying to keep on his tail, and he disappeared at nought feet." The Intelligence Officer decided that this one could be claimed only as " damaged."

Meanwhile the Interrogation Officer, whose job it is to question any Germans who land safely, was phoning round to find out where the one we had seen had come down.

After a while more of the night fighters glided in to land, and the crews followed one another in to make their reports. There were so many of them that three Intelligence Officers were hard at work taking down what they had to say. One had had two combats. In the first he had seen his bullets strike home and the enemy aircraft go in a steep dive. He was not sure about that one. Bits had fallen off the second bomber just before it went down, nearly vertically, but the Intelligence Officer only credited them as two " damaged " for the time being.

By this time the phones in the Intelligence Office were ringing almost without stopping. " This is the police station at So-and-so.

We have a German here." " This is H.Q. The score for the night so far is 7." " This is the Observer Corps. There is one down at So-and-so."

Then the tousle-headed pilot came in again, after a second patrol. He was told that the one down probably *was* his. The time and place where it crashed seemed to agree with his report. Then a squadron-leader came in reporting one definitely destroyed. " Just outside London a raider flew right in front of me," he said. " I gave him a long burst and he went down—straight down in flames."

H.Q. came on the telephone again. A voice reported that the score was now 15. Then another pilot, a flight-lieutenant this time, came in. He had got one. It had dived into the sea with both engines blazing. In the squadron hut a swastika was chalked up against his name on the blackboard.

Another flight-lieutenant, with the purple and white ribbon of the D.F.C. showing beneath his open flying-jacket, reported shooting at a raider south of London, and seeing it go straight down. Like the others who could not say definitely that the machine they attacked was destroyed, he was credited with one " damaged.". His hopes rose a few moments later when the H.Q. Intelligence Officer phoned to say there was one down which was probably his.

With the first streaks of dawn the last of the night fighters came back, including two crews who had been over enemy aerodromes trying to catch the raiders returning home.

An empty shell, all that is left of the famous church of St. Clement Danes after a recent raid. This was the third time that the church had been bombed. See also page 569.
Photo, Planet News

One of them, a tall fair-haired pilot in a heavy flying suit, got a Dornier 17. It was his second victory over France in a few days. " I followed him in to land," he said, " and nearly hit the ground doing it."

And to put the final touch to the night, the Interrogation Officer came back very pleased with himself. He had been speaking to the pilot of the German plane that everyone saw coming down in flames. The Ack-Ack gunners had been claiming this, but the German himself says that he was shot down by fighters. So that's another one to some pilot.

And so we went to breakfast with the station score at four destroyed and the tousle-headed pilot still allowed only one " damaged."

We Had a Little League of Nations in My Boat

Civilians, as well as the Empire forces, had adventurous escapes from Greece during the German advance. Among them was an acting British Consul, who sailed a small motor fishing-boat through the islands by night for six days. His story is told below.

THE acting consul, who served under Lawrence of Arabia in the last war, said that he had made a hobby of sailing round the Peloponnesus in peace-time and had become familiar with the innumerable beaches and coves where one could lay up a small boat. He continued :

" I had a nice little 25-ton Diesel engine fishing-boat, and I determined to gather together as many British subjects as I could.

" At dawn on Tuesday, April 22, we slipped out of a cove near Patras, having taken on board the remaining British subjects in Patras—three men and three women. We got early through the boom at Cape Araxas, and laid up at the little island of Oxia.

" It was my plan to spend each day hiding in coves providing good cover, and sailing only by night, since with the German bombers increasing in numbers and flying over continuously by day I had no hope of escaping their attentions except in the dark.

" On Tuesday night we ran from Oxia to Zante. Throughout Wednesday German bombers flew over the island, and in default of fighter opposition came down very low.

" We hid in the woods, wondering how long it would be before they spotted us. Nevertheless, we picnicked quite pleasantly —I had laid in plenty of tinned food—and in the evening stole down for a bathe.

" As soon as darkness fell we set off on the long run to Navarino. This took 12 hours, the last stretch being done by daylight.

" I picked up about a dozen people in Navarino Bay, but was told our Consul and several other British civilians were at

SPIRITUAL AND TEMPORAL JUSTICE were both involved in the heavy damage of the great raid on London. On the left, a view through the cloisters of Westminster Abbey ; right, the effect of a direct hit on the Old Bailey perfectly symbolizes the Hun attitude to the ideal of justice.
Photos, Planet News and Topical

I WAS THERE!

Kalamata, and I determined to drive there, though it was a poor road. I wasted half an hour bargaining for a car, but when it was obtained my driver certainly went fast. Before we were half-way to Kalamata I was more scared of him than of the Germans."

The consul went on to describe how he had arrived at Kalamata to find a considerable number of civilians there, as well as some Australian soldiers cut off from their units. Finally he drove back to Navarino with a mixed bag of 35, including the president of the Dodecanese Society.

From Navarino the craft made Iteolimani,

a tiny island near Cape Matapan, and from there they went to Anticythera, more than half-way to Crete. By this time German parachutists had already landed in Cythera. He concluded :

"On Sunday morning my little fishing-boat Hagias Trias—Holy Trinity—sailed into port at Suda Bay, in Crete, flying the consular flag. I had brought my boat through undamaged and, starting with six passengers, I had finished with 65 without loss of life. They were British, Greek, Australian and Yugoslav—a little League of Nations, in fact."—*Daily Telegraph.*"

We Were Lucky to Escape British Night Fighters

Evidence of the wholesome dread which British night fighters inspire in German bomber crews was afforded in broadcasts by German airmen during the first weeks of May, when the fighters achieved record successes.

A GERMAN bomb-aimer, in a talk on the German radio describing the great raid on London of May 10, betrayed some of his fears of the British night fighter. This is what he said :

"Where are the searchlights ? " we all asked when approaching London. Everything looked so gloomy, it was so deadly quiet. Our leader said : " No gun-fire. There must be night fighters somewhere."

We saw the Thames like a sparkling ribbon in the moonlight. No anti-aircraft fire. We are puzzled.

As we found our targets I pressed the button and the bombs started raining down. In a short time the whole area in the Thames was a sea of flames. We could recognize St. Paul's. There was still no defence. We flew on and returned to London from the north to have another look.

All of a sudden there was a cry, " Night fighters ! " and then we got it, but we escaped our pursuer, although we were hit.

Never mind. The main thing is we left London burning as never before.

The crew of another Nazi bomber were less jubilant over the destruction wrought in London. One of them said over the radio :

Suddenly somebody shouted, " Night

fighter, night fighter ! " Scarcely had we heard the cry when there was a violent splutter of bullets into the body of our plane. Another one. . . . A third . . .

In the next second we went down . . . down . . . and no one could make out what was above and what below. The pilot made frantic efforts to level us out, and succeeded at last. Nobody had any more interest in the fires down in London. For us it was to get away as quickly as possible and not to be caught again after our lucky escape.

A German airman broadcasting from Berlin on May 8 also described an encounter with a night fighter. He said :

We were over the North Sea when suddenly our radio operator shouted, " Night fighter ! " It was one of their new, very fast fighters.

We had hardly grasped the meaning of his words when a hail of bullets was pumped into our kite. Indescribable chaos surrounded us immediately. We were blinded by tracer bullets and deafened by the whistle of projectiles.

Our pilot tried an evasive manoeuvre, but time and again, with astounding courage and insistence, the excellent enemy pilot pumped more and more lead into us.

Six times he attacked us from below, but never allowed his machine to come within the range of our guns.

The bomb-aimer was wounded, and lay motionless near his sight. Our pilot attempted once more to shake off the British attacker, diving almost to sea-level . . . and at last succeeded. But one of our motors was out of action.

Still, we were now left undisturbed. We jettisoned our bombs, and flew home.

We had great difficulty in dressing the wounds of our comrade in the darkness, but we managed to make a successful landing, and soon our comrade was transferred to hospital.

Later we counted the hits which our machine had sustained. We found no fewer than 107 holes.

TRAIN OF BOMBS, on which the German ground staff rides astride, being brought up for the bomb racks of a German bomber which awaits its deadly load at an airfield in Northern France. Though heavy night raids by German bombers have inevitably resulted in considerable damage to property, the air defences of this country have improved to such an extent that the German Luftwaffe is suffering steadily increasing losses. How little the German airmen like facing our night fighters is shown by the excerpts from their broadcasts quoted in this page.   *Photo, Keystone*

▬▬▬▬▬▬▬▬▬▬▬▬▬▬▬▬▬▬▬▬▬▬ I WAS THERE! ▬▬▬▬▬▬▬▬▬▬▬▬▬▬▬▬▬▬▬▬▬▬

We Girls are Timber Measurers

Among the varied activities of the Women's Land Army, forestry has a place in this war as in the last. This entertaining account of felling and carting timber was written by M. Bicknell, and is published by arrangement with "The Land Girl."

As I write we are sitting in the wood; it is 9.30 a.m. and we are having our "half-past nineses." At the moment we are with a gang of five fellers, and each man is sitting against a tree gnawing a pear or sucking a plum, and they are laughing and chatting in the delightful way Yorkshire people have.

The Scots pine make a beautiful picture with their long, straight red stems and dark blue-green foliage. I love the smell of the pine; I love to hear the wind in the branches —it is like the sea. It is a sad sound, each tree making its tragic fall to the ground; but I remember that without pit-props we can have no coal, and without coal our factories would be silent and munitions could not be made and our armour would not be sufficient to win the war.

This wood has many black swamps and hundreds of thousands of mosquitoes torment us. The men provide us with foul-smelling scent which is supposed to keep them away from us—but, oh dear! just a minute while I scratch, or rather tear, at my legs. I have just been advised by one of the men to scrape my legs with holly, which is recommended to take out the poison!

The fellers are usually paid by the cubic feet they fell, but the method of payment has changed with our unit, and they are paid by the running foot, i.e. for every hundred feet of timber felled and dressed they get 1s. 8d. But much has to be done to a tree before it is ready for the men sawing up pit props. First a "fall" is put in, which is a large chunk chopped from the base of

A large number of the Women's Land Army are now busily at work in the Forest of Dean, and some of them are here seen weighing sawn logs.
Photos, Fox

the tree at the side they wish it to come down. Then they take a piece out all round, so that the tree is "teed up" upon its own base, which is a flat stool, ready for the saw. After the tree has been felled it has to be dressed or brashed out, which means the cutting off of all branches and notches. The brash is piled in long high lines each side of a broad row of felled trees; this is called a "breed," and it is usually between 30 and 40 feet wide. A gang of five men will work with about four or five breeds. This is where the feller's job ends, and the farmer comes with his horses and sniggs out the trees. "Snigg" is a Yorkshire word for dragging the trees out of the wood to the the men who saw them into props. They say "tosh" in Gloucestershire—I suppose each county has its own terms.

Our job, as timber measurers, is to be at work at 7.30 a.m. and measure fallen timber till 9.30 a.m., when we have our "half-past nineses." We begin again at 9.45 and stop at midday, when we have our dinner bags. Then we measure from 12.45 p.m. till 4.30 p.m., when it is "night" and our day's work is over.

Now that the men are paid by the running foot, we only have to measure the length of

LAND ARMY GIRLS "go to it" with a smile. Chopping, trimming and clearing trees, all part of their job when looking after forest land, is no work for weaklings, and these young women, though certainly of the fairer, are by no means of the weaker sex. In this page a woman timber measurer describes some of her experiences.

the trees, and quarter girth 20 per cent of them, i.e. measure the girth of the tree at half its length, so that we can find the average cubic capacity of timber felled.

Measuring hundreds of trees, day after day, is monotonous work, and at first the thought of doing this for the duration seemed

unbearable. Of course, we do have a few sums and plenty of adding up, and after a time we have found ways of adding some variety and interest to the day's work. Sometimes we brash out a tree or two for the men, but more skill is required to put in the fall and tee up the trees ready for the saw, and it is great fun trying to do this. We have not much time for using the axe now, because we have an extra gang felling. Sometimes we have loading to do: pit props are taken to the station in a lorry and loaded into railway trucks. This can be heavy work, but it is good fun riding on top of the load and pitching the props about.

I have also had the job of "snigging." Alas! I had a young 'un, a kicker and a bolter, and she got away while I was behind unfastening the snigging hook. But isn't a bolting cart horse a grand sight! Chains flying, head high, and the lovely sound of her heavy feet beating the moorland turf. Men shouting "stop that horse," and a small timber measurer in pursuit!

Siftings From the News

Eire is negotiating with U.S.A. for purchase of food and arms.

Australian Spitfire Squadron is being formed in Britain.

Colchester saved during February 76 tons of kitchen waste.

From May 1 all clothes of German workers were standardized.

Pan-American Airways have constructed nine 43-ton liners.

Millions of eggs for Britain are being bought in Middle West, U.S.A.

The S.S. (Nazi Black Guards) has appealed for volunteers.

Army deserter returned his uniform to his regiment marked C.O.D.

Canada's war bill for current fiscal year is about £322,000,000.

Sokol, or Slav youth movement, is to have headquarters in London.

U.S. Red Cross aid for Britain totalled £4,000,000 to end of April.

Hitler has instituted a corporation for German crews who scuttle their ships.

Up to April 6 Mediterranean Fleet successfully convoyed 2,750,000 tons of shipping.

R.A.F. fighter pilots now carry small collapsible rubber dinghy underneath parachute.

Soldier cost £600 to kill in Great War; today £12,000 to £18,000.

New British anti-tank weapons penetrated armour of German tanks in Balkans.

U.S. intercoastal lines are to furnish 50 large cargo vessels for U.S.-Red Sea voyages.

Two thousand British pilots annually will undergo preliminary training in U.S.A.

Spitfire presented by Royal Observer Corps destroyed three M.E.'s before succumbing.

Two Swiss ships loaded at Lisbon 71,000 parcels for British prisoners of war.

In first three months of 1941, 2,264 persons were killed on roads throughout Britain.

War Department vehicles were involved in less than 6 per cent of traffic deaths.

Germans use Norwegian prisoners for removal of time bombs dropped by R.A.F.

One ton of vegetables was produced in one year on an allotment 10 yards by 30.

Free Rumanian Legion to fight with Britain is to be formed by London Committee.

New Hampshire, U.S.A., sent three X-ray units to Red Cross for hospitals in Hampshire.

Three thousand enemy officers are now interned in India.

Dutch Indies have contributed 28 bombers and 79 fighters to Allied cause.

Belgian, Dutch and Yugoslav Ministers left Moscow because diplomatic recognition was withdrawn.

German E-boats have reached Mediterranean by descending the Rhône through France.

Ottawa has joined other cities in removing Lindbergh's books from its libraries.

The Editor's Postscript

As I write, not a modern Isaiah, nor a Jeremiah, could make even a remote guess at what will have happened by the time these paragraphs are printed. Not that the Hebrew prophets ever attempted the sort of stuff attributed to Nostradamus (1555) or the trumpery vaticinations of an Old Moore . . . but watch out for the I-told-you-soers ! One of them is alleged to have foretold that a big event would happen on May 10, but he did not know that a small event (his own death by enemy action) was scheduled for the 13th.

The big event was the descent of a beast from the blue. There are some photos of Rudolf Hess, Hitler's bloody-minded associate, that closely resemble a gorilla in the occipital-frontal process. His one unbroken eyebrow spanning his gorilla brow marks the base line of a brain capable of foulness worse than any gorilla's . . . nay, it is a libel on the anthropoid to compare them.

No one episode in any war has ever been so charged with the melodramatic. No incident ever awakened greater world interest : not even Napoleon's escape from Elba. Why this mass murderer is here among us is the subject of wildest speculation. I have no theories to put forward, but I'd rather have him under lock and key in England than at large among his fellow gangsters in Naziland.

That Hess came with any kindly intentions towards us is merely incredible. There can be no change of heart in any of these black-hearted scoundrels. That his is a case of dual personality ·(technically " schizophrenia ") like Dr. Jekyll and Mr. Hyde, as one writer suggests, is not entirely unthinkable, but you are a simpleton if you believe it. And, by the way, Jekyll changed to Hyde by means of a drug, which rather rubs the point off the Marquess of Donegall's " complete explanation of Hess." Possibly his amazing visit was an effort to save his hide . . . he is all Mr. Hyde and nothing of Dr. Jekyll . . . Hitler had " put him on the spot " and he made a bold " get away "—to the one free country in Europe !

Equally—and I should like to think this probable—dissensions among the infamous group of mass murderers may have prompted his flight, hoping, when the eventual showdown of Nazism takes place, that he may be alive to exercise for his own good such influence as remains to him on his black-hearted fellow countrymen. By the time this Postscript is printed my readers will know a great deal more about the Hess episode, which may have grown in importance rather than diminished. It is far more than any nine days' wonder. It may prove one of the major happenings in the War.

It has been suggested to me by a knowledgeable Anti-Nazi German that there may have been some genuine Anti-Comintern urge in Hess's visit. Conceivably his mad Fuehrer is aiming at a Nazi-Soviet military pact which would be hateful to the German Army chiefs, and also to Hess, who may still remain a genuine National Socialist. And as the only outcome of such an alliance would be the bolshevizing of all Europe, the German generals may have induced Hess to head a movement against a mad policy that would eventually obliterate the original aims of Nazism. With Hitler discredited before his people Germany might then be willing to make such terms as would dissolve the Hitler dream of world dominion and within her own domains and certain colonial acquisitions for *lebensraum* settle down to the energetic development of National Socialist ideals. Time will show if this is anything more than a mere guess at the explanation of the mystery. But in any case this solution

LORD BRIDGEMAN, new Director-General of the Home Guard, went to France in the present war as a staff officer and organized the defence of the perimeter of Dunkirk. *Photo, Planet News*

quite ignores our avowed aim of not ceasing the struggle until Nazism has been eliminated.

But so far as the creature himself is concerned let us remember the homely proverb : " You cannot make a silken purse out of a sow's ear." This man is no hero ; yet I'm glad that the Scottish shepherd refrained from puncturing his paunch with his pitchfork, which so many of us would have dearly liked to do. He'll be of use to the cause of Freedom, whose enemy he has been since the dawn of Nazism. I think there's wit enough among our leaders to see to that. And meanwhile the frantic lies of Goebbels endeavouring to minimize the Hess affair have done more than anything we could say to discredit German propaganda in the eyes of the whole world. So far, good !

The trend of policy of the decrepit Pétain and the dastard Darlan should remind us that France has never been a wholehearted ally of Britain—" perfidious Albion ! " If we achieved a union of sorts in 1914-18 it was rather a *mariage de convenance* than deep mutual affection. British admiration of France was mainly inspired by her continental leadership in democratic ideals— Liberty, Equality, Fraternity, all dishonoured by the vassals in Vichy—and her eminence in the realms of philosophy and the arts. Her catastrophic collapse and the aftermath of the Armistice have shown us how little we can now hope from her, apart from the cooperation of the patriot Frenchmen who have thrown in their lot with the gallant De Gaulle, who may yet have to help Britain— or at least to stand by—while she is forced to turn her arms in self-defence against her late Ally. An appalling thought when we recall the spirit in which we marched in September 1939.

But a France that is helping her own implacable enemy and ours to wage war upon us is no longer a disarmed and sympathetic spectator of the continuing struggle, but an active and dangerous foe. A Paris whose workshops are turning out tanks, guns, munitions, aero-engines, to batter our armies and kill our civilians is a hostile city and as deserving to be bombed as Hamburg, Brest, or Milan. Our gratitude and admiration for the Free French cooperation must not tie our hands or blind our eyes in dealing with the False French.

Meanwhile, what about Syria ? Today I happened to be dipping into the Letters of that amazing man Lawrence of Arabia, who away back in 1915, while still a subaltern, had a clearly conceived policy for the Near East which, had it been realized, would have changed the whole complexion of the present War. In March of that year he wrote from Cairo to D. G. Hogarth: " If Russia has Alexandretta it's all up with us in the Near East. And in any case in the next War the French will probably be under Russia's finger in Syria." It looked like that when he wrote. What mortal man could then have foreseen that it would be Germany's finger " in the next war" that would press the button in the Syria of a renegade France ? In the same letter, however, Lawrence says : " *One cannot go on betting that France will always be our friend.*" How right he was !

He also foresaw that France would jockey us into accepting the mandate for Jerusalem and Palestine. " Don't touch it with a barge pole " was his far-sighted advice. Here was genuine " prophecy." And what more prophetic than his closing words in this same letter written three years before the event ? " We must, I think, look for a renaissance of the Turk when he has lost Constantinople. They will be much more formidable militarily —and less so politically." It is not too much to say that when Lawrence of Arabia died as the result of a stupid motor-cycle accident twenty years later (May 1935) Britain lost one man of vision and experience—a realist whose counsel in this War would have enabled our Generals to change the whole course of events in the Near East. He was no lover of French imperialists.

JOHN CARPENTER HOUSE.
WHITEFRIARS. LONDON. E.C.4.

Registered at the G.P.O. as a Newspaper

The War Illustrated, June 13th, 1941

Vol 4

The War Illustrated

Nº 93

Edited by Sir John Hammerton

FOURPENCE

WEEKLY

"BOOTS, boots, boots, boots, moving up and down again . . ." sang Kipling a propos of the infantry of a former epoch, and this happy study of a cheery British infantryman cooling his feet after a march over scorching desert sand reminds us that, although mechanical transport has done away with a lot of unnecessary foot-slogging, in the last resort it is the infantry which decides a battle, and it does so on its feet. For this reason a good soldier bestows as much care upon his feet as upon his rifle.

Photo, British Official : Crown Copyright

Our Searchlight on the War

New Weapon Against Bombing

BRITISH, Canadian and American scientists have combined their researches to produce a new and powerful weapon against attacks from the air by both day and night. Details are naturally being kept secret, but in general terms the device involves the use of a great network of small, modern radio sets by which technical experts, posted all over Britain, will be able to detect the presence of enemy aircraft and to direct A.A. fire with great precision. An intensive drive was recently made in Canada for amateur and professional men, and over a thousand were rushed over here to operate the device. The Air Ministry is now looking for another 2,500 "Canadians of good common sense ready this minute to volunteer for overseas service." They will be trained in this work and will soon be holding key posts in the defence of Britain. In addition, a new scheme for training as radio operators young men over 16½ and under 18 was announced in London.

Keeping the Pigeons Dry

HOMING pigeons serving with the R.A.F. are being provided with a portable shelter which will add greatly to their comfort and safety. These birds accompany pilots on their flights, so that if a forced descent is made, and the aeroplane's radio is out of action, the pigeons form a vital link with the airmen's station. Forced descents on the water are sometimes made by aircraft returning by night from raids or patrol work. If the crew takes to its emergency dinghy the

ROBERT CROSS, coxswain of the R.N.L.I. Lifeboat City of Bradford II, has won seven medals in a career dedicated to the Lifeboat Service. He has been the Humber Coxswain since 1912. *Photo, Associated Press*

A METAL PIGEON CONTAINER of a new experimental type is now in use with the R.A.F. Its purpose is to keep the bird dry if the crew are forced to take to the dinghy. Pigeons are used for sending home messages from aircraft when wireless cannot be used.
Photo, British Official

pigeons, unless specially protected, get wet feet, which may cause their death. Specialists of the R.A.F. have therefore designed various kinds of container and these are being tried out. One, a cylindrical type, is not only watertight but buoyant, and so, while keeping its occupant warm and dry until with the coming of daylight the bird is released, the container can also be of assistance to an exhausted member of the crew swimming towards his dinghy.

Egyptian Quisling

A REWARD of £1,000 was offered by King Farouk's Government for information leading to the arrest of General Aziz el Masri Pasha, former Inspector-General of the Egyptian Army, and two Egyptian flying-officers, all of whom were said to have left Aimaza aerodrome, near Cairo, on May 16. The communiqué on this escapade stated that, thanks to the Air Control authorities,

the aeroplane was compelled to land, but the three occupants escaped and were thought to be hiding in Cairo, despite official warnings against harbouring the men. Examination of documents and maps abandoned in the aircraft showed that they had planned to fly to Beirut, perhaps as a first stage to Baghdad. Three days later it was announced in Cairo that desert patrols were searching for the fugitives, whose tracks had been traced to Fayoum Oasis, 80 miles south-west of Cairo. It was discovered that their car had broken down en route, and that General Masri got a lift in a passing Egyptian Army desert car to the oasis. Here he lunched comfortably in a well-known restaurant, since when no news of him or his companions has been received, or at least made public.

Nazis Stage Air Raids

FOR some time there has existed in this country a strong suspicion that the Germans were deliberately bombing the civilians in some occupied areas, hoping thereby to vilify the R.A.F. in the eyes of neutral and conquered countries. A resident of Brest who arrived in Lisbon told a newspaper correspondent there that it had often been observed that about half an hour after an attack by our machines on the port, a second attack would occur on the residential areas of the town itself, causing civilian casualties and the destruction of houses. But the following morning bomb splinters of German manufacture would be picked up, of a type that explodes laterally on contact but is not suitable for attacks on big objectives. For some weeks the R.A.F. have been systematically bombing the two German battleships Scharnhorst and Gneisenau, lying in Brest docks, and for such targets only armour-piercing and semi-armour-piercing bombs are carried. Moreover, neutral observers who have returned home from occupied France have testified that the bombing of military targets by the R.A.F. is so accurate that they were accustomed to watch attacks from the verandahs of houses in the town, without apprehension for their own safety. Reports from Belgium and Holland corroborate the use of this vile trick, and a plot to bomb the Vatican City and assign the blame to the R.A.F. was disclosed by Downing Street in April.

Lifeboat Hero

COXSWAIN ROBERT CROSS, of the Royal National Lifeboat Institution's Humber station, who already held seven medals, has been awarded a bar to his Bronze Medal by the Institution. The seven medals are the George Medal, the Institution's Gold Medal (the Lifeboat V.C.), its Silver Medal three times, and its Bronze Medal twice. The two named first were awarded for the same deed of gallantry—rescue of the crew of the Grimsby trawler St. Gurth. The trawler was seen to be drifting rapidly ashore with seas breaking over her. The wind had increased to gale force, with snow squalls, and the sea was very rough. Cross manoeuvred his vessel, the City of Bradford, on to the weather side of the trawler, and, nosing the

bow of his boat up to the forecastle of the trawler, he rescued one man. Several times the lifeboat was worked in, and eventually six men were got into the lifeboat; one at a time. After the sixth man had been rescued, the lifeboat's port engine stopped. With only one engine working Cross, after several more attempts, rescued the remaining three men. "The success of the rescue was almost entirely due to the courage, skill and endurance of Coxswain Cross," stated the "London Gazette." His latest award is for rescuing the crew of eight of a vessel grounded on a sandbank.

New Suits for High Fliers

NOW that aircraft are flying very much higher than they did at the beginning of the war, the crew are exposed to intense cold, even though summer heat may be experienced at ground level. To combat this, crews of the Bomber Command and other operational forces have been issued with special warm underclothing. So thick are these garments that they cannot be worn beneath ordinary uniforms, so crews are also being provided with roomy two-piece suits resembling the Army's battledress, except that they are in blue grey. The usual R.A.F. and rank badges will be sewn on.

NAZI AIR-BORNE TROOPS
One Division—Strength 7,000 Men
Infantry : 2 Regiments = 6 Battalions

I Battalion	Armament
3 Companies	Rifles
I Company	Machine-guns
I Gun Company	4 75-mm. guns
I Anti-Tank Company	4 37-mm. guns
I Company Light Infantry	

Artillery :   I Regiment
3 Batteries   24 75-mm. mountain guns

Anti-Tank :   I Battalion
3 Companies   37-mm. guns

Auxiliaries:
Reconnaissance Unit, motor cycles
Signals units, cycles and motor cycles
Engineers, Medical and Supply units.

Note.—These figures are estimated on the basis of the air-borne divisions used in the invasion of Holland. Germany then had 7 such divisions of highly trained men.

About 250 aircraft are required to transport I division in relays, making 2-4 journeys.

Parachutists precede all these troops to prepare the ground for them.

The Way of the War

THE WAR ENTERS A CRITICAL NEW PHASE

Under President Roosevelt's Inspiring Leadership All America Is United Against 'This Nazi Shape of Things to Come'

In 1919 America turned her back on Europe. President Wilson was disowned by his own people. The League of Nations, of which he had been the prophet and, more than any man perhaps, the parent, was rejected as a snare devised by wily foreigners to drag the New World into the disreputable politics of the Old. Back to the Monroe Doctrine ! was the cry. Off with the shackles imposed by Wilsonian idealism ! On to prosperity, and America for the Americans !

The years passed. Wilson died, a man broken in body and in mind. President followed President : Harding, Coolidge, Hoover . . . There was prosperity, oceans of it. Pockets were bulging. The Almighty Dollar never had so many well-paid, well-clothed, smugly complacent worshippers. Then came the crash . . .

One man saved the nation, gave back hope to the despairing. One man proved that he was worthy of being the captain of a great people. Since the day of his first inauguration—since March 4, 1933—Franklin Delano Roosevelt has occupied a position in America and in the world such as no American President has occupied before him, not Wilson or Lincoln, not Jefferson, not even Washington, the Father of the Republic. In the eight years that have passed since that historic day the United States have passed through what may well be described as a revolution. The national conscience has been awakened as never before, and the doctrine of more or less enlightened selfishness has given place to a concern for the under-dog—and for what may be described as the under-nation.

For F.D.R. is not and never has been an isolationist. Way back in 1916 he was Wilson's Assistant Secretary of the Navy, and what he learnt from Wilson he has never forgotten ; for all we know Wilson may have learnt something, much perhaps, from the young man who, though born into America's upper hundred, is a democrat through and through. Roosevelt's vision is not narrowed by the American shore ; he saw the red light across the Atlantic when it was but a glimmer, not yet fanned into a raging flame by the follies and worse of European policies. As late as 1937 the menace of Nazism was still not fully realized, even by those who were Germany's nearest neighbours ; Austria was still independent, Czechoslovakia was still free, Poland not yet threatened, Holland and Norway and the rest were sunk in the slumbers of an unreal neutrality. France was still France. Yet in October of that year he denounced at Chicago the " reign of terror and international lawlessness which has now reached a stage where the very foundations of civilization are seriously threatened . . . If these things come to pass in other parts of the world, let no one imagine that America will escape . . ."

Year by year the crisis grew, and the air was charged more and more heavily with the ominous thunder of the approaching war. At last the storm broke, and America's

millions awoke to a new interest in life. News of battles at sea and on land and in the air made interesting reading, and they rushed for the newspapers hot from the presses. In those days, not yet two years gone, the war to the great majority of the Americans seemed exceedingly remote. " It can't happen here," they said, " but it is darned interesting to read about . . ." But F.D.R., it is clear now, never shared that shortsighted outlook. He knew from the very beginning that this was a war between democracy and dictatorship ; and that this being so, the world's greatest democracy could not stand aloof, or, if at first, certainly not indefinitely. So step by step he led his country and his people into ever-increasing partnership with Britain and her Allied democracies.

We need not suppose that from the very first the President saw the last step, or even the last but one ; sufficient that he knew the next step and the one after that. Every step he took was carefully prepared for. Some of his supporters were fretful at his apparent

PRESIDENT ROOSEVELT in his " fireside chat " delivered at the White House on the evening of May 27 addressed himself immediately to the representatives in Washington of all the American countries, but 85 millions throughout the world heard his speech relayed by wireless. The most important passages are given in page 596.
Photo, Wide World

slowness. " We want action," they said, " and he gives us words, and more words." But F.D.R. is a past-master at timing and in reading the psychology of the American people, and when his friends grumbled and his foes raged, he just kept on smiling. He realizes how strange and far away the war must appear to the men arguing round the cracker barrels in the village stores way down in Tennessee or way up in the Middle West ; he knows full well and understands the passion that lies beneath the demand that never again shall American mothers' sons be sent across the Atlantic to die in a European quarrel. Because of this realization, this deep understanding, he has stressed all along the fact that Britain is fighting not only her war but America's.

With the American temper steadily rising, the President has kept ahead, even if only just a little ahead, of the great public. The man in the street, whether that street be in New York or in New Orleans, in Washington or San Francisco, relies on F.D.R. to put his own thoughts into speech. (Maybe he is not so quick to realize that those same thoughts would not have been his but for the President's prompting.) Save Britain ! Save the people of London, Liverpool, Bristol, Plymouth, and the other bombed towns ! Save China ! Save Latin America ! Save ourselves !

Roosevelt listens, and, having listened, makes another step towards—what ? War, perhaps ; and it says much for his masterly direction and inspiration of a great people that America has now come face to face with the possibility of war—and is not afraid.

" We do not accept and will not permit this Nazi 'shape of things to come ' . . . We shall actively resist wherever necessary and with all our resources every attempt by Hitler to extend his Nazi domination to the Western Hemisphere or to threaten it. We shall actively resist his every attempt to gain control of the seas."

A few hours before he made that forthright declaration, he had assumed powers under the Constitution such as have been no American President's before him. "I, Franklin D. Roosevelt, President of the United States of America, do proclaim that an unlimited national emergency confronts this country . . ."

That is as far as he has spoken. But as he sits at his desk in the White House smiling his famous smile and wisecracking with the reporters, what is going on behind the twinkling eyes in that restless, scheming brain ? He has said himself that no one can know what will happen tomorrow. But in the light of the words he has let fall or spoken with calculated deliberation, are we not entitled to believe that already he sees beyond the war to the day when Wilson's dream of a world of free peoples, ruled by law based on the consent of the governed, is no longer a dream—when the world will be a fit home for men fit to be free ?

E. ROYSTON PIKE

For 1750 Miles They Chased the Bismarck

"I have just received news that the Bismarck is sunk."   In these words Mr. Churchill announced
to an expectant House of Commons on May 27 the end of the chase of Hitler's newest and most
powerful battleship.   Below we tell the full story in the words of the Admiralty communiqués issued
shortly after the fight was fought and won.

AIR reconnaissance by Coastal Command aircraft revealed that a German battleship and cruiser, which they had previously located in the Norwegian port of Bergen, had sailed.

Certain dispositions were therefore ordered, and as a result H.M. cruiser Norfolk (9,925 tons), Capt. A. J. L. Phillips, R.N., wearing the flag of Rear-Adml. W. F. Wake-Walker, C.B., O.B.E., and H.M. cruiser Suffolk (10,000 tons), Capt. R. M. Ellis, R.N., were ordered to take up a position in the Denmark Straits. On Friday evening Adml. Wake-Walker reported sighting an enemy force of one battleship and one cruiser [Prinz Eugen] proceeding at high speed to the south-westward. Visibility in the Denmark Straits was bad and extremely variable. The range of the enemy was only six miles when he was first sighted, and storms of snow and sleet and patches of mist at times reduced the visibility to one mile.

Despite the difficulties of visibility, H.M.S. Norfolk and H.M.S. Suffolk shadowed the enemy successfully throughout the night.

Meanwhile, other units of the Royal Navy were taking up dispositions at high speed with a view to intercepting the enemy and bringing him to action with our heavy forces.

Early on Saturday morning H.M. battle-cruiser Hood (42,100 tons), Capt. R. Kerr,

nounced, received a hit in the magazine and blew up. H.M.S. Prince of Wales sustained slight damage. The chase was continued on a south-westerly course, with H.M.S. Norfolk and H.M.S. Suffolk shadowing the enemy and maintaining contact, despite all the enemy's efforts to shake off the pursuit.

It appeared at this time that the enemy's speed had been slightly reduced, and reconnaissance aircraft of the Coastal Command reported that she was leaving a wake of oil.

On Saturday evening H.M.S. Prince of Wales again made contact with the enemy and action was joined for a short time. The German ships at once turned away to the westward, and then swung round on to a southerly course, with our forces still in pursuit. Other

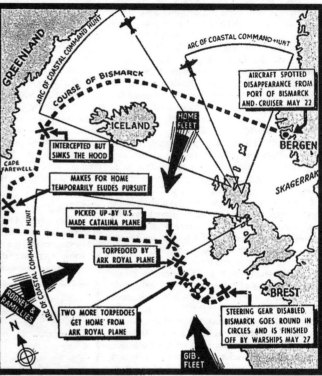

The Bismarck's course, from the moment that the Nazi battleship left Bergen on May 22 till her destruction 400 miles west of Brest, is here shown stage by stage.   *Courtesy of the "Daily Mail"*

of our naval forces were now approaching the enemy, and during the night naval torpedo-bombing aircraft from H.M. aircraft-carrier Victorious (23,000 tons), Capt. H. C. Bovell, R.N., delivered a torpedo attack on the enemy from a considerable distance, and one torpedo was seen to hit the Bismarck.

H.M.S. Norfolk, H.M.S. Suffolk and H.M.S. Prince of Wales continued to shadow the enemy successfully until shortly after 3 a.m. on Sunday. Touch with the enemy was now lost in low visibility. The enemy was then approximately 350 miles south-south-east of the southern point of Greenland. Searching dispositions were at once taken up by other units of the Royal Navy.

The main body of the Home Fleet, under the command of Adml. J. C. Tovey, K.C.B., D.S.O., with his flag flying in H.M. battle-ship King George V (35,000 tons), Capt. W. R. Patterson, C.V.O., R.N., was steaming at high speed in a south-westerly direction from northern waters.

Another force under the command of Vice-Adml. Sir James F. Somerville, K.C.B., D.S.O., with his flag flying in H.M. battle-cruiser Renown (32,000 tons), Capt. R. R.

McGrigor, R.N., was steaming north-westwards at high speed from Gibraltar.

H.M. battleship Rodney (33,900 tons), Capt. F. H. G. Dalrymple Hamilton, R.N., and H.M. battleship Ramillies (29,150 tons), Capt. A. D. Read, R.N., who were escorting convoys in the North Atlantic, proceeded to move in the direction of the enemy.

Extensive air searches were organized by Coastal Command and by the Royal Canadian Air Force stationed in Newfoundland.

It was not until about 10.30 a.m. on Monday that the enemy was again located. At that time the Bismarck was sighted by a Catalina aircraft of Coastal Command in a position about 550 miles west of Land's End.

This aircraft was attacked, and as a result lost touch with the enemy battleship half an hour later, but at 11.15 a.m. the Bismarck was sighted by naval aircraft operating from H.M. aircraft-carrier Ark Royal (22,000 tons), Capt. L. E. H. Maund, R.N. Only the battleship Bismarck was seen, and she was then steering an easterly course.

At this time H.M.S. King George V and H.M.S. Rodney were approaching the area, but were not yet sufficiently close to bring the enemy to action.

As soon as Bismarck was sighted by Ark Royal's aircraft Adml. Sir James Somerville detached the cruiser Sheffield (9,100 tons), Capt. C. A. A. Larcom, R.N., to make contact with and shadow the Bismarck. During the afternoon a striking force of naval aircraft was dispatched from Ark Royal to attack with torpedoes, but this proved unsuccessful. Shortly after 5.30 p.m. H.M.S. Sheffield made contact with the Bismarck and proceeded to shadow her. Within 20 minutes another striking force of naval aircraft was flown off by H.M.S. Ark Royal. This force attacked successfully, and one torpedo was seen to hit the Bismarck amidships.

H.M.S. PRINCE OF WALES, one of Britain's mightiest and newest battle-ships, slightly damaged by the Bismarck on the morning of May 24, 1941. She was launched in 1939, and her ten 14-in. guns are unique in power and range.
Photo, Keystone

ADMIRAL SIR JOHN TOVEY, in command of the Home Fleet which pursued the Nazis.
Photo, Planet News

C.B.E., R.N., wearing the flag of Vice-Adml. L. E. Holland, C.B., with H.M. battleship Prince of Wales (35,000 tons), Capt. J. C. Leach, M.V.O., R.N., in company, made contact with the enemy. Action was immediately joined. During the ensuing engagement Bismarck received damage and was at one time seen to be on fire. Hood, as has already been an-

How the Royal Navy Avenged the Hood

THE GERMAN BATTLESHIP BISMARCK was the last word in Nazi naval power and pride. She displaced 35,000 tons, carried eight 15-in., twelve 5·9-in. and sixteen 4·1-in. guns, and was launched in 1939. Under command of Admiral Luetjens (right) she met her doom in the Atlantic on May 27.
Photos, Wide World and G.P.U.

H.M.S. ARK ROYAL, one of whose naval operating planes sighted the Bismarck on the morning of May 26 and torpedoed her.

A second hit was obtained by a torpedo on the starboard quarter of the German battleship. It was subsequently reported that on being hit during this attack the Bismarck made two complete circles and that her speed was again reduced. During the evening some of our destroyers of the Tribal class (1,870 tons), under the command of Capt. P. L. Vian, D.S.O., R.N., in H.M.S. Cossack, made contact soon after 11 p.m. Between 1.20 a.m. and 1.50 a.m. on Tuesday the Bismarck was attacked with torpedoes by H.M. destroyers Zulu, Cmdr. H. R. Graham, D.S.O., R.N.; Maori, Cmdr. H. T. Armstrong, D.S.O., R.N.; and Cossack. Cossack and Maori each hit with one torpedo. After Maori's attack it was reported that there was a fire on the forecastle of the German battleship.

One hour after these attacks by our destroyers it was reported that the Bismarck appeared to be stopped She was then about 400 miles due west of Brest and had been pursued by our forces for more than 1,750 miles. It was subsequently reported that the Bismarck was again under way and had made good about eight miles in one hour, and that she was still capable of heavy and accurate gunfire. At daylight another striking force of naval aircraft was dispatched from Ark Royal, but this attack had to be cancelled owing to low visibility. Shortly after daylight Bismarck engaged our destroyers by gunfire. H.M. cruiser Norfolk was in action with the Bismarck almost immediately afterwards, and very soon the Bismarck was being engaged by our heavy ships. Details of this phase of the action have not yet been received. It is known, however, that H.M. cruiser Dorsetshire (9,975 tons), Capt. B. C. S. Martin, R.N., was ordered to sink the Bismarck with torpedoes. Bismarck sank at 11.01 this morning.

H.M.S. DORSETSHIRE, the cruiser which gave the Bismarck her *coup de grâce* with torpedoes. Right, above, H.M.S. ZULU, which, with her sister destroyers Maori and Cossack, chased the German battleship and attacked her between 1.20 a.m. and 1.50 a.m. on May 27.
Photos, Central Press, Wright & Logan, Planet News

So reads the Admiralty communiqué of May 27; a second issued on May 29 adds:

The torpedo attacks by naval aircraft and the destroyer attack during Monday-Tuesday night, in which H.M. Destroyer Sikh (Commander G. H. Stokes, R.N.) took part, in addition to the ships already announced, resulted in the speed of the Bismarck being greatly reduced and her steering gear being put out of action. Both her main and secondary armament, however, remained effective. The C.-in-C. Home Fleet, intended to close the Bismarck at dawn and sink her by gunfire from H.M.S. King George V and H.M.S. Rodney. This intention, however, was abandoned owing to uncertain and variable visibility, which made it necessary to await full daylight before closing the enemy.

Shortly before 9 a.m. H.M.S. King George V and H.M.S. Rodney engaged the enemy with their main armament. The gunfire of these two battleships silenced the enemy. The C.-in-C. then ordered H.M.S. Dorsetshire to sink the Bismarck with torpedoes. As already announced, the Bismarck sank at 11.1 a.m., on May 27. More than 100 officers and men from the Bismarck were picked up by our forces and are prisoners of war.

A Last Look Round the Bismarck's Victim

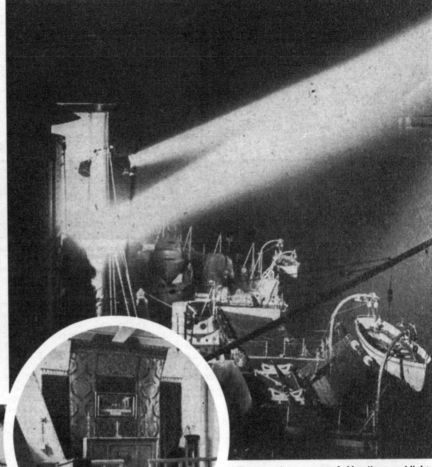

The ward room of H.M.S. Hood with its brilliantly polished tables, a vase of flowers suggesting the homely touch. Circle : the austere iron chapel relieved by a picture over the altar.

The amazing power of Hood's searchlights revealing a section of the deck. Note how the minutest detail stands out clear against the black night.

In the heart of H.M.S. Hood men are attending to the oil furnaces. The largest warship in commission, the Hood was laid down in September 1916 and completed in March 1920. On the right, Hood's men launching a paravane, the ingenious apparatus by which a mine is cut from its cable and deflected from a ship's side.

Photos, Central Press and Wright & Logan

Toll for the Brave of H.M.S. Hood

THE WORLD'S LARGEST WARSHIP, H.M.S. HOOD, was sunk by the German battleship Bismarck off the coast of Greenland on May 24. The Admiralty communiqué, referring to this loss, described the Hood as receiving an "unlucky hit in the magazine." H.M.S. Hood displaced 42,100 tons, full load, and had a normal complement of 1,341. Inset above, Vice-Admiral L. E. Holland, C.B., who flew his flag in H.M.S. Hood, and on the right, Captain Ralph Kerr, C.B.E., R.N., who was in command of the ship. The Hood's loss was soon avenged, for the Bismarck was sunk by us on May 27
Photos, Topical, Vandyk and Universal

And Still Tobruk Holds Out

This anti-aircraft gun, among the outer defences of Tobruk, is manned by a crew stripped to the waist and ready to give marauding aircraft a hot reception. The emplacement is protected by ammo. boxes filled with stones.

SUNKEN SHIPS are in the fairway outside Navy House in Tobruk, but a tattered White Ensign still flies from the original Italian flagstaff. The photograph top right shows one of the defenders of Tobruk engrossed in news from home.

German prisoners captured during operations around Tobruk are blindfolded before being escorted through the defences of the fortress.

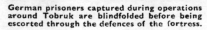

L IFE in Tobruk, which the Nazis have failed to take after weeks of intensive effort, goes on in a more or less normal manner despite the repeated dive-bombing attacks by Stukas which come over with monotonous regularity. An officer who recently returned from Tobruk to Cairo stated that the Imperial defenders were carrying on as usual : there was plenty of food and no shortage of beer or cigarettes, and a military band gave a daily performance of rousing music in the principal square. High tribute was paid to the work of the A.A. gunners and the R.A.F. patrols. A tribute of another kind is the strong defences which the Germans are constructing against the Tobruk garrison's forays.

The Germans have found Tobruk too hard a nut to crack, for the Navy successfully maintains sea communication with the seasoned soldiers who form its garrison. This trawler, en route for Tobruk, has a captured Breda gun in readiness to ward off all attempts at dive-bombing.

Photos, British Official   Crown Copyright

Hard and Bitter Was the Fight for Crete

By the end of April 1941 practically all the Empire Forces had been withdrawn from Greece. Their next stand was made in Crete. The battle for this island, so small yet so strategically important, was waged for 12 days from May 19. As will be seen from what is told below, it was a battle not only hardly fought but one in many respects entirely novel.

T HE battle for Crete began on May 19, when a great horde of Nazi bombers swept across the narrow sea from their aerodromes in Greece, and subjected Canea, the island's chief port and capital, Suda Bay, which the British Navy had been occupying as a base, and Candia (or Herak-

German parachute troops in Crete were supplied with food and ammunition in containers dropped by parachute from German aircraft.
Photo, E.N.A.

lion, to give it its modern name) — the three key points of the island—to an ordeal of intense bombing and ground strafing. But for some days before our reconnoitring aeroplanes had noticed very heavy concentrations of German aircraft on the aerodromes of Southern Greece, and our bombers had attacked them night after night, inflicting considerable damage.

On May 20 the first of the Nazi invaders made their appearance in the island—or, rather, above it, as they came by air. "An air-borne attack in great strength has begun this morning," Mr. Churchill told the House of Commons on May 20, " and what cannot fail to be a serious battle has begun and is developing. Our troops there—British, New Zealand and Greek forces—are under the command of General Freyberg, and we feel confident that most stern and resolute resistance will be offered to the enemy."

A little later in the day the Premier was able to give some further details of the battle. " After a

good deal of intense bombing of Suda Bay," he said, " and the various aerodromes in the neighbourhood, about 1,500 enemy troops wearing New Zealand battle-dress landed by gliders, parachutes, and troop-carriers in the Canea-Maleka area." The first parachutists landed at about 2 a.m. near Suda Bay and Maleka to the west, and later in the day more landings were effected near Canea and on the Akrotiri Peninsula. By nightfall some 3,000 had been landed altogether, chiefly round Maleka and Candia, and of these General Freyberg had reported that 1,800 had been taken prisoner, wounded, or slain.

At 4.30 the next morning the air-borne attacks recommenced. Another 3,000 men were dropped from the sky. Within two hours most of these had been accounted for The gaps in the Nazi ranks were swiftly filled by fresh troops, however, and fighting continued throughout the day. There was no staying the stream of German aircraft—great Junkers 52 troop-carrying planes, each with 14 or 20 fully-armed men in its cabin, and trailing behind them gliders—whole strings of them—each carrying 12 men apiece. Altogether the Nazis were said to have employed 1,200 troop-carriers, and at the height of the attack they were landing at the rate of one a minute. The British defenders, our fighter planes, and A.A. guns wrought havoc amongst the attackers ; numbers of the troop-carriers were shot down in flames, scores of gliders crashed to earth with a load of corpses. But still the Germans came on. They had apparently an inexhaustible supply not only of men but of planes.

By the night of May 21 the enemy attempted landings by sea, but these met with disaster.

NAVAL LOSSES IN CRETE

	Tons.	Guns			Torp. Tubes	Completed
		5-in.	4-in. A.A.	Smaller		
Cruisers						
Gloucester (Southampton Class)	9,400	12	8	20	6	1939
Fiji (Fiji Class)	8,000	12 3 in.	8	16	6	1940
York	8,250	6 4·7	8	18	6	1930
Destroyers						
Juno	1,690	6	—	6	10	1939
Kelly	1,695	6	—	6	10	1939
Kashmir (Javelin Class)	1,690	6	—	6	10	1939
Greyhound (Greyhound Class)	1,335	4	—	6	8	1936

A convoy making for Crete was intercepted by our naval forces. Two transports and a number of caiques—Greek fishing boats which the Nazis had impounded as troop transports—were sent to the bottom, together with an enemy destroyer which was acting as escort. On the next day an attempt on a much larger scale was made to carry an army into Crete, and a convoy of 30 vessels was encountered and scattered by our ships.

Speaking in the House of Commons on the afternoon of Thursday, May 22, Mr. Churchill said with perfect truth that " It is a most strange and grim battle which is being fought. Our side has no air support, because they have no aerodromes, not because they have no aeroplanes. The other side have very little or nothing of artillery or tanks. Neither side has any means of retreat." The same evening the British military spokesman in Cairo stated that the Imperial troops, assisted by Greek forces and Cretan hillsmen, had succeeded so far in

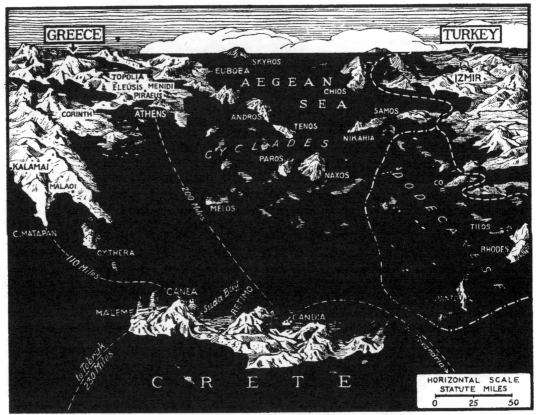

THE ISLAND OF CRETE, invaded by Nazi air-borne troops on May 20, lies at the southern end of the Aegean Sea and has an area of 3,195 square miles. (England has an area of 50,874 sq. miles). There are no railways, and few good roads. Heraklion (Candia) on the north coast is the largest city, with a population of some 34,000. The only other modern towns are Canea (27,000) and Retimo (9,000).   *Specially drawn for* THE WAR ILLUSTRATED *by Felix Gardon*

Flame and Fury of a New Kind of War

FALLUJA, IRAQ, showing the bridge on the Euphrates on the way to Baghdad. Fallujah was captured by our forces on May 22. After Crete, Iraq and Syria became the next Nazi objectives.   *Photo, " The Times "*

" keeping the situation well in hand." And a communiqué issued from British G.H.Q. in Cairo paid tribute to the splendid courage and dash of the defenders. But all the same it was revealed that the British fighters had had to withdraw from Crete, since the aerodromes available were so few and ill-equipped and were being continuously attacked by the enemy Stukas.

German attempts to land troops from the sea were still a failure—at least, in any considerable number. Though exposed to constant bombardment from the air by an enormous number of enemy planes, the Mediterranean Fleet under Admiral Cunningham maintained their patrol in those dangerous waters. It was not to be expected that they could do

so without loss, and the Germans were soon claiming that the Luftwaffe had sunk several British cruisers and destroyers, obtained direct hits on one of our battleships, and seriously damaged many other units of our Fleet. These claims were exaggerated as always, but the actual losses were severe enough (see table in previous page).

By May 28 the Germans claimed to have occupied Western Crete—prematurely, perhaps, although there was no disguising the fact that the situation was serious and becoming worse. It was claimed that our troops had inflicted very heavy casualties on the enemy, who had also lost a high proportion of his troop-carrying aircraft, yet it had to be admitted that not a day went by but fresh contingents of Nazi troops were landed in the island, and the defenders were subjected to almost uninterrupted dive-bombing attacks. A new note of horror was struck on May 24 when Heinkels pounded Canea, Retimo and Candia with heavy bombs.

Back and forth the battle swayed, and there were some places which changed hands time and again. But at one vital spot—the aerodrome at Maleme, 10 miles south-west of Canea—the Germans secured a foothold on May 21 and nothing could dislodge them. It was here that the main body of the enemy air-borne troops were landed, since it was so well situated for an attack on Canea and, still more important, Suda Bay, where British warships had been anchored.

H.M.S. GLOUCESTER (above), sunk in the battle for Crete. A cruiser of 9,400 tons, she was completed in 1939.
Photo, " Daily Mirror "

By now the Nazis in the island were reported to number between 25,000 and 30,000 men ; certainly they had sufficient to make an attack on Canea in force. Adopting battle formation, they marched against Canea and Suda Bay, and on May 26 a penetration of our positions was made. On the next day another attack enlarged this penetration, so that the Empire forces were compelled to withdraw to positions in the rear. Then on May 28 the German communiqué claimed that " German Alpine troops, despite the difficult terrain, broke down the stubborn resistance of British forces and insurgent bands [this term, by the way, refers to the Greeks and Cretans]. In a bold attack they thrust the enemy out of his position, took the capital, Canea, and pursued the beaten enemy." With Canea in their hands the Germans were able to bring their fire to bear on Suda Bay itself, and on May 29 it was announced by British G.H.Q. that " in face of further attacks by German forces, which have again been heavily reinforced, our troops have withdrawn to positions east of Suda Bay." Then on June 1 came the news that the Empire Force had withdrawn to Egypt.

IN CRETE the Germans used flame-throwers. Here they are seen manipulating this diabolical weapon in readiness for a forthcoming battle.   *Photo, Keystone*

What Remains Today of These Cities of Crete?

NEAR HERAKLION (Candia), a view through trees typical of the Cretan landscape. Right, between Heraklion and Retimo, and, beneath, Canea, the capital of Crete, which has been completely destroyed by 30,000 Nazi bombs.

Photos, Wide World, exclusive to THE WAR ILLUSTRATED

Not All Hitler's Terrorism Has Banished Life

Nurses of Great Ormond Street Children's Hospital, London, training in a Surrey wood. Above: young Bristolians think that craters merely add to the fun of things; and, right, a May-day dance in a bombed street to a military band, what joy!

Laughter from Britain's Towns and Countryside

Ploughing up the orchard, since every inch of land is wanted for food. Top centre: sailors and their girls don't care as long as they can dance on Plymouth Hoe. Oval: Monday was, is, and ever shall be washing-day, Adolf notwithstanding. Circle: a good shepherd has found a sheep that strayed and is bringing it back to the fold.

Photos, "Daily Mirror" and G.P.U.

The War in Abyssinia in Retrospect

The East African campaign of 1941 will be remembered as one of the most remarkable in British military history. A brief review of the operations conducted by General Cunningham and General Platt, which have resulted in the downfall of the Fascist East African Empire, is given below.

"THE victory at Amba Alagi has resulted in the surrender of the Duke of Aosta and his whole remaining forces, and must be considered to bring all major organized resistance in Abyssinia to an end." So said Mr. Churchill in the House of Commons on May 20, amid cheers. He went on : " No doubt other fighting will continue for some time in the south, but this certainly wears the aspect of the culmination of a campaign which, I venture to think, is one of the most remarkable ever fought by British or Imperial arms."

The East African campaign was, indeed, a remarkable one, and a model of concerted action on the part of widely separated columns which had to cover vast distances in the face of great physical difficulties, encountering strong resistance from time to time. Its successful termination in such a surprisingly short space of time was due, as the Prime Minister remarked, to " audacious action and extraordinary competence in warfare."

When Italy came into the war in June 1940 General Wavell had comparatively small and incompletely trained forces in the Sudan and in Kenya. Under the circumstances a long frontier was impossible to hold and a series of withdrawals took place, from Kassala, from Gallabat, from Moyale and from the northern frontiers of Kenya. Our military strategy in Africa had been based on the assumption that we should have the powerful support of colonial France, and after the French government had gone back on its promise, broadcast by M. Reynaud, to fight in North Africa if driven out of France, this strategy had to be completely replanned.

When British Somaliland was invaded by superior forces in August 1940 we were forced to abandon it. Axis propaganda made the most of our defeat. British prospects in Africa wore a far from rosy look. That corner of N.E. Africa comprising Abyssinia, Eritrea, Italian Somaliland and British Somaliland was held by a well-equipped force of 100,000 Italian metropolitan and 200,000 native troops which had at its disposal a considerable air force.

It was then that the British Government took what was among the most momentous decisions in the world's military history. Although Hitler had overrun France with his armed might and our island was under the threat of imminent invasion, large reinforcements in men and machines were sent to the aid of General Wavell. Some came from the Home Country, but many were sent from Australia and New Zealand to man the Libyan frontier, while Union forces moved up from the Cape to reinforce Kenya. There were, in addition, contingents of Indian troops and detachments of Free French forces who were upholding the honour of France by our side.

Time was needed to dispatch these forces and their supplies to Africa, and it was fully expected that Italy would launch a full-scale offensive before they could arrive. Egypt and the Sudan were threatened with attack from many sides, but for some reason neither Graziani nor the Duke of Aosta seemed anxious to undertake serious operations. By December the Italians had missed their greatest opportunity. In the second week of that month General Wavell launched his successful Libyan drive, and a month later British forces began their penetration into Eritrea and Abyssinia.

The Lightning Advance

On January 19, 1941, it was announced that Kassala, in the Sudan, had been retaken and that the Italians all along this front were in retreat. In three days they had withdrawn forty miles and the advance towards Keren was well under way. Meanwhile, our advanced forces from Kenya were making contact with enemy outposts in Italian Somaliland, and on January 24 it was announced that the Emperor Haile Selassie had re-entered Abyssinia to take his place at the head of the Ethiopian Patriot Army.

From the point of view of defence the nature of the country in East Africa seemed to offer every facility, but the Italians made little use of this advantage. On February 1 the British captured Agordat, in Eritrea, and two days later occupied Barentu. In Abyssinia the enemy were retreating towards Gondar, and on the Somaliland front South African and African troops, after capturing the important port of Kismayu on February 14, swept across the Juba river to Mogadishu.

March saw the biggest stand of the Italian forces at Keren, where they held what appeared to be an almost impregnable position. The battle for this fortress was bitterly contested, for here the Italians had assembled an army of some 40,000 men and, since the town was the key to the Italian defences in the north, they were determined not to yield it without a struggle.

A dramatic moment in the campaign came on March 16, when Berbera, in British Somaliland, after seven months in Italian hands, was captured by a British landing-party. This enabled another column to penetrate into Italian territory from the north and so maintain the pressure against the Italians from every possible side.

In Abyssinia, British and Patriot forces pressed forward from the Sudan through Metemma and Burye on to Debra Marcos ; from Italian Somaliland one column advanced along the Strada Reale, which runs via Neghelli to Addis Ababa, while another struck northwards to Daggabur and Jijiga, towards which town yet another column was advancing from the newly retaken Berbera. On March 24 a communiqué from Nairobi told how British Somaliland was once more under our complete control.

On Thursday, March 27, Keren fell after a tremendous assault in which Indian and Scottish troops particularly distinguished themselves, the latter swarming up the 6,000-ft. mountain of Sanchil, the most heavily defended Italian position. Harar and Diredawa were occupied about the same time and a few days later, on April 5, leading detachments of the Imperial forces entered Addis Ababa. The Duke of Aosta had left the city, and with the main Italian forces retreated northwards. Massawa fell on April 8, and the whole of the Red Sea was again safe for traffic.

Italy's African Empire had crumbled. Though two more stands were made, at Dessie and at Amba Alagi, the issue of the campaign was a foregone conclusion, for the Italians were penned into a hopeless position. The only thing the Duke of Aosta could do was to play for time and pin down British troops who were urgently needed elsewhere. Finally, unable to obtain reinforcements, he had to abandon the unequal struggle, and his request for an honourable surrender was granted. To the tune of "Cock of the North," played by South African pipers, he and his men marched down Alagi mountain. Local resistance continued in the Gondar and Lake Tana areas, but the campaign as such was over

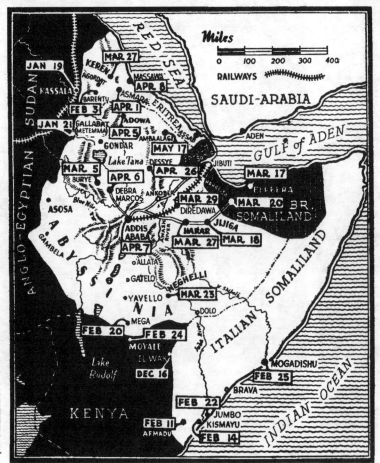

This map marks successive stages in the progress of the remarkable campaign in East Africa from the successful frontier raid at El Wak by South African and Gold Coast troops on December 16, 1940, to the action at Amba Alagi on May 17, 1941.

Map by courtesy of the "Daily Sketch"

Battlegrounds of the East African Campaign

THREE COUNTRIES OF A VANISHED EMPIRE, conquered in what Mr. Churchill has described as "one of the most remarkable campaigns ever fought by British or Imperial arms," are seen in this page. The top photograph shows planes of the South African Air Force flying over Eritrea, the rugged nature of the country being well typified by the rocky peaks in the background. Below, right, hundreds of Italian prisoners are marching under escort after their capture near Kismayu in Italian Somaliland. Left, British motor transport in the jungle country of the Gojjam district of Abyssinia. The physical difficulties which had to be overcome make the campaign all the more remarkable.   *Photos, British Official*

Our Diary of the War

SATURDAY, MAY 24, 1941 630th day

Sea.—British Navy intercepted German naval forces off Greenland on evening of May 23. H.M.S. Hood sunk. German battleship Bismarck damaged by Fleet Air Arm torpedo. British continued pursuit.

Air.—R.A.F. attacked enemy shipping off Dutch coast.

Africa.—Enemy troops and fort at Goang, in Gondar area, heavily bombed.

Near East.—More air-borne German troops landed in Crete. Hand-to-hand fighting between Maleme and Canea. During night of 23-24 R.A.F. heavily bombed enemy positions and aerodromes at Maleme.

Mass bombing by Germans of Canea, Retimo and Heraklion.

R.A.F. attacked German aircraft on aerodrome at Aleppo.

Iraq.—R.A.F. bombed insurgent positions at Qurmet Ali.

Home.—Night raid on West Country town.

General.—General Smuts appointed Field-Marshal.

SUNDAY, MAY 25 631st day

Sea.—Pursuit of the German battleship Bismarck continuing.

H.M. yacht Viva II reported sunk.

Air.—R.A.F. attacked shipping off Dutch, German and Danish coasts.

Africa.—Cairo announced surrender of over 8,000 troops north of Addis Ababa.

Near East.—Announced that King George of the Hellenes and the Greek Government had reached Egypt from Crete.

R.A.F. bombers and fighters heavily attacked enemy positions and aerodrome at Maleme, destroying at least 24 aircraft.

Iraq.—Rashid Ali revolt collapsing. R.A.F. bombed Ramadi, on the Euphrates, and aerodromes at Mosul and Baquba. Enemy aircraft attacked Habbaniyah.

Home.—Two Messerschmitts shot down.

MONDAY, MAY 26 632nd day

Sea.—Torpedo bombers of Ark Royal scored successive hits on German battleship Bismarck. Pursuit continued.

Africa.—Cairo announced that as result of recent fighting in Soddu area, Italians had lost four divisions.

Near East.—Fresh German air-borne reinforcements arrived at Maleme and strongly attacked British troops west of Canea, causing their withdrawal to new positions. R.A.F. renewed attacks on troop-carriers, beaches and aerodromes.

Iraq.—Lawful Regent, Emir Abdul Ilah, now back in Iraq. R.A.F. bombed aerodrome at Mosul.

Home.—Attack on Dover balloon barrage. East Anglian coast town bombed. Enemy fighter shot down in Channel.

TUESDAY, MAY 27 633rd day

Sea.—German battleship Bismarck sunk by naval torpedoes after pursuit of 1,750 miles.

Admiralty announced loss off Crete of cruisers Gloucester and Fiji, and destroyers Juno, Greyhound, Kelly and Kashmir.

Air.—R.A.F. made successful raid on Lannion aerodrome, Brittany. Enemy coastal shipping attacked. Night raids on Cologne and on aerodrome near Caen.

Africa.—Cairo announced enemy advance in Sollum area. At night our troops in Tobruk made small advance.

Near East.—Severe fighting continued in Crete; heavy attacks made on British forces in Canea area. R.A.F. heavily raided Maleme. R.A.F. bombed aerodrome at Aleppo.

Home.—Single aircraft dropped bombs on a town in East Scotland. Raider destroyed off Cornish coast.

General.—Roosevelt broadcast announcement of proclamation of unlimited national emergency.

WEDNESDAY, MAY 28 634th day

Sea.—Admiralty announced that British submarines had sunk Italian liner Conte Rosso, bound for Libya, and torpedoed three tankers, one being certainly destroyed.

Air.—Coastal Command bombed supply ship off Brest. At night Bomber Command raided targets in N.W. Germany.

Africa.—Cairo announced that British had withdrawn from Halfaya Pass, Libya. Benghazi raided by R.A.F. Coastal shipping damaged.

R.A.F. attacked enemy supply vessel taking refuge in Sfax harbour, Tunisia. Vichy Government lodged protest.

Round-up of Italians proceeding in Abyssinia. Garrison at Debra Tabor surrounded.

Near East.—Cairo stated that more airborne German troops had landed in Crete and made heavy attacks against Canea, compelling further withdrawal of British lines. Germans claimed capture of Canea. New British units stated to have reached Crete. Italian troops landed in eastern Crete.

R.A.F. attacked landing-ground at German-occupied island of Scarpanto.

Iraq.—British captured Khan Nuqta, half way between Falluja and Baghdad.

Home.—Bombs fell at night at many widespread places on coast. Two day and two night raiders destroyed.

THURSDAY, MAY 29 635th day

Sea.—Admiralty announced loss of H.M. cruiser York, bombed while out of action off Crete; and of H.M. destroyer Mashona, sunk by enemy aircraft after Bismarck action.

Africa.—Four enemy aircraft raiding Tobruk shot down. Operations in Lakes area, Abyssinia, proceeding well.

Near East.—Announced that British forces in Crete had withdrawn to positions east of Suda Bay. Germans claimed capture of Heraklion. Further enemy reinforcements were landed, necessitating new British withdrawals.

R.A.F. attacked aerodrome at Deir ez Zor, Syria.

FRIDAY, MAY 30 636th day

Africa.—S.A.A.F. continued to harass Italian force holding out at Gimma, Abyssinia. In Gondar area, forts at Azozo and Digya were attacked.

Near East.—Evacuation of British forces from Crete began. R.A.F. heavily bombed aerodromes at Maleme and Heraklion.

Iraq.—Cairo announced that British troops advancing northwards had occupied Ur. Other forces had reached Kadaimain, five miles north-west of Baghdad. Heavy bombing attacks on Washash and Rashid.

Home.—Sharp night raid on West of England town. Bombs also fell in Dublin, causing damage and casualties.

Three German bombers reported destroyed, two by H.M. ships.

THE BRISTOL BEAUFIGHTER (above) is a twin-engined, high speed, heavily-armed fighter monoplane produced by the Bristol Aeroplane Co., the firm responsible for the Beaufort, Blenheim and Bombay aircraft. The Beaufighter is suitable for use either as a day or night interceptor, and has proved a very useful weapon against the German night bombers. This is the first photo of a Beaufighter to be officially released.
Photo, British Official : Crown Copyright

Old Chungking Is Used to New Terrors

Chungking, capital of Free China, the most bombed city in the world, showing the river Yangtze and the mountains in the background. During two years of Japanese bombardment one-third of Chungking has been utterly destroyed and a third partly ruined. The population take the blitz as a matter of course, and crowd into deep cave-shelters, waiting sometimes for many hours in the dark until the All Clear signals the enemy's departure.

Citizens of Chungking, like those of London, have ceased to be perturbed by enemy frightfulness. Below is a post-blitz scene on the Hsiao-Liangtze road. But Chungking, one of the oldest cities in the world, has seen a lot of trouble in its time, and can go on taking it. In spite of Japanese aggression the city was modernized in 1938, when it became the capital.

THE BURNING CITY OF CHUNGKING, like a vast funeral pyre, after the Japanese raid of August 21, 1940. More than a square mile of buildings, including the congested shopping centre in the ancient walled part of the town, was set on fire. Right centre, citizens in a cave-shelter. When enemy raiders have crossed the border of the province one red lantern is hoisted on a mast, and two lanterns go up if planes are heading for Chungking.

Photos Associated Press and Wide World

For a Button or a Tank, Indent on Ordnance!

The Royal Army Ordnance Corps has developed almost beyond recognition since the last war, largely owing to the rapid growth of mechanization. It is a corps of which little is heard until something goes wrong, for which reason they were once called " apostles of disaster." Some idea of the vital services performed by the corps is given below.

Lieut.-General Sir Walter Venning, as Quartermaster-General to the Forces, holds a position fully as responsible as that of a commander-in-chief in the field, for his is the herculean task of seeing that our armies both at home and in the field are fully armed, equipped, fed, housed and transported. Under his control are the various branches of the army which cater for every need of the fighting men, and two important corps play a great part in seeing that the wheels of the army are kept turning smoothly : they are the Royal Army Ordnance Corps and the Royal Army Service Corps. The former may be looked upon as the army's universal provider ; the latter as a universal distributor, the army's " Carter Paterson." This article gives a brief résumé of the work done by that prodigious organization the R.A.O.C., while the R.A.S.C. will be dealt with in a later page.

The R.A.O.C. under various designations is one of the most ancient branches of the British Army. An Assize of Arms in 1181, giving a regular scale of weapons and equipment, is said to be the earliest example of what have now become enormous inventories. In England the Master-General of the Ordnance, from Henry VIII's time until the middle of the 19th century, was head of a board, partly military, partly civil, which managed all affairs concerning the artillery, engineers and field material of the army, and it is interesting to note that both Marlborough and Wellington were Master-General of the Ordnance.

Although the term ordnance was originally the general designation of all guns, howitzers and firearms of larger calibre than small arms, and the ordnance service was once concerned solely with artillery, the R.A.O.C. of today has become a sort of universal provider. Apart from rations and fuel, there is no part of the army's equipment and clothing, from a button to a tank, from a revolver to a howitzer, which is not issued, stored and serviced by the corps. The R.A.O.C. consists of three main divisions, each under its own director.

The Director of Ordnance Services deals with clothing, equipment and accommodation stores ; the Director of Ordnance Services (Weapons) sees that the army is provided with all its lethal weapons from rifles to long-range artillery, signal stores ranging from telephones to wireless sets, all bridging stores, every kind of vehicle, all types of ammunition and explosives, instruments such as compasses, binoculars and predictors, as well as miscellaneous stores like sandbags and barbed wire ; the Director of Ordnance Services (Engineering) sees that the army's technical equipment is kept up to date and in good working order. To aid in this the R.A.O.C. has two special units, the L.A.D.s (Light Aid Detachments), consisting of an officer and twelve other ranks, which deal with repairs requiring not more than a few hours' work, and R.A.O.C. divisional workshops, known as " Recksecks " (repair and recovery sections), in which a worn gun can be given new life or a wrecked Bren carrier

LT.-GEN. SIR WALTER VENNING, Q.M.G., supplies the army with everything from buttons to big guns.   *Photo, Topical*

renovated. Both these units are mobile and deal with varied tasks with unvarying success. Although these workshops have specialists competent to repair such things as compasses and telescopic sights, the bulk of the work carried out in them is the repair of motor vehicles. Apart from the mobile divisional workshops, the R.A.O.C. has its big stationary workshops and base repair shops.

Commenting on the miracles expected of the Ordnance Services, a correspondent of " The Times " remarked that on one occasion in France 50,000 men were instructed to wear white patches during night exercises. The R.A.O.C. produced the patches.

Repairs in the Field

The enormous development of mechanical transport has, of course, thrown a great burden upon the engineering side of the ordnance services and every campaign in the war has demonstrated the need for vehicle maintenance, on which the success of mobile columns so largely depends.

Whenever a gun or a tank or a lorry or a Bren-gun carrier falls out of action through some mechanical defect or is a slight casualty, the mobile repair shops or L.A.D.s must be there to haul it off the road and repair it as quickly as possible.

So important, indeed, is this question of vehicle maintenance that there was recently instituted in the Northern Command a special maintenance course for commanding officers, open only to officers of the rank of lieut.-colonel and above. At the end of the course the colonels are required to don overalls and assume positions which would once have been thought inconsistent with the dignity of two pips and a crown to detect faults in school vehicles. The result has been that older officers, brought up in the era of horses, have gone away filled with a new enthusiasm for the vehicles of their unit.

But though the R.A.O.C. today is largely manned by ex-garage hands and mechanically-minded youths, women also figure among the personnel. Members of the A.T.S. look after the clothing stores ; and civilian women, under R.A.O.C. officers, work in the laundries where thousands of blankets and sheets are washed.

This giant American boring and drilling machine now used in the British Army is one of the many instruments supplied by the Ordnance Services.   *Photo, British Official*

R.A.O.C.—the Army's Universal Providers

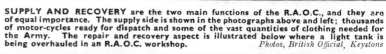

SUPPLY AND RECOVERY are the two main functions of the R.A.O.C., and they are of equal importance. The supply side is shown in the photographs above and left; thousands of motor-cycles ready for dispatch and some of the vast quantities of clothing needed for the Army. The repair and recovery aspect is illustrated below where a light tank is being overhauled in an R.A.O.C. workshop.   *Photos, British Official, Keystone*

MR. ROOSEVELT'S CALL TO THE AMERICAS
Significant Passages from the 'Fireside Talk' of May 27

WHAT we face are cold, hard facts. The first fundamental fact is that what started as a European war has developed, as the Nazis always intended it should develop, into a world war for world domination. Adolf Hitler never considered the domination of Europe as a end in itself. European conquest was but a step towards the ultimate goals in all other continents. It is unmistakably apparent to all of us that unless the advance of Hitlerism is forcibly checked now the Western Hemisphere will be within range of Nazi weapons of destruction.

Your Government knows what terms Hitler, if victorious, would impose. They are indeed the only terms on which he would accept a so-called " negotiated " peace. Under those terms Germany would literally parcel out the world, hoisting the Swastika over vast territories and populations, setting up puppet governments of its own choosing subject to the will and policy of a conqueror.

To the peoples of the Americas, triumphant Hitler would say, as he said after the seizure of Austria, after Munich, the seizure of Czechoslovakia : " I am now completely satisfied. This is the last territorial readjustment I seek." And he, of course, would add : " All we want is peace, friendship, and profit-able trade relations with you of the new world." And were any of us in the Americas so incredibly simple and forgetful as to accept those honeyed words, what would happen ?

In the Nazi Book of Conquest

Those of the New World who were seeking profits would be urging that all the dictator-ships desired was " peace." They would oppose toil and taxes for American armament. Meanwhile the dictatorships would be forcing the enslaved peoples of their Old World conquests into the system they are even now organizing—to build a naval and air force intended to gain a hold and be master of the Atlantic and the Pacific as well.

They would fasten an economic strangle-hold upon our several nations. Quislings would be found to subvert the Governments of our Republics, and the Nazis would back their Fifth Columns with invasion if necessary.

I am not speculating about all this ; I merely repeat what is already in the Nazi book of world conquest. They plan to treat the Latin American nations as they are now treating the Balkans. They plan then to strangle the United States of America and the Dominion of Canada.

UNDER the Nazis even our right of worship would be threatened. The Nazi world does not recognize any god except Hitler, for the Nazis are as ruthless as the Communists in the denial of God. What place has religion, which preaches the dignity of the human being and the majesty of human souls, in a world where moral standards are measured by treachery, bribery, and Fifth Columnists ?

Will our children, too, wander off goose-stepping in search of new gods ? We do not accept and will not permit this Nazi " shape of things to come." It will never be enforced upon us if we act in the present crisis with the wisdom and courage which distinguished our country in all the crises of the past.

THE war is approaching the brink of the western hemisphere itself ; it is coming very close home. The control or occupation by Nazi forces of any islands of the Atlantic would jeopardize the immediate safety of portions of North and South America and of the island possessions of the United States and the ultimate safety of the continental United States itself.

Hitler's plan of world domination would be near its accomplishment today were it not for two factors. One is the epic resistance of Britain and her Colonies and the great Dominions, fighting not only to maintain the existence of the island of Britain but also to hold the Near East and Africa. The other is the magnificent defence of China.

All these together prevent the Axis from winning control of the seas by ships and air-craft. The Axis Powers can never achieve their objective of world domination unless they first obtain control of the seas. This is their supreme purpose today, and to achieve it they must capture Great Britain.

> AS President of a united, determined people, I say solemnly : We reassert the ancient American doctrine of freedom of the seas, we reassert the solidarity of the twenty-one American Republics and the Dominion of Canada in the preservation of the independence of the hemisphere. We have pledged material support to the other democracies of the world, and we will fulfil that pledge. We in the Americas will decide for ourselves whether, when, and where our American interests are attacked or our security threatened. We are placing our armed forces in a strategic military position. We will not hesitate to use our armed forces to repel attack. We reassert our abiding faith in the vitality of our con-stitutional Republic, as the perpetual home of freedom and tolerance and devotion to the word of God.
>
> Therefore, with a profound conscious-ness of my responsibilities to my countrymen and my country's cause, I have tonight issued a Proclamation that an unlimited national emergency exists and requires the strengthening of our defence to the extreme limit of our national power and authority. The nation will expect all individuals and all groups to play their full parts without stint and without selfishness, and without doubt our democracy will triumphantly survive.
>
> I repeat the words of the signers of the Declaration of Independence, that little band of patriots fighting long ago against overwhelming odds, but certain, as we are, of ultimate victory : " With a firm reliance on the protec-tion of Divine Providence, we mutually pledge to each other our lives, our fortunes, and our sacred honour."

No spurious argument, no appeal to senti-ment, no false pledges like those given by Hitler at Munich, can deceive the American people into believing that he and his Axis partners would not, with Britain defeated, close in relentlessly on this hemisphere. But if the Axis fail to gain control of the seas they are certainly defeated, their dreams of world domination will then go by the board and the criminal leaders who started this war will suffer inevitable disaster. Both they and their people know this and they are afraid. That is why they are risking everything they have in conducting desperate attempts to break through to command the ocean.

Once they are limited to continuing the land war, their cruel forces of occupation will be unable to keep their heel on the necks of millions of innocent oppressed peoples of the Continent of Europe, and in the end their whole structure will break into little pieces. And the wider the Nazi land effort the greater the danger.

We do not forget the silent peoples. The masters of Germany—those, at least, who have not been assassinated or escaped to free soil—have marked these peoples and their children's children. But those people, spiritually unconquered—Austrians, Czechs, Poles, Norwegians, Dutch, Belgians, French-men, Greeks, Southern Slavs, yes, even those Italians and Germans who have themselves been enslaved—will prove to be a powerful force in disrupting the Nazi system. Yes, all freedom—meaning freedom to live and not freedom to conquer and subjugate other peoples—depends on the freedom of the seas.

THE Battle of the Atlantic now extends from the icy waters of the North Pole to the frozen continent of the Antarctic. Throughout this huge area there have been sinkings of merchant ships in alarming and increasing numbers by Nazi raiders and submarines. There have been sinkings even of ships carrying neutral flags. There have been sinkings in the South Atlantic, off West Africa and the Cape Verdes between the Azores and the islands off the American coast, and between Greenland and Iceland. Great numbers of these sinkings have been actually within the waters of the Western Hemisphere. The blunt truth is this—and I reveal this with the full knowledge of the British Government—the present rate of Nazi sinkings of merchant ships is more than three times as high as the capacity to replace them ; is more than twice the combined British and American output of merchant ships today.

We answer this peril by two simultaneous measures : First, by the speeding up and increasing of our great shipbuilding pro-gramme. Second, by helping to cut down the losses on the high seas.

I HAVE said on many occasions that the United States is mustering its men and resources only for the purpose of defence— only to repel attack. I repeat that statement now. But we must be realistic. When we use the word attack we have to relate it to the lightning speed of modern warfare. If you see your enemy coming to you in a tank or a bomber and hold your fire until you see the whites of his eyes you will never know what hit you. Our Bunker Hill of tomorrow may be several thousand miles away from Boston. Old-fashioned common sense calls for the use of strategy which will prevent such an enemy from gaining a foothold in the first place. We have accordingly extended our patrol in North and South Atlantic waters.

This America Will Do

OUR national policy today, therefore, is this : First, we shall actively resist, wherever necessary and with all our resources, every attempt by Hitler to extend his Nazi domination to the Western Hemisphere or to threaten it. We shall actively resist his every attempt to gain control of the seas. We insist upon the vital importance of keeping Hitler-ism away from any point in the world which could be used, or would be used, as a base for an attack against the Americas. Second, from the point of view of strict naval and military necessity we shall give every possible assist-ance to Britain and to all who, with Britain, are resisting Hitlerism or its equivalent with force of arms. Our patrols are helping now to ensure the delivery of needed supplies to Britain. All additional measures necessary for the delivery of the goods will be taken. The delivery of needed supplies to Britain is imperative. This can be done. It must be done. It will be done.

I Was There! .... Eye Witness Stories of the War

In Spite of Nazi Bombs We Got Away from Greece

Men of the Empire Forces in Greece who had tramped miles across the mountains were picked up by naval craft, merchantmen, and flying-boats all along the eastern shores of Greece. Reuter's correspondent who left with one batch of troops wrote this vivid account of the evacuation.

I WAS evacuated with a large force from a small port in the Peloponnese after spending a nightmare 24 hours lying under olive trees in a cornfield. We were subjected to continuous bombing and machine-gunning by Nazi planes. Many of my comrades had also been through Dunkirk.

I had left Athens at night with a convoy of lorries under sealed orders. As we roared towards Corinth in a ghostlike procession, I realized that a full-scale withdrawal was under way. We passed a mile-long column of British Imperial infantry marching in an exhausted state to their assembly post. More lorries and trucks joined in the convoy until one giant snake-like line was wending its way south.

In the grey light of dawn we passed through Burgos, where many British trucks had been left burning by the roadside as a result of Nazi machine-gunning. We swept on to the small port where we were to be picked up. Three ships lay sunk in the harbour. One ammunition dump was blazing furiously.

Thousands of troops were scattered in a wide area round the port. Acting on orders, they concealed themselves in woods and ditches in readiness for the embarkation which was planned at dead of night.

Throughout the day we underwent a terrific pasting from the German Air Force, which seemed to have scented the presence of large forces. First we watched Stukas bombing the harbour. Then the full brunt of the attack was turned on the valley. Large German bombers wheeled overhead unopposed. We were unable to use our anti-aircraft guns for fear of betraying our position. One bomber unloaded a stick of bombs 50 feet from our cornfield, killing a number of men. Then the bombers came down to a lower level and systematically machine-gunned the woods and bushes lying off the roadway. Explosive bullets zipped through the trees, plugging the ground all around us. Casualties were miraculously small.

Towards dusk we were given the order to form threes in the roadway and march towards the port. "In case of an air raid you will keep marching down the road. Any casualties will be taken with you. Anyone who shelters will be left behind. The embarkation is timed to the minute. Our ships will be there." With these instructions we started out on our way.

Never shall I forget that march. With perfect discipline thousands of troops went down the straight road to the sea, some of them singing. They were a perfect prey for Nazi bombers, but luck was with us. No planes appeared.

We found ourselves standing on the quayside. After what seemed an interminable time lighters appeared and systematically took off large batches of troops to the vessels lying outside the harbour. With at least 5,000 troops I was taken on board a warship. The organization was most impressive. Although it was by now the early hours of the morning every man was immediately given a hot meal and drinks. Then the men dropped down exhausted in odd corners throughout the ship.

Dawn found us steaming out to sea with a formidable escort of cruisers and destroyers weaving our way round vessels which were watching out for submarines and hostile aircraft. The ship was jammed with officers and men, many of them wounded. British and Imperial medical officers, after days of weary work at the front, spent all night

The story of the evacuation of R.A.F. personnel from Greece is told in this page. Above, ground staff of the R.A.F. are seen outside Athens en route for a southern port.
Photo, British Official

carrying out emergency operations. Nazi dive-bombers came over towards noon, but they were driven off by anti-aircraft fire. At least one plane was shot down.

Despite the gruelling time our forces went through they kept cheerful. When we reached a friendly port our vessel was quickly turned round and went back to pick up more.

Mine Were the Last R.A.F. Men to Leave

In addition to the Empire Forces, R.A.F. personnel had to be moved out of Greece when the position became untenable. The story of the escape of the last 2,000 was told by a senior staff officer who was entrusted with the organization of the evacuation.

THE last R.A.F. man to leave Greece was a staff officer, who himself got away under cover of darkness in a 25-foot boat crammed with 35 men. He said:

When it was clear we had to leave Greece the R.A.F. sent me to arrange for embarkation from the Peloponnese. I was supplied plentifully with money to buy or charter ships.

The total R.A.F. personnel to be evacuated, including flying men, was about 3,500. About 1,000 comprised the most highly trained men and officers who were evacuated with their own machines and Sunderland flying-boats from the port of Argos.

The remaining 2,500, who had been subjected to bombing and ground strafing for several days, were beginning to feel the strain. Of this number 500 were eventually evacuated

MERCHANT SHIPPING engaged in the evacuation of Allied troops from Greece was repeatedly attacked by German aircraft. Here, in the Greek harbour of Nauplia, whence 500 R.A.F. men were evacuated, lies a burned-out "Union Castle" steamer. *Photo, Associated Press*

SUNDERLAND FLYING-BOATS did good work in evacuating small parties of R.A.F. men from Greece. One of these great aircraft is here seen awaiting the arrival of a small boat. The Short Sunderland, a four-engined flying-boat, has a range of 1,780 miles. Its very effective armament has caused it to be dubbed the " Flying Porcupine " by German fighters.   *Photo, British Official*

from Nauplia, 1,000 from Kalamati and 400 from Gythian.

After destroying all our material and the bulk of our kit among the olive groves we hid near the shore.

One of the most touching parts of the whole affair was the help and kindness shown us by the Greeks in towns and villages. We might have been a conquering rather than a withdrawing force. Although we were going in the wrong direction they loaded us with food from their scanty stores, gave us flowers and provided us with billets.

Unhappily, a 2,000-ton ship which we had earmarked for the evacuation was found to be too slow to make a safe getaway from the range of Nazi planes during the night hours, but I secured a 500-tonner and aboard this we evacuated 600 men.

water bottles, given a steaming cup of hot tea and a cigarette, and within 15 minutes were as comfortable as could be. One of the nurses called up our friend, Mr. Bruce Smith, of the American Red Cross, and he appeared promptly to take us to an hotel for the night, the young doctor driving us there in his car.

I am quite sure that this was just the ordinary service that anyone would obtain. Certainly until the records were made out no one knew who we were, and where we came from. The admirable way in which this post functioned should be a sense of satisfaction to you in having developed such a smoothly functioning organization.

Your British First-Aid Posts Worked Well

The following tribute to the efficiency of British first-aid stations was paid by Dr. John E. Gordon, U.S. Liaison Officer with the Ministry of Health, after his personal experience in a recent air raid.

IN a letter to Professor F. R. Fraser, Director-General of the Emergency Medical Service, Dr. Gordon said:

Through courtesies extended to me from your office, and from many others concerned with the provision of medical care for air-raid casualties, I have from time to time during my stay in Great Britain visited various hospitals and first-aid stations. These observations have included those of London and other cities, such as Birmingham, Coventry, Nottingham, and Edinburgh. Everywhere I have been I have received the fullest cooperation and full details about organization.

Nevertheless, I think I learned more about the functioning of your first-aid posts in a few minutes the other Wednesday evening than in all my previous explorations. The system functioned so well that I wish particularly to express my appreciation not only of it, but of the personal service I received.

I was bombed out. The blast was terrific ; there was a veritable shower of glass, furniture was upturned, and altogether it was a pretty good show. Happily I suffered only a minor scalp wound and a few bruises. The door of my apartment was blown off, and lodged sideways in the doorway. I crawled out into the hall.

Within a minute perhaps, certainly no longer than two minutes, one of your first-aid workers, a young lady, popped in off the street, put a towel over my bleeding head, and with my colleague, Dr. Beeson, proceeded with us to the nearest first-aid post. She deposited us with the nurse in charge there, said a curt good-night, and I have not seen her since. She was just off about her business. At the first-aid post we had the finest attention from the four or five nurses and first-aid workers on duty.

A young doctor arrived promptly and made a few minor repairs that were indicated. We were then put to bed in the first-aid post between warm blankets—packed with hot-

All over Britain the First-Aid Posts have functioned well in the testing time. Here, in the City of Westminster, an ambulance has arrived during a raid. The injured stretcher cases are examined by doctors or nurses to decide whether or not they must be sent to hospital.
Photo, " News Chronicle "

I WAS THERE!

Our Big Convoy Came Proudly Over the Atlantic

Aboard a ship in one of the largest convoys brought safely over the Atlantic was the American reporter Quentin Reynolds, the first journalist to cross in a convoy. Here is the story of his voyage as published in the " Daily Express."

AT first it was just a faint grey smudge on the horizon. In mid-Atlantic a smudge on the horizon means a ship, and a ship that might or might not be a friendly one.

The mate kept his glasses glued to his eyes. The smudge grew darker, and then faintly—because it was blowing a gale and the horizon kept rising and falling—we could see the ship.

" How far from America do you think you are ? " the mate said, unexpectedly.

" I don't remember. About two thousand

Hudsons of the Coastal Command. The Admiralty and the Air Ministry were co-operating beautifully in protecting this precious war material we carried.

From the deck of our freighter the whole panorama of the convoy was spread out before our eyes. There were ships in every direction : large, proud-looking freighters ; small, battered tramps, jaunty despite their rusty paint ; enormous, armed merchant ships that had once been luxury liners ; and always the small, quick destroyers dashing inquisitively all over the sea.

Suddenly two of them wheeled and scurried a mile to port. Two Hudsons which had been flying high dropped over them. Perhaps 50 feet to the rear of one of the destroyers a huge fountain rose from the sea, seemed to hang in the soft air for a moment and then fell back reluctantly. A destroyer had dropped a depth charge.

The two destroyers (both American) dropped more depth charges. The two aeroplanes were very low now, buzzing angrily, looking for the submarine which had the temerity to consider attacking us.

Finally the two planes climbed joyously to a thousand feet and the destroyers, looking like sleek, grey cats, abandoned the chase and came back into formation.

Did they get the submarine ? I didn't know. I found later that the Admiralty had listed it as " probable." . . . .

Then the line of the horizon broadened and thickened and soon it wasn't a line at all ; it was land. The convoy was almost home. The sun shimmered on the soft green hills. We felt our way carefully, for this was mined territory.

We were only 20 hours from our home port. The night crept towards us stealthily as though it had some secret purpose of its own. It had. It had come to guard us from the Nazi dive-bombers on the last stretch of our trip. . . .

Far to the right searchlights poked long white fingers into the air. An air raid was on. The still, thin air carried the faint drone of Nazi aeroplanes to us ; the drone grew, and now they were above us, all unconscious of the prize that lay beneath protected by the friendly darkness of the night. The night ended and the dawn showed us England. Our ships, looking mighty proud, steamed past trawlers, pilot boats and harbour craft, disdaining to greet them with even a whistle toot.

GUN CREW at action stations on an ex-American destroyer, as one of the largest convoys, described in this page, is escorted across the Atlantic.   *Photo: Fox*

miles, I guess." When you are in a convoy no one knows your exact position but the captain.

" Well," the mate laughed, " you're nearer than that. Take the glasses and look at that destroyer if you want to see a piece of America seven miles away."

The glasses brought the destroyer close. It had four funnels. Only American destroyers have four funnels.

Other smoke smudges appeared, and they too materialized into ships. This rendezvous had been made before we left Canada. The word had gone out to the Admiralty : " Have escort at this position at noon on such a day." And here they were.

We would need them, we felt. We were nearing the most dangerous spot of water in the world. Until now we had only to worry about submarines and raiders. From now on we should have to be on the look-out for the long-range German dive-bombers and for mines.

But our convoy, the largest yet to attempt crossing, steamed merrily on. This was a strong life-line that Canada and America were tossing to their neighbour—England.

We had four big aeroplanes lashed to our deck. The smaller fighters were stowed in crates down in the holds. In addition to our planes our freighter carried an assorted cargo of tractors, drugs, cheese, and high explosives ; 500 tons of cordite, T.N.T. and dynamite—not the cargo of choice.

As we neared the English shores the character of our escort changed. Huge Sunderland flying boats encircled us during the daylight hours ; then there were Lockheed

ABBREVIATIONS USED BY THE FOUR SERVICES			
The Army: A—D			

A.A. Anti-Aircraft or Army Act.
A.A.G. Assistant Adjutant-General.
A.A.L.M.G. Anti-Aircraft Light Machine-Gun.
A.B. Army Book.
A.C.C. Army Catering Corps.
A.C.I. Army Council Instruction.
A.C.M.F. Australian Commonwealth Military Forces.
A.D. Air Defence.
A.D.C. Aide-de-Camp or Army Dental Corp.
A.D.O.S. Assistant Director of Ordnance Services.
A.D.R. Assistant Director of Remounts.
A.D.S. Advanced Dressing-Station.
A.E.C. Army Educational Corps.
A.F. Army Form.
A.F.V. Armoured Fighting Vehicle.
A.G. & Q.M.G. Adjutant-General & Quartermaster-General.
A.I.D. Army Intelligence Department.
A.I.L.O. Air Intelligence Liaison Officer.
A.L.G. Advanced Landing Ground.
A.M.G.O. Assistant Master-General of Ordnance.
A.M.P.C. Auxiliary Military Pioneer Corps.
A.O. Army Order.
A.O.C. Air Officer Commanding.
A.P. Ammunition Point, Armour Piercing.
A.P.M. Assistant Provost Marshal.
A.P.S. Army Postal Service.
A.P.S.S. Army Printing and Stationery Services.
A.Q.M.G. Assistant Quartermaster General.
A.R.H. Ammunition Railhead.
A.R.O. Army Routine Order.

A.R.P. Ammunition Refilling Point.
A.T.S. Auxiliary Territorial Service (Women's).
B.C. Battery Commander.
B.M. Brigade Major.
B.P.O. Base Post Office.
B.Q.M.S. Battery Quartermaster Sergeant.
B.S.M. Battery Sergeant-Major.
C.B. Counter-Battery or Confinement to Barracks.
C.B.O. Counter - Battery Officer.
C.C.S. Casualty Clearing Station.
C.F. Chaplain to the Forces.
C.G.S. Chief of General Staff.
C.I.G.S. Chief of the Imperial General Staff.
C.-in-C. Commander in Chief.
C.O. Commanding Officer.
C.O.M.E. Chief Ordnance Mechanical Engineer.
C.O.O. Chief Ordnance Officer.
C.Q.M.S. Company Quartermaster Sergeant.
C.R.A. Commander Royal Artillery.
C.R.E. Commander Royal Engineers.
C.R.O. Corps Routine Order.
C.S.M. Company Sergeant-Major.
D.A.A.G. Deputy Assistant Adjutant-General.
D.A. & Q.M.G. Deputy Adjutant & Quartermaster-General.
D.A.C.G. Deputy Assistant Chaplain-General.
D.A.D.O.S. Deputy Assistant Director of Ordnance Services.
D.A.M.G.O. Deputy Assistant Master-General of the Ordnance.
D.A.P.M. Deputy Assistant Provost Marshal.

D.A.Q.M.G. Deputy Assistant Quarter-master-General.
D.C.M. District Court-Martial.
D.D.M.I. Deputy Director of Military Intelligence.
D.D.M.O.I. Deputy Director of Military Operations & Intelligence.
D.D.M.S. Deputy Director Medical Services.
D.E.S. Director of Engineer Stores Service.
D.F. Direction Finding.
D.F.W. Director of Fortifications and Works.
D.G.A.M.S. Director - General of Army Medical Services.
D.G.R. Director of Graves Registration.
D.H. Director of Hygiene.
D.I.W.T. Director of Inland Water Transport Service.
D.M. Director of Mechanization.
D.M.I. Director of Military Intelligence.
D.M.O.I. Director of Military Operations and Intelligence
D.M.Q. Director of Movements and Quartering.
D.M.S. Director of Medical Services.
D.M.T. Director of Military Training.
D.O.S. Director of Ordnance Services.
D.P.S. Director of Personal Services. Director of Postal Services.
D.R.L.S. Dispatch Rider Letter Service.
D.R.O. Director of Recruiting and Organisation.
D.S.D. Director of Staff Duties.
D.S.T. Director of Supplies and Transport.
D.V.S. Director of Veterinary Services.

The Editor's Postscript

A NORTHERN IRELAND reader, like myself, finds Emerson one of the most stimulating, but not one of the most alluring of essayists—for he has no charm of style, no individual quaintness, rather a coolness, almost an austerity of manner, but such honesty of thought, such common sense and manifestation of goodness that his attentive reader feels himself forthwith a disciple listening to the voice of a master. A rare and eager spirit. I am glad that my Irish correspondent took the trouble to send me this passage from Emerson's essay on Compensation, for I agree with him that in so brief a space no more profound a study of the evils of Nazism could have come from any philosopher in the actual presence of those evil things—and it was written about a century ago. Read, marvel, and be encouraged!

◉

"The history of persecution is a history of endeavours to cheat Nature, to make water run uphill, to twist a rope of sand. It makes no difference whether the actors be many or one, a tyrant or a mob. A mob is a society of bodies voluntarily bereaving themselves of reason and traversing its work. The mob is man voluntarily descending to the nature of the beast. Its fit hour of activity is night. Its actions are insane, like its whole constitution. It persecutes a principle; it would whip a right; it would tar-and-feather justice, by inflicting fire and outrage upon the houses and persons of those who have these. It resembles the prank of boys who run with fire-engines to put out the ruddy aurora streaming to the stars. The inviolate spirit turns their spite against the wrongdoers. The martyr cannot be dishonoured. Every lash inflicted is a tongue of fame; every prison a more illustrious abode; every burned book or house enlightens the world; every suppressed or expunged word reverberates through the earth from side to side. The minds of men are at last aroused: reason looks out and justifies her own, and malice finds all her work vain. It is the whipper who is whipped, and the tyrant who is undone."

◉

It's turned twenty years since I went to Concord to see Emerson's home and his grave at Sleepy Hollow. Despite its memories of the Minute Men and the British reverse at Concord Bridge in the War of Independence and the modern Irish influx at Boston, there are no places in America where I am so conscious of the enduring English spirit as at Boston and Concord. And mention of the home of America's great essayist reminds me that the birthplace of our well-loved Charles Lamb—who differs from Emerson in almost every aspect—outside of which I stood in sorrow but yesterday, is now one of the pitiful ruins of the Temple, which is all in ruins through oft-repeated bombings. Even the church of the Templars, one of the most ancient shrines of London, has been gutted like St. Clement Danes near by in Fleet Street. London is now as rich in ruins as

Rome of the Caesars. I hope that the Vatican will escape, but I long for the cheap and gaudy stuff of Mussolini's Rome to feel the effect of our new " beautiful bombs."

◉

SPRINGTIME has come to London, everywhere the plane trees are greening, another week and they will be in full leaf. In many places the ruins wrought by planes of another sort will soon be so screened by the foliage of London's favourite tree that the abominable will yield place to the picturesque. Nature is always swift to cloak the follies of man . . . in the tropic lands especially. I remember going out to old Panama to see the ruins of the city that was sacked by Henry Morgan. There was little

GENERAL J. C. SMUTS, South Africa's Prime Minister and C.-in-C., received his appointment as Field Marshal in the British Army on May 24, 1941, his 71st birthday. South Africans subscribed over £140,000 for a birthday gift in the form of a contribution to the National War Fund for soldiers' dependants.   *Photo, Topical Press*

to see, as the periodical clearance of the jungle growth, a job for prisoners, was a little overdue. Left to the tender mercies of the jungle every stone would soon be swallowed up. Unnumbered towns once populous and wide spreading have been consumed by the jungle in Central America, just as the desert sand in Africa and Asia has deeply buried many another which some day will enrich world history when archaeology is more encouraged than the production of armaments.

◉

But I marvelled as I came up to town yesterday through the whole of south London at the scant evidence of destruction one could see, knowing too well what I could find in the centre, and at all points of the compass, within Greater London. I am certain, however, that London could take even worse than she has had and still carry on—bloody

but unbowed. It is towns like Liverpool, Birmingham, Manchester, Plymouth, where the blitz could concentrate on the vital centres of population and business, that show the results more painfully, if I may judge from what I'm told by visitors from all these places that have had to suffer in the Battle of Britain. Still we can all keep a stout heart until our R.A.F. has tipped the scale—and that will be sooner than we had hoped—in favour of our British air power . . . and then !

◉

OUR village seems suddenly to have burst into most colourful efflorescence. Walked up this afternoon as far as the church at the top of our only street that climbs to one of the finest views in Downland. Some of the cottages had displays of tulips that looked just like the colour pictures on the envelopes in which their bulbs are sold—pictures drawn by artists who never err on the side of understatement. The wistaria on a cottage brought memories of my verandah in Highgate, completely embowered with that loveliest of climbing shrubs, where through many a summer I spent delightful days in writing and reading, and where, as it happened, I had my first sight of a squadron of German planes attacking London on Saturday afternoon, July 7th, 1917 . . . a score or so that made as great a sensation then as two or three hundred today, though doing much less damage.

◉

But let's talk of the flowers and trees: lilacs in varying hues and some pure white are already in full bloom, the chestnuts that shade the road uphill are great masses of greenness and many of them have already lit their candles. My own apple orchard looks as though we had just had a snow fall, the grass strewn with fallen petals, though the trees seem to be as abundantly blossomed as they were before the biting wind set in from the south-west—our weather quarter here—and turned this May day into a good imitation of a blustering March coming in like a lion . . . grey sky and driving rain clouds and an aeroplane scudding over my study at this actual moment to remind me that on such a day twenty-five years ago no pilot would have cared to take the air. Progress ! [Heard an hour later that it had dropped bombs seven miles away near my chauffeur's evacuated house, blown out all the doors and windows and brought down the ceilings !!]

◉

I meant to mention that I do not recollect any springtime of my fifteen years of travel 'twixt London and the Sussex coast seeing such prodigal displays of primroses along the railway embankments. These are nearly over now, but they have been the welcome heralds of a re-birth of flower and frondage that tunes the soul to Nature's milder notes . . . while we await the coming of the Nazi swine ! But there are " steep places " near here and as the Nazis are already possessed of evil spirits we may see them do the Gadarene act, running violently to perish in the waters, when our H.G. ups and at them!

JOHN CARPENTER HOUSE
WHITEFRIARS, LONDON E.C.4.

Printed in England and published every Friday by the Proprietors, The Amalgamated Press, Ltd., The Fleetway House, Farringdon Street, London, E.C.4. Sole Agents for Australia and New Zealand : Messrs. Gordon & Gotch, Ltd. ; and for South Africa : Central News Agency, Ltd.   June 13th, 1941.   S.S.

Registered at the G.P.O. as a Newspaper

The War Illustrated, June 20th, 1941

Vol 4

The War Illustrated

Nº 94

Edited by Sir John Hammerton

FOURPENCE

WEEKLY

HAILE SELASSIE and GENERAL CUNNINGHAM, British Commander-in-Chief in East Africa, shaking hands on their victory. Time has its revenges, but surely none sweeter than the vindication of the rightful ruler of Abyssinia. On May 5, 1936, the Emperor was forced to flee from Addis Ababa after the brutal conquest of his realm by the Fascist bandits. On May 5, 1941, thanks to one of the most brilliant of British military operations, his throne was restored to him, and Mussolini's braggart interregnum ended.
Photo, British Official

Our Searchlight on the War

Britons' Escape Across Europe

In a recent speech in the House of Commons Mr. Eden related an incident to show how throughout Europe there are thousands, even millions, of people anxious to help the British and longing for their victory. Two British soldiers who had been captured in Northern France were sent to a prison camp in East Prussia. Managing to escape from there, they made a long and hazardous journey through Poland, across Hungary, through Yugoslavia and Greece, until they reached Athens. They knew no word of any language but their own, and yet, owing to their own fortitude and the secret help of sympathizers in all the countries they traversed, they were enabled eventually to rejoin their units, which by now were in the Western Desert. "Hitler," commented Mr. Eden, "though he may rule the lives of these people, cannot rule their hearts."

Postal Delays in Wartime

Considering the difficulties with which the Postmaster-General and his staff have to contend, our letters generally reach us with exemplary promptitude. Mails may, however, be considerably delayed by air raids and other wartime activities, and the Post Office has prepared a stamp of special design which will be impressed on inland correspondence that has been seriously delayed by enemy action. If the delay is slight the stamp will not be used, as this would only cause further delay, perhaps by missing connexion with a delivery. It is about the size of a halfpenny, and shows a bomb enclosed by the words "Delayed by enemy action."

Blockade Runner Caught

Boasting that "Germany always delivers the goods," Capt. Friedrich Brinkmann, master of the Nazi freighter Lech, arrived at Rio de Janeiro on March 3, having run the blockade from Bordeaux. The Lech, a motor-ship of 3,290 tons, started her homeward voyage on March 29, carrying a valuable mixed cargo which included 63 tons of nickel, 1,048 tons of dry salted hides, 1,260 tons of castor oil in drums, 1,500 tons of cottonseed cake, 5,891 kilos of mica, 25 tons of rock crystal, and 960 kilos of coffee. All these items, with the exception of the coffee, are of considerable value to German war industry, and it may be assumed that to the workers themselves the coffee would have been of equal importance. On May 24, however, the Admiralty announced that the Lech had been intercepted and seized by one of his Majesty's ships. When war broke out this vessel, outward bound from Hamburg, took refuge in Vigo, remaining there until 1940. She then unloaded her cargo and proceeded to Bordeaux, whence she sailed for Rio in February of this year. She is a valuable prize ship, and the report current early in May that she had been scuttled to avoid capture was fortunately untrue.

GERMAN MOTOR-SHIP, LECH, tried to run the British blockade but failed, being intercepted while on her way from South America to Occupied France with a valuable cargo.
Photo, Wide World

Iceland Independent

Stockholm was the first to announce on May 20 that Iceland had once more become a wholly independent State, her Parliament, the Althing, having decided to terminate the union with Denmark made in 1918. This Act of Union acknowledged the island as a sovereign state temporarily united with Denmark only through the identity of King Christian X. After December 31, 1940, the Danish Parliament and the Icelandic Legislature were empowered to demand that negotiations be opened concerning the revision of the Union Act. On April 10, the day after the German invasion of Denmark and Norway, the Althing took over all the powers exercised by the King, and also the conduct of foreign affairs, declaring that this was a purely temporary measure. Exactly ten days later British troops landed in Iceland to prevent a seizure by Germany, with the explicit assurance that they would be withdrawn at the end of the war. The Icelandic chargé d'affaires, Hr. Wilhelm Finsen, has stated that one of the reasons for the declaration of independence on May 20 was the difficulty of maintaining communications with Denmark. German propaganda, however, has put about a false story that it was issued under pressure from Great Britain. The British Government has not the slightest intention of interfering in the internal affairs of Iceland or in the relations between her and Denmark. The only reason for the military occupation of the island was to prevent its use as a most desirable German naval base.

'Crete News'

Two days before the invasion of Crete five New Zealanders based at Canea, who had been journalists in civil life, started a one-page news-sheet which they called "Crete News." They worked under difficulties, some of which were due to a shortage of type. There were no large-size "Hs" at all, so headlines had to be devised without using this letter; an "M" reversed was used for a "W." The first two issues had a circulation of about 3,000. Then Nazi dive-bombers got busy over Canea, and the circulation of No. 3 fell to 2,000. While three of the soldier "comps." were grimly setting up No. 4, their two companions having been detailed for urgent duty, bombs rocked the building and a burning house that collapsed at the end of the street cut off the press office. Pausing every now and again to rescue civilians from beneath the debris of wrecked buildings, the determined trio finished the setting and started printing. The following morning 600 copies of the fourth issue of "Crete News" were brought to Headquarters. "We couldn't print any more," apologized the three begrimed men, "for the plant has been burnt out."

Treasonable Listening-In

Death is the penalty risked by any German who may listen in to foreign broadcasts, and the first execution for this "crime" was carried out at Nuremberg on May 17. The victim was Johann Wild, a man of 49, and it was stated that he had not only listened but had passed on the information so received to others. The following day a Polish housemaid of 44 was sentenced to death at Grudziadz for listening to a B.B.C. Polish broadcast. Five persons to whom she had imparted the gist of the broadcast were given sentences ranging from five to ten years' imprisonment. Three Germans in Poland, who had listened to London broadcasts about Rudolf Hess, were let off comparatively lightly with sentences of three to five years, but the German judge commented that in future penalties would be much more rigorous as the British radio had become a serious menace to German rule in Poland.

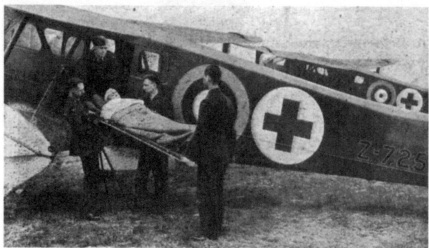

TWO AIR AMBULANCES have been presented to the R.A.F. by the Silver Thimble Fund. Over 17,000 thimbles have been melted down to provide hospitals, ambulances, and X-Ray sets for the forces, and during its first year's work the Fund raised £18,000, subscriptions having been received from all parts of the Empire.
Photo, British Official : Crown Copyright

The Way of the War

WHY, O WHY, DID IT HAPPEN IN CRETE?

Perchance Official Optimism Is a Greater Menace to Our Cause Than the 'Dangerously Unorthodox' Methods of the Nazis

LET us be fair. The Germans have learnt to use the air in war in a way never before attempted, hardly imagined.

Think how the Nazis employed their planes during the battle in Crete. They have used them as bombers and fighters, of course ; they have used them as scouts, as cavalry and as flying artillery, as troop-carriers and supply columns, even as light infantry. They have used them against other planes, against ships, against men on the ground. Never has the versatility of the aeroplane been so clearly demonstrated. It has been revealed as the speediest weapon in the modern armoury, as the most deadly, the most devastating, the most revolutionary—nay more, as the most powerful, since it can destroy armies, limit the operations of navies, drive opposing air fleets from the sky, terrorize peoples and wipe out towns.

"FANTASTIC " is the word most used to describe the fighting in Crete, and that its use is fully justified is plain from every story which has come from that strange battlefield. " Every man for himself is the order of the day" (reads just one account), " since parachutists have been dropping like confetti from clear skies, sometimes landing in the middle of our positions. Each man has been warned that he must be prepared suddenly to find a Nazi at his elbow, and to deal promptly with him.

" Strange as is the scene by day," it goes on, " it is fantastic by night. The sky is lit with flares and tracer shells, while searchlights of the Navy and ground defences pick out the swaying parachutists floating to earth." But however fantastic, the fighting is after all only a more concentrated repetition of the experiences of the last eighteen months.

RIGHT at the very beginning of the war the Germans used their aeroplanes to destroy the Polish airfields and as flying artillery ; they also employed them as terroristic weapons against the Polish towns. Rotterdam was but Warsaw carried to a higher degree of infernal perfection. In Norway the Nazis developed the aeroplane as a troop-carrier, thus enabling their front line to be speedily and continuously reinforced ; at the same time they smashed our bases, and through their command of the air prevented us from establishing new ones. A few weeks later the dive-bomber came into its own against troops massed on the plains of Flanders and Northern France, while parachutists, after making their debut in Norway, showed what they could really do in the five days' war in Holland. Then the Luftwaffe was flung against the R.A.F. over Britain, but here at last it more than met its match, since our aerodromes were numerous and well-defended, our fighters were better in many ways, our pilots altogether on top.

BUT, returning to Crete, it would seem that little attention had been paid to the lessons of the preceding months. Though we were in the undisturbed occupation of the great Greek island for six months we developed only one airfield and an emergency landing-ground, and built but two more. Even these were so poorly defended that quite early in the battle they were rendered untenable, and the British fighter force had to be withdrawn. True, Crete is a mountainous country, and there are few districts where a really good aerodrome could be constructed ; but, on the other hand, there are many stretches of country sufficiently level to provide safe landing for troop-carriers. The Germans realized this, and took full advantage of it. Moreover, just as in Greece a few weeks before, so in Crete ; as soon as the British were driven out of the island the Germans at once set about the construction of aerodromes and landing-fields.

A numerous and highly efficient ground staff was rushed to the island, and in a few days quite a number of air bases were in operation—bases from which all our positions in the Near East are now threatened. Still more significant, the attack on Crete was delivered from aerodromes which had been established in Greece and the Aegean islands since at the earliest May 1. Yet in Greece, as in Crete, it was the same story : our defeat was attributed in large measure to the impossbility of constructing aerodromes. Thus the Germans were able to do in three weeks what we did not find time or means to do in six months.

WE did not build aerodromes beyond a mere handful, we did not protect those we had built ; we did not mine them even when they had to be abandoned. We had nothing like enough planes—fighters, bombers, dive-bombers. So it was that we were unable to counter effectively the gliders trailed behind the Junkers, the cheap and flimsy troop-carriers which were crashed in their hundreds on the beaches and rocks of Crete ; crashed —but they got the men there all the same.

All that has happened in Crete might have been foreseen and, no doubt, was foreseen in many quarters. But even that able commentator, Air-Commodore L. V. Goddard, broadcast on May 22, when the battle for Crete had just begun, the soothing statement that " Never fear, air-borne forces by themselves will not capture that island. Please do not suppose that some new and unexpected danger to us has just emerged. We are prepared for air-borne forces. They are extremely vulnerable to good defences..." There can be no doubt that he was expressing the official view ; and even after the battle, after the air-borne forces *had* captured the island—largely because we had no " good defences "—a " high spokesman of the R.A.F." in Cairo declared blandly that " There is no chance of further German operations like those in Crete, in which they used 1,000 planes. Hundreds were destroyed . . .

" IF the Germans carried the Luftwaffe to the mainland of Africa or Asia Minor," he went on, " the situation would be largely reversed ; even should they attempt an air invasion of Cyprus they would not have the same vantage positions for bases as in the attack on Crete. . . ."

That is the sort of blind, incorrigible, ostrich-like optimism that loses battles, even wars.

E. ROYSTON PIKE

'DANGEROUSLY UNORTHODOX'—to quote a phrase from an Australian correspondent of "The Times," writing from Cairo—the German methods of making war may be, but at least they are victory-winning. Amongst them are the parachute troops, which have been used with great effect in all the German campaigns. This photograph from the "Berliner Illustrierte Zeitung" shows parachutists who, immediately after landing, have established a machine-gun post

New 'Cogs' in Hitler's Murder Machine

German soldiers landing a light gun. The enemy is continually trying to perfect his technique in the trans-shipment of men and weapons as part of his dream of world conquest. Left, Nazi paratroops being handed radio sets preparatory to boarding an aeroplane.

THE AMPHIBIAN GLIDER, many of which were used in Crete, several being towed at a time behind troop-carrying planes. Here is a one-seater glider adapted for descent on sea or land.

German observation and flak ship men patrolling the Aegean are now wearing camouflaged jerkins of oilskin painted with irregular blotches and designs. This simple disguise makes it difficult to identify these soldiers in the rock-girt islands of the Grecian Archipelago.

The Germans attacking Crete made use of smoke-screens. Here are troops advancing under such cover. The smoke-screen, or artificial fog, may be said to symbolize the whole Nazi movement. To create confusion and pollute the atmosphere has proved a strong weapon in Hitler's criminal strategy.

Photos, E.N.A., Keystone

This Is How They Got Away From Crete

"Dunkirk seemed a picnic by comparison." In these words one who went through both evacuations summed up the withdrawal from Crete. Below we tell the story, very largely in the words of men who were there, either as soldiers fighting their way to the coast or in the ships of the Royal Navy that effected their rescue.

"AFTER twelve days of what has undoubtedly been the fiercest fighting in this war," announced the War Office on the evening of June 1, "it was decided to withdraw our forces from Crete. Although the losses we inflicted on the enemy's troops and aircraft have been enormous, it became clear that our naval and military forces could not be expected to operate indefinitely in and near Crete without more air support than could be provided from our bases in Africa. Some 15,000 of our troops have been withdrawn to Egypt, but it must be admitted that our losses have been severe."

Many of the troops who had been defending Candia (Heraklion) and Retimo (Rethymo) were evacuated from those places by British cruisers, one of them the Orion, and destroyers.

"We entered the Aegean Sea as soon as darkness fell," said the staff officer in charge of operations on board one of the cruisers, "having successfully avoided the torpedo bombing attack which the Nazis launched to wind up the day's bombing. As we approached Candia we could see Very lights being fired from the front line. Otherwise there were no signs of activity. Although the Germans saw us enter the Aegean they took no further action, and we actually arrived at our rendezvous twenty minutes early, in spite of the delays caused by bombing.

"It was impossible for the cruisers to go close inshore, so destroyers loaded up with the men who were already drawn up by the quayside, transferred them to the waiting cruisers, and went back to pick up more until some 4,000 had been taken on board the two cruisers and five destroyers. Aboard our ship we had 1,100 men. The embarkation took three hours. The Army organization was perfect, and we were able to leave within one minute of our scheduled time, which was 3 a.m. We then made full speed, knowing that bombers would be waiting for us as soon as we rounded the eastern coast of Crete."

Sure enough, at 6 o'clock the next morning three Stukas delivered an attack; another attack came at 7.30, and a third at 9 a.m.

"All this time we were twisting and dodging, but although we successfully evaded most of the bombs it was impossible that all should miss us, as enemy machines attacked from every direction,

causing a number of casualties among the evacuated soldiers. The behaviour of the troops was magnificent. The wounded men never complained, while their more fortunate comrades used their Bren guns with such coolness that it was almost like a drill display. Others manned hoses and helped to get fires under control, and assisted in handling the ammunition supplies. I cannot tell you how really magnificent those chaps were."

"NOW do you understand?" Cartoon by Zec, from the "Daily Mirror"

Far more difficult was the evacuation of the men engaged on the main battlefield, in the Suda Bay region, at Canea and Maleme. They could not be withdrawn by sea, and so there was nothing for it but a 30-mile trek across the mountainous backbone of Crete to the southern shore. This, moreover, is almost harbourless, with steep cliffs rising precipitously from the sea.

It was a terrible march. For 48 hours they struggled across the mountains. They were hungry and thirsty, cold and weary beyond description. The weather was vile; now it rained, now it snowed, now it hailed. Then the sun broke through again, and it was baking hot. The enemy were close at their heels, kept at bay by only a tiny rearguard, and the sky was filled with Nazi planes which bombed them continuously.

FIGHTING FIT, this Maori who trained in England is typical of the Maori warriors who made bayonet charges at Suda Bay with the Australasian forces. *Photo, Wide World*

They had no protection from this air assault. The roads along which they staggered were nothing but tracks. They had no certainty of rescue even when they reached the coast. Still they kept on.

"Strange, unconscious discipline," wrote the "Daily Mail" Special Correspondent, "coordinated the whole column as they clambered painfully southward across Crete. Men marched with rocks cutting their boots and sweat running in their eyes. In blazing sunshine they climbed mile after twisting mile to surmount the great screen of jagged mountains which runs east to west across the island like a cockscomb. But when aircraft appeared they vanished instantly, for one man's movements might mean death for all. They grew desperately thirsty, for there are no streams in these barren uplands . . . Past burned-out lorries and dead Greeks, the column slithered down seawards. Ten miles from the shore they reached a region of eerie caves, and men stumbled into them and flung themselves in safety on the floor while the Luftwaffe turned on their evening blitz. As men's strength waned they jettisoned pyjamas and spare socks and anything that added weight and was not vital. Finally they lay down beside the road and waited their turn to cover in darkness the last mile and a half to the sea, where there was absolutely no cover."

Theirs was a weird experience indeed. Said one of the officers a day or two later:

"We lay end to end all along either side of the road to let the wounded through. They stumbled by, silhouetted against the dark night sky—a strange, contorted procession. You could hear their feet shuffling along the track and sometimes the sound of their breath coming in hoarse gasps. Sometimes there would be a gap, and then a single limping figure shouting as he tried to catch up. We waited five hours before we got the signal to move. Then we blundered on in the darkness on our way out to the warships and safety."

One of the ships engaged in the embarkation from the southern end of Crete on the night of May 29 was the Australian cruiser Perth, which embarked altogether 1,200 men.

"We moved in after nightfall," said her captain, "put three gangways down, and got 800 aboard in the first hour. Nearly every man, once he reached the cruiser, simply fell flat out on the decks. Our cooks made these 1,200 men 420 gallons of hot cocoa to help give them a boost."

As soon as the troops had been taken on board, the cruiser set sail, but before she reached port she was bombed solidly for seven hours one day, for thirteen hours on another. It was in this fashion that some 15,000 men were taken off Crete.

THE ISLAND OF CRETE, showing the mountainous character of the country, with alluvial plains along the northern coast, scenes of recent fighting. Crete, which has an area of 3,235 square miles, is 160 miles long. Cyprus, the Nazis' next objective, is somewhat larger, being 3,572 square miles in extent (see map in page 609).
Specially drawn for THE WAR ILLUSTRATED *by Felix Gardon*

Our Patrols Active in the Western Desert

This hairy Tommy has picked up a good souvenir, a German automatic rifle, and has awarded himself a foreign decoration for his astuteness.

Below, the commander of a British tank operating in the Western Desert scans the plains for a sign of the enemy.

Thirst is prodigious in the heat of battle, and nowhere more so than in the Western Desert. The watermen move up thousands of gallons of chlorinated water for the thirsty troops.

BEHIND the laconic communiqué, "Our patrols were active in the Western Desert," lies many a thrilling tale of enemy columns bombed and shot up on the move, of tank encounters in the desert sands and sharp, bitter skirmishes. The German army paper "Die Wehrmacht" pays tribute to our men at Sollum, saying : "British armoured patrols are hard to fight. Like ghosts, they suddenly appear from the darkness and attack before our machine-guns can open fire."

Left, an R.A.F. maintenance man overhauls the rudder controls of a Wellington bomber. Above, three British soldiers cast critical eyes over a captured German tank. In the circle are the remains of what was once a German lorry, one of a convoy shot up in the Western Desert.

Photos, British Official : Crown Copyright

How Britain Transports Troops by Air

TROOP-CARRYING AIRCRAFT are of vital importance in the Middle East, when bodies of men may have to be sent from one vital keypoint to another over country where no roads or railways exist. Among the best-known of British troop-carrying planes is the Bristol Bombay bomber-transport monoplane, one of which is seen above about to land at an aerodrome near a desert town. When used as a transport a crew of three is carried and there is accommodation for 24 fully-armed troops. In the circle officers and men are seen seated in the cabin of a Bombay. Seating can be removed to make room for ten stretcher cases or for war material.

Photos, British Official

Canada's Industries 'Go to It' With a Will

PUNCTURE-PROOF TANKS for Canadian-built Hurricanes are being covered with layers of rubber brought to Canada from British Malaya.

25-TON TANK, the 14,000 parts of which were made entirely in Canada, being inspected by (left to right) Mr. C. D. Howe, Canada's Minister for Munitions, Brig.-Gen. Stuart, Vice-Chief of General Staff, and Mr. J. L. Ralston, National Defence Minister.

Corvettes in great numbers, both for the Royal Navy and for the Royal Canadian Navy, are being built in the Dominion under the wartime ship construction programme. The one on the left is nearly ready for launching.

EVERY month from now on, as in the past, will see more Canadians with you to share in your defence.

During the year we shall dispatch to Britain a third infantry division, a tank brigade, an armoured division and many reinforcements.

Ships of Canada's Navy have, as you know, been engaged with your ships in the coastal waters of Britain. Other Canadian ships are taking their part in the duties of convoy on the great passage-way of the Atlantic.

In the Royal Canadian Air Force we have today 50,000 men ; every day that valiant brotherhood receives many new comrades in the proud partnership we enjoy with Australia, New Zealand and the United Kingdom in the British Commonwealth Air Training plan. This year that plan will double the number of its enlistments.

In this land over 50 training schools, 20 manning depots and 20 recruiting centres are already in operation. From this source is flowing to Britain an ever-growing stream of pilots, observers and gunners.

In this war of machines we are making machines of war for you as well as for ourselves. We will also continue to send you all the food which ships can be found to carry, but we will not stop there ; we recognize the tremendous financial burden you are bearing. That burden, as well, we are ready to continue to share in increasing measure.—*Mr. Mackenzie King, Prime Minister, in a broadcast from Canada on June 2, 1941.*

PRESIDENT AND PREMIER confer at Palm Springs, Georgia, where Mr. Mackenzie King (right), Prime Minister of Canada, called on Mr. Roosevelt and had an informal conversation during the latter's holiday there.

Photos, Sport & General, Planet News, Associated Press

After Crete—Will It Be Cyprus Next?

Hardly had the Germans established themselves in Crete when it was surmised that an attack on Cyprus would be the next item in Hitler's programme. Below we give some details of the island and its people, with some suggestion of its strategical importance.

IT was Benjamin Disraeli who secured Cyprus for Britain. That was in 1878, and from then until 1914 the island was a protectorate of the British Crown. Not until 1914 was the island definitely annexed as a Crown colony. Cyprus is described as Europe's third largest island ; other geographers will have it that Cyprus is in Asia. Certainly the nearest coasts are in Asia ; the mountains of Lebanon can be seen from Famagusta on a clear day. Its area is given as 3,572 square miles, which may be compared with Crete's 3,235 ; it is about 140 miles long by 60 miles wide at its greatest breadth.

The western half of the island is a tumbled mass of pine-clad mountains, and there are mountains, too, behind the northern coast. Between the two ranges is a broad plain known as the Mesaoria or Messaria, consisting for the most part of open, uncultivated downs, but with cornfields in the northern region. This big plain has been described by Sir Ronald Storrs, an ex-Governor of Cyprus, as one great airfield, a fact which, no doubt, the Germans have noted—and, let us hope, not only the Germans. Of rivers there are none worthy of the name ; nothing more than tiny, tinkling streams which at the height of the rainy season, i.e. December and January, become swollen torrents, emptying into the marshes near the sea. The coastline is broken by many bays and capes, but there are no natural harbours of any size. Famagusta is an ancient port, but it is capable of taking only small vessels. On the south coast there are good and safe open anchorages at Larnaka and Limassol. This time of the year is the island's hot season; from May to November little, if any, rain falls, and the soil becomes parched, cracked and dry.

At the last census in 1931, the population of Cyprus was given as just under 350,000, of whom 64,000 were Moslems (Ottoman Turks). The remainder were Christians : Greeks by race and speaking a Greek dialect. In the country districts there are Turkish villages and Greek villages, and seldom do the two races mix ; in the towns they live in separate quarters and are represented on the local councils proportionately to their numbers. Each village has its Mukhtar, or

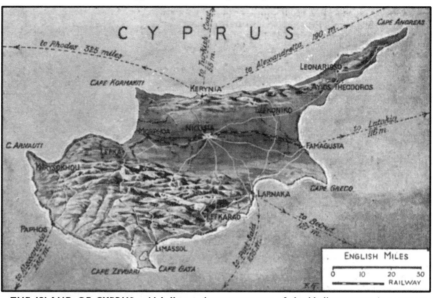

THE ISLAND OF CYPRUS, which lies at the extreme east of the Mediterranean, is a strong point in the defence of Syria and Palestine. Similar to Crete in terrain, its area is 3,572 square miles or slightly less than half the size of Wales. This map shows the distances to the Turkish coast and Syrian and Egyptian ports. *Specially drawn for THE WAR ILLUSTRATED by Felix Gardon*

headman, who is appointed by the Governor— since 1939 Mr. W. D. Battershill. The judicial system also recognizes the division between the two races.

There are only four towns of any size : Nicosia, the capital, which lies in the centre of the island, and the three seaports of Limassol, Larnaka and Famagusta. Most of the

Lt.-Gen. Sir J. H. Marshall-Cornwall, appointed General Officer Commanding-in-Chief the British troops in Egypt, is one of the greatest authorities on the Middle East.
Photo, Walter Stoneman

people are peasant farmers, producing crops of wheat and barley, cultivating their vines, and growing fruit and vegetables which find a ready market in Egypt. They are a picturesque folk ; the Greek in his white shirt, baggy black breeches, and wide straw hat, and the Turk in his bright-coloured shirt, white baggy breeches, fancy socks, and scarlet fez. The Moslem women still wear the yashmak.

A few weeks ago the island was bombed for the first time, by Italian aircraft, but since the invasion of Greece it has been the scene of intense military preparations. The R.A.F. has established bases there, and there are also seaplane bases ; the British garrison has been reinforced, and many of the Australians who fought in Greece have been transferred there. Recruiting for the Cyprus Regiment is in full swing. There are also a Cypriote Home Guard and A.R.P. organizations. Now the black-out is being tightened up, all the signposts have been taken down, and many of the people are evacuating the closely packed towns for the villages. For Cyprus is now on the edge of the war. At any moment it may be attacked by Hitler's dive bombers, troop-carriers and parachutists, coming, perhaps, from Rhodes, Crete (350 miles), or from the little island of Castellorizo, close to the Turkish coast (150 miles).

CYPRIOTE SOLDIERS, in readiness for a possible German attack on the island, are here seen undergoing training with a Lewis gun.
Photo, G.P.U.

IN FAMAGUSTA, a seaport of Cyprus. This is the main gate, typical of Roman and medieval architecture to be seen in the principal towns. *Photo, Dorien Leigh*

Britain's Friends Return to Power in Baghdad

After a month of intermittent fighting the revolt in Iraq collapsed at the end of May with the flight of Rashid Ali, and the pro-British Regent and party reassumed the Government. Thus in one corner of the Middle East, at least, the situation was once again rendered favourable to our cause.

RASHID ALI, the pro-Nazi usurper in Iraq, fled across the frontier into Iran on May 30, and with his flight the military revolt, which he staged on April 3 and which for a month past had taken the shape of war with the British forces, came to a summary end. He fled not a moment too soon, since one British column advancing on Baghdad from the north-west had arrived within four miles of the capital, while a second column approaching from the south-west had only three miles to go. Yet another British column advancing up the Euphrates had occupied Ur. Then a fourth column had entered Iraq from Transjordan.

Meanwhile, the legal Regent of Iraq, Emir Abdul Illah, had made a triumphal return to his country, and was already at Fallujah, 40 miles west of Baghdad, where he was greeted by deputations from the capital, and other principal centres, and immediately began the task of forming a new government. With him was General Nuri es Said Pasha, three times Prime Minister and negotiator of the Anglo-Iraq Treaty of Alliance. The Regent's return was announced to the people of Baghdad by tens of thousands of leaflets, dropped from the skies by R.A.F. planes.

Armistice in Iraq

Hostilities in Iraq ended with dramatic suddenness the next day when the authorities requested the British Ambassador, Sir Kinahan Cornwallis, to contact the British command at Habbaniyeh by means of the Embassy wireless and ask that British emissaries should be sent with terms for an armistice. The meeting was arranged accordingly, and at 4 a.m. on May 31 our emissaries were taken through the Iraqi lines to the Embassy. Sir Kinahan was roused and taken to the meeting-place, where from the Major-General commanding the British troops he received the terms which were to be presented to the Iraqi authorities. These required that all hostilities should cease forthwith; Iraqi troops should return to their peacetime stations; all British prisoners should be released; Axis prisoners, believed to number about 600, should be interned in Iraq, and Iraqi prisoners to be handed over to the Regent. All were agreed to, and the Armistice

ALEPPO is one of the most important towns of Syria. This air photo shows the ruins of its medieval castle and bridge. *Photo, Paul Popper*

was signed. Then on June 3 British troops re-occupied Mosul, the great oil-field centre, thus removing the last element of possible resistance.

Following the signature of the armistice about 500 British hostages—the men who stayed behind after all British women and children had been evacuated on April 29—who had been living in the British Embassy and the United States Legation at Baghdad for a month past, were set at liberty. Some 160 of them had enjoyed the hospitality of Mr. Knabenshue, the American Minister, and on their release they were loud in their praises of the way in which he had protected them

from the mob. When Rashid Ali threatened to bomb the Legation and the Embassy, the refugees offered to surrender themselves as prisoners of war. But Mr. Knabenshue, though well aware of the risk involved, refused to consider it, and when he was required to hand over his guests for intern-ment, he insisted that he must first receive written guarantee that they should be treated in accordance with international law. Finally, the Britons were allowed to remain in their refuge, sleeping on mattresses on the floor. Besides the courageous stand he made on their behalf Mr. Knabenshue shared all the inevitable discomforts his presence brought, and from first to last he insisted on taking all his meals with them. On the day the refugees went to the cellars—thinking every minute might be their last—they gathered round him to sing " For He's a Jolly Good Fellow."

Return of the Regent

On June 1 the Regent, Emir Abdul Illah, returned to Baghdad in state. The young King Feisal, who was reported to have been kidnapped by Rashid Ali, also returned to Baghdad on that date. Escorted by armoured cars, and accompanied by a number of in-fluential Iraqis who formerly held important administrative positions, and who, since the R.A.F.'s *coup*, had been cooperating with the British, the Regent reached the outskirts of the city, where he was met by a huge pro-cession of cars, carrying high Iraqi officials, the British Ambassador and American Minister and General Whitehouse, head of the British Military Command.

" I watched him and his cortège," wrote Reuter's Correspondent, " return triumphantly to the Palace amidst a swirl of white dust. As he entered the palace grounds six sheep were cere-monially sacrificed—a traditional Arab greeting for an honoured guest.

" A guard of honour lined up outside the palace building was inspected by the Emir, while a band played the Iraqi National Anthem. Then the royal standard was hoisted on the flagstaff just outside the palace. After acknowledging the felicitations of a large and enthusiastic crowd assembled outside the palace grounds, the Regent entered the building, where he received expressions of loyalty from the tribal sheikhs—picturesque figures with daggers and bandoliers: from heads of religious communities and the Apostolic Delegate, and from the entire Diplomatic Corps, with the exception of the Japanese and Italian repre-sentatives."

Good it was that the situation had cleared so dramatically in Iraq, following as it did so closely upon the collapse of the campaign in Crete. It was argued, indeed, that to a consider-able extent the position in the Middle East had been restored. But still all was not well in this corner of the globe. More and more Nazis were reported to be arriving in Syria. True, Vichy declared that it would be defended against all comers, and General Dentz made it known that " We will defend our pos-sessions with all our might." But such declarations were valueless, in view of Nazi penetration, and on June 8, British and Free French columns under General Wilson invaded Syria.

THE MIDDLE EAST, at present the most active war zone following the German capture of Crete and the invasion of Syria by the Allies—British, Imperial, Indian and Free French troops under General Wilson. This latter stroke, delivered early in the morning of Sunday, June 8, was made necessary by the infiltration of the territory by Nazi airmen and technicians, acting with the complicity of the Vichy Government. The most vital points in the area, so far as Britain is concerned, are Alexandria and Port Said at the entrance to the Suez Canal. *By courtesy of the " Daily Sketch"*

In the Land of the Caliphs—and Oil Kings

MOSUL, on the Tigris, which was occupied by British troops on June 3, 1941, lies 220 miles north of Baghdad. The surrounding country is rich in oil which the Nazis would like so much to seize.

BASRA (left) is Baghdad's trade outlet and chief port of modern Iraq. The Ashar Canal, which links the town with the Shatt-al-Arab, two miles away, is usually crowded with boats.

BAGHDAD, ancient domain of the Caliphs and capital of modern Iraq, is seen above from across the river Tigris. Though modernity is encroaching upon it, Baghdad still has many narrow streets with latticed windows overhanging the roadway like that seen top, right. The city, which under the Turks suffered an eclipse in power and prestige, has of late been regaining her old position as a great market of the Middle East.

Photos, Black Star and G.P.U.

The 'Unsinkable' Sinks: the End of the Bism

How the Bismarck was dispatched is vividly shown in this series of historic photographs taken from
H.M.S. Dorsetshire. 1, the crippled Bismarck outlined against the sky; 2, smoke pouring from the
great vessel after a torpedo had struck her amidships; 3, she sinks from view after being hit by the final
torpedo; 4, survivors swimming towards British warships;   *Photos, Keystone, "Daily Mirror"*

as Seen from the Deck of H.M.S. Dorsetshire

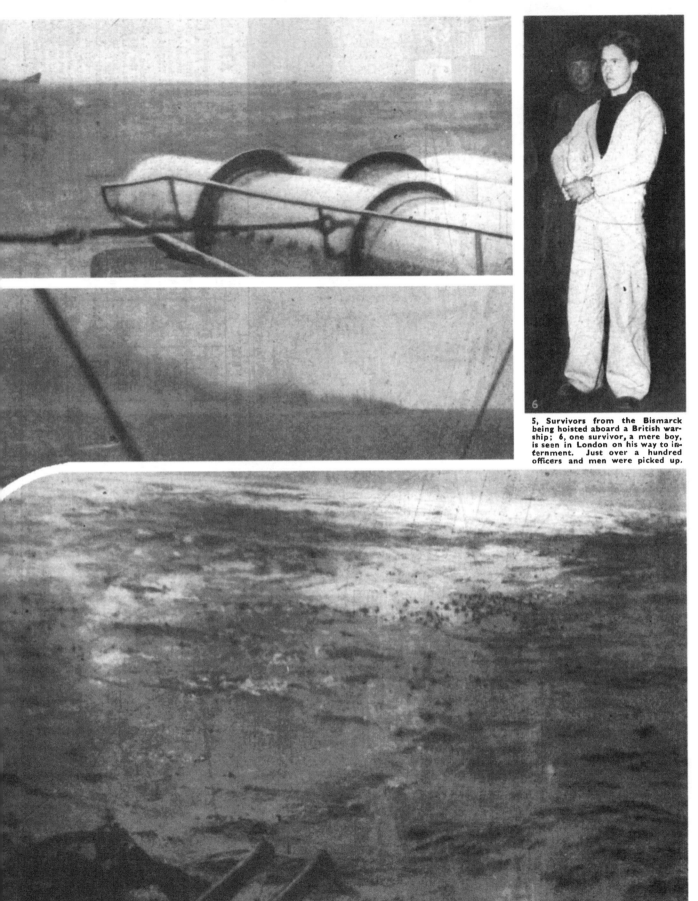

5, Survivors from the Bismarck being hoisted aboard a British warship; 6, one survivor, a mere boy, is seen in London on his way to internment. Just over a hundred officers and men were picked up.

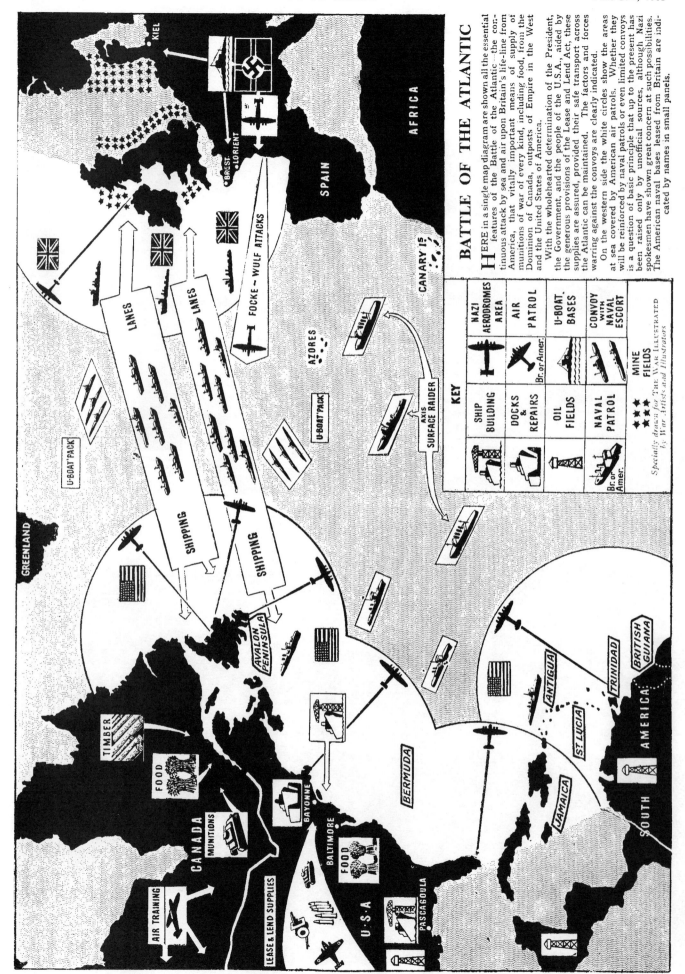

BATTLE OF THE ATLANTIC

HERE in a single map diagram are shown all the essential features of the Battle of the Atlantic—the continuous attack by sea and air upon Britain's life-line from America, that vitally important means of supply of munitions of war of every kind, including food, from the Dominion of Canada, outposts of Empire in the West and the United States of America.

With the wholehearted determination of the President, the Government, and the people of the U.S.A., aided by the generous provisions of the Lease and Lend Act, these supplies are assured, provided their safe transport across the Atlantic can be maintained. The factors and forces warring against the convoys are clearly indicated.

On the western side the white circles show the areas at sea covered by American air patrols. Whether they will be reinforced by naval patrols or even limited convoys is a question of basic principle that up to the present has been raised only by unofficial sources, although Nazi spokesmen have shown great concern at such possibilities. The American naval bases leased from Britain are indicated by names in small panels.

Specially drawn for THE WAR ILLUSTRATED *by War Artists and Illustrators*

Atlantic Outposts of the New World

With the Battle of the Atlantic approaching its climax, the importance of the islands which stud the surface of the ocean and serve as stepping stones between the Old World and the New becomes ever more manifest. Below we tell something of these islands which, not for the first time, have become entangled in the web of history.

SPEAKING in the United States Senate on May 6, Senator Pepper, a Democrat member of the Foreign Relations Committee, urged that " the United States should not only establish itself in Greenland, but, in conjunction with Britain, should seize Dakar, the Azores, the Canary Islands, and Cape Verde Islands, and assist in the defence of Iceland and Singapore."

Three weeks later Mr. Roosevelt in his "fireside chat" approved the suggestion in so many words when he stated that " the war is approaching the brink of the Western Hemisphere itself—it is coming very close home," and referred in particular to " the Atlantic fortress of Dakar and the island outposts of the New World—the Azores and the Cape Verde Islands." A little later in his speech he mentioned the last two groups which, " if occupied or controlled by Germany, would directly endanger the freedom of the Atlantic and our own physical safety."

Of these Atlantic outposts, the Azores and Cape Verde Islands belong to Portugal, the Canaries are Spanish, while Dakar is on the mainland of French West Africa.

The Azores form an archipelago of nine islands, divided into three distinct groups and stretching over a distance of some 400 miles. Altogether, they are only a little over 900 square miles in area, with a population of about 260,000. Though of little value commercially, strategically they are of vast importance, situated as they are in mid-Atlantic, about 800 miles from Europe, 1,600 miles from Newfoundland, 2,300 from New York, and rather more from the West Indies. They were first occupied by the Portuguese some 500 years ago, and for centuries they were a rendezvous for the Portuguese fleets making the journey between Lisbon and the East Indies, via the Cape of Good Hope. They are still a frequent port of call, and Horta Harbour in Fayal is a base for the American Clipper planes.

To the south-east of the Azores is Madeira (Cap Funchal), largest of a small group of islands, also Portugal's; its area is 314 square miles and its population some 211,000. Wine is its chief export, principally to Britain ; and because of its delightful climate and natural beauty the island has long been a favourite for European tourists. The shipping facilities are not of the best, however.

Some 1,100 miles to the south are the Cape Verde Islands—ten islands and five islets constituting a separate colony administered by a Governor ; the Azores and Madeira, by the way, are regarded as part of Portugal itself. The area of the Cape Verde Islands is given as 1,557 square miles, and they have a population of 162,000, negroes and mulattoes for the most part, descendants of the slaves brought to the islands before slavery was finally extinguished in 1878. The capital is Praya, in Santiago ; but the most important of the group is St. Vincent. Here at Porto Grande is one of the most important Atlantic

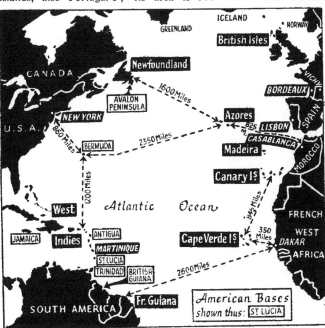

Portuguese troops, including units of anti-aircraft artillery, leaving Lisbon on their way to strengthen the garrison of the Azores. Dr. Salazar, the Portuguese Premier, though friendly to Britain, is striving to keep his country neutral. The Azores are about 800 mile west of the mainland of Portugal.

coaling and oil-fuelling stations ; before the war, indeed, it was used by practically all the ships on the run between South America and Europe.

Following Senator Pepper's speech and repeated allusions in the American Press to German intentions to occupy the Portuguese islands, Dr. Salazar, the Portuguese Premier, issued a Note declaring that up to the present there had been no request or suggestion whatever regarding the eventual use of ports or bases on Portuguese coasts or islands

by any belligerent or other Power, and that his government was concerning itself with the defence of the three Atlantic archipelagoes (the Azores, Cape Verde and Madeira), and were reinforcing the existing garrisons. President Roosevelt's references to the islands in his speech on May 27 were also received with considerable resentment in Portugal, suggesting that the Portuguese do not fully realize the dangers which threaten them. It is surely obvious that, in the event of a clash with Germany, Portugal would be quite incapable of putting up any effective resistance ; her safeguard today, as it has been for centuries past, lies in her alliance with Britain. The garrison of the Cape Verde Islands, it is interesting to note, was stated in 1937 to consist of three officers and 144 other ranks—hardly sufficient to beat off a single Nazi troop-carrying plane.

Between Madeira and the Cape Verde Islands lie the Canaries : 2,807 square miles, with a population of perhaps 660,000. The islands are regarded as an integral part of Spain, and they are divided into two provinces named from their respective capitals, Santa Cruz de Tenerife and Las Palmas. Las Palmas in the island of Grand Canary is the third most important port of Spain, and in tonnage the first. It has a deep harbour, capable of being used by the largest ships and also by seaplanes.

Importance of Dakar

Directly opposite the Cape Verde Islands, on the African mainland, lies Dakar, seat of the Governor-General of French West Africa, and an important naval base and military and air station, as well as a commercial centre. In its harbour are reported to be lying some of the principal ships of the French Navy, including the battleship Richelieu, the cruisers Georges Leygues, Montcalm, and Gloire, some destroyers, and several submarines. The Richelieu was severely damaged in the Free French and British attack on the port on September 23, 1940, but it is now said to have been repaired. These ships would be of inestimable value to Hitler in waging the Battle of the Atlantic, and the increasing subservience of the Vichy Government and the oft-shown anti-British attitude of Admiral Darlan makes it likely that he may well succeed in laying his hands upon them.

From Dakar Hitler might expect to seize with a minimum of difficulty the groups of islands which we have just described ; still more important, since Dakar is only just over 2,500 miles by air from the Brazilian coast, South America would be brought within range of his giant bombing planes.

It is not surprising, then, that the United States, through its President, has now made it clear beyond a doubt that a Nazi descent on Dakar, or even effective collaboration between the French authorities there and the Nazis, would be resisted by force of American arms. The same is true, indeed, of the other Atlantic outposts that have been mentioned. America, in effect, has declared that her safety zone extends to the opposite shores of the Atlantic, and that she will regard herself in danger—and act accordingly —if Nazi forces effect a lodgement on any part of the great arc which sweeps from New York through Canada to Greenland, Iceland, and then via Britain to the Portuguese and Spanish islands, and so on to Dakar. In all that vast area President Roosevelt, speaking for all the republics and countries of the Americas, has put up a " Keep Out " notice to Nazi trespassers.

The important strategic value of our bases loaned to the United States is increasingly emphasized by the Battle of the Atlantic. Other Atlantic keypoints are, so far, neutral. They are the Azores, Madeira and Cape Verde Islands, belonging to Portugal, and the Canaries (Spanish).
Map by courtesy of the " Star" ; Photo, Planet News

Our Diary of the War

SATURDAY, MAY 31, 1941   637th day
Africa.—Sfax harbour, Tunisia, bombed by R.A.F. Night attack on Benghazi.
S.A.A.F. bombed enemy motor transport, tents and buildings near Ghimbi, Abyssinia.
Near East.—British withdrawal from Crete continued, protected by R.A.F. and S.A.A.F. fighter patrols. Seven German bombers destroyed. Heavy night attack on aerodromes at Maleme and Heraklion.
Iraq.—Rashid Ali having fled to Iran, Iraqis signed armistice with Britain.
Home.—Night raid on Merseyside, points in N. Wales and in south and west of England. Three enemy bombers destroyed.

SUNDAY, JUNE 1   638th day
Sea.—H.M. armed merchant cruiser Salopian reported sunk.
Africa.—Two Junkers brought down over Tobruk. Night bombing attack on Benghazi.
Near East.—War Office announced that some 15,000 troops had been withdrawn to Egypt from Crete. Evacuation continued.
Iraq.—British troops entered Baghdad.
Home.—Heavy night raid on Manchester. Bombs also fell at widely separated places elsewhere. Enemy fighter shot down in sea.
Clothes Rationing Order announced to be in force.
Announced that London's War Weapons Week totalled £123,960,000.

MONDAY, JUNE 2   639th day
Air.—Coastal Command made daylight raid on shipping in Kiel Canal and objectives in Schleswig-Holstein. Supply ship sunk off Norway.
Night raids on Düsseldorf, Duisburg-Ruhrort, Berlin, and docks at Ostend and St. Nazaire.
R.A.F. fighters made sweep over Northern France and Channel, attacking motor transport, aerodromes and an E-boat.
Africa.—Our troops reported to be active at Tobruk and in Sollum area. Benghazi raided at night.
Operations continuing in Lakes area, Abyssinia. Stated that in Soddu area remainder of 16th Italian Colonial Battalion had been rounded up.
Near East.—State of siege proclaimed in Eastern Syria.
R.A.F. shot down Junkers troop-carrier off Malta.
Home.—Slight enemy activity off British coasts. Bombs fell at point in north-east. At night bombs fell at places in north and north-east England and in West Midlands. Three raiders destroyed.
General.—Hitler and Mussolini met at the Brenner Pass.

TUESDAY, JUNE 3   640th day
Air.—R.A.F. fighters attacked enemy troops in Northern France and shipping in Channel.
Africa.—Following reconnaissance by Maryland aircraft, R.A.F. bombers attacked enemy convoy, escorted by destroyers, off Tunisian

coast. One ship blown up, one left burning, others damaged.
Another night raid on Benghazi. Maritza aerodrome, Rhodes, attacked. S.A.A.F. attacked landing-ground at Ganbut, Cyrenaica.
Iraq.—British troops occupied Mosul. Martial law declared in Baghdad following serious rioting.
Near East.—Petrol dump at Beirut bombed by R.A.F.
Home.—Bombs fell by day at south-coast town and elsewhere. At night raiders were over districts in east, north-east and south-west England. Three night raiders destroyed.

General.—Lt.-Gen. Sir J. H. Marshall-Cornwall appointed G.O.C.-in-C. in Egypt.

WEDNESDAY, JUNE 4   641st day
Air.—R.A.F. continued attacks on enemy shipping and coastal targets. Three raids on Boulogne. Hits on Zeebrugge mole. During patrols over Channel and Straits one enemy bomber and three fighters were destroyed.
Africa.—Cairo announced that there had been stern fighting round Debarech, Abyssinia, recently captured by Patriot forces.
Near East.—Stated that German infiltration into Syria continued by land, sea and air.
R.A.F. bombed aerodrome at Kattavia, Rhodes by night.
Heavy night raid on Alexandria.
Home.—Bombs fell during day at a place on N.E. coast of Scotland. Heavy night raid on a West Midlands area. Other enemy machines reported over districts in north-east, East Anglia, and south-east.

Six day and five night raiders destroyed.
General.—Former German Kaiser, Wilhelm II, died at Doorn, Holland.

THURSDAY, JUNE 5   642nd day
Sea.—Admiralty announced sinking of H.M. trawler Ben Gairn and drifter Jewel.
Air.—Sunderland flying-boat shot down German seaplane in Atlantic.
Africa.—R.A.F. raided Benghazi by night, causing many fires and explosions.
Near East.—Italian aircraft at Aleppo aerodrome attacked by R.A.F.
Home.—Small number of enemy aircraft flew over parts of Scotland during the night, causing slight damage and few casualties.

PRESIDENT ROOSEVELT'S PROCLAMATION OF NATIONAL EMERGENCY

WHEREAS a succession of events makes it plain that the objectives of the Axis belligerents in such (the present European) war are not confined to those avowed at its commencement, but include the overthrow throughout the world of the existing democratic order and the world-wide domination of peoples and economies through the destruction of all resistance on land, sea, and in the air ;

And whereas indifference on the part of the United States to the increasing menace would be perilous, and common prudence requires that for the security of this nation and of this Hemisphere we should pass from peacetime authorizations of military strength to such a basis as will enable us to cope instantly and decisively with any attempt at the hostile encirclement of this Hemisphere, or the establishment of any base for aggression against it, as well as to repel threat of predatory incursion by foreign agents into our territory and society ;

Now, therefore, I, Franklin D. Roosevelt, President of the United States of America, do proclaim that an unlimited national emergency confronts this country which requires that its military, naval, air, and civilian defences be put on a basis of readiness to repel any or all acts or threats of aggression directed towards any part of the Western Hemisphere.

I call upon all loyal citizens engaged in production for defence to give precedence to the needs of the nation to the end that a system of government that makes private enterprise possible may survive.

I call upon all loyal workmen, as well as employers, to merge their lesser differences in the larger effort to ensure the survival of the only kind of government which recognizes the rights of labour or capital.

I call upon loyal State and local leaders and officials to cooperate with the civilian defence agencies of the United States to assure our internal security against foreign-directed subversion, and to put every community in order for a maximum of productive effort, a minimum of waste and unnecessary frictions. I call upon all loyal citizens to place the nation's needs first in mind and in action to the end that we may mobilize and have ready for instant defensive use all of the physical powers, all of the moral strength and all the material resources of this nation.

FRIDAY, JUNE 6   643rd day
Sea.—Admiralty announced sinking of three enemy supply ships and an armed trawler in the Atlantic after destruction of Bismarck.
Africa.—R.A.F. bombers made heavy night attack on the harbour at Benghazi and the aerodrome at Derna.
S.A.A.F. in action in Abyssinia.
Home.—Slight enemy air activity during daylight ; bombs dropped by single aircraft at two points in N.E. England.
By night bombs were dropped in S.E. and S.W. England, and in one London district by a single enemy plane.

SATURDAY, JUNE 7   644th day
Sea.—Admiralty announced loss of H.M. submarine Undaunted.
Air.—R.A.F. fighter aircraft carried out offensive daylight patrols over Straits of Dover and occupied territory.
Aircraft of Bomber Command attacked convoy of enemy supply ships off Holland, two ships being hit and set on fire and others damaged. Attacks were also made on a supply ship off Norway.
Night attacks were made by the Bomber Command on the docks at Brest and by the Coastal Command at Bergen.
Africa.—In Abyssinia E. and W. African troops crossed River Omo and captured 2,000 prisoners and 20 guns.
Artillery on both sides active at Tobruk ; vigorous patrolling in Sollum area.
Announced from Cairo that South African forces were in Egypt.
Near East.—Heavy night raids on Alexandria caused considerable damage and heavy casualties in residential quarters. One enemy aircraft shot down.
Home.—Night bombing attacks on convoy in Straits of Dover beaten off without damage to convoy or escort ; two German aircraft shot down.
General.—Announced that, by arrangement with French authorities, U.S. Navy will maintain daily patrol of Martinique and Guadeloupe.

When the first food ship for Britain under the Lease and Lend Bill arrived, it was welcomed by Lord Woolton, who is seen above (with stick) examining some of the eggs he is going to ration.   *Photo, Wide World*

Dumb Friends at the Noisy Front

"Peggy" is wondering what it's all about, after being rescued uninjured from underneath a mass of rubble which was her South London home. "Peggy's" house suffered a direct hit.

"Beauty" by name and nature, this wired-haired terrier wears the badge of the People's Dispensary for Sick Animals, and has been awarded a medal for finding animals buried under debris.

"Is he one of us?" says "Convoy," looking somewhat critically before making friends with the Indian Sepoy. This pet monkey, who "joined up" somewhere in Eritrea, has travelled thousands of miles with her dispatch-rider friend.

"All Clear!" howls "Dismal Desmond," though it is a bit boring to be fastened to this air-raid shelter in Kensington Gardens. Lovers of animals may rest assured that everything is being done by the P.D.S.A. and R.S.P.C.A. to alleviate their suffering as a result of the blitz. Right: "Joey," a young kangaroo mascot "attached" to the Australians in Malaya. Thought to have been left behind, he made sure of putting his kick into the war.

Photos, "Daily Mirror," Fox, and British Official.

No New Clothes Now Without Coupons!

PETTICOAT LANE, London's famous street market, as it appeared on the morning of June 1, 1941, when clothes rationing came into effect. Not many people, however, had brought their ration books with them.

STRIPPED FOR ACTION
From the cartoon by Zec, by permission of the "Daily Mirror"

Above, clipping coupons from a customer's book in a Knightsbridge store. *Photos, Associated Press, Fox, and Planet News*

RATIONING OF CLOTHING : NUMBER OF COUPONS NEEDED

On June 1, Mr. Oliver Lyttelton, President of the Board of Trade (below, left), announced his scheme for the immediate rationing of clothing, including footwear. Each person will have 66 clothing coupons to last for twelve months

MEN and BOYS	Adult	Child
Unlined mackintosh or cape	9	7
Other mackintoshes, or raincoat, or overcoat ..	16	11
Coat, or jacket, or blazer or like garment ..	13	8
Waistcoat, or pull-over, or cardigan, or jersey ..	5	3
Trousers (other than fustian or corduroy) ..	8	6
Fustian or corduroy trousers	5	5
Shorts	5	3
Overalls, or dungarees or like garment	6	4
Dressing-gown or bathing-gown	8	6
Nightshirt or pair of pyjamas	8	6
Shirt, or combinations—woollen	8	6
Shirt, or combinations—other material.. ..	5	4
Pants, or vest, or bathing costume, or child's blouse	4	2
Pair of socks or stockings..	3	1
Collar, or tie, or pair of cuffs	1	1
Two handkerchiefs	1	1
Scarf, or pair of gloves or mittens	2	2
Pair of slippers or goloshes	4	2
Pair of boots or shoes	7	3
Pair of leggings, gaiters or spats	3	2

CLOTH. Coupons needed per yard depend on the width.

WOMEN and GIRLS	Adult	Child
Lined mackintoshes, or coats (over 28 in. long) ..	14	11
Jacket, or short coat (under 28 in. long).. ..	11	8
Dress, or gown, or frock—woollen	11	8
Dress, or gown, or frock—other material ..	7	5
Gym tunic, or girl's skirt with bodice	8	6
Blouse, or sports shirt, or cardigan, or jumper ..	5	3
Skirt, or divided skirt	7	5
Overalls, or dungarees or like garment	6	4
Apron, or pinafore	3	2
Pyjamas	8	6
Nightdress	6	5
Petticoat, or slip, or combination, or cami-knickers	4	3
Other undergarments, including corsets.. ..	3	2
Pair of stockings..	2	1
Pair of socks (ankle length)	1	1
Collar, or tie, or pair of cuffs	1	1
Two handkerchiefs	1	1
Scarf, or pair of gloves or mittens, or muff ..	2	2
Pair of slippers, boots or shoes..	5	3

KNITTING WOOL. 1 coupon for two ounces.

Ancient Faith Triumphs Above New Ruin

ST. GEORGE'S R.C. CATHEDRAL, SOUTHWARK, was gutted by fire during one of the recent German air raids on London. But though the Germans have destroyed churches and cathedrals by the score, they cannot destroy the faith which brought them into being. Here, in front of a temporary altar, Archbishop Amigo, Bishop of Southwark, sang Pontifical High Mass on Whit Sunday, June 1, 1941. This impressive photograph bears out a saying by General Joffre in 1917 : " The German is the discipline of fear ; ours is the discipline of faith—and faith will triumph."

Photo, " News Chronicle"

They Have Won Honours in Freedom's Cause

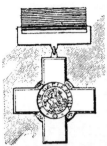

THE GEORGE CROSS

Mr. H. J. Savage, G.M., for putting out fire started by incendiaries in a railway wagon containing explosives.

Mr. Edward E. Hayes, A.R.P., G.M., for rescuing injured men from a burning ship at a London dock quay.

Mr. W. T. Whitlock, L.M.S. Home Guard, **G.M.**, for saving life of his Section Leader, although injured himself.

Mr. P. Whitting, late Dpy. Chief Warden, Hammersmith (now Pilot-Officer), **G.M.**, for splendid rescue work.

THE GEORGE MEDAL

Mr. C. J. Ditch, of the Gas Light & Coke Co., **G.M.**, for showing conspicuous bravery in tackling fire-bombs.

Mr. A. Webb, also of Gas Light & Coke Co., **G.M.**, for saving a comrade in danger of being burnt to death.

Mr. F. Harlow Tritt, A.R.P., G.M., for saving a family of four trapped under wreckage of a bombed house.

Mr. James Wood, A.R.P., **G.M.**, for working eleven hours with Mr. Tritt in their heroic task of rescue.

Mr. T. Higgins, Gas Light & Coke Co., **B.E.M.**, for putting out blazing gas-holder while bombs were still falling.

Mr. A. E. Page (M.M.), **G.M.**, for putting out fires in burning gas-holders by turning off red-hot valves.

Sister G. Seeley, R.R.C., for attending wounded at Dunkirk where she was herself injured.

Miss J. Westerby, Coventry A.R.P., **M.B.E.**, for making eleven journeys under enemy bombs.

Mrs. Jane Hepburn, A.R.P. ambulance attendant, **G.M.**, for rescuing soldiers injured in a raid.

Mrs. Dorothy Clarke, A.R.P., **G.M.**, first woman presented by the King with this medal.

Nurse Violet E. Reid, G.M., for rescuing other nurses after their hospital had been heavily bombed.

Nurse P. Marmion, of the Royal Chest hospital, **G.M.**, for rescuing patients on two occasions.

Sub-Officer G. Nicholls, of Peckham A.F.S., **O.B.E.**, for rescuing a trapped person.

Chief Fire Officer Collier, G.M., for devotion to duty, though hurt in Coventry raid.

Miss Ethel Martin, A.F.S. telephonist, **O.B.E.**, for remaining at her post during a heavy blitz.

Miss Margaret Hay, A.F.S., **O.B.E.**, for conspicuous bravery in a telephone room.

Patrol Officer G. H. Wright, G.M., for gallantry in fighting a fire at Plymouth.

Leading Fireman G. C. Lidstone, G.M., for gallant conduct at Plymouth.

Actg. Sqdn.-Ldr. A. H. Smythe, D.F.C., for bombing military objectives in Germany.

Sergt. Pilot K. Newton, D.F.M., for conspicuous courage in performance of air duties.

Sergt. G. R. Ross, of the R.N.Z.A.F., **D.F.M.**, for great skill in bombing the Scharnhorst.

Sergt. Pilot K. I. Street, D.F.M., for diving to three hundred feet in attack on Scharnhorst.

Pilot-Officer L. P. Massey, D.F.C., for locating and attacking a Heinkel 115 in the North Sea.

Wing-Cdr. L. Sinclair, R.A.F., **G.C.**, for rescuing an air-gunner from a burning bomber.

THE D.F.C.

Wing-Cdr. T. G. Pike, D.F.C., for intercepting and destroying at least four enemy aircraft at night.

Sergt. A G T. L. Mumby, R.A.F., **D.F.M.**, for skilful and courageous service in action against the enemy.

Sqdn.-Ldr. A. Hibberd, D.F.C., for bravery. He was killed in a car accident on his way to Buckingham Palace.

Sqdn.-Ldr. P. B. B. Ogilvie, D.S.O., for carrying out most valuable daylight reconnaissance work.

THE D.F.M.

I Was There! .... Eye Witness Stories of the War

How Our Catalina Shadowed the Bismarck

American-built Catalina flying-boats of the R.A.F. Coastal Command played a vital part in the tracking down of the ill-fated Bismarck. On occasion they encountered heavy fire from the battleship, as the following story by one of the pilots relates.

THE Bismarck was discovered in the Norwegian fiords and attacked in a storm by American-built Hudsons. Later on, when she was sighted by ships of the Royal Navy in the North Atlantic, shadowing was taken up by a Sunderland flying-boat, which subsequently witnessed the first engagement between the British and German forces. This Sunderland was relieved by a Catalina, which continued to shadow the Bismarck as she fled southward.

From this time onwards Catalina flying-boats cooperated with H.M. ships in keeping a watch on her every movement and device to evade close action. The Catalinas quartered the sea, so that there was the scantiest possibility of the Bismarck's avoiding detection for any length of time. As the captain of one of the flying-boats said, " We swept the seas in gigantic patterns, hopping from cloud to cloud."

But the Catalinas had to break cloud now and then. Their crews paid high tribute to the A.A. armament and the skill of the German gunners. A flying-boat might leave cloud for only a few seconds, but that was sufficient for the enemy guns to come into action and surround the aircraft with bursting shells.

The pilot of one Catalina which ran into heavy fire from the Bismarck told the following story :

We left our base at 3.30 in the morning, and we got to the area we had to search at 9.45. It was a hazy morning with poor visibility, and our job was to regain contact with Bismarck, which had been lost since early Sunday morning. About an hour later we saw a dark shape ahead in the mist. We were flying low at the time. I and the second pilot were sitting side by side and we saw the ship at the same time. At first we could hardly believe our eyes. I believe we both shouted " there she is," or something of the sort.

There was a forty-knot wind blowing and a heavy sea running and she was digging her nose right in, throwing it white over her bows. At first, as we weren't sure that it was an enemy battleship, we had to make

certain, so we altered course, went up to about 1,500 feet into a cloud, and circled. We thought we were near the stern of her, when the cloud ended and there we were, right above her. The first we knew of it was a couple of puffs of smoke just outside the cockpit window, and a devil of a lot of noise, and then we were surrounded by dark brownish black smoke as she pooped off at us with everything she'd got. She'd been supposed to have only eight anti-aircraft guns, but fire was coming from more than eight places—in fact she looked just one big flash. The explosions threw the flying-boat about and we could hear bits of shrapnel hit the hull. Luckily only a few penetrated.

My first thought was that they were going to get us before we'd sent the signal off, so I grabbed a bit of paper and wrote out the message and gave it to the wireless operator. At the same time the second pilot took control and took avoiding action. I should say that as soon as the Bismarck saw us she'd taken avoiding action too, by turning at right angles, heeling over and pitching in the heavy sea.

When we'd got away a bit we cruised round while we inspected our damage. The rigger and I went over the aircraft, taking up floor boards and thoroughly inspecting the hull. There were about half-a-dozen holes, and the rigger stopped them up with rubber plugs. We also kept an eye on the petrol gauges, because if they were going down too fast, that meant that the tanks were holed and wouldn't stand much chance of getting home. However, they were all right, and we went back to shadow Bismarck. There we

met another Catalina. She'd been searching an area north of us when she intercepted our signals, and closed. On the way, she'd seen a naval force, also coming towards us at full belt through the heavy seas. They were part of our pursuing fleet.

When we saw this Catalina I went close alongside. I could see the pilot through the cockpit window and he pointed in the direction the Bismarck was going. He had come to relieve us and it was just as well, because the holes in our hull made it essential to land in daylight.

We landed after half-past nine at night, after flying for just over eighteen hours. But one of our Catalinas during this operation set up a new record for Coastal Command of 27 hours on continuous reconnaissance.

This Pilot Officer is captain of one of the Catalina flying-boats which shadowed the Bismarck. His remarkable story is given in this page. *Photos, British Official : Crown Copyright*

I Saw One Vast Explosion—The Hood Had Gone

The end of the ' mighty Hood ' was described as an almost unbelievable nightmare by Reuter's special correspondent, who was on the bridge of one of our warships when the Hood went down with her guns still firing.

THE " Battle of the Giants " was the climax to a chase by Hood and Prince of Wales with their accompanying destroyers at top speed to prevent the Bismarck breaking out into the Atlantic to attack convoys. The pursuit began off Iceland, and continued hour after hour in the eerie half-light of the Arctic night.

The cruisers Suffolk and Norfolk, which had been shadowing the Bismarck since she left Bergen, kept Hood and Prince of Wales and others informed of her movements, and so helped them find their quarry.

It did not get dark at any time that night. Until two or three o'clock it was nearly as light as day ; then for the next few hours a leaden greyness settled down and it was like a dull winter's afternoon in Britain. It was expected to contact the Bismarck at about 2 a.m., but at the last moment she

altered course. For four more hours Hood and Prince of Wales continued on a course roughly parallel to the enemy's. Blinding snowstorms lashed the black sea, and at times visibility fell to a few yards. Then, as if Nature were taking a hand, this curtain suddenly lifted. There was the dark sea, and there in the sombre, murky light of dawn appeared two black specks on the horizon—the Bismarck and her accompanying cruiser.

For some minutes our ships steamed on towards the Germans to shorten the range. They, too, turned in towards their pursuers,

The American-built Consolidated Catalina Patrol Bomber Flying-boat, now in service with the Coastal Command, is fitted with rear gun " blisters," which, as can be seen, give the air gunner a good traverse.

Midshipman William Dundas, aged 17 (right), and Able Seaman R. Tilburn are two of the only three known survivors from H.M.S. Hood. They were landed in Iceland.

Photos, " News Chronicle " and " Daily Express "

so the world's biggest warships were thundering towards one another at a combined speed of probably over 60 miles an hour. The tension of waiting for the battle to begin became acute.

" Open fire " was ordered by signal, and almost simultaneously with the order orange-gold flame belched with a roar from Hood's forward guns. Within three seconds puffs of black smoke shot out from the Bismarck ; she had also opened up.

Prince of Wales's guns then began firing. Dense clouds of yellow cordite smoke enveloped her bridge, momentarily blotting out the view. To the left Hood, two or three hundred yards away, was still surging forward on a parallel course. Fountains of water shot up in her wake—the first about a hundred yards astern, the second fifty. Hood thundered on, leaving the subsiding water rapidly behind. The shell or shells appeared to fall just ahead of one of her after 15-in. gun turrets, and a large fire broke out, with thick black smoke. Hood continued to fire and to race forward.

What happened next was a sickening sight. There was a terrific explosion, and the whole of the vast ship was enveloped in a flash of flame and smoke which rose high into the air in the shape of a giant mushroom. Sections of funnels, masts and other parts were hurled hundreds of feet into the sky, some falling on the ship.

Hood's bow tilted vertically into the air, and three or four minutes after she was hit all that remained, apart from bits of wreckage, was a flicker of flame and smoke on the water's surface.

H.M.S. HOOD going into action in Denmark Strait : a last photograph of the battleship seen beyond the guns of H.M.S. Prince of Wales. *Photo, Wright & Logan*

A destroyer was diverted to rescue work, and picked up three of the ship's company—two seamen and a midshipman.

All this time Prince of Wales had continued firing at the Bismarck, and more than once spurts of water showed that she was straddled. Again the Bismarck's shells fell near the Prince of Wales, but no serious damage had been done. Then the Bismarck turned away, but only to be pursued all that day and night and next day over the Atlantic at high speed.

Our Guns Wrecked a German Armada Off Crete

The first German attempt at a sea-borne invasion of Crete was completely broken up by units of the British Navy, including H.M.S. Ajax. That night no Germans landed in Crete, as the captain of one British cruiser here makes clear.

WE arrived off Crete shortly before midnight on May 21 expecting that the enemy would try to land troops by sea.

We were steaming eastward when suddenly our destroyer screen opened fire on a darkened ship. Our destroyers' fire was very effective, and a great bonfire appeared on the ocean—apparently a merchantman ablaze.

The first ship sighted was the Italian destroyer, which was at very close range. Her identity was doubtful at first owing to her similarity to our own single-funnellers, but a searchlight picked out her flag and immaculate paintwork, which suggested many months in harbour.

We opened fire with our pom-poms, whereupon the Italian destroyer launched five torpedoes. During the ensuing avoiding action our fire was masked, but another cruiser was able to get a clear sight, and gave a full six-inch broadside, all of which were seen to hit.

A violent explosion occurred on board the enemy ship, and she went down. Throughout she never fired her guns.

The admiral then led the squadron through what appeared to be the middle of the convoy.

A large number of caiques (small Greek ships), probably 40, each carrying at least 100 Nazis, were then sunk by ramming. A small steamer was also sunk. We left her burning.

Some of the caiques tried to evade the attack by hiding the soldiers they were carrying below decks and flying the Greek flag. Others retaliated with rifle and machine-gun fire.

The sweep was continued northwards

until no more caiques could be picked up by our searchlights.

On a subsequent sweep we passed large numbers of Germans clinging to wreckage and shouting for help. But the possibility of enemy E-boats catching us at a disadvantage did not permit of our rescuing the survivors.

The havoc we wrought was so great that no Germans managed to land in Crete that night. It was mass execution.

Other officers who returned from the battle agreed that the whole Axis armada had been entirely at the mercy of the Navy's guns. One officer said :

We turned everything on them from pom-poms to six-inch guns and other heavy stuff. The night was filled with screams as the terrified Germans plunged into the sea.—*Reuter.*

Greek coasting vessels in Corfu harbour. Many such craft, each carrying a hundred Nazis, were rammed by our naval forces in the Crete battle. *Photo, Mrs. T. Muir*

We Saw Troop-Carriers Come in Over the Sea

How Nazi air-borne troops and parachutists, some of them on fire in mid-air, landed in waves over Crete, was told by one of a small British garrison who were cut off and had to make their escape by sea.

A BRITISH soldier, who came from Bromley, Kent, was in Heraklion (Candia) when the Germans began their invasion on May 21. He said :

At first we thought it was an attack on the aerodrome, but soon afterwards the German raiders were diving low and machine-gunning the town itself.

Then the parachute troops arrived. The skies seem to be hidden by them.

We saw the troop-carriers coming in low over the water and trailing their gliders—then gaining height and dropping their parachutists in the neighbourhood. We could see the troops quite clearly, and some

of them dropped to the ground and were killed instantly as their parachutes failed to open properly.

Others caught fire as they left the planes and became tufts of sparkling fire and smoke. They were burned to death as they fell, and their bodies thudded to earth, their parachutes disappearing in cinders.

A message came from the garrison for us to go to a certain point. We did so and found our way cut off by the enemy who had taken the position with their Tommy guns. All we could do was to turn back towards the fort which was held by Australians.

As more troops landed from the air they

consolidated their hold on the aerodrome and on the approaches to the fort, which became isolated. We were then ordered to leave the town and we broke into two parties. We were machine-gunned on our way to the sea.

We could see troop-carrying planes coming in towards the island 30 or 40 feet above the water, nine at a time—then another nine. They made towards the town and circled round, but the anti-aircraft fire was hitting them hard, and setting them on fire while they did so. Ten were shot down in the afternoon. One crashed into the water and there were no survivors. Another plane, with six or seven parachutes dangling like flies on a string behind it, disappeared into the sea. The parachutes were coloured black and white. The paratroops even fired their tommy-guns while they were coming down.

We set out to escape in our boats, and the Germans fired at us across the harbour—at this time the anti-aircraft gunners had run out of ammunition. But we got round the harbour in our boats.

No one talked or lit matches, and we took turns at rowing, keeping the land in sight all the time. Three hours later we heard the drone of engines, and two destroyers came up while a cruiser turned her searchlight on us. All guns were trained on us, and then they called to us.

I shouted, "We're English, sir," and the captain of one of the destroyers answered me. "What are you doing here?" "We were cut off by parachutists at Candia," I yelled back. "All right, pull in alongside the destroyer," came the answer. I and 12 others got aboard, while the others boarded other destroyers. All that night we spent cruising off Candia with the destroyers and cruisers. On the next evening we cruised around, looking for the expected invasion fleet between the Dodecanese and Crete, but all was quiet.

On Friday morning we found some barges which were trying to get through, but we just tipped them over, firing our pompoms at them in the meantime.

We saw the Germans and Italians floundering in the water, their faces black with oil. An Italian cruiser hoisted a white flag just as it was hit by one of our guns. The Germans and Italians were yelling for help, and wreckage was all over the place. Thousands were struggling in the sea without the slightest chance of rescue unless they were cross-Channel swimmers.—*British United Press.*

MASS ATTACK BY PARACHUTISTS, some of whom have reached land and are organizing themselves, while others slowly descend. Many thousands of such parachutists were employed in Crete. They are attached to the Luftwaffe, not the Reichswehr.　　　*Photo, E.N.A.*

Near Heraklion, Crete, this once remote and peaceful peasant hut is now engulfed in the horrors of Nazidom.　　*Photo, Wide World*

Siftings From the News

Hitler prohibited all travel, even for private purposes, by persons in his entourage, after Hess' escape.

Over 70,000 binoculars received as result of Ministry of Supply's appeal for the Services.

German lessons have been made compulsory in Greek schools.

Waiting list of 800 passengers for British Airways service from Lisbon to England.

More than 230 acres of London's Royal Parks have been "dug for victory."

Hours of work in the Civil Service are being increased to average 51 a week.

Rome taxi-drivers are forbidden to drive people to theatres, cinemas, racecourses or weddings.

Dutch are making cigars of beetroot pulp or dried cherry leaves.

Vatican City bureau has traced over 20,000 missing prisoners of war.

K.C.B. conferred on Czech Air Chief, Vice-Marshal General Karel Janousek.

"Great fire damage" admitted by General Milch, appealing to German A.R.P. workers.

Nazi newspaper boasted that Luftwaffe had destroyed Houses of Lords and of Commons.

About 1,300,000 prisoners of war stated by Nazi writer to be working in Germany.

Consumption of tobacco in Britain greatly increased since intensive enemy raids started.

Swiss newspapers prohibited in French unoccupied territory from May 15.

Sole public bar in Vatican City now closed to prevent its use for political conversations.

Germany requested withdrawal of U.S. ambassador in Berlin by June 10.

Three hundred heavy tanks are being built at shops of C.P.R. at Montreal.

War Office has released 10,000 cavalry swords for scrap metal.

Remains of enemy plane were found in ruins of 4-storey block of buildings.

General Bergonzoli ("Electric Whiskers") arrived with 2,000 Italian prisoners at Bombay.

All Dutch men and women from 18 to 25 have to serve six months with Labour Service.

Underground hangars are under construction near Warsaw by order of German authorities.

Nazi airmen are among patients in British hospitals being taught rug-making.

"Eagles Up" is name of film to be made on part played by American pilots in R.A.F.

Dionne Quins presented an ambulance to Ontario Red Cross on their seventh birthday.

Kurt Heinrich Reith, No. 1 Nazi in U.S.A., has been sent to Ellis Island pending deportation.

German Labour Front is to publish papers in Flemish and Dutch for imported workers.

Vichy stated Hitler had relaxed Armistice terms to let France build up a "Continental Air Force for the defence of the Empire."

Max Schmeling, former heavy-weight boxing champion, was reported killed in Crete.

The Editor's Postscript

UNDER the lead of the shameless Darlan, it is merely a question of time before we see the Vichy traitors actively take part in hostilities against France's former allies—an infamy which will smother in abomination the worst betrayals that Hitler's gangsters committed from the Anschluss to the slaughter of Poland. For Hitler had at least a majority of his fellow countrymen behind him in every one of his infamies, whereas the Vichy traitors in no sense represent the unhappy people of France and are merely a group of unscrupulous opportunists eager to hold and increase the simulacrum of power they possess, and ready to deliver their hapless fellow countrymen into perpetual German servitude so long as they can themselves retain positions of eminence in a servile State.

THE sole hope of a rebirth of France abides in De Gaulle. His latest recruit, Colonel Collet with his Circassian Legion, is a good omen. Let us remember that if all who muster to the banner of De Gaulle are no longer officially French, they are at least paladins of freedom, and if a France enslaved is ever to break her chains those are the men to whom she must turn. But there must be no more Dakars, the " Free French " must not hesitate to stand by Britain if she has to turn her arms against the vermin of Vichy, for she will be fighting in the only way that will ever in the lifetime of any of them lead to the restoration of a Free France.

THE " Winnipeg " incident, reported on the Wireless on May 31, when a Dutch warship discovered that this French vessel, fitted for 75 passengers, was crammed with six hundred, many of them Nazis proceeding to Martinique to organize that French colony for the Hitler-Darlan alliance . . . this sinister episode indicates how deeply Darlan has committed himself to his Nazi masters. He is obviously willing that they should have a Transatlantic foothold to menace the Democratic republics of the Western hemisphere. A little man in a big job—no wonder France collapsed with such as he in high places. I may have more to say about this most sinister personality of the War later on.

"TELL me the old, old story ! " . . . Let's have a few extracts from T. E. Lawrence, for whom I am developing a somewhat belated, but all the more sincere, admiration. In his after-War years in the Near East, when he was clearing up the mess in the Arab world, he reported to the Colonial Office, Oct. 24, 1921, from Amman, in Trans-Jordan, the Rabbath-Ammon of the Bible, an important base on the Hedjaz Railway as follows :

" The Armoured Cars were not fit for use. We obtained them with some difficulty from the War Office, in the expectation that they would assist in maintaining order in Trans-Jordania. They had not been out of Camp for weeks before my arrival. The cars were in fair mechanical condition. They had no covers or tubes, no mechanical spares, no lamps or batteries, no jacks or pumps, no petrol. For the two cars there were two

drivers and two gunners—not enough to man the cars or fight the guns, though in this case it was no matter since there were no gun belts, no ammunition, no gun spares. Of the two drivers, one was a ' second ' driver, intended to take over in an emergency. How good he is I do not know. The first driver, who is supposed to be qualified, can drive the car forward but is not good at reversing. He is practising this on the path between the tents. I think the Air Ministry should be informed of the condition of the section before they are called upon to pay the War Office for its maintenance charges."

That referred to British Units : the following to Arab units :

" Externally things are less satisfactory. At first people in Trans-Jordania said we were making an Army to smash them for our own purposes. Then as time went on they said we were

AIR MARSHAL A. W. TEDDER, who has been appointed Air Officer Commanding-in-Chief, Middle East, was born in 1890. He served in France 1915-17 and Egypt 1918-19, and was Air Officer Commanding R.A.F. Far East 1936-38.   *Photo, Bertram Park*

purposely creating an inefficient force to give us an excuse for sending British troops across. The reason for this has been the delay in supplying equipment and materials. Uniforms, saddles, machine-guns, rifles, have all been held up. Peake cannot show his men in public till they are reasonably smart and till they have rifles, for in Trans-Jordania every man of military age carries a rifle as a mark of self-respect, and Peake's, the so-called Military Force, is the only unarmed body of men in the country. 'When this is set right public suspicion will go to rest.

THE only comment on the foregoing is that in no country but one under democratic control would such a revelation of a confidential official report have ever been allowed as our Colonial Office did allow Mr. David Garnett to quote in his masterly volume of Lawrence's " Selected Letters."

But even more to the point today—for the British habit of muddling through is still obvious in the latest news from the Near East—is this revealing comment on our

quondam friends the French, written from Amman again on November 8, 1921 :

" We cannot afford to chuck away our hopes of building something to soothe our neighbour's feelings : and the French have made our job here as difficult as possible—if it is possible at all—by their wanton disregard of the common decencies observed between nations.

Please remind them that they shot Arab prisoners after Meisalun and plundered the houses and goods of Feisal and his friends. The dirty-dog work has been fairly shared, and I thank what gods I have that I'm neither an Arab nor a Frenchman—only the poor brute who has to clean up after them."

How true that is ! Britain is just the poor brute that will have to do the cleaning up once more. But what a mess it is going to be this time !

THIS is the last day of spring . . . and what a spring ! By one of those odd chances that are always happening to me I read in bed this morning some twenty pages of poetry in " The Oxford Book of Modern Verse "—this I often do before breakfast and the morning papers arrive, so that at least I begin the day without worrying about the War. Good idea, I think. Well here's a verse from " The Chestnut Casts His Flambeaux "—there's none of them so far on as that down in my corner of Sussex—by A. E. Housman :

The Chestnut casts his flambeaux,
    and the flowers
  Stream from the hawthorn on
    the wind away,
The doors clap to, the pane is
    blind with showers.
  Pass me the can, lad ; there's
    an end of May.

THE can has never attracted me, but I've been well-nigh driven to drink by the weather of late. Despite odd days— very odd days—of sunshine and biting winds, I do not recall a fouler May. But it has been only true to type, I gather, as I read in the local paper last week, under the heading "Fifty Years Ago," that a party of Huns—we knew them only as " Germans " then—had come on an interchange visit to some society or other for promoting friendship with a race that has proved itself incapable of friendship and their stay in the town was marred with such boisterous weather that they had to pass most of the time indoors. O, merry month of May ! I'm glad to see the last of you and none too hopeful that flaming June will make amends for your delinquencies.

SURPRISED to notice in the " Daily Mail " the other [morning that M. Camus, Chef de Cabinet of the Belgian Minister for the Colonies, " has died as the result of a recent air raid in London," as this information was given several months ago and I myself printed it on January 10. It seems strange that the official announcement should have been so long delayed. But actually it was officially announced in the first instance and the need at this late date of repeating it is not apparent. My own interest in the matter arises from my having been on a lower floor of the Carlton Hotel at the moment when M. Camus had the bad luck to be killed, when the fatal bomb fell that ended my very pleasant stay of more than two months at this famous hotel.

JOHN CARPENTER HOUSE.
WHITEFRIARS. LONDON. E.C.4.

The War Illustrated, June 27th, 1941   Registered at the G.P.O. as a Newspaper

Vol 4 The War Illustrated Nº 95

Edited by Sir John Hammerton

FOURPENCE   WEEKLY

FREE FRENCH TROOPS now operating in Syria include Circassian cavalry under the command of Col. Collet, who escaped from Syria to join General de Gaulle's army. Ignoring orders to resist any British attack, Col. Collet crossed into Transjordan territory there to rally other Frenchmen to the free cause. His patriotic gesture has influenced many of his comrades. These impressive Circassian cavalrymen, part of the French army of the Levant in occupation of certain Syrian towns, are now on the move against the Vichy defeatists.   *Photo, Mrs. T. Muir*

Our Searchlight on the War

Sun Rays for Night Fighters

BECAUSE they have to take their sleep in the daytime, night-fighter pilots have been deprived of their normal share of sunshine. To counteract this and to assist in maintaining their high level of physical fitness, Lord Nuffield has offered to provide them with facilities for sunray treatment. Each of the aerodromes at which night-fighter pilots are stationed will shortly be equipped with the latest type of collective irradiation apparatus. This type of apparatus enables the treatment to be enjoyed by as many as twelve pilots simultaneously.

Martinique in Custody

DETAILS of an "arrangement" between the U.S.A. and the Vichy government regarding the French islands of Martinique and Guadeloupe were made known on June 7. This agreement provides for certain guarantees regarding the movements of French vessels in United States waters and commits the French government to prior notification regarding any shipment of gold from Martinique. It also provides for the establishment of a daily boat and plane patrol of the islands. A naval observer stationed at Fort de France will check the patrols' observance. In return the United States will give certain forms of economic aid to both of the French islands.

Italy Tightens Her Belt

DESPITE the strict censorship on news going out of Italy, it has been learned that the country is suffering increasing economic difficulties owing to the war. Nickel-plating, except for surgical instruments, is forbidden "for the duration." Ceramics and aluminiumware are being standardized to cheapen production and make rationing easier. Since the supplies of coal coming from Germany are inadequate for Italy's needs, the Autarky Committee in Rome has been granting permits for the erection of hydro-electric smelting plants for the manufacture of pig-iron and certain alloy steels. Reserves of many imported raw materials coming by sea are already running low, among them stocks of textile fibres, hides for leathermaking, skins for furs, and foreign woods. The use of wheat flour or rationed fats or milk for the manufacture of biscuits has been forbidden from June 15.

Sinking of the Zamzam

DETAILS of the sinking of the Egyptian liner Zamzam by a German raider in the South Atlantic were given to a "Daily Telegraph" Special Correspondent by some of the U.S. passengers aboard her when they reached Lisbon. They told how the ship was fired on without warning at 5.30 a.m. on April 17 by the raider Tamesis. About a dozen shells hit the ship, but no loss of life was caused. Boats were lowered, and when all the passengers had reached the German ship the raider's crew boarded the Zamzam. The passengers were transferred to the supply ship Dresden, which cruised about for nearly five weeks before landing her passengers in France. After they had landed, 21 American ambulance drivers and a few others, including the Captain and Chief Engineer of the Zamzam, were detained by the Germans.

Nazis Adopt Roman Type

ON May 31 Berliners were amazed to see the *Angriff* printed in Roman type instead of the Gothic characters which the Hitler regime had hitherto made compulsory. The explanation given was that the Third Reich's new worldwide power would suffer, and the influence of the German press would be curtailed, if it continued to use the Gothic type which few people abroad can read. Other German newspapers are to follow the *Angriff's* example.

He Saved His Flock

A SHEPHERD's devotion to his flock was recognized by the award of the British Empire Medal to F. Mitchell of Abbots Leigh

SHEPHERD FRED MITCHELL, of Abbots Leigh, Somerset, awarded the British Empire Medal for bravery in saving his flock when fires spread in the lambing pens.
Photo, "Daily Mirror"

in Somerset. Incendiary bombs fell on the farm and set light to the lambing pens. Mitchell tried to cope with the outbreak single-handed, but it spread too quickly for him. So, although high explosives were falling in the vicinity, he entered the pens, snatched up the lambs one by one and carried them through the flames into the open fields.

The Warsaw Ghetto

VILLAINOUSLY treated as have been the Jews in Germany, the lot of their co-religionists in conquered Poland is even worse. The Nazis have aimed deliberately at their impoverishment and degradation, and by the establishment of separate Jewish districts, i.e. the Ghettos, have striven to separate them from their fellow citizens. The largest of the Ghettos is in Warsaw. Here, in a small area, the most neglected and the dirtiest in the city, 450,000 people are now compelled to live. There is only one square, and the only park is the Jewish cemetery. Even before the war the district was the most thickly populated part of Warsaw, but now the number of people per room has risen to six and, in some cases, to ten. The Ghetto is called "the closed contaminated area" and has been surrounded by walls. Within those walls the word of the German policeman is law, and the unhappy Jews are tricked and robbed and frequently mal-treated after the Nazi fashion.

Doctor Bombed out Four Times

A CERTAIN medical practitioner, a panel doctor, though bombed out four times, is still carrying on in his district. His surgery was totally demolished last winter. He then secured other accommodation in the same street, but six weeks later these premises, too, were damaged beyond repair. Undaunted, he opened a new surgery elsewhere in the street and that was demolished in the spring, together with all his furniture, drugs and medical records. Then his home in the neighbourhood was destroyed. He started again in a new surgery in the same street determined not to give up while there was still a spot available to him in the street where he had always carried on his practice.

G.P.O.'S DANGER SQUAD removing a 3-cwt. safe from a post office wrecked by a German bomb. These men rescue the contents of London post offices, safes, kiosks, and letter-boxes from raid-wrecked buildings, often at great personal risk. A dangerous job this squad tackled was to clear a letter-box almost on top of the time bomb which threatened St. Paul's. *Photo, Sport & General*

The Way of the War

SALUTE TO FREE FRANCE! VIVE DE GAULLE!

A Word in Appreciation of the Movement and the Man

ONE day in 1934 Alexander Werth, for long the "Manchester Guardian's" correspondent in Paris, was looking round a bookshop in the Boulevard St. Germain when the manager, M. Lucius, "round, bald and jovial," handed him a little volume in a green-and-buff paper cover. "Read this," he said; "it is important. De Gaulle—*c'est un type très fort.*" Mr. Werth confessed he had never heard of him. "He works over there," rejoined M. Lucius, pointing to the French War Office just opposite. And he added in a half-whisper; "Oh, but they don't like him there! He is too damned independent-minded."

That was seven years ago, and De Gaulle —he was only a colonel then—was practically unknown outside military circles. Even in those circles he was suspect : had he not ideas, unorthodox ideas, "unsuited to the French tradition"? Before long, however, his little book—it was *Vers l'Armée de Métier* (since translated into English under the title "The Army of the Future")— won a certain vogue, particularly when it was known that M. Reynaud had been supplied by De Gaulle with the facts and arguments which he used to advance the cause of a mechanized army. But the generals and the yes-men of "experts" and technicians who surrounded them looked askance at the plea for tanks and yet more tanks. What do we want tanks for, they asked, when in the next war all we will have to do is to sit comfortably and securely in *La Ligne Maginot* and let the enemy batter himself to destruction against its impregnable walls?

DE GAULLE'S warnings fell on deaf ears. Too late Reynaud was called to be premier ; too late he called De Gaulle to his side. At the front, as in the prime minister's cabinet, the General played a gallant and distinguished part, but the Battle of France was fought and lost. Reynaud went to the confinement prepared for him by his enemies ; De Gaulle, sickened, yet not disgusted into inanition, by the rottenness that he saw all around him, took a plane to England, and there became the rallying-centre of all that was still vital and honourable in French life. One June day he came to the microphone in London, and in burning words— words fired by a passionate patriotism—appealed to his fellow-countrymen not to despair. "The country is not dead! Hope is not extinct! *Vive la France!*"

Since that day a year has passed—and what a year! France has staged no dramatic "come-back"; the old men of Vichy are still in power, and if they have a policy, it is one of utter defeatism. "We must collaborate

with Germany," they plead mournfully; "otherwise we shall be ground into the dust, our sons and brothers will be kept prisoners beyond the Rhine, our fields and factories will rot and decay for lack of workers." In their heart of hearts some of them, at least, dread nothing so much as a British victory. For then would come a day of reckoning, and the guillotine might clang and crash again in the Place de la Concorde.

BUT De Gaulle—for him and the men who acknowledge his leadership the year that has just slipped away has been one of ever-increasing strength, moral and material. When the Battle of Britain was at its height last August the General was officially recognized by the British Government as "leader of all free Frenchmen, wherever they may be, who rally to him in support of the Allied cause," and an agreement was concluded between him and the British authorities concerning the organization, employment and conditions of service of the French volunteer force which was being assembled under his command.

That force has long since come into being, and on many a battlefield the soldiers of Free France have fought most gallantly and effectively. They have been in action against the common foe amid the torrid sands of the Sahara and on the rocky heights of Eritrea,

they marched and fought beside us on the road that led to Benghazi, a hundred-and-one of their ships of war are serving with our fleets, and in the air many a squadron of Free French airmen have helped clear the skies of enemy planes. And, to mention their most recent success, only the other day Free French troops poured across the frontier from Palestine into Syria, valiant comrades-in-arms of our own men, Britons and Australians, Indians and New Zealanders. "Our men went in singing the Marseillaise," said General Catroux, their commander— Georges Catroux, who as an Army Commander wears on his sleeve five stars, yet is happy and proud to serve under De Gaulle, whose sleeve bears only the two stars of a brigadier.

WHEN the Free France movement was born a year ago De Gaulle was still very largely an unknown quantity. Then and for months afterwards our Foreign Office hesitated to support him to the uttermost, since they clung to the belief that the Vichy government would sooner or later revolt against the Nazis. That belief, so pathetically misguided, is still not dead, neither here nor in America. Then the General was politically inexperienced—he was and is a soldier rather than a politician—and he was a newcomer to the world's stage. But today his position amongst his own people, as with us, is unchallengeable. "The psychological value of De Gaulle to us," said a foreign expert in a B.B.C. broadcast the other evening, "is that he provides a focus for all French people who are determined to carry on the fight. . . . He is one of the most distinguished Frenchmen who had the courage to sever all ties with their country, to accept the inevitable sentence of outlawry and even death. He is a first-class strategist, a man of the most uncompromising integrity, and enjoys the trust and friendship of the Prime Minister."

All over the world Frenchmen of valiant spirit are rallying to his standard. "Some come by canoe or by tramping for months through the jungle swamps. They come from Dakar, from France, Tibet and Indo-China. There are scientists, soldiers, priests and peasants, all guided by the same ideal. They are the cream of France." So writes a neutral journalist from Brazzaville, in French Equatorial Africa.

THE Free French movement is, then, no "ramp" run at the British taxpayer's expense, but something which is having a very real and solid effect on the prospect of winning the war. So on this first anniversary, *Vive De Gaulle! Vive la France Libre!*

E. ROYSTON PIKE

GEN. DE GAULLE broadcasting from the Free French headquarters in Cairo. On his right is Gen. Georges Catroux, Commander of the Free French Forces in the Middle East, and a great authority on French colonial matters. *Photo, Wide World*

'We Come to Proclaim Syria Free'

Although the invasion of Syria was determined by the resolve (stated by the British Government on July 1, 1940, after the collapse of France) not to " allow Syria or the Lebanon to be occupied by any hostile power, or to be used as a base for attacks upon those countries in the Middle East which they are pledged to defend, or to become the scene of such disorder as to constitute a danger to those countries," the Allies took with them the promise of independence.

FOR the second time in little more than twenty years Syria has been proclaimed free and independent.

The first time was after the last war, when, following upon the collapse of Turkey, the British and French governments jointly declared their intention of establishing in Syria, as in Mesopotamia, "national governments, drawing their authority from the initiative and free choice of the native populations." Inspired by this declaration, the leading Arabs of Damascus offered the crown of Syria to Feisal, son of King Hussein of the Hedjaz in Arabia. But Feisal's reign was short. After prolonged and acrimonious deliberation the peacemakers in Paris decided that Syria should be one of the mandated territories of the League of Nations, and awarded the mandate to France. Whereupon Feisal was driven out of Syria by the French, although his friendship with the British secured him the throne of Iraq instead.

France proceeded to reorganize Syria into four states : Syria proper, with its capital at Damascus ; the Lebanon, capital Beirut, which was also made the seat of the French mandate administration ; Latakia, the land of the Alouites ; and the Jebel Druse. One of the objects of this partition was to weaken the Syrian opposition to French rule ; but for many years that opposition continued—indeed, it has continued until this day. There were riots at the outset ; then in 1925 the Druses rose in open rebellion, and soon the whole country was aflame. Not until Damascus had been bombarded by the French troops and largely laid in ruins was the insurrection subdued. After this bloodshed there was an attempt at conciliation, but still the story of French rule was unhappy. France sent to Syria no adminis-

trator of the quality of Lyautey, her proconsul in Morocco. She drained the country of its money and resources, and contributed little or nothing in return. The officials at Beirut were chiefly concerned with keeping in check the tides of Syrian nationalism. Only in Lebanon were the French really at home, and that was because Lebanon is largely Christian and has had many cultural contacts with France for generations past.

By 1936 it was plain that the policy of conciliation had failed, just as the policy of repression had failed before it. Following another outbreak of riot and disorder, the French Government promised to grant Syria a status like that which Britain had just accorded to Iraq, and when M. Blum took office in June of that year treaties were negotiated with both Syria and Lebanon.

When the Mandate Should End

In effect, France agreed to end the mandate and abandon the country. Towards the end of the year treaties of friendship and alliance were signed in Paris between France and Syria and France and Lebanon, which provided that the two states should receive their independence after three years, although they should also conclude a 25-year alliance with France and permit the maintenance of French garrisons in certain strategic areas. Local autonomy was granted to Jebel Druse and Latakia.

The promise of freedom was illusory, however. Although the treaties were ratified by Syria and Lebanon, the French Government were in no haste to carry out their part of the bargain. Not until August 1938 was the next step taken, when it was declared in Paris that the transfer of functions from France to the Syrian administration should

BEIRUT, capital of the Lebanon, is the head-quarters of the High Commissioner of the French Levant, whose official residence is seen above. *Photo, Mrs. T. Muir*

be made in February 1939, and Syria was to be admitted to the League of Nations in the following September. But M. Bonnet, who was then Foreign Minister, refused to bring the treaty before the French Chamber for ratification, and the French High Commissioner in Syria, M. Puaux, made it known that he himself was in favour of prolonging the mandatory regime. There was a passionate outburst of nationalist feeling in Syria, whereupon the High Commissioner suspended the constitution. The state of high tension continued into the war period, and was by no means ended when France collapsed in the summer of 1940. On the contrary, the nationalists were encouraged in their demand for complete independence.

The French authorities, dispirited and disillusioned by the result of the fighting in France, were quite unable to maintain their position and prestige ; following the armistice with Germany and Italy, Syria seemed ripe for Axis penetration. Now, however, the situation is being transformed. Since it was plain that the French authorities were not in a position to defend their territory against Nazi aggression ; since, moreover, they had completely failed to win the confidence and support of the peoples entrusted to their rule—the Allies in the Middle East decided to act, and on June 8 an army of Free French, British, Imperial, and Indian troops crossed the frontiers from Palestine, Transjordan, and Iraq.

General Catroux's Proclamation

"Inhabitants of Syria and the Lebanon," proclaimed General Catroux, Commander of the Free French forces in the Middle East, " at the moment when the forces of Free France, united with the forces of the British Empire, her Ally, are entering your territory, I declare that I assume the powers, responsibilities and duties of the representative of *La France au Levant.* I do this in the name of Free France, who identifies herself with the traditional and real France, and in the name of her chief, General de Gaulle. In this capacity I come to put an end to the mandatory regime and to proclaim you free and independent. You will therefore be from henceforward sovereign and independent peoples, and you will be able either to form yourselves into separate States or to unite into a single State."

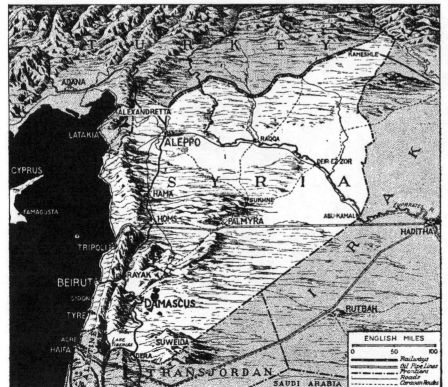

Syria's principal port of call is Beirut, towards which an Allied column moved north along the coastal road. In the north of Syria a British column from Irak proceeded in the direction of Aleppo, second largest city of Syria, on the airfield of which the Germans, with the connivance of Vichy, had landed numbers of bombers and transports.
Map in relief specially drawn for THE WAR ILLUSTRATED *by Felix Gardon*

Once Again the Bible Lands a Battlefield

IN ANCIENT SYRIA, battleground of the Middle Ages, a new Crusade against the Crooked Cross is raging. The Biblical scene above, near Aleppo, once the stronghold of Saladin's sons, shows the level plains hemmed in by steep escarpments, typical of the country. The Nazi-controlled aerodrome at Aleppo has been heavily bombed by the R.A.F. Along the valley of the Euphrates (centre) an Allied column is progressing, and another captured Sidon, seen below, on June 15.   *Photos, Mrs. T. Muir, Dorien Leigh*

'Closer, Get Closer Yet to the Bismarck!'

From 8.30 on the evening of May 26 until it was all over at about noon the next day—until, that is, the Bismarck had been fought to a finish and sent to the bottom—the officer whose story we give below was on the bridge of the King George V, Admiral Tovey's flagship. The official Admiralty account of the action appears in page 580, and other descriptions and illustrations will be found in pages 582, 583, 612-613, and 645.

THROUGHOUT the night on the Admiral's bridge of the King George V we sat, stood, or leant like a covey of disembodied spirits. It was dark, windy, rainy. None of us will ever know if it was cold. About two o'clock in the morning cocoa appeared. We drank it gratefully, but it might equally well have been pitch-tar; none would have noticed.

At last daylight, patchy rain squalls, a flickering sun, a tearing wind from the north-west and a rising sea. A little manoeuvring and then on tin hats. Norfolk appears to the eastward: "Enemy in sight twelve miles to the south of me," she says. A little change of course; Rodney opens out to port a little more. "Enemy in sight." Well, I couldn't see him; it is the aloft gun director who can see him. And then, veiled in distant rainfall, is a thick squat ghost of a ship, very broad in the beam, coming straight towards us, end on.

There is a sudden shift of wind and a squall of rain dashes across. The Commander-in-Chief, Admiral Tovey, saw it first and was giving orders to alter the course. He put on his tin hat, and out poured a little cascade of water all over him. He just grinned, quite undisturbed by that or, indeed, by any other incident of this five-day chase, which his brilliant judgement and leadership brought to a close in triumphant battle.

There is a sort of cracking roar to port: the Rodney has opened fire with her 16-inch guns, and an instant later the King George V lets fly with her 14-inch. The compass bounds out of its binnacle; my battle bowler tips over my nose and clatters down to the deck;

and a pile of signal papers shoots up like a fountain and swirls away in the tearing draught made by the great guns.

I have my glasses on Bismarck. She fires all four guns from her two forward turrets, four thin orange flames. The Germans have a reputation for hitting with their early salvos. Now I know what suspended animation means. It seems to take about two hours for those shots to fall! The splashes shoot up opposite but beyond Rodney's fo'c'sle. I'm sorry to say that we all thought, "Thank heavens, she's shooting at Rodney." My second thought was that I wouldn't care to be facing nine 16-inch and ten 14-inch guns; I just kept my binoculars glued to Bismarck. Rodney's first salvo produced great white columns of water 120 ft. high that would break the back of a destroyer and sink her like a stone if she steamed through one of them.

Rodney's Deadly Fire

The second splash I missed—all except one shot which seemed to belong to King George V and was a little ahead of Bismarck. Then I watched Rodney to see if she was being hit, but she just sat there like a great slab of rock blocking the northern horizon, and suddenly belched a full salvo. I actually saw these projectiles flying through the air for some seconds after they left the guns like little diminishing footballs curving up and up into the sky. Now, I am sure that four or five hit. There was only one great splash, and a sort of flurry of spray and splash which might have been a waterline hit. The others had bored their way through the Krupp armour belt like cheese; and pray God I

may never know what they did as they exploded inside the hull.

Bismarck turned north, steaming about twelve or fourteen knots. We kept turning in and out to confuse the enemy rangetakers, all the while closing the range rapidly. The Admiral kept on saying, "Close the range; get closer; get closer. I can't see enough hits!" And so we closed the range.

But although you couldn't see the hits they were there right enough. Somewhere about the eighth salvo there was a fire on the fo'c'sle which seemed to envelop the upper turret, and one observer tells me he saw a huge plate torn away from the tail of it. She turned away, then back, writhing it seemed, under the most merciless hail of high-explosive armour-piercing shells that any ship has, I suppose, ever faced. There was no escape for Bismarck; our fellows just went on pumping it out in a steady succession of shattering roars.

Smoke shot up, perhaps in an endeavour to screen herself, but it quickly blew away. And then I noticed her two rear turrets firing at us. There was a sort of shudder somewhere in our stern and I glanced that way for a hit—but there was no sign of it. A little later I heard the first whine of her 15-inch shell; it was a straddling shot over our fo'c'sle, one short and three overs. I wondered if the next would hit, and found myself edging into the doorway at the back of the bridge. It wouldn't have helped very much; it is only splash-proof plating, so I stepped forward again to see how Bismarck was getting along.

And an extraordinary sight met my eyes. The action had been going perhaps twenty minutes; some of her secondary armament and certainly two of the great turrets were still firing, perhaps a little wildly, for nobody on our side showed signs of a hit. There, racing across her quarterdeck, were little human figures; one climbed over the wire guard rails, hung on with one hand, looked back, and then jumped into the sea. Others just jumped without looking back at all—a little steady trickle of them jumping into the sea one after another.

'Lurching Black Ruin'

About this time the coppery glow of our secondary armament shells striking the armoured upper works became more and more frequent, and one fierce flame shot up from the base of the bridge structure enveloping it as high as and including the spotting top for a flickering second. Every man there must have been incinerated. There was no smoke; the heat had consumed it. Once I saw evidently a small-calibre shell afire, for a swift arc of flame shot high into the air and curved over the top of the mainmast. She still kept up some speed, but seemed heavy in the water and had a slight list to port.

Well, we just shot the guns out of her and left a smoking, lurching black ruin. It made one feel a little sick to see such a mighty powerful vessel brought to the state of an impotent hulk. Only her slow, wallowing speed seemed still to give her life, and those little jumping figures at the stern. It was like a dog that has been run over; someone had got to finish him off—because her colours are still flying at the mainmast head.

Our battleships turned away, and Dorsetshire closed in and finished her off with torpedoes. When we were about ten miles off, the hulk turned over to port, floated for a little bottom up, and then, with a lift of the bows, was suddenly gone.

ADMIRAL SIR J. C. TOVEY (left), Commander-in-Chief of the Home Fleet, takes a turn with the Captain (Capt. J. C. Leach) on the quarterdeck of H.M.S. Prince of Wales, the giant battleship which took part in the hunting of the Bismarck. *Photo, British Official : Crown Copyright*

Sheffield Shadowed the Bismarck

Top right, Captain C. A. A. Larcom, R.N., Captain of the Sheffield, who shadowed the Bismarck on the evening of May 26. Above, a Supermarine Walrus amphibian flying-boat being hoisted aboard H.M.S. Sheffield. In the foreground is a deadly type of A.A. heavy machine-gun battery.

Spray frames the forecastle and bridge of H.M.S. Sheffield as this 9,100-ton cruiser of the Southampton class ploughs through the seas. The barrels of her six forward 6-inch guns are visible below the bridge. Six more are mounted in the stern. H.M.S. Sheffield was completed in 1937. Her speed is rated at 32 knots, and she carries a normal complement of 700.

H.M.S. Sheffield making a black smoke screen. The different types of smoke screen and the way they are made is fully described in pages 296-297 of this Vol. In this photograph some of the Sheffield's eight 4-inch A.A. guns are visible to port and starboard.

Photos, British Official : Crown Copyright

Where Now Are 'Liberté, Egalité, Fraternité'?

Outside the Hotel Crillon in the Place de la Concorde, Paris, German troops parade, watched by an admiring crowd—of Germans.

The now familiar theatrical propaganda stunts of the Totalitarian states have penetrated into France. Outstretched hands greet Marshal Pétain at Le Puy with a regimented salute as he stands on the draped dais. The new slogan : " Family—Fatherland—Work " replaces the old " Liberty—Equality—Fraternity."

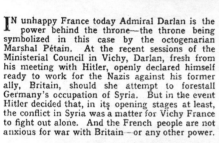

IN unhappy France today Admiral Darlan is the power behind the throne—the throne being symbolized in this case by the octogenarian Marshal Pétain. At the recent sessions of the Ministerial Council in Vichy, Darlan, fresh from his meeting with Hitler, openly declared himself ready to work for the Nazis against his former ally, Britain, should she attempt to forestall Germany's occupation of Syria. But in the event Hitler decided that, in its opening stages at least, the conflict in Syria was a matter for Vichy France to fight out alone. And the French people are not anxious for war with Britain—or any other power.

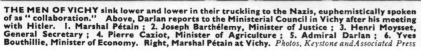

THE MEN OF VICHY sink lower and lower in their truckling to the Nazis, euphemistically spoken of as " collaboration." Above, Darlan reports to the Ministerial Council in Vichy after his meeting with Hitler. 1. Marshal Pétain ; 2. Joseph Barthélemy, Minister of Justice ; 3. Henri Moysset, General Secretary ; 4. Pierre Caziot, Minister of Agriculture ; 5. Admiral Darlan ; 6. Yves Bouthillie, Minister of Economy. Right, Marshal Pétain at Vichy. *Photos, Keystone and Associated Press*

Slow Progress in the Invasion of Syria

Early on the morning of Sunday, June 8, an Allied Army consisting of British, Anzac, Canadian and Indian troops and a Free French force, the whole being commanded by General Sir Maitland Wilson, crossed the frontier into Syria from the adjoining territories under British control. The situation after a week of rather confused manœuvre and fighting is summed up below. An article on the political background in Syria is given in page 628.

"OUR men went in singing the Marseillaise," General Catroux, Commander of the Free French forces in the Near East, announced over the Palestine radio on the day when the Allies invaded Syria. They were accompanied by wagons loaded with foodstuffs for the Syrian population, and their advance was heralded by loud-speaker vans from which came every few moments the announcement: "We are coming to chase out the enemy and wash out the shame of Vichy's capitulations. It is humiliating, perfidious Vichy which has precipitated war in the Levant."

Zero hour was at 2 a.m. on Sunday, June 8, and for hours before Bren-gun

[VICHY] FRANCE FIGHTS FOR HER FLAG
Cartoon by Zec from "The Daily Mirror"

has told how he came up with a famous English regiment supported by British and Imperial artillery and Indian sappers who had just occupied the town. Standing outside the deserted barracks where a crowd of smiling Arabs and Syrians gazed in bewilderment at the lorry-loads of dusky Indians, a British colonel described the operation. "We crossed the Jordan early on Sunday morning," he said. "We got bumped a bit from the enemy who was concealed on the ridges, with rifle, machine-gun and mortar fire and tanks, but we suffered only four casualties. Reaching the outskirts of Quneitra we sent in an officer on a Bren carrier with a white flag and asked for the surrender of the place. The officer was received by French officers who were very friendly and showed every wish to join the British, but who said their 'scoundrel' of a commandant had given them orders to fight on. The officer returned with the message that the commander refused to surrender and intended to fight. We shelled the enemy positions all night, and in the early morning we went in and found the troops had fled."

In their coastal advance the invaders occupied Tyre on the Sunday evening. There was a brush or two outside the town, a charge by Spahi horsemen broken up by the Allied fire, and then the British swept in. "I drove up," said the major who received

the town's surrender, "and Lebanese police came out. They gave me a cigarette and I handed mine round. They handed over their rifles saying they were tired of being French policemen, anyhow, and would prefer to become British police. I gave them back their rifles and said that suited me all right. Then we saluted and shook hands all round."

After Tyre the advance continued until the Litani River was reached. Here the French had taken up strong positions. The attack was delivered on the night of Tuesday, June 10. Alan Moorehead of the "Daily Express" was there and has described the fight.

"No car lights showed. We snuffed out our cigarettes. Hundreds of men, strapped with full marching kit, showed in faint outline on both sides of the road. They were lying in ploughed furrows and only a sudden laugh in the darkness or the tearing noise of a Bren-gun carrier or tank broke the tension of the electric moment when troops are waiting to go over the top. The column of vehicles stopped, moved on again, stopped again, and then the British artillery cut the stillness with the heaviest barrage ever seen in Syria. It was now early morning. There were two more barrages within an hour. All this time we were moving on the river. As the last barrage stopped, infantry and tanks charged along the river flat.

"Engineers breaking through a banana plantation dammed back a section of the fast, green stream and whipped a pontoon bridge across. Over it went tanks, guns, men and ambulances. They found themselves at first in an Italian fruit-tree garden lined with cypresses. French shots were smashing down the branches of banana and olive trees. Beyond the garden the British climbed sharply into the dark, wooded hills where the French 75 shells were coming from.

"Already there was chaos in the French lines. A British force of shock troops landed from the sea behind the French positions was wreaking havoc. This force had first rowed, then waded neck deep ashore not half a mile from the French

carriers, tanks, guns and lorries of every description had been taking up their places just behind the frontier.

"During the night of waiting," wrote Arthur Merton, "Daily Telegraph" Special Correspondent, "before the advance, officers and men were in a curious mood. There was no joking about this job, as there had been about the Libyan, Greek, and even Crete fighting; there was only a quiet resolution to see an unpleasant task through. But as a battery of guns jolted along the crews sang, appropriately enough, "South of the Border." The brilliance of the moonlight touched the whole scene with an eerie quality which gave to the watcher a sense of unreality. A force of English cavalry went by, with the clink of sword against stirrup. It was like a scene from an earlier war as they trotted along."

Australian infantry were the first to cross. Stealing swiftly and silently across No-man's land at 2.45 they captured two French police posts and a frontier post and then pushed on to assail the forts of Klair and Khaim, seven miles away, situated on promontories overlooking the plains of cultivated fields and olive groves. These subdued, the Australians proceeded along the road to Merj Ayun and beyond. Meanwhile, other columns were progressing to west and east along the coast from Nakura towards Tyre, and from the Jordan valley in the direction of Damascus. Yet other columns were reported to have crossed the frontier from Iraq and to be heading for Damascus from the east.

In the central sector Quneitra was captured early in the week. Reuter's Correspondent

SYRIA, showing principal Allied thrusts along the coastline by Tyre and Sidon, towards Damascus from the south, towards Deir ez Zor and Ras el Ain, indicated by black arrows. Airfields are also marked. Inset : Map of Damascus, Beirut and Lake Tiberias area, with names of places mentioned in the fighting up to June 12, 1941.

Stiff Resistance to the Allies' Advance

batteries." Meanwhile a second section of the sea force rounded on the river and dealt with the French machine-gunners under the fruit trees, while the third section turned northwards. Within 15 minutes of landing one soldier had smashed his way into the French barracks and hauled down the flag from the masthead. He brought the flag back to his captain.

Continuing along the coast, the British and Australians next attacked Sidon. For three days the ancient city was battered by gunfire and tank attacks, while in the orange groves there was the intermittent fusillade of machine-gun and rifle fire. There was bombardment from the sea, too, as British light cruisers and destroyers came into action.

A week after hostilities began the penetration was reported to be proceeding satisfactorily. The Allies were within 12 miles of Beirut, while Damascus was almost surrounded : the situation there, indeed, was such that the city could have been stormed, but the Allies, wise in their generation, were resolved not to repeat the

Sultan el Atrah Pasha, head of the Druse tribes, who led a Druse revolt against the French in Syria in 1926, is reported to have joined the Allies with 10,000 men.

mistake made by General Sarrail in 1925 when he bombarded this holy city of Islam.

From the beginning Vichy France had taken a very pessimistic view of the situation. Even on June 9 the Vichy News Agency reported that though the French troops in Syria were everywhere " putting up lively resistance against the British and de Gaulliste forces," the British forces were " markedly superior, especially in armoured equipment. The difficulties of defending the territories of the Levant for an army which has only weak forces at its disposal are pointed out in Vichy. Supplying this army, not only with arms and munitions but with food and fuel, is practically impossible." Confirmation of this state of affairs was provided by the prisoners taken. Thus one man, after describing the fighting north of Sidon as appalling, said that the French continued their resistance because they had been told that Britain was trying to annex Syria as a colony. " We have been fighting our best," he said, " even though headquarters does not seem to care what happens to us. We have had no food or water since we arrived at Sidon. We have been allowed no rest and been given no news except atrocity stories about what the British were doing to our men. Yet we have done our best, believing we were defending Syria."

These Free French soldiers who fought magnificently in the Western Desert are confident of victory. So are those now advancing into Syria under General Legentilhomme, seen on the left.

In those remarks lay tragedy. It was admitted by the Allies that the French resistance was far stronger than had been anticipated ; sufficient allowance had not been made for the traditional loyalty of the French soldier—native and colonial—to his officers and of the officers to their chiefs. Moreover, few of the rank and file, at least, had any knowledge of the extent of the German penetration into Syria. Then the British and still more the Free French were anxious to avoid shedding the blood of men who were once their allies and who, they hoped, would ere long be their allies again.

A camel on a desert aerodrome is a striking illustration of the contrast between old and new forms of locomotion. The new in this case is very new, for it is one of the latest Tomahawk aircraft now being used in Syria and elsewhere in the Middle East. (See also p. 487.)

Photos, British Official : Crown Copyright, Planet News

Outposts in Syria of Vichy France

ALEPPO, here seen from the air, is a city of about 180,000 inhabitants, the market-place of Northern Syria. Its most distinctive feature is the great fortress of the Saracens, seen in the foreground.

DAMASCUS, objective of the Allied Forces, lies on the borders of the Syrian desert in the Ruta, a large oasis. Capital of the Syrian Republic, it has a population of 194,000. Left, the fruit market showing produce from the luxuriant orchards which surround the town. Right, the Great Mosque, originally the church of Saint John Baptist, built by Theodosius I (346-95). After the conquest of the city by the Arabs the church was assigned to the Moslems and in 708 was transformed into the present mosque.

Photos, Paul Popper, Mrs. T. Muir, Dorien Leigh

The Fighting in Iraq: Scenes from the Short-

Ⓐ

FORT RUTBAH, an important point on the Kirkuk-Haifa pipeline, which was held by a garrison of Raschid Ali's troops, surrendered on May 9, after the R.A.F. had bombed the fort. Top left, a British armoured car inside the fort after the British entry. Above, Iraqi prisoners being interrogated. Right, a bomb exploding just outside the fort as a warning to surrender. The shed A, seen top, is shown in this aerial photograph. *Photos, British Official and British Newsreel Association*

British Campaign Against the Iraqi 'Quisling'

Here are some of Raschid Ali's army taken prisoner after being forced into the camp at Habbaniyah by low-flying R.A.F. planes. The oval shows the observer, pilot and air gunner of an R.A.F. bomber who rescued the pilot of another of our aircraft which had crashed near a body of Iraqi insurgents. Despite rifle and machine-gun fire from the enemy the injured pilot was transferred to the rescue plane and brought to safety.

An Ocean-Going U-Boat

**The Sinister Weapon with which Hitler
Hopes to Win the Battle of the Atlantic
by Cutting Our Life-Line with the
United States**

Specially drawn by Haworth for
THE WAR ILLUSTRATED

A TYPICAL UNDER-SEA RAIDER, the surface weight being about 740 tons, with a speed of 18 knots (8 knots below surface). The crew number 40. The Commander (A) is on the bridge of the conning tower and is examining a likely victim through his binoculars. He will try to calculate its speed and course so that he can take the U-boat underwater to a point which will give a good target for the torpedoes (see diagram 1), which have an effective range of 1,000 yards. Boats of this type may well constitute the "wolf-packs," based upon French ports, of which German propaganda has boasted.

The Controls

The hatch (B) leads down into the control-room. Here a petty officer (C) is raising one of the twin periscopes from its well in the floor. The navigator (D) is seen at his charts. This man plots the course and works the electric-signal board (E) whence the commander's instructions are relayed throughout the U-boat. Two men at (F) operate the diving rudders which control up and down movements.

Below surface the steering is carried out at (G), while surface steering arrangements are seen behind the Commander. (H) is the main switch-room and (I) the diesel engines, which drive the U-boat on the surface

and also keep charged the powerful batteries, small portion seen at (K), which in turn provide power for the electric motors, partly shown at (L), which propel the vessel under water. (M) is a store-room and (N) the pump-room. The metal bottles (O) contain the vital compressed air (also recharged by the diesel engines), which makes the ship buoyant by driving out water ballast from the external tanks seen at (P). The wireless cabin is at (Q) and Commander's cabin at (R).

Firing the Torpedoes

Torpedoes are seen being loaded into the four forward tubes at (S) and there are two similar tubes in the stern.

The large gun on the deck is a 4·1 inch and the small one a one-pounder A.A. gun.

The inset picture (2) shows a detail of the periscope eye-piece, which the Commander can turn round by means of the handles. When he has the target full in vision he grasps the pistol grip (T) and, pulling the trigger, fires off a torpedo.

The diagram, bottom right (1), shows how small a margin of error is permissible in aiming a torpedo.

Aircraft of the Coastal Command have taken a heavy toll of these U-boats, and diagram (3) shows the depth at which U-boats can be spotted from the air in different waters.

And in the Mediterranean up to a Depth of 80 Feet.

In the Western Approaches up to a Depth of 30 feet, the U-Boat is visible.

In the North Sea & Atlantic the U-Boat can rarely be spotted from the Air, even if the Periscope is well above Surface.

20% Error, no Shot.
10% Error in Calculation, more difficult.
Correct Calculation, perfect Shot.

New Methods for Fighting Britain's Fires

For too long the full extent of the menace of incendiary attacks upon our cities remained unrecognized. Now at length a re-organization of the fire-fighting services has been embarked upon which, had it been launched even a little sooner, would have saved the country much material destruction, not to mention the accompanying loss of life.

THE heroic manner in which the men of the fire services in this country, both regular and auxiliary, have acquitted themselves under an ordeal which could hardly have been imagined before the war, is common knowledge. The country has for these men nothing but praise ; criticism of the fire service there was, and it increased as the incendiary attacks of the enemy grew heavier and material destruction increased, but this criticism was directed entirely against defects in organization, and particularly against the system of basing the fire army of Britain on local authority areas, with its resulting delays and red-tape hindrances.

The need for replanning became more and more obvious with every raid, and the various anomalies of local control impeded the efficiency of the service as a whole. One serious drawback was the lack of national ranking in the fire service, so that a senior officer of one brigade might find himself with no authority at all over the firemen of another engaged in the same area.

Sometimes, when a call for aid was sent out, reinforcements arrived quite unfamiliar with the town or its water supplies, and then they were called upon to handle equipment of which they had had practically no experience. Sometimes a street in a city would be ablaze while pumps and crews stood idle in another part.

Then, again, many high officers in the service combined their appointment with other duties, which meant that they were unable to devote the whole of their energies to the brigades under their control, although an enormous responsibility might fall upon their shoulders at any moment should their area be heavily attacked. Moreover, the mobility so essential for the effective use of the fire-fighting services depends to a very large extent on the organization and administration of local brigades, and the control of their movements has to be closely co-ordinated, a process very difficult when responsibility is divided between the Government and numerous local authorities each with absolute control over its own brigades.

Small wonder then that public opinion demanded a radical reorganization of the country's fire-fighting services on a national basis. The great fire blitz of May 10 brought matters to a head, and Mr. Herbert Morrison, the Home Secretary, after conferring with representatives of local authorities throughout the country, announced that sweeping reforms were to be put into operation without delay. In the new home of the House of Commons on May 13, 1941, he told the House of the changes he contemplated, and concluded by saying : " The Government has decided to seek firm Parliamentary powers to place the whole fire brigade resources of the country under the general control of the Home Secretary and the Secretary for Scotland with a view to the regrouping of the resources into larger units for purposes of administration and control, with unity of command over each force, and to constituting mobile fire-fighting units for reinforcing purposes or other special duties."

All-England Fire Service

Details of the new scheme as far as it affected England and Wales were announced on June 9. A Fire Service Council was set up, with the Chief of the London Fire Brigade, Commander A. N. G. Firebrace, as Chief of the Fire Staff, and including also among its members the Home Secretary, Mr. Herbert Morrison, Mr. W. Mabane, M.P., Parliamentary Secretary to the Ministry of Home Security, and Miss Ellen Wilkinson.

The new fire forces are to be grouped on the basis of strategical and tactical requirements instead of on local authorities' boundaries, and in place of the existing 1,400 local fire brigades there will be 32 fire forces in England and Wales, plus certain others in the London region. The 32 areas have been selected for operational efficiency ignoring county boundaries. Each of the new forces will be under the command of a " fire force commander."

Supervision of the fire force in each civil defence region will rest with the Regional Commissioner under the direction of the

CDR. A. FIREBRACE, C.-in-C. of an army of 250,000 whole-time or part-time fire fighters under the new policy of putting this service on a national basis.   *Photo, Associated Press*

Secretary of State, but subject to this supervision the fire force commanders will have full administrative, executive and operational control of his force, and in the larger areas they will have deputies. At regional headquarters there will be a fire staff officer with a suitable staff, whose business it will be to undertake, under the Regional Commissioner, general supervision in the region. There are to be special staff and technical officers for such work as water supplies, control of transport, stores, communications, etc.

The fire force commanders and fire staff officers will be appointed by the Secretary of State guided by the recommendations of a selection board, and they will have to have had practical experience of fire-fighting, preferably under war conditions, or of the administration of fire brigades. Officer posts will be filled on the basis of merit by appointments both from the regular service and from the A.F.S., and Mr. Mabane, deputy chairman of the new Fire Service Council, stressed the point that promotion would be open to the A.F.S. no less than to the regulars.

Ready for Instant Action

New mobile divisions, self-contained in equipment and transport, are being formed, and these will be rushed to any heavily-bombed area at short notice. The first of these divisions has already been formed in London, and is ready for action. It is composed of about a thousand officers and men, and its equipment includes 64 pumps, lorries which lay hose at the rate of 20 m.p.h., repair vans, water towers, foam units, ambulances and field kitchens. It will take with it tents and baggage so that, if need be, the firemen will have their own quarters.

Nor has the problem of water reserves been overlooked. All open water, such as ponds, rivers, canals and swimming pools, has been surveyed and large numbers of water storage basins have been provided.

GRIMSBY FIRE FLOATS in action in the docks area. The A.F.S. in this town is in charge of the Mayor, Councillor C. H. Wilkinson (inset), who has been awarded the M.B.E. for gallant conduct in helping to rescue 31 men from a sinking trawler.   *Photos, G.P.U. and " Daily Mirror "*

Our Diary of the War

SUNDAY, JUNE 8, 1941   645th day

Sea.—Admiralty announced loss of H.M. drifter Thistle and H.M. trawler Evesham.

Air.—British bombers made widespread daylight attacks on enemy shipping off Norway, Holland, Belgium and France. By night R.A.F. bombed objectives in the Ruhr, including Essen and Dortmund.

Africa.—R.A.F. made prolonged night raids on Benghazi and Derna. Fleet Air Arm attacked Tripoli.

Near East.—British and Free French troops, supported by R.A.F., crossed Syrian frontier at dawn. R.A.F. made heavy raids on harbour and aerodromes in Rhodes during night of June 8-9.

Home.—Sharp raid on S.W. coast town.

MONDAY, JUNE 9   646th day

Sea.—Admiralty announced loss of A.A. cruiser Calcutta and destroyers Hereward and Imperial during evacuation of Crete.

Announced that two more enemy supply ships had been sunk in the Atlantic.

Africa.—In Abyssinia our troops continued their advance west of River Omo.

Near East.—Allied troops in Syria, supported by R.A.F. and R.A.A.F., progressed beyond Tyre and crossed River Litani.

Enemy aircraft attacked Haifa during the night; one plane shot down by A.A. fire. R.A.F. bombed aerodrome at Aleppo while Haifa raiders were returning; aerodromes in Rhodes also bombed.

Home.—A single enemy aircraft dropped bombs at one point in the north-east. H.M.S. Blencathra shot down an Me 109.

TUESDAY, JUNE 10   647th day

Air.—R.A.F. made daylight attacks on shipping off enemy coasts. By night strong force of Bomber Command attacked docks at Brest. Docks at St. Nazaire and aerodromes at Mandal and Stavanger also bombed.

Africa.—R.A.F. bombed the harbour at Benghazi, the aerodrome at Benina and landing-grounds at Derna, Gambut and Gazala. Fighter aircraft attacked enemy transport between Barce and Derna, destroying about 30 large tankers. Benghazi harbour and enemy aerodromes in Libya were also attacked during the night of June 10-11.

Near East.—Penetration of Allied forces into Syria proceeding satisfactorily. R.A.F. made heavy raids on aerodromes in Rhodes and at Aleppo.

Home.—Enemy activity by night was on a small scale, but in South Wales some damage and casualties were caused. One enemy bomber was destroyed.

WEDNESDAY, JUNE 11   648th day

Air.—R.A.F. attacked docks at Ymuiden and shipping at Zeebrugge. An enemy tanker carried out offensive patrols over Northern France and Belgium.

By night the Bomber Command made a heavy attack on the Ruhr. Attacks were also made on Cologne and docks at Rotterdam and Boulogne. The Coastal Command and Fleet Air Arm attacked docks at Dunkirk and seaplane base at Norderney.

Africa.—R.A.F. continued to attack enemy motor transport and troops in Libya.

Near East.—Allied forces in Syria continued to make progress. Our bombers attacked the aerodrome at Palmyra.

Tel Aviv was raided by enemy aircraft.

Home.—Night raiders dropped bombs in many districts of England, but casualties were not heavy except at one point. Leaflets were dropped on villages in east of England.

THURSDAY, JUNE 12   649th day

Sea.—Admiralty announced the loss of the monitor Terror and the gunboat Ladybird during operations off Libya.

German pocket battleship hit by torpedo from Beaufort bomber off Norway.

Confirmed in Washington that the American merchantman Robin Moor was torpedoed and sunk by a German U-boat on May 21.

Air.—R.A.F. attacked enemy shipping in the Channel.

Another heavy night raid by Bomber Command on the Ruhr. Coastal Command attacked docks at Brest and Antwerp.

Africa.—Announced from Cairo that Abyssinian Patriot forces have occupied Lekamti.

Capture of Assab by troops from H.M. ships and units of Royal Indian Navy announced.

Near East.—Allied forces in Syria, supported by R.A.F., made further important progress

in all sectors. Shipping in the harbour at Beirut was attacked by R.A.F. and Fleet Air Arm; one Vichy aircraft was shot down.

Home.—During the night enemy aircraft flew over eastern England. One destroyed.

FRIDAY, JUNE 13   650th day

Sea.—Cross-channel steamer St. Patrick sunk by dive-bombers near Fishguard.

Air.—Night raids over Ruhr continued, particularly in industrial district of Schwerte. Other forces attacked Brest docks.

Africa.—Belgian contingent advancing in Gambela area. Farther south operations progressing towards Jimma.

During night of 12-13 British troops at Tobruk considerably reduced salient held by enemy in outer defences.

R.A.F. destroyed 19 motor-transport vehicles between Gazala and Capuzzo. Heavy night raids on harbour at Benghazi and landing-grounds at Benina, Gazala and Derna.

Near East.—In Syria Allied forces made further progress in all sectors.

Nine Junkers, about to attack British naval forces near Sidon, driven off by R.A.A.F. fighters; three destroyed and others damaged.

Successful raids on aerodromes at Calato (Rhodes) and Aleppo.

Home.—Widespread but minor night attacks. Two day and seven night raiders destroyed.

SATURDAY, JUNE 14   651st day

Sea.—Admiralty announced further successful attacks by our submarines on ships and harbours in Mediterranean.

Announced that another enemy supply ship had been sunk in Atlantic.

Air.—R.A.F. fighters and bombers carried out widespread offensive operations over Channel and Northern France, including airfields at St. Omer. Cologne area heavily raided at night.

Africa.—Patriot forces completing encirclement of Jimma.

Near East.—Vichy troops reported to have evacuated Kiswe, 10 miles south of Damascus. In central sector British forces hold Nabatiye, 15 miles S.E. of Sidon. Abu Kemal, on Euphrates, captured by British armoured unit.

Home.—Bombs fell by day at a point in south-west. At night minor raids occurred in west of England. One day and one night raider destroyed.

RAID DAMAGE IN DUBLIN after the Nazis had dropped bombs in the early morning of May 31, 1941. A.R.P. wardens are searching the debris in North Strand where 20 people were killed. In protesting to Germany the Eireann Government announced that 27 people were killed and 80 injured, but the figures subsequently proved higher. With typical stupidity the Nazis tried to put the blame on Britain for this outrage before the bombs were proved to be of German origin. Eire, like other neutrals, has learned again that German aggression respects no frontiers.   *Photo, Planet News*

No Doubt About These R.A.F. Direct Hits

A direct hit from 8,000 feet on a German supply ship in Thyboron harbour, Denmark, proves the high accuracy of the new U.S. Sperry bomb sight installed in an R.A.F. reconnaissance Hudson. Only one salvo was needed to hit the target. The difference between the Sperry invention and the R.A.F. apparatus is that in the latter the aircraft is manoeuvred according to the orders of the bomb aimer. With the Sperry sight, which is built round the automatic gyroscopic pilot, the bomb aimer is able to control the aeroplane himself while taking aim. Circle, the bomb aimer in a Sunderland flying-boat manned by members of the R.A.A.F. setting his sights.

NEAR MANNHEIM this autobahn bridge has been extensively damaged by R.A.F. bombs. Of its two spans one has suffered a direct hit and, completely destroyed, has fallen into the river at A. Mannheim, situated on the Rhine not far from Heidelberg, is an important railway and industrial centre comprising oil-plants, docks, factories, power-stations and goods-yards. Following the wise policy of concentrating on military objectives only, the R.A.F. have continuously bombed Mannheim since June 1940.

Photos, British Official : Crown Copyright

Inquest on Crete: the Commons Debate

When the House of Commons met on June 10, 1941, it proceeded to discuss the Battle of Crete, concluded a few days before. What the M.P.s said takes up 100 pages of Hansard, but from the quotations given below it will be possible to follow the course of the debate and appreciate some, at least, of the questions which exercised their minds and tongues.

NOT a rancorous debate, but a useful one. That it should prove to be such was the anticipation of the first speaker, Mr. Lees-Smith, Labour Member for Keighley and a leader of what may be described as the unofficial Opposition. There were a number of questions in the public mind, he said, and it would be a good thing to give the Prime Minister an opportunity of answering them—or some of them.

Mr. Lees-Smith put some of the questions himself, but before doing so he asked the house to bear in mind that

" the overriding difficulty is not mistakes, but the simple fact that General Wavell has to conduct a number of campaigns simultaneously, in each one of which he is outnumbered and out-machined. The whole possibility of his avoiding serious reverses has depended upon the most precise timing, by which it has been necessary for him to bring one campaign to a conclusion and transfer his troops just before the other campaign reached its peak."

Turning to Crete, Mr. Lees-Smith did not question the decision to defend it. But he did ask why, when we had been in control of the island for about seven months, our Air Force had to be withdrawn at an early stage of the battle because of the lack of aerodromes ? Why we had evacuated aerodromes before making them unusable by the enemy ? Why the Germans were better equipped with tommy-guns than our own men, who had to rely largely upon those they captured from the enemy ? Finally, why was not more use made of the Cretan fighters as distinct from the Greeks ? To sum up, " the general impression which is widely felt is that this war in the Middle East was not viewed sufficiently as a whole, that there was insufficient long-distance foresight in the situation which might arise in Crete . . . that we were unprepared for the new technique which Germany had adopted, which we had to deal with by hasty improvizations."

' An Island Has Been Captured '

The next speaker was **Mr. Hore-Belisha**, the National Liberal Member for Devonport, who was Secretary of State for War from 1937 until January, 1940.

" For the first time in history," he said, " an island has been captured by an air-borne attack. That in itself is an occurrence—let us hope not a portent—on which we, situated geographically as we are, cannot fail anxiously to ponder."

Why was the Fleet called upon to operate in narrow waters, he asked, and the Army required to undertake so desperate a task in circumstances which neglected every dictate of experience ? Norway had shown under what a handicap the Fleet laboured within the range of the land-based Luftwaffe, and that an army cannot be maintained without aerodromes from which it could be given cover. Then more recent experiences had reinforced these tactical facts. Why were the lessons not applied ?

Mr. Hore-Belisha went on to urge that the Army, like the Navy, should be given its own air arm, and the Air Force should be provided with a corps of its own who would be available when they occupied new territory to prepare landing-grounds.

Soon it was **Mr. Beverley Baxter's** turn ; he is the Conservative Member for Wood Green, and a well-known journalist. He had some pertinent questions to ask : Who decided that we should have only so many planes in Crete ? Who decided that they should be withdrawn ? Who decided that we could afford to lose four cruisers and six destroyers better than 50 aeroplanes ?

A Service Member was the next to speak, **Lt.-Col. Macnamara**, Conservative Member

for Chelmsford. " It does not matter about Crete," he said, " provided we take the lessons it taught to heart." And those lessons were, first of all, the Navy cannot operate effectively in waters near the enemy land bases ; next, that air-borne troops can quite well land anywhere and, what is more, can be reinforced ; while the third lesson was that though our troops did not have very many casualties, men may apparently still be easily demoralized by dive-bombing and machine-gunning from the air, which does not give casualties but makes noise. " It sounds a strange thing to say, but I am sure it is true that one of the most effective weapons which have been used against us so far in all the theatres of war is noise."

Then he proceeded to ask a lot of questions. Is Eire properly defended ? If not, why not ? Are Ulster, Wales, Cornwall and the Scilly Isles studded with aerodromes, and are those aerodromes perfectly protected ? Are they underground ? Are there aeroplanes on the mountainside ? Is there an alternative aerodrome to every one of them ? Is every aeroplane kept in a blast-proof shelter ? Are the airmen trained as infantry

GROUP-CAPT. G. R. BEAMISH was the R.A.F. Officer commanding in Crete who endorsed the decision to withdraw the Air Forces from the Cretan aerodromes.

soldiers, to take part in the defence of their aerodromes ? Is every aerodrome a hundred per cent proof against gas ? Is it possible immediately to decontaminate every single aeroplane ?

Then **Lord Winterton** (Conservative, Horsham and Worthing) who has been a Member of the House since 1904, proceeded to review the present war in the light of the last, in which he served in Gallipoli, Palestine and Arabia.

He protested against the tendency to believe that because the Government had won a debate, we had thereby won a battle. " Facts sometimes become obscure in the tropical jungle of florescent rhetoric." Then after a tribute to the " popular Press," Lord Winterton went on with the dramatic words : " We can easily lose this war by our own faults as a nation, and lose it within the next three or four months . . . . this war will be won or lost within the next three or four months," he concluded, " in the factories, in the fields, and in the shipyards in this country, and on the seas around Britain."

Soon it was **Mr. Bellenger's** turn (Labour, Bassetlaw). He served in the Army in this war and the last. He gave the serving man's point of view, whether it be of dive-bombing :

" The troops at Dunkirk were not so much concerned with the dive-bombing, so long as they could see our aeroplanes "—or the lack of air support for the Army.

" Will we be able to maintain the morale of the troops on whom you depend for ultimate victory if you give them bayonets to fight against tanks, and tommy-guns, and if you deny them air support ? I can well imagine the feelings of the troops in Crete who knew that they were facing slaughter with no possible chance of success."

The last speaker in the debate before Mr. Churchill rose was **Rear-Admiral Beamish** (Conservative, Lewes). Naturally enough, perhaps, he stressed the fact of sea-power. " If it was not for sea power," he said, " there would be only one side in the Mediterranean at present. Yet in Crete, sea power had had its wings clipped ; in fact, its wings had been practically removed by asking the Navy to carry out work for which it was never designed. You may have as many aircraft carriers as you like," he went on, " but they are extremely vulnerable craft and are not designed for working close inshore for the protection of the Army." He proceeded to make a strong plea that the Army should have its own air force.

The Premier's Reply

Then **Mr. Churchill** replied. First he deprecated the debate, both on the ground that no full explanations could possibly be given without revealing valuable information to the enemy and also because the fighting in Crete was only one part of the very important and complicated campaign which is being fought in the Middle East. " The vast scene can only be surveyed as a whole, and it should not be exposed to a debate piecemeal, especially at a time when operations which are all related to one another are still incomplete."

Next, answering the question why there were not enough guns provided for the two serviceable airfields which existed in Crete, he said that a very great number of guns which might have been usefully employed in Crete have been and are being mounted in our merchant vessels, to beat off the attacks of the Focke-Wulf and Heinkel planes engaged in the Battle of the Atlantic. Moreover, he reminded the House, everything we send out to the Middle East is out of action for the best part of three months as it has to go round the Cape. The decision to withdraw the air arm from Crete, the Premier went on to reveal, was taken by the Commander-in-Chief of the Air Force, Middle East, on the recommendation of General Freyberg, concurred in by Group Captain Beamish, R.A.F. officer commanding on the spot.

Then dealing with the campaign in Crete, he said that it had been hoped that 25,000 or 30,000 good troops with artillery and a proportion of tanks, added to the Greek forces, would destroy the enemy parachute and glider landings and prevent the enemy from using the airfields and the harbour. In the event that had not been possible. He could not go into details, but he announced that 17,000 men had been safely evacuated from Crete, while our killed and wounded and missing and prisoners amounted to about 15,000. The Germans, for their part, had lost at least 5,000 drowned and 12,000 killed and wounded on the island itself, in addition to 180 fighter and bomber aircraft destroyed and at least 280 troop-carrying aeroplanes.

" I am sure," he said, " that it will be found that this sombre, ferocious battle which was lost, and lost, I think, upon no great margin, was a battle well worth fighting and that it will play an extremely important part in the whole defence of the Nile Valley throughout the present year."

First Photos of a 'Sombre, Ferocious Battle'

THE INVASION OF CRETE is here seen in the first photographs to be received in this country. They came from German sources as part of the Nazi war propaganda. The top photograph shows German parachute troops dropping from troop-carrying planes. Above, clouds of smoke rising from burning wharves and stores in the harbour at Suda Bay after a dive-bombing attack. This photograph reached London by Clipper mail after being radioed from Berlin to New York.

Photos, Keystone

New Machines and Old Ritual in Ethiopia

THE MARCHES COMPARED
British Advance to Amba Alagi, 1940

Rate of Advance	Place	Date	Distance
miles/day	Kismayu	Feb. 14	miles
	Juba crossed	Feb. 20	
	Brava	Feb. 25	
23 (50)*	Mogadishu	Feb. 25	250
31	Gabre Darre	March 9	370
25	Jijiga	March 17	200
5	Harar	March 26	50
6	Diredawa	March 31	30
	Bridgehead established at Awash	April 3	140
50	Addis Ababa	April 5	110
9	Dessie	April 27	200
7	Amba Alagi	May 19	150
		94 days	1,500 miles

*After crossing Juba

Italian Advance to Addis Ababa, 1935-36

Place	Occupation Date	Distance
Adigrat	Oct. 5, 1935	50 miles
Macalle	Nov. 8, 1935	
L'Amba-Aradam	Feb. 16, 1936	
Alagi	Feb. 28, 1936	75 miles
Quoram	Apr. 6, 1936	
Dessie	Apr. 15, 1936	100 miles
Addis Ababa ...	May 5, 1936	200 miles
	7 months	425 miles

EMPEROR HAILE SELASSIE arriving at his royal residence in Addis Ababa. Below, a primitive B.B.C. station somewhere in the African bush. Propaganda has been a valuable aid to our military operations in Eritrea and Abyssinia.

The return of Haile Selassie to the land of his fathers was celebrated with ancient religious ritual. Here are some of the officials of the Abyssinian Coptic Church awaiting the Emperor's arrival. Christianity was adopted by Ethiopia in the fourth century, the Copts being the early native Christians of Egypt.

South African mechanics making adjustments to a bomber. Abyssinia was for centuries a land of almost inaccessible mystery, but the Italian conquest and reconquest by British arms have opened up the country. In the top left-hand corner the speed of the British advance is compared with that of the Italians.

Photos, British Official: Crown Copyright; Associated Press

I Was There!.... Eye Witness Stories of the War

We Helped in the Sinking of the Bismarck

The terrible punishment which the Bismarck withstood before she was finally torpedoed and the rescue of a hundred or so survivors from the great German warship are here described by British naval officers and men who were "in at the kill."

AN able seaman, describing the action with the Bismarck, said: "We pumped everything we had into her. She withstood appalling punishment, and we were astonished that any ship could remain afloat in such fire.

We counted over 300 hits with our 8-in. shells. They killed many of the Bismarck complement, but still her guns replied. Bismarck gunners fired from individual control long after central controls were obviously wrecked.

An officer said:

She gave no sign of surrender and kept her battle colours flying and so our firing had to be continued. This was not pleasant.

The Bismarck was still firing in a desultory way when the Dorsetshire closed in to dispatch her by torpedo. But her salvos were whistling harmlessly overhead.

You could see that she was terribly distressed—on fire from stem to stern—flames on the forecastle, amidships, and on the quarter-deck. Dense smoke clouds rolled away, and her sides glowed red-hot as if she were a furnace inside.

An engineer then took up the tale:

We were determined that we would get her, and the engines took it wonderfully.

Down below men were waiting for the signal that would tell us that we had found the Bismarck. When it came, and our guns opened fire, there were cheers. We grinned at one another and said, "Let her have it."

And we did. Some of us were allowed on deck to see the end. When I first saw the Bismarck she was ablaze, and smoke was pouring from her over the tops of her masts. We could see salvo after salvo of shells bursting in her. Every time the guns fired men were waving their hats and shouting: "Give it to 'em," and cheering.

Then torpedoes finished the job. One burst on the stern. Steelwork and stanchions were hurled high above the masts. And men were hurled with them. She went down slowly, a blazing hulk.

A German gunnery officer, who was among those rescued, asked to send a message to the commander-in-chief of the action. It was this: "Your shooting was deadly. You knocked 17 bells out of us."

A British chief petty officer aboard the ship which brought the German prisoners back said: They were all dazed and looked "punch drunk." They said they had had "hell" from our ships, and most of them had bruises from being knocked about by the poundings and direct hits.

The final moments of the stricken German warship were described by another officer.

He said:

As the Bismarck heeled to port and slowly went down, we could suddenly see all over the hull hundreds of black dots. They were human beings, making a last effort to avoid death. As the vessel heeled over further the dots moved along the hull—anywhere out of reach of the water. The vessel took a last plunge and sank stern foremost, and the dots were seen in the water.

It was quite impossible to lower any boats in the heavy seas, and all we could do was to throw out long grasslines, which float on the surface, for survivors to grasp. We saved quite a number, but while engaged in this work we received warning that there were submarines in the vicinity and we must get under way.

At one time there were scores of men strung out along two long ropes, striving to get alongside. The waves were tossing them high out of the water and then plunging them into the depths.

Some were half-naked. Their faces were

Mr. A. V. Alexander, First Lord of the Admiralty, with senior officers of H.M.S. Rodney, at a British port after returning from the Bismarck action. The new battle honour is seen above their heads.
Photo, Keystone

streaked with oil, and when they reached the vessel many were so exhausted that they could not manage the final climb. Every now and then a man halfway up the rope would collapse and carry two or three of his comrades beneath him into the water.

Those we could haul aboard had their knuckles clenched and bleeding. They were frozen with cold and dropped like logs to the deck. Within a few minutes they were wrapped in blankets and bedding and they actually fell asleep as they talked to us below deck.

The lucky ones had very little to say for themselves. They were obviously grateful for all we were doing for them and told us they had had neither food nor sleep for four days.

There was no gloating over the sinking of the Hood, but they did seem to take a curious pride in the fact that so many of our vessels had been called out to put paid to the Bismarck.

We Fired the Torpedoes that Finished Her

When the chase of the Bismarck was ended and her guns were silenced, she still had to be sunk by torpedoes from the cruiser Dorsetshire, and here is the story of Lieut.-Commander G. R. Carver who fired those torpedoes.

WHAT it felt like to be the man who fired the torpedoes that finally sank the Bismarck was described by Commander Carver when Dorsetshire landed 83 survivors from Bismarck at a British port. He said:

The captain gave me the "stand by" order. I felt how terrible it would be to miss. It was my first chance of firing point-blank at an enemy.

We had closed in to short range, and the captain told me to give her two. I was astonished, when the torpedoes hit home, that the Bismarck hardly shuddered. We went around to the other side and I let her have another. When that one hit she began to list and quickly turned over to sink.

The water appeared to be full of struggling Germans, and we must have lost fathoms of rope which we trailed over the side to try to pick them up.

She was a terrible sight. Her top was blown clean away, flames were roaring out in several places, and her plates were glowing red with heat. Great clouds of black smoke were billowing from her and rising for a hundred feet or so.

When our torpedoes hit her the Bismarck settled down by the stern, and then heeled over to port. She had not blown up, but just went straight down on her side with her battle ensign still flying. It was a most impressive sight, and we watched in silence as she finally went under.

Dorsetshire's eight-inch guns had already contributed in a devastating way to the Bismarck's destruction. Prisoners who had been rescued said they were astounded by the rate and the accuracy of the shells.

Commissioned Gunner T. A. Pentney, a Londoner, described the action when they

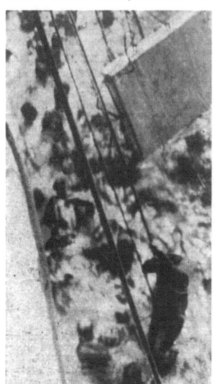

Survivors of the German battleship Bismarck, clinging to ropes, being hauled aboard a British ship. About a hundred were saved in this way after the Bismarck sank. *Photo, Keystone*

These smiling lads are the torpedo crew of H.M.S. Dorsetshire. They fired the torpedoes which sank the Bismarck, pride of Hitler's fleet. Right, Lieut.-Comdr. G. R. Carver, who gave the order to fire. H.M.S. Dorsetshire (Capt. B. C. S. Martin, R.N.) torpedoed the Bismarck after the German battleship's armament had been silenced by our guns. *Photos, "Daily Herald" and Keystone*

came upon the enemy steaming at about 10 knots in a rough sea. He said :

We opened fire at long range at 9.5 a.m., and kept up a ceaseless pounding until we had drawn into close range. By that time the Bismarck was in a hopeless state.

They fired four salvos at us at the beginning of the action, but they all roared overhead. Then her attention was fully occupied by the Rodney, which had come up and had started to pound her.

For many of the Dorsetshire's crew it was their first action, and as one lieutenant said :

I felt much better in a ship-to-ship fight than I thought I should. I was on the bridge and all I can say is that the enemy fought very well. I expected them to haul down their ensign, but they kept it flying to the very end.

The way this colossal German battleship "just rolled over like a giant porpoise and settled in a matter of moments " is still a matter of surprise to those who saw it.

But there was a private surprise for the Dorsetshire's officers. When the battle was over they listened to Lord Haw Haw on the radio. Lieut.-Commander (E.) J. F. Mansell, of Slough, said :

We heard him announce that H.M.S. Dorsetshire, steaming at 35 knots—a wonderful speed, anyhow—was on fire fore and aft before sinking at 2 p.m. on the day of the action. Which seems rather to put us in the Ark Royal class !

My Adventures After I Was Shot Down Over Crete

Winner of the D.F.C. and Croix de Guerre in France, Flight-Lieut. D. S. G. Honor has been awarded a bar to his D.F.C. for the exploit in Crete which is described below in his own words.

FLIGHT-LIEUTENANT HONOR was attacking Maleme Aerodrome on May 25 and had intercepted and shot down a Ju 52 and an S 79, when he was himself attacked from below. He said :

With my elevator and aerial control gone, I took what evasive action I could. Then a Messerschmitt 109 attacked me close to the cliffs of the bay. To stop attacks from astern I planed down and hit the water with the aircraft hood closed.

I went down with the machine 40 ft. into the sea without even a window open. Some-

how I got out and my " Mae West " brought me to the surface. Although battered by waves, I managed to get my trousers off. For at least four hours I tried to get ashore, and it took me an hour to do the last twenty yards. I was in despair of ever making it, but eventually drifted to a cave and climbed astride a stalagmite. Phosphorescent waves washed over me as I attempted to wring out my clothes. Having jettisoned my trousers I put my wet shirt over my legs and spent the night in the freezing cave.

After daylight I swam my way to a little headland, dried out my clothes in the sun, and footed it until I reached a goatherd's empty hut. On I tramped, and the next night I spent in a disused church, where I found some matches, an incense burner, and a stagnant well. I drank from this gladly, and at other times sucked pebbles to quench my thirst. Next day I found some lentils in another hut. After much more tramping I came on a little patchwork of green and gold fields with a small white house—a sight for sore eyes. It took me four hours to reach the village. The padre at the church gave me goat's milk, cheese and rye bread.

Here I was told another British pilot had been shot down that day. It turned out to be a sergeant pilot of my own flight. The padre gave me trousers and the sergeant and myself stayed the night.

Then there was a friendly discussion whether the villagers should turn us over to the enemy, as we were completely hemmed in. I asked for four hours to think it over, realizing that from their point of view it would be better to surrender us, as the poor devils had already had six of their villagers shot by Germans for supposedly withholding information. So we started our journey through the German lines. A Greek officer helped us. Before we went we were given tea, under-pants, food, water and a guide by the mayor of the village.

At night we saw Me 109's ground-strafing an aerodrome. When we heard an aircraft approaching the island we thought it was German until I saw the shape of a Sunderland. We started signalling with pocket torches, and I sent out messages in morse and was picked up. Actually my " R.A.F. here, R.A.F. here," in torchlight saved me, although it was a million to one chance, in the Sunderland pilot's words.

On the Ark Royal We Had an Exciting Day

The Mediterranean battle fleet—and the Ark Royal in particular—were assailed by Italian and German bombers for a whole day, but not a ship sustained a hit and several enemy aircraft were destroyed. Reuter's correspondent on board the Ark Royal sent this graphic dispatch.

WE were steaming between Cagliari, the Italian air base in South Sardinia and Sicily. The Italians were able to accompany their bombers with many squadrons of fast and well armed land fighters and could bring out Ju 87's and Me 110's from Sicily.

All ships were at the " stand-to " with fighters ranging in the sky and others were

drawn up on the flight deck in readiness to take off. A.A. guns were cocked grimly to the sky awaiting the expected attack.

Straining our eyes on the Admiral's bridge we saw five slim bird-like shapes coming swiftly towards us, almost skimming the wave-tops. With sharp deafening cracks our own guns snapped into action. Pompoms chattered, pumping two-pounder shells

FLT.-LT. D. S. G. HONOR shaking hands with the King at an Investiture. He tells in this page of his escape from Crete.
Photo, British Official ; Crown Copyright

I WAS THERE!

at the planes now about a mile and a half away. Every ship was brought to bear in the firing.

One of the foremost planes zoomed 100 feet into the air and then plunged nose first into the sea. The remainder dropped their torpedoes and sped away. Two crashed into the sea several miles astern. We were the target, but a skilful and quick turn saved the ship. Two pairs of torpedoes were seen to pass on either side of the ship.

The first round was to us. Again we waited. A fighter landed on the deck with its tail riddled and the rear-gunner lying back in his seat looking ghastly and half fainting. Doctors were waiting to attend the wounded gunner.

The second attack came on the starboard side. Three bombers came roaring through at a height of 5,000 feet. Shells screamed up from every ship in a terrific barrage. One plane sheered away from its formation after dropping its bombs into the sea and dived flaming after them astern. The remaining two kept on. Again we were the target ship. Almost screened by the exploding shells, the bombers drove over us and, with fascinated eyes, we saw the bombs released.

Down they rushed into the waves in a wide half-circle round the carrier and exploded with muffled booms under the sea. Regularly our own guns and those of other ships fired as enemy planes were seen diving out of the clouds shadowing ships, but we had a longer breathing space before the next attack.

Fighters roared down, landed, were rushed below in lifts and, after being re-fuelled and re-ammunitioned, streaked off again searching eagerly for enemies in the clouds.

Gradually the day wore on. Amid

H.M.S. ARK ROYAL, so often claimed by Axis propaganda to have been sunk, added fresh lustre to her name by her participation in the attack on the Bismarck. A correspondent aboard her tells in this page something of her part in an earlier fray. *Photo, British Official*

constant reports of bomber formations in the neighbourhood came an urgent one that bombers were closing in on the starboard. Presently a mighty chorus of guns thudded and then we saw four big black bombers, ghost-like and ominous shapes in the misty lower edge of the clouds. They were about 4,000 feet up. A destroyer on the far starboard vanished behind a wall of water as a stick of bombs crashed around her.

They were met with a veritable curtain of flying steel. One plane wobbled and banked sharply into the cover of the clouds. Others followed into the incessant murderous fire, but passed well ahead of us and jettisoned their bombs into the sea and tore away, pursued by a fighter.

With an hour of daylight left the last attack was made from the port side by three torpedo bombers, while at the same time a big force of thirty Stukas, protected by six Me 110s, were cruising in the clouds with the intention of making a simultaneous assault.

It was daringly carried out. With every ship spitting shells, pom-poms barking, and machine-gun bullets whistling round them in hundreds, the planes, wave-hopping, made straight for the Ark Royal. One turned towards a battle-cruiser ahead and we lost sight of it.

Our eyes were glued to a pair pressing home an attack on us. It seemed a miracle that planes could live in the deadly hail of bullets and shells. When the planes were about half a mile away we saw gleaming torpedoes splash into the sea. Both aircraft banked steeply and roared away as the torpedoes flashed towards us.

We felt the whole ship heeling over as it turned sharply to port to avoid the peril rushing upon her, her guns still blazing fast at the retreating planes. Breathlessly we waited. The torpedoes slid harmlessly past to starboard.

Six of our fighters dived among the Stukas with their machine-guns spitting venomously. One Ju 87 dived into the sea in flames, and two Me 110s staggered off to the shelter of the clouds with white smoke pouring from them. A terrific dogfight raged unseen to the ships below until the Stukas dropped their bombs into the sea and fled, leaving the fighters hard hit but victorious.

The Ark Royal's officers and men forget how often their ship has been sunk and hit by Axis propaganda, but she is still without a scratch as a result of enemy action. Thankfully we watched night closing in.

ABBREVIATIONS USED BY THE FOUR SERVICES

The Army: E—W

Continued from page 599

E.M.O. Embarkation Medical Officer.
E.S.O. Embarkation Staff Officer.
F.D.L. Foremost Defended Localities.
F.G.C.M. Field General Court-Martial.
F.M. Field-Marshal.
F.O.O. Forward Observation Officer.
F.S. Field Service.
F.S.R. Field Service Regulations.
G.A. Garrison Adjutant.
G.C.M. General Court-Martial.
G.O.C.-in-C. General Officer Commanding in Chief.
G.R.O. General Routine Order.
G.S. General Service or General Staff.
G.S.M. Garrison Sergeant-Major.
G.S.O. General Staff Officer.
H.D. Horse Drawn.
H.E. High Explosive or Horizontal Equivalent.
H.Q. Headquarters.
H.T. Horsed Transport.
I.A. Indian Army.
I.M.S. Indian Medical Service.
I.O. Intelligence Officer.
I.O.O. Inspecting Ordnance Officer.
J.A.G. Judge Advocate-General.
K.H.C. Honorary Chaplain to the King.
L.A.D. Light Aid Detachment.
L.M.G. Light Machine-Gun.
L.O. Liaison Officer.
L. of C. Line of Communications.
L/T. Line Telegraphy.
M.A.C. Motor Ambulance Convoy.
M.C. Motor Cycle or Movement Control.
M.C.O. Movement Control Officer.
M.D.G. Medical Director-General.
M.D.S. Main Dressing Station.
M.F.O. Military Forwarding Officer. [Works.
M.F.W. Military Foreman of

M.G. Machine-Gun.
M.G.O. Master-General of the Ordnance.
M.L.O. Military Landing Officer.
M.O. Medical Officer.
M.O.I. Military Operations and Intelligence.
M.P. Meeting Point or Military Police.
M.S. Military Secretary.
M.T. Mechanical Transport or Motor Transport.
N.C.O. Non-Commissioned Officer.
N.S.O. Naval Staff Officer.
O.C. Officer Commanding.
O.M.E. Ordnance Mechanical Engineer.
O.O. Operation Order.
O.P. Observation Post.
O.R. Other ranks.
O.T.C. Officers Training Corps.
P.C. Principal Chaplain.
P.M. Provost Marshal.
P.M.O. Principal Medical Officer.
P.O. Post Office.
P.O.W. Prisoners of War.
P.P. Petrol Point.
P.R.H. Petrol Rail Head.
P.R.P. Petrol Refilling Point.
P.S.S. Printing and Stationery Service.
Q.M. Quartermaster.
Q.M.G. Quartermaster-General to the Forces.
Q.M.S. Quartermaster-Sergeant.
R.A. Royal Artillery.
R.A.C. Royal Armoured Corps.
R.A.M.C. Royal Army Medical Corps. [Corps.
R.A.O.C. Royal Army Ordnance
R.A.P. Regimental Aid Post.
R.A.P.C. Royal Army Pay Corps.
R.A.S.C. Royal Army Service Corps.
R.A.V.C. Royal Army Veterinary Corps.
R.C.M. Regimental Corporal-Major (Household Cavalry).

R.E. Royal Engineers.
R.F. Representative Fraction or Range Finder.
R.M.A. Royal Military Academy (Woolwich).
R.M.C. Royal Military College (Sandhurst).
R.O. Routine Order.
R.O.O. Railhead Ordnance Officer.
R.P. Refilling Point or Rules of Procedure.
R.Q.M.C. Regimental Quartermaster-Corporal (Household Cavalry).
R.Q.M.S. Regimental Quartermaster-Sergeant.
R/T. Radio-Telephony.
R.T.O. Railway Transport Officer.
R.V. Rendezvous.
R.W. Royal Warrant for Pay and Promotion.
S.A.A. Small Arms Ammunition.
S.C. Staff Captain.
S.C.F. Senior Chaplain to the Forces.
S.L. Searchlight.
S.M. Sergeant-Major.
S.P. Starting Point.
S.Q.M.S. Staff Quartermaster-Sergeant.
S.R.H. Supply Railhead.
S.R.P. Supply Refilling Point.
S.S.M. Staff Sergeant-Major.
T.A. Territorial Army.
T.C.P. Traffic Control Post.
T.D. Tractor Drawn Territorial Decoration.
T.O. Transport Officer.
V.E.S. Veterinary Evacuating Station.
V.I. Vertical Interval.
V.O. Veterinary Officer.
V/T. Visual Telegraphy.
W.D. War Department.
W.E. War Establishment.
W/T. Wireless Telegraphy.
W.W.C.P. Walking Wounded Collecting Post.

The Editor's Postscript

SOMETHING that I wrote about prophecy in war-time a few weeks back has brought me a bunch of letters which but confirm my obstinacy in rejecting all prophecy and I shall pass these by without comment, excepting one. It contains a clipping from a local paper reporting at wasteful length a lecture under the heading " Amazing Biblical Prophecy " . . . a farrago of folly. But supposed by my reader to wipe my eye after my confessed incredulity concerning alleged Biblical prophecies of events in A.D. 1941. The speaker had the nerve to tell his simple-minded hearers that the second chapter of Joel provides a vivid description of a modern tank attack in a way which could not have been more graphically expressed by Richard Dimbleby reporting the descent of the mechanized Huns on Yugoslavia and Greece ! He read it, " and his audience was astonished." Well, read it for yourself and see. Joel (one of the shortest " Books ") is well worth reading anyhow as he had the stuff of the poet-prophet in him albeit of the Minor category. (A preacher for the Sunday was shown into an extremely small room at a Scottish manse one Saturday night. " Here's your bedroom," said the minister's wife, " we call it the prophet's chamber." "Aye," said the visitor dryly, " it must have been provided for one o' the *minor* prophets.")

ALL that Joel was after was to impress with brilliantly imaginative phrases the terrors of a threatening plague of locusts. " They shall run to and fro in the city ; they shall run up the wall ; they shall climb up upon the houses ; they shall enter in at the windows like a thief." Tanks ! The whole chapter is full of images that fit locusts (I have known them do these and even more surprising things in South America and in North Africa), but it has nothing on earth to do with the exploits of tanks in 1941. Yet that's the stuff which modern prophetmongers get the gullible to lap up.

THEY'RE all on the old tack about Armageddon, quite unabashed that they had worked it to death in 1914-18. " Armageddon would be fought in three spheres, the earth, the sea and the sky— the land warfare centreing and culminating in Palestine," said the learned lecturer. How's that for prophecy ? Again " No peace plan in the present conflict could be hoped for *because* the Bible prophesied that the conflict would grow more terrible and bitter." Anybody with a grain of sense can prophesy that, but it needs less than a grain of sense to identify the cockatrice and the flying fiery serpent of the Bible with—poison gas ! Which this interpreter does. Thus is the imagery of the fine poet-prophets of Israel distorted and fitted to the fiery fancies of those latter-day exponents, who do much harm in disturbing the minds of all who accept their sensationalism without turning to the sources on which it is based. " Always verify your references " was the sage advice of the famous Lord Salisbury. That is particularly necessary when considering Bible prophecies at secondhand.

I WONDER how many have taken the trouble, which I took this week-end, to get a line on a later prophet of a different sort— Nostradamus. A correspondent who has devoted himself through forty years to the study of things to come (I am convinced of his absolute sincerity, but of nothing more) tells me that he has never seen a copy of Nostradamus. Well, I got three editions from the London Library and settled down with them for two hours last night when all was quiet, no bombers going over. The earliest edition was 1720, the latest 1875, and the one to which I gave most of my attention was the Paris edition of 1840 fully annotated in pencil by some unknown English author who had himself written an

GENERAL CATROUX, in personal command of the Free French forces which marched into Syria on June 8, was formerly Governor of French Indo-China. Though senior in rank to Gen. de Gaulle, he volunteered to serve under him and was made High Commissioner of Free France in the Near East. *Photo, Planet News*

unnamed book on prophecy. There are many astonishing quatrains in the ten sequences of " Centuries " and as a literary curiosity Nostradamus is certainly worth more study than I have been able to give him.

ESPECIALLY am I impressed with his topographical knowledge—in itself surprising for a writer of the mid-sixteenth century—but I am certain from all I can gather in my cursory examination of this strange and intriguing book that he never heard of Hitler or of Vichy, and I have no use for a prophet who in 1555 pretended to know the future even beyond our own times but missed the significance of that man and that place ! I'd rather re-read Maeterlinck's " The Unknown Guest," which I'm taking to bed tonight, as I find the Belgian poet-essayist the most persuasive of all sensible students of the mysterious phenomena of premonitions and foretellings. Even when we may not agree with his conclusions we are held by the charm of his style.

THERE were two candidates for election in an American town. One abnormally tall, the other absurdly short. A supporter of the first said in a speech that while his rival had to stand on two packing-cases to be seen by the audience, his own candidate was so tall they had to dig a hole for him to stand in to address his hearers. " The truth," said the little chap, on hearing this, " is that my opponent has a hole dug for him because he's only happy when he's up to his neck in dirt." If we get much more of this ministerial talk, to which I have just been listening, about the " honour " of wearing shabby clothes we may arrive at the stage of being urged not to waste soap on cleaning our necks, to swear off hot baths, to avoid " hair cut and shave" until end of the War.

FACT is, there's no particular honour in presenting a beggarly and bedraggled appearance to one's fellowmen so long as we are able to live in our own homes and have not " gone to earth" like the fox. That way lies Bolshevism. The Bolshies, taking their cue from their leaders, who had assumed the outward guise of horny handed sons of toil, in order to " dress the part " have produced (as I am informed by various credible visitors to Stalin's Russia) a nation-wide populace who are habited as the now almost extinct denizens of the once notorious Glasgow slums. But the instant these same Bolshies, male and female, flooded into " conquered " Poland their fashion-starved women and lousy, dingy men swarmed like locusts on the dress and clothing shops, leaving not even an item of lingerie or clean linen behind them . . . incidentally paying for everything with worthless roubles.

TO be well dressed and clean are proper instincts in any civilized community, and to spread the idea that outworn clothes and abstention from refinements of toilette can pass for virtues is both dangerous and foolish. " Honest sweat" is still sweat and by any other name would smell as sour. Let's use these 66 coupons to best advantage and let's make ourselves as presentable as our means will allow. Don't begin to take a pride in appearing a down-and-out. Else we become down-and-outs in spirit as well as appearance. Nothing is better for our morale than to look our best . . . stopping always this side of dandyism.

IT was Diderot, I think, who propounded the theory that an actor who assumed the outward appearance of misery in the parts he played found himself in time feeling miserable . . . a proposition to which I do not fully subscribe, else we could not have a Grimaldi making his audience laugh while he himself was a victim of melancholy. I think I shall use some of my margarine coupons today in buying a few neckties. Think of the valuable paper that is being saved by them ! (Sez he to whom paper has become precious as life blood.) For which much thanks.

JOHN CARPENTER HOUSE. WHITEFRIARS, LONDON, E.C.4.

Registered at the G.P.O. as a Newspaper

The War Illustrated, July 4th, 1941

Vol 4

The War Illustrated

Nº 96

Edited by Sir John Hammerton

FOURPENCE

WEEKLY

HOTEL CENTRAL

IN DAMASCUS, where the British and Free French forces have been fighting against General Dentz, who is defending Syria for Vichy France. On June 19, General Sir Henry Maitland Wilson appealed to Dentz to declare Damascus an open city, and thus save bloodshed and destruction, but, having received no response our troops attacked and the city fell on June 21. Reputed to be the oldest city in the world, Damascus is full of picturesque contrasts. In this photograph laden camels roll along the electric-tram route.

Photo, Mrs. T. Muir.

Our Searchlight on the War

Goebbels Censored

ON June 13 Berlin readers of Goebbels' paper, "Voelkischer Beobachter," asked for it in vain at the news-stands, being told that the Gestapo had seized almost the entire issue at 6 a.m. Curiosity, whetted by this latest sign of the long-standing feud between Goebbels and Himmler, the Gestapo Chief, was allayed when a later re-printed edition was examined and it was reported that an article by the Minister of Propaganda himself had been omitted. The article was entitled "Crete as an Example," and jeered at British anti-invasion practice and the instruction of the population by means of 15 million pamphlets. All this, said Goebbels, was based on the assumption of the British Ministry of Information that the invasion of Britain would follow the same lines as that of Greece, whereas "the Fuehrer acts differently from what is expected." After saying that parachutists had now proved their value, Goebbels wound up: "Hitherto it has been Germany's lot to convince the world not by words but by facts. So we shall have to create these facts."

St. George Up-to-Date

THE British-American Ambulance Corps is benefiting by the sale throughout America of a poster stamp, representing a modern St. George and the Dragon, designed by the Polish painter and illuminator, Arthur Szyk. Grimly intent beneath his tin hat, a British Tommy bestrides an equally

MISS V. A. DRUMMOND, the only woman ship's engineer sailing the seas. Her professional skill and courage saved a British merchant ship when attacked by Nazi bombers.
Photo, "Daily Mirror"

exhibition here in July, 1940. His work is well-known in the States, for in the White House are thirty-eight of his paintings depicting the American Revolution, which were given to President Roosevelt in 1935 by Professor Moscicki, former President of Poland.

Anti-Jew Laws in France

MARSHAL PÉTAIN has recently signed a statute which places stringent prohibitions upon Jews in both Occupied and Un-Occupied France. Such individuals may not hold office in civil or municipal service; they are debarred from Army rank, whether commissioned or not, and they are excluded from all the liberal professions. They are not allowed to engage in any occupation which brings them in direct contact with the public, particularly as director, secretary or other administrator of a public company or a bank. They may not practise on the Stock Exchange, nor may they be employed in the film industry, the cinema, the theatre, at the Bar or in medicine.

Devices for Saving Pilots

BRITISH airmen who may have been shot down over the sea stand a better chance of survival than when the Battle of Britain was raging. At that time they depended on their life-jackets to keep them afloat until picked up, but since then several new devices have been put into use by the Ministry of Aircraft Production which will result in the saving of many valuable lives. One of the latest is a cushion which can be easily stowed inside even a fighter aircraft, since it measures only 15 inches square by 3 inches thick. Inside this cushion are packed an incredible number of appliances, comprising an inflatable rubber dinghy, a sea anchor, paddles, rations, distress signals, repair kit, baler, and a hand-pump for use if the automatic inflator fails to work. The dinghy, when properly inflated, will support a crew consisting of any number up to eight.

War Exports

LAST year 5,000,000 yards of gut for music-strings were exported from Britain to various parts of the world. The gut comes from Scottish sheep, and 25 yards of it, obtainable from a single animal, will furnish six "A" violin strings. New Zealand, it is interesting to note, is the biggest importer of 'cello strings, and Australia of those for the harp. One British firm last year sent abroad 4,000,000 gramophone records, which included many made by Mr. Churchill quoting passages from his own trenchant and inspiring speeches. Sales to America of rare books bring to Britain an annual income of over a million dollars.

Woman Who Saved a Ship

A COMMUNAL restaurant in Battersea, inaugurated on June 11, has been named after Miss Victoria Drummond, the only woman serving with the British Merchant Navy, the only woman with a Board of Trade

ENGLAND'S MODERN ST. GEORGE and the German dragon, a poster stamp issued in the United States and now being sold there in aid of the British-American Ambulance Corps. The traditional Saint is in the guise of a British soldier thrusting at the Nazi reptile. It is the work of Arthur Szyk, famous Polish artist, and is dedicated to Mr. Winston Churchill.

determined war-horse and drives his lance into the Nazi dragon, a revolting beast whose segmented tail is trimmed with swastikas and ends in the poisonous forked tongue of a serpent about to strike the saint from the rear. Sheets from the first and limited issue of the stamp were presented to King George VI, Mr. Churchill, President Roosevelt, General Sikorski and General de Gaulle. Proceeds from the sales will be divided between various war relief organizations run by the Ambulance Corps, including ambulances for the R.A.F., vitamin capsules for British children, motor ambulances to be used in desert warfare and medical and surgical supplies. Arthur Szyk has lived in England for about four years and held an

certificate for ship's engineering. Daughter of a lady-in-waiting to Queen Victoria, whose godchild she was, Miss Drummond, after serving her apprenticeship, rose to be second engineer. Captain Warner, the master of her ship, recently paid a tribute to her skill and fortitude. Here is what he said: "When the bombs were falling around us, with the ship thrown about by explosions, Miss Drummond had such control over her nerves that she inspired every man down below to give his best. We owe our lives and the ship to her in conditions that can only be called hellish." When after this nightmare voyage the vessel docked at Norfolk, Virginia, the story of the second engineer got about, and the local inhabitants enthusiastically collected £400 as a tribute to her heroism. It is this sum, handed by Miss Drummond to the Communal Kitchens Committee, which has now resulted in sixpenny lunches for Battersea workmen.

THE AIR BATTLE OF BRITAIN
CIVILIAN LOSSES
Casualties for 9 Months

	Killed	Injured	Total
Sept. 1940	6,954	10,615	17,569
Oct.	6,334	8,695	15,029
Nov.	4,588	6,202	10,790
Dec.	3,793	5,044	8,837
Jan. 1941	1,502	2,012	3,514
Feb.	789	1,068	1,857
March	4,259	5,557	9,816
April	6,065	6,926	12,991
May	5,394	5,181	10,575
Totals	**39,678**	**51,300**	**90,978**

Of the 5,394 killed in May: Men, 2,930; Women, 1,835; Under 16, 416; Unclassified, 213. Missing (in addition), 75.

THE NAZI LOSSES BY NIGHT, IN 1941

Jan.	15	April	90
Feb.	15	May	151
March	47	June 1-15	22

Total to Jan.-June 15 : 340
Probable total of Air Crew : 1,360

Air-Commodore Goddard, broadcasting June 15 on percentages of night raiders brought down, stated that: January 1941 showed substantial improvement on the previous six months; February and March, further improvement; April, twice as good as January; May, four times percentage of January.

TOTAL AIR LOSSES OVER BRITAIN
September 1939—June 10, 1941

Enemy		3,529
R.A.F.		882 (with 439 Pilots saved)

The Way of the War

GREATEST EVENT SINCE THE FALL OF FRANCE
A New Chapter Opens With Germany's Attack on Russia

By the Editor

THIS commentary on the War situation must differ radically from that which, at the moment of going to press, it replaces. The reason for a new angle of observation is too obvious to need stressing. The unprinted article made a rapid review of the strange tangle of recent events that had brought us to an opening into the dark forest of the future where many " paths of destiny " trailed away into gloom. Russia's preparations to meet a German onslaught was the theme. Before the ink was quite dry, however, Hitler had struck : his pact of eternal friendship between Nazis and Bolshevists had been dishonoured like every pledge, pact, and promise the Supreme Liar of all the ages had ever made. " Eternity " for this one had lasted barely twenty-two months ! His latest pact—with Turkey—specifies ten years. At the ratio of eternity to ten years we may regard the Turkish pact as already forsworn by Hitler.

ONLY those—and they were not a few—foolish enough to believe that so vast a military demonstration as that which Germany had prepared against her temporary friend was a bluff to disguise action elsewhere. With deep disgust one recalls the photograph in the first number of THE WAR ILLUSTRATED showing a smiling Stalin shaking hands with a happy Ribbentrop on the signing of the pact which plunged the whole world into war. Our pages give many glimpses of Stalin and Molotov rejoicing in association with the bloodthirsty leaders of Germany. These are worth looking at again after listening to Molotov's broadcast of Sunday morning June 22nd.

IN the suppressed article above mentioned I minced no words about Soviet Russia and her dictator's reasons for tieing up with the Nazi gangsters ; and in her plight today none but the most obtuse will deny that it " serves her right." Our own Leader has been an inveterate critic of Soviet politics, nor is he likely to change his opinion of the so-called dictatorship of the proletariat. The Chamberlain Government exhausted every reasonable means to secure Russian cooperation against the threatening Hitler War, and was entirely willing that the Soviets should work out their own national salvation within their own vast boundaries. To no purpose. Stalin shook hands with Hitler's minions under promises of territorial acquisition if he stood by while the Nazis started the world conflagration by destroying Poland. Stalin and his nearest associates were callously indifferent to the fate of France, Britain and all the other free nations of Europe. They made Hitler's subsequent conquests possible by their indifference.

WHY ? In the judgement of those who were best informed the whole Soviet structure at that time was too rickety to risk war with Germany. The sorry achievements of the Red Army in its onslaught upon Finland in the winter of 1939–40 will never be forgotten. Sir Stafford Cripps' mission to Moscow looked the other day as though

it might have given him material for a companion volume to Sir Neville Henderson's " Failure of a Mission," and even now it might be wrong to suppose that it was a success. The swift and imperious policy of Hitler in reaching out for big results may have had nothing at all to do with any Soviet change of heart resulting from the Cripps mission. It may be in the same order of things as the tearing of the scrap of paper in August 1914. Almost certainly it is.

" WE are both Orientals," said Stalin to Matsuoka when fixing up his recent pact with Japan. Wily Orientals ? Perhaps not so wily as they imagine. There is more deceit and cunning and sheer devilishness in the occidental ogre of Berlin than in any living scoundrel or gang of scoundrels the Orient can produce. And that is why Stalin finds himself today fighting for the life of his Soviet republics against the might of Nazi Germany, to whom he turned, with disdain of Britain when Britain, with Russia's collaboration, could have saved the world from the welter of blood and ruin into which it has been driven.

M. IVAN MAISKY, Ambassador of the U.S.S.R. in Great Britain since 1932, had a long interview with Mr. Eden on June 22, as soon as Hitler's onslaught on Russia became known.
Photo, G.P.U.

BUT there is this in the sea-change that has overtaken Democracy's relations with Bolshevism : Russia is now at war with Germany, and every nation, whatever its interior politics, its creed, or colour, that is crossing swords with Nazidom is helping Democracy to withstand and overcome its vilest foe. Thus, no matter the method or manner of Russia's arrival at Britain's side, our duty to support the Soviet in arms is clear and consistent. The cunning with which the Nazi attack on Russia has been designed is seen in the plan whereby all the Balkan nations that were Russia's potential allies were first put under Hitler's heel and even Turkey induced to sign a peace pact which

was the final signal for attacking Russia, just as the Nazi-Soviet pact was the prelude to the rape of Poland.

WE are none too well informed as to Russia's military potential, but as the Nazis have had nearly two years of unrestricted opportunity to discover that for themselves, we may take it that Hitler is confident the German machine can wreak swift destruction on the Soviet forces and then delve deeply into the Leviathan carcass of Russia for all that he requires in the way of wheat, coal and oil—especially " heavy oil "—to carry on the Long War which he must now envisage, having so patently lost the Short War he had banked upon when he unleashed his legions in 1939. For, though this fourth climacteric of the War, as the Prime Minister has just described it, will give it an entirely new direction, and tend to lengthen, not to shorten, its duration.

DOUBTLESS the scheme of things in the Nazi brain is so to subjugate the whole continent of Europe and to penetrate some way into Asia, crushing all who refuse to " collaborate " in founding his New Order—Bulgaria, Rumania, and Vichy France already actively participating—until he feels the stage is set for the *grand finale*—the victorious invasion of Great Britain and collapse of the British Empire. A grandiose plan and worth his trying—perhaps. But much will happen before our Home Guards are shooting down the paratroops as they descend upon our island. One thing may be enough to dissolve the dream : the mere massiveness of Russia. Just as the rapacious military Japanese will never conquer the peace-loving Chinese and their immense territories, so not even the mechanized might of Germany and her jackals may be able to overrun that sixth of the world which is Russia, whose 160,000,000 have at least achieved under Soviet rule a national consciousness that never existed under the Tsarist tyranny. The certainty of famine in the land, worse than any visitation of the past, will not improve matters for the aggressors, though Napoleon's retreat from Moscow is hardly an apt comparison of what awaits the mechanized hosts of Hitler.

ASSUREDLY this is one of the greatest hours of the Second World War—so momentous that all speculation as to its outcome is vain : the implications and repercussions of the Nazi move being so many and diverse. But it is a heartening fact that at this very hour Britain's power in the air is daily going from strength to strength. Those daylight sweeps in which our glorious R.A.F. are repeating over Nazi France their immortal victories of the Battle of Britain in 1940 are an earnest of the swiftly approaching day when by both day and night we shall have attained such aerial supremacy that the date of the threatened attack on this the final Fortress of Freedom will be subject to further postponement and so become one with the Greek Calends.

J. A. HAMMERTON

Malta is an Island of Heroes—and Heroines

For a year Malta has occupied what must be one of the most exposed positions in the British Empire. In that brief period the island has had nearly 700 air-raid Alerts and has been frequently bombed. Yet the spirit of the garrison is undaunted and the people as a whole have endured their time of testing marvellously well.

I_N Malta's history of more than 3,000 years, one of the most glorious pages is that which contains the story of the great stand made by the island against the Turks in 1565. Malta was then the headquarters of the Knights of St. John, who had established themselves there some 40 years before, after the Turks had expelled them from Rhodes. The Knights numbered fewer than 10,000 all told ; the forces which the Sultan sent against them were between thirty and forty thousand. For four months the siege went on, four months of almost continuous battle. The defence was heroic in the extreme, and it is on record that the Maltese women helped their men folk by rolling down great boulders on the heads of the invaders. At last, when they had lost many thousands of killed and wounded, the Turks withdrew.

Nearly 400 years have passed since that day of supreme trial, but the ancient warlike spirit of the Maltese is unsubdued. Since 1800 the island has been part of the British Dominions, and thousands of Maltese have served in the King's Own Malta Rifles and the Royal Malta Artillery, as well as the Royal Air Force. Much of the credit of their present great stand must be put down to the Maltese themselves, who have proved themselves to be very good shots ; with the Bofors gun in particular they are marvellous. "They are a lively, agile people—the Maltese," said a British anti-aircraft gunner broadcasting from Malta recently, "and the Bofors seem to suit them down to the ground. They do some first-class shooting with it, and there is no holding them back from any possible target."

In the Royal Navy it would be difficult to find a man who has not at some time or other visited Malta, since the island is one of our great naval bases. But it is also a fortress, and it says much for the military engineering of the old Knights of St. John that many of the works which they constructed centuries ago are still in use today.

Many of them date from the time of the Grand Master Jehan de la Valette, who after repelling the Turks in 1565 was responsible for the " city built by gentlemen for gentlemen," which bears his name and is today the capital of the island. The landward fortifications were largely cut out of the living rock, and, screened by an outer line of works including the parade ground and the great excavated granaries of Floriana, remain a masterpiece of military architecture, just as the planning of Valletta itself, with its uniform rectangular street lines and a central group of buildings, palace, arsenal and cathedral, reflect the greatest credit on the town planner of those distant days.

These rock-cut galleries, including some which were apparently used for the housing

of slaves, have been put to an excellent new use today as air-raid shelters. They have even been extended, as the soft sandstone has the quality of being easily worked. In these galleries deep underground the Maltese have learnt to take shelter, and so casualties inflicted by the numerous air raids have been very slight. Moreover, there have been very few fires caused by incendiary bombs, as the buildings are almost all of stone with stone roofs.

Since Italy declared war on June 10, 1940, Malta has been in imminent danger of invasion, and the threat has been intensified since the Nazi capture of Crete. But the island does not offer much scope for landing. There are, it is true, five bays where an attempt might be made, but for the rest the coast is broken and rocky, backed by high cliffs. The aerodromes built on the solid rock have been little affected by the bombing to which they have been subjected ; only the surface earth, a foot or so in depth, has been disturbed, and it has been an easy matter to fill in the craters.

To quote from a recent broadcast by the

During the last year Malta has had very nearly 700 air raids. That the Maltese have got quite used to them is indicated by this photograph of one of Valletta's main streets taken during a daylight raid.

fighting services are leaving no stone unturned to ensure that Malta shall give a good account of itself and make its present history more splendid even than its past.

"With God's help," the indomitable General continued, "I am confident that we shall succeed in so doing."

Acting Governor, Lieut. - General Sir William Dobbie: " Not only will we not give up Malta, but we have no intention of allowing it to be taken from us, whether by the Germans or the Italians. We have to face the possibility of invasion, but Malta is immeasurably more capable of resisting attack than was Crete. This opinion is fully shared by responsible officers. I am saying this with the quiet confidence that I consider the circumstances justify. I know that Malta will rise to the occasion whatever is required of it. The Government and

PEOPLE OF MALTA endure the incessant air attacks with fortitude. Centre, a Maltese coach-driver pacifying his horse during a raid. Above, a woman of 69, who has never left the island in her life, surrounded by some of Malta's younger generation.

Photos, Associated Press

After 700 Air Raids Indomitable Still

VALLETTA, Malta's capital, is one of the most bombed cities of the world. Crossing a bridge, some of its people contemplate the smoke from yet another raid. Right : workers clearing away the debris of a building destroyed by a heavy bomb.

Malta, which lies sixty miles from Sicily and about 180 from the African coast, still stands impregnably British in spite of innumerable Axis air attacks and the fulminations of the Duce. It has been in British hands since 1800, but was formally ceded to us in 1814, the year before Waterloo. And it will be British long after Italy's pinchbeck Napoleon has found his St. Helena or worse.

Valletta has been continuously bombed before and since Hitler became Italy's first dictator, but so strong are its defences that 20 per cent of the enemy aircraft were brought down. Now the Germans prefer to fly by night only and play the " tip and run " game. Other photos of Malta are given in page 496, Vol. III ; but the upper photo in that page shows a gateway in Floriana, close to Valletta, and not (as is stated) in Valletta itself.

Photos, Associated Press

Where Cretans Fought for Hearth and Home

DETAILS of the part played by Greek troops in the Battle of Crete are given in a telegram received at the Greek Legation in London from the Premier, M. Tsouderos,

The Greek forces which took part in the defence of the island numbered 15,000. In addition, Cretans of all ages, among them women, formed a militia and, says M. Tsouderos, fought with insuperable self-sacrifice for their hearths and homes.

"In Canea," his message continues, "where, as is known, a terrible and bloody struggle took place, and everywhere else the Germans paid with enormous losses for their effort to subjugate Crete, an effort which succeeded only because of the overwheming superiority in numbers of their machines.

"The Greek defence of Heraklion was particularly praiseworthy. For six consecutive days Greek soldiers kept up the fight and, proving much superior in courage, boldness and fighting capacity to the invaders, mopped up the German parachutists. This enabled the British troops to hold the aerodrome without diversion and to defend the coastal area of the town and remain masters of the situation.

"In one of many encounters all the parachutists were exterminated, but at the same time over 300 Cretans fell and a large number were wounded. British officers relate that young militiamen, boys of 17, were disarming Germans and using their arms skilfully like seasoned soldiers.

"At Retimo the sacrifices of the Greeks were also heavy. The Governor of Retimo, M. Tsagris, a former member of Parliament, and the chief constable of Retimo, are among the victims of the epic battle.

"Thus Crete has paid, as always, with heroism and self-sacrifice a bloody tribute to the shrine of liberty. Apart from the armed forces, which were decimated, thousands of non-combatants fell

CANEA, where "a terrible and bloody struggle took place," to quote M. Tsouderos, is the main seaport and capital of Crete, lying on the finest harbour of the island, Suda Bay. It had a population of about 27,000, many of whom, like the man above, were fishermen. It is now converted into a heap of ruins.

victims to the indiscriminate bombing and machine-gunning by the German planes. Most villages exist no more, and prosperous towns on the island like Canea and Heraklion have been turned into heaps of ruins."

Women of Crete in Uniform

THE courage of the Cretan women, some of whom fought side by side with their menfolk in defence of their homes, makes a glorious chapter in itself. Ten of them, wearing Greek uniforms and fully armed, were taken prisoner by the Germans. They were shipped to Athens, and then on Hitler's orders sent to Berlin, the Fuehrer having expressed a wish to see them. A more ominous note was struck by the report that the Nazis had been given orders to examine the shoulders of the Cretan women and girls to see if there were any tell-tale marks of rifle-butts.

Hundreds of Cretans fell during the bloody struggle for the island. Among them may have been this butcher of Heraklion, whose only enemy hitherto had been the flies.

Right, a general view of the town of Retimo, where casualties were heavy and included the Governor of Retimo, M. Tsagris. This view shows the Venetian fortifications and citadel.

M. Tsouderos, the Greek Premier, told how Cretans of all ages, women among them, formed a militia to fight the Nazis. In the oval is seen a typical Cretan peasant girl.

Photos, Wide World, E.N.A.

From Azure Skies Into the Cretan Hell

German paratroops descending near Candia, Crete. Clusters of four parachutes nearer the earth are supporting machine-guns and equipment. Right : enemy troop-plane afire after having been hit by our guns.

A LAND MINE exploded by British Royal Engineers to destroy Nazi supplies on Crete. On the left, a German troop-carrier has crashed in the vicinity of Heraklion aerodrome and is sending up a column of smoke and fire into which two enemy parachutists are falling.

Photos, British Official : Crown Copyright

How the Nazis Used Gliders in Crete

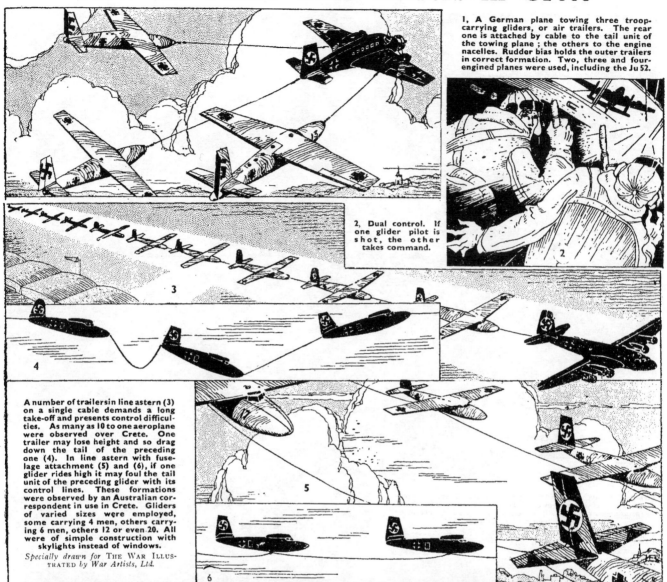

1, A German plane towing three troop-carrying gliders, or air trailers. The rear one is attached by cable to the tail unit of the towing plane; the others to the engine nacelles. Rudder bias holds the outer trailers in correct formation. Two, three and four-engined planes were used, including the Ju 52.

2, Dual control. If one glider pilot is shot, the other takes command.

A number of trailers in line astern (3) on a single cable demands a long take-off and presents control difficulties. As many as 10 to one aeroplane were observed over Crete. One trailer may lose height and so drag down the tail of the preceding one (4). In line astern with fuselage attachment (5) and (6), if one glider rides high it may foul the tail unit of the preceding glider with its control lines. These formations were observed by an Australian correspondent in use in Crete. Gliders of varied sizes were employed, some carrying 4 men, others carrying 6 men, others 12 or even 20. All were of simple construction with skylights instead of windows.

Specially drawn for THE WAR ILLUSTRATED *by War Artists, Ltd.*

MALEME AERODROME after the German invasion of Crete. It is cluttered up with Ju 52 transport planes, many of which were crash-landed in an attempt to get the aircraft down quickly at no matter what cost.
Photo, British Official : Crown Copyright

The Battle of Sollum Triangle Was a Draw

After some weeks of comparative inactivity, the battle in Libya flared up again on Sunday, June 15, when British and Indian forces delivered a lightning stroke against the Germans in the Sollum area. The following account of the fighting is based on reports from Reuter's Correspondent.

AT dawn on June 15 British and Indian forces advanced westward across the desert to attack Wadi Halfaya, better known as Hell Fire Pass, Fort Capuzzo and Sollum. A small armoured force followed the coast road, while infantry, supported by tanks and artillery, spread across the coastal plain which extends from the sea to the escarpment. Famous English and Scottish regiments attacked along the escarpment itself, and an armoured division made a wide sweep out into the desert with the audacious intention of attacking Sollum from the west, and so taking the Germans in the rear.

At the end of the first day's fighting our men had won a foothold on the slopes of Hell Fire Pass. At dawn the next day, under cover of a heavy ground mist, the attack was renewed ; and within two hours the Highlanders on the left flank had driven out the Germans from their fortified positions at the head of the pass. The Indians on the right had a harder task, and all through the day the Pass lived up to its name. Meanwhile, another column of British infantry, supported by a squadron of tanks, advanced along the ridge of the escarpment, past the Egyptian barracks which stand on the headland behind Sollum, until they saw glittering beneath them in the blazing sunshine the blue waters of Sollum Bay. Sollum itself was

taken, and those of its garrison who had survived were driven along the coast to join the battalion of Germans who had been occupying the shore. At noon this German force was completely cut off from support, retreat, or supplies, but nevertheless it continued to offer a stout resistance.

" Sitting a mile away from the bay," wrote Reuter's Correspondent, " halfway up the escarpment and between medium and light British guns, I watched the unhurried, relentless pounding of the trapped Germans. Hundreds of shells screamed overhead. The Germans were strung out along the edge of the bay for a considerable distance. While those farthest inland offered a spirited resistance with anti-tank guns and machine-guns, many of the Nazis on the beach stood in the water up to their necks, watching the bombs burst all around them. From where we watched it could plainly be seen that occasionally British shells were falling in the water, which must have given the Germans a trifling reminder of Dunkirk."

Perhaps the most striking feature of the battle was the fact that the British gained superiority in the air at the outset and never lost it. Asked how he had managed to attain such a phenomenal result, the senior air officer replied, " Shooting the sitting bird, sir. Shooting the sitting bird. We never let 'em get off the ground." From dawn to dusk British bombers, accompanied by fighters, raided every German aerodrome all the way back to El Agheila, 200 miles beyond Benghazi. Most of the vaunted dive-bombers were thus kept grounded, and Messerschmitts which made an appearance miles high above the battlefield were shot down. On one occasion a large force of Stukas did make an appearance, but they were at once attacked by a force of Hurricanes, and in a few minutes eleven of them were shot down for the loss of only one Hurricane.

Meanwhile, beyond the escarpment to the south, there had been taking place what Reuter's Correspondent described as " a fantastic Wellsian clash of metal monsters," as out of the incredible heat and choking dust of the open desert the British tanks smashed their way through into the Capuzzo region. The battle was fierce and furious, and on both sides the claim was made that large numbers of tanks were knocked out.

THE WESTERN DESERT, where the battle described here was fought by two mechanized armies in intense heat under a blazing sky.
Courtesy of the " Daily Telegraph "

At first the battle went well for the British, but on Tuesday, June 17, the Germans brought up large reinforcements and began to outflank our outflanking column. With the certain knowledge that they had not the necessary mechanical ground superiority both to consolidate their gains and repulse the Germans on the flank, the British were forced to withdraw from the Capuzzo area and Halfaya, and this withdrawal was followed automatically by one from the plain below.

When the operations began the British had had three separate objectives : (1) To capture and occupy the entire Halfaya-Capuzzo-Sollum triangle ; (2) to divert a threatened imminent attack on Tobruk ; and (3) to decoy the enemy armoured forces into the open for a trial of strength, which was expected to produce distinctly favourable results. Of these objectives the second was attained with complete success. The attack on the triangle was only partially successful, while a trial of strength showed that the Germans were even stronger than had been supposed in their mechanical arm. So the Imperial troops retreated 12 miles to their original line, abandoning the intervening territory to the Germans. The Battle of the Sollum Triangle ended in a draw.

German light tank captured by British armoured units near Sollum just inside the Egyptian-Libyan border, where a big battle was fought in mid-June. Several hundred Nazi prisoners and a number of enemy tanks and guns were taken. The Italians, fighting side by side with the Germans, also incurred heavy losses.

British tanks going into action against the Germans in the Western Desert. According to a Rome report (highly exaggerated as usual) about 1,000 British tanks took part in this action. The Nazis declared that there had not been a tank battle on such a large scale since Cambrai in 1917.

Photos, British Official : Crown Copyright

Stiff Resistance Fails to Save Damascus

Although the Allied forces in Syria made some progress along the coast and occupied Damascus, in the central sector they were strongly counter-attacked and for a short time were deprived of many of the positions which they had won. Below we tell of these developments in a campaign which has assumed a far more serious complexion than it originally presented.

Just a week after the Allies invaded Syria, the forces of Vichy France launched in the central sector a series of counter-attacks, while on the coast and in the neighbourhood of Damascus they put up an increasingly strong resistance. The main direction of the counter-attacks was against the Allied positions to the south and west of Mount Hermon.

"After several days' silence," telegraphed Reuter's Special Correspondent in the Metulla sector of the Syrian front, "punctuated with occasional bursts of artillery fire, the Vichy French forces opened a counter-offensive against the British troops in this sector at 3.30 p.m. today. The Vichy batteries directed a very intense fire on Merj Iyoun fort and the key crossroads leading to Kheim and Hasbaya. Then came a tank, machine-gun and infantry attack. The entire offensive was launched with great suddenness."

Moving up the road to some five miles north of Merj Iyoun, he contacted a British major. "We have continuous sniping from the mountains," said the latter. "I have reason to believe that a fairly large force is lurking there. Several times we have sent forward armoured vehicles, but they have been shot up." Shortly afterwards Merj Iyoun was recaptured by the Vichy troops, and about the same time Kuneitra, some 40 miles to the south-east, fell to an armoured column which claimed to have captured 100 prisoners and a quantity of war material. Kuneitra was defended chiefly by men of the London Regiment, who put up a stout resistance against superior enemy forces for 12 hours before they were forced to surrender.

Londoners' Stand at Kuneitra

"We were suddenly attacked by strong forces with 26 tanks," said a Free French officer who managed to make his escape from the town before its fall. "They converged on the town from every direction. The British garrison, with a few Indian sappers, coolly took up firing positions in the town and fought with amazing courage. A British sergeant with two men (all three come from the East End of London) dodged from cover to cover, throwing grenades. They put one tank out of action at point-blank range and damaged others. They went on fighting like this until wounded. The French used 75s and mortars, but the British fought like lions from house to house, never giving up until the last round of ammunition had been used."

But the triumph of the Vichy French forces was short-lived—little more than two hours, in fact. Hardly had their tanks reached the centre of the village when British reinforcements came into action. "The attack started with an artillery duel," said an Australian machine-gun officer who watched it from close by. "I was filled with admiration for the cool, meticulous way these men of a famous Home Counties regiment went into action. Scorning a barrage on the roadway, they did not pause, but pressed on steadily, approaching Kuneitra from the two flanks and down the centre roadway. It looked to me more like Salisbury Plain in peacetime manoeuvres. At dusk, after an attack lasting two hours, I saw a red Very light explode, indicating that Kuneitra was once more in British hands." At 8.45 p.m. the Union Jack and the Tricolour with the Lorraine Cross were once more unfurled above the town. Most of the Vichyites escaped along the Damascus road, but they left behind them nearly all the gallant Londoners whom they had taken prisoner.

SYRIA, showing the localities mentioned in the official communiqués of the fighting between the Allied forces and Vichy troops.
Map by courtesy of the "Daily Telegraph"

Kuneitra's recapture was announced on June 19, and at the same time it was made known that the strong Vichy force in Merj Iyoun, believed to be chiefly Foreign Legionaries, Chasseurs d'Afrique and Lebanese, had been surrounded by the Australians, while further important positions had been captured just south of Damascus. The Allies were, indeed, in the suburbs of the Syrian capital, and for some days past there had been fighting in the orange groves and amongst the canals which surrounded the district. Militarily speaking, Damascus was theirs for the taking, but General Wilson wanted to avoid hurting the susceptibilities of the Arab population. So it was that on the night of June 18 he sent a message over the Palestine wireless to General Dentz, the commander of the Vichy forces in Syria.

"My troops are on the outskirts of Damascus," it read. "I do not wish to cause any damage to that historic city. I therefore appeal to you to declare it an open town and to withdraw your troops from the city. Otherwise I shall have no alternative but to take such measures as are found necessary, and the responsibility for any damage to civil property and injury to the civilian population will be yours. I am transmitting this message by wireless because I have no other means of communicating with you. I shall expect your answer tomorrow by 5.30 a.m., and ask you to send it under flag of truce to the nearest Allied post on the Damascus front. The flag of truce will be respected."

No reply was received to the ultimatum, so General Wilson gave the order to advance. There followed a series of brilliantly executed operations against the defences south and west of the ancient city. A force of Free French tanks and two batteries, one Indian and the other British, attacked and drove off the French tanks which barred the Damascus end of the Kuneitra road. Indian troops secured the Mezze aerodrome, while their artillery heavily plastered Fort Gouraud on the north side of the Damascus–Beirut road. On the evening of June 20 the main Vichy forces withdrew from Damascus, but as they went they were spotted by Royal Australian Air Force fighters which swooped down and machine-gunned the long columns of motor transports.

The next morning the final Allied assault began. From the south General Legentilhomme's Free French made straight for the town, from the east swept up General Collet's Circassians, while Imperial troops—British, Indians and Australians—stormed Fort Gourard on the west. Then on Sunday morning, June 22, after a dramatic charge at Mezze by eight British 25-pounder guns with a couple of anti-tank guns firing over open sights, Vichy resistance collapsed. Shortly after 11 a.m. Damascus was occupied by Free French troops, led by General Collet.

"As a soldier," said their leader, General de Gaulle, "I think the fall of Damascus must be the end of Vichy resistance in Syria."

ARAB RECRUITS to the Allied cause, comprising desert Beduins, fellaheen from the fields, and townsmen, are lined up for their first parade on a barrack square in Palestine. A Palestinian force aided a British regiment to recapture Kuneitra from the Vichy troops.
Photos, British Official : Crown Copyright

Syrian Towns Lapped by the Tide of War

NEAR SIDON, in the Lebanon, stretches this fertile plain. Sidon was captured by Imperial forces on June 15 after a bombardment by our fleet.

SYRIAN TOWNS which have lately been in the news are Ezra (upper photo), which was retaken by Allied troops on June 17 after it had been lost to a Vichy counter-attack; Mezze, below, where the Damascus airport is situated, scene of heavy fighting, was captured on June 22; and Deir es Zor (right), on the Euphrates, through which British forces passed on their advance to Palmyra.

Photos, E.N.A. and Dorien Leigh

The War's Best Kept Secret Revealed

Above, W.A.A.Fs., with the aid of radiolocation, plot the movement of German raiders. Top left, Mr. R. A. Watson Watt, scientific adviser on tele-communications at the Ministry of Aircraft Production, who did so much to develop the science of radiolocation.

MAKING the first official disclosure of the new British device for beating the enemy bomber, Air Chief Marshal Sir Philip Joubert, who was Assistant Chief of Air Staff in charge of Signals, said : " I think and hope that it has been one of the best kept secrets of the war, and it is certainly one of the most important factors in our war organization.

"It was the need of the Royal Air Force to obtain early warning of enemy air attack that brought it into being by the development of what might be called a wireless trick in the laboratory into a practical weapon of war.

" Briefly it is a system whereby rays which are unaffected by fog or darkness are sent out far beyond the limits of our shores. Any aircraft or ship in the path of this ray immediately sends back a signal to the detecting station where people are on watch. These ether waves keep a 24-hour watch. They are always on duty.

"The use of the rays makes it unnecessary to maintain standing patrols of fighter aircraft for the protection of certain areas, and thus saves time, petrol, and energy. It is safe to say that the Battle of Britain was won by a combination of the fighting forces and radiolocation.'

LORD BEAVERBROOK broadcast on June 18 an appeal for technicians with radio and electrical experience " to assist in the great work."

"Demands for personnel come on us from the Air Force, the Army, and also the Navy. We want men of knowledge, men of technical skill, men of vision to take part in the improvement and upkeep of technical equipment. The repair and the maintenance of these devices is a task of the highest importance. So I appeal to you to come and help us ; you, the technician ; you, who have experience of radio and electrical devices ; you, who have enthusiasm for wireless development. I call you to the front line of human knowledge, where men are pushing forward into the unknown, call you to bring your insight and your vision to the battle for the future of the world."

IN AN OPERATIONS ROOM of the F... with information received from radiolo... presence and position of enemy aircraft...

aves in the Ether Are Beating the Nazi Bombers

well below ground, senior officers in the gallery watch the enormous map below them on which girl plotters move symbols indicating enemy aircraft in accordance
Royal Observer Corps. Left, a mechanic at the control desk of a transmitting station. The story of " radiolocation," the wireless means of discovering the
c by Air Chief Marshal Sir Philip Joubert on June 17, 1941.

MR. CHURCHILL ON THE INVASION OF RUSSIA

'A Prelude to an Attempted Invasion of the British Isles'

I HAVE taken occasion to speak to you tonight because we have reached one of the climacterics of the war.

In the first of these intense turning points a year ago France fell prostrate under the German hammer and we had to face the storm alone. The second was when the Royal Air Force beat the Hun raiders out of the daylight air and thus warded off the Nazi invasion of our island while we were still ill-armed and ill-prepared. The third turning point was when the President and Congress of the United States passed the Lease and Lend Enactment, devoting nearly £2,000,000,000 of the wealth of the New World to help us defend our liberties and their own. These were the three climacterics. The fourth is now upon us.

At four o'clock this morning Hitler attacked and invaded Russia.

All his usual formalities of perfidy were observed with scrupulous technique. A non-aggression treaty had been solemnly signed and was in force between the two countries. No complaint had been made by Germany of its non-fulfilment. Under its cloak of false confidence the German armies grew up in immense strength along a line which stretched from the White Sea to the Black Sea, and their air fleets and armoured divisions slowly and methodically took up their stations.

THEN suddenly, without declaration of war, without even an ultimatum, the German bombs rained down from the sky upon the Russian cities, German troops violated the Russian frontiers, and an hour later the German Ambassador, who during the night before was lavishing his assurances of friend-ship—almost of alliance—upon the Russians, called upon the Russian Foreign Minister to tell him that a state of war existed between Germany and Russia.

Thus was repeated on a far larger scale the same kind of outrage against every form of signed contract and international faith which we have witnessed in Norway, in Denmark, in Holland, in Belgium, and which Hitler's accomplice and jackal Mussolini so faithfully imitated in the case of Greece.

All this was no surprise to me. In fact I gave clear and precise warning to Stalin of what was coming. I gave him warning as I have given warnings to others before.

I can only hope that these warnings did not fall unheeded. All that we know at present is that the Russian people are defending their native soil and that their leaders have called upon them to resist to the utmost.

Hitler is a monster of wickedness, insatiable in his lust for blood and plunder. Not content with having all Europe under his heel or else terrorized into various forms of abject submission, he must now carry his work of butchery and desolation among the vast multitudes of Russia and Asia.

A Thousand Millions Are Menaced

THE terrible military machine which we and the rest of the civilised world so foolishly, so supinely, so insensately allowed the Nazi gangster to build up year by year from almost nothing—this machine cannot stand idle lest it rust or fall to pieces. It must be in continual motion, grinding up human lives and trampling down the homes and the rights of hundreds of millions of men. Moreover, it must be fed not only with flesh but with oil.

So now this bloodthirsty guttersnipe must launch his mechanical armies upon new fields of slaughter, pillage, and devastation. Poor as are the Russian peasants, workmen and soldiers, he must steal from them their daily bread. He must devour their harvests, he must rob them of the oil which drives their ploughs, and thus produce a famine without example in human history.

And even the carnage and ruin which his victory, should he gain it—and he has not gained it yet—will bring upon the Russian people will itself be only a stepping-stone to an attempt to plunge the four or five hundred million who live in China and the 350 millions who live in India into that bottomless pit of human degradation over which the diabolical emblem of the swastika flaunts itself.

It is not too much to say here, this summer evening, the lives and happiness of a thousand million additional human beings are now menaced with brutal Nazi violence. That is enough to make us hold our breath . . .

A Cataract of Horrors

NO one has been a more consistent opponent of Communism than I have for the last 25 years. I will unsay not a word that I have spoken about it. But all this fades away before the spectacle which is now unfolding. The past, with its crimes, even follies, and its tragedies, flashes away.

I see the Russian soldiers standing on the threshold of their native land guarding the fields their fathers have tilled from time immemorial. I see them guarding their homes, where mothers and wives pray—ah, yes, for there are times when all pray—for the safety of their loved ones, for the return of the breadwinner, of their champion and their protector.

I see the 10,000 villages of Russia where the means of existence was wrung so hardly from the soil, but where there are still primordial human joys, where maidens love and children play.

I see advancing upon all these in hideous onslaught the Nazi war machine, with its clanking, heel-clicking, dandified Prussian officers, its crafty expert agents, fresh from the cowing and tying down of a dozen countries.

I see also the deadly, drilled, docile brutish masses of the Hun soldiery plodding on like a swarm of crawling locusts.

I see the German bombers and fighters in the sky still smarting from many a British whipping, delighted to find what they believe is an easier and safer prey. And behind all this glare, behind all this storm, I see that small group of villainous men who planned, organized and launched that cataract of horrors upon mankind . . .

BUT now I have to declare the decision of H.M. Government, and I feel sure it is a decision in which the great Dominions will, in due course, concur. But we must speak out now at once, without a day's delay. I have to make the declaration. But can you doubt what our policy will be?

We have but one aim and one single irrevocable purpose. We are resolved to destroy Hitler and every vestige of the Nazi regime. From this nothing will turn us, nothing. We will never parley, we will never negotiate with Hitler or any of his gang. We shall fight him by land, we shall fight him by sea, we shall fight him in the air until, with God's help, we have rid the earth of this shadow and liberated its peoples from his yoke.

Any man or State who fights against Nazidom will have our aid. Any man or State who marches with Hitler is our foe. This applies not only to organized States, but to all representatives of that vile race of quislings who make themselves the tools and agents of the Nazi regime against their fellow-countrymen and against the lands of their birth. These quislings, like the Nazi leaders, if not disposed of by their fellow-countrymen—which would save trouble—will be delivered by us on the morrow of the victory to the justice of the Allied tribunals. That is our policy, and that is our declaration.

It follows, therefore, that we shall give whatever help we can to Russia and to the Russian people.

WE shall appeal to all our friends and allies in every part of the world to take the same course and pursue it, as we shall, faithfully and steadfastly to the end. We have offered to the Government of Soviet Russia any technical or economic assistance which is in our power and which is likely to be of service to it.

We shall bomb Germany by day as well as by night in ever-increasing measure, casting upon them month by month a heavier discharge of bombs and making the German people taste and gulp each month a sharper dose of the miseries they have showered on mankind.

THIS is no class war. This is a war in which the whole British Empire and Commonwealth of Nations is engaged without distinction of race, creed, or party. It is not for me to speak of the action of the United States of America, but this I will say : If Hitler imagines that his attack on Soviet Russia will cause the slightest division of aim or slackening of effort in the great democracies which are resolved upon his doom, he is woefully mistaken. On the contrary, we shall be fortified and encouraged in our efforts to rescue mankind from his tyrannies. We shall be strengthened, and not weakened, in our determination and our resources.

Russia's Danger Our Danger

HITLER wishes to destroy the Russian power because he hopes that, if he succeeds in this, he will be able to bring back the main strength of his army and air force from the east and hurl it upon this island, which he knows he must conquer or suffer the penalty of his crimes. **His invasion of Russia is no more than a prelude to an attempted invasion of the British Isles.**

He hopes, no doubt, that all this may be accomplished before the winter comes and that he can overwhelm Great Britain before the fleets and air power of the United States may intervene.

He hopes that he may once again repeat upon a greater scale than ever before that process of destroying his enemies one by one by which he has so long thrived and prospered, and that then the scene will be clear for the final act without which all his conquests would be in vain, namely, the subjugation of the Western Hemisphere to his will and to his system.

The Russian danger is therefore our danger and the danger of the United States, just as the cause of any Russian fighting for his hearth and home is the cause of free men and free peoples in every quarter of the globe. Let us learn the lessons already taught by such cruel experience, let us redouble our exertions and strike with united strength while life and power remain.

Broadcast on Sunday evening, June 22, 1941.

Hitler Takes the Road to Moscow

At dawn on Sunday, June 22, 1941, Hitler's armies invaded Russia, and in a few hours battle was joined on the huge front of more than 1,500 miles, stretching from Finland in the north to the Black Sea in the south. Below we tell of the opening moves in what Mr. Churchill in his broadcast (reproduced in the opposite page) well described as one of the great climacterics of the war.

"GERMAN people,"—it is the voice of Goebbels speaking over the German wireless at 5.45 on that fateful Sunday morning but the words are Hitler's— " in this very hour a movement of troops is taking place which in its extent and magnitude is the greatest that the world has ever seen.

" United with their Finnish comrades, the warriors who won the victory at Narvik are manning the shores of the Arctic Ocean. German divisions, commanded by the conqueror of Norway, together with the champions of Finnish liberty commanded by their Marshal, are protecting Finnish territory. From East Russia to the Carpathians fresh formations mass along the German eastern front. Along the lower regions of the Danube down to the shores of the Black Sea German and Rumanian soldiers are united under the Rumanian Premier, General Antonescu. The task of this front is no longer the protection of individual countries but the safety of Europe and the salvation of us all.

" I have decided " (concluded Hitler) " to-day once again to entrust the fate and the future of the German Reich and of our nation to the hands of our soldiers. May our Lord God aid us in this greatest of all struggles."

There was no declaration of war—Hitler has long dispensed with such formalities ; but the long statement which Goebbels read was a review of Russo-German relations which made it plain that for months past those relations had been strained. Hitler declared that his pact with Stalin of August 1939 had been made necessary by the " British policy of encirclement against Germany," although at the same time he had hoped that the tension between Germany and the Soviet might be permanently relieved. But, he complained, the Soviet rulers had throughout claimed far more than was laid down in the bond. They had occupied Lithuania and the other Baltic states, Bessarabia and Northern Bukovina ; they had demanded that Bulgaria should accept Russian protection and that the Soviet should be granted by Turkey a base on the Dardanelles—demands which Hitler refused. Then the Soviet had encouraged Yugoslavia in her resistance against the Reich and (so he alleged) attempted to form a Soviet Russian-Anglo-Saxon front. Now, he went on, something like 160 Russian divisions were massed on the frontier, and for weeks violations of that frontier had been taking place. " This has brought us to the hour when it is necessary for us to take steps against this plot devised by Jewish Anglo-Saxon warmongers, and the equally Jewish rulers of the Bolshevist centre in Moscow." So the mask was thrown off. The Pact with Russia was revealed as a mere

time-saving truce. The Bolsheviks were once again the enemy.

Russia's 180 millions were told of the German attack in a broadcast from Moscow by Mr. Molotov, the Foreign Commissar. " At 4 o'clock this morning," he said, " German troops attacked the Soviet Union, without any demands having previously been made upon us. The frontiers of our country were attacked at many points, and enemy planes bombed the cities of Kiev, Sebastopol, Kaunas, and others, killing and injuring more than 200 people. The attacks were launched from Rumanian and Finnish territory, both in the air and by artillery."

The attack, went on Mr. Molotov, had been made in spite of the existence of a treaty of non-aggression between the U.S.S.R. and Germany, and of the fact that the U.S.S.R. had always kept all its obligations. " The entire responsibility for this murderous attack therefore rests on the shoulders of the Fascist gangsters in Germany." Only after the onslaught had been launched did the German Ambassador in Moscow, Von Schulenberg, inform him that his government had decided to declare war on the Soviet Union.

" Now that our country has been attacked," continued Mr. Molotov, " the Government has ordered its troops, airmen and sailors to repel the attack and to drive the German troops from the soil of our country . . . The Soviet Government declares its unshaken confidence that its glorious army and air force will fulfil their duty of defending the native soil against the aggressor's shameless attack, and will inflict a shattering defeat on the enemy . . . Once in its history our country was attacked by Napoleon, and he was defeated here and suffered complete destruction. The same will happen to this megalomaniac Hitler."

BALTIC TO BLACK SEA. Where the German onslaught on Russia was launched. *Courtesy of the "Daily Mail"*

The first shots in the new war were fired at 4 a.m. when the German artillery came into action all along the frontier, shock troops advanced to the assault, and wave after wave of Nazi dive-bombers sped to attack the Soviet airfields, anti-aircraft gun positions, troop concentrations, and cities far behind the line. Soon came the report that Odessa, the great grain port on the Black Sea, had been attacked, " on the same scale as Rotterdam and Belgrade." From the far north there came no news as yet of the Finns having crossed the frontier, but at the opposite extremity of the huge front the Rumanians were reported to have gone into action, crossing the Pruth with a view to recapturing their recently-lost province of Bessarabia. Italy, too, declared herself to be at war with Russia.

German war correspondents at the front proceeded to give a running commentary on the course of events. · They described how

before zero hour in the villages in the area just behind the front " ghost-like movements " had been going on for hours as the German infantry marched into their positions. " The men had been given orders to creep forward like cats with their heavy war equipment, so as to be able to strike at and totally surprise the enemy at a moment's notice. The clearness of the night was emphasized by the bright rays of electric lamps burning cheerfully on the Russian side of the border. As yet there was no black-out in Russia."

At zero hour " red flares went up, and instantaneously the German infantry weapons began to fire with our second surprise, the assault gun, as it has been baptized. Only weak enemy fire meets the German soldiers—much too weak to stop our advance. Soon the enemy fire becomes weaker still ; their batteries have been hit. There is some resistance from a Russian pill-box beyond the frontier, but our soldiers advance in short dashes, jumping up when the enemy fire ceases, and falling again when it resumes. Only here is resistance met, and here it is soon broken." Then the Nazi bombers came up and dropped high explosives and machine-gunned the Russian airfields. "Apart from the airfields," said a German officer who was interviewed over the German radio, " we saw nothing but trees. The devil knows where the Russians went into hiding." With unfailing regularity throughout the day Goebbels' propagandists described how Soviet airfields were being smashed, how the main Russian air force had been smitten before it had been taken off the ground, and how the enemy positions were being deluged with bombs. Very much the same stories were being told by the Russian spokesmen, speaking from Moscow. . .

Where the Nazis Attacked

As far as could be gathered from the conflicting reports, the invaders were attacking in East Prussia, where the German onslaught was undertaken without artillery preparation so as to take the Russians completely by surprise ; in Poland, where the Germans were reported to have crossed the river Bug under cover of a fierce artillery barrage and to have made a deep penetration into Russian-occupied Poland ; and in the south, where under the command of Marshal List the joint German-Rumanian army was attacking the Bukovina and Bessarabia as the first step in the conquest of the Ukraine.

Hitler's first war communiqué stated that " Fighting has taken place on the Soviet frontier since the early hours of today. An attempt by the enemy to fly over East Prussia was repelled with heavy losses to the enemy. German fighters shot down numerous Red bomber planes." The Russian, issued from Moscow at 4 a.m. on June 23, was somewhat longer. " At dawn on June 22 (it read), regular troops of the German army attacked our frontier forces on the whole front from the Baltic to the Black Sea and were held by us during the first part of the day. At the beginning of the second part of the day German troops came in contact with the vanguards of the Red army. After stubborn fighting the enemy were repulsed, sustaining heavy losses . . . The enemy air force attacked several of our airfields and urban areas, but encountered everywhere vigorous resistance on the part of our fighters and anti-aircraft guns, which inflicted heavy losses on the enemy. Sixty-five enemy airplanes were shot down." So ended the first day. The battle of Slav and Teuton was joined.

Our Diary of the War

SUNDAY, JUNE 15, 1941   652nd day

Sea.—Admiralty announced that H.M. destroyer Jersey had been sunk by enemy mine.

Air.—R.A.F. bombers carried out successful daylight attacks on enemy shipping. At night strong forces raided the Ruhr and Cologne and Hanover districts. Small force attacked Dunkirk. Fighter aircraft raided aerodromes in France.

Coastal Command flying-boat routed four enemy aircraft near Gibraltar.

Africa.—British offensive against enemy positions south and south-east of Sollum. Enemy claimed to have destroyed 60 tanks. Bombing attacks by R.A.F. on Benghazi, Bardia, Derna, Martuba and Gazala.

Near East.—Allied forces captured Sidon. In central sector they reached Jezzin.

R.A.F. bombers raided Aleppo. Fighters carried out protective patrols over naval units on Syrian coast.

Home.—Place on East Anglian coast attacked by day. At night bombs fell at two points in southern England. One night raider destroyed.

MONDAY, JUNE 16   653rd day

Air.—R.A.F. fighters carried out sweeps over French coast and escorted bombers which attacked Boulogne. Ten enemy fighters and one seaplane shot down. Two British bombers and four fighters lost.

Night raids on Cologne, Düsseldorf and Duisburg. Fleet Air Arm attacked Dunkirk.

Africa.—Cairo announced surrender of Italian general and 2,000 troops in Soddu area, Abyssinia. Patriot troops engaging enemy in Jimma area.

Heavy bombers made night raids on Benghazi, Derna, Gazala and Bardia.

Near East.—Announced that Allied forces had captured Kiswe, south of Damascus. Heavy fighting reported in central sector. Vichy counter-offensive recaptured Ezra (in Jebel Druze) and Merj Ayoun.

Vichy destroyer sunk during air and naval engagement off Sidon.

Home.—Small-scale enemy activity at night over Britain. Four raiders destroyed.

TUESDAY, JUNE 17   654th day

Air.—R.A.F. carried out large-scale offensive over Channel and occupied territory. Sixteen enemy fighters destroyed ; ten British planes missing.

At night Cologne and Düsseldorf were heavily bombed and lesser attacks made on enemy ports and shipping.

Africa.—In Libya, after repulsing several tank attacks, British withdrew to avoid enemy encircling movement.

R.A.F. shot down 20 enemy aircraft in Western Desert. In Sidi Omar area 20 armoured vehicles were destroyed by bombs.

Near East.—Allied forces recaptured Ezra. Kuneitra taken by Vichy troops after 12-hour siege, but later regained by Allied reinforcements. Heavy fighting at Merj Ayoun. Counter-attack at Jezzin, east of Sidon, repulsed.

Home.—Small-scale night attacks, mainly over East Coast. One raider destroyed.

WEDNESDAY, JUNE 18   655th day

Sea.—Admiralty announced that submarines in Aegean and Mediterranean had sunk eight Italian vessels, including a tanker and three supply ships.

R.A.F. again attacked targets on French coast and shipping in Channel. Nine enemy fighters shot down with loss of four British.

At night Brest, Bremen and other German ports were raided.

Near East.—Further positions captured south of Damascus. Vichy force in Merj Ayoun now surrounded.

General.—Turkey signed Treaty of Friendship with Germany.

THURSDAY, JUNE 19   656th day

Air.—R.A.F. bombers and fighters again raided Northern France in daylight. Docks and shipping attacked.

R.A.F. bombers made night attack on targets at Cologne and Düsseldorf.

Africa.—Harbour and shipping at Benghazi bombed by R.A.F.

General.—Roosevelt ordered all German consulates to be closed and staff removed by July 10.

Near East.—Indian and Free French forces entered suburbs of Damascus. Australian patrols, advancing from Sidon, now within 13 miles of Beirut.

Home.—Slight night activity over Britain. Enemy lost one bomber.

General.—Berlin ordered all American Consulates in Germany and occupied territories to be closed by July 15. Rome issued similar Note.

FRIDAY, JUNE 20   657th day

Sea.—Enemy patrol vessel destroyed off Den Helder. Portuguese freighter Ganda torpedoed and sunk off Casablanca.

Air.—British bombers and fighters raided Northern France in daylight. Tenth successive night raid on Germany, Kiel being main target. Docks at Dunkirk and Boulogne also bombed.

Near East.—Allied forces gained more ground near Damascus. Free French forces withstood strong Vichy counter-attack. Australian troops reoccupied part of Merj Ayoun.

Imperial aircraft attacked motor transport convoys and shipping at Beirut. Navy shelled enemy positions along coast.

Home.—Three day raiders destroyed, one by H.M. trawler Capstone.

SATURDAY, JUNE 21   658th day

Air.—R.A.F. twice raided enemy aerodromes in France, destroying 26 Nazi 'planes. Two more shot down off East Coast. Britain lost one bomber, four fighters.

At night strong forces of Bomber Command raided Cologne and Düsseldorf. Lighter forces attacked Dunkirk and Boulogne.

Africa.—Patriot forces, led by British officers, captured Jimma, Abyssinia. Successful advances reported from other areas.

Near East.—Damascus evacuated by Vichy forces. British troops occupied the city.

Home.—Night raiders dropped leaflets over south and south-east areas. Bombs damaged south coastal town. One day and four night raiders destroyed.

SUNDAY, JUNE 22   659th day

Germany invaded Russia from frontiers of East Prussia, Poland and Rumania.

THE ALLIED POWERS were fully represented at a meeting in St. James's Palace on June 12, when the leaders of Britain, her Empire and the Allied Governments re-affirmed : " We fight on to Victory." Those seen above are : 1, Mr R. A. Butler ; 2, Sir Archibald Sinclair ; 3, Viscount Cranborne ; 4, Mr. Winston Churchill ; 5, M. Michiels (Netherlands) ; 6, M. Simopoulos (Greece) ; 7, Mr. S. M. Bruce (Australia) ; 8, Mr. W. J. Jordan (New Zealand) ; 9, M. Dupong (Luxembourg) ; 10, M. Soubbotitch (Yugoslavia) ; 11, M. Nygaardsvold (Norway) ; 12, M. Zaleski (Poland) ; 13, Mr. Anthony Eden ; 14, Mr. S. F. Waterson (S. Africa) ; 15, M. Gerbrandy (Holland) ; 16, M. Lie (Norway) ; 17, M. Pierlot (Belgium) ; 18, H. M. the King ; 19, M. Bech (Luxembourg) ; 20, M. Masaryk (Czechoslovakia) ; 21, M. Sramek (Czechoslovakia) ; 22, General Sikorski (Poland) ; 23, M. Spaak (Belgium) ; 24, M. Dejean (Free France) ; 25, M. Cassin (Free France) ; 25, Baron Cartier de Marchienne (Belgium) ; 27, Sir E. Bridges (Secretary of Cabinet) ; 28, Mr. Brendan Bracken (Parliamentary Private Secretary to Mr. Churchill).   *Photo, P.N.A.*

More and More Tools to Finish the Job

WHAT THE LEASE AND LEND ACT IS DOING FOR BRITAIN

Defence Materials transferred to Britain
Three Months to June 10

	millions
Ships and other craft	6½
Ordnance	5
Aircraft	2¾
Ammunition	2¼
Vehicles	½
Clothing, medical, chemical, etc., supplies	¾
Agricultural Products	2
Machinery, raw materials	¼

£17½ millions

Allocations for Further Aid :

	£ millions
Aircraft	475
Ordnance	220
Shipping	137½
Tanks and Vehicles	79½
Agricultural	70
Miscellaneous Equipment	64

£1,046 millions

The above represents part of the appropriation of £1,750,000,000 approved by Congress. The remainder, about £700,000,000, is being rapidly distributed as new contracts.

MR. CHURCHILL is seen in the top photograph inspecting an American tank, while that on the left shows Mrs. H. Gauntlett, member of the American Committee for the Defence of British Homes, presenting a revolver to a Home Guardsman attached to a London County Council Hospital. Below, workers of the Consolidated Aircraft Company at San Diego, California, are cheering the news that a Catalina Patrol Bomber spotted the Bismarck and was thus instrumental in bringing this battleship to her doom.

Photos, British Official : Crown Copyright ; Associated Press and Wide World

'None May Touch Me with Impunity' Their Motto

THE SCOTS GUARDS, like all the regiments of the Brigade of Guards, have a reputation they are determined at all costs to maintain. Above, members of the training battalion, referred to below, most of whom have been in the Army only a short while, are carrying out a strenuous course before being absorbed by service battalions. These men, carrying rifles and full equipment, who have already covered a considerable distance negotiating difficult obstacles, are making a jump worthy of the Grand National.
Photos, British Official : Crown Copyright

ON the great parade ground of their training centre somewhere in the London District the Scots Guards of 1941 drilled and marched, marched and drilled, with verve and splendid precision. Just like old soldiers in fact, though there was hardly a man there who was not walking about Glasgow in "civvies" little more than six months ago. Sixteen weeks at the depot, followed by another sixteen weeks here at the training centre—and they made a showing which was not unworthy of the great traditions of one of our greatest regiments.

Just how great, they have a daily reminder in the battle-honour which the R.S.M.—he of many medals and 27 years' service, so commanding in presence, so electrically efficient, so full of knowledge which he is so courteously ready to impart—proudly brought to my notice on the parade ground. The day I was there it showed "Festubert 1915," but it might have been the name of one of Marlborough's victories or Wellington's ; it might have been Inkerman or Tel-el-Kebir or Modder River, Mons, Ypres, or Somme. And in the Sergeant's Mess there was a living reminder of great days in the shape of five old Chelsea Pensioners adopted by the battalion for the duration of the war. There they sat in their be-medalled red coats, puffing their pipes and slowly quaffing their beer. "That old fellow over there," whispered the Major to me, "was my father's quartermaster at Suakin in 1885."

THOSE old soldiers must find the Army of today very different from the Army of their days ; it is even very different from the army we used to know when we wore khaki 25 years ago. The barrack huts are light and roomy, and there are no smoky stoves such as those round which we used to shiver ; central heating is now the rule in these Belisha militia-camps. Each man has his wardrobe, and there is a special store-room for suitcases ; hot water is on tap, and there are no cut-throat razors ; the cookhouse is glitteringly clean and the meals are served by A.T.S. girls in white overalls on the cafeteria principle. The food

looks good, and there is plenty of it (today's dinner is steak pie and two veg., rhubarb tart and custard) ; and if a man is still hungry after three good meals and a light supper he can get plenty more to eat at the NAAFI canteen, or at the canteens maintained by the various voluntary organizations. There is no waste, and the Colonel is justifiably proud of the home-made brawn, produced from scraps, and the electric potato peeler, and the profits derived from the sale of the peelings to pig farmers. The gymnasium is first-class, equipped with every muscle-building apparatus, and the instructors know how to make their "victims" laugh.

Then for the leisure hour there is a huge garrison theatre, equipped for both stage and cinema shows, where performances are given on every night in the week, the price of admittance being 6d., and 1s. for the officers. There is also a library under the control of the Quartermaster ; it consists of 3,000 volumes, he says, half of which are owned by the battalion and half are obtained through the County Library scheme. Each month 2,750 volumes are borrowed, dealing with every subject under the sun. The most popular books are those dealing with adventure ; little interest seems to be displayed in political questions, nor do the soldiers care to read about love. *E.R.P.*

The impeccable standard of the foot drill of the Brigade of Guards is maintained in wartime as in days of peace. The Adjutant takes the salute at a parade of Scots Guards in the training camp, where drill is still recognized to be the foundation of good discipline.

They Talk Over a Thousand Miles of Desert

BRITISH MOBILE RADIO CAR in action somewhere in the Western Desert. The nerve centre of operations, this type of car can remain in the desert as long as necessary 'and open up communications by Morse at the rate of about thirty words a minute, or by telephony. It has a range of over a thousand miles. In the background as far as the horizon are military tents, but no soldiers are to be seen. They have probably taken refuge from the intense heat.

Photo, British Official: Crown Copyright

Blow & Counter-Blow in the Grim Atlantic Battle

ANOTHER U-BOAT DOOMED, having been hit by our shells. Its conning tower has been wrecked, and the crew, assembling on deck, are about to abandon the submarine. Beneath, another photo of the submarine taken immediately before she sank for the last time.

SEA POWER is Hitler's most terrifying nightmare, for command of the oceans made sure of Britain's victory in the first World War as it will do in the second. Hence the Nazis are straining every nerve to destroy our shipping by submarine and plane, and the battle of the Atlantic goes on grimly day after day, night after night. This phase of the war is so critical for Hitler that he even risked and lost the Bismarck in the hope of cutting our life-line with America.

Unlike Germany, Britain has never hidden her serious losses, but thanks to the devoted courage of our seamen, the work of shipbuilders striving to make good our losses, and ever-increasing help from the United States, we shall win through. Moreover, U-Boat and Focke-Wulf aeroplane casualties are rising satisfactorily. Some submarines like that shown in this page are shattered by shell-fire, others are broken asunder by the depth charge ; and new devices are helping to smash the evil-power of Hitlerism in this vast arena of the war.

But, as Mr. Churchill said on June 19, the Battle of the Atlantic is a "continuous operation. Its seriousness has not by any means been removed by anything that has occurred as the year advanced." And the under-sea and aerial nature of this war of attrition makes spectacular surface victories like the destruction of the Bismarck a rare event ; but gradually and ultimately by the pooling of Anglo-American resources and the traditional courage and skill of our seamen in every department of marine operations the enemy will be worn down.

ON CONVOY WATCH, with their hands on depth charges, two sailors (circle) are ready to "roll out the barrel" full of really strong stuff in the event of a U-boat being about.

TORPEDOED, a cargo-boat laden with timber is settling down in the Atlantic, but her S O S has been answered by a British warship which has arrived in time to rescue her crew.

Photos. G.P.U., J. Hall, " Daily Mirror"

I Was There! .... Eye Witness Stories of the War

Our Air Defences in Malta are Pretty Good

*This vivid description of how Italian and German raids on Malta have been
beaten off by the island's A.A. defences was broadcast by an anti-aircraft
gunner who had been stationed there for three years.*

WE heard the news of the Italian declaration of war one night about seven, and the Italians arrived promptly at breakfast-time the next morning ; and they kept on visiting us at every mealtime —three times a day—for nearly two months.

At first they came over at eighteen thousand feet ; then they got bolder and came down to about ten thousand. We bagged one or two every other day, so they started coming in at about twenty thousand feet. The R.A.F. treated them pretty roughly and that had a good deal to do with it. In the end they gave up coming altogether.

The biggest day we had, although the fight only lasted about sixty minutes all told, was when the Germans came over in January to try to get the Illustrious, which had been damaged in a sea action. There were a lot of Junkers 88 and some Heinkels. It was about 10.30 in the morning when we sighted the first three ; then there were so many more that some of our chaps thought the whole Luftwaffe were on the way. They came over at about 18,000 feet till they were over the harbour, and then went into what was practically a vertical dive. They dived

in strings of about ten each time, one string from one direction, the next from another, and so on, and all focused apparently on the Illustrious. Of course, as soon as they came within effective range, all our guns opened fire in a barrage round the harbour, and soon you couldn't see a thing for smoke —white smoke and black smoke exploding everywhere, and the noise was terrific, what with shells, bombs, machine-guns and aeroplane engines.

Those Germans must have been brave pilots to come through that barrage. For a few seconds you couldn't see any of them while they were coming through. Then some of them did come through, still diving, down to about a hundred feet. By this time we'd stopped firing the barrage and each gun took on the planes that came into its own area, over open sights. The Number One of the gun chose his own targets. It reminded me of firing at clay pigeons with a shot-gun. The noise was even louder now. I couldn't even shout at my layer, but had to get hold of his head and turn it round to show him what I wanted hitting. I saw one of our shells burst on the tail

Many Axis machines now lie scattered over the island of Malta. Top, the engine and airscrew of one enemy raider ; above, the tailpiece of another, bearing Italian markings.
Photos, Fox

of a Junkers. He seemed to go out of control, recovered for a moment, and then dived down, on fire.

We were firing pretty solidly for half an hour. The attack finished and the last of the Germans trailed off. We were just congratulating ourselves that it was over for the time being when one of the gunners suddenly pointed into the sky—his mouth was open, but he couldn't speak. I whipped round and got the shock of my life—I saw them flying in again. But half a minute later I saw it was nothing more than a flock of seagulls. I believe those gulls did get a round or two.

The Germans came back again at about 12.30. We were expecting them and were quite ready. They didn't use quite so many planes in the second attack, but they behaved just the same way. In those two raids they lost twenty-nine, of which our fighters bagged a good many. The Germans were good ; but our chaps were better.

Of course, bombs were dropping thick in the harbour area, and there was so much noise that you'd think the Illustrious and the harbour must have been blown to pieces. But when I went to look round I couldn't see that they had hit the Illustrious at all, and the harbour itself was very little damaged.

The A.A. BARRAGE of Malta is seen bursting in the sky during one of the almost incessant air raids on the island citadel. That the Germans who come through our barrage are brave pilots is the conclusion reached by the A.A. gunner whose description of Axis raids on Malta is given in this page. See also pages 652-3.
Photo, Associated Press

AIR RAIDS ON MALTA
1 Year to June 10, 1941
Air Raid Alerts 694
Nazi Aircraft Destroyed ... 155
„ „ Damaged ... 60

Sir Edward Jackson, Lieutenant-Governor of Malta, on the anniversary of the first raids :

Is it not a very great thing that many hundreds of men and women have proved to themselves that they can look in the face of danger undismayed, have torn from them in an instant all they possessed except their courage and get up out of the dust and begin all over again ?
Who shall say that in the final account the material loss is not outweighed by the spiritual gain ?

IIIIIIIIIIIIIIIIIIIIIIIIIIIIIIIIIIIIIIIIIIIIIIIIIIIIIIIIIIIIII I WAS THERE! IIIIIIIIIIIIIIIIIIIIIIIIIIIIIIIIIIIIIIIIIIIIIIIIIIIIIIIIIIIIII

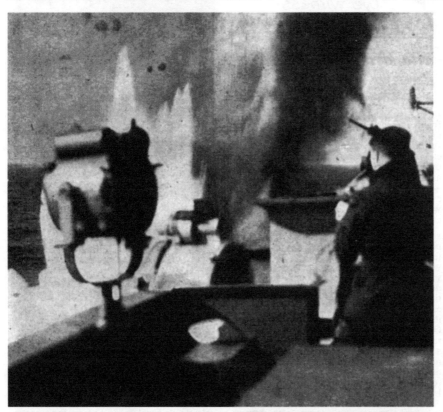

H.M.S. ILLUSTRIOUS, 23,000-ton aircraft carrier, was attacked by German bombers six times in the Mediterranean on January 10, 1941. Nearly 100 enemy planes were beaten off and nine of them shot down during the engagement. Several bombs struck the ship and started fires, but, above, a near miss fails to disturb the man at his action station.   *Photo, British Official : Crown Copyright*

Later the Illustrious went out at twenty-five knots under her own steam. The dockyard men had done good work.

There have been one or two more raids on the harbour and shipping since then, but they haven't been frequent. The defences of Malta are pretty good and the Germans usually kept at a good height when they came over by day ; and after a time they almost stopped bombing by day and just came over at night. They haven't done much damage in this way. I believe they have a healthy respect for the defences of Malta.

We Escorted King George over the Cretan Hills

A vivid account of the first Nazi air landings in Crete and of the fortunate escape of King George and his Prime Minister was given by two British officers who accompanied them.

THE two senior British officers who escorted King George were Major-Gen. T. G. Heywood, head of the British Military Mission in Crete, and Col. J. S. Blunt, Military Attaché in Crete. Major-Gen. Heywood said :

Last Sunday (May 18) the Germans made increasingly heavy air attacks on the aerodromes of Heraklion (Candia), Retimo and Maleme and on shipping and installations in Suda Bay. The next day their attacks were very heavy and they bombed a hospital severely.

Early on Tuesday there were more heavy bombings. At 8 a.m. I saw crowds of parachutists coming down in the area south-west of Canea. There were swarms of parachutists as well as troop carriers and gliders all round the south and south-west. Simultaneously, parachutists landed north of Canea and tried to land at Maleme.

The landing of the parachutists went on steadily for four hours until noon, with continual machine-gunning of the town and olive groves and dog fights wherever the parachutists landed.

The King fortunately had had a " hunch " and, leaving his house south-west of Canea the night before, had gone to that of the Prime Minister at Perivolia to be with him. At this point Col. Blunt took up the story. He explained that the King was in a house commanding a wide view of the countryside, guarded by an escort of Greek gendarmerie and a platoon of New Zealanders under the command of 2nd Lt. W. H. Ryan.

They were aroused by the roar of a squadron of Messerschmitts, and King George, Prince Peter, his cousin, and the Prime Minister came out to watch them. After the Messerschmitts came bombers, bombing targets where they thought there were troops. Col. Blunt went on :

Out of the smoke of the bombardment we saw a very large force of planes coming in from the north, and took cover in trenches. Large gliders appeared above the house, circling round for a long time, and we did not see them land, though others landed later at the bottom of the King's garden.

It was clear that a landing was going to take place, and shortly afterwards we saw troop-carrying planes flying from the west, very low and in chains of threes. They seemed endless.

Then the parachutists started coming down. In the same area where the King had been the day before a company of parachutists, estimated to number 150-200 men, came down.

It was a most extraordinary sight. Their parachutes were red or green. Through the glasses one could see the French chalk in which they were packed popping off as they came out of the containers. The nearest were about 800 yards away.

The parachutists seemed to come down all at once, and they descended rapidly. We saw many parachutes which did not open and let the men fall straight to the ground.

There was a great deal of machine-gunning from the planes, and firing by our anti-aircraft and by our troops in all directions. We decided that it was no use staying, as our house would obviously be attacked as a useful observation post.

With difficulty owing to the low-flying planes we collected our party. The whole thing happened so quickly that we could not get transport and took to the hills, literally with what we could carry in our hands.

We saw another flight of parachutists come down on our road, and had to climb a 1,500-ft. hill in the heat of a very hot day. Every five to 10 yards we had to take cover as hundreds of planes were whizzing about in every direction.

Col. Blunt explained that everyone was nervous of Germans in British and Greek uniforms, and parties indulged in much shouting before meeting, thinking the others were parachutists.

After climbing the ridges they arrived at noon at a cave, occupied by a Cretan

KING GEORGE, who narrowly escaped capture in Crete, as related in this page, was eventually evacuated from the island, protected by an escort of New Zealanders. The King of the Hellenes is seen thanking some of the escort, which was commanded by 2nd Lt. W. H. Ryan (right).
Photo, British Official : Crown Copyright

IIIIIIIIIIIIIIIIIIIIIIIIIIIIIIIIIIIIIIIIIIIIIIIIIIIIIIIIIIIIIIIIIIIIIIIIIIIIIIII **I WAS THERE!** IIIIIIIIIIIIIIIIIIIIIIIIIIIIIIIIIIIIIIIIIIIIIIIIIIIIIIIIIIIIIIIIIIIIIIIIIIIIIIIIIIII

shepherd and his family, beside a little spring. They sheltered there until three o'clock, when they continued their journey to Panagya.

From there Col. Blunt tried to get into touch with Canea. The situation, however, was confused with much fighting and he had to abandon the attempt.

Eventually he succeeded in telephoning to Suda to arrange for the embarkation of the King during Thursday night.

Throughout the three days' ordeal, he said, the bearing of everybody from his Majesty downwards was all that one could desire. His Majesty treated it like an outing and seemed bored at having to take cover from the planes. (*Reuter.*)

I Saw a Marine Corporal Firing to the Last

The magnificent work of the Royal Marines in Crete earned special recognition from General Wavell. A typical exploit was that told below of Lance-Corporal Thomas Neill, who kept his Bofors gun firing to the last.

DURING the withdrawal from Suda Bay the Royal Marines formed the rearguard, and some of them manned the anti-aircraft defences. On reaching Egypt, Marine Patrick Mahoney of Liverpool told this story. He said :

From the moment the Nazis started the attack on Canea, Lance-Corporal Neill, with three companions helping to operate an A.A. gun and two others passing ammunition, fired almost continuously.

Each time a group of Nazi dive-bombers came over us, Neill would let all but the last plane pass before opening fire, concentrating on that one. To my knowledge, he got nine within two days, and at least 20 within a fortnight.

after firing at the last plane of each group of bombers, he hopped on the lorry and moved the gun to a new position.

The German bombs kept bursting away on positions Neill had just left. His gun, camouflaged with brush, was kept in action continuously. On one occasion it shot down two out of ten bombers.

Mahoney concluded : I last saw Neill near Canea on May 27. He was with two companions, the only survivors from a gun crew of six, against a background of blazing trees set alight by a petrol dump which was blown up by the dive-bombers.

He was singing and shouting as he blazed away at the swooping planes. I hope he got away safely. (*B.U.P.*)

JONATHAN MILLS, ex-Seaforth Highlander, invalided out of the Army after Dunkirk, saved a mother and baby during a raid on a S.E. coast town. The story is told below.
Photo, L.N.A.

HEROIC MARINES IN CRETE

General Wavell to General Weston, of the Royal Marines, May 31 :—

You know the heroic effort the Navy has made to rescue you. I hope you will be able to get away most of those who remain, but this is the last night the Navy can come. Please tell those that have to be left that the fight put up against such odds has won the admiration of us all, and every effort to bring them back is being made. General Freyberg has told me how magnificently your Marines have fought, and of your own grand work. I have heard also of the heroic fight of young Greek soldiers. I send you all my grateful thanks.

The Nazis soon learned Neill's strategy, so they decided to get him by trickery. They kept sending over 10 to 20 planes, but behind this group three more.

Neill took his usual shots at the last machine in the first formation, and the following three planes plastered his position repeatedly with sticks of heavy bombs. But they failed to get him.

He countered the Nazi trick by some fast thinking, went on Mahoney. He attached his gun to a light lorry. Immediately

How I Got Mother and Child Out of the Ruins

After serving in France with the Seaforth Highlanders, Jonathan Mills was invalided out shortly after Dunkirk. He tells here how, when a S.E. coast town was raided a year later, he tunnelled his way through wreckage to the rescue of a mother and two children.

MILLS was about to leave for work when his house was shaken by the explosion of a bomb that had fallen streets away.

He ran to the spot and heard muffled cries coming from the ground floor back room of a shattered house. What happened next is described in his own words.

I dug a tunnel through the wreckage, propping up debris with pieces of wood.

As I crawled through the tunnel I came upon the handle of a pram sticking out of a heap of broken bricks. I tore away the bricks and uncovered the pram in which I felt a kiddy's leg.

There was a baby about a year old in the pram, and before I pulled it out I remembered to put my finger into its mouth and draw out dirt and dust to save it from suffocating.

After I had carried the baby to safety, I crawled back through the tunnel and came

upon a wrecked bed which had been overturned. I broke off the back of the bed, chopped through the springs, then slit up the mattress and pulled out the feathers.

There was a woman in the bed and one of her legs was pinned down by a length of twisted piping. This I cut through with a hacksaw handed down to me by other rescuers.

Now I reached down to the woman's head and managed to get a bottle to her mouth and let her have a wee drop. She said, " There's another baby there."

I smelt gas and shouted to get it turned off, and then, after I had given her another drop, they got the woman out.

Going forward, I found the other kiddy's cot, and as soon as I had got the child free a bit I sucked at its mouth and blew back again to see if there was any life in it, but unfortunately there wasn't. (*The Star.*)

L.-Cpl. NEILL, the story of whose exploits is related above, was one of those " magnificent Marines " who formed the rearguard of the evacuation from Crete.
Photo, G.P.U.

Siftings From the News

Double whisky and a peach now cost the same—2s.

Covent Garden dealer given three months for doubling wholesale price of oranges.

Another profiteer sentenced to three months and £100 fine for over-charge on sale of eggs.

Hitler reported to possess a 50-acre estate at Bogota, Colombia, as secret " hideaway."

U.S. Navy announced that mines were being sown in lower bay of New York harbour.

Test flight of new American R.A.F. bomber showed it to be as fast as most fighter planes.

" New Poor " of Hove, formerly one of wealthiest towns, now queue up for 9d. communal meals.

Australia is supplying 2,300,000 pairs of boots for oversea troops by February, 1942.

Expert survey of St. Paul's Cathedral revealed that general stability was unaffected by bombing.

President Roosevelt issued warning regarding alleged discrimination against negroes in defence industries.

Before the war we smoked 195-197 million pounds of tobacco annually ; present consumption is at rate of 230-240 million pounds.

" Battle of Britain " is to be published in U.S.A. in book form.

American women, now war-conscious, are abandoning extravagant style of dress in favour of sober fashions.

Five men were hanged in Polish market squares for smuggling sugar from Wartheland to Warsaw.

By end of June all British prisoners of war will have received a new outfit of clothes.

Forty-three women Fascists, thirty of British nationality, have been interned at Port Erin.

U.S. Maritime Commission disclosed that ship production has surpassed 1918 record.

During first year of war number of children under 14 found guilty of indictable offences increased by 41 per cent.

Axis ships seized in Mexican ports will be used on a new service between Vera Cruz and New York.

Buenos Aires ban on Chaplin's " Great Dictator," imposed at request of Italian ambassador, now removed.

Germans stated to be releasing 100,000 French prisoners of war.

The Editor's Postscript

An employee of the Amalgamated Press, now a leading seaman in the R.N.R., tells me, in a letter from the Western Desert, he was in the advance against the "Wops" when they were chased beyond Benghazi and, at the last point which the Italians abandoned there, copies of "The War Illustrated" came up with the supplies. "There was great competition for them and all who were able to secure a copy or get a loan of one regarded themselves as very fortunate." He himself had the good luck to find four different numbers in an Australian outpost. "W.I." certainly does get about.

Among the letters that have reached my desk recently from all parts of the Empire there is one that took about three months to get here. Less than two weeks would have sufficed before the War. It has come from the island of Malta and I am sure my readers will welcome some excerpts from it giving a lively glimpse of life in that little isle of heroes, about which we have not heard enough. The writer, a bright young Maltese, Miss X (I discreetly withhold her name) has many things to tell me.

"Once (she writes) you said that you could best identify the Nazi from the English planes by their drone. When we were staying at a seaside place, I used to distinguish the Italian planes from the English ones by their drone, too, especially during the night. On hearing the peculiar hammering noise of the enemy planes I used to tell those near me, 'They are coming. These are not ours, you know.' 'But how do you know that?' they would reply. 'Oh, because I know.' For them any plane had the same noise as any other.

As a spirited Maltese, rightly proud of her ancient island homeland—there is surely no other 90 square miles of land with such a long and inspiring history—Miss X goes on:

"I don't think there is enough written about our little island and its part in the War. We were and are subject to beastly air raids, of course not so intense as those on London, but our island is small, and in comparison we have suffered heavily, too. I wish to see printed some adventures experienced by Maltese people; there are many who could tell. I, myself, have been witness of some of the most thrilling 'dog-fights' ever seen in our blue sky. We are not afraid of the 'Ciccini Maccaroni'; we got used to their cowardice pretty quickly. They came, of course, because if they do not show off a bit they die. But how they go to 'the sunny-side up, up, up,' above the clouds! And on seeing our fighters they hurry off after having bombed and destroyed our coal mine, railway station and munition factories—when we have none of these. And they broadcast this great news from their Rome station, too. The silly asses! The British fighter pilots are grand. When I see one plane going right into an enemy formation, zooming upon them like a mad bull and scattering them right and left, I jump with joy and must hug somebody, since I can't hug plane and all. They are really wonderful."

So you see that the spirit of Malta is not unlike the spirit of London itself, and although our Maltese friends are now being bombed by airmen who are as ferocious as the little Wops were futile, I have no doubt that the Maltese—the island's population is

no more than that of Portsmouth—"can take it." My lively young correspondent will find when she gets this number of "The War Illustrated"—alas two or three months hence—that in giving Malta another show in our pages I have taken the opportunity to put right a very venial error that appeared so far back as No. 62, where the picture of the Porte des Bombes, on which the first bomb fell, was stated to be in Valletta. It is really in Floriana, a little to the south-west of the capital. There is an exactly similar gateway known as the King's Gate in Valletta. Myself, I have done no more than look at Malta from the deck of a P. & O., but I still cherish the hope of visiting the island to explore the remarkable remains of its Stone Age civilization, to the description of which I devoted many pages by Professor Peet in my

AIR MARSHAL SIR P. B. JOUBERT DE LA FERTÉ, new Coastal Command Chief, was seconded to R.F.C. in 1913. He is one of Britain's greatest authorities on long-distance flying over sea. Commanded R.A.F., India, 1937-39. *Photo, Howard Coster*

"Wonders of the Past." Malta's defence against the Hun promises to be one of the wonders of the present, and here's good luck to the Maltese—and to lively Miss X!

Calling all Gorillas . . . in Zoo or Jungle! An apology. To which I am constrained by a charming letter from Strone, a much loved haunt of my remote youth "doon the watter," at the mouth of Holy Loch. First, I must print the letter from Mrs. Lilian M. Russell, which has disturbed me to complete contrition for having in a thoughtless moment been guilty of a more than odious comparison:

"I was grieved to see your insulting references to gorillas in your issue of June 6th. I fear your knowledge of them must be derived from Du Chaillu's imaginings. Why attribute foulness to the gorilla? I have spent some four years in the gorilla country, the Gabun Province of French

Equatorial Africa, have known several young ones personally, and heard little but good of their elders. Far from being 'foul,' they are mono-gamists, and are reputed to live an exemplary family life. Nor are they savage: All agree that they never attack man unless first attacked by man. I knew an Englishman who on four separate occasions met adult male gorillas face to face on narrow jungle trails, and after a stare each went aside into the bush and let him pass. I saw a native hunter who had wounded one and had his leg and foot badly mauled when he was absolutely at the gorilla's mercy. A man would have killed his enemy; the gorilla was satisfied to punish him and let him go. Nor are their brows very low and ugly. I have seen a very large dead male who had a really 'good' face and well-shaped head. In the chapter on Gorillas in my book, 'My Monkey Friends' (pub. A. & C. Black), I give some account of young ones, and there are four photographs showing animals with brows which certainly convey no suggestion of foul ancestry. Surely *homo sapiens*, especially the white variety, is THE foul and brutal animal *par excellence*!

This needs no answer. I have always enjoyed every line of your postscripts until I came to this poor gorilla. One must stick up for one's cousins!"

Now, after that, I will never insult a gorilla again and I hereby apologize to the whole species (Sir Arthur Keith thinks there are not so many as 50,000 in existence: "a dying race"); but I did actually write: "nay, it is a libel on the anthropoid to compare them",—Hess and the Gorilla! For, besides reading Du Chaillu's account of his discoveries so long ago that his statements had not then been accepted by natura-lists, I have always been glad to make further book acquaint-ance with the Gorilla in later years. Though my intention to see an actual specimen at the London Zoo is still un-fulfilled, I did witness an amazing film of Gorilla-land in Paris ten or fifteen years ago and had the pleasure of publishing in my "Wonders of Animal Life" a chapter by Sir Arthur Keith which alone should have reminded me that our relative the Gorilla was at heart a gentle beast if unpro-voked but fierce and formid-able when attacked. The Nazi is a ferocious beast if unpro-voked and still more ferocious if his quarry attempts to defend himself. The Gorilla has one characteristic in common with Hitler, however, he's a vege-tarian.

I still think, despite Mrs. Russell's gallant defence of the greatest of the apes, that his beetling brows are rather suggestive of Hess's in the photograph I had in mind, though a re-examination of the gorilla portraits I published in "Wonders of Animal Life" proves to me that the frontal occipital process to which I referred is not entirely characteristic of the species. But I will say that Hess has a better nose than any gorilla. Only another word in self-defence: "gorilla" is a name that has long denoted savagery and dates back to Hanno, the Carthaginian traveller of 500 B.C., who first applied it to the "wild man" of Western equatorial Africa of whom he related hair-raising stories! But we live and learn and all of us who have had the misfortune to live in the era of the German Blonde Beast must cherish tenderer thoughts of gorillas and alligators, sharks and tigers.

JOHN CARPENTER HOUSE,
WHITEFRIARS, LONDON, E.C.4.

Registered at the G.P.O. as a Newspaper

The War Illustrated, July 11th, 1941

Vol 4

The War Illustrated

N°97

Edited by Sir John Hammerton

FOURPENCE

WEEKLY

RUSSIAN SOLDIERS under review on the Red Square, Moscow. On June 22 Hitler tore off the mask of friendship with Stalin and, true to his fulminations in " Mein Kampf," set forth to destroy Soviet Russia. The Nazi war-machine, consisting, it is said, of 100 divisions, was flung against the Russian frontier in one of the greatest political treacheries and military gambles in history. Hitler's objective is, of course, to break Russia before returning to attack Britain. According to Ribbentrop, the forces defending Russia consist of 160 divisions. *Planet News*

Our Searchlight on the War

Badge for the Wounded

KING'S BADGE for officers and men invalided out of the services.
Photograph, Ministry of Information

HIS MAJESTY THE KING has approved the institution of a badge for those invalided from the Naval, Military and Air Forces and the Merchant Navy and Fishing Fleet through wounds or war disablement attributable to service since September, 1939. The badge, designed by Mr. Percy Metcalfe, consists of the Royal and Imperial Cypher, surmounted by a Crown and surrounded by a circular band bearing the inscription " For Loyal Service." It is one inch in diameter, is made of white metal, and is fitted with a buttonhole attachment for men and a brooch attachment for women. The Ministry of Pensions will issue the badge automatically to everyone entitled to receive it.

Anti-Axis Moves in America

DRASTIC action has been taken by President Roosevelt against the ever-increasing Axis menace. On June 16 he issued an order for the immediate freezing of all German and Italian assets in the U.S.A. Two days later a Note was handed to a representative of the German Embassy, directing the closing of all German Consular establishments in the States and the removal of their German personnel from American territory by July 10. Other organizations similarly banished were the German Library of Information in New York, various " railroad and tourist agencies," and the Transocean News Service. The President's reasons for his action were succinctly stated in his Note to the German Embassy. The agencies of the German Reich " have been engaged in activities outside the scope of their legitimate duties. These activities have been of an improper and unwarranted character." On June 19 Hitler replied by ordering all American Consulates in Germany and occupied territories to be closed by July 15. Rome, Berlin's slavish echo, issued a similar Note regarding those in Italian territory, and on June 21 Washington added the final touch by including all Italian Consulates and official organizations within the original ban.

King Peter

YOUNG King Peter II of Yugoslavia arrived in England by air on June 21, accompanied by General Simovitch (Prime Minister), M. Nintchitch (Minister of Foreign Affairs), and M. Knezevitch (Minister

at Court). It is understood that a Free Yugoslav Government will soon be set up in this country. King Peter has stated that he intends forming a Free Yugoslav Air Force, flying American machines. " There are 300 young Slav pilots ready now to fight in the air to regain their country's freedom," he said. " With volunteers from America I hope this number will be quadrupled in a very short time." This seventeen-year-old King is already a trained navigator and intends to fly as such with his Air Force when it is ready for action. In the meantime he hopes to get his wings with the R.A.F.

Honours Across the Atlantic

ON June 17 the University of Rochester, New York, conferred the honorary degree of Doctor of Civil Law on Mr. Churchill by transatlantic short-wave radio. The President of the University, Professor Valentine, said in his address : " Winston Churchill, no longer historian and statesman, but symbol of Britain aroused, stout of heart, direct in speech, cheerful in reverses, calm in confusion—America admires you . . . May peace with freedom be your crowning work." The Prime Minister accepted the degree in a ten-minute broadcast. His final words were : " Divided, the dark ages return. United, we can save and guide the world." America's academic tribute was reciprocated on June 19, when Lord Halifax, as Chancellor of the University of Oxford, presided at Harvard over a special Convocation of the University for conferring the degree of D.C.L. on President Roosevelt. The President was unhappily prevented by indisposition from attending, but General Edwin Watson, his friend and Military Aide, appeared in his place. At the ceremony, which conformed as closely as possible with Oxford tradition, Lord Halifax, wearing his

KING PETER of Yugoslavia, here seen with the Duke of Kent, arrived in England with his Prime Minister on June 21, 1941.
Photo, British Official ; Crown Copyright

black and gold Chancellor's robes, was accompanied by six beadles. Accepting the degree by proxy, Mr. Roosevelt said in a message : " We would rather die on our feet than live on our knees. We, too, were born for freedom, and, believing in freedom, are willing to fight to maintain freedom."

Turkish Treaty With Berlin

WHAT was described as a " Treaty of Friendship " was signed on June 18 by Papen, German Ambassador to Turkey, and Sarajoglu, Turkish Foreign Minister, on behalf of their respective countries. Although Turkey put up considerable resistance against many weeks' pressure by the Axis forces encroaching on her western boundaries, she had eventually to accept this sinister offer. The British Government was from the outset kept informed by Ankara of the progress of negotiations, and the Treaty purports to leave unaffected the present commitments of both countries. The two main articles bind the signatories to " respect the integrity and inviolability of their national territory and not to resort to any measures, direct or indirect, aimed at their Treaty partner " ; and, in the future, " in all questions touching their common interests to meet in friendly contact in order to reach an understanding on the treatment of such questions."

OUR AIR WAR ON GERMANY
Period Sept. 3, 1939—May 30, 1941

Compiled from Official Communiqués of Attacks on Specified Targets

Railways and Communications	813
Docks and Shipping	931
Aircraft Works	88
Munitions Works and Military Stores	147
Electric Power Stations	93
Gas Works	17
Oil Refineries and Storage	386
Aerodromes and Seaplane Bases	270
Total	**2,745**

Attacks on Cities

Berlin (Aug. 8, 1940—May 16, 1941)	45
Cologne (May 20, 1940—May 28, 1941)	80
Duisburg (May 27, 1940—Feb. 15, 1941)	36
Düsseldorf (May 27, 1940—Apl. 11, 1941)	28
Essen (June 5, 1940—May 4, 1941)	35
Hamburg (May 18, 1940—May 16, 1941)	71
Hamm (June 2, 1940—Feb. 1, 1941)	82
Wilhelmshaven (Sept. 5, 1939—Apl. 26, 41)	49
Total	**426**

Places in the Ruhr

On August 9, 1939, Goering boasted as Reichs-minister for Air :

" I have convinced myself personally of the measures taken to protect the Ruhr against air attack. In future I will look after every battery, for we will not expose the Ruhr to a single bomb dropped by enemy aircraft."

The figures above give the R.A.F. answer. The vast web of destruction spread by British bombers is indicated by the fact that they have struck at over 270 target areas of military and strategic importance in Germany, and had in the period covered by the table made over 2,700 separate attacks on Germany alone.

BASEMENT TANKS for the use of fire-brigades are one of the measures adopted against incendiary attacks. Selected basements of bomb-wrecked buildings are cemented and turned into reservoirs, as above.
Photo, L.N.A.

The Way of the War

CHINA ENTERS HER FIFTH YEAR OF WAR
'In Asia and in Europe Two Fronts of the Same Struggle'

Just four years have passed since the Japanese invaded China. They called it an " incident," not a war. They expected to be home again within three or four months, with the bands playing and flags flying in honour of their victory. But they are there still. They are likely to remain there for some time to come. For China is still unsubdued. The " incident " has become one of history's greatest wars.

In those four years the Japanese have overrun—which is not the same thing as having completely occupied, still less as having conquered—ten of China's fifteen provinces, and those the most fertile, the most densely peopled. Her troops garrison not only Peking but China's four greatest cities—Shanghai, Tientsin, Hankow, and Canton. About half of China's 450 millions are under or within reach of Japanese rule. Great would seem to be the Japanese victory, yet it has been largely barren.

When the Japanese invaded China they gambled on a speedy and easy victory. They wanted quick returns in the shape of Chinese crops which they hoped to be able to sell on the world market, and with the proceeds to buy oil and cotton and all the other necessities of a highly industrialized, intensely militarized state. But the provinces Japan controls are so thickly populated that there is no great surplus available for export—famine in China is always only just round the corner—and the guerilla bands which roam the countryside see to it that the farmers are left with very little above what is necessary for their own bare subsistence. Then the expenses of the army of occupation are enormous, although so far as possible the invaders live off the country.

Meanwhile in the western provinces Chiang Kai-shek maintains his stubborn resistance. Under his leadership Free China is as resistant to Japanese blandishments as to their bayonets and their bombs. The provinces composing it are not only immensely rich in minerals and industrial reserves but they have been hitherto the most sparsely peopled; hence they provide plenty of elbow room for the hosts of Chinese who have flocked in from the Japanese-controlled areas so that they may continue to live under Chinese rule. It has been estimated that 100 million Chinese have gone off in search of new homes since the war with Japan began in July 1937. From the mountain regions of the north and the plains of the Yellow River and from the teeming cities on the coast, farmers and students — liable to be shot if the Japanese

catch them—mechanics, business and professional men, and ex-soldiers—they have all poured into Chiang Kai-shek's territory, where they play their part in a great human experiment only to be compared with Roosevelt's New Deal and Stalin's Five Year Plans.

In China's gallant struggle to survive, a great and valorous part is being played by her women. There are still millions of Chinese women who stump through life on deformed feet, but binding the feet of girl children is now very rare, and the unbound foot has become the symbol of woman's emancipation. The Japanese invasion has provided Chinese women with opportunities of service which they have gladly and capably seized.

Among the more spectacular " new women " in China are the 20,000 girls reported to be working among the guerillas. " I have known some of these girls," writes J. D. White, until lately Associated Press correspondent in China. " They were college and high school children when the war began. Many of them came from wealthy families, but they left luxurious homes and either fled before the Japanese advance or slipped through the lines afterward to live the life of a peasant. Today, instead of high heels, they wear straw sandals. Where they used to wear the latest Shanghai creations, they now dress in plain cotton gowns or slack suit. Where once they had good food, they now live frugally. They live among the farm folk in the interior, organizing them for resistance against the Japanese. They write and stage propaganda plays, do welfare work, teach first-aid, and nurse the wounded—in addition to holding down regular jobs in hundreds of new schools set up to teach the farming families to read and write."

More than 13,000 Chinese women are working in the new industrial cooperatives, of which nearly 20,000 of various types and sizes now exist. More than four million Chinese peasant women, it has been estimated, have had a whole new life opened up to them since the war began by learning to read. They are now looking forward to the vote which has been promised them after the war, when China " becomes a real democracy."

Personification of Chinese womanhood at war is Madame Chiang Kai-shek—known to everybody as "Madame." She and her husband are the inspiration of the New Life Movement, whose apostles vigorously wield their new brooms in every Chinese corner. Orders, regulations, and bans imposed are legion, covering (Hessell Tiltman tells us) such diverse subjects as the tidying of public streets, the prohibition of smoking and spitting in public and the attempted prohibition of tipping in hotels, restaurants, eating-houses and bathing-houses, the prohibition of " improper dress," instructions to housewives to wash window curtains, mosquito nets, chair covers and bedding " when soiled or dirty," " Swat that Fly " campaigns, an appeal to citizens to wash their hands and faces at least once a day, and a ban on books and pictures of a " whimsical or immoral nature."

Under Chiang Kai-shek's leadership today is an army of five millions—four million regulars and a million guerillas ; another million are in training camps, while ten millions more have received elementary military training.

These millions are fighting our battle as well as theirs. A million Japanese troops are hopelessly bogged in China. " From the very beginning," said Mr. Quo Tai-chi, recently, " we Chinese felt that we were fighting for others as well as for ourselves, for democracy and human freedom, no less than for our own national existence. The war in Asia and the war in Europe are two fronts of the same struggle." ROYSTON PIKE

CHIANG KAI-SHEK, Generalissimo of Free China. "China, like Britain," Mr. Quo Tai-chi, until recently Chinese Ambassador in this country, has said, "is 'blessed with a brilliant and great leader', to quote President Roosevelt's words, in her supreme crisis. We have our Chiang Kai-shek as you have your Churchill and as the Americans have their Franklin D. Roosevelt. Also our plain people, like your plain people, are indomitable in spirit, valiant in deeds, and immeasurable in fortitude."

180 Millions Under the Hammer and Sickle

Germany's attack on Russia has brought Britain and the Soviet Union closer together than they have been since the alliance of the Great War, when millions of Russian soldiers died in the common cause, was ended by the Revolution. Here we tell something of the country which, though not yet a formal ally, is our powerful associate in the war against Hitler's Germany.

ONE-SIXTH of the earth, more than eight million square miles of compact territory stretching across the north of the world from the Baltic to the Pacific. One hundred and eighty millions of human folk, 167 nationalities speaking nearly 200 languages and reading books and

principal organs of the Communist revolution and of the new state's administration. Election to them was indirect, and there was a pyramid of soviets, the members of one grade electing the members of the one immediately above, culminating in the All Russian Soviet Congress. But in 1936

practically universal suffrage; men and women of 18 and over may vote by secret ballot, and one deputy is elected for every 300,000 of the population. Eighteen is the minimum age for deputies, and the Supreme Council—the equivalent of our Parliament—is remarkable for the youth of its members. Thus in the first "Parliament" elected under the new Constitution, out of 1,143 deputies there were 13 under twenty, six between 21 and 25, and 479 under 30. The youngest deputy was a girl of 19, and altogether there were 187 women members.

Republics of the Union

The Council of Nationalities—over 50 are represented—is composed of nearly 600 representatives of the republics and autonomous regions comprising the Union. For the U.S.S.R. is indeed a union. At the time of the new constitution there were 11 republics. The first and by far the greatest in size and population is the Russian Soviet Federated Socialist Republic (R.S.F.S.R.), which has its capital at Moscow; the other S.S.R.'s were the Ukrainian, White Russian, Azerbaijan, Georgian, Armenian, Turkmen, Uzbek, Tadzhik, Kazakh, and Kirghiz. Since then, as the result of recent changes in the map of Europe, there have been five additions: the Karelo-Finnish, the Moldavian (Bessarabia), Estonia, Latvia, and Lithuania (see map).

The Supreme Council of the Soviet Union elects a Presidency or Presidium, whose chairman is the President of-the Union. The present holder of this office is M. I. Kalinin. The Supreme Council also elects the Council of People's Commissars which is the highest executive and administrative organ of state power in the Union. It consists of heads of the chief Government departments, and is directly responsible to the Supreme Council; its chairman is, in effect the Prime Minister.

SOVIET RUSSIA, showing its vast extent in Europe and Asia. The U.S.S.R. constitutes one of the largest political areas in the world, and its population is computed to be 180,000,000. All enemies of Hitler, they now take their stand beside the British Empire and the United States.

newspapers in nearly a hundred, whose theatre presents plays performed in nearly fifty tongues. A league of nations in actual being, a federal union already achieved. A country which has deliberately broken with the past and is striving to establish in a few years a standard of life and happiness which centuries of hope and effort have not yet secured for the countries of the West and East. A country whose aim is Socialism, whose creed is that of Marx and Lenin, whose banner bears the emblem of the hammer and sickle. All these are Russia—and very much more than these.

Soviet in Russian means council (or counsel), and it is upon the soviets—the local councils of peasants, workers (i.e. the artisans of the towns) and soldiers—that the new state has been built. The word came into prominence at the time of the first revolution in 1905, and in 1917, following the Bolshevist triumph of November (October according to the Russian Old Style calendar) the soviets were officially recognized as the

Stalin's new constitution did away with the Congress, and though it retained the Soviets, made election to them direct and reduced their mutual dependence.

"The U.S.S.R. (Union of Soviet Socialist Republics) is a socialist state of workers and peasants": so reads the first article in the new constitution. The ultimate authority is the Supreme Council of the U.S.S.R., which consists of two chambers: the Council of the Union and the Council of Nationalities.

The Council of the Union is elected by

The Supreme Council is in charge of national affairs as a whole, e.g. international relations, organization of defence, foreign trade, planning of the national economy and the State budget, administration of industrial and agricultural establishments and trading enterprise, and measures concerned with education, public health, labour, justice, and so on. For the rest, the republics composing the Union are sovereign and, theoretically at least, they have the right of withdrawal. They have their own constitutions and governments on the same lines as the Union.

Only one party is permitted to exist in Russia—the Communist Party. Once it was all powerful; it was, in effect, the Civil Service. Perhaps it is not so important as it was, but its Central Executive Committee, acting through its Politbureau of nine members, is still immensely powerful.

Particularly significant was the assumption by Stalin on May 7 last of the chairmanship of the Council of People's Commissars. Since 1922 he had been content with the office of Secretary General of the Communist Party, but now he became the Premier.

Russian newsvendor in a Moscow street. Above, peasants at work among the golden corn of the Ukraine soon to be deluged in blood by the enemy of all mankind. Right, Postage stamp bearing likeness of President Kallnin. *Photos, Keystone*

Names in the New War's First Communiqués

BREST-LITOVSK (right) fell to the Germans on June 24 ; the photo shows a Russian armoured car. An important trading centre east of Warsaw, Brest-Litovsk became famous in the last war by reason of the brutal treaty of peace forced on the Bolsheviks by the Germans in 1918.

TALLINN Harbour (below right) which was bombed and set on fire by the Nazis on June 24. The capital of Estonia, it is on the Gulf of Finland, and one of the Soviet naval bases ceded to Russia in 1940 by the Soviet agreement with that country.
Photos, Wide World & Keystone

CONSTANZA (above), in Rumania, is the largest oil port in Europe. Now in German hands as a result of Hitler's incorporation of Rumania in his " new order," it was heavily bombed by the Russians immediately the Nazis struck east.

"KIEV—the photo, right, shows the industrial quarter of Podol —on the Dnieper, is one of the richest and oldest cities of Russia. In the Ukraine, it is an important railway junction and air station, and the Nazis are making every effort to capture it as a stepping-stone to Odessa. Coal, iron ore, wheat, and oil are among the loot that Hitler hopes to seize in this rich province of the U.S.S.R.
Photos, Mrs. T. Muir and E.N.A.

Three Cheers for the Girls in Blue!

An officer of the W.R.N.S. taking the salute beside the figure-head of Queen Victoria standing in the grounds of their naval training college. On the left, a W.R.N.S. dispatch-rider turning a corner with the efficiency of a racing motorist.

Beneath are Wrens knitting while resting in hammocks in an air-raid shelter at a Naval college, the Alert having just been sounded.

HERE, in the headquarters directing the Battle of the Atlantic, a number of officers and ratings of the Women's Royal Naval Service work day and night at key jobs. Thus they release experienced men for service at sea.

The most secret signals about the ceaseless ocean struggle pass through their hands. By code and cipher they translate the messages which flash between warships and the base. Some of them work at charts, plotting the positions of convoys and warships with great efficiency.

Most of the signals which pass through their hands for coding or decoding concern routine movements of ships. But now and then come the brief wireless messages telling of some tragedy or success away out there at sea. Thus through their hands there passed the urgent signals which told the story of the hunt for the German battle-ship Bismarck and its final destruction. They had a "running commentary" on the engagement.

"They were the most thrilling hours of my life," said one woman who had been on duty in the decoding offices as the British warships closed in to finish the Bismarck. This was her response to the question whether she did not find life as a "Wren" rather dull after her distinguished career as an actress. For this woman has toured the world with famous theatrical companies, and has played with Dame Sybil Thorndike and Flora Robson; she is also well known on the West End stage, particularly at the "Old Vic." Now she is serving as a coding expert in the "Wrens."

AMONG the 250 women officers and ratings of the "Wrens" at these secret headquarters are others with interesting peacetime careers. Thus, the senior officer of this group was a noted concert singer and B.B.C. artiste. A dark-haired young woman who operates a teleprinter machine has had eight novels issued by leading London publishers. One of the "Wren" officers was a commercial and poster artist before the war; another was the almoner and secretary of a children's hospital; while a third was an investigator with the Economic Agricultural Research Institute at Oxford. Two of the "Wren" ratings in this group were teachers of art, while another—now a "Wren" plotter, meaning that she plots the movement of shipping on charts—was a librarian. Still another was a teacher of dancing.

They have come from many occupations and from widely scattered homes to take their part in the Battle of the Atlantic. One is a Canadian girl, daughter of a judge, and another was born in South Africa.

THE DUCHESS OF KENT and the Director of the W.R.N.S., Mrs. V. Laughton Mathews, one of the original Wrens of the last war, conversing with members selected for service abroad. They are wearing tropical uniform, and a squad has recently arrived in Singapore. On the right, a Wren issuing new boots to a sailor.

Photos, British Official ; Fox and Kosmos

The City's Answer to the Nazi Barbarians

IN LONDON'S GUILDHALL the Court of the City met on June 24 under the temporary roof to elect the sheriffs for the coming year in accordance with time-honoured custom. The Lord Mayor carried a posy of English flowers, and civic dignitaries transacted their business as they have done from time immemorial. This photograph symbolizes London's courageous spirit and the utter contempt of her citizens for the Nazi gangsters. It should be compared with that appearing in page 1 of Volume 4 of "The War Illustrated," taken just after the Guildhall was heavily damaged by Nazi bombs on December 29, 1940.

Photo, Keystone

What the Anzac Brigadier Said About Crete

Fresh from the fighting in Crete, Brigadier L. M. Inglis, of the Second New Zealand Expeditionary Force, has been called to London to advise the Cabinet and the General Staff on the lessons of the campaign. How important these lessons are may be gathered from this address made by Brigadier Inglis at the War Office on June 23.

O F Crete's garrison the bulk of the troops had been evacuated from Greece three weeks before the Cretan blitz began. They were inevitably under strength and they had suffered very heavy losses in equipment, especially in artillery, tanks, motor transport, and that sort of thing.

You will ask straight away : Why were not these deficiencies made up ? and that is just where we run up against the difficulty of the whole campaign—the problem of transport under conditions of air inferiority. Ships carrying and landing heavy equipment such as Bren carriers, tanks, guns, and so on, took a long time to unload and were particularly subject to bombing attacks in the restricted area of Suda Bay. The result was that these vehicles and equipment of all sorts were not easily landed, and they were not always in the best of condition when they got ashore. Trucks, tanks, etc., had to be landed from half-sunken ships, and were out of condition from the salt water. It took time and labour to condition them for the road when they were got ashore.

Again, a considerable number of the troops were of the noncombatant Services who had been evacuated from Greece. They had not been trained to arms, and though a number of them were organized into units and given arms, they were like all ill-trained, hastily organized troops, unable to contribute adequately to the defence. Of the Greeks many were very recent recruits, often to the noncombatant Services of the Greek army. All had been hastily organized or re-organized when they got to Crete, and they suffered from even greater deficiencies of equipment than we did. At Retimo they did some very gallant work in the recapture of the aerodrome, and elsewhere parties of them were constantly turning up and asking for Germans to fight ; but under the circumstances they could not be expected to maintain a sustained effort indefinitely. They had not the means to do it.

No Support in the Air

Really it comes back to this, that, so far as the Army was concerned, it had to try to defend Crete against forces supported by a very large and powerful air force without support from our own air forces. No air force sufficient to cope with the German air attack could have been based on the three Cretan aerodromes ; they were too small and too near the greatly superior numbers of German aircraft, so that had an attempt been made to maintain aircraft at those aerodromes they would have been blitzed out of existence very early in the piece. Egypt was too far away to permit of fighters based there operating in Crete. Ships with supplies were sunk because the enemy was able to bomb them freely. He got his troops into Crete by air because we could not oppose him in the air. He supported them by ground strafing from the air for the same reason ; and for the same reason again the Navy, which definitely saved the Army, could carry out that task only with heavy loss to itself.

I want to dispose of any idea that the troops did not fight in Crete. They did. The German himself has admitted heavy casualties and we know well enough that he got them. In one of my battalions, a platoon consisting

Brigadier L. M. INGLIS, one of the New Zealand officers who took part in the Crete fighting, came to London to advise on the lessons to be learned from the invasion of that island.   *Photo, Associated Press*

of an officer and eighteen men were concerned in a counter-attack in the Maleme direction. They killed over 140 Germans and took 27 prisoners, for which the officer apologized both to the Commander and myself. On the second day the platoon commander was wounded in three places ; on the second evening he made a rope sling to put over his left shoulder so that he could support his rifle on that, and he carried on with his platoon right through Crete, and some of the ammunition was taken out of him

after he got back to Egypt. That was typical of the sort of thing the men would do.

On one occasion thirty parachutists were dropped 250-300 yards away from one of my battalion headquarters. The Commanding Officer, the Regimental Sergeant-Major, the C.O.'s batman and three members of the Intelligence Section, armed with rifles, immediately " set sail " for the area where they had dropped. They had to go up one steep hill, down a steep gulley, and up on to the top of the other ridge where the parachutists were, but that party disposed completely of those thirty parachutists—the C.O. got eight and they did it at the cost of two casualties ; the R.S.M. was shot through the neck, but carried on right through the campaign. I tell you this because there has been an impression that parachutists are terribly difficult to deal with, and I think it is necessary that people should learn that if they do go for them and they can shoot, the parachutist when he comes down can be very quickly and effectively disposed of.

Full of Fight to the End

When the troops came off they came off in absolute cohesion and full of fight, in spite of the casualties they had suffered. Right at the finish of the afternoon one company was sent up a mountain to oppose an unexpected German attack round a flank and, although that company had been fighting for about eleven days, marching through Crete, and its feet were sore and it had not had much water for the last couple of days and very little rations—that company went up that mountain (which would take any of us two hours to climb in the ordinary way if we were going up it for fun) in half-an-hour, and did the job. The fighting troops did not come out of Crete in any beaten and cowed manner. The move-off was deliberate.

Then with reference to the suggestion that the bayonet is obsolete, I will give you an example of some bayonet work done in a certain village in Crete, the village of Galatas, near Canea, which was taken by the Germans after a concentrated dive-bombing blitz which rubbed out a great many of the defenders. Two companies of one of my battalions were put in in the dark ; they had not seen the village before ; they were put in one on each side of the road which curved about. The village was still full of stone houses and stone walls, and the Germans were armed with grenades. That village was retaken in twenty minutes solely by the bayonet, and you never heard such a row in your life as the screaming Germans made. I heard them. You could follow the progress of that attack right through by the shouting of our fellows and the yells of the Germans. The German soldier is well drilled to his task and he is physically fit, but he is not morally tough ; that is, the German soldier on the ground. He is not tough in comparison, and if he is gone for with determination he crumbles. Discipline and weapon-training are absolutely necessary for all troops who have to stand up to this full-scale air attack. Poorly-disciplined troops just disintegrate under it ; it gets them down. Those are very old lessons. Crete has just emphasized them again.

BAYONETS are not yet obsolete as effective weapons of war ; this was the conclusion reached by Brigadier Inglis. Here are some British soldiers, with fixed bayonets in a trench in Crete.   *Photo, British Official · Crown Copyright*

Russia and Germany Locked in Deadly Combat

Along a vast front of 1,800 miles the enormous masses of the German and Russian armies fought a furious struggle for supremacy. The Nazis were quick to claim that victory was shortly to be theirs, but as the battle went on they admitted that the Soviet resistance was stubborn and far heavier than had been anticipated.

O N the night of Sunday, June 22, the electric stars on the Kremlin ceased to shine for the first time for many years, and Moscow citizens realized that war with the hereditary Teuton enemy, so long postponed, had begun.

It was the city's first total black-out. Precautionary darkness, now so familiar in Western Europe, had been thrust by Hitler on the Soviet Republics. The people of Moscow were led to believe that a real raid was in progress overhead, but the droning in the sky was made by the high-flying Soviet machines, and the noise of exploding shells, the anti-aircraft defence firing with half-charges only. A.R.P. services functioned quickly and efficiently. Thousands of men and women civil-defenders took up their positions about the capital; wardens and firewatchers went to their posts. There was no sign of panic or fear, but everywhere a grim determination to face wounds and death rather than submit to the Nazi criminals.

Moscow radio warned workers of the need for carrying on, however violent the raids. Factories, railways and all other works must continue in spite of enemy bombs, it commanded.

1,800 Miles of Flaming War

Meanwhile, Hitler's colossal military machine was rolling east. Mechanized troops were flung across about 1,800 miles of frontier from the Baltic to the Black Sea in four great spearheads. In the north, advancing from East Prussia, with its flank on Memel, one struck through the Baltic states with Leningrad as its objective. The second

sector of the line extends south as far as Brest-Litovsk along the River Bug. It drove through the Baranovitch gap, north of the Pripet marshes, with Moscow as the goal. This was Napoleon's route in 1812.

The third is roughly from Przemysl to Czernovitch; it struck at Lwow north to Kiev, capital of the Ukraine. Then the fourth sector extends to Sulina, the Danube oil port, striking into southern Ukraine with Odessa as the target.

As the opposing armies came to grips, German and Russian aircraft ranged near and far with increasing ferocity, destroying tank formations and wreaking havoc in the cities behind the lines. Warsaw knew once again the horror of the exploding bomb as Red aircraft came over the ill-fated Polish city. Danzig, Koenigsberg, a shrine of Prussian barbarism, Lublin, and Constanza, the Rumanian oil-port, were heavily attacked. Nazi bombers, in their turn, dropped bombs on places as far apart as Tallinn on the Gulf of Finland, Sebastopol in the Crimea, and Kiev in Central Ukraine.

On June 24 the Russian official statement admitted that the Nazis had succeeded in penetrating the area of Bialystok, and had occupied Kolno, Lomza and Brest-Litovsk. In the course of violent fighting there, 5,000 Nazi prisoners had been taken and innumerable tanks destroyed. The corresponding German version of the fighting, while promising sensational victories, was confined to generalities, stating that the battle was going according to plan.

While assembling her war machine, Russia had to contend not only with Germany but with Nazified malcontents in Estonia; the Finns, her late enemy, said to be " defending " themselves; the Slovaks, who had declared for Hitler; the treacherous Rumanians; and the Swedes, whose " national independence " was reconciled with the passage of German troops across Swedish territory.

In the confusion of reports during the opening days one thing was absolutely clear. The Germans were not prepared for the stubborn resistance of the Russian troops, and the public were soon warned that the struggle with Russia would be no easy one.

Berlin radio, broadcasting a description of the fighting, admitted that the enemy were efficient, and had counter-attacked again and again,

Russian tanks appearing at times to come from all quarters and surrounding the advancing Nazis. On one occasion a Russian political commissar, barricading himself in a small farmhouse, held up single-handed a strong force of Germans for a considerable time. It was not until a detachment of Nazis stormed the place with hand grenades and

GERMAN ARMY LEADERS who are playing an important part in the Russian campaign. Left, Field Marshal List, blitzkrieg expert, commanding on the Rumanian front; centre, Gen. Von Reichenau, in command of the middle sector; right, Gen. Von Falkenhorst, leading the German armies in the northern sector.

Photos, Planet News and L.N.A.

dispatched this Russian stalwart that advance at this point could proceed.

A high level of courage would appear to be general throughout all branches of the Red Army, the Russian air force doing splendid feats of skill and endurance. Undeterred at times by superior numbers, many of the Soviet aviators attacked the Nazi planes and worsted them. Commander Sorokin, with only nine planes at his disposal, went into action against 15 of the enemy, bringing down six of them to four of the Russian. In the Stanislav area a Soviet unit destroyed 19 Nazi machines, and another aviation regiment lost only one machine to Germany's 13. The important fact thus emerges that the German High Command was dangerously optimistic in stating that the Nazis had gained mastery over the air.

On June 24 Moscow claimed that 76 enemy planes had been destroyed in the previous 24 hours, and that only in the north had the enemy made real headway. Employing the same tactics as they had used in France, separate groups of powerful tanks had broken through the Russian lines in the direction of the Polish-Lithuanian town of Vilna.

Hordes of Tanks in Action

Elsewhere, according to the Russian war communiqué issued by the Soviet Information Bureau on June 26, the Red Army was resisting the Nazi avalanche in immense battles between opposing tanks, and causing very heavy losses. In the Luck region, north of Lwow, the Russians had the advantage after twenty-four hours' continuous fighting. On the Bessarabian front they inflicted severe punishment on the Rumanians, stiffened by 40 German soldiers placed in each Rumanian regiment. Their many attempts to cross the River Pruth were beaten back, and the battle in this section may be said to have been a considerable victory for Russia.

Rumania, who hoped to keep out of the war by surrendering to Germany, now found herself driven to the slaughter, with Bucharest,

German soldier and Rumanian sailor on guard duty by the Black Sea. This photograph, from a neutral source, reached London a few days before Germany and Rumania marched against Russia.   *Photo, Keystone*

Fierce Fighting from Baltic to Black Sea

THE EASTERN FRONT showing the German lines of attack through the Baltic States towards Leningrad ; through the Baranovitch gap with Smolensk and Moscow as its objectives ; from Southern Poland in the direction of Kiev ; and from Rumania into the Southern Ukraine and Odessa.

Specially drawn for THE WAR ILLUSTRATED *by Felix Gardon*

Constanza, and the Ploesti oil plants fired by Russian incendiaries ; and to add to the vast confusion and terror innumerable Russian parachutists were landing behind the enemy lines.

On June 29 Hitler enjoyed a field day of "victory communiqués," but it is doubtful whether the German people, promised peace for so long but involved in more and more war, enjoyed them. The victory was still elusive. Two Russian armies were said to be encircled in the sector east of Bialystok, two hundred miles west of Minsk, and "in a few days would be forced to capitulate or be annihilated." It seemed that, although Minsk had not fallen, the town had been by-passed, and the Germans had reached the motor-road to Moscow. They were supposed to be within 500 miles of the Soviet capital.

According to Hitler, "the German air force delivered a crushing blow at the Russian air force. In air battles and anti-aircraft fire on land, 4,107 Russian planes had been destroyed. In contrast to these losses are the comparatively moderate German losses of 150 planes." The Nazis also claimed that 2,233 Russian tanks had been destroyed or captured.

'Manifest Lies and Humbug'

On June 30 the Soviet High Command replied to the German communiqué in vigorous and uncompromising language, as follows. "Hitler's victory claim is a manifest lie and humbug," it roundly declared. Here are some further extracts : "In spite of reinforcements by fresh tank units, all attempts by the enemy to penetrate in the direction of Novograd-Volynsk and Shepetovka were not only repelled, but our tank units and aircraft succeeded through a series of consecutive attacks in annihilating a great part of the enemy tank units and motorized troops."

Here is the Russian version of German losses. "As a result of stubborn and fierce fighting during the period of seven or eight days, the Germans lost no fewer than 2,500 tanks, about 1,500 airplanes, and over 30,000 prisoners of war. During the same period we lost 850 planes, up to 900 tanks, and 15,000 men missing or taken prisoner. The lightning victory which the German Command had expected has failed. Such is the real situation at the front."

It is, at least, clear that the Nazis tried to counter the disappointment of the German people by the old trick of exaggerating the enemy's losses and minimizing their own. All attempts to penetrate Russian territory proper would appear to have been frustrated. The Blitzkrieg was halted by terrific resistance and counter-attacks all the way from Brest-Litovsk to the Black Sea, and particularly in the Ukraine, Hitler's chief objective in the invasion of Russia. Here the Nazis employed their crack Panzer corps in an effort to break through to Kiev and Odessa. On June 29 the Ukraine front remained intact.

The first week of the Russo-German war proved several things of great importance in what is now almost a world-combine against Nazism. The Russians were fighting with indomitable heroism and patriotic zeal, they had an abundance of machines—tanks, planes and all other weapons of modern war, and they were determined to fight Prussian megalomania to the last.

There can be little doubt that Russia was better equipped for war than she was under the Czarist regime, and had not been beguiled by Hitler's "friendship" pacts into neglect of military precautions. Then it may be mentioned that, while her men were fighting and preparing to fight, 30,000,000 women rushed to defend the Fatherland in various wartime occupations.

Under Their Leadership Russia Went to War

MARSHAL TIMOSHENKO, who replaced Marshal Voroshilov as Soviet Commissar for Defence in May 1940, was previously commander of the Kiev special military area. He is seen, right, addressing officers and men of the Soviet army.

Marshal Klim **VORO-SHILOV,** below, was in 1940 appointed Chairman of Council for the Coordination of Defence, after having held the post of Commissar for Defence since 1925.

STALIN ("man of steel")—his real name is Joseph Vissarionovich Jugashvili —Premier and Dictator of Soviet Russia (centre).

Right, Marshal S. **BUDENNY,** a cavalryman and former N.C.O. in the Tsar's army, is First Deputy People's Commissar for Defence.

Below, Admiral N. **KUZNETSOV,** Chief Commissar for Soviet Naval Affairs, is at 39 the youngest commander-in-chief of any navy.

Lieutenant-General of Aviation Pavel Vasilievich RICHAGOV, above, is the leader of the Soviet Air Force. He bears the title of Hero of the Soviet Union.

Photos, Planet News and Wide World

Their Fathers Were Our Allies • The Sons Are

THE RED ARMY, according to Moscow figures given in 1938, has an effective strength of nearly 2,000,000, with something like 13,000,000 reserves, since some 800,000 men are called up for training every year. Its mechanized strength is not known, for after the Russo-Finnish war large-scale reorganization was effected. The whole of the vast territory of the U.S.S.R. is divided for military purposes into ten military districts. Much of the Soviet war material is good, but the question of maintenance and supply has yet to be answered. Below, Red Army troops on parade in front of the Kremlin. Right, Russian tanks on the move.

THE SOVIET N
It was announced
constructed and co
tains three old
refitted. A 35,000
laid down in Ju
have been laid
cruisers, some of
to possess a cons
marines. Belo

Our Comrades-in-Arms Against the Common Foe

ely an unknown quantity.
war that it would be re-
gthened by 1942-43. It con-
pleted 1914-15 and since
Tretii International, was
others are reported to
are probably seven old
refitted. Russia is said
of destroyers and sub-
oyers in the Black Sea.

RUSSIA'S AIR FORCE, like her other services, has
been built up in great secrecy. It is thought that
she has about 10,000 service aircraft available, with a
front-line strength of about half that total. There
is also a naval air arm, and an independent force
whose function is to defend important industrial
centres. Russia has also great numbers of trained
parachute troops. The performance of Russian planes,
to judge by the Finnish war, leaves much to be desired,
especially in the matter of speed. But new types
may have been produced since then. Above, a mass
parachute descent from Russian planes.

Vichy Troops Hard Pressed in Syria

With the fall of Damascus the progress of the Allies in Syria became more rapid, and the following week saw an advance of over fifty miles beyond the city to the north. Then, by the recapture of the key-town of Merj Iyoun in the central sector of the Syrian-Lebanese fronts, the coastal forces were enabled to continue their advance towards the important port of Beirut.

IT was Colonel Collet of the Free French Forces, accompanied by members of his staff, who made the first formal entry into Damascus pending the official entry of General Legentilhomme. Entry to the city was made without opposition, though up to the last minute Moroccan troops fought a desperate rearguard action in the suburb of Maidan.

Preceded by a British armoured car, Colonel Collet and his delegation made their way through Kadim, where a small action had been fought in the early hours of the morning, and entered the city by way of the suburb of Maidan. The small procession drove through the city, across the " Margi " or central square, and over to the Grand Serai on the right bank of the river Barada. On the first floor of this building, which corresponds to our City Hall, Colonel Collet was given an official reception by the Chief of State, Khaled Azm Bey, who was there with the entire Syrian Cabinet.

The Khaled related to those in the entourage of Colonel Collet how his government had for some time past pressed General Dentz, the Vichy High Commissioner, to declare Damascus an open city and spare it the horrors of war. This Dentz had refused to do, saying he would defend the city to the last street and the last house.

But the Allied forces were less ruthless than General Dentz. They spared the city as much as possible, and very little damage to property or loss of civilian life was reported. The civil losses were two people killed and eight wounded. Only one mosque was hit by our fire, and that was not badly damaged. But if we had been scrupulous in avoiding all unnecessary damage to this venerable city, such was not the case with the Germans, who, after we had occupied the town, raided it from the air, causing a large number of civilian casualties.

The first step towards Syrian independence, which had been promised by the Allies, was the severing of all ties with Vichy by the Syrian National Government in Damascus and the declaration of a general amnesty.

Meanwhile, fighting continued in other parts of Syria, one of the most stubborn actions of the campaign being that which centred around Merj Iyoun, a strongpoint of Vichy resistance which, after its initial capture by the Allies, had been retaken by Vichy troops. Imperial and British reinforcements were brought up and, after a hard struggle in which Australian forces again distinguished themselves, the town and important positions in that sector were recaptured. A correspondent with the A.I.F. has described the attack upon this town

as the climax of a heavy test of endurance to which the whole battalion was subjected.

." The men," he reported, " were secretly sent to a point from which they made a final dash towards the town through country which an officer, who is a veteran of the last war, described as ' tough as the cliffs of Gallipoli.' The distance was only three miles in a direct line, but the tortuous trail ' across stony ridges and gullies increased this to at least six miles. The men also had to ford the Litani river at a point where it is from 60 to 70 feet wide, wading against a current that was running at a speed of about five knots."

The Australian gunners, he said, were " proving themselves up to the hilt " in this campaign, and English Bofors gunners had also done extremely well. One Bofors section is said to have knocked out twelve Vichy tanks in the Merj Iyoun sector, and in one single bout of firing it destroyed two tanks and brought down one aircraft in twenty minutes.

Hard Struggle for Merj Iyoun

Merj Iyoun fell to the Australians' on June 24, after four days of bitter fighting, during which both sides suffered considerable casualties. Its recapture was of great importance to the Allies, since it secured a lateral road joining the coastal road about four miles south of Sidon, thus enabling the coastal forces to push onwards towards Beirut. A Victorian pioneer battalion, which, acting as infantry for the occasion, played a great part in the fighting for Merj Iyoun, had the honour of being the first to enter the town. They found the fort had been abandoned during the night, and they fought their way across the town, clearing up machine-gun posts and snipers left to cover the Vichy troops' withdrawal.

An Australian mechanized unit, too, did good work around Merj Iyoun, resorting for the time being to their old-time status of cavalrymen. They found that in the rocky country around Merj Iyoun their armoured vehicles could not operate satisfactorily, so they captured a number of horses from Spahis, mounted a detachment of cavalrymen and covered the flank of the advance.

So, while Allied troops were advancing northwards beyond Damascus, covering the fifty miles which lay between that city and Nebk in about five days, a further advance could be made by Australian troops along the coast road leading to Beirut, which was constantly bombarded from off shore by our naval forces. The coastal road is hemmed in by steep escarpments, allowing no room for deployment, and between Sidon and Beirut Vichy troops stood entrenched along the Damur river. But the moving forward of artillery to cooperate with the Navy in shelling these defences made the Vichy position precarious. On June 27 the Allies reached Saaydiye and Es Sayer, nine miles north of Sidon.

From the east, British troops advancing from Iraq reached Palmyra, 150 miles north-east of Damascus, and there encountered stiff resistance from a Vichy column. At Palmyra is an important aerodrome which, before the Syrian campaign opened, was being made use of by the Germans. The advance upon Palmyra has been made by two columns, one of which made contact with the Vichy troops about June 22, the other being close at hand. On the long route from Iraq these columns had been attacked at frequent intervals by hostile aircraft which delayed their progress. Saba Biyar, 60 miles south-west of Palmyra, was captured by British troops about June 28, and though the garrison at Palmyra still held out they were threatened from the east and south-west, and finally encircled.

PALMYRA, attacked by Allied forces advancing from Iraq, has a long history. It reached the height of its glory in the 3rd century under the famous Zenobia, Queen of Palmyra, and of its Graeco-Roman culture these ruins of the Temple of the Sun still bear witness.
Photo, Mrs. T. Muir

General de Gaulle's Men on the Syrian Front

FREE FRENCH FORCES of General de Gaulle have had their first big chance in the Syrian campaign, though their duty, which compels them to fight against their own countrymen, is an unpleasant one. Just before the advance into Syria Colonel Collet, founder of the famous Circassian squadron and an almost legendary figure to the troops in Syria, crossed the border into Palestine with many of his troops to join General de Gaulle's forces. 1, Some of the Circassian cavalry who came with him. These tough riders, who are mostly white Moslems originating from the Ukraine, wear the regimental sign seen (2) on one of their vehicles and on the shirt of the bearded driver. 3, Light tanks belonging to General de Gaulle's forces photographed in Palestine as they were preparing for the advance into Syria. 4, More Free French troops in Palestine on the eve of the Syrian campaign.

Photos, 1 and 2, British Official; 3 and 4, British Paramount News

Our Diary of the War

SUNDAY, JUNE 22, 1941 659th day

Air.—R.A.F. fighters and bombers made daylight raid on Northern France. Thirty enemy fighters destroyed for loss of two.

Bremen and Wilhelmshaven main targets of night raids. Others were Emden, Bremerhaven and Düsseldorf.

Russian Front.—Germany invaded Russia from East Prussia, Poland and Rumania. Simultaneously Luftwaffe bombed Soviet towns and airfields, including Kiev, Sevastopol and Kaunas.

Africa.—R.A.F. bombers attacked convoy off Libya, damaging one big ship. Night raid on Benghazi.

Near East.—Enemy shipping at Beirut attacked by R.A.F.; destroyer received direct hit and freighter was set on fire.

MONDAY, JUNE 23 660th day

Air.—R.A.F. made two sweeps over Northern France, destroying at least 19 enemy fighters for loss of three fighters and two bombers. Industrial plant near Bethune and many railway targets hit.

Strong forces raided Cologne, Düsseldorf and Kiel at night. Smaller attacks on Wilhelmshaven, Emden and Hanover.

Russian Front.—Soviet High Command claimed to have repulsed invaders at most points. In Polish sector Germans took Kolno, Lomza and Grodno.

Near East.—Cairo announced that Allied forces were in contact with Vichy troops west of Damascus; also that British had reached Palmyra, on oil pipe-line, where Vichy troops were resisting.

Imperial aircraft attacked many aerodromes at Baalbek, Talia, Rayak and Quseir.

Enemy raid on Alexandria, causing many casualties. R.A.F. attacked flying-boats in Syracuse harbour.

Home.—Two raiders destroyed, one by H.M. trawler Solon.

TUESDAY, JUNE 24 661st day

Sea.—Admiralty announced that 20,000-ton Italian liner had been torpedoed by British submarine in Mediterranean, and enemy supply ship sunk. Off Syrian coast naval aircraft sank Vichy destroyer, and our warships damaged two others.

Air.—Nine enemy fighters destroyed by R.A.F. during sweep over Northern France. Heavy night attacks on Cologne, Düsseldorf and Kiel.

Russian Front.—Germans occupied Brest-Litovsk, Kaunas and Vilna.

Africa.—Heavy raids during night of 23-24 on Benghazi and Tripoli.

Near East.—Palmyra under siege by Allied forces. British troops reoccupied Merj Iyoun. Australian troops in coastal sector made further advance.

R.A.F. bombed railway and aerodrome at Rayak, and citadel at Soueida. Fleet Air Arm attacked destroyers in Beirut harbour.

Home.—Night raiders over Merseyside. Four shot down.

WEDNESDAY, JUNE 25 662nd day

Sea.—Reported that Fleet Air Arm had sunk German sea raider Elbe.

Heinkel shot down by convoy A.A. fire.

Air.—Two R.A.F. sweeps over Northern France. Munition train blown up in Hazebrouck goods yard. Thirteen Nazi fighters destroyed; six British aircraft missing. Kiel, Bremen and Boulogne bombed at night.

Russian Front.—Having crossed R. Pruth and taken Bolgrad, in Bessarabia, German and Rumanian army held up by Soviet resistance. Intense air activity in south.

Russian aircraft bombed Turku, Lahti and Malmi airfield near Helsinki. Russian artillery shelled region west of Hango.

Africa.—British troops at Tobruk made further penetration into enemy salient in outer defences.

R.A.F. attacked shipping at Benghazi and landing-grounds at Gazala.

Near East.—Damascus bombed by Axis aircraft. Haifa and Acre also raided.

Home.—Two night raiders destroyed.

THURSDAY, JUNE 26 663rd day

Sea.—Reported that Dutch submarine had sunk two enemy supply ships.

Fleet Air Arm attacked Axis convoy off southern Italy, hitting three 20,000-ton ships.

Air.—During sweep over Channel and Northern France, R.A.F. shot down nine fighters. Main night attack directed against Kiel. Cologne and Düsseldorf also raided.

Russian Front.—Fierce tank battles near Minsk, White Russia, and in direction of Luck. Germans crossed R. Dvina, in Latvia, and captured Dvinsk.

In Bessarabia Russian stand was maintained and attacks on Cernauti repulsed.

Russians bombed Bucharest and Ploesti, and points in Hungary and Finland.

British advancing on Jimma, Abyssinia, occupied Dembi.

Near East.—Despite increased resistance, British troops made substantial gains west of Damascus.

FRIDAY, JUNE 27 664th day

Sea.—Announced that H.M. sloop Grimsby had been sunk.

Air.—Further R.A.F. sweeps over Channel and Northern France. Air-fields, troops and gun posts machine-gunned. Ship sunk off Dunkirk. Steel works near Lille bombed. Seven fighters destroyed. We lost 10 fighters.

Powerful night attack on Bremen and other targets, including Emden, Cuxhaven and Dunkirk. Twelve British bombers missing.

Russian Front.—Russians retiring to new positions in direction of Siauliai (Lithuania) and Baranowicze. Heavy fighting in Luck area, Poland.

Near East.—Allied forces closing in on Palmyra. Free French forces occupied Maaraba, north of Damascus.

Seven Italian fighters destroyed over Malta.

SATURDAY, JUNE 28 665th day

Air.—R.A.F. attacked power station at Comines, near Lille. Five fighters destroyed during sweeps over Northern France.

At night German convoy off Ameland was attacked.

Russian Front.—In northern sector Russians fought stubborn rearguard action. Heavy fighting in Minsk area. Large-scale tank battle raging in Luck area and intensive fighting in Lwow district.

In southern sector Russians claimed to be still holding frontier between Przemysl to Black Sea, having driven back troops who crossed R. Pruth.

Africa.—Benghazi and Tripoli heavily raided on night of 27-28.

Near East.—Allied forces occupied Nebec, between Damascus and Homs, and Saba Biyar, 60 miles S.W. of Palmyra.

S.S. ST. PATRICK, cross-channel steamer plying between Rosslare and Fishguard, which was dive-bombed and sunk by enemy aircraft on June 13, 1941. There were 66 survivors out of 89 on board, and the experiences of some of them are given below.
        Photo, Topical Press

WHEN the G.W.R. cross-channel steamer, St. Patrick (1,922 tons), was bombed in the early hours of June 13, the passengers were asleep. The vessel broke in two and there was no time to lower boats; the passengers, women and children included, rushed from their bunks and threw themselves into the water, where men searched for them in the heavy sea and dragged many on to rafts. All the women and children passengers are believed to have been rescued. One of the heroes of the St. Patrick was Jack Faraday, son of the master of the ship, Captain James Faraday. He was on leave from the Navy. When the ship began to go down Jack Faraday swam to a raft. Then realizing that his father was still on board he swam back once more to the sinking ship, unaware that Captain Faraday had been killed by the bomb as he stood on the bridge. The St. Patrick sank while the son was still searching for his father, and he was not seen again.

A stewardess, Miss Owen, told a "Daily Herald" reporter:

"Immediately the alarm sounded I began running round helping them to get their lifebelts on, and when the bomb struck most of them were up and ready.

"Amid all the terrible din my charges kept discipline and soon we were all on deck, waiting for the end.

"It came suddenly, the ship just breaking in halves and plunging to the bottom.

"One woman, in the excitement, lost her life jacket, and she clung to me, My lifebelt kept us both afloat until we were able to climb on a raft.

"Altogether, I and the woman without a lifejacket were two hours drifting about in the sea before we got on a raft."

The Army *Has* Its Own Planes Already

DURING the debate on the defence of Crete in the House of Commons on June 10, many criticisms were directed against the alleged lack of cooperation between the Army and the Royal Air Force. Mr. Churchill in his reply promised that there would be a much greater development of such cooperation in the future, although he did not concur in the view that the Army should have its own Air Arm in the same way as the Navy has the Fleet Air Arm. The standard British Army Cooperation plane is the Westland Lysander, shown in this page. It is used for photography, artillery spotting, communications and general reconnaissance work, and is the British counterpart of the German Henschel 126, to which it bears a superficial resemblance.

Left, a twin Browning machine-gun in the rear cockpit of a Lysander. Two fixed forward-firing guns are also mounted, one in each wheel fairing. Above, a container with food and supplies for a party of stranded troops is being fitted to the stub wing of a Lysander. Note the hinged window for landing lamp in the nose of the wheel fairing.

THE WESTLAND LYSANDER is a two-seater monoplane designed throughout for co-operation with an army in the field. It needs a comparatively small take-off run and so can operate from small flying fields. Although it has a speed of about 230 m.p.h., it can fly with full load as slowly as 55 m.p.h. It is one of the most easily recognizable of British aircraft on account of the prominent spatted undercarriage. Above the wheel spats in this photograph can be seen the detachable stub wings used for carrying light bombs or special equipment. Messages can be collected by means of a retractable hook.

Photos, Chas. E. Brown, Keystone and Sport & General

Learning to Win the War in the Workshops

Without the effort of the workers on the home front the daring and skill of our soldiers, sailors and airmen will be brought to nought by the lack of equipment. More "hands" are wanted for the workshops, and here our Special Representative passes on some of the information he received in a visit to a Government Training Centre where men and women are trained to take their places at the bench.

THERE are nearly 1,500 men and women here in this great workshop, or rather, series of workshops. They are of all ages from 18 to 60, and there may be one or two who are 60-plus. They have come from all walks of life. Some are artisans, skilled engineers who were thrown on the scrap heap in the years of depression, but who are now finding that the country needs their labour and their skill. Some used to belong to the white collar brigade, others tapped the keys of typewriters. Some have come from the country, and others have spent their lives in the crowded towns. Mostly they are British, but there is a large sprinkling of friendly aliens—French and Belgians, Poles and Czechs, Dutch and Germans. There's no petty discrimination here; if a man or woman is willing to work—to learn how to work—then they are all welcome. And there is no colour bar, as is evidenced by the presence of that strapping young negro at the bench over there.

This is one of the Government Training Centres which have been set up in London. It

and sheet metal working, electric and oxy-acetylene welding, draughtsmanship, electrical installation, and inspecting and viewing. Not all of these are taught at all the centres, and in certain areas other more specialized trades are taught in addition. The courses are of varying lengths, but most of them range from three to six month. Thus the fitter's course takes 14 weeks, and the instrument maker's 24 weeks; the course in draughtsmanship requires nine months—not surprising when one remembers the advanced mathematics and the high degree of skill involved.

The instructors are selected most carefully from men who are not only masters of their particular trades but have also got the knack of showing the novice how to get over his difficulties in learning it. On an average an instructor receives about £7 a week, and in these days they could probably earn very much more outside. The trainee learns as he goes, and the instructor is always there to answer questions; a frequent sight is a little knot of men and women trainees gathered

about the instructor who is explaining carefully and with the utmost patience the intricacies of a particular job. Very different, indeed, is this method of training from that which produced most of our engineers. "In my young days," says one instructor, "I was apprenticed for seven years to my trade; the first year we swept out the workshops, and for the rest we were left to pick up our knowledge the best way we could. If we asked a question we got our ears cuffed."

While learning, not only do the trainees get first-class tuition, but they are paid. The men trainees, aged 21 and over, receive 60s. 6d. per week; youths of 20 receive 39s. 6d., and those of 19, 34s. 6d. Women of 21 and over receive 38s. a week, while those aged 20 and 19 are paid 36s. 6d. and 35s. respectively. Men and women trainees living in lodgings away from home, if they continue to maintain a home in the district from which they have come, may receive a lodging allowance of 3s. 6d. a night. They may obtain meals, cheap and substantial, from the canteens established in the works.

Boys and girls aged 18 and under are not paid but are given an allowance. Boys of 18 receive 23s. a week, and girls 21s., while boys aged 16 and 17 receive 17s., and girls in the same age group 15s. If they are living away from home they receive a lodging allowance. They are also given a free midday meal.

During the course each trainee is required to undergo three tests; if they fail in any one of the three, then they are put back for further tuition, or in rare cases are refused further training. On passing each test the trainee, if he is a man, receives an increase of 5s. per week. If the trainee is a woman, however, she receives only 3s. a week. These differentiations in the pay of men and women are all the more surprising and all the more unjustifiable when it is realized that in the Centre, and as often as not in industry, men and women do exactly the same work.

is one of about 40 centres which are now in operation in most of the principal areas of industrial Britain. A few of the centres are restricted to the training of serving soldiers and a few are for men only, but the great majority accept both men and women trainees. They have been established by the Ministry of Labour and National Service to meet the urgent demand for skilled men and women for armament works and munition factories. So great is the demand and so urgent that it is necessary that many people not ordinarily engaged in war industries—many indeed who have never been engaged in industry at all—should fit themselves for this vital work. The jobs are there for those who have the skill, and these Training Centres have been set up so that as many people as possible shall obtain that skill.

The trades taught are fitting, machine operating, instrument making, panel beating

GOVERNMENT TRAINEES are seen in these photographs receiving instruction in their new jobs. They are so efficiently trained that in a short time they are well on the way to become skilled workers. Top left, a busy scene in the general fittingshop at a Ministry of Labour centre in the Midlands Above, girls attending a lecture on the use of measuring instruments.
Photos, Topical and Press Portrait Bureau

Yes, They 'Went to It'—the Derby—With a Will!

BRITAIN is at bay, fighting for her very life. She is struggling against a power which, already possessed of a mighty and. ruthless war machine, has the resources and slave-power of a continent at its command.

We need still more guns, still more tanks, still more planes, still more ships, if we are not to be defeated. Every day every man, every woman, every child if need be, should be working without respite to forge the weapons which alone will preserve us from domination and ruin. Yet, such is the selfishness of the few who cannot for one brief moment of their lives give up their "circuses," there are staged such scenes as those shown here—scenes which give some substance to the Nazi taunts against the "effete democracies."

PONDER well the top photograph. The owners of all these cars have used precious petrol to go to "the Derby." Look at the congestion on the roads (centre) and ask what would have happened if the military had suddenly to make use of them? Well, the answer is seen right, where a column of lorry-drawn tanks is held up. Centre right, R.A.F. Security Police are testing the petrol in the tank of a car driven to the Derby by an R.A.F. officer. Those who use Government petrol for pleasure trips are likely to have trouble.

Photos; Keystone, Topical, G.P.U. and Associated Press

They Have Won Honours in Freedom's Cause

Order of the British Empire

Capt. D. E. Rees, of the Merchant Navy, **O.B.E.** He has been torpedoed since this award.

Capt. W. W. Watson, of Wallasey, **O.B.E.,** for outstanding bravery on war service.

Petty Officer Michael Payton, M.B.E., for carrying out his duties with exemplary courage.

3rd Engr. W. Walker, of Grimsby, **M.B.E.,** for heroic work in engine-room of a torpedoed ship.

British Empire Medal

Flt.-Lt. J. E. McFall, D.F.C., for splendid reconnaissance work in the Libya fighting.

A. Cdr. L. H. Slatter, O.B.E., D.S.O., D.F.C., the **C.B.,** for distinguished services in East Africa.

Flying Officer C. H. Upton, D.F.C., for destroying more than nine enemy aircraft.

Flying Officer G. K. Larney, of No. 75 (New Zealand) Squadn., **D.F.C.,** for devotion to duty.

Flying Officer A. F. Weller, D.F.C., for bombing enemy planes and aerodrome at Benina.

Sergt.-Observer P. Hudson, D.F.M., for great skill in raiding enemy territory.

Flying Officer J. Cook, D.F.C., for conspicuous bravery in the Battle of Britain last September.

Pilot-Officer O. E. Wiltshear, D.F.C., for 26 trips over enemy territory as a rear-gunner.

Pilot-Officer C. R. Brown, D.F.C. for skill and courage in bombing military objectives.

Flying Officer W. D. B. Ruth, D.F.C., for gallantry displayed in flying operations against enemy.

Flying Officer M. H. Young, of Gloucester, **D.F.C.,** for outstanding devotion to duty.

Flying Officer G. E. Weston, of New Zealand, **D.F.C.,** for bombing a vessel in dock at Brest.

Dr. M. Manson, of Wood Green, **G.M.,** for saving the lives of people trapped in a tunnel.

Nurse M. E. Perkins, G.M., for heroic devotion to duty during a heavy raid on Coventry.

Nurse M. S. J. Newman, G.M., for great courage and skill during a raid on Southampton.

Nurse V. Howell, B.E.M., for coolness and presence of mind in rescuing a patient at Hendon.

F. D. Murphy, M.B., B.Ch., of Fulham Hospital, **O.B.E.,** for great ability and courage in a raid.

Dr. M. Kamill, of Clayponds Emergency Hospital, **G.M.,** for outstanding devotion to duty.

Mr. H. Sweetland, G.M., for saving a man injured in a raid at Deptford, though hurt himself.

Mr. Alfred Hobdell, L.M.S. employee, **B.E.M.,** for rescuing horses from burning stable.

Mr. Henry Hobdell, Alfred's father, **B.E.M.,** for gallantry during the same incident.

Mr. Arthur Paxton, who assisted the Hobdells, **B.E.M.,** for great courage and presence of mind.

Mr. J. Reynolds, A.R.P., **B.E.M.,** for rescuing six people from a bombed building in the Midlands.

Mr. S. Stillwell, A.F.S. messenger, **M.B.E.,** for devotion to duty in a London raid.

Distinguished Service Cross

Lieut. H. R. B. Janvrin, R.N., **D.S.C.,** for his part in the attack on the Italian Fleet at Taranto.

Fred Rusby, of Harwich, **D.S.M.,** for operating ship's gun against Nazi aircraft at Dunkirk.

Capt. W. H. Dawson, M.B.E., for gallantry and devotion to duty in the course of naval operations.

Lieut. H. B. Gordon, M.B.E., for showing great skill and courage in the course of his war duties.

Distinguished Service Medal

I Was There! .... Eye Witness Stories of the War

The Havoc Helped Us to Square the Account

Among the planes in use by night fighter pilots of the R.A.F. is the Havoc—an American-produced aircraft which, as the following story shows, has found high favour with our airmen.

A FLYING OFFICER broadcasting in May said :

One night recently I was cruising around in an American Douglas Boston 7— we call it the Havoc over here—in the neighbourhood of Brussels, watching a Nazi bomber we had just shot down blazing like a bonfire in a wood to the north of the city.

The bomber was a Heinkel 111 which was just returning from a raid on England, and though the Heinkel's a pretty good aeroplane, it is no match for the Havoc. My squadron is now fully equipped with Havocs and we like them immensely. They're nice to handle, easy to land at night, their performance is well up to anything the Hun is putting over at night, and we have implicit faith in their Wasp engines.

As one of my ground crew put it the other day : " If the Havoc is a fair sample of the tools America is sending us we ought to be able to make a fair job of this war when we get the complete set." Certainly, on behalf of my squadron, I'd like to thank Americans for sending us such first-rate aircraft and engines.

The night in question is a sample of the good work we're doing with them. Our objective was a Nazi aerodrome near Brussels, and soon after we had identified it the flare-path and obstruction lights were switched on and we saw one enemy bomber coming in to land with its navigation lights. I don't know whether the reception the pilot had had by the English defences had shaken his nerves, but he certainly made a mess of his approach, overshot badly and had to open up to go round again.

We thought we might help him down, so I closed in on him and our first two bursts of gunfire set one of his engines on fire. As he was going to land he wouldn't have wanted it anyway. The flames lit up the whole machine and enabled us to identify it as a Heinkel 111.

We then came round again and my rear gunner got in three good bursts which settled the job. I think the pilot must have intended climbing so that his crew could bale out, because we lost sight of him for a few moments, and when next we saw him it was as a glow of fire moving across the sky above us. Then, quite suddenly the blazing plane went streaking down, and crashed into a wood with a terrific explosion. The fire it started was seen by another pilot to be still burning half an hour later.

I don't know what damage that particular Heinkel had done in its attack on England that night, but that Havoc helped to square the account, and my crew will be very disappointed if it doesn't enable us to square a good many more.

Trying out the guns on a D.B.-7 night-fighter in preparation for raiders. This American all-metal, high-wing monoplane, which has a retractable tricycle undercarriage, also carries a light bomb load.

I Had a Shock When the 'Evacuees' Arrived

Many and varied are the experiences of recruits to the Women's Land Army when they are still ignorant of the technique and terminology of farming. This amusing little sketch by Joan Procter was contributed to " The Land Girl."

IMAGINE, if you can, the feelings of a raw Land Army recruit, fresh from the ordered routine of a Whitehall Government office, when the farmer said one evening : " I want you to meet Charlie at the gate at 6.30 tomorrow morning and cycle down to K——— station to meet 201 evacuees off the 7 o'clock train and bring them back here."

I decided to retire early that night, but was rudely awakened at 1 a.m. by the wail of the village air-raid sirens.

Immediately my thoughts flew to those miserable refugees who were travelling all night ; who, exactly, could they be ? Why 201 ? Would they all have luggage of sorts ? What language would they speak ? The drone of approaching aeroplanes was heard, and I had visions of my prospective charges being subjected at that very moment to merciless Nazi bombing attacks before they had tasted the beauties of this delightful corner of rural England, where I had the luck to be training. . . . But long before the All Clear sounded at 4.30 a.m. I had drifted into a dreamless sleep, and awakened at 6 a.m. refreshed and elated by the prospect of my unusual task on such a brilliant spring morning.

Charlie, the lanky, red-faced foreman, arrived at the gate punctually at 6.30 a.m., and we pedalled off together to the country station, three miles away, at the foot of the hill. I chattered gaily about the welfare of the approaching evacuees, but Charlie, having been on A.R.P. duty in a cramped emplacement beneath a cold moon for 4½ hours, took some time to warm up to the subject, and rather gave the impression that he had very little sympathy with Government evacuation schemes, and would not be unduly agitated if our evacuees had been subjected to the most ruthless bombing attacks *en route.* The journey was finished in silence and, of course, the train had not yet arrived, nor had the morning papers.

Last-minute ideas flashed through my mind. Could Charlie and I, with the aid of two bicycles, possibly cope with a crowd of 201 hungry strangers of all ages, and escort them on foot three uphill miles to the farm ?

Silhouetted against the dawning sky, a Havoc night-fighter on its way back to the base after scattering German raiders. Havoc is the R.A.F.'s name for the powerful U.S. machine called the D.B.-7. With twin-Wasp engines and easy manipulation the Havoc is proving popular with the R.A.F. ; as one of our flying-officers relates here, it is among the best American tools which our men are handling with ever-increasing effect.   *Photos, Keystone*

A LAND GIRL tells here how she went to deal with a sudden incursion of " evacuees." The photograph shows some of her comrades tackling more recalcitrant arrivals. *Photo, Fox*

Would they angrily demand food before attempting the journey, or would they be too weary to argue ?

Suddenly a puffing sound was heard round the bend into the station, the porters shouted " Here she comes ! " and Charlie and I

crossed the line to the receiving quarters. The train performed elaborate shunting manoeuvres, the doors were opened, and out poured 201 of the noisiest, skinniest, and most pathetically eager sheep that I have ever seen !

•

We Were in the First Sea-Air Battle in History

On May 22 hundreds of German bombers attacked the British Mediterranean Fleet off Crete, sinking two cruisers—Gloucester and Fiji—and four destroyers—Juno, Greyhound, Kelly and Kashmir. Here are eye-witness accounts of the battle by officers on board British warships.

DURING the night of May 21 reconnaissance reports indicated an attempt at a seaborne invasion of Crete had started, and it was this convoy of caiques which was completely broken up (see page 622).

Meanwhile other units continued at dawn to search northwards towards the island of Milo, in the west of the Cyclades group.

An officer who was on board one of these units gave this description of what happened :

The enemy began dive-bombing soon after dawn on May 22. At about 8.30 a.m. we sighted a caique, which we moved off to sink, but we became so heavily engaged by aircraft that we were only able to immobilize her by pom-pom fire and signalled a cruiser astern to finish her off.

The cruiser thus occupied got left astern, and received such concentrated attacks that we were compelled to return to her assistance. This enabled her to catch up with the remainder of the fleet, but drew all the attention of the aircraft to ourselves, and we were

attacked continually for two hours, from 9.40 a.m. until 11.40 a.m., by high and low dive-bombing.

Our guns were firing red-hot trying to shoot down the dive-bombers, and we had to change course almost constantly and swing our armament around to meet the simultaneous high-level attacks. Splinters fell about us like hailstones, tearing gaps in the super-structure, and near misses from heavy

bombs gave us a terrific shaking. One seaman counted the number of bombs aimed at us—186 in two hours.

Meanwhile, our heavy units patrolling the Ionian Sea entered the Kithera Straits (between Crete and the southern mainland of Greece) in order to support the hard-pressed light units, and further heavy bombing followed for the rest of the day by Dorniers, Heinkels, Junkers, and even specially converted Messerschmitt fighters.

Around 1.30 p.m. the destroyer Greyhound, which got astern, was sunk by concentrated dive-bombing. Two destroyers were sent back to pick up survivors from the Greyhound while two cruisers, the Gloucester and the Fiji, lent aircraft support. The Gloucester then received direct hits and sank at about 4 p.m. Shortly afterwards the Fiji, heroically endeavouring to stave off repeated unhampered air attacks, was likewise sunk.

During that night we returned to our base, and it was then that we heard that the destroyers Kelly and Kashmir had also been dive-bombed and sunk after bombarding Maleme aerodrome and searching for survivors from the Fiji. Another destroyer, the Kimberley (1,690 tons) did great work picking up about 250 survivors with whom she made port after a tremendous hammering from the air.

An officer in one of the battleships said that the air attack on May 22 was " probably the biggest of the war." He went on : From 1.30 p.m. until six o'clock there were hundreds of German planes over us. We were firing almost continuously, but the Germans seemed to spring out of the clouds like mushrooms, diving and dropping scores of bombs. This battleship received two hits aft, but the damage was superficial and the casualties light. The Germans tried a new trick of both high-level and dive-bombing simultaneously.

Bombs struck one of our destroyers, causing a tremendous explosion which blew the vessel wide open. Other bombs sent another destroyer down. I saw a stick of bombs fall upon one cruiser, hitting the magazine and setting her on fire from stem to stern. *Press Association and Associated Press.*

We Sat Knee-Deep in Water for 36 Hours

Survivors from a British ship which was sunk by a German raider in the Atlantic battled their way through heavy seas to safety. Their story was told by one of the passengers, an Indian traveller, Anil Chandra Mitra.

AFTER paying a tribute to the coolness and discipline of both officers and passengers during the shelling of their ship and afterwards, Mr. Mitra went on :

It was early in the morning when the ship's sirens announced the proximity of a raider, and within a few moments the raider's first shells were falling on our ship. While I was

standing on the deck at my boat station one shell burst close alongside the ship and a piece of shrapnel instantly killed the ship's officer standing at my side.

During a pause in the shelling the boats were lowered, but the first boat I entered sank within a few moments owing to it having been riddled with shrapnel. I swam to a second

Members of the crew of the American tanker Charles Pratt, torpedoed 200 miles off Africa watch a lifeboat set sail with survivors. They were picked up near Freetown. *Photo, Keystone*

boat, but found this, too, was sinking. Finally I reached a third boat in which people were crammed, including several women, while other women were in another boat not far away. The raider shelled our ship until she sank and then made off.

Our own boat was in a terrible state with about a dozen shrapnel holes through which the water poured continuously while large waves broke over the sides. We all sat knee-deep in water, baling in relays in bitter cold. We were thirty-six hours without drink.

Throughout the night we also had to care for two passengers who had been severely wounded by shrapnel. They died around dawn. Everybody remained calm, but we were all nearing despair when the miracle happened. We saw a friendly ship on the horizon which picked us up and carried us to safety.—*Reuter*

Air-Raid Warden HARRY BIRD won the British Empire Medal for helping to save many lives during an air raid. He relates his experiences in this page.

We Saved 45 People from Bombs and Floods

Endangered by flood, escaping gas, broken electricity mains, unsafe buildings and falling bombs, Warden Harry Bird and P.C. James Wilson Brown of Clapham, London, rescued forty-five people during an air raid. Their story is exclusive to THE WAR ILLUSTRATED.

WARDEN BIRD, describing the rescue work which earned him and P.C. Brown the British Empire Medal, said : Several high explosive bombs dropped in our area wrecked a number of houses, while some fell in the roadway, breaking a water main and fracturing electricity and gas mains. The water rushed down the street and very soon the street and the gardens at the rear of the houses were flooded. We heard the cries of people and we discovered that a number of them were trapped by the water, which was rising rapidly.

P.C. Brown and I went to their assistance. It was pitch dark. We found that some of the people were caught in their Anderson shelters with the water rushing in. They were in danger of being trapped. Others were marooned on top of their shelters. We started carrying the women and children to safety. As we walked up the steep gradient of the street, we had to walk carefully because of the rush of the water. For some of the people we formed a seat with our hands to carry them.

Gas was escaping from the broken mains. We were also in danger of receiving a severe shock from the broken electricity cables, for the water was " alive." Once or twice we had a slight shock, but our rubber boots probably saved us from anything worse. We also had to avoid the flooded bomb craters. Some of the houses we entered were in a dangerous condition. The walls might have collapsed at any moment. The lower rooms were flooded, and some of the smaller pieces of furniture were floating about.

To make matters worse, the Jerries came over again and dropped a few more bombs in the neighbourhood. One came fairly near, and we ducked under the water for safety's sake. Incidentally, the enemy helped us a bit by dropping some incendiaries in the district.

The light helped us to see what we were doing for a time.

The water was still rising, and before we were finished it was up to my chest. An old man, a cripple, was in bed in one of the damaged houses, and his wife refused to leave until we had got him out. We carried them both to a place of safety. P.C. Brown got a man out from under some debris, where he was trapped, but unfortunately he died later. It took us about three hours to get all the people, forty-five of them, to safety.

P.C. JAMES BROWN, who assisted Warden Bird to rescue 45 people from bombs and floods. He, too, was awarded the British Empire Medal.

Photos, South London Suburban Group

ABBREVIATIONS USED BY THE FOUR SERVICES
The Navy : A—W

A. Admiral.
A.B. Able Seaman.
A.C.N.S. Assistant Chief of Naval Staff.
A.F. Admiral of the Fleet.
A.G.R.M. Adjutant General Royal Marines.
A1. First-class at Lloyds.
A.M.C. Armed Merchant Cruiser.
A.P. Armour piercing.
A.P.S.L. Acting Paymaster Sub-Lieutenant.
A.S.L. Acting Sub-Lieutenant.
B. Boatswain.
C. Captain.
Cd. R.M.G. Commissioned Royal Marine Gunner.
Cd. S.B. Commissioned Signals Boatswain.
Cd. S.O. Commissioned Supply Officer.
Ch. Chaplain.
Ch. of F. Chaplain of the Fleet.
C.I. Chief Inspector, Royal Marine Police.
C.M.B. Coastal motor boat.
C.P.O. Chief Petty Officer.
Cr. Commander.
C.W.O. Commissioned Officer from Warrant Rank.
D.C. Depth Charge.
D.C.T. Depth Charge Thrower.
D.E.D. Director of Education Department.
D.N.A.D. Director of Naval Air Division.
D.N.E. Director of Naval Equipment.
D.N.I. Director of Naval Intelligence.
D.N.M.S. Director of Naval Medical Services, R.A.N.
D.N.R. Director of Naval Recruiting.
D/O.D. Director of Operations Division.
D.O.T.M. Director of Naval Ordnances, Torpedoes and Mines, R.A.N.

D. of N. Director of Navigation.
D. of P. D. Director of Plans Division.
D. of T.B. Director of Tactical Division.
D.P.S. Director of Personal Services.
D.P.T.S. Director of Physical Training and Sports.
D.T.S.D. Director of Training and Staff Duties Division.
D.Y. Dockyard.
E.A. Engineer Rear-Admiral.
E.C. Engineer Captain.
E.D. Education Department.
E. in C. Engineer-in-Chief of the Fleet.
E.L. Engineer Lieutenant.
E.L.Cr. Engineer Lieutenant-Commander.
E. V. A. Engineer Vice-Admiral.
G.S.P. Good Service Pension.
H.S. Hospital Ship.
I.D.C. Imperial Defence College.
L. Lieutenant.
L.A. Lieutenant-at-Arms.
L.Cr. Lieutenant Commander.
M.D. Medical Dept. or Mine Depot.
M.D.G. Medical Director-General of the Navy.
M. L. Minelayer.
Mon. Monitor.
Mid. Midshipman.
M.T.B. Motor Torpedo Boat.
M.V. Motor Vessel.
N.A.A.F.I. Navy, Army, and Air Force Institutes.
N.A.D. Naval Air Division.
N.E.D. Naval Equipment Dept.
N.I.D. Naval Intelligence Division.
N.O.D. Naval Ordnance Dept.
N.P.C. Naval Personnel Committee.
N.R.D. Naval Recruiting Dept.
N.Z.D. New Zealand Division.
O.D. Operations Division.
O.L. Ordnance Lieutenant.
O.L.Cr. Ordnance Lieutenant-Commander.

P. Boat. Patrol Boat.
P.C. Paymaster Captain.
P. Cr. Paymaster Commander.
P.D. Plans Division.
P.D.G. Paymaster Director-General.
P.L. Paymaster Lieutenant.
P.O. Petty Officer.
P.R.A. Paymaster Rear-Admiral.
P.S.L. Paymaster Sub-Lieutenant.
R.A. Rear-Admiral.
R.A.N. Royal Australian Navy.
R.C.N. Royal Canadian Navy.
R.G.B. River gunboat.
R.I.M. Royal Indian Marine.
R.M. Royal Marines.
R.M.O. Royal Marine Office.
R.M.P. Royal Marine Police.
R.S.M.S. Rendering Safe of Mines Squads.
S.A.N.S. South African Naval Service.
S.B. Signal Boatswain.
S.D. Signal Dept.
Sg. C. Surgeon Captain.
S.H.P. Shaft Horse Power.
Sg. L. Cr. Surgeon Lieutenant Commander.
Sg. R. A. Surgeon Rear-Admiral.
Sh. L. Shipwright Lieutenant.
Sig. L. Signal Lieutenant.
S.L. Sub-Lieutenant or Searchlight.
S.R.E. Scientific Research and Experiments Dept.
T.D. Tactical Division or Torpedo Depot.
T.L. Telegraphist-Lieutenant.
T.M.D. Torpedo and Mining Dept.
T.S. Training Ship.
T.T. Torpedo Tubes.
V.A. Vice-Admiral.
V.Y. Victualling Yard.
Wdr. L. Wardmaster Lieutenant.
W.O.O. Warrant Ordnance Officer.
W.T. Warrant Telegraphist.
W.W. Warrant Writer.
W. Wdr. Warrant Wardmaster.

The Editor's Postscript

" No retaliation," says the Archbishop of Canterbury, according to my daily paper. That anyone who has looked upon the diabolical handiwork of the Hun in London, Liverpool, Bristol, Coventry, Belfast, Glasgow, and a dozen other towns of the British Isles can say, or indeed contemplate, "no retaliation" leaves me marvelling at the degree of saintliness to which even an Archbishop may attain. If his grace of Canterbury has to be accepted as a Christian in the highest implication of a name that in Ancient Rome, when Christians were few, was a term of contempt, and which in the course of centuries has rightly become the symbol of all the virtues, then I fear that—in common with the vast majority of my fellow countrymen and all the ordinary men and women with whom I come in contact—I am no Christian in the best meaning of the word.

Yet I do not believe in retaliation ! Merely to do unto those bestial war-makers and mass-murderers what they have done unto us would be futile. Rather do I follow Mr. Bevin, albeit he does not have any outward aura of saintliness, in the fervent hope that we shall repay them with interest : "heap (real) coals of fire " upon the foulest race that has sought to dehumanize mankind. I trust the Archbishop in his saintly willingness to " take it " with meekness does not disapprove of the sort of retaliation that gives them a Bismarck for a Hood. " No retaliation " is merely an abuse of words when all peoples to whom liberty of conscience and freedom to live their own lives is p r i c e l e s s, have been so assailed by the most stupendous force for evil that has ever appeared on this globe—B.C. or A.D.

In front of my study window just now several squads of soldiers who have stopped here on manoeuvres all armed with tommy guns, are taking tea by the roadside under the tall elms. As I look at them I am impressed by the hint given by a young Nazi airman brought down somewhere in England last week who said that those saucer-shaped " tin hats " worn by our men are not so efficient as the German steel helmets. The British type looks better and provides more protection for eyes and nose, but seen from an aeroplane their broad brims tend to flatten out the whole headgear so that they appear to be large flat plates. The Nazi footsloggers are much less conspicuous in their brimless helmets. This sounds like sense to me.

And in the sunshine of this lovely summer afternoon every soldier that I can see might as well have a lady's vanity mirror stuck atop of his head—they are really like so many peripatetic heliographs reflecting pin points of light to any hovering Hun. The men would be better bare-headed—provided none of them were bald. Yet the tell-tale reflections could be avoided by covering the helmets with khaki cloth or dull paint. Two of the men I am looking at have them so treated, all the others seem to have performed the " spit and polish " act on them ! My effort last summer to set a local example by painting a dull lead mixture over all my resplendent cellulose and nickled car has scarcely had one follower. But I have one reward : I'm able to go in and out of a certain restricted area without hindrance as my lack-lustre car is so well known to the police ! All the same I still think that the authorities (whoever they are) should prohibit all cars that do not dim down their shining armour which makes them reflectors of light that can be seen miles away.

As I listened to the modest and most interesting broadcast today by Miss Jacqueline Cochran (Mrs. Odlum), that

SIR STAFFORD CRIPPS, to whose work as British Ambassador in Moscow Mr. Eden has paid tribute, saying that the country was deeply indebted to him for work done under conditions of the utmost difficulty. He was back in Moscow on June 27th.
Photo, Topical

charming young American lady, first of her sex to fly a big bomber from America to England, I could not help regretting that Lord Northcliffe had not lived until this day. Laughed at by many, who thought it a mere advertising stunt, when at the end of the Great War he offered £10,000 to any aviator who first flew the Atlantic, he hadn't to wait long before his prize was won in 1919, but what a joy to him, whose faith in the future of flying did so much to promote its progress, had he lived to meet the first American girl (she looks no more) that piloted a massive flying fortress across the Atlantic in nine or ten hours.

I fell for Miss Cochran (not Mrs. Odlum !) when I first saw her portrait in the papers. The dainty creature might have come straight from a beauty parlour instead of from so glorious an adventure. And the happy phrases in which she spoke of the job she had just done—and will do over again many a time, no doubt—must have endeared her to all who heard her recording. As she has been flying for nine years, she must have started in her college days. She told us there are some nine thousand American women who could be ranked as expert flyers : before the war is over I have no doubt British women will be giving them a close run. No wonder that ancient newspaper cliché " the weaker sex " has been entirely discarded by our journalists. And to think that anybody could have the nerve to announce " no cigarettes supplied to women " ! I'd like to hear Miss Cochran on that subject. Meanwhile, I've decided that my next visit to America will be by aeroplane.

The other night I was dining with a friend at his very posh hotel where the music in the lounge entirely disguised the fact that an Alert had sounded. When I eventually thought it was time to go and asked the porter to get a taxi, none was obtainable. It was raining as I went to the street door, where I learned that the Alert was on. Just as I got there the " midnight blue " sky blazed suddenly into light. " Is that a flare ? " I asked. " Oh, no," said Mr. Porter, " it's lightning." The crash of thunder that came as he spoke was more startling than any stick of bombs I have heard—*sans* whistle, however. But there was nothing for it but to foot it the half-mile or so to my own hotel. And let me tell you that you're a better man than I am, Gunga Din, if you can walk in tranquillity with an air raid on, and thunder and lightning and rain doing their stuff, innocent though that be, all at the same time.

I bumped into a dim figure in Berkeley Square, who asked me if he was heading for Oxford Circus, and was able to tell him that he would more likely arrive at the Circus yclept Piccadilly if he continued to follow his nose, which he could see only when the lightning flashed. I've been out in a good few blitzes, but this competition of the heavenly elements with those of hell's angels got me dithering, so that when two dripping A.R.P. men (hats off to those chaps every time) told me that my own hotel was " first on the right," my heart leapt up and in the bright interior of the familiar lounge I was soon calling for the waiter and emulating King Cole minus his fiddlers three.

In answer to many inquiries, I may mention that the reprint of my War-time Diary for 1939-40, entitled " As the Days Go By . . ." is now on sale. Its publication was delayed " by enemy action," as Messrs. Cassell & Co., who have issued the volume (price 7s. 6d.), had their historic publishing house at La Belle Sauvage, in Ludgate Hill, utterly destroyed by fire in a recent blitz. The fact that they and so many other famous publishers whose premises suffered a similar fate on the same night, or months before, are still carrying on at another address, is one of the many that must eventually make it clear to Hitler that he can do his damnedest in fire-bombing without extinguishing the energy and enterprise and eventual survival of a people whose spirit soars above all blastings.

JOHN CARPENTER HOUSE.
WHITEFRIARS. LONDON. E.C.4.

Registered at the G.P.O. as a Newspaper

The War Illustrated, July 18th, 1941

Vol 4

The War Illustrated

Nº 98

FOURPENCE

Edited by Sir John Hammerton

WEEKLY

BRITISH TROOPS IN SYRIA guarding a frontier position from behind a concrete tank trap. With the fall of Sidon, Damascus, and Palmyra, and the attack on Beirut, Vichy resistance in Syria is ending. But for a scrupulous desire to avoid loss of civilian life and the destruction of property the British and Free French commanders might have concluded the campaign long ere now. On July 1 the Vichy forces were said to be on the point of collapse, with the native population increasingly hostile towards Vichy France. *Photo, British Official : Crown Copyright*

Our Searchlight on the War

His Son's Medals

"YOU must be very proud of him," said King George to Mr. John McKellar whom his Majesty received at Buckingham Palace in order to hand him the D.S.O., D.F.C. and bar awarded to his only son, Squadron Leader A. A. McKellar, recently killed in action. His exploits in air fighting

JOHN McKELLAR gazes pensively at the medals awarded to his son, a Squadron Leader, who was killed after performing many fine exploits, some of which are related in this page.
Photo, Topical Press

included the following: He destroyed the first German raider that was shot down in an attack on this island; this was in the Firth of Forth raid of October 16, 1939. To him also fell the first raider to crash on British soil. He attacked a close formation of Heinkels head-on, and shattered three of them with one long burst of bullets. He shot down a German raider each day for eight days running during the Battle of London. He destroyed four Messerschmitt 109s in ten minutes. Small wonder that German pilots send each other agitated warnings: "Achtung! Schpitfeuer!"

P. G. Wodehouse in Germany

BROADCASTING from Berlin on June 26, Mr. P. G. Wodehouse, creator of the Wooster-Jeeves books, informed his listeners in New York that he had been released from

THE BATTLE OF THE ATLANTIC
Merchant Shipping Losses

	March	April	May	Totals
British				
Ships	83	71	73	227
Tons	338,105	338,186	355,105	1,031,396
Allied				
Ships	32	56	20	108
Tons	141,043	220,965	92,201	454,209
Neutral				
Ships	7	7	5	19
Tons	26,602	22,102	14,095	62,809
Totals Tons	505,750	581,253	461,401	1,548,414

Note : April and May figures are swollen by losses, mainly Greek, in evacuation from Greece. Figures for March and April are corrected to date, those for April including the addition of 24 ships (B.A. and N.), 102,167 tons, making the April total the largest for any one month of the war. May shows a slight improvement.
Enemy Losses : By capture, scuttling or sinking about 3,211,000 tons for the war period compared with 6,243,479 tons sunk by the enemy (4,024,913 tons British). Between May 10 and June 20, 1941, nearly 300,000 tons of enemy shipping were intercepted.
Mr. Churchill stated recently that "we have never fewer than 2,000 ships on the seas with 400 in the danger zone every day."

the Nazi internment camp near Breslau and was living for the moment in a suite on the third floor of the Adlon Hotel. Two German guards escorted him from the camp. "They took me around and showed me Berlin, which they had not seen themselves," he said. "We went to the Olympic Stadium, and to Potsdam, and back by steamer on the Wannsee." He may go and live on an estate in the Bavarian Alps belonging to a former Hollywood friend, for the only stipulation made by the police is that he must not attempt to leave Germany. Mr. Wodehouse stated that at the internment camp, to which he was taken from his house at Le Touquet when Germany overran France, he learnt to sew, darn, sole shoes and wash shirts, and that soling shoes is a "worthy occupation for philosophers." It has been announced that Mr. Wodehouse is to broadcast to the United States once a week on his experiences, and that his talks would be "general chats, entirely non-political."

Paderewski Dead

IGNAZ JAN PADEREWSKI, the great Polish pianist and statesman, died in New York on June 29 from pneumonia contracted while travelling to New Jersey to address a rally of 5,000 of his fellow countrymen. Always an ardent patriot, Paderewski came into political prominence in 1916, when he flung himself into the successful organization of a Polish army outside Poland. After the Armistice he returned to his native land. Received with tremendous enthusiasm, he formed an independent Government, holding office both as Premier and as Foreign Minister. He was also elected President of the new Republic, and under his energetic leadership the country was restored to order. But national unity in Poland did not seem to be a lasting possibility, and in 1920 his Government was defeated, and Paderewski returned to his music. Although he never went back to Poland, he never ceased to work for his unhappy people. When the news of his death was received, Gen. Sikorski, Polish Prime Minister, called a special meeting of the Cabinet in London, at which it was announced that a posthumous award of the highest military decoration, the "Virtute Militari," had been made to this great patriot, whose passing was an irreparable loss to the Polish cause.

Falangist Legion

THE recently appointed Falangist "Minister Secretary," Señor Arrese, is the author of a scheme for enlisting volunteers against Russia. "We must avenge our dead and permit our youth to join in the great European crusade," he said in the circular sent to all Falangist chiefs throughout Spain. Volunteers must be members of the Party, of good physical fitness, and between the ages of 20 and 28. They will enlist for the duration of the campaign, and while they are away their

jobs must be kept open for them and their full wages paid to their families. They will be commanded by officers who volunteer from the Regular Army. Young Falangists who allowed themselves to be exploited on June 24 in a German-staged riot outside the British Embassy in Madrid, will now have another outlet for their energies. This procession of Falange youths was led to the Embassy by a car in which was a German film camera and operators. Other cars decorated with swastikas and filled with Germans formed a rearguard. Excited by vituperative Nazi speeches, the Spanish youths presently began to throw stones at the Embassy, while the camera recorded the incident from its chosen point of vantage. General Franco has assured our Ambassador, Sir Samuel Hoare, that the Spanish Government strongly disapproved of the riots, and that the ringleaders would be punished.

Woman Pilot's Achievement

MISS JACQUELINE COCHRAN (in private life Mrs. Floyd Odlum, of New York), is the first woman to have piloted a bomber aircraft across the Atlantic. She arrived in England on June 20, stepping out of a Lockheed Hudson reconnaissance-bomber which was being delivered for service with the R.A.F. Her companion on the journey, Capt. G. Carlisle, captain and navigator, had engaged her as first officer, and although he was at the controls both when taking off and when the landing was made, it was Miss Cochran who flew the aircraft over 2,000 or so miles of ocean. This young pilot entered aviation in 1932. In 1937 she set up a new women's speed record of 304·62 m.p.h., and in the same year won the Harmon Trophy, which is awarded to the outstanding airwoman of the year. In 1938 she covered 2,042 miles in the Bendix Trophy Race in

JACQUELINE COCHRAN, American woman flier, was the first woman pilot to fly an American bomber over to England. Miss Cochran, after seeing London, reads a copy of "Time" in the Embankment gardens among City workers.
Photo, P.N.A.

8 hours, 10 min., 31 sec., and in 1940 maintained an average speed of 331 m.p.h. over a 2,000-kilometre course, setting up an unofficial world's speed record for the distance. Miss Cochran has had considerable experience in handling Lockheed aircraft and hopes to deliver more of them to the R.A.F.

The Way of the War

O, THOSE DULL UNINSPIRING COMMUNIQUES!

Why Should 'Their Battle Be More Full of Names than Ours'?

OURS is a very private sort of war, very private indeed. Our communiqués, whether their date-line is Cairo or London, whether they come from the Air Ministry or the War Office or from their Lordships of the Admiralty, never mention anyone below the rank of brigadier. Colonels and privates are beneath the ken of the bulletin compilers. Every battle is fought and won, or fought and lost to be won another day, by a host of unnamed warriors.

This bureaucratic penchant for anonymity has been carried to such lengths that seldom, very seldom, is the name even of a regiment mentioned. For weeks the world was given to understand that the Australians and New Zealanders were bearing the brunt of the fighting in the Western Desert; not until an outraged public " down under " protested against the grotesque partiality displayed in the communiqués was it revealed that men of England—I hasten to add, and men of Scotland, Wales, and Ireland, too— had played a manful and glorious part in the fighting. But even then we were left to guess at the identity of the various regiments.

At length, following upon the inquest on Crete, this policy of deliberate suppression was modified, at least in part. In the debate in the Commons Mr. Churchill gave the names of some of the regiments which had been engaged in the fighting and said that he had asked the Secretary for War "to endeavour to have mentioned more frequently the names of British regiments when this can be done without detriment to the operations." Ten days later the War Office announced at long last the names of a number of United Kingdom, Indian and Colonial units which, in addition to Dominion troops, had taken part in the recent operations in Greece, East Africa, and Crete.

FOR good reasons enough may we complain of what A. J. Cummings has aptly described as the " unimaginative dullness of our stereotyped communiqués." They make a very bad showing when compared with those of the enemy; to misquote Shakespeare, " Their battle is more full of names than ours." In just one of the Fuehrer's communiqués, for instance, that of June 30, we find personal mention of a couple of colonels, a lieutenant, a sergeant, a lance-corporal and four naval lieutenants. Admittedly, this would seem to be a new departure, one that has been copied from the Russians, but at least it shows that the Germans are not above taking a tip from the enemy.

As for the Russian communiqués, they are as full of names as a (pre-war) plum-duff of currants. Not for them the bald statements,

the irritating clichés, the dull brevity of our bulletins. They are crammed with detailed accounts of the fighting, and acts of individual heroism are singled out time and again. The man who compiles them—said to be Mr. Lozovsky, Soviet Vice Commissar for Foreign Affairs—evidently realizes that the Russian public expects something more than the commonplace little essays in evasion which fall so readily from the pens of our Civil Service scribes.

OUR heroes are anonymous until they have received a decoration. The Russian heroes are acclaimed on the very morrow of their deeds of prowess. " In air combats flyers of one aviation unit brought down ten enemy aircraft. The regimental commander, Major Kordekov, Hero of the Soviet Union, brought down two enemy bombers; radio operator and machine-gunner Shishkovitch brought down during the execution of his duties two enemy Messerschmitts. During the fighting Commander Sokokin with nine airplanes was attacked by 15 enemy aircraft; he brought down six of the enemy for a loss of four. Major Yachmenev was wounded in both legs, but refused to go to hospital and continued fighting." Compare this with even the best efforts of our Air Ministry.

Just as rich in personal details and even more informative are the accounts of the

deeds of the Russian soldiers. For instance, a Red Army infantryman, one Romanov, " stealthily approached an enemy scout motorcyclist and killed him. The commander of a subdivision of the same regiment, Junior Lieutenant Mezuev, although wounded, did not leave the field but continued fighting. . . . Gun Commander Junior Serg Trosimov, when his gun was surrounded by the enemy and his crew wounded, led three wounded Red Army members of his crew to shelter and calmly continued to direct the fire at the enemy. When further resistance became useless, as the enemy tanks had practically reached his position, Trosimov blew up his gun and skilfully escaped from encirclement . . . The commander of a battalion, Captain Koshel, skilfully organized machine-gun fire in battle. He quietly admitted the enemy to close quarters and opened cross machine-gun fire. Two enemy companies were annihilated."

THE Russians, it is clear, have no false modesty. They don't mind telling the world that not only have they heroes but that their heroes have names. Still more significant, even more strange, they recognize that not all the heroes are on the battlefield. Scanning this same communiqué we come across the name of " polisher Popov," who, we are told, after being wounded in the fighting in the Finnish War in the winter of 1940, on the outbreak of the new war came to the Ilyich plant in Leningrad and asked for a job. " ' At such a time,' he said, ' I cannot go on staying at home and drawing a pension. I have enough strength and experience to replace comrades who have gone to the front.' "

Then there is " mechanic Tiant who remained on duty for three days and nights until he had finished assembling important machinery. After that he rested for three hours and began helping his fellow-workers. . . . One of the workers in a Moscow factory, Comrade Zagouzoff, received the important task of making urgently 100 cylinders, which normally require about 500 working hours. Comrade Zagouzoff, working on two lathes simultaneously, did not leave his work for five whole days, until he had finished his job. The quality of the work was excellent . . . Foreman Antonov, jointly with his assistant Bashmanov, has designed an original appliance for raising the productivity of a certain machine which can do the work of five men called to the army . . . "

WELL done, polisher Popov, mechanic Tiant, foreman Antonov, and Bashmakov your mate ! But have we no John Browns, Bill Smiths and Peter Robinsons who have shown their patriotism in our workshops, just as their sons and brothers have shown it on the battlefield ? Have we no exemplars to make the "absentees" blush, wherever they live, whatever their class and station ? Of course we have. Then why shouldn't we know their names ? Why shouldn't we give honour where honour is due ? Why not, Mr. Bevin ? What about it, Lord Beaverbrook ?

WHO IS HE ? Talking to an eager audience of pit boys is the captain of the Catalina Flying Boat who sighted the Bismarck. We have published his story (see page 621); we have reproduced his portrait; but we are still not permitted to mention his name.

E. Royston Pike

Our Air Offensive Is Now Really Beginning

Following the invasion of Russia, the R.A.F. intensified their offensive against the Germans in Occupied France and in the Vaterland. Night after night, and—still more important, even more significant—day after day, our bombers and fighters carried the war well into enemy country.

"WE shall bomb Germany by day as well as by night in ever-increasing measure," declared Mr. Churchill in his great broadcast on June 22, "casting upon them month by month a heavier discharge of bombs and making the German people taste each month the sharper dose of the miseries they have showered upon mankind.

"Only yesterday," the Premier went on, "the Royal Air Force, fighting inland over France, struck down with very small loss to themselves twenty-eight of the Hun fighting machines in the air above the French soil they have invaded, defiled, and profess to hold. But this is only the beginning . . ."

For days and weeks before Mr. Churchill spoke the R.A.F. had been developing their air offensive in gathering strength. At first, months ago, there were "sweeps" across the Channel and up and down the French coast—"feelers" designed to discover the enemy's strength, small-scale raids resulting in shooting down quite a number of Nazi planes. These offensive patrols did so well that they were steadily increased in frequency and in the number of planes employed. With the coming of summer numbers of bombers were employed, escorted by hundreds of fighters. At first only the coastal regions were attacked, but now the R.A.F. is reaching ever farther and farther inland, until no part of the occupied territories is safe from their attentions. There is not an enemy aerodrome in north-western Europe which is not liable to be attacked at any hour of the day. German supplies have been hampered, their communications have been disrupted, and war production in the Nazi-controlled factories held up.

Unfortunately it is impossible to discriminate between friend and foe, and it was with a view to sparing the French workers (who, if reports speak true, are decidedly hostile to the Nazis, although they are compelled to work for them) that in a recent B.B.C. French broadcast an officer of the R.A.F. General Staff spoke direct to the French workers.

"The raids of the Royal Air Force," he said, "have wrought havoc on the armament factories in Germany and France. The Germans have therefore decided to evacuate their workers and to replace them by Frenchmen. Germany wants to attack your brothers with what your labour produces. The R.A.F. is resolved to attack all factories in occupied France. Therefore, go to the country to work there if possible. At least, evacuate your women and children from the neighbourhood of such factories. If you are compelled to stay in the factories, go to the shelters as soon as the Alert is sounded. Ask for good shelters, and if the Germans do not sound the Alert leave your working place whenever you hear the buzz of our planes. Should no security be given to you, then go on strike. The more pretexts found by you for stopping work the fewer bombs will be produced for your friends."

Day by day the score of Nazi planes downed by our pilots mounted. In the eight days between June 16 and 23, 114 German machines were accounted for by our fighters over Northern France. Many of the British pilots expressed surprise at the lack of spirit shown by the enemy. "They outnumbered us," said one Squadron Leader on returning to his base, "but did not attempt anything in the way of concerted attack. The Germans seemed to be looking for stragglers, and displayed a reluctance to attack the main formations." Maybe the Nazis have had orders to avoid combat ; more likely is it that their numbers were seriously reduced when the Luftwaffe found itself flung against the air armadas of the Soviet Union. Certainly, the invasion of Russia gave the R.A.F. a wonderful opportunity which they were quick to seize. The daylight sweeps beyond the Channel were intensified, and at night, in spite of the brief midsummer darkness, the Ruhr and the great ports and industrial centres of western and north-western Germany were hammered time and again. Bremen and Kiel, whence the German Navy is operating against the Russians in the Baltic, were battered afresh by night, and on June 30 they were attacked in the most daring fashion by day.

With what joyous relief our people watched the turn of the tide in the air war need hardly be stressed. Writing to the "Daily Express" from Dover on June 25, Hilde Marchant said : "These are the Dover days again—but this time the battle echoes from the other side. This time, when the people in the streets hear the sound of planes, they look into the sky and murmur a satisfied 'Ours.' This time the sound of heavy bombs drifts over the Straits from France's white coast, and these white cliffs and headlands lie safe and secure under the R.A.F.'s wings.

"Last September I sat on this cliff edge and watched the Battle of Britain. In those days we could only identify the R.A.F. when we saw six or nine planes tear into formations of 50 or more. That was a thrilling sight. But this sight today is even more glorious—to see the R.A.F. fly out in bold numbers and sweep over the Channel in their proud formations. Now the sirens on our coast are silent ; but they must be squeaking all day in those crumbling French towns . . .

"Day and night the heavy echoes come rolling over the Straits, and in the pubs and in the shops they say, 'Our boys are giving it to them again'

"The Nazi air force has not been seen or heard for weeks. And as a fresh formation passes over our heads at this moment one of the soldiers in the road says, 'The R.A.F. have got their tails up all right.'"

	LOSSES IN THE NEW AIR OFFENSIVE									
	June 1—30, 1941									
	GERMAN				Over Britain (Night)	R.A.F.				
	Over Britain (Night)		Over France etc. (Day)			Over France and Germany (Day & Night)				Pilots Safe
Date	B.	F.	B.	F.	F.	B.	F.	C.C.	R.	
June 1-10	15	2	1	7	1	15	3	4		
„ 11-15	9	2	2	4		20	1	4	1	
„ 16-20	6	3	1	36		15	18	2		2
„ 21-22	4	2		26	1	2	3			1
„ 22-23				31		3	2	1		1
„ 23-24				20		3	3			1
„ 24-25	4			9		3	2			
„ 25-26	2			13		2	5			
„ 26-27				10		2	3			
„ 27-28	1			8		12	9			
„ 28-29	1			5		1	3			
„ 29-30	1			7		14	1			
Totals	43	9	4	176	2	92	53	11	1	5

B = Bomber, F = Fighter, C.C. = Coastal Command, R. = Reconnaissance.   *From Air Ministry communiqués.*

R.A.F. ACES, veterans of the Battle of Britain, are now busily engaged in carrying the war into the enemy's camp. Here are some of them : I, Flt.-Lt. J. L. Kilmartin, D.F.C., who had already destroyed 12 enemy aircraft by the end of last September ; 2, Sqdn.-Ldr. D. R. S. Bader, D.S.O., the "legless wonder," who commands a Canadian squadron ; 3, Flt.-Lt. J. H. Mungo-Park, D.F.C., reported "missing" on July 1 ; 4, Flt.-Lt. H. M. Stephens, D.S.O., D.F.C. and bar, who once shot down five enemy planes in one day ; 5, Flying-Officer Newell Orton, D.F.C. ; 6, Sqdn.-Ldr. R. R. Stanford Tuck, D.S.O., D.F.C. and bar, who has shot down over 30 Nazi planes ; 7, Wing-Cmdr. J. A. Kent, D.F.C., A.F.C. ; 8, Wing-Cmdr. A. G. Malan, D.S.O., D.F.C. and bar, R.A.F.'s leading ace, with 35 Nazi planes to his credit.   *Photos, British Official, Associated Press, Planet News, and Central Press*

Now the Air Frontier Is Away Over France

HAZEBROUCK, the Grand' Place of which is seen in the top photograph, is a somnolent French provincial town, near Calais. As a German military base it possesses invasion significance, and is therefore under continual observation and bombardment from the R.A.F. Above is an aerial view of the marshalling yards there before being attacked, and in the photograph on the right we see the effect of bombs falling among the rolling stock. All the way from Calais to Brest Bomber Command is striking with increasing force.

Photos, British Official : Crown Copyright ; G. MacCormack

NORTHERN FRANCE and Southern England (left), showing the relative positions of aerial combat in September 1940 and June 1941. Gradually the R.A.F. are pushing back the Luftwaffe line and reversing the conditions of the Battle of Britain. Beneath is a once quiet corner of St. Omer, now a centre right in the R.A.F. scheme of things ; and an impression of nine bombs bursting on the concrete runway of the St Omer-Longueness aerodrome during a daylight sweep.

Photos, British Official : Crown Copyright ; A. J. Insall, Map by " Daily Mail "

They're 'On Top' in the Middle East, Too

While their brothers at home are establishing air supremacy over the Channel and Occupied France, the R.A.F. are maintaining their ascendancy in the eastern theatre of war. In the Middle East there are plenty of wide level spaces which can be used as landing-grounds, but the maintenance-men find the sand a curse. The Vokes Aero Filter (see page 293) has done much to combat the menace of sand in the engines and bearings, and this is supplemented by the use of vacuum cleaners, one of which is seen at the foot of the ladder in the top photograph, and in use in the other. Note the Nash and Thompson hydraulic turret with its two Browning guns in the nose of this Wellington bomber.

Photos British Official

Well May Russia Tempt the Greedy Nazis

By way of accompaniment to the description of the political organization of the Soviet State which appears in page 676 we print below an account of some aspects of Russia's economic life. Brief though it is, it may suggest not the least powerful of the reasons which have impelled Hitler to take the road to Moscow—the desire for oil and wheat and "living-space."

WHEN Napoleon went to Moscow in 1812 he wanted to teach Tsar Alexander a lesson. He had no intention of consolidating his conquest ; he went for prestige rather than for plunder. Now Hitler has taken the same road, but if Hitler gets to Moscow we may be sure that he will do his best to remain there. One more capital entered by his conquering legions can hardly be a great matter when practically all the capitals of Europe have echoed to the swaggering feet of his troopers. But Russia is rich—rich in natural resources and productive power ; rich, too, in human factory and farm fodder. Moreover, there is plenty of room in Russia since, taking the Union as a whole, there are only 18 people to a square mile. In Russia, and only in Russia, is there room for those 200,000,000 Germans who, if the Nazi boasts are fulfilled, will want their share of living-space before this century is out.

Russia was always a rich country, with her vast forests and the great plains of the black earth belt, waving with corn in the summer sunshine. But the Russia of Stalin is infinitely richer, and so infinitely more

desirable a prize than the Russia of ill-fated Tsar Nicholas. During the last ten or fifteen years the country has been transformed from one which was almost entirely agrarian to one which, though agriculture is still the mainstay of its life, is among the most highly industralized countries of the modern world. The transformation dates from 1928, when the first of the Five-Year Plans was inaugurated. Its aim, in Stalin's words, was to transform the U.S.S.R. "from an agrarian and weak country, dependent upon the caprices of the capitalist countries, into an industrial and powerful country, quite independent of the caprices of world capitalism." It was a deliberate attempt to beat the Americans at their own game—to accomplish in a single generation all and more than the countries of Western Europe and North America had been able to accomplish since the dawn of the Industrial Revolution.

Working in close and constant consultation with the All-Union Central Committee of Trade Unions (representing 18 million members), the Consumers' Cooperative Movement and the People's Commissars concerned with the home front, the plan was produced and put into operation by the State Planning Commission (Gosplan). The first Five-Year Plan, launched on October 1, 1928, aimed explicitly at the basic industrialization of the Union. In a country so essentially agricultural as Russia it was imperative that the means of production—"capital goods" in the economists' jargon—should be given

Anastas Ivanovich Mikoyan (left), People's Commissar of Foreign Trade, who received Mr. Laurence J. Cadbury (right) when the latter arrived in Moscow as a member of the British Economic Mission to Russia, in June 1941. *Photo, Planet News*

the priority over "consumer goods." It was a hard choice, and in the process the standard of living of the Russian workers, already low, was driven lower still, so that there was much grumbling and even open opposition. But when persuasion failed, compulsion was ruthlessly employed. Fortunately for the success of the plan the interest and enthusiasm of large numbers of the workers were effectively enlisted. They

subscribed to the state loans, they worked overtime without pay, they made short shrift of slackers in their midst ; moreover, they were encouraged to increase their output by the bigger rations granted to "shock workers" as well as by holidays at the seaside in the Crimea, and free railway passes. A new title, Hero of Socialist Labour, was created for those who distinguished themselves, particularly in the pioneering work, and another honourable appellation was "Stakhanovite," derived from the Donetz miner, Alexei Stakhanov, who invented

OIL AND WHEAT are two commodities which Hitler needs and hopes to seize from Russia by conquest. In Transcaucasia, between Baku on the Caspian Sea and Batum on the Black Sea, lie rich oilfields and many oil trains ply over the Transcaucasian railway (top left). Above is a scene in the fertile Ukraine towards the rich wheat belts of which the Germans have always cast covetous glances. But not only is the Ukraine a great source of Russia's wheat supply ; it provides her with a very large part of her mineral riches, including three-fifths of her pig-iron, iron ore and coal.
Photos, Wide World and Planet News

How the 'Plans' Have Made a New Country

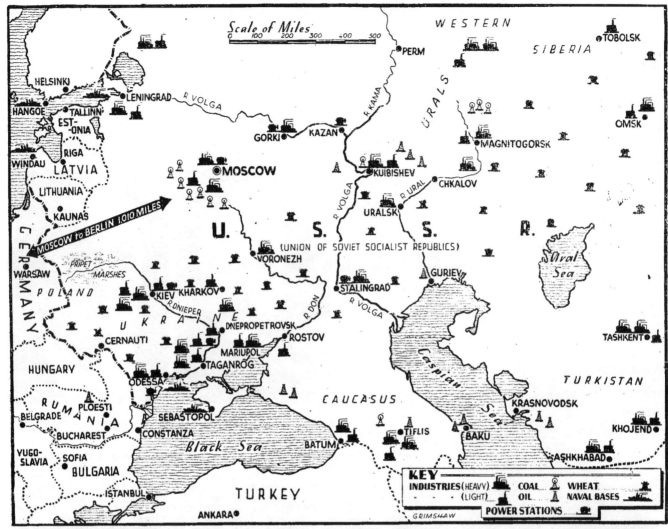

RUSSIA'S VITAL INDUSTRIES—coal, oil, wheat and electricity—are now widely dispersed all over the U.S.S.R. and not concentrated as formerly in one or two parts. This is her greatest strength against the invaders, for whatever the Nazi victories, even though they capture Moscow, they would not stop the heart of Soviet industry or the pulse of Russian patriotism. The map indicates Russia's immense retreating space, as far as the Urals and the Caspian Sea, if necessary, about 1,500 miles from the western frontier at Brest Litovsk.   *By courtesy of " Reynold's News "*

new ways for voluntarily increasing production.

In January 1933 Stalin summarized the results of the first Five-Year Plan. "When it began," he said, "we did not have an iron and steel industry, the basis of the industrialization of the country; now we have such an industry. We did not have a tractor industry; now we have one. We did not have an automobile industry; now we have one. We did not have a machine-building industry; now we have one. We did not have a big and modern chemical industry; now we have one. We did not have a real, solid industry for the production of modern agricultural machinery; now we have one. In output of electric power we were last on the list; now we are among the first on the list. In output of oil products and coal we were last on the list; now we are among the first on the list. We had only one single coal and metallurgical base, the Ukraine, which we could barely manage; we have not only succeeded in improving this base, but we have created a new coal and metallurgical base in the East which is the pride of our country. We had only one single textile industry base, in the north of the country; in the very near future we shall have two new bases of the textile industry, in Central Asia and Eastern Siberia. And we have not only created these enormous branches of industry, but we have created them on a scale and in dimensions which make the scale and dimensions of European industry pale into insignificance."

The second Five-Year Plan, which came into operation at the end of 1932, aimed not so much at the production of further capital goods as at an increase in consumer goods.

It also gave special attention to the collectivization of agriculture, and here it encountered stubborn resistance from the peasants, who since the days of the New Economic Policy (N.E.P.) forced upon Lenin in the early 1920's had been establishing themselves as virtual owners of their holdings. Peasant cultivation, it must be admitted, is most uneconomic; perhaps it had to go in Russia just as it was abolished in England 200 years ago. But even the most ardent wellwishers of the Soviet regime were aghast at the savage methods employed in the collectivization. By the thousand the peasants were driven from their holdings to take their places in the collective farms (Kolkhoz); and the more recalcitrant were expelled from the countryside and forced to labour in the timber camps in the frozen north. Particularly venomous was the onslaught on the better-class peasants—the kulaks—men who by their toil and enterprise in small matters had raised themselves above the economic level of their fellows. Despite the sternest repressive measures, resistance still continued; cattle were slaughtered on a huge scale, grain was hidden away so that it should not be seized by the officials sent from the towns; and the labour in the kolkhoz often suffered since the most industrious and keen farmers had been sent into exile. At length Stalin realized that his policy was too drastic and he gave orders to his emissaries to " go slow."

Henceforth, though there was no going back on the principle of collective farms, the individual peasants were permitted to own their own huts, to have a few personal belongings and a cow or two.

So the second Five-Year Plan ran its course and was succeeded by the third, which is due to be completed in 1942.

During the last few years the whole face of Russia has been changed. Whereas three-quarters of the total industries used to be concentrated around Moscow, St. Petersburg (Leningrad), and in the Ukraine, the Soviet policy is to distribute industry throughout its territory. Great new industrial towns have sprung up in all parts of the Union, sometimes in places where no human foot had ever trod. Only a few years ago Magnitogorsk was not even a village; today it is a great city of 150,000 people. Others that may be mentioned are Karaganda (166,000) in Kazakstan, Stalingorsk (76,000) in West Siberia, Igarka in East Siberia, and Korovsk, which is actually in the Arctic Circle. A prosperous cotton industry has been developed in what we still call Turkistan; wheat is grown not only in the Ukraine but in many regions in the centre, east and north of the Union; coal is supplied from Siberian mines and the Far East; rich metal deposits are being worked in the Urals, Siberia, and other parts of Asiatic Russia. The immense oil deposits in the Caucasus have been developed, as also in the Urals and in the Volga valley.

At Stalin's Battle-Cry All Russia Rallies

After a fortnight of fiercest fighting, Hitler's armies had overrun most of Stalin's recently-acquired territories, but had made little progress into Russia proper. Particularly incensed were the Nazis at the "scorched earth" policy called for by Stalin in his great broadcast of July 3—a policy which might well prove as disastrous to Hitler as the winter snows to Napoleon, 129 years ago.

STALIN broadcast to the Russian people on July 3. It was a speech grim in its realism, yet its frankness was matched by its courage and its note of supreme confidence.

"In spite of the heroic resistance of the Red Army," he began, "in spite of the fact that the best units of his air force have already been beaten and have found their grave on the battle-fields, the enemy continues to push forward and

General C. K. ZHUKOV, Chief of the General Staff of the Red Army (left) and Lieut.-Gen. F. N. MASON MACFARLANE, Military Attaché with the British Mission now in Russia.
Photos, Planet News and Walter Stoneman

to throw new forces on the front. Hitler's armies have succeeded in seizing Lithuania, the greater part of Latvia, the western part of White Russia, and part of Western Ukraine. The Fascist Air Force extends the operations of its bombers, and raids Murmansk, Orsha, Mogilev, Smolensk, Kiev, Odessa, and Sebastopol."

How could it have happened, he went on to ask, that the glorious Red Army had surrendered to the Fascist troops a number of the Russian towns ? "Are German Fascists armies really invincible as is continually proclaimed by the boastful Fascist propagandists ?" Swift came his answer.

"History shows that there are no invincible armies . . . Hitler's Fascist army can and will be defeated just as the armies of Napoleon and Wilhelm II were defeated.

"Our country," he went on, "has entered upon a death struggle with her most ferocious and perfidious enemy—German Fascism. He intends to seize our land, bathed in our sweat, to seize our wheat and our oil, the fruits of our labour. He intends to restore the power of big landowners, to restore Tsarism, to destroy the national culture and national States of the Russians, Ukrainians, White Russians, Lithuanians, Letts, Estonians, Moldavians, Uzbeks, Tartars, Georgians, Armenians, Azerbaidjanians, and other free peoples of the Soviet Union, to Germanize them, and to transform them into slaves of German princes and barons. It is therefore a question of life and death for the Soviet State, for the people of the U.S.S.R.—a question whether the peoples of the Soviet Union shall be free or reduced to slavery."

Soviet citizens must understand the full gravity of the danger threatening the country and put aside the " placid and carefree mentality " which had been theirs in the times of peaceful reconstruction. They must mobilize and reorganize their whole work on a new war footing. They should have no mercy for the enemy, nor should there be any place in their ranks for grumblers, cowards, panic-mongers, and deserters. They must organize

speedy transportation of troops, food-stuffs and munitions, as well as large-scale assistance to the wounded. They must produce more rifles machine-guns, guns, cartridges, shells, and aircraft, organize the defence of factories, power-stations, and communications, and arrange effective air-raid precautions in every locality.

"In the event of the retreat of the Red Army all railway rolling-stock must be brought away. We must not leave a single engine to the enemy, nor a single railway coach. We must not leave a single pound of grain or a single gallon of petrol to the enemy. The collective farmers must take away all their cattle and place their corn in the care of State organizations to be transported to the rear zone. All valuable materials which cannot be taken away must be resolutely destroyed.

"In the areas occupied by the enemy, foot and horse guerilla detachments must be created, as well as groups of *saboteurs* entrusted with fighting against the units of the enemy army, with the launching of guerilla warfare everywhere, with blowing up bridges and roads, with wrecking telephone and telegraph communications, and with setting forests, depots, and trains on fire. It is necessary to create in invaded areas conditions unbearable for the enemy and all his accomplices."

This was no ordinary war. It was not only a war between two armies, but a great war of the whole Soviet people against the German Fascist troops, a war for the liberation of all the peoples of Europe groaning under the Nazi yoke. " In this connection the historic utterance of the British Prime Minister, Mr. Churchill, about aid to the Soviet Union, and the declaration of the Government of the United States signifying readiness to give assistance to our country are fully comprehensible and symptomatic." Then Stalin concluded on a hopeful note. "Comrades !

Our forces are numberless. The overweening enemy will soon learn this to his cost. Side by side with the Red Army many thousands of workers, collective farmers, and intellectuals are rising to fight the enemy aggressor. The masses of our people will rise up in their millions. The working people of Moscow and Leningrad have already commenced quickly to form popular levies in support of the Red Army. Such popular levies must be raised in every city which is in danger of enemy invasion ; all working people must be roused to defend our freedom, our honour, our country, in our patriotic war against German Fascism."

Millions in Furious Battle

While the " Red Tsar " was speaking, the great battle round Minsk was at its height—a battle which was described as the greatest of all time, one in which millions of men were engaged over an area of hundreds of square miles. Great masses of infantry fought furiously in hand-to-hand combat, but there was a new feature in the hordes of tanks which charged each other like rampageous elephants. There was little that could be described as a front, and no line that could be clearly distinguished. Here at last "defence in depth " was being tried out against the thrusts of Hitler's Panzer divisions. Slowly the battle drifted towards the east, across the great plain, but it was continuous over an area half the size of England. At the very tip of the advance thundered the Nazi tanks which had broken through in the Minsk sector and triumphantly taken the road to Moscow. They sped along the highway, scattering confusion and death on either side ; but between them and the " deadly, drilled, docile, brutish masses of the Hun soldiery," as Mr. Churchill has called them, stretched 150 or even 200 miles of country—as far as, say, from London to York—which, though they had covered, they did not in any real sense of the term control.

This was a new kind of war, yet the Nazis who have specialized in military novelties found it not altogether to their taste. " Different methods from those used in France are being used in Russia," read an announcement from Berlin, " because large Russian units at the rear of the German forces are hiding in woods and marshes and are offering stubborn and at times powerful resistance. Thus there are two wars raging : one fought out by Panzers ; the other, a small scale war behind the German lines in which the Russians are trying desperately to impede the German

COMMITTEE OF DEFENCE, set up in Russia on June 30, are here seen on their way to the Red Square, Moscow. Left to right, M. Molotov (vice-chairman), M. Stalin (chairman), Marshal Voroshilov ; behind, M. Malenkov (left) and M. Beria, party chief for Georgia.
Photo, Planet News

Great Nazi Gains—But No Decisive Victory

advance by cutting their lines of communication."

The Nazis, it is clear, had expected that once the "line" was broken by their spearhead of tanks, then the Russians on either side of the gap would throw up the sponge. The Russians, however, let the German tanks go through; they admitted that the Germans had swept on 60 or 100 miles past Minsk. Then they said, in effect, "So what?" The spearhead had thrust deep, but the shaft was being gnawed and mauled by the huge Russian forces left behind and only just coming into action. Soon the Nazis began to show signs of anxiety concerning the fate of their advanced units. After all, Russia is not like France where petrol-stations are to be found in every village, at almost every cross-road. The question of supply and of refuelling units which had gone off "into the blue" must have taxed even the highly-efficient Nazi commissariat.

Great victories were claimed by the German High Command : 160,000 prisoners had been taken in the first ten days' fighting, and a huge quantity of booty, including 5,774 Russian tanks, 2,330 guns, four armoured trains, and 4,725 planes. Then it was claimed

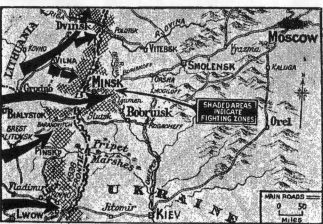

MINSK, capital of White Russia, with tanks passing Government House in Lenin Square. Fifteen miles over the Stalin Line on the road to Moscow, Minsk is the centre of one of the greatest battles ever fought.   *Photo, E.N.A.*

ness and absolute heroism of the Russians," described the battle as of the "civil war" type. "In the woods and fields Russian soldiers in civilian dress try to filter through the circle of Hitler's troops in order to contact the Bolshevik civil population and coordinate sabotage and auda-

cious coups behind the lines of the conqueror." The independence and capacity for initiativeness of these isolated guerilla bands was surprising, he went on; why, in some forts there had been found "almost undefeatable women, defending them with a fierceness hitherto unknown in normal beings."

After ten days of war a pattern of the battle began to emerge. To quote the apt imagery of Captain Liddell Hart, writing in the "Daily Mail," it might be described as a left-handed "five-finger exercise," stretching across the 1,800-miles keyboard of Russia's western frontiers, between the Black Sea and the Arctic Ocean. The thumb resting on the Black Sea coast was pressing upon Bessarabia in the direction of Odessa. The first finger was pushing south to the Pripet

CENTRAL WAR AREA of the Russo-German campaign with towns and districts on either side of the Russian frontier shaded to indicate fighting zones up to July 3, 1941.
By courtesy of the "Daily Telegraph"

marshes towards Kiev. The middle finger was pushing past Minsk on the road to Smolensk and Moscow. The third finger was operating in the Baltic States in the direction of Leningrad, while the little finger was pressing against the Arctic port of Murmansk in the direction of the White Sea. The main effort was that of the middle finger, made through Poland along the road that Napoleon took to Moscow. On the left flank the Germans had won considerable success in the Baltic States, since Lithuania had been overrun and Latvia penetrated. Leningrad was definitely threatened. But Hitler, so it was said, had expected to reach Moscow in three weeks; when half the time had elapsed he had still a long way to go.

LENINGRAD is seen in this map in relation to the Gulf of Finland and the Karelian Isthmus, with the German-Finnish line of attack.
Specially drawn for THE WAR ILLUSTRATED *by Felix Gardon*

that the Soviet Army had suffered bloody losses which were many times the number of prisoners taken. The Soviet resistance had been stubborn; surprisingly stubborn, indeed. "In many respects," said one German report from the front, "our present opponents are more formidable than our previous foes, not only from the point of view of numbers. Before, we fought soldiers possessing intelligence and experience. Now we have an opponent neither brave nor intelligent, but forming a collective, tough mass with the soullessness and indifference of a machine." Another German commentator complained bitterly that "the Red soldiers have a brutish obstinacy instead of intelligence and imagination." Then the Berlin correspondent of a Spanish newspaper, after referring to the "indisputable training and skilled stubborn-

MURMANSK, the most westerly base of Russia's Arctic fleet, which the German-Finnish forces captured on July 1, after dive-bombing the port with Stukas; they were soon ejected, according to Russian reports, and so a flank attack on Leningrad was prevented.
Photo, E.N.A.

First Photos of the Nazi Invasion of Russia

IN RUSSIA the Germans are hurling their masses against the Red Army in the hopes of a quick decision. Here are some of the first pictures received in London of the Nazi invasion. Above, Germans place a log bridge across a brook to enable supplies to be brought up.

Unchecked by a demolished bridge, German soldiers cross a Russian river in collapsible boats (right).

Below, according to the German caption, is a Nazi column marching into Soviet Russia. Coming from the opposite direction are Russian prisoners, their hands on their heads in token of surrender.

Photos, Associated Press and Keystone

From the Defensive to the Offensive: the R.A.F. Ta

Left, the crew c
Blenheim bon
loading their
returning from
over the Nor
search of enem
Right, a trio
Blenheims off t
foe.

Photos, Fox,
Press, L.N.A.,
Chas. E. Brown
and Associate

One of our young fighter pilots enjoys a refreshing cup of tea on his return from an offensive sweep over Nazi-occupied France.

Last summer people on the South Coast gazed apprehensively at the skies when they heard the drone of a plane. Now, like this young lady, they look up with a smile as our planes roar seaward to seek the enemy in his lair. If they are some of our new Spitfires (centre) well, it's just too bad for the Nazis.

the Air War Over the Water into Enemy Territory

Below, a pilot just back from a raid makes his report to an Intelligence Officer while his aircraft is quickly overhauled. The photograph in the oval shows a fighter pilot, who already has eight Nazi planes to his credit, adjusting his oxygen mask before going to look for some more.

Left, some of the pilots who, to use Mr. Churchill's words, have given the Germans " many a British whipping." With them are their animal mascots, including " William B. Goat."

At the Prow They Fly the Cross of Lorraine

THE Free French Naval Forces comprise more than a hundred ships of all categories. Many of them are actually in service and the others are being rearmed. Two of these vessels merit special notice ; one is the destroyer Triomphant, seen in this page, and the other is the submarine Surcouf. The Triomphant, a vessel of 2,569 tons, built more on the lines of a British light cruiser, has an exceptional turn of speed. Her maximum speed is 43 knots and she can maintain a steady 37 knots for long periods. Commissioned in 1934, she mounts five 5·5-in. guns, four 37 mm. and four 13 mm. A.A. guns as well as four D.C. throwers. She has nine torpedo tubes. The Surcouf is the largest submarine in the world. She carries a seaplane and mounts two 8-in. guns as well as two 37 mm. A.A. guns. She has a range of 12,000 miles at 10 knots (her speed submerged) and can cruise on the surface at 18 knots. She carries 22 torpedoes and her diving limit is over 70 fathoms.

The crews of the Free French Naval Forces, composed exclusively of French sailors, have been recruited from (a) the entire crews of ships who rallied immediately to General de Gaulle, e.g. the submarines Narval and Rubis ; (b) personnel who, at the time of the Armistice, were on ships in English waters and who eventually rallied to the F.N.F.L. ; (c) sailors from merchant ships, such as the trawlers of Newfoundland, anxious to serve in the Free French Navy, and (d) sailors from all over the world who decided to make their way to the side of General de Gaulle when their ships were disarmed.

ESTABLISHMENTS for training naval cadets have been set up ; cadets are divided between the "Ecole Navale," for officers, on board the President Theodore Tissier ; the "Ecole des Gabiers," for naval observers, on the schooner Etoile ; the "Ecole des Timoniers," for steersmen, on the schooner Belle-Poule, the "Ecole des Radios," for wireless specialists, on the battleship Courbet, etc.

The Free French Naval Forces, under the command of Vice-Admiral Muselier, have already won several distinctions for their work at sea. The commander of the submarine Rubis has been awarded the D.S.O., two of his officers the D.S.C., and five ratings the D.S.M.

Vice-Admiral Muselier has mentioned in the "Ordre de la Marine" the destroyer La Melpomène, the minesweeper Chevreuil, the patrol boat Poulmic, and the battleship Courbet, which has brought down five German bombers.

A French Fleet Air Arm is in process of organization, and close cooperation between the F.N.F.L. and the British Admiralty is assured by officers of the Franco-British naval mission.

One of the first orders issued by Vice-Admiral Muselier specified that the ships of the Free French Forces would fly the French national colours at the poop and a square blue pennant bearing a red cross of Lorraine at the prow.

Personnel of the Free French Naval Forces on parade. Their hatbands bear the letters F.N.F.L. (Forces Navales Françaises Libres).

Below, a sailor of the F.N.F.L. keeps a sharp look-out for enemy aircraft. Behind him flutters the emblem of Free France : the Cross of Lorraine and the motto "Honour and Fatherland."

In the circle below the Commandant of a Free French warship is fixing in his cabin the tail fin of a German bomb which fell on the vessel.

FREE FRENCH NAVY includes the destroyer Triomphant (centre left), an exceptionally fast ship with a maximum speed of 43 knots, and several submarine chasers, one of which is seen above. The average displacement of these craft is about 150 tons. They carry a 3-in. gun, anti-aircraft machine-guns and depth charges.
Photos, Forces Navales Françaises Libres

With Free France On the Ocean Wave

FREE FRENCH SAILORS at gun drill aboard one of their warships. It will be noticed that the gun-mounting is lettered Colonel D'Ornano, the gallant Free French soldier killed in a raid last January on Murzuk, Italian Libya. Since then the Camp Colonna D'Ornano, a military academy, destined to be the Saint Cyr of Free French Africa, was inaugurated in his memory at Brazzaville.

Photo, Forces Navales Francaises Libres

Our Diary of the War

SUNDAY, JUNE 29, 1941   *666th day*

Sea.—Italian 10,000-ton cruiser sunk by British submarine in Mediterranean.

Air.—R.A.F. fighters carried out sweep over coast of Northern France. Heavy night raids on Hamburg, Bremen and other targets in N.W. Germany.

Russian Front.—New German push towards Murmansk by troops from Norway. Germans also attacked from Karelian Isthmus.

Germans claimed to have crossed R. Dvina and to have captured Dvinsk.

Russians stated that advance of enemy tank columns in direction of Minsk and Luck had been stopped. Fierce fighting in progress. Germany claimed that armoured units had by-passed Minsk and pushed beyond.

Near East.—R.A.F. heavily raided Palmyra and aerodromes at Aleppo and Deir ez Zor.

General.—Lord Beaverbrook appointed Minister of Supply.

MONDAY, JUNE 30   *667th day*

Air.—R.A.F. bombers made two day raids on objectives in Germany, including Bremen and Kiel. Large force carried out sweep over Northern France.

Night attacks on Duisburg, Cologne and Düsseldorf. Four of our bombers missing.

Russian Front.—Fierce fighting in Murmansk sector. German attacks on Karelian Isthmus repulsed. Attempted naval landing frustrated.

Germans claimed capture of Latvian port of Liepaja (Libau). Russians reported heavy fighting in Dvinsk area.

Germans claimed to have occupied Minsk and to be advancing eastwards.

In southern Poland Germans reported capture of Lwow and Jaworow.

Africa.—Heavy and successful R.A.F. raids on Tripoli. Eight enemy aircraft shot down off coast of Cyrenaica.

Near East.—Free French forces repulsed strong Vichy counter-attack N.E. of Damascus.

Cairo reported that Palmyra was completely encircled. Heavy R.A.F. raids on Syrian aerodromes.

Home.—Night raid on South Wales towns. Bombs also fell in W. and S.W. England.

TUESDAY, JULY 1   *668th day*

Sea.—H.M. corvette Pintail reported sunk.

Air.—Day attacks by R.A.F. on Oldenburg, Borkum and Northern France. Night raids on Brest, Cherbourg and many aerodromes.

Russian Front.—In far north German and Finnish advance continued against strong resistance. Artillery duel at Hango, S. Finland. Riga reported to have fallen.

In southern Poland Germans announced capture of Luck. Russians claimed to have stopped enemy advance near Rovno.

Africa.—Night attacks by R.A.F. on Benghazi, Gazala and Tripoli.

Near East.—Imperial aircraft attacked Rayak and other aerodromes and military objectives in Syria, including Beirut harbour.

General.—Gen. Wavell, G.O.C.-in-C., Middle East, exchanged posts with Gen. Auchinleck, C.-in-C. India.

WEDNESDAY, JULY 2   *669th day*

Air.—Two daylight bombing raids on Northern France ; at least 17 enemy aircraft shot down for loss of 9 British. Night raids on Bremen, Cologne, Duisburg, Cherbourg and Rotterdam.

Russian Front.—Reported in Stockholm that Germans had captured Murmansk.

Germans claimed that many pockets of Soviet troops and tank units had been destroyed, and that in Bialystok area 100,000 men were captured and 400 tanks and 300 guns taken.

On Bessarabian front Russians repelled several enemy attempts to cross R. Pruth.

Naval base at Constanza shelled by Russian warships.

Near East.—Cairo stated that positions overlooking Palmyra, lost in counter-attack, had been regained.

Night air attacks on Vichy shipping in Beirut harbour and on flying-boats at Tripolis. Many aerodromes bombed.

THURSDAY, JULY 3   *670th day*

Air.—R.A.F. bombed railway targets in Hazebrouck-St. Omer area. Twelve enemy fighters destroyed. Britain lost 6 fighters and 1 bomber. Night raids on Essen and elsewhere in the Ruhr, and on Bremen and Bremerhaven.

Russian Front.—German advance continued in Karelian Isthmus.

Enemy drive from Dvinsk towards Leningrad developing.

North-east of Minsk German advance was slowed down. South of Pripet Marshes Russian resistance was stubborn. Violent tank battles in Borisov-Tarnopol sector. Enemy attempts to cross R. Beresina frustrated.

On Southern front German and Rumanian troops reported to have advanced into northern Bessarabia and to be pushing on to R. Dniester.

Africa.—Announced that 3,000 Italians and 1,200 natives had surrendered at Debra Tabor.

Heavy R.A.F. raids on Tripoli, Benghazi, Gazala, Bardia and Derna.

Near East.—Palmyra surrendered. Deir ez Zor and Tell Kotchek captured. Vichy submarine reported sunk off Beirut.

FRIDAY, JULY 4   *671st day*

Air.—Sixteen enemy fighters destroyed during offensive sweep over Northern France. Power station and chemical works at Bethune bombed. Day raids on Bremen and Norderney.

Heavy night attacks on Brest and Lorient, and smaller ones on Cherbourg, Abbeville and Rhineland.

Russian Front.—Soviet troops moving to new battle positions in Baltic States. In White Russia Germans claimed to have crossed R. Beresina at several points. Great tank battle in progress.

Heavy fighting in Rovno and Tarnopol sectors. Hungarians claimed to have forced Carpathian passes.

Africa.—Cairo reported that Gen. Gazzera, supreme commander of remaining Italian forces in Abyssinia, had surrendered.

Near East.—Imperial Air Forces attacked Vichy aerodromes and Beirut.

Home.—Night raiders bombed districts in Midlands and S.W. England. Three destroyed.

SATURDAY, JULY 5   *672nd day*

Air.—Steel works at Lille bombed during R.A.F. daylight sweep. Destructive night raid on many towns in Western Germany.

Russian Front.—Fighting reported at Murmansk, Kandalaksha and on Karelian Isthmus. Berlin claimed advance despite stubborn resistance.

Soviet forces repulsed repeated attempts to cross rivers Beresina and Drut. Germans claimed that forces east of Minsk had reached R. Dnieper.

In Ukraine Russians admitted that enemy tank thrust was developing in direction of Novgorod-Volinsk.

In Bessarabia Nazis crossed R. Pruth at several points, but further advance was held. Hungarians claimed capture of Stanislawow and Kolomea.

Near East.—New attack by Australians in Jezzine area, west of Damascus.

S.S. KEMMENDINE, 7,769-ton Glasgow liner, meets her doom in the Indian Ocean. The track of the Nazi torpedo is still to be seen as the explosion churns up the sea and sends a cloud of smoke and debris high into the air. The captain, Robert Reid, and his crew, taken aboard the German surface raider, were landed at Mogadishu, Italian Somaliland, in July 1940. Here they remained in captivity under the Italians until released by our victorious South African forces when they took this port. Inset, smoke and foam having subsided, the Kemmendine, her back broken, slowly disappears beneath the waves.

Photos, Keystone

They're Kept Busy Trying to Sweep Our Mines

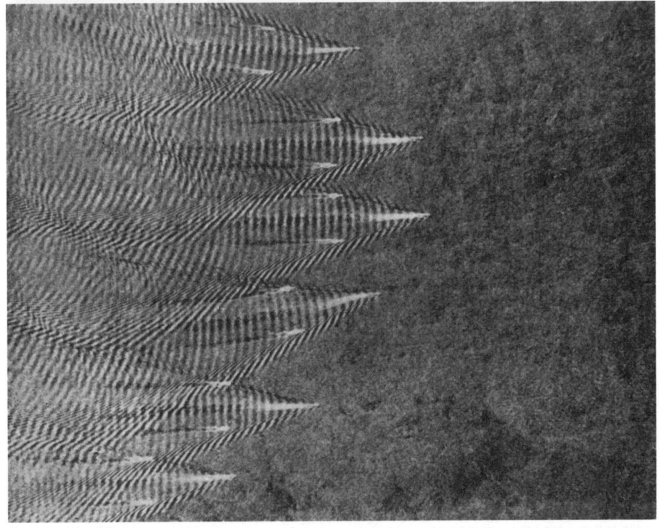

NAZI MINE-SWEEPERS from the air, with their paravanes trailing astern, make an intricate pattern on the sea. This photograph, taken by the R.A.F., shows how minesweepers comb the sea for submerged explosives. Above, a fleet of German minesweepers, escorted by a fighting ship, seen in the foreground, returning to the Flanders coast after operations in the English Channel. Mines, of course, are Britain's first line of defence against sea-borne invasion, and any attempt to land on these shores would have to be preceded by Nazi minesweepers.   *Photos, British Official and E.N.A.*

American Planes Sent Direct to Malaya

Here the unpacked machine is being swung by a crane into the hangar, where British and Asiatic mechanics will assemble it. The enclosed cockpit with sliding canopy can be seen.

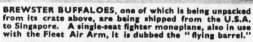

BREWSTER BUFFALOES, one of which is being unpacked from its crate above, are being shipped from the U.S.A. to Singapore. A single-seat fighter monoplane, also in use with the Fleet Air Arm, it is dubbed the "flying barrel."

Once the mechanics have put the aircraft together (above) they will go from their assembly lines (right) to the flying field for testing. The Buffalo has a top speed of over 300 m.p.h. and is extremely manoeuvrable.

LOCKHEED HUDSONS are also largely used by the R.A.A.F. serving in Malaya, and a flight of them is here seen over the Malayan forests. Note the power-operated gun turret near the tail. The Hudson has a range of 1,700 miles at an economical cruising speed of 170 m.p.h. Right, Bristol Blenheim bombers flying over the harbour at Singapore.

Photos, Associated Press, Planet News, Press Topics

New York's 'Rum Chasers' Hunt Nazi Pirates

U.S. REVENUE CUTTERS, sent to Britain under the Lease and Lend agreement, are now operating with the Royal Navy. One of these cutters, heavily armed for its size, is seen under Queensborough Bridge, with American sailors on board, shortly before leaving Brooklyn Harbour. Later on the journey British crews took over. The type of cutter shown has a standard displacement of 2,000 tons, carries a normal complement of 150 officers and men, and has a speed of 16 knots. With an average cruising radius of 8,000 miles, they are useful vessels for convoy work. Their nickname of " rum chasers " is derived from their employment against liquor smugglers in the days of Prohibition.　　　*Photo, Planet News*

Home Guards 'In Action' in War-Scarred London

Marked with a cross, by an officer-umpire, meant that this Home Guard had been put out of action. Circle, a defender in a man-hole has been caught by two attackers.

IN 'THE CITY' the Home Guards mount barricades during an exercise held on June 29. The General Post Office Battalion defended the square mile about Barbican, Moorgate, Cheapside and Aldersgate against "enemy" paratroops belonging to the L.M.S. Home Guards. In a war setting reminiscent of Ypres the attackers surrounded the telephone exchange building, hurling electric bulbs as hand-grenades, the defenders replying with balloons filled with water.

The G.P.O. men beat off the paratroops; and the exercise provided opportunities for nurses to display their skill. Here they are attending two "wounded" defenders amid the rubble of blitzed buildings.
Photos, "Daily Mirror," Keystone, Fox

I Was There! .... Eye Witness Stories of the War

I Warned the Man Who Sank the Robin Moor

The sinking of the American freighter Robin Moor in the South Atlantic on May 21 roused considerable feeling in the U.S.A. The stories of the two parties who reached S. Africa and S. America confirmed that it was a German submarine which torpedoed the ship.

WHEN all hopes of their rescue had been abandoned in Washington, thirty-five survivors from the United States freighter Robin Moor were landed at Cape Town by a British ship. A dramatic story of their encounter with the submarine was told by Chief Officer Melvin Mundy.

Describing their first meeting with the U-boat, Mundy said : I was on watch on the bridge in the early hours of the morning when I noticed a " blinker " light asking who we were. I replied, giving the ship's name.

I was very careful to signal the word " American " first, because I had a suspicion that it was a submarine. There was no immediate answer, so I sent someone down to waken the captain.

The captain ordered the signalman to ask, " Who are you ? " The answer came back immediately, " Submarine." A minute later the submarine flashed " LRL," which meant " I am pursuing you." A minute after that the submarine flashed, " Don't use your wireless."

We stopped our engines on the orders of our captain, Edward W. Myers, of Baltimore. Then the submarine flashed : " Send boat to me." The captain sent me to the submarine in our No. 1 lifeboat.

Aboard the submarine I was asked for the ship's papers and the nature of the cargo. I told him we had nothing but ordinary merchandise for South African ports, merchandise such as pleasure cars, but he would not listen to me. The submarine commander kept saying over and over again : " You have supplies for my country's enemy, and therefore I must sink you in twenty minutes."

I said we had eight passengers—that we didn't care about ourselves. I pointed out that one of the passengers was a little child. He only shook his head. I tried to impress him with the fact that we had women aboard, told him about a man and his wife who were

in their sixties and explained we couldn't get people like that into the boats in a hurry.

" Well, maybe I will give you thirty minutes," he told me. I begged him to take our ship to some neutral port. He absolutely refused. I warned him, " You may be sorry if you sink our ship."

The Robin Moor's lifeboats were launched and we were ordered to leave her lying as she was—a perfect target. A torpedo was fired and this was followed by thirty-three shells. The ship sank in twenty minutes.

The submarine officer promised to wireless our position, and handed over some black bread and tins of butter. My ankle was injured and I was handed some bandages with German markings.

Among the survivors to reach Pernambuco were Mr. Karl Nilson and Mr. Sanderlin, the first and second engineers of the Robin Moor. They made a joint statement as follows :

At dawn on May 21 a German submarine stopped the Robin Moor and immediately forbade the broadcast of all radio appeals for help, and ordered the crew to abandon ship under armed threats. We possess photographs of various scenes, which have been handed to Mr. William Phillips, Secretary of the U.S. Embassy.

We were nineteen days under a tropical sun, which caused terrible burns. When it rained we had to bale out the whale boats

Edward W. Myers, master of the 4,985-ton American freighter Robin Moor, sunk in the Atlantic by a German submarine on May 21.

with our hands already swollen by the oars. We had no food.

We were finally saved by the steamship Osorio, in which we were admirably cared for.

Some members of the Robin Moor's crew formed the impression that Germans were operating in a French submarine. Second Officer Taylor said :

On the side of the conning tower I plainly saw the words " La Touche " in raised letters, painted over in an attempt to hide them. There was also a painted cartoon of the head of a Guernsey cow. Near it was the inscription, " La Vache Qui- Rit " (The Laughing Cow).

The submarine commander was German all right, though he spoke English.

I Saw Chinese Soldiers Going Out to Die

This moving story by Agnes Smedley tells of the sufferings and privations of the Chinese soldiers, and also of the spirit that has enabled them to withstand the Japanese Army for four years.

ALL day long we had ridden along the Chinese defences in North Hupeh Province. When the shadows of the hills grew long we halted at a mud hut in a narrow valley which one of the armies was using as its first dressing station to care for the wounded.

There was but one door to the hut. Inside, on the earthen floor, lay a number of wounded men in a row ; in the fading light their dark forms were like a part of the mud walls and the earth floor beneath them. On a rude table near the door stood half a dozen half-filled bottles, a pair of black native scissors, a few rolled bandages, and some small squares of gauze. From a dusty rafter hung a big wad of unwashed local cotton. An army dresser sometimes reached up, took a bit of the cotton, dipped it in a small bowl of liquid, and washed the wound of one of the men lying on the floor. Then he took a bit of gauze and a bandage and bound the wound. He did not wash off the blood that had caked on the man's neck and face.

Marching feet beyond the mud hut disturbed me, and I turned to see a line of grey figures passing, with rifles and packs. I went slowly out. Soon they halted, removed their packs, sat down and rested, their rifles between their knees. Two of them went away and brought back a big wooden bucket of boiled water, and soon all had drunk. This was a company of troops moving up to the battlefield, and this was their last stop for rest.

I went towards them, and their commander arose quickly and saluted. He came up and we talked. " We are going up," he said. " Will you say something ? We have half an hour." Then he uttered a command, and all the soldiers arose and stood at attention. " Salute ! " shouted the commander. I returned the salute, but with better reason than they. " This is a foreign

ROBIN MOOR, despite the American flag painted on her side, was sunk by the Nazis. This photograph of the sinking ship was taken by one of her crew. The dramatic story of the Robin Moor's encounter with the German submarine is given in this page.

Photos, Wide World and Keystone

718   *The War Illustrated*   *July 18th,* 1941

|||||||||||||||||||||||||||||||||||||||||||||||||||||||||||||| **I WAS THERE!** ||||||||||||||||||||||||||||||||||||||||||||||||||||||||||||||||

friend. She works for our wounded. She will speak to us."

What does one say to men going out to die? The faces and eyes were solemn, serious—faces from another world than mine. But were they? Then I thought of my own people, of the people of England, of all the common people of the world who have watched and sympathized with China. And I told the soldiers of those people who hope for their victory, who give from small wages or salaries to send medical supplies to them. "We have not done enough," I said, "but we have tried to do something. I shall tell what I have seen here, how you look and fight, and of the spirit that moves you to continue fighting until your country is free."

I told them the names and the work of many organizations working for China, and of those that do work of humanity. In this I mentioned the name of President Roosevelt and of the Lord Mayor of London, who had issued calls for money for medical aid. Suddenly a soldier jumped to his feet:

"Long live Llod Mayo of London! Long live Llosevelt!" The entire company shouted after him. "Long live the——" The slogan leader had forgotten the names of the organizations I had mentioned, so he hesitated and then added: "All the people in the world who are our friends!"

The commander smiled proudly, turned to me, and said: "We must now move up."

"Salute!" he shouted, and all the men arose and saluted. They shouldered their packs and rifles and were ready. They began to march. With a heart heavy with misery I marched with them up into the ravine. On the crest of a rise the commander said: "Do not come farther!" I took his hand, shook my head, and together we walked in silence. The ravine grew

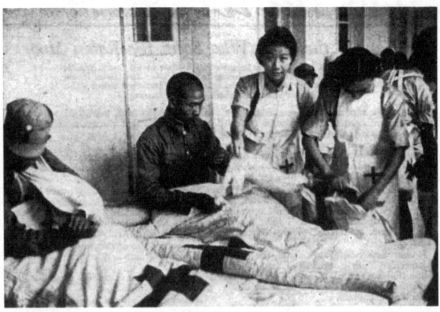

CHINESE NURSES, members of the Chinese " New Life " organization, attending to wounded soldiers at a Chinese hospital. In this page an American woman describes her experiences in war-ridden China. On July 7 the Sino-Japanese war entered its fifth year.
Photo, Wide World

dark, and again he halted and said: "Go back. Good-bye."

I stepped to the side and the men marched past me, each one turning his face to me. They were like shadows as they passed, and I reached out and touched them. Then they were all gone, and I stood until their figures blended with the darkness. Somewhere in the hills a shell burst and machine-guns hammered.—"*Manchester Guardian.*"

This Was One of Over 700 Raids on Malta

The spirit of the Maltese people, who have undergone so many air raids in the past year, is well exemplified in the following stories which appeared in the "Times of Malta." See also page 652.

I N one raid on Malta several houses were seriously damaged and a number of civilians had narrow escapes. Mr. E. V., a district commissioner, and Mr. G., an assistant commissioner, spoke highly of the behaviour of the people in the streets in which bombs fell, saying:

They were throughout cool, calm and collected, giving little trouble and making their own arrangements to move elsewhere from the damaged houses. In one house we found the family and the friends they had to tea when the raid started, were finishing their meal in the only room left whole in their home! A bomb hurtling down on a farm fell on a manure heap and killed some goats. The farmer's children were sheltering in a crude rubble shelter in the field near by, and came out none the worse for their experience.

One old lady who had an extraordinary escape said:

I was sitting on a chair in a corner of the room, when the house received a direct hit. The bomb burst on the roof, and the whole of it crashed down into the room where I was, but I was unhurt except for slight scratches.

Three Maltese Naval ratings heroically searched for survivors in damaged houses. One of them, J. C., an

Resolution tinged with scorn for the aerial invader stamps the face of this Maltese who has gone through hundreds of air raids.
Photo, Associated Press

18-year-old rating in a minesweeper, said: "I was sheltering behind a door with two comrades when we heard the whistle of falling bombs. We immediately flung ourselves face downwards in the street, and when we picked ourselves up we were enveloped in smoke and started calling out to each other to see if the three of us were safe. We then made our way to where the bomb had fallen, and people shouted to us that there was a boy in the house.

"I climbed in through one of the broken windows, tearing my uniform, and started searching among the debris, but could not find anybody. It was then realized that there had been nobody in the house. We made our way into all the houses which were damaged and where there might have been casualties. In one house we heard calls for help and, forcing the door open, found a man and his wife and child enveloped in smoke and too terrified to move. We calmed them, and then went from house to house, reassuring those who had been badly shaken."

The British Government have sent, through Lord Moyne, a message of admiration to the people of Malta, saying how they " continue to watch with profound admiration the heroic courage and unquenchable resolution of the garrison and people of Malta in battle." Above, bomb-shattered buildings in Malta.
Photo, Associated Press

Our Bomber Was in Flames Over Wilhelmshaven

Unlike the German bombers, who have only to cross the Channel to get to England, the R.A.F. have the North Sea as an obstacle on their way to and from Germany. A typically adventurous journey back from a raid was described by a Sergeant Pilot in a broadcast.

MY crew and I had just made a successful night raid on the docks at Wilhelmshaven and were barely ten minutes away from the target when we ran into heavy anti-aircraft fire. It wasn't as bad as I have known it, but one of the shells hit the starboard engine and soon after that the airscrew came away from the engine and flew off into space. I didn't actually see it go and the first I knew that something was wrong was when the aircraft swerved to the right—fortunately not a very violent swerve—and at the same time I heard the navigator telling me what had happened.

I looked down and there were sparks and flames shooting out of the engine cowling and for a second or two I thought that it was all up with us. I gave the crew the order to stand by to abandon aircraft, and then it passed through my mind that we ought to be able to make a forced landing in Germany. My next thought was that, either way, we'd become prisoners of war, and I didn't like the idea of that at all.

By now the crew were ready to bale out, and then I saw that the flames had disappeared. What put them out I don't know. The main thing is that they went out, and with the danger of fire over, there was a reasonable chance of getting back home. Anyhow it was worth the gamble and the crew were, like me, all in favour of having a shot at it.

At the time we were 8,000 feet up, facing a strong headwind which would soon have been too much for the single engine we had left—we would have gone so slowly that we might not have got there. So I came down to 3,000 feet in a gentle glide. I knew before we set out that at 3,000 feet the wind was less fierce. It was. The "Met" section was right as usual.

The next problem was up to the rest of the crew rather than to me—that was to try and lighten the machine. So I told the navigator, the wireless operator, and the rear gunner to jettison everything that could be spared out of the machine. This might lighten it and give us a chance to keep at a fairly good height. Just before this the navigator, who sits in front and below the pilot, had the bright idea of tying his oxygen tube round the left end of my rudder bar and pulling forward on it. This relieved me of a great deal of

strain, as before I had to correct the pull of our one engine all the time with the rudder. The navigator's brain-wave helped me out with the rudder and stopped me from getting cramp in the leg, though it didn't stop me from getting a nasty pain in the small of the back.

As soon as I was easier he got busy chucking things out of his own compartment. Guns, pans of ammunition and a good deal of our navigation equipment went into the sea. We kept just a few pans of ammunition as well as a couple of guns just in case we met an enemy. Next the crew tried to get rid of the armour plating behind me, but it wouldn't budge. Then they tried to unship part of the bombing apparatus, but that was

Every day an R.A.F. plane climbs to 25,000 feet over Britain to make meteorological observations. The author of this story probable owed his life to the "Met" section. *Photo, Keystone*

just as obstinate. By now we were down to 800 feet, but by getting rid of the guns and things we were able to keep at that height and later even climb to just over a thousand feet.

Still, there was always the danger of being forced down into the water, so the crew decided to get the dinghy ready in case it was wanted. We were keeping a reasonable air speed, but the one good engine was getting overheated. As dawn broke we could see no sign of land, but the navigator was confident it wasn't far away. He was right, although at five minutes past seven we had only thirty-five gallons of petrol left and still no land to be seen. And then, only a few minutes later, the grey outline of the East Coast came in sight. It was too early to count our chickens, but when we crossed the coast thirty-five minutes afterwards I knew we would be all right, if we could find an aerodrome. Then the navigator suddenly exclaimed: "It's all right, there's an aerodrome a couple of miles away." His navigation had been marvellous. He had reckoned with all the wobbling about I had done on the way and had brought us safely home. Down we went to make a perfect landing, four hours after the airscrew had said good-bye to the bomber. There was no petrol left in the tanks, but, as you can imagine, our spirits were high.

THE POETS & THE WAR
XLV
FAREWELL TO FEAR

The following lines were written by an airman after a recent crash :—

Three days ago
Eternity stood nigh me,
  Clean, white as snow
With nothing to deny me
  A passing mild,
Some little fame behind me
  For Wife and child
Before dull age could blind me.

Senseless I lie,
Five hours unconscious witness,
  To live or die ?
Nature's stern test of fitness.
  Of life the gift
Again so strangely given
  Gladly I lift
By some new strength reshriven.

Farewell to fear,
The doubts that ever tied me,
  The road is clear
With England's need to guide me.
  So high the quest
That every qualm is treason ;
  Life at its best
Is Faith beyond all reason.

—The Times

A bomber's engine being turned up for a raid over Germany. Above is told how a twin-engined bomber returned safely on only one engine.   *Photo, Fox*

Siftings From the News

Marlborough College has started a second-hand clothes shop.

Women's Land Army now has 14,000 members in regular employment.

Moscow citizens were ordered to hand over all radio and television sets for the duration.

German General Staff said to have allowed three months for the conquest of Russia.

Rumours that Gen. Gamelin and M. Daladier had escaped from prison denied by Vichy.

New York now has a Union Jack Club where everything British sailors want is available.

About 100,000 German evacuee children in Slovakia now within range of Russian bombs.

British prisoners of war have received through Red Cross 200 mouth organs "made in Germany," from pre-war stocks.

Canada is to recruit 3,000 women for a Canadian A.T.S.

"Oil is Hitler's soft economic spot," said Dr. Hugh Dalton.

Rumanians are forbidden, under severe penalties, to listen to enemy broadcasts.

Red Cross Penny-a-Week Fund has now passed the £20,000 a week mark.

Caravans, each housing five men, range over Essex to carry out emergency land work.

Inhabitants of Bergen are forbidden to open or look out of windows that give on the street.

Women are to be enrolled in the Royal Observer Corps, to replace men called up.

Nettles, dandelion roots, foxgloves and meadow saffron are being collected for medicinal purposes.

From £30 to £50 is paid by medical factories for one ton of dried nettles.

Hundreds of friendly alien doctors will shortly be allowed to practise in hospitals and A.R.P. services.

Polish workers in Germany have to wear a badge, virtually branding them as slaves.

Peru has prohibited the use of her territorial waters to any submarine of belligerents.

Tobruk garrison issues a daily newspaper entitled "Tobruk Truth or Dinkum Oil."

Goering is rumoured to have lost favour and been reduced in rank.

Prince Paul, ex-Regent of Yugoslavia, arrived with his wife in Kenya.

"Hitler's Headache," America's largest bomber, can fly 7,750 miles non-stop.

American newsreel companies are chagrined that the British Government has forbidden any attempt to photograph Hess.

The Editor's Postscript

SHAKESPEARE, as always, was right when he made Portia begin her defence of Antonio with " The quality of mercy is not strain'd." It's different, however, with the quality of humour. Sometimes I'm inclined to flatter myself that I have a sense of humour—having edited no fewer than forty volumes of selections from " Punch " might be some measure of evidence—but when I see five inches of valuable space occupied in one of our skeleton dailies this morning with a silly picture of a tank reared on its end balancing a large football on its nose, with the caption " Henderson used to train sea-lions," I certainly feel that the quality of humour is terribly " strained."

P. G. WODEHOUSE'S particular kind of humour, which derives so much from the highly ingenious hilarity of his dialogue, has never greatly appealed to me, though its "Entertainment value " is obvious. " Go and see your doctor " was the advice of the producer of an allegedly funny play, " Nothing but the Truth," when I told him that I sat it out with increasing impatience, and I shall not forget the causeless laughter that surrounded me on the dreadful night I spent at " French Without Tears." In both of these the quality of the humour seemed to me strained—through a horse's nosebag. But that's by the way . . . my sense of humour is no doubt at fault.

I SEE nothing funny, however, in the creator of " Jeeves " broadcasting to America once a week from Berlin, where he has been allowed the unusual liberty for an enemy alien of residing in a comfy little suite at the Hotel Adlon instead of remaining in an internment camp, like so many of his unlucky compatriots who were caught in the toils of war when France fell from us. It is difficult to see how this humorist of Anglo-American frivolous fame can have anything valuable to say to America once a week during his privileged captivity in Hunland. Not one word can he utter that has not been examined, approved, and sanctioned by some official Hun set over him, whose dearest delight would be to trip the humorist into some statement that would tend to put the censor's brother Huns in a good light with the broadcaster's American admirers.

ONE who was less of a " funny man " and more of a stubborn Briton would have scorned to enjoy a liberty denied to his fellow prisoners of war even at the cheap price of being entertaining at the microphone once a week. I feel sure that he can have no conception of the deep resentment aroused here in England by his action. At best it is a deplorable gesture from one who has enjoyed such popularity as a comic writer on both sides of the Atlantic. Surely not even those who admire his writings can find an excuse for such a solecism. To think of any Englishman living at the Adlon among the fashionable Huns at such a time as this is nauseating.

" WIVES and mithers 'maist despairin', ca' them lives o' men." That line from " Caller Herrin " comes to my mind whenever I hear of trouble in the fishing industry. The recent kick-up about profiteering there is characteristic of a commerce that has long exploited the men who do the fishing at risk of their lives and the housewives who buy the fish. I happen to know something of the methods of Billingsgate that were in force a few years ago, as two particular friends of mine (now both dead) were big men in the fishing industry—not in the hmckstering business that goes on at Billingsgate. One of them came to me a year or so before his death to ask if I could give him an idea how to get rid of three or four tons of good fish every week . . . not for profit, be it noted, but just to prevent its being used as manure ! Good sound fish for which men had risked their lives in the North Sea. Why did he have this surplus ? Because the method then (I know nothing of what is happening today) was for the trawlers to send their catches to Billingsgate to be auctioned, and as soon as the bidders had bought all that the trade needed there was a nod or a wink from a boss and no more bidding was heard.

HENCE the weekly three or four tons that went abegging from my friends' trawling enterprise. " Never buy up the whole catch " was evidently the motto, and you can see why. All my ideas for giving away the unbidden tons were thwarted. Even the idea of supplying them at the sheer cost of packing and transport to a great national charity was turned down on the ground that so many wealthy salesmen subscribed to the charity ! You twig the idea ?—

" give 'em fish for nothing and they'll not need our subscriptions." The charity went on buying its fish at trade price. The average market price realized (in those days) was 2¼d. per pound, out of which the fishing company and its employees who shared in the proceeds of each catch were rewarded for all their outlay of money and hard work ; but much of the fish bought at that price was sold in the shops at 2s. a pound.

THINGS may have changed out of all recognition since then, though it's only six years or so since the second of my friends in the fishing industry died—both of them told me the same story, with much more detail than I have space to relate—but it's just the standard story of the " ring " trick. In Buenos Aires when I was there the fruit ring used to tip hundreds of tons of fruit into the River Plate in times of plenty in order to keep up the price in the fruit shops, as the coffee kings at Sao Paulo used to dump ship-loads of coffee beans in the sea off Santos for the same reason. Some day —long after the War—social reformers may find some means of stopping that sort of sabotage on the people's food.

HEARD on the radio today that an Australian Air Squadron in Syria had encountered six of the futile Vichy fighters — the men not the machines, which were good American Glenn-Martins — and sent the whole lot down in flames. Less than an hour before I had been reading a letter written by T. E. Lawrence to his friend Lionel Curtis on March 19, 1934, soon after he had resigned from his job as aircraftman in the R.A.F., in which he said : " Our poorest squadrons could deal very summarily with France. When Germany wings herself—ah, that will be another matter, and our signal to reinforce ; for the German kites will be new and formidable, not like that sorry French junk." The programme which he then outlined in that inspired letter for Britain's air equipment would have been adequate to meet the German expansion which so soon followed.

WHAT a tragedy that he was allowed to throw away so many years of his precious life in his obstinate refusal of responsibility, squandering his organizing genius in the useful but uninspired pursuits of an aircraftman ! Little more than a year after he wrote that marvellous letter (wish I could reprint it all) his career of " tomfoolery," as his most understanding friend Bernard Shaw (T. E. Lawrence was then " T. E. Shaw " by deed poll) had justly named it, was at an end, and the restless, perplexing, irritating, and not very lovable man of genius was dead at 47. His many foolish-seeming years as a ranker in the Tanks and R.A.F. would have proved a priceless asset to him in a position of command, for which nature and his Arabian exploits had equipped him, and Mr. Churchill, who knew him well and fully appreciated his extraordinary talent, wrote : " I hoped to see him quit his retirement and take a commanding part in facing the dangers which now threaten our country." The pity of it !

GEN. SIR CLAUDE AUCHINLECK, C.-in-C. India since Dec. 1940, was on July 2, 1941, appointed G.O.C.-in-C. Middle East, changing places with Gen. Sir A. Wavell. General Auchinleck was commander of the Allied Forces at Narvik.   *Photo, Planet News*

JOHN CARPENTER HOUSE
WHITEFRIARS. LONDON E.C.4.

Registered at the G.P.O. as a Newspaper   *The War Illustrated, July 25th, 1941*

Vol 4   The War Illustrated   Nº 99

Edited by Sir John Hammerton

FOURPENCE   WEEKLY

'SCORCHED EARTH'—the policy adopted by China against the Japanese invaders—has now been decreed by Stalin as a most powerful weapon against the Nazis. "We must not leave a single pound of grain or a single gallon of petrol to the enemy," said Stalin in his broadcast of July 3; "leave only the scorched earth for the invader." Above, some of the Nazi vanguard, having reached Russian territory, where they hoped to find boundless loot, are looking in dismay at the smoke from raging fires which will cheat them of their booty.   *Photo, Wide World*

Our Searchlight on the War

Canadian Victory Torch

FLOWN in a bomber across the Atlantic to London the Canadian Victory Loan Torch, a massive golden emblem 4½ ft. high, was presented to Mr. Churchill on July 1. During Canada's great war loan campaign the torch travelled across the Dominion from Vancouver to Halifax, escorted always by three representatives of the Armed Forces ; and three young Canadian officers stood by in the garden of No. 10 Downing Street when the Prime Minister received it from Mr. Ian Mackenzie, Canadian Minister of Pensions. With the Torch came a scroll bearing the names of the Governor-General, the Canadian Prime Minister, the Premiers of the nine Provinces, and of distinguished citizens of 27 cities in which it was ceremonially received after its dedication at Victoria, British Columbia, on Empire Day. The Canadian campaign realized over £200,000,000 ; upon the Torch is the inscription : "Canada's Victory Loan 1941. Part of the Tools."

Norwegian Actors Defy Nazis

RESISTANCE to German bullying in Norway takes many forms, both passive and active. Conflict which has recently arisen between the Stage and the quislingist " Department for Culture and Enlightenment " had its origin in a refusal by Norwegian actors to cooperate with the Nazi-controlled Norwegian Broadcasting Corporation. The authorities retaliated by arresting some of the best-known actors and actresses who had refused to broadcast, whereupon a sympathetic strike was ordered by the Norwegian Actors' Association, and all theatres in Oslo and other cities closed down. The infuriated Nazis made further arrests, seized the funds of the Actors' Association so that no financial aid was forthcoming, and also took steps to " freeze " the private accounts of individual actors. Furthermore, in order to obtain complete control of the theatres, a licensing system was introduced both for theatres and actors ; each theatre

CANADA'S TORCH OF VICTORY being dedicated in Victoria, B.C., by the Premier of British Columbia, Mr. T. D. Patullo. After touring Canada it was flown to England and presented to Mr. Churchill, who, on the right, is reading a scroll signed by leading Canadians. Behind the Torch, which helped to raise £200,000,000 in War Loan, is Mr. Ian Mackenzie, Canadian Minister of Pensions.
Photos, Sidney Pott, P.N.A.

at Oslo refused to apply for a licence, four prominent directors were arrested. As a final turn of the screw the Germans now threaten to turn every theatre in Norway into barracks or storehouses.

Travelling in the Reich

SEVEN commandments for railway passengers in Germany have been drawn up by the authorities. It would seem that, owing to severe curtailment of services, travelling is now possible only in conditions of extreme discomfort. The first rule therefore is : " Do not travel unless you must ; if you do, don't complain." The second requires luggage to be of the smallest possible dimensions. The third urges that farewells be made outside the barrier, not on the crowded platform. Rule 4 is an instruction that the passenger who has been longest in any given compartment shall control the other occupants, settling differences of opinion as to seats, windows, disposal of

luggage ; order travellers to sit more closely wedged so as to make room for yet another ; ensure that all shall take their share of standing. Rule 5 deprecates the practice of elbow-digging and fighting for seats. In rule 6 passengers are requested not to bother guards or station officials. The final commandment curtly orders : " Observe the same rules on the journey home."

Hospital Ship as Hostage

SINCE the outbreak of war thirty-one deliberate attacks have been made by enemy aircraft and shore batteries on British hospital ships and carriers. Three of these ships were sunk, and many others were severely damaged, despite the fact that all were clearly marked and conformed in every way with the requirements of the Hague Convention. The Government, therefore, announced on July 3 that the Italian hospital ship Ramb IV had been detained and would be used as a hospital ship for British and enemy sick and wounded for at least six months. If by the end of that period enemy attacks on our own hospital ships have ceased, her return may be considered.

K.T. GIRL attached to the A.T.S. Her duty is to check gunfire by an ingenious photographic machine called Kine-Theodolite, hence the new flash-badge (inset) now worn by the K.T. section.
Photos, Fox

was put in charge of a " leader " responsible to the authorities, and licensed actors had to sign a new contract pledging themselves to collaborate with all State cultural institutions. Because the National Theatre

ABBREVIATIONS USED BY THE FOUR SERVICES

Home Defence and General

A. Ambulance.	**F.A.N.Y.** First Aid Nursing Yeomanry.	**N.D.C.** National Defence Corps or Contribution.
A.F.S. Auxiliary Fire Service.	**F.A.P.** First Aid Post (or Party).	**Q.M.** Queen's Messengers.
A.M. Air Ministry.	**H.O.** Home Office.	**R.C.** Red Cross.
A.R.P. Air Raid Precautions.	**K.S.K.** Ethyl-iodo-acetate (gas).	**R.O.C.** Royal Observer Corps.
A.R.W. Air Raid Warden.	**L.S.C.** London Salvage Corps.	**R.P.** Rescue Party.
Aux. F.S. Auxiliary Fire Station.	**M.A.P.** Ministry of Aircraft Production ; Medical Aid Post.	**RP/H.** Repairs Heavy (or Light).
B.B.C. Bromo-benzyl-cyanide (gas) or British Broadcasting Corpn.	**M.E.W.** Ministry of Economic Warfare.	**R.S.D.** Rescue Service and Demolition.
B.D. Bomb Disposal.	**M.H. or M.O.H.** Ministry of Health.	**S.B.** Stretcher Bearer.
B.T. Board of Trade.	**M.O.I.** Ministry of Information.	**S.F.P.** Supplementary Fire Party.
C.A.P. Chlor-acetone-phenone (gas).	**M.O.S.** Ministry of Supply.	**S.P.** Stretcher Party.
C.D. Civil Defence.	**M.U.** Mobile Unit.	**S.R.O.** Senior Rescue Officer.
C.D.V. Civil Defence Volunteers.	**M.W.B.** Ministry of Works and Buildings.	**S.W.** Shelter Warden.
C.N.R. Civil Nursing Reserve.	**N.A.A.F.I.** Navy, Army and Air Force Institutes.	**V.A.D.** Voluntary Aid Detachmt.
D.C. Decontamination.	**N.A.C.D.** National Association for Civil Defence.	**W.** Warden.
E.M.S. Emergency Medical Service.		**W.D.** War Department.
E.N.S.A. Entertainments National Service Association.		**W.I.** Women's Institute.
F. Auxiliary Fire Station.		**W.L.A.** Women's Land Army.
		W.O. War Office.
		W.R. War Reserve (Police).
		W.V.S. Women's Voluntary Services.

The Way of the War

THIS AMERICA IS NOT TOO PROUD TO FIGHT
'Life, Liberty, and the Pursuit of Happiness'

"AMERICA," said the President of the U.S.A.," is too proud to fight."

"America," said the President of the U.S.A., " will never survive as a happy and prosperous oasis of liberty in the midst of a desert of dictatorship. When we repeat the great pledge to our country and our flag it must be our deep conviction that we pledge, as well as our work, our will and, if it be necessary, our lives."

Two declarations, but what a gulf of time and circumstance separates Woodrow Wilson's speech on the morrow of the Lusitania's sinking in 1915 from Franklin Delano Roosevelt's broadcast of July 4, 1941 ! Woodrow Wilson, Mr. Churchill has told us, was first and foremost, all through and last, a Party man, one whose dominating loyalty was to the great political association which had raised him to the presidency. Next he was a good American, an academic Liberal, a hater of war and violence.

COMPARE this professor at the White House with the man who sits there today. F. D. R. is a Democrat like Wilson ; he too is a good American, a liberal in mind and spirit and life, though no one could call his liberalism academic. He too is a sincere hater of war and violence. But whereas Woodrow Wilson thought, or gave the impression that he thought, that peace could be secured by scholarly chidings, followed if they were not heeded by increasingly indignant protests, Roosevelt long ago reached the conclusion that, if America wants peace, then she must be prepared to fight for ·it.

Not until April 2, 1917, did Wilson deliver his war message to Congress ; and as late as the previous January he had told Colonel House that " There will be no war. This country does not intend to become involved in this war," and three weeks later still made his famous " Peace without Victory " speech to Congress.

THIS war is not yet two years old, but its 23 months have brought America, if not actually into the war, at least on to its very doorstep. In effect the United States stand now where they stood in 1917, when Wilson, driven at last from his ivory tower where for so long he had maintained a detachment as aloof as it was irritating —we may recall Theodore Roosevelt's bitter outburst, " For many months our Government has preserved between right and wrong a neutrality which would have excited the emulous admiration of Pontius Pilate, the arch-typical neutral of all time "—picked up the gauntlet flung down by the

Germany of the Kaiser. In 1939 as in 1914 America was neutral, but a very few months' experience of this war blasted her neutrality into a thing of shreds and tatters. Americans today are proud to hear their country called the Arsenal of Democracy. The dollar sign has been removed from the two nations' commerce, and American war materials of every kind are pouring across the Atlantic, not sold but leased and lent to Britain. The last time America went to war she had to build up an army from scratch ; she would have had to do so in 1939. But if she goes to war today there are a million and a half young Americans ready and eager to enter the battle. American ships by the hundred are bringing aid to Britain.

AMERICAN warships are patrolling the Atlantic as far west as the 20th degree. Their orders are to report if they sight a German hull rising above the horizon, but few expect them to content themselves with acting as messenger boys for our Navy. The America of the last war was inclined to shrug its shoulders at what Wilson in one of his utterances described as a " drunken brawl " on the other side of the Atlantic, but the Americans today have flung from them the cloak of isolationism and are

Oh! Say, does the star-spangled banner yet wave
O'er the land of the free and the home of the brave?

YES, indeed it does. A hundred and sixty-five years after the foundation of the American Union, it waves over one hundred and fifty millions whose hands we hold in brotherhood across the waves that once divided but now unite. *Photo, Associated Press*

stripped to brave the boisterous buffetings of war. American destroyers—true, the White Ensign flies at their masthead—are hunting Nazi U-boats ; American marines have landed in Iceland ; American bases have been established in British colonies. German and Italian funds, sent to America for safe custody, have been appropriated on the order of the President, and German and Italian consuls have been given their marching orders. American shipyards are filled with clatter and clangour as ship after ship rises above the stocks to take the places of those Hitler's submarines have sent to rust amid the weeds and obscene creatures of the sea bottom. American factories are working non-stop so that Britain shall have the planes, the ships, the guns, the tanks, the shells, and all the other paraphernalia of war that she must have if she is not to lose the fight that is America's fight, too.

A WEEK or two ago America celebrated Independence Day. On July 4 some 159 millions cast their thoughts back to that day in 1776 when the Fathers of the Union adopted the declaration born of Jefferson's brain and pen. In 1941 the anniversary was commemorated with even more than usual solemnity and patriotic fervour.

From the Atlantic to the Pacific, from the Canadian border to that of Mexico, men and women, boys and girls, assembled in city and town and village and listened to the new Chief Justice speak into the microphone from a park somewhere in the Rockies of Colorado. With one voice they repeated after him the pledge of allegiance to the United States flag. As one great multitude, joined in sympathy, made one in spirit, they were refreshed and inspired by Jefferson's noble sentences, surely contained among the title-deeds of humanity.

" We hold these truths to be self-evident, that all men are created equal, that they are endowed by their Creator with certain unalienable Rights, that amongst these are Life, Liberty, and the Pursuit of Happiness. That to secure these rights governments are instituted among men . . . "

SELF-EVIDENT truths. Perhaps they were in 1776, yet not so self-evident today, when the Nazis and their Fascist hangers-on spit on them with derision. Not so self-evident that this generation of Americans may not be called upon to maintain and proclaim them " with our work, our will, our lives." For these things, this America — the America of today—is not too proud to fight. Nor, when you come to think of it, are we.

E. Royston Pike

Soviet Soldiers Have Surprised the World

So disastrous to the Russian arms was the opening of the offensive against Finland in the winter of 1939-40 that the impression gained ground that the Red Army was by no means so great and powerful a force as we had been led to suppose. Even the eventual crushing of Finnish resistance did not suffice to stem the tide of disparagement. Thus it was that the magnificent stand of the Red Army against the Nazi invader came as a surprise to Western opinion.

IVAN has given Fritz a nasty jolt. "The German people," writes the military correspondent of the "Frankfurter Zeitung," "must understand that the Russian war is most complicated, not only owing to the enormous distance the German troops must cover, but also to the completely different attitude of the Red troops compared with the Belgian, French and Yugoslav troops. Soviet soldiers are unwilling to surrender or retreat when threatened by pincer movements, but stay as a threat to the Nazi rear so that the Germans cannot advance. The moral paralysis of the enemy which contributed so greatly to the victory in the West has not occurred in the East. It has often happened that German troops have been cut from their lines of communication, and the danger to our advanced tank troops is greater than ever before. The German nation must realize the difference between France and Russia."

German war correspondents have told time and again of Red soldiers fighting to the last. Outside Minsk, for instance, crews of wrecked Russian tanks, instead of surrendering, hid in the woods and ambushed the advancing Germans, doing considerable execution with their automatic rifles. For days after the fortress of Brest-Litovsk had been stormed by the Nazis there was fierce fighting in the streets of the town between the Germans and Red Army "suicide squads"; the final struggle was fought out hand-to-hand in the total darkness of the corridors of magazines situated 150 feet below the ground. One German Army cook has told how a fortnight later his detachment was still being fired on from houses, from behind doors, and that it was still dangerous for Germans to venture down the side streets except with armed patrols. The night after the capture of Minsk a single Russian tank made a sudden appearance in the middle of the city and kept all its guns firing until it was destroyed; then the crew emerged, and although their clothing was on fire, used their tommy-guns until they were mown down.

In the forests bordering the roads along which the German columns have marched, thousands of Russians have remained, emerging every now and again to take heavy toll of the Nazis in carefully-laid ambushes. Then a solitary Red Army infantryman stepped out from among the bushes and quietly strewed nails on the track. Before the advancing German motor cyclists realized what was happening, their tires had been punctured, and machine-guns concealed in the undergrowth opened fire. Such stories as these could be multiplied almost indefinitely; they are the tribute wrung from the enemy to the high courage, resolution and fortitude of the men of the Red Army.

Perhaps we should not be surprised at the high character revealed by the Russians, since (Max Werner tells us) there is no other army in the world which pays greater attention to education. The Red Army, he says, is something more than a mere military instrument; it is at the same time a school and a political organization. It is an educational institution which seeks to raise the general educational level of its men. It has innumerable schools and over 2,000 libraries, and every soldier has to have some general knowledge of both modern and classical literature. Then he goes on to quote a French military expert who declared some years ago that "the ordinary soldier in the Red Army has a level of education, discipline and professional earnestness unrivalled in any other army."

When Officers and Men Mix

"Theirs not to reason why" and "You are not paid to think" have no place in the Red Army. Every soldier is also a Soviet citizen in the fullest sense of the term, and he is taught not only how to fight but something of the greatness of the country and society which it is his proud privilege to defend in arms. In the Red Army there are differences of rank, but officers and men when off duty mix freely, sitting at the same tables for meals, sharing the same reading-rooms, the same sports and recreation, listening to the same lectures on military topics—yes, even engaging in military debates together. Yet discipline is strict and well maintained. A year ago saluting was re-introduced into the Red Army; as the "Red Star" remarked at the time: "The salute of lower ranks to the superiors expresses respect, love and confidence in military leaders." Another order by Timoshenko was that in future Red Army men who had been arrested for breaches of discipline should not be confined as heretofore in "guard houses resembling rest homes." Henceforth, "In the guard houses they may sleep only six hours, after which beds are to be removed. Prisoners are forbidden to sleep on the floor, play any games, smoke, or listen to the radio." Strict arrest was defined as solitary confinement, sleep on bare boards, hot meals every other day, bread-and-water and tea every day; simple arrest means bread, tea, water, and a hot meal and work every day.

Not the least of the virtues of the Red Army system is that there is nothing to prevent a private soldier working his way up to the highest ranks. Practically all the generals of the Red Army were once rankers.

What, then, may we expect of the Russian Army in its great life-and-death struggle with Hitler's hordes? Sir Bernard Pares gave the answer the other day in the "Manchester Guardian." "Great losses," he wrote, "perhaps great retreats, but in any case, a sturdy national resistance in which the soldier will feel that he has far more of a share in what he is defending than before the Revolution. The principal change that has taken place in Russia since then is a universal growth of public interest, of quick and firm initiative, and, above all, backbone. It would be quite absurd to think that a national army which I saw making such a glorious resistance in the last war, sometimes even without rifles or cartridges, will now show less vigour and courage with the enormous, if rough-and-ready, provision of mechanical defence that has been won for it by the Five-Year Plans."

RUSSIAN TANKS on parade in Moscow for the visit of M. Matsuoka in April 1941. The foremost tank bears the name "Stalin" on its side. According to Max Werner, the new Soviet tank for accompanying infantry has stronger armour than the similar French Renault tank and three times its speed. The new Soviet medium-heavy tank of 30 tons is stated to be armed with three cannon and four machine-guns.

Stalwarts of the Red Army Listen to Stalin

WHILE STALIN SPEAKS, members of the Red Army, assembled in the Kremlin, Moscow, bend forward to catch his words. In his great appeal to the Soviet peoples on July 3 Stalin called upon the Red Army and Navy and all the citizens of the Soviet Union to defend every inch of the Soviet soil, to fight to the last drop of their blood, to defend their towns and villages, and to show to the utmost their daring and ingenuity. Putting forward what has been called his " scorched earth " policy, he insisted that " it is necessary to create in invaded areas unbearable conditions for the enemy."

Photo, Planet News

R.A.F. Invasion of Hitler's Europe Has Begun

BOMBS BURSTING on the power station at Comines, Franco-Belgian frontier town. They are seen exploding on (1) the boiler-house, (2) pump-house, (3) water-circulating pipes, and (4) turbine-house. The right-hand photograph shows a Blenheim being loaded up with bombs preparatory to a daylight sweep.   *Photo, British Official : Crown Copyright ; and Barratt's*

THE great R.A.F. offensive over Northern France and Germany proceeds with increasing fury. From June 24 to July 10 no fewer than 128 raids were carried out in night and day operations.

German works and French arsenals under Nazi control felt the full weight of Britain's new striking power. Aircraft factories, chemical works, power stations, Nazi convoys hugging the French coast, are now under continuous bombardment. So great is the damage that many factories have been compelled to close down, and French workers, slave-bound to Hitler's war-chariot, are said to be striving for better shelter accommodation.

These formidable sweeps have become as regular as clockwork, and the ominous drone of our fighters and bombers is to be heard as every summer dawn and dusk comes up over the Channel. The aerial invasion of Northern France and of Germany itself, so long delayed for lack of material, is now part of a battle that will not cease until the Germans lay down their arms and surrender. Taking full advantage of the diversion of the Luftwaffe over the Russian front, Bomber and Coastal Commands, following the plan, consistently in operation since last summer, of disrupting the enemy's war machine, are " going to it " with a will, encouraged by their superior skill, the better quality of their machines, and the fact that these machines are piling up in vast numbers behind Britain's ramparts of liberty.

Succour for Our Men Down in the Channel

Racing along the Straits of Dover to pick up a pilot who has baled out is an R.A.F. rescue launch. On the right, the mast of the launch with her distinctive flag.

Flying-Officer captain of the high-speed rescue launch on the look-out. His peace-time job was that of a Bristol Channel pilot.

R.A.F. RESCUE LAUNCH speeds to pick up a pilot in the Channel; note the machine-gunner in his turret. The oval photograph shows an R.A.F. corporal and first-class coxswain seated in the ship's rescue craft. With continuous daylight raids over Northern France these R.A.F. launches are constantly on patrol, and many pilots have been saved by the skill and courage of their personnel. The photographs in this page were obtained while a Channel sweep by the R.A.F. was in actual progress.

Photos, " News Chronicle." Exclusive to THE WAR ILLUSTRATED

Speed the Tanks for the Victory Roll!

First of the tanks bought in the "Speed the Tanks" campaign leaves a London factory, where soldiers and civilians at the works subscribed £2,000 towards its cost. Left, "Waltzing Matilda," a name given by a Royal Tank Regiment unit as a compliment to the Australians who have done so well with this type of heavy tank in the Middle East. Right, a woman worker in a munitions factory pneumatic-drilling the steel sideplate of a tank. Beneath are some of Britain's new 16-ton tanks called the "Valentine." Strung out over a field these "land battleships" have a formidable appearance. The "Valentine" owes its name to St. Valentine's Day, for that date happens to be its birthday.

WALTZING MATILDA

THE War will be largely won in the factories, and every good and willing workman or workwoman is an artificer of victory. Britain, always slow to "get off the mark" in wartime, is none the less sure when she does get into her stride. After a year of organization the shortage of planes is being made good. Now it is "Speed the Tanks!" Just as we are getting planes in sufficient number eventually to overwhelm the Nazis in the air, so must we have a superabundance of tanks to destroy Hitlerism on land. On June 30 it was announced that Lord Beaverbrook had been appointed Minister of Supply to speed up the production of tanks. There is no question as to the splendid quality of our tanks of various types, for when it comes to building a machine Britain always leads the world. The question now is quantity. Then, "Speed the Tanks!"

Photos, British Official ; Topical, " Daily Mirror "

In Giant Battles Russia Stems the German Flood

Great tank battles and relentless guerilla warfare were features of the final stage of the orderly Russian withdrawal from the buffer states to the main defensive position along the Russian frontier of 1938. Here stubborn Soviet resistance frustrated the quick break-through anticipated by the German High Command.

AFTER a fortnight of intensive warfare, in which tremendous battles were fought by night and day over a front of 1,800 miles, certain facts emerged despite the fog of war and military censorship. When due allowance had been made for extravagant claims in the official communiqués of the adversaries, it seemed fairly clear that the quick break-through on which the Wehrmacht had reckoned had not yet materialized. The buffer states which Stalin had cleverly interposed between Russia and Hitler's anticipated eastern drive—the Baltic States, the annexed Polish territory and Bessarabia—these were in the main quickly overrun, as no doubt the Soviet High Command had expected them to be. Even so, they were not won except at the cost of heavy losses to the Nazis both in men and material.

Fighting a magnificent and highly-efficient rearguard action, the advance forces of the Soviet Army fell back from the frontiers of these buffer states upon the main forces waiting on the strongly fortified positions, popularly known as the Stalin line, though in no sense was it a rigid line, which marked the 1938 borders of the Soviet Union.

Nazi Prodigality of Men

Confident of quick victory, the Germans had flung into the battle masses of troops far more numerous than those employed on the Western Front during the last war. A complete army corps took part in the storming of Brest Litovsk, which fell on June 24, and this corps' advanced scouting unit consisted, we are told, of a whole division. But despite the prodigality with which the Germans flung their troops into the battle against an army which was not yet fully mobilized, the speed of their advance, though great in the first few days, was not commensurate with the rate at which they were losing men and material.

Over the immense battle line, stretching from the Arctic Ocean to the Black Sea, certain main German thrusts were perceived. In the south the Black Sea port of Odessa was an obvious goal, but the German and Rumanian forces thrusting across Bessarabia had a hard task in forcing the River Pruth ; and though it was crossed at several points during the first days of July, little headway was made in this sector, where Russian

counter-attacks succeeded in throwing back enemy formations in many places on to their original positions. In this sector heavy rainfall, too, checked the Germans, bogging tanks and transport.

In the extreme north, at the other end of the battle line, the Arctic port of Murmansk was the object of a strong Nazi thrust, but though the Germans claimed the capture of the port on July 1, their occupation, if capture it they did, was of short duration. The German advance here was embarrassed by the daring landing of a strong force of Soviet storm troops under cover of the guns of the Soviet Arctic fleet.

It was in the northern sector, too, that a battle of a different kind from that being fought elsewhere went on for a week along the Stalin Canal. At the beginning of the campaign it became obvious to the Russians that their submarine fleet operating in the Baltic would be trapped if the Nazi troops advancing north-east through Estonia and south-east through Finland should break through and capture Leningrad. It was therefore decided to evacuate the main submarine force through the Stalin Canal from Kronstadt to the White Sea. To interfere with this move, the Germans concentrated forces of dive-bombers to deliver an uninterrupted sequence of day and night attacks upon the canal. The Russians, on their side, flew continuous patrols above it, and although the German raiders did a certain amount of damage it was reported that the majority of the fleet got through safely.

Not only was the Nazi threat to Murmansk temporarily averted, but the thrust across the Karelian isthmus towards Leningrad seemed to have achieved no decisive results. In fact, the north-eastern thrust through Latvia to

Ostrov was by far the most dangerous menace to Leningrad, and here it was that one of the main German offensives developed. On July 9 the Germans claimed the capture of Ostrov, but Russian communiqués declared that on this front all German attacks had been repulsed with heavy losses.

The main German attack was through Minsk in the direction of Smolensk and

THE U.S.S.R. MISSION arrived in London for service consultations on July 8. Above, left to right, are M. Maisky, Soviet Ambassador in London, General Golikov, who headed the Mission, and the deputy-head, Rear-Admiral Kharlamov.   *Photo, Planet News*

Moscow. In this sector two distinct Nazi offensives developed, the northern through Lepel and the southern through Bobruisk, so that the German strategy became apparent as a pincers movement intended to close upon Smolensk. The southern thrust became the more dangerous of the two, the Lepel column having been successfully counter-attacked by the Russians. Here a complete German motorized division was wiped out, losing forty guns and a vast quantity of transport.

In the sector between Minsk and Bobruisk the Germans succeeded in crossing the historic Beresina River, but all attempts to force the line of the Dnieper were checked.

South of the Pripet Marshes the Germans strove hard to advance in the direction of Kiev. A German advance through Novgorod-Volynsk would, if pressed far, threaten the communications of the Russian forces operating in the Bukovina and Bessarabia ; but here again, although some mechanized forces of the German army might have reached the River Sereth, as they claimed, the Russians seemed to have broken up enemy attempts to break through in force.

By July 11 the Moscow communiqués were able to announce that the main German thrusts had been held, and that the Red Army had at last established a " fairly stable line " along the whole front.

German progress during the week July 4-12 fell short of what the Nazi High Command had expected. Learning from the experience of other countries, the Russians made no attempt to keep the German tank units always in front of them, but allowed the spearhead of the attack to advance and then attempted to cut it off from the supporting

RUSSIAN PLANE, photographed during the Soviet occupation of Bessarabia in June, 1940. Little is known of the actual strength and composition of the Red Air Arm, but reports so far indicate that it has cooperated well with the Army.   *Photo, Wide World, exclusive to* THE WAR ILLUSTRATED

Conflicting Claims in a Terrific Struggle

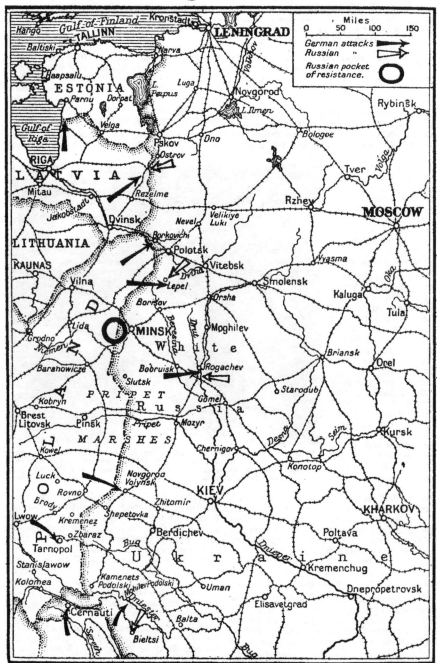

RUSSIA AT BAY. On this map are indicated the principal German thrusts and the Russian counter-attacks in progress when the war was some three weeks old. *Courtesy of "The Times"*

and that north-east of Dniester the Germans stood " immediately before Kiev." North of the Pripet marshes, the centre of the German offensive had been carried forward to more than 125 miles east of Minsk. This was the German story; the Russian was far different. The Soviet communiqué issued on July 14 claimed that " the first three weeks of

THE VOICE OF RUSSIA

Vengeance For London

WE do not fight this war alone, nor for ourselves only. Every Nazi killed by us, every tank smashed, every plane destroyed by us, is the reply to Hitler of the countries ravaged by the Nazis, of England determined to win, and of the liberty-loving people of the United States.

Every dead German, every smashed tank, every destroyed plane, is vengeance for London battered by a hundred raids, for our Allies in this war, and for those Germans who have fallen in the fight against Hitler.

That is the spirit that will make us resist to the utmost and will lead us to final victory—the spirit of solidarity with all freedom-loving people who are fighting for liberty against the twentieth-century Attila.—*Moscow Radio, July 5.*

Hitler's Mistakes

Hitler has made two great mistakes. His first error was to believe that Great Britain would capitulate. Instead, Great Britain has built up her forces until she is today mightier than ever.

Looking at what Hitler's Luftwaffe had done to beautiful London and other cities, the British set their teeth and aimed at one objective only—to smash Hitlerism. It is not for nothing that the English have coined the famous phrase, " Hitler's position is brilliant but hopeless."

Hitler's second great mistake was that he underestimated the strength of the Red Army.—*Alexei Tolstoy, in a broadcast from Moscow, July 7.*

'Sitting On Bayonets'

Napoleon said, " One cannot sit on bayonets." This is exactly what Hitler is trying to do.

We can mobilize another 10 million people if necessary, without any adverse effect on our man-power and material resources. That is why we are so calm in the face of difficulties.

Hitler says he wants to break the British Empire, and that the shortest route to London is via New York. The Germans also say they will soon be in Moscow. The British song has it, " It's a Long Way to Tipperary." And to Moscow the way is still longer.

The war has only begun. Hitler can win 100 battles; he will never win the war. We can fully guarantee that.—*Mr. Lozovsky, Vice-Commissar for Foreign Affairs, July 2.*

fighting testify to the undoubted collapse of Hitler's blitzkrieg. The best German divisions have been broken up by the Soviet troops. German losses in killed, wounded and prisoners so far amount to not fewer than 1,000,000 men. Our losses in killed, wounded and missing are not more than 150,000 to 250,000. According to verified figures our air force has destroyed more than 2,300 German aircraft . . . German troops have lost more than 3,000 tanks. During this period we lost 1,900 aircraft and 2,200 tanks.''

infantry. Defence in depth was exploited to the utmost, and everywhere the policy of Stalin's, that the enemy must find nothing, was being carried into effect. Herman Harvey, American N.B.C. correspondent, broadcasting from Moscow, said : '' Livestock is driven to the rear. The roads are jammed with tractors, trucks and agricultural equipment removed by the drivers from the front. What cannot be removed is destroyed. ' We will not leave a single horse, cow or sheep,' declare the peasants.''

On Saturday night, July 12, when the war was three weeks old, the German High Command issued another of its grandiose communiqués. In this it was claimed that in a daring assault the Stalin Line had been broken through '' at all the decisive points,'' that the German-Rumanian armies had thrown back the enemy beyond the Dniester,

NAZIS HUNTING RED SNIPERS on the Eastern front. This German photograph, which reached London after having been radioed by Dr. Goebbels' propaganda department to New York, is stated in the caption to show German shock troops searching for Soviet soldiers in Lithuania. Russian troops left behind the advancing German tanks have been waging a fierce guerilla war.

Photo, Wide World, exclusive to THE WAR ILLUSTRATED

Across the Frontier into Russia with the Nazis

THE SCORCHED EARTH policy in action, by which the Russians have not only raised a barrier of fire between their armies and the Nazi hosts, but have destroyed the loot which was Hitler's objective in striking against the Soviets.

NAZI TROOPS being landed at Kaunas (Kovno), Lithuania (top photograph). Centre left, is an impression of the German motor-cyclists racing along a street in Kaunas. Not far from the East Prussian border, Kaunas was an easy objective of the Nazi Panzer divisions in the first moves of the war on the east front, and fell on June 24, three days after Hitler attacked. The photographs in this page were German-radioed to New York and sent back by Clipper.

Tragic victims of the "bloodthirsty guttersnipe" whose lust for world-power has destroyed the happiness of millions. Look on this photograph of helpless men, women and children, herded together in attitudes of despair, trying to find safety in some ravine as Hitler's murder-machine thunders east, and never forget that this "martyrdom of man" is the wish and will of the Nazi system. But the world is closing in upon the killers. Russia's heroism and efficiency have "shocked" the Germans in more ways than one.

Photos, Wide World, exclusive to THE WAR ILLUSTRATED, *and Associated Press*

At the Front in Syria : First Photographs of Brit

WITH the acceptance and signing of the armistice on July 12, the Syrian campaign by the British and Free French forces against Vichy and its Nazi masters was concluded. The armistice was initialled by the light of headlamps in the officers' mess at the Sidney Smith barracks, Acre ; and all lovers of true France must be glad that this distressing conflict is now over. These successful operations, so vital to our Middle East position, have been brilliantly carried out by our Imperial forces with the comparatively moderate number of casualties of not more than 1,500 British, Australian and Indian soldiers.

THE photographs in these pages show various incidents in the course of fighting. 1, A British cavalry regiment patrolling the Litani river. 2, These British soldiers with their topees hung on the front of the lorry certainly have that victory smile. In the circle, 3, is the Matron of the Free French Nursing Sisters, Mme. L. A. Petyt de Mailly, attending to a minor wound at an advanced dressing station. Beneath, 4 and 5 respectively, are British tanks advancing into Syria, and the inhabitants of Damascus watching some of the Allied Forces passing through the city after its capture.

Photos, British Official : Crown Copyright

Troops in the Campaign Now Happily Concluded

Still the Atlantic Is One Vast Battlefield

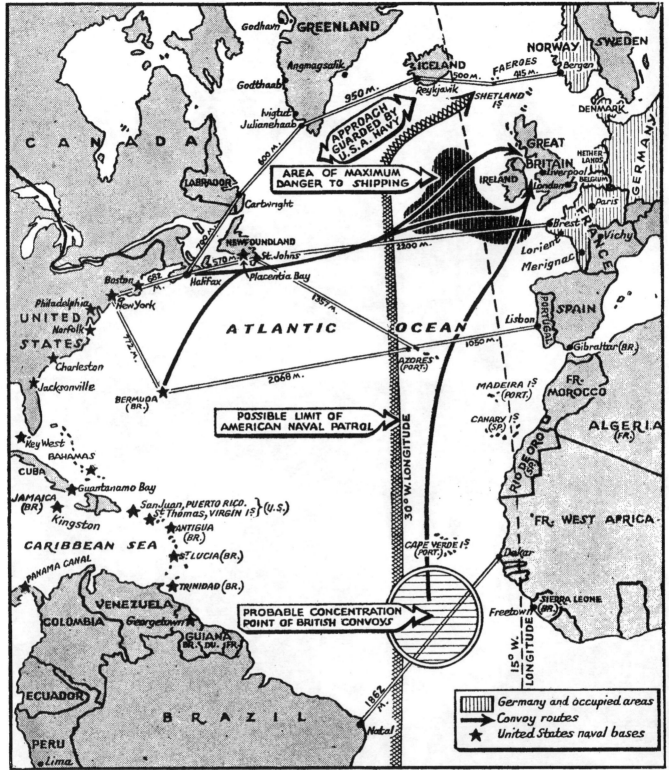

By courtesy of " The New York Times "

THE ATLANTIC CAMPAIGN is being fought out over the area shown in this map. What will decide victory or defeat in this great and remorseless battle in which the adversaries are struggling for control of the trade routes is neither the number of German submarines put out of action by the Royal Navy nor the number of British warships sunk by German mines, bombs, or torpedoes; it will be decided by the number of British merchant ships, from tramp to liner, which can sail the seas, bringing to Britain the things she vitally needs and taking away the goods which will help to pay for them.

German attacks on warships are incidentals in this battle; the main German attack is, and must

remain, an attack against convoys. Therefore it follows that in this campaign the riveter in the dockyard plays a part just as vital as the sailor who launches a depth-charge against an enemy submarine, for the speed at which ships can be built and repaired is as important as the number of U-boats sunk. By a deliberate act of policy in taking over Iceland, President Roosevelt has also taken over a greater measure of responsibility for the security of the Atlantic crossing, since he has ordered American naval forces to assure the safety of communications in the approaches between Iceland and the United States. Thus the activities of the American neutrality patrol now virtually extend right across the Atlantic, and more

of our own U-boat-hunting craft will be able to concentrate their efforts within a smaller range.

As will be seen from the map, the area of maximum danger to British shipping lies between the limit of the American naval patrol and the west of Ireland. This area lies comparatively near the occupied ports of Western France, and this is the reason for the reiterated R.A.F. attacks upon Brest and Lorient, the main bases of the German ocean-going U-boats, and the airfield at Merignac, near Bordeaux, base of the Focke-Wulf long-distance commerce raiders.

Both geographically and numerically Britain faces a naval problem it has never faced before, but American aid, already great, is growing fast.

America Joins Britain in Iceland's Defence

With the occupation of Iceland—the first territory outside the Western Hemisphere occupied
by United States troops—American warships entered the zone blockaded by the German Navy.
"Roosevelt is intruding into the battlefield," said one Nazi newspaper, while the official organ of
the German Foreign Office denounced his action as that of "an ally of Bolshevism, a Yankee
imperialist who has raped a small European nation."

AMERICAN forces have landed in Iceland. That was the announcement made by President Roosevelt in a special message to Congress on July 7. It followed hard upon reports that the Germans had been assembling at Narvik, in the north of Norway, an expeditionary force for a descent upon Iceland.

The United States, stated the President, could not allow the occupation by Germany of strategic outposts in the Atlantic to be used as air or naval bases for an eventual attack on the Western Hemisphere. A German occupation of Iceland would constitute a serious threat in three dimensions: against Greenland and the northern portion of the North American continent, including the islands which lie off it; against all shipping in the North Atlantic; and against the steady flow of munitions to Britain, which was a matter of broad policy clearly approved by Congress. For these reasons Iceland had been occupied, and for the same reasons substantial forces had also been sent to the bases acquired last year from Britain in Trinidad and British Guiana, in the south, to forestall any pincers movement by Germany against the Western Hemisphere.

Other points in the President's message were that the American Navy had been ordered to ensure the safety of communica-

tions between Iceland and the United States and all other strategic outposts; that Mr. Churchill had explained on June 24—two days after Germany attacked Russia—that the British forces in Iceland were needed elsewhere; and that America would observe a special request by the Icelandic Government that sufficient planes would be provided for defensive purposes.

Accompanying this special message were copies of communications which had been exchanged between Mr. Roosevelt and the Prime Minister of Iceland, Mr. Hermann Jonasson, on July 1, from which it was plain that triangular conversations had taken place between Britain, the United States, and Iceland on the subject. Mr. Jonasson had laid down certain conditions, as follows:

The United States promises to withdraw all military forces immediately at the conclusion of the present war, to recognize "the absolute independence and sovereignty of Iceland" and to use its influence to see that the eventual peace treaty will extend the same recognition, not to interfere with the Iceland Government during the occupation or afterwards, and to organize defence so as to ensure the greatest possible safety for the inhabitants with only "picked troops"; undertakes the defence of Iceland without expense to Iceland, and promises to further Iceland's interests in every possible way, including the supplying of "necessities" and the securing the necessary shipping. Iceland expects any declaration by the President to be in agreement with these promises, and considers it obvious that, if the United States undertakes the defence of Iceland, "it must be strong enough to meet every eventuality, particularly in the beginning; it is expected that as far as possible an effort will be made to prevent any special danger in connexion with the change-over."

Mr. Jonasson had added that Iceland had reached her decision as "an absolutely free and sovereign state," and considered it a matter of course that the United States would recognize Iceland's legal status, with both states immediately exchanging diplomatic representatives. In his reply, Mr. Roosevelt had stated that Iceland's conditions were fully acceptable and would be fully observed.

Commenting a few hours later on the President's message, Colonel Knox, United States Secretary of the Navy, announced that the President, as commander-in-chief of the American armed forces, had ordered the American Navy to take all necessary steps to keep the sea lanes open to the strategic outposts. He refused to say whether the orders implied that the Navy was prepared to shoot if necessary, but "the language of the message indicates that the policy goes farther than the original orders to the Navy"—those orders, it was understood,

being that the American warships should act merely as patrols, and if they spotted a German U-boat or raider to pass on the information to the nearest British force.

Speaking in the House of Commons on July 9, Mr. Churchill said that the new move was in complete harmony with British interests. "The United States occupation of Iceland is an event of first-rate political and strategic importance. In fact, it is one of the most important things that have happened since the war began." He went on to say that it was still proposed to retain a British army in Iceland—British troops landed in Iceland in May, 1940, and were later joined by Canadians—and "as British and United States forces will both have the same object in view, namely the defence of Iceland, it seems very likely that they will cooperate closely and effectively in resistance to any attempt by Hitler to gain a footing."

Then the Premier made a reference to the second principle of United States policy— "the declared will and purpose of the President, Congress and people of the United States, not only to send all possible aid in warlike munitions and necessary supplies to Great Britain, but also to make sure we got them. . . ." Apart from this, the position of the United States forces in Iceland would, of course, require their being sustained or being reinforced from time to time. "These consignments of American supplies for American forces on duty overseas for the purpose of the United States would have to traverse very dangerous waters, and as we had a very large traffic constantly passing through these waters it might be found in practice mutually advantageous that the two navies involved should assist each other as far as convenient in that part of the waters."

Commentators were swift to point out that the American occupation of Iceland meant that America now claimed the right to patrol the Atlantic up to and even beyond the 15th degree of longitude, which runs through Iceland. Hitherto the American patrol zone had been bounded by the 20th degree, but now not only Iceland but the Cape Verde Islands and Dakar were included as being outposts of the defence of North America.

IN ICELAND British troops have been reinforced by a very large contingent of Americans. These probably include U.S. Marines, like those seen above left, on manoeuvres at Timber Point, Long Island. The American forces will cooperate with the British, some of whom, manning a 6-in. naval gun, are seen above on the Iceland coast.   *Photos, British Official, and World Wide*

Our Diary of the War

SUNDAY, JULY 6, 1941   673rd day

Sea.—Admiralty announced that in Mediterranean three Italian ships had been torpedoed and sunk and armed merchant cruiser crippled.

Air.—R.A.F. made low-level attack on enemy patrol vessels in North Sea, destroyed four and damaged others. Steel works at Lille hit. Eleven enemy fighters shot down.

Night attacks on Münster, Dortmund and other industrial districts in Ruhr and Rhineland, Emden, Rotterdam and Brest.

Russian Front.—Stubborn Russian resistance in Murmansk area. Counter-attacks by Red Army in Ostrov, Polotsk and Borisov sectors. Heavy fighting in Novgorod-Volynsk and Tarnopol areas.

Africa.—Cairo announced surrender of nine Italian generals and capture of 5,000 more prisoners in Abyssinia.

Docks and shipping at Benghazi bombed.

Near East.—British mechanized units advancing from Palmyra towards Homs. El Boum, strategic village near Beirut, captured. Australians crossed Damour river and battered Vichy defences.

Heavy R.A.F. raid on Palermo ; five ships hit. Night attacks on Aleppo and Beirut.

Home.—Night raiders dropped bombs on coastal districts. Three destroyed.

MONDAY, JULY 7   674th day

Sea.—Convoy off Dutch coast attacked by R.A.F. ; six ships hit. One freighter and one escorting E-boat sunk off Calais.

Air.—R.A.F. made day attacks on aircraft works near Albert and power station and chemical factory near Bethune. Seven enemy fighters destroyed for loss of three.

Very heavy night raids on targets in Ruhr and Rhineland, particularly Cologne, Osnabruck, Frankfurt and Münster. Lighter ones on Channel ports and Den Helder.

Russian Front.—Moscow stated that enemy attacks in Baltic States were repulsed, and also his attempts to cross the Western Dvina. Germans claimed progress towards Upper Dvina and Dnieper.

In Northern Ukraine Russians claimed to have checked enemy advance in Novgorod-Volynsk sector.

Africa.—Day and night raids on Libyan aerodromes and on Tripoli harbour.

Near East.—Local gains north of Jezzin.

R.A.F. attacked Aleppo, Beirut, and Vichy flying-boats off coast of Syria.

Home.—Sharp night raid on Southampton causing casualties and much damage. Bombs also fell in south and south-east England. Six raiders destroyed.

General.—Pres. Roosevelt announced that U.S. naval forces had arrived in Iceland.

TUESDAY, JULY 8   675th day

Sea.—U-boat sunk by Fleet Air Arm off Gibraltar.

Air.—R.A.F. attacked power station and chemical works at Lille. Eleven enemy fighters destroyed ; we lost seven. Synthetic oil plant near Bethune heavily bombed. Seven fighters destroyed for loss of five.

Night raids on Hamm, Essen, Münster, Bielefeld, Leuna and Haugesund. Shipping off north and west coasts of France attacked.

Russian Front.—Moscow reported that enemy was being held or counter-attacked along whole front. Repeated attempts to cross Dnieper failed. Germans captured Salla, Finland.

Near East.—Resistance round Damour broken by Australian forces after severe fighting. British column advancing from Palmyra now 15 miles from Homs.

Home.—Widespread night raids over Britain ; main attack on Midlands. Five enemy aircraft destroyed.

WEDNESDAY, JULY 9   676th day

Air.—Heavy bombers made day attack on power station near Bethune. During operations 13 fighters were destroyed ; we lost eight. Night attacks on Aachen, Osnabruck, Bielefeld, Münster and Ostend docks.

Russian Front.—Moscow claimed victory in Lepel area. Germany claimed capture of Ostrov and two towns in Estonia.

Africa.—R.A.F. bombed Benghazi harbour and many Libyan aerodromes.

Near East.—Announced that General Dentz had sued for an armistice. Imperial forces occupied Damour.

R.A.F. bombed Aleppo, Beirut and Rayak. Raid on Syracuse, when three float-planes were destroyed and others damaged. Night raid on Naples.

Home.—Enemy activity over coastal areas. Four raiders destroyed.

THURSDAY, JULY 10   677th day

Air.—R.A.F. attacked shipping at Cherbourg and Le Havre ; six ships, totalling 20,000 tons, a total loss. Chemical works and railway sidings attacked at Chocques, near Bethune. Sixteen enemy fighters destroyed. Britain lost ten fighters and two bombers.

Night attacks on Cologne and elsewhere in Rhineland. Docks at Ostend, Calais and Boulogne also bombed.

Russian Front.—Furious battle still raging round Ostrov. Russians, counter-attacking at Polotsk and Lepel, claimed destruction of Panzer division. Another German division defeated at Borisov, and enemy held at Bobruisk and round Novgorod-Volynsk.

Africa.—Heavy raids on Benghazi harbour and Libyan airfields.

Near East.—Paris radio stated that Australian troops occupied Beirut.

Naples bombed for three hours at night.

Home.—Bombs fell by night at points in east and north-east of England, including sharp attack at one coastal place.

FRIDAY, JULY 11   678th day

Sea.—Three German freighters reported mined off Sweden.

Air.—R.A.F. bombed shipyard near Rouen. In another daylight sweep over Northern France nine enemy fighters were destroyed. Night raid on Wilhelmshaven.

Russian Front.—Pause in operations.

Near East.—Vichy announced that French Govt. had refused terms for armistice. Later Gen. Dentz agreed to negotiations and Cease Fire was ordered from midnight.

SATURDAY, JULY 12   679th day

Air.—During daylight sweeps railway and canal communications were bombed, shipping off Dutch coast attacked, and six enemy fighters destroyed. At night Bremen was attacked with exceptionally heavy bombs.

Russian Front.—Stubborn fighting took place, according to Moscow, in areas of Pskov, Vitebsk and Novgorod-Volynsk, but caused no important change.

Germany claimed to have pierced Stalin Line at several points ; that Leningrad was threatened, and occupation of Kiev imminent.

Near East.—Allied terms for armistice in Syria accepted by Gen. Dentz.

General.—British and Soviet Governments signed a military agreement.

CANADIAN TANK CREWS were among the latest contingent of Canadian soldiers to arrive in this country. Cheered by their comrades, a detachment of these men, among whom are many American volunteers, is seen marching into camp. These men form the advance guard of an increasing number of panzer troops now being trained in Canada to man the steadily increasing output of Canadian tanks.

Photo, Keystone

Britain's 'Recce' Troops Seen in Action

Above we have a glimpse of members of Britain's new Reconnaissance Corps (" Recce ") preparing to dislodge the enemy by means of a 3-in. trench mortar. Right, "enemy" troops, during field exercises, are firing at Reconnaissance troops advancing through a smoke screen.

FASTEST-moving unit in the British Army is the new Reconnaissance Corps, now an integral part of the Forces, with its own distinguishing badge. The men of the Army know it as the " Recce Corps." Formed at the beginning of 1941, it is a lightly-armoured and very fast-moving force, and its task is to provide a modern equivalent of the old divisional cavalry. Each scout company of the Corps carries with it a platoon of motorized infantry to be used against parachute troops or other enemy pockets of resistance and to give support until the main body of troops arrives. These infantrymen have to be more highly trained than infantry of the line, specialists in the art of guerrilla warfare and capable of acting on their own initiative. The Corps makes use of a variety of mechanized transport : motor-cycles, lorries, Bren-gun carriers, armoured cars and scout cars, and each unit is self-contained, with its own automatic cookers, repair outfits, petrol carriers and A.A. weapons. Like the British parachute troops the men of the Recce Corps are picked men and all volunteers. The Reconnaissance Corps will take its place in the van of the attack, spying out the land, holding up the enemy and sending back information by radio.

Recce cars, accompanied by Bren-gun carriers, are shown above careering over rough country during tactical exercises in Northern Ireland. Every man is so trained that he can take his turn in driving and maintaining Bren carrier, motor-cycle and armoured car, and he is taught to be familiar with every kind of automatic arms.

Photos, British Official : Crown Copyright

'RECCE' MOTOR-CYCLISTS, part of a motor-cycle detachment of the Reconnaissance Corps, raise clouds of dust as they speed into action during manoeuvres. Left, the new badge for officers and men of the Reconnaissance Corps : a spearhead flanked by lightning.

Assault from the Air

How German Parachute Troops Seize an Objective and Call Other Arms to their Aid, so Developing a Huge Offensive

Specially drawn by Haworth for THE WAR ILLUSTRATED

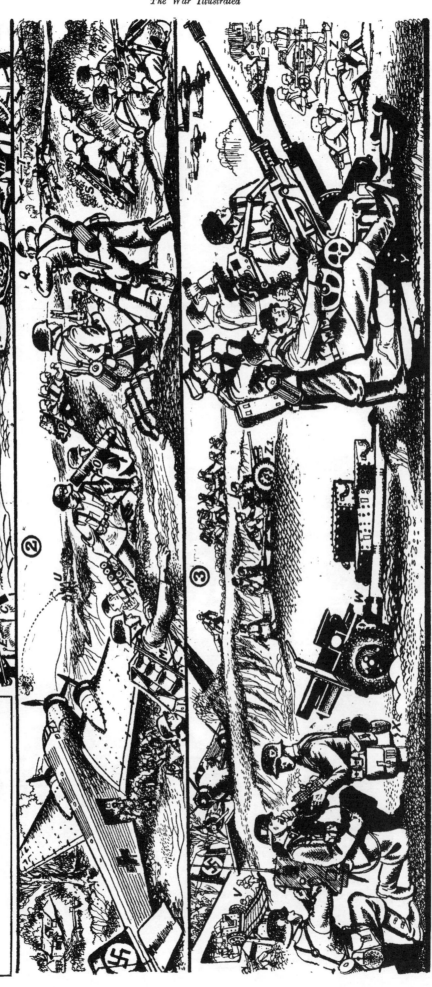

GERMAN PARATROOPS (Drawing I). The men have freed themselves from their parachute harness, and are running at their section leader's signal (A) to form round him. His parachute is of distinctive colouring, taking out a light bipod machine-gun (K). Signal light and he is armed with a machine-pistol (B) which fires 30 rounds contained in the clip (C). Six reserve clips are carried in the pouches (D). This weapon is normally fired from the hip, but if the extensible stock (E) is folded backwards a more accurate aim can be taken at extreme range of 200 yards from the shoulder. The rest of the men carry pistols, with spare ammunition in belt pouches, and small grenades in pockets (F).

His men assembled, the section leader makes for the containers parachuting near by (G G). The metal ends are knocked off and the body—canvas, stiffened with metal ribs—can be unlashed. These men are taking out a light bipod machine-gun (K). Signal light rifles (J) and stick-type grenades (K). Anti-tank pistols with cartridges and coloured smoke bombs are also included, and are used to form a predetermined code to call up reinforcements ; thus, a red smoke-bomb (L).

Drawing 2. A Junkers 52 troop-carrier arrives and troops are pouring from the machine. (M) carries the base-plate of a mortar, (N) mortar bombs in wicker containers, (O) the mortar barrel, (P) flame-carrying apparatus. (Q) mortar crew in action, (R) heavy type machine-gun mounted on tripod. This gun can be slung on the back when not in use (S).

Meanwhile, the dive-bombers are hammering at the opposition (T), preventing any interference whilst the air-borne troops are most vulnerable. If any headway is made, another signal is fired (U), this time with coloured lights, and so it goes on.

Drawing 3. Unloading a light infantry gun (V), shown in detail at (W). The feldwebel (X) or sergeant-major, after consulting his detailed map, is issuing instructions to wireless operators. Portable sets are brought into operation as early as possible, replacing smoke-bombs. The feldwebel is in touch with H.Q., with another assault party just over the hills, and reinforcing troop-carriers already in the air.

The gun in the foreground at (Y) is a 2 cm. A.A. gun. It can be used as an anti-tank gun, and in either case the portable range-finders (Z Z) are used. A 37 mm. anti-tank gun is being pushed into position at Z1.

Parachute troops, regarded as of doubtful theoretical value before the war, have proved of immense importance in the present conflict.

There Was No Sea-borne Invasion of Crete

Immediately it was clear that the Nazis were about to attempt an invasion of Crete, the Navy in
the Mediterranean received the order from the C.-in-C., Sir Andrew Cunningham, to prevent any
enemy soldiers, tanks, ammunition or supplies from reaching the threatened island by sea. How
the Navy performed its task is told here by Commander Anthony Kimmins.

WEDNESDAY, May 21. During the day the destroyer *Juno* was bombed and sunk, and as by now the Huns had gained a footing in Crete with air-borne troops, they felt that the moment was ripe to launch the main body by sea. Unfortunately for them, however, one of our reconnaissance aircraft sighted their ships just before nightfall as they were heading for Canea Bay. Rear-Admiral Glennie, flying his flag in the cruiser *Dido*, raced to the attack accompanied by other cruisers and destroyers.

The German convoy was escorted by Italian destroyers, and when Admiral Glennie's force suddenly crashed into them out of the dark they offered little resistance : they loosed off some torpedoes, but in a most erratic manner, so that they all missed. They seemed disinclined to defend themselves with gunfire and made off at full speed, but not before one of them had been sunk.

After that it was money for old rope : the transports were sunk by torpedoes and gun-fire. The moment our ships opened fire on the wooden schooners known out there as caiques, the Hun soldiers came tumbling up from between-decks and leapt overboard, all in their full heavy equipment. In several cases these caiques were rammed, and there is many a ship in the Mediterranean Fleet today with a proud dent in her stem. And so the whole of that first German landing force was sent to the bottom while our ships came away unscathed. First round to the Navy : things looked good.

But remember that this first attempt took place at night. The darkness which the Hun had relied on to protect his troops had in point of fact proved our greatest ally. Our ships had been able to dash in, do the job and retire before daylight returned and accurate bombing became possible. But the Hun is a quick mover, and ruthless as regards loss of life. The moment the news came through that disaster had overtaken his 'night attempt, he switched his tactics immediately and had a crack by day. The very next morning one of our reconnaissance aircraft reported a second troop convoy south of Milo island and heading for Crete.

Rear-Admiral King, flying his flag in the *Naiad*, raced in to intercept with a force of cruisers and destroyers on what at first sight would appear an easy task, because the only escorting warship was one Italian destroyer at the head of the convoy. But this time it was daylight, and above, taking cover in the glare of the sun and behind the thin wisps of cloud, the Luftwaffe was waiting. *Naiad* alone was treated to no less than 191 bombs that day, and by some miracle escaped with no more than superficial damage.

Once again the attempt failed ; the convoy was dispersed and many of the ships sunk, but not without casualties to our side. One could hardly expect otherwise with bombs raining down at that rate. At about two in the afternoon the destroyer *Greyhound*, which had spent the whole forenoon living up to her name—darting in and out of the convoy and catching one hare after the other—received a direct hit and sank with all guns firing. The destroyers *Kandahar* and *Kingston* raced to the assistance of their comrades, while the cruisers *Gloucester* and *Fiji* closed in to support. The Luftwaffe concentrated on the bigger targets of the cruisers, and wave after wave of dive-bombers came in. They concentrated first on the *Gloucester*. Wave after wave came over and occasional hits were scored, until, towards the end of the afternoon, a direct hit amidships finished her off and, with her ammunition almost exhausted, the *Gloucester* sank with her guns blazing upwards. From that moment the bombers concentrated on the *Fiji*. Before long, a direct hit forced her to reduce speed, and later she bought another packet and went down like her consort, fighting to the end. But the dive-bombers did not have it all their own way. Those men at the guns, exhausted as they were in the sweltering heat, never let up for one second. Any number of Junkers were seen to crash into the sea, and when squadrons returned a second time they were often at less than half their strength.

CRETE INVADERS clinging to an inflated raft after a convoy
of German transports had been dispersed and sunk by the
Royal Navy. Mr. Churchill said that about 5,000 Germans
were believed to have been drowned in attempting a sea-
borne invasion of Crete. *Photo, Associated Press*

Later that evening, in the fast failing light, *Kandahar* and *Kingston* managed to pick up about eighty per cent of the *Fiji* ship's company : a fine feat of seamanship. Of the *Gloucester* ship's company there's still no news, but the sea was calm and with a light breeze blowing their rafts towards the near-by island of Antikithera. So ended the second round.

Next morning at dawn the Huns made their third and final attempt to invade Crete by sea. The C.-in-C. had foreseen the possibility that some of the convoy, which had been dispersed during the day's operations, might try to sneak through under cover of night, and land their troops at dawn. The Fifth Destroyer Flotilla, under Captain Lord Louis Mountbatten, in the *Kelly*, had been asked by General Freyberg to bombard enemy-occupied positions in Crete, and were now ordered to remain close inshore and prevent the approach of enemy shipping.

Actually, only two enemy ships made the attempt and were sighted creeping towards the beach at the first streak of dawn. The Fifth Flotilla tore in to intercept and sank both of them. The first was full of Hun soldiers who—as before—leapt overboard in their full heavy equipment. The second was loaded with ammunition ; shells from *Kelly's* and *Kashmir's* 4·7s soon found their mark and set her on fire. As the fire spread and travelled down the ship, box after box of ammunition flared into the sky like a giant Roman candle.

Now remember that all this had happened close inshore in full view of the Hun air-borne troops, who had already felt the effect of the destroyers' guns. You can imagine their fury at seeing their much needed supports scuppered at the last fence. You can imagine the air sizzling with their impassioned signals for the bombers to concentrate on the destroyers that had been responsible.

And it wasn't long before they came. The first to arrive were the high-level bombers. They started at 5.30 in the morning and continued till 8. Hundreds of bombs were dropped, but both *Kelly* and *Kashmir* managed to escape unscathed. At 8 a large formation of dive-bombers took over and were more successful. The third wave got *Kashmir* with a thousand-pound bomb abaft the funnel. *Kashmir* broke in two and sank in a couple of minutes.

Shortly afterwards another thousand-pounder hit the *Kelly* abaft the engine-room ; at that moment she was steaming full out at 30 knots and heeling over under helm. All that could be seen from the bridge was the flying debris from the explosion, the plates of the ship's sides as they buckled back wrenched open by the force of the water, and the Junkers 87 diving head-long into the sea.

By this time a second wave were half-way down and Lord Louis instinctively yelled down the voice pipe, "Whatever happens—keep the guns firing !" As the words tumbled out of his mouth, he almost regretted them, for a quick glance down the deck showed that not a man had left his post and that every gun was firing harder than it had ever fired before.

But the speed of the ship and the force of the waters on the wrenched plates in her side were too much. She heeled further and further, and fifty seconds after being hit turned turtle. As she went, the men were literally swept away from their guns by the weight of water. One lad of 17, washed off by the sea as he was loading a belt into his gun, was still clasping the belt in his last desperate efforts to get it in.

And down below, those grand men, the engineers and stokers, remained at their posts to a man. In the engine-room they were still working the steam valves as she turned over, and it was only when she was completely inverted that the Engineer Commander gave permission to leave. Luckily an air lock had formed, and many were able to escape. Up top, those who had been washed off the bridge and decks saw the strange sight—as they came up to the surface—of the ship's propellers passing over their heads and still racing at full speed in the air.

Some three and a half hours later the destroyer *Kipling* managed to reach the scene and—in spite of further and continued dive-bombing—got *Kelly* and *Kashmir* survivors safely away.

But while those men—their eyes clogged up with oil fuel—were waiting and struggling in the water, the Hun pilots flew up and down while their rear-gunners machine-gunned them.

So ended the Huns' third and final attempt to invade Crete by sea. The Navy had been given the order, "There must be no sea-borne invasion of Crete." It was obeyed.

Battleship *v.* Bomber in the Mediterranean

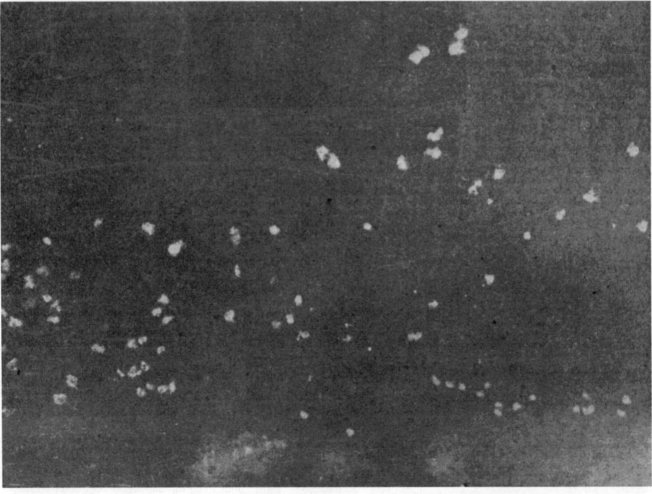

As the bomber dives, the battleship's anti-aircraft guns fill the sky with puffs of exploding shells. The photograph at top shows how skilful navigation can avoid the falling bombs. Before the war Germany thought that the bomber would neutralize the battleship, but sea power is the dominant factor in this war as in the last, and Britain still rules the crest of the wave—and under it for that matter.

Photos, Fox

I Was There! ....
Eye Witness Stories of the War

Ours Was a Quiet Passage From Canada

How the largest contingent of Canadian troops to arrive in Britain was brought safely across the Atlantic in June is described in the following dispatch from Reuter's special correspondent, who was in one of the escorting warships.

STANDING on the quarter-deck of a destroyer which had been my home for many days, I watched giant troopships, their rails packed tight with figures in khaki and Air Force blue, steam slowly past to their moorings. One of them flew the French flag and another the Dutch. They were carrying men from Canada, the Dominion's latest contribution in man-power to the Empire's war effort.

When I joined this destroyer I had no idea where we were bound or what our task might be. All I, or any of the ship's company, knew was that we were out on " a very interesting mission." We slipped out alone from a British naval base and steamed in solitude for some time until we had made rendezvous with a number of other destroyers. Not until we were all moving in formation far from land did we learn from our captain that our task was to escort Canadian troops to Britain.

As the hour for picking up our convoy approached excitement rose. Should we or should we not make the appointed rendezvous, a secret pinpoint on the vast chart of the Atlantic, in time to coincide with the arrival of the troopships?

" Objects bearing red four-five, almost indistinguishable," one of our look-outs reported. Surprised, for we were some time ahead of zero hour, we strained our eyes through glasses from the bridge, and slowly the " objects " took form. Grey blurs and intermingled smoke sorted themselves into our troopships, supported by the might of battleships and destroyers who had brought them from the Canadian coast.

From the senior ship of our escorting force lamp and flag signals followed each other in quick succession. Our yeoman of signals, glass at eye, had a hectic few minutes reading and decoding the instructions to us about our new positions. Then came the executive signal for us to form up in screen. The ship vibrated as we increased speed and jumped ahead. Then a rain squall bore down on us, blotting out every other ship from our view. When it passed we were all steaming ahead

in position—troopships, battleships, and screening destroyers, as if we had been doing it for hours.

In the clammy cold of the next afternoon I was on the bridge again. Suddenly a

With their eyes fixed on the convoy their ship is escorting these sailors on a British warship know no respite until their charges are brought safely home. In this page a special correspondent tells how his ship escorted a large Canadian contingent safely to Britain. *Photo, Planet News*

prolonged " honk " from the battleship's siren riveted our attention. " Emergency turn," she signalled. In a few seconds every ship was heading on her new course.

A submarine had been sighted on the surface, far off on the opposite side of the convoy to us. There was more flashing of

lamps, more hectic work for the signal yeoman. Several destroyers, with depth charges primed and set, dashed off to hunt. Our own luck was out, we must remain to keep the screen intact.

The submarine, on sighting us, had evidently made a crash dive. For half an hour she was hunted without avail. Until the convoy was well on a new course and out of harm's way the hunters kept her down to prevent her reporting us or observing our movements.

Next day I found an odd collection of rusty, salt-stained " battle bowlers " draped around the bridge and I took my own tin hat around with me with some affection. We

were approaching the area of possible aircraft attack, but we had our own air escort now. Visibility, too, was poor, and helped to screen us, and no hostile aircraft appeared.

So, in safety, we brought our charges home in a total of nearly one hundred and forty thousand tons of ships.

My Men of the Ladybird said 'Carry On, Sir'

The little gunboat Ladybird was for years one of the most famous ships in the Navy, and her last action at Tobruk was a worthy finish to her career. It is here described by her captain, Commander John Blackburn.

WE were anchored at Tobruk on May 12, when 47 Nazi bombers swooped towards us. My chief gunner's mate saw the first plane dropping out of the sun-

shine, and it laid a stick of bombs so near that their explosion flung the crew on the deck.

Then there was a terrific screech, and there came another lot, one of which got us right aft, almost immediately putting the deck under water. Then another bomb got us in the engine-room. The ship shivered from stem to stern and was obviously sinking, but my men urged me to carry on.

We were burning like hell amidships and fire was pouring out of the engine-room. I saw many of my men dash into that inferno and carry out the wounded while the forward six-inch guns, pom-poms and machine-guns sprayed a hail of metal at the Nazi planes.

The planes swarmed around us, dropping more bombs. By this time wounded men were helping to feed the guns as the planes swarmed around us. We got two of them. Rescue boats arrived from shore and took aboard the first of the wounded.

We still kept firing our forward guns, but Ladybird was sinking fast with the water sweeping closer to the bridge every moment.

Even then the sailors, gunners and officers, with fire all round them, and half the guns under water, said to me: " Carry on, sir,

H.M.S. LADYBIRD, sunk on May 12, 1941, in the manner described in this page, was a river gunboat of 625 tons. Launched in 1915, she is here seen at an early stage in her career. A later photograph is given in page 66 of this volume, where the part she played, together with her sister ship Aphis and the monitor Terror, in assisting our advance across the Western Desert, is fully described. *Photo, P. A. Vicary*

‖‖‖‖‖‖‖‖‖‖‖‖‖‖‖‖‖‖‖‖‖‖‖‖‖‖‖‖‖‖‖‖‖‖‖‖‖‖‖ I WAS THERE! ‖‖‖

please.'' They all stayed until, at the last minute, when the old ship was rolling for her final plunge, I ordered them to abandon ship. She went down with what guns we could man firing to the last.

The Ladybird had four men killed and 14 wounded. Her captain received this signal from Adml. Sir Andrew Cunningham, C.-in-C. Mediterranean : '' Great fighting finish worthy of highest ideals and tradition of the Navy and an inspiration for all who fight on the seas.''

A Nazi Shot Me Down Into the Channel

A fighter pilot rescued from the Channel by an R.A.F. rescue launch was two-and-a-half hours afloat in his dinghy, during which time he witnessed an aerial combat. Here is his story in his own words.

OVER Boulogne I got separated from my squadron in protecting a Blenheim which had itself got separated from its formation. On the way back I was repeatedly attacked from behind by Me 109s, one of which I shot down into the sea. Still being attacked I went down to sea level. There was then a loud explosion and petrol came streaming into the cockpit. Seeing flames and feeling uncomfortably hot, I decided to get out. I pulled up from the water to 15,000 feet, and after one unsuccessful attempt to get out I got clear.

When I hit the water, the shroud lines of the parachute fell on top of me. As I was entangled, I had difficulty in pulling up the dinghy, but I succeeded at last, inflated the dinghy and climbed into it. I could see no land on either side of me, and I started paddling with my hands towards the English coast, using the sun as a guide. The sea was calm, but the dinghy was half full of water all the time. I seemed to be making quite fair progress.

After about half-an-hour I saw a seaplane approaching from France, escorted by six single-seater aircraft. It was flying at sea level. The formation of fighters went right over me, the first two at about 50 feet and the other four at about 1,500 feet. I recognized them as Me 109s and got out of the dinghy and made myself scarce in the water. The whole formation then turned back towards the French coast, but returned again in about 20 minutes, passing about half a mile away from me. By that time I had resumed my place in the dinghy.

In the meantime I had seen a Lysander several miles away in the direction of the English coast at about 100 feet, but it had not seen me. After the enemy formations passed me the second time I saw the Lysander again, about five miles off towards the English coast, with an escort of Spitfires. I estimated my position at about. Mid-Channel out from Boulogne.

The Spitfires attacked some Me 109s at about 3,000 feet and I saw one Me 109 go into the sea immediately. I then saw a number of Hurricanes arrive and join the fray and attack some 109s which were lower down with the seaplane. Later I saw the seaplane go into the sea and blow up, leaving a column of black smoke. I also saw a Spitfire go into the sea.

All the aircraft then disappeared and I was alone again. I continued paddling until the English coast came into sight. I saw a motor launch too far away to see me. Later I saw two more patrolling around, apparently searching, and then went towards the place where the Spitfire had gone in. One of them came fairly close and I attracted its attention by splashing the water with my hand. I was told that the crew first discovered me through seeing the yellow dinghy and the splashing. I was hauled aboard the R.A.F. rescue launch, dried and made comfortable, given a drink and taken to Dover, none the worse for my adventure except being somewhat stiff and bruised. I was treated right royally by the Naval authorities at Dover and subsequently driven to my base.

We Went to Rescue Our Bombed Hospital Ship

An unsuccessful attack by Nazi bombers on the hospital ship Aba off Crete is here described by the '' Daily Mail '' Special Correspondent, who was on board a destroyer which answered the Aba's call for help.

WE had received a message from the hospital ship Aba that several bombers, after circling her, had dropped eight heavy bombs, which, fortunately for the helpless wounded she was carrying aboard, all fell wide of the mark.

We were a formation of destroyers with A.A. ships patrolling some 120 miles south when the call for help came, and putting on all speed we reached the scene shortly after another German plane had circled the ship at a height of only 1,300 ft.

With her hull glistening white and red crosses marking her at every angle of view, the Aba was a conspicuous sight, which no reconnaissance pilot could mistake.

Nevertheless, we had been escorting the ship only a short time when the object of this reconnaissance was made clear. A formation of eight dive-bombers was seen approaching and the destroyers immediately opened up with an umbrella barrage over the hospital ship.

As our own forward guns swivelled round they were just able to bear over the target, and round after round screamed over our heads as on the bridge we ducked under the terrific crack and blast of their firing.

R.A.F. RUBBER DINGHY supporting two airmen being drawn to one of the R.A.F. Rescue Motor Launches. This photograph shows how flying men who have baled out over the sea are saved. Dinghies carried by aircraft and dropped to men in the water are fitted with rations, paddles, etc. For other photographs see page 727.

A.A. Gunners, aboard a British destroyer, while on the watch for hostile aeroplanes, are testing their pom-pom, an ingenious and powerful form of multiple shell-firing machine-gun.
Photos, British Official ; Crown Copyright ; Sport & General

IIIIIIIIIIIIIIIIIIIIIIIIIIIIIIIIIIIIIIIIIIIIIIIIIIIIIIIIIIIIIIIIIIIIIIIIIIIIII **I WAS THERE!** IIIIIIIIIIIIIIIIIIIIIIIIIIIIIIIIIIIIIIIIIIIIIIIIIIIIIIIIIIIIIIIIIIIIIIIII

THE POETS & THE WAR
XLVI
EPITAPH ON A VERY YOUNG AIRMAN
By MAURICE HEALY

Think not of valour—the pain
  That never deflected my course :
Limbs would have mended again ;
  Wavering brings but remorse.
But think of the heart that lies cold—
  The singer, whose songs are unsung ;
For I, who shall never be old,
  Hardly knew what it was to be young.

*Published in U.S.A. by the
Refugees of England, Incorporated*

With my own ears plugged heavily with special wax, it was a shattering experience, especially when the tornado of hot air whisked off my steel helmet. Still those shells bursting high in the blue sky were obviously an even more shattering ordeal for the Germans, who changed their tactics, immediately broke up, and made individual bombing attacks on the A.A. cruisers.

With fierce fire these experienced vessels deterred them again and again. As we counted the aeroplanes manoeuvring in the sky like a bunch of frightened seagulls, the captain remarked to me, " These blokes haven't got the guts like those fellows we used to see." It was the same captain from whose bridge I had watched the bombing of the Illustrious on January 10.

Out of eight machines which circled about us only two put any dash into their attack. One turned several times like a fluttering leaf, then dived so steeply that it appeared absolutely vertical.

As he flattened out the pom-poms of an A.A. cruiser spat viciously after him. At the same time columns of water leapt into the air astern of the vessel and rose to a height above her masthead. By this time others, who had attempted shallower dives, dropping their bombs indiscriminately into the sea, were darting about just over the water in an effort to get so low that none of the guns of the ships could bear on them.

One seemed winged, and our signal yeoman was certain that it struck the water. For my part my eyes were glued in those few seconds to another dive-bomber who was certainly pressing his attack. He appeared out of control, so directly did he plummet on to the second A.A. cruiser.

A splutter of pom-pom fire hid the plane from our view. From where we stood it seemed probable this fellow, too, was winged. After that the raid collapsed suddenly.

The Raider Picked Us Up from the Zamzam

Considerable indignation was caused by the sinking of the liner Zamzam in the South Atlantic on April 17. All her passengers were saved, however, and one of the many Americans on board here tells his story of the incident.

SAILING under the Egyptian flag, the Zamzam was sunk by a German raider while on her way from Pernambuco to Cape Town. A large proportion of the passengers were Americans, among them being several missionaries and members of the British-American Ambulance Corps going out for service with General de Gaulle's forces in Africa.

One of the American passengers, Mr. J. V. Murphy, editor of the magazine " Fortune," describing the sinking, said :

The ship was four days from Cape Town when just before dawn on April 17 nine shells hit her.

Captain Smith tried to signal, but the ship's " blinker " had been shattered. He then ordered the Egyptian flag to be unfurled, grabbed a hand torch, and began signalling himself.

The firing stopped, but nine people had been badly wounded and many others hurt.

As the ship sank passengers were thrown into the sea. Doctors and orderlies attached to the ambulances dived overboard to keep women and children afloat, and towed pieces of floating wreckage to them to keep them up.

By 7.30 a.m. every one had been taken on board the raider, whose commander, Captain Rogge, expressed his regret for the shelling.

The next day all except two Americans and one Englishman, who were wounded, were transferred to a merchant ship. The captain of this vessel was not so polite. Speaking in English, he said : " Any monkey business and we'll answer with machine-guns ! "

The women were given cabins, while the men slept shoulder to shoulder in a single cabin. Survivors were on board this ship for 33 days before being landed at St. Jean de Luz.—*British United Press.*

AMERICAN SURVIVORS of the Egyptian liner Zamzam sunk by a Nazi raider in the South Atlantic on April 17. Landed in Unoccupied France, they were sent to San Sebastian, and are seen here on their way to a hotel, prior to returning to America via Lisbon.   *Photo, Associated Press*

OUR WAR GAZETTEER : RUSSIAN FRONT

BARANOVITCH GAP, key-point north of the Pripet Marshes, White Russia, about 500 m. from Moscow. This was Napoleon's route.

BARKOVITCHI, on the Latvian-Russian border, 25 m. N.W. of Polotsk, on the Dvina.

BOBRUISK, White Russia, town and river port on the R. Beresina, 105 m. S.E. of Minsk. Pop. 64,800.

BORISOV, White Russia, on the R. Beresina, 50 m. N.E. of Minsk. Near Borisov Napoleon made his disastrous passage of the Beresina. Pop. about 21,000.

BREST-LITOVSK, Poland, on R. Bug, due east of Warsaw. Great railway, road and water centre. Pop. 50,700. Scene of Russo-German peace Treaty of 1918.

CERNAUTI, Rumania, on R. Pruth, 167 m. S.E. of Lwow. Pop. 109,698.

CONSTANTZA, Rumania, large oil and grain port on the Black Sea. Pop. 61,412.

DNIEPER RIVER, rises in Valdai plateau near source of the Volga, runs through White Russia and Ukraine into the Black Sea. Length 1,340 m., navigable almost from source, and means of transport for Ukraine corn to Odessa.

DNIESTER RIVER, rises in Carpathians, traverses Poland, U.S.S.R. and falls into Black Sea. Length 750 m. Important waterway for trade.

DVINSK, Latvia, on R. Dvina. Important rail centre for traffic with Russia and Poland. Pop. 45,160.

GALATZ, Rumania, N. side of R. Danube, 10 m. above its junction with the Pruth and nearly 80 m. N.E. of Bucharest. Important oil, grain and timber port. Pop. 101,148.

HELSINKI (formerly Helsingfors), capital of Finland, 250 m. W. of Leningrad. Pop. 293,237.

KANDALAKSHA, White Sea port, 120 m. S. of Murmansk, in Russia's extreme north-west.

KARELIAN ISTHMUS, Russia, E. of Finland between White Sea and Lake Ladoga, area 53,890 sq. m.

KAUNAS (KOVNO), seat of Lithuanian Government, taken by Germans on June 24. Pop. 152,363.

KHARKOV, Ukraine, standing on three small streams that fall into the Uda, 250 m. S.E. of Kiev. Large industrial town and air station. Pop. 833,432.

KIEV, capital of Ukraine, city and river port on the right bank of the Dnieper, 280 m. from Odessa. It is the oldest centre of Christianity in Russia. Pop. 846,293.

KOLA PENINSULA, between White Sea and Arctic Ocean. The north shore is called the Murman Coast.

KRONSTADT, Russian seaport and State dockyard in the Leningrad area, 20 m. W. of and connected by canal with Leningrad.

LAKE LADOGA, between Russia and Finland, largest lake in Europe, a few miles north of Leningrad.

LENINGRAD (formerly St. Petersburg, then Petrograd), second largest city in U.S.S.R. It was the capital of the Empire and Republic till 1918. Pop. 3,191,304.

LEPEL, on the 1938 Russian-Lithuanian frontier, S. of Polotsk.

LUCK, Poland, on the R. Steyr, 51 m. N.W. of Kovel. Pop. 20,000.

LWOW, pronounced Lvoff, Poland. Important railway junction and industrial centre on R. Peltew, 135 m. east of Cracow. Pop. 317,700.

MINSK, capital of White Russia, N. of Baranovitch Gap, on the River Svisloch, a tributary of the Beresina. Has two universities and other cultural centres. Pop. 180,000.

MOSCOW, capital of U.S.S.R. and H.Q. of Soviet Government, 400 m. S.E. of Leningrad. Dominant feature is the Kremlin in the Red Square, where the embalmed remains of Lenin lie in a granite mausoleum. Pop. 4,137,018.

MURMANSK, Russia, seaport on Kola inlet of the Murman Coast, perpetually ice-free harbour. Pop. about 10,000.

NOVOGOROD-VOLYNSK, on the Ukraine front, 150 m. west of Kiev.

OSTROV, Russia, key-point on 1938 Russian frontier on Leningrad road between Dvinsk and Pskoff.

PLOESTI, Rumanian town situated in the centre of famous oilfields 35 m. N. of Bucharest.

POLOTSK, White Russia, 140 m. S. of Ostrov at confluence of Dvina and Polota Rivers, near Latvian border. Pop. 21,455.

PSKOFF, ancient town in western Russia, founded 965, 170 m. by rail from Leningrad. Pop. 52,600.

RIGA, Latvia, capital and seaport on the River Dvina, 9 m. from the Gulf of Riga. Pop. 393,211.

SMOLENSK, Russia, on R. Dnieper, 250 m. W.S.W. of Moscow. Pop. 104,100.

SULINA, Rumanian seaport on the mouth of the Sulina arm of the Danube. Pop. about 10,000.

TALLINN (formerly Reval), capital and seaport of Estonia, at mouth of Gulf of Finland. Pop. 145,000.

TARNOPOL, capital of the county of Tarnopol, Poland, 76 m. E.S.E. of Lwow. Pop. 31,000.

TULCEA, Rumanian port near Danube delta. Pop. about 28,000.

ZHITOMIR, Ukraine, on the R. Terterev, 80 m. S.W. of Kiev. Pop. about 70,000.

The Editor's Postscript

GREAT has been the change in our Southern sky during the last weeks; notably since the beginning of our daylight " sweeps " over the invasion ports and the sustained night bombing of German industrial centres. The drone of aerial engines has been so persistent of late that it is almost uncanny when none is heard. Time was, not so long ago, when one instinctively cocked an ear to make sure there was none of the once familiar broken pulsation of Heinkel or Junkers to be distinguished . . . so often that was heard and the thud of bombs came following after. Now the sky above my particular bit of the Southland reverberates so frequently with outward or inward planes by day and night that we don't bother about them except occasionally to admire the symmetrical beauty of a formation of two or three squadrons all keeping station and flying at a few thousand feet. A truly inspiring sight: the inspiration due in some measure to the knowledge that they are " Ours " !

DOUBTLESS the Huns can keep station quite as well so long as there are none of ours about. Our only danger under this plane-travelled sky is from an occasional sneak raider; but that has noticeably diminished of recent weeks, and I have seen too much of these lone raiders and their dirty work not to rejoice in the change that has come over our bit of " that inverted bowl they call the sky." Not that I imagine we have seen the last of the sneak raider or even of an enemy formation, for there's a lot of space up there in the sky, and, unlike Sir Boyle Roche's bird, neither Spitfire nor Hurricane can be in two places at once. But either can be in two different places so quickly now that we dwellers in the rural south feel much safer than we did not long ago. If Soviet airmen take good toll of the Nazi bombers they will hasten the day when Britain will again —as she did in 1918—rule the Western sky.

THE harvest is in full tide ot all the neighbouring farms just now. Every hour or so on hearing the clatter of motor machinery I find myself looking out expecting to see another Bren carrier rattling past my window, only to have a much more pleasing sight—another wagon with spilth of hay tugged by a tractor on its way to the uphill farm. And equally cheering is the picture of two or three summer-clad village children getting a ride on the tractor. Last year when travelling in East Anglia I was astonished to observe that the natural conservatism of the farmers made them still huddle their haystacks in their ancient corners instead (as it seemed to my non-agricultural mind) of dispersing them at wide distances from each other as a precaution against the possibility of fire raiding, which in the cities has proved so much more devastating than the high explosive. Before the War our dismal Desmonds were always warning us that the Hun would destroy our crops with his incendiaries. As a matter of historical fact, he did nothing of the kind, the total

crop areas that were destroyed amounting to a very few acres. But I'd be inclined to heed Desmond's warning, as it is foolish to bank on what didn't happen last year not happening this. Farmers should take—indeed, should be compelled to take—every reasonable precaution in storing their precious harvest so as to minimize injury to the whole if a haystack here and there gets an incendiary on it. [Just announced proper precautions have been outlined by Ministry of Agriculture.]

THE vagaries of the English climate are only rivalled by the prevarications of a Hitler. Within the last three weeks (as I write) we have experienced every variety of climate from Sub-Arctic to Eqautorial.

GEN. SIR ROBERT HAINING, who was Vice-Chief of the Imperial General Staff in 1940, has now been appointed Intendant General in the Middle East. His task will be to co-ordinate the administration of the various fronts in that theatre. *Lafayette*

In some parts of South America you can beat this inside twelve hours by taking a sort of perpendicular journey from the Andine heights down to sea level. I remember a lovely film of such a journey from Quito (which has just come into the news with the quarrel between Ecuador and Peru, provoked by Japanese it's said) down to the steaming rubber forests of Peru and Brazil. Myself I have travelled downstairs in Peru from Puño on Lake Titicaca to Mollendo on the Pacific 'twixt morn and evening, a drop of some 12,000 feet, passing through all sorts of climates in the descent . . . resulting in some hours of deafness. But I have seldom felt the weariness of the flesh in so pronounced a degree as in these blistering days of July down in the sunny south.

I HAD no complaint of heat or weariness this forenoon, however, as I hurried into my garden for a better view of as lovely a sight as I have seen of late—three of our big,

new, majestic four-engined bombers coming back from doing their stuff over hostile France or Hunland. A portentous vision in the sky! These mighty machines, their duty done, were flying low and leisurely on their homeward way, while the seven fighter-planes that accompanied them and continually made loops around the aerial Leviathans looked like mere toys by comparison. These were some of the big bombers that the inhabitants of towns on the South-East coast gathered together to cheer (see official reports) as they passed overhead. In our rural spot there were not enough of us to raise a cheer—you need a crowd for that—but all who saw them were, I'm sure, conscious of an elation of spirit as they passed over.

NONE of us—yes, I venture the assertion— said as they droned through the blue and glistening summer sky, " I hope they haven't been retaliating." Oh dear, no ! Most of us, I feel, being quite common unsaintly folk, just hoped that they had done all they were capable of doing in carrying terror and destruction into enemy concentrations, let these be " industrial targets," " marshalling yards," or just towns where our enemies were striving for our destruction. My own hope was that enemy towns had suffered. But then I was denied the refining influence of being reared in Tercanbury (a place I was reading about in Maugham's " Cakes and Ale " last night), whose Archbishop doesn't see eye to eye with me.

ANYHOW, the vision of these superb engines of retaliation had a most exhilarating effect on my heat-enervated frame and I got through the offices of my non-ecclesiastic day with an increase of confidence in our coming domination of the air. Three bombers no more ensure that than three swallows make a summer; but I know, and you know, that these three were only samples of innumerous big bombers that British and American brains and brawn have brought into being during the past twelve months of the War. May their numbers grow from more to more. But overhead as I write at the witching hour of 12.25 a.m. I hear the throb of engines that I'd bet are Nazis'. The Alert has not yet sounded and I'm carrying on. Perhaps tomorrow's papers will tell me something about " a solitary enemy plane," etc. [Turned out to be a heavy raid on Southampton.]

SUBSCRIBERS binding THE WAR ILLUSTRATED should note that we are nearing the end of the Fourth Volume, which will be completed with No. 100. I hope they are following my advice about the careful handling of the weekly parts now that the whole number is designed for binding. It is astonishing how well they look when guillotined and pressed in the bound volume. Approximately a quarter inch of the top and bottom margins and half an inch of the outer edges are removed in the process of turning your loose numbers into books. These WAR ILLUSTRATED volumes are going to be increasingly valuable in years to come, so that a little extra care in their preservation just now will be well repaid. Volume Four will contain all weekly parts numbered from 71 to 100.

JOHN CARPENTER HOUSE
WHITEFRIARS, LONDON. E.C.4.

Registered at the G.P.O. as a Newspaper

The War Illustrated, August 1st, 1941

Vol 4 The War Illustrated Nº 100

Edited by Sir John Hammerton

FOURPENCE

WEEKLY

RED ARMY TANKS, somewhere on the vast front which runs across Europe from the White Sea to the Black Sea. The skill and patriotic fervour of the Soviet armies now locked in a life or death struggle with the evil colossus of Hitlerism have astonished the world. In the obscurities and confusion of the conflict one fact emerges clearly: Hitler had underestimated the military efficiency and national consciousness of the totalitarian Slav. Nevertheless, it was his criminal destiny to strike east.
Photo, P.N.A.

Our Searchlight on the War

New Limbs for Old

THE vast experience gained by surgeons in the Great War of 1914-18 is proving very valuable today in dealing with men and women who have lost a limb through enemy action. It is a far cry from the old bucket and peg to the modern artificial leg or arm made of very light metal and equipped with control cords, springs and levers by means of which natural movements are possible. At Queen Mary's Hospital, Roehampton, a crippled patient is fitted with a temporary leg as soon as he is able to leave his bed, the aim being to restore the muscles of the stump and hasten its consolidation. When this end has been achieved the permanent limb is fitted. This is carefully made to match the sound limb, and the patient, who by this time has gained considerable

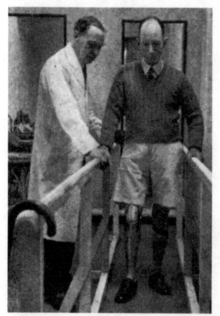

LEARNING TO WALK with the aid of an artificial limb, a patient of Queen Mary's Hospital, Roehampton, for limbless victims of the War, takes his first steps.
Photo, Topical Press

confidence, is able, after a little practice, to walk without a limp, to ride a bicycle, drive a car, and to engage in many active occupations. Most important of all to sensitive minds, he is able to avoid or banish any galling sense of inferiority or humiliation resulting from his disability, for the fact that he has an artificial limb is perceptible only to the sympathetic eye of an expert.

Norway in Scotland

HARD by an old grey Scottish town, surrounded by meadows and rolling hills, the Free Norwegian Army is in rigorous training against the day when its men will fight their way home. They arrived a year ago, stripped, angry refugees, and were welcomed by the Provost and the townspeople. About half the Force fought in the Norwegian campaign. Some of the others are men from whalers diverted to British ports when Hitler invaded Norway. All are now brown, fit and hard, appreciative of the constant kindness of the land that received them, learning to speak English, some courting Scottish brides. From one of the camps volunteers who took part in the Lofoten raid were selected, and to it came those who escaped to freedom with the returning boats. Major-General Carl G. Fleischer, Acting C.-in-C. of the Norwegian Army—for General Ruge has been a prisoner of war in

Germany since June 1940—may well be proud of the men under his command, growing daily in numbers and in military efficiency.

New Head of the A.T.S.

DAME HELEN GWYNNE-VAUGHAN, G.B.E., Director of the Auxiliary Territorial Service, has retired under the new age-limit rule. Her rank was that of Chief Controller, equivalent to that of a major-general. The choice of a successor has fallen upon Controller Jean Knox, who joined the Service in pre-war days and since March has held a special appointment as inspector, touring the country to investigate the personal side of A.T.S. life. Mrs. Knox, whose husband is a squadron-leader in the R.A.F., is 33.

Secret Anti-Nazi Radio

FROM a new and mysterious broadcasting station in Germany there have been recently transmitted violent, coarsely worded attacks on leaders of the Nazi Party. According to messages reaching London from a neutral source, the station, which is known as the Hess Station, represents the opposition alleged to exist within the Party itself, and which was associated with the name of Rudolf Hess. Broadcasts are made hourly from 5.53 p.m. to 1.53 a.m.

Famine Comes to Greece

GENERAL TSOLAKOGLOU, the Quisling Prime Minister of Greece, is regarded with contempt and hatred not only because of his treachery in signing an armistice on his part of the front against the Government's wishes, but also because of his incompetence in easing the plight of the stricken population. Starvation has come quickly to Greece, for the Nazis have stripped the country. Bread supplies are uncertain and inadequate. People are living chiefly on vegetables—if they can afford them. There is a great scarcity of fish owing to loss of boats in the evacuation. The Germans have taken over control of the major businesses, and have also commandeered all military hospitals in Athens. Greek wounded are turned out into the streets to make way for wounded Germans, and unless cared for by compassionate citizens, they would be left to die.

Marine With Nine Lives

ONCE again Marine Maurice Reidy, an assistant in the machine-room of the Amalgamated Press, whose personal account of the sinking of the Courageous was given in Vol. I, pp. 115-116, has cheated the enemy. He is now in a Middle East hospital recover-

MRS. JEAN KNOX, the new Controller of the Auxiliary Territorial Service, who was appointed on July 8 in succession to Dame Helen Gwynne-Vaughan. *Photo, Fox*

ing from wounds received when fighting in a rearguard action in Crete. Taken prisoner, he managed to escape and join the last boatload to leave the island. Mr. Reidy, who is 43 years old, was torpedoed in the Great War, and was also a survivor of Zeebrugge.

Saving Parish Records

LOCAL historians of the future will owe a debt of gratitude to the Provisional Committee for Micro-filming Parish Registers, of which the late Lord Stamp was head. A double page of a register can be photographed on a film measuring 1 in. by 1½ in., and if necessary the negative can be enlarged to 8 ft. 6 in. by 6 ft. 6 in. Between three and four hundred pages can be done in one hour. The records of more than 1,000 parishes have already been dealt with, but the Committee is hoping to include 11,000. The cost works out at about £2 for a small country parish, and £50 for a large one such as Stepney, where 10,000 exposures were made. It was Thomas Cromwell who ordered the keeping of parish records; the earliest date from 1538.

Dud Bombs on Russia

MOSCOW Radio announced on July 10 that of six bombs recently dropped by a Junkers on a little Russian village, only two exploded. On examination the other four were found to contain sand, and inside one was also a note. Written in German, in a woman's hand, were the words: " We are helping as we can." The Russian wireless commentator described this woman munitions worker as heroic. " She is the real representative of the German people. She displayed human feeling and risked being caught in order to save the innocent."

H.M.S. WATERHEN, the first Australian warship to be lost by enemy action. She sank after a bombing attack in the Mediterranean, as announced by the Admiralty on July 5. The Waterhen, a destroyer of the "Tribal" type, dated from 1918, displaced 1,100 tons, and was armed with four 4-in. and five smaller guns.
Photo, P. A. Vicary

The Way of the War

THE RUSSIAN PEOPLE ARE NOW OUR ALLIES
British Commonwealth and Soviet Union Together Against Hitlerism

STALIN smiled, Molotov smiled, Cripps smiled, as they watched the attendants affix the blue ribbons and blobs of red wax to the documents lying on the table—documents which had just been signed by Russia's Commissar for Foreign Affairs and Britain's Ambassador to Moscow. For they had been making history. Those documents declared in Russian and English that the Governments of Britain and the U.S.S.R. " mutually undertake to render each other assistance and support of all kinds in the present war against Hitlerite Germany," and " further undertake that during this war they will neither negotiate nor conclude an armistice or treaty of peace except by mutual agreement." Then chocolates were handed round and glasses of champagne, and Stalin, raising his glass, gave the toast of Anglo-Russian cooperation for victory.

So, after a lapse of more than a quarter of a century, Britain and Russia were allies once more. For, of course, it was an alliance, although some nervous nitwits at the Foreign Office—whose idea of Bolshevists is probably derived from the cartoons of a generation ago which showed them as fellows who never washed, with greasy beards and smoking bombs poking out of their pockets—gave out that Russia was not really an ally but a co-belligerent, an associate. . . . For this reason, but not for this reason alone, they banned the playing in the B.B.C.'s Sunday evening anthem parade of the " Internationale," which the Russians have had the bad taste to choose as their national anthem . . . Mr. Churchill gave short shrift to such bureaucratic boggling and bungling. " It is, of course, an alliance," he told the House of Commons on July 15. " The Russian people are now our allies."

FROM 1914 to 1917 the Russia of the Tsars was the ally of Britain and France in the Great War against the empires of Germany and Austria. During those three years the Russian soldiers fought with surpassing valour, endured most terrible hardships, suffered incomparable losses. The total figure was never published because it was never known, but Hindenburg estimated the Russian losses at between five and eight millions. In those days Germany was, indeed, fighting a war on two fronts, and it should never be forgotten that while Von Kluck was driving on Paris, the Russians invaded East Prussia so that two German army corps had to be detached from the Western Front and sent to the east. Hindenburg crushed the Russians at Tannenberg, but Tannenberg saved Paris and enabled Joffre to win the Battle of the Marne. For years the awful sacrifice continued, until

in 1917, when the horror and the uselessness of it all had penetrated into the consciousness of the meanest soldier, when the cream of the Russian forces had been wiped out, when those who were left could fight no longer with their fists and knives—then the front collapsed and the soldiers retreated on a rear foul with all the abominations of Tsarist misrule.

FOR a few months there was an attempt to maintain the war against Germany, since the provisional government of Kerensky and Kornilov felt themselves bound in honour to do all they could to help their allies, now bogged in the awful morasses of the western battlefields. The dawn of liberty in Russia was welcomed throughout the world by every man of liberal mind ; but the vision of a free Russia faded and died in the murk of the November days of revolution. Kerensky and the liberal regime crashed into ruin, and Lenin and Trotsky reigned in their stead. They made peace with Germany at Brest-Litovsk, a peace which in its vindictiveness was worse even than that of Versailles. But there was no peace in Russia, and for years the world stood appalled at the spectacle of Whites and Reds tearing each other in the bloody slime of civil war. And not content with letting the Russians fight out their quarrels amongst themselves, the Allies—Britain and France, America and Japan—sent armies to Russia to support one or the other of the White chieftains.

For years the civil war continued ; for years rape and rapine stalked the highways and murder and mutilation came hurrying after. 1918, 1919 and 1920 were years of incredible suffering ; years, too, of incredible achievement. At length the Reds were successful everywhere. Followed Lenin's death, Trotsky's exile, Stalin's rise to supreme power. Then came the Five Year Plans, the collectivization of agriculture, the " liquidation " of the kulaks, the industrialization of areas which hitherto had hardly been trodden by human foot . . .

During most of those years Britain and Russia were miles apart, separated not as in the Tsarist days by imperialistic fears but by ideological differences. Russia seemed so strange, so altogether different, so novel and in many ways so brutal. Always there have been in this country many who have seen in Communism *the* enemy, although there have been many, too, who have seen in Russia much to admire, grounds for hope.

AND now we are allies. Are we in the first flush of our enthusiasm to bury the red beneath thick applications of whitewash ? Rather we should aim at a truer synthesis, a more comprehensive vision. Let us remember that Russia means not only Stalin in the Kremlin but peasant Ivan in his humble hut—that she finds room for the missionaries of the godless cult and for Archbishop Sergius calling his people to pray for Holy Russia in the cathedral at Moscow. Let us have in mind not only the officers of the Ogpu driving their victims into impossible confessions, but the eager young Stakhanovites, the devoted girls teaching their letters to the nomads of the steppes, the city toilers who put up with every discomfort because they have seen a new heaven in a new earth, built here in Russia, where labour will be honoured, poverty abolished, together with unemployment, want and all the man-made ills of human flesh. Let us with proper humility admit that if we have much to teach Russia, Russia has much to teach us.

NOT so long ago the strain between Russia and Britain showed a tendency to diminish. There was even hope of a political alliance, until—alas for the happiness and lives of millions !—Litvinov's proposals for a combined front against the aggressors were rejected, and Russia and Germany signed a pact.

Now the wheel has turned full circle. Another pact has been signed. Hitler by his attack on Russia has presented us with an ally whose territory covers a sixth of the globe, whose people number 180 millions, one in twelve of the human race.

E. Royston Pike

THE ANGLO-RUSSIAN ALLIANCE was formally concluded at Moscow on July 12, but a Russian Military Mission arrived in London a week earlier. This photograph shows Admiral Kharlamov of the Red Navy chatting with Mr. Maisky (left).
Photo, Fox

Russia's Tank Corps Is the World's Largest

" The Germans sent 10,000 tanks against Russia," said Mr. Lozovsky, Soviet Vice-Commissar for Foreign Affairs, in a broadcast from Moscow on July 9, " hoping to repeat the experience of France. But they have encountered an opponent similarly armed." Russia's tank force, as will be seen from the chapter below, is indeed enormous. In preparing the chapter we have found Max Werner's " The Military Strength of the Powers " and " Battle for the World " (Gollancz) particularly useful.

How many tanks has Russia? We may ask the question, but it is a difficult one to answer. Certain it is that the figure is tremendous, greater—perhaps far greater—than that of any other military power.

As early as 1935 German sources put the strength of the Red Tank Corps at 10,000 ; by way of comparison we may mention that in the Battle of Cambrai in 1917—where British tanks achieved a break-through so startling and sudden that the High Command proved quite incapable of profiting by it, so that all the ground won was speedily lost—General Elles led some 350 tanks into battle. (But the Allies were hoping to have 30,000 tanks available for the great onslaught on Germany in 1919.) " As far as tanks are concerned," said General Loizeau, chief of the French Military Mission which attended the Kiev manoeuvres in 1935, " I think we shall have to put the Soviet Union in the first place. The Red Army has a whole arsenal of tanks of all sizes and types, beginning with speedy little whippets and ending with veritable armoured land cruisers." And General Guderian, who headed Hitler's tanks in their break-through on the Meuse in 1940, wrote that " the cavalry army of Budenny of 1920 has developed into the tank corps of Voroshilov in 1935," and went on to assert that " 10,000 tanks, 150,000 military tractors and over 100,000 military motor vehicles of various kinds, put the Red Army at the head of Europe in the question of motorization. Great Britain and France had been left far behind."

Four years later, in September 1939, Marshal Voroshilov reported to the Supreme Soviet that the Russian tanks were 43 times the 1930 total. What that total was he did not mention, but it cannot have been less than .500 and more probably was 1,000. Thus, at the outbreak of war in 1939 Russia may well have had between 40 and 50 thousand tanks ; and since they were then in mass production, the figure must have been increased since. Perhaps today Russia has 50,000 tanks.

Another witness to Soviet tank superiority is General Le Q. Martel, now commander of the Royal Armoured Corps, who in 1936 attended the Soviet manoeuvres in his capacity of Assistant Director of Mechanization at the War Office. In an address delivered in London on his return he recommended that the British Army should take the Red Army as its example in tank matters, and not the German.

" There are many officers," said General Martel, " who consider that the day of the tanks has already passed and that anti-tank weapons have now reached a stage where they will be able to deal with the tanks comparatively easily. If there are officers present here today who are of that mind, I would ask them to accompany me in spirit to the Russian manoeuvres which I had the great fortune to see last autumn. The total number of tanks employed on these manoeuvres was some 1,200 to 1,400 . . . These tank forces were most impressive, and the sight of these large numbers of tanks moving over the field of operations as opposed to a consideration of paper tank brigades with which we have so far had to be content, could hardly have failed to impress the most stubborn opponent of modernized warfare."

The Russians, he added, had made immense strides in the development of their tank army. Their conscript armies were drawn from raw peasants, yet in two years they turned them into a tank force that could drive and maintain their tanks in first-class condition.

All that we have learnt since about the Red Army supports General Martel's tribute to the efficiency of Russian training. In the Red Army, we are told, there are many tank drivers who have been 2,500 hours at the controls, tanks which have travelled nearly 4,000 miles, tanks which have travelled over 600 miles at a time without developing any mechanical defects, tanks which have travelled 300 miles through water. Tank drivers of the Red Army have been specially trained in driving through forests and swamps and the most difficult country. " Thanks to the simplest contrivances," says Voroshilov, " but thanks above all to the experience of their technicians and commanders, our tank drivers have succeeded in taking their machines through swamps without much difficulty although they were never made for that. They have crossed rivers, lakes and even bays. We have many capable tank drivers who control their enormous machines like virtuosi."

" The Russian guns, caterpillars and tanks appear to be completely new," reported the Berlin correspondent of a Swiss paper on July 7. " Immaculately painted, well looked after, cleanly finished, and well designed, the steel machines stand there produced by a state which 20 years ago hardly possessed its own machine and armament factories." The correspondent went on to state that the Soviet tanks included a giant 60-tonner, built on the French pattern, with three gun turrets, containing a howitzer, two light guns, and several machine-guns. Another German correspondent has asserted that at Lwow the Russians employed 120-ton two-decker tanks with crews of between nine and twelve men, armed with three 10.5 cm. guns and four machine-guns, with a speed of between 6 and 30 miles an hour. He asserted that the tank was " ill-designed and ill-manipulated, but very heavily armoured " and that it was captured only because it ran out of ammunition and fuel. Two Red tank models particularly mentioned are the Christie and the Vickers.

SOVIET TANK LEADER in the act of signalling. The numerical strength of Russian tanks is problematical. Some military experts say that the Soviets had as many as 50,000 when Germany attacked. There is no doubt, however, as to their efficiency and the skill and courage of their crews.
Photo, E.N.A.

Land Ships of the Red Armada Show Their Quality

Taking a ditch, this powerful Red Army tank demonstrates the revolution in land warfare since 1914. Against such monstrous and mobile machines all trenches and Maginot lines in lateral defence are obsolete, and the only method is defence in depth, which our Russian Allies have completely foreseen. Fast Soviet tanks can travel at 60 m.p.h. along roads and 40 m.p.h. across country. Russia was the first nation to go in for mass-production of tanks, and both in quantity and quality her machines won the admiration of French and German experts as long ago as 1935. In the top picture a column of Soviet tanks is seen taking up position.

Photos, British Official : Crown Copyright

Inside and Out: British Tanks in Detail

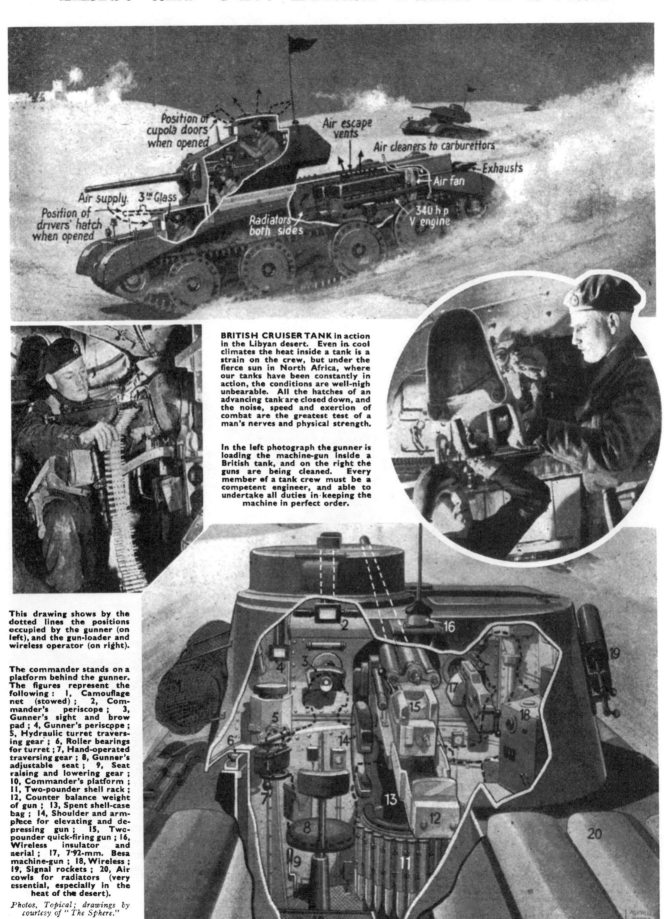

Position of cupola doors when opened

Air escape vents

Air cleaners to carburettors

Exhausts

Air fan

Air supply. 3ᴵᴺ Glass

Position of drivers' hatch when opened

Radiators both sides

340 h.p. V engine

BRITISH CRUISER TANK in action in the Libyan desert. Even in cool climates the heat inside a tank is a strain on the crew, but under the fierce sun in North Africa, where our tanks have been constantly in action, the conditions are well-nigh unbearable. All the hatches of an advancing tank are closed down, and the noise, speed and exertion of combat are the greatest test of a man's nerves and physical strength.

In the left photograph the gunner is loading the machine-gun inside a British tank, and on the right the guns are being cleaned. Every member of a tank crew must be a competent engineer, and able to undertake all duties in keeping the machine in perfect order.

This drawing shows by the dotted lines the positions occupied by the gunner (on left), and the gun-loader and wireless operator (on right).

The commander stands on a platform behind the gunner. The figures represent the following : 1, Camouflage net (stowed) ; 2, Commander's periscope ; 3, Gunner's sight and brow pad ; 4, Gunner's periscope ; 5, Hydraulic turret traversing gear ; 6, Roller bearings for turret ; 7, Hand-operated traversing gear ; 8, Gunner's adjustable seat ; 9, Seat raising and lowering gear ; 10, Commander's platform ; 11, Two-pounder shell rack ; 12, Counter balance weight of gun ; 13, Spent shell-case bag ; 14, Shoulder and arm-piece for elevating and depressing gun ; 15, Two-pounder quick-firing gun ; 16, Wireless insulator and aerial ; 17, 7·92-mm. Besa machine-gun ; 18, Wireless ; 19, Signal rockets ; 20, Air cowls for radiators (very essential, especially in the heat of the desert).

Photos, Topical ; drawings by courtesy of " The Sphere."

Four Weeks of R.A.F. Non-stop Fire and Fury

IN the 28 nights and days, June 15–July 12, covered by the map below, the R.A.F. were over Germany on 26 nights. Their targets ranged from Kiel in the N. to Magdeburg in the S. and as far E. as Leuna; only major attacks are shown. The attacks were especially concentrated on the industrial areas in the Ruhr and Rhineland, with particularly heavy attacks on Cologne, Duesseldorf and Munster. In daylight Bremen and Oldenburg were raided twice, and Kiel and Wilhelmshaven once each.

The air offensive over N. France on 23 out of the 28 days was mainly in daylight, large forces of bombers being escorted by fighters. Frequently there were two or more operations in one day. On three of the other five days fighters alone swept over the country. In the very successful double attack on Cherbourg and Le Havre, over 20,000 tons of enemy shipping were hit.

Aircraft casualties: Enemy, 295 fighters destroyed over France. R.A.F., 114 fighters (17 pilots saved) and 13 bombers.

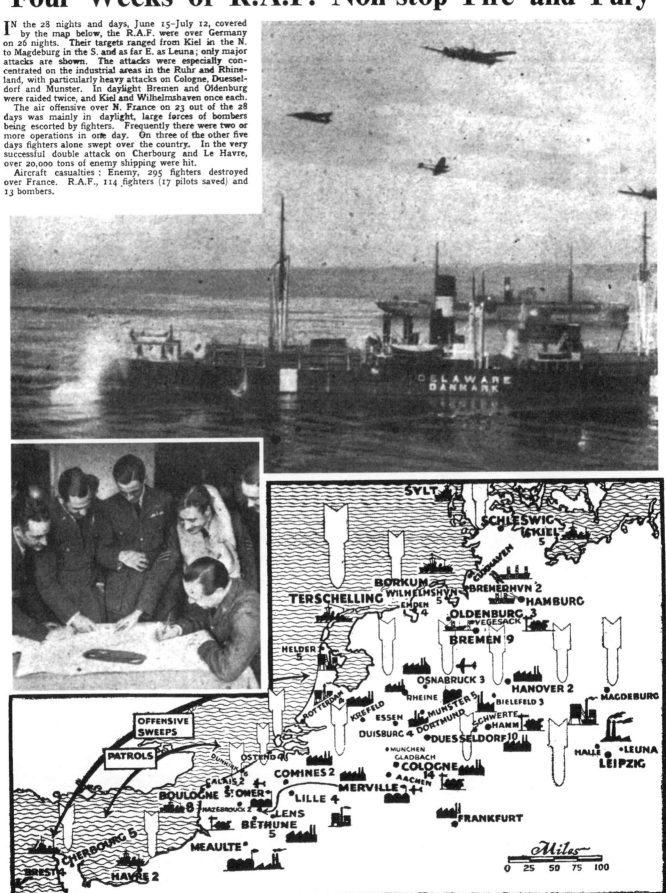

BOMBS ON THE NAZIS! Here we have striking proof of the R.A.F. non-stop invasion of Germany and German-occupied territory during the four weeks from June 15 to July 12. If a target was bombed more than once the figure beside it indicates the number of times. In the photograph at the top Blenheims are seen diving low over a Nazi convoy off the Dutch coast. One bomb has burst near the stern of the Delaware, a Danish vessel being used by the Germans. The smaller photograph shows some of the men who took part in the daylight sweep over French ports on July 10 reporting to the Intelligence Officer at their station.

Photos, British Official: Crown Copyright; Associated Press. Map, "News Chronicle"

Night and Day Convoys Come Safe to Port

INFERNO OF WAR over the Channel produced by burning flares and German coastal batteries concentrated on a British convoy.   A " nocturne " to be seen on the South Coast, it reminds us of the resolution and heroism of the men who go down to the sea in ships in wartime.   In the circle a bluejacket is signalling a convoy away;   and in the top photograph a convoy is seen beyond the King George V.   Escorted by this powerful new battleship, with her ten 14-in. guns and formidable defences against air attack, our merchantmen are scoring another point in the Battle of the Atlantic.

Photos, British Official: Crown Copyright; " News Chronicle " and L.N.A.

Nine Millions in History's Greatest Battle

As the first month of the Russo-German war drew to a close, the world's greatest armies grappled furiously in what might well be described as history's greatest battle. According to the Nazi prophets, the Red Army should have been crushed by now, but the hopes of an easy and speedy triumph faded in face of Stalin's scorched earth policy and the fierce resistance of the Russian armies and people.

"ALONG the entire eastern front," ran a statement issued by the German High Command on July 17, "a gigantic struggle for a decision is in progress. About nine million soldiers are opposed here in a combat which in extent surpasses all historical precedent and conception." It went on to claim that the Soviet Command had thrown into the battle their last reserves to try and halt the advance of the German and allied forces, and that "great successes are in the making."

The only success actually claimed in the statement was that the German and Rumanian troops had occupied Kishinev, the capital of Bessarabia, but far more extensive claims had been made nearly a week before—and had not been substantiated. On July 12 a special German announcement gave the news that the Stalin Line had been pierced by "daring assaults at all decisive points," and the next day the German News Agency boasted that "complete German victory is now assured. Leningrad is immediately threatened, and the occupation of Kiev is imminent. The road to Moscow is opened up, and there are no further natural or artificial barriers. Supply lines of the Panzer divisions are assured." These claims were premature, to say the least; the bright young men of Dr. Goebbels' propaganda department had overstepped themselves once more. Maybe they were relying on a repetition of the experience of past campaigns—that to secure just a foothold in the enemy's position was tantamount to having won it. The Russian resistance, however, was much more determined and prolonged than that which the Germans had encountered in Poland, France, and the Balkans. Once again the Russian soldier lived up to his reputation for stubbornness and tenacity; he refused to surrender, even when according to the text books he ought to have realized that it was the proper thing to do . . . Another reason may be advanced for

Goebbels' optimistic mendacity, and that is the effect on German morale of the enormous losses which could no longer be hid. The newspapers were filled with obituary lists, and at the stations in Berlin and other German cities huge crowds watched in silence the passing of the ambulance trains in an almost uninterrupted stream. The little doctor may well have come to the conclusion that something had to be done to raise the German people's morale.

Within a few hours the absurdity of the Nazi claims was so manifest that the propagandists in Berlin were forced to change their tune. Now they stressed the difficulties of the Russian campaign, and claimed not "open roads," but "break-through operations proceeding according to plan." On July 17 the German High Command issued a warning to the nation against over-optimism and an appeal for patience.

The unhappy position of the German soldiers was well described by A. T. Cholerton in a dispatch to the "Daily Telegraph" from Moscow. He spoke of them being choked and blinded by Russian dust, bombed and machine-gunned on bad, dyked roads, stubbornly counter-attacked by the Red Army, worn out by the night raids of Russian guerillas behind the front. He described how they were being told of the Anglo-Russian Pact by radio, leaflets dropped from the air, and secret means behind the lines. "They will now know, if they did not before, that however far they may get on any front, they will never get as far as peace until they give in and chase out their masters."

Then here is a significant broadcast from Germany addressed to the German people. "Our German infantry in many parts of the front are far behind our motorized units. The mechanized forces have penetrated deeply into Soviet territory and naturally the infantry are falling behind in many parts of the line. They are having to undertake forced marches to catch up.

"Very often there is no food for our brave soldiers because the field-kitchens cannot get

THE RUSSO-GERMAN FRONT with the positions of the opposing forces on July 17 is shown in the map, where black-arrows denote the main Nazi drives and the white arrows and oblongs the Soviet counter-attacks and defence. Above, left, are wrecked Russian planes, with a German aeroplane landing in the background. Above, right, a Soviet A.A. quadruple machine-gun in action. Wastage in planes on both sides has been enormous

Photos, British Official ; Crown Copyright ; Associated Press. Map by courtesy of the " Daily Mail "

Victories but No Victory for the Nazis

through. We have other worries as well. The Soviet civil population are burning down all their houses, and we cannot find quarters. So we often suffer in our tents from the extreme cold, and on many occasions we have shivered all night. It must be borne in mind, too, that this Stalin Line is a defence-line-in-depth, built up with the strongest fortifications."

By now the first month of the campaign was nearly ended, and the Germans had still not penetrated the Russian defence system, the Red Armies were still largely intact, and several hundred miles of country separated the most advanced of the Nazi tanks from Moscow.

In the north the main Russian positions were still intact, and the Finnish-German forces had made little progress. In Estonia, strong German forces were striving desperately to break through to Leningrad, but they were being subjected to ceaseless counter-attacks, particularly in the region about Pskov.

The Russian armies were here under the command of Marshal Voroshilov, who was reported to have nearly a million men at his disposal. Even on the coast Russian pockets kept up a fierce resistance ; little " Tobruks " stuck like thorns into the side of the Nazi advance, and the Red Navy smashed more than one attempt at a landing in the Gulf of Riga.

In the middle sector of the front—that most vital and hard-pressed sector where the great Russian armies stood at bay under Marshal Timoshenko—the Nazis could claim considerable progress, but only at a terrible cost following the launching of their resumed offensive on July 12. In places they were more than 200 miles beyond the old Russian

WHY WE STAND BY RUSSIA

" LET no one say we are now in league with Communists and are fighting the battle of Communism. More fitly can neutralists and fence-sitters be charged with fighting the battle of Nazism.

" If Hitler, in his insane megalomania, has driven Russia to fight him in self-defence, we bless her arms and wish her all success, without for a moment identifying ourselves with her Communistic creed."

—General J. Smuts

frontier, but Smolensk seemed to mark the limit of their progress—and Smolensk is 230 miles from Moscow. Then far behind the fighting front considerable Russian forces held out, although for weeks they had been completely surrounded—in the neighbourhood of Minsk, Bobruisk, and Bialystok in particular. This resistance, it was plain, was part of a prearranged plan ; the Russian forces engaged had been ordered to hold out to the last to give time for the millions of Russian reserves to be mobilized.

To the south the Germans claimed to have reached the outskirts of Kiev, but to their disgusted surprise the city was not surrendered. Marshal Budenny, in command in this sector, brought up his reserves and ejected the Nazi Panzer units which, so it was reported, had penetrated to the suburbs. The German News Agency claimed that " German infantry, under the protection of artificial fog, dynamited the Russians out of the earthworks, which had previously been partly shattered by artillery and which the German advance units had already passed." But, it was explained, the main fortifications extended for three storeys underground ; and as the Germans advanced the Red soldiers emerged from these labyrinths to attack the attackers in the rear. All the evidence went to show that Budenny was preparing to defend Kiev street by street and, if necessary, to burn it before it fell into the hands of the enemy. Still farther south hard fighting was reported to be taking place in Bessarabia, but nowhere, it seemed, had the old frontier into Russia been crossed.

In the first nine days of the campaign the Germans averaged an advance of about 20 miles a day ; during the next 18 days the advance to Smolensk averaged only about half that figure. Either Russian resistance was stiffening or the Nazi onrush was losing its impetus.

RED WARSHIPS in the Baltic, where most of the Russian fleet is based on Kronstadt. On July 12 units of the Red Navy destroyed in the Gulf of Riga four German destroyers and thirteen armed transports carrying troops and munitions for an attack on the Russian coast. The smaller photograph shows sailors aboard the Kalinin handling a torpedo. *Photos, British Official, and E.N.A.*

Harvest of Flames for Hitler's Barbarians

WAR AND PEACE make a grim contrast in this photograph, showing how the road was suddenly transformed into a highway of death and destruction as the military lorries arrived and unloaded a squad of machine-gunners. These Nazis have taken up their positions facing the enemy, while peasant women and children are trying to get out of the danger zone. In the top photograph a Russian village (note the traffic signs) is seen blazing furiously as part of Stalin's " scorched earth " policy. When the Huns arrive there will be nothing left but a heap of smouldering cinders.

Photos, Associated Press and Keystone

Into Damascus Clatters the Cavalcade of Free

ON THE ROAD IN SYRIA, a Bren-gun carrier manned by Indian soldiers. Derelict material left by the Vichy forces is seen by the wayside. Beneath, yeomanry and Bren-gun crews resting. In the centre, Free French soldiers, one of whom is the standard-bearer with the French flag of the Circassian cavalry, in Damascus, General Catroux and General Legentilhomme having just driven through the city.   *Photos, British Official : Crown Copyright*

n: British and Free French Share the Triumph

The car containing the two Free French Generals proceeding through Damascus from the station, followed by the standard-bearer. Below, Gen. Catroux inspects a Guard of Honour at Government House.

Peace in Syria After Five Weeks of War

On Sunday, June 8, General Sir Maitland Wilson's Army invaded Syria. Five weeks later, on Friday, July 11, the "cease fire" was sounded, and within a few days a convention had been signed providing for the termination of hostilities. So ended a campaign which, though it had to be fought, was one little to the taste of the belligerents on either side.

DAMOUR RIDGE, Vichy's last line of defence before Beirut, was assailed by the Australians at dawn on Sunday, July 6. The Vichyites were strongly entrenched and put up a fierce resistance so that the Australians had to go all out to win. "Reminiscent of Gallipoli" was how their commander described the fighting.

Before midnight on Saturday the Australian troops assembled on the southern bank of the Damour at a point some miles from where it joins the sea. At zero hour, shortly before dawn, they scrambled down into the gorge, and after half-an-hour's stumbling reached

costly struggle, since the legionaries and colonials fought to the bitter end.

By Tuesday, July 8, the Australians had occupied all their objectives south of Damour, and the attack on the town itself began. Once again there was fierce fighting, and the Vichyites in the orange and banana groves surrounding the town were heavily shelled before our men could get to them with the bayonet. "We are making progress," said the Brigadier commanding the coastal column, "but it is very slow. These Frenchmen are brave fellows. They just won't get out." But at 8 a.m. on July 10 the first of

possession of the strategic heights dominating the road to Beirut.

Communication with General Wilson was established in a roundabout fashion by way of the American Consul-General in Beirut, Washington, and London. The first proposals were rejected by Vichy on the ground that their acceptance would have involved the virtual recognition of General de Gaulle, but they washed their hands of an unpleasant business by stating that General Dentz was free to act "in the event of the British Government taking on itself responsibility for continuing the struggle." Thus empowered,

General Dentz made direct contact by wireless with the British authorities in Jerusalem on July 11, and it was at once agreed that fighting in Syria should stop. Hostilities actually ceased at 21.01 (G.M.T.) on Friday, July 11.

The next morning General de Verdillac, acting as Vichy's plenipotentiary, accompanied by a number of Vichy officers, proceeded to Acre, where at 10.30 in a room in the Sidney Smith barracks de Verdillac met General Wilson, accompanied by Lieut.-General Lavarack, his second in command, and General Catroux and other Imperial and Free French officers. The conference began at 11.30, and after a time the British withdrew, leaving Catroux and de Verdillac to thrash things out together. For hours they deliberated over the details, but everything was agreed at last, and de Verdillac initialled the terms.

The conference was resumed in the Sidney Smith barracks at 11 a.m. on July 14, and

NEAR TYRE, a new bridge is being thrown across the River Litani by British Army engineers in place of one destroyed by retreating Vichy forces. The Litani flows into the sea near Tyre, and came into prominence during the Syrian campaign. With other streams it formed a considerable obstacle to our mechanized units operating between Tyre, Merj Iyoun and Beirut.
Photo, Australian Official : Crown Copyright

the bed of the wadi. So far not a shot had been fired, but now the French watchdogs posted along the northern bank heard the troops splashing through the shallow stream, and with their yelping and barking gave the alarm. At once the French machine-guns and mortars opened fire, until the whole northern bank seemed to erupt in a sheet of flame. Many of the attackers fell, but the Australians plunged across the river and charged up the opposite bank just as their fathers had done on the bullet-swept slopes of Gallipoli. As they swarmed up the bank they slung their bayoneted rifles across their backs, until arrived at the top they got into some sort of order and then drove the French from their positions. At dawn the British artillery opened up, laying down a tremendous barrage in front of the advancing infantry ; warships, standing in close to shore, flung salvo after salvo into the French positions ; while at the same time planes of the R.A.F. and the R.A.A.F. drove the Vichy fighters from the sky. By the end of the day the Vichy resistance on the Ridge was smashed, but it had been a hard and

the Australians made their way into Damour, and their patrols pushed on along the coast road and were soon within sight of Beirut.

General Dentz, Vichy Commander-in-Chief, must have known that further resistance would be useless, but he hesitated to accept General Wilson's appeal that Beirut should be declared an open town so as to spare it the horrors and distress which would otherwise be inevitable. So the fighting went on for a day or two until overtures for a suspension of hostilities were begun.

None too soon, indeed, for the position of the Vichyites was critical. The Turks had refused to allow supplies for General Dentz to pass through Turkey, and reinforcements which were reported to have been assembled at Salonika failed to arrive : the British Navy was keeping too strict a watch. Beirut was threatened by the Australians, fighting their way along the coast from Damour. Two Indian columns had arrived within 50 miles of Aleppo, and a column of British infantry with Australian artillery had pushed its patrols to within easy distance of Homs. Near Damascus, British regiments had won

came to a successful end at eight o'clock in the evening. The convention—not "armistice," since technically there had been no war—consisted of 22 paragraphs, of which the most important provided for the occupation of the whole of Syria and Lebanon by the Allies ; the granting of full honours of war to the French forces ; the immediate release of any of the Allied forces who had been taken prisoner, including those who had been transferred to France, and the release of the French prisoners when the whole of the territory had been occupied and the clauses of the convention fulfilled ; the granting of the alternative of rallying to the allied cause or being repatriated to individual Vichyites, whether military or civil ; and the handing over of all war material of whatever description, public services, aircraft, aerodromes and equipment, ships, etc., intact.

When the last page of the document had been signed, General Wilson through an interpreter asked General de Verdillac to join him in a glass of wine, and "drink to a better day." The glasses were raised and emptied. The war in Syria was at an end.

Australians 'Mop Up' in a Crusaders' Fastness

AT SIDON Australian soldiers search for snipers amid the ruins of the old Crusaders' castle. The terms of the Syrian Convention signed on July 14, in their moderation and rectitude, are a credit to all concerned in this unfortunate episode. Mr. Churchill, who never fails to touch the inspired note in all the incalculable vicissitudes of the struggle against the evil of Hitlerism, reminded us of the discipline, skill and courage of our opponents in Syria. And they, too, must realize now that " we seek no British advantage in Syria . . ."

Photo, British Official : Crown Copyright

Our Diary of the War

SUNDAY, JULY 13, 1941   680th day

Air.—R.A.F. made night raids on industrial targets in N.W. Germany, particularly Bremen and Vegesack, docks at Amsterdam and Ostend, oil tanks at Rotterdam, and enemy aerodromes.

Russian Front.—Moscow stated that there were no significant changes to report. Finns claimed to have attacked Russian positions north and south of Lake Ladoga and penetrated far into their rear.

Africa.—R.A.F. successfully attacked convoy outside Tripoli, sinking two ships.

Near East.—Aerodromes on island of Rhodes bombed during night of 12-13.

Home.—Night raiders dropped bombs on some coastal districts and on one place in Midlands. Two enemy aircraft destroyed.

MONDAY, JULY 14   681st day

Sea. — C.-in-C. Mediterranean reported further successes by submarines. At least three troop and supply ships sunk, and probably two more.

H.M. sloop Auckland reported sunk.

Air.—All-day attacks on shipping and coastal targets, including Cherbourg, Le Havre and Hazebrouck. Seven enemy fighters destroyed; we lost two bombers and four fighters.

Night attacks on Bremen and Hanover and docks at Rotterdam.

Russian Front.—Moscow claimed to have sunk two U-boats. Soviet air force bombed Ploesti oil centre, Rumania.

Africa.—Night attacks on Bardia and Benghazi. Day raid on aerodrome at Zuara.

Near East.—Vichy Government officially announced approval and signature of terms for armistice in Syria.

R.A.F. made night attacks on aerodromes at Eleusis and Hassani (Greece) and Heraklion (Crete), and on docks at Messina.

Home.—Night raiders attacked east coastal town. Two day bombers destroyed.

TUESDAY, JULY 15   682nd day

Air.—Night attacks on Duisburg and other parts of the Ruhr.

Russian Front.—Moscow communiqué referred to heavy fighting in northern and central zones. Oil refineries at Ploesti bombed by Soviet aircraft.

Unofficial German announcement that troops had reached Kiev.

Africa.—Cairo stated that offensive patrols had been active at Tobruk, capturing prisoners and inflicting casualties.

Seven enemy aircraft shot down off Libyan coast.

Near East.—Allied troops formally occupied Beirut.

WEDNESDAY, JULY 16   683rd day

Air.—Great daylight raid on docks at Rotterdam, when 17 ships, totalling about 100,000 tons, were put out of action.

Night raids on Hamburg and other objectives in N.W. Germany. Boulogne docks bombed.

Russian Front.—Heavy fighting continued in Pskov, Smolensk, Bobruisk and Novgorod-Volynsk sectors. Russian air force again attacked oil centre at Ploesti.

Germans claimed to have flanked Lake Peipus and to be 130 miles from Leningrad; also that they have captured Kishinev, capital of Bessarabia.

Africa.—Pressure increasing on enemy forces holding Wolshefit Pass, near Gondar.

R.A.F. attacked convoy off Tripolitanian coast; one ship sunk, another damaged.

Japan.—Political crisis; Cabinet resigned.

THURSDAY, JULY 17   684th day

Sea.—H.M. auxiliary vessel Lady Somers reported sunk.

Air.—Five enemy fighters and a seaplane destroyed during offensive sweep over northern France.

Night attacks on Cologne and elsewhere in Rhineland. Coastal Command attacked shipping at St. Nazaire.

Russian Front.—Moscow reported violent battles at Pskov and Porkhov against German drive towards Leningrad.

German High Command spoke of gigantic struggle, involving 9,000,000 soldiers, in progress along whole of front.

Africa.—Another successful sortie into enemy positions south of Tobruk on night of 16-17.

R.A.F. heavily attacked Benghazi and Tripoli on nights of July 15, 16 and 17. Fleet Air Arm torpedoed a 6,000-ton tanker.

Home.—Two enemy fighters destroyed off south coast.

Sharp night raid on Hull, causing heavy casualties.

FRIDAY, JULY 18   685th day

Sea.—Admiralty announced that our submarines in Mediterranean had sunk two schooners and five large caiques, all carrying troops.

Air.—R.A.F. hit supply ship of 6,000 tons off Dunkirk. Weather precluded night raids.

Russian Front.—Germans officially claimed capture of Smolensk on July 16, and that Russian attempts to retake the town had failed. German-Rumanian communiqué stated that they held strategic key-positions in Bessarabia.

Moscow reported stubborn fighting in areas of Pskov-Porkhov, Smolensk, and Bobruisk, and on Bessarabian front, but no substantial change.

Africa.—Three simultaneous raids on broad front against enemy positions facing western perimeter of Tobruk.

Mediterranean.—R.A.F. heavy bombers attacked cruisers and destroyers in Palermo harbour, Sicily, on night of 17-18. Fleet Air Arm bombed aerodromes at Gerbini and Augusta.

Home.—Two bombers shot down off south coast.

Japan.—New Cabinet formed in which Mr. Matsuoka, Foreign Minister, was superseded.

General.—Agreement signed in London between Russia and Czechoslovakia restoring diplomatic relations.

SATURDAY, JULY 19   686th day

Air.—R.A.F. destroyed or disabled eight ships, totalling 48,000 tons, in convoys off The Hague and Isle of Norderney.

Night raids on Hanover and other industrial areas.

Russian Front.—Fierce fighting in Polotsk-Nevel, Smolensk and Bobruisk areas. Germans announced that Nazi and Rumanian troops from Bessarabia had forced Dniester river at several points.

Moscow announced destruction by aircraft of eleven enemy transports and an oil tanker in the Baltic.

Home.—Night raiders dropped bombs on two places in Midlands.

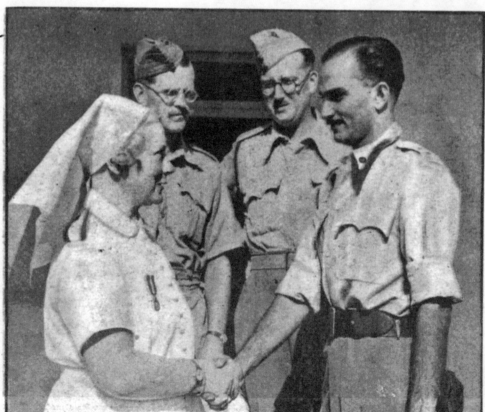

INDIA'S FIRST V.C. OF THIS WAR

SECOND-LIEUT. P. S. BHAGAT, of the 21st Bombay Sappers and Miners, received the Empire's most coveted order for gallant work in leading mobile troops to clear the road and adjacent areas of mines after Metemma had been captured on the night of January 31—February 1. For four days over a distance of 55 miles this officer, in the leading carrier, led the column, detecting and supervising the clearing of fifteen minefields. On two occasions when his carrier was blown up with casualties to others, and on a third occasion when ambushed and under close enemy fire, he continued with his task. Though exhausted with strain and fatigue and with one eardrum broken by an explosion, he refused relief but elected to carry on. His coolness and persistence in great danger over a period of 96 hours were of the highest order.

Left, Second-Lieut. Bhagat is seen shaking hands with the Matron of the hospital where he was treated for fever.

The British Empire is proud of this Indian hero, a member of our imperial brotherhood fighting against Hitlerism.

Photo, British Official

War Still Goes On in the Western Desert

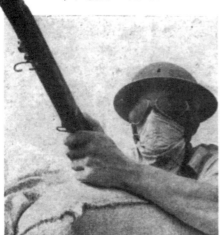

A British soldier wearing goggles and a handkerchief as a protection against the sandstorm sweeping across his outpost.

Tragic pawns in Hitler's megalomaniac game of chess. German prisoners captured in the fighting near Sollum sitting in attitudes of despair under the pitiless sun. Left : General Rommel (standing on tank, with field glasses), Commander-in-Chief of the Nazi African Corps, making observations somewhere in the Libyan war zone.

Above right, belts of ammunition captured by the British forces in the Western Desert. The circular photograph is of the Brigadier who was in charge of a successful attack on Fort Capuzzo, explaining the plan of the attack to his staff officers.

Photos, British Official : Crown Copyright ; Associated Press

Unseen Fingers Help to Track Down the Foe

RADIOLOCATION, described as the best-kept secret of the war, is one of the new marvels of science that are helping Britain to victory. Any plane, tank or ship in the path of the radio-ray flashes back a message. Thanks to radiolocation the night-bomber peril has been much reduced.

On the right we see some of the radiolocators who, day and night, man the instruments which have been installed all over the country.

Circle below : A radiolocation operator "twiddling the knobs" of an instrument not unlike the familiar wireless.

Right : Mr. C. O. Cummings (seated), who is in charge of the Civilian Technical Corps, signing up, at the British Consulate in New York, American radio men for service in England.

A sergeant and corporal at work with a Royal Army Ordnance Corps servicing lorry at a radiolocation site. On the left, mechanics testing a power unit.

Photos, G.P.U. and Keystone

They Have Won Honours in Freedom's Cause

King's Police Medal

Asst. Dist. Officer W. Mosedale, G.C., for saving twelve lives during a Birmingham raid.

Ch. Insp. R. C. Wainwright, B.E.M., for conspicuous bravery in many City of London raids.

P. C. Pritlove, King's Police Medal, for great resource and devotion to duty.

Fireman W. C. Skillern, G.M., for saving 21 women entombed in a London basement.

Royal Red Cross

Warden W. G. Smith, B.E.M., for helping to save four people from debris after an air raid in Hackney.

Mr. A. J. Sambridge, A.R.P., Hackney, **G.M.,** for rescuing a trapped woman from a flooded basement.

Postman F. G. Gurr, B.E.M., for clearing letters from post-boxes amid unexploded bombs and fires.

Mr. J. L. Pelham, Chief of Hendon A.R.P. Rescue Service, **M.B.E.,** for great courage and devotion to duty.

Mr. W. J. Holtham, G.M., for attending to gas-valves at Nine Elms though injured by exploding bomb.

Mr. N. Jaeger, A.R.P., **Bar to B.E.M.,** for rescuing trapped air-raid victims from a Lambeth lodging-house.

Prob. Nurse V. A. Clancy, B.E.M., for saving children from a Plymouth Hospital.

Dr. H. Billig, G.M., for attending casualties though suffering herself from a broken ankle.

Dr. A. J. McNairn, G.M., for displaying conspicuous courage when a Plymouth hospital was hit.

Sergt. M. H. Willans, A.T.S., B.E.M., for meritorious conduct with an Essex A.A. Battery.

Miss C. Bick, 15-year-old dispatch rider, **G.M.,** for bravery and devotion to duty at West 'Bromwich.

Matron G. E. M. Clubb, R.A.F. Hospital, **R.R.C.** First Class, for outstanding ability and courage.

P.O. the Hon. B. D. Grimston, D.F.C., for bombing enemy target under anti-aircraft fire.

Group Capt. G. M. Lawson, M.C., O.B.E., for great gallantry in the course of his air duties.

Air Comm. S. E. Goodwin, O.B.E., for conspicuous ability in connexion with his air duties.

Air Vice Marshal F. J. Linnell, C.B., for outstanding devotion to duty on all occasions.

Sqd. Ldr. J. R. Gordon-Finlayson, D.F.C., now **D.S.O.,** for completing 100 operational sorties.

Flt. Lieut. A. L. Taylor, Second bar to **D.F.C.,** for gallantry and resourcefulness of reconnaissance.

Flt. Lieut. W. F. Blackadder, of Edinburgh, **D.S.O.,** for heroism in air combat.

P.O. K. J. Holmes, of Hull, **D.F.C.,** for diving low to bomb the Scharnhorst and Gneisenau.

Flt. Lieut. R. P. R. Powell, D.F.C., for remarkable skill and courage in his air duties.

Sergt. D. F. Allen, G.M., for valiant efforts to save three men from a crashed-plane.

Actg. Flt.-Lieut. S. Smith, D.F.C., for bravery in attacking and bombing ammunition ships.

Flying Officer J. A. Hemmingway, D.F.C. for gallantry in the execution of his air duties.

Sqd.-Ldr. E. L. Magrath, M.B.E., in recognition of his distinguished services with the R.A.F.

Sgt. B. E. Dye, Bar to D.F.M., for exceptional skill and keenness in night-flying operations.

P.O. A. J. Hodgkinson, D.F.C., for destroying six enemy aircraft during night attacks.

Lieut. Kershaw, D.S.O., for landing under fire in Abyssinia and rescuing Captain Frost.

Capt. Frost, of the S.A.A.F., **D.F.C.,** for conspicuous courage in air fighting over Abyssinia.

Sqd.-Ldr. J. C. Willis, D.F.C., for brilliant service and courage in the Middle East.

Now We Know Why King Leopold Surrendered

On May 27, 1940, the Belgian Army, at the order of its King, laid down its arms. Following the
"Cease Fire," King Leopold was bitterly denounced by his Allies for his desertion, even betrayal,
of the common cause. But passing months have brought to light many facts which were not known
at the time—facts which go far to explain the King's action.

AFTER King Leopold surrendered with his army—or what was left of it—on that fateful May evening, he made no reply to the bitter accusations that were hurled against him. "*Votre sort est mon sort*" (Your fate is my fate), he told his soldiers ; and with that passed into captivity. Behind him clanged the gates of his château at Laeken, which now became his prison ; and there, in spite of the blandishments of the Nazis, who would have been delighted to have employed him as a royal Quisling, he has remained—silent and almost alone to this day.

Even at the time there were some who protested against the storm of opprobrium which hurtled about Leopold's ears. Mr. Churchill asked that judgement about the surrender should be suspended until the facts were known, and Admiral Sir Roger Keyes, who had been in close attendance upon the King, echoed his appeal. But the action was so sudden, so altogether unexpected, that there were few who put a rein upon their tongues. As the months have passed, however, King Leopold has attracted an increasing number of defenders. Thus in August 1940 Mr. John Cudahy, American Ambassador in Brussels, said that the King's decision to surrender would be applauded when the truth was known. "I think it will be shown that the Allies were informed, and fully informed, no less than three days before," he said. "Suppose you are in command of an army of half a million or more howling, panic-stricken civilian refugees. Suppose you have found that nothing can be gained for your army or for your Allies, and you say to yourself : 'I will be guilty of the taking of human life if I persist in this position,' and so decide as a man of Christian conscience that you have nothing else to do but to surrender. That was the position the King was in, and it will be shown by the facts when the facts are known."

Sir Roger Keyes, at the request of the British Government, left England by aeroplane to join King Leopold as Special Liaison Officer. Throughout the brief campaign in Belgium he was with the King at the headquarters of the Belgian Army, and at the same time was in close touch with British G.H.Q. and the Government in London. He remained with King Leopold until 10 p.m. on May 27, the day on which the King asked the Germans for an armistice. Thus he had unrivalled opportunities of observing the course of events.

When his country was invaded, Leopold had placed himself and his army under the French High Command, and the movements of his army conformed with their orders.

'No Right to Jeopardize British'

On May 20 the British Army and the French northern army were ordered to prepare to fight to the south-westward to regain contact with the main French army, and unless the Belgian army could conform to this movement it was clear that it would involve a breach of contact between the British and Belgian armies. On conveying the order to the King, Sir Roger was asked to tell the British Government and Lord Gort that the Belgian army had neither tanks nor aircraft, and existed solely for defence. He did not feel he had any right to expect the British Government to jeopardize, perhaps, the very existence of the British Army to keep contact with the Belgian army, but he wished to make it quite clear that if there were a separation between the two armies the capitulation of the Belgian army would be inevitable.

At the request of the French High Command the Belgian army was withdrawn on May 23 from the strongly prepared position on the Scheldt to a much weaker and longer line on the Lys, to allow the British Army to retire behind the defensive frontier line which it had occupied throughout the winter to

KING LEOPOLD of the Belgians seen at
the front during the invasion of the Low
Countries in 1940.   *Photo, Planet News*

army by May 27 was running short of food and ammunition and was being attacked by at least eight German divisions, including armoured units and waves of dive bombers.

On the morning of May 27 the King asked Sir Roger to inform the British authorities that he would be obliged to surrender before a débâcle took place. A similar message was given to the French. By the afternoon of that day the German army had driven a wedge between the Belgian and British armies. Every road, village and town in the small part of Belgium left in Belgian hands was thronged with hundreds of thousands of refugees ; men, women and children were being mercilessly bombed and machine-gunned by low-flying aircraft.

In these circumstances, at 5 p.m. on May 27, King Leopold informed the British and French authorities that he intended at midnight of that day to ask for an armistice so as to avoid further slaughter of his people. This message, like the earlier one on the same day, was promptly received in London and Paris, but all communications with the British Army were cut, and though wireless messages were repeatedly sent it is now known that these did not reach the Commanders-in-Chief.

Knowing these facts (concluded Sir Patrick Hastings), Sir Roger Keyes felt more than justified in suggesting a suspension of judgement on King Leopold. It was apparent that a very grave injustice had been done to the King of the Belgians, who had acted throughout in accordance with the highest traditions of honour and justice. Mr. Justice Tucker, approving the settlement which had been arranged, added : "All I need say is that this libel action, unlike some others, appears to have served a most useful purpose, and resulted in statements being made which will give very wide satisfaction."

By way of postscript, M. Pierlot, Belgian Prime Minister in London, said on July 15, "King Leopold was compelled by the military situation to surrender, but from the moment of surrender he considered himself a prisoner of war. He has maintained that position without wavering. He has not collaborated with his gaolers or assisted them in any way."

THE PALACE OF LAEKEN, one of the residences (and now the prison) of the King of the
Belgians, lies in a suburb to the north of Brussels. It was built in 1782, and for a time Napoleon,
who bought it, resided there.   *Photo, Topical*

And now the facts *are* known. They have been revealed in the course of a libel action brought by Sir Roger Keyes against a national newspaper in the King's Bench Division on June 13. Sir Patrick Hastings, K.C., Counsel for Sir Roger Keyes, in announcing that a settlement of the action had been arranged, described the course of events leading up to the surrender of King Leopold.

The Germans invaded Belgium on May 10, opened Sir Patrick ; and a few hours later

prepare for the offensive it was about to undertake to the southward.

On the evening of May 26 a break through the Belgian line by the Germans seemed to be inevitable, and the King moved the remaining French 60th Division in Belgian vehicles to a prepared position across the Yser, which by now was flooded over a wide area and its bridges mined.

Fighting on the Belgian front had been continuous for four days, and the Belgian

I Was There! .... Eye Witness Stories of the War

I Was in Moscow When War Was Declared

Here is a first-hand impression of Moscow after the German onslaught on Russia had begun. It was sent from the Soviet capital by Reuter's special correspondent at the beginning of July.

LIFE in Moscow continues amazingly normal, despite the fierce battles raging a few hundred miles away. Food and petrol are plentiful, and the shops are well stocked with every variety of goods. Through the Moscow streets, strangely combining the tawdry with the picturesque, the old with the spectacular, new army and official cars dash at top speed day and night. Often a thousand soldiers at a time march through to music. At numerous points voluntary mobilization centres have been established for women agriculturists and the Opolchentsy (Home Guard).

The walls are covered with eagerly-read posters depicting Hitler, like a Fascist rat, sticking his head through the German-Soviet Pact, and St. George, like a Red soldier, using his bayonet. There are also appeals to the women to relieve the men who have gone to the front. Stalin's speech is widely displayed, while the bookstalls sell Yaroslavsky's pamphlet on the significance of the war. The general tenor of all this is that this is a war of the Fatherland which is also defending the privileges acquired by the Revolution that German-led landowners and other exploiters will take away. This, anyway, is how the Soviet citizen takes it. Grimness, earnestness and confidence are written on all the male and female faces with unbounded pride in the Red Army.

The streets generally appear normal. The shortage of male civilians is not noticeable, owing to the unlimited man-power. On Sundays and in the evenings the streets are crowded with simply dressed girls in summer frocks, and youths. There is no drunkenness, the fruit-drink stalls being particularly popular. The cinemas and theatres are open, but amusements are much reduced. For example, the popular bathing beach of Khilki, on the Moscow River, was almost deserted on a Sunday afternoon.

So far there have been a number of air-raid warnings, but no raids. When the warnings sound the streets clear instantly with exemplary discipline, everybody taking shelter. The Russians are very interested in the newly arrived British A.R.P. and fire-fighting experts, Cols. A. Croad and G. Symonds, the latter the designer of the stirrup-pump, a specimen of which he brought with him. All are eager to hear anyone with British " blitz " experiences. Fire-fighting parties are being organized with the usual Soviet discipline.

Particularly remarkable is the utter silliness of the Russian-spoken German radio propaganda calling on Soviet soldiers to desert, and announcing that " Stalin and his Jews " are keeping the fastest planes in reserve to escape to New York, where they have " large bank deposits." This propaganda, broadcast by " Quisling " Russians, is an exact replica of the crude émigré anti-Bolshevik propaganda used in 1920. These German agents display a total unawareness of the changes of outlook of the Russian population in the past twenty years.

Russian sailors belonging to the warship Frunze under the Kremlin walls in Moscow. Top, three Soviet airmen go sightseeing in the streets of the capital.
Photo, Paul Popper

We Never Have a Square Meal in France Now

While the German troops in Occupied France live on the fat of the land the French go hungry. This letter, dated the end of April, from a worker living in a small town in Northern France to a friend in the unoccupied zone, gives an idea of the lives of tens of thousands of the French populace.

LIFE in France is becoming more and more difficult. Shopping is a real trial. Food, or rather how to get it, is almost the sole topic of conversation. That is not surprising when a square meal is an unknown thing. The bread ration for our family of three is 800 grammes, potatoes are unobtainable, of macaroni and the like we are only allowed one and a half kilos [1 kilogramme = 1,000 grammes = 2½ lb. approx.] a month for the three of us. Further, we get a little dried vegetables. This is not enough to live on. So far most people have been more or less successful in laying hands on something else besides the rations. We had a small reserve of macaroni and potatoes to help us through the winter. The spring has brought a marked impairment instead of an improvement in the food situation. Hitherto the supply of bread and meat was fairly adequate. But that has changed. This week all we have had for us three is 400 grammes of meat. Luckily we got a few eggs. But it has now been announced that eggs are also to be rationed, three per head and per month, we gather.

Everything is getting dearer. For unrationed goods in short supply prices are very high indeed. Carrots, when obtainable, cost 6 francs a kilo, small peas 12 francs a kilo, broad beans 10 francs, dates 26 francs, grape sugar 20 francs, eggs 20 to 22 francs a dozen. A worker, like myself, who earns 5 francs an hour, of course, cannot afford such supplementary food. He must fall back on sweet potatoes, turnips and beet-roots. Before the war this was cattle fodder. One cannot eat very much of such food. In addition, to prepare it fat is needed, and that is very scarce in France today.

We thought of cultivating a plot of land, to grow some food for the winter, which is going to be a very bad one. But there is a shortage of seed. The plot which was allotted to us was only suitable for growing potatoes. Sixteen kilogrammes of seed potatoes needed, but only got one kilogramme. This gives some idea of what the prospects are for the crop. With other sowing crops the position is similar.

My letter, you will note, is almost wholly taken up with food, the question that haunts us continually. If the stomach is satisfied everything will work. If the stomach is dissatisfied nothing will work.—*I.T.F.*

Squalor and poverty are now general in once gay and bountiful Paris, and the food queue has become the sign of Hitler's New Order. The city of epicures, for the French of all classes really understood and enjoyed food, is now haunted by the spectre of famine. There is a dearth of all the simple necessities of life.   *From " March of Time "*

766   *The War Illustrated*   *August 1st, 1941*

IIIIIIIIIIIIIIIIIIIIIIIIIIIIIIIIIIIIIIIIIIIIIIIIIIIIIIIII **I WAS THERE!** IIIIIIIIIIIIIIIIIIIIIIIIIIIIIIIIIIIIIIIIIIIIIIIIIIII

GERMAN AIR-BORNE TROOPS on the march in Crete. Some 130 troop-carriers landed within a few hours of the opening of hostilities on the island. How the Maoris and New Zealanders attacked them with bayonets is described in this page.   *Photo, Keystone*

For Days We Fought the Nazi Parachutists

How our troops in Crete tackled the Germans on the ground but were overwhelmed by their bombing planes is vividly described in this account of the fighting by a wounded Maori sergeant.

ON the afternoon when the first German parachutists began to land in the Canea area, a Maori battalion and a New Zealand battalion formed a thin line stretching for some miles from the sea towards the hills to check a possible enemy thrust towards Canea.

We lay on open ground until dusk and watched, until our eyes became tired, shower upon shower of parachutists floating to the earth before us. We were unable to move owing to the unremitting bombing and machine-gunning by the dive-bombers, but when the sun sank we fixed our bayonets and immediately it was dark charged.

Our first obstacle was a solid line of machine-guns, but these we quickly overran, and after a great fight lasting until dawn we annihilated nearly every German.

But with daylight waves of German airborne reinforcements began to arrive. Eventually parachute troops began to drop behind our lines, and bit by bit we had to give ground and fall back on fresh positions.

Within a few hours some 130 troop-carriers, escorted by clouds of fighters, had landed, and throughout the day we were attacked by over 200 dive-bombers.

We sheathed our bayonets and lay hidden in the rocks or drains—anything giving shelter from the relentless hail of bullets and bombs—while the dive-bombers had us at their mercy, as we had no air support. German reinforcements established themselves in the positions which we had cleared during the night. With darkness we again fixed our bayonets and charged, and again cut the enemy to pieces. This went on for four days and four nights.

Up in the mountains dead Germans lay in clumps where they had landed and were killed by Greek soldiers. In the battle area it was impossible to walk more than three yards without stepping on dead Germans. Two men out of every parachutist section were armed with rifles for sniping. The rest were equipped with tommy-guns. All carried plenty of rations.—*Press Association.*

We Cheered Like Mad for the British Navy

When the German supply and prison ship Alstertor was intercepted and scuttled at the end of June, 78 officers and men of the British merchant navy were rescued. Here is the story of their imprisonment and release, told by one of them, Chief Steward W. G. Johnson.

AMONG the prisoners on the Alstertor were survivors from the S.S. Rabaul and the S.S. Trafalgar. Mr. W. G. Johnson, proprietor of an Ilfracombe hotel and chief steward on the Rabaul, described how his own ship was sunk at 1 a.m. on May 14 by an ex-merchant ship armed with 6-in. guns. Twenty high-explosive shells were fired at point-blank range from half a mile. Eight of the crew and one passenger were killed ; the remainder left the burning ship on rafts and were picked up by the raider. He went on :

Many of us were wounded, including myself, and were attended to by the raider's doctor. We were very well treated, sleeping in bunks between decks. We were allowed on deck for four hours' exercise daily.

We were aboard the raider for 17 days and were then transferred to the cargo ship Japara. Conditions here were extremely unpleasant. Seventy-eight prisoners— 48 whites and the rest Chinese, Malays and Indians—were all jammed together in one hold, sleeping on sacks. The food and ventilation were bad. We were only allowed above decks for meals.

We stuck those conditions for 16 days. Then on June 15 we were put aboard the Alstertor, an ex-fruit ship, obviously fitted as a prison ship. There were extra stanchions and holds to take double tiers of hammocks.

Life here was much more comfortable, the white men being in one hold. I estimate the vessel would carry 350 men in this fashion.

The food was good and we took meals in another hold equipped with tables and forms. We were all given a tobacco allowance sufficient for an economical smoker, and permitted on deck 12 hours daily. The German naval lieutenant and the lieutenant in charge of us inspected daily the prisoners' parade. There was no harsh treatment, not even when I was caught throwing a bottle message into the sea. I was warned that if it occurred again we should all be kept below.

A British flying-boat bombed the ship on June 22. Our joy at being sighted was tempered by the horrid thought that we might be sunk by their own target. A bomb fell 50 yards away.

We grew sick with despair when nothing happened for the rest of that day and were resigned to the fate of internment for the rest of the war. We had given up all hope, for the ship was only 24 hours' steaming from Bordeaux when intercepted by British destroyers.

When suddenly the speed of the ship increased, the prisoners herded below sensed that rescue was near. Standing half-crouched under the clamped-down hatch, Johnson— his eye glued to a tiny rivet hole in the dimly-lit hold—"broadcast" a running commentary on the approach of the British warships.

We felt the vessel slowing down, he said. Then I saw the international code signal, "M.T.," run up the mast head.

"What does M.T. mean ?" I called to the men below.

Back came the answer, "Am Stopping Ship." Then I heard the guttural voice of a German lookout, recognized the German words for "British Warships" and shouted "Glorious news " to my fellow prisoners.

Madly happy, the men were still cheering when the hatch was opened and daylight flooded in. A German officer entered and said, "British warships have us fast. We are abandoning ship. You may have the big boat and rafts."

We got into the boat and on to the floats, concluded Johnson, cheering like madmen for the British Navy. As we got away the Alstertor was scuttled with time bombs, which threw debris all around us.—*Reuter.*

ALSTERTOR, German prison ship, settling down in the water after having been scuttled by her crew near Bordeaux. She was intercepted by British destroyers who rescued 78 officers and men of the British merchant navy. An eye-witness account appears in this page.   *Photo, Associated Press*

Our Fleet's Barrage Beat Off the Enemy's Air Attack

During the period May 5-12, our naval forces operating in the Central
Mediterranean sustained several enemy air attacks without damage. A
graphic eye-witness account of one night attack was written by Reuter's
correspondent on board H.M.S. Barham.

H.M.S. BARHAM full speed ahead in the Mediterranean. From the Barham's compass platform the writer of the article in this page describes how more than thirty warships in the Central Mediterranean beat off a torpedo attack by enemy planes. *Photo, Associated Press*

A HEAVY and most spectacular night
barrage was put up by more than
thirty warships in the Central
Mediterranean when for the first time in
this war enemy planes attempted a night
torpedo attack at sea against the British
Eastern Mediterranean forces. The firing
continued almost ceaselessly for forty-five
minutes.

The full moon was some twenty degrees
above the horizon when cruisers, escorting
a convoy, were seen to open fire a few miles
distant on our starboard quarter—I was on
board the Barham—whereupon our heavy
units blazed forth with all their armaments
from six-inchers downwards, while a strong
destroyer screen flung up an umbrella
barrage, protecting the battle fleet from a
possible high-level bombing attack.

When the battle fleet opened fire the raiders
apparently abandoned the convoy and,
splitting up into groups, attacked the fleet
from all angles.

From the Barham's compass platform I
had a magnificent panoramic view of the
fleet steaming in line ahead, belching flame
in all directions as the barrage, comprising
six-inch and four-inch guns, multiple pom-
poms and even Lewis guns, plastered a wide
area extending from the sea level to the sky.
Each battleship appeared to be aflame from
end to end, and was illuminated for seconds
at a time. Enveloped by clouds of smoke
from the guns, it looked like a giant set-piece
during a gargantuan firework display.

The whole ship shuddered violently under
terrific blast as the shells whistled away into
the distance, gun flashes temporarily blinded
me as the high angle barrage passed the
bridge with the reflection on the halyards,
giving the impression of masses of tracers

being hurled vertically to the mast. Speech
was impossible, and shouted orders were
drowned by the indescribable violence of the
barrage.

Meanwhile the sea, which was lit up by
the blaze of the guns, periodically became a
mass of small and large waterspouts as
splinters from the destroyers' protective
barrage fell all around us.

During brief lulls to ascertain the enemy's
line of approach I heard the water-cooled
pom-poms below the bridge hissing fiercely,
and there was a tremendous clatter of

thousands of empty shell cases of all calibres
being hastily swept aside before the next
barrage opened.

No torpedoes were seen anywhere near
us, though the last ship of the line was seen
to take avoiding action during the early part
of the attack.

The cease fire was given after 45 minutes,
and a thick wet fog suddenly descended on
the whole sea for the remainder of the night,
necessitating the use of stern lights in order
to avoid collisions. Darkness prevented
our ascertaining the results of the barrage,
but we did not suffer any casualties or
damage.

Siftings From the News

First goose-stepping parade since Armistice
watched in dead silence by 10,000 Parisians.

Alsatian boys and girls aged 14 have to
enrol in the Hitler Youth organization.

Glasgow Corporation has its own shops for
the sale of surplus produce from city parks.

Italy appeared under heading "Occupied
Territories" in list of international production
in German paper.

Tablet unveiled in St. Paul's, London, to Pilot
Officer W. M. L. Fiske, first American to die
for Britain in this war.

About 90 persons were arrested in Zürich
on charges of political espionage.

Spain seized Tangier lighthouse installation,
including wireless beacon, hitherto under
international control.

Two clerks in Nazi Consulates in U.S.A.
committed suicide sooner than return to
Germany.

All British nationals have been ordered to
leave French Riviera immediately.

Moscow propaganda describes Russian
pilots as "Soviet Falcons," Axis pilots as
"Fascist Vultures."

First rural Recuperation Centre for immediate reception of bombed-out people opened in
Lancs.

Thirteen Communists and Jews shot in
Belgrade "for preparing to commit acts of
violence and sabotage."

There are over 7,000 women workers on the
L.M.S. railway.

Largest fishing factory in North Norway,
owned by German company, destroyed by fire
one month after completion.

Russians spreading false rumours are liable
to five years' imprisonment.

Rome stated that Fascist casualties of
war numbered 255,361.

Britain is buying 150,000,000 tins of
sardines from Portugal.

Montenegro is to have a king ; meanwhile
a regent is being appointed by Italy.

Test parcel sent by the "Daily Telegraph"
through Red Cross took five months to reach
German prison camp.

Promenade concerts opened for first time
at Albert Hall on July 12, when the audience
numbered 4,000.

London firemen are allowed daily ration of
one pennyworth of meat at their canteens.

Reported that beer shortage may lead to
refusal of harvesters to work overtime.

Salary of top B.B.C. wartime announcers
is £1,000 a year.

The Editor's Postscript

WITH this number THE WAR ILLUSTRATED completes its Fourth Volume, most thrillingly varied of the series so far. Look back at Volume One in which the swift destruction of Poland and Finland's historic stand against Russia supplied the major subjects for camera and pen, with the glorious episode of the River Plate, and you will be surprised at the slow progress of the first four or five months of "phoney" War; surprised also to read of that "master mind of military France" named Gamelin; "the strong man of France," M. Daladier; and of the faith that still survived in a Maginot Line. Volume Two moved to a quickening tempo: the end of Finland's heroic stand, the unhappy chapter to which Narvik wrote finis, those more horrible chapters that opened with the invasion of Holland and Belgium and so quickly closed; finally, "Total War on the Western Front" which smothered our ally, France, in defeat and shame and left Britain with nothing more glorious to add to History's pages than the epic of Dunkirk. Six months of tremendous world-events . . . all at the call of Hitler !

VOLUME Three saw the Battle of Britain fought and won, so far as daylight raiding was concerned, with the Battle of the Atlantic engaged and menacing, while the new era of Fire over Britain, made possible only by the German occupation of fallen France, was raging as our Army of the Nile had begun its mighty wiping up of the disgusting Italians in North Africa. Look over those three volumes today and you will marvel at the endless interest of their graphic pages, certain to hold readers of all classes for generations to come.

VOLUME Four was destined, however, to be the most varied and arresting of the progression. No matter how many more or how few may yet be published, it is hard to picture any that will excel it in the variety and importance of its contents, which comprise a picture-record of what must prove one of the most historic periods of the world-wide conflict. The military success of Wavell's campaign which destroyed so large a proportion of the Italian Army; the vitally important battle of Cape Matapan; the heroic stand of Greece against Italian aggression; the sensational turn of affairs in Yugoslavia; the treachery of Bulgaria, Rumania and Hungary, leading to the Nazi domination of the Balkans; the abortive pro-Nazi revolution in Irak; the war in Syria, where the degenerate Vichy government forced the former allies of France to turn their arms against the hostile French forces under the command of General Dentz, and fortunately in so doing gave a new direction to Germany's Eastward thrust, little to the liking of Hitler and his thugs; the tremendous increase in Britain's air power, with its promise of the coming day when the command of the sky will have passed into the hands of Britain's incomparable Air Force; the sensational break between Germany and Russia, vastly extending the area and, as I have already indicated, the

probable duration of the War; America's no less sensational steps to make secure her means of cooperation with Great Britain—these are but a few of the many new chapters in the astounding history of the world that have been written in the seven months covered by this volume.

FROM another point of view Volume Four calls for remark: it has been produced in circumstances of exceptional difficulty which are already known to my readers. The acute paper famine has taxed the ingenuity of Editor and Publishers to the limit. Certain changes of format forced upon us will be apparent in the bound volume and actually add to its value as a contemporary historical record. But I think it

Another Splendid Volume for Your Bookshelf

The War Illustrated—Volume 4

To make THE WAR ILLUSTRATED of real permanent value you should have the weekly numbers bound as each volume is completed. Number 100 completes the Fourth Volume. The publishers have produced specially attractive binding cases. They are made of stout boards covered with durable Dark Red Cloth with side and spine bearing appropriate designs in two inks and blind blocking. You can obtain these cases, together with title page, index, frontispiece, etc., through your newsagent or bookstall for 2/6 each or direct from THE

WAR ILLUSTRATED (Binding Dept.), Bear Alley, Farringdon Street, London, E.C.4, when 7d. extra for postage must be enclosed for each case ordered.

Subscribers who would prefer an extra special binding for this work can secure our DE LUXE CASE, which is made of dark blue half leather with blue cloth sides, also blue leather corners, and spine blocked in gilt and blind. It can be obtained through your newsagents, price 6/6. (Postage 7d. extra if ordered direct from the Publishers.)

See Announcement in Number 91 for

PUBLISHERS' SPECIAL BINDING OFFER

The publishers will undertake to bind the weekly numbers of THE WAR ILLUSTRATED into volumes at a special inclusive charge of 6/- per volume for the Standard Binding or for the De Luxe Binding 10/6 per volume. These charges include cost of binding case, packing and return carriage. It is important that the details given in the announcement on the back cover of Number 91 of THE WAR ILLUSTRATED be complied with.

will be allowed, after one hundred weekly issues, that we have honoured my promise made to readers with Volume One, that no effort would be spared to maintain the publication on the lines on which it had been originally designed, and such modifications as have been forced upon us by "the fell clutch of circumstance" have in no wise impaired the usefulness or attractiveness of this, the only current picture-record of the War that has been kept afloat through a sea of troubles and may hope to survive until the bells of Victory peal in a world set free.

ALL which goes to show why the many thousands of my readers who are happy in the possession of the first three volumes should instantly set about the binding of Volume Four. Each new volume bound actually adds to the value of the preceding volumes. Large though the number is of those subscribers who do get

their loose numbers bound, they form a minority of our immense circle of readers, so that with our present restricted space we cannot give repeated reminders about bindings. The announcement in this page will appear only once again. It is up to them, therefore, to act upon it today.

ANOTHER important consideration is the increasing difficulty of securing binding materials, which may yet make it necessary to confine the acceptance of binding orders to those readers who have already bound earlier volumes. Don't delay, then, in acting upon this advice to which I must take this opportunity of drawing your attention; you will never regret putting this unique picture-record into permanent covers for consulting in years to come. It is sure to hold its place for many years as an historic product of the amazing times in which it has been compiled and circulated.

THE happy thought of an American publisher in presenting our Prime Minister with the manuscript of Arthur Hugh Clough's poem "Say Not the Struggle Naught Availeth," from which Mr. Churchill quoted with such dramatic effect in his historic broadcast to America, reminds me that I have a confession to make. The last and best known of the four quatrains which comprise the poem has been so often on my lips for more than half a century that I might well call it my favourite quotation. I have grown up with it, so to speak, but had never bothered to verify its origin. For which I am sincerely ashamed. I thought it was from Browning. What a bloomer that would have been in an "intelligence test"! I'd like to reprint the whole poem, as every line is instinct with thought and encouragement for the present time. (These Nazi bombers are droning over my cottage home as I write.) But I must at least give one of the other verses:

If hopes are dupes, fears may be liars;
It may be, in yon smoke concealed,
Your comrades chase e'en now the fliers,
And, but for you, possess the field.

THE last and best remembered verse which alone had stayed in my mind from youth to old age (measured by years alone and not by feeling !) runs:

And not by eastern windows only,
When daylight comes, comes in the light;
In front the sun climbs slow, how slowly !
But westward, look, the land is bright !

And now, I ask you, what do you think of a really brilliant cartoonist in a national daily who distorts the whole lovely image with a picture of Russian tanks labelled "Eastward look the land is bright"? By aiming at a clever switch of phrase he misses the whole pith of the quotation . . . but there, I'm going out into the moon-bright night, to see what's happening, as these infernal Nazis are still hovering around. And there are those who still babble about "rural peace" in England's countryside.

JOHN CARPENTER HOUSE.
WHITEFRIARS. LONDON. E.C.4.